The Mind in Sleep

THE MIND IN SLEEP

PSYCHOLOGY AND PSYCHOPHYSIOLOGY

Second Edition

Edited by

STEVEN J. ELLMAN
JOHN S. ANTROBUS
City College of the City University of New York

A Wiley Interscience Publication
JOHN WILEY & SONS, INC.
New York / Chichester / Brisbane / Toronto / Singapore

Library of Congress Cataloging-in-Publication Data

The Mind in sleep : psychology and psychophysiology / edited by
  Steven J. Ellman, John S. Antrobus. — 2nd ed.
    p.   cm. — (Wiley series on personality processes)
  ISBN 0-471-52556-1
    1. Sleep—Physiological aspects.   2. Dreams—Physiological
aspects.   I. Ellman, Steven J.   II. Antrobus, John S., 1932–
III. Series
QP425.M56   1991
154.6—dc20   90-39136
                                                            CIP

Printed in the United States of America

91 92 10 9 8 7 6 5 4 3 2 1

Dedicated
to the memory of
Arthur M. Arkin

who was our collaborator, beloved friend, and mentor. Our first edition was largely a result of his tireless efforts, and we hope this edition is a valuable testament to the man who was such a devoted researcher.

Arthur was the inspirational force for many initiatives in the doctoral programs of clinical psychology and experimental cognition at the City University of New York. He blended kindness of soul and clarity of thought in a way that allowed his penetrating rationality to gently guide those around him to new insights and left them refreshed and renewed rather than challenged and provoked. His wonderful tolerance of a person's personal and intellectual positions helped everyone around him to search for new ways to understand phenomena and themselves.

He was a psychiatrist who was a full-time faculty member in the Graduate School of Psychology at City University of New York and a faculty member of two doctoral programs in psychology. He was also an attending at various hospitals as well as a wonderfully empathic clinical psychiatrist. Only the writing of this tribute makes his achievements seem at all unusual, for Arthur made them all seem natural.

To anyone who knew him, it is not surprising that the experiments in sleep and dream research presented here include physiological, cognitive, and psychoanalytic perspectives. In his presence, cognitive and psychoanalytic researchers worked together and furthered each other's conceptualizations. Arthur was a man who could bring people and ideas together, and the world is much poorer and less integrated without him.

Preface to the First Edition

This book deals largely with four questions:

1. What goes on in the mind during sleep?
2. How do we come by such knowledge?
3. What relationships between physiological and mental events have been brought to light by electrographic and other controlled study of sleep mentation?
4. To what extent are the research findings of the past 25 years valid?

An indispensable component of the data base of scientific dream psychology is the dream report—that sleep experience or mentation sequence which the dreamer recalls as what he dreamt, and to which Freud (1900/ 1955a) referred as the "manifest dream." In 1953, a revolutionary advance in sleep and dream studies was initiated by the employment of new electrographic technology (Aserinsky & Kleitman, 1953, Dement & Kleitman, 1957a, 1957b). Prior to this time dream report data, with rare exceptions, consisted of whatever residual, often skimpy recall of dreams unreliably remained accessible to the subject on awakening the following morning, or after even longer intervals between dream events and recording them. Think what a marvelous technical advantage it is to have a dependable *objective* method capable of indicating to dream investigators when ongoing dreams were in progress! They would then possess the scientific luxury of the closest possible access to the living phenomena they were studying. Surely, reports of dreams in progress only seconds before laboratory awakenings would provide more faithful, comprehensive accounts of dreaming than reports obtained at some relatively remote time. And such a method has been precisely one of the cardinal contributions of modern psychophysiological electrography.

Has the only yield of this new line of work been greater availability of "fresh" dream reports? Surely not. The research accumulated since 1953 has demonstrated varieties of dreams which are associated in differential fashion with diverse physiological events, times of the night, individual subject differences, and so forth. It has also produced a large body of intriguing information in such areas as the effects of a host of experimental variables on dream content, the psychological and physiological effects of attempts to deprive subjects of that type of sleep in which most vivid dreams occur, and common sleep abnormalities such as sleeptalking, nightmares, and night terrors. Not unexpectedly, the findings have posed inescapable challenges to prevailing theories of dream psychology, dream interpretation, and philosophical thought concerned with mind–brain relationships.

Accordingly, the main goal of the book is to provide a comprehensive history and critical account of sleep mentation research since the introduction of the new electrographic techniques. Progress in this area has been marked throughout by vigorous scientific controversy, the main current outcome of which differs in major significant ways from such earlier formulations as: nocturnal dreaming is coterminal with REM sleep; or REM deprivation is the equivalent of dream deprivation and is especially harmful to the point that it is likely to result in psychosis. Such ideas have lingered in the minds of readers of the early literature of the 1960s who have lost touch with developments since.

Although other excellent books and reviews have appeared covering similar ground, they are out of date, do not provide coverage of equal scope, or else have not taken as a specific point of departure the dream or sleep mentation report itself within the operational context of eliciting and evaluating such material. This fundamental focus, this essential data base component has been the source of much critical research. At first glance, one might expect that obtaining sleep mentation reports by experimental awakenings is a perfectly straightforward uncomplicated matter from which useful, unequivocal scientific data could be easily produced. This is not altogether untrue but actually simplistic; methodological problems have plagued the field. Findings from one laboratory to the next have often shown great, even embarrassing disparities. Much of this has been due to differences in methods of evaluation of sleep mentation reports, and inadequate control of variables. Reliable findings and knowledge have been slow in coming.

The book is organized chiefly in accordance with topic headings covering areas of sleep mentation research which are of common interest. Separate chapters are devoted to methodology, critical reviews of REM deprivation studies, and relationships between sustained and short-lived physiological conditions and sleep mentation; the main findings of phenomenological studies of sleep mentation throughout the night and in various sleep stages; the effects of a host of experimental variables on sleep mentation; clinical phenomena such as sleeptalking, nightmares, and night terrors insofar as they reflect sleep mentation processes; and finally a section on implications of the work presented for clinical practice and cognitive psychology.

The main audiences for which the book has been prepared are scientists and scholars working in the field of sleep mentation including dreams, psychophysiologists, cognitive psychologists, graduate and advanced undergraduates in psychology, psychiatrists and neurologists, psychiatric and neurological residents desiring a comprehensive introduction to this new field, and possibly philosophers interested in the mind–brain problem.

ARTHUR M. ARKIN
STEVEN J. ELLMAN
JOHN S. ANTROBUS

Preface to the Second Edition

The present edition of this book deals with the same four questions that we posed in 1977. In addition, we focus more extensively on a related question, the psychological need for nocturnal dream experience. In each of the questions that we pose, there have been fascinating and thought provoking new findings that have appeared since 1977. The findings, however, have not been accruing with the same revolutionary speed of the first 20 years in sleep and dream research. We hope that the presentation of new findings will stimulate some of the revolutionary zeal of the earlier decades.

This volume again gives close attention to the methodology of sleep and dream research but also emphasizes theoretical integrations as well. It is our view that at this point in the field, new conceptual tools are as important as new findings. It may be that a limitation in the field of sleep and dream research has been the type of questions that have been asked. Perhaps new theoretical perspectives will open the way to new areas of inquiry. At any rate, we hope in this volume to do justice to past research in our reviews of the literature, and to help open the way to new research vistas by the presentation of some new questions and concepts.

Acknowledgments

Many people have been involved with the main research project that was the impetus for both editions of *The Mind in Sleep*. Clearly, the primary acknowledgment is owed to the late Arthur M. Arkin, who died in May 1982. We all deeply miss him still and we hope that this volume in some small way honors his memory.

I wish to thank Ms. Christina Sobin and Ms. Patricia Christina for their invaluable secretarial assistance. I wish also to acknowledge the helpful and extensive editorial contribution made by Frederick Korn, of Medgar Evers College of City University of New York. Dr. Korn reviewed much of the manuscript for the second edition and offered extensive suggestions on matters of style and mechanics. Though we bear responsibility for the final text, nonetheless this edition did enjoy in manuscript the benefits of Dr. Korn's expertise as a result of his training in the humanities.

S.J.E.

Contents

Introduction to the First Edition

ARTHUR M. ARKIN
City College of the City University of New York

Until 20 years ago the most influential body of scientific and scholarly thought about dreaming was derived from clinical observations. Freud's (1900/1953c) monumental Traumdeutung dominated the field and continues to be a major force. In addition, Jung, Adler, Stekel, and others had made highly significant contributions. To be sure, there had previously been a slowly growing scientific literature describing attempts to investigate dreaming by laboratory methods but, despite many provocative and even valid studies (Ramsey, 1953), it was not a field which commanded the interest of many research scientists.

In 1953, a new era in sleep and dream research began with the publication of Aserinsky and Kleitman's "Regularly Occurring Periods of Eye Motility and Concomitant Phenomena During Sleep." Their work demonstrated that during human sleep, recurrent episodes of distinctive electrographically recordable events were typically associated with dreaming experience as reported by subjects when awakened on such occasions. Actually Aserinsky and Kleitman were attempting to study the behavior of the eye during sleep, and for this purpose employed continuous electrical recording of eye movements (the electro-oculogram, EOG). They were struck by the occurrence of epochs of behavioral sleep featuring bursts of conjugate rapid eye movements, or REMs, in conjunction with low-voltage mixed brain-wave frequencies (LVM), and that following experimental awakenings on such occasions, subjects would regularly report the contents of a vivid dream.[1] By contrast, awakenings from sleep in the absence of the above electrographic patterns were said to result in little or no recall of sleep mentation. This finding was confirmed and extended in a series of studies conducted by Dement and colleagues (Dement & Kleitman, 1957a, 1957b; Dement & Wolpert, 1958b) and it was only a matter of a few years until scientists from all over the world, like enthusiastic treasure hunters, were absorbed in research on the psychophysiology of sleep and dreaming.

For the first time in history, a reliable, objective, quantifiable index of the occurrence of dreams seemed to be available. So enthusiastic was the dedication of the researchers that, in 1960, the Association for the Psychophysiological Study of Sleep (APSS) was founded. The unflagging labors of its membership have produced an enormous scientific literature on varied aspects of sleep and dreaming. Because research in this field is complex, expensive, and most arduous (even exhausting), preliminary findings were based on a relatively small number of selected subjects. As time passed, with the accumulation of new observations on larger and diversified subject populations, early conclusions underwent revision, sometimes to a drastic degree. We feel, therefore, that the time has come to prepare a definitive review of the current state of the art in that part of the field which is of central interest to psychologists: mental processes and their manifestations as they occur in sleep, that is, sleep mentation.

The presentation of any scientific field appropriately starts with its observational base. Accordingly, in the creation of his psychoanalytic work on dreaming, Freud utilized the following set of items:

1. The content of the dreaming experience as recalled and reported by his patient-subjects (including himself) usually on the morning following the dream. Freud referred to such reports as the *manifest* content of the dream; in laboratory research, the equivalent term is the *sleep-mentation report*.

2. The psychological context within which the dream occurred. This included the mosaic of the day's events previous to the dream as well as a multidimensional conception of the total life history and the specific psychological difficulties and personality of the dreamer. It was usually possible to discern some intelligible relationship

---

[1] Such epochs are referred to as stage REM sleep, whereas all other sleep is called non-REM or simply NREM.

between these psychological context materials and aspects of the manifest dream.

3. The psychological associations of the dreamer to the various components of the manifest content.

A psychoanalyst listening to an array of such information is often able to formulate interpretations of various aspects of the dream. Such interpretation might include making explicit the components of the dream which had previously been unintelligible or inaccessible to wakeful conscious understanding; or it might include articulating the complex psychological pathways traversed by unconscious elements in the course of acquiring final representation in the dream experience of sleep, what Freud called the *manifest* dream. The psychological totality of such unconscious elements—the "underlying" thoughts, urges, images, memories, fantasies, emotions, and so on—Freud defined as the *latent* content of the dream. The complicated intervening process through which the latent content became transformed into the manifest dream, he referred to as the *dreamwork*. (The details of dreamwork mechanisms such as condensation, displacement, influence of intrapsychic censorship, and so on are outside the scope of this discussion.)

Although other contributors to dream theory (Jung, Adler, Maeder, and others) differed with Freud in many respects, it is to be emphasized that they all used, along with Freud, the "manifest" dream report as their point of departure, as did Joseph, Daniel, Aesculapius, and Artemidorus.

In summary, modern ideas about dreaming have arisen from two main sources: clinical and laboratory investigation. In both cases, the fundamental observational base is the sleep-mentation report as it is produced in relation to multidimensional contexts. In the laboratory approach, the context includes the data derived from electrographic and behavioral methods as well as the laboratory situation itself. In the clinical approach, the context derives from the specific clinical theory, the method and personality of the investigator, as well as the particular clinical situation itself.

The sleep-mentation report occupies, therefore, a key position in any basic and applied science of dreaming, and a valid general science of dreaming must derive from the most complete investigation possible of the dream report within related standard contexts. In view of this consideration, it is essential to note that the samples of dreams available to us when we awaken in the morning, or which are remembered for a psychotherapeutic session, are always incomplete versions of a larger, more elaborate sleep experience. That is, an imponderable amount of forgetting of dream content occurs as well as subsequent distortion and editing in the ensuing wakefulness. By contrast, dream reports elicited in the laboratory are as "hot off the griddle" as we can get and even though they do not contain a "complete" record of sleep consciousness, they do provide us with the most direct possible access to dream content with minimal loss of information.

Laboratory studies have made clear that much more than dreaming goes on in the mind during sleep; rather, dreaming occupies an imprecisely defined area within a larger continuum of sleep experience. Thus, sleep mentation includes all sleep-associated cognitive processes: dreaming, thinking, unelaborated imagery, emotions, and so on. Inasmuch as laboratory method has unique advantages over other approaches to the problem, the principal focus of this book will be on sleep mentation as observed by laboratory method. All scientific scholarly and clinical approaches to dreaming must ultimately be consistent or capable of articulation with valid laboratory findings on reported sleep mentation.

As we present in detail in subsequent chapters, a fascinating finding obtained in the course of psychophysiological sleep research pertains to sequellae of deprivation of stage REM sleep. It should be noted, by way of introduction, that under baseline conditions, healthy subjects experience more or less stable proportions of the various sleep stages (including stage REM) during a night's sleep. For example, stage REM comprises 20–25% of the total nightly sleep of young adults. This observation, in conjunction with the demonstrated association between recall of vivid dreams and stage REM, led Dement (1960) to wonder what would happen if humans were prevented from experiencing REM sleep. Would this deprive them of all dreaming experience as well? Would the effects be deleterious? Accordingly, a laborious experiment was carried out requiring subjects to sleep a series of consecutive nights in the laboratory, during which their sleep was electrographically monitored.

First, a set of undisturbed nights were employed to establish baseline levels of stage REM. Then, on following nights, subjects were deprived of REM by awakening them each time they entered this stage. With succeeding nights, a striking phenomenon was observed: the number of awakenings required to deprive the subject of stage REM increased progressively. For example, on the first experimental night, a particular subject might be effectively stage REM-deprived by 7 awakenings, but by the fifth night, over 30 such awakenings would be necessary to bring about REM suppression. It seemed as though with increased amounts of deprivation, subjects made correspondingly increased "attempts" to obtain the stage REM being denied to them. Furthermore, when the subjects were allowed to sleep undisturbed once more during the next few consecutive nights, the proportion of stage REM was initially far in excess over that of baseline levels.

Could they be trying to make up their lost stage REM? Neither of the above results were obtained when an equal number of control awakenings from NREM sleep was made. Thus, the findings could not be attributed to mere deprivation of sleep per se but rather stemmed specifically from stage REM deprivation. Subsequently, additional studies revealed that when subjects were stage REM deprived, they tended to enter their first REM period of the night sooner than on baseline nights; and also, the frequency of REMs themselves (REM density) increased under conditions of REM deficit. These findings suggested that when subjects are REM deprived, a potential tendency to produce stage REM is established somewhat in proportion to the degree of deprivation. Furthermore, Dement (1960) noted that as REM deprivation progressed, subjects experienced distressing behavior changes and mental symptoms in their daily *wakeful* behavior. For example, intense anxiety, hunger, irritability, apathy, difficulties in concentration, undue suspiciousness, and hallucinatory tendencies were observable. It was concluded that humans have a biological "need" for a certain amount of REM sleep each night and that if this is suppressed, a REM "pressure" will arise, producing a rebound or compensatory increase of stage REM on subsequent undisturbed (or recovery) nights. Similar results have been obtained in a large number of studies on a variety of infrahuman mammals.

This demonstration of a biological "need" for stage REM in combination with associated psychological and behavioral disturbance suggested to Fisher and Dement (1963) that there might be validity to earlier speculations (Volkan, 1962) linking clinical psychosis to dreaming. For example, one often cited formulation defined psychosis as dreaming while awake (Jung, 1944). Thus, if REM deprivation results in increased REM "pressure," and if stage REM is that phase of sleep in which vivid dreams occur, might the behavioral disturbances associated with stage REM deprivation represent tendencies of dreaming experience to "spill over" into wakeful consciousness? And could stage REM deprivation, if continued long enough, result in clinical psychosis?

An ancillary question also arose: Besides a biological need for stage REM might there be a separate but related psychological need for nocturnal dream experience per se?

A further contribution on the significance of REMs was the demonstration of a high positive correlation between REM density (number of REMs per unit time) and the degree to which an awakened subject reports active involvement in or watching dramatic dream events containing much movement as opposed to reports of passively observing more or less static scenes (the latter being positively correlated with the absence of REMs; Berger & Oswald, 1962).[2]

---

[2]This conclusion has been brought into doubt in recent years. Three studies have indicated that the original finding reflected a time of night effect. Dreams occurring later at night are more likely to possess high visual activity. It was the sparseness of REMs in the first REM period that was responsible for the correlation; and when data from the first REM period are excluded, the relationship initially reported between REM activity and visually active dreams vanishes (Firth & Oswald, 1975; Hauri & Van de Castle, 1973b; Keenan & Krippner, 1970). On the other hand,

These three early conclusions—the close association between vivid dream recall and stage REM; the establishment of a biological need (and possibly psychological need as well) for this sleep stage; and the positive correlation between REM density and the subjects' active involvement in dramatic dreams—have provided stimuli for a vast amount of research, the critical review and discussion of which forms most of the substance of this volume. The relevant material lends itself for organization around the following topics.

METHODOLOGY

A striking and disquieting feature of reported results in sleep-mentation investigations has been the marked variability from one laboratory to the next. Much of these discrepancies are due to interlaboratory differences in the techniques of measurement of sleep mentation and the related difficult methodological problems. Accordingly, Antrobus and coworkers, in the chapter on measurement and design, deal extensively with the nature of these problems and describe the cautions and criteria necessary for adequate measurement, evaluation, and comparison of sleep-mentation reports.

An epitomizing example of such interlaboratory disparate results is provided by the variability of findings on NREM recall. Herman and co-workers explore this puzzle in depth. The question of whether NREM mentation actually exists, or should be taken seriously, has occasioned zestful partisanship in the field. And since several studies have proven that biases and expectancies of the investigator may critically influence the nature of the raw data obtained, it is good to have the information provided by well-designed work on the effects of experimenter bias on sleep-mentation reports. Thus, Herman and co-workers present their ingenious study in the second part of their chapter.

REVIEWS OF SLEEP-MENTATION STUDIES

First in order of the night's sequence, mentation associated with the transition from wakefulness to sleep seems an appropriate point of embarkation. Actually, much dreamlike experience occurs during this interval. Vogel has

---

Ellman et al. (1974b), comparing mentation reports from the same approximate time of the night, and keeping elapsed time of REMPs constant (2–4 min after REMP onset), found a weak but statistically significant positive relationship between the immediately prior presence of REM bursts and "dreamlike" mentation reports; and, with the prior absence of REMs, reports from equivalent durations of elapsed REMPs were less dreamlike (see Chapter 5).

been a leading investigator in this field and his work must be taken into account by all theorists interested in formulating models of sleep mentation. Vogel provides a comprehensive review of the phenomenology of sleep onset, a conceptual scaffolding and a discussion of the implications of the hypnogogic state.

In the chapter by Goodenough, we are given a detailed review of the topic of dream recall—an immensely complicated area. Factors affecting the amount and nature of what we remember of our dreams have long concerned clinicians, theoreticians, and philosophers. According to Freud and Bertram Lewin, variables related to intrapsychic "censorship" and repression are of cardinal importance. Do laboratory findings support this claim? If not, what are the most influential factors involved? Goodenough deals with these matters in a profound and gracious manner and relates them to more general concerns.

The chapter by Schwartz and coworkers is more difficult to introduce. Actually, we are not satisfied with its title; yet, we could think of none better. There is a heterogeneous assortment of topics which deserve review, or at least mention, in a book such as this. Methodological considerations not covered earlier, the content of children's dreams, dreams in relation to the menstrual cycle, dreams of the blind, work in the area of psychophysiological parallelism not extensively covered in other chapters, dreams in relation to psychopathological syndromes, and theories of relationships between wakeful life and sleep mentation are all touched on in varying degree. There is some overlap with material in other chapters, yet the emphasis is different. All, in some way, relate to phenomenology and qualitative aspects of sleep mentation. We could have included more—it was difficult to know when to stop.

PSYCHOPHYSIOLOGICAL MODELS OF SLEEP MENTATION

The earlier scientific work on sleep psychophysiology employed as an organizing principle the dichotomy between REM and NREM sleep. So distinctive and remarkable were the characteristics of REM sleep that it was referred to as a "third organismic state" of mammalian life, different from both wakefulness and ordinary sleep. The high positive association between dreamlike experience and REM sleep was an integral feature of this concept. As described by Pivik, Moruzzi proposed a useful scheme in which both REM and NREM sleep stages were viewed as possessing sustained, statelike properties during which sporadic, short-lived events occurred. The former were categorized as *tonic states* and the latter, *phasic events*. With the progress of investigation, reports appeared claiming that dreamlike mentation tended to be more closely associated with phasic event components of REM sleep rather than the tonic state aspects per se.

For example, an influential study claimed that intervals of REM sleep devoid of eye movements were associated with thoughtlike rather than dreamlike mentation, whereas the opposite was true when mentation reports were obtained in the presence of REM bursts. The question then arose as to whether the more useful organizing principle was the tonic state-phasic event dichotomy regardless of sleep stage, rather than the older REM-NREM sleep stage distinction. Was REM-phasic event sleep the "true dreaming sleep" and should REM nonphasic event and NREM sleep be lumped together as the relatively undreamlike sleep? Pivik conducts the reader through the relevant scientific territory in a masterful manner.

EFFECTS OF EXPERIMENTAL VARIABLES ON SLEEP MENTATION

The reader may well imagine that the new availability of detectable physiological events as likely indicators of dreaming provoked a frenzy of experimentation testing the effects of independent variables on sleep mentation. In her chapter, Cartwright considers in comprehensive fashion the effects of the laboratory situation and the person of the experimenter on sleep mentation. Taken up are such questions as whether dreaming is different at home as compared to the laboratory, and whether personal attributes of the experimenter are influential factors. In addition, she presents intriguing data from her own work.

Roffwarg and his colleagues deal with a painstaking investigation, still in progress, of the effects of sustained alteration of sensory experience on dream content. Specifically, if a person were to wear colored spectacles during the entire wakeful day, would this affect the sensory qualities of dreams in some systematic manner? If red goggles were so worn, would dreams be dominated by reddish colors, or would complementary greens suffuse visual dream life as if to compensate for the daily overdose of red? And would effects appear throughout the night's dreams, mostly the earlier or mostly the later ones? If effects are detectable, do they become manifest with the first night of dreaming after a red-goggle day, or is there a time lag? And, is there an analogous lag on termination of goggle wearing? That is, even after the subjects cease wearing goggles, do related color effects linger on for several nights afterward? All of these questions and many more are explored in depth.

In contrast to the previous two focused chapters of Cartwright and of Roffwarg and coworkers, Arkin and Antrobus attempt a panoramic review of the effects of external stimuli applied prior to or during sleep on ongoing mentation. Do we dream about scary or sexually exciting movies viewed prior to sleep? Do words uttered below waking threshold find their way into ongoing dreams? If so, do they appear unchanged or in "disguise" (that is, indirectly)? Is it possible to control dream content by posthypnotic suggestion? Does serious wakeful stress influence dream content? These are but a few of the questions taken up in this part of the book.

Finally, Arkin and Steiner's chapter is devoted to presenting what is known or claimed regarding the effects of various drugs on dream content. As we see, the assessment of such effects is difficult and the work done thus far, on the whole, leaves much unanswered.

EFFECTS OF REMP DEPRIVATION

As mentioned above, assessing the effects of REMP deprivation on a host of variables has understandably received much attention in the field. Accordingly, the three chapters in REM deprivation by Ellman, Arkin, and Hoyt are occupied by a comprehensive exploration of this realm. First, REMP deprivation research in humans and animals is generally reviewed by Ellman and coworkers. Methodological considerations and outcomes of studies are covered in detail. Next, we, the editors, present our own research on the effects of REMP deprivation on sleep mentation. If subjects are prevented from experiencing REMP sleep, does NREM mentation become more dreamlike? Does REM mentation acquire increased dreamlike intensity under conditions of REM deficiency? Is it psychologically important to have sufficient quantities of dream experience? This latter question is discussed further by Hoyt and Singer where the research dealing with wakeful effects of REMP deprivation is reviewed. For example, if we are deprived of REM sleep, do we experience intrusions of dream experience into wakefulness? If, as is claimed by some, psychosis is a form of dreaming in wakefulness, does REM deprivation seem capable of producing incipient psychotic states? How does REMP deprivation affect wakeful cognition generally? Hoyt and Singer also give additional discussion of the event to which experimental results are consistent with theoretical formulations regarding the functions of sleep.

CLINICAL PHENOMENA IN RELATION TO SLEEP MENTATION

In both common sleeptalking and the less common night terrors, subjects verbalize in close proximity to sleep. What might such verbalizations tell us about the content of sleep mentation? Does sleeptalking reflect ongoing dreaming? Does sleep speech betray personal secrets? Is a night terror an unusually intense bad dream? What physiological changes occur in the course of a night terror? Such questions are representative of those taken up in Arkin's chapter on sleeptalking, and the chapter by Kahn, Fisher, and Edwards.

IMPLICATIONS AND FUTURE DIRECTIONS

Arkin's chapter on contemporary sleep research considers the bearing of the new sleep-research findings on the ways in which dreams are utilized clinically. Are such findings inconsistent with attempts to interpret dreams? To what extent are changes in prevalent clinical theories of dream interpretation necessitated by experimental results?

The next chapter, by Antrobus, presents his ideas on relationships between sleep mentation and the general field of cognitive psychology. Is the latter enriched by experimental work on sleep mentation? And how might work in the cognitive psychology of wakefulness lead to better understanding of sleep mentation processes?

In concluding this section, we repeat that our chief concern has been the thorough presentation of the current state of sleep-mentation study as derived mainly from laboratory investigation. The field has not stood still. It has not progressed smoothly, building on a solid, well-established body of knowledge undisturbed by dissonant new findings and difficulties in replication of older ones. Much has happened to stimulate discussion, ferment, controversy, and revision; hence it is time to step back and critically review the field.

We end our introduction with a plea for the readers' indulgence. As we have indicated, the early reports of Aserinsky, Kleitman, and Dement were filled with germinal, provocative, exciting data and conclusions regarding specific relationships of sleep mentation to sleep stages, biopsychological needs for REM sleep, and the like. This body of information comprising the early history of our subject is like the hub of a wheel from which the various chapter topics radiate in spokelike fashion. As editors, we considered the possibility of reducing redundancy to a minimum by confining such historical material to one preliminary section and thereby eliminating as much repetition as possible from the introductory paragraphs of each chapter. When we attempted it, however, we had the feeling that an important element of unity was lost—the authors had taken their departure from the hub and used a review of it as an overture and frame for the succeeding material, each in their own way, to best achieve their overall goals. We therefore decided to retain this background material in each chapter, redundant though much of it may be.

A NOTE ON THE USAGE OF TERMS IN THIS BOOK

In accordance with the recommendations of Rechtschaffen and Kales (1968), we have employed the terms stage REM or REM sleep. The recurrent intervals occupied by such sleep are called REM periods and are often abbreviated as REMPs. Correspondingly, NREM or NREMP is also used.

Finally, in an effort to avoid the hydraulic implications of "REM pressure," we use instead the term REM deficit or deprivation.

ORIENTING REMARKS ON ELECTROGRAPHIC FEATURES OF THE SLEEP CYCLE

For the sake of completeness, we include a concise description of features of the sleep cycle. It has become standard laboratory procedure in sleep research to continually measure at least three electrographic parameters: the EEG, EOG, and chin EMG (Rechtschaffen & Kales, 1968).

The EEG is usually recorded from sites C3 or C4 as defined by the Ten Twenty Electrode System of the International Federation for Electroencephalography and Clinical Neurophysiology. The EOG is usually recorded from both eyes with electrodes applied to a site slightly lateral to and above the outer canthi. In both EEG and EOG, reference electrodes are attached to the contralateral and homolateral earlobe (or mastoid process) respectively. The EMG is recorded bilaterally from the muscle areas on and beneath the chin and it is often termed the mental or submental EMG.

We will now continue with the essential features and changes registered by these electrographic indicators during the course of a night's sleep of "normal" young adults (see Figures I.1–I.7).

When the usual subject is lying quietly in a darkened bedroom immediately after receiving permission to go to sleep, the EEG is likely to show prolonged intervals of more or less sustained alpha rhythm (8–13 Hz; 25–100 µv in amplitude), often with varying admixtures of low-voltage mixed frequencies (LVM); the EOG may contain REMs and eyelid blinks, and the tonic chin EMG is relatively high. This condition is termed stage W.

Presently, as the subject becomes progressively drowsy, there is gradual fragmentation of the sustained epochs of alpha frequencies giving way to shorter intervals of alpha, interspersed with LVM, and finally more or less complete disappearance of alpha and replacement by LVM with 2–7 Hz activity prominent. Vertex sharp waves may appear. REMs and blinks disappear from the EOG and are replaced by slow rolling eye movements (SEMs) or minimal or no eye-movement activity. The tonic EMG is generally below that of the preceding stage W. This condition is termed stage 1 NREM or sleep onset stage 1.

After 5–10 min of stage 1 NREM elapse, sleep spindles and K complexes appear. The former consist of recurrent groups of sinusoidal waves 12–14 Hz in frequency and at least .5 sec in duration. The latter are biphasic EEG forms exceeding 0.5 sec with initial negative sharp wave and succeeding positive components. EOG activity is minimal or absent and the EMG continues at a level lower than related stage W. Such an electrographic picture defines stage 2.

After a varying interval, high-voltage, slow waves occur. These occupy a range in excess of 75 up to 200 µv and are 2 Hz or less in frequency. At first they appear sporadically but gradually increase and come to dominate the EEG.

When such slow waves comprise 20–50% of the EEG, the sleep stage is termed stage 3; and when in excess of 50%, it is termed stage 4. The EOG and EMG continue more or less as before in both stages (sometimes called slow-wave sleep, or SWS, collectively). Stages 1 through 4 are also grouped as NREM or non-rapid eye-movement sleep.

Finally, sometime during the second hour of sleep, polygraphic changes occur which indicate the presence of REM sleep. The EEG consists of relatively low-voltage mixed frequencies with occasional bursts of lower than waking-frequency alpha and "saw-toothed" waves (averaging about 3 Hz). This configuration is correlated with intense CNS activation. The EOG by striking contrast to NREM sleep contains repeated clusters of one or more conjugate rapid eye movements. Finally, the EMG is at its lowest tonic level of the night. The latter corresponds to massive inhibition of muscular activity. Occasionally, brief episodes of increased EMG activity are interspersed with this general background.

These intervals of REM sleep are termed REM periods or REMP(s). The first REMP of the night is usually the shortest, tends to contain the smallest number of REMs, is occasionally omitted entirely, and compared to the subsequent REMPs of the night, is likely to be associated with less mentation and less dreamlike mentation. REMPs may last from a few minutes to times well in excess of a half hour. REMPs reappear on the average of 90 min throughout the night. With the passage of time they tend to become longer and the intervals between them shorter. Healthy young adults have 3–5 REMPs per night (7–8 hrs of sleep).

Following the termination of the REMP, stage 1 NREM typically reappears briefly, and is followed by stage 2. In the first half of the night, stages 3 and 4 succeed stage 2 as before; but in the second half, slow-wave sleep is usually insignificant in amount.

The events from sleep onset stage 1 NREM to the end of the first REMP comprise the first sleep cycle; and subsequent components of the sleep cycle are bounded by events from the end of one REMP to the end of the next, regardless of whether in the last half of the night slow-wave sleep occurs in between. Thus, the typical night of a healthy young adult is characterized by recurrent sleep cycles as described.

In summary, the chief typical electrographic features of the sleep-cycle stages are as follows:

Stage W or wakefulness (see Figs. I.1, I.2)
> EEG: More or less sustained alpha activity, and/or LVM
> EOG: Various amounts of REMs and blinks
> EMG: Relatively high tonic level

Stages NREM
> Stage 1 (Fig. I.2)
> > EEG: LVM, vertex sharp waves
> > EOG: SEMs or no EM activity
> > EMG: Lower than stage W
>
> Stage 2 (Fig. I.3)
> > EEG: Sleep spindles and K-complexes with a background of LVM
> > EOG: Absence of significant EM activity
> > EMG: Lower than stage W
>
> Stage 3 (Fig. I.4)
> > EEG: Moderate accounts of high-amplitude, slow wave activity comprising 20–50% of the epoch
> > EOG: as in stage 2
> > EMG: as in stage 2
>
> Stage 4 (Fig. I.5)
> > EEG: Large amounts of high-amplitude, slow wave activity comprising more than 50% of the epoch
> > EOG: as in stage 2
> > EMG: as in stage 2

Stage REM (Figs. I.6, I.7)
> EEG: LVM, saw-toothed waves, alpha bursts at slightly lower than stage W frequency
> EOG: Recurrent episodes of the conjugate REMs
> EMG: Lowest tonic EMG of the night.

ORIENTATION TO FIGURES

The series of tracings on pages 14–17 are all from the same night with a 25-year-old normal male college student as subject. The specimens were recorded on a Grass Model IV-C electroencephalograph. The paper speed was 15 mm/sec. The time constant for the EEG and EOG was 0.3 sec and the calibration was 1 cm = 50 μv. The time constant for the EMG was 0.03 sec and the calibration was 1 cm = 10 μv.

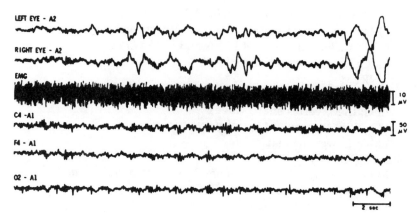

FIGURE I.1.   A tracing illustrating unambiguous stage W. Note high EMG, sustained alpha, and REMs. (From Rechtschaffen & Kales, 1968.)

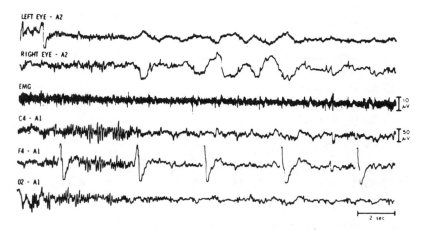

FIGURE I.2.   A tracing illustrating the transition between stage W and stage 1 NREM. Note low-voltage activity replacing alpha, high EMG, and slow eye movements. (From Rechtschaffen & Kales, 1968.)

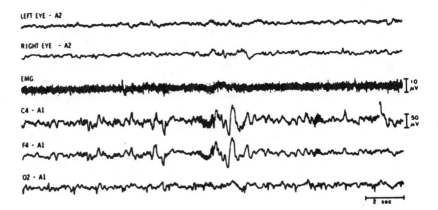

FIGURE I.3. A tracing of unambiguous stage 2. Note spindles and K-complexes. (From Rechtschaffen & Kales, 1968.)

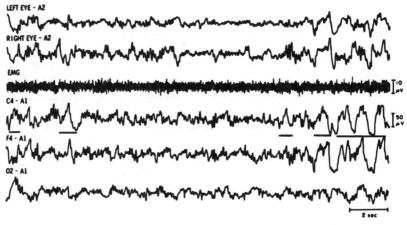

FIGURE I.4. A tracing of stage 3. Note approximately 28% high-amplitude, slow wave activity. (From Rechtschaffen & Kales, 1968.)

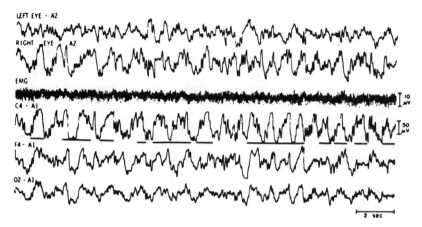

FIGURE I.5. A tracing of unambiguous stage 4. Note predominance of high-amplitude, slow wave activity. (From Rechtschaffen & Kales, 1968.)

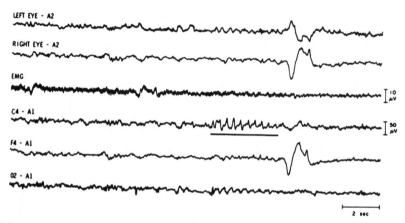

FIGURE I.6. A tracing illustrating transition from stage 2 to stage REM. Note REMs, relatively low-voltage mixed frequencies, saw-toothed waves in C4-A1 derivation (underlined), and decreased tonic EMG. (From Rechtschaffen & Kales, 1968.)

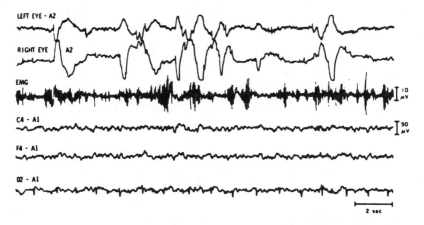

FIGURE I.7.   Unambiguous stage REM. Note REMs, low-voltage tonic EMG with phasic twitching, and relatively low-voltage mixed EEG frequencies. (From Rechtschaffen & Kales, 1968.)

Introduction to the Second Edition

STEVEN J. ELLMAN
City College of the City University of New York

We decided to let this Introduction stand alongside the Introduction to the First Edition, to preserve the original Introduction as Arthur Arkin wrote it and to give the reader a comparative overview of the changes in the field, as reflected in this new book. Research productivity during recent years has been relatively barren, considering the tremendous productivity of earlier decades. Nevertheless, research in the past 10 to 12 years has significantly altered many of the findings in the first edition and thus provided the rationale for this second edition.

Some of the same issues are still current in today's research. The gulf between psychoanalytic conceptions of dreaming and the findings of sleep mentation studies still remains. Freud's theorizing, which attached so much importance to the meaning of the dream, is today being brought into question. One purpose of the present volume is to bring together different researchers' views on the challenge to the meaning of the dream.

In the first edition, we indicated that we could clearly state at least three facts:

1. There is a close association between vivid dream recall and Stage REM (as opposed to other stages of sleep);
2. There is a biological need for REM sleep; if one is deprived of it, it will be made up for (REM rebound);
3. There is a positive correlation between REM density and subjects' report of active involvement in dreams.

In addition, we asked a question:

If REM sleep were eliminated, might there be a separate but related psychological need for nocturnal dream experience?

In attempting to provide an answer, we became involved in the question of REM intensity and dream activity or involvement.

Essentially, the first edition reported that we could not find evidence for the dream experience outside of REM sleep. In this edition, we present quite different evidence by Weinstein, Schwartz, and Ellman (Chapter 11) and by Antrobus and Fookson (Chapter 15), who have extended the view of mentation generated in REM sleep to other conditions outside of REM sleep, including certain waking conditions. The two groups of experimenters have attempted to present evidence for the activity of REM sleep being correlated with the active involvement of mentation reported from this state.

We have expanded this Introduction to include, in the final section, a brief overview of some of the issues in sleep research that are not covered in the book but bear on the type of mentation research that has been undertaken. Some issues in the neurophysiology and neurochemistry of sleep, which we believe have affected research in sleep mentation, are included.

The editors were heartened, when reading the new contributions to this second edition, at the new vitality in dream research.

During the past decade, the fastest growing area of sleep research has been the investigation of sleep disorders. Although surprisingly little research has been done on the mentation that accompanies sleep disorders, we believe this area will prove fruitful for future research. Spielman and Herrera provide an excellent overview of this burgeoning area of sleep research, which may spur some recognition of its implications for mentation research.

PART 1—METHODOLOGY AND SLEEP MENTATION STUDIES

A disquieting feature of sleep mentation studies continues to be the variability in results from one laboratory to another, but this variability is more explicable in light of new methodological considerations. Antrobus and his coworkers (Chapter 2) have added to their chapter in the previous edition, to help account for some of the unexplained variability. Much of their focus is on the underlying assumptions of different techniques of measurement. It is extremely difficult to undertake a sleep mentation study at this point in time and be casual about the type of instrument one will use to measure sleep mentation. This chapter highlights many of the issues that plagued not only sleep researchers but many cognitive and psychophysiological researchers as well.

PART 2—REVIEWS OF SLEEP MENTATION STUDIES

Chapter 3 includes Vogel's original chapter and an update by Bosinelli, an important researcher in this area. Vogel provided not only an excellent review of the sleep onset mentation but also an interesting theoretical model of sleep onset mentation and the role of sleep onset mentation in the process of falling asleep. Is it possible that this model, with some amendations, might be used as a way of conceiving of some sleep onset insomnia problems? Leaving aside this speculation, we regard the update of the sleep onset literature by Bosinelli as excellent. Bosinelli's update follows the chapter and is considered part of this new amalgam. Since Bosinelli's theoretical orientation is different from Vogel's, a comparison of interpretations of sleep onset mentation studies might be interesting.

We decided not to alter Chapter 4 because, in our opinion, this is both a classic chapter and an excellent representation of one interpretation of dream recall studies. Thus Goodenough in this chapter presents an interpretation of the reasons for forgetting dreams (REM sleep mentation). He also presents the corollary; a model for understanding dream recall, or why under some conditions dreams will be remembered. It is such a thorough review and integration that it challenges anyone who has an alternative view to do further research in the area.

Chapter 5 was difficult for Arthur Arkin to describe in the first edition and, although it is clearer and more comprehensible in its revised form, it is still difficult to describe. Perhaps it is most accurate to say that it contains everything we thought was left out of all the other chapters. This may be a slight exaggeration, but it is more true than not. Weinstein, in her update, reviews studies that have been published since our first edition, and she has revised the chapter to improve its organization. The chapter contains a wealth of information about issues of development, psychopathology, organic conditions, etc., as well as the normative content of dreams.

Chapter 6 is an update of Pivik's original chapter. He does a masterful job of presenting the state of the field and the relevant research that has been performed. At the same time Pivik was providing his update, Weinstein, Schwartz, and Ellman were writing Chapter 11, parts of which are directly relevant to the issues that Pivik is reviewing. Pivik has taken an excellent chapter and improved it.

PART 3—EFFECTS OF EXPERIMENTAL VARIABLES ON SLEEP MENTATION

Chapter 7, a revision of Cartwright and Kaszniak's original chapter, further clarifies the role of the experimenter and the laboratory situation in regard to sleep mentation studies. Chapter 8 is unchanged. In Chapter 9, Fiss explores one type of psychoanalytic approach to the study of dream or REM mentation, an approach that draws in part from the area of self-psychology and as such is introducing a modern psychoanalytic development to REM research.

PART 4—EFFECTS OF REM DEPRIVATION

Chapter 10 by Ellman and coworkers is a review of REM deprivation (REMD) literature. Interestingly, REMD has been used widely as a technique and thus continues to generate substantial amounts of research, particularly with animals. Thus the review includes the effects of REMD in animals when these studies include behaviorally dependent measures. Chapter 10 includes an update.

In the first edition, Arkin, Antrobus, Ellman, and Farber reported on an extensive study of the effect of REMD on mentation. This study, outlined in the Introduction to the First Edition, essentially produced negative results. Chapter 11 by Weinstein, Schwartz, and Ellman is an attempt to look at the same issues with new scales and different concepts. Arkin had begun to collaborate on this work right before his death. To briefly restate the issue, the authors were asking: Following REMD, does NREM mentation become more dreamlike? Arkin stated this question in terms of whether it is psychologically important to have the dream experience. There are, of course, different ways of stating this issue; in Chapter 11, they are explored. One might also ask: IF REMD takes place, do we experience REM "intrusions" in wakefulness? Lewin and Singer explore this issue in Chapter 12, which was intended to be an update but has turned out to be new material. In their chapter not only do they explore this issue, but they virtually give an overview and conclusions about the intriguing theoretical issue of the function of REM sleep.

PART 5—CLINICAL PHENOMENA IN RELATION TO SLEEP MENTATION

Chapters 13 and 14 are reprinted in their original form. Arkin's chapter on sleeptalking was a condensed version of his masterful book on that subject. Kahn, Fisher, and Edwards' chapter on night terrors and anxiety dreams presents a valuable perspective on this type of dream and sleep mentation. (There is a reasonable amount of new literature in this area that we were unable to cover.)

PART 6—IMPLICATIONS AND NEW DIRECTIONS

Chapter 15 by Antrobus and Fookson represents a new theoretical approach in attempting to explain the qualities of REM mentation. Antrobus and Fookson's artificial intelligence models are an interesting contrast to Ellman and Weinstein's attempt to explain some of the same phenomena through the use of psychoanalytic theory. Here the reader can compare an approach generated by Freudian thought, with a model that is stimulated by the concept of neural nets. Whether these two types of models can be reconciled, and how they can be compared, is an implicit issue in each chapter. Ellman and Weinstein also try to relate the biological function of REM sleep to dream formation.

NEUROPHYSIOLOGY AND REM SLEEP—A BRIEF REVIEW OF CONTEMPORARY RESEARCH

To entitle this section a review of recent neurophysiological studies is certainly misleading. We only mention recent neurophysiological studies to give the interested reader some introduction to the field and perhaps some sense of the interrelation of sleep mentation studies with studies of the neurophysiology and neurochemistry of sleep.

If we had written this brief review in 1968 it would have been a much easier task. At that time Jouvet (1968, 1972) had solved the problem and "isolated" the centers that control both REM and NREM sleep. Jouvet's research continued experimentation that helped to locate areas in the pons and hindbrain neuronal centers that controlled REM sleep. Aspects of a group of serotonergic nuclei called the Raphe nuclei controlled NREM sleep, and these nuclei, through the breakdown of serotonin, signaled the REM nuclei to commence firing. The nuclei responsible for the initiation and maintenance of REM were considered to be the locus coereleus (LC). Jouvet isolated those parts of this interesting area in the pons which controlled different aspects of REM sleep. For example, one area controlled the atonia of REM sleep, another area controlled the tonic EEG aspects of REM sleep, and yet another area controlled phasic events in REM (i.e., PGO spikes, rapid eye movements, etc.). These past few sentences are written in the past tense, because at least some of Jouvet's findings came into question as a result of subsequent research.

If we had written this introduction in 1977 it would also have been an easier task because the questioning of Jouvet's findings ushered in new research that seemed to indicate that a new REM center had been definitively located. Hobson and McCarley (1975, 1977) stated a model that posited the existence of what they called the REM-on cells in the gigantocellular tegmental field (FTG) of the pontine reticular formation. In direct contrast to Jouvet, they posited that the LC were actually off during REM sleep and these REM-off cells disinhibited or provided the conditions for REM-on cells to fire. This reciprocal-interaction model was stated in mathematical terms and has provided a focus of research to the present time.

Both of these hypotheses postulated different neurochemical substances underlying the initiation and maintenance of REM sleep. In addition, while both sets of investigators performed pharmacological and neurochemical experiments, they used different neurophysiological techniques. Hobson and McCarley utilized single-cell recording; Jouvet mainly performed lesion studies. To paraphrase a recent review by Hobson et al. (1985), it is clear that neither technique alone, and not even both techniques in conjunction, can provide evidence that can unequivocally support the hypothesis of a given area as the generator of REM sleep. In this recent review, Hobson et al. provided a summary of the traditional limitations of various neurophysiological techniques. Hobson, Lydic, and Baghdoyan (1986) also changed the earlier focus; that is, they shifted from postulating a brain center for REM sleep to the idea of distributed and somewhat dispersed "neuronal populations." A review of their arguments is beyond the scope of this Introduction but it is certain that the strong form of the previous Hobson and McCarley argument—that the FTG cells are the generator of REM sleep—has been abandoned.

Up to this point we have mentioned only two groups of investigators' work; but this scarcely does justice to experimenters such as Jones (1985) and Sakai (1985) who have shown that Jouvet was at least partly correct in postulating that the LC is an area responsible for the generation of at least some proportion of REM phasic events. Many other investigators are involved in studies of the neurophysiology and neurochemistry of REM sleep. The interested reader might start with a recent review edited by McGinty and Drucker-Colin (1985). Our purpose in presenting this limited review is to provide some slice of the controversies that continue in the investigation of neural mechanisms in sleep. We think it is particularly useful for the reader to get some feel for these controversies because physiological investigators sometimes hypothesize in a manner that makes the problem of sleep mentation seem to follow logically from their neurophysiological data. Although logically untenable, their position, and arguments frequently receive great attention.

It might be useful to cite an example: Hobson and McCarley (1975) developed a model of mentation based on their neurophysiological findings. Although they have stated their views in different ways, a frequent interpretation of their views (Vogel, 1978) is that REM mentation is simply a response to underlying neurophysiological activation. It is thus considered to be epiphenomenal and a response to the random firing of the FTG cells. Interestingly, Hobson and McCarley's ideas about sleep mentation received a good deal more attention than Vogel's rebuttal of their position, even though Vogel's position was firmly based on data from mentation studies. Thus, although Hobson and McCarley's ideas were interesting and provocative, in our opinion they ignored mentation data and their model allowed for no additional experiments to substantiate it. Even in his brief review, Vogel was able to meet both these criteria.

This evaluation of Hobson and McCarley's work should at least serve as a warning that the issue of the role of neural mechanisms is far from closed and that it is difficult to see mentation studies as simple extensions of neurophysiological models. Part of the difficulty in the history of sleep mentation is the frequency with which psychological hypotheses have been simply translations of a physiological model. The mentation investigator acts as if the physiological conditions were the necessary and sufficient conditions to explain all the variance in a mentation study. This was true in some investigators' versions of the phasic-tonic model; and as was stated in the first edition, from the "phasic-tonic model, there were no clear-cut predictions except for the hope that physiological conditions will be translated directly into psychological events." Thus, the dreamer was seen as a passive recipient rather than an active processor. Leaving aside the philosophical and theoretical difficulties in such an approach, the history of sleep research can be interpreted as advocating an alternative approach. A good many of the chapters in this book seem to go beyond this type of reasoning and offer interesting alternative frameworks. We believe they signal an important change in the field of sleep mentation.

1

Sleep Disorders

ARTHUR SPIELMAN
City College of the City University of New York

CHARLES HERRERA
Mount Sinai School of Medicine of CUNY

INTRODUCTION

Until a few decades ago, individuals with sleep disorders were essentially alone with their problems. They were literally alone at night because there were no means to monitor continuously the fluctuations in physiological processes that might be producing problems while they slept and they were figuratively alone because physicians paid only cursory attention to their complaints.

With the development of the electroencephalograph (EEG) in the late 1930s (Berger, 1969) it became possible to record the changes in brain-wave amplitude and frequency that occur over the course of the night. As clinicians began to see patients who required sleep laboratory monitoring of additional parameters, such as respiratory effort and airflow, oxygen saturation, expired gases, snoring sounds, body movements, cardiac rhythm, body temperature, and gastric acidity, the polygraphic monitoring of these functions changed the dimensions of the all-night recording. What for many years was the standard *sleep recording* consisting of EEG, eye movements, and chin muscle activity has become the *polysomnographic* (PSG) *recording* consisting of the three sleep variables, plus additional parameters specifically chosen to further characterize the individual's presumptive disorder.

While it was the absence of technical means to record the ongoing physiological functions that precluded the nocturnal characterization of the dysfunctions of sleep, the reasons for the medical neglect of these problems are numerous. Conventional wisdom has assumed that physiological functions slow down during sleep and this is a time for repair and restoration, not dysfunction and disease. Therefore, scant attention was directed toward the sleeping phase of the patient's life. As evidence to the contrary has accumulated, the relevant information has neither been disseminated widely to practicing physicians nor integrated into the core curriculum of medical schools. The absence of a clear and primary affiliation with one of the traditional departmental areas of medicine has also contributed to the isolation of the sleep disorders discipline. Major contributions to this new clinical discipline have come from individuals trained in such diverse areas as chronophysiology, endocrinology, neurology, neurochemistry, neurophysiology, physiology, psychiatry, psychology, and pulmonary medicine. Sleep problems produced by physiological dysfunctions in a wide range of organ systems as well as by diverse psychological dysfunctions have necessitated an interdisciplinary approach. An additional aspect of this identity problem has been the development of the clinical sleep disorders out of basic sleep research. Health practitioners, unaware of the clinical applications of basic sleep research findings, assumed that sleep specialists were exclusively engaged in research activities. Therefore, consultation and referral between front-line clinicians and sleep specialists have not been part of the normal relations that exist with other types of patients.

These factors are rapidly changing. There is now a growing awareness of the substantial prevalence of sleep problems, the identification of previously occult disorders with significant morbidity and mortality, the advent of sensitive polysomnographic assessment techniques, the development of effective treatments based on careful diagnostic determination, and availability of specialists in sleep disorders working out of sleep disorders centers. As a result, health practitioners have become aware of this developing field and patients with sleep disorders need no longer feel that they are alone.

The rapid growth of interest in sleep disorders is reminiscent of the excitement surrounding the discovery of Rapid Eye Movement (REM) sleep (Aserinsky & Kleitman, 1953). In 1953, Aserinsky and Kleitman's observation of the temporal association of rapid eye movements, a low-voltage, mixed-frequency EEG, and dreaming created a scientific revolution in psychophysiological studies. Investigators shifted professional commitments to this new area and the modern era of sleep research began. Kleitman's reflections on the reason that this discovery captured the imagination of the scientific community conveys the optimism of this group of early adherents. According to Kleitman, many of the researchers saw the REM sleep–dream association as an opportunity to get a detailed and faithful account of the dream experience not degraded by time. Kleitman believes that this group of clinical researchers hoped that as the "royal road to the unconscious" the dream caught in midstream during an awakening from REM sleep might yield information that would "cure the neurosis" (Kleitman, personal communication, 1982). While this wish has not been fulfilled, the intense focus on this area has yielded a veritable treasure trove of basic findings on the nature of the sleeping organism. The present chapter deals with the application of these sleep research findings in the development of the new field of clinical sleep disorders.

The large number of professionals who have become interested in this new discipline parallels the numerous investigators drawn to the discovery of the association of REM sleep and dreaming. Just as the ranks of basic sleep researchers swelled to mine the ore promised by the discovery of REM sleep, so has there been a corresponding influx of sleep disorders clinicians to forge these raw materials into useful products for the numerous patients in need of help.

SLEEP STAGE SCORING

In 1968 the publication of a manual defining sleep stages in normal human adults was a major advance for standardization of terminology and procedures (Rechtschaffen & Kales, 1968). Although a comprehensive description of the sleep stages and rules for scoring a sleep record is beyond the scope of this report, we will review some basic features of this visual scoring system and discuss the implications of using the system with sleep disorders patients.

Awake, Non-REM sleep, and REM sleep comprise the major divisions for scoring. The category of Non-REM sleep, not a stage score itself, is divided into four separate stage scores: 1, 2, 3, and 4. Stages 3 and 4 are also called slow-wave sleep. The scoring rules for awake and the Non-REM stages are essentially based on the frequency, amplitude, and wave-form morphology of the EEG (Figure 1.1). Identification of stage REM sleep entails the appearance of a mixed frequency EEG, tonically reduced chin electromyogram (EMG) activity, and rapid conjugate eye movements. One of these six stage scores is given for each 20- or 30-second interval, called an epoch. Most of what constitutes the scoring rules is not concerned with the depiction of the stages but rather focuses on the criteria needed to categorize the transitions between stages.

Awake – low voltage – random, fast

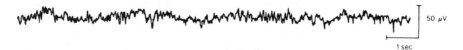

50 µV

1 sec

Drowsy – 8 to 12 cps – alpha waves

Stage 1 – 3 to 7 cps – theta waves

Theta Waves

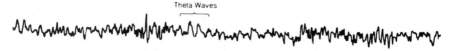

Stage 2 – 12 to 14 cps – sleep spindles and K complexes

Sleep Spindle

K Complex —

Delta Sleep – ½ to 2 cps – delta waves >75 µV

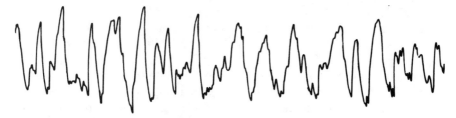

REM Sleep – low voltage – random, fast with sawtooth waves

Sawtooth Waves   Sawtooth Waves

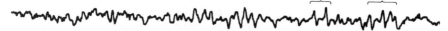

FIGURE 1.1. Human sleep stages. Adapted from the 1982 edition of *Current Concepts: The Sleep Disorders,* by Peter Hauri, PhD, The Upjohn Company. Reprinted with permission.

The early work in sleep research focused on descriptive studies of normal sleep patterns. These studies have shown that over the course of the night, there is an alternation of Non-REM sleep stages and REM sleep with a cycle of about 90 minutes. The majority of the slow-frequency and high-amplitude delta waves that characterize stages 3 and 4 sleep occur in the beginning of the night and REM sleep is more prevalent at the end of the night (Figure 1.2). Additional polygraphic features will be discussed subsequently in the context of the descriptions of the clinical entities.

The definitions of the sleep stages were derived from noncomplaining individuals and did not take into account the myriad aberrations present in the heterogeneous population of sleep disorders patients. While application of these conventions has proven useful in research and much clinical work, the assumptions and limitations of this approach may be profitably re-examined at this time.

In order for the current sleep stage scoring rules to be useful, codification by means of the matrix of correlative events comprising the EEG, eye movements, and EMG activity, must be reliable and valid. Questions arise when any one of these polygraphic features changes or the expected correlative relationship between them changes. We will begin by discussing features of the EEG that were not covered in the scoring manual. For example, EEG alpha frequency of 10 Hz, which is normally present during quiet wakefulness and episodically during REM sleep, may be relatively sustained and riding on the EEG delta frequency of 2 Hz during sleep (Hauri &

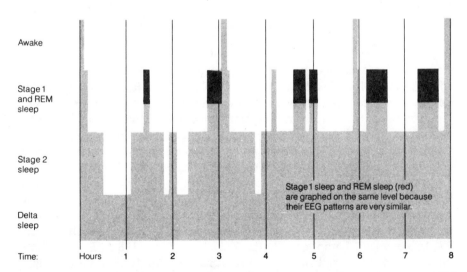

FIGURE 1.2. Typical sleep patterns of a young human adult. Adapted from the 1982 edition of *Current Concepts: The Sleep Disorders*, by Peter Hauri, PhD, The Upjohn Company. Reprinted with permission.

Hawkins, 1973). Is this change in slow-wave sleep fundamental? If so, a reconceptualization is required; if not, is noting this occurrence as alpha-delta sleep along with the traditional stage score a useful adumbration? If we ignore the alpha waves and score the stage based on the proportion of delta waves, reliability may not suffer appreciably, but the validity may be compromised by considering this combination of awake and asleep wave forms as stage 3 or 4 sleep. Another example of this problem is the presence of morphologically distinct sleep spindles concurrent with an otherwise clear cut REM period of rapid eye movements and a tonically suppressed chin EMG. Is this set of correlative features equivalent to the normative REM sleep and does the annotation "with spindles" to the stage REM designation convey a further understanding or flag our ignorance for future clarification?

In patients with senile dementia of the Alzheimer's type, Parkinson's disease, and other brain pathologies, the usually distinct features of the EEG such as spindles and EEG amplitude may be absent or reduced, rendering scoring more difficult and reliability impaired. Likewise, polydrug users may show excessive spindling, beta (>13 Hz), and alpha frequency throughout Non-REM sleep, complicating the decisions in scoring.

Polygraphic abnormalities that produce scoring complications are not confined to the EEG. For example, in drug-free narcoleptics and those taking tricyclical medications there are reports of the EEG and eye movements characteristic of REM sleep in association with a tonically active EMG and long periods of stage 1 EEG with a flat EMG (de Barros–Ferreira & Lairy, 1976; Raynal, 1976). Should this be scored REM sleep or is the designation of ambiguous sleep or REM sleep without EMG suppression sufficient to portray the significance of this finding? In a similar vein, a number of studies have shown that narcoleptics have increased amounts of stage 1 sleep (Montplaisir, 1976; Spielman et al., 1986). However, a case could be made for considering this stage a variant of REM sleep with EEG desynchronization but without eye movements or EMG suppression. The larger point is that once fundamental characteristics of a sleep stage are altered, as they often are in pathological conditions, then considering this new polygraphic configuration equivalent to the conventional sleep stage is an assumption the validity of which awaits further experimental testing.

As currently constituted, the scoring rules use the occurrence of very brief or microarousals to signal possible stage changes. However, recent research has shown that the number of microarousals may be a sensitive indicator of the overall efficacy of sleep (Bonnet, 1985; Rosenthal et al., 1984; Stepanski, Lamphere, Badia, Zorick, & Roth, 1984). In one study normal subjects were briefly awakened repeatedly throughout the night and tested the following day for performance capacity and subjective sleepiness (Bonnet, 1985). On the night of experimenter-induced disruption slow-wave sleep and REM sleep were reduced substantially but conventional scoring showed a reduction of merely 1 hour in total sleep time from baseline values. Following disruption subjects performed poorly, rated themselves as sleepy, and showed recovery sleep on subsequent nights. The magnitude of these effects was similar to that seen following total sleep loss of 24 to 48 hours. This work suggests that there are essential changes in the value of sleep that are not incorporated into the standard scoring system. Similarly, the lack of rules for sleep onset and the periodicity of REM–Non-REM cycles limits the comparability of studies using idiosyncratic definitions of these measures.

When the polysomnographic recording contains information on other physiological parameters, the number of potential combinations of this expanded correlation matrix becomes staggering. What has become standard practice is to retain the standard scoring system and annotate the additional physiological parameters that are assessed. For example, a condition called periodic movements or nocturnal myoclonus has recently been described in which some of the leg movements that occur are temporally tied to the appearance of alpha frequency in the EEG. Easily discernible, the number and density of these arousals is predictive of the kind of complaint and degree of daytime impairment (Rosenthal et al., 1984; Stepanski et al., 1984). Yet nowhere in the conventional scoring system is this finding incorporated. While one cannot fault the scoring system for leaving out features not discovered at the time of its publication, it is important to recognize that at present polysomnographic reports have become long lists of scores of physiological events that the individual sleep laboratory deems important. For example, some labs report total numbers of periodic movements; others indicate the number associated with arousals or break down these measures into the proportion in particular sleep stages. There is no question that the significance of these types of differences awaits the outcome of studies of the validity and usefulness of these distinctions. At present, the field must be content with the proliferation of multiple scores the value of which have not yet been definitively established. A major reconceptualization and synthesis is clearly needed.

The situation is even more critical in the PSG assessment of patients with sleep-related respiratory impairment. The number of variables of interest are numerous and include the number and duration of apneas (defined as the cessation of airflow of greater than 10 seconds) and hypopneas (defined as an incomplete reduction of airflow volume of at least 50%), the degree and pattern of oxygen desaturation and expired CO_2, the relative proportion of occlusive (obstructive and mixed apneas) versus nonocclusive (central or diaphragmatic apneas) disturbances, and the pattern of these changes in REM and Non-REM sleep. While some progress has been made toward standardization (Martin et al., 1984), an integration of these numerous and diverse findings or, short of this, a determination of the relative importance of different findings has yet to be made. Coordination is needed so that a core set of variables is standard reporting practice from sleep disorders centers. The current, and intolerable, state of affairs makes it difficult for a health care practitioner unacquainted with sleep to appreciate the significance of PSG findings. While it is appropriate for referring clinicians to rely on sleep specialists to interpret test results, the data base from which these conclusions are reached should have substantial overlap between different centers.

The high-speed computer analysis of the PSG for EEG power spectra and topographical mapping combined with other physiological parameters may lead to a radical revision of scoring practices and scoring categories, but this promise has yet to be realized.

SLEEP HISTORY

Until recently the thorough history was the exception in the clinical work-up of patients complaining of sleep problems. This was due to the considerable limitations in our knowledge of what information was relevant and what the differential diagnostic possibilities might be. Furthermore, the limited number of therapeutic options available often rendered the assessment an exercise in futility. The presumption that the results of the clinical evaluation were more than likely to be some form of symptomatic treatment vitiated the motivation for a systematic inquiry and resulted in a perfunctory assessment. The substantial corpus of work that has resulted from the emerging discipline of sleep disorders has begun to change the manner in which clinicians approach these problems.

The creation of the Nosology of Sleep and Arousal Disorder (Roffwarg, 1979) deserves much of the credit for the renewed zeal for the diagnostic enterprise. This landmark work, the product of a committee of experts chaired by Howard P. Roffwarg, has resulted in standardization of terminology and descriptions of the clinical entities. The text of the nosology reviews the relevant historical features of the disorders including course, age at onset, impairment, complications, predisposing factors, prevalence, sex ratio, and familial pattern. The nosology has made it possible to compare research and clinical work in different laboratories. Validity studies employing multivariate analysis and PSG data for the Disorders of Initiating and Maintaining Wakefulness (alternatively called the Insomnias) and two large cooperative case series studies have already demonstrated the coherence and usefulness of this classificatory system (Hauri, 1984; Coleman, 1983; Coleman, Roffwarg, Kennedy, et al., 1982).

Clarifying the Complaint

In most cases the patient's response to the opening question, "What is the problem?" will direct the inquiry to one of the four major diagnostic categories of the ASDC nosology (Table 1.1). Reports of the inadequacy of sleep point to the insomnias; daytime sleepiness is the hallmark of the disorders of excessive somnolence; problems with the timing, duration, and scheduling of sleep and wakefulness suggest the disorders of the sleep–wake schedule; and an assortment of abnormal events that occur during sleep or are exacerbated by sleep indicate the parasomnias. The character of the complaints associated with each major division will be discussed subsequently in conjunction with the specific disorders.

Because the organizational basis of the nosology is patients' perception of the problem rather than etiological factors, the complaint is the natural starting point for the diagnostic inquiry. Complaints such as tiredness and fatigue are common in patients presenting in sleep disorders centers and general medical practice. One medical survey ranked fatigue as the seventh most frequent initial complaint (National Center for Health Statistics, 1978). A prevalent problem, the wide range of disorders in which fatigue plays some role renders it a nonspecific symptom (Solberg, 1984). Experiential states sharing features with tiredness and fatigue include lack of energy, weariness, exhaustion, lethargy, lassitude, weakness, sleepiness, inadequacy, a desire for rest and reduced interest, motivation, and stick-to-it-iveness. A consensus definition and means of quantifying tiredness and fatigue have not yet been achieved. A survey of the available evidence from five studies of diverse medical settings not specializing in sleep disorders suggests that more than 50% of cases of fatigue have a psychological origin (Valdini, 1985). However, in all of these studies insomnia is assumed to be one of the indicators that signifies that the fatigue is psychologically caused. The shared experience of multiple centers specializing in the evaluation and treatment of sleep disorders indicates that approximately half of the cases of insomnia are produced by organic factors unrelated to psychiatric disorders or maladaptive conditioning (Coleman, 1983; Coleman et al., 1982). Therefore, one can conclude that a sizable proportion of patients presenting in medical settings with fatigue also have insomnia and that in half of these cases there is an unwarranted conclusion that the cause is psychogenic.

While we are casting a critical eye, let us look at practices in sleep disorders centers. It is possible that a subsample of cases with fatigue as a prominent symptom diagnosed as insomnia associated with psychiatric disorders or maladaptive conditioning (called psychophysiological insomnia), idiopathic disorders of excessive somnolence, and those associated with psychiatric disorders may have unsuspected organic conditions. However, two of the studies of fatigue (Allan, 1944; Morrison, 1980) and two reviews have concluded that when the duration of the fatigue is prolonged, especially longer than four months, there is an increased likelihood of a psychological etiology. Since the overwhelming majority of cases with insomnia and sleepiness seen in sleep disorders centers have a long history of the complaint, missing an organic basis for the complaint is less likely.

TABLE 1.1.   DIAGNOSTIC CLASSIFICATION OF SLEEP AND AROUSAL DISORDERS

A. DIMS: Disorders of Initiating and Maintaining Sleep (Insomnias)
   1. Psychophysiological
       a. Transient and Situational
       b. Persistent
   2. associated with Psychiatric Disorders
       a. Symptom and Personality Disorders
       b. Affective Disorders
       c. Other Functional Psychoses
   3. associated with Use of Drugs and Alcohol
       a. Tolerance or Withdrawal from CNS Depressants
       b. Sustained Use of CNS Stimulants
       c. Sustained Use or Withdrawal from Other Drugs
       d. Chronic Alcoholism
   4. associated with Sleep-induced Respiratory Impairment
       a. Sleep Apnea DIMS Syndrome
       b. Alveolar Hypoventilation DIMS Syndrome
   5. associated with Sleep-related (Nocturnal) Myoclonus and "Restless Legs"
       a. Sleep-related (Nocturnal) Myoclonus DIMS Syndrome
       b. "Restless Legs" DIMS Syndrome
   6. associated with Other Medical, Toxic, and Environmental Conditions
   7. Childhood-Onset DIMS
   8. associated with Other DIMS Conditions
       a. Repeated REM Sleep Interruptions
       b. Atypical Polysomnographic Features
       c. Not Otherwise Specified
   9. No DIMS Abnormality
       a. Short Sleeper
       b. Subjective DIMS Complaint without Objective Findings
       c. Not Otherwise Specified
B. DOES: Disorders of Excessive Somnolence
   1. Psychophysiological
       a. Transient and Situational
       b. Persistent
   2. associated with Psychiatric Disorders
       a. Affective Disorders
       b. Other Functional Disorders
   3. associated with Use of Drugs and Alcohol
       a. Tolerance to or Withdrawal from CNS Stimulants
       b. Sustained Use of CNS Depressants
   4. associated with Sleep-induced Respiratory Impairment
       a. Sleep Apnea DOES Syndrome
       b. Alveolar Hypoventilation DOES Syndrome
   5. associated with Sleep-related (Nocturnal) Myoclonus and "Restless Legs"
       a. Sleep-related (Nocturnal) Myoclonus DOES Syndrome
       b. "Restless Legs" DOES Syndrome
   6. Narcolepsy

7. Idiopathic CNS Hypersomnolence
8. associated with Other Medical, Toxic, and Environmental Conditions
9. associated with Other DOES Conditions
    a. Intermittent DOES (Periodic) Syndromes
        i. Kleine-Levin Syndrome
        ii. Menstrual-associated Syndrome
    b. Insufficient Sleep
    c. Sleep Drunkenness
    d. Not Otherwise Specified
10. No DOES Abnormality
    a. Long Sleeper
    b. Subjective DOES Complaint without Objective Findings
    c. Not Otherwise Specified

C. Disorders of the Sleep-Wake Schedule
  1. Transient
    a. Rapid Time Zone Change ("Jet Lag") Syndrome
    b. "Work Shift" Change in Conventional Sleep-Wake Schedule
  2. Persistent
    a. Frequently Changing Sleep-Wake Schedule
    b. Delayed Sleep Phase Syndrome
    c. Advanced Sleep Phase Syndrome
    d. Non-24-Hour Sleep-Wake Syndrome
    e. Irregular Sleep-Wake Pattern
    f. Not Otherwise Specified

D. Dysfunctions Associated with Sleep, Sleep Stages, or Partial Arousals (Parasomnias)
  1. Sleepwalking (Somnambulism)
  2. Sleep Terror (Pavor Nocturnus, Incubus)
  3. Sleep-related Enuresis
  4. Other Dysfunctions
    a. Dream Anxiety Attacks (Nightmares)
    b. Sleep-related Epileptic Seizures
    c. Sleep-related Bruxism
    d. Sleep-related Headbanging (Jactatio Capitis Nocturna)
    e. Familial Sleep Paralysis
    f. Impaired Sleep-related Penile Tumescence
    g. Sleep-related Painful Erections
    h. Sleep-related Cluster Headaches and Chronic Paroxysmal Hemicrania
    i. Sleep-related Abnormal Swallowing Syndrome
    j. Sleep-related Asthma
    k. Sleep-related Cardiovascular Symptoms
    l. Sleep-related Gastroesophageal Reflux
    m. Sleep-related Hemolysis (Paroxysmal Nocturnal Hemoglobinuria)
    n. Asymptomatic Polysomnographic Finding
    o. Not Otherwise Specified

Adapted from Association of Sleep Disorders Centers Classification Committee: Diagnostic Classification of Sleep and Arousal Disorders, first edition. Copyright 1979 by Raven Press. Reprinted by permission of the ASDC and Raven Press.

Nevertheless, the diagnostic evaluation of insomnia and the disorders of excessive somnolence should be informed by the physical causes of fatigue identified in medical settings outside of sleep disorders centers. In decreasing order of magnitude, infection, cardiovascular, endocrine, medications, and hematological factors comprised 81% of the physical causes of fatigue (Solberg, 1984).

Presented with the initial report of tiredness and fatigue, the clinician's job is to determine whether these complaints are reflective of either drowsiness, sleepiness, and daytime napping, suggesting the disorders of excessive somnolence, or lack of energy and reduced motivation, suggesting the insomnias. Another common difference between the complaints in these two diagnostic categories is that the patients with the disorders of excessive somnolence are often unaware of problems with their nocturnal sleep, whereas the insomnia patient is all too ready to blame the inadequacy of their sleep for a panoply of problems.

A number of approaches will improve the fidelity of the complaint. The sleep log, filled out daily, is of immense value. Designed so that a visual picture of the sleep–wake behavior can be discerned, the essential issues of the case often emerge from a pattern analysis. The best diaries are laid out so that the subjective estimate of the time of getting into and out of bed, time of sleep onset, and the timing and duration of daytime naps and nocturnal awakenings are indicated with symbols on a plot of the 24-hour day. Seven or 14 successive days are lined up vertically for a pictorial representation. With this type of richly detailed chart the clinician can, with a glance, determine the importance of factors such as the variability of retiring and arising times, the frequency and severity of sleep onset and sleep maintenance difficulties, and napping pattern. One feature of the diary that has been overlooked is the variability of the distribution of wakefulness within the sleep period. While it is well established that the variability of lights-out and lights-on times may contribute to the production and perpetuation of insomnia, there has not been a similar appreciation of the importance of the variability of nocturnal wakefulness. Development of a new behavioral treatment of chronic insomnia, called Sleep Restriction Therapy, was based, in part, on the recognition that too much time in bed promotes nocturnal wakefulness, which interferes with the self-sustaining properties of a consolidated sleep–wake cycle (Spielman, Saskin, & Thorpy, 1983, 1987).

Supplementing the diary with questions such as substance intake (e.g., sedative/hypnotic/alcohol/caffeine), amount of exercise, and estimate of total sleep time provides important ancillary information. A standardized diary is essential. Repeated analysis with the same layout builds a wealth of clinical experience and spares the clinician from the patient's own idiosyncratic diary, which is often unreadable and filled with superfluous details.

Interviewing the patient's bed partner can be valuable in some cases. If unsure of the patient's history, then the bed partner's report may corroborate the accuracy of the patient's reports and offers a different perspective. The presence of conflicting bedtime rituals and schedules, and information regarding the patient's snoring, body movements, and other sleep-related behaviors are often furnished by the bed partner. Furthermore, attitudes of the sleeping partner that may undermine treatment of the patient may be uncovered. The clinician may be able to nip in the bud the bed partner's resistance and facilitate a collaborative relationship.

Daytime Consequences

There is increasing recognition that the adequacy of sleep is best judged by its effects on daytime functioning and well-being (Institute of Medicine, 1979) rather than by proportion, amount, or sequencing of particular sleep stages. Thus broadly conceived, the entire gamut of sleep disorders can have profound effects on capacity, quality of life, and morbidity.

The importance of the subjective perception of sleep and the use of sleeping medications was underscored by a 6-year prospective study of more than 1 million people, which found that increased mortality risk was associated with individuals reporting (a) less than 4 hours of sleep per night; (b) more than 9 1/2 hours of sleep per night; or (c) using sleeping pills "often" (Hammond, 1964; Kripke, Simons, Garfinkel, & Hammond, 1979). Although a correlative study, which must be interpreted with caution, these results clearly identify the subjective report of low and high amounts of sleep and insomnia problems as key indexes of health.

Difficulty Initiating and Maintaining Sleep (Insomnias).   Individuals with insomnia may spend much of the waking day thinking, planning, and worrying about their sleep disturbance. As the day progresses, insomniacs become increasingly preoccupied with whether the coming night's sleep will be adequate. As night approaches, this anticipatory anxiety may become so intense that heightened physiological arousal may occur, thus making sleep even more difficult (Kales, Caldwell, Preston, Healey & Kales, 1976). Contributing to this intense preoccupation is the night-to-night variability of the sleep and corresponding daytime deficits in insomniacs (Karacan, Williams, Littel, & Salis, 1973). Because some nights will be disturbed with poor performance and mood the next day while other nights will be relatively undisturbed with compensatory increases in sleep and restored daytime capacity, the insomniac learns to expect that sleep and daytime functioning will vary widely. This uncertainty about the adequacy of the upcoming night's sleep perpetuates the anticipatory anxiety, which then becomes a self-fulfilling prophecy. Furthermore, the worry over the unreliability of sleep and the erratically occurring daytime deficits impairs

planning. Not knowing if disturbed sleep will sap motivation and impair concentration and mood, the insomniac is hesitant to plan demanding activities, such as complex cognitive tasks. This vacillation produces interpersonal and work-related problems.

Lacking mastery over sleep, individuals with insomnia feel out of control and their self-concept reflects this loss of autonomy. Although it is not clear how much characteristics such as complaining, worrying, irritability, and mild depression are the cause or the effect of insomnia, these features become psychological realities for these patients and personality patterns crystallize around these traits.

Sleep disturbance in young children and toddlers affects the child and the parents, and often leads to a vicious circle of consequences. All parents know the crankiness that an occasional night of disturbed or insufficient sleep will produce in their child. When a child's sleep disturbance is habitual rather than occasional the moodiness and restriction of attention color and constrain their experience and may produce long-lasting effects. But it is important to note that ministering to a sleepless child results in *parental* sleep fragmentation and sleep loss, which produces sleepiness, reduced motivation, and mild depression. The compromised condition of both the child and the caretaker will affect the quality of their interaction. While many different scenarios are possible we will depict only one possible outcome to convey the intra- and interpersonal consequences of a young child's sleep problem. The considerable prevalence and consequences of childhood sleep problems are reasons enough to draw out the implications of this problem. However, with a few small changes, the example is illustrative of how sleep disturbance in couples as well as parents and children may serve as a precipitating factor that becomes part of a self-perpetuating pattern (Wachtel, 1977).

The cranky demandingness of a little boy with a sleep disturbance can be conceptualized as having two aspects. One component is expressive in that it portrays his physical discomfort. The second part is communicative (or, alternatively, instrumental) in that it signals his need for others to soothe him because his own efforts are unsuccessful. Sapped of motivation and energy, the sleep deprived parent is not as responsive as usual and delays comforting the child until the demands reach a certain pitch. This type of interaction is repeated over and over and as a result the child learns a number of lessons as follows. First, discomfort is inevitable and must be endured because relief is not immediately available. Second, the child learns that different intensities of his communicative efforts produce different outcomes. At a lower intensity requests for help are useless, while at a higher intensity plaintive demandingness brings relief via the parents' ministrations. With repetition, the anticipation of discomforts and both hopeless and demanding complaining become ingrained parts of the child's behavioral repertoire. If other conditions are also met, then the beginnings of a depressive outlook are becoming established in the child. It is not hard to imagine that as the child's insomnia, moodiness, and complaining are repeated, the parents become discouraged and even more taxed. As a result, the parents become less responsive to the child and the vicious circle is completed. The self-perpetuating nature of this type of interaction underscores the long-range effects possible from a child's sleep disturbance.

In recent years attention has been focused on the decrements in alertness and performance on the day following nighttime sedative-hypnotic administration. The hangover effects documented in systematic studies include deficits in reaction time, memory, calculation, and sleepiness (Carskadon, Seidel, Greenblatt, & Dement, 1982; Johnson and Chernik, 1982; Oswald, Adam, Borrow, & Idzikowski, 1979; Roth, Hartse, Saab, Piccione, & Kramer, 1980). These effects have been attributed, in part, to the presence of active metabolites in the blood up to several days after a single dose of certain benzodiazepines (Greenblatt, Divoll, MacLaughlin, Harmatz, & Shader, 1981). For example, the major metabolite of flurazepam, the most popular hypnotic, has a half-life of 40 to 150 hours (Greenblatt, Allen, & Shader, 1977). This makes it difficult for an insomniac who relies on a hypnotic with moderate or long half-life to distinguish between daytime deficits due to sleep disturbance or hypnotic use. The issue of reduced alertness is not confined to patients taking hypnotics. While it is not true of the majority of insomniacs it has been shown that a proportion of this patient group have a degree of daytime sleepiness that is considered pathological (Sidel & Dement, 1982).

Disorders of Excessive Somnolence.   These disorders have a profound impact on patients' physical, psychological, and social functioning. The cardiopulmonary effects of obstructive sleep apnea are well documented. In addition to the morbidity of systemic and pulmonary hypertension; increased vulnerability to stroke, cardiac arrhythmias, cardiomegaly, and reduced right ventricular ejection fraction, there is the risk of sudden death (Guilleminault & Dement, 1978). In narcolepsy, which is the second most common cause of daytime sleepiness, lifelong stimulant use is likely and may contribute to hypertension and swings in mood due to tolerance effects and the onset and offset of action of these psychoactive drugs.

The social and psychological impact of sleepiness, the feature common to the disorders of excessive somnolence, cannot be underestimated. Sleepiness is a global condition that affects vigilance, attention, cognition, motivation, mood, and performance. Certain tasks are more vulnerable to the disruptive effects of sleepiness than others. Studies have shown that sleepiness has a profound impact on driving. One study showed that almost 73% of narcoleptics have fallen asleep while driving and more than 39% have had auto accidents due to falling asleep (Broughton & Ghanem, 1976).

These are impressive statistics and underscore the intensity of the drowsiness that cannot be suppressed in life-threatening situations. While characterization of the severity of a disorder is multidetermined (Spielman, 1984), in our view, the presence of near-obligatory sleepiness while driving must be given overriding consideration in an individual who must drive. Other sedentary activities that demand concentration and reflection are especially vulnerable to the insistent intrusion of sleepiness and sleep. In contrast, if a task involves physical activity, sleepiness may be masked. The partial clouding of consciousness that accompanies sleepiness reduces the range and sharpness of cognitive processes. Work functioning and relationships may suffer. Therefore, the history of the current complaint should ascertain the severity of sleepiness in a representative sample of activities and the social and economic consequences of these deficits.

The psychological consequences of pathological sleepiness are far reaching. One of the features of sleepiness that creates psychological problems is that sleepiness is a normal experience. Determining the level of sleepiness that demarcates normal from abnormal sleepiness is no easy matter for the patient. Therefore, patients are often unable to label their sleepiness as a medical symptom or as a pathological physiological process. Furthermore, there is a lack of social awareness of the medical implications of sleepiness so that the patient has no frame of reference for viewing drowsiness as a symptom of a medical disorder. On the contrary, there is ample social context that views sleepiness as representing psychologically meaningful behavior such as boredom, dissatisfaction, a dissolute life-style, and laziness. In short, sleepiness has not been legitimized as a symptom of physical illness.

Disorders of the Sleep–Wake Schedule.   The consequences of sleep–wake schedule disturbances are varied. Patients with delayed sleep phase disorder are habitually up late at night and cannot get up in the morning (Weitzman, Czeisler, & Coleman, 1981). Lateness and morning performance decrements may be interpreted by employers as reflective of poor motivation or expressions of hostility. Individuals with this problem often seek out jobs with late or flexible hours. In this and other insomnia disorders the difference between sleep during the workweek and weekend or how well one sleeps on long vacations helps assess the contribution of job-related stress and socially imposed sleep–wake schedules on the insomnia. Patients with work shift or other causes of frequent changes in their sleep–wake schedule must contend with lack of regularity in their circadian periodicity that can interact with the mild sleep loss that they invariably suffer (Johnson, 1974). This may result in considerable performance decrements. Night tours of duty and other schedules that preclude the individual's family or social participation may be a hardship. Gastrointestinal problems are common in these conditions.

Disorders Associated with Sleep, Sleep Stages, or Partial Arousals (Parasomnias). The group of problems subsumed under the rubric of parasomnias are diverse and the consequences of these conditions are varied. Each condition produces its own set of unique problems—for example, dental deterioration due to bruxism, injuries resulting from somnambulism or sleep-related head banging, and dirty laundry generated from enuresis. In addition to the specific effects of the problem these patients are often embarrassed and suffer social or familial stigma. In one memorable and extreme case, a woman's night terrors were so loud and frequent that her neighbors took legal steps to evict her. Whether the nocturnal event is bruxism, a sleep-related seizure, somnambulism, or another event, the noise and movements produced by the patient may disrupt the sleep of the bed partner.

In summary, assessment of the daytime consequences of the sleep disorder is of central importance in determining its severity, the indications for treatment, and for establishing a base rate against which treatment outcome can be compared.

DISORDERS OF INITIATING AND MAINTAINING SLEEP (INSOMNIAS)

To understand this group of conditions it is essential to keep in mind the differences between complaint, disorder, and pathogenetic process. The patient's subjective report of difficulty falling asleep, difficulty staying asleep, early morning awakenings, unrefreshing sleep, sleeping lightly, needing sleeping pills in order to sleep, and daytime consequences such as fatigue, impaired concentration, and mood disturbance, comprise the major insomnia complaints. These descriptions are not equivalent to the disorder of insomnia. Like the report of pain in medical examinations, a patient's complaint of unsatisfactory sleep should be the starting point of an investigation that leads to a formulation of the case summarized in a diagnostic conclusion that suggests appropriate treatment. A disorder of insomnia is one of the diagnostic categories used in a nosological scheme such as that adopted by the Association of Sleep Disorders Centers (Roffwarg, 1979). Because the etiology and pathogenesis of the vast majority of sleep disorders is unknown, the Association of Sleep Disorders Centers nosology is based on descriptive features. Therefore, to depict these conditions comprehensively requires going beyond diagnostic statements, toward speculation as to the origins and pathological processes responsible.

In the evaluation of insomnia it has been proposed that in addition to the standard survey and problem-solving approach, a schema for classifying case material into predisposing, precipitating, and perpetuating factors is useful (Spielman, 1986). This categorization aims to highlight the features of a case that set the stage for, contribute to, trigger, and are currently producing, the insomnia. Formulations based on this schema allow for the most comprehensive treatment planning. This schema helps focus attention on perpetuating factors in addition to precipitating circumstances. Traditionally, precipitating circumstances are viewed as the best clue to the origin of the insomnia. This other point of view posits that in a sizable proportion of cases of chronic insomnia the factors that triggered the insomnia are no longer operating to maintain the sleep disturbance. The insomnia has become functionally autonomous from its origins and other factors are currently responsible for sustaining the insomnia. In these cases, the perpetuating factors are the necessary and sufficient factors that must be addressed in treatment. Clinical experience suggests that the most common perpetuating factors are excessive time in bed, napping, variable retiring and arising times, drug and alcohol use, and conditioning.

Because predisposing conditions serve as contributing factors or establish a propensity for the genesis of the insomnia, then neglecting these conditions in treatment planning will weaken the intervention or will leave the patient vulnerable to relapse or recurrence of the insomnia. In addition, if the patient learns how the predisposing factors operate, then if these factors surface in the future the patient will be able to take corrective steps and avert an insomnia.

Categorizing the insomnias as primary or secondary is another approach toward specifying the processes responsible for the sleep disturbance. In the secondary insomnias there exists a clinical entity that has a deleterious effect on sleep. For example, the pain of arthritis, the irregular nocturnal respiration of chronic obstructive pulmonary disease, the reduced mobility of Parkinson's disease, and nocturnal asthma are disorders with processes that interfere with sleep. The treatment of certain medical conditions, such as beta-blockers for cardiac arrhythmias and theophyline for pulmonary conditions, may also secondarily produce sleep problems. Another group of secondary insomnias includes conditions that while regularly associated with insomnia there is only a presumption that a mechanism of the condition produces the sleep disturbance. Major depressive disorders exemplify this group, in that insomnia is such a regular and characteristic feature of these conditions that it is one of their diagnostic criteria (American Psychiatric Association, 1982). However, the insomnia of depression is merely presumed to be produced by some as yet unspecified process that is an inherent part of the depression. The primary insomnias involve abnormalities of the processes inherent to sleep in the absence of disorders or treatments that affect sleep. For example, the sleep disturbance due to rotating shift work, spending too much time in bed, irregular sleep–wake habits, napping, or discrete lesions of hypnogenic CNS sites directly affect the basic biological and behavioral substrates that control the timing, triggering, and duration of sleep.

While daytime consequences such as fatigue, inability to concentrate, and worrying about sleeplessness are common, there is the occasional patient who reports no daytime consequences of the insomnia but rather just the discomfort of trying to fall asleep. In this case appropriate behavioral or cognitive restructuring approaches may be needed. The target of this treatment should not be to improve sleep but to eliminate or shift the wakefulness and reduce the distress associated with trying to sleep.

A comprehensive survey of drug usage is an integral part of a complete history. When the drug is started, the type, intake regimen, dosage, response, and side effects should be ascertained for each prescription, over the counter, and illicit drugs, as well as certain dietary substances (e.g., caffeine and alcohol) ingested. Performance deficits and mood disturbance on the morning following bedtime ingestion of sedative-hypnotics should be routinely assessed. Assessing the drug hangover contribution to morning tiredness, lethargy, and dysphoria is an important part of taking a drug history. On the other side of the coin, the newer, short half-life, benzodiazepine hypnotics, marketed to avoid drug-hangover effects, have been reported to produce an early morning insomnia, which may also be part of the presenting symptom complex of insomnia (Kales & Kales, 1983). Alcohol is one of the most commonly used substances in the evening and is often taken to help induce sleep. Clinical experience has shown that alcohol does facilitate sleep induction but produces a marked sleep maintenance insomnia.

Numerous studies have shown that there is a discrepancy between an insomniac's report of sleep latency and total sleep time and polygraphic determination of these parameters (Carskadon et al., 1976; Frankel, Coursey, Buchbinder & Snyder, 1976). However, high correlations between reported and recorded parameters such as sleep latency and total sleep time demonstrate there is a correspondence between the severity of the complaint and the polygraphic findings (Carskadon et al., 1976; Frankel et al., 1976; Spielman et al., 1987). Unlike the procedure in some quantifiable lab tests the table of normative sleep values that are available have not generally been used to determine if a patient's average amount of sleep or speed of falling asleep are within the normal range. Sleep clinicians do not rely on the normative values because sleep of noncomplaining individuals varies widely. In fact, while a number of controlled studies have shown that the sleep of insomniacs and controls differs, other studies have demonstrated a large overlap (Carskadon et al., 1976) in the sleep of these two groups. Therefore, the complaint and history of trouble sleeping and daytime consequences must be relied upon to focus the inquiry. Recognizing the importance of the history and what to ask is essential in the assessment of insomnia (Guilleminault, 1982; Roffwarg & Altshuler, 1982).

The PSG recording permits objective documentation of the sleep problem, including comparison of recorded and reported sleep parameters and measurement of key physiological processes (Guilleminault, 1982). Sleep, by its very nature, prevents awareness of events that occur during sleep. Respiratory irregularities, periodic movements, and other episodic events may be entirely occult and their significance may only emerge following an all-night PSG assessment. However, insomnia is such a common health complaint that PSG evaluation is impractical in all cases, and unnecessary in most. The clearest indications for PSG assessment include the following: chronic insomnia, especially in cases that have been unresponsive to treatment; suspected sleep apnea or nocturnal myoclonus; insomnia with concurrent medical conditions; and ruling-out sleep apnea prior to the initiation of hypnotic drug therapy in vulnerable individuals such as the elderly and those with pulmonary problems. In patients reporting no sleep at all, a PSG recording can be of use, by way of reassurance, in objectively demonstrating that they indeed do sleep. A PSG recording, in a patient who complains of abrupt awakenings from sleep with difficulty breathing, will assess whether nocturnal anxiety or some physiological event such as a respiratory disturbance, cardiac arrhythmia, gastroesophageal reflux, or body movement is precipitating the arousal. The advent of PSG recording has uncovered many occult somatic causes of insomnia, and even seemingly clear cases of psychologically based insomnia may have physiological determinants (Roffwarg & Altshuler, 1982). Screening recordings may uncover atypical polysomnographic features, such as alpha frequency EEG activity interspersed throughout the non-REM sleep stages. This alpha-delta activity may be associated with the complaint of light or nonrestorative sleep (Hauri & Hawkins, 1973). The PSG may serve a role in evaluating the patient with insomnia and concurrent depression. A short REM sleep latency (i.e., time from sleep onset to the first appearance of REM sleep of less than 50 minutes) has been shown to be one of the biological markers of primary depression, increases the diagnostic certainty of a biological depression, and contributes to the indications for antidepressant drug therapy (Kupfer & Thase, 1983).

What follows is a review of the most common insomnia disorders organized according to the ASDC nosology. We have chosen this diagnostic framework over the primary/secondary and predisposing/precipitating/perpetuating schemata because of its widespread use.

Psychophysiological Insomnia

Transient and Situational.   Undoubtedly the most common sleep disorder familiar to most people, psychophysiological insomnia results from diverse factors such as the stress accompanying the anticipation of an exam, excitement of the thrill of victory, and sleep schedule shifts from "jet lag." This type of short-lived sleep problem, often called "the insomnia of everyday life," fades as the instigating events recede into the past. It may last up to 3 weeks and is rarely seen in sleep disorders centers because of its transience.

While the controversy continues regarding the place of sedative-hypnotics in the treatment of sleep problems, there are clinicians who believe that drug therapy is specifically indicated in the early stages of insomnia (National Institutes of Health, 1984). They reason that prescribing a sleeping pill for a few days or up to a week will allow the patient to function and derail the problem before it becomes established. One potential problem with this approach is the inadvertent transformation of an acute situational sleep disturbance into a chronic pattern by the prescription of hypnotics. For example, in a typical case the physician may prescribe a month's supply of the sleep medicine and when the patient attempts to discontinue the drug after 3 weeks the sleeplessness, nightmares, and daytime anxiety that are part of the withdrawal process cannot be tolerated. If the patient resumes taking the drug, the withdrawal insomnia rapidly resolves and the good sleep and improved functioning convince the patient that the original insomnia is still present and necessitates continued hypnotic use. This process has many patients mistakenly believing that they still have insomnia and drug dependence is the result.

Persistent.   Individuals who transform mental distress into somatic tension and those who are prone to ruminating about sleep may develop a chronic sleep problem. Maladaptive associations may become established linking the bedroom environment and sleep-time rituals with the distress and arousal accompanying the insomnia (Bootzin, 1973). Repeated over time, this process of classical conditioning results in the once-neutral stimuli involved in retiring becoming capable of triggering distress and arousal that then perpetuate the insomnia in a vicious circle. A clue that this maladaptive conditioning has occurred is the history of less difficulty sleeping in beds and environments outside of the habitual sleep situation. A particularly telling example of this occurs when patients spend their first night in the sleep laboratory and on the following morning they report that they have not slept as well in years. This good night's sleep is obtained despite, and perhaps because of, the unusual procedures and strange environment that in many normal control subjects results in a poor night's sleep. This "reverse first-night effect," while not always found, may be present in a subsample of psychophysiological insomniacs (Pena, 1978). Patients with psychophysiological insomnia may also report that when they are not trying to sleep, for example while watching TV, they fall asleep rapidly.

If thinking about sleep becomes enmeshed in a vicious circle that triggers insomnia, conditioning may perpetuate the insomnia (Kales et al., 1976). For example, after a few nights of disturbed sleep the thought of not sleeping produces anxious worrying which is arousing and interferes with sleep. This increased difficulty sleeping further heightens the anticipatory anxiety and sustains the vicious circle. Stimulus Control rules (Bootzin & Nicassio, 1978), such as using the bed only for sleeping, and getting out of bed if awake for more than 10 minutes, are ways of countering the conditioning that have been hypothesized to sustain insomnia.

Insomnia Associated with Psychiatric Disorders. In this entity a diagnosable psychiatric condition is present that is presumed to play a role in the insomnia. Abundant evidence has documented the high prevalence of insomnia in psychiatric patients (Kales et al., 1976; Sweetwood, Kripke, Grant, Yager, & Gerst, 1976). While only eight separate disorders described in the American Psychiatric Association DSM–III use insomnia as a defining criterion, sleep disturbance is known to occur in diverse psychiatric disorders. Identification of the psychological problems may suggest an approach, such as psychopharmacotherapy, that addresses both the sleep and psychological difficulties. For example, the finding of a shortened REM sleep latency on a PSG recording in a patient with a sleep maintenance insomnia who is minimizing his or her depressive symptoms would suggest further psychological assessment and might result in antidepressant drug therapy. It is essential to determine the daytime consequences of insomnia. Tiredness, fatigue, reduced concentration, mild dysphoria, anticipatory anxiety, and irritability often accompany the complaint of sleep difficulties. Ascertaining how much of these experiences are due to disturbed sleep and what portion are the result of psychosocial problems is one of the prime objectives of a good evaluation. Patients with a psychiatric disturbance may confuse cause with effect in attributing their daytime distress to insomnia, when the insomnia may be the result of the daytime distress.

Insomnia Associated with Use of Drugs and Alcohol. The sleep of the chronic sedative-hypnotic user is different from the nondrug user. Reduced stage 3/4 and REM sleep, alpha and beta frequencies occurring in the EEG throughout sleep, and a proliferation of 14 Hz sleep spindles may be seen on the PSG record. As discussed previously, the sleeping difficulty produced by acute drug withdrawal insomnia may prevent the patient from discontinuing sedative-hypnotics. Tolerance develops with chronic drug ingestion and symptoms return. Dosage then must be increased to accomplish the same effect. Varying dosage, switching among different sleeping pills, as well as maintaining a constant dosage results in episodes of insomnia related to tolerance and withdrawal effects. With the new shorter-acting benzodiazepine hypnotics, early morning insomnia has been reported, presumably because the action of the drug wears off (Kales & Kales, 1983).

If a patient's entire complaint is that he or she cannot sleep without sleeping pills, then tapering the drug and assessing the patient's response in the drug-free period is warranted. If following an appropriately long trial the patient develops daytime symptoms or sleep difficulties continue, then an assessment of the role of the previously habitual sedative/hypnotic in the regulation of psychological problems is relevant.

Insomnia Associated with Sleep-Induced Respiratory Impairment.   Respiratory disturbances, while not one of the most common causes of insomnia, do occur and increase in incidence with age (Bliwise, Carey, & Dement, 1983; Bliwise, Carskadon, Carey, & Dement, 1984). The potential medical consequence of this condition is an important indication for thorough assessment. The PSG recording will characterize whether the sleep-induced breathing dysfunction is of the central type, also called diaphragmatic type (due to reduced respiratory drive) or the obstructive type (due to an occlusion in the upper airway). The diaphragmatic type is more common in the patients complaining of insomnia. The complaint of the patients with these conditions may be snoring, waking gasping for breath, or there may be no subjective awareness of irregular breathing. In fact, experience has shown that the majority of patients complaining of insomnia and reporting nocturnal awakenings with difficulty getting a deep breath have no respiratory findings on PSG recording. These episodes are often a variant of anxiety attacks. A careful inquiry into deaths or the onset of major medical problems in family or friends coincident with the development of the nocturnal bouts may uncover the proximate etiological factor.

Insomnia Associated with Sleep-Related (Nocturnal) Myoclonus and "Rest-less Legs."   Patients with the condition of "restless legs" report that they have an irresistible urge to move their legs because of a difficult to describe, uncomfortable feeling in the thigh muscles, sometimes with muscular twitching. These symptoms are more frequent in the evening when sedentary or lying down. Characteristically, these patients report that the distressing feeling abates when they move their legs and returns when they become stationary. Sleep onset difficulties is the most common complaint in this condition (Coleman, 1982). Treatment with benzodiazepines, vitamin E, or opioids has been reported as somewhat effective.

Periodic movement in sleep has been shown to be present in a sizable number of patients with insomnia. The movements themselves are often limited to the foot and leg, and are slow writhing in character, not rapidly myoclonic. The signature of this condition is activity in the anterior tibialis muscle in 1- to 2-second bursts occurring every 20 to 40 seconds, periodically. Temporally associated with these muscle bursts may be a short train of alpha activity in the EEG indicating cerebral activation without behavioral arousal. Patients are characteristically unaware of these stereotyped movements. Patients with "restless legs" commonly have nocturnal myoclonus. Both of these conditions increase their incidence with age.

Periodic movement is readily distinguished clinically from a sleep start or hypnic jerk. The typical sleep start occurs when the individual is trying to fall asleep. The movement is a true clonic contraction, often generalized to the entire skeletal musculature. The individual is made aware of this gross body movement because it often produces full wakefulness.

The remaining insomnia entities are either relatively uncommon, more appropriately understood in the context of specific disease processes, or relatively poorly described. Outside of the insomnia diagnoses that are formally part of the Association of Sleep Disorders Centers nosology the following diagnostic entities, which are subsumed under the rubric Disorders of the Sleep–Wake Schedule, also correspond to particular insomnia complaints.

Disorders of the Sleep–Wake Schedule

Delayed Sleep Phase Syndrome.   Delayed sleep phase syndrome is characterized by exclusively sleep onset insomnia in conjunction with difficulty waking at a socially acceptable time in the morning (Weitzman et al., 1981). The patient's need to wake early in the morning to get to work or school results in the foreshortening of the sleep period and, over time, sleep loss accumulates. As a result, difficulty waking in the morning as well as daytime sleepiness increases over time. Their sleep problems may disappear—for example, on vacation—when no externally imposed sleep schedule is present. Under these conditions falling asleep is no longer difficult because they choose to go to bed later. In addition, there is no trouble waking because, having no difficulty maintaining sleep, they remain asleep until they receive their full complement of sleep.

The pattern of self-described "night owls" may extend back into early childhood. Treatment specifically designed for this condition consists of shifting both the bedtime and wake-up time to a later time each day (Weitzman et al., 1981). For example, if the patient's regular retiring time is 4 A.M. and he or she arises at 11 A.M., then on the first day of treatment the sleep period will be 7 A.M. to 2 P.M. and on the second 10 A.M. to 5 P.M. This 3-hour shift continues each day until the schedule approximates the patients's desired retiring and arising time. Another treatment for this condition involves a night of total sleep deprivation once a week followed by a 90-minute phase advance (i.e., setting the bedtime and wake-up time earlier) on the subsequent night (Thorpy, Korman, Spielman, & Glovinsky, 1988).

Irregular Sleep–Wake Pattern.   In this condition variable retiring and arising times, excessive time in bed, and daytime napping produce a disorganized pattern and upset the regularity of the sleep–wake rhythm. Wide fluctuations in the timing and amount of sleep result. Sleep Restriction Therapy (Spielman et al., 1983; Spielman et al., 1987) or sleep hygiene

(Hauri, 1982) recommendations to go to sleep and get up at the same time every day, discontinue napping, and curtail the time in bed may be the initial interventions suggested. However, noncompliance with these recommendations may indicate that motivational issues underlying the disorganized behavior have not been addressed. These sources of resistance should be explored within the circumscribed sleep treatment or in a more traditional psychotherapy setting.

The treatment of insomnia is problematical and, considering that 17% of the population continue to have a serious insomnia problem (Mellinger, Balter, & Uhlenhuth, 1985), current approaches are either only partly effective or have not been given adequate trials. The importance of this topic demands a comprehensive review and we will wait for another time to address this area (Spielman, Caruso, & Glovinsky, 1987). For now, we will comment on some of the issues.

The major modality of treatment for insomnia is sedative-hypnotic administration. Although the introduction of the benzodiazepines as hypnotics had major advantages over the barbiturates and other compounds, problems remain. A recent consensus conference concluded that while the short-term use of hypnotics is safe and effective, long-term use is controversial (National Institutes of Health, 1984). The efficacy of chronic use of hypnotics has not been established. Furthermore, in addition to the development of tolerance the problem of drug withdrawal may keep patients on these compounds long after they are indicated. For example, many patients start taking a hypnotic while in the hospital or at the onset of some life stress. After discharge or weeks later when the stress has subsided, they may try to stop the hypnotic, but the inability to cope with the acute and severe sleep disturbance that is part of the drug withdrawal effect may result in their taking another dose of the hypnotic. The immediate resolution of both the physiological withdrawal and accompanying sleep disturbance convinces them that an insomnia persists and they need to be on the hypnotic. Of course, this may not be the case. Patients find that if they are able to get through the disruptive withdrawal period they sleep as well, if not better, than when they were on the drug. This is how many a transient insomnia that has been treated with hypnotics results in a patient's dependence on sleeping medication.

The development of new benzodiazepines with different half-lives and other pharamacokinetic properties gives the clinician a broader range of alternatives. Clinical judgment as to the needs of the patient become the basis on which different drugs are chosen. For example, for exclusively sleep onset problems or to avoid daytime drug hangover a drug with a rapid onset and short duration of action, like triazolam, may be the rational choice (Greenblatt, Divoll, Abernathy, & Shader, 1982). Similarly, for patients with compromised metabolical clearance, such as the elderly or those with liver or kidney problems, a short-acting drug may be needed (Green-blatt et al., 1981). Individuals with exclusively sleep maintenance problems or those who are sensitive to withdrawal effects may benefit from longer-acting compounds, such as temazepam or flurazepam. The property of sedative-hypnotics to blunt the arousal response, and thereby prolong sleep-disordered breathing, renders them contraindicated in patients with sleep-related respiratory irregularities.

A number of behavioral treatments have now been shown to have effi-cacy in insomnia. Stimulus control instructions have received the most extensive experimental testing (Bootzin & Nicassio, 1978). The treatment involves adhering to a set wake-up time in the morning, not napping dur-ing the day, and only getting into bed when the patients feel sleepy. They are instructed not to use the bed for anything other than sleeping. If they do not fall asleep rapidly, within about 10 minutes, they must get out of bed and go into another room. When they feel sleepy they can return to bed. In addition to systematic experimental evaluation, stimulus control instruc-tions have been widely used clinically and adopted as part of what are considered sleep hygiene recommendations (Hauri, 1982). Biofeedback of different EEG rhythms and muscle activity has also been shown to improve sleep (Hauri, 1981). However, this approach has not been widely used clinically in the population of insomniacs at large. A new approach, called sleep restriction therapy, requires patients to curtail the amount of time spent in bed at the start of treatment (Spielman et al., 1987). The mild sleep loss at the beginning of treatment consolidates sleep. As the patients sleep 90% of the time in bed they are then given increases in the amount of time in bed. These procedures result in consistent amounts of sleep from night to night. Chronotherapy, previously described in the section on delayed sleep phase syndrome, is a treatment for patients presenting with a sleep schedule disturbance and exclusively sleep onset problems (Weitzman et al., 1981).

The treatment of insomnia represents a challenge. While both behavioral and pharmacological approaches are being developed the pursuit of more precise pathophysiological mechanisms of this set of disorders is sorely needed.

DISORDERS OF EXCESSIVE SOMNOLENCE

This group of disorders, as discussed earlier, may have a major impact on mood and the ability to function. The daytime sleepiness that is character-istic of the majority of these disorders produces deficits in vigilance and cognitive processes. Whether the patients are in a perpetual haze of drowsiness, struggling to stay awake, or having frank sleep episodes during the day, the quality of their lives is compromised. Until relatively recently, physicians lumped sleepiness together, calling it narcolepsy. With better diagnostic techniques and specific treatments, a number of discrete entities have been described and narcolepsy is no longer a synonym for the sleepy patient. The sleep apnea conditions have been responsible for the recruitment into sleep disorders medicine of many physicians of diverse specialties, such as pulmonary medicine, otolaryngology, pediatrics, and internal medicine. The multidimensional consequences of sleep apnea have awakened us to the pathophysiological processes present in sleep. Prior to our understanding of the diverse morbidity associated with sleep apnea, clinicians were akin to the fabled blind East Indians holding onto different parts of the elephant. Neurologists focused on the sleepiness and called it narcolepsy; psychiatrists and psychologists were concerned with the reduced motivation and irritability and called it depression; internists and cardiologists dealt with the blood pressure and right-sided heart changes and called it hypertension, cardiomegaly, and reduced cardiac output; and otolaryngologists inspected the upper airway and called it snoring with a deviated septum, or a craniofacial abnormality. In the recent past, the disease entity of obstructive sleep apnea brought together these diverse observations, cured the clinician's blindness (or at best, provincial myopia), resulting in tremendous strides in evaluation and treatment.

To introduce this most important set of disorders, we will begin with a very brief introduction to the regulation of breathing in sleep. Respiratory control is different in sleep compared with waking; more vulnerable behavioral mechanisms are absent and ventilatory regulation is left to involuntary neurological and chemical (baroreceptor and chemoreceptor) mechanisms. As a result, during sleep in nonpathological conditions, ventilation decreases, pCO_2 rises, and PO_2 falls. Furthermore, during REM sleep, the diaphragm alone does the work of creating negative intrathoracic pressure because of the normally occurring flaccid paralysis of the intercostal and accessory muscles. Therefore, in sleep, there is an accentuation of the adverse impact of factors such as reduced patency of the upper airway due to bony and soft tissue configurations; diseases such as chronic obstructive pulmonary disease and asthma; obesity; medications with respiratory depressant properties; and postural changes associated with recumbency. An apnea is commonly defined as the cessation of airflow greater than 10 seconds in duration and a hypopnea as a reduction in tidal volume. Two of the consequences of irregular respiration are hypoxia—a reduction in the partial pressure or oxygen tension in the blood stream, and hypercapnia—an increase in blood levels of carbon dioxide. Apneas can be classified as obstructive or occlusive; nonocclusive, also referred to as diaphragmatic or central; and mixed. Physical occlusion in the upper airway during sleep results in obstructive apnea in which respiratory effort continues but airflow is blocked. Absent respiratory effort characterizes the nonocclusive apneas. Mixed apneas are a combination of the two, with a nonocclusive component followed by an obstructive component.

Obstructive Sleep Apnea

The significant potential for death during sleep and substantial prevalence of Obstructive Sleep Apnea (OSA) have stimulated much work in this area. Good reviews are available that comprehensively describe the symptoms, course, vast array of treatments, and proposed pathophysiological mechanisms in this disorder (Guilleminault & Dement, 1978; Lugaresi, Coccagna & Mantovani, 1978; Saunders & Sullivan, 1984).

The key clinical symptoms of OSA are loud snoring during sleep and sleepiness during the day. Snoring is produced during respiration due to the rapid movement of tissues in the upper airway. Snoring indicates that there is a partial obstruction of the airway. Although not all individuals who snore have OSA, virtually all patients with OSA snore. The snoring in patients with OSA has a typical pattern. A number of breaths with loud snoring may culminate in a snort that is followed by silence. The silence typically lasts 30 seconds, but may vary from 10 to 120 seconds or more. This is followed by a number of deep breaths with loud snoring, and the pattern then repeats. This pattern is so characteristic of OSA that from this signature alone one can be relatively certain of the underlying process. The loud snores result from partial obstructions; the snort or beginning of silence indicates that airflow has ceased, and the resumption of loud snoring results when the complete obstruction has cleared and air exchange resumes.

Daytime sleepiness produced by OSA may be profound. As detailed earlier, the consequences of sleepiness include performance decrements and mood disturbance. Far-ranging psychological problems result from reduced concentration and work capacity, irritability, emotional lability, decreased libido, and low self-esteem. Patients are at risk of automobile accidents because of drowsiness or frank sleep episodes while driving. The development of a standard, objective, physiological test of sleepiness has documented the pathological level of sleepiness present in these patients throughout the day (Mitler, 1982). The severity of sleepiness is one of the important indications for treatment.

Although Gastaut and his group were the first to describe the syndrome polysomnographically (Gastaut, Tassinari, & Duron, 1965), it was Charles Dickens in 1837, in the *Posthumous Papers of the Pickwick Club*, who described an incredibly fat boy named Joe who was persistently somnolent during the day. Burwell and colleagues coined the term Pickwickian Syndrome to refer to patients with daytime somnolence, obesity, CO_2 retention, and cor pulmonale (Burwell, Robin, Whaley, & Bickelman, 1956). Our present understanding of the different entities and pathophysiology of obstructive sleep apnea has far outdistanced the usefulness of the Pickwickian category. However, it remains in use, often referring to those patients who, following treatment such as tracheostomy, continue to have reduced CO_2 drive and CO_2 retention.

Recumbency during sleep, in and of itself, contributes to hypoxia, due to reduced functional residual capacity and the increase in venous admixture. If you add repetitive apneas in sleep, which may amount to hundreds over the night, the combination produces further falls in oxygen saturation. Frequently, although not invariably, systemic hypertension is present in obstructive sleep apnea syndrome. In more severe cases, pulmonary hypertension occurs as well. Obesity is common in OSA and results in reduced patency of the upper airway, increased diaphragmatic effort necessary to inflate the lungs, and sharper drops in oxygen saturation due to the reduced residual lung volume. Case series have shown that men with OSA outnumber women by 20 to 1, although this ratio decreases in later life to 5 to 1 as more women develop OSA after menopause (Guilleminault & Dement, 1978; Lugaresi et al., 1978; Saunders & Sullivan, 1984). The syndrome is most prevalent in the middle years between 40 and 60. The incidence of OSA is estimated to be 1% to 5% (Lavie, 1983).

The site of the obstruction is commonly in the oropharynx, but hypopharyngeal involvement also occurs. As increased negative pressure is created intrathoracically on inspiration, the lateral and posterior walls of the upper airway collapse because during sleep there is reduced or absent tone of the pharyngeal musculature. As the apnea continues, complex changes, including increased hypoxia and increased respiratory effort, lead to a transient arousal with return of the pharyngeal muscle tone. Decreased caliber of the airway space may result from localized adipose tissue and craniofacial abnormalities such as micrognathia or an acute angle of the base of the skull with the neck. The exacerbation of snoring and apneas while sleeping in a supine posture has been hypothesized to be the result of the tongue falling back into the pharynx and contributing to the occlusion. Sleep deprivation and medications that are sedating and suppress respiratory drive, such as opiods and hypnotics, make sleep apnea worse by increasing the arousal threshold. Since a transient arousal is one of the key elements that terminates an apnea, conditions that make arousal more difficult will prolong the duration of the apnea.

Treatments have developed rapidly for OSA. Tracheostomy, which creates an artificial airway bypassing the site of the obstruction, is a definitive treatment that eliminates the obstructive events and reverses the daytime sleepiness and associated medical symptoms. However, permanent tracheostomy has a certain degree of morbidity, and is not an acceptable treatment to many patients. Weight loss has been shown to reverse the syndrome in patients without bony structural abnormalities of the upper airway. However, considerable numbers of patients cannot lose weight or keep it off.

A major advance was the adaptation of a surgical procedure designed to reduce snoring. Fujita and colleagues (Fujita, et al., 1981) developed this procedure, called uvulopalatopharyngoplasty (UPPP), which, in addition to reliably eliminating snoring, often reduced the number and severity of apneic events. However, studies from many centers have shown that a reasonable level of success is achieved in only about 50% of cases. A screening measure to increase the success rate of UPPP was conceived by Borowiecki and colleagues (Borowiecki & Sassin, 1983) and systematically assessed by Sher and colleagues (Sher, Thorpy, Shprintzen & Spielman, 1985). Performing a Müller maneuver, which involves inspiring against a closed nose and mouth with a fiberoptic endoscope in the naso-pharynx, allows a determination of the site of the obstruction. According to Sher et al., (1985), if little or no collapse is present in the hypopharynx and the majority of the collapse is at the level of the soft palate in the oropharynx, then UPPP is likely to be successful.

Most recently, the use of nasal continuous-positive airway pressure (C-PAP) has become the major modality of treatment of OSA (Sullivan, Berthon–Jones, Issa, & Eves, 1981). A nasal mask is fitted on the patient and a pump delivers a continuous stream of air to produce a positive pressure which stents the upper airway in attempting to prevent obstruction. The problems with nasal C-PAP include return of the apnea if the device is not used, blockage of the nose and upper respiratory infections rendering the device ineffective, and the unwillingness of some patients to sleep with a mask on their face and to endure the annoying noise from the compressor operation. However, the immediacy of the improvement with this relatively benign procedure represents a major advance.

Other treatments that may have some value but are not widely employed are protriptyline (Acres, Brownwell, West, Sweatman, & Krygér, 1982) devices to keep patients off their back (Cartwright, Lloyd, Lilie, & Kravitz, 1985), and nasopharyngeal tubes (Karetsky, Scoles, Fourre, & Nahmias, 1985).

Narcolepsy

Within the relatively new discipline of sleep disorders, the venerable disorder of narcolepsy holds a special place. Clinically characterized more than 100 years ago, it has been called the sine qua non of sleep disorders. Until recently, the term narcolepsy was synonymous with sleepiness, its major symptom. However, we now know that a number of conditions can lead to pathological sleepiness and therefore the term narcolepsy is reserved for a particular syndrome with distinct characteristics. Because of its historical importance, we will structure this section around a chronology of the advances made in the understanding of narcolepsy.

Inappropriate daytime sleepiness in combination with loss of motor activity was described first (Westphal, 1877). The term narcolepsy was coined in 1880 to reflect both sleepiness, the major symptom of the disorder, and cataplexy, the unique symptom of sudden muscle weakness in response to emotion (Gelineau, 1880). The presence of hallucinations and paralysis during the transition of sleep and wakefulness were appreciated early, while the problem of disturbed nocturnal sleep was described only recently (Montplaisir et al., 1978). The age of onset peaks in the late teens and then again in the twenties. Onset after 50 is extremely rare (Billard, Besset, & Cadilhac, 1983). The initial symptom is most commonly daytime sleepiness, and cataplexy may not appear for many years. While sleepiness, once present, is virtually an everyday occurrence, the frequency of cataplexy varies from multiple episodes every day to one episode in a lifetime. The course of the disorder may vary in severity, but it is not progressive. The condition is lifelong, with no substantiated cases of remission.

In the early years of its description, the lack or warning, suddenness, and the obligatory nature of the sleepiness were emphasized, and naps were characterized as "sleep attacks." While some sleep episodes are peremptory, in the vast majority, drowsiness precedes the nap and alerting measures, such as walking, can be initiated to delay or avoid the sleep episode.

Cataplexy can affect all limbs and result in global paralysis. More commonly, the sudden muscle weakness amounts to no more than a weakness in the knees, neck, and facial muscles. Cataplexy typically lasts for a second or less than a minute. The most frequent precipitating events are emotional arousal such as anger, laughter, or sexual arousal during intercourse (Guilleminault, 1976).

In the 1940s, the development of the amphetamines, with their alerting properties, offered the first effective treatment for sleepiness. Newer analeptic compounds, such as methylphenidate and pemoline, have become available that have somewhat fewer side effects and a longer and more graded duration of action.

The beginning of the search for more precise objective techniques to characterize sleepiness was undertaken at the Mayo clinic. Continuous measurements showed that pupil diameter was smaller and unstable in narcoleptics compared with nonsleepy normals (Yoss, Moyer, & Ogle, 1969). The early pupilometric work was limited by the imprecision of the diagnostic criteria for narcolepsy available at that time, and samples of so-called narcoleptics probably included patients with sleep apnea and other conditions that produce sleepiness. Work continues along this line of investigation with more sophisticated pupilometric hardware and a more rigorous and limited definition of narcolepsy (Pressman et al., 1984).

The discovery of REM sleep in normals in 1953 set the stage for the finding that has become the centerpiece of most conceptualizations about narcolepsy. A study made brief mention that REM sleep appeared shortly after sleep onset in narcolepsy—an unusual time in the sleep cycle for its occurrence. Systematic polygraphic investigation of the sleep of narcolepsy followed and showed that so-called Sleep Onset REM Periods (SOREMPs) were a fundamental characteristic of the disorder (Rechtschaffen, Wolpert, Dement, Mitchell, & Fisher, 1963), occurring at the beginning of the nocturnal sleep period as well as during many daytime naps (Dement, Rechtschaffen, & Gulevich, 1966). This finding gave tremendous impetus to diagnostic, therapeutic, and pathophysiological work. For the first time, a laboratory test could be used to confirm the clinical impression of narcolepsy. This resulted in the further refinement and delimitation of the diagnostic criteria of the syndrome. Not pathognomonic of the disorder, SOREMPs can occur in patients with sleep apnea, sleep–wake schedule disturbances, and major depression. In addition, SOREMPs may be present in infancy, during drug withdrawal, and in experimental REM and total sleep deprivation. If one can exclude these disorders and conditions, then the finding of a SOREMP can assist in the diagnostic process. As first used diagnostically, the nocturnal sleep recording of a daytime nap was scrutinized for SOREMPs. However, the sensitivity of this finding was unsatisfactory; it yielded too many false negatives. In approximately half of sleep onsets, a SOREMP will occur in a narcoleptic. The development of the standardized format of the Multiple Sleep Latency Test (MSLT) (Mitler, 1982), with five nap opportunities during the day, has improved the diagnostic process. The criteria of at least two SOREMPs and an average sleep latency of less than 5 minutes have proven to be sensitive and specific for narcolepsy. These two criteria enable the clinician to be confident that the specific pathophysiological process of narcolepsy and the pathological degree of sleepiness are both present.

Although not the exclusive domain of narcoleptics, the occurrence of SOREMPs did suggest a pathophysiological explanation for the auxiliary symptoms of cataplexy, sleep paralysis, and the hallucinations that occur during the transition from either wakefulness to sleep (hypnogogic) or sleep to wakefulness (hypnopompic). Neurophysiological research has shown that during normally occurring REM sleep, there is an active inhibition of most of the skeletal musculature, resulting in a flaccid paralysis (Jouvet & Michel, 1959; Pompeiano, 1967). Psychophysiological research has described the regular occurrence of dreaming in association with REM sleep. The dislocation of the REM-sleep period at sleep onset in narcoleptics suggested that an abnormality of REM-sleep mechanisms may play a role in the disorder. In line with this reasoning, cataplexy and sleep paralysis were understood as disturbances in the timing or triggering of the normal REM-sleep process of muscle atonia, while hallucinations at the transition of sleep and waking were attributed to the activation of dreaming in this transitional state leading to dissociative phenomena.

Some investigators have claimed that an entity called independent narcolepsy exists in which exclusively non-REM sleep occurs at sleep onset (Roth, Bruhova, & Lehovsky, 1969). However, most clinicians throughout the world reserve the diagnosis of narcolepsy for those patients exhibiting SOREMPs.

Prior to the discovery of SOREMPs in narcolepsy, tricyclical antidepressant drugs, with their powerful REM sleep-suppressant capacity, were used successfully as a treatment of the auxiliary symptoms, and had little effect on sleepiness. The monoamine oxidase inhibitors are unusual in that they have a dual effect (Wyatt, Fram, Buchbinder, & Snyder, 1971). They are alerting in addition to their anticataplectic activity (Mitler, 1976), and are unusual in that they have this dual effect.

The relatively recent discovery that dogs and a few other mammals have a condition that resembles, in most respects, this disorder in humans offers the hope of important strides in our understanding of the basic processes of this disorder (Baker & Dement, 1985). Long suspected to be in some measure an inherited disorder in humans, the disease in different strains of dogs shows different modes of genetic transmission (Mefford et al., 1983). The canine model of narcolepsy has also yielded findings that in specific brain sites there is reduced turnover of dopamine and the proliferation of cholinergic receptors (Kilduff et al., 1986).

The most recent lead in the mystery of narcolepsy comes from Japanese investigators who, along with others, have shown that nearly all narcoleptics have the same Human Leukocyte Antigen (HLA) halotype. The HLA antigen DR_2 positive has now been shown to approach a frequency of 100% in mongoloid, Caucasian, and Negroid narcoleptics (Honda et al., 1986). While this halotype is not specific for narcolepsy in that about 30% of Caucasians are DR_2 positive, it is the highest association yet reported between a disorder and an HLA antigen. In addition, it offers a new direction for research into the possibility that narcolepsy may be an autoimmune disorder (Langdon et al., 1986). Intensive investigations are currently under way to elucidate the meaning of this finding.

In summary, the progress in understanding narcolepsy has proceeded through stages of clinical description, objective laboratory markers, symptomatic treatment, animal models, and neurochemical and blood assays. The future promises an understanding of the origin and pathophysiology of the disorder and better treatment. With luck, prevention and possibly a cure may be found for this debilitating disorder.

Other Conditions

A number of other conditions are also associated with daytime sleepiness. Hypersomnolence, a term reserved for excessive amounts of sleep over the 24-hour period, is a prominent symptom of Klein–Levin Syndrome (Critchley, 1962). The hypersomnolence in this condition is episodic and may last for days, during which time behavioral disturbances such as increased aggressivity, hypersexuality, and excessive eating may also be present. Asymptomatic periods last for weeks or months in between what may be the two or three symptomatic episodes. The etiology of this syndrome is unknown. Descriptions of Klein–Levin are few because it is rare, occurring mainly in adolescent or young men, and the symptomatic bouts are brief. Prolonged use of long-acting soporifics, anxiolytics, alcohol, and antihypertensives can cause excessive daytime sleepiness.

DISORDERS OF THE SLEEP–WAKE SCHEDULE

Measuring time has a mathematical, albeit geometrical, emphasis to it. Humans measure it in a circular way and our timekeeping devices are, for the most part, round simply because it is easier to measure time this way. The geometrical nature of time may have its roots in the cosmic origin of our solar system. The earth, moon, and other planets are all round, not triangular, square, or elliptical. Earth, with all of its inhabitants, makes a complete trip on its axis every 24 hours and around the sun every 365 days. Where we are in relation to this ever changing position on the circle is indicated by the hands of the clocks we wear.

The human species, similar to all organisms, has a rest–activity cycle. After exhaustive investigation, authorities agree that this cycle is under the endogenous control of the central nervous system. It is an inherent quality in every living organism to exhibit oscillations in biological functions. Obvious examples of these rhythms are the cardiac and respiratory cycles, which occur without conscious effort but exhibit features such as period length, frequency, amplitude, and an intrinsic oscillatory capacity. The term circadian (circa = about; diem = one day) was coined by Halberg to describe the period length of many biological rhythms (Halberg, 1969). The earth spins on its axis once every 24 hours, experiencing alternating periods of light and darkness, upon which signals many organisms predicate their rest–activity cycle. Signaling is not the sole determinant of an organism's activity schedule; when external time cues are removed, and under conditions of temporal isolation, the organism's mean 24-hour cycle will persist. Despite an environment entirely devoid of any time cues such as light, the endogenously driven cycles persist with a great deal of regularity. Biological rhythms display a wide range of frequencies besides the circadian. Ultradian rhythms are those with a period length of less than 24 hours, such as the 80- to 100-minute alternation between REM and NREM sleep that occurs during sleep. Infradian rhythms have a greater than 24-hour period length; for example, the menstrual cycle. ACTH and cortisol secretions are lowest in the late evening hours, exhibit some increase in the latter part of sleep, and peak after wakefulness. This pattern suggests a coupling mechanism between the sleep phases and hormonal output. With environmental manipulation, it is possible to uncouple these rhythms transiently.

In 1729, a French astronomer, de Mairan may have been the first to suggest that environmental time cues are not the only determinants of an organism's behavior (de Mairan, 1729). Placing a heliotrope plant in a closet insulated from daily variations in light, de Mairan found that the plant continued to open and close its leaves on schedule. De Candolle studied the same plant species in total darkness, and found that its periodicity of daily leaf movements ceased to be 24 hours (De Candolle, 1832). This plant, like other biological organisms, when removed from environmental time cues, alters the length of its cycle. The heliotrope plant's free-running period decreased by 1.5 to 2 hours. Other studies demonstrated that organisms set free from external time cues will develop daily cycles greater or less than 24 hours, and that these periods are species-specific and genetically determined. Differences between species are accounted for by each organism's unique need to adapt and survive changes in its environment. The endogenous rhythms persist from youth to senescence and remain remarkably stable through successive generations, despite widespread variations in environmental factors. Under consistent experimental conditions, many organisms can maintain new cycle lengths for years.

The question as to whether humans are subject to similar changes in the rest–activity cycle had to await the innovative work of Aschoff and Wever, who isolated six human subjects in a cellar in Munich (Aschoff, Gerecke, & Wever, 1967). Deprived of all environmental time cues such as fluctuations in light, temperature, and humidity, subjects, similar to other mammalians, had an ongoing rhythmicity in rest–activity and body temperature cycles. The period length of their new cycles was 25.3 hours, with the daily sleep episode occurring an average of 1.3 hours later each day. Societal norms require most of us to synchronize our rest–activity cycles around a 24-hour day. Human rhythms may be more attuned to factors of social entrainment than to light–dark cues and, when freed from these constraints, such as on weekends, may develop longer rest–activity periods.

The organizational, physiological, and anatomical correlates of this system have undergone scrutiny (Kronauer, Czeisler, Pilator, Moore–Ede, & Weitzman, 1982). Studies have shown that the normally predictable relationship between the rest–activity cycle and body temperature rhythm can be disrupted at times (called internal desynchronization) via denial of exposure to environmental time cues. Aschoff and Wever's subjects displayed a rest–activity cycle of 33 hours and a 24.5-hour body temperature rhythm. It has been hypothesized that these two rhythms are under the control of two separate but interrelated pacemakers labeled X (body temperature) and Y (rest–activity). The rhythms that humans display are partly the result of signals relayed from both sources. These two oscillators, as demonstrated by Aschoff and Wever, can temporarily dissociate with slow-wave sleep and growth hormone following the Y pacemaker and cortisol secretion and REM sleep following the X.

Initial studies by Richter identified an area in the ventral hypothalamus as being involved in the regulation of circadian rhythms in rats (Richter, 1922). Other investigators identified a monosynaptic projection, the retinohypothalamic tract, which began in the eye and terminated in the suprachiasmatic nucleus (SCN) of the hypothalamus. Destruction of this area seems to affect Y-driven functions more than X, suggesting that the X pacemaker lies outside the SCN. The importance of the SCN role as coordinator of circadian rhythms lies in its persisting circadian neural activity after anatomic isolation from nearby hypothalamic tissue.

Biological Rhythms, Hormonal Secretions, and Aging

This is an area worthy of more attention, both from the research and the clinical points of view, because of the evidence that rhythmic changes are associated with aging. Pittendrigh found that the free-running period of the circadian rest–activity cycle shortens with advancing age in rats (Pittendrigh & Daan, 1974). Tune's survey of 509 subjects showed that older subjects went to bed earlier and awakened sooner than the younger group (Tune, 1968). The amplitude of circadian rhythms decreases with age in humans (Loggan & Tredre, 1967).

Often considered a very stable circadian rhythm, temperature curves do change with normal aging. Weitzman studied six normal men aged 53 to 70 and six men aged 23 to 30 during entrained and temporal isolation conditions, and found a reduction in the amplitude and period of body temperature rhythms during both conditions in the older group (Weitzman, Moline, Czeisler, & Zimmerman, 1982). Such a shortening of the period length would affect the phase relationship between temperature and the sleep–wake cycle. The older group showed a greater elevation in temperature during sleep and a lowering of the temperature amplitude during entrainment and free running. These findings suggest that the aging process brings with it changes in fundamental properties of biological rhythms which may set the groundwork for the vulnerability to disease.

Hormonal Aspects

Several studies refute the clinical myth that all neuroendocrine functions deteriorate with age. The 24-hour pattern of adrenal cortical steroids remains stable throughout aging, and stimulation of the adrenal gland by ACTH produces an augmented cortisol secretion in older men and women (Blicher–Toft & Hummer, 1977; Vermeulen, 1976). Older patients with depression frequently exhibit a hypersecretion of cortisol during their illness, and it has some usefulness as a diagnostic and monitoring tool (Carrol, Curtis, & Mendels, 1976). These hypersecretory patterns return to normal when the depression remits. The number of episodes of growth hormone (GH) secretion, its mean amount, and sleep-related secretion decrease with aging (Prinz, Blenkarn, & Linnoila, 1976).

Presently available data indicate that prolactin secretion, T4 and basal TSH does not appear to be affected by age (Murril, Barreca, & Gallaminia, 1977; Vosberg, Wagner, & Boeckel, 1976). Overall, investigations into the changes in circadian hormonal patterns that occur from maturity to senescence are in the embryonic stages.

Jet Lag

Most individuals have a set time for sleep initiation and termination, a type of self-entrainment of the rest–activity cycle. Although variations may occur on weekends, they are relatively slight in comparison with what happens after a rapid change of time zone, that is, after a flight from New York to Japan. Jet lag does not occur in north–south travel, as time zones are not crossed, and may not happen if time zone changes are small, such as New York to Chicago. Symptoms include inability to maintain sleep; frequent, unwanted arousals; and excessive daytime somnolence (McFarland, 1975). Many individuals report difficulty with cognitive performance, being unable to focus their thoughts on the matters at hand. Irritability, malaise, and stomach problems are also reported. In general, clinical information suggests that the healthier, younger traveler will adjust more quickly and be affected less severely than his or her older counterpart whose biological clock has lost some of its plasticity, especially if concomitant medical illnesses exist.

Advice to travelers to slowly change their sleep schedule before leaving to conform with the demands of the new time zone will prevent or diminish the problem at the destination. However, the disruption in routine and life-style prior to leaving may be unacceptable. Other recommendations include an effort to seek out and engage in the time cues of the new environment as quickly as possible in order to expedite functional adaptation to the new time zone.

Shift Work

It is estimated that approximately 17% of the U. S. population is employed in some type of rotating shift work (Rutenfranz, Knauth, & Colquhoun, 1976). Obvious examples include health care professionals, hospital employees, postal workers, truck drivers, airline pilots, air traffic controllers, police, firefighters, and sanitation workers. Considerable numbers of workers in steel, textile, petrochemical, and automobile industries are shift workers. When shifts are changed, many workers experience symptoms similar to someone with jet lag, the common denominator being a rapid shift in their place on the circle of time. A 3-week period may be needed to adapt functionally to a rotating shift. When it is done in a shorter time period, absenteeism increases, worker satisfaction and productivity decrease, while the number of accidents and other morbid events increases. More attention, however, is being paid to this problem by U. S. industry. As with jet lag, the impact of shift work is probably more profound on the middle-aged and older group, who may require an even longer period to adjust to rotating shifts.

Frequently Changing Sleep–Wake Schedule

As noted above, many jobs require relatively infrequent changes in work schedule, such that the disruptive effects are short-lived and not serious. Workers whose livelihood dictates acceptance of a frequent and too rapid change in schedule are prone to fall victim to the complications described previously. Family life can be affected adversely as the worker's sleep schedule degenerates into a group of naps distributed throughout the 24-hour day. The internal desynchronization of circadian rhythms may result in lability of mood, impaired motor performance, and serious effects on cognitive functioning during situations that require a constant degree of vigilance.

Delayed Sleep Phase Syndrome

As discussed earlier, in the context of insomnia, this newly described disorder is characterized by a difficulty in falling asleep and difficulty in awakening (Weitzman et al., 1981). The patient notes a profound inability to begin sleep until late at night; for example, 3 to 6 A.M. Despite societal/work demands that the day begin around 7 or 8 A.M., the patient is unable to arise, is chronically late for work, and misses important appointments. Daytime sleepiness may be present, especially in the early part of the day. On weekends, patients try to catch up on lost sleep by sleeping late in the afternoon. On extended vacations, when they are left to determine their own sleep–wake schedule, they go to sleep late and get up late in the day, but have little difficulty falling asleep, no problem waking, and are alert. Despite the use of soporifics or alcohol, phase advancement (getting to sleep earlier) of the sleep–wake cycle is difficult for these individuals. Chronotherapy, discussed earlier, consists of further delaying the onset of sleep (getting to bed late) by 3 hours each night until the patient's sleep is moved to the appropriate time. Another entity called Advanced Sleep Phase Syndrome may be relevant to the aging individual. Although few cases of this syndrome have been described adequately in the literature, the middle-aged and older group have been frequently described as advancing their sleep phase by getting into bed earlier at night and out of bed earlier in the morning.

The Non-24-Hour (Hypernycthemeral) Syndrome

This often intractable but fortunately rare syndrome is frequently associated with patients who exhibit a severe degree of psychopathology in the form of personality disorders (Kokkoris et al., 1978). Their sleep period length of 25 to 27 hours is out of synchrony with the 24-hour solar day and resembles the temporal pattern seen in normal individuals devoid of time cues as in temporal isolation. Unresponsive to societal influences and other time cues for rest–activity cycle adjustment, their subjective day begins a few hours later each 24 hours. This regular rotation in the sleep–wake schedule keeps them out of step with a world that is regimented to clock time.

DISORDERS ASSOCIATED WITH SLEEP STAGES OR PARTIAL AROUSALS (PARASOMNIAS)

This classification consists of a group of heterogeneous disorders that occur during sleep or during a partial arousal from sleep (Broughton, 1968) or are exacerbated by sleep. Considering them true disorders of the sleep–wake cycle would be somewhat inaccurate; to exclude them as purely psychiatric or mental issues would ignore the very real impact they have on the rest–activity cycle. We have chosen to address sleep-related asthma, cardiovascular symptoms, and gastroesophageal reflux in another section. They represent a continuum of chronic illnesses which have different phases or expressions during sleep but often result in a chronic disturbance of the sleep–wake cycle. Some of the conditions within the parasomnia rubric are dissociated behaviors in which behavior that is normal during wakefulness occurs in sleep and is, because of that context, abnormal. Sleepwalking and enuresis are examples of this. Other phenomena, such as nocturnal seizures, bruxism (tooth grinding), or jactatis capitis nocturna (head banging), are patently abnormal whenever they occur.

Sleepwalking (Somnambulism)

Behavioral manifestations of sleepwalking are diverse, ranging from confused wandering to seemingly purposeful but repetitive motor acts such as rearranging furniture, urinating, and so on (Kales, Jacobson, Paulson, Kales, & Walter, 1966; Kales, Paulson, Jacobson, & Kales, 1966). These episodes usually occur in the first 3 hours of sleep. The duration of these episodes is often brief (the patient sits up in bed for a few seconds), but some episodes can last as long as minutes, with the patient leaving the home in bedclothes. The sleepwalker has a limited capacity to respond to the environment and may be difficult to arouse. If awakened, the patient reports sparse mental content. The sleepwalker is characteristically able to return to sleep rapidly, and in the morning may not recall the nocturnal event.

There are reports that stress, fatigue, febrile illness, nighttime medications, and sleep apnea increase the frequency of episodes (Charney, Kales,

Soldatos, & Nelson, 1979; Kales, Kales, Soldatos, Chamberlin, & Martin, 1979). In addition, sleepwalking may be triggered in susceptible individuals by partly arousing them from sleep. Prevalence has been estimated at 10% in childhood and 2% in adults. When sleepwalking persists into adulthood, psychopathology is often present. Studies have shown that sleepwalking, as well as nocturnal enuresis and sleep terrors, runs in families (Kales, Soldatos, Bixler et al., 1980; Kales, Soldatos, Caldwell et al., 1980). Polysomnographically, episodes emerge out of stage 3 and 4 sleep. Differential diagnosis often involves epilepsy. While the two disorders can coexist, sleepwalking is most often not of an epileptic origin.

Sleep Terrors (Pavor Nocturnus, Incubus)

Night terrors are probably best described by Coleridge as he recounted his own sleep terror: "Distemper's worst calamity . . . when my own loud scream has waked me." The signature of this disorder is the sudden occurrence of a loud vocalization (Fisher, Kahn, Edwards, & Davis, 1973; Kales, Kales, Kales et al., 1980). The arousal from sleep is abrupt and frightening, with autonomic system activity producing diaphoresis, hyperapnea, and tachycardia. Sitting up in bed, writhing, or sleepwalking are common. Attempts to console patients during these episodes are fended off. After an initial state of confusion, the patient rapidly returns to sleep. If the episode is terminated and the individual wakes up, there may be reports of minimal mental content, but no thematically elaborated dream will be recounted. As with somnambulism, the episodes occur shortly after sleep onset, within the first 2 to 3 hours of the night, and in the morning there may be amnesia for the event.

Night terrors typically occur out of stage 3 and 4 sleep. Furthermore, there is some evidence that with greater amounts of stage 4 sleep preceding

TABLE 1.2.   DISTINGUISHING CHARACTERISTICS

Night Terror	Nightmare
Occurs in wakefulness with alpha rhythm	Occurs in sleep
Preceded by stage 4	Occurs in REM sleep
Intense: Vocalization, fright, motility, autonomic discharge	Less intense: vocalization, fright, motility, autonomic discharge
Mental confusion	No mental confusion
Difficult to arouse	Easy to arouse
Occurs early in the night	Occurs later in the night
Sparse mental content	Elaborate mental content
Some amnesia	Less amnesia
Uncommon to rare	Not uncommon

the episode, the night terror is more intense (Fisher et al., 1973). Although the prevalence of night terrors has been estimated at 2% in childhood, informal surveys of physicians and psychologists have suggested that the occurrence of at least one episode in early childhood may be closer to 33%. As with somnambulism and enuresis, the disorder becomes less prevalent with age. In adults in whom night terrors have been persistent since childhood or begun later in life, there is evidence of psychopathology characterized by inhibition of outward expression of aggression and phobic tendencies (Kales, Kales et al., 1980).

Features that help distinguish the night terror from the nightmare are listed in Table 1.2. Enuresis will not be reviewed because it is comprehensively reviewed in various medical textbooks.

Nocturia/Urinary Incontinence

Just as nocturnal enuresis is a transient disorder of childhood, urinary incontinence is an embarrassing and socially unacceptable malady of the aged. Unavoidable, unwanted, chronic bed wetting in almost any situation is found in 5% to 15% of those in acute care facilities (Libow & Starer, 1985). Incontinence refers to the uncontrollable, frequent, and unexpected inability to control the process of urination, as contrasted to nocturnal enuresis, which only occurs during sleep. Out of shame, ignorance, and the medical profession's unwillingness to address the problem, the aged are left to their own devices to deal with this problem. Some series report up to a 75% incidence of cognitive impairment coexisting with urinary incontinence. Urinary incontinence exacts a heavy toll on family members or caretakers for those individuals living at home. Urinary incontinence is an important risk factor for placement in a long-term care facility. Long-term institutionalization currently costs $25 billion per year in the United States. Today, techniques are available for the proper evaluation and treatment of urinary incontinence. Evaluation consists of a physical exam, measuring residual volume of urine in the bladder after voiding, urinalysis, and sometimes urodynamic studies. Management includes correction of precipitating events, such as infection, removing offending drugs, and bladder retraining.

No studies have been done to evaluate the pathophysiology of bladder dysfunction during sleep in the middle-aged and older population. Medications such as diuretics, when given toward evening, have a propensity to produce nocturia, forcing the patient to wake up frequently to void, thus fragmenting the sleep pattern. Numerous nursing home residents are found in the morning with their beds saturated from urine, often producing bedsores. Other medications that exacerbate or produce incontinence are sedative hypnotics, tricyclical antidepressants, neuroleptics, anticholinergics, and certain cardiac medications that inhibit bladder contraction.

Bruxism

Bruxism is the term for teeth grinding during sleep. It can be found in almost all age groups, and may be a symptom of states of anxiety or depression. Dental damage can result if left untreated.

SLEEP AND AGING

The transformations in sleep that occur over the course of life are profound and among the best documented in sleep research. The subjective and polygraphic changes that take place between the middle to later years have been extensively reviewed (Dement, Miles, & Carskadon, 1982). The present report will focus on sleep as it relates to physiological changes, pathological processes, increased therapeutic interventions, and social/ psychological factors that are the concomitants of the aging process.

Large surveys of the population have consistently found that complaints of sleep disturbance increase with age (Cooper, 1977). Likewise, the use of sedative-hypnotics in older individuals is disproportionate in relation to their proportion of the population. Individuals over 65 years of age, who comprise 13% of the population, consume 25% of the sedatives prescribed for sleep problems. Among the institutionalized elderly, who number about 1.4 million, as many as 98% have standing orders for bedtime sedation. An astounding 25% to 50% of these institution-bound patients receive these sleeping pills nightly. While the indications for and efficacy of chronic administration of sedative hypnotics is an active area of debate, their nightly use in the elderly patient poses special problems. Firstly, the elderly consume more nonsedative drugs than younger individuals, thereby running increased risks of drug interactions. Secondly, the aged person's diminished capacity to metabolize and excrete drugs leads to prolonged and unwanted drug effects, such as daytime sedation and deficits in cognitive functions. Thirdly, the increased incidence of sleep-related respiratory disturbances in older persons increases their vulnerability to the respiratory suppressant properties of sedative-hypnotics. These and other factors suggest caution against the reflexive use of sedative-hypnotics in the elderly patient complaining of disturbed sleep.

The three factors that converge on the sleep of the elderly are physiological aging processes, specific sleep pathologies that occur as a function of age, and medical illnesses and treatment.

The mythology surrounding the aging process and the role sleep serves alleges that a concomitant of the normal aging process is a reduced need for sleep in the elderly. While it is true that the amount of time spent asleep diminishes as a function of ontogenetic changes from infancy through adolescence, maturity, and senescence, the decline in later life is small, if present at all (Miles & Dement, 1980). Decline in well-being and functional capacity resulting from sleep-related disorders of respiration and motor activity in the elderly underscore the continuing need for good sleep in this group. It has long been recognized that as we age, we experience more frequent nighttime arousals, early morning awakenings, difficulty maintaining sleep, and shortened total nocturnal sleep time. In addition, the elderly spend more time in bed, have increased sleep latency and brief, involuntary, and often embarrassing daytime naps. The consistent results of these surveys form a consensus that the prevalence and severity of sleep problems comprise a major problem for the ever-expanding elderly population.

Although the aged continue to sleep 7 or more hours, it is no longer consolidated into one long bout as it was during their youth. Older individuals wake more frequently and for longer periods during the night, which results in fragmentation of sleep. In addition, increases in the time spent in bed and the increased frequency of napping further distributes sleep throughout the day. As a result, the sleep efficiency during nocturnal sleep, which is the ratio of time asleep to time in bed, is reduced from above 90% (characteristic of younger adults) to below 85% in older individuals. The other polysomnographically documented change is the decline in stages 3 and 4 sleep, which is more severe in men than women.

When considering these changes in sleep, the distinction between the ability and need to sleep must be clearly understood. The ability to sleep refers to sleep characteristics such as the amount, composition, and pattern of sleep and wakefulness throughout the night. In contrast, the need to sleep is measured by the daytime functions that sleep serves, such as alertness, cognitive capacity, and the regulation of mood.

There is no question that the aging process and the disorders that become more prevalent with age result in fragmented sleep and the reduction in "deep" sleep stages 3 and 4. While it is true that this decreased ability to sleep does not automatically mean that the elderly have a sleep problem, the fundamental question is to what degree the day is affected by the night. It is well established that reduced amounts of sleep and increased nocturnal awakenings in the elderly and younger individuals are associated with drowsiness, performance decrements, and impairments in mood and the sense of well-being. These symptoms, as well as undesired napping, are the appropriate standards by which to judge the need for sleep.

The resolution of these problems by such nondrug approaches as sleep restriction therapy (Spielman et al., 1987), a new modality currently being tested in the elderly, and medical treatments for organically based insomnia are evidence for the continued need for adequate sleep. It is a disservice to those elderly individuals whose quality of life suffers from correctable insomnia to relegate their disordered sleep to the status of "normal changes."

In response to their distress, the elderly consume sedative hypnotics, over-the-counter preparations, and alcohol. The use pattern of soporifics in the aged is essentially linear in relation to age. The older the group, the more its members consume sedatives. There are legitimate objections to excessive reliance on a drug-oriented approach to sleep disturbances in this population. First, the physiological changes in sleep that occur as a part of the aging process are not returned to the patterns of youth by soporifics. Sedatives reduce the amplitude and amount of stages 3 and 4 sleep and often REM sleep. Second, the many discrete entities that have been identified as producing disturbed sleep are not eliminated by sleeping pills. In fact, sleeping pills may adversely affect already compromised physiological functions that have caused the sleep disturbance. For example, the well-known CNS depressant properties of soporifics will dampen the already deficient respiratory drive in insomnia associated with nonocclusive sleep apnea. The arousal mechanism that compensates for sleep-related breathing disturbances is compromised by sedative hypnotics.

Surprisingly, few studies have been done on the efficacy of sedatives in the older age group. One study prescribed flurazepam for six elderly females for seven consecutive nights (Frost & Delucchi, 1979). Although improvement was demonstrated in both the time it took to fall asleep and duration of sleep, daytime performance was not measured. In addition, two patients complained of daytime somnolence. No sedative hypnotic has proven efficacy beyond 6 or 7 weeks, yet treatment is often continued on a chronic basis. Of more relevance is the paucity of data concerning prolonged use in the aged. Prescribing patterns, although improving because of educational endeavors, still employ prolonged use without any measurement of efficacy, side effects, or interactions with other drugs. Physiologically, the aged person's ability to excrete and metabolize drugs may be compromised by illness or by the aging process itself, predisposing the individual to prolonged and unwanted drug effects, namely daytime sedation, impaired cognition, and motor performance. One wonders if the increased incidence of accidents and hip fracture in the elderly could be related to unwanted daytime sedation.

Concomitant with the aging process are a significant number of pathologies that affect sleep. These disorders are more prevalent and serious in the middle-aged and older group whose nocturnal problems are exacerbated by congestive heart failure, emphysema, pain, and so forth. The aging process brings with it physiological changes, many of which result not so much in an absolute decrement in functional capacity but in a compromise of speed and grace. Motor performance slows down, reaction time increases, yet the main goal can still be achieved if patience is applied. Organ systems are affected differentially by aging. For example, degenerative joint disease occurs universally and is often called osteoarthritis, rheumatism, or simply arthritis. It affects both sexes, and its incidence increases with age. Though not crippling, the chronic pain, discomfort, and difficulties with mobilization can disrupt the sleeping process. Patients may complain bitterly to their health care provider about frequent nocturnal awakenings and inability to return to sleep. As discussed more elaborately in the section on insomnia, poor sleep often begins with temporary stressors which often abate after 1 or 2 months (death in the family, acute illness, financial setbacks, etc.) but leaving an insomnia that has become autonomous from its origins (Spielman, 1986). The elderly are subject to more stressors than their younger counterparts, such as death of a spouse, retirement, concerns about failing health, the empty nest syndrome as the nuclear family is separated, financial concerns, and so on. Although attention is paid to the clinical complaint, appropriate treatment prescribed, and good results obtained, such as the amelioration of pain, nevertheless, the patient may be left with a set of poor sleep habits and complaining of an inability to initiate or maintain sleep.

Musculoskeletal Pain/Arthritis

Fibrositis is the term applied to a vague clinical entity consisting of nonarticular pain of the musculoskeletal system that is more prevalent in the aged individual. Lumbosacral musculature is most often involved with the patient complaining of stiffness and tenderness, fatigue, and mood swings. These complaints are more intense upon awakening. Soft tissue sites involved are the occipital crest, trapezius, erector spinae, the lumbar triangle, the anterior superior spine, midthigh and gluteus, medial knee, and adductor tubercle. Terms used to describe this syndrome, such as neurasthenia, anxiety neurosis, hypochondriasis, psychogenic rheumatism, and finally neurotic depression, presume a psychogenic component but do not adequately address the unusual spectrum of symptoms manifested nor their relation to the sleep–wake cycle. Complaints of disturbed sleep are common in these patients, and Moldofsky and colleagues have described criteria for this entity (Moldofsky, Scarisbrick, England, & Smythe, 1975). Polysomnographic evaluation of sleep in 7 of 10 of these patients revealed NREM sleep disturbance in the form of alpha intrusions into stages 2, 3, and 4. It is postulated that the association of an arousal rhythm (alpha) in NREM sleep periods may constitute an internal arousal mechanism that competes with NREM sleep, producing the symptoms of fibrositis.

As a disease that expresses itself in later life with pain, deformity, and limitation of joint motion, the early form of osteoarthritis may not show up via conventional laboratory tests. At autopsy, degenerative changes of weight-bearing joints can be found in 90% of individuals by age 40. Radiographic changes occur later in life, mostly at the weight-bearing joints. The standout feature is pain, generally caused by activity and relieved by rest. Joints involved are the knees, hip, spine, and distal/proximal interphalangeal joints of the fingers, with women affected 10 times more frequently than men. As it progresses, pain often disrupts the sleeping process. Once established, treatment revolves around relief of pain and preservation of joint mobility. Frequently, stabilization of the condition is too late to relieve the insomnia. Though reasonably free of crippling pain, patients still cannot initiate and maintain a stable rest–activity cycle.

Cardiovascular and Cardiac Disorders

The prevalence of essential hypertension increases with age such that 30% of males and 50% of females over 65 will have systolic blood pressures of 160 or greater (165 being the cutoff for HBP in the aged) or diastolic pressure of 95 or greater (upper limit of normal). Current treatment emphasizes pharmacological intervention, yet most antihypertensives have central nervous system side effects in this age group and may disrupt the sleeping process. Beta-blockers, reserpine, clonidine, and alphamethyldopa may produce psychosis, affective disorders, mood disturbance, and insomnia. Diuretics can produce nocturia, resulting in frequent unwanted awakening and difficulty reinitiating the sleeping process.

Congestive heart failure, which is more prevalent among the aged and describes the heart muscle's inability to maintain adequate circulatory integrity, often leads to troubled sleep. Nocturnal dyspnea is indicative of left ventricular dysfunction, as fluid accumulation in the lungs produces a feeling of asphyxia. Patients wake up with a feeling of air hunger (Simpson, 1969).

The pain of angina pectoris, a symptom of compromised coronary artery circulation, may produce prolonged sleep latency and reduced stage 3 and 4 sleep (Karacan, Williams, & Raylor, 1969). Such pain is anxiety provoking at any time and, when it occurs at night, disrupts the sleeping process. Patients who undergo coronary artery bypass surgery, a common form of intervention for patients with angina, often have their sleep–wake schedule disrupted by hospital routine. Postoperatively, they spend time in intensive care units where understandably little attention is paid to the sleep–wake cycle. The older patient may have difficulty readjusting biological rhythms after discharge, finding it difficult to re-establish his or her previous schedule. Issues such as postoperative depression, fear of death during intercourse, anxiety over medical bills, and reduced self-esteem are all issues that can exacerbate and perpetuate a hospital or medical-induced sleep disturbance, and are often ignored by the health care team.

Chronic Obstructive Pulmonary Disease

Obstructive airway disease is the major cause of pulmonary disability in the elderly, with Chronic Obstructive Pulmonary Disease (COPD) and asthma comprising a great majority of the clinical entities involved. COPD victims are usually males over 50 with a long smoking history whose major symptoms are shortness of breath upon exertion. The natural history of this entity is characterized by a long period without symptoms, finding a peak incidence in the fifth decade. Complaints of poor sleep are common in this group. One study documented less than 6 hours sleep among 20 patients (Giblin, Garmon, Anderson, Kline, & DeLancey, 1980). They had frequent awakenings and subsequent increased levels of stage 1 sleep (probably secondary to the numerous arousals). Marked decrements in REM and stages 3 and 4 sleep were found. Other studies have shown that oxygen desaturation is worsened in REM sleep, with SaO_2 17.5% lower than the waking state (Fleetham et al., 1982). These periods of desaturation are not secondary to sleep apnea. Reports suggest that the degree of hypoxemia in wakefulness corresponds with a worsening dip in SaO_2 during sleep. Alveolar hypoventilation in COPD patients increases from wakefulness through sleep and reaches a zenith during REM sleep. Prolonged hypoxemia often leads to pulmonary hypertension, heart failure, and cardiac arrhythmias. Nocturnal low-flow oxygen has prolonged (Nocturnal oxygen therapy trial group, 1980) survival and reduced morbidity in one major study. This is a controversial area because oxygen may prolong apneas in patients with OSA syndrome. Therefore, concurrent recordings of sleep and respiration during a trial of low-flow oxygen may be indicated in some patients who have COPD and a suggestion of OSA.

Treatment with bronchodilators, which are sympathomimetics and have stimulant effects, may further disrupt sleep. Glucocorticoids have well-known negative effects on sleep and are often used when bronchospasm exists. The difficulty for the patient and health provider is to reach an acceptable balance between life-prolonging treatment and their unavoidable effects on sleep. If both patient and provider are aware that sleep disruption may be prolonged, other forms of sleep-promoting measures can be employed. Some of these are sleep hygiene, more appropriate timing of medications, and avoidance of sleep-promoting medications that can blunt respiratory drive. What is achieved for the patient is his or her assurance that the physician is aware that the sleep complaint is not psychogenic and has a very real organic basis. Such reassurance may reduce anxiety to the point where better sleep may be obtained.

Asthma

Asthma is characterized by airway hyperreactivity. In the aged, it is most often precipitated by a viral upper respiratory infection. When wheezing begins, it often requires steroids to control bronchospasm. These patients often have attacks of nocturnal dyspnea and report poor sleep. Sleep studies have shown that asthmatic episodes can occur in REM sleep, but most often occur in NREM sleep. As happens with patients with COPD, the medications needed to control the symptoms may disrupt sleep, and although used on a short-term basis, may be the precipitant that leads to a prolonged sleep complaint. Bronchodilators have a spasmolytic effect on the gastroesophageal junction, possibly accounting for the high incidence of reflux in asthmatics, and may lead to nocturnal bronchoconstriction. The incidence of gastric aspiration into lung tissue increases as we age and acts as another source for bronchial irritation. Mucous plugging can compromise airway tone, and even healthy younger individuals are found to have decreased mucociliary tone at night. Further compromise is noted as we age, lending some credence to excess plugging as a contributory factor.

It has been suggested that nocturnal decrease in cortisol and epinephrine secretion removes two bronchial protectors of airway hyperreactivity, allowing vagal tone to predominate and produce nocturnal wheezing. Although there is some evidence to support a role for the circadian rhythmicity of these secretions and bronchospasm, it remains clear that nocturnal asthma is a multifactorial problem that may result in disturbed sleep.

Gastrointestinal Disorders

Nocturnal awakening secondary to epigastric pain is considered the most important symptom of duodenal ulcer disease. It is clinically accepted that pulmonary aspiration and subsequent pneumonia occur during the hours of sleep, especially in the middle-aged and older groups, and that gastric acid secretion is pathophysiologically involved. Although extensive investigations into the circadian rhythms of gastric acid secretion have not been performed, available data indicate a peak from 10 P.M. to midnight and a trough between 8 and 10 A.M. Studies done in the mid-1970s did not reveal any relationship between acid secretions and stages of sleep (Orr, Hall, Stahl, Durkin, & Whitsett, 1976). They did demonstrate that acid inhibition did not occur at the time of highest secretion, shortly after the onset of the first sleep period. Recent successes in treating these patients with nocturnal acid suppressors, rather than 24-hour therapy, suggest some rhythmic vulnerability in the pathogenesis of duodenal ulcer disease.

Gastroesophageal Reflux

Gastroesophageal reflux is even more common than peptic ulcer disease, especially among the older population, and is often diagnostically confused with chest pain of cardiac origin, gall stones, hyperventilation, cervical disk disease, and peptic ulcer itself. Patients who complain of heartburn often have nocturnal reflux, with an excessive amount of time required to clear the acid secretion. Entities such as pulmonary aspiration, esophageal ulcer, and strictures may be the results of prolonged exposure of the epithelium to nocturnal acid secretion.

Ulcer Disease

States of acid hypersecretion occur in duodenal ulcer, esophageal irritation, gastric irritation, and gastric ulcer. Nocturnal acid secretion is known to be excessive in these conditions and may be partly responsible for the chronic, gnawing pain that occurs. Gastric ulcer is more likely to occur in the aged, with the ratio of duodenal ulcer to gastric being 2 to 1 in the elderly, a distinct reversal of the 10 to 1 ratio of youth. Symptoms are atypical with unusual pain and catastrophic clinical consequences, such as bleeding or perforation. Duodenal ulcer patients secrete 3 to 20 times as much nocturnal gastric acid as do normals (Stacher, Presslich, & Starker, 1955).

Orr studied patients with ulcer disease, but could not demonstrate any significant relationship between sleep stages and acid concentration, output, or serum gastric levels (Orr et al., 1976). The study was short and the patients not very ill, so it is difficult to draw further conclusions concerning sleep stages and exacerbation of ulcer disease. Although it is currently recommended that blockers of acid secretion, such as Tagamet and Ranitidine can be used nocturnally, these drugs may produce insomnia and profound changes in mental status in the elderly. In particular, the first generation histamine–2 blockers have a propensity toward drug interactions.

Chronic Renal Insufficiency

Although there is a significant decline in renal function with age, many forms of chronic renal impairment are secondary to other age-related infirmities. Benign prostatic hypertrophy, which is ubiquitous in older males, may lead to hydronephrosis if left untreated. Other examples include renal failure secondary to drug toxicity, atherosclerosis, or tumor. The older person's thirst sensation is often compromised, leading to dehydration and further impairment of renal function.

Patients who undergo chronic dialysis often complain of disturbed sleep, with both the patient and their spouses victimized by the illness and procedure needed to keep it under control. Laboratory studies of uremic patients demonstrate long periods of awakening from all sleep stages (Karacan, Williams, Bose, Hursch, & Warson, 1972). Total sleep time is less, and there are less than normal amounts of stages 3 and 4. The severity of the sleep disturbance correlates with the blood urea nitrogen, which is not excreted normally in patients with impaired renal function. Blood purification by various forms of dialysis improves the disturbed sleep, and as their cycles achieve more stability, stages 3 and 4 increase (Passouant, Cadilhac, Baldy–Moulinier, & Mion, 1970).

METABOLICAL DISORDERS

Hypothyroidism

Failure of the thyroid gland, with its central role in regulation of many metabolical processes, is more common in the older age group than younger adults. The difficulty in making a clinical diagnosis is that symptoms are not so dramatically different than in normal older individuals. Some of these are changes in weight, changes in skin turgor, fatigue, tiredness and irritability, and depression.

Kales found no difference in REM percentage, total sleep time, sleep latency, and number of REM periods between a control group and seven hypothyroid patients studied via overnight polysomnography (Kales et al., 1967). The amount of time in stages 3 and 4 were markedly reduced in hypothyroid subjects, but this condition returned to normal after treatment with dessicated thyroid.

Subjectively, patients complain of sleepiness and inability to function well during the day. There are no studies concerning the effects of hypothyroidism on sleep in the aged population. One can only speculate whether the known reduction in stages 3 and 4 in the elderly is somehow related to a change in the functional economy of an aging thyroid gland or even perhaps that our current reference standards for testing are due for reappraisal.

Hyperthyroidism

In the older population, an overactive thyroid gland is usually due to multi-nodular goiter, as opposed to the diffuse enlargement of Graves disease in a younger population. Symptomatic presentation can be dramatically different in apathetic thyrotoxicosis in an older adult, somewhat opposite of what would be expected in a state of chronic glandular hypersecretion. Instead of overactivity, nervousness, and feelings of being energized, we see apathy, depression, inactivity, weight loss, anorexia, and constipation. Left untreated, patients sink into a coma and die. The profound tiredness and fatigue seems to resemble hypersomnolence, drug abuse, or drunkenness.

Hyperthyroidism increases stage 3 and 4 sleep and accounted for up to 70% of total sleep time in one study, with the normal percentage being closer to 25% (Dunleavy, Oswald, Brown, & Strong, 1974). With restoration of thyroid function to normal levels, sleep stages reverted back to normal. As in hypothyroidism, only speculation exists as to other effects hyperthyroidism may have on the aged sleep process. For example, do hyperthyroid states restore the percentage of deep sleep to normal in an otherwise healthy aged individual? Information to answer this question does not exist.

Diabetes Mellitus

The aging process brings with it a certain degree of glucose intolerance, namely a defective mechanism by which to metabolize carbohydrates. Approximately one-half of patients over 70 years of age would achieve "abnormal results" 2 hours after ingestion of an oral glucose load and be considered mildly diabetic, resulting in a misrepresentation of the incidence of true diabetes mellitus, which is elevation of fasting blood sugar. The abnormal utilization of carbohydrates in the older adult is not characterized by a paucity of insulin or elevated fasting blood glucose values, but rather involves a decrease in peripheral sensitivity to insulin, albeit a problem with cell receptors.

True diabetes mellitus is known to affect 25% of individuals over 85, with a clinical presentation dissimilar to that of youth. Changes in renal function elevate the level at which glycosuria is found as high as 300 mg/dl (nl 70–140). Symptoms such as polyuria and polydypsia are infrequently reported. Neurological findings of peripheral neuropathy, cranial nerve palsies, and nonketotic hyperosmolar coma predominate as presenting signs and symptoms. In contrast to youth, the aged diabetic has considerably higher levels of blood glucose, frequently above 700, and a plasma osmolality of 350–400 (nl 285–295), reflecting profound intravascular volume depletion. The majority of elderly diabetics are not insulin-deficient and can be managed with diet and oral antihyperglycemics. This group is considered type II, noninsulin-dependent, adult-onset diabetics, in contrast to the type I, insulin-dependent "juvenile" onset diabetic.

The development of peripheral and autonomic neuropathy is associated with duration of insulin dependence and the degree of control achieved. Autonomic neuropathy is associated with irregularities and instability of the autonomic nervous system's ability to control heart rate, blood pressure, and bladder function. Assuming the upright position from the supine can produce severe hypotension as well as syncope and cardiac arrhythmias.

Guilleminault studied 12 type I and 7 type II diabetics with 2 to 3 nights of polysomnography, daytime pulmonary function tests, and tests of vagal responses (Mondini & Guilleminault, 1985). Five of the type I subjects had sleep-related respiratory dysfunction, mainly central and obstructive sleep apnea. Daytime pulmonary function tests were normal. Five of the subjects were felt to have autonomic neuropathy and 3 of them had apnea. The fourth had breathing irregularities in stages 3 and 4 sleep. One type I patient with sleep-related respiratory irregularities did not have evidence of neuropathy. Only one type II patient, an overweight male, had evidence of apnea, mostly obstructive, with mild oxygen desaturation. The type I patients had blunted cardiac responses to the apneas. The association between autonomic neuropathy and an excessive 3-year mortality rate, when compared with control groups, suggests a relation between sleep death and autonomic dysfunction in type I diabetics.

Another study of the same subjects found much wider variations in blood pressure during REM than what is usually found, possibly attributable to the presence of autonomic neuropathy.

NEUROLOGICAL CONDITIONS

Senile Dementia of the Alzheimer's Type and Sundowning

Senile Dementia of the Alzheimer's Type is a progressive, degenerative disease of insidious onset, involving many areas of cognition in an otherwise alert individual. The presenting symptom is generally a difficulty with recent memory and remembering names. Certain patients, however, will exhibit problems with primary language or visuospatial abilities. Eventually, the patient will have deficits in many spheres of daily living, such as dressing, feeding, and toileting, and will require a great deal of familial or outside assistance or even placement in a long-term care facility (Katzman, 1986).

Patients with Senile Dementia of the Alzheimer's Type and other dementing illnesses often have major disruptions of the sleep–wake cycle, including fragmentation of nocturnal sleep and napping during the day, difficulty initiating and maintaining sleep, decreased amounts of the deeper stages of sleep, stages 3 and 4, as well as large decrements in the percentage of REM sleep (Prinz et al., 1982). It should be emphasized that these changes bear some resemblance to the alterations in sleep that occur in the elderly; however, these changes are pathological in their extremity.

Sundowning, a clinical phenomenon not part of the normal aging process, is a disruptive behavioral pattern associated with sleep or the timing of the usual sleep period. As an eponym used to describe episodes associated with dementing illness, sundowning encompasses a spectrum of unusual but transient behavior whose etiology is poorly understood and whose treatment currently relies on the long-term use of physical or chemical restraints. Partly to reflect the time of day in which it is observed and the disorientation that is an integral part of its clinical presentation, it is often referred to as nocturnal senile confusion. Other terms commonly used include nocturnal hallucinosis, nocturnal wandering, nocturnal delirium, and nocturnal agitation. All of these terms describe various facets of the syndrome that may be observed in isolation or in combination with one another.

The anecdotal descriptions of sundowning most commonly exhibit the following characteristics. With the onset of early evening hours, these patients change from relatively docile, cooperative, manageable individuals into agitated, confused, verbally or physically aggressive individuals. They wander from room to room, speaking nonsensically and cannot be placed in bed at their usual time. Sundowners do not usually exhibit clouding of consciousness or speech impairment; their behavior indicates a state of inappropriate hyperactivity without any single or obvious stimulus (Prinz & Raskind, 1978; Winograd & Jarvik, 1986). Somewhat unpredictable, sundowning can occur throughout the 24-hour day in varying degrees of severity and duration. Some patients have trouble initiating the sleeping process for 3 or 4 hours due to complications of excess motor activity and irritability. They fall asleep at 1 or 2 A.M. and remain in bed until 6 or 7 A.M. Others fall asleep with relative ease, only to awaken 3 or 4 hours later in a state of profound confusion and hallucinosis. Although the literature is sparse, it suggests that sundowning often begins in the moderate stage of the disorder (Lowenstein, Weingartner, Gillin, Ebert, & Mendelson, 1982). It is postulated that many of the manifestations of sundowning, with its disturbed sleep physiology, represent a breakdown of the previously stable control of sleep–wake cycles, secondary to anatomic damage to the various centers involved in the initiation and maintenance of the sleep–wake cycle (Sterman & Shouse, 1985). Intervention is called for before the situation becomes dangerous to the patient, family members, or other patients. Stabilization is achieved through pharmacotherapy, either neuroleptics or sedative/tranquilizers. Studies to date do not demonstrate one treatment as more efficacious than another (Barnes & Raskind, 1980). If episodes of sundowning are unresponsive to treatment, patients are often placed in nursing homes where this disruptive behavior is better tolerated.

Parkinson's Disease

This degenerative disease of the central nervous system is predominantly a bane of the geriatric population. In its early phases, diagnosis is often missed as the patient's lack of initiative, blank expression, abulia, motor slowness, and intellectual apathy are dismissed as "old age." As it progresses, a tremor may be noted in the upper extremities, the gait is shuffling, the patient is stooped with diminished arm swing, the face is expressionless, and there is significant difficulty in beginning movements. When James Parkinson first diagnosed this syndrome, no formal physical examination was performed (Parkinson, 1817). In order to display the characteristic retropulsion of these patients, Dr. Parkinson would poke them gingerly with his cane to initiate gait and hurriedly run ahead to stop them before an accident ensued. Once started, these patients have difficulty stopping their gait.

The substantia nigra, a dopamine-containing segment of the basal ganglia, undergoes progressive degeneration that is not halted by current drug therapy. Although the discovery that these parts of the brain contain neurotransmitters, such as dopamine, which are involved in motor coordination, logically led to the discovery that replacement with L-dopa could ameliorate symptoms, the pathological destruction of tissue continues. Unfortunately, all medications used are fraught with side effects. L-dopa, a replacement analogue for dopamine, causes nausea and gastrointestinal upset, hallucinations, and dyskinesias, to name a few unwanted side effects. Anticholinergics can cause increased mental confusion, blurred vision, dry mouth, and bladder paralysis. The search for agents with more efficacy and fewer side effects continues.

Nocturnally, these patients have trouble with sleep initiation and maintenance. L-dopa's role in sleep is controversial (Matsumoto & Jouvet, 1964). It has been described as (a) not changing sleep patterns, (b) increasing REM sleep and decreasing deep sleep, (c) decreasing REM sleep, and (d) decreasing REM sleep only when excessive amounts of L-dopa are prescribed. Other work states that the number of sleep spindles and their duration increases in patients with Parkinson's disease (Askenasy & Yahr, 1985). Amantidine, which stimulates the release of dopamine at specific nerve terminals in the brain, improved sleep quantitatively in patients with Parkinson's disease, but polysomnographically only increased the number of sleep spindles. Yahr demonstrated a disturbed sleep pattern in patients before dopaminergic replacement (Askenasy & Yahr, 1985). Sleep was light and fragmented, with increased muscle activity. With dopaminergic replacement, the sleep pattern was improved, muscle activity normalized, and clinical improvement was noted as well. The five patients studied showed improvement in sleep efficiency. Kales studied six patients with Parkinson's disease in the sleep laboratory prior to the administration of L-dopa (Kales, Ansel, Markham, Scharf, & Tan, 1971). These patients had prolonged sleep latency and frequent long nocturnal arousals, as compared with a normal elderly control group. Treatment with L-dopa for longer than 2 weeks resulted in no change from REM baseline values, and sleep induction and efficiency were unaltered by treatment.

Although insomnia may be a prominent complaint in patients with Parkinson's disease, authorities recommend dopaminergic replacement for its clinical efficacy in reducing the rigidity and other problems of these patients. It may not improve sleep in some patients and its side effects may make the insomnia worse. As in other insomnias, poor sleep hygiene, excessive time in bed, and going to bed too early may all be involved in the perpetuation of poor sleep in these patients.

Migraine

The diagnosis of migraine headaches is usually made in the second to fourth decade of life. Clinically, migraine is representative of a diffuse alteration in vascular physiology, and headaches occur when the central nervous system is involved via distention of its blood vessels. Other symptoms are related to vessels in spasm, producing paresthesias as the episode begins. In the older age group, headaches themselves may not be as prominent a feature as visual and sensory alterations. Paresthesias often spreads slowly from one anatomical location to another, with subsequent feelings of numbness replacing them. Speech impairment may occur after the sensory modality has returned to normal. Those in the older age group often trace their headaches or visual/sensory symptoms back to youth, although a firm diagnosis may not have been made. Treatment revolves around anticonvulsants such as Dilantin or beta-blockers such as Inderal, both known to affect sleep architecture.

Migraine patients often awaken nocturnally or in the morning with a headache. Available data support the occurrence of nocturnal migraines during REM sleep, with 17 of 19 nocturnal migraine episodes either beginning in REM sleep or shortly before or after a REM period (Dexter & Weitzman, 1970). Other treatments, such as serotonin antagonists, produce insomnia so severe that patients discontinue the medication.

Institutionally Induced Insomnia

Currently, 1.3 million people are quietly spending the rest of their lives in long-term care facilities, including nursing homes (Butler & Lewis, 1982). This is more than the number of people who occupy acute care beds on any given day. Although they currently represent 15% of the population, 40% of all hospital admissions are for people over 65 (the age for Medicare eligibility). Their average length of stay is longer, they consume more drugs, utilize more resources, and have prolonged periods of recovery. The aging process compromises our previous vigor, creating a vulnerability to disruptions, and extending our adjustment period to changes in the rest–activity cycle.

Hospitals are no place for anyone interested in or needing a good night's sleep. Patients are awakened for vital signs, temperature recording, and toileting. While younger patients, whose sleep is more efficient, can recover quickly and do not need prolonged sedation, their older counterparts have more difficulty. An insomnia begun in the hospital is often perpetuated on the outside by a prescription of sedatives that may lose their effectiveness after one month. Meanwhile, the insomnia that was transient becomes chronic, and the patients complain bitterly that they have not slept well since they went into the hospital.

SUMMARY

The application of basic sleep and medical knowledge to the domain of the sleeping patient has resulted in rapid progress in delineating disease entities, pathophysiological mechanisms, and improved treatments. The need for this type of interdisciplinary approach is evidenced by the increasing numbers of sleep disorders centers and certified sleep specialists, called clinical polysomnographers, in the past 12 years. The initial groundwork of common language, shared classificatory system, proven techniques, standards of clinical knowledge and professional institutions to maintain high standards, promote research, and facilitate communications of findings have been established. In the future, systematic training programs of clinical sleep disorders will be available, and the interdependence of basic and clinical research will foster collaborations and focus research endeavors. We have devoted special attention in this review to clinical issues related to sleep and aging because we believe that in the future, this area will serve an ever-increasing role in the elucidation of basic sleep mechanisms, clarification of concepts such as the ability to sleep and the need for sleep, and will become the major focus of the clinical practice of sleep disorders.

PART 1

METHODOLOGY AND SLEEP MENTATION STUDIES

2

Measurement and Design in Research on Sleep Reports

JOHN S. ANTROBUS
GEORGE FEIN
LARRY JORDAN
STEVEN J. ELLMAN
ARTHUR M. ARKIN
City College of The City University of New York

In the broad sense of the term, the "measurement" of the characteristics of sleep reports ranges from the clinical "interpretation of dreams" to formal psychometric scaling procedures. The notion that the interpretation of dreams constitutes a form of judgment or multidimensional measurement of the characteristics of the sleeper and the sleeper's cognitive processes has not been developed in the research literature and for that reason is not discussed further in this chapter.

In this chapter we consider certain issues regarding the subject's report of the sleep experience, particularly the method of eliciting the sleeper's report, the optimum number of reports to obtain, order effects in the sleep report, memory and attention during sleep, and postawakening biases in the report. We then consider methods for improving judgments based upon sleep reports. Finally, we compare the merits of several research designs together with their statistical models for determining the association of sleep-report variables (judgments) and physiological events and states.

For our purposes, the measurement of the characteristics of sleep reports includes any systematic procedure whereby judgments about certain qualities are made by an individual, upon awakening, about an experience, a private event, which in the individual's judgment occurred while asleep. A subsequent judgment may often be made by a second person or judge, based on the verbal report, or occasionally on a drawing, produced by the awakened sleeper.

For the purpose of analyzing the measurement issue in this area, it is useful to classify the judgments or measures on two factors: (a) whether the judgments are made only by the sleeper or jointly in a sleeper–second-judge sequence; and (b) whether the judgments are to be compared with an independent criterion such as stage REM versus NREM sleep.

THE SLEEPER AS DREAMER AND JUDGE

Let us begin with a look at the subject who is awakened from sleep and asked to report on whatever was going through the subject's mind before being awakened. *We propose here that the "verbal report" itself be regarded as a set of judgments, albeit unsystematic judgments, about the subject's private experience prior to awakening.* The subject judges the names of the persons, objects, and events "seen" and "heard"; he judges the color and brightness of the images, kinesthetic sensations, and intentions of the dream characters. Second, the subject judges how many of these judgments–statements are required for a report that will satisfy the experimenter. Thus, remembering a very long dream sequence, the subject may summarize the visual detail in order to report the plot within a reasonable interval of time. Recalling almost nothing, the sleeper may stretch one or two vague images into several sentences. This tendency will attenuate the distinction between REM and NREM reports. It may be counteracted by asking the subject for as much detail as possible.

Finally, we present evidence that suggests that, at least in REM sleep, the subject may make judgments while asleep about the relevance of the sleep experience to the experiment (or psychotherapy), and thus make the experience more available for subsequent recall.

As scientists, who also dream, we would like to take the subject's report at face value as an accurate description of the sleeper's prior state. Yet there are clear limits to our gullibility. Interestingly, in the two cases in which discrepancies exist between the sleeper's report and independent evidence concerning the validity of the report, we rule the report in error. There is the child who believes that there was a bad man in the room and we know there really wasn't. Then there is the subject who claims being awake and thinking despite the fact that posture and EEG indicate sound sleep. We reject the subject's judgment about wakefulness. After reading Goodenough's (1967) account of a subject who said he was *thinking* and who gave a vivid account of going to the rear of the classroom, operating a pinball machine which spilled out all its contents, and then observing an oil well under the machine, we are also disinclined to accept the subject's judgment that he was thinking rather than dreaming. But, in the absence of an independent measure of the sleeper's thought and imagery, we too easily tend to take the report uncritically.

Experimenter Bias

One plausible, potential factor affecting subjects' report-judgments is experimenter bias. Inasmuch as this issue is a complex one, we make only a passing comment here. Since the beginning of sleep-mentation research we have been concerned about the possibility that the experimenters might unintentionally communicate to the subject something about the experimenter's knowledge of the EEG waking criterion. Thus, the experimenter might inadvertently alter the inflection or loudness of voice, or be more likely to repeat a question if aware that the subject was awakened from stage REM rather than from NREM sleep. Fortunately, this problem can be managed by tape-recording the awakening stimulus (usually the subject's name) and all subsequent questions.

Dependence of Judges on Subjects' Judgments

In most sleep-mentation studies, the standard requests utilized are: (a) "Tell me everything that was going through your mind"; and, when the subject finishes, (b) "Was there anything else?" Since the questions are open-ended, the subject is quite free to decide how much information to provide. For example, if the subject is struck by an odd or bizarre combination of elements in the dream, little information may be provided about the hallucinatory quality of the experience. Now let us suppose that we wish to have an independent set of persons judge or rate the strength of such different qualities of the sleep experience as: vividness of the visual imagery, bizarreness, and hallucinatory quality. This second set of judges must base their judgments upon the judgment-reports of the subject. Like the subjects' judgments, those of the independent set of judges are about the private experience of the sleeper, but the qualities judged are generally more abstract. If the subject has made a number of judgment-reports or simple statements about the bizarreness of the experience, the judges will have a reasonable basis for making a more abstract rating of this quality. If there is no specific statement about the vividness of the visual imagery, then a judgment about this quality may be inferred from the number or, perhaps, relative frequency of concrete nouns, action verbs, and so on in the original report. If no specific mention is made about the hallucinatory quality of the experience, then the judges may have little choice other than to infer its absence. In other words, the validity of the judges' judgments is totally at the mercy of how much information is contained in the judgment-reports of the subject.

Open-Ended versus Specific Questions

Foulkes (1966) and other investigators have attempted to rectify this matter by asking the subject to make judgments in the form of simple descriptive statements about several specific qualities of interest to the investigator. Following the first two questions mentioned above, the subject may be asked, "How vivid was the visual imagery?" "How much emotion . . . ?" and "How real . . . ?" As the procedure is repeated, the subject eventually learns to report on each of these dimensions when responding to the first question, that is, without a reminder from the specific questions. In a recent study, we also asked the subject to make a numerical rating of the magnitude of these qualities. Although the results have not yet been formally analyzed, the numerical response appears promising.

How Many Questions?

In the course of replicating the Molinari and Foulkes (1969) phasic-tonic study, Foulkes and Pope (1972) produced some evidence suggesting that judgments and ratings are more valid when based only upon the response to the first two questions. When judges in the Foulkes and Pope study were given subjects' responses to one open-ended question plus five specific questions regarding the sensory quality of the sleep experience, there was no distinction between the phasic and tonic sleep reports. When, however, they used only the responses to the initial open-ended questions, they obtained a statistically significant difference between the two. Foulkes and Pope asked whether the significance is spurious or whether subjects' responses tend to be more similar from condition to condition when they are question-cued about specific qualities of their sleep experience. Obviously, further examination of the matter is appropriate.

We decided to study the discriminability of stage REM and stage 2 reports among the 20 subjects in the Arkin, Antrobus, and Ellman study reported in Chapters 11 and 15. We compared responses to only 2 open-ended questions versus all 5 questions, the last 3 of which were: "How vivid and clear was the sleep experience you just described?," "What feelings were you aware of in the course of the sleep experience?," and "To what extent did the experience seem like it was really happening?" Each subject contributed one stage REM and one stage 2 report from each of the first 2 baseline nights. Each report was rated on the basis of the response to the first 2 baseline nights. Each report was rated on the basis of the response to the first 2 questions and on the response to all 5. The entire pool of 160 reports from 80 awakenings was rated for magnitude of dreaming on an 8-point forced-normal distribution. Eight judges were arranged so that each judge rated 80 reports, 40 2-question reports, and 40 5-question reports, from 80 awakenings. That is, no judge rated a 2-question and a 5-question item from the same awakening.

Judges rated the 5-question responses higher on dreaming than the 2-question reports (5.1 and 4.7 respectively; $F = 13.6$; $p \leq .01$) on an 8-point scale, collapsing sleep stages. The difference between stage REM and stage 2 reports was 0.87, identical for the 2- and 5-question responses ($F = 27.7$; $p \leq .01$). In short, the main effects for sleep stage, number of questions, and order of session were statistically significant, but no interaction existed between number of questions and sleep stage. That is, the discriminability of sleep stage was independent of the number of questions asked.

Order Effects

Whenever possible, sleep studies are designed so that all subjects go through all experimental conditions. The data are analyzed by means of a randomized block analysis-of-variance solution which is a powerful statistical procedure, but one which is quite sensitive to violations of the statistical assumptions upon which it is based. Violations of compound symmetry of the variance-covariance matrix (Winer, 1971) are commonly caused by a host of order effects which properly should be checked before proceeding with the analysis of variance. Failure to satisfy the assumptions results in significance levels that purport to be better than they really are, and the bias increases as the sample size decreases.

Antrobus, Arkin, and Toth (1972) found that word count of subjects' reports decreases as a function of number of baseline nights in the lab (see Figure 2.1). Employing a partial sleep-deprivation procedure bounded by a pair of pre- and a pair of postdeprivation baseline nights, we found that word count decreased from the first to the last baseline night; the drop being larger for stage REM awakenings than for stage 2. Since we decided to modify the procedures after running only 10 subjects, the decrements,

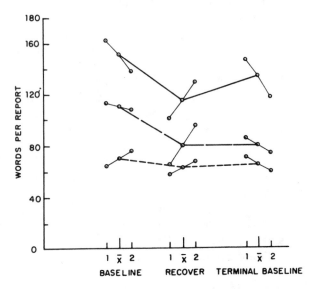

FIGURE 2.1. Word count per report from REMP, NREMP 5 min. after REMP and NREMP, 15 min. after REMP, before, during, and after recovery from REM deprivaton.

while sizable, were not statistically significant. Changes in fatigue or motivation seemed likely reasons for the decrement in word count. Fatigue was ruled out, however, because the last two nights were preceded by normal home sleep so that the decrement could not be attributed to sleep loss or similar short-term experimental effects.

First-Night-Report Effect. The final version of this experiment (see Chapters 11 and 15) was designed to give more careful attention to order effects, particularly inasmuch as each of 20 subjects went through both stage 1 REM and stage 2 deprivation. Night 1 was preceded by 3 adaptation nights in which no awakenings for sleep reports were made. Night 3 was preceded by at least 3 nights of normal home sleep, but night 5 was preceded by a laboratory recovery night, which in turn was preceded by 3 nights of either stage 1 REM or stage 2 deprivation. Postadaptation laboratory nights 1 and 2, 3 and 4, and 6 and 7 were established as first, middle, and terminal baseline nights. The reports were rated on an 8-point scale for dreamlike quality. (For a complete description of the procedures and results, see Chapter 11.) The mean ratings by night, early and late half of the night, and sleep stage are presented in Figure 2.2.

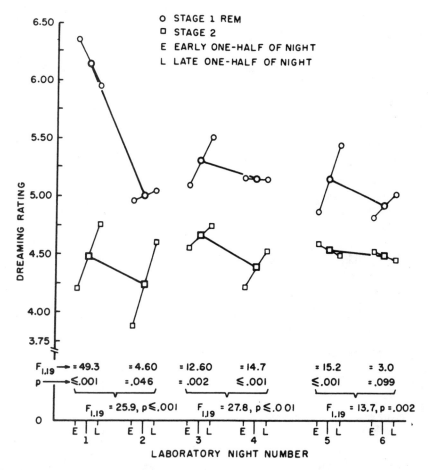

FIGURE 2.2. Dreaming ratings for 20 subjects by number of nights in the laboratory, and early versus late halves of the night.

Some of the order effects in Figure 2.2 are among the strongest effects of any kind reported in the sleep-mentation literature. They have important implications for the interpretation of the stage 1 REM–NREM effect and for the design of sleep-mentation studies. First, we see that within each of the three pairs of nights, dreaming is always lower in the second member of the pair (mean of stage 1 REM, and stage 2 awakenings). Since normal home sleep did not precede night 5, a statistical test on the difference between first and second members of a pair was carried out only on nights 1, 2, 3, and 4 ($F_{1,19} = 18.38$; $p \leq .01$). By far the largest within-pair drop occurs within stage 1 REM from night 1 to night 2.

The within-night, within-sleep stage effects are not particularly consistent. In general, dreaming is higher during the second half of the night. The order is reversed within the first night, stage 1 REM, so that the largest contrast in dreaming between stage 1 REM and stage 2 occurs during the first half of the first night (see Figure 2.2). Within stage REM only, there is a strong negative linear trend across the three night pairs, but the linear trend for pairs of nights averaged across sleep stages is not significant ($F_{1,19} = 1.48$; $p = .24$).

Looking at the whole-night differences between stage 1 REM and stage 2 dreaming scores, we find the largest contrast occurring during the first night. Figure 2.2 shows how the significance levels vary if we were to carry out tests on different baseline nights. F drops from 49 on night 1 to $F = 4.6$, barely significant at the .05 level, on night 2; and just under the .10 level of significance on night 6.

Throughout this chapter we insist that statistical tests of significance are only gross estimators of the size of experimental effects. We want to know the *magnitude* of the differences between stage 1 REM and stage 2, not simply that the differences are significantly different from zero. If we collapse the design to a simple sleep stage × subjects randomized blocks design and compute omega, the size of effect variable proposed by Hays (1973), omega drops from .68 on night 1 to .10 on night 6. That is, the REM–NREM effect accounts for 68% of the night 1 variance, or variability among scores, but only 10% of the night 6 variance.

The strongest effect in the data appears to be a "novelty" effect associated with verbal report-response. This novelty effect appears strongest within stage REM; it appears largely dissipated by the second night in which reports are elicited. Being absent from the laboratory appears to revive the novelty motivation (night 7); but sleeping in the laboratory without being asked to report "What was going through your mind. . . ?" (night 1 versus night 7) may further enhance the effect. The decrement in dreaming may be caused by an effort or cost of attending to one's REM mentation such that the negative cost effect accumulates over time in REM sleep.

Interaction of Order Effect with Sleep Stage

We may now return to the original issue of distinguishing what goes on within the sleeper's experience from possible biases in the verbal report-description of the experience. By bias, we refer to variation in the attention, selectivity, motivation, alertness, and memory for the original sleep experience. The problem may be limited somewhat by looking only at the difference in the responses to two states or stages of sleep. Biases that are common to both states may thereby be canceled out. Since, however, we do not have an independent measure of the sleeper's internal experience, we cannot easily determine whether the response biases are equal in the two states. In the case of the first night effect and first half-night effect in Figure 2.2, such simple motivational response sets as the subject wanting to perform well and please the experimenter by giving thorough detailed report cannot by itself account for an effect that occurs in only stage REM. Perhaps the finding by Williams, Hammack, Daly, Dement, and Lubin (1964) is pertinent: Compared to NREM sleep, subjects in REM sleep show a large drop in response threshold to a "significant stimulus" (response avoids loud noise) relative to a stimulus that was not paired with the noxious noise. The significance or consequences of responding to the stimulus were "interpreted" by the sleeper during stage REM sleep whereas the physical qualities of the stimulus were the sole determiners of probability of response within NREM sleep. To interpret the relevance of the perceptual and cognitive elements of one's sleeping experience in terms of a potential future request for a verbal report-response is an operation similar to that required of Williams et al.'s (1964) sleepers—an operation that might well be characteristic of stage REM sleep.

The quality of stage REM sleep may differ on night 1 in some way that distinguishes it both from preceding nights in which no reports were elicited and from subsequent nights when dreaming scores were lower. One might expect more signs of phasic events, for example, during night 1 (see Chapter 7). But just as the physiological description of stage REM sleep has not advanced our understanding of the cognitive processes by which the dream is constructed, so too, the identification of physiological characteristics unique to the first night effect might neither add nor detract from a cognitive explanation of the process. The most promising way to test the preawakening explanations of the first-night effect is to manipulate, by means of instructions, the subject's expectation of the night that sleep will be disrupted.

Memory and Dream Modification

If the first-night-report-effect operates within sleep, it will be essential to determine whether the effect is simply to improve attention to and recall of the stimulus events of the sleep experience of whether the elementary events of the sleep experience, like dreams, are themselves altered in some way. We may think of the sleeper as carrying through time an open-ended box of continuously decaying memory where the rate of decay or loss at one end of the box is approximately equal to the rate of entry of new items. Let us suppose that the first-night-report-effect operates by increasing the length of the box, that is, the number of events in memory or available for report. If the sequence of events generated in the dream is determined in part by the presence of the preceding dream events in the box, then the dream should become more consistent from one moment to the next as the size of the memory box increases. In this case, not only recall of the sleep experience, but the nature of the experience itself would be affected by the first-night-report-effect.

On the other hand, the elements of the sleeper's experience available to the sleeper immediately before the awakening stimulus may be the same on all nights; night 1 may differ only with respect to what happens *after* the awakening stimulus. For example, on night 1 the subject may awaken faster and reach a higher level of arousal before giving the report. Such a possibility could be tested by showing subjects a 5-sec visual or audio-visual movie sequence immediately upon awakening and determining whether their description-reports of the sequence showed the same night-to-night order effect as the stage REM report trend.

Long-Term Order Effects

The long-term order effects are somewhat puzzling because of the tendency of stage 2 dreaming to move in the opposite direction from stage REM dreaming (see Figure 2.2). Perhaps the small positive slope within stage 2 should await replication before interpretation. The net result of the respective positive and negative slopes is a sizable linear decrease in the difference between stage REM and stage 2 as the subjects move through the three baseline night pairs (1 and 2, 3 and 4, and 5 and 6). As the trend continues, the stage REM–NREM effect disappears below statistical significance.

Pre- and Postawakening Biases: Summary

We have argued that order effects possibly involving a sense of novelty or other motivational factors may be associated with postawakening processes such as the retrieval of the sleep experience (visual and auditory images) as well as the manner in which these images are judged and reported by the subject. We have stated that the motivational factor may also operate within sleep, at least stage REM sleep, to improve the amount of imagery events stored and possibly even the manner in which the images are generated. We have suggested some research routes to determine whether the first-night-report-effect is a pre- or postawakening effect or both.

The Real Effect versus Bias

In general, it seems reasonable to assert that postawakening effects would constitute "response bias" whereas preawakening experimental effects, unless they are specific to the experimental procedure, belong to a larger class of factors which affect the sleeper's perceptual-cognitive sleep experience. Let us look at the implications of these alternatives. If the first-night-report-effect operates only as a postawakening one and is restricted to stage REM, and if the effect of order on stage 2 awakenings is trivial, then the first night and other order biases can be removed by comparing the two stages only after the bias asymptotes, for example, after several nights of laboratory awakenings. Even then we cannot be assured that the bias is equal in both sleep stages, but we can be assured that we have removed a very large source of differential bias. We would, thereby, sacrifice considerable detail in the stage REM report in order to make a less biased estimate of the magnitude of the true difference in dreaming, or any other scale, between stages REM and 2. If all of the order effect is response bias, then the asymptote in Figure 2.2 implies that there is no real difference in REM and NREM mentation.

If the first-night-report-effect operates only during the preawakening interval, we would assume that the instructional stimuli which elicit the motivation are part of a larger class of stimuli which could be described experimentally. If the class can be abstracted and defined operationally as a variable, then we might conclude that the effect of stage REM on dreaming or visual imagery is contingent upon the state of that motivational variable; or, that dreaming is a joint function, possibly both linear and interactive of sleep stage and motivation. In other words, the REM/NREM effect on dreaming may not stand alone, or, if it does, only rather weakly.

If the first-night-report-effect operates only during the postawakening interval, we could conclude nothing about the size of the REM/NREM effect on dreaming or other variables unless we found a way to measure and match across the two stages the magnitude of the motivation effect or remove its influence by means of some covariance procedure.

Consequences for Research Design

If a particular effect does actually exist among a population of subjects, we want our experiment which uses only a sample of subjects to pick up, or be sensitive to, this effect. The probability that the experiment will do so is called the power of the experiment. Statistical power is a function of one's significance level, the size of the real effect in the population and, in general, one's sample size. With respect to the difference between stage REM and stage 2, it is clear that the largest difference occurs within the first night, and in particular, the first half of the first night. We have, therefore, optimum statistical power or sensitivity, if we make awakenings only from one night, or for the matter, only from the first half of the first night. Not only is the statistical power lower on all other nights, but it decreases as we combine data from the first night with those of any other night (see Figure 2.2). Of course, the interpretation of all data so gathered must be qualified by the issues raised in the preceding section.

Individual Differences

Individual differences are the brick and mortar of personality theory. Attempts have been made to demonstrate a link between individual differences in sleeping fantasy and daytime fantasy, schizophrenia, and adjustment (Cartwright, 1972; Fisher & Dement, 1963; Foulkes, 1966; Singer & Schonbar, 1961). For those investigators interested in effects that hold across subjects in general, such individual differences constitute a random, nuisance variable. Because misconceptions exist respecting the size and consequences of the nuisance, we would like to devote some space to its consideration.

The statistical model underlying the typical sleep-mentation study is

$$X_{ij} = \mu + \tau_j + \pi_i + \tau\pi_{ij} + \varepsilon_{ij},$$

in which:

X_{ij} = the imagery score of the ith subject under the jth sleep stage;

μ = the mean score of all possible subjects under all j conditions, a constant;

τ_j = the mean of all possible subjects in the jth condition, not just the subjects in the particular sample;

π_i = the mean of the ith subject;

$\tau\pi_{ij}$ = the interaction of the ith subject in the jth sleep stage;

ε_{ij} = all residual unidentified variability, essentially differences between different awakenings under the same condition (j), of a specific subject (i). Where subjects are observed only once in each treatment condition or sleep stage, no separate estimate of ε_{ij} is available (Hays, 1973; Winer, 1971).

In personality research (Singer & Schonbar, 1961) in which the interest is in individual differences in imagery regardless of sleep stage (that is, averaged across sleep stages), the component of interest is π_i. In testing personality models, however, some investigators explicitly refer to individual difference within a specific treatment condition, such as stage REM or REM deprivation. Such individual differences are the sum of $\pi_i + \tau\pi_{ij} + \varepsilon_{ij}$. That reports from a specific condition be reliably different from reports averaged across all conditions assumes that the treatment-by-subject term, $\tau\pi_{ij}$, is appreciably > 0. For example, are individual differences in REM imagery reliably different from individual differences in imagery averaged over all states? With the exception of Foulkes and Vogel's (1965) comparison of REM and sleep onset imagery, to our knowledge, no one studying individual differences has ever tested this assumption in sleep mentation.

We examined individual differences in the effect of stage REM versus stage 2 (REM/2) on dreaming during the first two control nights of our recent study and found that r ranged from .92 to $-.44$ for the 20 subjects, with 4 subjects lying between .1 and $-.44$.

Do all subjects do their own thing? If so, what does the test of the main effect (across subjects) of sleep stage on dreaming mean? The main effect is essentially the effect of the hypothetical "average subject." Under conditions of substantial $\tau\pi$ effects, some investigators have given up testing the main τ effect and proceeded to test a main effect separately on each subject ($\tau + \tau\pi$). This approach is reasonable only if some method of combining the results of several subjects is available, or of independently distinguishing subjects who respond differently to the treatment conditions. It seems to us that the randomized block analysis of variance (ANOVA) combined with estimates of both ω_τ^2 and $\omega_{\tau\pi}^2$ (Fleiss, 1969) remains the best solution. Thus, individual differences in the sleep stage effect may account for 30% of the dreaming variance ($\hat\omega_{\tau\pi}^2 \text{May} = .3$), but it is still worthwhile to know whether the main sleep stage or "average subject" effect ($\hat\omega_\tau^2) = 0$ or .5. Conversely, if $\hat\omega_\tau^2 = .5$ and $\hat\omega_{\tau\pi}^2 = .1$, the "average subject" tells nearly the whole story!

Before estimating the size of ω_τ^2 and $\omega_{\tau\pi}^2$, however, it is appropriate to test the null hypothesis for each. It is possible, as we shall see, for there to be large "individual differences" in scores which are simply due to ε_{ij}, while true individual differences, π and $\tau\pi$ remain essentially = 0.

Since we were not interested in π in the study described in Chapter 11, we eliminated the term and held response scale magnitude constant for all subjects by judging each subject's reports independently on a forced-normal distribution with subject mean and variance = constant. $\tau\pi_{ij}$, however, was free to vary. In designs in which there are no replications in the design, $\tau\pi_{ij} = 0$ may be tested by Tukey's nonadditivity test (see Winer, 1971). Where replicated observations exist, as in our recent study with 6 control nights, $\tau\pi_{ij}$ can be tested directly by the randomized blocks ANOVA or by examining the night-to-night stability of individual differences in dreaming during stage REM versus stage 2. Taking the latter route, we first computed the signed difference in dreaming between stage REM and stage 2 separately one each of 6 control nights and then correlated the differences between all pairs of nights. The mean of the 15 correlations was .03! Apparently, the interaction of REM/2 and dreaming, $\tau_j\pi_i$, is reasonably close to 0. Since visual imagery, hallucinatory quality, and so on correlate strongly with dreaming, it is a reasonably safe hunch that $\tau\pi = 0$ for these variables also.

Because this finding is at variance with the working assumptions of many investigators, it should be replicated and the limits within which it holds should be identified. Note that this result carries absolutely no implication about the significance of the π_i component. This analysis suggests that more attention should be given to our working assumptions about the magnitude of the components of the individual differences in sleep mentation. In the meantime, the main implication of the zero treatment-by-subject interaction is that *the "average subject" model fits nearly all subjects.* There is, therefore, no need or advantage of making separate tests of the REM/NREM effect for each subject. From a statistical point of view, if $\tau_j\pi_i = 0$, then a simpler statistical model may be employed for the randomized blocks design: $X_{ij} = \mu + \pi_i + \tau_j + \varepsilon_{ij}$ (see Winer, 1971). In this model,

$MS_{\text{Treatment} \times \text{Subject}}$ or MS_{Residual} is an estimator simply of σ_ε^2. To the extent that the treat-by-subject interaction = 0 for other treatment effects, such as REM deprivation versus control night, the various subject interactions may be pooled to give a single pooled MS_{Residual} which is a stable estimate of σ_ε^2. Further, the computations of the error terms for factorial models are greatly simplified if all MS_{Residual}s estimate the same σ_ε^2.

Subjects versus Nights

This is perhaps a good point to draw attention to an important procedural issue in sleep mentation research: whether to put one's money into subjects or nights. The traditional sleep experiment tends to run a few subjects over and over again. Is this preference for nights over subjects the "best" experimental strategy? Is it the most powerful in the sense of being most likely to identify relationships that do, in fact, exist in the population of subjects at large—within the constraints of an investigator's time and resources? The strategy with the greatest power or sensitivity is the one with the smallest error team. Since most sleep studies run each subject through all or most conditions, variation from subject to subject, the π_i effects, are eliminated from the error term which is then associated only with $\tau\pi_{ij}$, the treatment-by-subject interactions and ε_{ij}, residual unidentified errors of measurement and variation from occasion to occasion within a subject, order effects, variations in experimental procedures, and so on. We have just presented evidence that the $\tau\pi_{ij}$ effects are negligible, at least for dreaming and sleep stage, thereby assigning all unidentified variation to the ε_{ij}. If multiple awakenings are made on each subject, then the expression on page 94 changes so that X_{ij} becomes $\overline{X}_{ij}$ = the mean dreaming score of the ith subject in the jth sleep stage, and ε_{ij} similarly becomes $\overline{\varepsilon}_{ij}$ which is generally smaller than ε_{ij}. Using the familiar

$$\sigma_{\overline{\varepsilon}}^2 = \frac{\sigma_\varepsilon^2}{N},$$

the estimate of the error term, $\hat{\sigma}_{\overline{\varepsilon}}^2$, can be reduced by half by doubling the number of observations. If $\sigma\tau\pi_{ij}^2$ is close to 0, then $\hat{\sigma}_\sigma^2$ should be reduced equally well either by increasing subjects or awakenings within the same subject(s). That is, 40 nights on one subject is as good as 40 subjects, one night each.

As a check on this conclusion, we examined 19 studies of the dreaming-sleep stage relationship in order to see how subject sample size and number of observations per subject was associated with power. Sample size ranged from 3 to 25. Number of awakenings per subject was essentially independent of sample size. We were able to construct a 2 × 2, dreaming/not dreaming-by-stage 1 REM/NREM table for each study, and for each study computed a phi coefficient. We then plotted one against the other (see Figure 2.3). The range

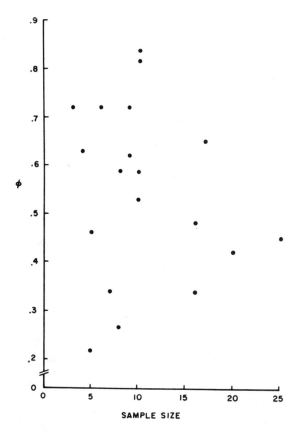

FIGURE 2.3. Phi coefficients of association between dreaming and stage. REM versus NREM sleep plotted against sample size for 19 studies.

of phi with the small sample sizes runs from .22 to .84 (Wolpert & Trosman, 1958) with sample sizes of 5 and 10 respectively. As the sample size increases to 25, the largest sample size we could locate (Orlinsky, 1962), the range of phi narrows sharply. The entire plot appears to point toward a best estimate for phi of approximately .45.

Figure 2.4, which plots phi coefficients against number of awakenings per subject, shows little consistent effect of number of awakenings upon the stability of phi from one study to another. The modest negative slope of the plot (r = −.19) is completely consistent with the first-night-report-effect in which the maximum degree of association between dreaming and sleep stage was on the first half of the first night. Unlike the previous distribution, there is no tendency for the variability among studies to decrease as more awakenings are made per subject.

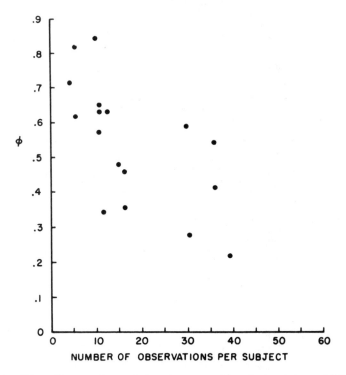

FIGURE 2.4. Phi coefficients of associations between dreaming and stage 1 REM versus NREM sleep plotted against number observations per subject.

The chief conclusion to be drawn from this analysis is that increasing the number of observations-reports by increasing the number of observations per subject does not increase the statistical power of the design, but increasing the number of observations by increasing sample size does. Furthermore, sample sizes less than 20 are completely useless for the purpose of estimating the strength of the relationship between sleep-stage and sleep-report variables. Inasmuch as the indices of association between sleep stage and dreaming most commonly quoted are the highest estimates and are based upon studies of only 5 subjects, this analysis calls for a large downward shift in our estimates—unless, perhaps, we restrict our estimates to the first laboratory night.

Our analysis suggests that the preferred design observes each of 20–40 subjects on only 1 night each. We cannot make this suggestion a firm recommendation, however, until some of the assumptions about the first-night-report-effect are tested. In the meantime it is clearly advisable to analyze reports separately by laboratory-night order and perhaps by early versus late half of the night. It is entirely plausible that some of the discrepancies among different studies come from the fact that some used only 1 or 2 nights, thereby obtaining high estimates of degree of association and others used many nights, thereby obtaining low estimates. We should like to note parenthetically that there is a tendency ($r = -.25$) for phi to decrease with sample size (see Figure 2.3). We interpret this as an inclination of experimenters to stop running subjects if their initial results are strong.

JUDGMENTS BASED UPON SLEEP REPORTS

The purpose of judging, measuring, or scaling different qualities of sleep reports is to directly or indirectly obtain a description of the sleep report or experience. When a judge, other than the subject who made the sleep report, makes a judgment based upon that report, the judge generally makes an implicit or explicit judgment about the private experience of the sleeping subject prior to the subject's awakening. Notable exceptions are simple counts of the total number of words and other syntactic classifications. Nevertheless, when a judge counts the total number of humans or architectural objects in the report, the judge is, in our opinion, assuming that these events occurred in the original sleep experience. For the most part, therefore, judgments based upon sleep reports are judgments about characteristics of sleep experience or what we have come to call sleep mentation. The discussion of the first-night-report-effect in the previous portion of this chapter suggests some ways to test the presumed invariance between the mentation and report.

Global Ratings versus Counts of Simple Events

Judgments about qualities of sleep reports vary from global judgments of complex, loosely defined classes such as dreaming to a count of the total number of concrete (visualizable) nouns in the report. In general, the greater the detail with which a scale is defined, the less latitude there is for the judges to impose their own personal set of assumptions and response biases. For example, should a report of a "red car" receive the same visual-imagery rating if it is the only visual object in a one-hundred-word report as it would if it made up the entire report? Some judges may tend toward a proportional rating whereas others may judge the absolute number of visual items. To what extent should reports of color and movement be weighted against the number of different objects or number of words in the report? Despite the prominent role of visual imagery in discriminating between stage REM and NREM sleep reports, the private "rules" by which judges weight these various properties have never been investigated. Perhaps the time has come for us to combine some of the techniques of psycholinguistics for the analysis of sentence structure with the methods developed by Paivio (1971) for scaling visual imagery.

Although high interjudge reliabilities tend to be associated with precise definitions, global judgments about dreaming, visual imagery, and related scales have generally yielded high interjudge agreement even when the judgment class is defined in no more than a single sentence.

The single major limitation of the global rating is that the meaning of the quality judged lies unarticulated in the head of the judge. The very fact that the experimenter cannot describe the rules of definition to the judge suggests that even the experimenter may be unable to define explicitly the quality under study. It is our position that the psychophysiological model of sleep mentation will not be complete until we are able to define precisely the nature of judgment operation performed on the sleep report.

The difficulty with the precise, countable qualities, on the other hand, is that standing alone they tend to be of only trivial interest. The variables of greatest interest to many investigators are multidimensional in nature. Accordingly, rules, arbitrary or empirical, must be devised for combining elementary classes into the larger judgment classes of interest to the investigator. Even a simple quality such as visual imagery may consist of some weighted combination of a count of several elementary judgment classes: concrete nouns, visual modifiers of the nouns, action verbs, and spatial prepositions. *A Psycholinguistic Scoring Manual for Mentation Reports* (Antrobus, Schnee, Offer, Lynn, & Silverman, 1976), currently being tested in our laboratories shows that a count of the number of words in any of these four classes is highly correlated with a global rating of Visual Imagery and is also a good discriminator of REM/NREM sleep stages.

It seems impossible, however, to define complex constructs such as dreaming, bizarreness, or regressive thought in terms of a count of words standing in isolation. Rather than instructing judges to make a direct judgment concerning the presence of a complex, abstract class, it seems better to define several less abstract classes of events which constitute regressive thought. Thus Vogel, Foulkes, and Trosman (1966) defined regressive thought as a report which had one or more of six qualities such as: single isolated images, incomplete or fragmentary scenes, inappropriate or distorted imagery, magical or omnipotent thought.

Scoring Unit

The Gottschalk–Gleser (1969) content analysis scales are, to our knowledge, the most elaborate scoring system to be applied to the analysis of sleep reports. The system provides for the scoring of several affects: anxiety, hostility directed outward, and inward and ambivalent hostility, as well as a social alienation-personal disorganization (schizophrenic) scale.

The Gottschalk–Gleser scales were developed for the analysis of verbal behavior in a psychiatric-clinical psychology setting where the basic operating assumptions are psychoanalytic. But regardless of his affiliation with the psychoanalytic model, the reader will find the author's detailed description of their procedures and explicit consideration of their assumptions and the testing of some of these assumptions most instructive. Instead of using the entire sleep report to obtain a global judgment, Gottschalk, Winget, and Gleser (1969) divide the report into a sequence of clauses which are then used as a basis for all subsequent judgments. Although the authors describe several procedural rules for defining the clauses, they do not indicate the reliability of this operation. Although the clause may be the best unit for judging complex qualities such as anxiety and hostility, we have found that the individual word is a satisfactory scoring unit for visual imagery. The variable bizarreness, on the other hand, which has figured prominently as a characteristic of dreaming, would seem to require the entire sleep report as the scoring unit. Objects and events in a dream often assume their bizarre quality because they are improbable in the larger context in which they appear. A suitable scoring unit must therefore preserve an adequately large context. Certainly, the analysis of sleep reports could benefit from a comparison of different sizes of coding units.

Word Count

Consideration of the size of the scoring unit inevitably raises the issue of the effect of the length of the total sleep report on judgments made from the reports. In our own data, word count shares a significant portion of the variance of most of our scales. In our most recent study (see Chapter 15, this volume) we estimated the correlation of dreaming with word count from the pooled regression coefficient in an analysis of covariance design: $r = .35$; $r^2 = .12$. That is, when treatment conditions were held constant, word count shared 12% of the between-treatments term, holding subject and time of night constant, word count shared .41–.48 of the variance of dreaming. The proportion was invariant for nights 1 and 2 of our recent study despite the fact that the mean word count dropped by one-third from night 1 to 2. Word count shared .35 to .60 of the variance of 7 out of 10 of the global ratings we employed. Nevertheless, there is a sizable portion of predictive variance that a simple word count does not share. If we use the scales to discriminate the 2 stages of sleep from which the reports were gathered, dreaming accounts for .48 of the REM/NREM variance whereas word count manages only .32. If we first partial out the word count variance, dreaming adds .173 to word count. To put it another way, the correlation of dreaming with stage 1 REM/NREM, corrected for word count, drops to $\sqrt{.173} = .42$ from .69, using a set of 115 Stage 1 REM/NREM report pairs.

Whether one corrects a variable for word count depends entirely upon the quality or purpose of the construct under study. In general, if one wishes to isolate particular components of a complex variable, it is entirely appropriate to clean up a variable by partialling out other unwanted variance. Let us suppose, however, that sleep reports consisted almost entirely of descriptions of visual imagery; that is, the correlation between visual imagery and word count was .90. To partial out word count would simply wipe out almost all the visual-imagery variance! Obviously, a word count correction should be used cautiously.

The chief consideration, in our opinion, is whether the variation in word count is attributable only to the amount of material available in memory immediately prior to awakening. In this case one assumes that memory and speech functions at the time of making the report are the same for all subjects under all conditions. If, on the other hand, subjects are more articulate and fluent upon awakening from REM sleep, one could measure this articulacy by instructing subjects to describe a briefly presented, post-awakening, audiovisual event. Such an independent word count could be used to statistically correct for variation in waking report fluency. Yet if such waking fluency were an integral part of the preawakening cognitive processes, the statistical correction would be inappropriate. At best one might parcel variance into a fluency-memory component and a visual-imagery component.

A major consideration with respect to whether one should or shouldn't partial out word count is whether one regards the variable in question, say visual-imagery, as an intensity or total-magnitude variable. If we are concerned with the cognitive processes involved in generating, storing, and retrieving visual or auditory images, we may want a total-magnitude judgment and would, therefore, not partial out word count. On the other hand, if we want to find out whether people are more anxious in REM than NREM sleep or whether one set of subjects is more anxious than another, then we might prefer an intensity variable. Thus, Gottschalk, Winget, and Gleser (1969) argue that anxiety and similar variables should be independent of word count. Although the Gottschalk et al. (1969) scoring procedure has been applied to the analysis of sleep reports, it was originally developed for the analysis of psychotherapy protocols. The fluency factors which determine total word output in the waking state differ considerably from the consolidation and retrieval factors which presumably account for differences in the word count of reports from sleep states. We are asking simply that the assumption of independence of word count, which Gottschalk, Winget, and Gleser (1969) make for the analysis of waking protocols, not be applied uncritically to the analysis of sleep reports. The assumption of independence does seem plausible for anxiety and hostility where we are looking at an average quality of an experience, but a total count of recalled items seems more appropriate as a measure of visual imagery. The soundness of these options is open to empirical test. For example, if anxiety has higher predictive validity when corrected for word count, the independence assumption is supported.

Gottschalk, Winget, and Gleser (1969) point out that the reliability of their scales begins to decrease rapidly as the word count falls below 100. They recommend that their scales not be applied on samples of fewer than 70 words. The scales would be unsuitable, therefore, for sleep reports particularly from NREM sleep or from any sleep stage after multiple nights in the laboratory. In our recent REM-deprivation study, we found that word count decreased from a mean of 84 words/report on night 1 to 67 on night 2. Gottschalk and Gleser's reliability problem would appear to stem from their use of the word-count correction. When a variable, such as dreaming, is correlated with word count, decreasing the range of word count by using samples of more than 75 words will decrease rather than increase all measures of reliability. We must conclude, therefore, that correction for word count may lower predictive validity simply because of decreased reliability.

Explicit Assumptions

One of the most refreshing things about the construction of the Gottschalk–Gleser scales is their attempt to make explicit assumptions by which they infer an affect such as anxiety or hostility from speech. Although the assumptions are based upon the psychoanalytic model, some nonpsychoanalytic investigators may find the assumptions quite acceptable while, conversely, some psychoanalysts may disagree with certain features. The great virtue of the Gottschalk et al. (1969) effort is that we know what the authors think it is measuring and we have an informed basis for accepting or rejecting their scales. Let us illustrate this point by once again referring to their anxiety scale. One of their key assumptions is that:

> the more anxiety a person is experiencing, the more likely he will speak of incidents in which he reports being directly threatened. . . . When the anxiety is somewhat less potent, the subject is more likely to express it indirectly by externalization or displacement and, hence, more likely to refer to others as being hurt or in a dangerous situation, and even more remotely, in terms of inanimate objects being injured or destroyed. (Gottschalk et al., 1969)

The authors then assign interval weights of 3, 2, and 1, respectively, to the three ordinal classes of self, animate others, and inanimate others. Thus "Boredom and finances, that's what's killing me," and "He was so mad he might have killed me," receive a weight of 3 under death anxiety. "He took his own life," and "They caught a beauty of a trout," are weighted 2, and,

"The baby pulled the doll apart," and "The whole motorcycle was demolished," are each weighted 1. An additional arbitrary weight of 1 is added to an item which is amplified by a modifier. Thus, "I am terribly afraid of being hurt," receives an additional point for the presence of "terribly." This weighting system is repeated across the sub-subtypes of scaled anxiety. Although the authors state that each subtype receives equal weight because the scores of each subtype are summed to create a total score, the subtypes are, in fact, weighted by the proportion of variance they contribute to the variance of the total score and this proportion, in turn, is determined empirically by the frequency of clauses scored in each subclass. This latter particular procedure is, therefore, neither arbitrary nor objectionable. The assumption that anxiety is a decreasing negative function (weights 3, 2, and 1 plus 1/0 for an amplifying modifier) is, however, very much in need of empirical justification. Fortunately, the assumptions are sufficiently explicit so that they can be independently tested. Gottschalk and his colleagues have vigorously sought out empirical support for their scales, but, alas, most of their studies test the predictive validity only of the total-scale scores. In a general sense, all of the scales seem to be doing what they are supposed to but only independent tests of the various assumptions will make it possible to improve the weights of the component parts of the scales. In our opinion, he advantage of a weighted over an unweighted system must be reliably demonstrated. If weighted scores are to be used, the weights must be determined by a discriminate function analysis or multiple regression. Finally, the relative advantage of alternative scaling models must be estimated from the proportions of predicted variance accounted for, ω, rather than from simple significance tests.

We recommend that investigators studying imagery and thought during sleep follow the example of Gottschalk, Winget, and Gleser (1969) in making explicit all of the assumptions underlying their judgment and scaling processes. Only by so doing can measurements based upon sleep reports have a public meaning shared by all investigators and their readers. Otherwise the meaning of a scale remains the private subjective property of the judges who scored the reports, whose assumptions are hoped to be somewhat similar to the general public's.

Validity

For the purpose of considering the validity of sleep-mentation judgments, we find it useful to divide the judgments into two classes. The first are concerned primarily with whether the persons making the sleep (particularly REM) reports have certain personality characteristics such as hostility or anxiety. Such judgments may be validated in the same manner as any other measure of individual differences as described in every textbook in psychometrics. The second attempts to compare the cognitive and affective qualities of certain physiological states such as stage REM/NREM. The validity issue is somewhat simplified by the opportunity to use the physiological states, discrete or continuous, as criteria variables. Research strategies and statistical models appropriate to this second effort are the subject of the next section.

MULTIDIMENSIONALITY OF VARIABLES: RESEARCH STRATEGIES

Research on sleep mentation has, from the outset, involved multidimensional variables both on the physiological and cognitive side of the fence. Not only were the sleep stages defined jointly by EEG and eye movements and subsequently EMG, but the EEG variable involves a combination of frequency, pulse duration, and amplitude. Dreaming, the most commonly used cognitive variable in sleep research, remains an obscure multidimensional conglomerate of an hallucinatory belief in the actual occurrence of an imagined experience which, in turn, tends to be an extended visual, sometimes bizarre, drama. The first question asked of that rapid-eye-movement interval of sleep called stage REM was of its association with dreams (Aserinsky & Kleitman, 1953; Ladd, 1892). The high degree of association repeatedly observed in the initial studies of the late 1950s promoted the compelling assumption that there was a one-to-one association between the two. As subsequent research forced the abandonment of the one-to-one model, it became necessary to broaden the search. Several variations on both the cognitive and physiological side of the fence needed consideration.

The research problem became essentially a multivariate one. Yet, investigators have continued to employ univariate models, at least in their data analyses. In an effort to clarify some of the issues involved, we would like to propose four research strategies relevant to the multivariate, psychophysiological study of sleep mentation:

1. One physiological variable, one cognitive variable, repeated measures on each subject; for example, stage REM, dreaming: phasic-tonic sleep, bizarreness;
2. Multiple physiological variables, one cognitive variable, multiple measures on each subject; for example, sleep stage and phasic tonic sleep, dreaming;
3. One physiological variable, multiple cognitive variables, repeated measures on each subject;
4. Multiple physiological variables, multiple cognitive variables, multiple measures per subject.

In general, most investigators think in terms of strategy 4, but research with strategy 1! Strategy 1 encourages the endless collection of countless psychophysiological relations but allows no way to distinguish unique associations from redundant ones. In his excellent review of "Mental Activity During Sleep," Rechtschaffen (1973) concludes that those few variables which are reliably associated with dreaming and related cognitive variables appear simply to be sharing variance that has previously been identified in what are regarded as more fundamental associations. He cites the association of dreaming within stage REM to low-rectal temperature, pointing out that both variables are associated with REM activity, and the association of dreaming with REMS within the sleep stage is stronger than the association with rectal temperature. Rechtschaffen rightly recommends that future studies in this area must examine several variables jointly and use some kind of statistical technique to correct for the overlap among the physiological-predictor variables. Specifically, he suggests the use of partial correlation. For example, the correlation of rectal temperature with dreaming should be statistically corrected for the correlation of both with rapid eye movements.

Because of the multiple-measures-per-subject feature there is no single existing statistical data-analysis method suitable for strategy 4. Canonical correlation comes closest since it identifies the relationship between two sets of multivariables—physiological and cognitive. Since a canonical correlation analysis generally requires a minimum of 40 independent observations per variable, working with only 5 variables in each set, we would require either one set of scores from each of 400 subjects or 400 observations on each subject. In the latter case, several subjects would be required for replications.

To avoid the blind piecemeal approach of strategy 1 and the statistical problems as well as the high cost of strategy 4, we recommend the middle ground of strategies 2 and 3—together with a strong background in neurophysiology! Before proceeding to examine these strategies in detail, let us say in passing that factor analysis is not appropriate as a formal analysis of data that crosses such diverse domains as cognition and physiology. If such a statistical procedure were attempted, it would tend to produce separate cognitive and physiological factors. Factor analysis is useful for reducing a large number of correlated variables to a small number of orthogonal vectors, but provides no unique shortcut to "truth." Thus, if one constructs separate scales for the measurement of purple, violet, and yellow dreams, one will obtain a "purple versus yellow dreams factor," and in grape country it might embrace a Bacchus scale! Since one can, in effect, create a factor simply by intensively building or sampling variables in the area of one's interest rather than systematically sampling within the domain of inquiry, one's factor analysis may simply mirror one's prior personal conception of the domain under study.

Having so said, we would nevertheless encourage investigators to make free use of factor analysis and canonical correlation as an intermediate step in data analysis, simply to identify patterns of organization among variables in the two domains. Appreciation of such patterns can make the subsequent steps in formal data analysis more efficient and intelligently focused.

Criterion Variable

In strategies 2 and 3, the weights given to the multivariables in one domain are determined by, or anchored to, a single empirical point, the "criterion" variable, and thereby relatively immune to the response variable sampling problems of factor analysis. These strategies, therefore, require the judicious choice of a criterion. Should a better criterion turn up, the research must be done all over again. As the multivariate experiment increases in sample size, more and more cost and effort hang on the adequacy of criterion variables derived from the sleep reports. If the choice of a cognitive variable (strategy 2) is a poor one, there is always some consolation in knowing one can obtain judgments or ratings on an indefinite set of variables once the sleep reports have been obtained. This is not true when the criterion is a physiological variable, in which the measurement of each variable requires a unique electromechanical system and the total number of such systems is limited to the number of channels on one's polygraph. Despite the greater potential freedom of choice, there must be sufficient consensus among sleep researchers as to the significance of a given criterion so that it will be employed by several investigators.

When a single-criterion variable is employed it should, if possible, derive its significance from some more fundamental or larger system of variables. REMs and PIPs (phasic integrated potentials) derive their importance from their presumed relation to the PGO (parietal-geniculate-occipital) neural system. Visual imagery derives its significance from the fact that vision is one of the fundamental sensory modalities. The virtue of recall of any content as a dichotomous all-or-nothing variable is that it avoids the arbitrary selection of any dimensions within the recall universe. It is thus a crude first approximation to any variable which might be derived from "content." The significance of dreaming comes from its universal use in the vernacular of all cultures since the beginning of recorded history. More precise psychophysiological models, however, might well employ more specific cognitive criteria, for example, primary visual experience (Molinari & Foulkes, 1969) might be an appropriate criterion for a psychophysiological model of right hemispheric dominance in sleep (multiple-EEG predictors); bizarreness might be more appropriate for measures of phasic activity, including PIPs and REMs (Rechtschaffen, 1973).

Strategy 2—Statistical Models: Cognitive Variable, Continuous; Physiological Variables, Discrete or Continuous.   Again, because of the multiple-measures-per-subject feature, if a large number (20–100) of awakenings are obtained from each of, for example, 5–40 subjects, no single statistical model is available to handle the analysis. The simplest alternative is to carry out separate multiple-linear-regression (MLR) solutions for each subject, entering the physiological "predictor" variables in the same order for all subjects, carrying out incremental F tests on each added variable using a liberal alpha level because of the small N per subject. The order should be determined by a psychophysiological model rather than by an empirical criterion as in the case of stepwise MLR. The significance of the combined F tests from all subjects may be estimated by the chi-square test for combined tests (Winer, 1971, pp. 49–51). Fisher z transformations can be used to estimate the average incremental contribution, R^2, of a particular variable.

Because this model handles correlated physiological variables, it permits the investigator, by means of the incremental F test, to look at the correlation between, say, dreaming and penile erection, with sleep stage partialled out.

Strategy 2—Cognitive Variable, Continuous; Physiological Variables, Discrete and Orthogonal. This method of analysis was employed by Pivik (1971) when he examined the joint effects of sleep stage and phasic-tonic sleep on several cognitive variables. Pivik treated four sleep stages × phasic-tonic sleep as orthogonal independent variables in a randomized blocks ANOVA design. Thus, the main effect of phasic-tonic sleep is independent of sleep stage and, therefore, analogous to the effect of phasic-tonic sleep with sleep stage partialled out. This orthogonal design is a powerful technique as a test of significance, but since the two "independent" variables are, in fact, strongly dependent or correlated in normal sleep, the analysis does not present as accurate a picture of their joint action as does MLR in the statistical models discussed above.

Strategy 3. Question 3 asks the psychophysiological question from the other end: *not*, "What are the physiological correlates of a particular cognitive variable, such as dreaming?" but, "What are the cognitive correlates of a particular physiological criterion variable, such as stage REM versus NREM sleep?" We remind the reader that the two questions are identical so long as we confine ourselves to simple bivariate relationships, such as correlations and differences between means. The purpose of our discussion, however, has been to assess the improved power of multivariate models and to compare the relative merits of three different classes of multivariate psychophysiological models: where the physiological, cognitive, or both domains involve two or more variables considered jointly, as in partial, multiple, or canonical correlation.

The selection of a single physiological-criterion variable against which to describe the joint association of several cognitive variables is just as critical as the choice of the cognitive criterion for question 2. Two dichotomous variables, stage REM/NREM and tonic-phasic sleep, have been acknowledged for several years as fundamental physiological classifications of sleep. They are possibly the strongest candidates for criterion variables associated with characteristics of sleep mentation. Although details in the measurement of these states are under constant revision, there are sufficient occasions during sleep which can be unequivocally classified that stage REM/NREM sleep is quite suitable as a criterion variable. Within stage REM, REMs themselves are acquiring longevity as a measure of phasic-tonic sleep. Other physiological criteria should probably be evaluated under strategy 2 before being used to supersede REM/NREM sleep as a physiological criterion.

Statistical Models: Dichotomous Physiological Criterion; Multiple, Continuous Cognitive Variables, Correlated Pairs.   Each subject contributes data from both, say, stage REM and stage 2 awakenings. If there are a large number of awakenings per subject, and multiple-cognitive scores derived from each awakening, a complete multiple-regression solution may be obtained for each subject, similar to the solution on page 108 of this volume. Not only are the 50–100 observations/subject impractical, however, but the order effects of motivation (pp. 90–91, this volume) may wash out real effects that exist. If each subject is run 1 or 2 nights, the scores from each sleep state should be averaged over all awakenings so that each subject contributes a stage REM and a stage 2 score for each cognitive measure. The difficulty encountered in handling these data is that not only are the cognitive variables correlated, but the two members of the pairs are correlated (stage REM with stage 2).

It is instructive to examine briefly why multiple-linear regression (MLR) doesn't quite do the job. If half of the subjects were observed only in one physiological state, such as stage REM, and the remaining subjects in stage 2, the multiple-linear-regression (MLR) model would provide an ideal solution. The physiological state would constitute a dichotomous criterion variable and the multiple-cognitive measures—the "predictors"—one set of predictor scores for each subject. But if every subject provides two sets of predictor scores, that is, paired scores, the assumption of independence of the N observations is violated so that MLR analysis cannot be used, at least in its usual form.

Hotelling's T^2 (Timm, 1975) is the appropriate multivariate statistical test where each subject contributes a set of paired scores, for example, one set from REM and one from NREM reports. That is, each subject contributes scores on several variables and each variable is measured once in REM and again in NREM sleep. In most REM–NREM mentation studies, multiple reports are obtained from within REM and NREM conditions. If the investigator wishes to reduce certain sources of measurement error by obtaining multiple awakenings, or measures, within each of the two states, within each subject, then the mean of each measure within each sleep condition and subject can be used, instead of the single measure. Hotelling's T^2 test, in effect, computes the weights for the multiple-paired differences between REM and NREM variables, to determine the maximum discrimination between the conditions. If the obtained T^2 is statistically significant, it is appropriate to proceed with individual correlated T^2 tests to determine which individual variables are independently statistically significant. More importantly, for our purposes, a test proposed by Rao (1973) tests for the significance of partialled variables. As the last section of this chapter shows, Rao's test permits a test of such questions as: If we partial out or statistically control for the difference between REM and NREM reports in Word Count, does Dreaming account for the significant portion of the residual REM–NREM variance? Or, does Total Recall Count, or Total Recall Frequency (number of words specifically concerned with describing the preawakening mentation) discriminate REM from NREM better than Total Word Count (all words in the report) and does it do better than the global variable Dreaming?

The fundamental issue examined in the last section of this chapter is whether or not Dreaming is a multidimensional structural variable. If it is, then different physiological and environmental factors may be independently responsible for its different structural properties and the search of the past 35 years to find antecedents for Dreaming as a univariate dimension are doomed to failure. Thus, it is essential to determine whether the antecedents of Bizarreness are the same as the antecedents of Visual Imagery and whether the factors that determine the length of a mentation report, that is, the amount of information reported, is independent of both. If most characteristics of sleep mentation reports are heavily dependent on the amount of information in the verbal report, then the primary search for the antecedents of the report should be directed toward factors that affect verbal production, short-term memory, and perhaps the overall activation of the cognitive system (see also Chapter 15).

COMPARISON OF WORD FREQUENCIES BY COGNITIVE CLASSES IN REM AND NREM SLEEP REPORTS*

This study was prompted by my longstanding dissatisfaction with the use of the global construct "dreaming" to adequately describe the distinctive cognitive characteristics of stages 1 REM and NREM sleep mentation. Dreaming has variously been defined as a multi-variate term based on visual imagery, a storylike quality, a hallucinatory quality, and a bizarre

---

*This section is reprinted from *Psychophysiology*, 1983, 20, 562–568. Copyright 1983 by Society for Psychophysiological Research. Reprinted by permission.

juxtaposition of elements. Foulkes (1966) proposed a rational though somewhat arbitrary weighting of these elements in a single rating scale, but their weighting in most studies remains a private matter in the heads of the judges who exchange sleep reports for global ratings of dreaming or dreamlike quality. The remarkable ability of this poorly defined, subjective rating to distinguish REM from NREM reports has effectively discouraged investigators from examining its separate parts and defining these parts in terms of more public properties. If a judge can distinguish REM from NREM sleep stages by reading the sleep reports, then it should be possible to identify and count the words in the classes that the judges use. Total word frequency seems like an appropriate starting point. Progressively more sophisticated classes can be constructed if necessary until the upper limit of discriminability is reached. To this end several measures of global Dreaming are employed as reference points.

The primary purpose of this study, however, is to test the general assumption that the fundamental cognitive differences between the neurological states REM and NREM are at the level of general processes such as attention and memory consolidation. It assumes that the countless REM/NREM differences such as visual imagery, anxiety and dreamer participation that have been reported in the literature are all secondary to differences in these more fundamental processes. Unfortunately, until recently, no suitable stastical model has been available to compare multiple dependent variables on the dichotomous REM/NREM criterion variable. Once a sleep subject is wired to the polygraph we obtain multiple reports from him/her in both stages of sleep. The multiple linear regression model permits tests of the additive effects of multiple independent variables using dichotomous or continuous criteria, but each subject may enter the model only once. In practice one could enter a subject's REM data or NREM data but not both. Hotelling's one-sample T^2 test, applied to this case of matched-pair multiple observations (see, e.g., Timm, 1975, pp. 226–229),

$$T^2 = N\overline{d}' \, S_d \overline{d}$$

where $\overline{d} = [\overline{d}_1, \ldots, \overline{d}_p]$, $\overline{d}_j = \Sigma_{i=1}^{N} d_{ij}/N$, d_{ij} = difference between REM and NREM on the jth variable for the ith subject, and S_d = the sample variance-covariance of the differences, is precisely the needed statistical test. Less well known is the incremental test for determining whether one variable significantly adds to the REM/NREM difference already described by the first dependent variable. Without such an incremental test we would be restricted to a set of correlated t tests and have no way to rule out the possibility that they were all describing the same difference. Rao (1973, pp. 551–556, 552–564) developed such a multivariate, one-sample incremental F test:

$$F = \frac{(N-p)}{(p-s)} \frac{(T_p^2 - T_s^2)}{[(N-1) + T_s^2]} \sim F(p-s, N-p)$$

where N = sample size, p = number of variables in the larger model, and s = the number of variables in the smaller model. The F statistic is derived from the fact that

$$F = (N - p)T_p^2/(N - p)p \sim F(p, N - p) \text{ and } F = (Ns)T_s^2/(N - 1)s \sim F(s, N - s).$$

When s = 1, T = the t of the familiar repeated measures t test. When s or p > 1, T^2 may be conveniently computed by computer using a one-sample MANOVA model and using the F test for Roy's Maximum Root criterion (see SAS User's Guide: Statistics, Version 5, 1985, pp. 431–506). For the convenience of the reader a worked example of the first incremental test is provided in the Appendix.

Method

REM/NREM Reports. A pool of 73 REM/NREM reports pairs was assembled from eight studies carried out in five different laboratories with each subject contributing only one pair. All NREM reports were obtained from Sleep Stage 2. Since Antrobus, Fein, Jordan, Ellman, and Arkin (1979) have shown that the REM/NREM difference is sharpest on the first night that reports are obtained, all report pairs were selected from the first night following one or two adaptation nights. It is not assumed that results obtained in this study generalize to other night orders.

Report Scales. A Psycholinguistic Coding Manual (Antrobus, Schnee, Offer, & Silverman, 1977) was developed for reliably counting the words in several classes relevant to sleep mentation reports. Each category was given a formal definition followed first by unequivocal and then borderline examples together with comment. A separate test set of 50 reports was compiled and scored by experienced people. All persons using the Manual were obliged to score the Test Set and obtain a correlation > .90 with the Total Recall Freq. criterion, the most complex of the variables. The list of variables employed in this study, together with their interjudge reliabilities based on the Spearman-Brown correction formula for four judges, are given in Table 2.1.

Total Word Frequency = the count of all words emitted to the two questions, "What was going through your mind just before I called you?" and "Was there anything else?" or "Can you give me any more detail about that?" Total Recall Frequency = Total Word Frequency minus "ahs," "uhms," repeated and corrected words, and all commentary on the experience, the report, or the current status of the subject. Visual Imagery was assessed in four frequency classes: nouns of objects that could be seen in waking life, verbs that described visible action such as running, modifiers such as adjectives, and adverbs that added visual information to the report. Prepositions that provided visual information about position in space were classified as Spatial Relations. Two classes of auditory imagery were employed: Explicit

TABLE 2.1.   RELIABILITIES OF VARIABLES

Variables	Transformations	Reliabilities
Total recall frequency	$\log(X + 1)$	.97
Visual nouns	$\log(X + 1)$	.93
Visual modifiers	$\log(X + 1)$	.92
Visual action	$\log(X + 1)$	.93
Spatial relations	$\log(X + 1)$	.88
Explicit speech	$\log(X + 1)$	.84
Implicit speech	$\log(X + 1)$	.90
Waking perception	$\log(X + 1)$	.89
Dreamer participation	$\log(X + 1)$	.93
Global dreaming	Forced normal	.96

or quoted Speech, and Implicit Speech where the subject reports characters talking "about" something in particular.

Two additional word frequency variables were added because it was anticipated that they would be largely independent of Total Recall Freq. and yet distinguish REM from NREM sleep. Waking Perception was a count of all words referring to awake, waking, drowsy or not asleep. Previous research has shown these words to be more frequent in Stage 2 than in REM (Antrobus et al., 1979). The second variable, Dreamer Participation = the count of the use of the first person singular to describe the dream action. For example, "I was flying through the air. . . ." The subject as participant rather than observer ("I was watching. . .") has been proposed as a measure of the sleeping subject's lack of awareness of unresponsiveness to the external (bedroom) environment and thus a measure of the magnitude of the tendency to dream.

Global Dreaming.   Two measures were obtained by independent sets of four judges each: 1) Dreaming-Forced Normal Distribution. Judges were instructed to use their own private weighting of the characteristics: visual imagery, bizarreness, hallucinatory quality, and storylike quality. Judges were instructed to sort the reports into 8 piles, each .75 z scores wide so that the number in each pile did not exceed a specified maximum. 2) Paired Comparison Dreaming: Judges were given the reports in REM/NREM pairs and instructed to judge which of each pair was most dreamlike (Score = number of REM reports judged as Dreamlike, maximum = 4).

Scale Transformations.   Since word frequencies are generally positively skewed across subjects, judges and occasions, all scores were normalized by the $\log(X + 1)$ transformation and then summed across all four judges. Subsequent transformations are evaluated in the next section.

Results

Reliabilities.   The mean r for all possible judge pairs was computed using the Fisher Z transformation and the reliability of the mean of the four judges was determined using the Spearman–Brown equation (see Table 2.1). The reliability of the Total Word Frequency was not computed on the entire sample but was estimated as = 1.0 since there were no disagreements between two judges in the Total Word Frequencies in a sample of 10 reports.

REM/NREM Associations.   In order to determine the effectiveness of simple structural variables for discriminating REM from NREM sleep, it is first necessary to determine how well global judgments of dreamlike quality do the job.

Rating Variables. If Global Dreaming is independent of REM versus NREM, the expectation of the mean difference in Global Dreaming (REM minus NREM reports) = 0. For any given REM/NREM report pair, a difference > 0 indicates that Global Dreaming, averaged over judges, is greater in the REM than in the NREM member of the pair. A difference = 0 indicates that the judges are tied, etc. The mean judgment of four judges correctly classifies 93% of the reports, ties on 1% of the reports, and misclassifies 6% (see Table 2.2). Note that these percentages are unaffected by the transformations imposed on the scores. The obtained F of 95.52 far exceeds the critical value of 3.98 and R^2 indicates that this particular Dreaming measure accounts for, or shares, 57% of its variance with the dichotomous REM/NREM variable. Although the paired comparison version of Dreaming correctly classifies only 90% of the reports, it ties on 6%, makes only 4% misclassifications, and yields an F of 252.41 and accounts for 78% of the REM/NREM variance. One might assume that this larger F is the consequence of the greater sensitivity of the paired comparison judgment processes. For example, a judge might rely on word length to make most discriminations but if two reports are equally long the judge might then take an alternate variable into account and consider, for example, which pair is more bizarre or which has more visual imagery. On the other hand, the greater R^2 of the paired comparison judgment may be due to the smaller variance of the dichotomous judgments, even when summed over four judges. The possible sums are 4, 3, 2, 1, or 0. To test this notion, both Dreaming variables are trichotomized so that higher scores in REM = 1, lower = −1, = = 0. The trichotomized Dreaming variables yield Fs of 254.23 and 267.57, both close to the paired comparison F. In Table 2.3, Test 5 shows that the trichotomous, paired comparison F is not significantly greater than the trichotomous, forced normal F, thereby discounting the hypothesis that judges use more sophisticated comparison rules in the paired comparison judgment situation. Nevertheless, all subsequent tests involving global ratings of Dreaming will use scores based on the forced

TABLE 2.2.   ASSOCIATION OF REPORT VARIABLES WITH REM/NREM
DIFFERENCE

| Variables | Percentage in REM | | | F | R Square |
	More	Equal/ Tied	Less		
	Rating Variables				
Dreaming: global, forced normal, log	93	1	6	95.52	.57
Trichotomous (>, =, <)				254.23	.78
Dreaming: global, paired comparison, log	90	6	4	252.41	.78
Trichotomous				267.57	.79
	Word Frequency Variables				
Total recall frequency, log	92	1	7	97.78	.58
Trichotomous				196.01	.73
Visual nouns, log	81	11	8	66.82	.48
Visual modifiers, log	36	21	16	29.10	.29
Visual action, log	69	23	7	33.40	.32
Spatial relations, log	64	29	7	26.50	.27
Explicit speech, log	12	83	1	8.38	.10
Implicit speech, log	34	61	5	12.99	.15
Sleep/wake perception, log	14	61	25	3.80	.05
Dreamer participation, log	56	34	99	23.70	.25

Note. All values based on the sum of four judges.

normal distribution of judgments because these judgments are made independently on each report rather than on the greater amount of information available in a REM/NREM report pair. The high order of associations under examination makes the F tests highly sensitive to tied scores which, in turn, are more probable when reports are judged independently than in pairs. The forced normal version of global judgment is, for this reason, most comparable to the word frequency variable, whether in the log or trichotomous form.

At this point it is appropriate to determine whether the trichotomous versions of the best discriminators of REM versus NREM are more powerful than the log versions. Tests 5 and 6 in Table 2.3 show that the trichotomous transformations are significantly better for both Dreaming

TABLE 2.3.   SELECTED INCREMENTAL MANOVA TESTS

Variables Based on Independent Reports: Transform = log Sum of Judges (X + 1)	
1. Increment due to Total Recall Freq. over Total Word Freq.:	
Total Word Freq. + Total Recall Freq., log	$T(2/71) = 97.88$
Total Word Freq.	$T(1/72) = 45.50$
Increment	$F(1/71) = 31.65**$
2. Increment due to Total Recall Freq. over Dreaming, Forced Normal:	
Dreaming + Total Recall Freq.	$T(2/71) = 106.25$
Dreaming	$F(1/72) = 95.52$
Increment	$F(1/71) = 4.58*$
3. Increment due to Dreaming, Forced Normal, over Total Recall Freq.:	
Total Recall Freq. + Dreaming, Forced Normal	$T(2/71) = 106.25$
Total Recall Freq.	$F(1/72) = 97.78$
Increment	$F(1/71) = 3.56$
4. Increment due to Waking Perception over Total Recall Freq. + Dreaming, Forced Normal:	
Total Recall Freq. + Dreaming + Waking Perception	$T(3/70) = 108.37$
Total Recall Freq. + Dreaming	$T(2/71) = 106.25$
Increment	$F(1/70) = 0.83$

Comparison of Judgments of Dreaming Based on REM/NREM Paired Reports versus Independently Judged Reports	
5. Increment due to Dreaming: Judged Pairs over Independently Judged Reports:	
Independently Judged Reports + Judged Pairs	$T(2/71) = 275.05$
Independently Judged Reports	$T(1/72) = 267.57$
Increment	$F(1/71) = 1.57$

Comparison of Transforms: Log versus Trichotomous (More, Equal or Less on REM Compared to NREM) for Variables Based on Judgments of Independent Reports	
6. Increment due to Trichotomous over Log Transform: Dreaming	
Dreaming, log + Dreaming, Trichotomous	$T(2/71) = 256.41$
Dreaming, log	$T(1/72) = 95.52$
Increment	$F(1/71) = 68.60**$
7. Increment of Trichotomous over Log Transform: Total Recall Freq.:	
Total Recall Freq., log + Total Report Freq., Trichotomous	$T(2/71) = 200.20$
Total Recall Freq., log	$T(1/72) = 97.78$
Increment	$F(1/71) = 43.08**$

Variables Based on Independent Judgments, Transform: More,
Equal or Less on REM Compared to NREM

8. Increment due to Trichotomous Dreaming, Forced Normal, over Trichotomous Total
   Recall Freq.:

Total Recall Freq. + Dreaming	$T(2/71) = 255.77$
Total Recall Freq.	$T(1/72) = 196.01$
Increment	$F(1/71) = 15.89^{**}$

9. Increment due to Trichotomous Total Recall Freq. over Trichotomous Dreaming:

Dreaming + Total Recall Freq.	$T(2/71) = 255.77$
Dreaming	$T(1/72) = 254.23$
Increment	$F(1/71) = 0.34$

10. Increment due to Trichotomous Dreaming over Trichotomous Total Recall Freq. +
    Trichotomous Waking Perception:

Total Recall Freq. + Waking Perception + Dreaming	$T(3/70) = 271.74$
Total Recall Freq. + Waking Perception	$T(2/71) = 211.21$
Increment	$F(1/70) = 15.17^{**}$

11. Increment due to Trichotomous Total Recall Freq. + Trichotomous Waking Perception
    over Trichotomous Dreaming:

Dreaming + Total Recall Freq. + Waking Perception	$T(3/70) = 271.74$
Dreaming	$T(2/72) = 254.23$
Increment	$F(1/70) = 14.96^{**}$

12. Increment due to Trichotomous Waking Perception over Trichotomous Total Recall
    Freq.:

Total Recall Freq. + Waking Perception	$T(2/71) = 211.21$
Total Recall Freq.	$T(1/72) = 196.01$
Increment	$F(1/71) = 4.03^{*}$

13. Increment due to Trichotomous Waking Perception over Trichotomous Total Recall
    Freq. + Trichotomous Dreaming:

Total Recall Freq. + Dreaming + Waking Perception	$T(3/70) = 271.74$
Total Recall Freq. + Dreaming	$T(2/70) = 255.77$
Increment	$F(1/72) = 3.46$

14. Increment due to Trichotomous Dreamer Participation over Trichotomous Total Recall
    Freq.:

Total Recall Freq. + Dreamer Participation	$T(3/70) = 213.19$
Total Recall Freq.	$T(1/70) = 196.01$
Increment	$F(1/72) = 4.55^{*}$

15. Increment due to Trichotomous Dreaming over Trichotomous Dreamer Participation
    + Trichotomous Total Recall Freq.:

Dreamer Participation + Total Recall Freq. + Dreaming	$T(3/70) = 269.02$
Dreamer Participation + Total Recall Freq.	$T(2/71) = 213.19$
Increment	$F(1/70) = 13.70^{**}$

16. Increment due to Trichotomous Dreamer Participation over Trichotomous Total Recall
    Freq. + Trichotomous Dreaming:

Dreaming + Total Recall Freq. + Dreamer Participation	$T(3/70) = 269.02$
Dreaming + Total Recall Freq.	$T(2/71) = 255.77$
Increment	$F(1/70) = 2.83$

$^{*} p < .05.$ $^{**} p < .01.$

(F (1/71) = 68.60, $p \leq .01$) and Total Recall Freq. ($F(1/71) = 43.08$, $p \leq .01$), increasing the proportion of shared variance by .21 for Dreaming and .15 for Total Recall Freq., even though the proportion of correct matches with REM/NREM is unaltered by the transformation. Although it may seem reasonable to drop the log transform versions of the variables at this point, they will be retained on the grounds that other experimental designs may use continuous independent variables and not wish to throw away the information contained in the log versions. For example, Fein, Floyd, and Feinberg (1981) have been able to differentiate different orders of Stage 2 by their EEG power distributions. In the near future we may correlate sleep report variables directly with different segments of the EEG power spectra and ignore the grosser "stage" classifications.

Word Frequency Variables. Table 2.2 shows that Total Recall Frequency accounts for .58 of the REM/NREM variance and correctly classifies 92% of the reports, more than any other word frequency variable. The four visual imagery, and two speech imagery, word frequency variables are constructed from words included in Total Recall Freq. Since their associations with REM/NREM are weaker than the Total Recall Freq. association, it is unlikely that they provide any unique addition to this association. None of the incremental F tests (not listed in Table 2.3) carried out on the six imagery word frequency variables, separately or collectively, approached significance at the .05 level. Because of the large number of reports with no reference to waking or sleeping, Waking Perception, log, correctly classified only 25% of the REM/NREM reports and its association with REM/NREM was not quite significant at the .05 level. Test 11, Table 2.3 shows that Waking Perception, trichotomous, plus Total Recall Freq., trichotomous, are associated more strongly with REM/NREM than is Total Recall Freq. alone. Since the F for Waking Perception, trichotomous, is 2.33, less than the incremental F, one may conclude that Waking Perception acts as a suppressor variable in the regression equation. That is, the report pair with the greater number of words is generally the REM report, unless the words refer to sleeping or waking, in which case the report with more words may come from Stage 2.

Comparison of Dreaming and Word Frequency REM/NREM. In the log form, Total Recall Freq. is associated more closely with the difference between REM and NREM than is Dreaming (see Test 1, Table 2.3), whereas Dreaming makes no significant addition to Total Recall Freq. (Test 2). Test 3 shows that Waking Perception does not significantly add to the discriminability of Total Report Freq. over Dreaming.

In its trichotomous form, Dreaming, forced normal, is associated significantly better with REM/NREM difference than Total Recall Freq. (see Test 7, Table 2.3), even though only 1% more of the pairs were correctly classified. Further, Dreaming adds significantly to the association of Total Recall Freq. + Waking Perception with REM/NREM (Test 9).

Nevertheless it is equally true that Trichotomous Total Recall Freq. plus Trichotomous Waking Perception add significantly to the association of Trichotomous Dreaming with REM/NREM. The reliability of this latter test is somewhat tenuous, however, inasmuch as the unique contribution of Trichotomous Waking Perception is not quite significant at the .05 level (see Tests 10–12).

Dreamer Participation performs somewhat like Waking Perception (see Tests 13–15). It improves on the correlation of Total Recall Freq. with REM/NREM, but there is still a part of the REM/NREM variance that Dreaming picks up better than Dreamer Participation + Total Recall Freq., and there is no significant addition of Dreamer Participation to the combination of Total Recall Freq. + Dreaming. But while the edge of Dreaming is statistically significant, it is very small in magnitude.

Discussion

The major purpose of this paper is to determine whether an examination of REM/NREM reports from a perspective other than that provided by presumably complex but poorly defined judgments such as dreaming could yield useful information about the cognitive processes that precede the report. Although there are slight differences in the transformations carried out on the variables examined and in the tests of association employed, it is quite clear that the global judgment of Dreaming adds little, if anything, to Total Recall Content with respect to the association with the sleep stages REM and NREM. This conclusion is remarkable because Dreaming, regardless of how it is defined, has been the best single discriminator of REM/NREM reports. Visual Imagery generally runs a close second with Bizarreness coming up third (Antrobus et al., 1979; Foulkes, 1966). That none of the traditional "content" variables adds substantially to Total Recall Frequency suggests that the fundamental cognitive difference between Stage 1 REM and Stage 2 is the ability of the subject to recall and describe the events of which he/she was aware prior to making the report. That Dreaming and Visual Imagery also distinguish REM and NREM reports may be attributed to the fact that visual imagery, storylike quality and bizarreness are qualities of sleeping and drowsy cognition. Since the ability to recall is enhanced in Stage 1 REM, more dreaming, visual imagery, bizarreness and storylike sequences are reported from REM awakenings.

The possibility that REM is distinguished from NREM, in this case, Stage 2, by cognitive variables other than recall or memory is in no way excluded by these findings. Antrobus et al. (1979) have argued that the longer REM report is partly attributable to better selective attention to private events and to better ability to follow instructions from the previous waking state. To put it another way, the cognitive processes within REM are more likely to be influenced by the goals or motives established in the waking state. Evidence for this position was provided by the tendency for the REM/NREM difference in dream reporting to disappear over 14 nights of reporting.

The alternative to models that emphasize differences in selected cognitive processes is one that says cognitive processes in REM are simply more like waking cognitive processes than are NREM processes. But since people in REM sleep are not as fully alert as when awake, the cognitive processes tend to be flawed, like the speech of an inebriate (Kleitman, 1952). Until much more data on the reports of people who are lying on their beds with their eyes closed for sustained intervals is available, little more can be said on this matter.

The uncritical acceptance of the now classic association of dreaming with REM sleep may have prematurely closed the door to the search for alternate dreaming-physiological models. I am repeatedly impressed that REM reports are not as bizarre as what I call "late morning, weekend, home

APPENDIX COMPUTATIONAL EXAMPLE OF INCREMENTAL TEST FOR INCREMENT DUE TO TOTAL RECALL FREQUENCY OVER TOTAL WORD FREQUENCY

Mean	Source	df	Smaller Model Sum of Squares	Mean Square	F	T^2
			Total Word Frequency			
0.7927	Model	1	45.87355	45.87355	45.50	45.50
	Error	72	72.58464	1.00812		
	Total	73	118.45819			
			Total Recall Frequency			
7.0285	Model	1	3606.27328	3606.27328	97.78	97.78
	Error	72	2655.58186	36.88308		
	Total	73	6261.85515			

Larger Model:
Total Word Frequency + Total Recall Frequency

	Sum of Squares and Cross Products	
	Total Word Freq.	Total Recall Freq.
Total Word Freq.	72.58464	288.46345
Total Recall Freq.	288.46345	2655.58186

$T^2(2/71) = 97.88 = F(1/72)$ for Roy's Maximum Root criterion, $F(2/71) = 48.26$

Incremental Test

$$F(2 - 1/73 - 2) = \frac{(73 - 2)(97.88 - 45.50)}{(2 - 1)[(73 - 1) + 45.50]} = \frac{3,718.98}{117.5} = 31.65$$

dreams." Perhaps in the REM-alpha soup of late morning sleep or the sleep onset period studied by Foulkes (1965) we may rediscover some of the characteristics of dreaming that we have tended to ignore because of the compelling simplicity of Stage 1 REM as the definition of the physiological dreaming state. Reliance on a single global measure of variation in sleep cognition is equally restrictive in that the defining cognitive processes remain forever in the heads of the judges employed. It is entirely possible that different characteristics of what might otherwise be called dreaming may vary independently with other physiological parameters of sleep. Antrobus, Ehrlichman, Wollman, and Wiener (1983), for example, have found that a difference in hemisphere activation affects the log word frequencies of several imagery classes but not Total Recall Freq.

PART **2**

REVIEWS OF SLEEP MENTATION STUDIES

_3_

Sleep-Onset Mentation

GERALD W. VOGEL
Georgia Mental Health Institute
and
Emory University School of Medicine

More than a decade elapsed after the initiation of modern laboratory studies of sleep and dreaming (Aserinsky & Kleitman, 1955; Dement & Kleitman, 1957) before the systematic investigation of the psychophysiology of sleep onset (SO) was undertaken (Foulkes, Spear, & Symonds, 1966; Foulkes & Vogel, 1965; Pope, 1973; Vogel, Barrowclough, & Giesler, 1972; Vogel, Foulkes, & Trosman, 1966). The findings of these studies were important not only in their own right but because they required alteration of the early generalizations to the effect that REM sleep accompanies dreaming and NREM sleep accompanies either no mental activity, or, as was later reported, more thoughtlike mentation (Foulkes, 1962; Monroe, Rechtschaffen, Foulkes, & Jensen, 1965). In this chapter I review these findings and some of their implications.

DESCRIPTION OF MENTAL ACTIVITY AT SLEEP ONSET (SO)

Reports of SO mentation were retrieved by "awakening" subjects from one of four consecutive electroencephalographic/electrooculographic stages which cover the transition from wakefulness to sleep. (Foulkes & Vogel, 1965). Usually several SO awakenings of each subject were made each night, each awakening from a randomly selected EEG/EOG SO stage as the subject returned to sleep from a previous awakening. The four SO EEG/EOG stages, in order from wakefulness to sleep, were: (a) alpha EEG, usually continuous, with one or more rapid eye movements a few seconds prior to the "awakenings" (alpha REM); (b) alpha EEG, often continuous, with pronounced slow eye movements (alpha SEM); (c) descending stage 1 EEG; and (d) *descending* stage 2 EEG or .5–2.5-min duration. Subjectively these four successive EEG/EOG stages were usually rated as ranging in succession from awake and alert, or awake but drowsy, through drifting off to sleep, to light sleep. There were individual differences in the match between these subjective states of consciousness and EEG/EOG stage but all subjects did report a steady progression toward sleep with successive SO EEG/EOG stages. Moreover, with each successive EEG/EOG stage there was a steady decline in control over the course of mental activity and an awareness of the immediate environment and a steady rise in the frequency of hallucinatory experience, though again with large individual differences in the EEG/EOG stage at which these changes typically occur.

Recall of at least one item of mental content at SO was very frequent in all four EEG/EOG stages, more so than during REM sleep (83.3%; Dement, 1965a) and during NREM sleep (23–74%, depending on the study; Foulkes, 1967b). Pooled recall percentages of awakenings with content by SO stages were as follows: alpha REM, 96.2%; alpha SEM, 98.1%; S-1, 97.9%; S-2, 89.7% (Foulkes & Vogel, 1965). The length of SO reports (word count of alpha SEM and stage 1 reports) was not significantly different from the length of REM reports from the same subjects (Foulkes et al., 1966). Thus these data indicated that an awakening from SO is at least as likely to produce as long a report of recalled mentation as an awakening from REM sleep.

The mentation recalled from SO was not simply flashing lights or primarily auditory imagery, or affectively intense and unpleasant as had been indicated by folklore or by earlier anecdotal reports of SO mentation, some of which were obtained by morning questionnaires rather than from on-the-spot awakenings at SO (Critchley, 1955; McKellar, 1957). Like REM mentation, most SO mentation collected "on-the-spot" consisted of meaningful sensory imagery, and again like REM mentation, the imagery was visual (Foulkes & Vogel, 1965). In fact, visual imagery was present in 78–89% of reports depending on the EEG/EOG stage of the awakening. Though auditory imagery occurred occasionally (range of 14 to 37% of reports from each stage), as did undistorted bodily sensations like touch and movement (range of 22 to 32% of reports from each stage), gustatory imagery was never reported and olfactory imagery was very rare (2 to 4%). The systematic data collected on the spot also revealed that affect was usually not intense nor unpleasant, usually peaked during alpha SEM, and thereafter decreased. If anything then, the SO period can be called a period of relatively flat affect. (Of course, that makes some kind of adaptive or teleological sense since it is hard to imagine that SO could proceed successfully to deep sleep with intense affect.)

Since dreaming has previously been assigned exclusively to REM sleep, the most unexpected finding in the initial laboratory study of SO (Foulkes & Vogel, 1965) later replicated in three other studies (Foulkes et al., 1966; Pope, 1973; Vogel et al., 1972), was the presence of substantial dreaming during SO. Dreams, defined as hallucinated, dramatic episodes (not as single scenes or flashing lights or nonhallucinated images) occurred in the following percentages of awakenings from EEG/EOG stages; alpha REM, 31%; alpha SEM, 43%; stage 1, 76%; stage 2, 71%. Again, though all subjects dreamed, there were large individual differences in dream frequency and in the EEG/EOG stages at which dreaming became abundant.

That these [reports classified as dreams] were something other than engrossing waking fantasies was indicated by the following facts: (a) by definition, these experiences had to partake of an hallucinatory quality which is lacking in even the most engrossing of waking fantasies; (b) subjects generally described such experiences as more like night-dreams than any form of waking fantasy; (c) subjects described their state prior to awakenings producing such content as "drowsy," "drifting off to sleep," or "light sleep;" and (d) such content showed distortions and symbolic transformations of a type generally assumed to be absent in voluntary daytime fantasy. To illustrate these four points, let us consider . . . an alpha SEM dream. (Foulkes & Vogel, 1965, p. 237)

"I was looking at sort of a low lazy-Susan type of thing which was on the floor under a typewriter stand. I was in a very peculiar vantage point. I was looking down between the legs there, and never got above this. It was made out of crystal, and it was a platter type of arrangement. In the middle there was a stem and a little ball on the top, and I first saw there was blood in the little glass thing. In the middle it was full of blood; and then as it developed, the blood turned into what looked like sort of cocktail sauce that's served with shrimp; and then as it developed more, little shrimp started appearing around the little glass where the sauce was; and then as it developed more, more shrimp appeared on the platter below; and just as you called, a dog was walking over there and was just about ready to help himself to a few of the shrimp. This was mostly in vague symbols because there was nothing realistic about this at all. The dog was strange too, because his head, you know where his snout comes down to his nose, this part was all, like it was sawed off. In other words, his face was completely squared off and he didn't have any nose, I remember when I saw the dog coming out, I looked at him, made me feel uneasy . . . ." (Foulkes & Vogel, 1965, pp. 237–238)

The occurrence of dreams like this one—long, vivid, visual, hallucinated, bizarre—suggested that SO reports might be very similar to REM reports. Three later studies showed this to be the case (Foulkes et al., 1966; Pope, 1973; Vogel et al., 1972). One study compared REM reports with alpha SEM and stage 1 SO reports and found there were no significant REM-SO report differences in length of report, and in reliably rated sexual content, aggressive content, hedonic tone, and dreamlike fantasy (DF) (the last was measured on an 8 point scale by which the formal properties of reported content were rated in terms of increasing dreamlike properties, ranging from no content to conceptual, everydayish content; to conceptual, bizarre content; to perceptual, nonhallucinatory everydayish; to perceptual, hallucinating everydayish; to perceptual, hallucinating, bizarre content; Foulkes et al., 1966). The finding of similar REM-SO DF scores has also been twice replicated (Pope, 1973; Vogel et al., 1972).

In another study (Vogel et al., 1972), using a different approach, trained judges attempted to discriminate unlabeled REM from unlabeled stage 1 SO reports on the basis that REM content would be more "dreamlike" or regressive than stage 1 content; that is, compared with stage 1 SO reports, REM reports would have some combination of being "more visual, more perceptual, more affective, less thoughtlike, less hedonically neutral, less concerned with contemporary life and more concerned with past life; more bizarre, implausible or novel; more 'lived in;' under less volitional control; accompanied by less awareness of the environment; and/or more often hallucinatory [p. 450]." Results showed that although the nine judges were able to discriminate stage 1 SO from REM reports with an overall 70% correct hit ($p < .001$), there was considerable overlap. Approximately 25% of SO reports were called REM reports and approximately 50% of REM reports were called SO. Looked at in terms of regressive or dreamlike mentation, these results confirmed studies indicating that REM reports are often less implausible and more banal than originally thought (Dorus, Dorus, & Rechtschaffen, 1971; Snyder, Karacan, Thorp, & Scott, 1968); more to the point of this review, they again confirmed that SO mentation was often as regressive as the most regressive REM mentation—a fact now shown in four separate studies, two of which indicate that the most dreamlike, regressive mentation is retrieved from SO about half as often as from REM sleep (Foulkes et al., 1966; Vogel et al., 1972).

PSYCHIATRIC IMPLICATIONS OF SO MENTATION

Because of the similarities between dreams and psychoses (Freud, 1900, 1955a), psychiatrists have for a long time hypothesized that the physiological correlates of dreaming might be similar to, or clues to, the physiological correlates of psychoses (Jackson, cited in Jones, 1961). With the initial discovery that REM sleep was a reliable correlate of dreaming and the subsequent early generalization that it was the only correlate of dreaming, this hypothesis took the form that some unique property of REM sleep might be a correlate of psychosis (Fisher & Dement, 1963). Oversimplified, the notion was that psychosis might be a psychological expression of an intrusion of the REM state into wakefulness. Several different experimental approaches to this hypothesis have failed to find support for it (Vogel, 1968) and, although some controversy still exists about this question (Wyatt, Termini, & Davis, 1971), the bulk of the evidence is still against it (Vogel et al., 1972). However, the finding that dreaming frequently occurred during SO in the absence of REM sleep suggests that the failure to find a link between REM sleep and psychosis may not be a complete refutation of the dream-psychosis hypothesis. In other words, if there is some physiological foundation to the psychological similarity of dreaming and psychosis, it may lie in a physiological correlate of SO dreaming or in a common physiological correlate of SO and REM dreaming rather than in a unique property of REM sleep.

In this regard it should be repeated that stage 1 EEG, which is so similar to a stage REM EEG, is not a strong, or at least a unique, physiological correlate of dreaming because: (a) dreams (hallucinated dramatic episodes) were reported from high percentages of SO awakenings from EEG stages other than stage 1 (31% of alpha REM; 43% of alpha SEM; and 71% of stage 2); Foulkes & Vogel, 1965); and (b) dreams were also reported, though infrequently, from NREM sleep (Vogel et al., 1972). Nor is regressive content (i.e., bizarre, implausible content), regardless of whether or not it is hallucinated (dreamed), limited to the stage 1 EEG pattern, of SO or REM sleep. Although regressive content reports occurred in a significantly greater percentage of reports during SO stage 1 than during the other SO stages ($p < .002$), (51.2% of stage 1 reports had regressive content in comparison with 19.2% of alpha REM reports, 27.8% of alpha SEM reports, and 26.9% of stage 2 reports), only 37.1% of all regressive content reports from SO occurred during stage 1 (Vogel et al., 1966). Furthermore, regressive content, independent of hallucinations, was reported from only 50% of stage REM awakenings (Vogel et al., 1972). In short, neither REM sleep nor a stage 1 EEG is a relatively unique physiological correlate of regressive content or of dreaming.

PSYCHOPHYSIOLOGICAL IMPLICATIONS OF SO FINDINGS

Although the search for other physiological correlates of dreaming and regressive mentation occurred about the same time as the discovery of dreaming at SO, it was independently initiated from an entirely different area of sleep research. What follows is a brief review of this new direction to the search for the physiological correlates of dreaming and of regressive mentation during sleep, and its relation to SO studies.

The new approach was initiated by Moruzzi's (1963, 1965) physiological distinction between tonic and phasic physiological events during REM sleep. Tonic events are continuous ones, for example, the relatively low-voltage, mixed-frequency EEG or the persistent loss of muscle tone. Phasic events are brief and intermittent, like the rapid eye movements, the PGO spikes, changes in autonomic discharge, spike discharges at the extraoccular muscles or the middle ear muscles. Moruzzi's tonic-phasic distinction was soon supported by Pompeiano's (1970) evidence that the vestibular nucleus controls phasic but not tonic events. From the psychological side Aserinsky (1967) suggested that the tonic-phasic distinction might be paralleled by psychologically different kinds of dreams, a suggestion taken up by Molinari and Foulkes (1969), who reasoned that since phasic events occurred not only during REM sleep but also in NREM and SO, they might provide a stronger and temporally more precise parallel to regressive mentation than REM sleep (Moruzzi & Foulkes, 1969). Thus, the phasic-tonic distinction came to supercede the old REM-NREM dichotomy as a hypothetical parallel for regressive-nonregressive content. In very recent investigations not yet replicated, several different phasic events have been reported to be correlates of regressive mentation. These included the following:

1. In visually hallucinated content retrieved from REM sleep, thinking was less likely to occur during REM bursts than during REM quiescence (Molinari & Foulkes, 1969); the absence of thought or cognitive elaboration was even more strongly related to EEG sawtooth waves, which are unique to REM sleep and often occur during REM bursts (Foulkes & Pope, 1974); and very recently, Pope (1973) generalized and extended this finding to SO by observing that SO theta bursts, which are in the same frequency range as sawtooth waves, were associated with discontinuity in the content reported.

2. Another indicator of phasic activity is the phasic integrated potential (PIP) of the periorbital EMG, which is believed to be a correlate of the ponto-geniculate-occipital spike, the presumed generator of many phasic events (Rechtschaffen et al., 1970). These workers found that both REM and NREM content reported from PIP awakenings was more bizarre than that reported from non-PIP awakenings in the same sleep stages (Watson, 1972; Rechtschaffen et al., 1971), although the REM finding was not confirmed (Foulkes & Pope, 1973).

3. Pivik and Dement (1970) found that in the human, momentary suppressions of the EMG occur during SO stage 1 and during NREM which were coincident with phasic H-reflex inhibition. Finally, Pivik's (1971) study of the relationship between the phasic EMG suppressions and NREM mentation found that the EMG suppressions were related to increased aggression and auditory imagery.

In summary, if replicated, several lines in the current investigation of the phasic-tonic dichotomy may provide stronger, and temporally more precise, physiological parallels to regressive-nonregressive mentation than the old REM–NREM dichotomy, to which the finding of SO dreaming originally stood as an isolated exception.

PSYCHOLOGICAL ORGANIZATION OF SO

The finding that SO dreams and REM mentation were not correlated with a particular EEG stage—in effect that SO dreams and regressive mentation were not simply EEG stage epiphenomena—not only stimulated the search for other physiological correlates of dreaming and regressive mentation, but it also initiated a search for psychological variables which might be related to SO dreaming and REM mentation.

An early unsuccessful candidate for a correlate of SO regressive content was hallucinatory activity. A priori, it made sense that subjects should have had regressive content when they hallucinated. But the fact was that they often did not. Only 42% of all hallucinated SO reports had regressive content and only 49% of all regressive content reports occurred in the presence of hallucinatory activity (Vogel et al., 1966).

More success was obtained with the relation between regressive content and loss-of-waking control over mentation and reality orientation (Vogel et al., 1966). In this regard, I repeat the findings. During SO subjects first lost their control over the course of mentation; either slightly later or simultaneously they lost awareness of the environment (did not know they were in bed in the laboratory) and only after these two losses, did they begin to hallucinate (believe that mental events were really happening in the external world). In psychoanalytic terms, one might say that over the course of SO there was a progressive withdrawal of interest in (decathexis of) the psychological functions which maintained waking contact with reality: first, a decathexis of the volitional control over mentation; then a decathexis of perception; and finally, with hallucination, a decathexis of reality testing.

Empirically, there was a positive relation between the degree of decathexis (withdrawal) and the pooled frequency of regressive content reports. Regressive content occurred in 6% of reports with no decathexis of these functions; in 12% of reports with only loss of control over mentation; in 31.3% with loss of control over mentation and loss of awareness of environment; and in 50.7% with complete decathexis, that is, with loss of control over mentation, loss of awareness of environment, and loss of reality testing (hallucinations). Altogether, 94% of regressive-content reports were accompanied by some degree of decathexis of contact with reality and only 6% of regressive-content reports were not accompanied by some decathexis (Spearman $r = 0.44$; $p < .001$). This figure was high enough so that it was concluded that during SO some decathexis of waking contact with reality was a necessary condition for regressive content, and the 6% exceptions to this rule were interpreted as the result of a decathexis too subtle for the gross instrument (question with four-point scale) to detect.

And yet this conclusion stood in puzzling contrast to the fact that reports with the greatest loss of control (hallucination) often had nonregressive content (for example, 58% of all stage 2 reports were hallucinated, nonregressive–content reports). Thus, if some loss of contact were necessary for regressive content, why should reports with the greatest loss of contact often have had nonregressive content?

The suggested resolution of this paradox involved the considerations about the following modal (typical) relation in each EEG stage between kind of content (regressive or nonregressive) and the degree of decathexis of waking controls. In each alpha stage the modal report had nonregressive content with either no decathexis of waking control or only a partial one, a combination called a relatively intact ego (I). The percentage of I reports in each alpha stage was significantly higher than the percentage of I in all reports ($p < .001$), and progressively decreased during successive EEG/EOG stages (75% of reports in alpha REM; 63% in alpha SEM; 20% in stage 1; 15.4% in stage 2).

In stage 1 the modal report had regressive content and a partial or complete decathexis of waking controls, a combination called a destructuralized ego (D). The percentage of D reports in stage 1 was significantly higher than the percentage of D in all reports ($p < .002$), and it increased with successive stages to a maximum in stage 1 after which it decreased (19.2% of reports in alpha REM; 27.8% in alpha SEM; 51.2% in stage 1; 26.9% in stage 2).

In stage 2 the modal report had a complete decathexis of waking control and paradoxically a return to nonregressive content, a combination called a restructuralized ego (R). The percentage of R reports in stage 2 was significantly higher than the percentage of R in all reports ($p < .001$) and progressively increased with successive EEG/EOG stages (5.8% of reports in alpha REM; 9.2% in alpha SEM; 28.8% in stage 1; and 57.7% in stage 2). Thus the modal SO report was I during alpha EEG; D during stage 1; and R during stage 2. An example of the I-D-R sequence follows:

- Alpha SEM: intact ego (I): "I was thinking of sending a clipping to a Russian pianist and I saw an envelope with 15 cents postage." (The subject was a concert pianist. The content was not regressive. The subject reported that during the SO experience he had lost volitional control over content, was unaware of his surroundings, but knew that the image was in his mind and not in the external world.)
- Stage 1: destructuralized ego (D): "I was observing the inside of a pleural cavity. There were small people in it, like a room. The people

were hairy, like monkeys. The walls of the pleural cavity are made of ice and slippery. In the midpart there is an ivory bench with people sitting on it. Some people are throwing balls of cheese against the inner side of the chest wall." (The report contains bizarre, implausibly associated elements, distortions, and so on. The subject reported that during the SO experience there was a complete loss of contact with external reality—including hallucination—during the reported experience.)

• Stage 2: restructuralized ego (R): "I was driving a car, telling other people you shouldn't go over a certain speed limit." (In this report the content is again plausible and realistic. There was a complete loss of contact with external reality (including hallucination) during the reported experience.)

Though the above sequence was the modal psychophysiological parallel during SO, that is, I during alpha EEG, D during stage 1, and R during stage 2, there were, among all the reports, numerous departures from this modal psychophysiological parallel. However, the departures seemed to fit in a pattern which suggested that the psychophysiology of SO could be understood as follows: at each SO each subject progresses through the I-D-R psychological sequence and also progresses through the four EEG/EOG sleep stages. Usually the members of the two sequences match in the modal manner, but in some instances they do not, though each sequence still progresses through its individual stages in the typical order. Two kinds of data supported this interpretation. First, in some subjects D usually occurred earlier (during alpha EEG) while in others D usually occurred later (during stage 2). Among the 9 studied subjects there were 2 subjects in which most of the D reports were in alpha and a higher than expected frequency of R in stage 1. On the other side, one subject's highest frequency of D was in stage 2 and a lower than expected frequency of R was in stage 2. Second, if the ego states I, D, and R were assigned numbers 1, 2, and 3, and each subject's mean ego state was calculated for each EEG stage, all subjects showed a monotonically increasing curve of mean ego state across the four EEG/EOG stages. Of the 27 comparisons of consecutive EEG stages (9 subjects, 3 comparisons between 4 successive EEG stages), 23 were in the expected direction ($p < .001$). The 4 exceptions were in 3 subjects and 3 of these exceptions concern minimal differences between alpha REM and alpha SEM.

In summary, the psychophysiological data about SO can be interpreted as follows: viewed psychologically SO is a sequence of three ego states (I, D, and R), and viewed physiologically it is a sequence of four EEG/EOG states. The elements of the two sequences have a typical match with I during alpha EEG, D during stage 1, and R during stage 2. But each sequence can and does occur independently of the other, thus accounting for departures from the ideal psychophysiological parallel.

The finding of a sequence of ego states—or psychological changes—that were relatively independent of EEG stages suggested that the individual differences in the frequency of SO dreaming and in the (EEG) interval from wakefulness to dreaming might be more readily explainable in psychodynamic terms than in terms of a psychophysiological parallelism. Thus, the finding that withdrawal from contact with reality preceded regressive mentation suggested that the withdrawal helped induce the regressive content for two reasons. First, SO withdrawal from sensory input (represented by loss of awareness of environment), indicated sensory deprivation and that encouraged the emergence of regressive content. Second, SO "withdrawal" from the usual directed thought of wakefulness (represented by a loss of control over course of mentation), indicated a reduction of the usual waking inhibition of regressive content or of regressive thought connections. Thus, both these aspects of the withdrawal during SO allowed or encouraged the emergence of regressive content (D state). Accordingly, the regressive mentation during SO is not necessary for SO, nor is it the result of endogenous activation of archaic modes of thought. Rather, it is simply an unavoidable side effect of the reduction in focused thought and sensory input which is essential for SO.

> Furthermore, because the D state is so quickly and regularly followed by a restitution (R) (to nonregressive content), it appears that the tendency toward regression which is represented by D, threatens the ego and produces the need for defense. Thus, at this point in the SO period, the ego, in order to sleep, needs a defense which will allow it to continue to withdraw and yet overcome the threatened chaos (D) induced by the withdrawal. The finding that the loss of reality testing is necessary for the return to nonregressive content (at the end of SO) suggests that the inactivation of reality testing is a part of the needed defense which will resolve the conflict and allow the restitution represented by R. (Vogel et al., 1966, pp. 246–247)

In other words, potentially threatened by the emergence of regressive content, but needing to continue the withdrawal (which only adventitiously fostered the emergence of the regressive content) in order to sleep, the ego gains some control by constructing its own reality in a primitive manner, reminiscent of the defensive renunciation of reality testing used in psychosis.

This psychodynamic view of SO provided an explanation of an empirically significant characteristic of hypnagogic dreaming, namely, the individual variations in the length, frequency, and EEG stage of SO dreams (Vogel et al., 1972).

The suggested explanation was

> . . . that during SO individuals differ in their tolerance of the potential threat of regression induced by the withdrawal and that these differences are responsible for the variations in the length, frequency, and EEG stage of hypnagogic dreams. This notion is consistent with our clinical impression that the subjects who are free to experience and enjoy their own fantasies had

earlier and richer hypnagogic dreams than more anxious and rigid subjects. It appears likely that the more rigid subjects were more threatened by an impending regression and so held on to external reality longer or withdrew in some special way so as to minimize the regression. This is also compatible with the clinical phenomena of hypnagogic dreamlike experiences which abruptly awaken anxious patients who are particularly prone to insomnia. (Vogel et al., 1966, p. 247)

PERSONALITY CORRELATES OF SO MENTATION

Some empirical support for the above psychodynamic view of SO has been obtained by the study of personality correlates of individual differences in SO dreaming (Foulkes et al., 1966). In this study subjects contributed both SO (alpha SEM and descending stage 1) and REM reports, which were reliably rated for their word count (length), manifest aggression, sexuality, hedonic tone, and dreamlike fantasy. Personality variables were measured by the California Personality Index (CPI) and by reliable ratings of thematic apperception test (TAT) responses, in terms of aggression, sex, hedonic tone, and imaginativeness.

SO and REM reports did not differ significantly in mean length, dreamlike fantasy (DF), aggression, sexuality, and hedonic tone, thus confirming the essential similarity of REM and SO reports. There were, however, some differences in distribution of kinds of reports which were not revealed by the group averages. The frequency of REM bizarre, hallucinatory reports was twice that of the SO frequency. Indeed, REM reports tended to be at either extreme of the dreamlike fantasy scale, having either no content or bizarre hallucinatory content, whereas SO reports were evenly distributed at all points on the DF scale with substantial individual differences in the frequency of hallucinated, bizarre reports. There was no significant intrasubject REM and SO correlation in DF, sex, aggression, and hedonic ratings. It seems then that different psychological mechanisms must determine the mental qualities of SO and REM reports.

This was borne out by the finding that several indicators of waking fantasy were related to SO fantasy (DF rating) and not related to REM fantasy (DF rating). SO fantasy correlated positively and significantly with TAT word count, sex, imagination, and not with REM fantasy. REM fantasy and SO fantasy did, however, both correlate with TAT, aggression, and hedonic tone. By inference, the psychological mechanisms responsible for SO fantasy are strongly related to the mechanisms responsible for waking fantasy and independent of the mechanisms responsible for REM fantasy. Investigation of these mechanisms was begun by a study of the personality differences between SO dreamers and nondreamers (Foulkes et al., 1966). In support of the above psychodynamic view of SO, it was found that SO dreamers were less rigidly defensive than SO nondreamers. On the CPI administered to college students, SO dreamers were more self-accepting, less rigidly conforming to social standards, and more socially poised than SO nondreamers, who, in contrast, scored high on items characteristic of the authoritarian personality (rigid, intolerant, conformist). And none of the personality variables which correlated with SO waking fantasy was related to REM fantasy, which was found in a separate study to be bizarre and vivid in subjects with psychopathology (Foulkes & Rechtschaffen, 1964).

Thus, SO and REM fantasy are independent of each other and independently related to different personality variables. SO fantasy is positively related to a flexible, nonrigid, nondefensive ego which is free to engage in waking fantasy, while REM fantasy is more related to psychopathology. One might reasonably conclude from this that SO fantasy is positively related to ego strength, while REM fantasy is positively related to ego weakness. However, that must be a mistaken oversimplification because SO and REM fantasy are not negatively correlated. They are unrelated.

An explanation for this paradox may be as follows. SO fantasy is related to waking fantasy and both of these are inhibited by rigid defensiveness, while REM fantasy is related to psychopathology. But defensiveness and psychopathology are not correlated; that is, some rigidly defensive subjects have severe psychopathology (like the "frozen" paranoid); some do not (like the inhibited but well functioning obsessive-compulsive); and some undefensive subjects may have severe psychopathology (like the disorganized schizophrenic), and some do not (like the poised, self-acceptant adult). In a sample of functioning college students, such as the one used in the Foulkes (1966) study, subjects with little defensiveness would more likely be poised and self-acceptant rather than disorganized and disturbed. Hence, such a sample would suggest that high SO fantasy would relate equally well to ego strength and to lack of defensiveness. But it is my hunch that a broader range of subjects including those with undefended disturbances would show that SO fantasy is related to waking fantasy and that both are related to lack of defensiveness independent of ego strength.

Whether or not this explanation (of the paradoxical lack of a negative correlation between REM and SO fantasy) is correct, the central empirical findings whose implications I want to pursue are: (a) that SO and REM fantasy are independent of each other; and (b) that each is related to different waking personality variables.

If each subject's REM and SO fantasy were correlated, then one could easily imagine a common mechanism or control determining each subject's SO and REM fantasy. But the lack of a relation between a subject's REM DF score and SO DF score implies that SO and REM fantasy must be under separate controls. Thus the evidence implies that there are two independent systems for the production of fantasy including regressive mentation. Let us consider some psychoanalytic implications of this conclusion.

In psychoanalytic terms there are several reasons for classifying SO fantasy—and particularly its regressive mentation—as initiated by ego regression and for classifying the REM fantasy (and its regressive mentation) as initiated by unconscious wishes and needs of the id. (Of course, in psychoanalytic terms both ego and id participate in both SO and REM fantasy. The question here concerns the initiator.) SO fantasy can be classified as initiated by ego regression because it is initiated volitionally; is related to waking fantasy under volitional control; becomes more regressive as the ego's "nutriment," sensory information is reduced. REM fantasy, on the other hand, can be classified as initiated by unconscious wishes and needs because it is never volitionally initiated; is not related to waking mentation under volitional control—on the contrary it is related to nonvolitional waking mentation, namely, psychopathology; is almost invariably associated with the physical signs of sexual arousal (Karacan, Hursch, Williams, & Thornby, 1972); and arises with increased endogenous activation (Berger, 1969). Thus, the laboratory evidence that there are two independent, different systems for fantasy production supports psychoanalytic theory, derived from clinical observations, that regressive mentation can result from two such independent, different systems. Further, within my limited knowledge of the psychoanalytic literature, the SO–REM dichotomy is the first systematic, laboratory, empirical evidence supporting the proposition that psychopathology is more related to the system producing nocturnal dreams than to the system which controls waking fantasy. Perhaps, modern psychoanalytic ego psychologists to the contrary, Freud's (1955a/1900) original topographic model is more consistent with these findings than later elaborations of the structural model. Certainly contemporary structural views that psychopathology and the nocturnal dream can better be explained as a result of ego regression than of unconscious "activation" are not supported by this laboratory evidence (Arlow & Brenner, 1964).

CHAPTER 3 UPDATE: RECENT RESEARCH TRENDS IN SLEEP ONSET MENTATION

MARINO BOSINELLI
University of Bologna

The psychophysiological determinants of sleep onset (SO) mentation still present dark areas that need exploring.

In 1978 Vogel proposed a model in which mental processes during SO could be explained by a psychological-psychodynamic interpretation, and also stressed the independence of psychological and physiological-EEG events. According to this model the SO mentation follows the sequence Intact-Ego→Destructuralized-Ego→Restructuralized-Ego, where the loss of control over mentation and the loss of contact with the environment would produce the regressive destructuration, with no need to postulate the activation of archaic contents. The following loss of reality testing would determine the restructuration of the dream experience. The SO dream would thus be initiated by Ego regression, while the REM dream by the Id.

Antrobus's (1978) commentary on this model, besides advancing some methodological considerations, claimed that one could not exclude the possibility that psychological SO events might be correlated with physiological events different from the EEG ones.

Research work on SO mentation after 1978 can be grouped according to two orders of problems: first, as an analysis of the variables that define the SO process and the precise moment in which sleep begins; second, as a study of mental experiences in SO, their interpretation, and their relationship with mentation in other sleep stages.

The following factors have been shown to "facilitate" the SO process: use of intermittent tones or association of tones and counting (Webb & Agnew, 1979); a visual/verbal polygraphic feedback or utilization of a ritual, such as reading, and so forth (Leonard, 1983). As to detection of SO, data are not wholly consistent. Campbell and Webb (1981) found that only 52% of subjective signals of wakefulness correspond to an EEG-defined wake condition. According to Fellman and Strauch (1983), there is a good concordance between EEG recordings and subjective SO quality only when stage W is included. In general, when subjects are asked to give a different motor response for each different level (such as W, stage 1, stage 2), it is rather difficult to establish a significant relation between response and EEG data with respect to lighter stages: Antrobus and Saul (1980), for example, using insomniacs and good sleepers, observed that the bias in classifying subjective waking condition as sleep was higher in stage 1 than in stage 2. According to Redington, Perry, Gibson, and Kamiya (1981), subjects were able to identify stage 1 in 86% of cases (this result was not improved by feedback), while the baseline for stage 2 was 55% and improved up to 71% with feedback. Bonnet and Moore (1982) calculated the SO threshold at 2–4 min after the first sleep spindle. According to Gibson, Perry, Redington, and Kamiya (1982), correct behavioral identification of W–1–2 stages occurred in 61% of cases, with some preference for lighter stages; identification of the difference between stage 1 and stage 2 was more difficult than between W and stage 1. The following physiological variables, along with behavioral and EEH data, were considered useful to detect SO: the toe temperature peak (Brown, 1979), and the abdominal and thoracic respiratory changes (Naifeh & Kamiya, 1981; Ogilvie & Wilkinson, 1983, 1984).

Other interesting data emerging from this field of study may be noted: for example, the evidence that affectivity is not only infrequent during SO mentation, but also shows a tendency to decrease; moreover, when affectivity is present, it constitutes an obstacle to falling asleep (Antrobus & Saul, 1980; Gibson et al., 1982).

The SO mentation problem still shows controversial aspects. In his book of 1978, Foulkes stressed the importance of the formal disorganization ("intrasentence," i.e., intraimage) of many stage 1–SO experiences, such as incomplete images, superimposed images and so forth. His interpretative model is not yet openly cognitive. A psychophysiological-cognitive trend may be found in an article on insomnia by De la Peña (1978), from which many useful suggestions for studying SO dynamics can be drawn. In his view, the psychophysiological mechanism may be a function of the degree of "mismatch" between optimal and de facto information load during SO process.

Further research has provided empirical data on SO mentation content, recall frequency, and the relationships among SO, REM, and NREM mentation. Bosinelli, Cavallero, and Cicogna (1982), for example, found that REM mentation did not show a significantly higher frequency of Ego presence than did SO mentation. However, these results, which were analyzed according to a psychodynamic model, might be questionable because they were collected from unmatched-for-length reports (Foulkes & Schmidt, 1983). Antrobus (1983) established that the quantitative parameter of Total Recall Frequency represents the most effective technique for the analysis of the psychological differences between REM and NREM sleep (TRC in REM mentation > TRC in NREM mentation). In general, Antrobus believed that the cognitive difference between REM and NREM sleep depends on the level of general processes, such as attention and memory; furthermore, REM situation is favored by its cortical activation and high perceptual threshold. The Foulkes and Schmidt (1983) study analyzed REM, stage 2–SO, and stage 2–NREM dream reports from a cognitive point of view and found that the percentage of recall was 93% in REM, 88% in SO, and 67% in NREM. When each report was divided into "temporal sequences," results showed the following percentage of reports with more than one temporal sequence: 80% in REM, 47% in SO, and 40% in NREM. The reports collected by Foulkes and Schmidt were then analyzed according to two modalities: comparison between reports unmatched for length (different number of units) and comparison between reports matched for length (equal number of units). Only the differences between reports matched for length were judged to be true qualitative differences. As a result, unmatched multiunit reports showed many interstage differences which disappeared in the comparison between matched reports. The following data were considered as a qualitative residue: more per unit self-representation in REM versus SO mentation; denser per unit overall characters in REM versus NREM mentation. Foulkes and Schmidt's results seem to support the hypothesis, shared by Antrobus, of a common dream production system: accordingly, most interstage differences in dream "quality" derive from interstage differences in dream "quantity." As far as the residual, real qualitative differences are concerned, Foulkes and Schmidt believe that they can be better interpreted in terms of production mechanisms, rather than in terms of retrieval mechanisms, as suggested by Antrobus.

In his conceptualization of 1985, Foulkes reconsidered the SO mentation problem and proposed an interpretation of the regressive experiences during stage 1–SO, without taking into consideration a psychoanalytical model. Such disorganized contents would be determined by the absence of the control operation of the Active-I, while the mental productive activity would be, at the beginning, only reduced. This could thus produce intrusive elements, fragments, regressive experiences. This kind of experience could not be easily restructuralized since such a rapid restructuration could subvert the transition process. On the other hand, a real dreamlike activity could include an emotional accompaniment which would hamper the passage into sleep. Here, once again, there is evidence of the idea of a scarce emotionality in SO mentation and of its tendency to produce disturbing effects (cf. Antrobus & Saul, 1980; Gibson et al., 1982; Lehmann, Meier, Meier, Mita, & Skrandies, 1983).

According to the data presented by Lehmann and Koukkou (1983), three classes of experiences occur most frequently during SO: reality-remote visual imagery, experiences concerning body-image, and reality-oriented thoughts. These elements are correlated with EEG data and it seems possible to interpret them accordingly to the state-dependency concept, which allowed the authors to propose their state-shift-theory (Koukkou & Lehmann, 1983; Lehmann & Koukkou, 1981).

The study of SO mentation may also include the search for material that might represent the input for dream production. Utilizing a free-associative technique in an experimental setting, Cavallero, Cicogna, and Bosinelli (1986) and Cicogna, Cavallero, and Bosinelli (1986) found that the selectivity of the mnemonic sources associated to the dream content is higher in SO dreaming than in REM dreaming. A modification of Tulving's memory stores classification was utilized. Following this technique, the memory traces associated to SO mentation are mainly represented by strict episodes, while those elicited by REM dreams are equally distributed in the three categories of Strict Episodes, Abstract Self-References, and Semantic Traces. Strict Episodes and Day Residues are significantly more frequent in the associations to SO dreams. On the other hand, the ratio number of associations/number of thematic units does not differ in the two conditions (SO = 1.25; REM = 1.20). Taking into account the distinction between single-unit reports and multiunit reports, Cicogna, Cavallero, Bosinelli,

Battaglia, and Natale (1987) observed that the category of Strict Episodes associations to SO dreams is the most frequent for the single-unit reports, while in the case of multiunit reports this difference decreases. In general, it is possible to maintain that REM dreams (single- or multiunits) are consistently stable in the kind of mnemonic sources they have access to SO mentation, when well formed and temporally extensive, shares with REM dreams the same kind of mnemonic input.

Summarizing the data and their interpretation, it may be noted that the differences between SO mentation and mental activities in other sleep stages (especially REM) are today frequently interpreted in quantitative terms, even when they appear in qualitative phenomenic aspects. However, it should be pointed out that: First, residual qualitative differences can also be observed, and they are not easily attributable to pure quantitative factors; second, agreement has not yet been reached on the interpretation of observed differences (state-dependency and psychophysiological shifting: Lehmann & Koukkou, 1981; Koukkou & Lehmann, 1983; processes like attention and memory consolidation: Antrobus, 1983; cognitive production mechanisms: Foulkes & Schmidt, 1983; Foulkes, 1985; selectivity in the material that constitutes the dream input: Cicogna et al., 1986).

It may be useful to indicate here some topics on which future research work might be centered. For example, a renewal of research work on stage 1–SO mentation may be useful. In fact, most of the awakenings utilized in studies on SO mentation are performed in stage 2, quite different from REM sleep from the EEG point of view, whereas stage 1–SO is the most REM-like period as far as EEG characteristics are concerned, but less REM-dreamlike than stage 2–SO from the mental activity viewpoint. Moreover, it would be worthwhile to enlarge the range of the sleep stages to be studied, and to systematically collect experiential reports from stages 3– and 4–NREM, which are the least REM-like sleep periods, according to EEG criteria.

Another problem concerns the precise interpretation of SO mentation, discussion of which has by no means been exhausted, particularly with reference to the following hypotheses: (a) a state-dependency hypothesis; (b) a psychological-cognitive hypothesis ("congruity" problems) or even a psychological-psychodynamic one ("conflictual" problems), both based on the psychological problematicity of the passage from waking to sleep; (c) an hypothesis stressing, still mainly in psychological terms, the usual proximity of the SO process to a long wake period, burdened by a high load of information (De la Peña, 1978). So, keeping in mind these three factors (state, passage, long preceding waking period), at least two kinds of research work could be proposed. As far as SO mentation in a strict sense is concerned, a comparison might be made between the mental activity in a "classic" SO period (i.e., after many waking hours) and the mental activity in an "advanced" SO period. The latter could be obtained by awakening the subject after 5–6 hours of uninterrupted sleep, then by maintaining the waking state for about 10–15 min, and finally by allowing the subject to fall asleep again ("advanced" SO process). Even some research control in REM sleep might be done: For instance, a comparison between the REM dream production in REM periods with latency = 0 (as may occur in depressed or narcoleptic patients: cf. Berger, Reimann, Wiegand, Joy, & Höchli, 1986; Roth, 1978; Schulz, 1981), with short latency (first REMP), and with long latency (last REMP).

If we consider, finally, the psychophysiological approach, we must conclude that the correlates between mentation and EEG data are still unclear, particularly in view of high intersubject variability. So a neuropsychological approach, based on the hemispheric activation patterns, could be undertaken. Bertini, Bosca, De Gennaro, Perrotta, and Solano (1986) showed that, after inducing a hypnagogic, that is, dreamlike mentation (reverie), and then giving the subjects a unilateral tactile test (shape recognition), a relation between such hypnagogic mentation and a right hemisphere activation could be observed.

On the other hand, hemodynamic research work has demonstrated that, while during wakefulness there is a "hyperfrontal" distribution pattern of the cerebral blood flow, during SO condition, besides a general reduction of the blood flow, a hemodynamic "repatterning" can also be detected. In fact, such reduction is more evident in the brainstem-cerebellar, right inferior, temporal, and bilateral frontal regions, than in other regions, occipital included. A final interesting point is represented by the interhemispheric hemodynamic differences (Ingvar, 1979; Sakai, Stirling Meyer, Karacan, Derman, & Yamamoto, 1980; Sakai, Stirling Meyer, Karacan, Yamaguchi, & Yamamoto, 1979).

Perhaps the possibilities of finding some small but satisfying psychophysiological correlate are not yet completely exhausted.

4

Dream Recall: History and Current Status of the Field*

DONALD R. GOODENOUGH
Educational Testing Service

It has long been a matter of common knowledge that we dream far more than we are able to remember the morning after. In the words of Freud (1955a/1900):

> . . . we are so familiar with the fact of dreams being liable to be forgotten, that we see no absurdity in the possibility of someone having had a dream in the night and of his not being aware in the morning either of what he has dreamt or even of the fact that he has dreamt at all. (p. 43)

The widespread belief that dream recall is difficult derives from the everyday observation that many once-recalled dreams are impossible to

*This work was supported in part by grant MH 21989.

recover even a few moments after they are vividly in our recollection. During the last two decades it has become increasingly evident how much of our nightly dream life is lost to recall by morning. Since the discovery by Aserinsky and Kleitman (1953) of REM sleep, many studies have been done on the frequency of dream reporting following awakenings from different types of sleep. Snyder (1967) has summarized this work in his excellent review. The consensus of these studies is that dreams can be recalled from about 80% of REM-period awakenings and from a somewhat smaller, although still substantial percentage of NREM awakenings. Since approximately two hours of a normal night are spent in REM sleep, it is clearly possible to collect a large number of dream reports from awakenings during the night. In contrast, ordinary morning recall of a dream occurs in the typical person at the rate of about once every two days (Webb & Kersey, 1967).

One way to account for this huge discrepancy is to suppose that dreams are produced by the awakenings themselves and therefore the more frequent the awakenings, the greater the number of dreams recalled. Such a view has had its historical proponents (e.g., Goblot, cited in Giora, 1973). While arousal (hypnopompic) experiences may occur under certain conditions (Goodenough, Lewis, Shapiro, Jaret, & Sleser, 1965a), the view that all or even many dreams are produced in this way is not taken seriously by current authors for a variety of reasons (Rechtschaffen, 1967; Stoyva & Kamiya, 1968).

An alternative explanation is that most dreams are simply not remembered by morning. In fact, the evidence consistently supports the view that dreams are difficult if not impossible to recall unless the sleeper awakens during or shortly after the dream experience itself. While dream reports may be collected in 80% of awakenings from REM periods, percentage recall drops dramatically if the awakening is delayed for even a few minutes after the end of REM sleep (Goodenough et al., 1965a; Wolpert & Trosman, 1958). Even a slight delay in the process of awakening, produced experimentally by the use of a gradual (as contrasted with an abrupt) awakening procedure, is enough to decrease the frequency of dream reporting substantially, particularly among people who rarely recall dreaming in the morning under everyday conditions (Goodenough et al., 1965a; Shapiro, Goodenough, & Gryler, 1963; Shapiro, Goodenough, Lewis, & Sleser, 1965). Given all the evidence, the common conclusion that the vast majority of dream experiences are forgotten seems inescapable.

The key question remains as to why dreams are so much more difficult to recall than waking experiences. The answer to this question could be very useful in the attempt to understand memory processes more generally, or so it has seemed, at least, to those involved in the area. It is not surprising, therefore, to find a substantial body of literature on dream recall and a wide variety of proposed answers. Very little research has been directed at this question directly, however. Most studies of dream recall have been concerned with the conditions under which dreams are initially reported, with the conditions under which the rerecall of once reported dreams occurs, or with individual differences in frequency of dream reporting. While these issues may be important in their own right, they are of primary interest in this review to the extent that they bear on our key question.

My purpose in this chapter is to review the most prominent of the theories offered to account for differences in ease of recall between dreams and waking experiences, to summarize the evidence relevant to these theories, and to suggest an arousal-retrieval model as an alternative explanation for some of the generalizations that are emerging from the evidence.

THE DEFINITION OF DREAM-RECALL FAILURES

The fact that dream recall has attracted a fair amount of research attention over the years certainly is not due to a ready access to empirical information in the area. All research approaches attempted so far are beset with difficulties. The major problem involves the definition of recall failures. Defining dream recall failures depends directly on our ability to identify when a dream experience occurs. If we can tell when dreams occur, then there is no problem in defining recall failures. If we cannot tell, then we cannot easily define recall failures. We may "see no absurdity" in supposing that a dream occurred without the dreamer's recall of it as Freud suggested, but we cannot be certain whether we are dealing with a recall failure or whether the claim that no dream has occurred is in fact correct.

The problem of determining when a dream occurs has been dealt with in a variety of ways. At one extreme, it has been argued that dreams go on continuously during sleep. In this view, failures to report a dream are obviously always failures of dream recall (ignoring for the moment the possibility that subjects may lie about their dream experiences). At the other extreme, some theorists have insisted that the concept of a dream experience is meaningless (e.g., Malcolm, 1959). This view renders the problem of dream-recall failure meaningless as well. One simply equates dreaming with the dream report as does Erikson (1954): "A dream is a verbal report of a series of remembered images, mostly visual, which are usually endowed with affect [p. 17]." Neither one of these extreme positions has many adherents among contemporary sleep researchers.

The proposal by Dement and Kleitman (1957b) that REM sleep be used as an objective, operational definition of the dream state had a dramatic and well-known impact on theories of dreaming. Initially the REM criteria of dreaming seemed to solve the problem of defining dream-recall failures. If REM sleep is the dream state, then one simply awakens the subject from a REM period (or some time thereafter) and counts a failure to report as a failure to recall. Unfortunately this simple solution does not look as appealing today as it once did. A variety of evidence has accumulated since the discovery of REM sleep to indicate that the REM definition of dreaming is inadequate. It seems clear that dreams may occur in NREM sleep, and that REM sleep may occur under conditions which make it unlikely that dreaming can occur (that is, decorticate individuals or neonates). The evidence on these points has been reviewed in detail by a number of authors (e.g., Foulkes, 1966; Rechtschaffen, 1967; Stoyva & Kamiya, 1968). We are left, then, with a reasonable doubt that REM sleep coincides completely with dreaming sleep.

While the uncertainty that exists in defining the dream state represents a substantial problem, it has not paralyzed research efforts. Many current theorists view the concept of the dream experience as a construct which can be approached through sets of converging operations, including physiological ones as well as verbal reports (e.g., Rechtschaffen, 1967; Stoyva & Kamiya, 1968). Similarly, the concept of dream-recall failure may be viewed as a construct. Hypothetical properties may be assigned to the construct, and deductions made on the basis of these properties may be examined empirically. A construct of dream-recall failure of this sort serves a useful function. It has a clear role in generating research hypotheses. In addition, a recognition of its status as a construct may inhibit the uncritical use of data on dream reporting to draw inferences about dream recall failures.

The problems involved in drawing inferences about recall failures from data on dream reporting may be illustrated in the literature on individual differences. In most such studies people either are asked how often they typically dream or are required to keep a diary of the dreams recalled each morning over some representative period at home. Home dream reporters and nonreporters are then selected from the extremes of the resulting distribution of people, and compared on some variable of interest.

The problem of defining dream-recall failures certainly arises in these studies. There are several possible ways to account for differences between home dream reporters and nonreporters without assuming that recall is involved. For example, it has been suggested that some people typically fail to report dreaming merely because their alarm clock is usually set to go off in the morning during NREM rather than during REM sleep (Webb & Kersey, 1967). Since the probability of reporting a dream is lower during NREM sleep, this view raises the question as to whether individual differences in home dream reporting may be due to recall at all. There is a considerable amount of evidence on this point. It is clear that home nonreporters have about the same number of REM periods as home dream reporters (Antrobus, Dement, & Fisher, 1964; Goodenough, Shapiro, Holden, & Steinschriber, 1959; Lewis, Goodenough, Shapiro, & Sleser, 1966). The evidence indicates, however, that the total amount of time spent in REM sleep is slightly but significantly related to the frequency of home reporting (Antrobus, et al., 1964; Baekeland, 1970). This relationship suggests that the probability of the alarm clock going off in the morning during REM sleep may be somewhat greater for home dream reporters than for nonreporters. This issue has been examined directly. Neither Antrobus et al. (1964) nor Cohen & MacNeilage (1973) found any consistent difference between home dream reporters and nonreporters in the tendency to awaken in the morning from REM sleep in the laboratory. At this point, the evidence is not very persuasive that substantial individual differences exist in the likelihood of awakening from REM sleep in the morning, but the issue is not completely settled.

There are additional grounds for suspecting that individual differences in home dream reporting do not necessarily reflect differences in dream recall. In one laboratory study of subjects identified as home nonreporters (Lewis et al., 1966), some nonreporters claimed that they were awake and thinking rather than asleep and dreaming each time their REM periods were interrupted by an experimental awakening. They were able to recount the content of their thoughts. These thoughts were bizarre and dreamlike in many ways, raising the possibility that something about the process of labeling their experiences as dreams, rather than recall of their experiences, is responsible for their claim to be "nondreamers." Other subjects among the home-nonreporter group were able to report only an occasional vague fragment of sleep mentation even when awakened from REM periods. In the absence of a definitive method of determining when dreams occur, it is not clear for these latter subjects whether they may be correct in their claim that they rarely dream, even though they have REM periods.

The point should be emphasized that many home nonreporters did recall dreams with no apparent difficulty under relatively ideal conditions in the laboratory (that is, following abrupt awakenings from REM sleep). Even a slight departure from these conditions was enough to significantly decrease dream reporting, however, as would be expected on the assumption that recall difficulties are involved for these people. The evidence from other studies indicates that people who claim that they rarely dream at home are likely to find it particularly difficult to rerecall dreams that they have once reported (Baekeland, 1970; Barber, 1969). It is clear, therefore, that many nonreporters are nonrecallers of dreams.

It is obvious that there are problems involved in attempts to apply the construct of dream-recall failure to the study of individual differences. Since recall factors may not be the sole determinants of home dream reporting, the correlates of individual differences in frequency of home dream reports may be hard to identify. It should not be surprising, therefore, to find only low relationships among variables in this area, and many failures to replicate findings from one study to the next. Just such a picture emerges from the literature. In spite of the problems, the studies of individual differences in dream reporting have produced some interesting results. Moreover, some of these results are relevant to questions about why dreams are more difficult to recall than waking experiences. It seems reasonable to conclude that the construct of dream-recall failure can usefully be applied, even in a research area as problem ridden as is the study of individual differences.

TWO TYPES OF THEORY ABOUT WHY DREAMS ARE HARD TO RECALL

All attempts to explain why dreams are so difficult to recall begin by emphasizing either some characteristic of dream experiences, or of sleep more generally, that is distinctively different from waking life. It is possible to distinguish two classes of explanation in terms of the characteristic so emphasized. One class may be called content centered. This class of explanation focuses on some feature of the content of dream experiences which may make them more difficult to recall than the usual waking experience. A second class focuses on some property of sleep which impairs memory for experiences without regard to content. The ability to recall any experience during sleep, whether endogenously or exogenously produced, is said to be impaired. Something in the memory process is thought to be deficient during sleep.

The distinction between content-centered and memory-process theories of dream forgetting is a very useful one. It serves as a convenient framework for the discussion of alternative explanations of dream forgetting. However, its use is not confined to this didactic function. It is possible to gather evidence which bears on one or the other of these two formal classes of theory without consideration of the specific class members in terms of their substance. In the organization of the discussion to follow, this distinction is therefore given a major role.

Content-Centered Explanations of Dream-Recall Failure

Before examining the literature which bears on specific content-centered theories of dream recall, the evidence on this general class of theory will be considered. The evidence that would be most directly relevant to content-centered theories of dream recall would certainly involve a comparison between dream experiences that are recalled and dream experiences that are not recalled. Unfortunately the content of a dream experience that the subject never recalls is no more available to us than it is to the subject. The only data we have are in the form of the subject's best recollections of some of the dreams. We can compare initial reports of dreams which are subsequently rerecalled or not rerecalled. We can also collect dream reports from subjects who typically fail to report dreams, and compare these with reports from subjects who typically do report dreaming. Both of these techniques involve certain difficulties, but the data are of interest to content-centered theorists.

One study of home dream reporters and nonreporters is particularly relevant to the content-centered class of theories (Barber, 1969). In this study it was possible to collect five dreams from most subjects by waking them at home with a telephone call, although more calls were naturally required for the nonreporters than for the reporters. As might be expected, subsequent rerecall of these initially reported dreams was more likely for the home reporters than for the home nonreporters, but the study did not stop at this point. The novel feature involved teaching the dream reports to subjects other than the ones who produced the dreams. These new subjects were then tested for recall of the dream reports they had learned. Dreams produced by home nonreporters turned out to be more difficult to recall than dreams produced by reporters, not only by the subjects who originally produced the dreams, but by other people as well. These results suggest that at least insofar as once-reported dreams are concerned, there is something about the content of nonreporters' productions that makes them less recallable.

While Barber's (1969) results are interesting, they do not require a content-centered theory of dream recall. As Barber recognized, some forgetting of the dream experience no doubt went on before the subjects reported their dreams initially. This fact leads to a rather simple interpretation of Barber's results. One may begin with the plausible assumption that the subjects who often totally fail to remember dreams (nonreporters) also tend to remember only vaguely the dreams that they do report. There is no reason to believe that the recall of dreams is an all-or-nothing affair. For people who find it easy to recall, more dreams should be reported and the dreams they are able to recall should be more vividly told. In the dreams collected from each nonreporter we may have, then, a set of narratives that are somewhat vaguer and less easily rerecallable than is true for the set of dream narratives collected from the reporters.

In view of the possibility that a very simple explanation of the results may suffice, it seems imprudent, in the opinion of this reviewer, to draw any far-reaching conclusion from these data concerning the content-centered class of theories. More studies of the content of dream reports in relation to rerecall are needed. It is important to recognize, however, that certain kinds of content differences may be expected and may be of trivial consequence.

We turn now to a consideration of the most prominent specific theories within the content-centered class.

The Role of Dream Salience in Recall.   The relationship between item salience and recall is well known in classical memory theory. The greater the novelty, bizarreness, affectfulness, or intensity of an experience, the more salient it appears to be, and, other things being equal, the more likely it is to be recalled.

The salience concept appeared very early in the literature on dream recall. For example, according to Strümpell (cited in Freud 1955a/1900):

> When we are awake we regularly forget countless sensations and perceptions at once, because they were too weak or because the mental excitation attaching to them was too slight. The same holds good of many dream images: they are forgotten because they are too weak while stronger images adjacent to them are remembered. (p. 43)*

Calkins (1893) early discussed the role of dream intensity in recall, while Radestock (cited in Freud, 1955a/1900) believed that the most peculiar dreams are best remembered. Among recent theorists, Cohen (1974) and Goodenough, Witkin, Lewis, Koulack, and Cohen (1974) have also emphasized the role of salience in dream recall.

The evidence leaves no doubt that salience is an important factor in the rerecall of once-reported dreams. Long dream reports are much more easily recalled than short ones (Baekeland & Lasky, 1968; Meier, Ruef, Ziegler, & Hall, 1968; Strauch, 1969; Trinder & Kramer, 1971), and dream reports with great dramatic intensity are better recalled than bland reports (Strauch, 1969; Trinder & Kramer, 1971). Emotional intensity has also been related to morning recall in the data of Meier et al. (1968) and Goodenough et al. (1974), but not in the study by Baekeland and Lasky (1968).

There are other hypotheses that may be generated on the assumption that salience of the dream experience is related to morning rerecall of dreams reported immediately after experimental awakenings during the night. One set of hypotheses rests on the known relationship between certain physiological variables during REM sleep and the salience of the dream report obtained at REM-period awakenings. Dement and Wolpert (1958b) provided the earliest demonstration that salience in dream reports can be predicted from REM characteristics. These authors found that frequency of eye movements during REM sleep is related to activity in dreams reported from REM-period awakenings. This finding has often been replicated (e.g., Berger & Oswald, 1962; Goodenough, Lewis, Shapiro, & Sleser, 1965). Eye-movement activity during REM sleep has also been related to dream bizarreness (Goodenough et al., 1965b), and to intensity and emotionality (Hobson, Goldfrank, & Snyder, 1965; Karacan, Goodenough, Shapiro, & Starker, 1966; Molinari & Foulkes, 1969; Takeo, 1970; Verdone, 1963, 1965). Moreover REM-period respiration rate and irregularity have

---

*The extensive review by Freud (1955a/1900) of the early work on dream recall has been used as the source of material for the early non-English literature in this summary.

been related to dream intensity and affect, at least under some conditions (Fisher, Byrne, Edwards, & Kahn, 1970; Goodenough, Witkin, Koulack, & Cohen, 1975; Hauri & Van de Castle, 1970b; Hobson et al., 1965; Knopf, 1962).

Given these data and the fact that the most salient dream reports of the night are most easily rerecalled, it would not be surprising to find that, among the dream reports given during the night, the ones remembered next morning tend to come from REM periods with frequent eye movements and with the most rapid and irregular breathing. In line with this expectation Baekeland and Lasky (1968) found that eye-movement activity is significantly related to morning rerecall. This finding has since been replicated (Goodenough et al., 1974). In the latter study, evidence was also found that morning rerecall was better for dream reports collected during the night when the report came from a REM period with relatively irregular respiration. It is interesting to note that in this study the relationship between REM-period respiratory irregularity and morning rerecall was significant only among those subjects who responded to stress when awake by increased breathing irregularity. No such relationship was found among subjects who did not respond in the respiratory channel when awake. Such a finding suggests that his respiratory correlate of emotion is congruent in waking and dreaming states and adds credence to the idea that the relationship between REM-period breathing irregularity and morning recall can be understood in terms of emotional salience.

Since salience plays such a well-documented role in the rerecall of once-remembered dreams, the question should be raised as to whether this principle might be used in interpreting findings from various studies on the initial recall of dreams. In fact, a variety of initial-recall data can be understood in terms of salience theory.

In view of the relationships between REM-period eye-movement activity, breathing rate, breathing irregularity, and salience of dreams that are reported, it seems plausible to assume that these REM-period characteristics are related to salience of the dream experience itself, whether or not the dream is ever recalled. If this assumption is correct, and if salience is an important factor in the initial recall of dreams, then failures to remember dreams immediately after REM-period awakenings ought to occur more frequently for REM periods with little eye-movement activity, low respiration rates, and relatively regular breathing. The evidence tends to support these expectations.

Snyder (1960) was one of the first to explore the relationship between REM-period characteristics and dream recall. He showed that respiratory irregularity was related to immediate dream recall, a finding which was replicated by Shapiro, Goodenough, Biederman, and Sleser (1964) and by Goodenough et al. (1974), although not by Hobson et al. (1965). Significant relationships between respiratory rate and REM-period dream reporting have been found by Hobson et al. (1965) and Goodenough et al. (1974), although not by Shapiro et al. (1964). In the case of eye-movement activity, significant relationships with dream reporting have been found by Goodenough et al. (1965b), Hobson et al. (1965), and Verdone (1965), but not by Goodenough et al. (1974). Takeo (1970) found no relationship between eye-movement activity and frequency of dream reporting, but dream reports obtained from REM periods with great activity tended to be more complicated and distinct. The data from these studies can be understood by assuming that during REM sleep the most salient dream experiences are the best recalled on awakening.

There is a fair amount of data on the relationship between measures of autonomic functioning during NREM sleep and dream reporting. These data have been summarized repeatedly in the recent literature (e.g., Cohen, 1974; Rechtschaffen, 1973) and, therefore, are not reviewed here. There is some evidence that transient autonomic changes in NREM sleep are related to dream reporting. It is possible to explain these relationships in terms of salience theory (Cohen, 1974). Often, however, these relationships are interpreted in terms of frequency of NREM dreaming rather than in terms of frequency of dream recall. This shift in interpretation as we move from REM to NREM sleep merely underlines the fact that we are dealing with *constructs* of the dream experience and of dream recall failure. In either REM or NREM sleep, the relationship of autonomic activity with frequency of dream reporting may either reflect an underlying relationship with the occurrence of dream experiences or with the frequency of dream recall, and we cannot tell for certain which of these interpretations is correct.

Studies of individual differences in the frequency of dream reporting are also interesting to examine within the framework of salience theory. The suggestion has been made that nonreporters may have less salient dream experiences and have difficulty in dream recall for this reason (Cohen, 1974). Several studies have been done on eye-movement activity during REM sleep in dream reporters and nonreporters, with results that are inconclusive. Baekeland (1970) found that home dream reporters had greater eye-movement activity during REM sleep than home nonreporters, as might be expected if salience is involved. However, Lewis et al. (1966) found no significant relationship between eye-movement activity and frequency of home dream reporting; and Antrobus et al. (1964) actually found greater eye-movement activity in nonreporters than in reporters. The weight of this evidence does not favor the salience explanation of individual differences.

Studies which have compared home reporters with nonreporters in the content of reported dreams in the laboratory are also relevant here. These studies have been summarized by Cohen (1974) and are not reviewed in detail here. As Cohen suggests, there is some evidence from these studies to indicate that dream narratives of nonreporters are less salient in some respects than the dream narratives of reporters. As suggested in the preceding section, however, most of these data may mean simply that the nonreporter not only recalls fewer dreams, but when remembering one, memory of the details is less vivid.

In summary, it seems safe to conclude that salience is an important factor determining which dreams will be recalled by a given person. Salience may play some role in individual differences as well. The theory of dream salience has been offered as an alternative to repression theory in the explanation of dream-recall failures (Cohen, 1974; Meier et al., 1968). Since salience theory suggests that the most ordinary, mundane experiences are the ones most likely to be forgotten, the contrast with the types of dreams that might be considered good candidates for repression is inviting. It should be noted, however, that repression theory does address itself to the question of why dreams are more difficult to recall than waking experiences as well as to the question of why some dreams may be more difficult to recall than others. Salience theory seems to help only in our attempt to answer the second of these questions.

Dream Disorganization.   Strümpell (cited in Freud, 1955a/1900) listed disorganization of dream experience as one of the factors considered important in accounting for dream-recall difficulty. There is no doubt that dreams can be chaotic and disorganized experiences. If chaos results in forgetting, then we can easily account for the fact that many dreams are difficult to recall. In fact, however, there is no evidence that dream organization plays a major role in recall. The organization factor has been studied extensively by Barber (1969). She did not find a significant relationship between ratings of organization in initial dream reports and subsequent recall of the reports. Nor were there significant differences between home reporters and nonreporters in degree of dream organization. To further study this issue Barber gave her subjects two types of dream reports to learn: ordinary dream reports and reports for which degree of organization was experimentally increased by changes in the structure of the narratives. No significant difference was found between these two types of dream materials in their recallability. The evidence from these several approaches consistently suggests that organization does not play a substantial role in dream recall.

The Role of Dream Kinesthesia in Recall Failure.   Rorschach (1942) is responsible for one little-known but interesting content-centered theory of dream-recall failure. He focused on the fact that the sleeper perceives his own movements in the dream but these movements are not usually overt. Like kinesthetic imagery in the waking state, dream recollection is inhibited by actual body movements, in Rorschach's view. If the dreamer does not move his body or open his eyes, dreams may be retained on awakening, but a movement at arousal is often sufficient to blot out the kinesthetic recollection. Rorschach's view has recently been reemphasized by Lerner (1967).

There is no doubt about the effect on dream recall of distraction. It is a common experience that even momentary distractions at the time of awakening may blot out the recollection of a dream experience. For example, Calkins (1893) early noted the importance of attentional factors:

> To recall a dream requires usually extreme and immediate attention to the content of the dream. Sometimes the slight movement of reaching for paper and pencil or of lighting one's candle seems to dissipate the dream-memory, and one is left with the tantalizing consciousness of having lived through an interesting dream-experience of which one has not the faintest memory. (p. 312)

The effect of distractors has been shown very clearly in experiments by Cohen and Wolfe (1973). They collected dreams from home diaries under two conditions. In the distracting condition the subjects were required to telephone the local weather information number at awakening and to record the predicted temperature range at the top of their diary sheet before writing their dream descriptions. Control subjects were asked to lie quietly in bed for a similar period of time before recording their dreams. The distracting telephone call dramatically decreased the number of dreams whose content the subjects were able to report.

That small distractions at awakening do have large effects on dream recall is interesting. It seems doubtful, for example, that telephone calls of the sort used in the study by Cohen and Wolfe (1973) would have such profound effects on waking experiences as they appear to have on dreams. The dramatic effect of distraction is one of the phenomena which must be taken into account by any comprehensive theory of dream recall. There are a number of alternative explanations that are possible, however. For example, according to Whitman (1963), the forgetting of dreams is partly an ego problem at the moment of awakening, "involving the turning of cathexis outward to the sensory or motor demands on the dreamer, thereby depriving the ego of sufficient searching energy to focalize on the dream [p. 65]."

It is possible to view distraction as one of the energy-depriving demands. In addition, Cohen (1974) has suggested that the large effect of distraction on dream recall may be a consequence of state-dependent learning of the dream experience. How this process may work is not entirely clear, however. Still another explanation of the effect of distraction is attempted subsequently in the framework of the proposed consolidation theory of dream recall failures.

In summary, while it is clear that distraction at awakening does impair dream recall, as suggested by Rorschach, the kinesthetic theory is only one among several ways of accounting for this phenomenon. The theory suffers from the fact that no other deductions have been suggested in the area of dream recall. As a consequence, Rorschach's views have not generated much interest among workers in the area.

Disinterest in Dream Content.   Another factor suggested by Strümpell to account for dream-recall failures was lack of interest in the content of dream experiences. In stronger terms, Schachtel (1959) has emphasized the lack of importance assigned to dream content in modern western civilization. According to Schachtel, there is a rejection of the useless, irrational dream thoughts when the dreamer enters the logical, reasonable, efficiency-oriented waking state.

Frequency of dream reporting is clearly related to how interested we are in our dream life and how strongly we are motivated to work at the recall process. Psychoanalysts have often commented that patients who rarely recall dreams before entering therapy can do so when motivation increases after entering analysis (e.g., Stekel, 1943). Cohen and Wolfe (1973) have manipulated motivation by varying the instructional set given to their subjects. They were able to collect more dreams by the home diary method from subjects for whom the importance of dreams as emphasized than from control subjects. In another study Reed (1973) was able to collect more dreams from his students when they were highly motivated to report than when interest in the project was not so high.

Evidence which is consistent with the hypothesis that motivational variables play a role in dream recall has also been found in studies of individual differences in dream reporting. According to Strauch (1969), and Cohen and Wolfe (1973) home dream reporters tend to feel that their dreams are meaningful and important, whereas nonreporters more often express disinterest in their dream life.

It seems clear that how much a person wants to remember his dreams may influence how many dreams he can actually report. The importance of motivation may be based on the fact that dream recall requires so much attention at the moment of awakening. In the opinion of this reviewer, however, motivational factors can only account for a limited range of phenomena in the area. Anyone who has struggled to remember a dream or who has observed others do so, would probably reject the idea that dream recall is difficult merely because dreams are uninteresting experiences.

Repression.   The Freudian view that repression plays a major role in dream recall failures is also, of course, a content-centered theory, and it has been by far the most influential of all explanations. Lewin (1953) and Kanzer (1959) are among the strongest modern advocates of a repression model. Lewin has expressed the view that *all* dream recall failures are due to repression, a position upon which even Freud appears not to have insisted. For Kanzer, repression of dreams so clearly follows from the nature of dream content that his attention is directed at the question of why dreams are ever recalled, rather than to the problem of recall difficulty. In the recent literature Whitman (1963), Wolpert (1972), and Goodenough (1967) have discussed repression as one of a multiplicity of factors that may be responsible for dream recall failures.

The evidence for the repression explanation of dream-recall failures came initially and still comes primarily from clinical sources which suggest that dreams are often recalled at the moment when resistance to the dream content is lifted during the course of analysis. One interesting study by Whitman, Kramer, and Baldridge (1963) has combined the clinical and laboratory approaches by using subjects who were concurrently visiting a therapist and participating in laboratory dream collection procedures. In some instances, a dream was reported either to the laboratory experimenter or to the therapist, but not to both. Failure to report the dream to one or the other of the two listeners seemed to be a function of the way in which the dream content bore on the developing relationship between the subject and the person to whom the dream was not told. These recall failures were attributed to repression by Whitman et al. (1963).

A number of recent authors have shared Whitman's interest in the communication of dreams to different persons (Kanzer, 1959; Winick & Holt, 1962). In the opinion of this reviewer, Whitman's approach to the study of motivated, content-centered recall of dreams is one of the most promising to appear in the literature. Unfortunately, however, we have only a few instances of selective reporting from Whitman's work, and while these cases are dramatic, they are hardly more than anecdotal in nature.

A number of studies on individual differences in dream reporting have appeared which are based on repression theory. These studies begin by postulating a dimension of individual differences in the organization of defenses against ego-threatening information. At one extreme of this dimension, people are said to be characteristic users of repression, and at the other extreme, users of sensitization or intellectualization as preferred defenses. In this view, nonreporters should be repressors if repression plays a major role in the production of dream recall failures. Three lines of work may be distinguished which take this general approach. One line involves the use of personality questionnaires to identify repressors. Another makes use of projective techniques. Still another involves the use of cognitive style dimensions which are thought to be related to repression as a defensive style. Field dependence, leveling versus sharpening, and convergent versus divergent thinking are among the cognitive dimensions that have been examined.

Field dependence was the first of the cognitive styles to be related to dream recall. The first studies in this area were conducted before the discovery of REM sleep. It had been suggested that field-dependent persons are likely to use repression as a predominant defense (Witkin, Dyk, Paterson,

Goodenough, & Karp, 1962/1974), and it seemed reasonable, therefore, to expect that field-dependent subjects might have particular difficulty in dream recall (Witkin, 1970). To explore this possibility, Linton and Eagle (cited in Witkin et al., 1962/1974) examined the relationship between frequency of home dream reporting and field dependence. In these studies field-dependent subjects tended to be home nonreporters. Schonbar (1965) was subsequently able to replicate this finding. However, no significant relationship has been found between field dependence and frequency of home reporting in a number of other studies (Baekeland, 1969; Bone, Thomas, & Kinsolving, 1972; Montgomery & Bone, 1970; Starker, 1973).

In view of the fact that people apparently may be nonreporters for a variety of distinctly different reasons, it is not too surprising to find that attempts to replicate the relationship between field dependence and home dream reporting are not very consistent. Fortunately, more detailed laboratory studies are available that clarify the situation. An unpublished finding from an early study of 46 home dream reporters and nonreporters conducted in our laboratory is relevant here (Lewis et al., 1966). Comparison of the 8 most field-dependent and the 8 most field-independent subjects in the sample showed that 7 of the 8 dependent subjects were nonreporters, in contrast to only 3 of the 8 independent subjects. This difference was only marginally significant ($p < .05$; one-tailed test). It is important to note, however, that the field-dependent nonreporters all came from one subgroup who were able to recall their dreams immediately after abrupt REM-period awakenings. The field-dependent home nonreporters, like the field-independent home reporters recalled some dream content for approximately 80% of their REM-period awakenings. However, with a gradual awakening method, produced by slowly increasing the intensity of a bell until the subject awakened, the percentage of awakenings from which dream content could be collected dropped to about 60% for the field-dependent subject. In contrast, the method of awakening had no significant effect among field-independent subjects. The results of this study suggest that among the several types of home nonreporters that may be distinguished by analysis of laboratory awakening, only one type is field dependent. In addition, the results suggest that field-dependent people have no difficulty in recalling their dreams under relatively ideal conditions (that is, abrupt awakenings from REM periods), but dream reporting is dramatically reduced by departures from this ideal (for example, gradual awakenings, ordinary morning recall at home).

The results of several other studies are consistent with this view. In one study subsequently described in more detail, frequency of dream reporting from REM-period awakenings was significantly reduced by stress among field-dependent subjects, but no stress effect was found among field-independent subjects (Goodenough et al., 1974). In another study, Baekeland and Lasky (1968) found no relationship between field dependence and initial reporting of dreams following REM-period awakenings, but subsequent morning recall of these once-reported dreams was significantly less frequent among field-dependent than among field-independent subjects. These laboratory studies support the conclusion that dream recall is disrupted by a variety of conditions among field-dependent people.

While it seems reasonable to conclude that field independence is related to dream recall, the question remains as to whether repression has anything to do with this relationship. We have had an opportunity to examine dreams collected from field-dependent and independent subjects at abrupt REM awakenings. We have not been impressed by any dramatic content differences that might account for the greater difficulty to recall among field-dependent people. It is possible, of course, that the critical content features are subtle ones. Clearly, however, the factor responsible for the poor dream recall among field-dependent people has not yet been persuasively demonstrated.

Turning now to similar research with other cognitive style dimensions, one investigation of leveling-sharpening in relation to individual differences in home dream reporting has been done on the premise that levelers tend to use a repressive defensive style (Lachmann, Lapkin, & Handelman, 1962). The study produced positive but somewhat equivocal results. Convergent and divergent cognitive styles have been studied extensively by Hudson (1966), who noted that some people (divergers) do better on open-ended intelligence tests than on conventional objective tests, while other people (convergers) are superior on conventional tests. As is the case for field-dependent persons and for levelers, it has been proposed that convergers typically resort to repression as a defense (Hudson, 1966) and it has therefore been hypothesized that convergers will tend to be nonreporters. Austin (1971) did find that convergers reported dreaming less often than divergers immediately after REM awakenings in the laboratory. Holmes (1973), however, failed to find an overall relationship between frequency of dream reporting and convergence-divergence. As in the case of leveling-sharpening, the results available to date with the converger-diverger dimension appear suggestive but inconclusive.

Turning now to more traditional personality-test measures of repression, Levine and Spivak (1964) have examined their Rorschach index of repressive style in relation to frequency of home dream reporting. In women, the hypothesized relationship was found: repressors tended to report fewer dreams. In men, however, just the opposite result obtained: repressors tended to report more dreams.

Equivocal results have also emerged from questionnaire measures of repression. Expected correlations between home report frequency and an interrelated cluster of repression-relevant questionnaire scales (repression-sensitization, anxiety, neuroticism, and ego strength) have occasionally been found, following the work of Schonbar (1959), but these findings have not been confirmed in other studies (Bone, 1968; Bone & Corlett, 1968; Bone, Nelson, & McAllister, 1970; Cohen, 1969; Domhoff & Gerson, 1967; Foulkes & Rechtschaffen, 1964; Foulkes, Spear, & Symonds, 1966; Larson, 1971; Pivik & Foulkes, 1968; Puryear, 1963; Singer & Schonbar, 1961; Tart, 1962).

In summarizing the findings from these personality tests, it seems prudent to say that the role of repression as an explanation of individual difference in frequency of dream reporting has not been clearly established. Even if it can be shown that one or more of these measures is related to dream reporting, it may be that the relationship is due to differences among the subjects in the importance which they attach to inner-life experiences, a factor which is known to be related to individual differences in dream reporting, as discussed previously, and which may underlie questionnaire and projective-test responses leading to repressor-sensitizer scorings.

Laboratory studies which have examined the effects of presleep stress on dream reporting may also have some bearing on the repression issue. These studies are based on the assumption that more dreams will occur which are good candidates for repression under conditions of stress than under neutral conditions (Goodenough, 1967; Witkin, 1969a; Witkin & Lewis, 1965, 1967). Cartwright, Bernick, Borowitz, and Kling (1969) found less dream reporting at REM awakenings following the viewing of a sexually exciting film. They attributed these effects to the influence of repression. Foulkes, Pivik, Steadman, Spear, and Symonds (1967) also found reduced dream reporting following presleep stress-film viewing, but Foulkes and Rechtschaffen (1964) did not. Karacan et al. (1966) also failed to find the expected stress-film effects, but this study was complicated by the fact that a penis gauge was used in all sleep sessions. There was reason to believe that the gauge in itself may have been stressful, overwhelming any possible film effects.

Two recent studies have examined individual differences in the effects of stress on frequency of dream reporting. These studies have compared subjects with an hypothesized repressive style, for whom the stress effect should be pronounced, with control subjects. In one of these studies, briefly referred to previously, presleep stress films significantly decreased the frequency of dream reporting from laboratory REM awakenings in field-dependent subjects, but had no effect among field-independent subjects (Goodenough et al., 1974). Since field-dependent subjects are presumed to be repressors, the fact that the stress films were particularly effective for them is noteworthy. However, no evidence could be found that the stress-produced dream-report failures came from REM periods characterized by physiological arousal as might have been expected (Goodenough, 1967; Koulack, 1970).

In another study, Cohen (1972) examined the effect of stress on home dream reporting in home reporters and nonreporters. In the stress condition used by Cohen, subjects watched a "fake" experiment in which an accomplice, ostensibly in the subject role, apparently received painful treatment. The subjects were led to believe that they themselves would participate in this experiment a few days later. Dream reports were collected from home diaries kept of the morning following this experience and following control (nonstressful) conditions. Cohen found that dream reporting was less frequent under stress conditions for home nonreporters and better under these same conditions for home reporters relative to the control condition. As Cohen pointed out, his results are also consistent with repression theory.

While the studies of stress effects on dream reporting have produced results that are consistent with repression theory, a rather simple alternative explanation seems possible. Both Goodenough et al. (1974) and Cohen (1974) have emphasized the possibility that anxiety-produced distractions at awakening may have been responsible for the lower frequency of dream reports on stress nights. This interpretation is in line with the known importance of distraction in producing dream-recall failures.

In summary, while repression may be responsible for some instances of dream-recall failure, the role of repression has not been persuasively demonstrated in solving the problem of why so many dreams are so difficult to recall.

Memory-Process Explanations of Dream Recall Failure

To this point, the discussion of dream-recall theories has focused on content-centered explanations of dream-recall failures. We now consider the second major class of theories about dream recall, the "memory-process" class. As suggested earlier, this class of theories is content free—that is, the ability to recall any experience during sleep is said to be impaired, whether the experience is an endogenous dream or one produced by an exogenous stimulus. In considering content-centered theories it was appropriate to limit the review to studies concerned with the frequency of dream reporting under various conditions. In considering memory-process theories, however, the literature concerning the effects of sleep on memory for events other than dreams is also of interest.

In fact, the acquisition of information is very generally impaired during sleep. This conclusion is so much a part of common experience that it must have been evident early in the history of thought on dream recall. Incidental observations to this effect are repeatedly found in the psychological literature. For example, in their study of retention over periods of sleep, Jenkins and Dallenbach (1924) found that in the morning their subjects sometimes could not remember that tests were given to them during brief nighttime awakenings. During his studies of respiration in sleep, Magnussen (1944) also observed that his subjects frequently failed to recall the fact that they had awakened during the night and had spoken a few words or had performed simple tasks during these awakenings.

These casual observations have been amply supported by more systematic studies of sleep learning conducted during the past 20 years. Since the classical studies by Simon and Emmons (1956) and by Emmons and Simon (1956), it has commonly been concluded that learning does not occur during sleep. In more recent years, however, there has been some revival of interest in the possibility of sleep learning, due primarily, perhaps, to persistent claims of success by Russian workers (e.g., Rubin, 1968). It is important to note that Simon and Emmons did find some learning during EEG stages of sleep which were defined as light or transitional at the time, but which we now know would include REM sleep. While the literature suggests that some sleep learning may be possible during REM, or even during NREM periods, it is clear that learning is at least substantially impaired during all states.*

At one time it was popular to regard sleep as a state of deafferentation. Difficulties in sleep learning were thus understood as failures of stimulus registration. Recent research suggests, however, that auditory stimuli can be discriminated and are effective in evoking responses which have been learned when awake (e.g., Minard, Loiselle, Ingeldue, & Dautlich, 1968; Oswald, Taylor, & Treisman, 1960; Williams, Morlock, & Morlock, 1966). It also seems clear that rewards and punishments are effective in motivating performance during sleep (Williams et al., 1966; Wilson & Zung, 1966). These findings suggest that impaired learning during sleep is due to some defect in memory. If we accept this conclusion, then some kind of memory-process theory must be entertained. If sleep impairs recall of all experiences, including dreams, then a theory explaining the more general phenomenon is required. At best, content-centered theories could account for only a limited set of data.

The literature on individual differences in dream reporting also contains some evidence which is relevant to memory-process theory. Home dream reporters and nonreporters have been compared on standard tests of memory in the waking state in a number of studies (e.g., Barber, 1969; Cohen, 1971; Puryear, 1963). Intelligence has been examined in many other studies (e.g., Antrobus, et al., 1964; Ramsey, 1953; Schonbar, 1959; Singer & Schonbar, 1961). There is no persuasive evidence from these studies that nonreporters are less intelligent or are lower in specific waking memory abilities. Of course, these findings do not rule out the possibility that some sleep-memory-ability factor may be found that distinguishes dream reporters from nonreporters. However, they do suggest that whatever the memory dimension may be during sleep, it is not the same dimension tapped by waking memory tests.

---

*For an excellent review of learning during sleep, see Aarons (1976).

Specific theories about the nature of the memory process impaired during sleep are considered in the sections below.

Some Classical Memory Phenomena in the Recall of Dreams. It is not surprising to find that the classical laws of memory apply to the recall of dreams as they do to memory for other types of material. It is important, however, to examine the available data on dream reporting in order to see how much can be understood from this perspective. Attention was drawn in a very dramatic way to the role of these factors in the study of dream reporting by Meier et al. (1968). These authors studied morning rerecall of dreams that were initially reported during the night. As might be expected, the duration of the interval between the initial report and the morning rerecall was an important factor in determining which dreams were lost. Many more of the dreams reported later in the night were recalled by morning, in contrast to dreams reported earlier in the night. In addition, the number of dreams reported during the night was significantly related to the percentage recalled the next morning. For nights when few dreams were reported, these dreams were much easier to recall the next morning than was the case for nights when many dreams were reported.

The results of Meier et al. (1968) have been confirmed and extended in several studies. The relationship between number of dreams reported and morning recall has also been found by Trinder and Kramer (1971), Strauch (1969), and by Goodenough et al. (1974). The recency effect has been noted by Trinder and Kramer (1971), Strauch (1969), and by Baekeland and Lasky (1968) for home nonreporters (but not for subjects who claim that they recall dreams at home almost every morning). Strauch as well as Trinder and Kramer not only found that the last dream of the night is favored, but also found that the first dream report of the night is more easily recalled than reports in the middle positions of the nightly set of dreams.

In this connection, it is interesting to note the results of a different kind of study done in our laboratory (Goodenough, Sapan, Cohen, Portnoff, & Shapiro, 1971). In this study subjects were awakened briefly several times each night, and at each awakening a different word was shown. Next morning the subjects were asked to recall the words. We found that for words, the effects of list length, primacy, and recency appear to be comparable to the effects that have been found for dreams. We did not anticipate these results, perhaps because we did not have a "set" to think of the words shown to the subject at widely separate times during the night as a serial list. However, it is clear that either the dreams of the night or the words of the night may be viewed as a serially occurring list of items with effects on memory that are well known to classical learning theorists.

In summary, serial effects may play an important role in determining which dreams of the night are recalled. However, they do not help us in the attempt to understand why dreams and other types of sleep experiences are more difficult to recall than waking events.

State-Dependent Learning.   Another type of memory-process explanation considers dream-recall failures as special cases of state-dependent learning. In this view, any information acquired in the sleeping state is difficult to retrieve from memory storage in the waking state (but theoretically it might be retrieved at a later time during the sleeping state). The concept of state-dependent learning has been used primarily to account for the fact that responses acquired while under the influence of certain drugs can be elicited at a later time when the individual returns to the drugged state, but cannot be elicited under nondrug conditions (e.g., Overton, 1966). If the sleep state is also characterized by state-dependent learning, then it may be possible to account for difficulties of dream recall.

Theories of this general type were popular in the early literature. For example, Strümpell (cited in Freud, 1955a/1900) called attention to the fact that dreams often involve details of waking life which are torn out of the contexts in which they are usually remembered when awake. Given this characteristic of dream content, he believed that recall difficulty was a natural consequence. Similar ideas have been expressed by many theorists since Strümpell. For example, Bonatelli (cited in Freud, 1955a/1900) believed that "the alternation in coenesthesia between the sleeping and waking states is unfavorable to reciprocal reproduction between them [p. 45]." Similarly Prince (1911) proposed that the forgetting of dreams may be a special case of amnesia for experiences in dissociated mental states. Jung (1939) also suggested that the fantastic arrangement of ideas in dreams makes them difficult to connect with waking consciousness. More recently Blum (1961) has suggested that specific contextual circuits are inaccessible during dreaming. Schachtel (1959) has offered a similar argument that "it seems obvious that the experience and memory schemata developed and formed by man's life in his society are much less suitable to preserve the fantastic world of the dream than to recall conventional waking experience [p. 307]." This tradition is represented in the current literature by Evans and his colleagues (Evans, Gustafson, O'Connell, Orne, & Shor, 1966, 1969, 1970) and by Cohen (1974).

As far as this reviewer is aware, only one series of studies has been directed specifically at this issue (Evans, 1972; Evans et al., 1966, 1969, 1970). In these studies, subjects were given verbal suggestions during REM sleep of the sort, "Whenever I say the word 'itch,' your nose will feel itchy until you scratch it." Some subjects carried out the suggestion in response to the cue word during REM sleep. That is, they scratched their noses when the experimenter said, "itch," without waking up. The subjects typically had no waking recall of the suggestion the next day, nor did they respond appropriately to the cue word when awake. The most interesting aspect of this work is that the subjects did respond on subsequent nights to the cue words, indicating that the appropriate response was learned, but could only be elicited in the REM state in which the learning had occurred. These experiments did not work in NREM sleep. For REM sleep, at least, Evans et al. (1969) offer the possibility that "acquisition of new experiences must occur within a particular context of other ongoing experience, aspects of which are necessary at a later time to act as a 'triggering mechanism' for the subsequent recall of the acquired behavior [p. 667]."

It is interesting to note that these findings are related to hypnotic phenomena in several ways. First, the results could be obtained only for good hypnotic subjects (poor hypnotic subjects were apparently awakened by the suggestions). Second, for one subject at least, a posthypnotic suggestion to recall when awake was effective. The complex nature of the relationship between hypnosis, REM sleep, and the ability of the subjects to remember the response contingency is discussed in detail by Evans (1972). While this line of work is intriguing, it is uncertain whether a state-dependent learning model of sleep is necessary to account for the results, as Evans has pointed out.

It seems likely that state-dependent theories would gain more widespread acceptance if it could be shown that habituation readily occurs during sleep. Habituation to a repetitive stimulus should not be difficult during continuous sleep if the only problem in sleep learning is a state dependency. However, the data on habituation do not appear to support a state-dependent theory very strongly.

In discussing the literature on habituation, it is important to distinguish between habituation of the awakening response itself, and habituation of other responses like the K complex, orienting responses, and the like, which may occur without awakenings. This distinction is important because it is only in the latter case that learning may be said to occur entirely during sleep.

Many studies have been done on habituation of awakening responses. It is evident that a stimulus which may awaken a person when novel, tends to lose its effectiveness on repeated presentation. Data on this point are reviewed by Oswald (1962). Habituation during sleep of responses that are not accompanied by awakening appears to be relatively ineffective, however. Unfortunately, the data on this point are not absolutely clear. By the very nature of the habituation phenomenon, many stimulus presentations are necessary, and some of these are likely to produce awakenings even if the response being studies is not a necessary arousal accompaniment. In fact, several studies have reported some evidence of habituation for K complexes, for galvanic skin responses, and for heart-rate responses during sleep (e.g., Firth, 1973; Oswald et al., 1960). However, no evidence of habituation has been found in other studies (e.g., Johnson & Lubin, 1967; Roth, Shaw, & Green, 1956; Tizard, 1968). In still another study, habituation of the orienting response was found to be impaired in a drowsy state as compared with an alert state (McDonald, Johnson, & Hord, 1964). It is probably a conservative conclusion to say of these data that if habituation occurs during sleep, it is much slower and more difficult to demonstrate than is habituation during the waking state.

In summary, while a state-dependent learning theory of dream-recall failure is attractive, the evidence for an explanation of this sort is not very compelling at this time.

Impairment in Memory-Trace Consolidation.   Another type of memory-process explanation involves the assumption that consolidation of memory traces is impaired during sleep. The concept of memory-trace consolidation has had a long history among learning theorists (Muller & Pilzecker, 1900). In the most general terms, the consolidation concept implies a multistage memory trace. For some period of time after an experience occurs, the trace of that experience is carried in a temporary, short-term form. The more-or-less permanent traces in long-term memory take time (and perhaps a favorable state) to become effectively established. As information is transferred from the short-term to the long-term form, trace consolidation is said to occur.

During the history of thought concerning consolidation, a number of variants of the concept have been proposed, and several very different forms have been applied to sleep-related phenomena. It is essential to distinguish among these forms in order to avoid confusion in any discussion of consolidation mechanisms during sleep.

The traditional conception of consolidation was developed in the attempt to account for retrograde amnesias produced by a variety of agents, including electroconvulsive shocks, blows to the head, and certain drugs. In this view the long-term trace may take an hour or more to become fully established. During the process of consolidation, a disrupting agent may destroy the trace or a facilitating agent may enhance trace establishment, but susceptibility to these agents diminishes with time. Several applications of this concept have been applied to sleep phenomena.

Some theorists, attempting to understand the adaptive function of REM sleep, have proposed that the transfer of daytime experiences to long-term memories and/or integration of the temporary memories of these experiences into long-term storage occurs during dreaming (e.g., Dewan, 1968; Fishbein, 1969; Greenberg, 1970; Greenberg & Leiderman, 1966; Shapiro, 1967; Stokes, 1973). In this view, memories are held in short-term storage for hours before the REM periods of the night produce their consolidation. The extensive experimental literature on the possible consolidation function of dreaming are not reviewed here because a mechanism of this sort is irrelevant to an understanding of dream-recall failure.

Another application of traditional consolidation theory has grown out of sleep research on the interference theory of memory. The study of forgetting over periods of sleep attracted early learning theorists because it seemed reasonable to suppose that cognitive activity ought to be minimal during sleeping states. If such activity interferes with memory, then one might expect forgetting to be slight if sleep intervenes between learning and tests of retention. In fact, the early research on this issue suggested that memory tends to be better over periods of sleep than over comparable periods of waking activity (Jenkins & Dallenbach, 1924; Newman, 1939; Van Ormer, 1932, 1933). More recent studies have largely reemphasized this conclusion, particularly for NREM sleep (Barrett & Ekstrand, 1972; Ekstrand, 1967; Fowler, Sullivan, & Ekstrand, 1973; Hockey, Davies, & Gray, 1972; Lovatt & Warr, 1968; Yaroush, Sullivan, & Ekstrand, 1971). It has been suggested by some authors that the less rapid decay of memory during sleep may be due to a facilitation of consolidation during NREM periods rather than to a reduction in interference (Fowler et al., 1973; Graves, 1936; Grieser, Greenberg, & Harrison, 1972; Heine, 1914; Richardson & Gough, 1963). In this view, consolidation must continue for a considerable period, since subjects typically do not go to sleep until many minutes have elapsed after the end of learning trials. As is the case for the consolidation concept as a REM-period function, difficulties in dream recall cannot be understood in terms of this application of consolidation theory.

The traditional view of the consolidation concept has also been applied in just the opposite way by some authors who have suggested that consolidation may be impaired by NREM sleep. This view is implicit in the work of several authors. It has been suggested, for example, that the transfer of information from short- to long-term memory storage is less effective as arousal level decreases (e.g., Kleinsmith & Kaplan, 1963; Walker & Tarte, 1963). It is not easy to characterize REM sleep in terms of its location on a hypothetical arousal continuum. However, during NREM sleep, at least, these theories imply a reduction in effectiveness for the process of long-term memory storage. Hebb (1949) also suggested a consolidation explanation in his discussion of sleep learning problems. In Hebb's theory, memory is a two-stage process: a short-term memory store in the form of reverberating circuits; and a long-term store involving the more permanent growth of "neural knobs." The structural changes involved in the growth of these knobs is believed to be difficult, at least during the synchronized EEG stages of sleep more or less characteristic of many NREM periods. The idea that dream-recall difficulty may be due to consolidation difficulties is explicit in the writing of a number of researchers in the field (e.g., Goodenough, 1967; Goodenough et al., 1971; Portnoff, Baekeland, Goodenough, Karacan, & Shapiro, 1966; Rechtschaffen, 1964; Wolpert, 1972).

The idea that dream-recall difficulty might be due to ineffective consolidation was first suggested by observations indicating a rapid decay in the probability of eliciting the report of a dream after the end of REM periods in the absence of an awakening. It was found that many fewer dream reports are obtainable from NREM awakenings a few minutes after REM periods end than from REM period awakenings (Dement & Kleitman, 1957b; Goodenough et al., 1965a; Wolpert & Trosman, 1958). It was also found that more dreams can be collected from NREM awakenings shortly after REM periods end than can be obtained after longer delays. These data were originally interpreted to mean that memory for the dream may persist after some minutes of NREM sleep. However, the decline in dream reporting after REM ends may not be part of a forgetting curve. It may reflect, instead, a decrease in NREM dream frequency. The evidence for this conclusion is summarized elsewhere (Goodenough, 1968). In brief, there is good reason to suspect that dreams are never recalled unless the dream experience is interrupted by an awakening.

Given the evidence on rapid loss of dreams, it was easy to imagine that consolidation is impaired during sleep. According to Rechtschaffen (1964), for example:

> Dreams are remembered if there is an awakening following the dream, because consolidation can take place during this wakefulness. However, if the dream is followed by NREM sleep, it is forgotten because of the lack of opportunity for consolidation. (p. 165)

There are other sorts of data that can be understood in terms of traditional consolidation theory. Length of time awake at REM awakenings has been related to the rerecall of the dream experience. The longer the subject remains awake after initially reporting a dream, the more likely is dream-recall the next morning (Baekeland & Lasky, 1968; Strauch, 1969). The authors of both studies have interpreted the time spent awake as "consolidation time," under the assumption that more effective consolidation of the long-term traces will occur as a function of more time awake after the dream experiences.

The relationship between length of time awake after an experience and subsequent memory of the experience is not unique to dreams. The same relationship holds for word stimuli (Goodenough et al., 1971; Portnoff et al., 1966). In these studies, subjects were awakened several times each night, and immediately after each awakening a word was shown by means of a bedroom slide projector under incidental learning conditions. These studies clearly demonstrate that when the subjects spontaneously remain awake for a relatively long period of time after the words are shown, they are more likely to remember the word the next morning than when they return to sleep more quickly.

This series of studies also produced data that appear to contradict an interpretation in terms of traditional consolidation theory. The studies were designed to determine whether the critical variable that affects memory for the words might be the level of arousal during the minutes that followed the word presentation. For this purpose, on half the trials the subjects were kept awake for about 15 min after the words were shown by requiring them to work on a motor task. Next morning, memory for the words shown under this enforced waking condition was compared with memory for the words shown on trials when the subjects were permitted to return to sleep immediately. Over the range of times examined, longer periods of waking "consolidation time" did not affect retention as was expected. These findings suggest that the relationship between spontaneous time awake and retention must be due to level of arousal at, and/or very shortly after, the work presentation. If the subject is highly aroused at this point in time, then sleep onset is likely to be delayed for some minutes, but delay in sleep onset beyond a few minutes is not in itself sufficient to improve retention. In fact, some evidence was found that instructions to the subjects designed to vary level of arousal within a period of seconds *after* the word presentation did have an effect on subsequent retention. High-arousal instructions tended to favor retention (Goodenough et al., 1971). Thus, while evidence of an arousal-retention relationship was found, the time during which arousal is effective may be on the order of seconds after the stimulus rather than many minutes after it, as assumed in traditional consolidation theory.

Another problem in the attempt to understand dream recall difficulty in terms of traditional consolidation theory was pointed out by Foulkes (1966), who emphasized the retrieval problem:

> There must be something still unknown about the way in which these traces are "filed" that renders them generally inaccessible to consciousness unless wakefulness intervenes very soon after the original impressions are experienced. (p. 55)

As this statement indicates, Foulkes has emphasized the possibility that recall difficulties may be due to retrieval of the trace from long-term storage at the time of recall, rather than to an impairment in consolidation. From everyday experience we may share with Foulkes (and with Freud, 1955a/1900) the impression that dream recall failures are typically retrieval failures. In many cases, we cannot recall a dream for the moment, but can vividly recall the dream at some later time. Kanzer (1959) has discussed this phenomenon at length. Such cases are troublesome for traditional consolidation theory.

An Arousal-Retrieval Model.   The results of these studies suggest still another application of multistage memory theory that involves what might be called a "rapid" consolidation concept (Koulack & Goodenough, 1976). As before, it is assumed that the effectiveness of information transfer from short- to long-term storage is impaired at low levels of arousal and particularly during sleep. However, the duration of the short-term memory is assumed to be on the order of seconds rather than many minutes or hours.

While the existence of a short- as distinct from a long-term memory system is not universally accepted, it seems fair to say that the evidence for a short-term memory form which lasts for a period of seconds is more persuasive than is the evidence for a short-term memory form which lasts for much longer periods. Much of the material for consolidation theory has come from studies on the effects of electroconvulsive shock on memory. In the view of some authors, however, the evidence for a short-term store would support a process lasting less than a minute (Spevack & Suboski, 1969). A short-term memory form of this duration is consistent with a variety of other data, as well. The work of Peterson and Peterson (1959) provided a dramatic impetus to research on theories of short-term memory. In much of the recent work in this area, buffer memory stores have been proposed with very limited capacities in terms of chunks of information and/or time span (e.g., Atkinson & Shiffrin, 1968; Waugh & Norman, 1965).

In many of the recent multistage memory theories, it is assumed that cognitive processing of information in the short-term store facilitates the transfer of information to long-term memory storage. These processes include repetition or recycling of information through the short-term store as well as more complex activities such as recording, reorganization of the information for insertion into long-term storage, and the like. Within this framework it is easy to imagine that sleep impairs or even prevents such processing.

The fact that dream-recall failures are often retrieval failures is easily handled in this view. One may suppose that the information processing steps impaired by sleep are critically involved in the "filing," coding, or addressing of new information for ready retrieval from long-term storage. Thus information may be transferred to long-term storage during sleep, but in a form that is difficult to access.

In this view, dream-recall failures should occur unless the sleeper awakens within a matter of seconds after the dream experience occurs. If arousal takes place during the life of the short-term trace, then the content of the dream experience which immediately preceded the awakening may be retrievable from the short-term store directly. Given this retrieval cue as an entry into the long-term store, the dreamer may then be able to recall some of the preceding content of that dream experience. If the awakening is delayed until the short-term trace has expired, then retrieval may no longer be possible, or it may be much more difficult. Ralph Waldo Emerson (1884) has expressed this state of affairs at awakening in much clearer terms:

> Dreams are jealous of being remembered; they dissipate instantly and angrily if you try to hold them. When newly awakened from lively dreams, we are so near them, still agitated by them, still in their sphere—give us one syllable, one feature, one hint, and we should repossess the whole; hours of this strange entertainment would come trooping back to us; but we cannot get our hand on the first link or fibre, and the whole is lost. There is a strange wistfulness in the speed with which it disperses and baffles our grasp. (p. 10)

That distractions at awakening have such a devastating effect on dream recall can also be understood in terms of an arousal-retrieval model. It is easy to suppose that incoming events may compete with the dream experience for attention in the limited-capacity processing system during the critical period after the awakening when effective transfer to long-term memory storage must take place if the dream is to be subsequently recalled.

An arousal-retrieval model also appears to be useful in accounting for a variety of data on sleep learning. There seems to be little doubt that sleep learning is facilitated if the stimuli to be learned are followed within a few seconds by even a transient arousal. This conclusion has been emphasized in a series of studies by Koukkou and Lehmann (e.g., Lehmann & Koukkou, 1973). They found that their subjects could remember sentences read to them during sleep. However, the amount retained was a function of the duration of transient waking alpha induced by the stimuli. Koukkou & Lehmann (1968) suggest that ". . . the duration of the EEG wakefulness pattern after the presentation of the test sentences reflects the time available for long-term storage of the memory material in retrievable form [p. 461]." In other studies (Jus & Jus, 1972; Jus et al., 1969), words and tones were presented during sleep, and recall of these stimuli was also found to be significantly related to the duration of arousal produced. A consolidation explanation of the phenomenon was proposed. In still another study by Evans and Orchard (1969), subjects were presented during sleep with learning materials in the form of "A for apple," "B for ball," and so on, and were subsequently asked to recall the word associated with the letter. In cases of successful recall, alpha responses were found to occur within 30 sec of the stimulus presentations.

SUMMARY AND CONCLUSIONS

Many of the theories which have been advanced to account for difficulty in dream recall can be traced back at least to the beginnings of psychology as a discipline. Despite the fact that dream-recall failures were sufficiently interesting to invite extensive speculation, it was not until the discovery of REM sleep that systematic research in the area became common. During the past 20 years, evidence has accumulated which now makes it possible to evaluate many of these theories.

It is evident that serial position and dream salience are important factors in determining which dreams of the night will be recalled. These factors appear to play the same role in dream recall as they do in the recall of waking experiences. However, they are not very helpful in the attempt to understand why dreams are harder to recall than waking experiences.

In the attempt to understand dream-recall difficulty, several generalizations require central consideration. First among these is the fact that recall difficulties are encountered for any experience during sleep, whether a dream or an experience produced by exogenous stimulation. This generalization is a central one because it limits the type of theory that can account for the effect of sleep on recall. Theories which explain dream-recall difficulty in terms of some factor in dream content are not necessarily incorrect, but they are obviously insufficient to account for the effects of sleep on recall of other experiences. At the least, it is necessary to postulate some effect of sleep on memory processes more generally.

Two additional key generalizations concern the conditions under which sleep experiences can be recalled. One is that dreams or any other type of sleep experience seem to be recalled with ease only if the sleeper is awake within a matter of seconds after the experience occurs. Another is that distractions at the moment of awakening impair dream recall. Conversely, recall is improved if attention is focused on the dream for a period of some seconds after awakening.

We can account for a variety of facts in terms of the need for attention to the dream at awakening. For example, it has been found that interest in dream life is related to dream recall. It seems reasonable to suppose that the effect of interest may be mediated by attentional processes. The fact that salient dreams are most easily recalled may also be due to their attention-demanding quality. Moreover, the fact that stress impairs dream recall may be understood in terms of an anxiety-based distracting effect which interferes with attentional processes at awakening.

An arousal-retrieval model (Koulack & Goodenough, 1976) has been employed in the attempt to understand why sleep experiences seem so difficult to recall unless waking attention is focused on the experience during the period immediately after the experience occurs. It is assumed that cognitive information processing is required to effectively transfer information from short- to long-term memory storage in retrievable form. It is further assumed that sleep or distraction will impair this type of processing. Because of this impairment, transfer to long-term storage of retrievable information about sleep experiences cannot occur effectively unless a distraction-free waking state occurs during the life of the short-term memory trace.

An arousal-retrieval theory of this sort may be capable of accounting for the striking effects of sleep on memory.

5

Qualitative Aspects of Sleep Mentation

LISSA N. WEINSTEIN
Teachers College, Columbia University

DAVID G. SCHWARTZ
Private Practice, New York City

ARTHUR M. ARKIN
City College of the City University of New York

Following the progress of mentation research to 1978, our original review emphasized the qualitative aspects of sleep mentation in relation to a heterogeneous assortment of variables. In an attempt to be comprehensive, important methodological papers, sleep stage correlates, sleep mentation in association with psychopathologic syndromes, and sensory and physical impairments were addressed.

Various developmental epochs were reviewed, as well as material on dream sequences and the organization of dreams, papers on the Pötzl phenomenon, and ESP studies utilizing dreams. These reviews are reproduced in shortened form below; new trends in mentation research are reviewed at the end of the chapter.

METHODOLOGICAL ISSUES

Since the demise of introspectionist psychology, the study of private experience has labored under the burden of methodological difficulties. The central problem of the methodology of dream research is that the dream is not a publicly observable event; verbal report is the primary indicator of an already past experience. Rechtschaffen (1967) pointed out that the correspondence between verbal reports and actual dreams can be diminished by recall and by those "processes which intervene between the recalled dream and the . . . dream report" (p. 5), such as choosing words to describe the dream. To minimize the distortions of the dream experience, dream researchers take various precautions, such as excluding subjects with gross memory defects and structuring the experimental situation so that subjects are encouraged to report freely.

Stoyva and Kamiya (1968) applied some contributions from the philosophy of science and methodological theory (Campbell & Fiske, 1959; Garner, Hake, & Eriksen, 1956) to give a more detailed exposition of the logic of dream research, paying particular attention to the role of physiological indicators in validating inferences concerning private experiences. They argued that the dream should be viewed as a hypothetical construct imperfectly indexed by verbal report, motor behavior, and physiological measures, which themselves are the convergent operations that corroborate inferences we make concerning the dream experience itself. Inferring that there was a dream experience of a particular quality constitutes a most probable hypothesis to explain the correlation of a verbal report with various physiological signs. The dream is an event separate and distinct from REM sleep and from what subjects say, although it is correlated in time with both of these variables. Stoyva and Kamiya (1968) went on to show that this view of the logical status of dream experience places the study of dreaming alongside other unobservable phenomena and/or dimensions of private experience, such as mood, state of consciousness, and subatomic particles.

One particularly exciting aspect of dream research is that it produces psychophysiological data, that is, data that correlate a mental or "mind" event with a physiological or "body" event. This feature also engenders problems that are relatively peculiar to psychophysiological research—for example, what Hauri (1975) calls "individual response specificity," or the fact that "most individuals [manifest] specific and unique [relationships between] psychological and physiological variables" (p. 277). Thus, for some subjects, emotionality in a dream may manifest itself in heart-rate variability; for others its physiological correlate may be lowered GSR.

Another problem is the phenomenon of forgotten content. Many dream scales score such reports as "zero." However, Hauri (1975) noted that Shapiro, Goodenough, Biederman, and Sleser (1964) reported that when subjects said they were dreaming but had forgotten the content, breathing irregularity during the REMP was always highest. Informally, Hauri and Van de Castle (1973b) found that "no-content reports" are associated with either very high or very low arousal. Hauri (1975), therefore, recommended that no-content reports should be eliminated from data analyses.

Finally, Hauri (1975) noted the more traditional pitfalls of human behavioral research that have stymied progress, particularly the use of rating scales to assess verbal reports. By 1975, approximately 150 scales had been developed, few of which provided adequate reliability and validity data, and many of which tended to measure similar but not identical constructs. These factors made it difficult to evaluate seemingly comparable data from different laboratories. In addition, he noted that studies of dream content from different subject groups often failed to use adequate control procedures such as assessing for the length of the dream report in evaluating the prevalence of particular content themes and failing to match controls with patient or experimental groups on potentially relevant variables.

THE NORMATIVE CONTENT OF DREAMS

What do people dream about in the course of their "garden variety" dreams? Hall (1966) and Hall and Van de Castle (1966) carried out monumental, systematic, content-analytic studies, under varying conditions, of people of both sexes, all ages, different cultures, and different personality types. The reader is referred to their work and to other studies of dream content based on daytime recall outside of the laboratory (Hall, 1966; Hall & Nordby, 1972; Hall & Van de Castle, 1966; Winget & Kramer, 1974).

Snyder (1970) conducted one of the few studies intended simply to determine how dream experience differs from waking experience. Subjects were 58 college and medical students, which limits the generalizability of the findings, as does the author's failure to report the details of the data analysis and interjudge reliability. Mentation reports were classified as dreams only if: (a) the words conveyed some sense of complex, organized, perceptual imagery; and (b) the imagery had undergone some temporal progression or change. Isolated images and fragments were discarded. Of REM awakenings, 75% produced narratives involving progression of organized and complex visual imagery with great variability in word count and detail.

Both Snyder's and Hall and Van De Castle's comprehensive work indicated that the manifest dream content is, on the whole, continuous with everyday life, and is a faithful reflection of external reality. In Snyder's (1970) words: "In almost every instance the progression of complex visual imagery . . . was a realistic facsimile of the visual perception of external reality; it was representational" (p. 133).

One's self rarely appeared alone, distorted, or as one was in childhood. Rather, the self pervaded the dream almost always in interaction with people sometimes known, and sometimes not known, to the dreamer. The usual mode of interaction was talking. From this, Snyder (1970) concluded that auditory imagery was almost as common as visual (76% and 100%, respectively). Furthermore, contrary to Freud's assertion that speech in dreams tended to have only something of the character of waking speech, dream speech tended to be actual and hallucinatory. Other sense modalities such as taste and smell were uncommonly represented.

The incidence of cognitive elements can be described as a range of occurrence percentages (figures are approximate as they were read from a bar graph): volition (10–50%), inferential reasoning (7–40%), memory processes (1–10%), reflexive contemplation (17–75%). In general, all four cognitive elements were least frequent in short dreams and most seen in dreams of over 300 words.

A perennial favorite is the question of dreaming in color. Snyder found that 61% of dreams were in color and that this proportion increased for longer dreams. This figure is consistent with those published by Kahn, Dement, Fisher, and Barmack (1962). The incidence of brilliant "technicolor" was greatest when awakenings were made during an ongoing REMP, intermediate during a body movement, and lowest one minute after a body movement associated with REMP termination. Thus, the recall of color fades rapidly with time.

Dysphoric emotions outnumbered pleasant ones by two to one. Fear and anxiety exceeded anger. Of the pleasant emotions, friendliness was the most common; erotic feelings were rare and representations of sexual relations even rarer. Violent aggressive reaction appeared in less than 4% of the total sample. The most common emotional tone was blandness or general nebulousness.

Relatively few dreams were disjointed or chaotic; dreams that were "crazy" and impossible or even unlikely were uncommon. Dream scenarios were largely mundane. The majority of dreams were moderately clear; some were extremely lucid and some unclear and vague. In terms of complexity, much variability was observed and seemed subject to demand characteristics. About half of the dreams showed only slight temporal progression; sagas were rare and about 50% of the dreams were sedentary. "Typical" dreams, such as loss of teeth, death, or nudity with embarrassment, were rare.

In short, the impression left by this study is that dreams are "not so dreamy after all." How can one account for the difference between these findings and the general impression of dreams as strange and uncanny? Snyder (1970), following Hacker (1911), believed that dreams recalled at home are remembered precisely because they contain emotion intense enough to leave an impression—it is these dreams that have contributed to the popular conception. In addition, the actual experience of dreaming can be approached from the point of view of what the manifest content means to the dreamer as well as the "raw content itself." We suspect that these uncollected data might have been found more interesting and less mundane than the manifest content upon which Snyder based his conclusions.

DEVELOPMENTAL CHANGES IN DREAM CONTENT

Freud (1955a/1900) regarded the theory of dreaming to be his most important contribution to psychology, and it is no surprise that his ideas on this subject have been a prime organizer of dream research. Unfortunately, Freud said little about the quality of children's dream experience. Arguing both from clinical observation and by deduction from theory, Freud suggested that the dreams of preschool children are relatively blatant and undisguised expressions of wish fulfillment. Foulkes and his associates (Foulkes, 1967, 1971; Foulkes, Larson, Swanson, & Rardin, 1969) took this as a starting point for several studies. Before examining them, it is worth noting that the problems of translations and recall in the collection of sleep mentation are potentially greater with children, who may be even more reactive to the novel experimental situation. In addition, their memorial and linguistic capacities, even in waking, are not fully developed.

In the first EEG study of older children's dreams, Foulkes, Pivik, Steadman, Spear, and Symonds (1967) examined the REMP mentation of 6–12-year-old boys. Children were given the Children's Apperception Test (CAT) and Otis Quick Scoring Mental Ability Test. Mentation reports were rated along dimensions such as spatial and temporal extensivity, unpleasantness, parental warmth, hostility, and guilt. The authors described the dream content they collected as mundane, nonbizarre, and dominated by references to current concerns.

The content ratings of the children's dreams were compared with analogous data collected from young adult males by Foulkes and Rechtschaffen (1964). Compared to young adult males, 6–12-year-old boys' dreams were more concerned with nuclear family members; male peers played a larger role and female peers a smaller role than with young adult males; the children had fewer dreams with extrafamilial known adults, indoor settings, and social plots. Supernatural figures or other symbolic personages or animals occurred more frequently in the dreams of children. School-related plots were virtually nonexistent.

Foulkes and Rechtschaffen (1964) obtained several significant correlation parameters of dream reports and dimensions of their subjects' TAT scores. These relationships were *not* found between the children's dreams and corresponding categories from the CAT protocols. Foulkes et al. (1967) interpreted this to indicate that "styles of mental approach are not nearly so stable or consistent across the sleep-wakefulness border for children as they are for adults" (p. 463). They also concluded that earlier reports (DeMartino, 1955) that described children's dreams as traumatic were most likely the result of atypical sampling of total dream experience. The authors noted a relative paucity of blatantly wish-fulfilling dreams. In general, children's dreams were not so clearly differentiated from those of young adults.

Foulkes (1967) further examined the dreams of four of the subjects from his original study in order to shed light on the qualitive aspects of dream experience. He found that the waking styles of the four subjects were continuous with aspects of their dream experience. Foulkes (1967) took these data to be consistent with Foulkes and Rechtschaffen's (1964) and Verdone's (1965) finding of an association between vivid and bizarre dream content and waking personality disturbance in young adults.

From these data (Foulkes, 1967; Foulkes et al., 1967) the author concluded that the dreams of preadolescents are not predominantly of an obviously wish-fulfilling nature and that during REM sleep the latency child does not always think in a highly disguised form; on the contrary, he asserted that realism is an impressive feature of the dreams of the male child, although as the child comes closer to conceiving things he fears, dreams become less straightforward. However, we take issue with the generalization that realism and lack of disguise typify the preadolescent's dream life. Although this may be true, the type of data described herein do not constitute evidence for inferring it. To know whether the content that a subject reports is in fact "disguised"—whether it represents something that is literally not the same—it is necessary to know how the subject experiences the content, that is, to know whether the cognitive and affective reactions to the content are consonant with its denotative meaning. The ordinariness of manifest dream material is no guarantee that it does not mask extraordinary conscious or unconscious experience. Some children may provide more effectively defended or expressively inhibited disguises than others. The sort of free-association procedure that might address this question was specifically eschewed.

Dreams of Preschool Children

When do children begin to dream? Kohler, Coddington, and Agnew (1968) studied 2-year-old children selected because of superior verbal ability. They concluded that some 2-year-old children can have nocturnal dreams and that such material, when it occurs, is associated with REM sleep.

As indicated, one place to evaluate Freud's "blatant wish-fulfillment" hypothesis is in the dreams of preschool children. This has been the stimulus for research in two other studies by Foulkes and his associates (Foulkes, 1971; Foulkes et al., 1969). Together these studies examined the REMP mentation collected from children aged 3½–5 years. In Foulkes et al. (1969) children were also assessed using Laurendeau and Pinard's tests of precausal thinking and the Blacky test. The children's parents were given the Traditional Family Ideology scale (a measure of authoritarian attitudes).

The two studies produced consistent data. The most striking findings were the infrequency of recall and the brevity of young children's dream reports. Although there was a considerable range among subjects, it was clear that most preschool children frequently do not report anything when awakened from REM sleep. When young children do report a dream, the report is very brief compared to reports of older children and adults. Foulkes (1971) described these dreams as generally impoverished in motoric, affective, and cognitive content. However, what content there is, is realistic with respect to setting and plot and bears demonstrable relationship to the subjects' behavior in the period preceding mentation collections (Foulkes, 1971). Foulkes also pointed out that the young children's dreams were not so dramatic, traumatic, or dreadful as other observers (Hall, 1966) had stated. He ascribed the discrepancy between the "prosaic" dreams he obtained using EEG awakening techniques (Foulkes, 1971) and earlier reports (DeMartino, 1955; Hall, 1966), as the result of a more representative sampling of normal children. Noting the possible objection that the laboratory setting may have had an inhibitory effect on dream reporting, Foulkes (1971) responded that there is evidence from young adults that dreams collected at home and in the laboratory do not differ in intensity (Weisz & Foulkes, 1970), and there is "no reason to believe that youngsters are more facile at situational suppression of their nocturnal fantasies, than are college students" (p. 63). Foulkes et al. (1969) also doubted the likelihood of the possibility that the preschool children lacked the vocabularies and concepts to accurately report the nature of their dream experience, because there was a positive significant correlation of recall with the descriptive ability scale of the Blacky test.

Foulkes et al.'s (1969) and Foulkes's (1971) conclusions regarding the dreams of preschool children were as follows: In general, they may be regarded as reflecting more the influence of ego processes than of "destructive id impulses" and as such their content is prosaic and realistic, reflecting current waking-life concerns. This reflection of current concerns is incomplete in that certain important concerns, such as parents, are omitted from dream content. Nevertheless, the authors felt that dream content is very much continuous with, and mirrors, current waking life.

Again, we would suggest that this conclusion is premature. The actual data sample that Foulkes et al. (1969) and Foulkes (1971) generalized from was very small and potentially systematically biased. Of the 12 children, one-third reported no dreams at all. Unless we are to assume that one-third of preschool children have no dream experience, our conceptions of what elicits defensive forgetting or denial in children would suggest that the missing data may be predominantly unpleasant, unrealistic, or anxious material. In this context, it is interesting that the authors noted that when atypical (that is, usually "omitted") categories of dream content appear, they are in the context of anxiety.

The authors showed, however, that there are important continuities between styles of waking functioning and patterns of dreaming, extending the findings of Foulkes and Rechtschaffen (1964). Such continuities were also in evidence in data collected by Foulkes et al. (1969) from institutionalized emotionally disturbed male adolescents and normal male adolescents. The institutionalized adolescents' dream reports were longer and were rated as more imaginative and more unpleasant; they contained more physical aggression but less verbal aggression, less heterosexual content, and less relation to everyday experience. Correlations between aspects of dream content and scales of the California Personality Inventory supported the notion that less well adjusted subjects had more vivid and bizarre dreams.

The firm findings that emerge from the studies reviewed are: Until adulthood, recall frequency and dream report length increase with age; waking personality styles are strongly related to individual differences in patterns of dreaming and this correlation increases with age; presumably important areas of waking concern are omitted from the manifest content of children's dreams. In its simplest form, Freud's (1955a/1900) expectation of blatant wish-fulfillment in children's dreams is given little obvious support. However, psychoanalytic conceptions of development were represented in the content of dreams.

PSYCHOPATHOLOGICAL SYNDROMES

The Dreams of Schizophrenics

The excitement generated by the discovery of a relationship between REM sleep and dreaming partly stemmed from the hope that grounding dreaming in the solid rock of the nervous system would lead to a better understanding of the nature of psychopathology. This hope developed from the idea that there are important connections and similarities between the experience of normal dreaming and of waking consciousness in schizophrenia. One aspect of this hypothesis is that the symptoms of schizophrenia and the content of dreams are both seen as behavioral and experiential manifestations of a wish-dominated, nonlogical, nonrealistic subjectivity that is usually inhibited during wakefulness. A second aspect is that if the quantity of primary-process ideation is more or less constant for a given individual (as Freud, 1955a/1900, believed), then an individual who discharges some of it during wakefulness would experience less ideation of this type during sleep. It would be predicted that such an individual's dream life would be relatively less populated with bizarre, blatantly wishful, and nonlogical elements than the nonschizophrenic.

Dement (1955) conducted the first EEG study of schizophrenic dreams. Two basic findings emerged. During REM sleep, the schizophrenics gave fewer actual dream reports. One-half of the schizophrenics frequently reported dreams of isolated inanimate objects, devoid of any overt action, while the medical student controls reported no dreams of this type.

These data seem to confirm the hydraulic model of dream function alluded to above. However, Dement's (1955) study is illustrative of the very difficult methodological problems besetting dream research with schizophrenics. He described his schizophrenic subjects as having been selected from a hospital population on the basis of their being manageable and "at least to a slight degree communicative." Further, Dement (1955) noted that "certain of the schizophrenics consistently replied negatively to interrogation [with] a monotonous stereotypy [apparently not] a true verbalization of inner experiences" (p. 267). This would imply that the strangely barren reports of the schizophrenics may as much reflect their negativism and residual symptomatology as their actual experience prior to being awakened. Thus, it may be that the reporting style of chronic schizophrenics when awakened from REM sleep may obscure the experience to which it is supposed to correspond.

Cartwright (1972) used the Foulkes DF scale to assess the REM and NREM mentation of eight schizophrenics and two groups of normals (high and normal scorers on the K-corrected schizophrenia scale of the MMPI). The data she reported seemed to support a compensation model. Unfortunately, the study was beset with several serious methodological problems, which were carefully reviewed by Pivik (1974). These included the use of different awakening procedures for the schizophrenics and the normal groups, inadequate statistical analysis, and the misdiagnosis of three of the schizophrenic patients.

Okuma, Sunami, Fukuma, Takeo, and Motoike (1970) collected dreams, using the REMP awakening technique, from subjects who were diagnostically similar to Dement's (1955) original group. Their subjects were chronic hebephrenic schizophrenics, hospitalized an average of 9.9 years each. These patients were described as communicative, although having hallucinations and delusions. Ten days prior to the study all subjects were taken off drugs. The normal controls consisted of college students and male psychiatrists.

The schizophrenic population displayed a style of response to dream collection that might be indicative of a relative diminution of the vividness, clarity, and cinematic qualities associated with REM dreams, and/or of the inability or unwillingness to translate a perceptual dream experience spontaneously into a verbal report. The authors also noted the possibility that a differential level of wakefulness for the schizophrenics might produce the response style observed. The latency from the experimenter's request to describe their dream to the beginning of a dream report was significantly longer for schizophrenics, the average amount of time spent spontaneously reporting a given dream was significantly shorter and less variable than controls, and the average word count of such reports was significantly lower for schizophrenics.

Following the initial dream narrative, subjects were asked a series of supplementary questions to collect information missing from the spontaneous reports. Schizophrenics required significantly more of these questions. In the morning, schizophrenics had a significantly lower incidence of such recall of the dreams reported the previous night than controls. The conceptual richness of dreams was assessed by counting the number of independent clauses in each report. Controls averaged significantly more independent clauses per dream. Examination of dream content revealed that schizophrenics had a significantly lower incidence of dreams that could be classified as bizarre, coherent, or complex. However, data on the incidence of bizarreness, clarity, coherence, and complexity are difficult to interpret, since these variables are confounded with dream length, which significantly differed between the groups being compared.

As Okuma et al. (1970) pointed out, the simple and abbreviated dream reports they obtained from schizophrenics may have been the product of various interdependent factors. For example, the fact that schizophrenics' morning recall of their dreams of the previous night was relatively poor, may have been the result of the vagueness or unclarity of the dream itself or of deficits in waking cognitive functioning. The relatively low variability of the schizophrenics on most of the parameters described above suggests that some stereotyped process was influencing their reporting.

It is possible that the apparent lack of clarity and simplicity of schizophrenic dream reports were artifactual products of the schizophrenics' tendency to withhold a full accounting of their experience. Snyder's (1970) data suggested that the relationship between coherence and dream length is negative in normals; that is, shorter reports tended to be more coherent. Therefore, we can feel more confident in stating that schizophrenics' dreams are less coherent than controls', independently of their other formal characteristics.

The advantages of Okuma et al.'s (1970) study included the use of a relatively homogeneous group of schizophrenics and the examination of behavioral styles as well as presented dream content. One disadvantage was the selection of psychiatrist controls, a subject group that we can assume a priori to be significantly more articulate, psychologically minded, and intelligent than the average chronic hebephrenic schizophrenic, a fact that might influence dream reporting in unknown ways.

One problem for all dream studies with psychopathological populations is teasing apart the influences of waking cognition from nocturnal dream phenomenology. The validity of current findings such as Okuma et al.'s

(1970) would be enhanced by more careful assessment of waking cognitive deficit. The results of such assessment procedures should be correlated with aspects of sleep mentation so that their influence might be controlled using analysis of covariance techniques.

Kramer and Roth (1973) compared EEG-collected REMP dreams of 10 depressed patients to those of 13 schizophrenics, using the Hall–Van de Castle (1966) scoring system. Schizophrenics had a higher frequency of dream recall than depressed patients. The most frequent character for schizophrenics was a stranger; for depressed patients it was a family member. For both schizophrenic and depressed patients, groups of characters were more frequent than individuals, but this effect was more pronounced for the depressed patients. Schizophrenics' dreams contained more aggressive than friendly or sexual interactions; depressed patients' dreams were more evenly divided among these categories. The most frequent emotion in schizophrenics' dreams was apprehension. Depressed patients showed a relatively even distribution of different emotion, with the least frequent emotion being happiness and the most frequent, anger. As Weisz (1975) pointed out in his review of Kramer and Roth's (1973) study, their work had several important methodological shortcomings. For example, we are not told diagnostic subtypes; it is not clear that raters were blind to the diagnosis of the patient, although they may have been blind to the experimental hypotheses.

Kramer, Trinder, and Roth (1972) reported data similar to Kramer and Roth (1973), comparing male paranoid schizophrenics' dreams before and after drug treatment with those of normal college males; however, the value of that study was seriously flawed by the fact that controls' dreams were *not* collected using EEG techniques and patients' dreams were.

In his review of manifest-dream studies, Kramer (1970) stated "the dreams of schizophrenics may . . . be generally characterized as unrealistic, affectively neutral, openly hostile . . . less blatantly sexual than waking life and with the dream action focused on the dreamer who finds himself most of the time with strangers" (p. 154). Some of these assertions, such as the claim that schizophrenics' dreams are unrealistic, have been directly contradicted by more recent research (Okuma et al., 1970). However, more important, even where these generalizations are supported, these aspects of schizophrenics' dreams do not necessarily differentiate them from normals' dreams. Snyder (1970) found that emotions are generally infrequent in manifest dreams of normals, but when they do appear, they are predominantly unpleasant, with fear and anger most common. Unidentified characters (who may be strangers) are also frequent in the dreams of normal young adults, and the dreamer himself is the most pervasive presence in the dream (Snyder, 1970).

Because of the methodological difficulties alluded to, any generalization concerning the actual dream experience of schizophrenics in comparison with normals is premature. Some support has been given to the expectation, based on the compensation model of dreaming and schizophrenia, that REM dreams of chronic schizophrenics are relatively impoverished and empty, compared with normals'. However, this finding needs to be replicated with careful assessment and control of the effects of waking cognitive deficits on dream reporting.

Depression and Dreaming

In this section, nonlaboratory studies of dreaming, and depression, and EEG studies, are briefly reviewed. Dreams of patients in treatment and of remitted patients are discussed.

Beck and Ward (1961) studied 287 randomly selected psychiatric patients. Subjects were assessed for depression by a battery of psychological tests and were evaluated by two independent judges. Patients reported their most recent dream. This was scored either positive or negative for masochism, defined as being: deprived, disappointed, thwarted, exploited, disgraced, rejected or deserted, blamed or ridiculed, punished, physically injured or discomforted, lost something, or showed a distorted body image. A strong association was noted between masochistic dream content and both the prevalence and severity of depression. These findings could not be attributed to differences in age, sex, race, IQ, or socioeconomic status. However, masochistic content was not diagnostic for depression as it was also found during symptom-free periods in nondepressed masochistic characters (Beck and Hurvich, 1959). Thus, Beck and Ward (1961) may have tapped into an underlying personality trait related to depression, rather than identifying a dream style peculiar to depressed patients. The study suffered from using only recalled dreams, scoring all reports with a subject and a verb, a lack of qualitative measures, and a reliance on manifest content.

Langs (1966) found that a depressive group of patients reported the shortest, fewest, and most barren dreams, concluding that the dreams reflected a decathexis of the external world and external objects. He did not find a predominance of masochistic themes. However, the author noted that this may have occurred because the control group included women with depressive features, who would have been noncontrol depressed subjects in the Beck and Ward (1961) study. Problems with the study were a neglect to match dream reports for length and a failure to age-match the groups.

Kramer, Baldridge, Whitman, Ornstein, and Smith (1969) studied the manifest dream in male paranoid schizophrenics, male psychotically depressed patients, and male nonpsychiatric medical inpatients. Dreams were rated for hostility (both toward the dreamer and away from the dreamer), plausibility, and the relationship of the dreamer to other dream characters.

The mean word count of the depressives' dreams was midway between that of the schizophrenics and the medical patients. The degree of hostility was also intermediate for the depressed group; it was equally likely to be turned against the dreamer as against others. The dreams of depressives showed only family members more than half of the time, those of schizophrenics showed mostly strangers, and medical patients' dreams were largely of friends. Dreams of depressives scored midway between those of schizophrenics and controls on plausibility and were more often plausible than not. One serious question about the validity of this study is raised by the atypically low recall of nonpsychiatric medical patients.

In general, laboratory studies have been in agreement with nonlaboratory studies. Despite methodological problems such as the use of mixed groups of depressives (Kramer, Whitman, Baldridge, & Lansky, 1966), problems of dream reporting in the absence of a decrease of REM time, inadequate controls (Kramer et al., 1969), and a paucity of statistical analyses (Langs, 1966; Van de Castle & Holloway, 1970), some firm findings have emerged. Depressives' dream reports are shorter than controls (with the exception of Kramer et al., 1969). They show a greater incidence of family members (Kramer et al., 1969; Kramer & Roth, 1973; Langs, 1966). They seem to have a higher incidence of depressive themes than a comparison group (Kramer et al., 1966) and more masochistic content (Beck & Ward, 1961), although this may be related to a stable character trait rather than to clinical depression.

How does the mentation of depressives alter with improvement? Most studies see the dreams of remitted depressives remaining similar in some aspects to that of patients. Miller (1969), comparing dreams from 16 deeply depressed and 13 improving patients, concluded that when patients improve, their dreams become more troubled and may begin to deal with problems. However, definitions of patient groups were not clearly stated; thus, comparisons with other studies are difficult. However, some support for Miller (1969) was found in Kramer, Whitman, Baldridge, and Ornstein (1968) and Kramer, Sandler, Whitman, and Baldridge (1970).

Hauri (1976), in a well-controlled study, examined the sleep of patients remitted from reactive depression. Eleven remitted patients with at least one psychiatric hospitalization and a final diagnosis of severe reactive depression and 11 control subjects slept in the laboratory for 3 nights and were awakened from both REM and NREM sleep. They were given the Beck Depression Inventory and Nowlis Mood Adjective Checklist. Careful control of subject selection, time of night, and length in sleep stage assured that observed differences could not be attributed to sleep pattern differences.

In most respects, the remitted depressive dreams were similar to the control dreams in terms of recall, vividness, intensity of feeling, and hedonic tone. The main differences were that the remitted patients more often had dreams dealing with the past, which contained more childhood elements. For both REM and sleep onset mentation, the patients' reports had fewer words. After rating the 42 matched pairs of REM narratives of more than 70 words in length, the patient dreams scored significantly higher on the Beck and Hurvich masochism scale and on Gottschalk and Gleser's covert hostility out, which measures hostile acts in the environment not involving the dreamer. Thus, Hauri (1976) concluded from their dreams that remitted patients see the world as more threatening, hostile, and violent, although not necessarily directed against the dreamer.

Comparing mentation from the three sleep stages (REM, NREM, and sleep-onset), Hauri concluded that depressives might have a cognitive style such that the reporting of both realistic and fantasylike material would be difficult. This would lead to the conclusion that remitted patients have more material in NREM sleep than do controls. Hauri and Hawkins (1973) showed that the percentage of phasic REM correlates with clinical state as assessed by the Beck Depression Inventory. Thus, the sleep parameters of remitted patients may remain atypical in some ways, as does their mentation.

Dreams and Organic Brain Disease

Greenberg, Pearlman, Brooks, Mayer, and Hartmann (1968) studied the dreaming of 14 hospitalized patients afflicted with Korsakoff's psychosis. They were interested in whether the lesions involved in the disease have any effect on sleep mentation.

The patients were divided into 2 groups: acute (ill less than 1 year), and chronic (ill more than 1 year). Their age range and degrees of memory impairment were not significantly different. The patients, all severe alcoholics, had no alcohol for 2 weeks prior to the study. After establishment of a stable baseline, 7 patients were then studied for another 2 to 3 nights, with awakenings from REM and NREM sleep over varying elapsed durations. With regard to mentation, out of 34 awakenings in 7 patients, only 1 vivid unequivocal dream report and 1 elaboration of a stereotyped kind of mentation given on another awakening were elicited. Acute patients also reported 2 possible dreams in which confabulation was likely. In the remainder, recall was absent. NREM awakening produced either no-content reports or brief thoughts about home.

Kramer and Roth (1975) reported on the REM dreams collected in 17 hospitalized patients with a chronic organic brain syndrome. In general, the results of the foregoing investigations are in accord with that of Torda (1969) for 6 patients afflicted with postencephalitic memory loss. That is, organic cerebral syndromes are associated with dream recall which is much less frequent, shorter, simpler, reality bound, and lacking in emotional depth.

To what extent this poverty-stricken state of REM mentation is a result of cognitive deficits secondary to brain-tissue damage, as opposed to loss of affective impetus, is difficult to assess. Greenberg et al. (1968) noted that two Korsakoff patients, who had provided mundane laboratory dream reports, had intense, affect-laden, and dreamlike experiences under the influence of nitrous oxide and were able to give detailed description and remember them for some time after completion of the experiment. The authors ascribed this to the increase in emotion during nitrous oxide administration, and this was thought to overcome the hippocampal-cortical block to which the memory impairment has been partly attributed.

War Neuroses and Dreaming

Freud (1955b/1917) interpreted the repetitive dreams of patients suffering from war neuroses as unsuccessful attempts of the ego to master a prior traumatic episode. Greenberg, Pearlman, and Gampel (1972), who suggested that one function of dreaming is "to reconstitute characteristic defenses in relation to recent waking experiences which have stirred up old unresolved conflicts" (p. 27), hypothesized that the recurrent nightmares were evidence of dreaming that did not fulfill its function. They predicted that war neurosis patients would have a greater "pressure" to dream, manifested as a shorter REM latency and longer REM time.

Patients suffering from war neurosis slept for at least 3 nights in the laboratory. On half the nights, they were awakened at the end of each REMP for dream content. A 5-minute verbal sample was collected from each subject before sleep and when awakened in the morning and scored for defensive strain—a composite score derived from 3 factors (degree of emergence of traumatic material, the relative prominence of safe versus unsafe interpersonal interactions, and the extent of emergence of threatening ego-alien impulses). On the basis of defensive strain scores, and without knowledge of the REM latencies, the presleep mentation samples of 7 patients were ranked as either high or low latency nights. It was predicted that high defensive strain scores would be associated with shorter REM latency and that decreased defensive strain from evening to morning would correlate with a high percentage of stage REM.

In the 9 patients, average REM latencies were less than 40 minutes on 14 of a total of 29 nights. Sleep onset REM occurred frequently. Such short latencies have previously been found only in adults who were narcoleptic (Rechtschaffen & Dement, 1969). Independent judges were able to rank defensive strain to predict REM latency at better than a .05 level of significance. The changes in REM time with change in defensive strain scores were not as clear-cut as the latency measures and no statistics were reported.

Methodological problems include the low incidence of actual nightmares in the laboratory (suggesting that measuring the phenomenon by allowing subjects the security of sleeping in the lab may have altered results), the absence of reliability data for the defensive strain measure, and the possibility that 5 minutes does not provide an adequate sampling of behavior to assess psychological state. However, this remains a suggestive study, providing evidence that a psychological parameter can be correlated with a physiological variable.

Laboratory Studies of Patients in Therapy

The technique of dream interpretation and interest in dream mentation has historically been tied to clinical therapeutic work. Yet, little use has been made of the sleep laboratory to test hypotheses about dream formation. Laboratory findings have shown that people dream far more frequently than the usual one or two dreams reported in psychotherapy. To examine whatever systematic biases exist in the patient's recollection of a particular dream in the morning, Whitman, Kramer and Baldridge (1963) studied 2 subjects who spent 2 nights per week in the lab for 8 weeks. Subjects were allowed 5 minutes of REM sleep. They were then awakened for a dream report and associations to the dream were taken. After the dream nights, the subjects were interviewed by a psychiatrist, either 1 hour or a full day after the night of dreaming.

For both patients, the nature of the subject's relationship to the experimenter or the psychiatrist largely determined who was told what. This was true for both major changes in content (omission of one or more dream scenes, change of situation, omission of prominent details) and partial omissions. These findings suggested that the unreported dream may be the one containing evidence of major interpersonal conflicts.

The authors concluded that the accuracy of the retelling of most of the reports indicates that ordinary forgetting plays only a minor role. The amount of dreaming recalled 1 hour after awakening differed only slightly from that recalled a full day later. During the night, dreams were fragmented. By the time they were told to the psychiatrist, they included a greater degree of thematic coherence.

Besides dream content, the process of awakenings, the stated interest of the therapist in the dreams, the therapist–patient relationship, and the time of night were all relevant in decreasing order to recall. In addition, the process of being awakened and asked to give mentation reports must influence the amount of remembering that occurs—a kind of rehearsal effect. These findings are relevant to the use of dreams in psychotherapy.

Another approach was used by Freedman, Luborsky, and Harvey (1970) and Greenberg and Pearlman (1975), namely to correlate REM parameters with the content of a single session. Freedman, Luborsky, and Harvey (1970) found few consistent results, perhaps due to the fact that their one subject was taking a number of drugs that may have affected the amount of REM sleep.

Greenberg and Pearlman (1975) attempted to correlate REM latency and REM time with stress in the psychoanalytical session. A patient in psychoanalysis was seen in the sleep laboratory on 24 separate nights, 1 night a week, with a month between each group of 4 nights. The laboratory session was scheduled on the night after an evening analytical hour, which was then followed by a morning analytical hour.

A measure of defensive strain was utilized to score the analytical sessions. This included 3 separately scored subsections (the degree of emotional disturbance produced by the material in the hour, the relative prominence of safe and threatening self–other fantasy constellations, and the flexibility of defensive functions), which were then summed to produce the defensive-strain score. It was hypothesized that a high defensive-strain score would indicate a need for REM sleep or a pressure to dream, which would be manifest as shortened REM latency. Changes in strain from the evening to morning hours were rated with the prediction that low REM time would be associated with increase in strain and high REM time, with decrease in strain. All ratings were done by the authors.

There was extreme variability in the physiological parameters. In contrast, a control subject showed a relatively consistent REM latency. Clinical scores also showed great variability. There was an inverse relationship between the defensive-strain measure of the Friday session and REM latency. Higher defensive-strain scores were followed by shorter REM latencies. The examiners were able to predict which 8 nights would have the most REM time and which 8 nights would have the least REM time on the basis of changes in the defensive-strain scores.

Melstrom and Cartwright (1983) investigated the effects of psychotherapy on laboratory-collected dreams. They hypothesized: (a) the experiencing level of REM sleep dreams would increase pre- to posttherapy and would increase more in successful psychotherapy patients; (b) dysphoric affects would decrease pre- to posttherapy more in successful than in unsuccessful patients; (c) DF scores would increase pre- to posttherapy more in successful than in unsuccessful patients; (d) pretherapy dream-experiencing scores would correlate positively with ratings made by intake interviews of patients' access to their inner lives; (e) after treatment, the sequence of dreams across the night in successful cases would show progressive decreases in rated anxiety and progressive increases in rated experiencing level in contrast to the sequence of dreams in unsuccessful cases.

Ten subjects who applied for psychotherapy were assigned to a REM-awakening condition, and 4 subjects were assigned to a yoked NREM awakening condition. The length of psychotherapy varied from 11 to 74 sessions in the REM group and from 5 to 65 sessions in the NREM group. Subjects were adapted to the lab prior to beginning psychotherapy. Therapy was rated on a 9-point scale after termination by the therapists. On the basis of a median split, subjects were divided into successful and nonsuccessful groups. Dreams were rated independently by 5 judges for anxiety, guilt, experiencing level, and dreamlike fantasy.

Contrary to prediction, the successful patients showed a near-significant increase in dream anxiety. In addition, they had a much higher overall level of dream anxiety than did the unsuccessful patients. A comparison group showed no change in dream anxiety. Both successful and unsuccessful patients had a significant increase in dream experiencing posttherapy but there was no difference among the groups. Successful patients remained unchanged in their degree of dreamlike fantasy after therapy while unsuccessful patients showed an increase. There was a positive correlation between interviewers' ratings of access to inner life and their dream experiencing scores posttherapy. Dream anxiety scores did not decrease across the night more in successful than in unsuccessful cases.

These results, largely contradictory to the original hypotheses, also contradicted previous findings that successful patients have less anxious dreams after therapy. Limitations of this study include the lack of free association and the focus on manifest content, both of which limit understanding of the unexpected results. In addition, all the patients in the study were considered to be poor psychotherapy risks and the therapy was short-lived, making comparisons with longer-term analytical therapy unfeasible. However, as the authors suggested, it may be that the original hypotheses were simplistic and that anxiety is a facilitation factor that aids adaptation. At any rate, further work would be needed to illuminate the findings that successful therapy increases dream anxiety.

In conclusion, the small amount of work done has yielded interesting data and observations, but attempts to relate the content of therapy sessions and REM parameters remain merely suggestive. As Knapp et al. (1975) stated: "Psychoanalysis allows in some ways a more complete knowledge of a human being than any other form of encounter, but its very comprehensiveness militates against structuring a simplified model for testing its conclusions" (p. 420).

DREAMS AND THEIR RELATIONSHIP TO PHYSICAL CONDITIONS

Dreams of the Blind

Prior to the era of electrographic research, Blank (1958) reviewed the topic of dreaming in the blind. The dreams of the congenitally blind are devoid of all visual imagery. With few exceptions, visual imagery was said to remain for varying periods, even into adulthood, when blindness occurred between the critical ages of 5 and 7 years. However, even among these subjects, the capacity for visual imagery tends to deteriorate with time and visual dreams eventually become a rarity. According to Blank, with the exception of the absence of vision, dreams of those whose blindness antedates the critical period do not differ in essential respects from those of the sighted and contain auditory, tactile, kinesthetic, gustatory, olfactory, and temperature sensations in decreasing order.

In general, laboratory studies are in agreement with Blank (1958) on the relative incidence of nonvisual sensory material (Amadeo & Gomez, 1966;

Berger, Olley, & Oswald, 1962). REMs were not detectable in 5 of 8 subjects studied by Berger et al. (1962) and in one subject observed by Offenkrantz and Wolpert (1963). Their REM periods were otherwise "normal." In both studies, absence of REMs and absence of visual dream imagery coincided, supporting the hypothesis that REMs were essential to and closely corresponded to visual dream events. By contrast, Amadeo and Gomez (1966) reported that 7 of 8 subjects with congenital blindness consistently showed REMs during REM periods, albeit at a lower frequency and amplitude, compared with sighted subjects. REM awakenings yielded reports of elaborate nonvisual dreams. They concluded that REMs and visual dreaming were not related in a one-to-one manner and that REMs were merely the expression of the increased neural activation associated with REM sleep. In support of the latter notion, they described experiments on 3 blind subjects in whom, while awake, REMs were twice as frequent during experimentally produced states of increased attention in contrast to wakeful rest.

These discrepancies were apparently resolved when Gross, Byrne, and Fisher (1965) demonstrated, by visual inspection of the eyelids of 5 sleeping blind subjects, and also by means of ceramic strain gauge recording of eye movements, that those blind subjects who seemed to lack REMs had a great deal more REM activity than was revealed by standard EOG recording. Thus, it appears that with suitable techniques of detection, all blind subjects with intact extraocular muscle systems will have abundant REM activity, though possibly reduced in amplitude, and such REM activity may occur independently of visual imagery.

Kerr, Foulkes, and Schmidt (1982) attempted to look at the dreams of the blind from a cognitive perspective, examining the formal characteristics of their dream reports. They had 4 sighted, 4 congenitally blind, and 2 adventitiously blind subjects sleep in the lab 1 night a week for 8 weeks. Subjects were also administered a number of tests of cognitive ability. Of these tests, only a vividness of imagery scale distinguished the sighted and congenitally blind subjects; all 4 blind subjects rated their auditory imagery as more vivid than did the sighted subjects. Report rates for different awakening categories were not different for groups with different visual states.

When blind and sighted subjects were compared for each sleep stage on 22 response categories focusing on the sensory quality and content structure of their dreams, the two groups showed little difference in these comparisons. Except for the presence of visual imagery, the dreams of the congenitally blind were formally similar to those of the sighted, and the dreams of the late adventitiously blind were indistinguishable from the sighted. The authors concluded that visualization does not have a special role in dream generation. Because the dreams of the blind were as complex as those of the sighted, the authors argued that the integrative mechanisms responsible for both the momentary and the sequential coherence of dreaming cannot depend on a system specific to visual encoding. Dream coherence is seen as depending on a stage of dream generation prior to the selection of particular outputs in modality-specific representational systems. The dreams of the adventitiously blind (who were able to "see" people in their dream whom they had met after the onset of blindness) suggested that dreams represent life as we imagine it, not as we "see" it, thus transcending current perceptual knowledge. It was concluded that dreaming is a cognitive constructive process rather than a reproductive perceptual one.

Extensive coverage of the dreams of the blind and blind deaf may be found in Kirtley's (1975) study.

Dreams of the Deaf

Mendelson, Siger, and Solomon (1960) reported on the daytime dream recall of deaf adults. The population consisted of three groups: the congenitally deaf, those whose deafness was acquired before the age of 5, and those who became deaf after the age of 5. Both the congenitally deaf and the deaf-before-5 group were reported as high in dream occurrence frequency, color content, vividness of recall, and three-dimensional quality. By contrast, the deafness-after-5 group was strikingly lower in these categories. In all deaf subjects, the perception of motion in the dreams, other than movement involved in communicative signing, was described as low. It is of interest that the language of signs was their usual means of communication in dreams. However, in dreams accompanied by intense anxiety, there was a striking prevalence in the congenitally deaf of primitive signs (gestural communication employed by parental figures in early childhood before the standard language of signs was learned); gestures of this sort usually conveyed strong affective qualities. The suggestion was made that the greater vividness and color representation in the dreams of the deaf served a compensatory function. The main detraction from this work was its lack of a normal control group.

The only laboratory study of the dreams of the deaf is that of Stoyva (1965). This work was instigated by an earlier classic report that in deaf subjects, a close relationship exists between EMG potentials of the arm and finger muscles and subsequent recall of dreams (Max, 1935, 1937). It was concluded that in the deaf who use sign language, finger-EMG activity was associated with high dream recall. By contrast, no such association was found in 11 hearing subjects during 33 similar observations.

Stoyva (1965) repeated this work with electrographic technology. He was interested in two questions: (a) Does the EMG activity with finger movements of the deaf indicate NREM mentation? (b) Are the deaf different from hearing controls with regard to finger-EMG activity in relation to frequency of episodes, their nightly distribution, or association with specific sleep stages? He found that the rates of dream recall from REM sleep were similar in the deaf and hearing groups. Finger-EMG activity in

NREM sleep was not associated with mentation. In both deaf and hearing groups, a consistently accelerated rate of finger-EMG activity was observed during REM as opposed to NREM sleep. Contrary to expectation, rates of finger-EMG activity were similar among the deaf and the hearing subjects. Stoyva concluded that his findings did not support the motor theory of thinking.

Dreams of the Physically Disabled

We are unaware of any systematic laboratory studies of subjects with major motor paralysis. Newton (1970) published his observations on 27 quadriplegic and paraplegic men based upon post-sleep-period dream recall.

The mean proportion of dreamed self-propelled physical activity for disabled and normal subjects was not significantly different; nor was there any correlation between dream physical-activity scores and a Rorschach index of body-image integrity. On the other hand, it was found that immediately after the onset of the paralysis there was an upsurge of dreamed physical activity in excess of that of the normal controls and that with the passage of time, its level decreased and remained stable at lower than normal levels.

Dreams and the Menstrual Cycle

A psychoanalytical approach to female sexuality would predict temporal correlations between women's feelings, wishes, and experiences of themselves, and the phases of the menstrual cycle. Benedek and Rubenstein (1939) conducted a classical study of these issues using neurotic subjects in psychoanalysis. They reported that changes in the menstrual cycle were paralleled by changes in the thematic content of free associations and dream material.

Other investigators failed to support some of Benedek and Rubenstein's (1939) assertions (Davis, 1929; Terman, 1938). Swanson and Foulkes (1968) attempted a partial replication of their study using electrophysiological techniques. In contradistinction to Benedek and Rubenstein (1939), they hypothesized that, during menses, a time of relative sexual deprivation, overt heterosexual drive expression would be greatest, as sexual wishes were being frustrated in waking life.

Dreams were collected from 4 normal undergraduate women during 1 night per week, sampling several REMPs during the night, for 11 consecutive weeks. Following each night, subjects rated their most recent dream on a variety of dimensions, such as distortion, hostile press, sexual press, and sexual need.

Judges' average ratings of dreams on a manifest sexuality scale were highest during menses for 3 subjects. Once again, a stronger relationship was obtained between dream content and subjects' waking reactions to cyclical changes than between dream content and cyclical changes themselves. Peak hostility ratings of dreams were highest for 3 of the 4 subjects during menses. The authors suggested that this might be a reflection of the unpleasantness, physical discomfort, and activity restrictions generally associated with menstruation. No other rated dimensions of dream content were significantly related to cycle phase.

The authors concluded that their data contradicted Benedek and Rubenstein's (1939) assertions of a direct connection between hormonally regulated phases of the menstrual cycle and arousal of the sexual drive in women. The authors concluded that, for these subjects, inner-experienced reaction to the menstrual cycle was a better predictor of dream unpleasantness than cycle phase itself. However, Swanson and Foulkes's (1968) data must be viewed with caution because of the very small sample used and because of the limited statistical analysis. Nevertheless, their study suggested that psychological correlates of organic states may mediate and possibly override the influences of physiological variables that we might intuitively expect to be quite powerful in determining dream experience.

Pain in Dreams

In a clinical population, we *have* observed dreams that involved the experience of pain. Usually, when this is the case, the pain is short-lived and the dreamer awakens. Much more common are dreams in which pain normally would have been felt if the dreamed episode had occurred while awake, but was nevertheless absent. The phenomenon is an interesting example of dissociation between vivid dreamlike experience and normally expected (but absent) sensory concomitants.

Arkin et al. (1975), in an attempt to assess the frequency of references to physical pain sensation in dreams, collected 119 REM reports from 20 college students under baseline conditions following 3 days of REM deprivation. There was only one ambiguous reference to pain in the entire sample. Thus the age-old test of whether an event is real ("I had to pinch myself to see if I was dreaming") suggests that pain is incompatible with the reality of dreaming.

BODY MOVEMENTS AND SLEEP MENTATION

Large Movements

Wolpert and Trosman (1958) attempted to look at differences between mentation from 2 points in the REMP. They believed that a gross body movement signaled a change in dream activity and betokened a completed dream episode. Ten male subjects were observed for a total of 51 nights. Awakenings were made during ongoing stage REM sleep, during stage REM sleep followed by a gross body movement, during stage 2 within 5 minutes after REMP termination, and during stage 2 at least 10 minutes from the last eye movement. Dream-recall data were divided into detailed and single or fragmented recall.

They found dream recall high from stage REM and lower from periods of stage 2 sleep. But the amount of recall from ongoing stage REM awakenings was 82.5% as compared with 69.1% from stage REM followed by a gross body movement. NREM recall was higher from the 5- as opposed to the 10-minute post-REMP awakenings. Although in both REMP conditions recall was quite high, the authors did not present specific data that a gross body movement was associated with the "natural" end of a dream scenario. Rather, the lower incidence of REMP recall succeeding such movements was understood by the authors to be a sign of completion of a previous dream event sequence and of very rapid memory decay.

These results are partly consistent with Dement and Wolpert (1958b), who found apparently unrelated fragments were associated with electrographic evidence of body movements. Of the 10 REMP awakenings that were performed just after a gross body movement, 3 yielded no content, 3 provided usual REMP dreams, and 4 contained spontaneous comments very suggestive of completion of dream episodes ("I had just come to the end of a dream"). Dement and Wolpert (1958a) concluded that body movements during dreams tend to signal a change in dream activity or termination of an event sequence.

Small Movements

REM sleep is accompanied by much fine-muscle activity, some, but not all, of which is related to concurrent dream activity. Also, dreamed motor activity need not be reflected in the EMG. Wolpert (1960) found, in some subjects only, that there was an impressive relationship between specific EMG patterns and specific dream content just before awakening. Anecdotal reports of Dement (1972) and McGuigan and Tanner (1970) replicated the findings.

The most systematic attempt to study this issue was made by Grossman et al. (1972) and a comprehensive review of motor patterns in human sleep has been published by Gardner and Grossman (1976). Ten young adult subjects who were good dream recallers were observed for 4 to 8 nights in the laboratory, during which REMP awakenings were carried out. Reports were independently judged for dreamed muscular movements. The movements of each upper and lower extremity were separately monitored. When both upper and lower extremities were active, the mean number of movements was 2.15; when either upper or lower extremity girdle was active, the mean was 1.16; and when none was active, the mean was 0.89. The last value indicates that many false positives (EMG activity without concomitant dreamed movement) occurred. An analysis of variance revealed, however, that despite the false positives, the results given here were significant.

In a second analysis, more upper than lower extremity dreamed actions occurred after upper extremity preawakening movements; the converse was true with subjects with lower extremity movements. It was concluded that a significant relationship exists between actual and dreamed action with respect to amount and girdle location.

THE WAKING STATE

One method that has been used to clarify the relationship between physiological and psychological events is the study of mentation collected from different sleep stages. The literature on sleep-stage correlates of mentation has been reviewed in Chapters 3, 7, and 16. This section reviews literature on waking.

The waking state has generally been assumed to provide a baseline index for rational-reality-oriented nondreamlike mentation. Foulkes and Fleisher (1975), impressed by surprising results from an earlier study (Foulkes & Scott, 1973), attempted to systematically look at cognition during relaxed wakefulness. Twenty subjects were questioned during 45- to 60-minute sessions on their last mental experience at intervals from 1 to 9 minutes about the prevalent modality (auditory or visual) of their thought, and whether they believed the experience was really happening, they were just thinking, they were aware of being in the laboratory, and they were voluntarily controlling their thoughts. Subjects were monitored on EEG and EOG during the sessions. Reports were judged for regressivity of content. Of 120 arousals, 118 yielded reports of content. Of these, 68% yielded some type of visual imagery and 16% involved auditory imagery experiences. Endogenous imagery was reported as having hallucinatory qualities in 19% of the "awakenings." Following Vogel, Foulkes, and Trosman (1966), Foulkes and Fleisher (1975) quantified the regressive quality of the reports. They evaluated two functions: maintaining contact with reality, and maintaining nonregressive content. Neither function was found to be invariably present in waking mentation. One-quarter of the reports were judged to be regressive and about 50% of the reports showed a lack of reality contact. Hallucinatory ideation and regressive ideation were relatively independent report characteristics.

EEG activity and EOG patterns were examined in relation to the mental content of the reports. All EEG and EOG patterns indicated that subjects were awake, except for one EOG pattern with slow eye movements, which can be seen at sleep onset. However, this pattern was quite rare.

Singer (1976) suggested that the subjects were oriented toward regressive and hallucinatory mentation by being told that this was a sleep study. Kripke (1972) for example, had shown that the 10- to 20-cycle-per-day oscillations expressed during sleep by the cyclic occurrent of REM periods may be preset during waking. Lavie and Kripke (1975) also reported periodicity of daytime fantasy, and it is therefore possible that the Foulkes and Fleisher (1975) data reflected ultradian rhythmic effects in interaction with other wakefulness factors.

However, the idea of waking mentation as a baseline is brought into question if a high percentage of waking thought shows characteristics of dream mentation when assessed by identical scales and if demonstrated differences are primarily quantitative rather than qualitative. Perhaps dreams are better conceptualized as the end point on a continuum and the dream state could be tapped in a variety of ways, including meditation, hypnosis, introspections, and relaxed wakefulness.

CHANGES OF DREAM CONTENT

Czaya, Kramer, and Roth (1973) studied the pattern of the development of a REM dream. They woke 4 male subjects at varying intervals during the second and fourth REMP of the night. Self-rated emotion, recall, anxiety, and pleasantness showed significant linear increases in intensity as a function of time, as did clarity. For emotion, anxiety, and pleasantness, in addition to a linear trend, there was a leveling-off and decline in intensity of the dream at 20 minutes, followed by an increase at 30 minutes. In an extension of their 1973 study (Kramer, Czaya, Arand, & Roth, 1974), all dream reports were rated by two independent judges. Content was scored for characters, descriptive elements, and activities using Hall and Van de Castle (1966) categories. Results were essentially the same, showing that the development of psychological parameters in the REMP is the same whether defined by subjects' rating of their experience, judges' ratings of content, or manifest scoring of content categories.

In summary, research has shown that there are significant differences in the development of certain parameters of dreams during the course of the REM period, while NREM dreams do not seem to undergo similar intensification (Tracy & Tracy, 1974).

DREAMING AT DIFFERENT TIMES OF THE NIGHT

Various physiological parameters of sleep (REMP length, REM density, body temperature, and quantity of delta sleep) reliably covary with time of night. Since relationships between these physiological variables and dream content have been hypothesized, it is important to know how time of night independently relates to dream content in order to assess its possibly confounding effects. More theoretically, Freud (1955a/1900) had argued that the cessation of sensory input during sleep permitted the retrieval of early memories in the form of images. The obvious corollary is that more regressed memories would occur after greater or more prolonged blocking of external sensory input, hence later in the night.

Based on these notions, Verdone (1965) studied intraindividual differences in the temporal reference of manifest dream content, with respect to amount of time spent in bed, physiological variables, and aspects of dream content, such as vividness and emotionality. Verdone awakened subjects 5 and 12 minutes after REMP onset. The subjects self-rated their mentation upon awakening on goodness of recall, plausibility, and several aspects of temporal referents. Body temperature and heart rate were recorded every 2 minutes in REM sleep.

Dream reports whose elements were relatively recently encountered in reality by the subjects were labeled contemporary reference (CR); reports whose content corresponded to more remote events were labeled noncontemporary reference (NCR). NCR versus CR status was also evaluated with respect to the "age of the single oldest element in a dream." Ratings of all variables (including time in bed) were dichotomized around each subject's median, so that NCR reports did not represent a "qualitatively unique entity." The relationships among the dichotomized ratings of sleep and dream variables were assessed using the Cochran test.

Significantly more NCR reports were elicited later in the night. NCR reports were also significantly related to goodness of recall, vividness, implausibility, emotionality of dream reports, and total amount of REM activity in the REMP and in the last 2 minutes of the REMP. Prior duration of REM sleep within a specific REMP was not significantly associated with temporal reference. Significantly more well-recalled, vivid, and emotional dreams were elicited relatively later in the night. Thus, dreams reported later in the night were more regressed with respect to temporal reference and more dreamlike in the sense of Foulkes (1966). However, the small number of subjects and disregard of correlations between variables across subjects make these results less generalizable. Verdone (1965) noted that, because of the dichotomizing of variables, it is not possible to assess the linearity of the relationships obtained. In response to this problem, he plotted curves for temporal reference against time in bed. The following trends were visible: during the first 3.5 hours of the sleep period dream reports referred to elements encountered in reality in the last week; during the next 4 hours, temporal reference moved back in time toward more remote events following a negatively accelerated curve, until approximately 7.5 hours of the sleep period had elapsed, when a reversal of this trend occurred toward more recent temporal reference.

As part of an effort to better understand the sources of difference between REM and NREM mentation, Pivik and Foulkes (1968) awoke 20 male subjects on 2 nights, 4 awakenings per subject, spread across the night. The first awakening was 30 minutes after sleep onset; each subsequent awakening was made 30 minutes after the first, second, and third REMPs, respectively. Mentation was scored on the Foulkes DF scale. The authors asserted that both recall and DF ratings increased with time of night and concluded that late-night NREM mentation reports are not very different from early-night REMP reports. However, since no REMP reports were collected from these subjects and no statistical analysis of the relationship between mentation quality and time of night was presented, it is difficult to assess the meaning of these data with respect to the issue of progressive or continuous changes in mentation quality with time into the sleep cycle. Furthermore, the possible effect of time of night is confounded with sleep stage in Pivik and Foulkes's (1968) study, in that stage 4 awakenings predominated for the first NREM awakening of the night and were virtually absent from later awakenings. Data are available that support Pivik and Foulkes's (1968) conclusion that stage 2 mentation reports from the latter portion of the night are more dreamlike than those elicited earlier (Chapter 13 in the first edition).

In summary, we feel that little can be said firmly about the changes in mentation quality across the night, except that the first awakening, be it REM or NREM, produces less dreamlike mentation than the second.

THE TIME INTERVAL IN DREAMS

How long does a dream take? Until modern electrographic research, the generally accepted answer was that what was experienced as an extended time interval in dreams corresponded to an actual process that was completed almost instantaneously. This opinion was largely based upon an anecdote related by Maury (1861) about one of his own dreams in which he had been watching condemned people being guillotined. His turn came to mount the scaffold and at the moment of feeling the blade on the back of his neck, he awoke in terror only to find that the top of the bed had fallen, struck him on the back of the neck, exactly as had the blade in the dream, and awakened him. He inferred that the entire dream had taken place between the time the falling bed had struck his neck and the time of his awakening—a fraction of a second.

Not until the research of Dement and Kleitman was there solid evidence of a positive relationship between the length of actual dream experience and the length of electrographic evidence of dream experience. Subjects were awakened either 5 or 15 minutes after REMP onset and asked to decide from their dream experience whether they had been awakened after 5 or 15 minutes of dreaming. Four out of 5 subjects were able to guess correctly with highly significant accuracy. There were also significant correlations in all 5 subjects between the word count of the dream narrative (an index of dream duration) and the 5- versus 15-minute REMP awakening categories.

Koulack (1968) attempted to determine the frequency with which percutaneous subawakening—threshold electric shocks to the median nerve—were incorporated into the REM experience. The procedure entailed stimulating the sleeper either immediately after or 3 minutes after the stimulation for mentation. If there was clear evidence that the stimulus had been incorporated into the dream events, the subject was then asked to estimate whether the dream-incorporated event had occurred 30 seconds or 3 minutes prior to the awakening buzzer. Of the 12 instances where the presence of the stimulus could be clearly identified, 92% of the subjects' judgments correctly corresponded to the actual time interval between stimulation and awakening.

Thus, the evidence points to the conclusion that the time sense in dreams corresponds to time intervals in reality over a considerable temporal range.

Sequential Dreams

To what extent are the contents of dreams of the same night or across nights related? We would expect some degree of consistency between waking adaptations and defenses and those in sleep because the same person produces both, as Offenkrantz and Rechtschaffen (1963) have noted. Yet several questions remain. If a night's dreams do center around a psychological conflict, why would they be represented so variously? And why are certain contexts chosen over others?

Dement and Wolpert (1958a) collected 38 REM dream sequences from 8 subjects. Their criterion for relatedness was the appearance of identical or similar characters, plots, actions, environments or emotions. Within the 38 sequences, each dream seemed to be a relatively self-contained production, somewhat independent of its precedent or consequent dream. Nevertheless, the manifest content of nearly every dream showed some obvious relationship to one or more dreams on the same night. Considerations of dream content on an individual basis may not reveal a common underlying theme, which emerges when the entire sequence is examined. Despite the degree of relatedness observed, the authors stated that one cannot conclude that this relatedness is the norm outside of the laboratory. They hypothesized that the mentation awakening report provides "day residue" material for the next dream.

Trosman, Rechtschaffen, Offenkrantz, and Wolpert (1960), studying the dream sequences of 2 subjects intensively, concluded that within nights, unambiguous relationships among the contents of reports were rarely observed. However, across nights, the appearance of unique features of similar points in a sequence, lateral similarities between events from one night

to the next, and the combination of similar qualititative dimensions suggested an organization of REM mentation into regular patterns. Lateral
similarities were also noted by Offenkrantz and Rechtschaffen (1963). Finally, assessment of "latent" dream content through the use of psychological tests, subjects' associations following awakenings, and the authors'
psychodynamic inferences also suggested cyclic relationships. However,
the authors' conclusion that there is a recurring nightly sequence of tension
accumulation due to psychic conflict, discharge, and attempted conflict
resolution is based on posthoc analyses. A similar sequence was noted by
Breger, Hunter, and Lane (1971) in a study of the effect of stress on REM
dreams. Offenkrantz and Rechtschaffen (1963), basing their conclusions on
the posthoc analysis of one intensively studied individual, agreed with
Trosman et al.'s (1960) sequence, claiming it is "correlated" with a psychological sequence in which the organization of a particular dream seems to
depend on the results of the dream work of the preceding dream.

Rechtschaffen, Vogel, and Shaikun (1963) studied the interrelationship
of both REM and NREM content. They looked only at obvious relationships
among the manifest content—identities or repetitions of manifest themes
or elements. Because there is no way to judge the baseline occurrence
of the elements, statistical procedures were impossible, and the authors
relied on a common-sense judgment of whether the probabilities of the
co-occurrence of elements exceeded randomness. They found that identical or closely related content elements were often repeated in reports from
NREM awakenings throughout the night. Specific manifest elements
from NREM awakenings were reported in accounts from REMP awakenings and vice versa. Moreover, the identical or closely similar elements
appeared in different contexts, and thus cannot be dismissed as recall of
previous reports since they were not part of a continuous story. Some
elements appeared initially during NREM sleep, prior to the first REMP—
thus providing evidence that NREM images need not be recalled from
previous REMPs. To follow up these results, Rechtschaffen, Vogel, and
Shaikun (1963) compared REM and NREM mentation. Although results
were less striking than the previous study (perhaps because subjects were
not chosen on the basis of their having good NREM recall), in several
subjects there were unique NREM elements that recurred in different contexts at different times of the night.

In sum, several factors speak against the possibility that recurring elements are merely recollections of earlier reports. First, there are wide
differences in the mentation contexts of each item repetition. Second,
dreams referring to the subject rendering aloud a mentation report are
rare, although it is an invariant, repetitive, prominent occurrence in all the
experiments. If repetitive elements were recollections of reporting, we
would expect that dreams of the subject talking into a microphone would
be more common.

In conclusion, Rechtschaffen, Vogel, and Shaikun (1963) stated that the manifest structure of sleep mentation is marked both by an apparent lack of observable connections between different episodes of mental activity on some nights and by the repetition of elements in varying contexts in different episodes on other nights. On those nights when themes and images persist through both NREM and REM periods, the dreams do not arise *sui generis* as psychologically isolated mental productions but emerge as the most vivid and memorable part of a larger fabric of interwoven mental activity during sleep.

A number of general criticisms lessen the scientific validity of these studies, namely the small sample sizes, the use of posthoc analyses, and the less than optimally reliable methods of rating the dreams.

DREAM SEQUENCES AND DREAM MEANING

Kramer, Hlasny, Jacobs, and Roth (1975) and Roth, Kramer, and Arand (1976) attempted to prove that dreams have meaning and possess some kind of orderliness. They reasoned that if dreams have meaning for the individuals within a group (traitlike component) and within an individual at different times (statelike component), then dreams should be psychologically related to the individual's current wakeful concerns.

Judges, who were provided with randomized series of REM dreams obtained from several different subject populations, were asked to sort the dreams: (a) so that the REM reports would correspond to their actual sequence of occurrence both within and across nights; and (b) so that all the dreams of one individual would be together. Results indicated that, overall, these two sorts were possible. This implied that dreams have stable traitlike features and statelike features. In another study, the experimenters demonstrated positive correlations between content ratings of REM mentation and those of contiguous wakeful mentation. This implied that dreams were related to wakeful life in an orderly manner.

These results remain both intriguing and puzzling. The work on sequential content of dreams (see previous section) showed that while relationships were often discernible across nights, this was by no means as regular an occurrence as these studies suggest. Perhaps, if Kramer et al. (1975) and Roth et al. (1976) had provided us with the specific cues the judges utilized, the apparent inconsistency could be resolved.

DREAM INTERRUPTION AND MEANING

Among the experimental approaches to the issue of meaning in dreams, an interesting technique has been to measure dream content changes if the dreamer were repeatedly frustrated in his attempts to complete his fantasy. Rechtschaffen and Verdone (1964) repeatedly awakened subjects 3 minutes after REMP onset and found evidence of "mounting frustration, hostility and paranoia" about not being permitted to complete "tasks" recurrently depicted in dreams. The investigators noted the interrupted sequences tended (more so than completed REM dreams) to depict striving to overcome obstacles to dream event completion. No statistical data were given.

Fiss, Klein, and Schollar (1974) also reported differences between interrupted and completed dreams. Although dream reports following interrupted REMPs were equal in length to dream reports after completed REMPs, they were more vivid, dramatic, emotional, and conflictful, and seemed to facilitate the emergence of unconscious material. In addition, they were less bizarre, narrated with greater articulate clarity, and accompanied by more intense REM activity, less frequent body movement, stage 2 "intrusions," and alpha bursts. Fiss et al. (1974) concluded that REM sleep and dreaming are two functionally dissimilar organismic states. Because the interruption in REM time was slight, they assumed that the experience of dreaming was what mattered most and that the dream was squeezed into a shortened REM period. Results were interpreted as indicating a need to complete a psychological task. However, Fiss and co-workers' assumption that dream physiology and psychology are independent is unwarranted. Their interrupted REMP procedure clearly led to more physiologically intense REM periods. One might easily hypothesize that it was the alteration in physiological patterning that influenced the dream's intensity and not the reverse.

AUDITORY-AROUSAL THRESHOLDS

Zimmerman's (1970) study of sleep mentation and auditory-arousal thresholds (AAT) examined individual differences in relation to both the amount of and qualitative differences in NREM mentation. Sixteen subjects were assigned to a light-sleeper group (LSG) based on previously determined auditory arousal thresholds, and 16 subjects were assigned to a deep-sleeper group (DSG). They were awakened for mentation reports twice during REM sleep and twice during NREM sleep. After each mentation report, subjects responded to a questionnaire measuring 16 dream content dimensions. Two independent judges also rated the mentation reports on an expanded questionnaire that included measures of aggression, sexuality, and imaginativeness.

For both the judges' and the subjects' ratings, differences in the REM mentation of the LSG versus DSG were negligible. Although all subjects after all NREM awakenings claimed to have experienced prior mentation, the LSG subjects reported *dreaming* after NREM awakenings significantly more often than the DSG subjects. Among LSG subjects, REM and NREM mentations were not statistically different on the dimensions of dreaming versus thinking, perceptual versus conceptual, volitional control, awareness of presence in bed, belief in the reality of the sleep experience, and distortion of dream content. By contrast, the REM–NREM differences on each of these dimensions among DSG subjects were significant.

Zimmerman proposed that dreaming is a function of cerebral arousal in the absence of reality contact and that dreamlike mentation occurs whenever cerebral-arousal levels exceed a certain critical point. Arousal levels below this critical point are deemed sufficient to produce thoughtlike mentation. Although both kinds of sleep entail loss of reality contact, stage REM is more conducive to dreaming than NREM sleep because of its much more intense cerebral arousal, plus greater occlusion of reality, whereas arousal levels of NREM are generally lower and more variable.

Did Zimmerman's (1970) study support his conclusions? Baseline arousal levels of LSG subjects seemed significantly higher than those of the DSG. This was shown by their low auditory-arousal threshold, greater frequency of spontaneous awakenings in undisturbed sleep, greater frequency of gross body movements, faster resting heart and respiratory rates, and higher body temperatures (Zimmerman, 1967), as well as by LSG subjects' evidencing of strikingly more and vivid NREM dreaming than the DSG. Among the subjects of Zimmerman's (1970) study, if one tried to make a prediction as to whether a report was from REM or NREM sleep, significantly better results would accrue by taking the LSG versus DSG criteria into account, than on the basis that REM equals dreaming and NREM equals not dreaming. However, only by taking the interaction of AAT with subject variables into account could accurate prediction be made as to which sleep stage mentation originated from. This finding is in agreement with Cartwright (1972) and Pivik and Foulkes (1968), who noted other relevant individual difference parameters that influence mentation.

THE PÖTZL PHENOMENON

In their original work on peripheral stimulation, Pötzl, Allers, and Teler (1960/1917) showed pictures to subjects and found that there is a delayed entry into consciousness of those parts of the picture not consciously perceived at the time of stimulus reception. These originally unconscious elements will usually manifest in an altered state of consciousness. Pötzl claimed that three factors determine later dream formation: a sensory factor, which is the unconscious registration and fragmentation of the percept; a motor factor dealing with the role of incomplete eye movements; and a symbolic factor, similar to Freud's (1955a/1900) concept of an unconscious wish.

Fisher (1959), in a partial replication of Pötzl's work, exposed subjects to geometric forms, 4-digit numbers, or words at a speed of .001 second. After exposure, subjects were given a period during which they drew their images. They were then asked to make comparisons between their drawings and the percepts. Some were also given suggestions to dream.

Basically, the drawn images had one of three characteristics. They were occasionally photographic or distorted representations of the preconscious percepts resulting from tachistoscopic presentation. Images could also be condensations of a childhood memory with the exposed figure. Fisher concluded that both the visual raw material for later dreams, as well as the latent dream thoughts, were present in the imagery period after the stimuli were shown.

On the basis of his findings, Fisher expanded Freud's original notion of day residue to include sensory events and environmental stimuli. While Freud (1955a/1900) believed that an unconscious wish cannot emerge into consciousness unless it is covered by day residue, Fisher added that visual scenes associated with the unconscious wish will fuse with the preconscious visual percepts associated with the day residue. The day residue percepts are not repressed because they were never capable of entering consciousness.

Fisher's revised model is as follows: During the day, in temporal association with the day-residue thoughts, there are percepts. Some immediately attain consciousness. Others are retained in the preconscious, incorporated as memory images. Still other percepts attain consciousness, lose attention cathexis, and fall back to the preconscious. Simultaneously, the unconscious wish makes contact with the day-residue thoughts and the surrounding subthreshold or peripheral imagery. The intensity of the unconscious wish is transferred to these images and they undergo distortion. During sleep there is a second activation of the unconscious wish and an arousal of some of the same memory images associated with the wish during the day. These images are the raw material for the sensory structure of the dream and are fused and condensed with infantile-memory images. They attain consciousness in a delayed and fragmented manner when they reach hallucinatory intensity.

DREAMS AND ESP

Freud (1953a/1922) had made observations on patients in treatment that strongly suggested the possibility that telepathic phenomena could become manifested in dreams. Ullman and Krippner (1974) published positive findings in support of the hypothesis. Briefly, the typical experimental design has involved 2 subjects: an agent and a receiver. The receiver sleeps in the laboratory in the standard manner. The agent, isolated in a separate room, selects one of 12 sealed envelopes, each of which contains a small reproduction of a well-known painting—the "target." The agent then gazes at the picture for about 30 minutes, writes down personal associations, and attempts to influence the receiver's dream content accordingly. The experimenter, unaware of the specific target selected by the agent, awakens the receiver 5 to 10 minutes after REMP onset and obtains a mentation report in the standard manner. The method of assessing the degree of correspondence between the target and the receiver's dreams involves the ranking, separately by the subject and 3 independent judges, of all 12 potential targets against the REMP mentation reports.

The findings have repeatedly demonstrated that such rankings are correct to a statistically significant degree. Furthermore, there are many anecdotal examples of striking correspondences between target and dream.

This work, like so much other research in the area of the paranormal, is intriguing and exciting but requires careful replication in other laboratories and by other investigators with positive results. Two attempts to replicate this work have not been encouraging. Globus, Knapp, Skinner, and Healy (1967) stated that they could find no substantial evidence in favor of ESP manifesting itself in dreams, but also indicated that posthoc analysis revealed some slightly suggestive evidence in favor of it. Belvedere and Foulkes (1971), on the other hand, reported an outright failure to replicate the findings of the Ullman and Krippner (1974) research.

NEW TRENDS IN MENTATION RESEARCH

In revising Chapter 6 from the previous edition, we realized that while it contained a vast compendium of reference information, there was little thematic continuity in the review of the studies of qualitative aspects of sleep mentation. While, in part, this reflected our editorial efforts, it also spoke to the paucity of models for dream content research up until 1978. Prior to this time, research was dominated by the exciting discovery of REM sleep, and the majority of studies were of psychophysiological parallelism. By 1982, however, Foulkes was to state:

> Psychophysiological correlational research now appears to offer such a low rate of return as not to be a wise place for dream psychology to continue its limited resources. Dreaming is a mental process and it must be studied as we now study other mental processes. Whatever the brain events accompanying dreaming, what the dream is is a mental act. (pp. 249–250)

Of course, this view did not go unchallenged, and studies of the isomorphism between physiological and psychological events were undertaken, although far less frequently than in earlier years (Kushniruk, Rustenberg, &

Ogilvie, 1985; Moffitt et al., 1983). Hobson and McCarley (1977) took a diametrically opposed view to cognitively oriented researchers, claiming that dreaming was an epiphenomenon, a random synthesis of neurological activity that could tell us little about cognition or the specific meaning of the dream to the dreamer. In a somewhat different vein, Herman and Roffwarg and colleagues (Herman, Erman, Boys, Peiser, Taylor & Roffwarg, 1984; Roffwarg, Herman, & Lamstein, 1975) continued to report positive one-to-one correspondence between eye movement activity or middle-ear muscle activity and dream content.

In general, in an effort to develop a psychology of the dream itself, dream content research since 1978 has moved toward the study of cognitive factors in dream formation. We report here on several lines of research that seem representative of new directions in the areas of sleep stage differences, self-representation in dreaming, and dream ontogeny.

Sleep Stage Differences

Differences between REM and NREM sleep are no longer examined in terms of dream content (i.e., vividness, bizarreness, or the relative presence or absence of primary process material). Rather, researchers inspect formal properties of mentation from different sleep stages. These properties are not reliant on subjective judgments such as "dreamlikeness," but can be defined by overt features of the report.

Antrobus (1983) attempted to compare several word frequency measures of characteristics of REM and NREM dream reports. His thesis was that the fundamental cognitive dissimilarities between REM and NREM sleep are differences in attention and memory consolidation, while differences in visual imagery, self-participation, and anxiety are secondary.

REM/NREM report pairs were scored for total recall frequency, visual nouns, visual modifiers, visual action, spatial relations, explicit speech, implicit speech, waking perception, dream participation, and global dreaming. Antrobus found that a simple word-count measure discriminated REM from NREM reports as well as global ratings of dreaming. While incremental repeated-measures multivariate tests showed that global measures of dreaming contributed some unique variance to the REM/NREM discrimination, the unique portions were very small. He concluded that the cognitive differences between REM and NREM lie in the ability of the subject to recall and describe what was experienced prior to awakening. Visual imagery and dreaming are seen as characteristic of all drowsy cognition. In REM a subject simply remembers more images than in other sleep stages.

Foulkes and Schmidt (1983) also attempted to distinguish mentation from different stages of sleep. Twenty-three adult women each slept for 3 nonconsecutive nights in the laboratory, and had 4 awakenings per night from the REM, NREM, or the sleep onset period. After giving a spontaneous report, subjects were questioned as to the order of the reported dream events. Judges scored the reports for activity units (whatever activities could have occurred synchronously and were not described successively), setting, and characters.

Previous findings of interstage differences in dream recall and length were replicated. A sample of 18 REM, 12 NREM, and 15 SO dreams that excluded any purely thoughtlike or single-unit reports were examined for thematic continuity/discontinuity, character density (the proportion of units for which the self or other character was scored), the percentage of units without a scored setting, the percentage of units lacking both a scored setting and scored character, the mean number of temporal units for which a setting persisted, and the mean number of units for which a character persisted. The authors concluded that although REM reports usually contain more temporal units, when NREM reports have as many temporal units, they are very similar to REM reports. Thus, many interstage differences in mentation are secondary to stage differences in dream length; it is unnecessary to postulate different dream production systems to account for these dissimilarities.

However, even when reports were matched for length, there were residual stage differences. Characterization (defined as the per-unit representation of self or others) was the central differentiating feature of REM reports, and we agree with the authors that this would be an unlikely candidate for selective forgetting and that differences in the accessibility of memory alone could not account for this finding. Foulkes and Schmidt (1983) argued that either memory is organized differently on arousals from different stages or there are true qualitative differences in what is available to memory on these arousals.

Several studies (Cavallero, 1987; Cavallero & Cicogna, 1984; Cicogna, Cavallero, & Bosinelli, 1986) addressed themselves to the controversy raised by Antrobus (1983) and Foulkes and Schmidt (1983): Are differences in stage characteristics attributable to memory processes or to a different availability of mnemonic sources for the process of dream production? Interestingly, in these studies, the use of free association has been revived, not in order to reveal underlying dream meaning but rather as a method for gathering information on memorial processes associated with dreaming.

Cicogna et al. (1986) postulated that the differences between SO and REM reports are due to the nature of the mnemonic material that is available when a dream is generated. Following Vogel (see Chapter 3) they hypothesized that during sleep onset there would be significant disorganization and a subsequent attempt at cognitive reorganization using available memory traces. This led to the prediction that references to autobiographical episodes would be more frequent in SO than in REM and that free association referring to autobiographical episodes would be more frequent than other types of memory traces during SO.

A total of 20 REM and 20 SO reports from 10 male subjects were used. After a standard mentation interview, the experimenter replayed the recorded dream to the subject. Each single thematic unit (defined as a brief dream segment that expressed a concept or action that appeared complete) was replayed separately and the subject offered associations. Associations were classified into: (a) strict episodes (discrete episodes in the life of the dreamer with precise spatiotemporal coordinates); (b) abstract self-references (memory traces not connected to any particular spatiotemporal context); and (c) semantic traces (elements of general knowledge of the world).

Results replicated earlier findings of quantitative differences in SO and REM in dream length. SO and REM elicited similar amounts of associative material. There was a significant interaction between sleep stage and the type of memory trace activated. Strict episodes were significantly more frequent in SO than in REM; abstract self-references were significantly more frequent in REM than in SO; semantic traces showed no significant differences. The distribution of memory types within the two stages also differed: During sleep onset, strict episodes were significantly more frequent than abstract self-references and semantic traces. Within REM there were not significant differences among memory categories.

The authors interpreted their results as supporting the hypothesis of a differing availability of memory traces in SO and REM, as recall differences alone would not account for stage-specific selectivity in the types of memory traces.

Cavallero (1987) examined whether the relationships between sleep stages and specific types of memorial processes would persist over time. If delayed associations to SO and REM dreams still differed in terms of memory categories, it would suggest that observed differences reflected dissimilarities in the structure and content of the SO and REM reports rather than in the mnemonic elements involved in the production of the two types of dreams. Cavallero did not find that differences in memory categories continued over time. Rather, far fewer associations of all types were given to dreams replayed to the subject after a delay of 2 months from the original mentation collection. In particular, strict episodes were retained less than any other types of memories. Thus, after a delay, there were no differences between REM and SO reports in the types of associative memories accessed. The author concluded that the temporal distance from the stimulus event had a determining influence on the possibility of access to the mnemonic sources of the dream, and that memories are reorganized under the sway of intervening new experiences.

In sum, recent research supports the idea that there are different cognitive correlates of sleep onset and REM. In many cases, these differences are attributable to differences in report length; however, there are also nontrivial differences (i.e., in characterization and the access to specific types of memories) that cannot be attributed merely to report length.

Self-Representation in Dreaming

Several authors (Bosinelli, Cavallero, & Cicogna, 1982; Purcell, Mullington, Moffitt, Hoffman, & Pigeau, 1986; Weinstein, Schwartz, & Ellman,
1989) have attempted to examine differences in self-representation and
self-reflectiveness (an awareness of dreaming while it is ongoing) during
different sleep stages.

Bosinelli et al. (1982) used Foulkes's (1982) Scoring System for Latent
Structure (SSLS) to study the degree of self-participation in dreams reported
during SO and REM. Foulkes's complicated technique of identifying and
scoring the discrete elements of dream reports is a psychodynamic and psycholinguistic system meant to be applicable both to the manifest content and
to free association in dreams. The SSLS subdivides the dream reports into
linguistic units. Because of its complexity, the system will not be reviewed in
this chapter; however, it does represent an exciting effort to wed cognitive
theory with more classical Freudian ideas. However, as Bosinelli et al.'s
(1982) study shows, it is an extremely difficult system to operationalize.

Bosinelli hypothesized that the level of Ego activity would be greater in
REM than in SO, that the ratio of interactive sentences (those where the
verb indicates the presence of relative movement between the subject and
the object of the relationship) with the Ego present would be different in
REM than in SO, and that the ratio between interactive sentences with the
Ego not present and interactive sentences with the Ego present would be
significantly different in REM and SO. None of these predictions was borne
out. The authors did find that the relative incidence of a defective Ego
(defined as an interactive sentence where the Ego is personally involved as
a subject, but where the object of the action is not knowable), was greater in
SO than in REM. As the authors state, it is difficult to interpret these
findings without an analysis of the structure of free associations accompanying these states.

The data contradicted Bosinelli, Cicogna, and Molinari (1973), who
found a significant difference in self-participation between phasic REM
reports and SO reports. The discrepancy was attributed to changes in
methodology: in the initial study a global score was assigned to the last
element in the dream; in the later study the frequency with which specific
sentences appeared in the report was the unit of analysis. In addition, the
later study did not differentiate REM-phasic from REM-tonic awakenings.

Purcell et al. (1986) had college students who were high in dream recall
and students who were low in dream recall sleep in the lab. They made a
total of 4 awakenings per night from REM, SO, or stage 4 sleep. Dreams
were scored for word count and given a rating on a 9-point scale of self-
reflectiveness (SR). REM dreams showed greater SR than SO dreams. High-
frequency recallers had higher SR scores than low-frequency recallers. The
overall correlation between word count and SR scale score was significant.

It was stronger for high-frequency recallers, but varied negligibly across sleep stages. Purcell et al. (1986) concluded that the SR scale is "a normally distributed continuous variable which can discriminate between dreams as a function of sleep stage and recall frequency and which is moderately correlated with an omnibus variable: report length in words" (p. 434). They felt that the SR scale contributed unique variance to the dream, because it reflected higher cognitive activity and self-awareness. Their data suggest that self-reflection is a different dimension than the more global "thoughtlike" reflection, since self-reflection is high in REM and lower in NREM, although NREM is usually seen as more thoughtlike. The authors also noted that recall frequency is an important variable, since good recallers had a higher frequency of SR in all sleep stages.

It is noteworthy that the two preceding studies were not measuring exactly the same phenomenon. Different aspects of self-observation were measured. A third study of self-reflection and its relation to sleep parameters is described in Chapter 11. Our own research suggests that there are also intrastage differences in subjects' awareness of their dream activity and in their feeling of self-participation in a hallucinatory experience. While the variable of self-reflection needs to be more consensually defined so that results from different studies are comparable, results to date suggest that the representation of the self in dreaming is a unique component of the dream experience, one that is separable from other factors such as dream-likeness or even simple word count. In addition, the relationship among recall, the accessibility of mnemonic traces, and the experience of the self in dreaming needs to be explored further. It may be that the integration of enhanced associative productions is one factor in recall. Fiss (1986) has also championed the study of the experience of the self in dreaming, albeit not from the perspective of sleep stage correlations, but as a bridge between the laboratory study of dreams and the clinical study of the Ego's attempts at adaptation and maintenance of self-cohesion.

Lucid Dreaming

Starting with Tart's (1979) paper on attempts to consciously control nocturnal dreaming, an entire literature has quickly grown examining the phenomena of "lucid" dreaming. The term refers to people being consciously aware that they are dreaming while the dream is ongoing. The literature on lucid dreaming has recently been reviewed by Gackenbach and LaBerge (1988), and no attempt will be made at comprehensive coverage here. The first major methodological problem of the study of lucid dreaming is the extent to which subjects understand the definition of lucid dreaming and the degree to which they can separate lucidity from a retrospective clarity upon morning recall. Particularly in the study of individual differences in lucid dreaming, subjects are often classified as to the frequency of lucid dreaming. Yet indices of home dream recall and dream diaries do not always correlate with lucid dreaming verified in the laboratory (Kueny, 1985). Finally, as Snyder and Gackenbach (1988) noted, such variables as social desirability response bias and dream recall frequency need to be used as covariates in any analysis so that spurious correlations with personality variables that correlate with social desirability can be ruled out.

Interestingly, the phrases used to verify lucidity (i.e., "I realized it was just a dream") bore considerable similarity to the processes we termed reflective self-awareness (Weinstein, Schwartz, & Ellman, 1988), namely, an awareness that one was having an internal, mental experience with no external referents. However, we found that during periods of phasic REM, there is a suspension of self-reflection—a state of mind directly opposite to that suggested by lucid dreaming. (Lucid dreaming shows a significant correlation with phasic REM and follows a parallel development to eye movement patterns within REM sleep; LaBerge, 1985). How could we reconcile this apparent contradiction? Chapter 11 reports on a series of studies suggesting that the tendency to suspend self-reflection (i.e., to be completely immersed in the dream) is a tendency that is determined both by the underlying physiological conditions at the time of the mentation report and by the preexisting personality characteristics of the subject. Subjects who tended to respond in a socially desirable manner were more likely to report that they knew they were dreaming, even when independent raters evaluating the same mentation reports judged the subject to be deeply immersed in the dream. We suggest that a tolerance for anxiety-producing thoughts discriminated those who responded to phasic activity with immersion in the experience; a relative intolerance for reporting anxiety-laden cognitions characterized those who were more reflective. In fact, high anxiety has been associated with lucid dreaming frequency for males (all of the subjects in our studies were male).

In sum, while lucid dreaming is a fascinating subject, individual difference variables such as social desirability response style and arousal and anxiety need to be carefully measured before the significance of this phenomenon can be clear.

DEVELOPMENTAL ASPECTS OF DREAM FORMATION

While some of Foulkes's work on children's dreams has been reviewed earlier, Foulkes's later emphasis (Foulkes, 1982) was an exploration of the relationship between cognitive development and dream ontogeny. The reader is referred to Foulkes (1982) for a more complete exposition of his thinking.

While at ages 3 to 4 high rates of REM dream reporting were associated with an expansive/expressive style, by ages 5 to 6, high rates of REM recall were correlated not with personality factors, but with cognitive variables, particularly tests measuring visuospatial aptitudes (i.e., block design, Kagan's Matching Familiar Figures). After this age, visuospatial tasks were more strongly correlated with REM report rate than verbal or memory measures. This pattern suggested to Foulkes that dream generation depends in part on specific cognitive skills, so that the cerebral activation of REM sleep can be accessed for the symbolic reconstruction of reality and the formation of dream narratives.

Dreaming, now defined as a cognitive act, is seen as part of overall cognitive maturation. A Piagetian framework is proposed where dreaming can begin only after the advent of symbolism in the middle preoperational period. Dreams from children in the 3- to 5-year age group exemplify the same cognitive limitations as their waking ideation, namely an inability to imagine transformations, a low degree of awareness of their own actions, a limited ability to construct narratives, and a tendency to focus on the immediate environment. Interestingly, Foulkes noted a developmental continuum in the ability to represent the self in dreams. It was only after children passed beyond egocentrism (during middle latency) that there was noteworthy self-participation in dreaming. In conclusion, dreaming is seen as continuous with waking cognitive development. Attempts to view children's REM mentation in terms of the parameters of adult dreams or in terms of wish fulfillment were not useful.

Some of the problems with Foulkes's work have been dealt with earlier. Let us briefly add that it might be useful to further analyze the qualitative nature of the visuospatial tasks that correlated with dream recall. For example, poor block design performance could reflect poor motor coordination, a deficit in abstract reasoning, a perceptual limitation, or a perceptual motor deficit. In addition, more complex visual memory measures that look at visual encoding, organization, and retrieval might be promising. However, Foulkes's work offers a new way to conceptualize a dream ontogeny and presents a Piagetian developmental perspective that supplements earlier Freudian notions.

CONCLUSION

A great deal has changed since we last reviewed sleep mentation studies. Previously, the literature was largely concerned with models of sleep physiology and mentation (i.e., the REM–NREM dichotomy or the phasic–tonic dichotomy). There was no psychological model of dream formation, apart from analytical formulations. In the ensuing years, researchers have made strides toward ameliorating this problem. A more process-oriented approach has come to the fore, and the relationship between psychological and cognitive variables without recourse to dream physiology has become more common. Particularly promising lines of research are those that explore the way self is cognized in dreaming, and the access to memorial associations in different sleep stages.

However, we wonder whether the pendulum has simply swung in the opposite direction. From a physiologically dominated model, we now are developing a pure psychological model. Yet one important question remains: How do different individuals cognize physiological events? This question cannot be answered outside of multifactor approach to dream formation, which examines both levels of a physiological stimulation and how such events are represented—by different individuals, with different psychological and cognitive makeups. An attempt at formulating such a model is presented in Chapter 16.

6

Tonic States and Phasic Events in Relation to Sleep Mentation*

R. T. PIVIK
University of Ottawa

Research fields often progress by a reconceptualization of known facts. Before sleep research embarked upon a new era in the early 1950s, sleep had been viewed as a unitary state. As data from the new research gradually accumulated, it became apparent that this monistic legacy would have to be discarded and replaced by a dualistic view of sleep. By the early 1960s, sleep was seen as the cyclic alternation between two states that

*Preparation of this paper was supported by grants from the United States Public Health Service (MH04151); the State of Illinois, Department of Mental Health (448-13-RD); and the Ontario Mental Health Foundation. The author gratefully acknowledges figures supplied by Dr. David Foulkes, Dr. Allen Rechtschaffen, and Dr. Howard Roffwarg. The author also acknowledges the helpful comments given by Dr. Rechtschaffen and Dr. Foulkes on earlier drafts of this chapter.

were physiologically and neuroanatomically distinct entities—rapid-eye-movement (REM) and non-rapid-eye-movement (NREM) sleep periods (Dement, 1964b; Hawkins, Puryear, Wallace, Deal, & Thomas, 1962; Jouvet, 1962; Snyder, 1963). Yet another manner of viewing sleep events was to emerge which took concrete form in Moruzzi's (1963, 1965) distinction between the long lasting, sustained (*tonic*) and short-lived, sporadic (*phasic*) events of REM sleep in the cat—a distinction which was subsequently expanded to include NREM sleep events as well (Grosser & Siegal, 1971).

In this chapter I review the development of sleep psychophysiology in the context of the state and tonic-phasic models with the intention of imposing some historical perspective on the empirical developments and providing a current view of progress made in the attempt to understand the mesh between the psychology and physiology of sleep.

THE REM–NREM DICHOTOMY

The new sleep research began in the spring of 1953 when Aserinsky and Kleitman announced their discovery of periods of physiological activation during sleep. Although this activation was evident in several physiological measures, its most striking manifestation was in the occurrence of peculiar rapid eye movements. This eye-movement activity was so prominent and characteristic of these episodes that they soon came to be called REM periods, and the remainder of sleep, NREM periods (Dement & Kleitman, 1957b). In the initial publications (Aserinsky & Kleitman, 1953, 1955; Dement, 1955), the physiological measures differentiating REM from NREM sleep apart from eye movements included a low-voltage EEG and increased heart and respiratory rate. Over the course of the next several years the physiological distinctions between the two kinds of sleep were more highly accentuated and the state boundaries more emphatically drawn. Thus, in contrast to NREM sleep, REM sleep showed marked activation in several systems, including changes in heart rate and regularity (Snyder, Hobson, Morrison, & Goldfrank, 1964), respiration (Aserinsky, 1965b; Snyder et al., 1964), blood pressure (Snyder, Hobson, & Goldfrank, 1963), brain temperature (Kawamura & Sawyer, 1965; Rechtschaffen, Cornwell, & Zimmerman, 1965; Reite & Pegram, 1968), and blood flow (Kanzow, Krause, & Kuhnel, 1962). In association with these signs of activation was a condition of tonic muscular and reflex inhibition (Berger, 1961; Hodes & Dement, 1964; Jacobson, Kales, Lehmann, & Hoedemaker, 1964; Pompeiano, 1966, 1967). Notable exceptions to the apparent static characterization of NREM sleep are the greater activation of the electrodermal response in the human during NREM Stages 3 and 4 relative to REM sleep (Asahina, 1962; Broughton, Poire, & Tassinari, 1965; Johnson & Lubin, 1966), and the episodic occurrence of sleepwalking and sleeptalking (Jacobson, Kales,

Lehmann, & Zweizig, 1965; Kales, Jacobson, Paulson, Kales, & Walter, 1966; Rechtschaffen, Goodenough, & Shapiro, 1962), and night terrors (Broughton, 1968) during these NREM stages of sleep.

Among the early studies which served to strengthen the REM–NREM dichotomy, one weighing most heavily was Dement's (1960a) dream-deprivation experiment. This study demonstrated that curtailment of REM sleep eventuated in the partial recuperation, or rebound, of the apparent REM sleep debt incurred by the deprivation procedure, thereby suggesting a need-fulfilling role for REM sleep.

The consensus of these data, bolstered by neuroanatomical evidence from animal studies (Jouvet, 1962; Jouvet, Dechaume, & Michel, 1960; Jouvet & Jouvet, 1963), was to overwhelmingly endorse a two-state tonic model of sleep, the full implications of which might be appreciated in the following characterization by Snyder (1966), "The physiological characteristics of this phenomenon prove so distinctive that I consider it a third state of earthly existence, the rapid eye movement or REM state, which is at least as different from sleeping and waking as each is from the other . . ." (p. 121).

MENTAL ACTIVITY AND TONIC SLEEP PHENOMENA

The psychological differences between REM and NREM sleep proved to be as dramatic as the physiological distinctions. The early studies (Aserinsky & Kleitman, 1953; Dement, 1955; Dement & Kleitman, 1957b; Dement & Wolpert, 1958b) found a high incidence of dream recall from REM sleep awakenings (greater than 70%), and a relative mental void in NREM sleep (consistently less than 10% recall). Even during this first wave of studies, however, some reports surfaced which suggested a considerable amount of NREM mentation (Goodenough, Shapiro, Holden, & Steinschriber, 1959). These reports continued to mount, so that by 1967, Foulkes was able to cite data from nine studies subsequent to 1959 across which NREM recall ranged from 23 to 74%. Part of the discrepancy in NREM recall values between the early and later studies could be attributed to differences in what investigators were willing to accept as a dream. Dement and Kleitman (1957b) demanded a coherent, fairly detailed description, whereas Foulkes (1960, 1962) and the majority of subsequent investigators have been willing to admit more fragmentary, less clear impressions of mentation as dreams. However, despite the consistency and strength of the NREM recall results, the reluctance of investigators to accept these data at face value remained widespread (Foulkes, 1967b). The reasons for this hesitancy were not without apparent empirical bases. For example, comparisons between REM and NREM mentation with respect to amount of recall and qualitative characteristics seemed to indicate an absolute, even fundamental, REM–NREM distinction. In addition to the quantitative data already cited, the greater degree of subject variability in the incidence and quality of NREM reports appeared to attest to the ephemeral nature of NREM mentation. However, REM–NREM differences in recall are usually presented in terms of average recall values which mask intersubject variability. A closer examination of the data reveals that there has always existed a great deal of subject variability in recall of mentation from both REM and NREM sleep. The early Dement and Kleitman (1957a) study had a range of REM recall values extending from 57.1 to 90%, with a median value of 80%. Subsequent studies have reported variability of comparable magnitude for REM recall, for example, Foulkes (1962) and Pivik (1971) have reported median recall values and ranges of 85%, 64–100% and 94.5%, 62.5–100%, respectively. With respect to NREM mentation, the latter two studies reported median recall values and ranges of 71%, 44–100% and 44.3%, 19–90.9%, respectively. These figures suggest that recall from REM sleep is not much less variable than that from NREM sleep. Although such variability was overlooked for REM recall, it served to emphasize the unreliability of NREM reports, thus contributing to the characterization of such reports as capricious or artifactual events.

Qualitative distinctions between REM and NREM reports do exist, and those differences which Foulkes noted in 1962 have been upheld by subsequent investigations (Foulkes & Rechtschaffen, 1964; Pivik, 1971; Rechtschaffen, Verdone, & Wheaton, 1963):

> Reports obtained in periods of REM activity showed more organismic involvement in affective, visual, and muscular dimensions and were more highly elaborated than non-REMP reports. REMP reports showed less correspondence to the waking life of the subjects than did reports from spindle and delta sleep. The relatively frequent occurrence of thinking and memory processes in spindle and delta sleep was an especially striking result. (Foulkes, 1962, pp. 24–25)

Although, as Foulkes (1962) indicated, NREM mentation is relatively more thoughtlike than that elicited from REM sleep, NREM reports of dreaming are as frequent (Goodenough, Lewis, Shapiro, Jaret, & Sleser, 1965) or more frequent (Bosinelli, Molinari, Bagnaresi, & Salzarulo, 1968; Foulkes, 1960, 1962; Pivik, 1971; Pivik & Foulkes, 1968; Rechtschaffen, Vogel, & Shaikun, 1963; Zimmerman, 1968) than NREM thinking reports. Nevertheless, the differences between reports from the two kinds of sleep are of sufficient magnitude that judges can discriminate between them, given that a method of paired comparison is used (Bosinelli et al., 1968; Monroe, Rechtschaffen, Foulkes, & Jensen, 1965). Exclusive attention to this REM–NREM discriminability neglects the degree of variation in incidence and quality which has been demonstrated among NREM sleep stages (Pivik, 1971; Pivik & Foulkes, 1968; Zimmerman, 1970). Most neglected in this respect is NREM sleep onset mentation, which compares favorably in incidence, hallucinatory dramatic quality, and length of report with REM mentation (Foulkes, Spear, & Symonds, 1966; Foulkes & Vogel, 1965; Vogel, Foulkes, & Trosman, 1966). Moreover, REM and sleep onset stage 1 reports share specific perceptual and emotional qualities which considerably blur the discriminability between them (Vogel, Barrowclough, & Giesler, 1972).

Investigators impressed with the differences between REM and NREM mentation offered various explanations for the latter, the most reasonable of which suggested that NREM reports were: recollections of mental activity from a previous REM period; artifacts of arousal, that is, hypnopompic experiences; or reports confabulated by subjects in an effort to please the investigator. In his review, Foulkes (1967b) was able to effectively counter each of these claims with empirical evidence which had been previously available. What, then, might be the reasons these data were ignored or slighted? Foulkes (1967b) listed three probable reasons which grew out of the then prevailing theoretical thinking:

1. While the low-voltage, random EEG of REM sleep is compatible with the existence of ongoing thought processes, the high-voltage, low-frequency EEG of NREM is not.

2. A report of a mental experience is not credible unless supported by public behavioral or physiological observation.

3. REM sleep is so vastly different physiologically from NREM sleep that there must also be a vast psychological difference between the two, such as vivid dreaming versus little or no mental activity.

It would seem that the first two statements could be considered variants of the third, suggesting that the REM physiology, perhaps in conjunction with the early reports indicating a unique relationship of REM sleep to dreaming, had been the primary restraining force behind the hesitancy of investigators to accept the reality of NREM mentation. In support of this notion, and of most direct relevance to the need for a public event to which Foulkes referred, is the observation that the most convincing arguments for the authenticity of NREM mentation come from situations in which the presence of preawakening stimuli, either naturally occurring (e.g., sleeptalking, Arkin, Toth, Baker, & Hastey, 1970b; Rechtschaffen et al., 1962) or experimentally induced (e.g., incorporations, Foulkes, 1967b; Foulkes & Rechtschaffen, 1964; Rechtschaffen, Vogel, & Shaikun, 1963), in postawakening NREM reports provides an event to which the mentation can be time locked.

The demand that observational psychological data conform to observable physiological events forced psychophysiologists to sift through the physiology of sleep in search of public physiological events with which to correlate and validate the already observed psychological data. One bonus which resulted from this search was a more complete and extensive description of the physiology of sleep.

PHYSIOLOGICAL CORRELATES OF MENTATION

The great variability in both incidence and quality of sleep mentation within sleep stages prompted investigators to look for physiological variations within sleep stages which might covary with the mentation. An extensive review of the current status of these psychophysiological correlations has been completed (Rechtschaffen, 1973), and it is more to the point of this chapter to concentrate on the distillates of that review than to duplicate the effort.

At a very general level, the EEG can be used as an index of both recall and quality of mental activity during sleep. Specifically, the more desynchronized the EEG, the greater the recall and the more dreamlike the recalled material. Thus, awakenings from low-voltage, mixed-frequency EEG (stage 1) are productive of the greatest amount of recall and recall of the most vivid and bizarre quality (Dement, 1955; Foulkes & Vogel, 1965; Vogel et al., 1966). Furthermore, with EEG slowing and increased voltage there is a corresponding decrease in recall (Pivik, 1971; Pivik & Foulkes, 1968) and the quality of the recalled material is generally less dreamlike (Pivik, 1971).[1] The positive correlation between degree of EEG activation and recall squares well with other work indicating increased recall across the night (Foulkes, 1960; Goodenough et al., 1959; Shapiro, Goodenough, & Gryler, 1963; Verdone, 1963), since there is a considerable reduction in the amount of slow-wave, high-amplitude activity in the second half of the night. This intrinsic confounding of sleep stage and time of night presents an enduring obstacle to attempts to arrive at independent correlations of either with sleep mentation. (See Fig. 6.1.)

At a more detailed level of analysis the deficiencies of the EEG correlation with recall and quality of sleep mentation are evident. As already pointed out, there is much variation in both the incidence and quality of mental activity within a sleep stage where a given EEG pattern is essentially constantly maintained. Likewise, where marked differences in EEG pattern exist, relatively slight differences in recall may be obtained. For example, two studies (Pivik, 1971; Pivik & Foulkes, 1968) report recall differences of only 6.3 and 7.3 percentage points, respectively, between stage 2 (spindles and K complexes on a low-voltage, mixed-frequency background EEG) and stage 3 (spindles and K complexes on a high-voltage,

---

[1]Tracy and Tracy (1974) have found, however, that differences in recall and qualitative differences in mentation between stages 2 and 4 become negligible when time within the stage prior to the awakening is controlled.

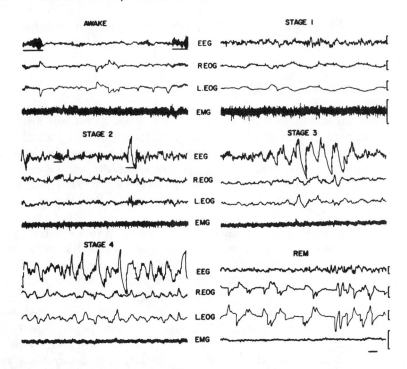

FIGURE 6.1. Representative samples of awake, NREM, and REM sleep EEG patterns with accompanying eye movement (EOG) and electromyographic (EMG) activity. The wakefulness pattern in this case consists of a low-voltage, mixed-frequency EEG upon which bursts of 8–12 cps alpha activity (underlined) are periodically superimposed. Rapid eye movements and highly activated EMG are typical of wakefulness. Stage 1 is also characterized by a low-mixed-frequency voltage, mixed-frequency EEG, but the accompanying eye-movement patterns consist of slow, pendular movements. EMG activity may be at a level comparable to that of wakefulness, but generally undergoes a slight reduction at sleep onset. Prominent characteristics of stage 2 are the occurrence of 12–14 cps sleep spindles (underlined) and generally high-amplitude, biphasic K complexes (underlined). The EOG tracings of stages 2, 3, and 4 do not represent eye movement activity, but rather are reflections of EEG activity. The EMG patterns of these NREM sleep stages are subject to much variability, but their general reduction relative to that of wakefulness is typical. Outstanding in the EEG tracings of stages 3 and 4 is the occurrence of high-amplitude, slow (1–2 cps), delta-wave activity. The EEG and EOG patterns of REM sleep are similar to that of wakefulness, but the tonic EMG inhibition is unique to this stage of sleep. Calibrations: 1 sec; 50 μv.

low-frequency background EEG). Conversely, marked similarities in EEG patterns, as is the case for sleep onset stage 1 and REM sleep, may result in discriminable content reports (Vogel et al., 1972).

Recently, emphasis has been placed on another tonic EEG correlate of sleep mentation, namely, interhemispheric variations in EEG symmetry during sleep, particularly during REM sleep (Figs. 6.2 and 6.3). This approach

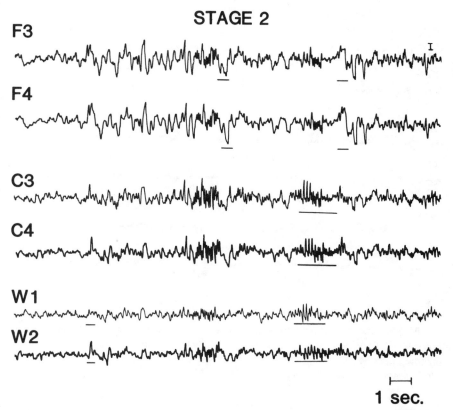

FIGURE 6.2. Asymmetries evident in homologous EEG recordings during stage 2 sleep prior to computer processing. Note the amplitude differences within homologous pairs (underscored) as well as amplitude differences across recording sites. Derivations: left and right frontal, central, and parieto-temporal (Wernicke's area), respectively, all referenced to linked mastoids. Calibration = 50μV. Reprinted by permission from R. T. Pivik, F. Bylsma, K. Busby, and S. Sawyer (Interhemispheric EEG changes: Relationship to sleep and dreams in gifted adolescents. *Psychiatric Journal of the University of Ottawa,* 1982, 7, 56–86).

draws on neurophysiological and psychophysiological studies in waking subjects in which it was demonstrated that specific cognitive processes are accompanied by differential hemispheric EEG activation. For example, linguistic and analytical processes are thought to be mediated by the left hemisphere, and visuospatial and holistic processes by the right hemisphere. Accordingly, during performance on selected spatial and verbal tasks, higher alpha amplitude has been reported over the right hemisphere on verbal tasks and over the left hemisphere on spatial tasks (Doyle, Ornstein, & Galin, 1974; Galin & Ornstein, 1972). Since alpha activity is considered to be inversely related to attention or effort, increased alpha activity is thought to indicate decreased cerebral involvement in a given task or behavior.

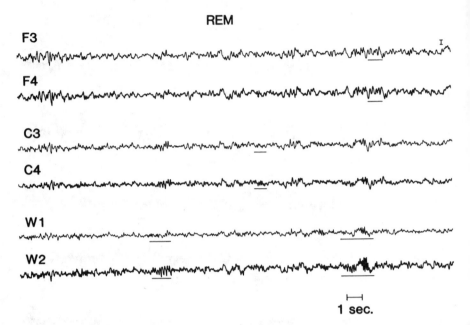

FIGURE 6.3.   Example of amplitude asymmetries (underscored) during REM sleep. Calibration = 50μV. Reprinted by permission from R. T. Pivik, F. Bylsma, K. Busby, and S. Sawyer (Interhemispheric EEG changes: Relationship to sleep and dreams in gifted adolescents. *Psychiatric Journal of the University of Ottawa*, 1982, 7, 56–86).

This concept of increased EEG power-indexing decreased cortical activation and, by inference, less hemispheric involvement, has been generalized to other EEG frequency bands and has been used to interpret studies utilizing total EEG power recorded from homologous sites. The application and interpretation of this approach to REM sleep-associated mentation reflects the perceived basis and general characterization of this mentation. If the REM dream is considered primarily as a series of perceptual events associated with and perhaps triggered by (Hobson & McCarley, 1977) neural elements with a heavy visuomotor loading, then it would be expected that REM sleep would be a right-hemisphere phenomenon, i.e., there would be greater activity of right hemispheric EEG during REM sleep (Broughton, 1975). If, however, the REM dream is viewed primarily as a cognitive, analytical event into which sensory expressions—largely visual—are incorporated, then during REM sleep greater activation of the left hemisphere should occur. Investigations seeking to characterize the lateralization of EEG activity during REM sleep have been inconsistent in their findings, with many affirming (Angeleri, Scarpino, & Signorino, 1984; Goldstein, 1979; Goldstein, Stoltzfus, & Gardocki, 1972; Hirshkowitz,

Turner, Ware, & Karacan, 1979; Hirshkowitz, Ware, & Karacan, 1980; Murri et al., 1984; Rosekind, Coates, & Zarcone, 1979), but with an increasing number failing to confirm (Antrobus, Ehrlichman, & Wiener, 1978; Cohen, 1977; Gaillard, Laurian, & Le, 1984; Herman, 1984; Moffitt et al., 1982; Pivik, Bylsma, Busby, & Sawyer, 1982) REM sleep as a right-hemisphere state. In response to inconsistencies in the nature of hemispheric activation of EEG assessed during REM sleep, Herman et al., (1983) have suggested that "perhaps EEG desynchronization is not the optimal method for observing the role of the right hemisphere in dreaming" (p. 177).

The majority of studies considering the issue of interhemispheric EEG balance during REM sleep have not related lateralized EEG measures to concomitant sleep mentation; that is, content arousals have not been made in most studies. Rather, the inference is made that dreaming is a consistent feature of this state. It is interesting, therefore, that with few exceptions (Angeleri et al., 1984) studies that have sought to characterize the lateralized nature of REM-sleep mentation have noted inconsistencies across subjects with respect to EEG activation correlates of visuospatial (right hemisphere) or verbal (left hemisphere) functioning at this time (Cohen, 1977; Moffitt et al., 1982; Pivik et al., 1982; Figures 6.4 and 6.5). The issues and interpretation of data derived from studies examining interhemispheric EEG balance during sleep are far from straightforward. For example, hemispheric balance during REM sleep may vary with subject characteristics, scalp recording sites, and EEG frequency band (Pivik et al., 1982). Furthermore, a lack of interhemispheric asymmetry has been observed in association with dreamless reports and higher arousal thresholds (Angeleri et al., 1984). Such considerations and observations, together with results indicating that the notion of dreaming as a unilateral, right-hemisphere phenomenon is inadequate to explain existing data, suggest that the characterization of the hemispheric specialization of cognitive processes during sleep will be as difficult to establish as have been the same relationships during wakefulness.

Apart from the EEG, two major classes of physiological measures have been studied in relationship to mental activity during sleep, namely, autonomic variables and motoric phenomena. Several autonomic variables have been examined in this regard and, in general, tonic levels of such activity during REM or NREM sleep have proven to be poor correlates of mental activity. Of the studies correlating heart rate (Fahrion, Davison, & Berger, 1967; Hauri & Van de Castle, 1970a; Knopf, 1962; Shapiro, Goodenough, Biederman, & Sleser, 1964) or respiratory rate (Kamiya & Fong, 1962; Knopf, 1962; Hauri & Van de Castle, 1970a; Hobson, Goldfrank, & Snyder, 1965; Shapiro et al., 1964) with REM sleep mentation, only respiratory rate was found to relate to qualitative (Kamiya & Fong, 1962; Hauri & Van de Castle, 1970a; Hobson et al., 1965) or quantitative (Shapiro et al., 1964) aspects of the mentation. It is notable that the positive relationship observed by Hobson et al. (1965) obtained for both REM and NREM mentation. Although

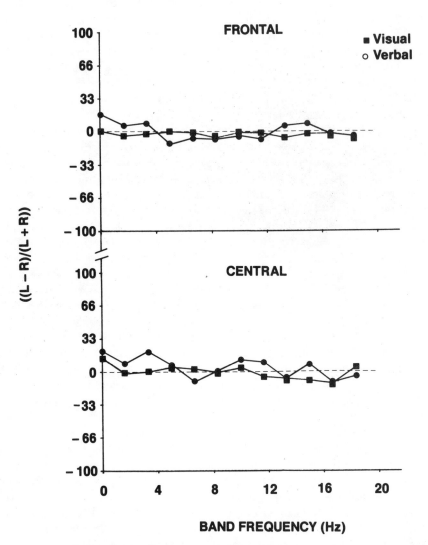

FIGURE 6.4. Within subject (DN) comparisons of interhemispheric ratio data associated with sleep mentation rated as exclusively visual or exclusively verbal. The data in this figure and Fig. 7.5 show near-hemispheric balance of frontal and central EEG activity, and not right and left hemispheric dominance, respectively, in association with visual and verbal REM sleep mentation. Reprinted by permission from R. T. Pivik, F. Bylsma, K. Busby, and S. Sawyer (Interhemispheric EEG changes: Relationship to sleep and dreams in gifted adolescents. *Psychiatric Journal of the University of Ottawa*, 1982, 7, 56–86).

Subject : D.R.

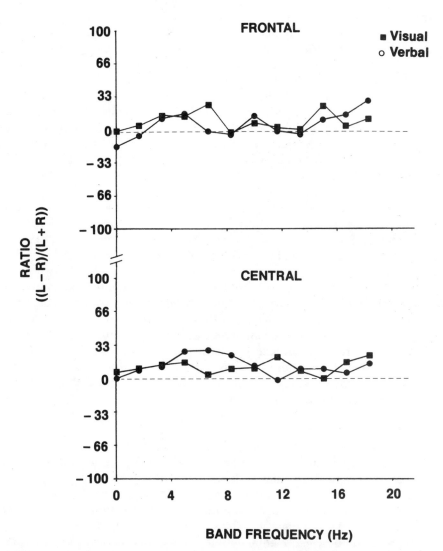

BAND FREQUENCY (Hz)

FIGURE 6.5.   Within subject (DR) comparisons of interhemispheric ratio data associated with sleep mentation rated as exclusively visual or exclusively verbal. Reprinted by permission from R. T. Pivik, F. Bylsma, K. Busby, and S. Sawyer (Interhemispheric EEG changes: Relationship to sleep and dreams in gifted adolescents. *Psychiatric Journal of the University of Ottawa*, 1982, 7, 56–86).

cardiac and respiratory rate do not relate well to ongoing mentation, variability in these measures does relate positively to dream emotionality (Fahrion et al., 1967; Hauri & Van de Castle, 1970a).

The most dramatic autonomic display in NREM sleep is provided by the "storms" of electrodermal activity that occur during stages 3 and 4 (Burch, 1965). Despite the intensity of this activity, Hauri and Rechtschaffen (1963) found no relationship between spontaneous or evoked electrodermal responses and mental activity during NREM sleep. The only positive relationship between mental activity and GSR that has been reported was obtained during REM sleep. Hauri and Van de Castle (1970a) found that GSR activity in the last minute preceding content awakenings related positively to dream emotionality. These authors emphasized, however, that, unlike NREM GSR storms, REM GSR potentials consisted of small, unipolar, isolated deflections that are more like waking reactions to emotional stimuli.

Penile erections occur regularly during REM sleep and only rarely during NREM sleep in man and monkey (Fisher, Gross, & Zuch, 1965; Karacan, Goodenough, Shapiro, & Starker, 1966). If a strict psychophysiological parallelism obtained, the data from these studies would suggest that 80 to 95% of REM dreams would contain overt sexual elements. This is clearly not the case. Hall and Van de Castle (1966) found overt sexual interactions in only 12% of the dreams they examined. Nevertheless, some variations in tumescence during REM sleep relate to variations in both recall and specific qualitative aspects of dream content. Karacan et al. (1966) obtained significantly greater recall from REM-period awakenings accompanied by sustained erections than from those associated with partial or no erections. Fisher (1966) was able to show a strong relationship between highly erotic sexual content and sudden increases in tumescence. When Fisher examined the relationship between presence and degree of tumescence and corresponding presence and intensity of sexual content, he found the strongest relationship to be between highly erotic sexual content and sudden increases in tumescence. This latter observation points to a general principle to be derived from these autonomic studies, that is, a better psychophysiological correlation is obtained when periods of rapid physiological change have been related to sleep mentation than when correlations are attempted between tonic levels of these variables and such mentation. Better relationships are found between mental activity and cardiac and respiratory variability, sudden GSR deflections, and sharp increases in tumescence than between mental activity and tonic activity of any of these autonomic measures. In the discussion of motoric events and sleep mentation that follows, we will find that this observation continues to hold true.

Except for twitches and body movements, the tonic activity of trunk and limb muscles remains essentially constant during sleep (Jacobson, Kales, Lehmann, & Hoedemaker, 1964). The muscles of the face and neck, however, undergo significant tonic inhibition which begins prior to and extends throughout REM sleep (Berger, 1961; Jacobson et al., 1964). The question of whether the pre-REM decrease in facial and submental muscle activity reflects the onset of REM sleeplike mental activity has been examined with some rather surprising results. Contrary to expectation, awakenings from low-EMG pre-REM periods yield not only less recall than those from NREM sleep associated with high EMG levels (Larson & Foulkes, 1969), but the recalled material is of a less dreamlike quality (Larson & Foulkes, 1969; Pivik, 1971).

The psychophysical correspondence improves when more discrete muscle activity is considered. For example, some, but not all, discrete twitches of peripheral musculature have been appropriately related to specific dream content (Grossman et al., 1971; McGuigan & Tanner, 1970; Stoyva, 1965a; Wolpert, 1960). Much greater success has been obtained in studies relating another index of discrete motor activity, namely, eye movements, to REM sleep mentation. These studies have described the eye-movement–dream-content relationship from two perspectives, one suggesting a very precise correspondence between the two variables, and another noting a general, nonspecific association. The former, more specific, view is embodied in the scanning hypothesis, that is, the notion that the eye movements are elaborated in the service of scanning the dream imagery. The development and current status of this controversy, which has endured for years, were extensively reviewed by Rechtschaffen (1973), who concluded that the issue was still in doubt. A recent, well-controlled and executed study of the scanning hypothesis (Herman, Erman, Boys, Peiser, Taylor, & Roffwarg, 1984) generally concurs with Rechtschaffen's conclusion, that is, the latter authors were unable to demonstrate a significant eye-movement–dream-imagery relationship based on an analysis of these variables alone. However, when the interviewer's confidence in his prediction was high— reflecting his belief that the narrative was reliable—a significant relationship did emerge. Many complexities and nuances are involved in the experimental study of this relationship, and these issues are considered in detail in these latter two references. The second, nonspecific view is supported by data relating the presence of eye movements to the vividness and emotionality of the dream (Hobson et al., 1965; Verdone, 1963), to the dreamlike nature of the report (Ellman et al., 1974), and to activity within the dream (Berger & Oswald, 1962; Dement & Wolpert, 1958b; Pivik & Foulkes, 1968)—although the latter relationship between activity in the dream and eye movement density has been questioned (Firth & Oswald, 1975; Hauri & Van de Castle, 1973; Keenan & Krippner, 1970).

Apart from the strong nonspecific relationship of eye movements to dream content, it is important to note that many measures that have been related to mental activity in REM sleep have also been shown to occur in close temporal contiguity to the eye movements. These measures include cardiac and respiratory variability (Aserinsky, 1965b; Baust & Bohnert,

1969), penile erections (Karacan et al., 1966), GSR activity (Broughton et al., 1965), and changes in muscular and reflex activity (Hodes & Dement, 1964; Pivik & Dement, 1970). This confluence of physiological activity highlights the necessity to seek out instances where these measures are dissociated in order to establish specific, unconfounded psychophysiological correlations—an effort which is yet to be realized.

Fortunately, in scientific research the best predictor of future results is not always past results, for the efforts to determine physiological correlates of sleep mentation had been largely negative or inconclusive. Although much had been learned about the descriptive physiology of sleep, the strongest psychophysiological association remained that between eye movements and dream content in REM sleep, with only frail hints of possible physiological correlates of NREM mentation. The situation was not very different from that which existed just after Aserinsky published his initial (1953) report. The need for revitalization and redirection was apparent, and the beginnings of such changes became evident in Moruzzi's (1963, 1965) tonic-phasic distinctions for REM sleep. Moruzzi (1963), on the basis of observations derived from the descriptive physiology of sleep in the cat, suggested that REM sleep be considered not as a homogeneous entity, but as the irregular alternation between periods of sustained (tonic) activity and periods of activity upon which are superimposed "sudden [eruptions] of an ensemble of phasic events" (pp. 291–292). Moruzzi's notion served as a conceptual focus for the ongoing stream of European animal research (Gassel, Marchiafava, & Pompeiano, 1964a, 1964b; Jeannerod, 1965; Jouvet, 1965b), whereas the earliest explicit expression of such a distinction on this side of the Atlantic was in terms of both animal and human research (Aserinsky, 1965a, 1965b; Dewson, Dement, & Simmons, 1965). The real surge of research utilizing these concepts began in the late 1960s with the appearance of several papers applying the tonic-phasic distinction to both physiological and psychophysiological studies of sleep (Aserinsky, 1967; Ferguson et al., 1968; Molinari & Foulkes, 1969; Pivik & Dement, 1968; Pivik, Halper, & Dement, 1969a).

Although the tonic-phasic distinction was originally confined to the REM period proper, it became apparent that phasic variations also occurred during NREM sleep. In the human, such variations have been noted in vaginal blood flow (Cohen & Shapiro, 1970), penile tumescence (Fisher et al., 1965; Karacan & Snyder, 1966), respiration (Hobson et al., 1965), and vasoconstriction (Johnson & Karpan, 1968). Even eye movements have been observed during NREM sleep (Jacobs, Feldman, & Bender, 1971). In the cat, transient increases and decreases in brain temperature during slow wave sleep have been reported (Rechtschaffen et al., 1965), and limited amounts of ponto-geniculooccipital (PGO) spike activity occur regularly outside the definitional confines of REM sleep (Dement, 1965a; Michel, Jeannerod, Mouret, Rechtschaffen, & Jouvet, 1964; Thomas & Benoit,

1967). This latter event, the PGO spike, has been singled out for intensive study during the past few years. When first described (Jouvet & Michel, 1959), PGO activity appeared to be merely one more sleep event among many which were useful in differentiating REM sleep from NREM sleep. Data soon accumulated, however, suggesting that this event deserved special attention. For example, during REM sleep this activity was prevalent throughout the visual system (Bizzi & Brooks, 1963; Michel et al., 1964; Mikiten, Niebyl, & Hendley, 1961; Mouret, Jeannerod, & Jouvet, 1963), and was present in the pontine region designated by lesion studies as necessary for REM sleep (Jouvet, 1962). Moreover, PGO spiking occurred sporadically throughout NREM sleep and regularly anticipated REM sleep onset by 30–40 sec of intensified activity (Michel et al., 1964). As demonstrated below, PGO activity has assumed a major role in studies attempting to elucidate the nature of tonic and phasic processes during sleep.

THE TONIC-PHASIC DICHOTOMY

What was the importance of Moruzzi's (1963) suggestion? Was his tonic-phasic terminology merely a descriptive clarification of the differentiation of sleep events based on their temporal extensity? If so, then it did not represent anything new, for the terms are common ones in descriptive physiology, and, within psychophysiological sleep research, investigators had long been looking at correlations between relatively long-lasting events (EEG defined sleep stages, autonomic levels) or short-lived changes (autonomic variability, muscle twitches) and sleep mentation. Clearly then, at the empirical level, the basis for a tonic-phasic distinction could be traced back to the early Aserinsky–Dement and Kleitman studies. However, Moruzzi was postulating more than a descriptive differentiation; he was suggesting that, along tonic dimensions, REM–NREM differences were largely ones of degree and not of kind, and, furthermore, that the episodic intrusions of phasic events within REM represented activity which was fundamentally different from the tonic background upon which it was superimposed. Although at the time the proposal was initially made it was lacking a solid empirical foundation, the primary demand upon the model was clear, that is, that a dissociation between events defined as tonic and phasic be demonstrated. More a plea for physiological parsimony than an intended corollary to the model was Moruzzi's further hope that the phasic events of REM sleep be unified under the workings of a single system.

Evidence in support of both of Moruzzi's propositions was forthcoming from investigators employing a variety of experimental approaches including lesioning techniques, pharmacological intervention, and behavioral manipulation. Lesions of different brain stem nuclei, for example, were shown to result in the selective elimination of either tonic or phasic components of REM sleep. Bilateral destruction of the nucleus locus coeruleus eliminated the tonic muscular inhibition of REM sleep leaving PGO spiking and eye-movement activity intact (Jouvet & Delorme, 1965). Conversely, after complete ablation of the medial and descending vestibular nuclei, the integrated bursts of PGO spiking, eye movements, transient EMG and reflex inhibition, and autonomic changes were no longer present in REM sleep (Morrison & Pompeiano, 1970; Pompeiano, 1967). The only evidence of phasic activity remaining after this lesion was the sporadic occurrence of isolated PGO spikes and eye movements.

The results of these vestibular lesion studies were important in demonstrating the separateness of tonic and phasic events, but were also relevant to Moruzzi's second proposal that the widespread phasic activity might originate from a single, common generator. The tendency for phasic activity to occur in clustered bursts during REM sleep in both the human and cat suggested this might be the case, and the comprehensive elimination of such bursts of activity through selective vestibular lesions indicated a fundamental role for these nuclei in the generation of these events. It was postulated, however, that the primary source of phasic activity was located in the pontine reticular formation, and that this pacemaker normally interacted with the vestibular nuclei to trigger the intense, integrated bursts of phasic activity. The isolated PGO spikes and eye movements which survived the vestibular lesioning were thought to represent the activity of this pontine center.

Further proof of the independence of tonic and phasic events was provided by studies demonstrating that phasic events could be displaced from REM sleep. It was observed that the suppression of REM sleep, by means of either forced awakenings at the onset of each REM period (Dusan-Peyrethon, Peyrethon, & Jouvet, 1967; Ferguson et al., 1968; Ferguson & Dement, 1968) or the administration of biochemicals (Delorme, Jeannerod, & Jouvet, 1965; Dement, Zarcone, et al., 1969; Ferguson et al., 1969) resulted in the enhancement of PGO spiking during slow wave sleep. The latter studies using biochemical methods of intervention reported a displacement of spiking not only into slow wave sleep, but into wakefulness as well. Dement and his colleagues (Dement, 1969; Dement, Ferguson, et al., 1969; Ferguson et al., 1968, 1969) made use of these results to take another look at the REM deprivation-compensation phenomenon. Typically, the suppression of REM sleep is followed by partial compensation of the REM sleep loss. However, by behaviorally or pharmacologically manipulating the number and distribution of PGO spikes, these investigators were able to regulate and even obviate the compensation phenomenon. For example, by making awakenings at the onset of spike intensification preceding REM onset, thereby depriving the animal of a few seconds of NREM sleep in addition to the normal curtailment of REM effected during REM deprivation, it was possible to enhance the amount of rebound over that produced by the classical REM deprivation procedure.[2] In another procedure, animals were gently aroused but not fully awakened during the pre-REM period of intensified spiking. This manipulation deprived the animals of REM sleep while potentiating NREM spiking, and was not followed by a rebound. Furthermore, a count of the number of PGO spikes elaborated during the deprivation procedure and recovery period revealed a nearly exact quantitative compensation for PGO spikes prevented by the experimental manipulation. These studies, by showing the intimate relationship between PGO spike activity and REM deprivation phenomena, imparted a functional significance to the PGO spike independent of the tonic processes of REM sleep.

Although these data provided an especially powerful justification for a concentrated study of the PGO spike at the physiological level, the intuitive appeal of this event as an investigatory tool for the study of the psychophysiology of dreaming seemed equally compelling. Specifically, in addition to being concentrated in REM sleep where reports of dreaming are most prominent, PGO spikes are strongly identified with the visual system, occur in association with quite generalized increases in unit activity (Hobson & McCarley, 1971), and have been observed in the presence of hallucinatory-like behavior during wakefulness in cats (Dement, Zarcone, et al., 1969; Jouvet & Delorme, 1965)—observations which are in harmony with our conception of dreaming as an hallucinatory mental experience of a highly visual nature occurring during sleep. Psychophysiological correlations such as these, together with the physiological data suggesting that PGO spikes represented a primary triggering process for phasic events in general and were crucially involved in the REM deprivation-rebound phenomenon, prompted investigators to view the feline PGO spike as the standard phasic event against which all others were to be evaluated. This concept has constituted the explicit basis upon which much of the subsequent research into the psychophysiological processes of dreaming has been conducted. This hypothesis that the PGO spike is an intimate correlate of dreaming in the human is based largely on general similarities between the two in distribution and intensity within the sleep cycle, as well as the shared accentuation upon the visual modality. A more empirical test of the correlation would be an examination of the correspondence between known properties of PGO spike activity and reported results from investigations of sleep mentation.

Setting aside for the moment the obvious pitfalls involved in suggesting cross-species analogy in distribution and function between a little understood physiological event and an even less well understood psychological

---

[2]For reasons which are unclear, the enhanced rebound after spike deprivation could only be obtained in animals on scheduled cycles of sleep and wakefulness. When the manipulation was applied to animals sleeping ad libitum, the rebound was similar to that obtained after classical REM deprivation procedures.

process, let us examine five possible points of correspondence which lend themselves to comparative analysis, all having to do with distributional patterning of PGO spikes and sleep mentation:

1. PGO spikes are highly concentrated in REM sleep, a time when dreaming is most prominent.

2. Measured at the pontine level, spikes increase in amplitude and frequency within a REM period (Brooks, 1968), a pattern that finds a parallel in the increased intensity of dreaming as a function of REM time (Foulkes, 1966; Takeo, 1970). Interestingly enough, if the measure of spike activity were taken at the level of the lateral geniculate nucleus, the correlation would be reversed, since LGN spikes decrease in frequency and amplitude as a function of REM time (Brooks, 1967).

3. Spiking during NREM sleep is most intense in the 30 to 60 sec preceding each REM period, but mental activity is not suddenly enhanced during ascending stage 2, which temporally corresponds to this time of increased spike activity in the cat (Larson & Foulkes, 1969; Pivik et al., 1969a) and may suffer qualitatively and quantitatively relative to post-REM stage 2 (Pivik et al., 1969a), which would correspond to a time marked by the virtual absence of spike activity in the cat.

4. Deprivation of REM sleep in the cat increases the density of spiking within REM sleep during the ensuing rebound, and increases the incidence of NREM-spike activity during the deprivation manipulation (Dement, 1969; Dement, Ferguson et al., 1969a; Dusan-Peyrethon et al., 1967; Ferguson et al., 1968; see also Chapter 11). Correspondingly, it would be expected that REM deprivation in the human would intensify REM dream content during the recovery period and enhance NREM mentation during the deprivation procedure. With respect to the former, both negative (Antrobus, Arkin, & Toth, 1970; Carroll, Lewis, & Oswald, 1969; Firth, 1972; Foulkes, Pivik, Ahrens, & Swanson, 1968) and positive (Greenberg, Pearlman, Fingar, Kantrowitz, & Kawliche, 1970; Pivik & Foulkes, 1966) results have been reported. Studies looking for the postulated intensification of NREM mentation during REM deprivation have been few, and the results negative (Antrobus, et al., 1970; Arkin, Antrobus, Toth, & Baker, 1968; Foulkes et al., 1968; see also Chapter 11), but these results are based upon either small numbers of awakenings or did not sample from all NREM sleep stages and are accordingly limited in their generality.

5. PGO spikes are virtually absent at sleep onset, whereas several reports (Foulkes & Vogel, 1965; Foulkes et al., 1966; Vogel et al., 1966; Vogel et al., 1972) are consistent in demonstrating a great deal of very dreamlike activity occurring at this time in the human.

Considering the impressiveness of the animal physiological data, this preliminary review of psychophysiological correspondence is disappointingly unimpressive. The lack of a strong relationship between the spike and content data might reflect a true noncorrelation of the two variables, or indicate a need to refine our method of dream collection and analyses, or point to the need for a better physiological measure. However, the five general comparisons listed above constitute at best a once-removed and largely inadequate test of the spike-content relationship, or the tonic-phasic model as it applies to sleep mentation. A more direct test of the model as it applies to REM sleep (Aserinsky, 1967) suggested that a comparison among content reports elicited from intra-REM awakenings made during periods of ocular motility (phasic), ocular quiescence (tonic), and NREM sleep might reveal greater qualitative similarity between the REM tonic and NREM reports than between those from REM tonic and REM phasic arousals. This suggestion is a more explicit statement, presented in terms of human psychophysiological research, of what Moruzzi (1963) proposed for animal physiology, and, like the latter proposal, it totally disregards any possible distinctions within NREM sleep or between REM and NREM sleep deriving from the presence of phasic activity in NREM sleep. In both cases the disregard did not represent an oversight of available data, but a real absence of data, that is, no consistent, discrete physiological measure of phasic activity during NREM sleep. It is this reason too that prevented application of the tonic-phasic model to NREM mentation.

THE TONIC-PHASIC MODEL AND REM SLEEP MENTATION

Investigations that have sought to differentiate phasic from nonphasic periods in REM sleep (see Table 6.1) have relied upon the presence or absence of eye movements for such differentiation, sometimes in conjunction with additional measures (Foulkes & Pope, 1973; Watson, 1972). Several additional physiological measures have been affiliated with the feline PGO spike and examined as presumptive NREM PGO analogues, and a complete cataloguing of these measures, together with pertinent literature and relevant descriptive information, is presented in Table 6.2. In some instances the strength of the PGO association is enhanced by direct observation of the event in both man and cat (MEMA, PIP, EMG, and spinal-reflex inhibition; see Figures 6.6 and 6.7), but in all cases there is a basis for the association through correlational inferences, that is, distribution in sleep, response to experimental manipulation, or association with other known PGO correlates.

The tendency toward the use of ever more temporally discrete physiological indices and recognition of the moment-to-moment variability of the dream experience prompted the use of a more microscopic methodology in

TABLE 6.1.   REM RECALL AS A FUNCTION OF PHASIC (EYE-MOVEMENT-RICH)
AND TONIC (EYE-MOVEMENT-POOR) CONDITIONS

Investigator	Number of Subjects	Percentage Recall Number of Arousals		P-T Percentage Recall Differences
		P	T	
Pivik, Halper, and Dement (1969a)	9	100, 18	79, 29	21
Molinari and Foulkes (1969)	10	80, 20	100, 20	−20
Medoff and Foulkes (1972)	2	81.8, 22	55, 18	26.8
Pivik (1971)	10	90.5, 42	82.5, 40	8
Foulkes, Shepherd, Larson, Belvedere, and Frost (1972)	14	74.1, 81	66.7, 81	7.1
Watson (1972)	4	96.3, 48	90, 48	6.3
Foulkes and Pope (1973)	14	95, 78	87, 54	8
Bosinelli, Cicogna, and Molinari (1973)	10	95, 40	87.5, 40	7.5

the collection of dream reports in which attention was focused upon the last experienced preawakening mental event—a technique that had been used extensively in tests of the scanning hypothesis (Roffwarg, Dement, Muzio, & Fisher, 1962). Also, being cognizant of the experimental demands upon the subject (rapid arousal from sleep, attentiveness to the mental experience with special emphasis upon detail and temporal relationships), some investigators have taken to careful preselection of subjects (Foulkes & Pope, 1973; Molinari & Foulkes, 1969; Watson, 1972).

Conceptually and methodologically the field was ready for testing the viability of the tonic-phasic model, at least for REM sleep, and the first studies explicitly directed toward this purpose began appearing in the late 1960s (Molinari & Foulkes, 1969; Pivik et al., 1969a) and have continued to mount. The single most important variable left to be determined was the dimension or dimensions along which the tonic-phasic differentiation would be expressed. From the data tabulated in Table 6.1 it is clear that at least in REM sleep this expression is not in terms of incidence of recalled mentation, although the presence of phasic activity does seem to somewhat enhance recall. Among the several qualitative features of mentation that have been examined, the list of those that have proven to be nondiscriminating is extensive, with some surprising entries. For example, the presence or absence of phasic activity is not a strong predictor of the hallucinatory (Molinari & Foulkes, 1969; Pivik, 1971; Pivik et al., 1969a) or emotional (Pivik, 1971) quality of mentation, or felt bodily presence or subjective depth of sleep (Molinari & Foulkes, 1969; Pivik, 1971). Furthermore, all the studies listed in Table 6.1 agree that the presence of visual or auditory

TABLE 6.2. CATALOGUE OF PRESUMPTIVE PGO ANALOGUES IN THE HUMAN

Investigator	Event[a]	Recording Source	Duration	Distribution
Medoff and Foulkes (1972) Foulkes and Pope (1973) Pope, 1973	Theta burst	Frontal EEG	2–3 Hz trains	REM–NREM
Pivik et al. (1969a) Weisz (1972)	K complex	Central EEG	500–700 msec	NREM Stage 2
Antrobus et al (1973)				
Pessah and Roffwarg (1972a) Pessah and Roffwarg (1972b) Roffwarg et al. (1973)	MEMA[b]	Compliance of tympanic membrane	500–1000 msec	REM–NREM
Rechtschaffen and Chernik (1972) Rechtschaffen et al. (1970) Rechtschaffen et al. (1972a) Rechtschaffen et al. (1972b) Watson (1972)	PIP[c]	Periorbital region	20 msec	REM–NREM
Wyatt et al. (1972) Pivik and Dement (1968) Pivik et al (1969b)	EMG inhibition	Submental musculature	≤ 100 msec	REM–NREM
Pivik and Dement (1970) Pivik (1971)	H-reflex inhibition	Soleus muscle	7–10 msec	REM–NREM

[a] Refer to Notes to table for a more complete description of these events.
[b] Middle ear muscle activity.
[c] Periorbital integrated potential.

Notes:

Theta bursts: See Figure 6.8 legend.

MEMA: Middle-ear muscle activity is reflected in movement or variations in compliance of the tympanic membrane which alters the existing baseline sound-pressure level in the external auditory canal. This change is detected by a probe fitted into the canal and translated into an impedance change which is registered on a paper writeout.

PIPs: Periorbital phasic integrated potentials are fast potentials, probably of muscular origin, recorded using integration techniques from surface electrodes placed around the eye.

Reflex inhibition: Electrical stimuli delivered to the tibial nerve through surface electrodes placed over the popliteal fossa elicit action potentials in musculature of the lower leg both directly and through a monosynaptic spinal pathway. The direct response is altered only by peripheral movements, whereas the reflex response is altered by central excitatory and inhibitory influences on controlling motoneurons.

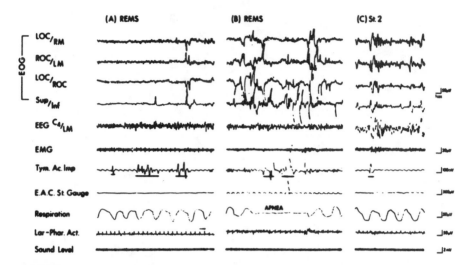

FIGURE 6.6. Polygraph sections containing representative appearances of MEMA in REM and NREM sleep. (A) REM sleep: MEMA with and without concurrent rapid eye movements. (B) REM sleep: MEMA associated with a period of apnea. (C) Stage 2 sleep: MEMA simultaneous with a K complex and slight laryngeal activation. Electroculogram (EOG) horizontal leads: LOC/RM, left outer canthus referred to right mastoid; ROC/LM, right outer canthus to left mastoid; LOC/ROC, left outer canthus to right outer canthus. EOG vertical leads: SUP/Inf, supraorbital ridge referred to infraorbital ridge. Electroencephalogram (EEG) leads: C4/LM right central to left mastoid. Electromyogram (EMG) leads: masseter muscle referred to submentalis placement. Tympanic acoustic impedance (Tym. Ac. Imp.) deflections underlined, 100 mv = 12.5 acoustic ohms. External auricular canal strain gauge (E. A. C. St. Guage) mounted on ear mold. Laryngopharyngeal activity (Lar. Phar-Act.) recorded from laryngeal prominence of thyroid cartilage. Sound level monitored from sleep room (2 mv = 7.7 dB). Activity from possible sources of MEMA-like artifact is absent during acoustic impedance deflections, indicating that they represent true MEMA. Reprinted by permission from M. A. Pessah and H. P. Roffwarg (Spontaneous middle ear muscle activity in man: A rapid eye movement phenomenon. *Science*, 1972, *173*, 773–776). Copyright 1972 by the American Association for the Advancement of Science.

imagery does not differentiate between "tonic" and "phasic" reports, although "phasic" reports are associated with a greater incidence of both kinds of imagery. The absence of a significant positive correlation between the presence of phasic activity and visual imagery is especially surprising in view of the concentration of such activity in the visual system. It should be noted that the relationship between auditory imagery and phasic activity in the auditory system (MEMAs; see Figures 6.6 and 6.7) is undergoing detailed scrutiny, with strong positive preliminary results (Roffwarg et al., 1973; Roffwarg, Herman, & Lamstein, 1975).

On the positive side, content elicited subsequent to "phasic" arousals contains significantly more hostility (Pivik, 1971; Watson, 1972), movement

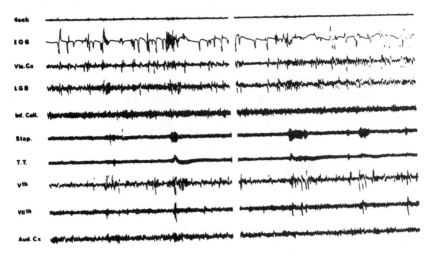

FIGURE 6.7.   MEMA during REM sleep in the cat. Middle-ear muscle activity recorded from tensor tympani (T. T.) and stapedius (Stap.) derivations occurs in conjunction with spiking in visual and auditory cortices, lateral geniculate body (LGB), motor nuclei V and VII, and "bouffee" type clusters of eye movements. Reprinted by permission from M. A. Pessah and H. P. Roffwarg (Spontaneous middle ear muscle activity in man: A rapid eye movement phenomenon. *Science*, 1972, *173*, 773–776). Copyright 1972 by the American Association for the Advancement of Science.

(Bosinelli et al., 1973), and self-participation (Bosinelli et al., 1973), but less conceptual, thoughtlike material (Bosinelli et al., 1973; Foulkes & Pope, 1973; Molinari & Foulkes, 1969; Pivik, 1971). Molinari and Foulkes (1969) found they could differentiate between content elicited from REM phasic and tonic arousals by classifying the reports as primary visual experiences (PVE) or as secondary cognitive elaborations (SCE). Reports were scored for PVE when the very last experience consisted of passively received, nonintellectualized, "thoughtless" imagery (like watching a clock), and for SCE when this experience included evidence of active conceptualization, cognition, or verbalization (like watching a clock, but considering the indicated time; or thinking about time in the absence of any imagery). REM phasic reports were found to be associated with PVE, whereas the content from REM tonic awakenings and from three categories of NREM sleep (ascending stage 2, and sleep onset stages 1 and 2) were characterized by mental activity of the SCE type. This initial study concentrated upon the last experience related in subjects' spontaneous reports. The within-REM findings were subsequently replicated (Foulkes & Pope, 1973), but it was also found that if, following the spontaneous report, subjects were specifically asked about the presence of SCE-type material, the response was generally affirmative (Foulkes & Pope, 1973; Medoff & Foulkes, 1972). In other words, although PVE was a very prominent aspect of REM phasic content, conceptual activity was nevertheless present at this time and could be elicited upon direct questioning.

In the latter two studies, a third awakening category within REM was included consisting of periods of frontal EEG sawtooth waves [2–3 Hz notched waves generally preceding eye-movement bursts (Berger, Olley, & Oswald, 1962)] in the absence of eye movement activity (see Figure 6.8). Content elicited in association with sawtooth waves was similar to REM phasic awakenings in terms of incidence of PVE ratings, but, unlike the latter, was found to be more discontinuous with respect to the preceding content (Foulkes & Pope, 1973).

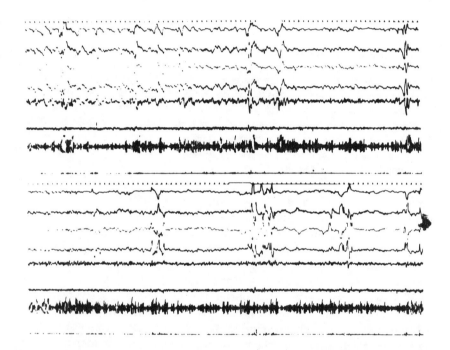

FIGURE 6.8.   NREM and REM polygraphic tracings indicating band-pass filtered EEG thetawave (5–6 Hz) activity and its relationship to other psychophysiological variables. In both the upper (NREM stage 2 just preceding stage REM onset) and lower (stage REM) records, polygraph channels are as follows: time marker (small blips are second indicators); Channel 1: right horizontal electrooculogram (EOG); Channel 2: left horizontal EOG; Channel 3: right infraorbital vertical EOG; Channel 4: left infraorbital vertical EOG; Channel 5: unfiltered F_4 EEG; Channel 6: submental electromyogram (EMG); Channel 7: filtered F_4EEG; Channel 8: periorbital phasic integrated potentials (PIPs). Note the concordance of theta bursting in ascending stage 2 with PIPs and EEG K complexes and that the EMG suppression heralding REM onset (at the large minute mark on the time marker) is initiated (almost invariably in our experience) concurrently with a theta burst. In the REM tracing, theta bursts precede and/or accompany other phasic events—REM bursts and PIPs.

Watson (1972), like Foulkes and his collaborators, also made use of three different awakening conditions within REM, but employed a different measure of phasic activity in conjunction with eye movements—the periorbital integrated potential (PIP) (see Figure 6.9). Arousals were made when PIPs were present with and without eye movements (PIP–REM and PIP conditions, respectively), and in the absence of both kinds of activities. Subjects rated the last experience on both PIP and PIP–REM awakenings as very or moderately bizarre significantly more often than they did the last experience on control awakenings. Furthermore, compared to control conditions, the last experience on both phasic conditions was found to be more discontinuous and more bizarre relative to the immediately preceding experience. Watson interpreted his results as indicating that PIPs, with or without eye movements, "are associated with bizarreness and discontinuity in the stream of dream mentation" [p. iii]. The Foulkes and Pope (1973) study discussed above included analyses for bizarreness and discontinuity but did not corroborate Watson's findings on either scale. These differences might be the result of the two studies having used different measures of phasic activity (PIPs versus REM bursts and sawtooth waves), but it is unlikely since PIPs and sawtooth waves have been related to each other

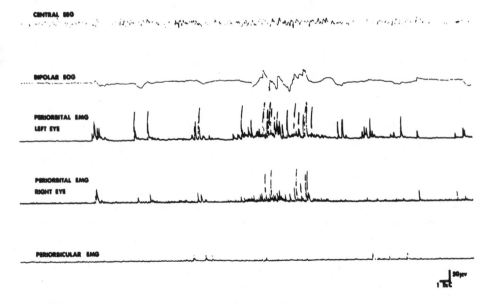

FIGURE 6.9.   Illustration of PIP activity during REM sleep. Note the occurrence of PIPs with and without eye-movement activity, and the relative asynchrony between PIPs and integrated phasic muscle activity recorded from the periorbicular (lip) region.

(Rechtschaffen, Molinari, Watson, & Wincor, 1970), and both have been related to eye movements.

The inconsistencies may reflect a combination of methodological and analytical differences (for example, clarification and extension of spontaneous content reports in Watson's study were not conducted by an interviewer blind to the awakening condition; many of the quiet awakenings of Foulkes and Pope may have been contaminated by PIPs; interrater reliability on the bizarreness scale in the Foulkes and Pope study was less than that achieved in the Watson study) or, perhaps, indicate more fundamental difficulties, such as the reliability of the psychological scales used.

THE TONIC-PHASIC MODEL AND NREM SLEEP MENTATION

The observation that PGO activity occurred intermittently during NREM sleep in the cat spurred the search for analogous measures in the human. It was hoped that a positive correlation between such activity and NREM sleep mentation would obtain, thus providing the "public physiological" landmark needed to lend credibility to, and promote more efficient study of, such mentation. Apart from the previously cited studies using autonomic variability as the physiological index, another measure that received considerable attention was the K complex (see Figure 6.1). K complexes are most easily detectable during stage 2 sleep, and are by definition (Rechtschaffen & Kales, 1968) absent from REM sleep. Nevertheless, the distribution of these events before the REM period (Dement, 1967) and their response to experimental manipulation (Pivik & Dement, 1968) suggested they might reflect PGO spike activity. Pivik et al. (1969a) reported that high K-complex frequencies (determined on the basis of preawakening 3-min counts) were associated with either the absence of recall or with recall of the most dreamlike quality, whereas the lowest rates of K complexes were associated with "conceptual mentation, both mundane and bizarre, and perceptual mentation of a nonhallucinatory quality [p. 215]." Later, Weisz (1972) conducted a study in which awakenings were made in ascending stage 2 following a single K complex or sleep spindle; he found no significant differences between the two classes of awakenings although a variety of variables were examined, including recall, SCE, PVE, distortion, and active participation. Antrobus, Ezrachi, and Arkin (1973) made stage 2 awakenings after REM and after sleep onset and found no relationship between a dreamlike rating on several scales and incidence of K complexes.

If these largely negative K-complex findings are discarded, the case for the feasibility of the tonic-phasic distinction for NREM sleep mentation is reduced to three lines of work, each using a different presumptive PGO index (PIPs, phasic reflex inhibition, and theta bursts) and overlapping only slightly in the portions of NREM sleep sampled.

It has already been indicated that PIPs occur in both REM and NREM sleep (see Table 6.2), and it is notable that the initial sleep mentation-PIP studies were conducted in NREM sleep (Rechtschaffen et al., 1972a, 1972b). In these studies stage 2 awakenings were made under four conditions: (a) control, consisting of the absence of PIPs or tonic periorbital EMG activity for 1 min; (b) phasic–tonic (P–T), a mixture of PIPs and tonic activity; (c) tonic (T), brief burst of tonic activity without PIPs; and (d) phasic (P), 3–5 sec of PIPs alone. The two studies were consistent in finding that, relative to control conditions, there was an increased likelihood of recall under P–T conditions, and that phasic reports (P and P–T) were more lengthy and more highly distorted.

Another test of the NREM tonic-phasic model made use of transient inhibition of the spinal monosynaptic H reflex as the index of phasic activity (Pivik, 1971; see Figures 6.10 and 6.11). Awakenings were made during all NREM sleep stages except sleep onset stage 1 under phasic (inhibition of a single-reflex response) or tonic (absence of such inhibition for at least 2 min) conditions. Of a considerable battery of variables (visual, auditory, or kinesthetic imagery; recall; hallucinatory quality; and sleep depth among others) only two—auditory imagery and hostility—significantly discriminated between phasic and tonic reports, with higher scores on both variables under phasic conditions. However, an unexpected clustering of variables emerged from the analyses. With respect to amount of recall, tonic-phasic distinctions obtained for NREM stages 3 and 4, but not for NREM stage 2 and REM sleep. Recall in the former NREM stages, generally the worst among all sleep stages, was markedly enhanced under phasic conditions, that is, stage 3, phasic, 55.6%, tonic, 40.6%; stage 4, phasic, 58.1%, tonic, 38.3%. Qualitatively, there was a reversal of the tonic-phasic correlates which, however, preserved the above sleep stage groupings. NREM stages 3 and 4 tonic and REM and stage 2 phasic awakenings were characterized by content having more visual imagery, movement, and higher dreamlike fantasy ratings, and being more hallucinatory; NREM stages 3 and 4 phasic and REM and stage 2 tonic arousals were rated more thoughtlike, with stage 4 phasic arousals receiving the highest percentage of such ratings. Although these results need to be cross validated, the internal consistency of the pattern would suggest that they are not capricious fluctuations. Remarkable, too, is the fact that these NREM differences in recall and qualitative characteristics are based on the occurrence of a single observable phasic event lasting only 7–10 msec.

Although PIPs and phasic EMG inhibitions occur at sleep onset (Pivik et al., 1969b; Rechtschaffen et al., 1970), the only study that has attempted to relate a measure of phasic activity to mental activity at this time is one by Pope (1973), using theta bursts as the phasic index (see Figure 6.7). In keeping with previous reports of sleep onset mentation (e.g., Foulkes & Vogel, 1965; Vogel et al., 1966), all three categories of awakenings (category

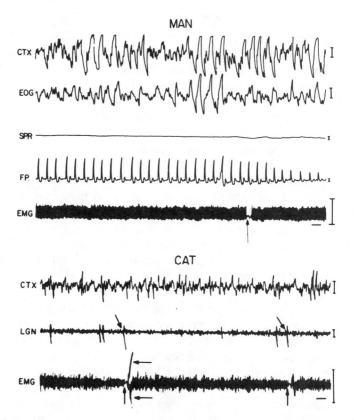

FIGURE 6.10.   The occurrence of phasic EMG suppressions in man and cat. In the upper tracings the single vertical arrow indicates the occurrence of a relatively long sustained phasic EMG suppression during non-REM stage 4 sleep in man. CTX, monopolar central (C₃/A₂) EEG; EOG, bipolar horizontal electrooculogram; SPR, spontaneous skin potential; FP, finger plethysmograph; EMG, bipolar submental electromyogram. In the EMG tracing of the cat, two phasic suppressions can be seen (vertical arrows). A biphasic muscle twitch (horizontal arrows) occurs near the end of the first suppression. Note the close temporal correlation between geniculate spiking (arrows, LGN derivation) and phasic EMG suppressions. CTX, visual cortex; LGN, lateral geniculate nucleus; EMG, electromyogram recorded from the posterior cervical muscles. Calibrations: 1 sec; 50 µv. Reprinted by permission from T. Pivik and W. C. Dement (Phasic changes in muscular and reflex activity during non-REM sleep. *Experimental Neurology*, 1970, *27*, 115–124).

1: 15 sec following EEG alpha loss; category 2: theta burst following alpha loss; and category 3: 15 sec following a theta burst) produced a high incidence of recall (93–100%). Moreover, theta-burst awakenings contained significantly more PVE than pretheta reports and substantially, but not significantly, more than posttheta reports. As the sleep-onset period progressed from pretheta through theta and posttheta conditions, mentation

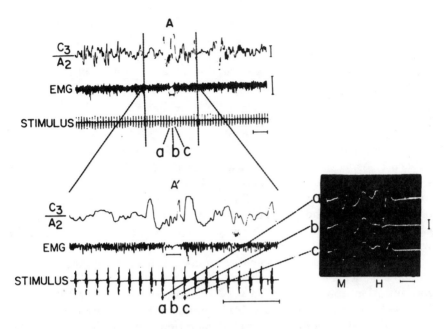

FIGURE 6.11.   A phasic EMG suppression (underscored) and associated EEG recorded at standard (A) and enhanced (A′) speeds together with the muscular responses elicited by the three consecutive stimuli (a, b, c) overlapping the suppression. The muscular responses (a, b, c) pictured to the right of A′ correspond, respectively, to the lettered stimuli in A′ directly under the suppression. In the tracings of the muscular responses, note the stability of the direct response (M wave) and the inhibition of the H reflex in tracing b, the stimulus for which occurs coincident with the phasic EMG suppression. Calibrations: A and A′, 1 sec, 50 μv; oscilloscope tracings, 10 msec, 500 μv. Reprinted by permission from T. Pivik and W. C. Dement (Phasic changes in muscular and reflex activity during non-REM sleep. *Experimental Neurology*, 1970, 27, 115–124).

became increasingly more discontinuous in nature. Although these three conditions did not differ significantly with respect to this variable, a declension of theta into high- and low-amplitude categories proved to be discriminating, with high-theta reports being significantly more discontinuous.

OVERVIEW AND SPECIAL CONSIDERATIONS

Ideally, models endure only so long as they sustain a heuristic influence; but it is often the case that such concepts linger on far beyond their use, hindering rather than stimulating, finally dying from neglect, without public or official recognition of their demise. One of the reasons models or theories persevere in the face of glaring inadequacies is the apparent necessity of having something "better" with which to replace them. The 2-state model—

the limitations of which were clearly evident in the mid 1960s—languished in a state of depreciated heuristic usefulness, and was finally laid to rest in the early 1970s (Dement, 1973). The continuing influence of the heir-apparent tonic-phasic model is undeniable, but the value of singling out phasic events for study at the psychophysiological interface is as yet unclear. The work that has been completed provides some guidelines that are clearly indicated, and others which are suggestive at best. It is clear, for example, from the measures that have been taken, that phasic activity is not the determinant of sleep mentation per se. Phasic activity does appear to facilitate recall (see Table 6.1), especially during slow wave sleep (Pivik, 1971) but recall is relatively profuse under tonic conditions. In the only study to date in which tonic-phasic distinctions in recall have been examined in REM and the bulk of NREM sleep in the same subjects (Pivik, 1971), only 1 subject out of 10 exhibited a significant tonic-phasic recall difference across all sleep stages, with greater recall under phasic conditions.

With respect to phasic-tonic discriminators at the qualitative level, the results are meager and sometimes conflicting, with suggestions toward a concentration upon discontinuity, SCE, auditory imagery and hostility in NREM sleep, and discontinuity, bizarreness, and PVE in REM sleep, However, even under the most optimal of conditions, that is, during REM sleep when recall and detailed elaboration are at their best, the presence of phasic events proves distinctive only part of the time. The increased bizarreness of PIP-associated REM reports observed by Watson (1972) is experienced on only 55% of such reports, which, although significantly greater than comparable control values, still leaves 45% of PIP and PIP-REM reports of apparently nondistinctive quality. Similarly, Watson's discontinuity effects were present on less than 40% of PIP or PIP-REM awakenings. Pivik's (1971) results indicating auditory imagery and hostility as significant tonic-phasic discriminators are likewise based on the presence of these characteristics on less than half of the phasic arousals. The results of Foulkes and Pope (1973) suggesting PVE as a REM tonic-phasic discriminator are on more solid footing, with the median-subject PVE value being 100% on REM-burst arousals relative to 63% on control arousals. Except for the latter data, we appear to be dealing with a rather weak effect.

Before concluding that phasic-tonic distinctions apply even to REM sleep mentation, a reassessment of the validity of the bases for our expectations regarding the relationship between presumptive PGO measures and sleep mentation might be useful. The major expectation was for dramatic differences to obtain at the psychological level to match those indicated physiologically and anatomically in the cat. In point of fact, the bases for the latter differences are not clearly established. The separate anatomical mediation of tonic and phasic events (Pompeiano, 1966, 1967) has been questioned (Perenin, Maeda, & Jeannerod, 1972) and the notion of the PGO spike as a unitary event (Bizzi & Brooks, 1963; Malcolm, Watson, &

Burke, 1970)—an idea which would fit well with the impression of spikes as intrusive or disruptive events—may be open to review (McCarley, Hobson, & Pivik, 1973). However, from a psychophysiological standpoint, the synaptic processes underlying PGO-spike generation may not be as important a determinant of the resultant effect of such activity as is the *intensity of phasic activity relative to the existing level of background activity.* Reasonable expectations regarding possible measurable effects of phasic activity must consider both the amount of activity and the physiological context within which these events occur. For example, relative to their occurrence in REM sleep, phasic events in NREM sleep occur with vastly diminished intensity and against a dramatically different background in terms of both gross EEG activation and level of unitary activity. It should not be surprising, therefore, that significant REM-NREM differences in both amount and quality of mentation are observed (Foulkes, 1962; Pivik, 1971; Rechtschaffen et al., 1963a).

Many factors contribute to the makeup of the physiological background against which phasic events are elaborated. EEG sleep stages constitute what might be called predictable sources of variation in background activity—predictable because there is a regularity to their occurrence within and across subjects. A less predictable determinant of background activity which is only infrequently considered (Hauri & Van de Castle, 1973; Monroe, 1967; Pivik, 1971; Pope, 1973; Zimmerman, 1970) is that originating from individual differences in physiological stability. The degree to which this factor may influence experimental outcomes is not well defined, but its potential for doing so may be illustrated by considering data from two subjects in a recent experiment utilizing reflex inhibition as the measure of phasic activity (Pivik, 1971). Subject A exhibited a spinal reflex the amplitude and waveform of which in NREM sleep remained virtually unchanged for periods of time ranging from 15–45 min, whereas these measures of reflex stability in Subject B underwent such constant fluctuations that tonic-phasic distinctions were rendered nearly meaningless. At one level of analysis these physiological differences were apparently meaningful, that is, Subject B had 100% recall from REM arousals and 84% recall from NREM arousals, while Subject A had recall percentages of 62.5 and 19.9% for REM and NREM, respectively.

Another intensity-related aspect of phasic activity especially evident in the human is the apparent asynchrony of the presumptive PGO analogues. The lack of a tight temporal linkage among MEMA, PIPs, theta bursts, and phasic EMG and reflex inhibition has been commented upon only in passing fashion in the literature (Rechtschaffen, Michel, & Metz, 1972; Roffwarg et al., 1973). This lack of concurrence—least prevalent within REM sleep during bursts of eye movements and most evident during NREM sleep—raises the possibility of multiple phasic-event systems driven by separate generators which become jointly active only during intense bursts of activity. Differentially active phasic-event systems might find expression at the psychological level as variations in salience of event-specific qualitative correlates, and such an interpretation can be easily applied to existing data. For example, at sleep onset, theta bursts correlate with mental activity characterized by PVE and discontinuity; during slow wave sleep, and stage 2 to a lesser extent, phasic reflex inhibition indicates thought-like, auditory imagery; and during REM PIPs and theta bursts are related to mentation that is relatively bizarre and distorted. The resulting mélange of event and state-specific content correlations, although not an implausible possibility, certainly lacks parsimonious appeal. Pessah and Roffwarg (1972b), in dealing with the apparent problem of a lack of synchrony between MEMA and PGO spikes in the cat, present a cogent discussion of considerations permitting the maintenance of a single generator theory in the face of asynchronous phasic events. They suggest that the partial asynchrony:

> . . . does not necessarily indicate that the primary brainstem discharges, which originate activation in the different systems, are not synchronous. It indicates only that the end motor responses recordable with our transducers . . . are not simultaneous. It is conceivable that impulses transmitted in parallel from a unitary generator into several neuronal channels may eventuate as *apparently* asynchronous peripheral phasic events as a result of a mixture of a partial and complete inhibitions variously affecting different motor pathways . . . (Pessah & Roffwarg, 1972b, p. 776).

Attributing these asynchronous phasic manifestations to the activity of a single master generator does not clarify the existing confusion in the psychophysiological data. A situation of event-specific, state-specific content correlations might still obtain if the psychological concomitant of generator activity was a function of the most highly activated end organ. On the other hand, if the psychophysical link is to activity of the generator itself there should be some unique, enduring psychological characteristic which would clearly differentiate "phasic" content from "tonic" content. Such a characteristic is yet to be demonstrated.

CONCLUSION

The early notion of sleep as a relatively uncomplicated state in which mind–body relationships might be profitably studied inbred an oversimplified view of sleep psychophysiology which, although perhaps useful in terms of stimulating interest and promoting popularity in those initial years, was found to be inadequate to the task of answering questions raised by the data. It was replaced by a view that fractionated sleep into tonic and phasic components and made use of the microscopic dream report in conjunction with microphasic physiological measures. The yield from this new view with its new methodology has not been as fruitful as hoped. Perhaps, as Bosinelli et al. (1973) suggest, we may be approaching a physiological limit in this kind of research where, in attempting to match the temporal discreteness of our physiological measures, we are demanding an impossible degree of introspective precision from subjects. Perhaps there is a qualitative aspect of dream phenomenology which is the phasic-event correlate par excellence (Bosinelli et al., 1973; Rechtschaffen, 1973; Watson, 1972); or it may indeed be as Foulkes (1973) portends that "what differences may emerge between phasic and non-phasic moments . . . will have to be relatively subtle, and revelatory of a slightly different 'mix' of dream functions, rather than any kind of qualitative alternation" (pp. 25–26).

Research utilizing the tonic-phasic model of sleep mentation has reached a point of diminishing returns. Whether this situation represents a temporary condition or is a signal of the impending demise of the model is a question for time and discerning research to answer.

PART 3

EFFECTS OF EXPERIMENTAL VARIABLES ON SLEEP MENTATION

7

The Social Psychology of Dream Reporting

ROSALIND DYMOND CARTWRIGHT
Rush–Presbyterian–St. Luke's Medical Center
Chicago

ALFRED KASZNIAK
University of Arizona

A question that was raised very early in experimental sleep work concerned whether the dream reports collected from rapid eye movement (REM) sleep periods under laboratory conditions constitute a representative sample of more "natural" dreams. Can we safely generalize from the laboratory to dream life as the latter occurs under more usual conditions? Studies comparing samples of home and laboratory dream reports from the same subjects pointed out a number of areas of differences. Dreams collected in the laboratory were reported to be less aggressive and sexual, and less characterized by either success or misfortune. In other words, these dreams were found to be less dramatic than those dreamed at home (Domhoff & Kamiya, 1964; Hall & Van de Castle, 1966). Dreams collected in the laboratory were also reported to deal with the laboratory situation itself, which is clearly not a usual dream topic (Dement, Kahn, & Roffwarg, 1965; Domhoff & Kamiya, 1964; Snyder, 1970; Whitman, Pierce, Maas, & Baldridge, 1962).

HOME–LABORATORY DIFFERENCES

These home–laboratory differences raised a number of issues: What accounts for them? Can they be overcome? Do they matter? Does the experience of coming into the laboratory, with all its attendant novelty and feelings of anxiety, affect not only what is dreamed, but how it is dreamed? If the nature of the process itself is changed, this might well invalidate these reports as a basis for understanding dream function and content as they occur more typically. Perhaps, though, the laboratory may affect only the manifest dream content, and that only temporarily, in terms of providing different grist for the same dream-process mill. If the process itself is not affected but works on this new experience in its characteristic way, inferences based on these dreams should not differ from inferences based on home dreams.

One possibility is that the reported dream differences are not due to any basic differences but are the result of comparing noncomparable samples. During a typical laboratory night in which dream content is to be retrieved, 3 to 6 REM sleep periods are interrupted and the subject is asked for a report. Usually all, or all but one, of these awakenings will yield a report of a dream. These reports are then compared with the home dream reports of the same subject. However, home dream reports are usually based on diaries written after the final morning awakening. Most often these yield only one dream per night. The dream recalled at home is most likely to be the final one of the night. Based on laboratory experience, this last dream is characteristically the longest, most bizarre, and most exciting (Snyder, 1970). Since it is also the one closest to the morning awakening, it is also the one most easily recalled (Meier, Ruef, Ziegler, & Hall, 1968; Trinder & Kramer, 1971). It is, however, an unrepresentative sample of the night as a whole. This difference in sampling accounts at least in part for why laboratory-collected dreams appear pale in comparison with home dreams.

In addition to the difference in the nature of the dreams sampled under the two conditions, there are differences in the method and circumstances of their retrieval that may have effects of their own. The context for laboratory subjects is that they are sleeping "in public." The environment is strange and the condition of being wired for EEG recordings is unique. On top of this, the subjects are awakened unexpectedly and intermittently throughout the night by a voice over an intercom requesting them to report their dreams orally from their bed in the dark. These reports are then tape-recorded remotely. In the home environment these subjects are in private; their surroundings are familiar; the awakenings are spontaneous or at a selected time under the subject's own control. The dream reports are usually written, which involves much more formal language structure than is typical of oral speech, particularly when one is sleepy. Perhaps the findings that home dreams are more sexual, aggressive, and dramatic mean only that the last dream of the night, when written out in private and in narrative form, has these qualities.

To test this last possibility, Weisz and Foulkes (1970) undertook a well-controlled study to compare home and laboratory dream reports when they were collected under uniform sampling and reporting conditions. If under these circumstances the differences in reports were negligible, the question of representativeness would be settled. Their subjects were given the same reporting instructions under both home and laboratory sleep circumstances. Each had an alarm clock with which to make his or her own awakenings, and a tape recorder with which to report dreams, for 2 nights in each location. The alarm was set for 6:30 A.M. and the oral report to the tape recorder was made in privacy. The order of the nights was counterbalanced, with 6 subjects sleeping first at home and then in the lab, and the other six sleeping first in the lab. Under these circumstances the dreams were found *not to differ in the level of their vivid fantasy*. This vivid fantasy factor is the one found by Hauri, Sawyer, and Rechtschaffen (1967) to account for most of the variance in dream ratings. It is made up of two components: the *unrealisticness or imaginativeness* of the reports, and their *intensity or dramatic quality*. Weisz and Foulkes (1970) concluded that the laboratory does not alter the basic nature of the cognitive process of dreaming. However, they did support the earlier studies of Domhoff and Kamiya (1964) and Hall and Van de Castle (1966) by finding that even under these matched reporting conditions home dreams were significantly *more aggressive* in content than those the subject recorded in the laboratory. Although this study gave a partly affirmative answer to the question, "Are the dreams dreamed in the laboratory equally dreamlike to those dreamed at home?" This may hold only under these atypical reporting circumstances in which the social elements of the reporting situation are minimized. Ordinarily these factors are prominent, so that the dream report must be looked at as a social communication. Subjects often remark before sleeping in the laboratory that they hope they do not shock us or embarrass themselves by their dreams. They frequently demonstrate that they feel uncomfortable about being "caught in the act" in a way they have no chance to prepare for and have not experienced beforehand.

The power of the particular subject–experimenter relationship to affect the REM-period content reports was demonstrated in a study by Whitman, Kramer, and Baldridge (1963). Here, 2 patients, who were in psychotherapy as well as subjects in a sleep laboratory, reported their dreams to both the experimenter at the time they were dreamed and to their psychotherapist later in the day. Whitman et al. (1963) reported that these subjects "unconsciously selected" the dreams reported to these two different recipients to be appropriate to the interpersonal situation as they saw it. To his male therapist, the male subject told dreams that cast him in an admirable heterosexual light and failed to report those reported during the laboratory night that had homosexual connotations. The female subject did not report to her male laboratory experimenter competitive dreams that she had about him, but did report these later to her therapist. On the other hand, she did report to her experimenter dreams that included some erotic feelings about her therapist, although she omitted these when reporting her dreams to the psychiatrist. It appears that the subject–experimenter relationship may well have an impact on what dreams are dreamed as well as on their availability for later retrieval. If this is a replicable finding it raises the further issue of whether this effect is temporary and subject to adaptation with further laboratory experience.

Dement, Kahn, and Roffwarg (1965) reported evidence that dream reports showing adaptation to the laboratory occurred within the first night. Incorporation of laboratory elements was strongest in the first and least in the last report following a REM-period awakening. This reduction was progressive over subsequent nights. Dreams that involved direct references to the laboratory dropped from 43% of those recalled from the first REM period of the first laboratory night to 16% of those reported from the sixth awakening on night 1. Comparing nights, the first yielded laboratory dreams on 25% of the occasions and the sixth only 7%. In contrast, Whitman, Pierce, Maas, and Baldridge (1962) reported that there was no reduction in the anxiety about laboratory sleeping as expressed in the dreams of 10 subjects over 4 nights of dream reporting. The data analysis of Whitman et al. (1962) was more clinically interpretive, whereas the Dement et al. (1965) data were based on an objective scoring of the manifest dream elements. In a later paper (Fox, Kramer, Baldridge, Whitman, & Ornstein, 1968), the authors concluded that "since the experimental situation includes an affective human relationship . . . adaptation in any meaningful sense may not occur . . . attempts must be made to control this variable and to account for its influence in any dream content material being evaluated (p. 701). A finding from a recent study (Trenholme, Cartwright, & Greenberg, 1984) suggests that the life circumstances of the subjects at the time they are dream-monitored are an important modifier of the influence of the laboratory on the dreams. This study compared the dreams of two groups of women undergoing a divorce to a control group of stably married women. It was found that the real-life stress of divorce took precedence over the more modest stress of laboratory dream monitoring. The control group had a higher proportion of dreams that incorporated elements of the experimental conditions (28%) than did the divorcing groups (12%). When subjects have enough real stress in their own lives their dreams appear to be less affected by the experimental conditions.

In a study designed to manipulate dream content experimentally, hetero-sexually oriented males were exposed to an erotic movie as a presleep stimulus (Cartwright, Bernick, Borowitz, & Kling, 1969). They reported that no directly sexual dreams were recalled by any of the 10 subjects studied for the next 4 consecutive nights. There were other changes in the dream content reported by these subjects that showed that the film did have an impact on the dream reports, but not the one anticipated. For example, fewer dreams were recalled in comparison with the number retrieved on the night before seeing the film. There was also a significant decrease in the percentage of dreams involving opposite sex characters and an increase in the proportion of dreams involving only one character. All of these results were seen as pointing to an increase in the strength of the usual defense against the expression of sexual fantasy in the laboratory despite an experi-mental manipulation designed to enhance it. At what point this censorship operated, and how consciously, it was not possible to say. Did the censor-ship prevent these dreams from being formed at all? Once dreamed, was there inhibition on their retention? Or, when sexual dreams were dreamed and recalled, was the reporting process affected? In any case, fewer dreams of all kinds were reported; those that were had a different character after the exposure to the film than before, and the change was in the direction of fewer heterosexual situations appearing in the reported sleep fantasy.

The possibility of using these data as a basis from which to gain some further insight into the variables affecting laboratory dream reporting oc-curred some 3 years later when a group of homosexual males agreed to participate in a study of the psychological and physiological concomitants of their sexual arousal response. This made it possible to collect data com-parable with the heterosexual sample and to look into the effects of labora-tory circumstances on dream reporting in 2 groups for whom different predictions would be made about their response to the same social situa-tion. If the homosexual subjects were equally sexually aroused by the film before sleep, and also showed an absence of sexual dreams and an increase in the failure to recall, this could mean that the laboratory exerts a gener-ally dampening effect on more primitive dreams and that this is exagger-ated when impulse levels are heightened. If, however, the inhibition on sexual dream reports was related more specifically to the embarrassment of the heterosexual subjects in reporting to a sexually attractive female exper-imenter, the homosexual subjects would be expected not to show this effect. To test the influence of the sex of the experimenter, in relation to the sexual orientation of the subject, on the amount and kind of dream reports col-lected before and after sexual stimulation, half the homosexual subjects were assigned to a male and half to a female experimenter for their 5 nights of REM reporting.

It was predicted that the homosexual subjects would be less embarrassed to report to the female experimenter than to a male and would show less dream inhibition than the heterosexual subjects. It was also predicted that if sex of experimenters contributes to the variance in dream reports, those homosexuals assigned to the male experimenter might show effects parallel to those observed in the first group with the female. In addition to testing for a general laboratory effect across both groups, and a specific within-group sex-of-experimenter effect, there was another variable involved that might lead to some between-group differences in dream reporting. This was a difference in the definition of what constitutes appropriate role behavior in that particular interpersonal context.

The subjects in the first study were all medical students drawn from the institution where the study was being conducted. All were heterosexual in identity and practice, as established by a detailed psychiatric history interview conducted by a senior faculty member of the department of psychiatry. Those in the second sample were selected to match the subjects in the first group in age and educational level, but none were medical students nor had they any connection with that university. Their primary identity as far as the study was concerned was their sexual identity and not their occupational role. All were drawn from the same chapter of the Gay Liberation Front at another university. These subjects were also interviewed by the psychiatrist, who established them to be homosexual in sex-role identity and practice. Both groups were given the Minnesota Multiphasic Personality Inventory (MMPI), and the results showed that aside from being somewhat more anxious and feminine, the gay subjects did not differ significantly from the heterosexuals on the clinical scales.

To the medical-student group the experimenters occupied the complementary role of faculty members in the same institution, and as such had other actual, or potential, relationships with these subjects that might affect their careers. This reinforced the need of the subjects to behave like "students," and no doubt created a demand for them to watch their step and look like good prospective doctors in our eyes.

To the homosexual subjects the experimenters had only a passing importance as members of the straight society and researchers in the area of sexual identity. The study provided them an opportunity to educate some potentially influential people and to help change the image of the homosexual from that of "pervert" to sexually liberated, and even nobly misunderstood, person. Evidence of this view came from the buttons worn to the laboratory reading "Gay Is Good" and the like, the small talk instigated during the presleep preparation period, and the dream reports themselves. For them, the situation seemed to be: "Tell it like it is to show the straight folks what it means to be gay." In sum, the role behaviors elicited in response to the study were potentially different for the two groups. For the first group there may have been some conflict between the student and the subject role behaviors, since both were associated with the same persons and place. While expressing sexual fantasies is clearly appropriate behavior for a subject in a sex study, it is not appropriate for a medical student when dealing with professors in the hospital context. For those in the second group, who were not known to the experimenters except in their homosexual identity roles, expressing their sexual fantasy material was the appropriate, expected behavior. The first group had reason to be closed, the second, open.

If these inferences were valid and both groups were sexually stimulated by the film, the motivation to report fully should have been greater for those in group 2 than group 1, particularly after having been exposed to the movie. The amount of dreaming directly involving sex should have been increased for the homosexuals and decreased for the heterosexuals. Also, the amount of dreaming in which the subject was in an occupational versus a sexual identity role should have differed, with the heterosexual subject producing more occupational and the homosexuals more sex-role-related dreams.

The question of whether the two groups were in fact equally aroused by the movie is a valid one in light of the fact that the same movie stimulus material was used for both groups and this material involved only heterosexual activity. Both groups were monitored before, during, and after the film for their response in terms of a number of physiological measures: heart rate, plasma levels of 17 hydroxycorticosteroids, pupillary dilation, and subjective and objective measures of penile erection. Each subject was asked after seeing the film if an erection had been experienced and to estimate its extent on a 4-point scale in which zero equaled no response and 3 a full erection. Nine of the heterosexual males and 8 of the homosexuals reported erections above the level of zero. Of the 10 homosexual subjects, 8 wore a penile strain gauge. This more objective measure showed 7 of the 8 in sample 2 to have moderate to full erections (Kling, Borowitz, & Cartwright, 1972). The relation of the verbal to the plethysmographic report showed the verbal to be, if anything, an underestimate for those where the two measures could be compared. When asked to identify the scene or act in which their erections took place, the homosexuals differed from the heterosexual subjects in the reported stimuli. The gay subjects most often ignored the female and responded to the male actor in the movie and in this way redefined the stimulus as appropriate to them.

What are the effects of this arousal in the dream reports? Can observing a heterosexual interaction stimulate a homosexual dream expression? Two dreams illustrate that this does in fact occur.

Homosexual Subject D, Night 3, REM 4:

I was back in that room, or that sort of garden and Hefner was there . . . Hefner and I had been talking philosophy . . . we wandered back into that restricted courtyard and then we went through the door there, and there was this man sort of fiddling around with this young girl and the other young girl looking on. I thought: He's so jaded this is what he has to do to amuse himself. And there are two guys who eventually started giving each other blow jobs and I, I joined in, finally.

Homosexual Subject I, Night 4, REM 6:

I was talking to some people, I think it was around Dearborn Street and they were sitting there. There was a beautiful blond boy who was sitting with a very fat girl who was actually very interesting. And I don't know if I was coming by on my bicycle or if I was just walking along, but anyway, they said hello and I said hello and we started to chat . . . and the girl asked me which I would rather go to bed with and I said, "Well, probably your friend." And she just sort of smiled. . . . All of a sudden the boy was in my arms. The girl didn't seem to mind at all, and he was kissing me very violently—no, passionately—and sort of arranging himself in various positions. Finally he turned over . . . and I started to lick his back, very sensuously. I did that for a while and he really seemed to like it. He was sort of in my power.

Did the homosexual group follow the heterosexual in having less recall following the film? The most commonly accepted figure for the percentage of REM-period awakenings leading to a report of a dream is 83.3%. This was derived by Dement (1965c), who pooled the samples from several studies to obtain a total of 200 subjects awakened from more than 2,000 REM periods. In this study each REM report for the 20 subjects was individually coded and rated blindly by a judge naïve to the study hypotheses. The rates of recall for our two samples showed the heterosexuals to have a prefilm recall rate almost exactly at the norm quoted herein. The decrease in recall rate following the film for the heterosexual subject group, who reported to a female experimenter, was not observed in the second group. The homosexuals showed a higher rate of recall both before and after the movie regardless of the sex of their experimenter. The difference between the two groups in recall rate on night 2 was significant, and within the homosexual group the pre- to postfilm recall rate was not reduced. Thus the dampening effect on recall following an increase in sexual stimulation was not replicated, showing this not to be a general effect for all subjects but to be specific to the medical student group.

The best baseline data on the number of sexual dreams occurring in laboratory and home dreams of the same subjects are those reported by Domhoff and Kamiya (1964). They reported that 12 males, who slept in the laboratory once a week for a total of 10 nights and wrote down any home dreams recalled during that period, had only 2 sexual dreams (2%) in the laboratory, in contrast to 11 (9%) at home. This difference, while small, was significant. The 10 medical student subjects reported only 1 sexual dream out of the total of 31 collected on their first night of awakenings before seeing the film. This gives a 3% figure comparable with the Domhoff and

Kamiya rate just quoted. The dream itself demonstrates the fear of being caught by authority figures while responding to a sexual situation.

Heterosexual Subject J, Night 1, REM 2:

> This time there was music in the living room of our apartment and I had my girlfriend there, and I had undressed her and we were just about to make love when there was a knock at the door and it turned out that it was her parents, of all people. . . .

For the homosexual sample the prefilm number of directly sexual dreams was identical—1 out of 39 awakenings that yield some content, or 2.5%. However, the nature of the dream is much more matter of fact.

Homosexual Subject D, Night 1, REM 4:

> I was making love. It's hard to remember the details. I remember I was right on top at the same time . . . there is nothing I can add right now.

Following the movie both groups of subjects slept for 4 more consecutive nights of REM awakenings. Of the 157 reports with some dream recall reported from the heterosexual sample, none contained any overtly sexual content. Of the 190 postfilm dreams contributed by 5 of 10 homosexual subjects, 6 dealt with direct, unambiguous sexual activity. All of these occurred, however, with the subgroup of subjects who reported to the male experimenter. This made the comparison 5.4% for the homosexuals reporting to the male, compared to 0% for the heterosexuals, and 0% for the homosexuals reporting to the female. These results are rather meager, but suggest that, contrary to expectation, the potential sexual element in the experimenter–subject relationship had opposite effects for the two samples. Heterosexual subjects suppressed reporting sexual material to a female and gay subjects suppressed to the female, but expressed more freely to a male (potential sex partner).

More evident was the amount of homosexual content that was not directly sexual in nature but defined identity. The dreams of all subjects for all nights were categorized according to the primary social role of the dreamer in each dream. The differences in the frequency with which these categories were used by the two samples can be seen in Table 7.1.

The three differences that had been anticipated were all found to be significant. The most common way heterosexual subjects define themselves in their laboratory dreams is as students or doctors. This is particularly true in situations that might hold sexual potential. The homosexuals present themselves more often as "friends" to other males or as "sexual," in this case, gay people. Many of the "friend" dreams involved others known to be Gay Liberation members. The role-frequency analysis confirmed the

TABLE 7.1. THE ROLE OF THE DREAMER TO OTHERS IN THE DREAMS
FOR 5 NIGHTS

| | Heterosexual Subjects | | Homosexual Subjects | | |
Role	F	Percentage	F	Percentage	Z
Alone	22	12.4	29	13.4	—
Family member	16	9.0	25	11.5	—
Friend	19	10.7	43	20.1	2.76^a
Onlooker	16	9.0	10	4.6	—
Sexual identity	9	5.0	28	13.0	2.82^a
Sports participant	16	9.0	4	1.8	3.27^b
Stranger	19	10.7	17	7.9	—
Student or student doctor	34	19.5	15	6.9	3.21^b
Subject in experiment	8	4.5	24	11.1	2.45
Victim, escapee	11	6.2	10	4.6	—
Employee	8	4.0	11	5.1	—

$^a p$ .05
$^b p$ .01

saliency of the occupational role of the medical students and the sexual-identity role of the homosexuals across all the nights.

A few examples will illustrate this difference. The first two demonstrate how the medical students employ a professional identity to deny sexual curiosity, whereas the next two illustrate the motivation of the homosexuals to be known as gay in order to educate others. In the first dream the subject goes through a patient's room while she is in bed, and she protests that he has no legitimate reason to be there. In the film a young man is taken to a prostitute's bedroom. In the dream the subject denies the similarity and says: "I am not staying. Just passing through."

Heterosexual Subject S, Night 5, REM 7:

I was walking through a patient's room in order to get to another one and she had just returned from the operating room and had on one of those little short robes. She was indignant because I had gone through her room and made some remark about it not being a thoroughfare.

The second dream can be read as a response to watching the movie in which a couple are "making a baby." Again this subject says, "My interest in observing this is legitimate."

Heterosexual Subject J, Night 4, REM 4:

I had just walked into a room where a young man and a young woman were changing the diapers on a new baby. I don't know whether I was supposed to be a doctor but it was obviously a hospital. She wasn't, you know, in bed or anything, you know. She was standing up. Neither one were in hospital robes but they did have a new kid and I seemed to be very interested in the, in the, kid, you know, the way it looked and the fact that it was healthy and so forth.

The role of the dreamer as doctor appears to be used defensively to prevent his sexual interests from being recognized by others, whereas the role of the dreamer as homosexual expresses his wish to make known his sexual identity.

Homosexual Subject P, Night 1, REM 3:

It was a really dramatic scene in which I don't know what doctor, some doctor I haven't met here—well it's like I had already finished the experiment or something like that and this doctor was a lady doctor who was terribly scandalized by the fact that I was homosexual. And she said, "If I had known what you were for," and I said, "That's not true and that's not the approach you should take and, uh, you don't understand what it's all about." And I was very gentle and kind and all that, and she sort of broke down and started crying. And I just explained the way things were, just pointing up the fact that some people make money the center of their lives, and some people make intellect the center of their lives, and some make taking care of their children the center of their lives. And in the end a lot of them make this some sort of monomania. And with homosexuals oft times the center of their lives can just be sex. But at the same time they might be quite intelligent, and they may be intelligent as far as money matters are concerned, and so on and so forth, but they can never forget, never, never, never (very dramatic) uh, that they are homosexual and that sort of broke both, broke both of us up.

Homosexual Subject M, Night 3, REM 1:

It was sort of a press conference. And we were talking about the fact that Gay Liberation was trying to do something good for the community with regard to a certain person. And we weren't getting any support. In fact members of the community were trying to destroy the organization. I was standing in front of a large machine of some sort which reminded me a lot of these newspaper racks that they have in libraries where the newspapers are on poles and hang like flags. Anyway, we were in front of a rack and we were illustrating various points of the press conference by pulling out the rack and there were pictures on there. This was after there had been some bloodshed and a lot of trouble. And people were saying things like, "Oh what a shame it was, you know, that we didn't see these events sooner so we could have prevented them . . . .

The impact of the film in making the homosexual subjects more self-revealing in the research context and the heterosexual subjects less so was also evident in the role analysis. When the three anonymous categories (alone, onlooker, and stranger) were combined, the groups did not differ on night 1. Twenty-five percent of the homosexuals' and 26% of the heterosexuals' dreams fell into these categories. On night 2, following the movie, the homosexuals' use of these categories was reduced to 15% and the heterosexuals' increased to 46%, a significant difference in proportion.

Three content-analysis scales, adapted from those developed by Whitman, Pierce, Maas, and Baldridge (1961) were applied by the rater to each REM report. These 6-point scales measured the degree of homosexuality between two or more men, the degree of heterosexuality, and the degree of intimacy. The mean score for each subject on each night was obtained, as was the group means of these scores. These appeared to confirm that the change from pre- to postfilm nights was in the opposite direction for the two samples. The heterosexual subjects reduced their scores on all three scales, showing the dream interactions to be less intimate with both opposite- and same-sex characters; the homosexual subjects moved toward higher intimacy and closer relations following the film. This was particularly true for those subjects reporting to the male experimenter.

All the evidence is consistent in pointing to a single interpretation: The dream reports of the two groups of subjects were affected by the experimental situation quite differently, and these differences were congruent with what the subjects felt to be approvable behavior in their subject role. The demand characteristics of the laboratory were clearly different for these two groups, and their dreams were shaped in response to these. For the first group the demand to report to professors was met with a need to hide their sexuality from these authority figures. For the second group the demand to report to straight researchers was met with the need to be open to help us understand them. Two examples illustrated this difference. Both dreams took place in a bathroom adjoining a bedroom and involved an older woman. This was the actual situation in the sleep laboratory at the hospital where these subjects were seen. The subjects' rooms had been converted from cubicles that had originally housed bathtubs in an old ward bathroom. The bathroom itself was still in use and the subjects entered their bedrooms through this bathroom. The director of this laboratory, the senior author, is a woman older than the subjects. In the first dream the subject, having been standing erect but innocent all night, was caught by an older authority figure.

Heterosexual Subject G, Night 3, REM 3:

I had been to see my old girlfriend, the one from New York. She was living at a dorm at _____, and we often had a habit of staying too late. Well, in this case I overdid it and the ladies closed the door, and for some reason instead of asking to get out I went with her upstairs and stayed in the bathroom of the little, you know, cubicle she was living in with another girl. The other girl didn't know I was there, so apparently I just slept in their standing up all night long. The next morning there was an inspection of the room and I was caught. Ah, L_____, the girl I was going with, was gone and I had no explanation of how I got there, so I was in kind of a tough spot. The lady who was doing the inspection was very nice about it. In fact she wasn't the least surprised when she opened the door and found me standing there. And that was it.

In the second dream the subject cooperated and was helpful to the older woman's interests in male sexuality.

Homosexual Subject D, Night 2, REM 3:

A bathroom has some "male enlightenment." There was this old lady going through some things of her father, who had died, and she was looking for a book called *Male Enlightenments*. The room looked like the master bedroom of my mother and stepfather. She was cute but real old and was trying to get this book *Male Enlightenments* in order to learn some sex techniques. It was funny because she was too old for that sort of thing. I liked her and found some things for her that she was looking for.

The findings do not support the interpretation that the laboratory has any generally dampening effect on intimate dreaming or dreams with strong affects, nor that there is a sex-of-experimenter effect on these dreams that can be interpreted outside of the interpersonal context. Whether the laboratory has the effect of reducing or heightening certain types of dreaming and whether the sex of the experimenter reduces or increases reporting depends on how the experience is defined as a whole and how the possible responses to it are valued by the subject. Dream reports in the laboratory tend to support the subject's waking motivations and enhance a sense of self-worth in that context.

These data support the position, taken by Whitman, Kramer, Ornstein, and Baldridge (1970), that even under sexual arousal conditions the interpersonal situation of the sleep laboratory cannot be ignored. Are these reports representative of dreaming under home conditions? If not, what can be done about it? The best analogy may be to the behavior elicited in psychotherapy. In that situation as well, the verbal behavior that emerges is responsive to the interpersonal context of patient and therapist and thus differs from that observable under the more neutral conditions of everyday life. Dreams collected in the laboratory must be understood as behaviors in their own right, not as pale shadows of the more "real" home dreams. All dreams have both trait and state characteristics, and as such must be interpreted in the light of the emotional state the individual brings to the situation as well as the particular emotional context of the experimenter relationship and the motivations operating at the time. This makes the manipulation of the laboratory factors a fruitful field for research into dream processes as yet almost completely untouched.

Acknowledgments

This work was carried out at the Department of Psychiatry, University of Illinois College of Medicine, as part of a collaborative study with Marjorie Barnett, Gene Borowitz, and Arthur Kling. It was financed by grants MH 18124 and MH 23450 from the U. S. Public Health Service. The authors are indebted to Nancy Chiswick, Linda Kamens, Sarah Labelle, Harvey Lucas, Frances Morowski, and Phyllis Walesby, all of whom acted as laboratory assistants and judges.

8

The Effects of External Stimuli Applied Prior to and During Sleep on Sleep Experience

ARTHUR M. ARKIN
JOHN S. ANTROBUS
City College of the City University of New York

Throughout the long history of the interpretation and study of dreams much observation and discussion have been devoted to the effects of presleep experience on dreams, including the events of the previous day and of sensory stimulation during sleep. The cognitive response of the sleeper to presleep and concurrent sleep sensory stimulation provides us with one of the powerful research tools for the study of how sleep mentation, including dreams, is generated. Since the rules and principles that describe the generation of dreaming belong to more general theories of thought and cognition, presleep experience and sensory stimulation during sleep provide a unique and therefore valuable testing ground for such theories. In the 19th century, sleep-stimulation anecdotes were commonly cited as support for the associationist theory of thinking. For example, the introduction of perfume into a sleeper's room on a hot night was said to be capable of eliciting dreams of tropical romance. Among the secondary benefits of this main research thrust are enlightenment about sensory thresholds, perceptual vigilance, and individual differences during sleep, as well as effects of presleep posthypnotic suggestion as manifested during sleep.

The literature prior to the advent of electrographic technology has been thoroughly reviewed by Freud (1953c/1900) and more recently by Ramsey (1953). Although these reports include many dramatic instances of factors that influence dream content, the observations lack the systematic controls and protections against observer bias that are now required of experimental studies.

The first question asked by contemporary work was whether sleep mentation can be reliably and systematically modified by external stimulation. That is, may we demonstrate such phenomena experimentally? As we shall see, Dement and Wolpert (1958b) and others answered this question with a qualified "yes," that it is possible to observe the phenomenon frequently under laboratory conditions. The second question, in our judgment, is: Can we take these observations beyond a set of interesting curiosities and use them to further our understanding about how the dream is constructed? As this review shows, we will be a long time in arriving at an answer.

We will develop the topic as it has been researched during the current electrographic era along the following lines:

1. The effects of stimuli applied *during* sleep on dream content (flashes of light, tones, water sprayed on the skin, tape recording of one's own voice versus that of others, names of persons emotionally close to the sleeper versus indifferent names, and so on);

2. The effects of variables impinging on the subject *prior* to sleep, ranging in time from occurrences during the day (including Freud's "day residue" concept), to events experienced at sleep onset including the hypnagogic phase;

   a. Studies involving experimental procedures carried out in "normal" wakeful consciousness (specific films, specific drive arousal and frustration, studying, exercise, planned day-time experience, free association at sleep onset, and so on);

   b. Studies involving presleep hypnosis with posthypnotic suggestions to dream about selected topics or specific content.

EFFECTS OF STIMULI APPLIED DURING SLEEP

Although the studies described under this heading share a common feature—all pertain to the effects of external stimuli applied during sleep on concurrent mentation—they also have many differences: There was considerable variation in the nature of the stimulus, the sleep stage in which it was introduced, and the focus of attention of the investigator. Regarding the latter, some workers were interested in more basic primary and secondary perceptive processes in sleep, whereas others sought to examine higher order cognitive operations. Also, some studies were specially designed to assess the effects of external stimuli whereas others only provided incidental observations obtained during the pursuit of other experimental goals. We describe each such category of research separately.

Effects of Sensory Stimulation Introduced During Sleep

The first systematic experimental study of the effects of external stimuli on sleep mentation to utilize electrographic technology was that of Dement and Wolpert (1958b). In an experiment with 12 volunteer subjects, stimuli consisting of either a 1000 Hz tone, a series of light flashes, or a spray of water on the skin were applied during ongoing stage REM. These stimuli were usually below waking threshold. The subjects were then definitively awakened by a loud bell. The mentation reports elicited following each condition were examined for evidence of: (a) unambiguous *incorporation* of the preawakening stimulus into an ongoing dream; and (b) *modification* of ongoing dream content in some appropriate, recognizable manner other than direct incorporation.

The water-spray stimulus was the most effective by far in producing both types of results. An example of the former outcome was a report in which the subject dreamt of being "squirted" by someone; and of the latter, dreams about sudden rainfalls, or leaking roofs. Following the stimulus of the 1000 Hz tone, a subject reported experiencing the sudden intrusion of a brief roaring sound into the dream. The subject was frightened and thought that either an earthquake was occurring or that a plane had crashed outside of the house in the dream. And after stimulation with light flashes, dream modifications included a sudden fire, a flash of lightning, seeing shooting stars, and a more direct indication of incorporation in which the subject dreamt of the experimenter shining a flashlight into the subject's eyes. Finally, the most frequent incorporations occurring after the sounding of the awakening bell were dream content of the ringing of a telephone or doorbell just as the subject awoke.

The results of 98 tests were available in which the various experimental stimuli, themselves *insufficient* to awaken the subjects, were applied during ongoing stage REM. Fourteen of 33 followed the water spray (42%); 7 of 30 followed light flashes (23%); and 3 of 35 (9%) achieved direct incorporation.

Because of the short latency between stimulation and awakening, those instances in which subjects *were* aroused to full wakefulness by the experimental stimulus or by the awakening bell provided the best opportunity to evaluate the effectiveness of stimuli in modifying ongoing dream content. Of 15 such occasions following the water spray, 6 (40%) showed such modification; whereas of 204 occasions following the bell, only 20 (10%) revealed similar results. Finally, of 5 instances following the 1000 Hz tone, none of the reports disclosed evidence of dream modification.

Thus the findings of this initial experiment demonstrated that external stimuli presented during stage REM could be perceived by the subjects without apparent awakening. Further, they showed that the phenomenon might be similar to waking perception of the stimulus event; or, on the other hand, that such percepts could be transformed in some fashion according to the context of the concurrent mentation of the sleeper.

Is it not interesting and puzzling that this study showed such a relatively small overall proportion of stimulus incorporation (24% of all tests) and experimental modification of dream content (12% of all tests)? Taken at face value, the results suggest that ongoing REM sleep mentation is relatively impervious to intrusions from concomitant external sources. Another partial explanation is that the experimenters' judgments of the reports were unduly conservative and literal, thus leading to an underestimate of the magnitude of incorporation of external stimuli and their potential for modification of dream content.

Why the dreamer is more likely to respond to some stimuli, and only on some occasions, is quite relevant to notions of perceptual vigilance during sleep and to models of dream formation. Parametric studies of the effects of stimulus intensity, stimulus modality, and familiarity or history of experience with the stimulus are called for.

Thus, it is not clear why the water spray should have been superior to auditory and visual stimuli in the experimental situation.* It is of interest, however, that a parallel clinical situation occurs in enuresis in which

---

*More recently, Dement (1972) cited work of his students on the effects of external stimuli on dreams. Unfortunately, the original work is unavailable to us and we can only describe Dement's summary. A number of subjects (total not given) were awakened during REM sleep prior to which tape recordings of stimuli, introduced about 10 seconds after REMP onset, had been played at subwaking threshold levels. The stimuli included 12 familiar and evocative sounds such as a rooster crowing, a steam locomotive, a bugle playing reveille, a barking dog, traffic noise, and a speech by Martin Luther King, Jr. By contrast to the earlier study (Dement & Wolpert, 1958b), a striking proportion of the sound stimuli influenced dream content: 56%. The locomotive sound was the most effective, and traffic noise the least.

dreams about moisture, liquids, and so on are common despite the occurrence of enuretic episodes in NREM rather than REM sleep. The most reasonable explanation is that the sustained stimulation of the urine to the skin affects the content of succeeding REM-sleep dreams in the same manner as did the water spray in the above experimental situation.

Results qualitatively similar to those observed by Dement and Wolpert (1958b) have been reported by others. Thus, using stimuli applied to other types of sensory systems, Baldridge (1966) and Baldridge, Whitman, Kramer, Ornstein, and Lansky (1965) have published preliminary findings on the effects of thermal stimulation on dreams; incorporations were said to occur in 25% of the occasions. Examples were a dream containing a reference to getting food from a refrigerator following cold skin contact, and another referring to a warm day following a warmth stimulus. In addition, the effects of kinesthetic stimuli (produced by raising and lowering the upper part of a hospital bed) were said to be followed by dreams that were distinguishable from those associated with control nonmovement awakenings. Mentation reports following motion often involved not only specific movement activities but dreams of falling, flying, riding a motor scooter, and other indications of increased activity on the part of the dreamer, as well.

Along related lines, incidental observations, made in the course of studies designed for other purposes, indicated that external stimuli, such as tones used to experimentally awaken subjects, are more likely to be incorporated into REM sleep, transformed, or misperceived when either the subject's awakening threshold was high or the stimulus was initiated at low intensities and permitted to increase gradually (Goodenough, Lewis, Shapiro, Jaret, & Sleser, 1965a; Goodenough, Lewis, Shapiro, & Sleser, 1965b; Rechtschaffen, Hauri, & Zeitlin, 1966). Their findings suggest the importance of stimulus-threshold factors in determining outcomes—a factor not yet systematically investigated.

In the course of designing research in this area, Koulack (1969) properly utilized a technique that would simultaneously ensure cortical registration of the stimulus in all stages of sleep and minimize the production of concurrent arousal bursts of alpha frequencies or body movements. Goff, Allison, Shapiro, and Rosner (1966) had shown earlier that percutaneous electrical stimulation of the median nerve at the wrist sufficiently intense to elicit a thumb jerk during wakefulness, is capable of producing cortical responses in all stages of sleep. Accordingly, Koulack (1969) utilized this technique, excluding from his main analysis all stimuli associated with EEG alpha frequencies or body movements. Thus, subjects received percutaneous electrical stimulation to the wrist as described, during REM sleep under 5 different conditions, each with awakenings for mentation reports as follows: C_1, no stimulation with awakening 3 minutes after the first REM; C_2, stimulation at first REM with awakening 30 seconds afterward; C_3, stimulation at first

REM with awakening after 3 minutes; C_4, stimulation 3 minutes after the first REM, with awakening 30 seconds later; and C_5, stimulation 3 minutes after the first REM and awakening delayed for 3 minutes after stimulus termination. Each wrist was stimulated at least once in each condition and conditions were randomly ordered. Stimuli without awakenings were also applied during NREM sleep. Fifteen awakenings were made for each of 10 adult male subjects, 3 in each of the conditions, during 4 to 9 nights each slept in the laboratory. Subjects rated their own dreams on a number of ad hoc rating scales and mood adjective checklist dimensions. Postexperimental interviews were conducted to secure associations to the dreams and additional content. The chief focus of interest was whether the somatosensory electrical stimulus would produce direct and/or indirect stimulus incorporations into the ongoing dream. From both sets of data, direct and indirect dream incorporations were scored by a judge who was unaware of the specific association between the experimental awakening category and the subjects' productions. A second judge, totally unaware of the experimental details, scored edited nocturnal interviews in 7 content areas (such as self-participation or self-activity). In all, 28 subdivisions of such scored material were obtained. Reliability for each judge was evaluated by extent of agreement with the author and was reported as at least 96%. By direct incorporation, Koulack (1969) meant "some sort of direct representation of the stimulus situation in the dream" (p. 719), whereas indirect incorporation referred either to events suggestive to the rater of the stimulus situation or to occasions when subjects were able to connect associatively with the stimulus during the postsleep interview, when such associations related to the more general laboratory or stimulus situation.

The specific hypotheses to be tested were:

1. Stimuli applied during REM sleep in a sequence of six shocks at 2.5-second intervals would be manifested in mentation reports in both direct and indirect fashion, as indicated by comparison to reports elicited from nonstimulated conditions in the same subject.
2. Stimuli would enhance self-participation and self-activity in the dream.
3. The greatest dream modification would occur with introduction of stimuli at the beginning of the REM period as opposed to later on.
4. Stimuli presented in NREM sleep would either initiate REM periods or reduce latency to stage REM.

In accordance with Koulack's (1969) prediction, each stimulation condition occasioned significantly more direct and indirect incorporation than occurred with C_1, but contrary to expectations the stimulation conditions did not produce different outcomes among themselves. Maximum indirect incorporation (42%) was attained in C_3, whereas maximum direct incorporation (40%) occurred in C_5. Expectations that stimuli would produce increased presence and activity of oneself in the dreams; that effects would be greatest when stimuli were applied early as opposed to later in the REM period; and that stimuli would initiate or hasten the onset of REMPs were not supported. In addition, direct incorporation was more likely when associated with alpha bursts. Unfortunately, potential gains over other studies in obtaining refined data under improved conditions of stimulus control were not realized because of methodological difficulties. Specifically, Foulkes (1970), in criticizing the work, commented that although the study appeared to demonstrate incorporation of somatosensory stimulation in REM dreams, the lack of control data for stimuli in other modalities made assessment uncertain. Also, a separate control group would have been a useful supplement to using each subject as a self-control (the control baseline having been the number of "incorporations" during the C_1 procedure). Additional problems in evaluating the study included inadequately described dream-scoring categories, inclusion among indirect "incorporations" of any material relating to the general laboratory situation, inadequate stage REM control awakenings, and a confounding of results of stimulations associated with REM-phasic versus nonphasic differences with early (C_2 and C_3) versus late (C_4 and C_5) conditions.

Children as Subjects in Sensory-Stimulation Experiments in Sleep

Might the maturational level of brain development affect the outcome of external stimuli applied during sleep? One could imagine reasons for predicting either a greater or smaller effect in children than in adults. Relevant information is provided by Foulkes, Larson, Swanson, and Rardin (1969), who sought to determine whether external stimuli were incorporated into children's dreams partly to assess validity of their laboratory dream reports and partly out of the inherent interest residing in the question. After two children between $4^1/_2$ and $5^1/_2$ years of age provided two fairly clear-cut but unplanned examples of stimulus effects on dream content, attempts to investigate this possibility more systematically were carried out on four additional children whose age ranged from 4 to $4^1/_2$ years. On one experimental night each, drops of water, puffs of air, puffs of cotton, and an emory board were all lightly applied to the skin of each subject during REM sleep. Only one subject (female) appeared to incorporate a stimulus, and this was on 3 of the 4 occasions. The cotton puff was followed by a dream of her sister playing with a cuddly toy lion; the air puff, a dream of a family outing in a boat on a lake, with the wind blowing on her face; the water, a dream that she was with her siblings and spraying a hose. The emory board produced no obvious effect on dream content. In no instance were sleep EEG patterns disrupted and in all cases, stimulation was terminated a few seconds prior to awakening. The results as a whole support the contention that stimulus incorporation is indeed possible in the dreaming child but does not permit meaningful comparisons with results on adults.

Subsequently, Foulkes and Shepherd (1972) performed a more ambitious study. The subject pool consisted of 30 children, 16 of whom were 9 to 10, and 14 were 3 to 4 years of age. Awakenings were made after external stimulation on nights 2 and 9 of a long-term study schedule on the content of children's dreams..Mentation reports were obtained from both REM and NREM sleep. The stimuli were a cotton puff dabbed on the face, induced limb movement, and a water spray to the skin, each preceding awakening by 5 to 15 seconds.

Fifty-six usable mentation reports were categorized by two independent judges as displaying direct incorporation (related to the subject as a dream character), indirect incorporation (unrelated to the subject), or no incorporation. The incorporation rates were as follows: cotton puff: both judges, 0%; limb movement: Judge 1, 8.5%, Judge 2, 5.6%; water spray: Judge 1, 15.6%, Judge 2, 10.4%. Of Judge 1's six successfully detected-water stimulations, four were categorized as indirect, and two direct; four were in REM and two in NREM sleep. The results were deemed to be generally consistent with those of Dement and Wolpert (1958b).

(It should be noted that, in this instance, "direct" versus "indirect" incorporation are used in a somewhat different sense than that of Koulack, 1969 and that of Dement and Wolpert, 1958b.)

Effects of Verbal Stimulation

What would happen if, instead of primarily stimulating sensory components of perceptual systems, one chose to observe the effects of verbal stimuli? One might expect in this way to involve more complex cognitive processes. One of the most useful and impressive studies in the entire field of sleep mentation is Berger's (1963) work on experimental modification of dream content by meaningful verbal stimuli. His purpose was to determine whether verbal stimuli would be incorporated or misperceived in some fashion and appear in ongoing dream events, and also whether such occurrences would be related to the emotional significance of the stimulus to the subject. The stimuli were tape recordings of four first names of persons. By suitable objective methods, two were predetermined to possess strong emotional significance for the subject and two were emotionally neutral. The latter were equal to the emotional names in the number of syllables but maximum in phonic contrast.

The experimental plan called for the presentation of a single name 5 to 10 minutes after each REM-period onset. On each succeeding occasion, a different name was chosen on a random basis from the set of four specifically selected for each subject. The stimulus was sounded at an intensity sufficient to initially provoke a just discernible change in the EEG without awakening the subject.

Such EEG changes usually consisted of a flattening of the EEG trace; of "humping"; of low-voltage, fast activity for 1 to 2 seconds or, only rarely, 1 or 2 seconds of alpha rhythm. Four male and 4 female, "normal" young adults served as subjects.

An approximate total of 10 dreams was obtained from each subject during 4 to 6 nights of sleep. There were 89 usable reports with approximately equal proportions following emotional and neutral stimulus names. In contrast to the study of Dement and Wolpert (1958b) in which the subjects were aware of the nature of the experiment, not one in Berger's (1963) study seemed to have an awareness of the true aims of the project (as evidenced by their replies to relevant questions put to them, and their expression of genuine surprise upon being informed at the end of the experimental schedule).

The results were assessed by testing the prediction that both an independent judge and the subjects themselves (for their own dreams) would be able to correctly match each of the four stimulus names with its corresponding mentation report significantly more often than would be expected by chance alone. The assessors were told in advance that "the type of connection to look for is between the dream content and the sound of the name—or any other you may think fit." Both the subjects and the judge did indeed make correct matchings at statistically significant levels (range of $p: \leq .05$ to $\leq .001$) and, furthermore, there was a strikingly high level of agreement between them regarding the specific matches. (The subjects had been instructed to state whether their matchings were based either upon a perceived connection between the stimulus names and the reports, or whether they merely made their choice as a guess; the independent judge had been instructed to rate matchings at four levels of confidence, the last level a guess.)

Of the 89 mentation reports used in the assessment, 48 (54%) were scored overall as possessing a "definite connection" to the stimulus name. The manner of the relation varied, however, and appeared to be separable into four different categories, assonance (by far the most frequent), association, direct, and representation. Details are furnished in Table 8.1.

Berger (1963) indicated his awareness of problematic aspects of the categorizations of his data, stating for example, that

. . . in order to examine the forms in which the stimuli were incorporated into the dream, one must decide which dreams were in fact modified by the stimulus. [For various reasons] there appear to be no adequate criteria by which one can make such judgements and one must rely upon a reasonable, subjective analysis of the dream. The analysis [of the modes of incorporation of the stimuli into the dreams] is therefore only a tentative one and it must be

TABLE 8.1.   MODES OF RELATIONSHIP BETWEEN STIMULUS NAME AND MENTATION REPORT

Category	Number of Reports	Stimulus Name	Features of Mentation Report Illustrative of Relationship Category
Assonance	31	Robert	Rabbit; was slightly frightened and distorted
		Naomi	An *aim* to ski; friend who says "*Oh, show me*"
		Gillian	Came from *Chile* (that is a Chilean); *linen*
		Andrew	*Land*, cent*rifuge*, h*and*
Association	6	Maureen	Relevant dream content: being handed back his math book which had been marked in a peculiar manner, similar to the way the English master used to mark books at school. Subject's spontaneous associations upon hearing the tape recording of mentation report but still unapprised of the specific corresponding stimulus name: the name of English master had been *More*; *Maureen* (current girlfriend) studied math
Direct	8	Eileen	The subject thought to have shouted out the name of current girlfriend, "Eileen" in dream
Representation	3	Leslie	The subject dreamed of an Indian woman with glasses; subject's boyfriend an Indian named Leslie who occasionally wears glasses
	Total: 48 out of 89 reports		

continually borne in mind that examples quoted may have been arrived at fortuitously. (p. 730)

Thus, relationships categorized as assonance were based upon phonic features that the stimulus name and mentation report held in common. Most frequently these resembled the "clang associations" of descriptive psychiatry. More often the dream items repeated single features of the stimulus word-vowels and consonants, either singly or in combination.

Occasions illustrative of the association category arose only during the course of subjects listening to the recordings of their own mentation reports. This provoked spontaneous associations in the subject that were clearly related to the stimulus name where the mentation report contents themselves had not been previously revealing.

Direct relationships included all instances in which the stimulus was directly incorporated into the dream as an externalized or internalized voice.

Representation was the category reserved for occurrences in which the person bearing the emotional stimulus name appeared either directly in the dream or else "in a disguised or transformed" manner.

In presenting his results, Berger (1963) made the following additional observations and remarks:

1. There were no appreciable differences in the number of correct matchings made for emotional or neutral stimuli or in relation to the sex of the subjects, or between subjects. This result was contrary to one of his hypothesized predictions to the effect that emotional stimuli would be matched more frequently with the proper mentation reports than neutral ones. However, Berger did state that sexual symbols of a Freudian psychoanalytic type tended to appear mainly in association with emotional rather than neutral stimuli.

2. Although the perception of the stimulus name, as manifested by apparent incorporation into dream events, was usually as a single assonant word, such perception frequently occurred as a series of words composed of assonant vowels and consonants. Occasionally, the stimulus word was perceived as a type of auditory "Gestalt" of parts or whole words spoken in succession. For example, "Peter" was thought to have been manifested in the dream as "*t*hree *t*icks" against the name of a firm to whom bills had been paid. On still another occasion, incorporation of the stimulus appeared to be manifested by repetition of one or more letters of the stimulus name in the dream narrative. Thus, "Kenny" was the stimulus to the following dream sequence in which such repetitions occurred: "I was at a *c*oncert . . . some *S*cots *c*haracter was—I think he was mainly a *c*omedian . . . the scen*ery* was some ro*ck* with a *c*rack in it." Berger indicated that the

manner of incorporation, the relationship between the stimulus name, and its pattern of appearance in the dream, was consistent with Freud's formulations concerning primary process mentation.

3. Incorporation of the stimulus into the dream events was not associated with the presence of alpha rhythm in the EEG following presentation of the names, nor was there any relation to the frequency of GSR fluctuations. By the same measures, no differences in arousal were detected in response to neutral versus emotional names. Thus, the likelihood of incorporation bore no relationship to concomitant levels of arousal.

4. Another interesting phenomenon was the high frequency with which subjects spontaneously described the incorporated stimulus as it appeared in the dream events as especially "strange," "odd," "sudden," and "vivid."

Berger's (1963) chief conclusions were that "perception of the external world, be it impaired, does occur during the REM periods associated with dreaming" (p. 739). When the stimulus achieves registration, the sleeper usually does not recognize that it originates in the external world but tends on the contrary to perceive it as if it were part of ongoing sleep-mentation experience. When this occurs, the stimulus, as a rule, appears in a dream with various degrees of transformation. Finally, although Berger stated that perceptual awareness of the stimulus is coincident with its cortical analysis, it is neither generally dependent upon the significance of the stimulus names to the subject, nor upon levels of arousal associated with the stimulus. This latter conclusion is somewhat at variance with implications of an earlier study of Oswald, Taylor, and Treisman (1960) in which K complexes were more likely to be provoked by sounding the subject's own name, a stimulus of greater emotional significance, as opposed to the names of others. Perhaps the most important difference between the conditions of the two studies is that Berger (1963) tested his subjects during stage REM whereas Oswald et al. (1960) made their observations during NREM.

Castaldo and Holzman (1967, 1969) performed an interesting variant of Berger's basic approach. A total of 19 subjects participated in the original and a replication study. Five minutes after REM period onsets, sleeping subjects were exposed to tape recordings of isolated words uttered by the subjects recorded at a prior time. All stimuli were made intense enough to produce EEG evidence of registration but not sufficiently intense to awaken the subjects. Shortly afterward they were definitively awakened and mentation reports were obtained following which an interval of free association was elicited. The control condition was a tape recording of another person's voice matched for sex, age, intonation, and the same words played under the same conditions with the same consequent procedure and in counterbalanced order.

Two judges independently rated the mentation reports by means of Likert-type scales which measured aspects of the behavior of dream characters. These aspects included amounts of activity, passivity, helpfulness to others, being helped by others, independence, competence, competitiveness, and assertiveness. The authors stated that the intercorrelations between the scales were quite low, attesting to their statistical independence.

The striking new finding was that reports elicited after recordings of the subject's own voice were judged to be much more likely to contain dream content in which the subject was active, assertive, and independent; whereas in the control condition, hearing another's voice tended to be followed by dreams in which the subject was passive and unassertive. Furthermore, the free association interval following completion of the report was likely to continue into wakefulness whatever active or passive trends had been experimentally initiated while dreaming. In addition, as with Berger's (1963) study, the dreams contained varying degrees and kinds of stimulus incorporation in which repetition of content elements, condensation, and assonance were common forms of response and/or transformation. An example of condensation is provided by a dream containing three references to "pennies," which were in response to the stimulus words "fountain pen," and after a 1-second pause, "kneecap." Another point of agreement with Berger's (1963) study is the demonstration that neutral verbal stimuli are capable of dream incorporation.

Finally, the results indicated quite remarkably that sleeping subjects are better able to discriminate between their own voices and those of others, than while they are awake. This conclusion was drawn on the basis that 89% of the subjects ($N = 20$, combining both the initial experiment and its replication) gave a differential dream incorporation response to the stimuli as compared to only 38% in another group of subjects tested in wakefulness for differential recognition of tape recordings of their own voices versus those of others.

The Effects of External Stimuli on NREM-Mentation: Sensory Stimulation

The first comment in the literature on this point appears in the report of Dement and Wolpert (1958b), mentioning that despite stimulus application during NREM sleep, no dream recall could be elicited following awakenings on any occasion. (The protocol called for 15 stimulations per subject during NREM sleep, 5 times each for the 3 stimulus conditions.) One cannot help but speculate, considering that the study was published in 1958, whether this starkly negative result was partly influenced by the already congealed belief that NREM dreaming was either nonexistent or inconsequential.

Subsequent commentary appears sporadically in the literature as parts of papers devoted to other topics. Thus Rechtschaffen, Verdone, and Wheaton

(1963), in the course of a paper on sleep mentation in general, mentioned that 2 of 7 subjects tested showed evidence of incorporating external stimuli into NREM sleep reports. A convincing example was provided in which an experimental tone sounded twice was represented in stage 2 mentation by a whistling noise repeated on two occasions and interwoven into a dream scene containing dialogue with another dream character. In a subsequent paper on auditory awakening thresholds, Rechtschaffen and Foulkes (1965) commented on the great rarity of incorporations of external stimuli into NREM sleep. Further mention of laboratory observation of incorporation of external stimuli into NREM sleep was made by Foulkes (1966).

Thus, it may be said that no truly systematic study of this problem has been published as yet.

Verbal Stimulation During NREM Sleep

Even though mentation reports were not elicited by Oswald et al. (1960), their study is worthy of description here because it involves the effects of tape recordings of persons' names within NREM sleep upon K complexes—an indication of cortical response to external stimulation. Oswald et al.'s (1960) goal was to test the hypothesis that a sensory stimulus causing arousal from sleep is preceded by cortical analysis of the personal significance of that stimulus. The data consisted of electrographic and behavioral responses during NREM sleep of human sleep-deprived subjects to tape-recorded playbacks of their own first names versus the names of others throughout the night. Evidence supporting their hypothesis was derived from the findings that:

1. K complexes occurred significantly more often on stimulation with their own names versus those of others or their own names played backward; and this was observed even in the absence of overt behavioral responses.

2. Polyphasic K complexes appeared significantly more often after hearing one's own name played in the forward direction rather than the smaller, less elaborate K complexes that were more prone to occur following one's own name played in reverse.

3. Overt awakening responses were significantly more likely after hearing one's own name than after someone else's.

4. Names played forward were significantly more likely to evoke a GSR than when played in reverse.

5. It was possible to repeatedly observe persistent lack of response with repetitive playback of the names of others and the sudden sequence of K complexes, GSR, behavioral response, and waking alpha rhythm, beginning as little as .5 second following playback of one's own name. Thus, absence of some electrical response of the brain to repetitive

stimulation need not signify cortico-fugal inhibition of afferent inflow to the cortex, but, rather, failure of response may indicate that the stimulus, as a *result* of cortical analysis, is deemed unimportant.

To bring Oswald et al.'s (1960) contribution up to date, we briefly describe a recently reported study of McDonald, Schicht, Frazier, Shallenberger, and Edwards (1975) on the effects of tape recordings of personal names on certain electrographic measures during sleep. Unfortunately, mentation reports were not obtained. Thirteen paid male undergraduate subjects spent 2 nights in the sleep laboratory. Besides the EEG and EOG, the finger plethysmogram (FP) and heart rate (HR) were monitored. The stimuli consisted of tape recordings of 25 monosyllabic male nicknames (Al, Bill, Jim, Dave, Mike, and so on), among which was the subject's own name. This tape was played a total of 6 times throughout all periods of wakefulness and *all* stages of sleep such that subjects received their own name stimulus 12 times and other names 288 times. Interspersed with the names on the tape were brief 500-Hz tone signals played a total of 156 times. The main relevant results were that subjects responded differentially in stage 2 to recordings of their own names, others' names, and the tone stimuli, respectively, in descending order. These effects were manifested in the FP and HR measures, and to a lesser extent by the K-complex response. Similar results were observed in stage REM for the FP measure, and to a lesser extent in HR. Differential results were not observed in stage 3–4. The results were deemed consistent with those of Oswald et al. (1960), in that both studies demonstrate information processing during sleep. However, they differ in certain details. First, Oswald et al.'s findings pertained only to stage 2 whereas McDonald et al. (1975) extended the finding to stage REM, and also showed that FP and HR reflect the stimulus conditions more sensitively than the K-complex indicator. Second, contrary to Oswald et al. (1960), names of others rather than one's own were associated more often with K complexes. To round off this digression on information processing during sleep, we should like to cite the other half of the paper of McDonald et al. (1975). This consisted of an independent study on autonomic concomitants of a wakeful conditioned auditory stimulus presented during sleep. It was found that sleepers were able to retain the wakeful ability to discriminate between the conditioned stimulus and another nonconditioned auditory stimulus. This discrimination was indicated by differential FP, HR, and K-complex responses in stages 2 and 4; neither K complexes (not normally present in stage REM), nor differential FP or HR responses occurred in stage REM, however. In agreement with Williams, Holloway, and Griffiths (1973), who wrote an excellent review of information processing during sleep, McDonald et al. (1975) believed that information stored in long-term memory remains most available for processing during sleep in stage 2, least in stage 4, and to an intermediate degree in stage REM, particularly if the content is sufficiently meaningful. In addition, stimulus preprocessing and short-term memory storage are demonstrable in all stages of sleep as indicated by the persistence of the FP and HR orienting responses and their potential for habituation throughout.

Not until 1970 was a systematic study performed in the topic area involving the elicitation of NREM as well as REM mentation reports. Using 10 male psychiatric residents as subjects, Castaldo and Shevrin (1970) administered specially designed subwaking threshold stimuli which nevertheless produced convincing EEG signs of stimulus registration. As in 2 earlier experiments by Castaldo and Holzman (1967, 1969), the following stimulus word sequence was employed: "fountain pen," and following the 1-second pause, "kneecap." This stimulus assembly had been previously shown to produce frequent psychoanalytic-type primary and secondary process associative responses. Typical of the former would be a rebus combination of the "pen" and "knee" part of the stimulus into "penny"; and typical of the latter would be associations conceptually related to the stimuli such as "ink" and "paper" for "fountain pen," and "leg" and "bone" for "kneecap." The authors predicted that following such stimuli, stage 2 mentation reports would tend to contain conceptual types of responses as opposed to REM reports, which would include more rebuslike responses. No effects of the stimuli were discernible after stage REM awakenings, but stage 2 reports possessed a greater number of words conceptually related to the stimulus word on experimental nights in comparison to the control nights (during which awakenings were carried out without prior auditory stimulation). That is, as expected, stage 2 was associated with conceptual-type responses to the stimulus. Noteworthy is the lack of REM rebus effects previously observed by Shevrin and Fisher (1967) in response to presleep subliminal stimulation with drawings of a pen and a knee. A further description of presleep stimulus studies is contained in the following section. Castaldo and Shevrin (1970) concluded that their results support the hypothesis of different levels of thought organization associated with REM and NREM sleep.

A more recently published work relevant to REM versus NREM responses was that of Lasaga and Lasaga (1973). Eight young adult females served as subjects in a laboratory study of short-term memory during sleep. Inasmuch as the method involved administration of tape-recorded words, phrases, and numbers to the subjects in all stages of sleep and testing for the efficiency of memory of these stimuli shortly afterward, many opportunities arose to observe incorporation of external events into sleep mentation. Accordingly, many incorporations were reported to occur in stages 2, 3, and 4, as well as REM. On such occasions, besides instances in which the entire stimulus was correctly perceived and recalled, the experimenters observed incorporations of only part of the stimulus (like "my boyfriend" recalled as "friends"), substitutions of another word or words, similar in sound and length to the original stimulus ("your mother" recalled as "you're marvelous"), or else complete distortions of the experimental stimulus. In general, the authors stated that their observations resembled those of Berger (1963).

Although not fitting precisely into our expository categories, a unique experiment of Rechtschaffen and Foulkes (1965) is important to describe. Mentation reports were elicited out of both REM and NREM sleep from subjects whose eyes were kept open artificially throughout the night and before whom visual stimuli were displayed prior to awakenings. A total of 7 subjects were studied, all of whose eyes had been taped open at the time of retiring. Three of the 7 also had a pupillary dilator instilled in amounts sufficient to maintain suitable pupil diameter but insufficient to prevent wakeful identification of ordinary common objects (inasmuch as accommodation was also partially impaired). The visual stimuli included a book, a black X, a moving handkerchief, a coffee pot, and a "do not disturb" sign. The results were that at no time was there evidence of any incorporation into sleep mentation regardless of sleep stage.

It is to be recalled that Dement and Wolpert (1958b) found occasional instances of light flashes influencing dream content, showing that visual sensory stimulation is capable of producing positive effects. It would have been interesting to have used similar stimuli in the Rechtschaffen and Foulkes (1965) study for comparison. It seems on the face of it that perception of light flashes need not involve higher order cognitive resources nor coordinated activity of the oculomotor nuclei in tracing moving patterns. Most of the stimuli used by Rechtschaffen and Foulkes, by contrast, probably would have required the functional availability of higher visual neural circuitry.

In concluding this section, it is safe to say that cognitive responses of some form may occur in both REM and NREM sleep as a result of external stimulation. In addition, such responses when they do occur often involve some transformation of stimulus content or pattern, which then seems to "fit in" with ongoing sleep mentation. One must be cautious about accepting the validity of the concept of such stimulus incorporation into dreams. In wakefulness, stimuli are often misperceived and misinterpreted. We do not then say that such stimuli were "incorporated" into our wakeful sequences of consciousness. Many of the reported findings could be explained on whatever bases throw light upon wakeful misperception or misinterpretation, on the sleepers accurately perceiving only a part of a stimulus and elaborating a response to that part only, or upon postperception transformation or elaboration of sensory elements more accurately registered initially. As yet we have no way of distinguishing between these and other alternatives as well.

It is to be noted that considerable variation exists from study to study as to method, definitions of stimulus "incorporation," and experimental results obtained. What is needed is a group of experiments that will provide us with systematic knowledge of the relationships between stimulus-produced modification of dream content and sensory-stimulus threshold factors; effects of "simple" sensory versus more complex stimuli such as verbal material; individual subject differences in tendencies to have dream modifications and subjects' tendencies to misperceive and misinterpret similar stimuli during wakefulness; and factors related to specific sleep stages, time into sleep stages, and time of night.

Sleep Mentation as Affected by Conditioning Techniques

Inasmuch as several papers have been published demonstrating the feasibility of eliciting conditioned responses during sleep (both classical and operant types) (Gradess, Stone, Steiner, & Ellman, 1971; Granda & Hammack, 1961; McDonald et al., 1975), it is curious that thus far, no reports have appeared describing attempts to condition dream content. Work along these lines is in progress (Antrobus, Arkin, & Ellman, 1976; see also Antrobus & Fookson, Chapter 15, this volume).

THE EFFECTS OF PRIOR-TO-SLEEP STIMULUS FACTORS ON SUBSEQUENT SLEEP MENTATION

We will now review a group of studies where the effects of prior-to-sleep stimuli or the prior-to-sleep environment on dreaming was investigated. The experimenters test the assumption that dream content will respond to biochemical tissue deficits, drives, or the arousal of strong emotions. In a sense, this area of investigation includes controlled study of the role of "day-residue material" in dream content. The day residues in dreams refer to dream components that represent an event, experience, or thought of the previous day, and it was Freud's belief that in every dream, it is possible to find a connection with an experience of the previous day.

The variety of presleep stimuli has been broad and it seems reasonable to group the studies together, when possible, by similarities in the nature of the stimulus employed. Strictly speaking, the category of the effects of sustained alteration of presleep sensory input on sleep experience belongs here. However, this is the subject of a magnificent experimental study and discussion in Chapter 8 of this volume.

Effects of Biological Drive Frustration on Dream Content

Three reports are available dealing with the effects of frustration of biological drives ordinarily satisfied by oral intake of food or drink. In one study, Dement and Wolpert (1958b) deprived 3 subjects of all fluid for 24 hours prior to retiring in the laboratory. All subjects were quite thirsty at bedtime. Mentation was sampled from REM sleep on 5 separate nights for each subject yielding a total of 15 mentation reports. The authors concluded, on the basis of their own categorizations, that no content directly portrayed the subject as thirsty or in the act of drinking. Ten dreams were said to be devoid of any direct reference to thirst or drinking whereas 5 were categorized as possibly containing indirect references. An example of the latter was the following mentation report: "While watching TV, I saw a commercial. Two kids were asked what they wanted to drink and one kid started yelling, 'Coca-Cola, orange, Pepsi, and everything.'" In actuality, the remaining dreams so categorized were similar in the manner of expression of thirst-related material and the reader might well think that the authors were too stringent in their criteria, possibly resulting in unwarranted exclusion of dreams with material reflecting thirst.

By contrast, Baldridge (1966) and Baldridge et al. (1965) mentioned as preliminary findings the occurrence of dreams with "obsessive reference to food" in some subjects following 24-hour food deprivation. With other subjects under similar experimental conditions, dreams possessing angry content were observed.

Finally, Bokert (1968) performed a more elaborate study to determine the effects of thirst and a related verbal stimulus on dreams. REM sleep reports were obtained under the following conditions from 18 subjects, nurses on night duty, who slept in the laboratory by day:

1. Sustained daytime deprivation of food and fluids with ingestion of a salty meal just prior to sleep, to enhance thirst (thirst-alone condition);

2. The same procedure repeated except that in addition, just prior to stage REM awakenings, the subjects receiving the subwaking-threshold tape-recorded verbal stimulus, "a cool delicious drink of water" (thirst-verbal stimulus condition);

3. A control condition in which the subjects were given a nonsalty meal prior to sleep without prior deprivation of food and fluids.

Each subject experienced all three conditions and hence served as their own controls. The hypotheses to be tested were:

1. Under conditions of thirst alone, dreams would contain a greater amount of thirst-related content than in the control conditions.

2. Under conditions of thirst-verbal stimulus, dreams would contain a greater amount of thirst-related content than both thirst-alone and control conditions.

The REM reports were judged for thirst-related content by three "blind," independent judges (interjudge reliability = .93). Thirst-related content words in mentation reports were those that could be placed in the following categories:

1. Words related to thirst sensations (like "thirsty," "parched," "dry," "salty taste");
2. Words related to thirst satisfiers:
   a. liquids ("water," "beer," "soda," "fruit juices," "milk," and so on);
   b. foods with high water content ("watermelon," "ice cream," "apples," "tomatoes," and so on);
   c. water in its natural state ("snow," "rain," "ice," "river," "lake," and so on);
3. Words related to activities or behavior associated with thirst (for example, all forms of the verb "to drink," "sip," "gulp," "quench," "suck," and so on);
4. Words related to places associated with thirst (like "bar," "fountain," "ice-cream parlor," "oasis," "kitchen," and so on);
5. Words related to persons associated with thirst (like "bartender," "soda jerk," "waiter" or "waitress," "counterman," and so on);
6. Words describing inanimate objects associated with thirst (like "glass," "bottle," "cup," "refrigerator," "straw," and so on).

The results were as follows: In accordance with expectations, the average number of thirst-related words in the mentation reports from either thirst condition exceeded that of the control. Specifically, the average was 2.11 for the thirst–verbal stimulus condition, 1.67 for the thirst–alone condition, and .53 for the control condition ($n = 35, 41$, and 41 dreams, respectively). To control for dream length, the averaged ratings of the three judges were used to obtain the proportion of thirst words in the total verbal output of each dream report. Transforming the data into radians, an analysis of variance was performed which resulted in a significant difference between both thirst conditions and the control ($p < .025$). Interestingly, it was found that the positive effects were observed to a significantly greater degree in the later REM periods of the night rather than the earlier ones—a finding consistent with the progressive increase of the somatic need for water with the passage of time. Additional experimental findings were:

1. The thirst-verbal stimulus condition produced significant variation in subjects' responses. Under this experimental condition:
   a. Subjects who appeared to incorporate part of the verbal stimulus into their dreams had a greater amount of additional thirst-related content than subjects who did not incorporate the stimulus. (Incorporation was defined as the appearance in the dream of parts of the verbal stimulus such as "drink," "drinking," "drank," and "water.")

b. Incorporator subjects also had more thirst-related content in the thirst-verbal stimulus condition than in the thirst-alone condition.
2. Dream content was related to aspects of postsleep behavior. Thus, subjects reporting gratifying dreams (containing themes of drinking and/or eating), actually drank less and rated themselves as less thirsty following sleep than those whose dreams were devoid of such content.
3. The thirst-alone condition was associated with increased REM activity.

Among Bokert's (1968) conclusions were that experimentally intensified somatic needs were capable of modifying dream content accordingly. Furthermore, a key notion related to both Freud's (1953/1900) proposition that dreams represent attempted unconscious wish fulfillments, and some cognitive models of dreaming, which state that the dream may generate a partial solution to a problem, is that the need, state, or problem should be partially reduced by the act of dreaming. Bokert is one of the few workers to directly test this notion, and the implied prediction finds some support in the finding that subjects who gratify their thirst in dream fantasy succeed in reducing their thirst need in postdreaming reality. In addition, the results were deemed consistent with Freud's contention that dreams represent an attempted unconscious wish fulfillment, but Bokert also speculated that it was possible for conscious wishes to be so represented independent of reinforcement from repressed unconscious infantile tendencies. Regarding both Freudian and cognitive models, however, one should not lose sight of the limited generality of the findings; effects were detectable solely in a subgroup of subjects.

Finally, Bokert (1968) also asserted that the relatively unimpressive results of Dement and Wolpert (1958b) were due to excessively narrow criteria for thirst-related content which did not allow for a wide range of cognitive representatives of thirst in the dream.

Effects of a Presleep Cognitive-Affective Deficit—Social Isolation—on Dreaming

In an unusual experiment, testing the effects of a cognitive-affective deficit rather than a physiological one, Wood (1962) worked with 5 young college graduates who spent 5 nights in the laboratory. Their second day was spent in solitary confinement. On the average, his subjects showed 60% more REM time but less REM activity in response to this condition. The associated dream content both paralleled and differed from the nature of the presleep wakeful behavior. Just as the day was spent in physical inactivity, the subsequent dreams were also physically inactive; but the physical inactivity tended to involve groups of people standing around talking in a sociable fashion—a contrast to the isolation.

Many procedures, and especially many drugs, are capable of suppressing REM sleep; by contrast, only a few drugs are capable of producing increases in REM time percentage (increases that are slight). With the controversial exception of wearing prism lenses which alter optical verticality during wakefulness, and the finding of Rechtschaffen and Verdone (1964) that money incentives are capable of producing slight increases of REM time, the results of Wood (1962) are perhaps unique in reporting an independent variable producing substantial increases. Inasmuch as this outcome preceded publication of the standard scoring manual of Rechtschaffen and Kales (1968), it would therefore be important to either rescore Wood's records or else replicate the experiment.

The Effects of Viewing Films on Subsequent Sleep Mentation

Just as simple sensory stimulation during sleep requires lower order cognitive functioning than complex verbal stimuli, so experimental presleep tissue deficits such as thirst seem to impose a more direct, uncomplicated variable for the mind to deal with than elaborate, thematic-affect-arousing dramatic displays such as films. Might such experimental conditions as the latter be more likely to produce effects on dream content that could serve to enlighten us about dream formation processes? As we shall see, the results once again are mixed.

We therefore turn now to a group of seven studies which have in common the employment of a presleep condition of sustained visual stimulation by means of films. Each study compared mentation reports following a bland, neutral film with those following an affect-arousing one, which, depending on the study, might provoke anxiety, aggression, or sexual excitement, and correlated the findings in various ways with psychological data. Thus, Foulkes and Rechtschaffen (1964) observed 24 adult subjects who slept in the laboratory for 2 counterbalanced nights following an adaptation night. On experimental nights either a violent or nonviolent film was shown prior to retiring. Five nightly awakenings for mentation reports were made according to the following schedule: 2 NREM, one well prior to the first, and one well after the fourth REM period of the night; and from the early portions of each of the first 3 REM periods.

The results were that the violent film was followed by longer and more imaginative REM sleep reports, and the subjects themselves rated these reports as more vivid, clear, and more emotional than after the nonviolent film. That is, the violent film, far from producing dreams judged to be more violent, aggressive, or unpleasant, was followed by dreams that were exciting and interesting, but without influence over specific drive expression or hedonic tone. This nonspecific increase in intensity of dream experience was observed only in the later stage REM reports and not in either NREM or first-REM-period awakenings. Furthermore, incorporations from either film were rare (5% of 179 reports). Finally, no significant differences were found for either film condition on frequency of stages REM or NREM mentation recall, and on latencies to sleep onset or the first REM period.

A somewhat different result was obtained by Foulkes, Pivik, Steadman, Spear, and Symonds (1967) in a study on the effects of presleep films on children's dreams and sleep. Thirty-two boys were employed as subjects, 16 of whom averaged 7 1/2 years of age and 16, 11 1/4 years. Prior to sleep they were shown either a film with much aggressive content or one with interesting, albeit rather bland, content, in counterbalanced order. One film was a violent western and the other dealt with baseball. Subjects were awakened for REM sleep reports on experimental and control nights, the results of which were categorized on the basis of whether incorporation of the film content into REM sleep mentation had been judged to have occurred. In addition, content analyses, degree of mentation recall, and sleep-cycle parameters were assessed. The results were that 14 of 179 REM sleep reports (8%) were judged to have incorporated elements of the presleep stimulus film. Neither the aggressive nor the neutral film was more likely to have yielded incorporations. And, finally, measures of dream intensity in general and hostile-unpleasant content in particular were *less* following the aggressive film.

Of special interest was the *greater* frequency of "bad" dreams (subjects' own judgments) following the neutral film. In addition, neither film condition typically affected standard parameters of the sleep cycle. Mentation recall was also not significantly affected by the presleep conditions. In effect, then, the likelihood of children's incorporation of material from presleep films was close to the 5% observed for adults (Foulkes & Rechtschaffen, 1964), thus finding against the hypothesis that children would possess a greater tendency to employ in a direct, unambiguous manner proximate presleep stimuli in synthesis of their dreams. The decrease in dream vividness and unpleasantness following the aggressive film in children is a finding opposite to that for adults. In explaining this difference, Foulkes et al. (1967) noted that the adults were more emotionally involved in the nonviolent film they had seen (a romantic comedy) than in the violent one, whereas the boys were more attentive to the depictions of hostility. Thus, the combined results suggest that greater interest in the presleep film, regardless of the specific content, is likely to be followed by less vivid dreams. In other words, the observation that less intense and unpleasant dreams followed the better attended, violent film in children was deemed to support the notion that viewing dramas of violence provides emotional catharsis in which aggressive tendencies could be momentarily dissipated and not find expression in the subsequent dreams.

More extensive results with regard to incorporations were apparently obtained by Witkin (1969a) and Witkin and Lewis (1967). Twenty-eight men who worked by night and slept by day underwent the following non-consecutive 5-night experimental schedule: 1 adaptation night and 1 night each for seeing films of human birth, human subincision, a neutral film, and receiving psychological suggestions aimed to alter bodily sensations. In some instances, a sixth session was added in which a film was shown of a mother monkey eating her dead infant, following which subjects were required to verbalize their ongoing reverie until they fell asleep (Bertini, 1968). On each night, subjects were awakened for REM sleep-mentation reports. In the following morning, each subject received an extensive inquiry about each mentation report and the entire laboratory experience. Also, each subject received a comprehensive clinical evaluation.

The presleep input was regarded as a source of "tracer elements" whose transformations during subsequent mentation samples could be studied. This voluminous data is still being slowly processed but the authors have volunteered the following impressions, which must be regarded as highly tentative:

1. Anxiety-arousing films tend to be followed by increases in anxiety ratings of mentation reports.

2. Presleep stimulus material often appeared in dreams in transformed presentations in striking accord with classic Freudian dreamwork mechanisms.

3. Dreams following the neutral film had less obvious sexual symbolism.

4. The laboratory situation, including features of interpersonal relationships, appeared in the dreams.

5. Individual stylistic features in the manner of processing presleep stimuli were discernible.

6. The "tracer elements" reappeared in various guises in the sequential REM periods of the night.

7. There was a higher frequency of "forgotten dreams" on nights following affect arousing stimuli.

8. Dreams following stress films contained features that led to childhood memories (sometimes to one's earliest memory).

9. The sense of conviction as to the relationship between presleep stimuli and their transformed presentation in dreams was maximized by associative material elicited during the following morning.

The authors concluded that presleep stimuli in the laboratory undergo complicated transformational processes, circulate through a network of "cognitive structures," including earliest memories, and continue to influence associations in the following morning, all in a cogently discernible manner. One must await publication of the final fully processed results of this study before firm conclusions may be drawn.

From the same laboratory, two subsequent studies appeared, in which specific attempts were made to arouse intense presleep anxiety for the purpose of detecting effects on sleep mentation and electrographic parameters. Thus, Karacan, Goodenough, Shapiro, and Starker (1966) utilized 16 paid, "normal" college males, who spent 6 nights in the laboratory. After an adaptation and a single baseline night, each subject, prior to retiring, viewed over the next 4 nights, 2 emotionally stressful and 2 neutral films, 1 on each night. Besides the standard EEG, EOG, and EMG recordings, this study was distinctive by virtue of its monitoring REMP erections. The anxiety content of REM reports was assessed by an adaptation of the Nowlis and Nowlis (1956) adjective checklist given to subjects to rate their own sleep experience following each awakening, and also by the Gottschalk, Winget, and Gleser (1969) anxiety scale. The results were that no significant differences in anxiety content were observed among film nights; however, dreams high in anxiety content were associated with lack of, or nonsustained erections, without relationship to the nature of the presleep film.

In the second, more recent study, Goodenough, Witkin, Koulack, and Cohen (1975) obtained clear-cut positive results on a special subgroup of subjects. The authors reasoned that subjects who were demonstrably more responsive to stress during wakefulness would be more likely to have affect-laden dreams following presleep stress. Specifically, it was hypothesized that with all subjects during REMPs, REM activity, dream affect, respiration rate, and degree of irregularity would be higher on nights after viewing stress films as opposed to nights after viewing neutral films; and that in subjects who showed greater respiratory response to stress films during wakefulness the above effects would be more intense; also, respiratory rate and irregularity were expected to be highly correlated with affect in dream reports.

Accordingly, 28 "normal" male night workers who slept by day were selected as subjects. Each subject slept in the laboratory 5 days each at least 1 week apart. The first session provided for adaptation to the experimental situation and the remaining were used for data collection. During these 4 experimental sessions, 2 stress films (depicting birth and subincision of the penis), and 2 neutral educational travelogues (depicting London and the western United States) were shown to each subject in counterbalanced order.

The data from 366 useful REM-period awakenings (yielding 264 dream reports, a 72% recall rate) consisted of 3 sets of observations:

1. Sleep electrographic recordings of the EEG, EOG, EMG, and respiration (thoracic and abdominal components independently measured). (In addition, wakeful measurements of respiration were made during the viewing of the films. This procedure enabled the experimenters to determine and compare the nature of the respiratory responses to the stress films, the neutral films, and the REM sleep experience; and to separate the subjects into a group of wakeful responders and nonresponders.)

2. REM mentation reports elicited 5 to 10 minutes after REMP onset (scored by a blind judge for anxiety, hostility-out, hostility-in, and

ambiguous hostility on the scales devised by Gottschalk, Winget, & Gleser, 1969).

3. Mood adjective checklist scores (modified from Nowlis & Nowlis, 1956) obtained in response to a baseline control condition, each film condition, and to each REM sleep experience after experimental awakenings.

In comparison to the neutral films, stress films, while being viewed, produced significant wakeful, dysphoric, anxious mood reactions and delayed sleep onset. Viewing stress films likewise resulted in significantly increased dream anxiety and also increased REM-period respiratory irregularity primarily among those subjects who, in the waking state, showed irregular breath patterns in response to stressful film events. In addition, dream affect tended to be related to REM-period respiratory irregularity among those subjects who were wakeful responders to the stress films. This tendency reached statistical significance, however, only on the Gottschalk, Winget, and Gleser (1969) hostility measure. The authors concluded that the data supported the hypothesis of congruence between wakefulness and the REM dream regarding the relationship between affect and respiratory irregularity. Thus, laboratory findings partly documented the everyday experience that daytime stress often tends to be followed by emotional dreams.

Arousing a completely different drive state, the effects of presleep sexual stimuli were studied by Cartwright, Bernick, Borowitz, and Kling (1969). The experimenters observed 10 young adult students over 5 consecutive nights with the following procedure: Reports were collected from all REM periods on 1 initial baseline night without presleep stimulation, and on succeeding nights 2 pornographic films were shown prior to retiring. The records disclosed no evidence of sleep-cycle changes. After the erotic film there was a significant decrease in ability to recall dream content; the number of dream characters per dream was reduced and the number of 2-person dreams was increased; also the amount of symbolic representation of the film content was higher than would have been anticipated if the subjects had not been exposed to an erotic movie. This last conclusion was based upon comparison with a similar sample of reports elicited from comparable subjects not seeing a sex film. And finally, the amount of direct incorporation from the laboratory setting was greater than from the movie.

Rather than using an absorbing, attention-arousing, presleep visual stimulus, such as a film, Shevrin and Fisher (1967) showed 10 adult females a special subliminal visual stimulus previously demonstrated capable of eliciting primary and/or secondary process-types of cognitive responses. Specifically, drawings of a fountain pen in juxtaposition to a knee were presented in tachistoscopic fashion. As mentioned above, a primary-process type of response would be exemplified by images or words related to the stimuli on the basis of their sounds rather than meanings, and a secondary process type of response on the basis of a conceptual relationship to the stimulus. A typical primary process response is "penny" (pen-knee) and a secondary process response is pencil, ink, bone, or leg, accordingly.

These drawings were flashed before the subjects prior to retiring, and samples of mentation, free imagery, and free association were obtained immediately after the stimulus, and upon awakenings from stages REM and 2, subsequently. It was hypothesized that REM mentation reports would contain more evidence of primary process thinking, and stage 2 more evidence of secondary process when each was compared to the other. The hypotheses were supported neither by mentation report nor free imagery analysis, but positive findings were obtained from free associations carried out following all three conditions: presleep and stages REM and 2; and, furthermore, as predicted, rebus responses were more likely from stage REM, and conceptual responses more likely from stage 2. These results are consistent with those of Witkin and Lewis (1967) who also found that free associations elicited on the following morning could be traced to stimuli derived from presleep conditions. Considered together, the observations indicate that perceptual material may be placed into "intermediate-term" memory storage prior to sleep, undergo various transformations and be available for retrieval subsequently under special postsleep conditions; but why primary and secondary process derivatives of the original percepts are detectable in free association only, rather than in mentation reports and free imagery, is a puzzle. Certainly in view of Fisher and Paul's (1959) replication of the Pötzl phenomenon, one would have expected clear positive effects in REM mentation reports.

Clues about the status of presleep perceptual material during sleep are provided by an interesting study of DeKoninck and Koulack (1975). Hoping to learn whether dreaming facilitates adaptation to stressful experience, they presented a film featuring body mutilation to a group of subjects before sleep at night and again the following morning. It was hypothesized that subjects who exhibited a greater mastery of the presleep stress, as manifested by less emotionality following the morning showing of the film, would be those who had more anxiety-infused dreams and more dream content related to the film. In order to manipulate the degree of incorporation of film elements and anxiety content of the dreams, a part of the sound track of the film, containing the verbalized self-reproaches of a man guilty of the negligence causing the mutilations, was played during REM sleep. The experimental design provided for separate examination of the effects of the film alone without sound-track stimulation; the effects of the sound track alone without previous viewing of the film; and the effects of combined viewing of the film and sound-track stimulation. This part of the procedure involved 16 "normal" college males. In addition, a separate control group of 8 comparable subjects saw the film twice, each showing being separated by 8 hours of wakefulness. Wakeful emotionality was scored by means of a modified Nowlis and Nowlis (1956) mood-adjective checklist. Mentation reports were analyzed by two "blind" independent judges using the aggressiveness, friendliness, anger, happiness, sadness, and confusion scales of Hall and Van de Castle (1966). Laboratory-incorporation categories of objects, persons, locations, and situations; film-element incorporations with categories similar to those used for laboratory incorporation; and sound-track incorporations were scored as direct when the subject heard in the dream a voice containing key words uttered in the portion of the sound track played during REM sleep, and as indirect when the subject heard a sound or voice in the dream. In addition, judgments were also made of whether the subject was a dream participant, and also the degree of vividness and bizarreness of the dream.

The results were as follows:

1. The hypothesis that the film would induce stress was supported by comparison of the mood-adjective checklist scores before and after the film. There was a significant increase in anxiety and depression, and a decrease in surgency and social affection.

2. Compared to the baseline, the film with the sound-track stimulus during REM sleep showed a significant increase in the amount of film-element incorporation; whereas the film alone (without the sound-track stimulus) produced no marked difference. This difference in the amount of incorporation occurred mainly in the REM periods of the second half of the night. There was only one instance of a direct incorporation throughout. No effects could be attributed to the sound-track stimulus in sleep alone without previous viewing of the film. In some respects, the augmenting effect of the sound-track stimulus resembles that observed by Bokert (1968) for a subgroup of his subjects; that is, for some, the sound stimulus did produce thirst-stimulus incorporation, and with it an increase in thirst-related dream content.

3. Neither film with sound-track stimulation nor the film alone produced increases in the anxiety content of the dream. And this result resembles previous studies showing unimpressive or limited effects of affect-arousing films on dream content.

4. Contrary to expectation, subjects who exhibited more emotionality at the morning presentation of the film tended to be those who had more dream incorporation of film elements. Thus, film incorporation was associated with less, rather than greater, mastery over the experimental stress.

5. The film was followed by a significant increase of sleep-onset latency, averaging 16 minutes, showing that the stress had physiological as well as psychological effects.

In conclusion, the authors viewed the findings in terms of two rival hypotheses, both of which assert that dreams serve adaptive functions. One states that we dream about stressful events to acquire mastery over them; the other contends that we dream about events with qualities opposite to those of the reality stress in order to psychologically compensate for them. The authors feel that their experiment does not permit a clear-cut decision as yet.

The Effects of Task Performance on Subsequent Sleep Mentation

The first two categories of presleep-stimulus conditions thus far considered placed the subject in a more or less passive role; that is, the subject had merely to endure drive frustration, perceive stimulus conditions imposed by the experimenter, submit to being wired up, sleep, dream, and report. By contrast, the succeeding group of 5 studies all required some kind of task performance prior to sleep.

In the first study, Orr, Dozier, Green, and Cromwell (1968) asked 7 high-school students to awaken themselves in the laboratory at a preselected time after falling asleep. The target times ranged 250 to 350 minutes after sleep onset. Each subject spent 5 consecutive nights in the laboratory; the first 3 were control and the last 2 were experimental nights. Four of the 7 subjects were successful in awakening within 16 minutes of the target time, but the number of subjects was too small to reach statistical significance. At the moment of awakening from these "hits," 6 stage REM dreams were available to recall. One contained a reference to a specific time (but other than the time of the specified target); 2 involved meeting a time commitment; and the others all contained indications of anticipation and apprehension. Such occurrences were not observed on the control no-presleep-task nights of successful subjects; and on none of the nights of the unsuccessful ones. In addition, on experimental nights, the successful subjects had less total sleep and recalled more dreams than on control nights and in comparison to the unsuccessful subjects. The results of the study are at best suggestive but deserve replication with a larger sample and careful mentation-report analysis. It is possible, for instance, that not only may dreams contain more references to time on experimental nights, but other aspects of their organization and content, such as sequential coherence, may also show changes.*

---

*That sleep is compatible with cognitive processes subserving awareness of temporal sequencing is indicated by studies of Dement and Kleitman (1957b) who showed that subjects awakened after 5 and 15 minutes of REM sleep are able to discriminate between correspondingly shorter or longer intervals of dreaming. Congruent results were reported by Koulack (1968) in a study employing subwaking-threshold percutaneous electrical stimuli to the median nerve during REM sleep. Subjects were awakened either 30 seconds or 3 minutes after the stimuli and correct time-category discriminations were demonstrable.

In four remaining studies, Baekeland (1971); Baekeland, Resch, and Katz (1968); Hauri (1970); and Cartwright (1974a) required their subjects to perform specific behaviors prior to sleep. The presleep activity selected by Baekeland and co-workers in both experiments was 30 minutes of free association. Over all, they compared the REM sleep reports of 27 experimental subjects to those of 17 controls of whom no presleep task was required. In addition, both subject groups were each further subdivided in accordance with degrees of field dependence versus independence, a cognitive-style index. The free-association interval was divided into thirds and the subjects' subsequently tape-recorded REM mentation reports were divided into nonredundant idea units in accordance with predetermined syntactical rules. Each idea unit in turn was related to the contents of the presleep free-association interval in accordance with a categorization system providing for direct unambiguous incorporation, transformation of free-association elements into the REM reports, and lack of apparent relationship.

The main findings were that presleep mentation as revealed in the free-association interval was richly represented in REM sleep mentation. The proportion of dream-idea units related to the free-association content ranged from 0.69 in the first REMP to 0.38 in the fourth. In general, the proportion of REM-mentation idea units scored as transformations of free-association elements exceeded the proportion of those scored as incorporations. In addition, cognitive-style factors appeared to play a role. Specifically, the field-independent group had the richest dream content, the greatest number of transformations of presleep free-association items in their dreams, and the greatest tendency to produce such transformations throughout the night. By contrast, the field-dependent subjects' dreams were less likely to show transformations beyond the first REMP. Also, elements derived from the first third of the presleep association interval were more discernible in the reports of field-dependent subjects than those derived from the last third. Finally, in comparison to the control subjects, who were not made to carry out presleep tasks, the experimental subjects of whom free association *was* required, recalled more dreams that tended to be higher in references to the experimental situations, degree of unpleasantness, and self-participation. The results were deemed consistent with the idea of a partial causal connection between presleep mentation and REMP reports.

In one of the few studies that examined the effects of presleep conditions on both REM *and* NREM sleep mentation, Hauri (1970) employed 15 adult males as subjects in the following experimental schedule 1 night weekly: 1 adaptation night and 1 night, each in a counterbalanced order, with a 6-hour presleep condition of physical exercise, pleasant relaxation, or challenging mental-task performance. After 3.5 hours of uninterrupted sleep, subjects were awakened twice each for REM and NREM sleep mentation reports. These were rated by the subjects themselves immediately after rendering each report, and also by independent judges in accordance with a previously standardized procedure. The subjects' own ratings revealed a unique finding: a tendency for stage REM mentation to possess less content relating to whatever activity subjects had been involved in prior to sleep. That is, in REM sleep mentation, there was less physical activity after presleep exercise, and less thinking and problem solving after presleep mental effort. The reduction in physical activity was likewise noted in NREM sleep mentation following exercise; but somewhat in contrast, after presleep mental effort, NREM mentation featured a feeling tone of increased tension and greater attempts to influence one's stream of sleep experience. Because of the sparseness of NREM report content, only the stage REM reports were suitable for the judges' ratings method; and the main significant result of their ratings was that the number of social interactions per character after the mental-effort night was greater than for the other 2 conditions, and that more solitary activity was depicted after presleep exercise and relaxation. In all, only 29 out of 164 mentation reports (17.7%) contained an unambiguous incorporation of some aspect of the experimental situation; and with 1 exception, the presleep experimental activity never "openly intruded into sleep mentation." Furthermore, a judge, highly sophisticated in dream theory and dream analysis, was unable to distinguish which mentation reports were associated with which presleep condition. Finally, incorporations often seemed concerned with short but psychologically important events of the previous day, whereas longer-lasting events did not appear in sleep mentation in proportion to their wakeful duration alone. Hauri (1970) was impressed by the results of the subjects' own ratings of their REM reports as supporting the notion that dream life is complementary to waking life. He commented on the similarity between his finding and those of Wood (1962), Kramer, Whitman, Baldridge, and Lansky (1966), and Cartwright et al. (1969). In brief, this model of REM dreaming holds that dream content compensates for whatever characteristics of behavior dominated the presleep condition by depiction of scenes of an opposite or different nature. For example, Wood found that when subjects spent their days in social isolation, their dreams contained greater amounts of socially active and physically passive dream content, such as group conversation, sitting, and "socializing." Similarly, Hauri (1970) found that REM dreams contained less physical activity after exercise and less thinking and problem solving after studying. Of special interest is that this relationship held only for REM dreams, whereas NREM mentation tended to continue in sleep imagination the behaviors prevailing prior to sleep. Thus, after studying, the associated wakeful, tense, emotional atmosphere carried along into the NREM mentation of the night, instead of being "left outside the door" after sleep onset and being succeeded by a type of sleep experience different from that occupying preceding wakefulness.

The last study of the effects of a subject-performed presleep task on subsequent sleep mentation is that of Cartwright (1974a), in which the influence of a conscious wish on REM reports was assessed. She was interested in carrying out an experiment that would also throw light on the meaning and functions of dreams. Thus, she attempted to locate a specific area of psychological tension within each subject, to endow it with saliency by bringing it to the subject's attention, and induce a need to resolve the tension just prior to sleep. Regarding these considerations, Cartwright made two general predictions:

1. Dreams following focused awareness of the specific relevant area of tension would tend to possess content elements capable of being related to this tension area.
2. Such dreams would tend to represent a result inversely related to the nature of the resolution as hoped for during wakefulness.

To test these predictions, she employed 17 paid volunteer, college men and women who were self-professed good sleepers. They each slept 2 nights in the laboratory; the first was an adaptation night and the second was for the introduction of the independent variable. During the presleep interval of the latter night, a self- versus ideal-self-trait discrepancy item was identified by an adjective Q-sort technique.

The item with the highest degree of discrepancy between self as actually perceived and self as the subject wished to be was selected as the target presleep-stimulus adjective. By means of the same procedure, 2 control words were selected: a word with a similar degree of self-ideal-self discrepancy but not used as a stimulus adjective and another word without self-ideal-self discrepancy, also not used as a stimulus.

Subjects were then permitted to go to sleep and instructed to verbalize to themselves repeatedly the target-stimulus adjective as they drifted off. Thus, "I wish I were [target word]" e.g. "I wish I could be more *poised* . . ." or more *persevering*, or not so *irritable*, and so on were the kinds of the self-administered presleep stimuli employed. Throughout the night, the subjects were awakened for REM mentation reports, following which they were permitted to resume sleep but were reminded on each such occasion to continue self-administration of the stimulus adjective.

Each REM sleep report was rated separately by a "naive" judge for the presence of each of the selected 3 adjectives on the basis of the following category system:

1. Adjective describes self.
2. Opposite adjective describes self.
3. Neither adjective nor its opposite describes self.
4. Adjective describes other dream character.
5. Opposite adjective describes other dream character.
6. Neither adjective nor its opposite describes other dream character.

These design features provided the experimenter with an opportunity to discover whether the technique and the instructions to wish for personality change were effective in producing significant incorporation of the trait or its opposite in the dream; whether other personal traits equally characteristic but not brought to the subject's attention were also incorporated into the dream; and whether the manner in which the target trait appeared in the dream represented continuity with waking thought, that is, was consistent with the conscious wish to be different, or whether some other outcome was represented. The results were that 15 of 17 subjects had some evidence of the target word or its opposite being descriptive of the dream characters in 1 or more of their mentation reports ($p < .01$). By contrast, neither of the 2 nontarget words were incorporated to a significant degree. This result indicates, therefore, that the procedure was effective in securing representation in the dreams of items related to the tension area. However, when the instances of incorporation were categorized in accordance with the scheme presented above, only the target words that were the opposite in quality to that wished for reached statistical significance. That is, although the target words tended to be incorporated, few subjects had dreams in which the ideal, wished-for trait was ascribed to the self; rather the opposite held true—only 2 subjects had instances in their dreams in which their self characters possessed the ideal trait as wished for in wakefulness. The overall results persuaded Cartwright (1970) to conclude that under the experimental conditions described, dream mentation, though responsive to presleep instructions to attend to specific traits (the wished-for personal quality), revealed differences in affective values compared to those stated in wakefulness.

The final study reviewed in this section consists of two fascinating related experiments which are unique because they employed naturalistic stressful presleep stimuli—"sensitivity" group therapy and major surgery (Breger, Hunter, & Lane, 1971a). Four experimental and 2 control subjects (college students, 3 males and 3 females) participated in the group-therapy project in accordance with the following schedule: 4 initial laboratory baseline nights for all subjects; for the experimental subjects, 2 laboratory nights following stressful therapy sessions during which the subjects and their personal problems were the focus for group discussion; for the control subjects, 2 laboratory nights, 4 weeks after the initial baseline. On all laboratory nights, REM sleep-mentation reports were collected throughout. On all subjects, personality data were derived from a brief initial interview and the MMPI. In addition, the contents of all group sessions were tape recorded. All mentation reports were evaluated by means of rating scales for incorporation of presleep-condition components, for thematic dimensions of the dreams, for cognitive-affective characteristics and by means of a qualitative psychological analysis. A total of 147 dream reports were collected from all 6 subjects.

The chief results were that the material aroused during the stressful group sessions was said to be represented and worked over in the dreams according to each subject's individual style. The incorporation ratings showed that the central content of each dream of the experimental subjects was related to the material discussed in the preceding group session. The manner of both the incorporation and representation processes tended to be indirect, allusive, symbolic, and derivative. Dream events often indirectly paralleled wakeful events and blended with both chronologically older similar anamnestic material. In comparison to their baseline nights, the control subjects' ratings all changed in the direction of pleasanter interactions, more adequate and successful roles for both dreamer and others, and more desirable dream outcomes; whereas for the experimental subjects, the trend was either absence of such change or change in the opposite direction with respect to the same parameters. This differential result was attributed to the impact of the group-therapy experience.

The surgery study involved 5 volunteer patients, males and females, all under age 65, who were awaiting major surgery; and 2 control subjects. Each surgical subject spent 4 preoperative nights in the laboratory (with a 1 day interval between the last preoperative night and the actual surgery). Postoperatively, each subject experienced 3 laboratory nights 1 to 5 weeks afterward. The control subjects underwent a similar nightly schedule but without comparable stress. All subjects were awakened for stage REM mentation reports throughout. In addition, each subject received an intensive clinical and psychological-test evaluation. Psychological analysis of dream content was said to reveal much incorporated stress—related material both directly and symbolically. Examples were references to repairing mechanical objects or removal of objects from enclosures.

The degree of incorporation was quite marked when the personal meaning of the surgery and individual modes of coping and psychological preparation were taken into account. Of greatest significance regarding the amount of incorporation was the level of preoperative emotional arousal rather than the degree of daily preoccupation with the surgery itself. That is, the dreams, rather than simply reflecting waking experience, seemed to express attempts to deal with unassimilated affect-arousing information. For example, 3 subjects had actual unexpected stressful experiences with drainage tubes. In each instance, ensuing dreams incorporated and dealt with the incident in a central way. Thus, one such preoperative dream of a male patient exhaustively depicted insertion of tubes into a woman and himself for medical tests, and interwoven with this material were overt descriptions of the subject having sexual relations with her.

In addition to data contained in the case-study material, mentation reports were rated by judges in accordance with 13 scales as follows: degree of incorporation of presleep stimuli (2 scales); thematic dimensions (2 scales: quality of interactions, and the role of the dreamer); formal qualities (6 scales: anxiety, cognitive disturbance, implausibility, involvement, primitivity, and recall); and surgery-related content (3 scales: body imagery, castration, and hostility). The results were said to indicate that the general effect of surgery-related stress was to increase dream anxiety, fragmentation, bizarreness, involvement of dream characters, hostility, concern about the integrity and health of the body for all patients, and worry about specific injury for the males. Some similar elements appeared in the dreams of all patients presumably because of the situation they all had to contend with. Thus, dreams commonly depicted defective objects, references to the acts of cutting, extirpated objects, construction of some innovation or new object, and so on. Such elements were classified as psychological transformations of items of wakeful concern. Also, the individual coping style and psychological meaning of the surgery imparted a characteristic specificity to the dreams of each patient. In general, the same characterological sources for coping strategies manifested in wakefulness appeared in dreams. Fears and conflicts symbolized in dreams rarely occurred without an attempt to resolve or cope with them in some way. A characteristic way in which preoperative stress affected dreams was by repetition of elements and themes. This occurred with nonstress-related components of the preoperative dreams as well as those related to stress and often resulted in constriction of dream content. Also, specific dream symbols or themes were consistently used by certain subjects to represent their central concerns.

Lack of "disguise" was not correlated with increased dream anxiety since few dreams included an actual representation of surgery, whereas some of the most frightening dreams were the most disguised—disguised in the sense that although the subject experienced anxiety in the dream, and in wakefulness as well, the dream content referred to matters other than surgery explicitly. For example, on one preoperative night, a subject dreamed about being threatened by a fellow patient with a gun while they were both involved with cars in a parking lot. In a summary comment, Breger et al. (1971a) stated that "in dreams of all the subjects, the individual fears and conflicts are expressed in altered form. That is, the stress-related stimuli appear to be recoded, symbolized, displaced, or condensed so that their expression is at least one step removed from the primary source of the stress" (p. 182). Furthermore, as in the results with the group-therapy study, stress-related input was said to be integrated with, or assimilated into, an organized network of older memories which also appear in the dream content. The authors concluded that their data support the hypothesis that it is affect-related or emotionally arousing information of personal relevance that one tends to dream about. Furthermore, the ensuing transformational processes were deemed consistent with the notion that dreams serve an adaptive function. By means of the transformations and the integration with memories, the psychologically noxious stimuli are believed to be converted into forms that are familiar to the dreamer, and make available psychological resources for coping with the threat.

Aside from criticisms, many of which the authors anticipated and commented upon themselves, the most serious problem with both of these studies stems from the method by which the major analysis of the study was carried out. This portion of the work consisted of dream-by-dream, case-by-case, posthoc studies in which the dream reports of each subject were "analyzed in the context of the presleep experience." The flavor of the analyses may be conveyed by the following excerpt from the case of a male patient about to have surgery for a recurrent peptic ulcer:

> In Dream 5, he must remove the wood-eating moths that could destroy or damage trees, symbolizing the ulcerated condition of his stomach. Also: tree trunk = the trunk portion of the body = the trunk of Dream 2 [a storage trunk], all referring to the part of his body to be operated on. (Breger et al., 1971a, p. 131)

The authors were well aware of the subjectivity in this approach and attempted to check on their analyses by the independent content ratings as described earlier. Although these posthoc analyses are certainly the most interesting part of the study, containing abundant clinically persuasive and dramatic substantiations of the authors' hypotheses, they do not constitute the kind of scientific support that might be provided by independent "blind" analyses of the reports with prior specification of analytic rules and guidelines.

The Experimental and Laboratory Situation as Presleep Conditions Influencing Dreams

This topic certainly deserves review under the general heading of this chapter, but all of the relevant work is ably presented and discussed by Cartwright in Chapter 7 of this volume.

Hypnosis and Posthypnotic Suggestion as a Presleep Condition Affecting Sleep Mentation

In all of the following studies attempts were made to test the traditional view that suitable subjects tend to incorporate and transform material contained in presleep posthypnotic suggestions into their nocturnal dreams. The literature of the pre-electrographic era has been thoroughly reviewed by Tart (1965). In addition a valuable more recent critical review has been contributed by Walker and Johnson (1974).

The first formal work since the advent of modern techniques was carried out by Stoyva (1961). He employed 16 highly hypnotizable subjects, each of whom received presleep suggestions on 6 or more experimental nights, with or without standard hypnotic-induction procedures. Reports were obtained from stages REM, 2, 3, and 4. Mentation following both presleep conditions contained references to the suggested topics but a larger proportion of hypnotized subjects (44%) reported frequent dreaming on the suggested topic than when they had received suggestion without hypnosis (25%). This effect was manifested in all sleep stages. Stoyva concluded that although hypnotic trance with posthypnotic suggestion was not a requisite for incorporation of presleep suggestions, it increased the probability of such occurrences.

Two subsequent studies were performed by Tart (1964) and Tart and Dick (1970). The first employed 10 highly hypnotizable subjects who received presleep posthypnotic suggestions to dream about a dramatic, anxiety-tinged, threatening narrative in which the subjects were instructed to imagine themselves the central characters. Thirty-eight REM sleep reports were collected after varying intervals of stage REM had elapsed. Fifty percent of the subjects were judged not to have dreamed at all, in accordance with the posthypnotic suggestion. Those remaining subjects who could fulfill the instructions had dreams that possessed a wide range of evidence of influence, from only a few elements being affected to "almost total control" over the content of the sleep experience. However, the posthypnotic suggestion to dream on a certain topic was deemed to have an inhibiting or suppressing effect on natural dream processes. Tart (1964), therefore, concluded that dreams following posthypnotic suggestions designed to influence natural nocturnal dreaming are best viewed as the outcome of interactions between hypnosis factors and those involved in production of natural stage REM dreams. In addition, conspicuous by their absence were instances of psychological transformations of hypnotically implanted presleep stimuli that were reported in previous studies (reviewed by Tart, 1965). Finally, it was concluded that equating of dreams occurring in hypnosis and sleep, either spontaneous or in response to specific suggestions, is invalid on psychophysiological and psychological grounds.

In the second study, Tart and Dick (1970) employed 13 highly hypnotizable subjects who were given presleep posthypnotic suggestions to dream in great detail about a presleep narrative they heard prior to retiring. In the course of a 2-night protocol, 2 different stimulus narratives were employed, 1 per night in counterbalanced order. Rather than permit wide variation in the time elapsed since onset of each REM period sampled for mentation (as in the Tart, 1964, study), all subjects were awakened whenever 5 to 10 minutes of REM sleep appeared during the night. Tart sought to control his data analysis by having 2 independent judges score every dream report obtained in the study against *both* stimulus narratives without knowing which narrative had been employed on the specific night of the report elicitation. Thus, half the dreams were scored against the wrong stimulus narrative to serve as a control for possible overlapping between spontaneous dream content and presleep narrative. A predetermined scoring system was devised to enable measurement of the degree to which the 2 stimulus narratives affected the dreams following their use on different respective nights. The narratives had been broken down into small specific action-contentlike elements and all dreams were examined to assess the extent to which dream reports contained elements relating to both narratives. The total number of possible description items in the narratives averaged 41.5 (40 and 43, respectively, for Narratives 1 and 2).

When a total yield of 78 dream reports were scored against the stimulus narrative actually employed on the associated experimental night, the mean number of narrative elements appearing in the associated dreams ranged from 2.5 to 4 (interjudge reliability coefficient = .98). By contrast, when the same dream reports were scored against the narrative not used on the experimental night concerned, the corresponding mean score ranged from 0.41 to 0.44 ($p \leq .01$, one-tailed test).

In addition, a more global, thematic analysis of the same narrative-dream-report pairings was carried out, unlike the atomistic, fine-grained initial procedure described above. Two independent judges (reliability coefficient = .85) indicated that specific effects of the narratives were manifested in the dreams of 11 of the 13 subjects. Of the entire pool of dreams, 64.5% possessed thematic qualities clearly related to the associated stimulus narrative, 12.5% had only a tangential relationship, and 21% were apparently unrelated. Eight of the 13 subjects reported at least 1 dream of which the narrative appeared to be the dominant dream content organizer. The authors concluded that although posthypnotic suggestion is a powerful technique for influencing dream content, other nonhypnotic self-training methods described in their discussion are also capable of similar influence.

Barber, Walker, and Hahn (1973) criticized Stoyva (1961) for using repeated, authoritative suggestions for his hypnosis group and a permissive manner for his nonhypnosis control group, pointing out that this could have confounded hypnosis factors with the forcefulness in which suggestions were given to either group. In addition, he felt that Tart and Dick (1970), restricting their subject population to highly hypnotizable subjects, imposed upon themselves severe limits as to the generality of their findings. With the design features mentioned above, he hoped to control for these factors, and others. Accordingly, Barber et al. (1973) carried through an elaborate well-controlled study on 77 randomly selected females, half of whom were exposed to a presleep hypnotic induction procedure and half not. In addition, all subjects were given either authoritative, permissive, or no suggestions at all to think and dream about a specific topic: the death of President Kennedy.

In the laboratory, mentation reports were elicited from each REM period and at least once during NREM sleep 45 min after the previous REM-period termination. The results were that presleep suggestions altered the dream content of 25% of the subjects regardless of whether hypnosis had been used. This significantly exceeded the performance of the control subjects receiving no suggestions. Furthermore, the style of the suggestion did play a role after all. That is, presleep suggestions had the greatest effect on dream content of hypnotized subjects when given authoritatively and on that of the nonhypnotized when given permissively. Finally, because subjects were randomly selected, it was possible to demonstrate that incorporation of suggested material was not related to the hypnotizability.

Miscellaneous Studies

In Chapter 13 of this volume, the effects of a variety of experimental procedures on sleep utterance are described. However, it is necessary to relate a fascinating study of Evans (1972) and Evans, Gustafson, O'Connell, Orne, and Shor (1969, 1970), which deals with the effect of suggestions administered during REM sleep on sleep behavior. Although elicitation of mentation reports was not part of the procedure, the work has distinct relevance for the topic of mental processes in sleep.

Intrigued by promising exploratory observations, Evans (1972) and Evans et al. (1972) studied the effects of verbal suggestions presented during alpha-free stage REM on specific subsequent sleep actions. Nineteen male nursing students slept for 2 nights in the laboratory. Typical examples of the suggestions were "Whenever I say the word 'itch,' your nose will itch until you scratch it"; or "Whenever I say the word 'pillow,' your pillow will feel uncomfortable until you move it." Tests were made of each cue word on at least two different occasions during the same REM period in which the suggestion had been administered (immediate), during all subsequent REM periods of the same night (delayed), and during REM periods of the second night (carry-over). Suggestions were given only once at the first presentation and never repeated throughout (that is, only the cue words were employed on subsequent occasions).

The results were that over the 2 nights, 416 trials were made and 89 correct responses were observed. On the average, 19 subjects responded to a mean of 21% of all cue words (the highest response rate by a subject was 48%). Continuation of REM sleep without alpha was compatible with reception of the cue words as well as execution of appropriate responses shortly afterward. After subjects were awakened in the morning they remembered neither the cue words nor their motor responses.

Perhaps the most striking finding was that these responses could be called forth on subsequent occasions, delayed and carry-over, as well as on a night *five months* after the single initial suggestion was given and without intervening practice. The lack of demonstrable wakeful recall is therefore best characterized as state-dependent amnesia rather than forgetting, because the availability of the response was preserved and was demonstrable provided that the initial condition of the suggestion was employed for testing. In addition, there were indirect indications that successful responses might be occasions in which the cue word was incorporated into ongoing dream sequences. Although hypnosis was not used as part of the initial procedure, the best performance was given by subjects who were most highly susceptible to hypnosis as determined at the other times.

DISCUSSION

By now, the reader will no longer be surprised by comments as to the broad range of variability in reported outcomes in the sleep-research literature. As remarked elsewhere (Chapter 2 of this volume), the arduousness and expense of experiments in this field has often constrained researchers to "make do" with relatively small numbers of subjects. Let us begin therefore by listing the various known sources of variability in experimental results, all of which limit the degree to which findings may be generalized.

Individual Differences

Differences in cognitive style, responsiveness, and personality characteristics have been shown to affect the manner and frequency with which external stimuli are incorporated and transformed in sleep mentation (Baekeland, 1971; Baekeland et al., 1968; Breger et al., 1971a; Goodenough et al., 1975; Witkin, 1969a; Witkin & Lewis, 1967).

Criteria for Defining the Response

The proportion of occurrences categorized as incorporations or dream modifications according to Dement and Wolpert (1958b) is low compared to that reported by Bokert (1968). This difference is partly attributable to the comparatively strict, conservative criteria employed by the former. Also, some studies utilized subjects to judge their own mentation reports as well as independent judges, and some relied only on judges used in a somewhat inconsistent manner across studies.

Type and Intensity of Stimulus

Dement and Wolpert (1958b) found that water sprayed on the skin during REM sleep, and presleep stimuli, which tended to arouse strong anxiety, were more likely to be incorporated into or modify dream content (Baekeland, 1971; Baekeland et al., 1968; Breger et al., 1971a; Goodenough et al., 1975; Witkin & Lewis, 1967).

Time of Awakening

Some studies awakened subjects for REM sleep reports in a consistent manner within 5 to 10 minutes after REM-period onset and others in a comparatively unsystematic manner. Dement and Wolpert (1958b) awakened their subjects 5 to 20 minutes and Tart (1964) 6 to 32 minutes after REM-period onset. The same variability is true regarding total sleep time and clock time elapsed with respect to mentation report schedules.

Technique of Elicitation of Sleep Mentation and Associated Cognitive Activity

Besides differences in the manner of awakening subjects, it was noted in at least three different investigations that a body of spontaneous associations elicited before (Baekeland, 1971; Baekeland et al., 1968) or after collection of mentation reports (Berger, 1963; Shevrin & Fisher, 1967; Witkin, 1969a; Witkin & Lewis, 1967) enabled judges to discern much more easily, and convincingly, evidence of a relationship between experimental stimuli and sleep mentation. In general, however, apparently successful detections of such relationships were made on the basis of posthoc findings rather than in terms of systematic analysis.

Perhaps one unfortunate characteristic of the experiments testing effects of stimuli applied during sleep has been the general insistence by investigators that only mentation reports following EEG evidence of stimulus registration would be included in the data analyses. This decision has resulted in neglect of opportunities to observe the effects of stimuli that leave the EEG undisturbed. In line with this thought, evidence from several studies demonstrates that it is indeed possible for the sleeper to discriminate between external stimuli in the *absence* of signs of increased activation (Gradess et al., 1971; Granda & Hammack, 1961; Oswald et al., 1960; Williams, Morlock, Jr., & Morlock, 1966). Perhaps experimental techniques used thus far have mostly permitted us to observe outcomes of forceful intrusion of external stimuli into ongoing sleep mentation within a context of arousal rather than a deft blending or merging of the two without arousal. This remark is supported by Berger's (1963) observation of the high frequency with which mentation seemingly derived from external stimuli seemed to disturb dream continuity, and Koulack's (1969) finding that stimulus incorporation was more likely in association with alpha bursts.

Despite the inconsistencies and misgivings mentioned above, the group of studies as a whole permit us to conclude that incorporation of, and sleep mentation modification by, external stimuli (applied prior to or during sleep), has been demonstrated as a genuine, frequently occurring, but by no means inevitable effect. Furthermore, depending upon the factors already cited that promoted variance, the manner of incorporation differed over a wide range. Thus, the most frequent kind of relationship observed between verbal stimuli introduced during sleep and associated sleep mentation was that of assonance. However, direct unambiguous incorporations, although uncommon, were also seen as well as other stimulus transformations involving indirect representations. It is noteworthy that with stimuli applied prior to sleep the reverse was found, with relationships based upon assonance seeming to be relatively infrequent in comparison to indirect representations. At any rate, the overall results lend themselves to the following partial formulation: During sleep, the immediate content of awareness is largely determined by internally produced ongoing stimuli; and, in addition, components of cognitive resources are continuously available for detection and analysis of signals from external sources (Oswald et al., 1960). These cognitive components are responsible for three types of decisions following such signal detection and analysis: awakening, ignoring the stimulus, or incorporation and/or modification of sleep mentation in a variety of ways (Berger, 1963; Dement & Wolpert, 1958b). Actually it required no fancy experimentation to tell us this. After all, adults rarely fall out of bed; soldiers, during bombardments, do awaken in response to sudden lulls; sleeping mothers do selectively respond to an infant's cry; and so on. In addition, similar phenomena are observable during wakefulness. The clichéd but valid example involves being lost in a vivid daydream while driving, and preserving adequate cognitive resources for accomplishing both concurrently.

CONCLUSION

Despite the number of carefully executed and sophisticated studies on the experimental manipulation of dream content, the results have told us relatively little about how dreams are constructed. The findings seem rather meager next to the rich elaborate causal links that one may construct posthoc. Knowing the dream, and presleep or sleep stimulus, and knowing something about the cognitive style, personality, and associative patterns of the dreamer, one can frequently make extensive cogent inferences connecting these various sets of items. But posthoc inferences cannot substitute for systematic and predictive studies.

If there is any validity to these posthoc analyses, and our hunch is that there is much that is valid, then we need to do the hard work of spelling out the associative rules that join stimulus to dream response. Until we can articulate these rules, our understanding of the process may remain very rudimentary indeed. In particular, we feel that there is considerable predictive potential in the construction of associative memory networks. There is a variety of association, sorting, and clustering techniques that seem potentially useful. Many of them have been extensively developed by psycholinguists and students in the fields of memory and computer simulation of intelligence. For example, the surgical operations performed on Breger et al.'s (1971a) subjects are concrete examples of the intersection of cutting and fixing procedures. Both cutting and fixing activity appeared in these subjects' dreams but tended to be portrayed in other nonsurgical forms of cutting and fixing. Was a direct, unequivocal depiction of surgery barred from dream experience because it was too threatening or were the situations actually dreamed simply more familiar, or derived from "older" memories, and hence more likely to be dreamed about?

The implicit-association model employed thus far is that of classical conditioning; that is, the sound of a bell or sensation of water sprayed on the skin activates memory components of previous pairings of such stimuli with percepts of contiguous events. Yet many of our models of dreaming emphasize goal and motive. Operant-conditioning relationships, in which the stimulus is associated with avoidance, escape, or rewards, seem much more appropriate avenues to the study of effects of external stimuli on dreaming. For example, subjects might be taught, while awake, that pointing to a particular visual stimulus or operating a lever controlling a mental content-bearing visual display will terminate a mildly annoying noise. Or, subjects could be taught to reliably associate photographs depicting ubiquitous cognitive-affective categories with specific, easily recognized sound patterns, receiving small but significant sums of money as reinforcement. Such cognitive-affective categories might include heterosexuality, homosexuality, interpersonal hostility and cruelty, body mutilation, appetizing food, childbirth, death, excretory processes, and depictions of the subjects' earliest childhood memories. Then, after such pairings are well established and maintained by intermittent reinforcement, sleeping subjects would receive the specific sound pattern stimulus, or else the annoying noise stimulus mentioned earlier, and awakened shortly afterward for mentation reports. We might then predict that such stimuli would elicit dreaming of the particular reinforcement-bearing stimulus or common associates thereof. In such a fashion, a large variety of operant-conditioned stimuli could be employed, each representative of major cognitive-affective categories. Eventually, one might be able to construct an experimentally based catalogue of transformational patterns linking external stimulus to dream component. Such a catalogue would doubtless have to be developed with due regard and special provisions for the effects of individual differences, nature of stimulus, stimulus threshold, sleep stage, time of night, and phasic-tonic contexts in association with which the stimulus was applied and from which the subject was awakened. Eventually a catalogue of this type could form the basis of more elaborate systematic studies and hypotheses testing regarding dream formation.

In conclusion, we feel that the size and complexity of human memory has discouraged investigators from the difficult task of developing specific testable models of dream formation. Considerable innovation in both experimental design and data analysis are now in order.

9

Experimental Strategies for the Study of the Function of Dreaming

HARRY FISS
University of Connecticut
School of Medicine

My primary concern in this chapter is to advance a theory of dreaming. While no one would seriously argue the point that science can progress only to the extent that it advances theory, in psychology no such consensus exists when it comes to the question of whether a theory should properly be a *psychological theory* about a *mental state*, when the theory is based primarily on *psychological concepts* and *psychological data*. Today's *Zeitgeist* would have us believe otherwise. A case in point is the widely held belief that dreams are instigated and shaped not by psychological but by biochemical, that is, cholinergic, events originating in the hind brain (Hobson & McCarley, 1977). Regardless of the merits of this popular notion, which has been extensively reviewed elsewhere (Fiss, 1983; Labruzza, 1978; Vogel, 1978), it is my purpose here to demonstrate: (a) that the dream can most definitely be studied in its own right, independently of its neurophysiological basis, whatever that may be; and (b) that the dream *should* be studied as a separate psychological process quite apart from REM sleep. This is not to say that an interactional approach, taking account of both psychological *and* biological determinants simultaneously, would not yield equally valid results. My contention is only that a primarily psychological model, as proposed here, is more likely to yield results relevant to the clinician's interests. It is, after all, the dreamer who dreams, not his or her brain. Polanyi (1965) once wrote that "a neurophysiologist observing the events that take place in the eyes and brain of a seeing man would invariably fail to see in these events what the man himself is seeing" (p. 807). I would like to rephrase Polanyi's statement as follows: A neurophysiologist observing the events that take place in the brain of a dreaming person would invariably fail to see in these events what the person is dreaming.

Evidence to the effect that dreams are phenomena existing in their own right is plentiful. Dreamlike thinking in the waking state has been observed by Fiss, Ellman, and Klein (1969) and by Fiss, Klein, and Bokert (1966), who have shown that REM sleep mentation, rather than being automatically switched off upon awakening, persists or "carries over" into the waking state. Studies showing that REM-like mental activity occurs in non-REM sleep also refute a REM definition of dreaming (Foulkes, 1962; Foulkes & Vogel, 1965). Slap (1977) observed dreamlike episodes in naps. Cartwright (1966) reported striking and consistent similarities between subjects' REM dreams and their waking (drug-induced) hallucinations. She also found that the drug experience may actually have served as a substitute for dreaming: The night following the drug experience, there was a sizable reduction in the time spent in REM sleep. Similar substitution phenomena have been reported by Feinberg, Koresko, Gottleib, and Wender (1964), Kramer, Whitman, Baldridge, and Ornstein (1970), Kupfer, Wyatt, Scott, and Snyder (1970), and Okuma, Sunami, Fukuma, Takeo, and Motoike (1970). These findings are all consistent with the view that "mind" is an emergent property of cerebral activity with causal efficacy in its own right (Arkin, Antrobus, & Ellman, 1978).

In short, the content and quality of dreaming—what we dream about—should be regarded as being as legitimate a subject for scientific investigation as is the physiological substratum of the dream experience. I say this with great deliberateness, since the canons of scientific rigor say nothing about the subject matter of science. Whether an investigation satisfies these criteria depends solely on the soundness of its methodology, and not on whether its unit of study is a single brain cell, an entire person, or even groups of persons.

Finally, a word about function. Dream theorists commonly distinguish between how the dream is constructed and what the dream does (its function or consequences). However, many theorists, notably Foulkes (1980), contend that the function of dreaming cannot be studied without first understanding how dreams are organized. In this chapter I intend to show that dream formation and dream function can and should be treated as separate issues. Again, this is not to deny that the two issues are related. If Freud, for example, had not assumed that dreams represent disguised instinctual wishes, he could not have proposed that they have a sleep-protective function (a notion much in dispute today). One can even go so far as to say that the mechanisms of dream formation are *preconditions* for the function of dreaming. Still, this does not alter the fact that dream function can be studied independently of dream formation. As I suggested elsewhere (Fiss, Klein, & Schollar, 1974), dreams, instead of concealing conflicts, often *reveal* them; that is, they help bring conflicts into focus and enable subjects to communicate them and work them through. Yet, the very same study that led to this conclusion shed virtually no light on the possible mechanisms responsible for this revelatory dream quality. It should be apparent, therefore, that focusing on dream function without taking account of dream formation is an entirely legitimate choice.

DO DREAMS SERVE A FUNCTION?

Having decided in favor of a function-oriented approach to the experimental investigation of the dream as an autochthonous psychological process, I now ask whether dreaming serves any function at all—whether it is in any way important. (This is not to say that all dreams are likely to be significant. Like any waking thought, some are undoubtedly trivial. This, however, does not in any way negate the importance of the process itself.) To answer this question, Fiss et al. (1974) carried out an investigation that, though summarized in the first edition of *The Mind in Sleep*, bears recapitulating. The paradigm for this investigation was an earlier study by Fiss and Ellman (1973), in which 4 subjects (Ss) were awakened on 2 consecutive nights during every REMP after approximately 10 minutes of REM sleep. These nights were preceded by 4 consecutive uninterrupted baseline nights and were followed by 2 uninterrupted recovery nights. During the first recovery night, all 4 Ss had significantly shorter-than-normal REMPs. This finding, obtained without depriving these Ss of their normal total amounts of REM sleep, was interpreted as a conditioned avoidance response and raised the question of whether it would be possible to train Ss to compensate for lost *dream* time. Would Ss be able to learn to cram as much dreaming as possible into these shortened REMPs, to "accelerate" their dreams, so to speak? The Fiss et al. (1974) study on the effects of repeated REM interruptions on dream *content* addressed itself to this question.

   In this investigation, 2 Ss, 1 male, 1 female, spent 15 consecutive nights in the sleep laboratory, for a combined total of 30 nights. The 15 nights consisted of 6 baseline nights of uninterrupted sleep; 4 nights during which every REMP was interrupted after approximately 10 minutes of REM sleep; 4 nights during which the Ss were allowed to complete their REMPs before being awakened; and 1 final uninterrupted recovery night. The interruption and completion nights were counterbalanced to control for order effects. As in the Fiss and Ellman (1973) study, REM deprivation was controlled by requiring Ss to remain in the laboratory until they had accumulated as much REM time as they had averaged during their baseline nights. In addition to the electrophysiological recordings and dream reports obtained following each awakening, we collected life history and projective test data as well as dream associations.

The results were as follows: (a) the dream reports collected during REM interruption nights were on the average as long as the dream reports elicited during the REM completion nights; in fact, the interruption reports were slightly but not significantly longer. (This was a rather striking finding, considering that the interrupted REMPs were only about half as long as the completed REMPs.); (b) the REM interruption reports were significantly more dreamlike—more vivid and affect-charged—than were the REM completion reports; (c) the REM interruption procedure helped bring the Ss' major conflicts and preoccupations into sharper focus, whereas the REM completion procedure did not; (d) in comparison with the completed REMPs, the interrupted REMPs contained significantly more eye movement activity but also significantly *fewer* indicators of arousal (alpha, body movements, non-REM intrusions).

These findings led to the interpretation that the Ss did apparently learn to compensate for lost dream time by intensifying their dream experience and by compressing more and more of their dream activity into the experimentally shortened REMPs. Thus, our principal hypothesis was confirmed. However, the results also showed that experiencing vivid, emotional, and even conflictual dreams does not necessarily disrupt sleep, as one might expect. On the contrary, the results strongly suggest that we dream in order to focus or concentrate our attention periodically on what troubles us most, perhaps even to work out some kind of solution. Rather than the dream's being a guardian of sleep, it seems that *sleep may be the guardian of the dream*, as Greenson (1970) once proposed. (It is worth noting here that Greenberg, Pearlman, Fingar, Kantrowitz, and Kawliche (1970) came to a similar conclusion on the basis of results obtained in a study of the psychological effects of REM *deprivation*, an experimental technique quite different from our REM *interruption* method.) Obviously, dreaming serves a vital function. But what exactly *is* this function?

Promising and provocative as the findings of the REM interruption study may be, they cannot provide a definitive answer to this question because an answer would require a demonstration that dreams actually influence what an individual does: that they *transform* or *change* a person in some predictable fashion. The study described subsequently, by Fiss and Litchman (1976), employed a paradigm that makes such a demonstration possible. It is a test of the hypothesis that dreaming serves an *adaptive* function. (This is not to imply that there are not other functions that dreaming may serve.)

THE DREAM ENHANCEMENT PARADIGM

The belief that dreams are adaptively useful goes back to the ancient Greeks and continues to be held by virtually every therapist. It is a belief that was expressed by Jung (1933), Adler (1936), Erikson (1954), French and Fromm (1964), Breger, Hunter, and Lane (1971), Jones (1970), Spitz (1964), and many others following the tradition of ego psychology. Some went so far as to attribute artistic creations and scientific discoveries to dreaming (Krippner & Hughes, 1970). Yet, despite this wealth of speculation, a rigorous test of the adaptational hypothesis of dreaming is hard to come by, probably because "the question of what psychological functions are involved in dreaming requires experimental manipulations which may be very difficult to carry out" (Arkin et al., 1978, p. 230).

Indirect evidence of the adaptation hypothesis is plentiful. New, difficult, or stressful stimuli, such as maze learning (Lucero, 1970), inverting prisms (Zimmerman, Stoyva, & Metcalf, 1970), perplexing tasks (Lewin & Gombosh, 1972), or traumatic experiences (Greenberg, Pillard, & Pearlman, 1972), have all been shown to increase REM sleep. Grieser, Greenberg, and Harrison (1972) showed that REM-deprived Ss have poorer recall and cope less effectively with stressful stimuli than do Ss who are not REM-deprived. However, while all these studies suggest that REM sleep has adaptive value in that it facilitates learning, memory consolidation, and information processing, they tell us nothing about whether *dreaming* has these functions, since in all these studies the psychological process of dreaming is confounded by the physiological event of REM sleep. The Fiss and Litchman (1976) study got around this difficulty by focusing on dream content. It did so by means of an experimental method of raising dream consciousness, which we termed "dream enhancement."

The Technique of Dream Enhancement

Dream enhancement (DE) is a unique, intensive crash program, designed literally to immerse Ss in their dreams. DE is a method of experimentally heightening dream awareness and serves a number of functions: It is a way of maximizing dream recall and minimizing dream forgetting, and it encourages Ss to focus their waking attention on their dream life. It consists of the following steps.

1. *Inducing a positive dream set.* Ss are told, before the experiment, that dreams are valuable and meaningful experiences that can have a lasting, positive influence on their waking life, and that concentrating on one's dreams (making a special effort to remember them, reflecting on their meaning and relevance to one's personality and adjustment problems) can be a rewarding experience.

2. *Making a positive dream suggestion.* Ss are instructed, before going to sleep, to dream about a specific problem they are having, to include a possible solution to it, and to repeat the suggestion several times before falling asleep. (Barber, Walker, & Hahn, 1973; Cartwright, 1974; Fisher, 1953; Newman, Katz, & Rubenstein, 1960; Stoyva, 1961; and Tart, 1964 have all demonstrated that it is possible to influence dream content by suggesting to the dreamer that he or she dream about a specific topic.) In using the DE technique, the attempt is made, whenever possible, to tailor the dream content suggestion to a subject's major complaint. For example, if a subject perceives his or her major problem as being difficulty in communicating with others, we would instruct the subject to try to have dreams in which he or she is successfully communicating.

3. *Recording dreams at night.* Ss' sleep is monitored on a polygraph for the purpose of obtaining continuous EEG (electroencephalographic), EOG (electro-oculographic), and EMG (electromyographic) recordings, in accordance with criteria standardized by Rechtschaffen and Kales (1968). During each REMP, Ss are awakened by having their first name called out over the intercom and are asked to "tell me what was going through your mind." Following the dream report, which is tape recorded, they are asked, "Anything else?" No further prompts are used.

4. *Spontaneous dream recall.* Following the final awakening in the morning, a recording is made of all the dreams Ss are able to recall spontaneously.

5. *"Forced" recall—dream playback.* Ss listen attentively to all the dreams recorded during the laboratory night. This constitutes the principal and most innovative feature of the DE procedure.

6. *Dream discussion.* Ss are asked a few standard questions intended to stimulate them to reflect upon the meaning and importance of each dream. For example: What does this dream mean to you? What does it reveal about you as a person? Does it help you understand or solve your problem, and if so, how? At no time, of course, are Ss offered any interpretations. However, they are encouraged to continue to reflect throughout the day upon their previous night's dreams, to keep a log of their associations, and to try to engage in dream-preserving daytime activities (e.g., making a drawing or a painting of the dream).

Measuring the Effects of Dream Enhancement

Five instruments commonly employed in clinical research are used to evaluate the effects of the DE procedure: Four are measures of psychopathology or symptom distress and one is an objective index of insightfulness or self-awareness. The psychopathology measures are the *SCL–90*, a symptom distress checklist covering the most common complaints of psychiatric patients; the *Target Complaints* (Battle et al., 1966), which also measures symptom distress but is individually tailored to each S's unique or special symptom; the *State-Trait Anxiety Inventory (STAI)*; and the *Beck Depression Scale*. For measuring the degree of self-awareness or insightfulness we used the *Experiencing (EXP) Scale* (Klein, Mathieu, Gendlin, & Kiesler, 1970). This is a seven-point, annotated, and anchored rating device, progressing from markedly impersonal or superficial discourse at the lowest end to increasingly elaborate, introspective self-description at the upper end. It yields a modal rating, characterizing the average level of self-understanding, and a peak rating, describing the highest EXP scale level reached. The scale was blindly administered by 2 independent judges whose overall reliability exceeded .80. It is used to rate psychotherapy protocols as well as 10-minute monologues (free association periods) elicited from Ss after each final awakening.

The Subjects

Our Ss were 3 young, adult outpatients who presented clearly definable psychological conflicts and were, according to their therapists, at an impasse in therapy. S1 was a 27-year-old female with a 1-year history of anxiety and depression and extremely low self-esteem. S2 was a 30-year-old unemployed father of 5 children; his presenting complaints included anxiety, depression, and severe marital difficulties. S3 was a 27-year-old male who was experiencing a great deal of difficulty in adjusting to his recent divorce. None of the Ss was on any kind of medication, nor did any of them present a major psychiatric disorder.

Results of the Pilot Study

To get a feel for the procedure and to see whether we would get an effect at all, we did a trial run with S1, consisting of 14 nights: an adaptation night with no REM awakenings, 2 baseline nights with REM awakenings but no postsleep playback, 9 nights of REM awakenings with playbacks (DE nights), and 2 post-DE nights with REM awakenings only.

The results of this pilot run were all in the predicted direction. On the SCL–90, comparison of pre- and post-DE profiles showed a marked reduction not only in overall symptom distress but also among those factorized scores peculiar to S1—anxiety, depression, and feelings of inadequacy. Parallel declines over time were evident in her Target Complaints, STAI, and Beck scores. The EXP ratings, based on therapy protocols before, during, and after DE nights, showed a similar pattern. Moreover, EXP ratings reached a peak after maximum DE. The EXP ratings also matched the therapist's report that during the DE procedure S1 made a major breakthrough in therapy.

DE Study Proper

Though encouraged by these preliminary findings, we had no way of knowing, of course, whether they resulted from the experimental manipulation itself or from potentially confounding extraneous variables such as the extra attention given to the S, her expectation that the DE procedure would benefit her, or even the mere passage of time. To control for these variables, we redesigned the study for Ss 2 and 3 as follows. Each S was run for a total of 7 nights: 1 adaptation night and 6 nights accompanied by DE. However, for 3 nights, Ss were awakened from REM and for 3 nights they were awakened from non-REM sleep (the control condition), in counterbalanced order. Since there was no reason to assume that either the attention or expectancy variable would interact differentially with regard to either REM or non-REM–DE, any differences between the two DE conditions could be reliably attributed only to differences in the kinds of mental activity evoked by them. The tightened-up design also had the advantage of making it possible to determine whether any obtained DE effects were the outcome of merely focusing on one's fantasy life in general or whether they were the result of concentrating on REM mentation in particular.

Table 9.1 summarizes the results for S2 and S3 on all 4 psychopathology measures. Note that *on all measures, both Ss showed greater improvement, that is, greater decreases in symptom distress scores following REM–DE than following non-REM–DE,* regardless of order of conditions. It should be pointed out that neither S was aware of any differences in the two awakening conditions, though their spontaneous comments suggested that they both felt their REM dreams were considerably more enlightening, stimulating, and therapeutically beneficial than their non-REM dreams. S2, an extremely passive man, gave a particularly striking illustration of this. His chief complaint had been an inability to assert himself in the face of adversity. During the experiment, he showed a great deal of concern about being "hassled" by the gas company about outstanding bills. During REM–DE Night No. 1 he reported a dream about killing a lion during a lion hunt. The following day he acted in a most uncharacteristic fashion by "raising hell"

TABLE 9.1. RESULTS ON PSYCHOPATHOLOGY MEASURES

Condition	Target Complaints		General Symptomatic Index (SCL)		Positive Symptom Total (SCL)		STAI-State		STAI-Trait		Beck Depression Score	
S2:												
Pre-NREM–DE	101		1.0		53		52		63		24	
Post-NREM–DE	92	– 9%	1.0	0%	50	– 6%	54	+	57	– 10%	22	– 9%
Pre-REM–DE	63		1.6		67		46		55		12	
Post-REM–DE	38	– 40%	1.3	– 19%	54	– 19%	31	– 33%	37	– 33%	6	– 50%
S3:												
Pre-REM–DE	58		1.4		56		35		43		3	
Post-REM–DE	42	– 28%	0.2	– 86%	10	– 82%	27	– 23%	34	– 21%	0	– 100%
Pre-NREM–DE	43		0.1		11		29		30		4	
Post-NREM–DE	40	– 7%	0.1	0%	9	– 18%	42	+	30	0%	4	0%

in the utility office and getting his gas bill straightened out, something his wife would normally have been compelled to do. Though there were no other dramatic instances of this kind, the experience had a most cohesive effect on his self-image, as corroborated by his therapist.

Table 9.2 summarizes both Ss' ratings on the EXP scale. Analysis of these ratings showed a pattern similar to that presented by the psychopathology scores: Ss 2 and 3 achieved their highest modal and peak ratings in the REM–DE condition; that is, they both demonstrated a higher level of self-awareness during REM–DE than during non REM–DE.

Obviously, these results need to be replicated on a much larger scale. They are at least consistent enough, however, to warrant the assumptions that directing one's waking attention to REM-related mental activity may have greater adaptive value than directing one's attention to non-REM mentation, and that REM dreams, in contrast to other types of fantasy activity, may play a unique role in maintaining adequate ego functioning. Related work reported by Cartwright, Tipton, and Wicklund (1980) lends even stronger support to these assumptions. Although their Ss did not serve as their own controls, as ours did, and were not "immersed" in their dreams to the extent that ours were (no playback and no continuous all-day dream monitoring), their findings are based on a substantially larger N and are remarkably consistent with ours. They show that patients trained in attending to their REM dreams remain longer in treatment and make better progress (as determined by somewhat different outcome measures) than patients trained in focusing on their non-REM dreams or patients not trained in attending to any of their dreams. Thus, the ancient notion of the adaptive value of dreaming does seem to have some empirical validity. However, given the complexity and arduousness of such a validating task, it is hardly surprising that the attempts to carry it out have been so few and so late in coming.

TABLE 9.2.   MEAN EXPERIENCING RATINGS FOR S2 AND S3

Condition	Mode	Peak
S2:		
Adaptation	2.0	3.0
Non-REM–DE	2.0	3.0
REM–DE	3.3	4.2
S3:		
Adaptation	1.5	3.5
REM–DE	2.7	4.8
Non-REM–DE	2.0	3.5

THE DREAM INCORPORATION PARADIGM

A second major paradigm successfully used in studying the function of dreaming has been the incorporation paradigm, in which dream content, rather than being highlighted, is influenced by some specific presleep stimulus and the effects of this influence on postsleep behavior are investigated. In this type of approach, dream content is not so much an independent variable as it is an *intervening* variable that mediates the effects of presleep manipulation on postsleep activity. It has proven particularly effective in studying *specific* adaptive properties of dreaming because each manipulation can be tailored to the function in question. Thus, in a study on the relationship between dream content and one's capacity to cope with stress (mastery function), Cohen and Cox (1975) subjected their Ss, prior to going to sleep, to a stressful failure experience: They gave them a task to do in a way that made them feel inadequate (by treating them impersonally, giving them no explanations, etc.). Ss who incorporated the negative presleep condition into their dream content felt better about it the next day and were more willing to tackle it again than those who did not incorporate it.

A related study by Greenberg and Pearlman (1975) demonstrated that dreaming about a problem raised during a presleep psychoanalytical session predictably influenced the degree of defensiveness ("defensive strain") evidenced during a subsequent psychoanalytical hour. These findings are consistent with the ego psychological view of Hartmann, Rapaport, and others that adaptation involves not just a general "synthetic" function (Nunberg, 1931) but *multiple* ego functions, some "autonomous" (e.g., mastery) and some evolving from conflict (as in defense). The dream study described herein addresses itself to the adaptive ego function of memory consolidation.

A Study of the Mnemonic Function of Dreaming

The aim of this study by Fiss, Kremer, and Litchman (1977) was to demonstrate that the dream experience has a memory-consolidating function all its own, independent of REM sleep. That REM sleep facilitates recall was demonstrated earlier (Grieser et al., 1972). The question we asked was: Would dreaming about a presleep stimulus also facilitate its recall?

Method.   The Ss for this study were 6 adult, nonpatient volunteers (3 male, 3 female), ranging in age from 24 to 35. They were selected for good dream recall, had no sleep disorder, and were not taking any hypnotic or other psychoactive medication.

Each S was run for 2 consecutive nights, during which standard polygraphic recordings were obtained. Each night, Ss were awakened from every REM period of more than 10 minutes. Upon awakening, Ss reported their dreams, which were tape recorded. They were awakened 4 or 5 times per night.

On night 1, the Adaptation-Control Night, Ss were simply awakened periodically for dream reporting. On night 2, the Stimulus Night, Ss read a brief story immediately before going to bed. The story described a vivid scene in which a sea monster attacks a sinking ship. Ss were instructed to continue to visualize the scene as they fell asleep and to try to incorporate the story into their dreams. In the morning, after their final dream report, Ss were asked to try to recall the story. This request, as we had hoped, took the Ss by surprise. The Ss then rated the amount of conscious thought that they had given the story during the previous night.

Each S's recall was scored on the total number of story-idea units remembered. All dreams were transcribed and coded; they were then scored for story incorporation by two raters who were unaware of the night on which the dreams were produced. Various measures of dream incorporation were developed, the most reliable of which proved to be a content checklist. The checklist contained an exhaustive listing of story elements that might be incorporated into dream content directly, symbolically, or thematically. Each dream was scored according to the total number of incorporative elements it contained. Interrater reliability for this procedure, computed from scores of the two independent raters, was 0.84. Polygraphic records were scored for sleep latency and eye movement density. The sleep latency measure was used, in conjunction with the Ss' self-ratings, to assess the extent to which the subjects rehearsed the story while awake.

Results

1. Stimulus Night dreams received significantly higher checklist scores than Control Night dreams ($\overline{X} = 3.75$ for story elements occurring in Control Night dreams, 5.22 for story elements in Stimulus Night dreams). The consistently higher scores on the Stimulus Night provided evidence that the story *was* actually incorporated into the subjects' dreams.

2. To determine whether dreaming about the presleep stimulus facilitated its recall, we computed the correlation between incorporation scores and story recall scores. The incorporation score given each subject was the *difference* between his or her mean checklist scores on the Stimulus and Control Nights; the greater the difference, the greater the degree of incorporation. This difference score was used to control for the chance occurrence of story elements in dream content. We found a large and significant correlation between dream incorporation and story recall ($r = 0.84$, $p < .05$). These findings supported the hypothesized relationship between incorporating a stimulus into dreams and recalling it (Table 9.3).

TABLE 9.3. PREDICTION OF STORY RECALL FROM DREAM INCORPORATION AND DREAM PRODUCTIVITY

	Dream Incorporation	Dream Productivity	Story Recall
Dream Incorporation		0.52	0.84*
Dream Productivity			0.80*
Story Recall			

Multiple $R = 0.94$*; Multiple $R^2 = 0.88$.

3. An interesting but unexpected finding was the significant correlation between dream productivity per se and story recall. Using the number of discrete dream episodes reported as a measure of dream productivity, we found a significant correlation between story recall and dream productivity on the Stimulus Night ($r = 0.80$, $p < .05$). Dream productivity on the Control Night was unrelated to story recall ($r = 0.37$, n.s.).

4. Dream incorporation and dream productivity were not themselves significantly correlated ($r = 0.52$, n.s.). However, in a multiple regression analysis, the two predictors (dream incorporation and dream productivity) taken together accounted for a higher portion of the variance in story recall than either predictor taken singly (Mult $R = 0.94$, $p < .05$). With these two indexes of a subject's intervening dream experience, we were able to account for 88% of the variance in subsequent recall of a presleep experience. The content-related measure (dream incorporation) contributed greater predictive power than did the more general measure of overall dream productivity.

5. We also attempted to determine whether the differences in story recall could be explained on the basis of story rehearsal. A low and insignificant correlation was found between Ss' self-ratings for story rehearsal and their recall scores. A nonsignificant correlation was also found between sleep latency and story recall. Thus, being awake after reading the story did *not* help Ss recall it. These findings clearly indicated that waking rehearsal of the story was not an important factor in determining its subsequent recall. An index of REM physiology (eye movement density) also showed no consistent relationship with story recall. Dream content and dream productivity were better predictors of story recall than either REM-related physiological events or story rehearsal.

In summary, the presleep stimulus *did* influence Ss' dreams, and this dream incorporation, not the story rehearsal, was related to subsequent recall. Furthermore, recall was correlated with dream productivity but not with physiological activation during REM sleep, as reflected in eye-movement density. Apparently, having richer, more varied dreams and dreaming about a specific subject can together facilitate recall. The results clearly showed that dreaming has a mnemonic function analogous to, but not identical with, the mnemonic function of REM sleep.

DREAM INCORPORATION, WISH FULFILLMENT, AND THE REGULATION OF DRIVE

Freud (1905/1953), in the case of Dora, suggested that the meaning of a dream could be "of as many different sorts as the process of waking thought. . . . In one case it would be a fulfilled wish; in another a realized fear; or again a reflection persisting on into sleep; or an intention; or a piece of creative thought" (p. 68). Freud never seriously entertained this notion of multiplicity of function and continued to favor his wish-fulfillment hypothesis. But it seems to be implied in his statement that dreams can serve both the pleasure and the reality principle, that they can not only discharge but also control and regulate drive, and that they can be adaptively, even creatively, integrated into waking life.

The opportunity of putting this possibility to an experimental test presented itself to me a few years ago when a population of alcoholic patients became available for study at one of our affiliated hospitals. Since Ss who are addicted to a substance such as ethanol can be expected to be in a state of intensified drive, they seem particularly well suited to an investigation involving the wish-fulfilling and drive-controlling function of dreaming. Yet, only a small number of studies have actually been conducted on the subject of dreaming in alcoholics. Most of these were undertaken for the purpose of comparing the manifest dream content of alcoholics with that of nonalcoholics (Hall, 1966; Moore, 1962; Scott, 1968). In an investigation using a *normal* population, Bokert (1968) found that thirst-related dream content was inversely related to feeling thirsty and to the amount of water consumed the next morning. Bokert deprived his Ss of food and fluids and gave them a salty meal prior to sleep. Following a night of laboratory dream collection, Ss who had dreams containing themes of drinking drank less and rated themselves as less thirsty in the morning than did Ss who had no such dreams. The present investigation addressed itself to the question of whether the dreams of substance abusers serve a function similar to the dreams of Bokert's thirsty, normal Ss; however, it was undertaken to study the relationship between dream content and *craving*. Would alcoholics who dream about drinking evidence less craving than alcoholics who do not?

Dream Content and Response to Withdrawal from Alcohol

The Ss for this investigation (Fiss, 1980) were 20 alcoholic, inpatient volunteers who had just completed a week-long detoxification program. None of them was organic, psychotic, or mentally retarded and none showed any physiological signs of withdrawal. Also excluded were patients with insomnia and a history of polysubstance abuse. Only those who reported recalling more than one dream per week were selected. As a group they were fairly homogeneous with respect to socioeconomic background: Virtually all were unmarried, unemployed, had comparable drinking histories, and lacked education beyond 12th grade. Their median age was 41. Twelve were male, 8 female.

Starting on the seventh day following Ss' admission to the treatment unit, tape-recorded clinical interviews focusing on dream content were conducted for 5 consecutive mornings shortly after awakening from sleep. Ss were asked if they recalled any dreams from the previous night and, if so, were requested to report them in as much detail as possible. Additional questions were asked only for the purpose of clarification. The final question was: "Do you recall anything else?" If the answer was "no," the interview was terminated. After the dreams collected from the patients had been carefully transcribed, each dream was blindly and independently scored, by two trained judges, for length and drinking themes and on a selected number of content scales described by Winget and Kramer (1979). Only scales yielding rater reliability scores in excess of .70 were used for data analysis.

On the third day of dream collection, and again shortly before being discharged from the program, Ss were administered the Ludwig–Starke Craving Questionnaire (L–S) and the Profile of Mood States (POMS) and were evaluated by their counselors on a modified version of the Global Assessment Scale (GAS), a 100-point scale of overall psychological adjustment.

Analysis of the data revealed, first, that dream recall was extremely high for these Ss: All but two of them (90%) recalled one or more dreams in the course of the study. This suggests that REM rebound effects may persist long after withdrawal symptoms have disappeared. Researchers interested in Ss who are exceptionally good recallers might thus be interested in collecting dreams from alcoholics during the early stages of ethanol withdrawal.

Analysis of the correlations performed between dream content and overall mood and adjustment (POMS and GAS scores) revealed that nearly 20% of them were significant, with dream length ($r = .54$, $p < .05$), dreamer involvement ($r = .63$, $p < .03$), affect intensity ($r = .62$, $p < .03$), intropunitiveness ($r = -.65$, $p < .02$), and hedonic tone ($r = .42$, $p < .05$) being among the best predictors of response to treatment, as shown on the GAS.

We also did a median split comparison between Ss' dream content scores and treatment outcome, and found significant relationships between intropunitiveness and GAS scores ($t = 2.73$, $p < .03$) and between interpersonal closeness, dream length, and dream complexity and the POMS Total Mood Disturbance Index ($t = 2.21$, $p < .05$; $t = 2.69$, $p < .04$; $t = 2.49$, $p < .05$). In other words, alcoholic patients are most likely to respond positively to treatment if their dream narratives are long and elaborate, if they appear as active participants in their dreams, if the characters appearing in their dreams represent people with whom they have close relationships, if aggression is expressed externally in their dreams rather than directed inward, and if the feelings expressed in their dreams are both intense and pleasant. Evidently, dream content has the potential for being an extremely useful tool for the prediction of treatment outcome. Is this so because "effective dreaming may be likened to effective psychotherapy" (Jones, 1970, p. 133)? The results of the dream enhancement and dream laboratory training studies described earlier (Cartwright, et al., 1980; Fiss & Litchman, 1976) suggest that Jones may indeed have a point here.

Of greatest interest to us, however, was the relationship we found between dream content and craving. A median split of the L–S scores revealed that more than *80% of the high cravers dreamed about drinking, while only 30% of the low cravers dreamed about drinking*—a difference significant at the .03 level, according to the Fisher Exact Test.

This finding—that patients who dreamed about drinking (incorporators) showed higher levels of craving than those who did not (nonincorporators)—puzzled us because it contradicted the results of Bokert's study. It then occurred to us that there may have been important qualitative differences in the manner in which drinking themes became incorporated into dream content. When we checked into this possibility, we discovered that the dreams of the low cravers all contained themes of drive gratification (e.g., drinking at a party and having a good time), and the dreams of the high cravers all contained defensive or conflictual themes (e.g., loss of a love object as a consequence of being caught drinking). This suggested that our response to an intensified drive state may be determined not only by *how much* drive material we incorporate into our dreams, but also by *how* we incorporate it. However, it still remains to be explained why, in contrast to the dreams of Bokert's Ss, most of our Ss' dreams about drinking were nongratifying. The answer probably lies in differences between the two populations. Bokert's Ss were nonalcoholics who thirsted for and dreamed about water, not liquor. They may have been motivated by different wishes. For them, dreaming positively about drinking may have had the aim of relieving discomfort. Our Ss, on the other hand, may have dreamed about drinking in a negative way in order to maintain sobriety— a major adaptive task.

Again, we can see how important consideration of meaningfulness and intentionality are in any clinically relevant experimental dream psychology. It is also clear that the study of dreaming during and after withdrawal, not just from alcohol but from any addictive substance, be it drugs, tobacco, even food, can be an extremely useful model for investigating the drive-regulatory and wish-fulfilling function of dreaming.

CONCLUSION

I have described two basic paradigms that have proven useful for an experimental psychology of dream function: one highlighting, the other influencing dream content. Both have been shown to be effective tools for investigating the effects of dream content on postsleep behavior, and both represent a departure from the more traditional strategy of influencing dream content by means of presleep manipulations. Rather than concentrating on the "day residue," our approach focuses on the "*night residue.*"

As with all methodologies, the heuristic value of the approach outlined in this chapter depends on its capacity to generate useful future research. A few examples will have to suffice.

Dream Content and Stress Management

This is one area in which further research is definitely indicated. Although the effects of stress on dream content have been amply documented (Breger et al., 1971), little is known about the effects of dream content on the ability to cope with stress. Using the dream incorporation stratagem employed by Cohen and Cox (1975), one could pick up where Breger et al. (1971) left off and study not the effects of the stress of surgery on dream content, as they did, but the effects of dream content on one's reaction to surgery; for example, would dreaming about an impending operation influence a patient's anxiety about the actual event and possibly even his or her recovery from it? If so, in what ways? Precisely such a study is currently in progress. Once a relationship is established between dream content and adaptation to stress, a further step would be to try to reduce stress by means of maximizing dream awareness. Will DE reduce preoperative anxiety, help Ss cope more effectively, and facilitate recovery from the surgical procedure? Will dreams have this adaptive effect regardless of the manner in which the stressful event is incorporated? Or will the effect depend on whether incorporation is positive (themes of mastery, intact body image, and so on) or negative (themes of deterioration, failure, inadequacy)? It is entirely possible that dreaming about a stressful situation even in negative terms can be adaptive, since the dream can be conceptualized as an attempt to turn a passive into an active experience.

Dream Content and Therapeutic Management

A still open question is whether dreams, to be adaptively useful, must be communicated, or whether they fulfill their function as private, unreported experiences. And if they have to be communicated, is it enough simply to report them? Or do they have to be reported to particular individuals and laboriously worked over with them before they can be successfully integrated into our lives? The DE procedure, as it stands now, is too complex to provide any answers to these questions. It would seem desirable, therefore, as a logical first step, to refine the procedure in order to ascertain which of its components are the actual therapeutic ingredients. To accomplish this, we have begun to investigate whether the DE effect occurs by merely having Ss listen to a playback of their recorded dreams *without* reflecting on their meaning, as they did in the study by Fiss and Litchman (1976). Perhaps dreams need only to be brought into awareness without being worked over. The implications of these considerations for the process of psychotherapy are not inconsequential. If dreams merely need to be dreamed and recalled without additional efforts on the part of patient and therapist, then the importance of interpreting may have been overvalued. And if REM dreams are adaptively more useful than non-REM dreams, as Cartwright et al. (1980) and Fiss and Litchman (1976) suggested, then therapists and patients should perhaps concentrate more on REM dreams, especially since REM dreams can easily be discriminated from non-REM dreams even when Ss are asleep (Antrobus, 1967). Finally, the therapeutic manipulation of dreaming is now a distinct possibility, as Garfield (1974) has long suggested. Thus, the sleep lab has possibilities not only for purposes of research and assessment, but also as a therapeutic agent. It may even teach us about the therapy process itself. If, as Fiss and Litchman (1976) and Cartwright et al. (1980) showed, dreaming is conducive to increased self-awareness, then the sleep lab should be able to teach us something about the process of acquiring insight—the very core of therapeutic personality change.

Dream Content and Self-Esteem

Not only self-awareness but also self-esteem is open to investigation with the experimental strategies that have been outlined. With so much current emphasis on the self, research on this personality dimension may do much to advance the scientific status of self-psychology. An experimental investigation which, like the Cohen and Cox (1975) study, would seek to relate dream incorporation of an especially frustrating presleep experience (for instance an incomplete Zeigarnik-type task) to changes in self-esteem, would certainly be a step in the right direction.

Dream Content and Nicotine Addiction

This is another area worthy of further exploration. What is the nature of the relationship between tobacco withdrawal symptoms and sleep and dream variables? Is there a progressive change over time in the frequency, intensity, and quality of sleep and dream characteristics during the transition from heavy smoking to abrupt cessation? Is there a causal direction to this change, so that one may perhaps determine the extent to which sleep physiology and nocturnal mental activity *influence* the course of the nicotine withdrawal syndrome? Might the success or failure of nicotine abstinence efforts depend on dream content changes, as perhaps in the study on withdrawal from alcohol (Fiss, 1980)?

These are only a small sample of the types of experimental questions that a function-oriented experimental dream psychology is capable of raising. They obviously cover a vast territory, extending from the analytical couch into behavioral medicine and even public health issues. They are operational enough, however, to be capable of being answered. When these answers are in, we shall have a more fully balanced conception, both biological and mental, of why we dream.

PART 4

EFFECTS OF REM DEPRIVATION

10

REM Deprivation: A Review

STEVEN J. ELLMAN
ARTHUR J. SPIELMAN
City College of the City University of New York

DANA LUCK
St. Vincent's Hospital and Medical Center

SOLOMON S. STEINER
City College of the City University of New York

RONNIE HALPERIN
State University of New York at Purchase

In this chapter we deal primarily with the "psychological" and behavioral effects of deprivation of rapid eye movement (REM) sleep. Our chapter largely overlaps with an article by Vogel (1975) which also reviewed the behavioral effects of REM deprivation (RD). Since our manuscript was in preparation when Vogel presented his review in 1974, we decided to continue our work, but we must acknowledge our debt to the comprehensive and scholarly effort performed by Dr. Vogel. His review clearly influenced us, although, naturally, he is in no way responsible for the views contained in this work.

In 1960, Dement performed a study in which he asserted that he was dream-depriving subjects. In fact, what he did was awaken people at the beginning of each REM period (REMP) and, using today's terminology, performed the first RD experiment. Dement's (1960a) use of the term "dream deprivation" reflected early views that dreaming, or perhaps all sleep mentation, is confined to REM sleep (Dement & Kleitman, 1957).

However, a variety of developments have led a number of investigators to maintain that not all sleep mentation is confined to the REM period (REMP) and that the biological-behavioral significance of REM sleep might be better conceptualized somewhat apart from the dream experience. The findings of Foulkes (1962) and others (Foulkes, Spear, & Symonds, 1966; Foulkes & Vogel, 1965; Kamiya, 1961), that awakenings from non-REM (NREM) sleep yield mentation reports that are at times quite dreamlike, make it clear that RD is not necessarily dream deprivation. The necessary link between REM sleep and dreaming has also been weakened by both phylogenetic and developmental studies. Almost all mammalian species that have been studied have manifested a type of sleep that can be identified as REM sleep. In addition, numerous studies have shown that infant mammals have much more REM sleep (in both absolute and percentage terms) than adult mammals (Roffwarg, Muzio, & Dement, 1966; Roffwarg, Dement, & Fisher, 1964). Thus, the discovery that REM sleep occurs in virtually all mammals (Snyder, 1969) and that infants can spend 8 to 12 hr a day in REM sleep has led some researchers to hypothesize that the functional significance of REM sleep should not be linked solely, or perhaps even primarily, to dreaming. Dement's dream-deprivation experiment then failed to assess, as he had intended, the basic function and significance of dreaming. However, his experiment was a germinal one in the history of sleep research, and few, if any, experiments have had as great an impact on the field.

Although the theme of this book focuses mainly on sleep mentation, we have chosen to include animal studies in this chapter, since, in our view, animal and human RD studies are in many ways inextricably interwoven. After Dement's (1960a) initial RD experiment in humans, he and his collaborators performed extensive RD studies in cats and rats (Cohen & Dement, 1965; Cohen, Mitchell, & Dement, 1968; Cohen, Thomas, & Dement, 1970; Dement, 1965b; Dement, 1969; Dewson, Dement, Wagener, & Nobel, 1967; Ferguson & Dement, 1967, 1968, 1969). On the basis of his animal studies, Dement developed a position that we label a "motivational" hypothesis. Essentially, it is his view that REM sleep is an occasion for the discharge of drive behaviors (Dement, 1969). From this point of view, RD should lead to a higher probability of discharge of drive behaviors in the waking state.

This assumption is compatible with a hydraulic model, and many authors (Holt, 1976; Sheffield, Roby & Campbell, 1954) in other areas have contended that a hydraulic model is not able to explain various behaviors that have been traditionally studied by investigators interested in "learning and motivational" variables. It is beyond the scope of this chapter to attempt to evaluate these arguments, but it is important to report that Dement, to our knowledge, has never presented his hypothesis in a formal manner where he fully spells out the implications of his assumptions.[1] Rather, it has seemed to us that his theoretical position has served as a working hypothesis, and as such has stimulated a good deal of research. Thus, he and his collaborators have looked at the effect of RD on subjects' perceptions on projective tests, on what might generally be termed drive behavior in animals, and on the sleep cycle of schizophrenic patients. Whatever one's view of Dement's hypothesis, to gain a fair representation of his work and the work that he has in part stimulated, it has seemed necessary to us to include animal studies in our review.

Although in our brief historical introduction we have used Dement's work as an illustration, we might just as easily have pointed out that researchers (Dewan, 1969; Greenberg & Pearlman, 1974) who have linked REM sleep with learning and memory variables have used their hypotheses to generate experiments in both humans and animals. At this point, the most extensive studies in this area have been in rats and mice.

We will not systematically attempt to evaluate the various theoretical views put forth to explain the behavioral significance of REM sleep, but it is worth noting that these views have rarely been parochial and narrowly focused. Rather, they have often been global (Ephron & Carrington, 1966; Roffwarg et al., 1966), and have attempted to explain elements of psychopathology, mammalian development, drive behavior, learning, memory, and so on. Most (if not all) of the theoretical views about REM sleep attempt to explain RD effects, and most of the views that have led to the experiments we review in this chapter have been concerned with data that have been generated from animal and human subjects. We might parenthetically add that this is symptomatic of a good deal of sleep research but is probably most often the case in the RD literature.

This chapter contains a comprehensive review of the RD literature and, as such, provides background material for Chapter 11 of this volume, in which the effects of RD on sleep mentation are discussed.

In the first section of this chapter we discuss RD in humans, and in the second section, RD in animals. Each section has subdivisions concerned

---

[1]We recognize that Dement has published articles in which he has made predictive statements; however he has not, to our knowledge, published a statement of his drive-discharge hypothesis, in which he fully and formally makes a theoretical statement (that is, spells out his postulates and the predictions from these postulates).

with methodology and with the effects of RD on various behavioral and psychological variables.

THE EFFECTS OF RD IN HUMANS

Sleep-Cycle Changes

In his first RD experiment Dement (1960a) used a "pre–post design" that has frequently been employed in subsequent RD studies. First, the subject is allowed to sleep uninterruptedly for several nights; this baseline (BL) condition provides a standardized sample of the subject's sleep patterns. Following BL nights (five in Dement's study), RD nights are initiated during which the subject is awakened every time upon entering REM sleep. RD nights are followed by recovery (R) nights during which the subject is again allowed to sleep uninterruptedly, as in the BL sequence. In the typical control condition, the subject is awakened during NREM sleep the same number of times as awakened in the RD condition. Thus, in this experiment, the subjects serve as their own control (that is, the same subject goes through both RD and control conditions). Usually, a week or two separates the RD and the control conditions. Since there have been several variations of Dement's original design, we attempt to set down some basic methodological criteria for adequately assessing RD studies.

Two obvious factors in a pre–post design are adequate BL or premeasures, and adequate R, or postmeasures. Various investigators (Agnew, Webb, & Williams, 1966; Dement, Kahn, & Roffwarg, 1965; Rechtschaffen & Verdone, 1964) have shown that on the first night in a sleep laboratory, subjects show lower REM sleep values in absolute and percentage terms than on subsequent BL nights. Kales et al. (1969) have shown, as have others (Fiss & Ellman, 1973), that only by the third BL night can one obtain stable BL values. Given that this is the case, it is clear that studies which utilize pre–post designs must have at least three BL or adaptation[2] nights to adequately assess the effects of their manipulation on R nights. In addition, the mean of the third and all subsequent BL nights should be used for statistical comparisons.

At least two R nights are needed to assess the effects of RD in studies utilizing four RD nights or less. The need for at least two R nights is

---

[2]Here we are using the terms *baseline* and *adaptation nights* interchangeably, since from a subject's point of view they are identical. On an adaptation night, a subject is treated just as on a BL night, except that no recording is performed. This is a relatively inexpensive way to acclimate subjects to a laboratory. All RD (and sleep) studies should inquire about drug and alcohol habits of subjects. Clearly, for one to two weeks preceding RD and throughout the study, a subject should be drug-free, inasmuch as many drugs influence REM sleep.

particularly important because during RD studies, subjects are frequently deprived of some delta (stages 3 and 4) sleep (Agnew, Webb, & Williams, 1967). If delta deprivation is great enough, then on the first R night one may see a delta rebound that can displace a potential REM rebound. The REM rebound would then take place on the second R night. As a related point, since BL and R nights are often compared, every attempt should be made to allow subjects approximately the same total sleep time in both conditions. In response to Dement's (1960a) first RD experiment, Barber (1960) has pointed out that control and RD conditions should be counterbalanced. (See Chapter 11 of this volume for a specific example of how counterbalancing can be accomplished.)

As a last general methodological point in human studies, the criteria used for RD can be important. Frequently, a drop in EMG levels (muscle atonia) is an early sign of a REMP, and studies that do not employ EMG measures may allow a subject up to several minutes of REM sleep before an awakening (Kales, Hoedemaker, Jacobson, & Lichtenstein, 1964). Some investigators do not utilize EMG recordings (Cartwright, Monroe, & Palmer, 1967), while others (see Chapter 11 of this volume; Kales et al., 1964) do.

It is quite important to clearly specify the criteria used for RD, particularly in studies reporting negative findings. Moreover, some type of REM-density measure[3] (number of eye movements per unit time) should be calculated for scoring of REM sleep during R nights, since it is possible that high-REM density may substitute for overall REM-time measures of REM rebound. (This point is presented in more detail subsequently in the chapter.)

Dement (1960a) found that for each additional night of RD, more awakenings were required to keep subjects from entering REM sleep. On R nights, they demonstrated elevated amounts of REM sleep (REM rebound), while in the control condition (NREM awakenings), subjects did not display a REM rebound. Thus, they seemed to display a "need" for REM sleep in the sense of attempting to compensate or make up for lost REM sleep. Three other suggestive results have come to be associated with the effects of RD:

1. REM rebound can last for more than one R night (and for as long as four to five R nights).
2. Latency to the first REMP after sleep onset is reduced on the first R night (REMP latency refers to the time interval between onset of sleep and the first REMP of the night).

---

[3]REM density is defined as REM-phasic events per unit of REM time. As an example, one may compute the average number of REMs per REM sleep time. Actually, this measure of REM density is usually calculated by computing the number of 2-sec epochs in a REMP that contain one or more REMs. Latency to the first REMP denotes the interval between sleep onset and the first REMP of the night.

3. During RD, the number of eye movements per REM time (REM density) increases (Dement, Cohen, Ferguson, & Zarcone, 1970; Ferguson & Dement, 1968). This can also occur on R nights.

Kales et al. (1964) were the first researchers to attempt to replicate Dement's (1960a) findings. Two subjects were REM deprived for six nights and showed a large REM rebound during R (REM was elevated 40 to 70% over BL). Kales et al. (1964) also REM deprived the same subjects for 10 nights and produced an even larger REM rebound. Unfortunately, Kales and co-workers did not specify how many BL nights were employed in the study, nor subject the results to statistical analysis. He reported (as did Dement) that as RD nights progress, the number of awakenings needed to prevent a subject from entering REM increases. This increase is nonmonotonic, although from the first night to the tenth night, mean awakenings increased from 20 to about 40 per night. When Kales et al. (1964) used a NREM awakening control, subjects showed no increase in REM sleep. As in Dement's (1960a) study, conditions were not counterbalanced. Snyder (1963) briefly reported similar results in two subjects, that is, an increased number of awakenings as RD nights progressed, and a REM rebound during R.

Sampson (1965) maintained that Dement's (1960a) findings might be a result of "dream" or REM interruption, as opposed to RD. He proposed to separate these two possibilities by utilizing a method he called "partial sleep deprivation." Sampson allowed subjects to sleep only 2.5 hr per night for five consecutive nights, reasoning that since very little REM (an estimated 10 to 15 min) occurs during the initial 2.5 hr of the night, this procedure would REM-deprive subjects without interrupting REMPs. For comparison, the same subjects were REM-deprived for five successive nights by awakening them at each REMP onset. Sampson found that both procedures, partial sleep deprivation and dream interruption, produced a REM rebound. While there was no significant difference in REM rebound, there was a trend in the direction of larger REM rebound following recovery from dream interruption. In addition, dream interruption produced a REM rebound in all six subjects, while partial sleep deprivation produced a REM rebound in only four out of six. Of the two subjects that did not show a REM rebound, one was not adequately assessed during R. The second clearly did not display a REM rebound on any of the three R nights following partial sleep deprivation.

One might argue that a NREM rebound displaced a REM rebound in this subject, since partial sleep deprivation, as its name implies, deprives subjects of both REM and NREM sleep. However, this seems to be an unlikely possibility since, even with total sleep deprivation, one can usually see a REM rebound during the second R night, and this subject showed no effect in three R nights as a result of partial sleep deprivation.

Dement, Greenberg, and Klein (1966) performed two types of studies demonstrating that extended partial RD has a cumulative effect, and that RD effects are reversed only by REM rebound. In the first experiment, after 10 BL nights, two subjects were deprived of about 25% of their REM sleep each night for 19 nights. On the first R night, both subjects displayed REM levels that were higher than on any BL night. For one of the two subjects, the effects was small (less than 10 min), and the authors offered as a possible explanation that BL REM levels were spuriously high. From the data they presented, there is no reason to assume this, since subjects had 10 BL nights. Moreover, their statistical treatment of the data (simple probability statement) does not allow one to generalize beyond the population of BL nights they sampled. In the second study, after 10 BL nights, two subjects were REM-deprived for five nights; on the five subsequent nights, they were allowed REM levels *equal* to those of their BL night. The next five nights were "normal" R nights, and both subjects displayed REM rebounds. The conclusion the authors reached is that REM rebound is necessary to dissipate excess REM, or, stated another way, RD effects can be stored over time.

Agnew et al. (1967) performed an interesting study comparing stage 4 to stage REM deprivation. Their study is difficult to evaluate because all sleep data is presented in percentages, and there is no way to ascertain whether total sleep time on BL and R nights was held constant. Unless one knows this data, the possibility of artificially high REM rebound totals is present if total sleep time was greater on R as opposed to BL nights. Obviously, REM rebound could be reported as spuriously low if total sleep time on BL nights is greater than on R nights. Controlling for total sleep time is essential because after the fourth hour of sleep REM percentage[4] increases (Verdone, 1968). Therefore, it is likely that the longer one sleeps, the higher the percentage of REM sleep. Nevertheless, Agnew et al. (1967) reported that selective RD leads to REM rebound, while selective stage 4 deprivation leads to a stage 4 rebound. RD produced a selective rebound in that there was no stage 4 (or any other sleep stage) rebound after RD. On the other hand, even though the authors stated that during stage 4 deprivation there was virtually no RD (a drop of only 2% per night), on the second and third R nights, subjects displayed elevated REM percentages (REM percentage went from 21 on BL night to 26% on the second and third R night, respectively). This finding may be explained as a partial RD effect. Thus, if a subject displays a percentage loss of 2% per night, then this loss over seven (stage 4) deprivation nights would be anywhere from 40 to 50 min of REM sleep. This is roughly equivalent to one-half night of RD. This conclusion is a tentative one, since we do not know the absolute values of total sleep time.

Ferguson and Dement (1968) and Dement et al. (1970) suggested that, in RD studies, what is made up is not REMP time per se, but rather phasic

---

[4]REM percentage is defined as REM time over total sleep time.

events. If this is correct, then it is logically possible to have no elevation in REM time, but a REM rebound in the sense that there are more phasic events per unit time. Although these results are in large part derived from animal studies, and are not replicated, nevertheless it seems to us important in any RD study where rebound is a dependent variable, to report on any measure of phasic activity that is available. Clearly, if phasic events are a crucial element, then the reporting of REM rebound results is not complete without including some measure of phasic activity.

Agnew et al. (1967) reported only group data, but in the other four studies[5] we have just reviewed, 20 subjects were administered some type of RD, and 19 of these subjects displayed elevated REM levels on either the first or second R night.[6] In all of the studies, there was an increase from the first to the last deprivation night in the number of awakenings[7] needed to accomplish RD. However, in two studies (Agnew et al., 1967; Kales et al., 1964), total sleep time from BL to R was not mentioned, and in two studies (Dement et al., 1966; Sampson, 1965), there was no NREM awakening control group. Neither of the experiments (Dement, 1960a; Kales et al., 1964) that used the same subjects in both deprivation and control conditions counterbalanced these conditions, although Dement (1960b) stated that he had counterbalanced conditions and it had no effect on the results obtained. (To our knowledge, he has not published these results.)

Individual Differences in REM Rebound

Witkin (1970) stated that the effects of RD have been inconsistent, and that "published reports on REM sleep deprivation in which individual subjects have been included provide striking individual differences in . . . number of awakenings required to maintain REM sleep deprivation and in the extent of subjects' indulgence in REM sleep during recovery . . ." (p. 158). What Witkin called "striking individual differences" can alternatively be seen as the type of normal error variance encountered in most experiments. The case for individual differences depends on the demonstration that unaccounted-for variance can be explained by an independent variable

---

[5]Dement and Fisher (1963) reported that in studies they conducted, 20 out of 21 subjects displayed REM rebound. We have not included this report because they did not present their data but only summarized their findings.

[6]One subject in Dement's (1960a) initial dream-deprivation study displayed REM rebound on the second R night. This result can be explained by the fact that this subject reported drinking alcohol before the first R night, and alcohol is a known REM suppressant.

[7]Agnew et al. (1967) used subawakening threshold electric shocks to the foot as their method of sleep stage deprivation, instead of the usual mechanical awakening at each stage onset.

other than RD. Witkin cited Cartwright et al. (1967) as presenting evidence that differences in response to RD can be accounted for by "psychological" variables. (In addition, Witkin cited the Pivik and Foulkes (1966) study, reviewed in another section of this chapter.) The issue of individual differences in response to RD is a controversial one, and because of this, we review Cartwright's studies in some depth.

In their first study, Cartwright et al. (1967) found that REM-deprived subjects on their first R night could be classified as displaying three different response patterns: "disruption," "compensation," and "substitution." The disruption pattern is defined as a subject having many stage 2 intrusions during REMPs, making the sleep record difficult to score by conventional criteria. The compensation pattern is one that Dement and others have typically reported following RD: subjects have an increase in total REM time (REM rebound) and a shortened latency to the first REMP. Cartwright et al. (1967) stated that subjects in the substitution group *do not* show a REM rebound following RD. If one elicits mentation reports at REM onset during RD, these subjects also report more dreamlike mentation on Foulkes's (1967a) DF scale than do compensator subjects.

In a subsequent study, Cartwright and Ratzel (1972) stated that "the variable which seems likely to be crucial in determining subjects' response to REM deprivation is the degree to which their dream-like activity is restricted to REMPS" (p. 277). In short, substitutors seem to have the ability to have dreamlike fantasies that in some way substitute for REM rebound. Cartwright and Ratzel found that subjects who have low onset fantasy (LOF), on the DF scale, for dream reports obtained at REM onset will, as a result of RD, display significantly higher REM rebound, and will have more marked changes in waking behavior than subjects who are high in REM onset fantasy (HOF).[8] In the language of Cartwright et al.'s (1967) previous study, HOFs tend to be substitutors and LOFs tend to be compensators.

Although during the R night the LOFs had a significantly higher percentage of REM sleep than the HOFs (34% versus 24%, respectively), the two groups did not differ with regard to percentage of REM sleep on the BL night, nor did they differ on the RD nights, on measures such as the number of awakenings needed to accomplish RD, total sleep time, or minutes of REM sleep.

In the data presented, both groups seemed to show some rebound on the R night, as compared to their own BL night; HOFs had about 4% more REM, while LOFs had about 10% more REM. The authors did not state whether the HOF REM rebound was statistically significant (comparing BL and R nights).

On pre–post deprivation test measures, LOFs, as predicted, showed a significant change in the WAIS and on two Rorschach measures (M+ scores

---

[8]Subjects in this experiment are rated on a Foulkes DF scale; generally, one can say that low scores indicate less dreamlike reports than high scores on the scale.

and M : sum C scores). Both Rorschach postdeprivation changes were interpreted to mean that the LOF group became more sensitive to internal stimulation. Interestingly, the LOF group showed a 10-point postdeprivation *rise* in IQ score. Most of this rise, according to Cartwright and Ratzel (1972) "could be accounted for by a change in the Picture Arrangement score," (p. 279) (a performance subtest).

In our opinion, Cartwright and collaborators (Cartwright, et al., 1967; Cartwright & Monroe, 1968; Cartwright & Ratzel, 1972) dealt with fundamental questions that explore the relationship between psychological variables and psychological states. However, there are a number of statistical and methodological questions, any one of which by itself might appear trivial, but when taken together raise some questions about the conclusions one can draw from the present study. The most obvious methodological question arises from the fact that the study employed only one BL night and R night. As noted earlier, to evaluate RD effects, one needs an extended number of BL and R nights. The authors did not use an EMG lead in monitoring their subjects; this may not have had any notable effect on their procedure, but their scoring of necessity differed from the Rechtschaffen and Kales (1968) manual. Moreover, some investigators have reported that the most complete RD in humans is accomplished only with the aid of submental EMG recording.

It is important to note that the authors did not include a measure of REM intensity in their results. These points gain some importance when one takes a close look at some of the data. HOFs on RD nights had an average of 23.2 min of REM, while LOF subjects had an average of 18.4 min of REM. Across three RD nights, the mean REM-time difference between groups is 14.4 min. Put in percentage terms (which may be somewhat misleading), the HOF group had 20% more REM time on deprivation nights than did the LOF group. (Although the difference in REM time was not statistically significant, this is in part due to sizable night-to-night variation.) Moreover, in comparing HOF and LOF groups, the HOF group required an average of 10 more awakenings per night (or 30 over three nights) to achieve RD ($p = .10$). The fact that the HOFs required more awakenings and had more REM sleep on deprivation nights would seem to indicate at least as great (or perhaps greater) REM "pressure" on deprivation nights, as the LOF group evidenced. It would be interesting to know whether the number of awakenings for the HOF group increased as deprivation proceeded, as one would expect in conventional RD experiments.

If we take some of these factors into account, it is possible that the HOFs are not "substitutors," but rather they did not manifest REM rebound in this study because:

1. They had more REM time on deprivation nights.
2. They may have had more intense REMPs on the R night (higher percentage of REMs per unit time).

3. HOF subjects, in addition, may have had somewhat delayed REM rebounds which would not have been seen in this study, since only one R night was allowed.

The authors presented no data about the second point, but it would be crucial to know whether REM intensity differed between groups, since Ferguson and Dement (1968) and Dement et al. (1970) asserted that REM intensity is as important as total REM time in assessing the effects of RD.

Nakasawa, Kotorii, Kotorii, Tachibana, and Nakano (1975) also found that personality variables correlated with subjects' responses to what they called partial RD. For example, introverts tended to show less REM rebound than did extroverts. This study is difficult to interpret because: (a) subjects were allowed only one R night; and (b) the R night was terminated by the subject whenever he awakened spontaneously. It is possible, then, that introverts, who the authors reported are more "neurotic and nervous" than extroverts, also tend to be poorer sleepers. Monroe (1967) showed that poor sleepers tend to be more neurotic. The lowered REM rebound may simply be a result of introverts' getting up earlier in the morning (resulting in less total sleep time), and therefore displaying less REM rebound. In this type of experiment, the total sleep period for all subjects should be held constant. Prolonged discussion of these results may be premature, since the authors were comparing only 10 extrovert with only four introvert subjects.

As a final point in this section, we can say that we share Witkin's (1970) interest in the question of individual differences in response to RD but, in our opinion, there is no firm data for nonpsychotic subjects that has established that there are *systematic* individual differences in response to RD. We can only repeat an earlier statement: One would expect differences in any study; the question is, can these differences in RD studies be explained by a specifiable independent variable? At this point, there is only interesting preliminary data that certainly does not conclusively support Witkin's statements about individual differences in response to RD.

Fantasy and Sleep Mentation

Unfortunately, it seems as if two questions have been joined in evaluating the issue of the effect of RD on psychological variables:

1. Does RD have deleterious effects, that is, can RD trigger or lead to psychosis or "regressive" behavior?
2. Does RD affect psychological variables in the waking state?

Dement (1960a) and Dement and Fisher (1963) initially indicated that four or more nights of RD led to tendencies such as anxiety, irritability, and inability to concentrate. They found what they regarded as particularly striking psychoticlike effects in two subjects who were REM-deprived 13 to

15 nights. These two subjects were REM-deprived by hand-awakenings and by ancillary administration of amphetamine, a drug that suppresses REM sleep (Rechtschaffen & Maron, 1964). Vogel (1975), Albert (1975), and Dement (1969) have all concluded that these studies were methodologically unsound for the following reasons:

1. NREM control awakenings were often not used.
2. Neither subjects nor experimenters were "blind" with respect to the condition.
3. Most frequently, anecdotal rather than systematic psychometric data was reported.

In addition, the use of a pharmacological agent is a confounding variable.

Although findings of the harmful effects of RD have not been accepted, investigators have been attempting to assess the effects of RD on such variables as fantasy, motor performance, and so on. In two early studies, both Kales et al. (1964) and Sampson (1966) found that RD did not affect performance on tests such as digits forward and backward (Wechsler adult intelligence scale, WAIS) and other types of objective tests.[9] Kales et al. (1964) reported that there were no behavioral changes that could be attributed to RD, while Sampson (1966) reported (in agreement with Dement's (1960a) findings) that REM-deprived subjects developed intense hunger; that is, all subjects reported increased appetite and assorted other types of oral phenomena (increased smoking, desire for special foods, etc.) Subjects also displayed disturbances in their sense of reality or in their "feelings of reality" (p. 316). Sampson did not report how he quantified the increase of oral phenomena, nor did he run a NREM control condition. Clemes and Dement (1967) studied the effect of six days of RD (six subjects), using mainly unstructured psychological tests (for example, Holtzman ink blot, TAT-"type" tests, and the Welsh figure preference tests) to evaluate the effects of RD. This study employed a NREM condition and counterbalanced conditions. They found that a number of variables on the Holtzman ink blot and "story (TAT-type) test" were affected by RD. Intensity of need and feeling, as measured by the "story test" and "pathognomic verbalizations" in response to the Holtzman ink blot test showed significant increases, whereas form appropriateness and movement perception in the latter showed decreases following RD. The authors viewed these results as a further confirmation of Dement's (1965b) cat experiments (reviewed below) which were reported to show that cats increased "drive"

---

[9]Minnesota Multi-Phasic Personality Inventory (MMPI), Nowlis adjective check list, Clyde mood scale, Stroop color work test, word association test, and a complex serial-subtraction test.

behavior following RD. The interpretation of increases of intensity of need, of feeling, and pathognomic verbalization were thought to be signs of increased "drive" to focus subjects on internal as opposed to external events. In a similar way, this changed focus leads to less form appropriateness following RD. Fewer movement responses following RD were seen as "a reduced ability to control" internal perceptions. They quoted Holtzman to the effect that a person needs good "ego control" functions to perceive movement in the ink-blot designs. The contention is that in humans, tests that are not subject to practice effects and tests that are able to measure fantasy production are most likely to detect the effects of RD. The authors cautioned that their study needs replication because only six subjects participated in the experiment.

At this point in history, one could say that the different test results in the Kales et al. (1964), Sampson (1966), and Clemes and Dement (1967) studies were dependent upon the use of different psychometric measures.

Lerner (1966), in a study that did not utilize polygraphic recordings, concluded that RD enhances the perception of human movement on the Rorschach. From this, she reasoned further that some aspect of REM (or dreaming that takes place during REM) is important in facilitating appropriate body image. Without going further into Lerner's conclusions, from our point of view, her study contained none of the necessary controls that would allow her to make a statement about the effects of RD. Moreover, since she REM-deprived subjects with amphetamine, one does not know whether her effects are due to RD or are the effects of the drug per se.

Greenberg, Pearlman, Fingar, Kantrowitz, and Kawliche (1970) found (in four subjects) that RD causes changes in subjects' (three out of four) responses to projective tests "that show a clear pattern for (almost) each subject." The authors' view seemed to be that defense mechanisms for three out of four subjects were disrupted by RD. Thus one saw more feelings and wishes in the RD as compared with the BL condition. This conclusion would seem to fit in with "classical Freudian" theory but the authors maintained that their results were better explained by other information processing types of hypotheses. At any rate, this study is difficult to evaluate since there were no quantitative data presented, there were only four subjects in the study, and in general the study was presented as a pilot experiment. A related issue was pursued by Greenberg, Pillard, and Pearlman (1972) in a study in which they attempted to evaluate the differential adaptability to stress following REM deprivation. Nine subjects were used in that study and the authors concluded that REM-deprived subjects displayed less adaptability to stress than NREM control subjects. Cartwright and Ratzel (1972) found that RD enhances only M+ responses, and only for those subjects who displayed a REM rebound (LOFs). Substitutors (HOFs) did not show this enhancement. More importantly, what was considered as responsiveness to inner versus outer stimulation (the M : C ratio) was unchanged in HOFs, but changed significantly in LOFs. In other terms, these subjects became significantly more responsive to internal stimulation. In addition, LOFs' IQ (WAIS) scores became significantly higher, while HOFS' WAIS scores did not significantly change. Since we have previously discussed the methodological problems of this study, it is clear that the Cartwright and Ratzel (1972) findings need to be replicated. However, we think that because these findings correlate changes in REM rebound with changes in waking behaviors (Rorschach and WAIS), these findings deserve more serious consideration than studies that may simply rely on the comparison of two groups, one of which remains unchanged.

Agnew et al. (1967) found that RD (seven nights) caused six subjects "to become less well integrated, less interpersonally effective . . . [and] to show signs of suspicion. [They] seemed introspective and unable to derive support from other people" (p. 856). Their conclusions were based on results derived from the MMPI, Taylor manifest-anxiety scale, Cattell's 16 PF test, and the Pensacola Z scale. They compared stage 4 and RD conditions and found that psychological changes were unique for each deprivation condition. Agnew et al. (1967) did not present any statistical data on psychological variables.

This study is in contrast to that of Johnson, Naitoh, Moses, and Lubin (1974), who found no differences between subjects undergoing REM and stage 4 deprivation. They used a number of performance tests and, in addition, a mood scale and the primary affect scale, and the Rorschach as scored by the McReynolds Rorschach concept evaluation test (CET). Although Albert (1975) in a RD review presents the Johnson et al. (1974) study as a RD article, it must be pointed out that Johnson et al. administered the Rorschach test after a night of total sleep deprivation following two nights of RD. Clearly, this is a confounding variable if one wants to make statements about RD.

Although the Clemes and Dement (1967) and Cartwright and Ratzel (1972) studies produced seemingly opposite effects on one measure, the authors utilized the same type of concept to explain this result. Thus, Clemes and Dement (1967) found decreased movement responses on the Holtzman, while Cartwright and Ratzel (1972), on a similar test, found that RD in some subjects (LOFs) leads to an increased number of movement responses. Both papers explained these changes in terms of subjects' increased focus on internal events. It is, of course, possible that Clemes and Dement's subjects were HOFs and this could account for the discrepancy, except that Cartwright and Ratzel did not find a decrease in M responses in HOFs. However, the Clemes and Dement subjects underwent six days of RD, as compared to three days of RD for Cartwright and Ratzel's subjects. It is possible that there is an interaction between subject type and amount of RD. Regardless of whether this accounts for the differences reported (actually, the Clemes and Dement, 1967, effect was not a strong one), the point should nevertheless be made that if one deems RD to be a psychological–biochemical manipulation, the amount of RD has to be carefully considered. It may be the case, as in many drug studies (Sharpless, 1970), that differing amounts of RD, with some dependent measures, may have opposite effects.

Pivik and Foulkes (1966) were the first to systematically investigate the effect of RD on dream content. They found that RD increased the intensity of REM mentation reports (as scored on the Foulkes DF scale). In this experiment, REM mentation reports were elicited after the subject had been deprived of REM sleep for 5 RD awakenings. Thus, RD and the mentation awakenings were performed within the same night. Subjects were initially selected on the basis of the MMPI (Bryne repression-sensitization scale). The experimenters chose 20 subjects: 10 "repressers" and 10 "sensitizers." Only the repressers were "significantly" affected by RD, although this may be misleading since:

1. They obtained statistically significant results when both groups were combined.
2. As many sensitizers as repressers (six subjects in each group) showed change in the predicted direction.
3. The DF scale is one that was designed to rate NREM content and, as such, may not be as sensitive to more detailed REM reports (or, in other terms, the scale has a low ceiling for REM reports).

Given this, together with sensitizers having initially higher REM reports, it may be that the DF scale was simply not sensitive to some of the more intense REM mentation reports from sensitizers.

In a second study, termed "a cross-night replication" of the Pivik and Foulkes (1966) study, Foulkes, Pivik, Ahrens, and Swanson (1968) looked at the effect of RD on REM reports elicited from the night after the RD night. They found that there were no significant differences between mentation reports collected the night after either the NREM-deprivation control or the RD condition. The conditions were counterbalanced and mentation reports were rated blindly. The study, however, suffers from the fact that there was no REM rebound and no shortened latency to the first REMP following RD. Order effects occurred regardless of condition, so that on Night 4, there was always more REM sleep than on any other night.

Their procedure contained neither adaptation nor BL nights, nor an adequate number of R nights. Therefore, there may have been interactions between first-night effects and RD or NREM control effects. Counterbalancing would not control for these interactions, nor could they be taken into account by sophisticated data analysis. Also, subjects were allowed only 6 hr of total sleep time, thus cutting off a period of time where substantial amounts of REM would have occurred. Here, again, the effects of reduced total sleep time interacted with deprivation conditions.

What are the effects of all these possible interactions? At this point, no one really knows, but the authors have concluded that their failure to find significant REM rebound may bring into question the generalizability of RD effects. Moreover, they refer to Cartwright et al.'s (1967) and Cartwright and Monroe's (1968) experiments as evidence that RD effects are not as generalizable as one would believe from the past literature. We have discussed the Cartwright and Ratzel (1972) experiment previously (see page 000) and we can only suggest that the Foulkes et al. (1968) data are not comparable to any past RD experiments where RD effects have been found. Because of methodological differences, this experiment makes no interpretable comment on the RD literature and does not adequately asses the effect of RD on mentation since it is not clear that RD was the major variable being manipulated.

In our view, the better and/or the more interpretable studies in this area are the RD experiments that have reported positive results (Agnew et al., 1967; Clemes & Dement, 1967; Dement, 1960a; Dement & Fisher, 1963; Lerner, 1966; Pivik & Foulkes, 1966). However, the area is a difficult one to summarize because of two general factors: (a) the small number of subjects that are used in almost all studies; and (b) the fact that no two studies have utilized the same methodologies, the same RD procedure, the same number of RD nights, the same controls, the same dependent variables scored in the same way, and so on. Moreover, there is now enough suggestive data to indicate that individual differences should clearly be taken into account when looking at the effect of RD on waking psychological variables.

Schizophrenia

We have already joined Vogel (1975), Albert (1975), and Dement (1969) in stating that no RD study[10] has shown that RD is in any way injurious to one's mental health. There are, however, several studies that have investigated the possibility that certain schizophrenics have a unique (or at least rare) reaction to RD. Two distinct types of results have emerged when investigators have looked at the effect of RD in a "schizophrenic" population: a "normal" REM rebound, or no REM rebound. Zarcone, Gulevich,

---

[10]In an experiment dealing with the effect of RD on four schizophrenics' responses on the Rorschach, Zarcone, Zukowsky, Gulevich, Dement, and Hodes (1974) found that schizophrenics' maladaptive-regression scores and blatant primary process responses (level 1) increased. Nonschizophrenic hospitalized patients (a control group of five) did not show increases following RD. However, they had no NREM awakening control, and therefore one cannot say their results were due to RD.

Pivik, and Dement (1968), Zarcone, Gulevich, Pivik, Azumi, and Dement (1969), and Zarcone et al. (1975) stated that actively ill schizophrenics do not display REM rebound, while "inactive" or schizophrenic patients in remission manifest a larger than normal (control group) rebound.

Azumi, Takahashi, Takahashi, Maruyama, and Kikuti (1967) reported a similar result; they studied only three patients, and two of the three did not display REM rebound. Gillin et al. (1974), in a relatively well-controlled study, found that patients who were diagnosed at the time of the study as not psychotic demonstrated a REM rebound, while actively ill patients did not. Vogel and Traub (1968c) and de Barros-Ferreira, Goldsteinas, and Lairy (1973) reported that REM-depriving chronic schizophrenic patients produced a REM rebound.

These studies have been reviewed extensively, and we may summarize and paraphrase both Vogel (1974) and Gillin and Wyatt (1975) by stating that the results from these experiments (excluding Gillin et al., 1974) are not definitive. The work of Vogel and Traub (1968c) and de Barros-Ferreira et al. (1973) does not comment specifically on the actively ill versus remission issue, since their patients were clearly not actively ill schizophrenics. Vogel and Traub confounded their RD procedure by using amphetamine (a REM suppressant that produces a rapid REM rebound; Rechtschaffen & Maron, 1964). In addition, the patients were continued on psychoactive medication (as was true in the study by Zarcone, Gulevich, Pivik, Azumi, & Dement, 1969), which might affect REM rebound. (In cats, REM rebound is affected by phenothiazines, Cohen et al., 1968; while in normal humans, low doses of phenothiazines do not affect REM rebound, Naiman, Poitros & Englemann, 1972). The Zarcone, Gulevich, Pivik, Azumi, and Dement (1969) and Azumi et al. (1967) studies do not present statistical comparisons and utilize few subjects without a control group. Vogel has "analyzed" their data, but the statistical test he used is a low-power nonparametric test. Furthermore, it is not common statistical practice to conclude, as he has, that the hypothesis of Azumi et al. (1967) and Zarcone, Gulevich, Pivik, Azumi, and Dement (1969) is contradicted because their data do not reach statistical significance. It can only be said that one is not able to reject the null hypothesis. As Gillin and Wyatt (1975) have stated, in the Vogel and Traub (1968a) and de Barros-Ferreira et al. (1973) studies, total sleep time increased from BL to R periods.

In a carefully controlled study, Gillin et al. (1974) found that although BL measures of total sleep time and REM sleep did not differ significantly between actively ill and nonpsychotic groups, first R night values of total sleep time and REM sleep did differ significantly. Thus, the nonpsychotic group showed a rise in absolute amounts and percentage of REM sleep on the first R night, while actively ill patients showed a slight nonsignificant decrease in REM time. In this experiment, the major confounding variable is that the nonpsychotic group averaged 53 min more total sleep time on the first R night compared to BL nights, and 71 min more total sleep time on the first R night than did the actively ill group.

This raises at least two possibilities:

1. The actively ill group is simply showing signs of poor sleep and is therefore not able to produce a "classic" REM rebound, and/or the poor sleep of the actively ill group leads to "fragmented" or disrupted REM rebound.
2. The nonpsychotic group is not showing a clear REM rebound, but is showing elevated amounts of REM sleep solely because they had more total sleep time.

One could argue that RD is such a stressful procedure for the actively ill group that the sleep during the first R night is disrupted to some extent. One possibility is that, for actively ill patients, previous RD creates a situation in which one sees effects on the first R night that are analogous to first-night effects in the laboratory in normal subjects (that is, total sleep time and REM time and REM percent are reduced, ostensibly because of some factor, like stress or anxiety). The analogy is that since actively ill patients are easily "disrupted," any strong change in laboratory conditions will bring about something that looks like a first-night effect. If this were the case, then one would expect that REM rebound would occur on a later R night (Gillin et al., 1974, had five R nights), but there were no R nights during which actively ill patients showed statistically significant elevations of REM sleep. There was, however, a small, nonsignificant rise in REM time, REM percentage, and total sleep time on the third R night. In addition, "REM latency for the actively ill patients was low on the third night," and in fact, it was significantly lower than for the nonpsychotic ill group, who, even on the first and second R nights, showed two signs typically associated with increased REM pressure—seemingly large (but nonsignificant) increases in REM density, and shortened REM latency.

There is, then, the alternative possibility that actively ill patients show REM rebound in a fragmented fashion. Using the Gillin et al. (1974) study as an example, it is possible that the rise of REM density and the shortening of REM latency on the first two R nights, coupled with the rise in REM time on the third night, are actually manifestations of REM rebound. This would suggest that, somehow, phasic events (REM density) and amount of REM time might be alternative mechanisms for manifesting REM rebound, and in some way, these mechanisms summate. This type of possibility is a remote one, but gains some slight support if one considers the de Barros-Ferreira et al. (1973) study that maintains that schizophrenics' sleep patterns are difficult to score by conventional criteria, and that there is an intermediate phase (IP) of sleep that contains elements of REM and NREM sleep.[11] It may be that this IP or fragmented phase of sleep is in part yet another vehicle for the manifestation of REM rebound. Thus, perhaps one should attempt to combine REM density measures, REM time measures, and IP sleep measures to obtain a better picture of REM rebound in the actively ill patient. Although we have presented this possible explanation, it is at best a weak alternative, since there is as yet no evidence or way of determining how phasic events summate with amounts of REM, nor is there good evidence for the IP of sleep being a manifestation of REM rebound.

An alternative explanation of the Gillin et al. (1974) results is that neither the actively ill group nor the nonpsychotic control group displayed a REM rebound. This interpretation is based on the fact that the nonpsychotic group had more total sleep time on R nights than the actively ill group. Gillin and co-workers rejected this alternative, since both REM time and REM percentage increased significantly on the first R night for the nonpsychotic group. Moreover, an analysis of covariance, in which total sleep time was covaried out, yielded statistically significant differences. The question of an increase in REM percentage is one that has to be evaluated with reference to normative data from subjects age-matched with the patients who participated in the Gillin et al. (1974) study. Verdone (1968) published data which shows that by simply allowing subjects to sleep for longer than the 6 to 7 hr BL sleep in the Gillin et al. (1974) study, REM percentage would be expected to rise approximately 2%. This is true, since there is proportionately more REM sleep in the last two-thirds, as opposed to the first third, of the night. We are thus led to question whether a 5.3% rise is significantly different from a 2% rise in REM sleep.[12] Covariance procedures do not provide a full answer, since covariance methods partial out linear trends, and the amount of REM increase as a function of time increase is not strictly a linear relationship. A simple comparison is available by equating total sleep time of the R and BL nights and comparing REM percentage for this time period.[13] Gillin et al. (1974) performed this type of comparison, and they claim to have found significant differences ($p < .05$ one-tailed t test).

Their use of a one-tailed t-test brings up a more general point, for although Gillin et al. (1974) in their statistical comparisons utilize a

---

[11]Other authors (Cartwright et al., 1967) have maintained that nonpsychotic subjects also show an ambiguous, or IP, phase of sleep, in response to RD.

[12]The control group in the Gillin et al. (1974) study exhibited a 5.3% rise in REM % on R Day 1, as compared to BL. Based on Verdone's (1968) normative data, one would expect the control group's increased TST on R Day 1 to have resulted in a 2% increase in REM.

[13]To illustrate this concretely, one would equate the total sleep time on the first R night with the total sleep time on BL nights (391 min for the control group), and then for this sleep period, compare amounts of REM (REM percentage).

variety of conventional multivariate analyses, they frequently compare differences between groups by utilizing a number of one-tail t tests. We would criticize both the use of multiple t tests and the use in this experiment of any one-tail test. As Cohen and Cohen (1975) pointed out, it is preferable never to utilize one-tail tests, but if they are utilized, there should be some clear prediction based on indications in a given literature that would warrant the use of one-tail tests. The latter hardly seems appropriate in a controversial area in which two of the four previous experiments have produced contradictory results to the Gillin et al. (1974) findings. Thus, in the analysis where Gillin and co-workers attempt to equate total sleep time between groups, their result does not reach significance ($p = .10$, two-tail t test). In addition, since the use of multiple t tests affects (raises) the p level of the overall experiment, if one were to calculate the experiment-wise p level, a number of their results would no longer be significant. This criticism, however, should not diminish the more sophisticated anlyses that Gillin et al. (1974) have undertaken, since they have employed analytic techniques that have rarely been utilized in sleep studies.

We may add here parenthetically that we have not discussed a report by Zarcone et al. (1975) that appeared after the Gillin et al. (1974) article. In this article, Zarcone and co-workers presented statistical analysis of data on nine schizophrenic and seven control subjects, and essentially confirmed results from their previous studies. Since we have already commented extensively on the Gillin et al. (1974) report, we will only say here that some of the difficulties we noted in the Gillin et al. (1974) experiment are also present in the Zarcone et al. (1975) report (multiple t tests, the possibility of total sleep time[14] confounding their results, and so on). Their report does contain an important discussion of the conditions under which REM rebound occurs, and a discussion that compares these conditions with RD in "actively ill" schizophrenic subjects. Despite methodological flaws, this is one more report that tends to confirm the Zarcone, Gulevich, Pivik, Azumi, and Dement (1969) initial findings.

The question of whether actively ill schizophrenics display a REM rebound is part of a larger question of the relationship of REM sleep and schizophrenia, and we have deliberately not pursued questions that would

---

[14]Although in the Zarcone et al. (1975) experiment total sleep time was not significantly different between control and schizophrenic groups, the analysis is not adequate since, as we have pointed out, REM percentage is not a strict linear component; therefore, the possibility of interaction terms being significant still exists. In addition, control subjects' first R-night total sleep time was significantly different than their BL total sleep time. This was not true for the actively ill group. This is clearly the more important comparison since REM rebound is determined by the difference in REM percentage between R and BL nights.

lead to investigations that do not involve RD. In our opinion, Vogel (1975) confused several issues when he stated:

> As I understand it, the hypothesis that lack of REM rebound is a distinctive feature of schizophrenia is based on three poorly supported propositions, viz., a) decreased REM time in acute and actively symptomatic chronic schizophrenics; b) large REM rebounds during the waning phase of depression; and c) abnormally low REM rebound in schizophrenic patients following experiment REMD. (p. 755)

It seems to us that the first two points could be false, and if the third is true, the hypothesis still be true. We say "might," because the question would center on whether lack of REM rebound distinguishes actively ill schizophrenics. Thus far, in our opinion, the Gillin et al. (1974) study is the only one that has presented reasonably solid evidence that any independent variable is related to the absence of REM rebound following RD. Their finding of a correlation between field independence and REM rebound is some confirmation of a similar finding by Cartwright et al. (1967) in non-schizophrenic subjects. As Gillin and co-workers pointed out, their field independence finding was posthoc and should be interpreted with caution. In a similar way, their investigations, while exemplary, are by no means definitive for the reasons we attempted to spell out earlier in this section.

RD and Depression

Vogel has been among the main researchers who have consistently pointed out that there is no well-documented evidence that RD is in any way deleterious. In a recent series of investigations, Vogel and collaborators (Vogel et al. 1975; Vogel & Traub, 1968a, 1968b, 1968c) have maintained that RD is in fact helpful in the treatment of endogenous depression. The study looked at the effect of RD on 34 endogenous and 18 reactive-depressives (as rated by two independent clinicians on a scale derived from Mendels & Cochrane, 1968). Since the effect was limited to endogenous depressives, we can summarize the results by saying that RD was more efficacious than the control condition (NREM awakenings) when clinical improvement was measured by Hamilton (1960) or global scores of depression (Vogel et al., 1975). There was not significant improvement on self-rating depression scales or psychomotor tests (Zung self-rating depression scale, WAIS, and a letter-cancellation test). Vogel et al. (1975) argued that these tests did not correlate with clinical improvement in other studies. While it is true that there were significant differences between RD and control conditions (including subjects who were in the control condition for three weeks and then switched to the RD condition), 16 out of 34 subjects showed no clinical improvement. Of these 16 patients, 4 were transferred to another ward, and for some reason, only 9 subsequently received clinical doses of imipramine hydrochloride (mean of 259 mg per day) over a 4-week period. Of these 9 patients, only 1 improved with imipramine administration, and the authors consider this evidence that patients who do not respond to RD also do not respond to imipramine. In brief, since imipramine is a powerful REM suppressant, the contention is that imipramine works through its REM suppressing action, and if suppressing REM by awakenings does not alleviate depression, then imipramine also should not alleviate depression. A further contention then is that there are two subcategories of endogenous depression, one that responds to REM deprivation and another that is responsive to electroconvulsive treatments (ECT). This is based on Vogel et al.'s (1975) finding that ECT did not reduce REM time in depressed patients, and that 6 of 7 patients who did not respond to RD or imipramine (and 1 additional patient who received only RD), did respond to ECT. As a last point Vogel cited the antidepressant-drug literature and maintains that the improvement rate of REM-deprived patients is equal to the improvement rate in most studies that evaluate the efficacy of antidepressants.

The Vogel et al. (1975) study is in many ways a model clinical study in its use of double-blind and crossover techniques, and in its attempt (unlike the RD-schizophrenia studies) to quantify diagnoses and clinical improvement. It seems to us that Vogel and co-workers would agree that while their investigation is a pioneering effort and of great interest, many of their conclusions and internal analyses are posthoc and need replication. Despite this, the study is an important one, for it points to a specification of the mechanisms of at least one type of endogenous depression.

The Effect of RD on Cognitive Functions

A number of workers have attempted to explore the hypothesis that REM sleep is necessary for some aspect of information processing in humans. Two distinct questions have been asked:

1. Is REM sleep a time during which recently learned information is consolidated into long-term memory?
2. Is REM sleep necessary for learning or consolidation of information obtained shortly after the REMP?

Studies investigating the first question employ a paradigm in which training is followed by RD; retention is then assessed. Studies investigating the second question administer training to subjects after RD and then assess learning and retention variables.

Empson and Clarke (1970) presented tape-recorded verbal information to subjects prior to a night of RD- or NREM-control awakenings. Subjects were tested for retention and distortion immediately upon awakening in the morning. RD subjects had lower retention scores and more distortion than NREM controls. The authors note that the study is confounded by total sleep time, since REM-deprived subjects had less sleep and more slow-wave sleep than NREM controls.

Grieser, Greenberg, and Harrison (1972) suggested that RD only affects retention of ego-threatening material. Subjects were selected for high-ego strength, and the task utilized was the Zeigarnik effect. RD subjects had impaired retention compared to NREM controls solely for ego-threatening material. The major problem in this study is the discrepant BL performance between experimental and control subjects.

The study by Lewin and Glaubman (1975) investigated the effects of RD on rote learning (serial memory, clustering memory) and creativity tasks (Guilford's word-fluency test, Guilford's utility test). RD produced a decrement in one of two creativity tasks, and an increment in one of six rote-learning measures. The authors did not control for order effects in that RD and NREM conditions were not counterbalanced.

Ekstrand, Sullivan, and Parker (1971) tested the hypothesis that spontaneous recovery of a retroactively inhibited response was facilitated through RD (one night). They found no significant results when they compared RD subjects to NREM controls.

Experiments by Allen (1974) and Muzio, Roffwarg, Anders, and Muzio (1971), using a task learned prior to RD, also yielded negative findings. In general, there are no positive findings that lead us to believe that RD affects retention of previously learned tasks.

Chernik (1972), Feldman and Dement (1968), and Feldman (1969) have investigated both the question of whether RD affects recently learned material and whether REM sleep is necessary to consolidate information obtained shortly after the REMP. All three papers reported that RD immediately following a verbal learning task did not impair retention (when RD subjects are compared to NREM-control subjects). In addition, Chernik (1972) found that neither a performance task nor a self-administered mood scale were affected by RD. She stated that her findings did not support Greenberg and Pearlman's (1974) hypothesis that REM sleep was necessary for incompletely learned tasks. (See the animal learning section of this chapter for discussion of Greenberg and Pearlman's hypothesis.) In studies pertaining to the second question, Chernik found that in a verbal learning task acquired immediately after RD, consolidation was unaffected by RD. Feldman and Dement's (1968) findings in similar studies were inconsistent. (It should be noted that Chernik, 1972, did not record and did not control for the interactive effects of administering more than one task to the same subjects.)

At this point in time, there is no replicable data to support the hypothesis that REM sleep is necessary for the retention of information learned immediately following the REMP. We conclude, from the studies cited in this section, that the case for a relationship between RD and human information processing is a weak one. However, since those studies reporting negative findings are not methodologically sound, we do not feel that one should reject the possibility of such a relationship.

The Effect of RD on the Sleep Cycle—Animal Methodology

Although some of the methodological considerations that were raised in the preceding section are relevant to animal RD studies, most experiments that use nonprimate species employ methods that differ substantially from human RD studies. There are at least two factors that are related to developing special RD techniques for nonprimate species:

1. Almost all nonprimate species manifest polyphasic, as opposed to diurnal, sleep cycles (this means that if one wants to deprive a rat or cat of all REM sleep, one must monitor the animal 24 hr a day, as opposed to an 8- or 10-hr interval required to REM-deprive human subjects).
2. The length of the sleep cycle in most species used in RD studies is substantially shorter than that of humans. It follows that the number of awakenings necessary for RD in the rat or cat is at least 5 to 30 times the number of awakenings necessary for human RD (Morden, Mitchell, & Dement, 1967; Siegel & Gordon, 1965; Steiner & Ellman, 1972b).

These two factors have induced sleep researchers to automate RD. The methods utilized have been: (a) the flower-pot or platform method, in which an animal lives on a stand during the time it is being REM-deprived; and (b) techniques that "consolidate" the animal's sleep time by forcing the animal to stay awake at times outside of the selective RD period (Cohen, Thomas, & Dement, 1970; Dewson et al., 1967). Frequently, the animal is kept awake by putting it on a treadmill, requiring it to move continuously or suffer some aversive consequence. During time off the treadmill, animals are polygraphically monitored and selectively REM-deprived by hand awakenings.

Using the platform method, the animal is placed on an appropriate small platform which is elevated above water. Each time the animal is about to enter REM sleep, it experiences loss of postural muscle tone and falls off the stand and into the water, or loses its balance and simply wakes up trying to remain on the stand. The platform technique entails difficulties that require controls differing from those in human studies. The most obvious factor, and perhaps the most difficult, is that the animal must continuously live on a stand for a prolonged time. A frequently used control for this is a large platform in which the animal is presumably able to obtain REM sleep but has to live in an environment similar to that provided by the small platform.

As Vogel (1975) pointed out, since the platform method is the one most often used in animal RD studies, it demands close attention. Two questions about the platform method can immediately be asked:

1. Can the small-platform condition selectively deprive the animal of REM sleep?
2. Can the large-platform condition allow the animal significantly more REM sleep than the small-platform condition while remaining an adequate control for the platform environment? Specifically, does the large-platform condition control for loss of total sleep time, stress, weight loss, and activity, while allowing the animal to obtain significantly more REM sleep than on the small platform?

To answer the first question (and part of the second), polygraphic recordings must be taken while the animals are on the platforms. Seven studies (Duncan et al., 1968; Fishbein, 1970; Jouvet, Vimont, & Delorme, 1974; Mark, Heiner, Mandel, & Godin, 1969; Mendelson, Guthrie, Frederick, & Wyatt, 1974; Mouret, Pujol, & Kiyuno, 1969; Pujol, Mouret, Jouvet, & Glowinski, 1968) report such data: four studies in rats, two in cats, and one study using mice.

In both cat studies, the mouse study, and one rat study (Pujol et al., 1968), no adequate large-platform comparison data is available, and therefore it is difficult to evaluate this technique in these studies. In the only study in which recordings were sampled from mice (Fishbein, 1970), animals were on small platforms (3 cm) for three to five days, while five subjects were placed on large (8 cm) platforms, and recordings were taken for several days. Fishbein did not specify on what day REM time was reduced, nor what time period he was citing in presenting his data.

In four studies,[15] rats were the subjects, and in all, after two to three days, animals on small platforms showed significantly less REM sleep than animals on large platforms. However, there was considerable variability among the studies in every sleep measure. For example, Duncan et al. (1968) reported that the five-day mean REM percentage on small platforms was 20% of BL, while large-platform REM values were 50% of BL. While Duncan and co-workers presented grouped data (mean of five RD days), Mendelson et al. (1974) compared animals after 24 or 72 hr on the small- versus the large-platform condition and found that after 24 hr of RD, recordings from large and small platforms yielded REM levels that were virtually equal (REM = 9.6%, or 60.2 min of REM on the small platform;

---

[15]To summarize, for one rat study no large-platform polygraphic data is available (Pujol et al., 1968), four studies are reviewed, and the sixth study is the Mark et al. (1969) report, which is not included here because recording was taken only from 10:00 A.M. to 4:00 P.M. We feel that due to the possibility of circadian alterations, this sampling procedure is not adequate.

REM = 10.5%, or 58.5 min of REM on the large platform). By the fourth 24-hour period (between 72 and 96 hr of RD), animals on the large stand showed REM levels that were virtually equal to BL (REM percentage was somewhat elevated), while subjects on the small stand had significantly lower REM levels when compared to the BL and large-platform subjects (small-platform REM = 8.5%, with 46.6 min of REM time, as compared to large-platform REM = 18.3%, with 105.6 min of REM time). There were no significant differences reported for any group on measures of total sleep time or NREM sleep. Vogel (1975) concluded from these data that:

> in studies of rats, using the platform technique for 24 hours or less, dependent variable differences between experimental and control groups cannot be due to REM sleep differences. But in rat studies using this technique for about four days, dependent variable differences . . . could be due to REM sleep deprivation assuming that confounds are controlled. (p. 750)

Vogel's conclusions were reasonable, given the data he was considering, but Mendelson et al. (1974) did not report on a number of factors that Ellman and Steiner (1969a, 1969b) found to be of importance in RD platform studies.[16]

We found that, first, if one is using the platform method, the weight of the animal in relation to the size of the stand is a crucial variable. Furthermore, specifying the weight of the animal at the beginning of the experimental procedure is not satisfactory, since most behavioral experimental procedures from the time of surgery often last 4 to 10 weeks. During that time, our strain of rats (male albino Sprague-Dawley) can gain 100 to 140 gm. The crucial weighing time is immediately before animals are placed on platforms; subsequent weight measurements should then be continued throughout. We found that during the first day, four 300-gm rats on stands with a diameter of 7 cm displayed mean REM levels (RD 32 min, 5% REM time, versus BL 111 min, 14% REM time) below the four-day levels of Mendelson et al. (1974). Moreover, there was nothing approaching statistical significance when one compared BL (home cage) versus 7-cm platform condition on either total sleep time or NREM sleep (7-cm platform groups, 82% of BL total sleep time).

Second, it seems that the REM reduction observed by Mendelson et al. (1974) during the first 24-hr period is comparable to a first-night effect in human studies. We found that if one adapts subjects (by placing them on the stand) for four days, 10 to 14 days before experimental procedures are performed, then during the first 24-hr experimental period, large-platform subjects' REM levels (95 min) go up to 85% of BL REM levels (111 min).

---

[16]When we refer to Ellman and Steiner, we are referring to two presentations to an APSS meeting (Ellman & Steiner, 1969a, 1969b), as well as an article by Steiner and Ellman (1972a), and more recent unpublished work from our laboratory (1972b).

Furthermore, in most rat and cat sleep experiments, lighting conditions during the experiment are carefully specified. Unfortunately, of all the sleep-cycle studies we reviewed, lighting conditions before the experiment have only been specified by Mendelson et al. (1974). This is a possible confounding variable, since Fishman and Roffwarg (1972) showed that some changes in lighting conditions lead to sleep-cycle changes lasting 2 to 4 weeks. Standard lighting conditions should be obtained 2 to 4 weeks before the experiment is begun.

A methodological paper by Mouret et al. (1969) highlighted some of the difficulties of the platform technique and will therefore be described in detail. Rats weighing 250 to 280 gm at the time of operation were placed on either small platforms (4.5-cm diameter) or large platforms (11.5-cm diameter). In the first experiment, animals were recorded continuously during 91 hr on the platforms, and for the following 4.75 hr in their home cages. The animals on small platforms were totally REM-deprived, while the animals on large platforms obtained 25% of BL levels of REM sleep. During the 4.75 hr of recovery, both groups exhibited a REM rebound that was markedly smaller in the large-platform group. In a second experiment, two groups of animals were again placed on small and large platforms for 91 hr, followed by 4.75 hr of R. In this study, recording cables (for EEG and EMG) were attached only during R. Animals on the small platform had approximately the same amount of REM rebound during R as in the first experiment, while animals on the large platform had no REM rebound. Evidently, animals on the large platform were not REM-deprived under these circumstances. Apparently, the burden of the attached recording cables in a necessary condition for RD to be accomplished in rats of this weight on such large platforms. This is a dramatic finding in view of much work where recording is performed only in pilot experiments. It is possible that pilot studies provide markedly different levels of RD, since in the experiment proper versus pilot study, recording cables were not connected to the animals. Furthermore, in two reports (Fishbein, 1970; Stern, 1971a), investigators dismiss nonsignificant differences between small- and large-platform groups because they assume that large-platform animals are partially REM-deprived. But this may not be the case, if experimental conditions are not the same as pilot conditions. The Mouret et al. (1969) study strongly underscored the absolute necessity for polygraphic recording during all experimental conditions.

The most frequent criticism of the platform technique is that it provides nonspecific stress to the animal, which may be a confounding variable. However, if there is no difference on stress measures or NREM-sleep measures in small- and large-platform conditions, and REM measures do differ, then the differential effect of these conditions on a given dependent variable must be due to differences in REM levels. In rats, three studies reported no differences between animals on large and small platforms on a variety of measures of stress (Ling & Usher, 1969; Morden, Mullins, Levine, Cohen, & Dement, 1968; Stern, 1969), whereas a fourth study (Mark et al., 1969) found that animals on small platforms had increased adrenal hypertrophy, as compared to large-platform animals, only on day 4 of the platform condition. From the fifth to the tenth days, there were no stress differences between animals on the large and small platforms. Therefore, the preponderance of evidence indicates that animals on small and large platforms are stressed to the same extent.[17]

In his review, Vogel (1975) included total sleep time as a measure of stress. Vogel (1975) concluded that if one compares small-platform subjects to baseline subjects, studies that give statistical significance report that total sleep time is significantly reduced in the small-platform condition. This is not the case in the Mendelson et al. (1973, 1974) experiment—cited by Vogel (1975) as a superior RD study—that reported no significant differences in total sleep time between any conditions. Moreover, the fact that differences in total sleep time are sometimes found is not surprising, given: (a) the methodological considerations that were raised previously; and (b) that, in our opinion, NREM sleep totals, rather than total sleep levels, is the more useful measure. In any RD experiment, what one attempts to do is to leave NREM sleep intact while eliminating REM sleep. If one is successful in doing this, then obviously there will be less total sleep time. Interestingly, in some experiments (a group in one of our experiments, and in the Mendelson et al., 1974, study) subjects had more NREM sleep in the small-platform condition (in the first 24 hours) than in the large-platform or BL condition.

Although we agree with many of Vogel's (1975) points, we disagree with some. We believe that comparisons between small- and large-platform conditions can yield significant differences after one day:

1. If the appropriate large-platform control is used (the appropriate large platform is one that should minimally REM-deprive the animal; Plumer, Matthews, Tucker, & Cook, 1974, argued that most studies have utilized large platforms that produce contaminating RD in their control animals); and
2. If animals' weights are matched to stand size and an adaptation procedure is used, then sizable REM reductions in the first 24 hours on the small—but not the large—platform conditions can be obtained. (In fact, measures sensitive to REM-sleep changes, such as intracranial self-stimulation measures, can be affected by 22 hours of RD; Steiner & Ellman, 1972a).

---

[17]It should be added that animals on both the small and large platforms there were significantly more stressed than nonplatform controls, as shown in experiments (Ling & Usher, 1969; Mark et al., 1969; Stern, 1969).

Let us now try to summarize the effects of RD on the sleep cycle. Fishbein (1970; see previous comments) showed that mice could be REM-deprived differentially, but he did not test for REM rebound. In an unpublished report, he has shown that mice, after one day of RD, will display a statistically significant REM rebound (30 to 40%) above BL levels. In rats, the experiments that have employed continuous recording and large-platform controls (Mendelson et al., 1974; Mouret et al., 1969; Steiner & Ellman, 1972a) have all demonstrated REM rebound. In an early study, Morden et al. (1967) concluded that RD by hand arousals yielded REM rebounds equivalent to those obtained during deprivation by platform methods (no recording in platform groups). Morden et al. (1967) employed a yoked NREM-awakening control group and a large-platform control group. Steiner and Ellman (1972a) also found that hand awakening and platform RD methods yielded similar results, although the hand awakening condition yielded a (nonsignificant) lower rebound. Siegel and Gordon (1965), using reticular stimulation to REM-deprive three cats, found that a combination of 12 hr of reticular stimulation and 12 hr of sleep deprivation (referred to as a brick technique) yielded a large REM rebound (59%). Each subject had a different number of RD days, and there was no recording in what they called their sleep-deprivation condition. Foote (1973), in an experiment in which he partially REM-deprived cats, showed (over a 16-hr period) a high negative correlation (r ranged from −.22 to −0.86) between amounts of REM recorded in deprivation and R nights. He used a slow-wave sleep-deprivation control, and also controlled for number of arousals.

Dement and his colleagues (Cohen & Dement, 1966; Dement, 1965b; Dewson et al., 1967; Ferguson & Dement, 1967) performed RD studies on cats. In a variety of experiments, they attempted to explore some of the limits of the REM rebound phenomena. In one such experiment, RD continued for 70 days, and it was found that number of awakenings and amount of compensation plateau after 30 days (Dement, 1965). They mentioned that, within a given sleep cycle, REM time never reached more than 70% of total sleep time, during R conditions. In most of their cat RD work (Cohen et al., 1970; Cohen, Duncan, & Dement, 1967; Dewson et al., 1967), animals were placed on a treadmill for (typically) 16 hours a day, and off the treadmill for 8 hours. The treadmill ostensibly sleep, deprives cats, but no study has reported polygraphic evidence to support this claim. During the 8 hours off the treadmill, RD procedures are performed. This method was designed so that during the 8-hour off-treadmill condition it would comprise a typical RD study, with BL, deprivation, and R periods as well as (at times) a NREM awakening control. The trouble with the entire procedure is that (granting that animals are sleep-deprived), it is difficult to assess how the sleep deprivation on the treadmill and RD interact. Also, it is likely that the treadmill does not fully sleep-deprive subjects (Ferguson & Dement, 1967; Levitt, 1967). If so, the problem of varying amounts of sleep deprivation coupled with RD is even harder to assess. Despite these issues, it is clear that Dement's (1965b) plateau is showing something about the upper limits of REM rebound, and any bio- or neurochemical theory of REM has to explain this data.

Neural Excitability

Many experimental approaches indicate that, following RD, central nervous system excitability in the waking state is increased.

In a series of studies, Cohen and collaborators have demonstrated in the rat (Cohen & Dement, 1965) and the cat (Cohen et al., 1967; Cohen et al., 1970), that RD lowers electroconvulsive shock (ECS) thresholds. Owen and Bliss (1970) also found that rats on small stands had decreased seizure thresholds. While they ran a number of control groups, they did not obtain polygraphic recording. Handwerker and Fishbein (1975) found that mice placed on small pedestals have reduced ECS thresholds. No control groups were tested, and no polygraphic data was reported. One contradictory finding has emerged from this line of research. While Cohen and Dement (1968) found that RD of mice prolongs the tonic phase of the behavioral convulsion, Handwerker and Fishbein (1975) found that RD shortened the tonic phase.

When all the studies are taken together (including an additional study with mice by Hartmann, Marcus, & Leinoff, 1968), the results are, in the main, consistent and therefore compelling. One can probably conclude that RD lowers ECS thresholds. However, in all of these studies, the lack of polygraphic data does not allow one to comment on how much of a reduction in REM sleep is necessary to produce lowering of ECS thresholds.

In a study of the effects of RD on intracranial self-stimulation[18] (ICSS) in rats, Steiner and Ellman (1972a) found that, following RD, ICSS thresholds were lowered and response rates were increased. This study employed two groups of large pedestal controls. Polygraphic sleep recording confirmed that subjects on the small pedestals were deprived of "almost all REM sleep."

In several experiments, RD has been shown to sharpen and intensify neural excitability in sensory systems. In a well-controlled study in the cat, Dewson et al. (1967) demonstrated that RD shortens the refractory period of cortical responses to auditory stimuli. Kopell, Zarcone, de la Peña, and Dement (1972) studied auditory-evoked potentials during attention tasks, and concluded that following RD, there is greater selective attention when compared to a NREM-awakening control. No measures of waking auditory-evoked potential were obtained in subjects who slept normally. Accordingly,

---

[18]Sometimes called the Olds phenomenon after Olds (1956), who discovered that rats (and other mammals) find electrical stimulation to certain parts of the brain reinforcing. Put in other terms, animals will work to provide themselves electrical stimulation to some areas of the brain.

interpretations were confined to the difference between RD and NREM awakening conditions.

Satinoff, Drucker-Colin, and Hernandez (1971), in RD of cats by the platform technique, measured evoked potentials following brief electrical stimulation. No control groups were run, and no polygraphic sleep data was presented. They concluded that RD does not lead to a general increase in neuronal excitability, but rather to paleocortical excitability and an increase in some type of inhibition which results in sensory filtering.

In summary, various measures of central nervous system excitability are increased following RD. Thresholds of ECS, as well as ICSS, are reduced. Cortical refractory periods are shortened, and selective attention and cortical excitability are enhanced.

Animal Learning and Retention Studies

In evaluating the effect of RD on learning and retention, one must consider: (a) whether appropriate controls are utilized (for example, in animal research, a large-platform control); (b) whether polygraphic recordings were obtained during the experiment and not simply in a pilot study; and (c) whether distinctions are made between learning-retention and performance variables.

As Vogel (1975) pointed out, in retention tasks in which animals are trained before RD and tested immediately following RD, even if an animal shows a deficit, it may be that some performance variable, as opposed to a retention variable, is being affected (perhaps because of the animal's state and so on). To explore this possibility, one would want to test the animal at some later point. To quote Vogel (1975), "If a performance deficit appeared immediately after REMD but was absent in later testing, then one would have to conclude that REMD impaired performance but not memory of the task" (p. 752). Vogel stated that "[only] Fishbein has used such a control for performance deficit" (p. 752). However, Wolfowitz and Holdstock (1971) and Sagales and Domino (1973) also used this type of control. Although there are several somewhat different variations, the positions in this area that have been spelled out most clearly assert that REM sleep serves as an information-processing state. Thus, Greenberg and Pearlman (1974) saw REM sleep as a state that plays an important role in processing what might be labeled as new or unusual information. While Greenberg and Pearlman hypothesize that REM may be important in both acquisition and retention, Fishbein has stressed the role of REM sleep in retention, and Stern has focused on REM sleep playing a part in the acquisition and retention of any task in the animal's repertoire.

Greenberg and Pearlman (1974) have roughly divided learning situations into ones that are involved in survival value for an organism (REM-independent), and other learning situations where the organism is required to assimilate "unusual information" (REM-dependent). It was Greenberg and Pearlman's (1974) view that the "assimilation of unusual information requires REM sleep for optimal consolidation" (p. 516). Greenberg and Pearlman regard the distinction they have made as similar to that of Seligman's (1970) distinction between prepared (REM-independent) and unprepared (REM-dependent) learning. (Greenberg and Pearlman's work goes beyond the experiments summarized in this section and they have performed a variety of studies in human as well as animal subjects. One experiment that we have not included in this section is one by Greenberg, Pillard, and Pearlman (1972) that deals with the effect of RD on stress. In this study they conclude that RD interferes with adaptation to stress.) Pearlman's experiments involving the effect of RD on latent learning[19] and latent extinction[20] are attempts to operationalize and test the REM-independent, REM-dependent distinction. In one experiment in which he looked at the effect of RD on latent learning, Pearlman found that REM-deprived animals did not show an improvement in learning when a reinforcer (food) was introduced into a latent learning situation. On the other hand, control animals (immersed in cold water for 20 minutes to 1 hour) displayed the normal improvement one would expect in this kind of situation. Such learning was compared to a simpler type of food exploration "learning," in which animals were simply allowed to explore a rectangular box with a niche. He found that RD did not affect this type of "learning." In another study, Pearlman (1973) found that while latent extinction was affected, ordinary extinction was not affected by RD. In addition, he reported that immediate RD affected latent extinction, while RD begun 5 hr after preextinction trials took place did not affect latent extinction. Thus, he concluded that RD affected latent extinction, but not normal extinction, and that latent extinction was affected when RD was administered within a certain time period.

In a study that specifically focused on both the method and timing of RD administration, Pearlman and Greenberg (1973) REM-deprived three groups of rats immediately after they had learned a shuttlebox-avoidance task. They REM-deprived another group 2 hr after the task. The three groups that were REM-deprived immediately after the task were deprived by one of the following techniques: (a) the flower-pot method; or (b) administration of a drug that suppressed REM sleep (5 mg/kg of imipramine or 35 mg/kg of pentobarbital). Another group was simply put back in its home cage after the task. Twenty-four hours after the completion of the task, all animals were tested for retention of the task.

The authors were attempting to show that any method of RD, if applied at the appropriate time, will lead to a learning or retention deficit (in rats, it

---

[19]Latent learning refers to learning that has not been manifested in performance. However, performance appears upon introduction of reward contingencies.

[20]Latent extinction refers to extinction without responding. This results from an experience without reinforcement contingencies.

is apparently within 2 hours of the task being learned). In fact, the groups that received what the authors call immediate RD did show a greater retention deficit than either of the other two groups. All of the Pearlman studies suffer from the fact that polygraphic recordings were not taken; and no platform-control condition was utilized.

The experiment (Pearlman & Greenberg, 1973) in which two different pharmacological agents were used to REM-deprive animals, included neither a saline condition (that is, control injections with saline), nor administration of different drug dosages. Both of these procedures are typical controls in pharmacological experiments (Fingl & Woodbury, 1970). In addition, it would have been preferable to have a control condition with a drug that is not a REM-depriving agent. Of course, this is asking for a large number of controls in a given experiment, but unfortunately, if one is using pharmacological agents, then appropriate pharmacological controls are necessary.

Pearlman and Becker (1974), in a study that did employ a saline-control group, found that RD (alternatively 5 mg/kg of imipramine hydrochloride and 4 mg/kg of chlorodiazepoxide hydrochloride) immediately following training, impaired acquisition of a bar-press response. This was true whether training involved the presence of a bar, a visible trained rat who was bar pressing in an adjacent cage, or a visible naive rat in an adjacent cage with no bar. However, the most significant impairment occurred in those subjects trained through observation of a previously trained rat. Also, REM-deprived animals had impaired acquisition of a DRL (different reinforcement of low rates) 20-second bar-press response when switched from a continuous-reinforcement response schedule.

In a similar study by the same authors (Pearlman & Becker, 1975), a cooperative-learning task was impaired by immediate RD, as compared to a saline control group. In both experiments, polygraphic recordings were not obtained for experimental animals. In addition, it is difficult in this type of study to differentiate more general drug effects from those related to RD. Moreover, different drug dosages were not employed. This is a crucial control in any drug study.

Stern, on the basis of research that he and Hartmann have conducted (Hartmann & Stern, 1972; Stern, 1971a), has also concluded that RD impairs learning and retention tasks. Stern (1971b) has reported that RD interferes with the acquisition of passive and active avoidance responding and with the acquisition of an appetitive alternation-discrimination task. In these studies, Stern did not find differences between animals on small stands and large stands, but only between small-stand and home-cage animals. Stern's (1971b) contention is that failure to find learning differences following treatment between animals on large and small stands can be interpreted as a failure of 50% vs. 80% RD to produce differential behavioral effects. This may be the case, but the question is circular unless Stern can specify under what RD conditions learning differences can be found.

Moreover, it is not necessarily the case, as Plumer et al. (1974) and Mendelson et al. (1974) have shown, that large-stand animals have to be deprived of 50% of BL REM sleep values.

Hartmann and Stern (1972) also performed a RD experiment in which 1-dopa (or catecholamine restoration) partially reversed the interfering effects of RD on acquisition and retention. Stern (1971b) has also found that RD does not affect habituation and that this response is not relevant to the question of the effect of RD on learning. In this experiment, Hartmann and Stern did not utilize a large-platform control group, making the experiment difficult to evaluate.

Fishbein, in several studies in mice (Fishbein, 1970, 1971; Fishbein, McGaugh, & Schwarz, 1971; Linden, Bern, & Fishbein, 1975), looked at the effect of RD on retention. Because he and his coworkers employed complicated paradigms, we discuss the design of these experiments with the aid of a schematic diagram. In one experiment (Fishbein, 1971; see Figure 10.1a), animals were first put in a one-trial passive avoidance (PA) situation, and were then immediately placed on RD platforms. Animals were tested for PA retention 1 hour or 1 day after RD. In a study with a similar design (Fishbein et al., 1971; see Figure 10.1b), he again put animals in a PA situation, and then put animals on RD platforms. In this study, at varying points[21] after RD, animals were administered ECS.[22] All animals were then tested for retention 1 day after RD.

In the first experiment (see Figure 10.1a), Fishbein (1971) found that 3 days (but not 1 day) of RD impaired retention 1 hr, but not 24 hours after RD. In the second study (Fishbein et al., 1971; see Figure 10.1b), animals were REM-deprived for 48 hr, and when ECS was applied within 3 hr of the RD, retention was impaired. Fishbein et al. (1971) concluded that RD is unique in keeping "the memory trace of a previously learned experience . . . susceptible to disruption (for) several days" (p. 82). The question as to why ECS must be applied less than 3 hours after RD to disrupt the memory is answered by assuming that, at some time after 60 min and before 3 hours, the memory is converted into a relatively permanent form (long-term storage), and is no longer susceptible to disruption.

Fishbein (1970), in another experiment, used a different paradigm, in which RD preceded a PA task (see Figure 10.1c), and in which animals were given retention tests at varying times[23] after experience with the task. In this experiment, he found that RD interfered with the retention of the task when retention was tested more than 1 hour after RD, but retention was not

---

[21]ECS was administered 5 min, 30 min, 1 hour, 3 hours, 6 hours, or 12 hours.

[22]ECS is commonly used in memory studies (McGaugh, 1966), and when it is applied at the appropriate time, total or partial amnesia occurs.

[23]The retention tests were given within 5, 30 seconds; 1, 2, 15, 20, 45, 60 minutes; and then 1, 3, 5, or 7 days after the task.

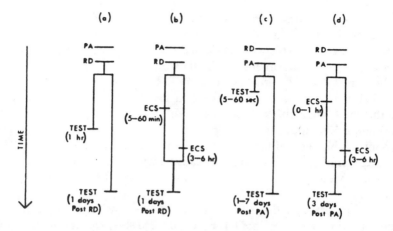

FIGURE 10.1. The diagram is a schematic of the four paradigms used by Fishbein et al. (1971) (a) Animals were REM deprived after passive avoidance (PA) training. One branch represents animals tested for retention of the PA task 1 hour after REM deprivation (RD), while the other branch represents animals tested 1 day after RD. (b) Animals were REM deprived after PA training and given electro-convulsive shock (ECS) at varying times after RD. Depicted on the left branch are several groups of animals that received ECS 5 to 60 sec after RD. The right branch depicts groups that received ECS from 3 to 6 hours after RD. All groups were tested for retention of the PA task 1 day after the termination of RD. (c) In this design, RD preceded PA training. One branch represents the groups retested for PA retention 5 to 60 sec following PA training. The other branch represents groups retested for PA training 1 to 7 days following PA training. (d) As in Figure 10.1 (c), RD preceded PA training. The left branch represents groups that received ECS 0 to 1 hours following PA training. The right branch represents the groups that received ECS 3 to 6 hours after PA training. All groups were tested for PA retention 3 days following the PA training.

affected if the retention test was presented within 1 hour of RD. The paradigm just described was then coupled with ECS (Linden et al., 1975; see Figure 10.1d). ECS was given at varying times[24] after PA training. They found that when ECS is given within 3 hours of RD, long-term memory is impaired. However, when ECS is given more than 3 hours after RD, long-term memory is not impaired. Again, 3 hours appears to be the crucial time, since ECS is not effective when it is given more than 3 hours after RD.

Wolfowitz and Holdstock (1971), in work that was similar to that of Fishbein (1971), reported the same effects in rats.

Sagales and Domino (1973), in looking at the effect of RD in mice on both acquisition and retention, found that RD does not affect acquisition and retention of an active-avoidance task. Their results concerning the effects of

---

[24]Immediately; 5, 15, 30, 45 minutes; 1, 3, 6 hours.

RD on retention (8 days after acquisition) are contradictory: In one study, they reported that RD impaired retention, while in a second study, RD did not impair retention. This work is flawed because no recordings were taken to verify whether experimental animals were actually REM-deprived, and whether stress control animals were not REM-deprived.

Fishbein's (1971), and Wolfowitz and Holdstock's (1971) experiments have the same difficulties that are present in other RD-learning-retention experiments. The appropriate (large-platform) control group was not used, and polygraphic recordings were not taken during the experiments. However, these studies are important because they focus on some other difficulties in conceptualizing the relationship between REM sleep and memory consolidation.

As we understand the REM memory-consolidation hypothesis, new memory traces are kept in labile form until REM sleep occurs. At that point, some process associated with REM facilitates the consolidation of a labile memory trace. Clearly, there can be gradations of this hypothesis. In the strong form, one would maintain that some manifestation of REM sleep is necessary for all long-term memory consolidation. In some weaker form of the hypothesis, one would maintain that REM sleep is not necessary for, but to some extent facilitates, long-term consolidation.

In terms of this discussion, let us assume that the studies that maintain that RD impairs retention have been well controlled, and that the results are, in fact, due to RD. The question still arises as to whether a memory consolidation hypothesis in the strong form is the only, or even the best, explanation of this data. To point out some of the difficulties, let us briefly review two of Fishbein's experiments. In one experiment (as schematized in Figure 10.1a), Fishbein REM-deprived animals after a PA task and then found that retention was impaired when animals were tested shortly after RD, but retention was not impaired when retention tests were performed 24 hr after RD. (The explanation put forth was that RD kept the trace in labile form so that retention was impaired when testing was done shortly after RD.) When the animals were allowed REM sleep, the trace was consolidated, and therefore retention was not affected when animals were tested a long time after RD. Compare this experiment with one in which RD preceded the PA task (see Figure 10.1c). In this experiment, short-term memory was not affected, but long-term memory was impaired.[25] Here the explanation was that RD set up conditions in which a labile trace could not be converted from short- to long-term memory.

In our opinion, from a memory-consolidation standpoint, these two experiments yield contradictory results. Our reasoning is as follows: If RD

---

[25]We are aware that many authors make finer distinctions about short- and long-term memory consolidation, but we feel that our distinctions are adequate for the purposes of this discussion.

keeps a memory trace in labile form, then in both experiments the animals are in the same state following RD (see Figure 10.2). Our simple diagram indicates that both experiments should produce animals with labile memory traces at Time A. Since in both experiments animals that are tested a long time after RD are allowed to have REM sleep, what happens to the memory trace should happen uniformly in both experiments, but, in fact, this is not the case. Fishbein (personal communication, April, 1976) has indicated to us that in his (as opposed to Pearlman and Greenberg's 1974) view, the strong form of the REM-memory-consolidation hypothesis is not tenable, and some change in the conditions necessary for long-term consolidation must take place, even during RD. Although this is a view that seems to be closer to the data, it is not clear at this point what the testable implications are for this weaker form of the REM-memory-consolidation hypothesis. An alternative view that might explain the results of both experiments involves a state-dependent learning effect. In both paradigms, retention deficits depend on the animals being tested in a state that differed from the one during which acquisition took place. Of course, the question still remains whether or not it was RD that influenced even these variables.

The question of why ECS disrupts retention (Fishbein et al., 1971) 0 to 3 hours after RD but not 3 or more hr after RD, is, in our opinion, also not necessarily related to memory-consolidation variables. One might alternatively consider that RD lowers ECS thresholds and that in Fishbein's (1971) experiments, what one is comparing is a large amount of ECS in the RD condition, as opposed to a smaller amount of ECS in the control condition. Cohen and his collaborators (Cohen et al., 1967; Cohen et al., 1970; Cohen

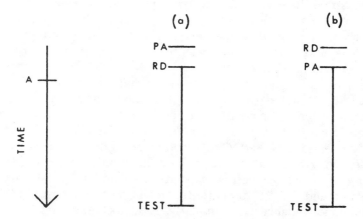

FIGURE 10.2. (a) and (b) refer to the Fishbein et al. experiments depicted in Figures 10.1(a) and 10.1(c) respectively. In design 2(a), PA training preceded RD and the PA retention test followed after some specified amount of time. In design 2(b), RD preceded PA training and the PA retention test follows.

& Dement, 1965) have shown that RD lowers ECS thresholds, and a number of studies have shown that RD increases neural excitability (see previous section of this chapter). Even more importantly, Handwerker and Fishbein (1975) have shown that while RD lowers ECS thresholds, 3 hr later they are back to pre-RD or normal levels. Thus, one can say that in RD-ECS studies, when time of ECS administration has been varied, the effective magnitude of the ECS treatment has also been varied. This is the case, since the stimulus (amount of current) is held constant, while threshold (over time) varies as a function of time from RD. Thus, if one applies ECS immediately after RD, greater neural excitability will result than if one applies the same amount of electricity 3 to 4 hours after RD. We can conclude that in RD-ECS studies, effective amounts of ECS and time of administration are confounding variables.

The possibility also exists that RD plus ECS will disrupt many tasks that are not well learned or "overlearned." Thus, it might be important to perform a Fishbein-type experiment in which the animal is allowed 3 hours of sleep following PA training and before RD begins. Immediately after RD, the animal would receive ECS and then be given retention trials short and long periods of time after RD. In this experiment, since the animal would be trained 3 hours before RD, one would expect that memory consolidation would take place before RD begins. If in this experiment RD plus ECS affected retention, then the conclusion would be that RD is effective not because it keeps memory traces labile, but primarily because it increases neural excitability and leads to a general disruption of some aspects of the animal's behavior.

Up to this point, we have reviewed studies that only report positive results. There are, however, several reports in the literature that have failed to demonstrate that RD affects either acquisition or retention in animal-learning experiments. For example, Joy and Prinz (1969) utilized a pole-climbing task, and found that neither acquisition nor retention was affected by RD. They did find that when retention tests were given after RD, only then was retention affected. The conclusion the authors draw is that retention following RD is not disrupted when animals are tested under acquisition conditions, but if the retention conditions differ from acquisition conditions, then retention is affected. For the purpose of this review, we say they concluded that RD sets up conditions that induced a type of state-dependent learning. Albert, Cicala, and Siegel (1970) also concluded that REM-depriving rats did not affect the acquisition of two different tasks requiring an avoidance response (shuttlebox- and one-way avoidance). They also found that RD did not affect retention of responses in the one-way running-avoidance task. Similarly, Holdstock and Verschoor (1973) found that RD did not affect retention of a learned position response in a T-maze situation. In two related experiments that were reported in very brief fashion, Miller, Drew, and Schwartz (1971) concluded that RD does not affect retention in a 1-trial PA task.

REM Deprivation and Motivation

Although Dement and his co-workers frequently referred to the effect of RD on "motivational" or "drive" states, there have been surprisingly few studies that have systematically tested the effect of RD on behaviors such as eating, drinking, or aggressive and sexual behaviors. Dement (1960a) and Dement and Fisher (1963) initially referred to the effects of RD on human subjects, and we have previously discussed the limitations of these observations. Dement (1965b, 1969) later reported that RD seemed to lead to hyperphagia and hypersexuality in cats. The effect of RD on eating was apparently negligible unless the cats were deprived of food for a period of time before testing. If REM-deprived and control cats were food-deprived, the REM-deprived group ate significantly more than control animals. After RD, it was also reported that 6 out of 12 cats became hypersexual in a manner that was never seen in BL condition or in control animals. (To our knowledge, these observations have never been written up in a full experimental report, so even the mention of these data must be considered anecdotal.)

Two papers using different dependent measures indicated that RD increases aggressive behavior in rats. Morden, Mullins, et al. (1968) found that RD increases shock-induced fighting, while Sloan (1972) found that RD increases aggression in rats as measured by the Klein-Hall rat aggression scale. Both of these studies had appropriate large-stand control groups, but neither study took polygraphic recordings during experimental procedures. Ferguson and Dement (1969), in a study that REM-deprived rats 80 to 100 hours and then injected them with amphetamine, found that the rats displayed what they termed stereotypic aggressive behavior (in virtually all animals), and "abnormal" sexual behavior (in 9 of 25 animals). Large-stand control animals did not exhibit the same effects. There was no polygraphic recording performed during the experiments. Morden, Conner, Mitchell, Dement, and Levine (1968) also found that RD increased sexual behavior (large-stand control, but no recording).

Although there are a small number of studies, all of them found that both sexual and aggressive behaviors are facilitated by RD. Unfortunately, none of this work employed polygraphic recordings, but all have used some form of platform control. Steiner and Ellman (1972a) and Cohen et al. (1972) both looked at the effect of RD on intracranial self-stimulation[26] (ICSS) behavior in rats. Steiner and Ellman found that RD lowers hypothalamic ICSS thresholds and raises ICSS response rates. They also showed that nonconvulsive ICSS can reduce REM rebound by 52%. Steiner and

---

[26]ICSS, or self-stimulation, is defined as an animal performing work for an electrical stimulation to the brain. Olds (1956) and many subsequent investigators (see review by German & Bowden, 1974) have mapped a variety of areas in the brain that are self-stimulation sites.

Ellman utilized polygraphic recordings and two types of large-platform control (one a yoked large-platform control), and two methods of RD (platform method and hand awakening). As a control for the hand awakening RD method, they employed a NREM awakening control condition. Since Steiner and Ellman (1972a) and Cohen et al. (1972) demonstrated a reciprocal relationship between REM sleep and ICSS, this is additional evidence that in some way RD facilitates motivational states. The result that self-stimulation of a "motivational" area reduces REM rebound was looked at in a parallel way by Putkonen and Putkonen (1971), who showed that elicitation of hypothalamic rage reactions reduces REM rebound. Although the evidence is sparse at this point, there are no data to contradict the assertion that RD facilitates aggressive, sexual, and ICSS behavior and that ICSS and hypothalamic-elicited rage reactions can substantially reduce REM rebound.

The question of course arises: How can one reconcile evidence linking REM sleep and motivational states with Pearlman and Greenberg's (1974) statements that RD does not affect motivation, or what they called REM-independent behaviors? Their assertion (which rested on the citation of unpublished data) consisted of looking at the effects of RD on rats' bar-press behavior for food. There is little data linking RD and eating, but the Dement (1965) study stated that, in effect, one has to prime the animal or starve it to see the effect of RD on eating behavior. This should not be terribly surprising since, under normal circumstances, there is a rapid ceiling effect in eating behavior. Since Dement (1965b) had already published that normal eating was not affected by RD, Greenberg and Pearlman's (1974) and Pearlman's (1971) similar comments did not come as a surprise. Nevertheless, based on the data from studies looking at sexual, aggressive, and ICSS behavior, what they had called REM-independent behaviors seem not to be REM-independent at all, but rather to be facilitated by REM deprivation.

Dement (1969), in fact, hypothesized that REM sleep also provides a type of periodic drive discharge; thus, RD should lead to drive facilitation. Ellman and Steiner (1969a, 1969b) put forth a similar hypothesis, in which they postulated that during REM sleep, at least some elements of the ICSS (or positive reinforcement) neural network are activated. They further hypothesized that activation of the ICSS network lowers the threshold for a number of "drive" behaviors, or what they have termed stimulus-bound behaviors (SBB).[27] Thus, RD causes a lowering of threshold for the ICSS system, and in turn for SBB sites. This hypothesis attempts to explain why thresholds for

---

[27]Stimulus-bound behaviors are those goal-directed behaviors that can be elicited by electrical stimulation to the brain. By goal-directed, we mean that an animal will work to achieve, and can display, a number of alternative motor movements to achieve a given consummatory response. This definition separates stereotypic behaviors from goal-directed behaviors that can be elicited by electrical stimulation.

sexual, aggressive, eating, and ICSS behaviors are lowered following RD. It also explains why one may see different drive behaviors activated in different animals, since the threshold for any drive behavior can be influenced by at least two internal factors: the threshold at a given site of the specific behavior, and the threshold of the ICSS network. Thus, in a free-moving animal, one may see many drive behaviors or no drive behaviors, activated following RD. However, if one took central-nervous-system measures for eliciting drive or SBB, then all SBB should show a lowering of activation thresholds following RD. In a similar way, priming the animal by starving it would potentiate the effects of RD for a given behavior or behaviors.

The Ellman-Steiner (1976, May) hypothesis may also help explain why RD facilitates some behavior, while impairing the acquisition and/or retention of some tasks. It may be that RD impairs performance by lowering the threshold for a variety of behaviors, thus lowering the probability that the "correct" (from the experimenter's point of view) behavior will be emitted. This might explain why (except in Stern's (1971) studies) behaviors that are not well consolidated are affected by RD, while behaviors that have been more practiced tend not to be affected by RD. In addition, we speculate that the reason why RD is efficacious in alleviating endogenous depression is because RD lowers ICSS and SBB thresholds. In a simplistic way, one can view endogenous depression as a raising of threshold for a variety of drives or SBBs (like sex, aggression, eating, and so on). By REM-depriving depressives and lowering ICSS (positive reward) and SBB thresholds, one is increasing the probability of evoking "drive" behaviors (like eating and sex).

It is clear from our review that RD studies share much of the promise and, hopefully temporary, limitations of other areas in sleep research. Despite the methodological difficulties encountered in many RD studies, it seems clear to us that this technique will continue to be of value in helping to understand the many seeming paradoxes uncovered by the discovery of REM sleep.

CHAPTER 10 UPDATE: REM DEPRIVATION

STEVEN J. ELLMAN
ARTHUR J. SPIELMAN
LAUREN LIPSCHUTZ-BRACH
City College of the City University of New York

This update of the REM deprivation (REMD) literature focuses only on animal studies, as human studies are reviewed elsewhere (see Chapter 11). Since 1977 the controversies about the technical aspects of REMD have not subsided. In the past (before 1978), virtually all of the REMD studies that were performed utilized the platform method (see below in this chapter). This method has been constantly criticized as a method that confounds REMD with other conditions such as stress. The control for the platform method of REMD, which is the large-platform control, has been criticized by a number of authors as being an inadequate control. This has led to other methods being proposed to accomplish REMD. In our update, we first go over some of the methodological issues that have continued to be issues in this literature and then look at two main areas of the REMD literature: studies that involve motivational variables and studies that involve learning variables.

METHODOLOGICAL ISSUES

Essentially, there have been either modifications of the original platform technique or a new technique called the pendulum method. To quote a brief description of the pendulum technique from Van Luijtelaar and Coenen (1986), "Rats in their home cages are placed in a slowly moving swing which produces regular and continuous postural imbalance and subsequent awakening at the two extremes of oscillation. This permits brief periods of slow wave sleep but prevents PS (REM Sleep). Control rats are placed in an identical device but adjusted so as to fall short of actual imbalance" (p. 608).

The modifications of the platform technique have included the multiple platform method (see later in this chapter), the cuff pedestal technique, and the rotating carousel procedure. The multiple platform method was designed to allow animals more movement while continuing to live on a platform during REMD or during the control condition. This method allows rats to move from pedestal to pedestal. The cuff pedestal technique as described by Hilakivi, Peder, Elomaa, and Johansson (1984) was designed to allow the animal to stay on the same stand during control condition runs. Essentially, the cuff pedestal allows the investigator to enlarge the REMD platform during control condition runs or manipulations. It thus permits more exact control when one is performing an experiment where the subject acts as its own control.

The carousel procedure, recently introduced by Rechtschaffen and colleagues (Rechtschaffen, Gilliland, Bergmann, & Winter, 1983), involves placing two animals on separate sides of a partition that divides a round disk that serves as the floor. Below the disk is a shallow pool of water. Computerized analysis of EEG and EMG allows on-line determination of sleep stage. This apparatus has been used for total sleep deprivation and selective deprivation of high voltage NREM sleep and REM sleep. We confine our discussion to the REM deprivation experiment (Kushida, et al.,

1986). When the animal to be REM-deprived enters REM sleep, the computer program automatically rotates the carousel at a slow speed. To avoid falling in the water both rats must walk on the disk. This contingent carousel movement REM-deprives one animal and subjects the yoked control animal to comparable forced activity. REM-deprived animals had REM sleep reductions of 99.2% from baseline while total sleep time was only reduced by 17%. Results of this procedure include elevations of energy expenditure and food intake and a progressive decline in body temperature. Most striking was the finding that on an average of 37 days in this protocol, REM-deprived rats died or were sacrificed when death seemed imminent. The implications of this line of research are far-reaching; however, we will reserve a more complete review until the full report of these findings is published.

The single and multiple platform and cuff pedestal techniques of REMD were recently compared by Van Luijtelaar and Coenen (1986). They compared what they called the classical method (small platform as REMD condition, large platform control), multiple platform method, and the pendulum method. These authors performed many analyses but found few significant differences between the techniques. Given the extraordinary number of statistical analyses they performed, their findings must be viewed with some restraint. They themselves pointed out that the basic assumptions of analysis of variance were violated. Moreover, they used both scheffe and orthogonal comparisons for the same data; obviously one or another of these analyses is inappropriate. At any rate, to quote the authors' results, "In conclusion it can be said that all three PS (REM) deprivation techniques examined here produce clear and significant deprivation levels." They also concluded that "during rebound sleep very few technique differences are found." Although they found that the pendulum technique produced many more awakenings than the platform technique, they did not think it produced more sleepiness—this despite the fact that in human studies there is evidence that awakenings are a major determinant of sleepiness (Bonnet, 1985, 1986; Carskadon, Brown, & Dement, 1982; Glovinsky, Spielman, Carroll, Weinstein, & Ellman, 1988). The five arguments they used to deal with the sleepiness issue would involve lengthy analysis to deal with each in detail, but essentially they argued that rats' performance following REMD does not seem to reflect the performance of a sleepy animal. To quote, "Perhaps the strongest argument can be derived from work of our own group with a shuttlebox avoidance task (1982). While platform rats (rats REM deprived by platform method) show a poor performance in a two-way active avoidance task, pendulum deprived rats show a perfect avoidance indistinguishable from control groups" (p. 607). The authors maintained that if the pendulum made the rats sleepy one would predict just the opposite. This is a somewhat naive view of avoidance in rats, and of REMD. It could be that "real" effects of REMD are to increase activity (see van Hulzen & Coenen, 1981). Thus the "real" REMD method produces a more activated animal and one that makes poor discriminations during avoidance. One can then say with the pendulum technique that the sleepiness caused by the technique dampens the amphetamine-like state caused by REMD and allows the animal to look more "normal." This of course is as speculative as the authors' assumptions. It seems at best circular to investigate the effect of REMD on avoidance learning and then to argue on the basis of the results that the effect on avoidance shows that REMD took place. One could only do this if the effects of REMD were quite well known.

The question that one may pose at the end of this section is how one is to determine which technique produces "true" REMD. In our opinion, that question has not been answered. We believe that all techniques should be compared to REMD by hand awakenings. Included in this assessment, one would attempt to evaluate the effect of awakenings themselves; thus there would be a condition where NREM awakenings would be assessed. These NREM awakenings would be performed without NREM deprivation (or at least as little deprivation as possible),. This, it seems to us, is the technique that should be considered the baseline technique. It may be that REMD itself is stressful or that awakenings per se are stressful, but at this point in time we still do not know the answers to these basic questions. We would maintain that the technique that comes closest to the hand awakening technique is the "true" REMD technique. We believe this to be the case since hand awakenings involve only one condition common to all techniques, that is, the awakening itself. All other techniques involve some other manipulation. A comparison with the hand awakening technique allows one to sort out the additional manipulations involved in other techniques.

MOTIVATIONAL STUDIES

In discussing results from one of their studies, Hicks et al. (1981) suggested, "Perhaps the most prudent course to adopt in future research would be to avoid the use of the concept of 'motivational behaviors' for it seems too broadly conceived to be of real scientific value (p. 240)." We certainly agree that it is a broad term and we also agree with Hicks et al. (1981) when they stated: "The possibility clearly exists that REMD may effect . . . more than one CNS (central nervous system) network system." Despite the possibility—indeed, in our minds the probability—that REMD affects more than one CNS network, we have maintained that between separate sites or systems there is a link between these networks. This link in our hypothesis is made via a positive reward or self-stimulation neural system which is also part of the REM sleep neural network. Thus, given our theoretical position (see Chapters 10 and 16) we have wanted—perhaps more accurately, felt obliged—to use the term *motivational*. Despite our theoretical position, we must state that the term *motivational* is one that lacks a rigorous definition. For the purposes of our theoretical position, we have restricted our use of the term to those behaviors that can be elicited by brain stimulation (for a definition of stimulus bound behaviors, see Chapter 10). In addition, we have only been interested in stimulus bound behavioral sites that also elicited self-stimulation. Thus, we are interested in behaviors that can be elicited by brain stimulation that results in stimulus bound behaviors, and we have artificially defined motivational behaviors in this way. In any case, despite our restrictive definition, we have included behaviors that normally are included in conventional definitions. The behaviors that we include are intracranial self-stimulation (ICSS), aggression, eating, and sexuality. We might note that Vogel (1975) used the term motivational in reference to REM sleep. While we have been interested in his hypotheses, we have had some difficulty applying his thoughts to our motivational model.

Intracranial Self-Stimulation

Since Steiner and Ellman (1972) reported that REMD lowers intracranial self-stimulation (ICSS) thresholds and raises ICSS response rates, there have been several attempts at replicating these results. Steiner and Ellman also reported that 1 1/2 hours of ICSS reduces REM rebound by about 50%. There has only been one attempt at replicating this result. The first replication attempt of Steiner and Ellman's findings was performed by Cohen, Edelman, Bowen, and Dement (1972). This study is frequently not cited since it was published only in abstract form. It was an essential replication of the Steiner and Ellman study and replicated the increase in ICSS response rates, reduction in ICSS threshold, and reduction in REM rebound. These results led Ellman et al. to postulate that the REM and ICSS systems were functionally reciprocal and might actually involve the same neural networks (or overlapping neural networks). These assumptions or hypotheses have been tested in a variety of ways and to some extent these results are reviewed in Chapter 16 by Ellman and Weinstein. Kovalzon and Tsibulsky (1980) published a partial replication, indicating that ICSS leads to an increase in response rates. Their method for obtaining thresholds was quite different from Steiner and Ellman's and as such was not comparable. Two more studies were performed looking at the effect of REMD on ICSS. Both of these studies utilized the pendulum technique of REMD and both found neither lowering of threshold nor increase of ICSS response rates. Van Luijtelaar, Kaiser, and Coenen (1982) concluded that their failure to replicate previous results was due to the method of REMD. Marti-Nicolovius, Portell-Cortes, and Morgado-Bernal (1948) concluded that this was a possibility, but they also allowed for the possibility that different ICSS sites were used and that REMD might have different effects, depending on the ICSS site that was utilized. This of course is a possibility and, in a number of ICSS studies, Ellman and Steiner have frequently found that different ICSS sites can yield quite different results (see Chapter 10). In addition to the possible effect of different neural sites, other differences from the original Steiner and Ellman study include the method of stimulation (60 cycle vs. monophasic square wave), as well as the method of shaping and the method for obtaining thresholds.

The effect of these differences is difficult to ascertain without a controlled study, but there were yet other differences that escaped mention. The original Steiner and Ellman experiments were done with the idea of REMD technique differences very much in mind. It was because of that consideration that these studies employed two methods of REMD: the platform technique and hand awakenings. This fact lends more credibility to Steiner and Ellman's results. It was also not mentioned by Van Luijtelaar et al. (1982) that ICSS lowers REM rebound. This omission is significant since they attempt to implicitly bring into question the idea that REMD facilitates "motivated behavior." The lowering of REM rebound is as least as important a result as the changes in ICSS and yet it is not mentioned. Perhaps most important in looking at this issue are results that have been reported but not fully published that further link REM sleep and ICSS. When rats are allowed ICSS, ad-libitum REM sleep is greatly reduced (Spielman, 1973; Spielman, Mattiace, Steiner, & Ellman, 1973; Spielman et al., 1974). Moreover, this reduction is not followed by REM rebound, thereby demonstrating the type of reciprocal relationship between REM and ICSS that Ellman had initially postulated (see Chapter 16). This study is of course not a REMD experiment, but it is an experiment that offers converging evidence for the "motivational" hypothesis. It also points out something that is generally relevant; given the present amount of controversy about the technique it is important to have converging data from studies that do not utilize REMD to bolster one's theoretical position.

Aggression

Although we have spent some time reviewing the REMD-ICSS experiments, these studies are by no means the most important studies in this section. Perhaps the most consistent finding following REMD is an increase in aggression. Morden, Conner, Mitchell, Dement, and Levine (1968) found that REMD facilitates shock-induced aggression and this finding was replicated by Mollenhour, Vorhees, and Davis (1977). Both Dallmeier and Carlini (1982) and Tufik (1981) found that REMD increases or facilitates apomorphine-induced aggression. This facilitated aggression lasts after REMD is discontinued. Peder, Elomaa, and Johansson (1986) have found that REMD increases aggressive behavior (rat boxing in males and females) and that the size of the enclosure is not a crucial factor in this facilitation. Interestingly they found that in female rats genital exploration was increased by REMD. Since this result came in a posthoc analysis it must be seen as a tentative finding. In this series of studies, the deprivation techniques that were utilized were either the small stand or the cuff pedestal technique. Utilizing these two techniques, all the results were in agreement.

Eating, Food Seeking, Food Restricting

Elomaa (1981), Elomaa and Johansson (1980, 1981) and Johansson and Elomaa (1986) performed a series of studies that looked at the effect of REMD on total food intake, meal size, and meal patterning. They also investigated the effect of REMD on counteracting the effects of food restriction. Their findings indicated that REMD affects the patterning of meals and causes a shift in the light-dark cycle with respect to eating. They did not find that REMD affects overall eating in terms of quantities ingested. They were cautious about their conclusions, given that Hicks et al. (1981) found that REMD increases "the likelihood of winning in a food competition, that is in a task which combines hunger and aggression" (p. 246). Of course it is hard to compare a study that utilizes a food competition paradigm to a study that looks at eating responses alone. Hicks et al. (1981) conducted their experiment in part to test a hypothesis that Ellman et al. had previously put forth: "Further their hypothesis stipulates . . . 'priming the animal by starving it would potentiate the effects of REMD for a given behavior or behaviors'" (see Chapter 10). We have modified our theoretical position since then, but their experiment would still lend confirmation to our present position. Although REMD stimulated potentiated food competition responses after REMD, the animals did not return to baseline levels. This was unlike ICSS results, and it led Hicks et al. (1981) to question the term motivational behavior, since these different behaviors did not respond in the same way following REMD.

We have a different perspective and suggest that although recovery gradients should of course be considered, this does not obviate the fact that these behaviors interacted in the predicted manner. This correct prediction lends support to the idea these neural systems are strongly related. Although we would predict that starvation would potentiate a number of "motivational behaviors," we would not predict that food intake would be facilitated by REMD. (For discussion, see Chapter 16.)

LEARNING STUDIES

We have reviewed the logic of some learning paradigms in our chapter and so in this update we will state only the results from these studies. We have attempted to integrate some of the REM augmentation results in our theoretical position (see Chapter 16).

Smith and Young (1980) and Smith and Butler (1982) found that REM is necessary for the acquisition of shuttlebox avoidance responses in two different types of paradigms. They also found that amygdaloid stimulation reverses these results as would be expected if REMD impaired acquisition. Koridze and Nemsadze (1983) and Oniani (1984) found that REMD did not effect learning if one took into account their measure of emotionality. If animals were emotional, acquisition would be impaired; if animals were not emotional, acquisition of passive avoidance responses would not be impaired. All of the above learning studies used the same REMD methods and utilized rats as the experimental subject. Van Hulzen and Coenen (1982) found that REMD with the platform technique impaired shuttlebox avoidance, but REMD with the pendulum technique did not impair shuttlebox avoidance. They concluded that it is the REMD technique that is crucial. This seems unlikely, given Koridze and Nemsadze (1983) and Oniani's (1984) findings. It may be that emotionality is the crucial intervening variable in the learning experiments, but this awaits further study.

11

Sleep Mentation as Affected by REM Deprivation: A New Look

LISSA N. WEINSTEIN
Teachers College, Columbia University

DAVID G. SCHWARTZ
Private Practice, New York City

STEVEN J. ELLMAN
City College of the City University of New York

Despite the inconclusive results of studies of the effects of deprivation of rapid eye movement on (REM) sleep mentation (Arkin, Antrobus, Ellman, & Farber, 1978; Dement, 1978 [cited in Arkin et al., 1978]; Foulkes, Pivik, Ahrens, & Swanson, 1968; Pivik & Foulkes, 1966; Sampson, 1966), we felt that prior research had not sufficiently addressed the question of individual differences. Our opinion was supported by evidence (Cartwright & Monroe, 1968; Cartwright, Monroe, & Palmer, 1967; Cartwright & Ratzel, 1972; Nakasawa, Kotorii, Kotorii, Tachibana, & Nakano, 1975) that subjects who failed to respond to REM deprivation (RD) tended to be more introspective and more influenced by their inner thoughts and fantasies as measured by both projective and standardized tests. We attributed the paucity of findings (as in other areas of dream content research) to the narrowness of prevalent research models, which posit an isomorphic relationship between sleep physiology and dream content (Berger & Oswald, 1962; Hobson & McCarley, 1977; McCarley, 1983). Although each of these models has an unstated assumption that physiological stimulation will be directly translated into mental imagery, the models differ in how direct they believe the correlation between sleep physiology and mentation to be. All of the models neglect psychological hypotheses, however, and do not consider how the physiological stimuli are actively processed. Several authors have explicated the theoretical and empirical limitations of this physiological approach (Ellman, Chapter 7 of first edition; Vogel, 1978; Wasserman, 1984).

In the first edition, Arkin, Ellman, Antrobus, and Farber succinctly stated the rationale for the expectation of changes in sleep mentation following RD. We were influenced in our thinking also by the work of Dement and his colleagues (Dement et al., 1969; Ferguson et al., 1968; Ferguson & Dement, 1968), who attempted to explore the tenacity of the association of phasic and tonic events of REM sleep. Their results implied (a) that REM sleep is not a unitary entity, but rather a convergence of several processes which usually occur together but can be dissociated, and (b) that the crucial variable in the occurrence of REM rebound was not REM time per se, but phasic activity. If Dement and his colleagues were correct, if phasic activity following RD is displaced into non-REM (NREM) sleep, then changes in mentation following RD would best be assessed with scales that could sensitively discriminate phasic from tonic awakenings during REM sleep.

The following experiments were part of an ongoing attempt to develop an alternative multifactor approach to the study of sleep mentation, where physiology is seen as the first step in a complex process, which eventuates in the dream report. In Experiment 1 we developed scales that would discriminate phasic from tonic awakenings in REM sleep. We then used these scales to test hypotheses about personality factors and the response to RD.

Clearly, the choice of which aspect of sleep mentation to study was critical. Previous studies of psychophysiological correlations during sleep were limited by their focus on dream content because the amount of scorable content varies with the subjects' capacities to express themselves linguistically. As Antrobus (1984) and Foulkes and Schmidt (1983) noted, many correlations between aspects of dream content and REM versus NREM awakenings are artifactual: they are caused by an unexamined correlation between dream scale scores and a simple word count.

We chose to examine changes in self-reflection during dreaming. Our interest in these changes grew initially out of psychoanalytic thinking on the experience of the self. Apart from a few studies (Bosinelli, Cicogna, & Molinari, 1974; Purcell, Mullington, Moffit, Hoffmann, & Pigeau, 1986), self-awareness during sleep has been largely ignored in the literature, in part because of the assumption that dreams are nonreflective and isolated from other systems of consciousness (Rechtschaffen, 1978). One advantage of studying self-reflection is that there is no a priori reason to believe that it correlates with word count. In addition, a critical review of the literature on phasic–tonic correlations in REM sleep led us to hypothesize that the loss of reflective awareness was a central aspect of the dream experience—one that would correlate highly with the occurrence of phasic activity. The animal models underlying our research are discussed in Chapter 16.

PSYCHOANALYTIC CONTRIBUTIONS

How we come to experience events as external and compelling, as opposed to having merely thoughts or fantasies (i.e., products of our minds), has long been the subject of psychoanalytic thought. Arlow and Brenner (1964), Rapaport (1951/1967), Rubinfine (1961), and Schafer (1968) all have focused on the diminished capacity to test reality in dreaming, when the ability to distinguish the real from the intrapsychic returns to a state characteristic of infancy. Early in a person's development, wishes and memories of past satisfactions are confused with reality, particularly in states of need or high excitation. With the increasing operation of delay and inhibition as the person ages, thought processes evolve into forms of trial action, and internal experience is less frequently confused with external perception. Central to this development is the capacity for reflective awareness. In adulthood, various factors determine the ebb and flow of reflective awareness. This awareness is more likely to be suspended when endogenously generated excitation is allowed increased access to consciousness, for example, when opportunities for motility are decreased and external stimulation is limited.

Freud (1905/1953) emphasized that during sleep unacceptable wishes are expressed in dream content, albeit in disguised form because of the lowered intrapsychic censorship. Later theorists (Jacobsen, 1964; Schafer, 1968) suggested that one wish fulfilling aspect of fantasy is the momentary and gratifying loss of reflective awareness. The dreamer forgoes the tedious, effortful expenditure of energy necessary to maintain the distinction between thought and action. A common clinical observation is that the tendency to "lose oneself in an experience" differs widely among individuals, varying with such diverse parameters as psychopathology, external events, level of somatic stimulation, cognitive style, and quality of associated mental contents. At one end of the continuum—in sexual pleasure, meditative states, strenuous physical activity, or psychotic states—a person has low self-awareness and is quite lost in the experience. At the other extreme, while participating in an activity that causes anxiety, a person may suffer painful states of self-awareness. Reflective awareness also oscillates in dreams. An increase in reflective awareness can serve to lessen the subjective intensity of the dream experience. Recent research on cognition in dreaming has focused on self-reflectiveness as an example of higher-order cognitive processing (Purcell et al., 1986). Purcell et al. noted that self-reflectiveness varied between different sleep stages, being present more often in REM than in stage 2 and stage 4 dreams. The authors concluded, although from a perspective different from that of analytic writers, that dreaming varies along the continuum of a self-reflective process.

THE PHASIC–TONIC MODEL

In early research, an equation was made between the activation of REM sleep and dreaming. As high rates of NREM recall were consistently reported (Foulkes, 1962; Herman, Ellman, & Roffwarg, 1978) and a high percentage of REM sleep in infancy was found (Roffwarg, Muzio, & Dement, 1966), another model, based on Moruzzi's (1963) distinction between tonic and phasic events in REM sleep, replaced the original REM/NREM dichotomy (Grosser & Segal, 1971). This latter model asserted that REM sleep was not a unitary entity and stressed the continuity of phasic and tonic phenomena throughout all stages of sleep.

Although numerous studies employing lesioning techniques, pharmacological techniques, and RD procedures have supported Moruzzi's (1963) model by demonstrating the physiological independence of the phasic and tonic aspects of REM sleep, the mentation data have been far more equivocal. (See Chapter 6 for a critical review of these studies.) Briefly, studies of the mentation correlates of phasic activity within REM sleep have attempted to support a key element of Moruzzi's model—that the phasic event is qualitatively different from the tonic activity that surrounds it. Methodological problems (i.e., failure to control for time into the REM period or time of night, small subject pools, poor interrater reliability, failure to use interviewers who were blind to the awakening conditions, and the possibility that tonic intervals were contaminated by unmeasured phasic activity) made interpretation of these studies difficult. Bursts of rapid eye movements were associated (a) with reports of dreams characterized by increased activity (Berger & Oswald, 1962; Dement & Wolpert, 1958), increased vividness and emotionality (Hobson, Goldfrank, & Snyder, 1965; Verdone, 1963), increased "dreamlikeness" (Ellman et al., 1974), increased bizarreness (Kushniruk, Rustenberg, & Ogilvie, 1985), and increased aggression (Pivik, 1971), and (b) with reports of dreams that were less conceptual and thoughtlike and that were accompanied by a greater feeling of self-participation on the part of the dreamer (Bosinelli et al., 1974; Bosinelli, Molinari, Bagnaresi, & Salzarulo, 1978). Molinari and Foulkes (1969) found that REM phasic arousals were correlated with the presence of primary visual experience, defined as watching an event in an intellectually passive manner without apparent reflection or cognitive elaboration upon the visual imagery. This post hoc analysis was partly confirmed by Foulkes and Pope (1973), although their reported correlations were considerably lower than those of Molinari and Foulkes. Phasic activity in the form of periorbital integrated potentials was associated with more bizarreness and discontinuity in the dream report (Watson, 1972), as was middle-ear muscle activity (Ogilvie, Hunt, Sawicki, & Samahalski, 1982).

Few of these studies attempted to build upon one another to develop a psychological construct that would unify the diverse measures seen to correlate with phasic activity. Only Antrobus (1984) attempted to compare the efficacy of various dream scales in discriminating phasic from tonic awakenings on the same data, and no attempts were made to assess the redundancy of various dream scales. In reviewing these studies, one fundamental characteristic of mentation from phasic intervals was that the reported experience was unaccompanied by reflective cognition and was felt by the dreamer to be real, immediate, and involving.

We were interested in whether changes in reflective awareness during dreaming bear any relation to underlying sleep physiology. Our hypothesis was that phasic activity lowered the threshold to the loss of reflective awareness and increased the likelihood that the dream would be experienced as real and compelling.

Experiment 1

Mentation reports from the first two pairs of baseline nights were used. Of the 630 mentation reports rated, 149 were from stage REM (69 tonic; 80 phasic); 406 were from stage 2 (135 tonic; 271 phasic); and 75 were judged as having no content and were excluded from the data analysis. There was no significant difference in the number of missing reports between subject groups or in the Sleep State × Subject Group interaction.

Upon being awakened, a subject was given the following structured interview:

1. What was going through your mind just prior to being awakened?
2. Any more to this?
3. How clear and vivid was the experience you just had?
4. What feelings or emotions did you experience?
5. How real was the experience you had just prior to being awakened?

Each report was rated on eight dream scales by two independent judges who were blind to sleep condition and subject characteristics. Five of the scales—Reality, Affect, Self-Representation, Temporal, and Global—had been constructed to measure the extent to which the subject experienced his or her dream as involving, real, and external (i.e., as indicating a suspension of self-observation).

Replies to question 5 were rated (on a 7-point Reality scale) for how real the subject judged his or her report to be; replies to question 4 were rated for the subject's judgment of the intensity of affect (7-point Affect scale). From the first three questions, raters judged whether the subject seemed to be immersed in a mentation experience that involved a loss of reflectivity (dichotomous Global scale). Any assessment on the subject's part was ignored. From the first two questions, raters judged whether the subject spontaneously utilized a grammatical form that implied a cognitive process, for example, "I was thinking . . . dreaming . . . ," and so forth (dichotomous Self-Representation scale). A failure to utilize this expression was taken as evidence of a lower degree of self-observation. From the first two questions alone, raters judged whether the report showed inappropriate shifts in verbal tense, which were assumed to reflect greater involvement in the experience (dichotomous Temporal scale).

Three dream scales used in previous studies were also scored: Foulkes's (1966) Dreamlike Fantasy (DF) scale, Molinari and Foulkes's (1969) dichotomous Secondary Cognitive Elaboration versus Primary Visual Experience (SCE/PVE) scale, and Foulkes and Pope's (1973) 5-point scale of sensory versus conceptual prominence in the reported dream. Interrater reliability for the scales ranged from .82 to .96. Reliability to assess temporal drift ranged from .85 to .93.

The eight dream scales were intercorrelated across all sleep conditions to assess whether they were redundant. These correlations tended to be low and positive; the highest correlations were among the DF, Global, and Reality scales and between the Sensory and SCE/PVE scales. We decided to treat each of the eight scales as an independent variable.

Each subject was administered the Imaginal Processes Inventory and the Minnesota Multiphasic Personality Inventory (MMPI). We were interested in whether reporting style or the subjects' capacity to tolerate anxiety-producing thoughts would affect their ability to distinguish phasic from tonic intervals during REM sleep. One measure of this variable, the Guilt Daydreaming scale of the Imaginal Processes Inventory (Singer & Antrobus, 1973), was chosen on the basis of an analysis of the individual scale items and its overall high correlation (.52) with the Social Introversion scale of the MMPI, which Jackson and Messick (1967/1972) showed to be a social desirability response indicator.

Eight three-way univariate analyses of variance (ANOVAs) were conducted with the eight dream scale scores as the dependent variable. The independent variables were: (a) REM (or NREM) condition, (b) phasic (or tonic) condition, and (c) time of night (before or after 50 percent of the subject's total sleep time for the night had elapsed). Duncan's range test was used to identify which cell means differed if the overall F test was significant.

Efficacy of Mentation Scales in Discriminating Phasic from Tonic Awakenings. As shown in Tables 11.1 and 11.2, the Global, Reality, Sensory, DF, Temporal, and Affect scales all showed highly significant main effects of REM condition. REM dreams scored higher than NREM dreams. The SCE/PVE scale showed significant main effects for time of night: late dreams evidenced more primary visual experience. The interaction between REM condition and phasic condition was significant for the Self-Representation (SR) and Global scales but fell just short of significance for the Reality and Sensory scales. On the Reality, SR, Sensory, and Global scales, REM phasic reports were scored highest. The difference between REM phasic and REM tonic reports was significant for the Global scale ($p < .05$, Duncan's range test).

Scales' Discrimination of Phasic from Tonic Awakenings Within Subject Groups. In trying to understand the findings shown in Tables 11.1 and 11.2, we reasoned that the eight scales were differentiated by the extent to which they required an introspective report by the subject. Some scales required the subject to exercise a conscious self-judgment (i.e., "How real did it feel?" or "What emotions did you have?"). Other scales were rated purely on the basis of the subject's verbal report, so that no reflection was necessary. It is possible that asking the subject to make a judgment about his or her own sensations mitigated the experience of becoming absorbed in the dream, in that the very act of judging forced the subject to take the dream as an object of consideration.

Subjects who tended to respond in a socially desirable manner and to tailor their responses in order to appear "normal" were unlikely to be accurate reporters, particularly if they considered a seemingly real, hallucinatory experience to be unacceptable. Those subjects who were least influenced by demand characteristics were more likely to show a differentiation between phasic and tonic REM reports if such reports actually had different psychological correlates. We were able to identify two such subject groups by looking at scores on measures that rated the subjects' tendencies to tailor responses to fit what they believed would put them in a favorable light. An additional set of eight three-way ANOVAs was conducted with subjects split on the median of the scores on the Guilt Daydreaming scale of the Imaginal Processes Inventory. The results are shown in Tables 11.3 and 11.4.

TABLE 11.1. MENTATION SCALES THAT DISCRIMINATE AWAKENING CONDITIONS

Sleep Condition	Mentation Scale							
	Global	SR	Reality	Sensory	DF	SCE/PVE	Temporal	Affect
REM vs. NREM	$F = 24.36$ $p < .0001$	*	$F = 11.10$ $p < .0009$	$F = 12.67$ $p < .0004$	$F = 19.77$ $p < .0001$	*	$F = 6.05$ $p < .014$	$F = 12.65$ $p < .0004$
Early vs. Late	*	*	*	*	*	$F = 5.96$ $p < .014$	*	*
Phasic vs. Tonic × REM vs. NREM	$F = 4.27$ $p < .039$	$F = 3.95$ $p < .047$	$F = 3.77$ $p < .053$	$F = 3.60$ $p < .058$	*	*	*	*
Early vs. Late × REM vs. NREM	*	*	*	*	*	*	*	*

* = Nonsignificant.
F = results of analysis of variance; p = probability of accepting the null hypothesis.

TABLE 11.2. CELL MEANS FOR ANALYSES OF VARIANCE (ALL SUBJECTS)

Interaction	Awakening Condition	Mentation Scale							
		Global	SR	Reality	Sensory	DF	SCE/PVE	Temporal	Affect
REM vs. NREM	REM	.81^a	.40	5.00^a	2.53^a	6.56^a	.77	.29^a	4.05^a
	NREM	.59^b	.36	4.19^b	2.09^b	5.82^b	.76	.19^b	3.33^b
Early vs. Late	Early	.68	.41	4.44	2.23	6.05	.82^a	.24	3.53
	Late	.60	.31	4.36	2.19	5.98	.72^b	.20	3.51
REM vs. NREM × Phasic vs. Tonic	REM Phasic	.88^a	.46^a	5.19^a	2.59^a	6.75	.75	.29	4.16
	REM Tonic	.71^b	.33^a	4.67^{ab}	2.43^{ab}	6.34	.77	.29	3.93
	NREM Phasic	.56^c	.39^a	4.02^b	2.22^c	5.79	.75	.19	3.24
	NREM Tonic	.59^{bc}	.33^a	4.40	2.01^c	5.90	.81	.20	3.50
REM vs. NREM × Early vs. Late	REM Early	.80	.39	4.73	2.65	6.56	.80	.34	4.10
	REM Late	.82	.41	5.24	2.42	6.56	.72	.24	4.01
	NREM Early	.52	.27	4.21	2.05	5.74	.83	.20	3.30
	NREM Late	.64	.42	4.18	2.11	5.88	.72	.19	3.35

Note. Cell means with similar superscripts are not significantly different.

TABLE 11.3. MENTATION SCALES WHICH DISCRIMINATE AWAKENING CONDITIONS IN DIFFERENT SUBJECT GROUPS

Sleep Condition	Mentation Scale							
	Global	SR	Reality	Sensory	DF	SCE/PVE	Temporal	Affect
More Introspective Reporters								
REM vs. NREM	F = 16.0 p <.0001	F = 4.39 p <.037	F = 11.64 p <.0008	F = 9.11 p <.0028	F = 20.59 p <.0001	*	F = 11.45 p <.0008	F = 23.13 p <.0001
Early vs. Late	*	*	*	*	*	F = 3.80 p <.052	F = 6.84 p <.009	*
Phasic vs. Tonic × REM vs. NREM	F = 1.26 p <.26	F = 1.72 p <.19	F = 5.70 p <.018	F = 1.08 p <.29	F = 2.80 p <.09	F = .05 p <.81	F = .23 p <.63	F = 2.42 p <.12
Early vs. Late × REM vs. NREM	*	*	*	*	*	*	*	*
Less Introspective Reporters								
REM vs. NREM	F = 8.60 p <.004	*	* p <.04	F = 4.21	*	*	*	*
Early vs. Late	F = 3.10 p <.07	*	F = 4.22 p <.04	*	*	*	*	*
Phasic vs. Tonic × REM vs. NREM	F = 2.73 p <.10	F = 2.14 p <.14	F = .03 p <.87	F = 2.37 p <.12	F = .22 p <.63	F = .99 p <.32	F = .18 p <.67	F = .00 p <.95
Early vs. Late × REM vs. NREM	*	*	F = 7.40 p <.007	*	*	*	*	*

* = Nonsignificant.
F = results of analysis of variance; p = probability of accepting the null hypothesis.

TABLE 11.4. CELL MEANS FOR ANALYSES OF VARIANCE BY SUBJECT GROUP

Interaction	Awakening Condition		Mentation Scale							
			Global	SR	Reality	Sensory	DF	SCE/PVE	Temporal	Affect
		More Introspective Reporters								
REM vs. NREM	REM		.86a	.47a	5.04a	2.68a	6.75a	.76	.31a	4.49a
	NREM		.60b	.34b	3.91b	2.13b	5.62b	.76	.14b	3.07b
Early vs. Late	Early		.67	.43	4.27	2.34	6.03	.84a	.25a	3.70
	Late		.67	.30	4.19	2.19	5.86	.71b	.13b	3.28
REM vs. NREM	REM	Phasic	.93	.53	5.75a	2.75	7.13	.75	.30	4.78
x Phasic vs.	REM	Tonic	.78	.41	4.06b	2.59	6.28	.78	.31	4.13
Tonic	NREM	Phasic	.59	.32	3.87b	2.06	5.64	.76	.14	2.99
	NREM	Tonic	.61	.36	4.81b	2.25	5.59	.78	.13	3.24
REM vs. NREM	REM	Early	.86	.44	5.25	2.72	6.83	.78	.39	4.69
x Early vs.	REM	Late	.86	.50	4.83	2.64	6.67	.75	.22	4.27
Late	NREM	Early	.58	.23	3.80	2.23	5.65	.87	.18	3.23
	NREM	Late	.60	.40	3.98	2.05	5.61	.69	.11	2.96
		Less Introspective Reporters								
REM vs. NREM	REM		.77a	.38	4.96	2.39a	6.39	.77	.27	3.65
	NREM		.58b	.34	4.44	2.05b	6.00	.75	.24	3.55
Early vs. Late	Early		.70a	.40	4.67a	2.18	6.22	.81	.26	3.72
	Late		.54b	.32	4.45b	2.09	5.94	.73	.23	3.39
REM vs. NREM	REM	Phasic	.85	.40	4.75	2.48	6.38	.75	.28	3.55
x Phasic vs.	REM	Tonic	.68	.27	5.21	2.30	6.40	.76	.27	3.76
Tonic	NREM	Phasic	.57	.35	4.21	1.96	5.92	.73	.23	3.47
	NREM	Tonic	.61	.42	4.85	2.24	6.15	.85	.26	3.71
REM vs. NREM	REM	Early	.74	.34	4.11b	2.57	6.29	.83	.29	3.49
x Early vs.	REM	Late	.79	.33	5.60a	2.24	6.48	.69	.26	3.79
Late	NREM	Early	.46	.31	4.57b	1.90	5.81	.80	.21	3.35
	NREM	Late	.67	.43	4.34b	2.17	6.14	.75	.27	3.70

Note. Cell means with similar superscripts are not significantly different.

When the subjects' response styles were taken into account, the Reality scale showed a highly significant interaction of REM condition and phasic condition. This subanalysis indicated that phasic REM activity was associated with the subjective feeling that the dream was "really happening" but that the observation of these associations was interfered with by the operation of a response bias when assessment was carried out via a self-evaluation question.

The occurrence of a dream report in which an external observer independently judged the subject to have been unreflectively immersed in a dream (Global scale) was also clearly associated with phasic REM activity. This relation was more reliable across subjects, in that it was statistically significant for the 20 unselected subjects but was weaker when compared with the Reality scale for more introspective reporters. The SR scale was the least sensitive of the four measures that were able to discriminate phasic REM awakenings (it is a dichotomous as opposed to a 7-point scale and attempts a more limited assessment). However, the SR scale was not a good discriminator of REM versus NREM but simply discriminated the interaction of REM condition with phasic condition, suggesting that the loss of self-observation is independent from the more general category of "dreamlikeness" that distinguishes REM from NREM.

The intensity of affect and the degree of temporal incoherence were not reliable correlates of phasic activity. This lack of correlation was consistent with the hypothesis of a primary correlation between the suspension of self-observation and phasic activity.

Only one of the scales previously shown to discriminate phasic from tonic awakenings within REM sleep did so in our study. Molinari and Foulkes's (1969) SCE/PVE scale failed to discriminate REM awakenings in our sample or in that of Bosinelli et al. (1978). In 1970, S. Ellman wrote, in an unpublished critique, that Molinari and Foulkes had neglected to control for time into the REM period. When we controlled for this variable, the scale could no longer differentiate REM awakening categories. The DF scale also failed to discriminate phasic from tonic awakenings. Our hypothesis is that the DF—a composite of four independent factors (how real, perceptual, and bizarre the dream is, and whether content is present) which are combined and statistically treated as an interval level measurement—will be less sensitive because of these limitations.

In summary, our results provided evidence that the primary psychological correlate of phasic REM activity is the experience of the dream as real; as a consequence, the dreamer reports mentation in a manner that communicates his or her immersion in the dream event. These results are in agreement with the findings of other authors (Bosinelli et al., 1974; Foulkes & Schmidt, 1983), who have noted a relatively higher incidence of the self-character in REM reports versus sleep onset and NREM reports.

Experiment 2

Once we had developed scales that discriminated phasic from tonic awakenings better than any previously cited in the literature, we wanted to use them to evaluate changes in mentation following RD. Mentation reports from the first deprivation nights and the recovery nights were used in Experiment 2.

Each subject contributed approximately eight reports per night (six NREM, two REM), for a total of 309 reports from the first two deprivation nights and 314 reports from the two recovery nights. Each report was scored on the four scales that had been effective in discriminating phasic from tonic awakenings in Experiment 1. The DF and the SCE/PVE scales were included for further validation, and we predicted that they would not show changes following RD. For each subject a mean rating for each of the six mentation scales was computed for each of the six sleep conditions: REM, REM tonic, REM phasic, NREM, NREM tonic, and NREM phasic. These scores were computed for the first deprivation night in each series (REM deprivation versus NREM deprivation [NRD]) and for the recovery night in each series. A three-way, repeated-measures ANOVA was conducted with the six dream-scale mean scores as the dependent variable. The three independent variables for each repeated-measures ANOVA were RD versus NRD, REM versus NREM, and phasic versus tonic. The analysis included a blocking factor that split subjects into more versus less modulated reporters based on their scores on the Guilt Daydreaming scale of the Imaginal Processes Inventory. The three-way analysis was done, comparing the first deprivation night in each series and comparing the recovery nights. Duncan's range tests were conducted if the overall F test was significant. Planned comparisons were done on NREM mentation following RD and following NRD on all six dream scales.

Analysis of the First Deprivation Night.   As shown in Table 11.5, the Global scale showed a significant four-way interaction among deprivation condition, REM condition, phasic condition, and subject factors: dreams from REM phasic awakenings following RD seemed significantly more real than those following NRD, but only for the less introspective reporters. The SR showed a significant three-way interaction among deprivation condition, REM condition, and subject factors, so that REM mentation following RD showed significantly more suspension of reflective awareness than REM mentation following NRD. As with the Global scale, this interaction was true only for the less introspective reporters. The Reality scale showed a significant three-way interaction among deprivation condition, REM condition, and phasic condition, so that REM phasic reports following RD were rated as more real than those following NRD. The Sensory scale showed a

TABLE 11.5. ANALYSIS OF VARIANCE FOR THE FIRST DEPRIVATION NIGHT

Source of Variation	Mentation Scale F Ratio					
	Global	SR	Reality	Sensory	DF	SCE/PVE
RD vs. NRD	.01	1.01	.57	.47	2.26	.57
RD vs. NRD × More vs. Less Introspective Reporters	1.33	.39	1.82	.27	.59	.86
REM vs. NREM	80.08***	6.15*	8.50**	35.29***	57.64***	6.85*
RD vs. NRD × REM vs. NREM	5.05*	.47	.11	10.95**	.07	2.37
RD vs. NRD ×REM vs. NREM × More vs. Less Introspective Reporters	1.18	.05	1.53	2.22	.01	1.50
RD vs. NRD × Phasic vs. Tonic × More vs. Less Introspective Reporters	2.52	4.51*	1.36	.41	1.46	.08
RD vs. NRD × REM vs. NREM × Phasic vs. Tonic × More vs. Less Introspective Reporters	1.18	2.16	7.32**	1.62	1.55	.02
RD vs. NRD × REM vs. NREM × Phasic vs. Tonic × More vs. Less Introspective Reporters	4.62*	.00	.01	1.74	.45	.07

$* p < .05$ $** p < .01$ $*** p < .001$

significant two-way interaction between deprivation condition and REM condition, so that REM reports were rated as having more sensory elements following RD than following NRD. The DF scale and the SCE/PVE scale showed no significant effects of RD versus NRD.

Analysis of Recovery Night Mentation

Effect of RD on NREM Mentation.   Comparisons of mean ratings of stage 2 mentation on the recovery night following stage 2 versus stage REM deprivation nights were significant for the Global scale ($t = 2.08$, $p < .025$, one-tailed test), the SR scale ($t = 1.964$, $p < .05$, one-tailed test), the Sensory scale ($t = 1.95$, $p < .05$, one-tailed test), and the DF scale ($t = 1.86$, $p < .05$, one-tailed test). There was no significant difference among subject groups. There also was no difference in stage 2 mentation following stage REM versus stage 2 deprivation on the Reality scale or the SCE/PVE scale.

Effect of RD on REM Mentation.   As shown in Table 11.6, the Global scale and the SR scale showed significant three-way interactions among deprivation condition, REM condition, and subject factors, so that REM mentation following RD was rated as much *less* involving than after stage 2 deprivation, but only by the less introspective reporters. There were no significant results of RD versus NRD on the Reality scale. The Sensory scale showed a significant three-way interaction among deprivation condition, REM condition, and phasic condition, so that REM phasic mentation following RD was rated as *less* sensory than that following NRD. This effect was true for all subjects but was largely carried by the less introspective reporters.

DISCUSSION

We predicted that on recovery nights there would be greater suspension of reflective awareness from mentation reports collected in NREM sleep following RD but not following NREM control deprivation. This suspension occurred for all subjects, primarily on those scales that discriminated phasic and tonic awakenings on baseline. This result was the first to show that RD had an effect on mentation or cognitive processes in a well-controlled, double-blind paradigm and is particularly significant after 10 years of researchers' failed attempts to find results in this area.

Because of our interest in individual differences that might influence the response to RD, and because subject variables were one determinant of the ability to discriminate phasic from tonic awakenings on baseline, we split subjects on the median of their scores on the Guilt Daydreaming scale. Subjects who were likely to be more introspective and to report or focus on

TABLE 11.6. ANALYSIS OF VARIANCE FOR THE RECOVERY NIGHT

Source of Variation	Mentation Scale F Ratio					
	Global	SR	Reality	Sensory	DF	SCE/PVE
RD vs. NRD	.12	.07	1.33	.79	1.00	.03
RD vs. NRD × More vs. Less Introspective Reporters	3.80	4.42*	.07	3.22	.01	4.27*
REM vs. NREM	1.02	.05	.56	4.52	2.09	1.27
RD vs. NRD × REM vs. NREM	2.84	5.12*	.25	.03	2.65	.16
RD vs. NRD ×REM vs. NREM × More vs. Less Introspective Reporters	7.28**	4.29*	.13	2.53	.00	1.43
RD vs. NRD × Phasic vs. Tonic × More vs. Less Introspective Reporters	.05	.05	.10	.44	3.55	1.06
RD vs. NRD × REM vs. NREM × Phasic vs. Tonic	2.21	.06	.57	6.21*	2.58	1.90
RD vs. NRD × REM vs. NREM × Phasic vs. Tonic × More vs. Less Introspective Reporters	.06	.26	1.80	2.93	.46	.57

*$p < .05$ **$p < .01$

anxiety-producing percepts showed no differential pattern of response to stage REM deprivation versus stage 2 deprivation in their REM mentation. Subjects who tended to avoid such percepts showed a characteristic pattern of response to RD, which was significant only on those scales that successfully discriminated phasic from tonic awakenings during baseline.

On the first RD night, these subjects found REM, and particularly REM phasic mentation, to be extremely involving, often reaching ceiling values on the scales. On RD nights, subjects were allowed a minimal amount of REM phasic activity, since it is eliminated by the deprivation procedures. The subjects did not show this pattern after NREM control deprivation, which did not deprive them of REM phasic activity. On recovery nights following RD, these subjects had significantly less involving REM mentation. During recovery from RD, an increase occurs in the absolute amount of phasic activity within REM sleep. Thus, at a time when one would expect all subjects to experience their dreams as extremely intense and real seeming, a subgroup paradoxically showed an increase in reflective awareness, and invoked the disclaimer, "I was only observing; I knew it was just a dream." The subjects were not simply responding to stress, as shown by the absence of a similar pattern during recovery from NRD. The subjects were responding specifically to the patterning and intensity of phasic activation, as indicated by the fact that the effect was significant only using scales that were good phasic–tonic discriminators for the less introspective reporters during baseline nights.

A heightened tendency to lose self-awareness in NREM sleep following RD would be predicted by the fact that increased REM pressure caused the REM phasic phenomenon to spill over into NREM sleep. The internal analysis that focused on subjects for whom intense dream and fantasy mentation led to anxiety had surprising results. The increase in these subjects' reflective awareness during recovery following RD was so powerful that the effect was significant for all subjects—only when we graphed the data did we recognize that the effect was being carried by a subgroup.

Experiment 2 was undertaken both as an attempt to validate the ability of our scales to discriminate phasic from tonic awakenings and as an effort to clear up some of the inconsistencies of the previous RD literature through the correction of major methodological flaws and through the use of improved mentation instruments. Our data can be considered a confirmation of Pivik and Foulkes's (1966) results. If one reconceptualizes the Guilt Daydreaming scale as a measure of a subject's ability to report accurately and tolerate anxiety-producing thoughts, then our more introspective reporters are roughly equivalent to Pivik and Foulkes's (1966) sensitizer subjects. In both studies, subjects who tended to avoid anxiety-producing thoughts increased some quality of their REM mentation following RD. Although we did not find changes in REM mentation using the DF scale, one could view the DF scale as a less sensitive indicator of the suspension of reflective self-representation and hence a poorer discriminator of phasic versus tonic awakenings then either the SR or the Global scale. What our data add to the earlier results is that the increased dreamlikeness of REM mentation was due to an augmentation of some properties of REM phasic mentation.

In the first edition, Arkin, Ellman, Antrobus and Farber failed to find an effect of RD on mentation using the same data as in the present experiments. The differences are due to a combination of factors. Arkin et al. used a forced normal distribution to rate the mentation reports. Although we found a significant difference in NREM mentation following stage REM deprivation versus stage 2 deprivation on the DF scale, there were no other significant findings using this scale. Our other scales were more sensitive discriminators of phasic versus tonic awakenings, and the results following RD were consistently found with these scales. Finally, Arkin et al. did not evaluate individual differences, a factor that proved crucial in our analysis.

CONCLUSIONS

Taken together, the results of our two experiments suggest that there was a reliable psychophysiological correlate of phasic activity, which could be most clearly demonstrated when intervening psychological processes manifested on self-report inventories were taken into account. In addition, we demonstrated changes in mentation following RD, not in terms of dream content but rather by focusing on how the fantasy is experienced by the subject.

Arkin, concluded, in the first edition: "Although several physiological states are capable of supporting dream-like mentation, they do not respond to REM deprivation with detectable increases in such mentation" (p. 478). Our own results suggested a different conclusion: depending on a combination of factors (the level of physiological stimulation, sleep stage, and the subject's capacity to report or tolerate inner experiences), RD will, for some subjects, give rise to a subjective experience of more involving mentation and for other subjects, an experience of less real-seeming mentation. Our original intention had been to examine the utility of a multifactor model of dream construction. An isomorphic model, which predicts that higher levels of stimulation would engender more involving mentation, could not predict that the suspension of reflective awareness would be inhibited in subjects who were averse to allowing socially unacceptable thoughts into consciousness. For these subjects, more stimulation (measured here as higher levels of phasic activation) led to an experience that they related as less real-seeming.

The question remains as to why the suspension of reflective awareness might be anxiety-producing and cause some subjects to defensively insist that the dream experiences are simply thoughts. To understand this, a more psychodynamic understanding of the construct is suggested. Schafer (1968) conceptualized the suspension of reflective awareness as one form of the loss of self–object differentiation, which can be either a pleasurable and wished-for experience or, under different circumstances, a frightening assault on one's identity. Insofar as one's wishes and fantasies are experienced as real and as having real consequences at higher levels of phasic stimulation, they are more likely to be responded to with anxiety or to be denied, particularly by those subjects who are less introspective or less tolerant of anxiety-producing thoughts while awake. This interpretation is, of course, speculative but it could be tested with large numbers of subjects and in-depth personality assessment in an extension and replication of the present study.

12

Psychological Effects of REM ("Dream") Deprivation upon Waking Mentation

ISAAC LEWIN
Bar–Ilan University

JEROME L. SINGER
Yale University

In updating the first edition's review of the psychological implications of interruptions or reductions in the EEG state 1 of REM sleep stages, we have felt it necessary to reexamine some of the major hypotheses concerning the functional role of this REM–non-REM distinction in sleep patterns. The literature over the past decade permits identification of the following proposals, which we shall examine briefly, in relation to available recent literature.

1. Non-REM and REM sleep differences as nonfunctional evolutionary remnants in human beings,
2. REM as a general arousal mechanism,
3. REM as a specific factor maintaining binocular vision efficiency,
4. Jouvet's genetic programming hypothesis,
5. REM sleep as enhancing "divergent thinking" and "assimilation of unprepared learning,"
6. REM sleep as compensation for real search activity,
7. REM sleep and depression; therapeutic implications.

Each of these theoretical standpoints is defined, its rationale is specified, and related later research is examined.

NON-REM AND REM SLEEP

The essential activities of life, those necessary for individual survival as well as those designed for the survival of the next generation, do not occupy the full 24 hours of the day, for most animals. The rest of the time is therefore spare, and may be used by animals for exploratory behavior, playful behavior, or what has been sometimes termed "luxurious behavior." However, at least during some hours of such spare time, for certain animals more and for others less, being idle may have detrimental consequences. For animals that are visually light-adapted, walking during dark hours may be dangerous and even fatal. Less serious but still vital is the problem of energy conservation: Leisure activity should be limited to the amount of energy reserves that might be accumulated during hours of goal-directed behavior. It might be assumed that an innate behavioral tendency (instinct, drive, motive, etc.) has been evolved appropriate to the species' requirements, in order to "keep the animal out of trouble." This tendency usually involves keeping out of sight and keeping still, and may be termed "the innate enforcement immobilization theory of sleep." Such a hypothesis was suggested almost 60 years ago by Hollingworth (1927), long before the different stages of sleep were discovered. During recent decades Meddis (1977, 1983) has been its major proponent, along with Webb (1975, 1979, 1983), who has adopted a more hesitant stance on this position.

This hypothesis rests mainly on negative findings: Many research efforts to disclose the functional properties of sleep as a vital process have brought negative results. Within this general framework, REM sleep does not deserve any particularly important status. Meddis hypothesized that REM sleep is evolutionarily the more ancient type of sleep and that it is less effective, especially as it is not appropriate for homeothermic species such as birds and mammals. He attempted to support his argument with the inappropriateness of REM sleep as a regulator of body temperature in mammals. During REM sleep, the organism does not respond with its regular adjustment mechanisms to thermal stress, panting by nasolabial sweating, nasolabial secretion, peripheral blood flow changes, shivering, and so forth. (Parmeggiani, 1977; Toutain & Ruckebusch, 1972; Walker, Glotzbach, Berger, & Heller, 1977). In response to thermal stress, Parmeggiani, Cianci, Calasso, Zamboni, and Perez (1980) showed that cats sleeping in a cold environment reduced their total sleep time mostly at the *expense* of REM sleep; this was not followed by REM rebound during later sleep in thermoneutral environment, at least not until the amount of prior REM sleep deprivation exceeded about 40 to 50%. Similar findings have also been found in humans. REM sleep was reduced while sleeping in the cold and a 20% reduction of REM sleep over 16 nights did not bring about subsequent rebound (Buguet, Roussel, Watson, & Radomski, 1979). There is not yet any good explanation of why the usual rebound effect does not occur in this situation. Is the REM reduction here the "natural" effect, not imposed by outside-of-the-system forces?

If the evolution of non-REM type of sleep is most advanced in homeothermic animals and may provide for long periods of immobility while regulating their body temperature appropriately, what is the function of REM in these species? Why did it survive, evolutionarily, and why is it interspersed among periods of the more advanced non-REM sleep?

Two answers seem to be appropriate. The first answer rests on the observation that REM sleep episodes very often are finished with brief awakening in several mammalian animals: the rat, hedgehog, rabbit, and rhesus monkey. This phenomenon has not been found in the cat. Humans also do not usually wake often after REM episodes; they are, however, more likely to wake from REM sleep than from non-REM sleep (Langford, Meddis, & Pearson, 1972; Meddis, 1977). This phenomenon of brief awakening at the conclusion of REM episode led Snyder (1966, 1970, 1971) to his sentinel hypothesis of REM sleep, that is, the role of REM sleep is to activate the animal periodically to monitor the environment during the long period of reduced vigilance of the non-REM sleep.

Within the framework of this theory, another possible answer to the questions of why REM sleep survived after the appearance of the supposedly more advanced non-REM sleep, and why REM is interpersed among periods of non-REM sleep, may be found in the suggestions of Walker and Berger (1980) and Horne (1977). These authors suggested that REM sleep, relative to non-REM sleep, contributes to energy conservation through the reduction of metabolism. Each REM episode lasts as much time as the animal is able to undertake before its body temperature might fall below a dangerous level, depending on body size (Meddis, 1983).

According to this theory, because modern human life does not require much of this kind of immobilization, both non-REM and REM sleep will presumably disappear eventually, in the normal course of the evolutionary process. In the meantime, we are left with a need or drive that entails a strong and elaborate mechanism to enforce sleep, even though its original evolutionary purpose has already been abolished. It is a "gentle tyrant" (Webb, 1975). According to this standpoint no real, vital, lasting, detrimental effect (physiological or psychological) is to be found as a consequence of REM sleep deprivation. However, if some evidence does emerge, it might be attributed only to a consequence of a vestigial nonfunctional drive mechanism that evolution has not had time to correct by abolishing it. As this theory stands now, it is hard to refute and, of course, hard to test properly.

REM SLEEP AS A GENERAL AROUSAL MECHANISM

One possible assumption is that the central nervous system requires a regular flow of stimulation for its ongoing functioning, especially during its developing stages. Continuous *low-level* stimulation may be harmful. Thus, REM sleep may serve as a general arousal mechanism for the central nervous system, which operates without the involvement of the organism's peripheral sensory and responsive systems. This may be beneficial in times when actual perception and behavior and highly restricted, in the fetal condition, during regular sleep (whatever the main reason for the development of the sleep itself may be), and in times when the situation calls for the extension of the hours of sleep. This ties the phenomenon of REM sleep with the findings and theory of stimulus deprivation or the restriction of normal stimulation. This is essentially the viewpoint recommended by Ephron and Carrington (1966) and by Roffwarg, Muzio, and Dement (1966).

Several well-known facts fit nicely into this theory. One is the regular interspersion of REM sleep into the continuous non-REM sleep. Other findings congruent with the hypothesis of REM sleep as the general arousal mechanism involve ontogenetic changes in the proportion of REM/non-REM sleep. In all mammalian fetuses the REM sleep ratio is relatively higher, compared with their adults (Jouvet, 1978; Jouvet–Mounier, Astic, & Lacote, 1970). In humans, for example, REM sleep may be noticed as early as at 6 months postconception, before any detection of non-REM sleep. Later in fetal development, it occupies almost 90% of the overall sleep time. In premature infants of 32 to 36 weeks' gestation, REM constitutes 75% of total sleep. This drops sharply to about half of the overall sleep time at birth, and to about 30% at the age of 3 months (Williams, Karacan, & Hursch, 1974).

Moreover, it has been shown that in infancy the amount of REM sleep and quiet wakefulness reciprocate each other (Denenberg & Thomas,

1981), and it is suggested that the latter subsumes the former, both acting to stimulate the CNS. Support for the general arousal hypothesis may be obtained from experiments that indicate that REM deprivation heightens cerebral excitement during subsequent wakefulness in rodents (Dewson, Dement, Wagener, & Nobel, 1967) as well as in humans (Kopell, Zarcone, De La Pena, & Dement, 1972).

A direct test of the effect of REM deprivation on brain size in the early development of rats is related to the idea of REM sleep as an arousal mechanism important in the early development of the central nervous system. In a series of experiments conducted recently by Mirmiran and colleagues (Mirmiran & Uylings, 1983; Mirmiran, Uylings, & Crown, 1983), the previously discovered results of enriched environment and brain size (Bennett, Diamond, Krech, & Rosenzweig, 1964; Campbell & Spear, 1972; Rosenzweig, Mollgaard, & Bennett, 1972) were used. In one experiment, Mirmiran et al. (1983) used daily injections of clonidine to induce REM deprivation in young rats, and well-balanced control groups were used. The effect of enriched environment on brain size was then measured. It was found that the environmental enriched effect upon cortical growth (increase in total brain weight, mainly due to heavier cerebral cortex) was neutralized by the concomitant pharmacological suppression of REM sleep prior to weaning. Presumably REM deprivation counteracted the effectiveness of subsequent environmental enrichment on cortical growth. It seems that both prior and concomitant REM sleep is a necessary condition for the environmental stimulation to have its effect on brain growth.

It seems to us that an interesting and unsuspected corollary may be deduced from the hypothesis of REM sleep as a general arousal mechanism, one that has not been followed up as yet. This is the hypothesis that *total* sleep deprivation in the normal adult may yield quite different, and even less detrimental consequences (at least if not excessively prolonged), compared with REM sleep deprivation alone. After all, REM sleep in the arousal mode is supposed only to free the organism from the "side effects" of non-REM sleep.

REM SLEEP AND BINOCULAR VISION EFFICIENCY

A specific derivative of the hypothesis of REM as an arousal mechanism is Berger's (1969) suggestion that a function of REM sleep is innervation of the oculomotor system, a means of maintaining binocular vision efficiency. This is based on the assumption that non-REM sleep may cause deterioration of depth-perception capacity, owing to lack of stimulation. At first it seems as if there is empirical support for this suggestion. Berger and Scott (1971) demonstrated more accurate depth perception after awakening at the end of REM periods than after awakening at the beginning of REM periods. In an experiment by Lewis, Sloan, and Jones (1978), subjects performed more accurately in tests of binocular depth perception when awakened after REM periods than when awakened before REM periods. The data of Wallach and Karsh's (1963) research in the waking state were seemingly supportive, indicating that 8 hours of monocular occlusion (a patch over one eye) resulted in decreased accuracy on stereoacuity, a finding that they attributed to "disuse" of the occluded eye.

However, more careful series of experiments by Herman, Roffwarg, Rosenmann, and Tauber (1980) showed the inadequacy of this assumption. These authors included in their study both REM deprivation and awake-state visual deprivation, and they measured mainly stereoacuity rather than the complexity of binocular and/or monocular cues in an actual depth situation. They succeeded in replicating the Wallach and Karsh original findings, but it seemed that these were not the results of disuse but rather the results of misuse (Herman, Tauber, and Roffwarg, 1974): Monocular patching in the awake state, which is actually single-eye vision, causes nonsymmetrical activation of visual input to centers regulating disparity detection. On the other hand, limited but still symmetrically represented input disrupts stereoacuity much less. There is some degree of degradation after sleep.

However, the most relevant results of Herman et al. (1980) were those related to REM deprivation. They clearly indicated that a whole night's REM sleep deprivation (by awakenings) is not detrimental to binocular depth perception the next morning. In their tests, they also found that binocular depth perception at the end of REM periods is not significantly different from depth perception at the beginning of REM periods. Moreover, significantly better stereoacuity was found following REM sleep deprivation than following a normal night's sleep!

How are we to reconcile the Herman et al. (1980) study with the Berger and Scott (1971) study? One interesting possibility lies in the differences of the achievement measured: Herman et al. used an apparatus that strictly measured stereopsis, to the exclusion (as far as possible) of the possibility of judgments based upon accurate monocular cues as well as those based upon binocular cues other than stereopsis, whereas Berger and Scott's apparatus did not preclude cues such as size constancy or accommodation. It may be possible, therefore, to assume that REM sleep, by its nature a visualization of the "dream world," contains some central (and peripheral) stimulations similar to awakening depth perception, but does not contain all the visual details included in waking depth perception. Specifically, the "disparity detectors" in the visual cortex are not operating in the dream experiences in a parallel way as in awakening retinal disparity. Accordingly, REM may induce both an improvement in one class of depth cues, namely oculomotor cues, and a simultaneous deterioration of stereoscopic acuity. Much more research is needed, before considering such a hypothesis as tenable.

JOUVET'S "GENETIC PROGRAMMING"

Based on a number of brain lesion experiments performed on cats, Jouvet (1978, 1980) suggested his "genetic programming" hypothesis for REM sleep function. He proposed that REM sleep facilitates the transcription of genetic material associated with innate behavior patterns and with adjusting and modifying these programs in the light of recent experiences and learning. Therefore, chronic REM deprivation, for example, by bilateral brain lesions in the pons area, will inhibit the accomplishment of the appropriate modifications of these genetic programs. Thus, a given behavior pattern found in chronic REM-deprived animals will show a greater between-animal invariability, for example, more stereotypical behavior, in comparison with nondeprived animals.

Vogel suggested a hypothesis similar to Jouvet's. Vogel (1979) argued that REM deprivation elicits fixed-type, stereotypical, and drive-related behavior, which indicates that REM sleep modulates drive-related behavior.

Some experimental findings from outside Jouvet's laboratory, using different kinds of rodents and different REM deprivation techniques, may be cited to support Jouvet's hypothesis. For example, it was found that REM-deprived animals eat during the usual sleeping times (Elomaa & Johansson, 1980a), show more than the usual aggressiveness (Hicks, Moore, Hayes, Phillips, & Hawkins, 1979), and show greater than usual exploratory or locomotor behavior (Hicks & Adams, 1976; Hicks & Moore, 1979; Moore, Hayes, & Hicks, 1979). In humans, it was reported that REM deprivation heightens sexual interest (Zarcone, De La Pena, & Dement, 1974).

The most convincing support for Jouvet's hypothesis comes from Sastre and Jouvet's (1979) observations. These authors made bilateral lesions in cats' brainstems in the nucleus locus coeruleus alfa, which is in the lower part of the pons. This lesion suppresses the muscular atonia, otherwise characteristic of the REM sleep of the cat, and so REM sleep is no longer accompanied by a continuous motoric inhibition. After recovery from the operation, these cats engage frequently, during the otherwise regular REM sleep, in a variety of stereotypical drivelike behaviors, such as "imaginary" predatory attacks, rage, flight, grooming, and exploration. These authors termed such actions "oneiric behavior." It is as if these cats "act out" their dreams, which would otherwise only have been experienced "internally."

Cohen (1979), after having viewed a film of the behavior of these cats, found it compelling and concluded that these cats must be dreaming. Hendricks, Morrison, and Mann (1980) showed that Jouvet and Sastre lesions may lead to a similar release of locomotor activity during wakefulness, not only during REM sleep. They argued therefore that the "oneiric behaviors" cannot be interpreted as an "acting out of dreaming." It seems to us that their results added to the original Sastre and Jouvet findings but did not necessarily disprove the oneiric idea altogether. Such a lesion might possibly disturb and reduce the intensity of REM sleep, in addition to its atonia negation, so that oneiric responses are "pushed" to be expressed not only during REM sleep but also during waking. Indeed, the lesion also disrupts the regularity of the waking behavior. Many investigators continue to assume greater differences than can be shown between waking and sleep mentation (see Hoyt & Singer in first edition).

REM SLEEP AS AN ENHANCING FACTOR
FOR DIVERGENT THINKING

Since the discovery of the REM sleep phenomenon and the initiation of REM deprivation studies, the possibility of relating REM sleep to learning and memory functions has been suggested in several variations. However, it has become clear that a distinction should be made between the suggestion that *prior* REM sleep prepares the organism for subsequent learning and the proposal that *subsequent* REM sleep may have a certain facilitative effect on prior learning. McGrath and Cohen (1977) compiled a detailed evaluative review of both animal and human studies and came to the conclusion that only the latter suggestion could be accepted. We may add here that research since the publication of the McGrath and Cohen paper supports the overall negative evidence of the first suggestion. As to the second suggestion, which implies that learning followed by REM deprivation will result in a decrement in learning, McGrath and Cohen concluded that the evidence tended to be positive, "with qualification." With animals, there were generally positive results; with humans, the results were somewhat equivocal.

From McGrath and Cohen (1977), as well as from a later review by Cohen (1979) and later research findings, it seems that the most promising approach today as to the cognitive function of REM sleep is that suggested by Greenberg and Pearlman (1974), and by Lewin and his colleagues (Lewin, 1980, 1985; Lewin & Glaubman, 1975; Lewin & Gombush, 1973). It is interesting to note that although Greenberg and Pearlman and Lewin and his colleagues employed different terminology and theoretical orientations, their actual proposals seem to be quite similar, as do their empirical results.

Greenberg and Pearlman (1974) emphasized considerations about animal evolution and adaptation. They proposed that REM sleep is not functionally oriented toward the consolidation of the learning of habitual responses, but rather toward the consolidation of learning, which involves the integration of unusual behavior. They drew mainly upon the theoretical approach by Seligman (1970), which posed different degrees of "biological preparedness": For some stimuli–response connections and some ways of behavior toward the environment, organisms are hereditarily prepared, and learning is achieved readily and quickly, with very little amount of practice; for other ways of behavior, for which organisms are less prepared, learning takes place after much practice and recurring experiences. Indeed, for still another class of learning tasks, organisms may actually be hereditarily contraprepared.

Greenberg and Pearlman's suggestion is that REM sleep is necessary for the learning, consolidation, and assimilation of unusual information, in the realm of unprepared and contraprepared ways of behavior. Pearlman reviewed the evidence for this hypothesis both in animal research (Pearlman, 1979) and with humans (Pearlman, 1982). Again, when speaking about learning, whether simple or complex, experimental evidence seems more supportive in the case of animals than with humans.

Lewin, Bergman, Glaubman, Melamed, and Yehuda (1973), on the other hand, spoke of divergent thinking as the major characteristic of REM sleep mentation that is related to human waking mentation. Informally speaking, their notion is based both on the phenomenological aspects of dreaming and on the psychophysiological nature of the REM state. The environmentally uncontrolled imagery and the imaginative nature of the dreaming experience, together with the high arousal of the central nervous system while sensory and motor interaction with the environment is in ebb, provide the rationale for the divergent thinking hypothesis. A more formal rationale for human REM deprivation studies was suggested by Lewin (1980, 1985) within a general classificatory system for cognitive processes. A model of mental space was created by the Cartesian multiplication of the following three dimensions, which are assumed to be independent of each other: (a) media of inner representation (imagery vs. verbal or a specific combination of these two); (b) degree of voluntary control and goal-directedness (going from a free-floating mental state to a high level of control and directionality); (c) degree of adherence to rules (going from imagination, that is, decreased consideration for known physical and logical restrictions, to reality and logically bound sequences of thought or intended action). In this space model, dream experience is located in the areas of: (a) mostly imagery representation; (b) relatively uncontrolled, free-floating mentation; and (c) highly imaginative, frequent violations of rules of reality and logic. It is assumed that underlying psychophysiological and neurochemical processes in the brain that operate during REM sleep create the proper basis for this combination. This combination (imagery × uncontrolled × imagination) is closely akin to the concept of divergent thinking, and it may operate to free the cognitive processing from proceeding in a definite, previously established routine. Thus, it should be detrimental when a solution to a problem is best achieved by previously learned procedure, but should be beneficial whenever a new and fresh outlook is needed, whenever originality and creativity are called for. (See also the discussion in Chapter 15, in which the "general activation-low rate of externally generated information" hypothesis is proposed as one means of accounting for comparable rates of recall frequency counts in REM and in understimulated waking mentation states.)

Even though this specific combination of divergent thinking occurs regularly during REM sleep periods, it may also occur irregularly during waking periods, depending on internal psychological and physiological conditions as well as on external circumstances. On the other hand, slow-wave (delta) sleep periods, that is, stage 4 EEG and most of stage 3, are improper for divergent thinking; stage 2 and part of stage 3 constitute possible though not especially effective periods for divergent thinking, certainly less efficient than some waking states (especially those that are characterized by high and dense alpha EEG waves).

Note that, in the literature of REM deprivation, some attempts have been reported to test the hypothesis that specific waking activities may compensate for REM sleep (i.e., they should lead to less REM rebound). The most direct and complete experiment of this sort available in the literature is that of Cartwright and Monroe (1968). Some "preliminary" studies on this problem were reported by Fiss (1980) and Koulack (1973). However, the accurate characteristics required for such a task in order to compensate for actual REM sleep were not well defined nor were they theoretically specified. Here, for the first time, we may have an elaborate theoretical consideration from which specific operational definitions may be derived.

As related to REM deprivation studies, the foregoing considerations (Lewin, 1980, 1985; Lewin et al., 1973; Lewin & Glaubman, 1975; Lewin & Gombash, 1973) should lead to the following hypotheses: (a) When a person is confronted with problems that call for creativity and originality, subsequent REM deprivation should be detrimental; (b) REM deprivation subsequent to a stable learning situation involving tasks that require strict routine adherence should be beneficial; (c) effects of (a) and (b) would be strongest in an experimental procedure where the task assigned is immediately followed by sleep, and achievement is measured right after awakening. In this way, occasional waking divergent thinking episodes would be minimized.

These hypotheses served as the basis for the Lewin and Glaubman (1975) experiment. Before going to bed, subjects were assigned 4 tasks on which testing took place the following morning shortly after awakening. Tasks were carefully selected, ranging from those closely adhering to facts through those "going beyond the information given" (Bruner, 1957): serial memory, clustering memory, word fluency, and Guilford's Utility Test

(Guilford, 1967). Scoring of this test provides a good evaluation of the amount of divergent thinking, flexibility, originality, and creativity. Equivalent forms of each test were employed on the REM deprivation night and the control night; to overcome the problem of individual differences, subjects served as their own controls. Findings showed marked REM deprivation effects on both the extreme types of tests: REM deprivation lowered creativity, but at the same time heightened rote memory (i.e., REM sleep lowered rote memory of tasks memorized just before going to sleep). The two intermediate tasks—clustering memory (which requires less adherence to original serial order, as in learning) and word fluency—were not affected by REM deprivation.

Even though Lewin and Glaubman's (1975) experiment was carefully balanced, one drawback still remained: In order to equate as accurately as possible the control nights to the experimental nights in number of awakenings and length of time being awakened each period within the same limits for total amount of sleep, the REM deprivation night in each subject always preceded the control night, that is, order effect was not balanced. However, in 1978, the original Lewin and Glaubman experiment was both replicated and extended, with similar experimental conclusions, by Glaubman et al. (1978). In this experiment, in addition to balancing for order effect, new cognitive tasks were employed and subjects were sampled from different age groups. These changes from and extensions of the original experiment contributed to the validation of the conceptual interpretation of the results (Sidowski, 1966).

Another line of thinking seems lately to bring support to the divergent thinking hypothesis. It starts with an information-processing model for the function of REM sleep, which had been suggested as early as 1969 (Breger, 1969; Dewan, 1969, 1970). Dreams in this model serve as a sort of nightly house-cleaning period during which the useless information accumulated during the previous day or days is cleared up to make room for new input while that worth saving is "consolidated" (Fishbein, 1969; Fishbein & Gutwein, 1977). However, as mentioned earlier, this kind of thinking did not gain much empirical support from experiments with humans. However, Crick and Mitchison (1983) proposed ideas that converge on both the Lewin et al. (1973) and the Greenberg and Pearlman (1974) hypotheses, although framed in physiological terms and computer analogue language. They proposed that the function of dream sleep is to remove certain undesired modes of interaction in the work of cells in the cerebral cortex. It was suggested that in viviparous mammals the cortical system is subjected to unwanted or "parasitic" modes of behavior which arise as the system is disturbed either by the growth of the brain or by the modifications produced by experience. Such modes are detected and suppressed by a special mechanism that operates during REM sleep and has the character of an active process that is opposite to learning.

Support for this kind of thinking is suggested by a computer simulation study which was conducted by Hopfield, Feinstein, and Palmer (1983), using a network of 30 to 1,000 "neurons"; the computer had an associative memory that allowed it to learn and store many memories. In this process, spurious memories were not only created, but they could also be evoked. Applying an unlearning process enhances the performance of the network in accessing real memories and in minimizing spurious ones. This finding seems to us similar to the assumption that creativity is related to the freeing of mental activities from "functional fixedness" (Duncker, 1945), from fixed *Einstellungen* (Luchins, 1942), producing the same effect as divergent thinking (Lewin, 1980). It is encouraging as a first step toward an accurate evaluation of the logic of such hitherto seemingly loose ideas.

REM SLEEP AS COMPENSATION FOR REAL SEARCH ACTIVITY

A hypothesis that is completely different from the "divergent thinking" and the "assimilation of the unprepared" hypothesis was suggested by Rotenberg and his colleagues (Rotenberg, 1984; Rotenberg & Arshavsky, 1979; Rotenberg & Biniaurishvili, 1973) it is called the search activity hypothesis. These authors suggested the necessity of distinguishing between two types of behavioral reactions to emotional stress. One is a search activity, "directed at changing or supporting (contrary to the perturbing effect) the situation, or changing the attitude to the situation in the absence of a definite forecast concerning the result of such activity." The second type of behavior is the renunciation of search, which assumes the form of passive avoidance ("freezing") with distinct signs of fear and anxious tension or a reaction resembling "imagery death" in a situation which cannot satisfy the subject and the overcoming of which requires search activity. These authors looked at REM sleep as a consequence of the renunciation of search, as a compensation (in imagination) for the lack of search activity in the real, waking state. Search activity is accompanied by reduction in REM sleep time.

Rotenberg and his colleagues brought support to their hypothesis from their own research in both animals and humans, and they made an effort to interpret results in the literature in this light. Individual differences in reaction to stress in REM time, whether an increase or a decrease in REM, were interpreted as individual differences in an effort to cope or to resign in the face of difficulty. On the other hand, they were ready to attribute adaptive function to REM sleep in humans. This seemingly paradoxical assumption was suggested by attributing the adaptivity of REM sleep to its "activation of primary, imaginative thinking in the dreams." Unusual situations call for (momentarily, at least) the renunciation of search activity, which "activates the REM sleep-dream mechanisms which compensate for this unproductive passive-defense reaction." The extent to which this increase in REM will bring about adaptive waking behavior depends on the type of problem as well as on "the extent to which the REM sleep-dream system performs (efficiently) its compensatory function."

This assumption may seem self-contradictory to some readers, but it reflects what are sometimes the known facts about REM. This standpoint may be one way to reconcile the supposedly beneficial effect of REM *sleep* in creativity tasks with the beneficial effect of REM *deprivation* in the case of depression.

REM DEPRIVATION AND ENDOGENOUS DEPRESSION

When REM sleep was discovered, most, if not all, REM deprivation studies started with the idea of looking at some detrimental effect that such experimental manipulation might cause. Gradually, however, such expectations met with serious disappointments. Although some researchers had data suggesting that REM deprivation might have some limited detrimental effect (Lewin & Glaubman, 1975), this new hypothesis was not readily accepted. With respect to the area of psychopathology, some early researchers were very cautious about subjecting patients to REM deprivation situations lest real harm be caused. Early reports showing lack of REM rebound after REM deprivation of chronic schizophrenics (Feinberg, 1969; Mendelson, Gillin, & Wyatt, 1977; Zarcone et al., 1968), came as a surprise.

Real surprise, however, has been created by the finding that REM deprivation has a beneficial therapeutic effect in the psychologically depressed (Vogel, 1979). This finding has been substantiated, mainly in the area of endogenous depression (Elsenga & Van den Hoofdakker, 1982/1983; Fahndrich, 1982; Vogel, 1979, 1983; Vogel, Vogel, McAbee, & Thurmond, 1980), but also with schizophrenic depressed patients (Fahndrich, 1982). Moreover, there are good reasons to believe that the effect of the various antidepressant drugs is via a mechanism of causing REM sleep deprivation (Vogel, 1983). Similar therapeutic effect may be gained by awakening REM deprivation and by drugs; the efficacy of antidepressant activity, across drugs, is directly related to capacity of drugs to produce large and sustained reductions of REM sleep. Endogenous depressives who do not improve after treatment by REM deprivation do not improve by drug therapy, especially by tricyclic antidepressants, for example, amitriptyline. Fahndrich (1983) experimented with 60 depressed patients, first treated with sleep deprivation and afterward with clomipramine or maprotiline, and found a significant correlation between positive effect of sleep deprivation and response to clomipramine, and negative effect of sleep deprivation and response to maprotiline. If these results can be replicated, they carry implications for depressive therapy: Sleep deprivation and/or a serotonergic antidepressant agent is the proper treatment for some patients, but a nonadrenergic agent may be more appropriate for others. Even though this research used total sleep deprivation, it will be argued later that the effect of total sleep deprivation may be indirectly caused mainly by the loss of REM sleep.

Gillin (1983) reviewed more than 70 research reports relating to deliberate sleep-waking manipulations that presumably have antidepressant effects. These research reports may be classified into five types:

1. Total sleep deprivation;
2. Partial sleep deprivation during the first part of the night;
3. Partial sleep deprivation during the second part of the night;
4. Intervention during a phase prior to sleep periods; and
5. REM innervation.

The effects of total sleep deprivation are the least documented: Of 852 depressed patients studied, 57.9% improved following treatment of total sleep deprivation. Partial sleep deprivation during the second half of the night seems to be as good as total sleep deprivation, and better tolerated. The effect of shifting the pattern of the sleep–wake cycle (going to bed earlier and arising earlier) is less well documented but seems to have a positive effect, even though the actual time in bed is not reduced. The effect of REM deprivation is slower than that of total sleep deprivation, but it has the most lasting clinical value of all the forms. From the theoretical standpoint, it may well be claimed that all other manipulations of the sleep–wake cycle produce their effects by indirectly causing REM deprivation: Total sleep deprivation obviously eliminates REM; the second half of sleep has much more REM than the first half; and going to bed earlier and arising earlier excludes much of REM sleep, at least until many nights later when the patient might adapt (see also Rudolf, Schilgen, & Tolle, 1977; Wehr, Wirz–Justice, Goodwin, Duncan, & Gillin, 1979; Weitzman, 1981).

The practical problem of which therapeutic procedure to choose has, of course, other considerations. Elsenga and Van den Hoofdakker (1982/1983), for example, investigated the differential efficacy in the treatment of endogenous depressives of an antidepressant drug—clomipramine (CL)—alone, compared with CL in combination with sleep deprivation. In a third group, placebos were combined with sleep deprivation. Each treatment group contained 10 hospitalized patients. Evaluation included self, blind, and nurses' ratings of anxiety and depression, taken twice daily during the 15 experimental days, and the Hamilton Rating Scale for Depression, which was administered on the first day of the experiment and after 1 and 2 weeks of treatment. The combination of CL with sleep deprivation seemed to be the most effective, although toward the end of the second week the difference between such combinations and CL alone seemed to decline and eventually disappeared. This experiment used total sleep deprivation (2 nights per week) and it might be hypothesized that the combination with CL induced somewhat more and better overall REM deprivation.

Closely related to the therapeutic effect of REM deprivation in depression is still another fact: It seems that REM latency, that is, the time between going to sleep and the first subsequent appearance of REM sleep, is shorter in depressive patients. Berger, Lund, Bronish, and von Zerseen (1983) measured REM latency in 8 healthy subjects and 45 patients with major depressive disorders, subdivided into endogenous, neurotic, and unclassified groups. Measurements were taken under baseline conditions and after administration of physostigmine. Subjects slept in the laboratory for 5 consecutive nights. In depressed subjects, REM latency during baseline nights was significantly shorter than in controls. This short REM latency was similar for all depressed patients. Physostigmine infusion caused a significant shortening of REM latency in comparison with baseline conditions in control subjects, but not in the depressives, who were instead awakened by the infusion. Again, no difference was found in this respect among the three subdivisions of the depressives. From this finding, it may be concluded that depressives on the whole have a stronger "need" for REM sleep, and that their REM "need" strength approaches the limit. From the REM deprivation studies mentioned earlier, it seems that this strong need is concomitant with the depressive state and that eliminating one of these produces change in the other.

Short REM latency is related to depressive moods not only in severely disturbed patients, but also in those within the "normal" range, as found by Cartwright (1984), who monitored for 6 nights the sleep patterns of 29 women undergoing divorce. The more traditional women were more depressed and had shorter REM latencies. Depression was also related to an irregular eye movement density sequence throughout the night.

How are we to integrate all these facts of the relationship between REM and depression with the other facts that show adjustment function to REM, limited and restricted as it may be?

One answer to this question may be to relate the beneficial therapeutic effect of REM deprivation to another set of facts, found in research mainly with rodents, that points to heightened motivation as a result of REM deprivation. Research shows that REM deprivation diminishes fear in rats (Hicks & Moore, 1979) and enhances drive-motivated behavior, such as intracranial self-stimulation (Cohen, Edelman, & Brown, 1972; Steiner & Ellman, 1972; but see contrary findings by Portell–Cortes, Nicolovius, & Bernal, 1983; negative results were also reported in the study of Van Luijtelaar, Kaizer, & Coenen, 1982), eating behavior (Elomaa & Johansson, 1980a), aggressiveness (Hicks et al., 1979; Modern, Conner, Mitchell, Dement, & Levine, 1968; Mollenhour, Voorhees, & Davis, 1977; Sloan, 1972), and exploratory or locomotor behavior (Albert, Cicala, & Siegel, 1970; Elomaa & Johansson, 1980b;

Hicks & Adams, 1976; Hicks & Moore, 1979; Moore, Hayes, & Hicks, 1979). In short, these are indications that REM deprivation enhances drive-related behavior. If depression may be viewed as apathy with regard to normal drive and motivation, then REM deprivation in these patients may restore their normal level of motivation and drive strength, thus bringing their behavior to the normal level.

However, the foregoing is by no means the only answer to the theoretical question of REM and depression. In the previously reviewed Rotenberg hypothesis, REM sleep, especially in excess, acts as a compensation for real search activity. REM deprivation may force the organism, animal as well as human being, back to real life.

Another line of reasoning was suggested by Greenberg, Pearlman, Schwartz, and Grossman (1982). On the basis of their preliminary exploration as well as on theoretical considerations, these writers suggested that REM sleep acts to connect present with past emotionally meaningful portions of a person's memory store; REM deprivation, therefore, produces disconnection between such experiences. For depressed patients, this can positively affect their behavior. Indeed, the relation of REM sleep as enhancing negatively affected thought and REM deprivation as enhancing positively affected thought was found in other studies, for example, Cartwright (1982), Glaubman et al. (1978). This may be related to Beck's (1967) cognitive theory of depression as well as to the theories of Abramson, Seligman, and Teasdale (1978) and Seligman (1975).

The last suggestion to be discussed here is based on the idea that depression is concomitant with severe disturbance in the sleep cycle, and that REM deprivation may restore the proper balance in such sleep disturbance. There is evidence to suggest that the whole sleep process is disordered and disturbed in depressive patients, and it may even be one of the major causal factors in depression. The main features of such disturbances are: (a) decreased slow wave, or quiet-sleep activity (i.e., delta phases, stages 3 and 4 sleep); (b) reduced REM latency; (c) an altered REM sleep activity distribution; and (d) frequent complaints of insomnia and daytime sleepiness (Borbily & Wirz–Justice, 1981; Kupfer, Spiker, Coble, & Shaw, 1978; Kupfer, 1984; Vogel et al., 1980).

Vogel et al. (1980) suggested that the depressive abnormalities represent a damaged, weakening sleep cycle "oscillator" and its correlate, a circadian rhythm disturbance, and that REM sleep deprivation reduces depression to the extent that it stimulates the oscillator and corrects one manifestation of the rhythm disturbance. On the other hand, Borbily (1983) and Kupfer (1984) suggested a two-process model of sleep regulation: a sleep-dependent process (process S) which is mainly reflected by EEG slow-wave activity, and a sleep-independent circadian process (process C). Kupfer applied an automated REM and delta analysis, which had allowed the precise testing of this two-process model. He also analyzed 41 depressed patients, and came to the conclusion that a weakened process S, the sleep-dependent process, is the major disturbance in depressiveness. It is manifested as a deficiency in slow-wave density and a shifting of REM sleep. The severity of such disturbance in baseline measure also predicted the amount of improvement after treatment with amitriptyline, that is, the increase in slow-wave sleep distribution and the reorganization of REM sleep activity. It was also found that such changes consolidated the REM sleep periods during the night, thereby allowing improved dream recall, which has been considered an early sign of clinical improvement in depression.

On the whole, the psychopathological research in REM deprivation and its therapeutic effect represents a challenge for sleep, dreaming, and REM deprivation theory, and carries the promise of enrichment of such theory.

PART **5**

CLINICAL PHENOMENA IN RELATION TO SLEEP MENTATION

13

Sleeptalking

ARTHUR M. ARKIN
City College of the City University of New York

In this chapter I am concerned chiefly with the scientific literature on somniloquy which has come to my attention or has been published since my first review (Arkin, 1966). Readers interested in details of the descriptive psychiatry of sleeptalking and in the history of related scientific psychoanalytic and philosophic commentary are referred to this earlier paper.

Sleeptalking (somniloquy) is defined as the utterance of speech or other psychologically meaningful sound in association with sleep, without simultaneous subjective critical awareness of the event.

HOW COMMON IS SLEEPTALKING?

It is generally agreed that sleep speech is more frequent than is appreciated, largely because potential observers are usually asleep when episodes take place (Arkin, 1966; Arkin, Toth, Baker, & Hastey, 1970a), and the sleeptalkers themselves tend to have no memory of the event. The most recent known attempt to estimate the incidence of somniloquy was made by Gahagan (1936), who asked 228 male and 331 female college students to fill out an extensive 23-item questionnaire pertaining to such sleep characteristics as dreams, recurrent dreams, sleepwalking, sleeptalking, and the like. Of this group, 65 and 57% of the females and males, respectively, reported a history of sleeptalking (combined percentage 61%). Of those so reporting, 176 (51% of erstwhile sleeptalkers) stated that sleeptalking had persisted until the time of the survey. Gahagan believed that the elusiveness of the phenomenon makes any figure, based on self-report, lower than the real incidence. For this reason Gahagan (1936) concluded that a "history of sleeptalking should be considered normative, i.e. modal" (p. 234).

In our own laboratory investigations (Arkin et al., 1970a), it was usually an easy matter to obtain experimental subjects volunteering a current sleeptalking history. Our pool of paid subjects consisted of 17 females and 26 males. Two were high school students, 1 was a medical technician, and 1 was a professional subject in the teaching of medical hypnosis, and the remaining 39 were college students or recent graduates. With a few exceptions, our subjects volunteered in response to advertisements for sleeptalkers, posted at the placement bureaus of several colleges in New York City.

Baseline records of undisturbed nights' sleep were recorded with 13 subjects. This yielded a total of 206 speeches uttered during 53 such nights (mean = 3.9 speeches per night). Ten subjects spoke 1 or more words at least once, one merely moaned, groaned, and emitted other types of sounds, and the remainder failed to vocalize in any significant manner.

In an independent study, MacNeilage (1971) found that of 5 subjects who volunteered a history of sleeptalking 4 somniloquized at least once in 6 nights, and uttered a total of 28 speeches and 54 nonlinguistic vocalizations in the same period.

ARE SPECIFIC ORGANISMIC FACTORS ASSOCIATED WITH SLEEPTALKING PROPENSITIES?

More than 70 paid adult volunteer subjects who alleged that they had spoken in their sleep at some time in their lives were interviewed. It was our impression that sleeptalking per se was not associated with any specific psychiatric syndrome. The symptom occurred in a wide range of personalities, namely people with borderline schizophrenia, psychoneuroses, and character neuroses of various types, overt homosexuality, and those with insignificant or no easily detectable psychopathology. Sleeptalking is apparently so widespread that it was difficult to locate individuals in a college population who have *never* been told by someone, at least once in their lives, that they had talked in their sleep. Comparison of the sleeptalkers with a nonsleeptalking control group from the same college populations (by means of a life-history questionnaire and interview) revealed no psychodynamic or genetic patterns typical of sleeptalkers in contrast to the nonsleeptalkers. This conclusion found considerable support from an independent study of Bone et al. (1973), in which 27 males and 39 female sleeptalking college students were compared to 12 male and 19 female nonsleeptalkers by means of a test of 16 personality factors. Differences were revealed for only two factors: female sleeptalkers scored higher on radicalism ($t = 2.95$; $p = .01$); and male sleeptalkers scored lower on superego strength ($t = 2.08$; $p = .05$). These results seem more or less consistent with our earlier conclusion that sleeptalkers do not differ from nonsleeptalkers in any gross, striking manner; and that the two groups are more similar than different (Arkin, 1966). However, MacNeilage (1971), MacNeilage, Cohen, and MacNeilage (1972), and MacNeilage and MacNeilage (1973) found a significant association on questionnaire responses between subjects' estimates of their sleeptalking propensities and their estimates of their dream recall. That is, while subjects with high recall of dreams may or may not sleeptalk, subjects who recall few dreams are much less likely to be sleeptalkers (MacNeilage, 1971).

Finally, several investigators have reported that subjects with somnambulism and night terrors also tend to talk in their sleep (Fisher, Kahn, Edwards, & Davis, 1973a; Gastaut & Broughton, 1965; Kahn, Fisher, Edwards, & Davis, 1973; Kales & Jacobson, 1967).

Thus, the future possibility of finding subtle psychological differences between sleeptalkers and "silent sleepers" cannot be excluded.

DO AVAILABLE LABORATORY STUDIES THROW ANY LIGHT ON THE ISSUE OF SPECIFIC PHYSIOLOGICAL FACTORS?

MacNeilage (1971) selected 5 subjects who were good dream recallers and who had claimed that they talked in their sleep at least occasionally. In the laboratory, over a period of 6 nights, 3 subjects talked in their sleep on 27 occasions, 1 talked only once, and 1 not at all over the same period. (The latter 2 were grouped as nonsleeptalkers.) The speech musculature of the sleeptalkers displayed much more frequent and intense occasions of electromyographic activity through the night (although only a small proportion of such occurrences was associated with actual vocalization).

Considering the information available from all known studies, the importance of physiologic factors is strongly indicated by the striking individual differences among subjects, with respect to quantity of sleep speech, the sleep stages with which the somniloquy tends to be associated, and the content and degree of linguistic correctness of the speeches. The details of these differences become apparent as we proceed. However, samples are too small and the variability of the phenomena too large to permit definitive statements to be made as to degrees of association between possible specific organismic factors and the above parameters.

WHAT ARE THE ELECTROGRAPHIC CONCOMITANTS OF SOMNILOQUY?

In general, the electrographic characteristics of most sleep speech occurrences are consistent with those criteria described for "movement arousal" episodes (regardless of sleep stage) by Rechtschaffen and Kales (1968; Arkin et al., 1970c; Cohen, Shapiro, Goodenough, & Saunders, 1965; Gastaut & Broughton, 1965; Kamiya, 1961; MacNeilage, 1971; Rechtschaffen, Goodenough, & Shapiro, 1962; Szabo & Waitsuk, 1971; Tani, Yoshii, Yoshino, & Kobayashi, 1966). This does not make the two identical, however. For example, the question is still unanswered as to why some such movement arousals are accompanied by vocalization and others are not. Also, there is great variability in electrographic concomitants of sleep-speech episodes both within and across subjects. Because of this variability, meaningful quantitive comparison is difficult and most commentary in the literature, with a few minor exceptions (Cohen et al., 1965; MacNeilage, 1971; Tani et al., 1966), describes what seems typical on the basis of inspection of large numbers of records rather than precise measurements.

WHAT ARE THE RELATIONSHIPS BETWEEN SOMNILOQUY EPISODES AND THE VARIOUS STAGES OF SLEEP DURING WHICH THEY ARE PRONE TO OCCUR?

There is general agreement that most sleeptalking occurs in association with stage NREM sleep although a definite, albeit smaller, proportion of episodes occur in association with stage REM.

Furthermore, I wish to emphasize again that among our own subjects, individual differences were marked; that is, some were loquacious, others somewhat reticent; some spoke entirely in association with NREM sleep, others both in association with NREM and stage REM (our most prolific sleeptalker spoke predominantly in association with stage REM). Rechtschaffen et al. (1962) also noted that stage REM episodes occurred with subjects who also produced NREM incidents. The results of reports in literature are presented in Table 13.1.

The data of Tani et al. (1966) and our own (Arkin et al., 1970a) in the table are the results from baseline nights of undisturbed sleep. The experimental conditions for the entire populations of the other studies were heterogeneous, including baseline nights, nights with experimental awakenings and possibly other types of unspecified manipulations.

In summary, about 80% or more of sleep-utterance episodes are associated with NREM sleep and 20% or less with stage REM.

TABLE 13.1. SOMNILOQUY IN ASSOCIATION WITH SLEEP STAGES

Study	Number of Subjects	Total Number of Episodes	Percentage by Sleep Stage (rounded off)	
			NREM	REM
Kamiya (1961)	Not specified	98	88	12
Szabo et al. (1971)	10	Not specified	100	0
Gastaut and Broughton (1965)	Not specified	Not specified	92	8
			By sleep stages	
			1 = 33	
			2 = 33	
			3 = 17	
			4 = 9	
Rechtschaffen et al. (1962)[a]	28	84	92	8
			1 = 0	
			2 = 63	
			3–4 = 29	
Rechtschaffen et al. (1967)[a]	28	28	86	14
			1 = 0	
			2 = 43	
			3–4 = 43	
Tani et al. (1966)	3	8	0	100
MacNeilage (1971)	4	28	82	18
			1 = 11	
			2 = 68	
			3 = 3	
Arkin et al. (1970a)[b]	10	206	52	48
			1 = 4	
			2 = 19	
			3 = 13	
			4 = 16	
Arkin et al. (1970a)[b]	9	105	81	19
			1 = 1	
			2 = 27	
			3 = 26	
			4 = 27	

[a]Because of the possibility that the distribution of sleep speech episodes among the various sleep stages was biased by data from a minority of the subjects, Rechtschaffen et al. (1962) recalculated their results on the "basis of one incident selected at random from each subject. This calculation reduced the number of incidents to 28, of which 4 (14%) were in REM periods, 12 (43%) were in Stage 2, and 12 (43%) were in Stages 3 and 4 [p. 420]."

In attempting to arrive at a comparable value of the central tendencies of the data from our own subjects (Arkin et al. 1970a), we determined the average percentage (*across* subjects) of sleep speech episodes in each sleep stage (not tabulated). The results were as follows: NREM Stage 1, .9%; Stage 2, 21.5%; Stage 3, 21.5%; and Stage 4, 28.5%; total NREM 72.3%; Stage REM, 27.7%. Omitting the exceptionally prolific Stage REM sleeptalker mentioned above yielded NREM Stage 1, 0.1%; Stage 2, 22.5%; Stage 3, 23.9%; and Stage 4, 31.4%; total NREM, 77.9%; Stage REM, 22.1%.

[b]The first entry with 10 subjects contains an unrepresentative high percentage of Stage REM-associated sleep speech. This "disproportion" is the result of our most voluble sleep-talker who contributed 101 speeches to our total sample of sleep speeches collected under conditions of baseline undisturbed sleep. The subject spoke mostly in association with Stage REM and uttered 79 of our 99 Stage REM speeches. The second entry with 9 subjects omits the contribution of this unusual subject and the results more closely resemble those of the other studies.

DOES SOMNILOQUY TEND TO OCCUR AT CERTAIN TIMES OF THE NIGHT AND/OR IN ASSOCIATION WITH SPECIFIC PORTIONS OF THE SLEEP CYCLE?

Rechtschaffen et al. (1962) concluded that "the chance sleep-talking would occur during any one particular hour of sleep was about as great as the chance that it would occur during any other hour" (p. 421), and that "NREM" sleeptalking never initiated REM periods" (p. 421). In attempting to evaluate our observations (Arkin et al., 1970a) with regard to the same question, the entire nightly sleep period and each REM period and NREM period of the night were each divided into tenths and the occurrences of all sleep speech in each such time interval were tabulated for each baseline record for all subjects on whom baseline sleep was recorded. This procedure failed to disclose any well-marked tendencies and these results were, therefore, consistent with those of Rechtschaffen et al. (1962). There was a suggestion, however, of slight increases in frequency during the second 10th and the eighth 10th of the entire sleep period and also the last 10th of each NREM and REM period. Moreover, we observed 16 instances of sleep speech and 12 additional nonspeech vocalizations in NREM sleep just preceding stage REM sleep, many of them occurring at or immediately before REM sleep onset. Thus, although one cannot say that NREM speech "initiated" the REM sleep in any causal sense, it is clear that the above temporal sequence is observable.

The lack of any tendency of sleep-speech episodes to cluster in some specific portion of the night provides an interesting contrast with "night terrors," which do indeed tend to occur more frequently during the first two hours of sleep (Fisher et al., 1973a). Thus, two syndromes both characterized by sleep-associated utterances nevertheless display different temporal patterning.

WHAT IS THE DEGREE OF CONCORDANCE BETWEEN THE CONTENTS OF SLEEP SPEECH AND THE MENTATION RECALLED BY THE SUBJECT UPON BEING AWAKENED IMMEDIATELY AFTER THE UTTERANCE? AND HOW IS THIS RELATED TO THE SLEEP STAGE AND TIME OF NIGHT IN ASSOCIATION WITH WHICH THE UTTERANCE OCCURRED?

Kamiya (1961) reported that a comparison of sleep-speech content and mentation elicited upon waking the subject afterward failed to disclose any obvious relationship. The data, however, were too meager to support definite conclusions.

Rechtschaffen et al. (1962), in a more extensive work, mentioned that of two awakenings following stage REM-associated speech, the content of one mentation report bore an unambiguous relationship to the sleep speech (classified as first-order concordance below). In addition, 9 of 12 (75%) awakenings following stage NREM-associated speech resulted in the recall of at least some cognitive content which the subject believed had occurred just prior to the awakening. In 7 of these 9 NREM awakenings (58.3%), a relationship between the content of the mentation report and the sleep speech could be inferred (presumably classifiable as either first or second order concordance below). The remaining 2 sleep speech-mentation report pairs (16.7%) seemed devoid of concordance.

In their study of episodic phenomena during sleep, Gastaut and Broughton (1965) agreed with Rechtschaffen et al. (1962) that the content of several of their observed REM sleep speeches "related to dreaming." By contrast, however, Gastaut and Broughton (1965) associated NREM speeches with a "lack of recalled dreaming," and concluded that the speeches "are not exteriorized symptoms of true oneiric activity" (p. 208). Furthermore, they expressed a belief that NREM sleep speech is "liberated from low level continuous mental life during sleep" or else stems from "simple perceptual confusion during abrupt awakening" (p. 208).

Neither Kamiya (1961) nor Gastaut and Broughton (1965) mentioned the number of sleep-speech-mentation report pairs on which they based their conclusions.

Arkin (1967) and Arkin et al. (1970b) published their findings based on 166 sleep speech-mentation report pairs uttered by 28 paid chronic sleeptalking subjects in the laboratory. The content of each sleep speech was compared to its associated wakeful mentation report with regard to similarities and differences in *manifest* content alone. Each such associated pair was scored as showing:

1. *First-order concordance* when they possessed in common one or more words, phrases, or other clearly identifying feature, e.g. REM-sleep speech, ". . . telling her how I can tell . . . that really likes"; associated mentation report, "I was thinking how I can tell philosopher better than the other—how much more I liked them," and so on;

2. *Second-order concordance* when they possessed in common some specific feature of mental content or subject matter but did not share identical words, phrases, and so on, e.g. stage 3 sleep speech, "No good as a dry dock"; associated mentation report, "This . . . one passage where it says . . . the hull of a ship, single mast, single boom for a cutway sail," and so on;

3. *Third-order concordance* when the only element of concordance between the sleep speech and mentation report was the latter's containing a reference to someone (usually the subject) vocalizing. Thus a postutterance mentation report describing someone as "talking,"

"saying," "asking," and so on was scored separately as third-order concordance if recall of an event involved vocalization without additional specific commonalities, that is, if criteria for second- or first-order concordances were not fulfilled;

4. *No discernible concordance* when concordance was not discernible on the basis of the manifest content of both speech and report, despite mentation having been recalled, and criteria for third-order concordance were not fulfilled.

5. *No mentation recalled.*

The most relevant results are presented in Table 13.2.

For the population examined in Table 13.2 one may conclude (disregarding stage 1 NREM pairs because of their small number) the following:

1. Sleep utterance-mentation-report concordance tends to be greatest for stage REM, least for stage 3 to 4 and intermediate for stage 2.

2. Recall of mentation after sleep utterance is most likely after stage REM, least for stage 3 to 4 and intermediate for stage 2.

3. No discernible concordance between sleep utterance and recalled mentation is most likely with stage 3 to 4, least with stage REM and intermediate with stage 2.

Comparison with the results reported by Rechtschaffen et al. (1962) shows that in our data a somewhat smaller proportion of concordance and a higher proportion of no recall were found in NREM pairs. It should be noted, however, that only 12 NREM awakenings were performed by them and the differences could be related to differences in size of sample. Their findings on REM sleep speech are consistent with ours but their data contained only 2 stage REM pairs. The REM sleep-speech findings reported by Gastaut and Broughton (1965) are likewise consistent with ours, but they did not mention the number of speech-report pairs in their paper.

With regard to the speech associated with night terrors arising in association with stage 4, Gastaut and Broughton (1965) were impressed by the nearly complete tendency for amnesia during full wakefulness for the mental content associated with the episode. However, some instances were described which might be included in our categories of first and second order concordance, but no differential proportions were mentioned. By contrast, our data contain a sizable number of instances of recall as well as concordance. This may be explained on the basis that our sample contained many instances of stage 4-associated sleep speeches which were bland in quality and apparently not infused with anxiety—a type of nocturnal episode which is quite different from a night terror. This indicates the importance of stressing once more that sleep speech is not a unitary

TABLE 13.2. SLEEP UTTERANCE: MENTATION REPORT-PAIR CONCORDANCE IN RELATION TO SLEEP STAGE

Sleep Stage	Total Number of Utterances	Order of Concordance[a]				None Discerned	No Recall
		First	Second	Third	Combined		
REM	24	8 (33.3)	5 (20.8)	6 (25.0)	19 (79.2)	4 (16.7)	1 (4.2)
2	85	15 (17.6)	7 (8.2)	17 (20.0)	39 (45.8)	28 (32.9)	18 (21.2)
3–4	52	5 (9.6)	4 (7.7)	2 (3.8)	11 (21.1)	21 (40.4)	20 (38.5)
1 NREM	5	3 (60.0)	1 (20.0)	0.0	4 (80.0)	0.0	1 (20.0)

[a]Percentage of total utterances in parentheses.

phenomenon but rather one in which important subject differences exist as well as differences within the same subject from one sleep speech to the next, depending on a number of factors. This view is further borne out by a recent study of Fisher et al. (1974), presenting findings contrasting to those of Gastaut and Broughton (1965). In their study with 11 subjects, 58% of night-terror arousals were followed by recall of mentation described as occurring prior to full achievement of subjective wakefulness, after termination of the attack. In addition, many striking instances of first- and second-order concordance were observed between "night-terror speech" and the following mentation report. In conformity with our own results, such concordance was more likely in episodes with milder levels of arousal (Arkin et al., 1970b, 1972).

Finally, MacNeilage (1971) observed only one instance of a direct relationship (first-order concordance) between a sleep speech and a mentation report in a population of 16 pairs. This speech was associated with stage "Alpha," considered by MacNeilage to be a "transitional" phase between sleep and wakefulness. In addition, she found that 44% of mentation reports following sleep speech contained verbal content (third-order concordance?), most of her sample occurring in association with stage 2.

WHAT ARE THE CHARACTERISTICS OF THE SLEEP UTTERANCES THEMSELVES?

It is not possible to give a brief description of sleep utterances because they possess almost as much variability as those of wakefulness (Arkin, 1967). Although the majority of sleep speeches contain at least a few words, some consist of only one, such as "good," "no," "okay," "yes," or "Mm-*hm*," others are of paragraph length, occasionally in excess of one hundred words. Most speeches last a few seconds or less, but longer ones may continue for a minute or more. The range of clarity extends from unintelligible mumbles to crystal-clear words. The belief is widespread that most sleep speech is indistinct. We have been repeatedly surprised, however, by utterances which, unclear when heard over the intercom, turned out to contain some clear *sotto voce* or whispered speech on the tape recording. Often, speeches contain silent pauses, in which case the context suggests sleep dialogues with hallucinated partners, sometimes resembling one side of a telephone conversation. Another frequent occurrence is sudden interruption of a speech in the middle, followed by sustained silence or an apparently meaningless mumbled petering out. The hearer is left with a feeling that a thought has been fragmented or left incomplete.

Of major interest are the structural features of sleep speech. Evaluation of these aspects were perforce based upon fragments of varying completeness.

When associated with REM sleep, they were somewhat more likely to be correct in syntax, inflection, and word structure. Almost all cases of marked abnormality were associated with NREM sleep and could be arranged on a continuum from no or mild disturbance to sheer gibberish, in which clang associations and recurrent utterances were prominent with occasional "neologisms." The latter especially occurred in association with stage 3 to 4 in the first half of the night, and often had an explosive quality with rapid emission of words. It is particularly the sleep speeches with degrees of disorganization which bear striking resemblances to aphasic utterances and, in a sense, may provide a physiological model of aphasia (Arkin & Brown, 1972).

Turning to the content of sleep speech, one is struck first by the *rarity* of secrets. This provides a contrast to widely held popular belief and frequent use of sleeptalking in literature as a technical means by which the "real truth" comes to light. (Witness Othello's convinced response to Iago's account of the alleged sleeptalking of Cassio.) From a moral point of view, however, most of the somniloquy observed in the laboratory is prosaic and would not ruffle the strictest censor. In our entire population, only 5 or 6 speeches uttered by 4 males and 1 female contained references to what might flout conventional sensibilities. One made an oblique reference to male homosexuality. The other 5 utilized crude slang expressions for the female genital, sexual intercourse, and feces. But the majority of intelligible, clear utterances sound like fragments of overheard, unremarkable daily conversations. References to gossip, school matters, newspapers, entertainment, art, science, the experimental situation itself, food, philosophical discussion, and the like were all common.

Another item of interest is the affective qualities of somniloquy. Not infrequently, sleep speeches involve tense, anxious, and dramatic fragments. Doubtless many of these are examples of a variety of NREM night terrors and REM nightmares (Fisher et al., 1973a). The most common affect, however, is one of conversational blandness appropriate in quality to the content of the speech but of somewhat diminished intensity. But the range is broad. Subjects chuckled, laughed, sang, whimpered, sounded petulant, sulky, childish, irritable, sarcastic, displayed intense anger with shouting, anxiety of all degrees, sobbing with both fear and remorse, and finally an inchoate, nonspecific high-intensity affect accompanying the discharge of the outburstlike vocalizations mentioned above with clang associations and recurrent utterances.

Finally, another group of sleeptalking phenomena resemble words and sounds one utters in solitude while awake. Exclamatory words, phrases, sounds of surprise, curiosity, pleasure, agreement, and so on are common. In addition, one encounters utterances resembling wakeful vocal self-priming or stimulation as if someone were following a recipe or other stepwise task, and wondering aloud what to do next.

ARE TECHNIQUES AVAILABLE BY WHICH SLEEPTALKING MAY BE EXPERIMENTALLY INFLUENCED?

Following the introduction of modern electrographic technique, I became intrigued by the possibility of gaining control over sleeptalking with the object of obtaining first hand, "hot off the griddle," reports of ongoing sleep mentation (much as a television commentator gives an on-the-spot account of an event). I hoped in this fashion to get a report of a dream in progress influenced as little as possible by interference from cognitive factors operating during retrospective recall after awakening.

The basic feature of the technique in the first attempt consisted in hypnotizing sleeptalkers prior to retiring for the night and giving them posthypnotic suggestions that they would sleep and dream normally in the laboratory, just as they do at home, but that the occurrence of a natural dream would be a posthypnotic signal for them to talk in their sleep and describe the dream as it was going on without awakening. In addition attempts were made to increase the amount of sleeptalking by giving posthypnotic suggestions to talk in their sleep more than before. The subjects were then aroused out of the hypnotic trance to normal wakefulness, whereupon they were permitted to go to sleep. Needless to say, results fell short of the ideal goal specified in the posthypnotic suggestion. Out of 8 subjects, a striking result was obtained with one, a less striking but convincing result was obtained in a second, an equivocal result in a third, and either no effect or a diminution of sleeptalking in the remainder, to the point of total suppression (Arkin, Hastey, & Reiser, 1966b). With our best subject we obtained the results demonstrated in Table 13.3.

The mean frequency of sleep speech over 9 first baseline nights was .8 per night (total speeches = 7) all of which occurred in the first half of the night, all of which were associated with NREM sleep, and 71% of which were more than 15 min from the nearest REM period. By contrast, the mean frequency of sleep speech over 23 nights employing posthypnotic suggestion was 10.0 per night (total speeches = 230). Of this latter total, 27% occurred in the first half of the night, and 73% in the second; also, 35% were associated with stage REM, and an additional 4% occurred at either REMP onset or termination. Of the remaining 61% uttered in association with NREM sleep, 64% occurred less than 15 min from the nearest REMP. The mean frequency of sleep speech over the 6 terminal baseline nights was 7.8 (total speeches = 47). Of this latter total, 79% occurred in the first half of the night and only 10.6% over the entire night were in association with stage REM; and of the 89.4% occurring in association with NREM sleep, 57.4% were more, and 42.6% less, than 15 min from the nearest REMP.

Thus, all procedures utilizing posthypnotic suggestion resulted in a marked increase in mean total number of speeches per night, a shift in

TABLE 13.3. RESULTS OF POSTHYPNOTICALLY STIMULATED SLEEPTALKING WITH OUR BEST SUBJECT

Experimental Condition and Number of Nights	Mean Episodes per Night	Percentage First Half Night	Percentage During REM Sleep	Percentage NREM Sleep	Percentage NREM More Than 15 Minutes from Nearest REM Period	Percentage NREM Less Than 15 Minutes from Nearest REM Period
First baseline, 9	0.8 (N = 7)	100.0	.0	100.0	71.4	18.6
All posthypnotic hypnotic suggestion, 23	10.0 (N = 230)	27.0	39	61.0	36.0	64.0
Terminal baseline, 6	7.8 (N = 47)	79.0	10.6	89.4	57.4	42.6

location of the bulk of speeches from the first to the second half of the night, initiation of speeches during REM sleep, and an increase of NREM speeches closely associated with the nearest REM period. Tart (personal communication, 1974) has independently demonstrated the effectiveness of this technique for the experimental production of sleeptalking.

In addition, a certain number of awakenings following sleep utterances were performed on 9 experimental nights separate from the above. After 8 REM-associated speech awakenings, recalled mentation displayed first order concordance in 87.5% of the cases; and after 35 NREM associated speeches, wakeful mentation reports displayed 20% first order concordance. The quality of speech, number of words, and emotion resembled that of many of our spontaneous sleeptalkers not subjected to the hypnosis technique. However, the proportions of first order concordance were somewhat higher with the posthypnotic subject than with the spontaneous sleeptalkers not subjected to the hypnosis technique: stage REM 87.5; versus 33.3% respectively; NREM 20 versus 13.6% respectively.

In another experimental study, a significant increase in sleeptalking was observed during recovery nights following two prior consecutive nights in which subjects took a dextroamphetamine spansule (15 mg) and pentobarbital (100 mg) prior to sleep (Arkin, Antrobus, Toth, & Baker, 1968). Although at that time our result was attributed to the increased "REM pressure" usually following presleep ingestion of this drug combination, it is now known that other stages of sleep are also affected by this procedure. Whatever the underlying mechanism, it is, nonetheless, an instance of experimental stimulation of somniloquy.

Aarons (1976) reported preliminary findings on attempts to condition sleep vocalization by escape-avoidance techniques. Using 3 paid male students (ages 22–23) who were apparently in good mental and physical health and without a history of sleeptalking or other sleep disturbance, the EEG, EOG (electro-oculogram), submental EMG, respiration, and voice were monitored for a total of 3 control-adaptation and 8 experimental nights. The basic strategy was that of shaping and developing operant responses of avoidance behavior. The termination of various combinations of noxious light and sound stimuli applied during sleep was first made contingent upon *any* vocalization and by gradual steps changed to requiring increasing overt verbalization as the desired operant response. The goal was the elicitation of speech of sufficient duration, intensity, and clarity to be easily comprehensible without awakening the subject. For a number of reasons, the procedure was not strictly uniform. In general, most of the experimental nights were carried out without informing the subjects of the desired goal, but in the latter part of the series, they were explicitly told that the purpose of the experiment was to produce sleeptalking and that if they spoke, the unpleasant stimuli would cease. No subject vocalized during the control night whereas all vocalized during experimental nights, in a large variety of ways. Thus, groans and unintelligible mumbling, clearly enunciated coherent words, phrases, and sentences were all observed. In addition, there was a similarly broad spectrum of affective tone and content both related and unrelated to the experimental situation. One subject increased in responsiveness over 3 nights and another decreased over 4. Total responses per session were obtained over a range of 28 to 100% of the stimulation trials with 57% transient awakenings. Responses, in weighted percentage for response sample size accompanied by alterations of the EEG but without alpha evidence for awakening, were distributed by sleep stage as follows: stage 1 NREM, 62% ($n = 10$); stage 2, 88% ($n = 40$); stage 3, 70% ($n = 27$); stage 4, 96% ($n = 22$); stage REM, 40% ($n = 10$). Aarons regarded his study as possessing numerous limitations, however, and was cautious about making generalizations. More experimentation is necessary to assess the extent to which the reported conditioned sleep speeches resemble spontaneous somniloquy observed in "natural" sleeptalkers as to content, electrographic correlates, and concordance with mentation reports elicited immediately afterward. Moreover, the effects of aversive techniques in training subjects to talk in their sleep may have powerful biasing influences over each of these parameters.

Still more recently, Bertini and Pontalti (1971) claimed to be able to train nonsleeptalkers to "free associate" in response to white noise during wakefulness. After this response was well established, the subjects were exposed to the same white-noise stimulus in the laboratory during REM sleep and were said to free associate in response without awakening. On the other hand, Hauri (1972) attempted to replicate this work and failed to produce sleeptalking during stage REM. Subjects often reported that they "heard the white noise in their dreams, but when they realized that they were now supposed to talk, they 'lost' their dream experience" (Hauri, 1972, p. 61). Hauri did report, however, that spontaneous sleeptalking increased during the experiment, especially in stages 2 and 3.

Finally, in the course of our own work, it was observed that frequent awakening of subjects and requiring them to perform verbal tasks aloud (giving mentation reports or performance of mental arithmetic aloud) resulted in the appearance of spontaneous sleep speech in two separate populations of nonsleeptalker subjects who were selected only on the basis of being light sleepers and good dream recallers (for another project) (Arkin et al., 1970a, 1970b; Farber, Arkin, Ellman, Antrobus, & Nelson, 1973). It is of interest that such sleeptalking experimentally produced in nonsleeptalkers, occurs most frequently in stage 2 sleep. (They also occurred often in stages 3–4 and stage REM.) Electrographically, phenomenologically, and contentwise, the episodes were undistinguishable from those of chronic sleeptalkers. In addition, it was observed that frequent awakening of chronic sleeptalkers for mentation reports resulted in increases of sleep speech (Arkin, Farber, Antrobus, Ellman, & Nelson, 1973).

IS IT POSSIBLE FOR AN EXPERIMENTER TO ENGAGE IN CONVERSATION WITH A SLEEPTALKER WITHOUT AWAKENING THE SUBJECT?

The old clinical and scientific literature contains many accounts of "conversations" between somniloquists and a wakeful companion for which the sleeptalker either has complete or partial amnesia (Arkin, 1966). Knowing of my interest in sleeptalking, at least 6 intelligent conscientious couples in recent years have volunteered that they can regularly engage their respective partners in prolonged sleep conversation with the sleeptalker experiencing complete lack of recall in the morning. Attempts to observe this phenomenon in the laboratory have met with partial success (Arkin, Hastey, & Reiser, 1966a). The reason for this qualified comment is that, thus far, the dialogues recorded do not seem as sustained as those described in the anecdotal reports of the above reliable persons. It is possible that the laboratory, its equipment, and an experimenter who is not an intimate of the subject may have an inhibiting effect.

There are two techniques which may be useful: the "answering method" and the "provocation method." Using the former, the experimenter waits patiently for the sleeping subject to talk and attempts to answer audibly in the same spirit, intensity, and on the same topic as if conversing empathically with a wakeful partner. In so doing, the experimenter should strive to "feel his way" into the experiential world of the subject at the instant and respond accordingly for as many interchanges as possible. With the latter technique, the experimenter softly speaks to the at-the-moment "silent" sleeper using the subject's or another's name, word, or topic which the experimenter knows is of interest to the subject. When the sleeptalking is thus initiated, the experimenter continues with the answering method.

In general, during the actual vocalization, the accompanying electrographic background, when readable, is that of stage 1 NREM.

RATHER THAN BEING A VALID REFLECTION OF SLEEP MENTATION, IS IT POSSIBLE THAT SLEEPTALKING MERELY INDICATES THE MENTAL CONTENT OF THE MOVEMENT-AROUSAL EPISODE (AS DEFINED BY STANDARD CRITERIA) AND IS ESSENTIALLY UNRELATED TO SLEEP MENTATION AS SUCH?

The results of studies in several different laboratories have a bearing on this question.

First, with regard to stage REM-associated sleeptalking, the high proportion of concordance between sleep-speech content and the usual relatively elaborate REM sleep-mentation reports described as dreams by the subject, provides convincing evidence that REM-associated sleep speech arises out of and reflects previous ongoing REM sleep mentation. On the other hand, the same conclusion with regard to NREM-associated utterances cannot be drawn so easily. This caution is required by the lack of well-established electrographic correlates of NREM sleep mentation in contrast to those of stage REM. That is, in the latter instance, electrographic signs of stage REM permit a reasonably valid inference that dreamlike mentation was in progress immediately prior to the actual onset of the sleep utterance and continuous with it, whereas this would not be the case with NREM sleep.

An effort was made by us (Arkin, Antrobus, Toth, Baker, & Jackler, 1972) to approach this problem by comparing NREM mentation reports elicited immediately after NREM-associated sleep utterance to reports elicited during NREM "silent sleep." We sought to evaluate the following hypothesis: Many NREM-associated utterances are the outgrowths of previous streams of *ongoing* NREM mentation which, from time to time, find expression in overt vocalization of the subject. Evidence that this could indeed occur would be important because we would then possess a spontaneous subject-emitted, objective indicator of the presence and content of some NREM mentation. Support for this hypothesis would require the following 3 findings:

1. An analysis of the general content of mentation reports elicited immediately after NREM-associated utterances would reveal no significant differences from reports elicited from NREM "silent" sleep, that is, sleep without proximate sleep vocalization.

2. There would be no significant differences in the total word counts of the mentation reports elicited from these two conditions; and also no significant difference in proportion of reports categorized by judges as lacking in content altogether.

3. By contrast, on awakening the subject after NREM sleep utterance, the frequency with which the subject recalls an imagined occurrence in which the sleeper was vocalizing would be *greater* than after an interval of NREM silent sleep. Examples of such occurrences would be those in which the subject reports, "I was (or we were) talking, discussing, teaching, arguing, conversing, and so on" in an imagined incident prior to being awakened.

We obtained our data from the first 23 of the 28 subjects utilized in our study of the degree of concordance between the content of sleep speech and the associated wakeful mentation (Arkin et al., 1970b). Only their NREM reports were employed and from this pool, we set up pairs each consisting of one report associated with sleep utterance and one associated with silent sleep. Both members of a given pair came from the same subject, from the same night, and were also chosen to minimize the difference in time elapsed between the two reports. This procedure yielded a total of 74 pairs of reports for initial data processing. (Of the 23 subjects, 4 yielded 1 report pair each; 7, 2 each; 4, 3 each; 3, 4 each; 4, 6 each; and 1, 8 pairs.)

Content analysis and total word counts were made on the entire population of report pairs. The content analytic categories included visual content, action, number of characters, self-representation, bizarreness-incongruity, interpersonal action, emotion, references to the laboratory-experimental situation, references to work and/or school, mentation absent or unscorable, subject vocalizing, and other verbal categories. Eight of the 11 reliability coefficients for 2 dependent judges ranged from .70 to .89. The coefficients for the remaining 3 categories (emotion, bizarreness, and visual content) were below acceptable levels, but were deemed spuriously low largely because of the low frequency and the low overall amount of variability of these items in the entire report population (Arkin, 1973b). No significant differences were found between the mean total-word counts, frequency of mentation recall, the content analysis categories in the 2 groups of reports with *one* clear exception: Reports after sleep utterance were much more likely to contain an indication of the subject vocalizing in an imaginary sleep experience (33.8% after sleep utterance versus 12.2% from silent sleep). An additional 6.7% of both groups of mentation reports contained references to other verbal categories (such as "others vocalizing," anticipated vocalization," and so on). This brought the total proportion of reports containing references to verbal content to 40.5% after sleep speech and 18.9% from silent sleep, a difference of 21.6%. It was therefore concluded that many NREM-associated sleep utterances arise out of ongoing streams of NREM mentation and provide valid indices of NREM mental content because the 2 types of reports were indistinguishable with the sole exception as described. These results are closely consistent with those subsequently reported by MacNeilage (1971). Her findings were that the proportions of reports judged as reflecting dreams, coherent dreams, containing visual content, and finally physical activity were uniformly but only slightly higher after sleep utterance than after silent sleep (mean difference, 5.5%; range, 1.5–7.7%). This difference is presumed to be statistically insignificant inasmuch as levels were not reported. By contrast, the percentage of reports elicited after sleeptalking categorized as possessing verbal content was 43.8 as opposed to 23.1 for the controls, a difference of 20.7%. The figures from the two laboratories were therefore in close agreement.

Finally, Fisher et al. (1974), in a study of night terrors (which feature speech and vocalization), report that on several occasions, awakened subjects described mentation prior to the spontaneous terrifying arousal which possessed content out of which the night terror seemed to develop, for example, one subject remembered political discussions preceding a night terror of falling off a cliff in a baby carriage. These observations accord without conclusion that many NREM sleep speeches are outgrowths of previous ongoing streams of NREM mentation.

A CONCEPTUAL SCHEME FOR THE FORMULATION OF SLEEP UTTERANCE AND RELATED PHENOMENA

Preparatory discussion of two considerations are necessary to make my exposition clear. First, in what senses may we say that when a subject somniloquizes, he is in fact "talking in his sleep"; and second, how shall we view the concept of psychic dissociation which, as mentioned in my previous papers (Arkin, 1967, 1974b), seems useful in accounting for sleep utterance.

At the outset it is necessary to note that a universally accepted, unambiguous definition of sleep has not yet been formulated. Although polygraphic parameters, particularly those derived from the combined use of the EEG, submental EMG, and EOG, have been used by sleep researchers for providing the most pragmatic criteria yet available, there are, nevertheless, exceptions and transitional states not conveniently subsumed under them. For our purposes, it will suffice to cite two recent authoritative views. Thus, Dement and Mitler (1973) indicate that the cardinal feature of wakefulness is the efficiency of discriminatory reactivity to the environment or perceptual "environmental engagement." They ask us to imagine an individual whose eyes are taped open and who is required to make a motor response to light flashes whenever they are presented. At some point, the individual fails to respond. The moment of sleep onset is taken by the authors as coinciding with this moment of "perceptual disengagement" as betokened by the response failure—and such response failure may occur in the presence of a wakeful EEG. They continue by remarking upon their existing uncertainty concerning the precise temporal relationships between loss of discriminatory reactivity and the usually accepted EEG signs of sleep.

Likewise, Johnson (1970) evaluates the evidence for unique correspondence between electrographic signs and mentally defined states. Reviewing the then present state of the art in electrographic assessment of sleep and states of awareness as described by a mentation report, actually he considered the state of consciousness to possess priority over electrographic measures and, further, that the assessment of the state of consciousness was a prerequisite to interpretation of the EEG.

Earlier in this chapter, it was established that the typical episode of somniloquy occurs within the electrographic context of a movement arousal episode. Rechtschaffen and Kales (1968) classify such events in a pragmatic, somewhat arbitrary manner. If their duration exceeds half of the duration of the epoch simultaneously obscuring the EEG and EOG tracings, they are categorized as (MT) muscle tension. In such cases, they are counted neither as unambiguous sleep nor wakefulness because of currently insufficient knowledge of their behavioral correlates. If, on the other hand, half of the epoch or less is occupied by a movement-arousal incident, its sleep-stage classification depends upon the electrographic characteristics of the readable remainder of the record. The category "movement arousal," therefore, is not necessarily considered incompatible with ongoing sleep but is recommended to the experimenter as a herald of some impending change in whatever sleep state had obtained before its occurrence.

Moreover, in many instances observed in our laboratory the EEG was artifact-free at the exact moment of utterance and fulfilled the criteria of unambiguous sleep. Similar findings have been reported by others during episodes of somnambulism; that is, coordinated motor activity was maintained in the presence of electroencephalographically unambiguous slow-wave sleep (Broughton, 1973; Jacobson & Kales, 1967; Kales & Jacobson, 1967).

The relevant point to be gleaned from these previous comments is that despite certain electrographic signs of increased arousal, a subject may nevertheless be, or remain, *psychologically* asleep, especially if such occurrences are immediately preceded and rapidly followed by unambiguous electrographic correlates of sleep. This latter sequence actually describes the electrographic structure of a typical sleep-utterance episode. In other words, psychological and electrographic sleep may often be slightly out of phase. Further support for this suggestion arises from the demonstration that when subjects are awakened, there is a time lag in the full recovery of wakeful critical reactivity even though typical electrographic signs of wakefulness prevail. Experimental results of others reviewed by Tebbs (1972) demonstrated that postawakening performance decrements may range from 25 to 360% below full wakeful levels, and that although the rate of recovery is most rapid during the few minutes following the awakening, complete recovery may require as long as 25 min. Findings consistent with these have been reported by Feltin and Broughton (1968) and Scott (1969). In addition, Broughton (1968) has demonstrated the carryover of NREM sleep components of the occipital visual evoked potential, or increased latencies and decreased amplitudes of later components into immediately-following wakefulness.

The second relevant area to be discussed is that of psychic dissociation. In a recent paper, Hilgard (1973) published a neodissociationist theory which accounts nicely for somniloquy. Its basic assumption is that unity in personal cognition is precarious and unstable. Self-perception and conception of self as agent, maintained largely through continuity of memory, is a function of the "executive ego." The latter normally has ascendancy over a hierarchy of cognitive subsystems themselves mutually autonomous and concurrently interactive in varying degree. Each subsystem, which may operate outside of awareness, has an input and output system with feed-back enabling it to seek or avoid input and enhance or inhibit output. These formulations provide a conceptual scaffolding for the following phenomena observable in connection with sleep utterances:

1. They express input from endogenous sources; that is, vocalization appears to arise spontaneously requiring no external stimuli.
2. They often accompany and/or reflect the content and the subject's imagined participation within streams of mentation associated with sleep. This is demonstrated by variable degrees of concordance with recalled mentation elicited during immediately subsequent wakefulness.
3. The content of the sleep speech may be ample and yet bear no discernible relationship to the equally ample content of the immediately following mentation report. This suggests the possibility of multiple dissociated concurrent streams of mentation.
4. There is a lack of simultaneous critical awareness of external reality at the moment of the occurrence. That is, when accompanied by sleep consciousness the subject treats the sleep-imagined experience associated with the sleep utterance as if it were real. Furthermore, when receiving a threshold arousal stimulus, the subject describes experiences and behaves in accordance with customarily expected characteristics of one who has been asleep and has just been awakened.
5. There is a strong tendency for amnesia which is more marked for mentation accompanying NREM than REM sleep utterances.
6. Lack of associated recalled mentation is often total; that is, the subject may deny recall of any preawakening experience whatsoever. Inasmuch as this outcome is usual when sleep utterances possess marked degrees of linguistic disorganization, the possibility exists that such speech emissions may occur in the absence of awareness.
7. The psycholinguistic integrity of the emitted speech tends to possess broadly varying degrees of disturbance, often resembling ictal automatism or types of aphasia (Serafetinides, 1966). Thus, we might express somniloquy in terms of Hilgard's (1973) theory as follows: During slumber, the sleep executive ego acquires ascendancy over its wakeful counterpart. Its related subordinate semiautonomous cognitive systems include those mediating imagery, covert utterance, overt utterance, moral codes, and memory which in turn is subdivided into echoic, short-term, and long-term components. Accordingly, our definition of somniloquy may now be reformulated as follows: *somniloquy is the output of the overt-utterance system during psychological sleep (v.s.) occurring in varying degrees of dissociation from the memory and*

imagery subsystems along a continuum from minimal to apparently complete dissociations, while at the same time with little or no dissociation from individual moral-code subsystems.

This last item indicates that sleep speech, no matter how dissociated from other cognitive structures, has, nevertheless, little autonomy from moral-code subsystems judging from the rarity of exposure of secrets under conditions which would seem to actually facilitate revealing them. This provides an interesting sidelight upon the tenacity of moral-code systems in their role of modulation of psychological outputs.

14

Night Terrors and Anxiety Dreams*

EDWIN KAHN
Queensborough Community College

CHARLES FISHER
ADELE EDWARDS
Mount Sinai Medical Center

A distinction has been made between the night terror which occurs with very rare exception out of stages 3 and 4 sleep, and the more common anxiety dream or nightmare which arises from REM sleep.[1] The night terror

*This research was supported by United States Public Health Service Grant MH03267.

[1]In their original publication (Fisher et al. 1970), the authors described an exceptional form of frightening arousal occurring in association with stage 2 sleep. The concomitant anxiety tended to be more severe than REM anxiety dreams but much less than that related to stage 4 night terrors. Prior to awakening, similar to the latter, there was no change in heart or respiratory rate but after awakening, only moderate increases were observed. One such stage 2 episode was described as an occurrence of moaning followed by spontaneous awakening with a report of content about receiving a severed human leg as a Christmas gift.

is usually an event of the early part of the night when most stage 4 is present, while the nightmare can take place in any REM period. Also the night terror is physiologically much more intense than the REM nightmare (heart rates have almost tripled for the night terror while in the REM anxiety dream the greatest heart rate acceleration at our laboratory was from 76 to 92 beats per min). The lesser intensity of the REM anxiety dream may be at least partially explained by the fact that during REM the physiological activation provides a buffer which prevents extreme terror. Finally, night terrors occur in an arousal state (arousal out of stages 3 and 4 sleep) while anxiety dreams occur during sleep, in the midst of an ongoing REM period and terminate on arousal.

The following is a summary of our laboratory's findings on night terrors, detailed accounts of which have been reported elsewhere (Fisher, Byrne, Edwards, & Kahn, 1970; Fisher, Kahn, Edwards, & Davis, 1973a; Fisher, Kahn, Edwards, Davis, & Fine, 1974b; Kahn, Fisher, Byrne, Edwards, & Davis, 1970; Kahn, Fisher, Edwards, & Davis, 1973).

The severe stage 4 night terror consists of perhaps the greatest heart rate acceleration possible in man (in a typical severe arousal heart rate accelerated from 64 bpm to 152 bpm within 15 to 30 sec) with screams of enormous intensity, cursing, motility, increases in respiratory rate and especially amplitude, and a sharp increase in skin conductance. The episode is of brief duration, heart rate decelerating 45 to 90 sec after the moment of onset, and returning to normal baseline levels within 2 to 4 min. Most subjects characteristically fell asleep shortly after an episode, and in several with multiple terrors it was not unusual for another one to occur 15 to 30 min later when they were back in stage 4. There seemed to be a sex difference in incidence; although considerably more women responded to our newspaper ad soliciting nightmare sufferers, 10 of the 12 night-terror subjects were men.

Although arising out of stage 4 (approximately two-thirds of the night terrors occurred during the first NREM period when most stage 4 occurs) the episode actually takes place as part of an arousal response, characterized by a waking EEG pattern (see Broughton, 1968, below). When the night terror occurred in the first NREM period, the mean time from sleep onset to the first night terror was 44.5 min showing how early in the night these episodes will occur.

One consistent finding was that the intensity of the night terror was correlated with the amount of stage 4 preceding the attack; that is, the more stage 4 the more severe the episode. Thus, for *each* of the three subjects with the most frequent arousals, amount of preceding stage 4 correlated significantly with the heart-rate change at arousal and this relationship was further confirmed for the other subjects with fewer arousals. It was speculated that with increased duration of stage 4, sleep becomes "deeper," and with deepening sleep there is an increasing potential for loss of ego control, eventuating in the uninhibited release of terrifying repressed impulses.

Since night terrors occurred out of stage 4 it was hypothesized that a way to curtail them would be to administer a drug that suppressed stage 4. Kales, Preston, Tan, and Allen (1970) reported that diazepam had such an effect; therefore it was tried. In 4 of 6 subjects it was found that 5 to 20 mg of diazepam taken at bedtime suppressed night terrors, which returned when the subject was taken off drug or given placebo. In the remaining 2 subjects, diazepam reduced night terrors; however, the reduction persisted during the off-drug period. One subject differed in that night terrors occurred during each NREM period, so that toward morning when stages 3 and 4 were absent, night terrors occurred out of stage 2. Diazepam suppressed this subject's stage 2 as well as stage 4 night terrors, indicating that the drug could exert its effect independent of sleep stage.

In other findings, night terrors were elicited in 2 of 3 subjects when buzzers were sounded in slow-wave sleep. The buzzer-elicited night terrors were, on the average, of the same severity as those arising spontaneously. Clinical EEGs performed on 3 of the subjects with the most frequent night terrors (in 2 it was recorded just preceding and during severe night terrors) indicated no pathology in the tracing. Sleep heart rates for night-terror subjects were in the normal range and were significantly lower than for subjects who had REM nightmares or anxiety dreams, the latter showing elevated sleep heart rates.

The night terror is one of three major stage 4 sleep disorders, the others being somnambulism and enuresis. Broughton (1968) and Gastaut and Broughton (1965) formulated some unifying ideas about these three disorders by considering them disorders of arousal. The authors noted that each of these disorders occurred during arousal from delta sleep, associated with alpha EEG, body movement, mental confusion, and disorientation, relative nonreactivity to external stimuli, and amnesia for the episode. They also took the position that because of amnesia it is virtually impossible to demonstrate that preceding NREM content is the trigger of night-terror attacks. Any content could be determined by the physiological changes occurring during arousal, for example, respiratory changes giving rise to feelings of suffocating and choking, increases in heart rate giving rise to fear of death, this formulation being a restatement of the old James–Lange theory. Gastaut and Broughton (1965) further speculated that thoughts may be rationalizations of the autonomic components of the attack or that during the postarousal period a return of waking conflict occurs through a clouded sensorium. Therefore, in these authors' view it is unlikely that the night terror is triggered by ongoing NREM mentation.

In our investigation of night terrors it was observed that distinct content was often reported following these episodes. To help resolve the question of whether or not the night terror can be initiated by ongoing NREM mentation, a thorough review of our night-terror arousal interviews was made to determine the frequency and nature of the reported content.

THE EXPERIMENT

Method

Twelve adult stage 4-night-terror subjects (10 males and 2 females) were studied for a total of over 250 nights. A night terror was defined as a NREM arousal when heart rate reached a level of 108 bpm or more during any 15-sec postarousal interval.* By this definition we have observed over 275 night terrors at the laboratory. About half of the night terrors came from Subject 1, who was studied during 98 nights.

The subjects slept undisturbed while EEG, eye movement, heart rates, and respiratory rates were recorded. When a spontaneous awakening occurred, subjects were interviewed by the experimenter for content through a two-way intercom. A tape recorder was operated through the night to record all arousals and interviews.

Half of the subjects on some nights were studied on diazepam and other drugs in attempts to suppress night terrors. Drug as well as baseline nights were combined in this study so that a greater number of night terrors could be sampled. There was minimal effect of drug on amount of recall and content.

Abstracts of the arousal interviews were prepared which eliminated irrelevant detail. Each arousal was then labeled as recall, vague recall, or no recall by two judges working independently of each other.

Further details of method and subjects can be found in our earlier report (Fisher et al., 1974).

Results

Table 14.1 presents the number and percentage of instances of recall, vague recall, and no recall for all spontaneous night-terror arousals in 8 subjects who had at least 3 night-terror episodes. Of the 4 remaining

---

*Editors' note: In the papers referred to earlier in which the authors provide more extensive detail than is possible here, a separate category of "milder arousals" was described which was defined by heart rates of less than 108 bpm. The associated findings in this group, especially regarding the nature of recalled mentation, presented some important differences in comparison with those of the more severe night terrors. For example, the content resembled many of the sleep speeches recorded by Arkin and co-workers (see Chapter 13 of this volume) uttered by subjects defining themselves as chronic sleeptalkers rather than night-terror sufferers.

TABLE 14.1. NUMBER AND PERCENTAGE RECALL, VAGUE RECALL, AND NO
RECALL OF NIGHT TERRORS (HEART RATE > 108 BPM)

Subject	Number of Nights	Number			Percentage		
		Recall	Vague Recall	No Recall	Recall	Vague Recall	No Recall
1	92	112	13	38	69	8	23
2	32	5	6	10	24	28	48
3	31	12	2	11	48	8	44
4	48	6	1	0	86	14	0
5	9	0	0	33	0	0	100
6	13	3	0	0	100	0	0
7	4	2	0	1	67	0	33
12	16	12	0	5	71	0	29
					58^a	7^a	35^a

[a]Percentage means.

subjects with fewer arousals, 2 had 100% recall for 2 and 1 night terrors, respectively, and the other 2 subjects had no recall whatsoever for the same number of night terrors. Recall for night-terror arousals was 58% (65% when including vague recall), calculated by the mean of subject percentages.

Some of the most severe night terrors involved being crushed or struck by some sudden force, things closing in or being entrapped in a small area, being left alone or abandoned, and choking on or swallowing something, such as electrode wires. In Subjects 1 and 2 there was a tendency to better recall the most severe night terrors. It seemed that these two subjects were more fully aroused by the more severe terror and thus were more alert and better able to report detailed content, whereas in milder arousals the subjects were groggy, confused, and unmotivated, and recall was impaired.

To illustrate more clearly the content associated with night-terror episodes, examples are given of six of the subjects' night-terror reports.

Subject 1, the most extensively studied subject, had repetitive and frequent night terrors of choking on something, such as the electrodes, tapes, and so on, and also had several very severe night terrors of being trapped in a small space. After one of the severest night terrors observed at the laboratory (heart rate went from 56 to 164 bpm within 1 minute) the subject gave the following report:

Somebody said . . . somebody . . . oh shit . . . somebody said something, I don't even remember what this person said. All of a sudden I felt on all sides of me like, uh, metal, or stone doors. In other words I was someplace, probably in a basement, and like on every side of me was, except one, which I could sort of see maybe a window, every side was like stone or something, stopped up, almost like when I was in a tomb. *And so I started . . . uh, screaming.* I didn't realize that there was still a . . . an opening of some kind.

The screaming probably coincides with the onset of the arousal reaction. Note the brief content of someone speaking *before* the terrifying imagery appeared and the subject's statement that the content caused the screaming. Other night terrors of this subject who, it is to be noted, was violently opposed to the United States policy of involvement in Vietnam, were swallowing and choking on an American flag (occurring at the height of the protest movement), choking on something that had been cut and severed, perhaps belonging to the experimenter: "I swallowed the whole thing." The subject also recalled being squeezed between a bus and wall.

After one of the night terrors where heart rate went from 60 to 120 bpm, Subject 1 reported "One of the people here asked to have the light on . . . So I said it was okay. There was a hard time finding it. It was very dark. I thought they wanted to . . . And that's where I got panicky . . . I don't know what it was that really frightened me, the boxes themselves in front of me. . . ." Although the content is not especially clear, from the above report it seems that some unavailable thought associated with ongoing NREM content ("And that's where I got panicky") instigated the episode.

Much of Subject 1's report content was repetitive and brief, like the choking on wires and being entangled in electrodes, the repetitiveness giving the impression of postarousal elaborations of the intense autonomic responses. However, as noted in the illustration above, other contents were distinct and specific and seem to rule out postarousal elaborations.

Subject 4, in a disturbing arousal that did not, by the heart-rate criterion, reach night-terror intensity (heart rate went from 48 to 92 bpm) reported the feeling of a snake in bed. He screamed to his girlfriend, who he imagined was lying beside him, "Lights! I got a snake or something here!! Get the lights on, please, can you get the lights on? *Can you get the fucking lights on,* goddamnit! Are you awake?"

After the episode Subject 4 reported:

I felt like I was going to have a nightmare . . . I had sensations there was something on the bed like a snake . . . it was damned low and moving up towards me, moving up the bed . . . The potential fear . . . might be the most interesting thing, namely, you build up a certain panic about *not being able to turn the lights on;* that seems to be one of the most important goals in a situation like that. Otherwise I thought I was with Mary Liz because I was actually talking to her, telling her to turn on the lights.

It would appear that the mental content of the snake, or something, in the bed triggered this episode.

In other night-terror arousals this Subject 4 often felt that he was being threatened or victimized by the sleep laboratory or others. In one very severe arousal, in which he ripped off the electrodes, he reported he was on a car trip requiring a reservation or tickets, such as to the Rose Bowl. He was with his sister and brother-in-law and suddenly felt as if someone was going to do something to him, like hit him over the head, shoot him, or humiliate him in some way. He wanted to get out of the situation and rip off the electrodes. This subject, who was sophisticated about the distinction between stage 4 and REM sleep, then asked, "Was it a stage 4 night terror . . . cause there was a lot of dream content there?"

Subject 2 had excellent recall for very severe arousals. In one the subject believed he had rolled over into the "wrong slot" and was about to be stepped on by the experimenter who was coming into the room (heart rate went from 80 to 160 bpm). The subject screamed during this episode:

AOH! AAH!—HEY HEY, WATCH—WATCH—WATCH—WATCH—WATCH —Watch!! What's with me? Hold it . . . Hold it . . . Hold it . . . It wasn't me now! IT's NOT ME ANYMORE!! Oh, shit, you are *stepping on me now,* Dummy!! Hey, I switched . . . I'm here now. I'm here now. I'm in the middle position now. There you go. Okay?

After the night terror, and the heart rate returned to normal, the subject gave the following description of the arousal:

In the room, you know, and, like someone was going to step on me . . . It was like—just like—It was a mixup like, you were doing—You weren't doing me harm purposely, you know what I mean? You follow me? . . . Well, someone was coming in. I didn't know who was coming to fix something up here and, I was like in the wrong slot. And you didn't realize I was in this wrong spot and *you were stepping on —you were stepping on me,* or something like this, and then I'm trying to tell you like I'm here. I'm over here. I'm over here, or something like this, I don't know. But it was violent there for a couple of seconds, yes. It was. Because I had a burst of energy . . .

In another of Subject 2's night terrors the room was shrinking and coming down on the subject, and in a third the subject experienced being left alone by someone on a rowboat in the middle of nowhere on a rough ocean, the other person disappearing in the distance. The latter was so severe that the subject ripped the electrodes off and we have no record of the heart-rate acceleration.

Subject 6 had two very severe arousals, ripping off the electrodes and later recalling vivid and detailed content. In one, the hull of a ship came down on and caught the subject beneath it, not crushed but trapped. In the other, the subject fell off a cliff while sitting in an English baby carriage on an endless fall, feeling helpless and shocked. Preceding the fall there was a political discussion with a neighbor whose radical political beliefs the subject strongly disagreed with. It also turned out that this neighbor owned an English stroller resembling the one the subject was trapped in during the night terror. The subject reported, "Falling, calling for help, and then waking up occurred at that very second."

Subject 3 reported in about half of the arousals strong physiological sensations, such as heart pounding and difficulty breathing. Although Subject 3's recall was, in general, poor, several "dreamlike" contents were reported, like warriors or soldiers on horseback rattling their swords, while the leader talked to the group and the horses were about to charge. In one night terror in which heart rate went from 50 to 128 bpm, the subject screamed, "Help! Hey! Help! Hey get! It's near my throat! Thing's choking me! Something is stuck in my throat!" During the postarousal interview the subject reported, "*Something is choking in my throat* . . . It is choking in my throat, whatever the fuck is in there . . . I just want to know why, I'd like to know what the hell is in my throat. *It just woke me up that's all!*" The subject's last statement may be taken as evidence that content initiated the arousal.

Subject 12 often reported dreamlike imagery; for example, in one night terror, Martha Raye at age 20 was helping the experimenter put electrodes on the subject, who wanted to tell them that the stuff on the head was too tightly fit. Suddenly no one was there and the subject awoke frightened. Subject 12's most fearful arousal, during which the electrodes were ripped off, was that a shelf in the room was closing in. The theme of a threatening person in the room appeared quite frequently in this subject's night terrors.

Discussion

The results reported indicate that recall of content associated with spontaneous arousal from night terrors is much better than has been reported by Broughton (1968). The degree of recall, a mean of 58%, is similar to the 70.0 and 61.5% recall at nonspontaneous awakenings from stages 3 to 4 sleep in normal young adults reported by Foulkes (1962) and Arkin, Toth, Baker, and Hastey (1970a, 1970b), respectively.

An important problem, of difficult resolution, is the temporal relationships of the content recalled from stage 4 night terrors; that is, does the psychic content refer to events that took place during the prearousal period of stages 3 to 4 sleep just prior to the sudden onset of the night terror; or the postarousal period lasting not more than 1 to 2 min and characterized by marked autonomic activation, sleeptalking, and other utterances such as cries, screams and cursing, and return of motility? Recalled content may refer to one or both periods in a given instance.

Broughton (1973) believed that any content retrieved from night terrors is probably postarousal, either an elaboration of the intense autonomic changes that occur or a return to waking conflict. In our study, during the postarousal period some content may have been elaborated, as Broughton emphasized, like fears of dying associated with pounding of the heart (Subjects 1 and 3), or of choking in response to respiratory difficulty (Subject 1). Elaborated content may also occur in response to environmental circumstances, like Subject 1's frequent report of being left alone or abandoned. Most often, it is impossible to decide whether such content (dying, choking, or being abandoned) represented pre- or postarousal events.

However, a considerable amount of the content reported by our subjects was extremely vivid and so clearly described that it is difficult to imagine that it was postarousal mentation. Furthermore, in several instances, the subjects reported that it was because of the content that they became panicky, aroused, and began screaming (like Subject 1's report of being in a tomb, Subject 1 in the dark, and Subject 3 choking on something). Now that the existence of NREM mentation has been firmly established, there is little reason to doubt that such prearousal NREM content could initiate night-terror episodes.

Arkin et al. (1970a) and Arkin, Antrobus, Toth, Baker, and Jackler (1972) have extensively studied mentation reports following NREM-sleeptalking episodes. They believe that the sleep speech often reflects the content of NREM sleep mentation, since content reports immediately after NREM sleep speech and NREM silent sleep show no differences except that there are more references in the former to the subject's talking. They also demonstrated concordance between sleep speech and recalled mentation, which, according to their argument, suggests that this recalled mentation frequently reflects ongoing NREM mentation. We have illustrated several instances of concordance between sleep speech and reported mentation during night-terror episodes (Fisher et al., 1974). However, we doubt in the situation of night terror or sleeptalking episodes, whether this constitutes proof of prearousal content as Arkin seems to contend, since the concordance could simply reflect mentation during the screaming and/or speech episodes which take place during arousal periods and not NREM sleep.

In 2 of 3 subjects, night terrors have been induced by sounding a buzzer during slow-wave, stages 3 to 4 sleep (Fisher et al., 1970). One other subject reported that night terrors while in the army were set off by someone slamming the barracks door, or by other noise. These night terrors, induced by external stimuli, are perhaps the best evidence for mental activity playing no role in precipitating the episodes (Broughton, 1970). It might be postulated that in predisposed individuals, terrors can be "set off" by either of two types of stimulation: (1) endogenous, in the form of mental activity occurring in NREM sleep; and (2) exogenous, in the form of a loud noise or other external stimulation.

One subject, Subject 5, had no recall from 33 arousals classified as night terrors. It is interesting that Subject 5 was the only subject of 3 (Subjects 1,

3, and 5) in whom it was impossible to induce night terrors with a buzzer. In fact, the subject could not be aroused from stages 3 to 4 sleep even with an extremely loud buzzer. This finding supports Zimmerman's (1970) hypothesis that NREM recall is related to amount of cerebral activation; that is, Subject 5, as evidenced by the high-arousal threshold, was a very deep sleeper (much less cerebral activation) with an NREM recall of zero.

A frequent very frightening content was that the room was closing in or shrinking; for 3 subjects the room was closing in, a fourth imagined being enclosed by the hull of the ship, and a fifth reported a shelf in the room getting closer. This may be typical of night terrors at home or especially stimulated by the experimental situation, because the sleep room was quite small, located in the basement, with no outdoor view.

In 4 of 6 subjects with the most reported content, aspects of the sleep laboratory occurred in over 50% of the reports. Therefore, this has not been a study of night-terror content in general, but in a particular situation, that is, a laboratory. Nevertheless, there was very considerable overlap between content noted in the laboratory and that reported to have occurred at home before the investigation or during nonlaboratory nights during its course. Thus, Subject 1, whose most frequently reported content at the laboratory was choking on the wires or electrodes, reported that night terror content at home also involved choking, but not on wires. At home the subject would choke on or swallow such things as nails, a shirt, part of the subject's own throat, an itemized list for a tax return, and so on. His wife reported that he sometimes spit when he awakened as if he had swallowed something and wanted to get rid of it. This shows for Subject 1 that although the laboratory influenced the details of the content, the underlying theme may not have been different from what it was at home.

The REM nightmares show a gradual acceleration of heart and respiratory rates during sleep immediately prior to spontaneous arousals (Fisher et al., 1970; Kahn et al., 1972); however, the acceleration is not nearly as great as for the stage 4 night terror. For example, in one of the most severe REM nightmares observed at the laboratory, heart rate went from 76 to 92 bpm and respiration from 18 to 30 breaths per min in the several minutes of REM sleep preceding spontaneous arousal. The stage 4 night terror has *never* manifested *any* physiological change just prior to the sudden onset of the episode. This finding suggests that in the stage 4 night terror the frightening content does not build up gradually as in the REM anxiety dream; rather it occurs suddenly, immediately igniting the arousal reaction. There may be ongoing neutral NREM thoughts which then touch upon an intense conflict area of the subject, producing simultaneously a terrifying image or thought and the intense arousal reaction, as in the example of Subject 6's night terror about the English stroller.

Of the three classical characteristics of nightmares discussed by Jones (1911, 1959) and others—intense dread, paralysis, and oppression on the chest—only the first, intense dread, has been found in this study to be a consistent characteristic of night terrors.

None of the night-terror content involved fear of paralysis. Liddon (1967) noted that during REM sleep there is a loss of muscle tone, and that this lack of tone may be related to the traditional report of paralysis in the nightmare. He further noted that some of the symptoms of narcolepsy are sleep paralysis, hypnagogic hallucinations, and sleep-onset REM periods (see Rechtschaffen & Dement, 1969) and speculated that those persons experiencing frightening dreams of paralysis, who had been described in the literature as victims of the nightmare, actually suffered from narcolepsy. It is of interest that in our studies the one content report of paralysis associated with considerable fear came from a sleep-onset REM period from Subject 3, who consistently had sleep-onset REM periods but none of the other symptoms of narcolepsy.

SUMMARY

In their studies on stage 4 night terrors, Broughton and Gastaut took the position that ongoing NREM mentation did *not* trigger these episodes. In this study we made a careful review of our night terror data and found content recalled from 58% of 272 night-terror arousals in 8 subjects. A distinction was made between "prearousal" and "postarousal" mental content. In many instances it is difficult or impossible to determine whether the reported content refers to one or both of these periods. Some content was brief and repetitive and may have been postarousal elaboration of the intense autonomic response, but much was vivid, unusual, and sometimes detailed, more likely originating in the prearousal period. Also, in several instances the subject reported that the frightening content caused him to scream and ignited the episode.

PART 6

IMPLICATIONS AND NEW DIRECTIONS

15

Parallel Distributed Processes and Dream Production

JOHN S. ANTROBUS
City College of the City University of New York

JEFFREY FOOKSON
New York University

The Distributed Recurrent Activation Model of Imagery and Thought—Schemata (DREAMIT-S), which is introduced here, develops the **tonic** activation component of the Activation-Synthesis model (Hobson & McCarley, 1977) further and introduces a specific neurocognitive linkage between cortical and cognitive activation. In so doing, it suggests an alternative account for the production of bizarre mentation to that proposed by the Activation-Synthesis model. Most of this new model development is based on the recent development of connectionist models, particularly the Parallel Distributed Processing (PDP) models of McClelland and Rumelhart (1986).

This chapter describes several cognitive characteristics of dreaming sleep that have long evaded explanation, proposes the features of connectionist models that suggest potential solutions to these problems, and then describes several simulations of the characteristics. Several implications for the "interpretation of dreams" and suggestions for further research complete the chapter.

The traditional structural characteristics of dreams are their vivid visual imagery, bizarreness, storylike thematic quality, and hallucinatory or credibility quality. Other, even more basic characteristics, perhaps shared by waking mentation, are the schematic unity of each temporal moment of the dream, and the capability of the higher levels of the central nervous system to produce perceptionlike images in the absence of external stimulus input. In emphasizing the hallucinatory quality of dreaming we have so focused on the sleeper's gullibility that we have forgotten to ask how one part of the cognitive system can produce accurate facsimiles of perceptual events that in the waking state require input from the sensory systems. The solution to these questions suggests a different perspective to the hallucinatory experience of visual imagery and bizarreness in sleep.

THE SCHEMATIC CHARACTERISTIC OF DREAMING

Although the notion of the schematic quality of conscious experience has an intuitive validity, the concept was too vague and elusive to play a strong theoretical role in cognitive psychology (Alba & Hasher, 1983; Anderson & Bower, 1973) until Rumelhart, Smolensky, McClelland, and Hinton (1986) demonstrated their connectionist schemata (SCHEMATA:RSMH) model. Their schema is a pattern of activation among a distributed set of schemata, which in turn may be the consequence of a pattern of lower-order subschemata, and so on until units with fixed properties such as the line detectors in the visual cortex are reached. Conversely, a pattern of activation among schemata may constitute a higher order schema.

A fundamental assumption of this approach is that schemata are not fixed features or memory units as in list-processing models of artificial intelligence, but rather patterns of activation among lower-order units. Objects' meanings and names may be computed from clusters of features as in conventional models, but the features are constructed from subfeatural or microcognitive units that are not accessible to introspection. These reductive levels of description putatively extend down to the individual neuron but, fortunately, the lowest levels of description need not be explicitly included in models that are focused on higher level processes.

The units in a connectionist schemata model must be defined at a level that is one or two levels subordinate to that of the overall schema to be computed. The units may be selected to represent the objects, features, or subfeatures of the domain to be modeled. At any point in time each unit has a particular level of activation, which it passes on to other units as a function of the $\pm$ weights that connect it to those units. Because the SCHEMATA:RSMH model cannot learn its own weights, they must be estimated by some procedure that is independent of the schemata-producing process of the model (see Rumelhart, Smolensky, McClelland, & Hinton, 1986).

As the activation from each unit contributes to the activation or inhibition of other units in the network, some units inevitably become more activated than their neighbors. Over successive cycles the most strongly activated units build up the activation of units to which they are connected by positive weights and these subgroups of units begin to act collectively to activate and inhibit other subgroups of units.

It is these coalitions of tightly interconnected units that correspond most closely to what have been called schemata. The stable pattern as a whole can be considered as a particular configuration of a number of such overlapping patterns and is determined by the dynamic equilibrium of all of these subpatterns interacting with one another and with the inputs. Thus, the maxima in the goodness-of-fit space corresponds to interpretations of the inputs or, in the language of schemata, configurations of instantiated schemata. In short, they are those states that maximize the particular set of constraints acting at the moment (Rumelhart, Smolensky, McClelland, & Hinton, 1986).

SCHEMATA UNDER STATES OF HIGH SENSORY THRESHOLDS

In SCHEMATA:RSMH, perceptual processing is initiated by activating a subset of units from an outside source. But this source of initial activation is not available for nonperceptual processes, for example, the production of imagery during states of high sensory threshold such as REM sleep. This problem is solved by giving each unit in the network a decay function so that, once activated, it will retain a fraction of its activation across succeeding cycles.

In the first model described here, the Distributed Recurrent Activation Model of Imagery and Thought—Schemata (DREAMIT-S), the weights estimate some of the spatial and temporal asymmetries of the external world. If, for example, A normally $\rightarrow B$, which typically $\rightarrow C$, then a cluster of units representing A should have positive weights to the units representing B. The B units should similarly have positive connections to C units, but inhibitory or negative connections to A units, and C should similarly inhibit B. In this fashion, temporal sequences can be modeled in a distributed fashion. To model such a sequence, the weights *might* be symmetric within each cluster ($w_{ij} = w_{ji}$), but asymmetric between clusters. This asymmetric characteristic violates the basic assumption on which SCHEMATA:RSMH was constructed.

NOVELTY

Another characteristic of a connectionist schemata model that is of particular significance for a model of dream production is that the production of a schemata is heavily influenced by its distributed context. For example, the schemata of a table may vary with the type of room and building in which the table exists. In a modular model, this contextual influence may be "top-down" from units in a higher-order module, or it may be from other units within the same module. Secondly, if contextual constraints are sufficiently strong, a complete schema can be produced with relatively little external input. To the extent that schemata are tailor-made to their contexts, they are, like dream images, always somewhat unique. This ability to construct novel schemata is a necessary requisite for modeling the bizarre mentation of dreaming sleep.

VISUAL IMAGERY

The ability of PDP nets to respond equally well to top-down and bottom-up input (Hinton & Anderson, 1981) is an essential characteristic of any cognitive model that must account for the production of output in the absence of sensory input. To the extent that sleep mentation, and even waking fantasy, is generally independent of concurrent external stimulation, such mentation must necessarily be produced by something other than the conventionally defined bottom-up process that originates in sensory receptors or the projection areas of the cortex. As Feldman (1981) pointed out:

> [the connectionist] model gives us a particularly simple way to describe visual imaging. It is what happens when the perceptual net operates top-down without sensory input. . . . Notice that a visual image (just like a percept) is a state of activity of the network and the issue of iconic versus propositional representation . . . doesn't arise. There is considerable evidence that visual images are mostly reconstructed from highly abstracted internal descriptions. . . . Visual imagery is just one instance of the ability of the neural networks . . . to be operated with input and output connections suppressed. We refer to this as simulation and posit it as the fundamental mechanism underlying memory reorganization, planning, and other higher mental activities. (pp. 60–61)

BIZARRENESS AND DREAMIT-S

Bizarre mentation includes improbable conjunctions of image parts, of relations between image and name or meaning, or improbable sequences of event characteristics. Bizarreness is always defined relative to some waking perceptual norm. For this reason, a model of bizarre mentation must be able to first simulate "normal" waking perceptual responses, and then shift to the occasional production of a "bizarre" event only when parameters that characterize REM sleep are in operation. Because SCHE-MATA-RSMH, upon which DREAMIT-S is modeled, has no procedure to simulate the fine tuning of weights that takes place in waking perception, satisfactory waking simulations cannot be achieved by DREAMIT-S. The simulation of bizarreness must therefore be handled by another model, DREAMIT-BP (Backpropagation), which is able to simulate perceptual learning.

DREAMIT-S: SIMULATION OF A STATIC SCHEMATA

DREAMIT-S was constructed by Fookson and Antrobus (1990) to simulate some of the characteristics of REM and NREM sleep and of waking menta-tion, both as a closed system and, in a very limited fashion, as a perceptual system. It consists of a network of 180 compound units, plus several control units, processed on the Rochester Connectionist Simulator, Version 4.1, run on a SUN Workstation. Units influence one another by passing their activa-tion throughout the network according to the pattern of positive or nega-tive weights that describes the relation of each unit to every other one. Inasmuch as the weight matrix represents the memory structure of a partic-ular individual rather than a hypothetical group average, the weights, w_{ij}, are conditional probabilities, estimated by the author, to approximate the probability that unit j is active given that unit i is active.

The weights are then modified in 35 brief perceptual-conceptual-motor response simulations, so that seeding between 1 and 3 perceptual units would yield the appropriate conceptual and/or motor responses. Imaginal processes and dreaming sequences are subsequently simulated by seeding or priming the same units and then running the network through 20 to 30 cycles as a closed system.

Both unit activation and weights are continuous functions. In order for units to represent both the depolarization and the hyperpolarization and negative afterpotential of sets of neurons, units are permitted to take on both positive and negative values. A squash function squashes the positive values downward and the negative values upward toward the resting po-tential, or off state, of the unit. Since weights take account of the temporal order of events, w_{ij} does not necessarily equal w_{ji}. Each unit represents a cluster of neurons which, in turn, is capable of representing a particular perceptual, cognitive, or action attribute. DREAMIT-S consists of 180 units that represent visual features, visual percepts of objects and events, names, action or command units, motor execution units, roles and subroles, states, values, and modifiers of all of the above. It includes a very small linguistic production module but no linguistic encoding units.

SIMULATION OF A MENTATION MOMENT IN TIME BY DREAMIT-S

The "moment in time" schemata simulations are useful in that they replicate the basic characteristics of SCHEMATA:RSMH and demonstrate specific limitations of a single layered network as a model of stream of imagery and thought over time.

A slice in time is represented by the pattern of activation of the units in the network at a given point in time. This "moment" simulation follows the schemata simulations of Rumelhart, Smolensky, McClelland, & Hinton, (1986) of various rooms, in that one or more units are "seeded" with an initial level of activation, though not clamped, and the net is allowed to move through a number of cycles until it reaches a stable state. For example, seeding units that represent *math* and *professor* will, over several iterations, activate the role unit, *I-as-student,* and the units *college, concentrate,* and *try-to-understand,* and inhibit all the units concerned with sports, family, and friends. Seeding the network with *Mom* will activate the role unit *I-as-son* and units that represent the *home, kitchen, eating,* and Mom's features, *smile, blond,* and eventually *father* too. Rumelhart et al. have argued persuasively that these clusters of activated units simulate the associative characteristic of human schemata.

As described earlier, the SCHEMATA:RSMH model iterates to a schematalike solution and then stops. It does not change until it is perturbed by new "perceptual" input. It is, therefore, unable to simulate the continuous aspect of the flow of imagery and thought that is characteristic of dreaming and waking fantasy.

Turning to theories and research in visual perception for a foundation for the simulation of the temporal sequencing of images, we find that the field is restricted almost exclusively to the study of stationary visual stimuli. If we turn to traditional conceptions of dream formation we find them dominated by motivational variables that are removed by many steps from the production of visual features, event sequences such as limb movements, or shifts in visual perspective or orientation. There is, therefore, little solid empirical basis on which to build a model of image sequencing.

Let us conjecture what kinds of information might drive image sequences. Consider, for example, an imagined game of catch where the dreamer is a participant. The visual images themselves may determine, in part, the sequencing of the images. The ball must move in an orderly fashion, and this order is based on the prior perceptual learning of the dreamer. But a fast moving ball does not create a clear visual image in waking perception so it is unlikely that an image of the fast moving ball can be created, at least from the information in visual memory. If the continuity of the imagined sequence depends only on the "visible" features of the image such as form, texture, and color, it will falter at this point. Fortunately, information about the trajectory of the ball is computed in spatial modules and is probably available to sustain the continuity of an imagined sequence, even in the absence of imaged visible qualities.

But even visible and spatial information are not sufficient to generate an imagined game of catch. Conceptual knowledge is also necessary to the game. Conceptual information is necessary for the image of a moving ball to produce the image of a player catching the ball and then throwing it to another player. This example illustrates how different classes of information, possibly in different memory modules, are necessary to generate a simple imaginal sequence.

This emphasis on the role of perceptual learning in image construction differs from that of traditional approaches to dream interpretation, which emphasize personal motives and personality styles of perception and behavior. These approaches assume, but never make explicit, the processing links between motive and image. Clearly, this is a requirement for any comprehensive model of dreaming. Although the manner in which motivational, stylistic, spatial, and visual features are combined to create the dream sequence will not be solved by the end of this chapter, the simulations presented will, we hope, help to draw the theoretical issues more clearly and will demonstrate a fundamental role for perceptual learning in the production of dream image sequences.

Simulation of Temporal Sequences by DREAMIT-S

Although the joint contribution of motivational, conceptual, spatial, and visible information to a succession of schemata is a plausible psychological notion, it is not compatible with the SCHEMATA:RSMH model, which computes to a single schema state. For a schemata model to move through a succession of states, it must be inherently unstable. As previously stated, the weights must be asymmetric, biased in the direction of learned, ordered sequences. But if the successive steps of a sequence consist of the ordered activation of individual units, then the model will be a conventional linear, nonparallel, nondistributed model. By contrast, the successive steps in a sequential schemata model should consist of schema states. That is, DREAMIT-S must be not only sequential but parallel and distributed as well.

The most active image sequences in DREAMIT-S are illustrated by a subset of units that can simulate a game of catch between two players. Seeding the network with *ball* and *Harry*, the first player's sporting friend's name, will activate *I-as-ballplayer* and the subrole unit *as agent*, followed by the activation of a distributed sequence of units concerned with *throw*(ing the)-*ball, other-player as recipient*, and the inhibition of the units that initiated the sequence. Motivational influence is simulated so that activating *concentrate* decreases the probability that the ball will *go wide* and that *Harry* as *recipient* is obliged to *run* to *catch-the-ball*. Once Harry has caught or picked up the ball and has the *ball-in-hand*, a nondistributed step, the subrole *I-as-recipient* is activated, and one of a set of alternative motor commands is given, depending on how well Harry is known to be able to throw the ball. Clearly, DREAMIT-S is able to simulate a sequence of schemata.

Although DREAMIT-S is able to simulate the distributed and sequential flow of imagery and thought, it has serious limitations that restrict its usefulness as a model for the production of REM and NREM imagery. First, it is a one-layered model and therefore cannot represent nonlinear relationships among its units. That is, the +/− weights between each pair of units do not allow the model to represent interactive relationships. For example, *A* can send activation to *B*, but it can't handle an interactive relationship such as sending activation to *B* if and only if *C* is also active. Thus, activating *I'm hungry* should activate *Mom* and the *kitchen* only when *at home* is also activated. However, because DREAMIT-S is a single-layered model, activating *I'm hungry* activates *Mom, kitchen*, and *home* even though the subject is in the college *cafeteria*. This restriction of the single-layered model to linear relationships causes the network to occasionally come apart. This issue is discussed in some detail in connection with learning the "exclusive or" problem and multilayered networks (Rumelhart, Hinton, & Williams, 1986).

The second limitation of DREAMIT-S as a single-layered model is that it has no satisfactory, nonarbitrary way to learn or otherwise determine the weights of the network. DREAMIT-S weights were assigned as conditional probabilities, and then "fine-tuned" by running the network in short "perceptual" sequences. Once the weights were adjusted so that satisfactory perceptual sequences could be simulated, the network was run for longer imaginal sequences of 10 to 20 iterations. These sequences were "imaginal" in that they were seeded only on the first cycle, and then run for extended iterations as a system that was closed to external input. Despite the perceptual fine-tuning of the weights, it was difficult to determine whether a bizarre relationship at the 20th iteration was due to anything other than small errors in the assignment of weights.

These two limitations persuaded the authors to develop DREAMIT-BP as an alternative model, which will be introduced after briefly describing several additional positive features of DREAMIT-S that have not yet been incorporated into DREAMIT-BP.

Simulation of REM and Waking versus NREM Mentation

Following Antrobus (1983), who showed that Total Recall Count (TRC) is the major discriminator of REM and NREM mentation reports, and

Antrobus's (1986) argument that distributed cortical activation is the major neurophysiological antecedent of TRC, DREAMIT-S was designed to control and vary distributed activation to all units in the network. Control units were constructed to represent the sleep state shifts in subcortical activation that, in turn, control the shifts in distributed activation to the cognitive units.

Distributed Activation

DREAMIT-S uses several methods to modulate the overall level of network activation as well as the pattern of activation among sections of the net. A general pontine reticular formation (PRF) control unit multiplies the input to each unit from all other units by a value equal to or less than 1. This Sigma-Pi type unit (Rumelhart, Hinton, & McClelland, 1986) can thus simulate the lowered general activation of NREM sleep by lowering the value below 1.0, which represents full waking activation. Implementation of this feature of the simulator requires that each compound unit be constructed from 5 subunits, separate excitatory and inhibitory units, and an output unit, for a total of 900 units.

The effect of decreasing this excitatory control unit < 1 is to slow the rate at which a mentation sequence moves and also to decrease the total number of units that are active at any one point in time. If we further assume that memory decay is some positive function of number of cycles of the simulator, then as the imaginal sequence slows down, less information is available for recall and verbal report. If we further assume that retrievability is a function of the number of active content-addressable cues in the association module, then the reduced number of activated units at any one point in time would further reduce the amount of retrievable information.

Further modulation of the network could be provided by a feedback loop from a generous sample of network units to the control sites so as to maintain the average level of activation in the network within a fixed range. It is assumed that this average level in REM and NREM sleep is determined in part by the organism's goal of maintaining sleep.

Additional modulation of the net is provided by the rate at which each unit naturally decays. To the extent that role and motivational states change more slowly than images, role and motivational states are set with slower decay rates than other units.

Two additional control features are added, to simulate the putative effects of afferent and motor inhibition in REM sleep on REM mentation. Following the Activation-Synthesis model, it is assumed here that: the cortex gives motor commands in REM dreams but the motor execution is inhibited at the spinal level, and further, any proprioceptive feedback from even truncated movements is inhibited before it reaches the cortex. One consequence of this activation–inhibition pattern is the illusion of motor paralysis in the dream.

To simulate this effect, a "spinal" sigma-pi control unit can inhibit afferent feedback from units in the network that represent motor execution commands. Thus, the *I-throw-ball* command, in the absence of activation of motor feedback, inhibits the activation initially sent to *ball-going* and it may secondarily activate *I can't throw* and *I-can't-move*, a common experience in REM sleep dreams. This paralysis and the panic response to it are often regarded as one of the bizarre characteristics of REM dreams. Depending on the context of the network at large, the catch-playing may come to a stop at that point, or the *other-player-agent* may eventually be imagined to possess the *ball* and continue to throw it, even though the ball was never seen going toward him.

Simulation in a Closed System:
Bias, Personal Concerns, and Motivation

Cognitive models are most precise when there is a short distance between the input to and output from the external, sensory world. The behavior of a closed cognitive network over many cycles is therefore difficult to test with precision. One interesting characteristic of a closed network is that it is strongly influenced by the sampling density of the objects or events that it represents. The network tends to compute to states that are representative of events that have been sampled with the highest frequency. An early version of DREAMIT-S was built around a role of *I-as-student*. The role included concentrating on lectures, doing homework, and so on. But even though we seeded, or primed, the network with references to baseball, dinner, or a girlfriend, DREAMIT-S kept returning to the student routine. As the network was expanded, however, to give more equal representation to alternative roles and activities, DREAMIT-S produced a wider variety of outputs to different initial seeds. It would seem, therefore, that high unit sampling density might be one way in which personal concerns, interests, or even motivational states, may be represented in a neural network. As with a delusional system, the more one thinks out all the ramifications of a particular event, the more one learns new connections between that event and other events in one's life. Eventually, anything one thinks of eventually reactivates the central delusion and is modified or biased by it.

Such a bias can also be represented by deliberately assigning a positive resting bias activation level of a unit to some value greater than zero. Thus, to become fully active, the unit requires less activation from surrounding units. For example, assigning a positive bias to *run-from* or the *fix* unit will increase the probability that these units—and units that they in turn activate—will become fully activated.

From the perspective of dream interpretation, an interpreter uses the mentation report to infer the biases in the sleeper's cognitive network. The size of the bias units creates some formidable problems for the would-be interpreter. The dreamer may have run from a barking dog during the preceding afternoon but may then dream of running from, instead, her shouting boss. In a study of a logger and a trainman awaiting surgery for vascular obstructions, both dreamed about unclogging objects in their occupational environments, but neither dreamed about repairing their much less visually familiar vascular obstructions (Antrobus, 1977; Breger, Hunter, & Lane, 1971). In each case the motivational bias, to unclog, was linked to the highly familiar occupational activity biases of the two workers. Reports such as these imply that action biases created in recent waking-state episodes may persist into the sleep state, but, for reasons not understood, the units that represent these goals may be unable to activate the object units, particularly the visual units, to which they were attached during the waking episode. The goal units may well activate some of the features of the objects in the waking episode, but not enough to fully activate a visual representation of that object.

This completes a brief introduction to the accomplishments of DREAMIT-S. We remind the reader that its inability to represent nonlinear relations and to learn its own weights is a major limitation of the schemata model. We turn now to DREAMIT-BP, a back-propagation model that has none of these limitations.

DREAMIT-BP

In contrast to the 180 units of DREAMIT-S, DREAMIT-BP has only 10 or 12 units and these units are not intended to represent any particular real-life objects or features. Further, it does not at this time include the control units that permit the simulation of shifts in sleep states. Its chief value presently is to provide some insight into how the learning of perceptual sequences in the waking state may account for some of the features of dreaming that we label "bizarre."

DREAMIT-BP is a three-layer model that first acquires its weights in a learning mode representative of waking perceptual learning. It is then run in an imaginal mode that is intended to represent the closed system characteristics of the dreaming sleep state. In the learning mode, stimuli are presented to the input layer. This information is propagated forward, recoded to an intermediate "hidden" layer, and then propagated forward and recoded again to an output or response layer. At this point, the output is compared to the "correct" output, and the "error" information is propagated back so that the weights linking the hidden to output layers and input to hidden layers are adjusted by small increments so as to reduce the final set of errors (see Rumelhart et al., 1986). After many, say 1000, such training trials, the weights tend to settle to values that yield accurate responses to all of the stimuli. The use of the two sets of weights permits this model to learn nonlinear relations between the input and output, something not possible with a single-layered schemata model such as DREAMIT-S.

In the imaginal mode, the stimulus for the input layer is the response produced by the output layer. The response is folded back to the input layer so that the output equals the input. In this form the model is like a two-layered model. It is similar to the schemata model in that each unit is connected to each other unit, but only via the units of the hidden layer rather than directly.

The Simulation of Bizarreness

DREAMIT-BP is particularly interesting because of its ability to simulate the most common classes of bizarreness in dreaming: discontinuities and improbable combinations. Discontinuities occur where a sequence of images appears to be interrupted and followed by an event that would have a low sequential probability in normal waking perception. For example, a subject may report the "sudden" appearance in the kitchen of a person who is deceased or otherwise absent from the normal waking environment. Improbable combinations are the occurrence of two or more objects or features whose co-occurrence in waking perception is low. For example, an imaged person may be carrying false teeth that are too large to put in his mouth.

In the perceptual mode, DREAMIT-BP learns a sequence of events such as $A \rightarrow B \rightarrow \ldots \rightarrow N$, where each letter event is represented by a binary string such as 101101. For reasons that are described below, each binary digit is doubled, so that the $A \rightarrow B$ sequence might be represented by $110011110011 \rightarrow 110011001111$. The simulation of the imaginal mode begins only after the perceptual learning phase is successfully completed. That is, when DREAMIT-BP produces B in response to A, and C in response to B, and so on.

A simulation of imaginal events is defined by the production of responses to internally produced events. Imaginal responses may be initiated by seeding or priming DREAMIT-BP with one of the stimulus events in the learning set, or simply by a random value such as 101010101010. Note that while the initial stimulus is in binary code, DREAMIT-BP's responses are continuous values. For example, a "good" response to 110011110011 might be:

.935 .941 .057 .064 .973 .982 .012 .009 .989 .984 .945 .954,

in that all of the values fall in the .000 to .100, or .900 to 1.000 ranges. This is also a "correct" response in that all of the values approximate the 110011001111 values in the learning set. A "soft" response is one where at least one of the values falls in the .101 to .300 or .700 to .899 range, and a "noisy" response is one with values in the .301 to .699 range.

In summary, after DREAMIT-BP is initiated by one external stimulus, each response that it produces becomes the internal stimulus for the succeeding response, and that response is the internally produced stimulus for the succeeding response. Note that this internally produced, "imaginal" stimulus may or may not approach the quality of the corresponding external stimulus in the perceptual learning set. The question of interest here is whether, in the imaginal mode, DREAMIT-BP produces responses or sequences that mimic some of the characteristics of dream imagery.

DREAMIT-BP passed its first test by producing a high proportion of good responses in the imaginal mode. Even when run to 5000 steps, there was no decline in the average quality of its responses. This contrasted sharply with DREAMIT-S, which degenerated into chaos after 50 cycles.

Temporal Discontinuity

DREAMIT-BP reliably produces good responses in the imaginal mode where the imaginal event consists of previously well learned responses to stimuli in the training set. But what does it produce in response to a stimulus for which no response has been learned? Our prediction was that this situation would lead to a discontinuity in sequencing. To test this hypothesis, DREAMIT-BP was taught 4 7-event sequences, so that the last response event in each learning sequence was not presented as a stimulus for a subsequent response event. In the imaginal mode, DREAMIT-BP was presented with any event in the early part of any sequence. It then accurately produced each successive event in the sequence down to the final response. At the end of the learned sequence set, DREAMIT-BP produced 2 or 3 noisy responses and then a good response that belonged to one of the learned sequences. The good response was followed by the rest of the events in their proper sequential order. At the end of the learned set, 2 or 3 noisy responses occurred again, followed by a good response and the correct subsequent members, and so on.

It is important to note that the output did not degenerate progressively, following the production of a noisy response. DREAMIT-BP essentially "found" the event that was the most appropriate response to the stimulus in the learning set that was most similar to noisy response. For example, if the learning set had included the sequences (A) 111111000011 $\rightarrow$ (B) 111100001111, and (C) 111100000011 $\rightarrow$ (D) 111100001100, and, further, if in the imaginal mode DREAMIT-BP produced the noisy response (rounded to one digit):

.8 .9 .8 .9 .9 .9 .5 .6 .5 .6 .7 .8,

it was more likely for its next response to produce a good approximation to B than to D, simply because the noisy self-produced stimulus was more similar to stimulus A than to C in the original training set.

In summary, where a sequence of perceptual events was well learned, the sequence was faithfully reproduced in the imaginal state, but where perceptual learning provided no reliable succeeding response, DREAMIT-BP, after several ambiguous responses, resumed the production of good imaginal responses but in a sequence with a new starting point. This is, by definition, a temporal discontinuity.

Not only did DREAMIT-BP resume the production of good responses, but the point of resumption tended to be relevant to the preceding context. The first 4 digits of each event in the training set were constant within a given sequence, and they were identical in the stimulus and response members of each sequence. For example, the first 4 digits for the 7 stimuli and responses of the first sequence set were *0011*; for the second sequence set they were *1100*. Thus the 4 digits constituted a context for the remaining 8 digits in each stimulus and response event. In the training phase, DREAMIT-BP was taught to always reproduce the first 4 "context" digits of the stimuli in its responses. Consequently, when, in the imaginal mode, DREAMIT-BP came to the end of a learned sequence, it tended to at least stay in context. That is, it tended to reproduce the first 4 digits of the final stimulus in the learning set event, though any of the latter 8 digits might be noisy. In summary, when temporal discontinuities occurred, they tended to retain the context of the preceding sequence.

Improbable Combinations

DREAMIT-BP logically permitted two classes of improbable combinations: (a) between features that were invariant in the learning phase, and (b) between features that varied considerably in the learning phase. The invariant feature combinations were the 6 identical digit-pairs, *11* or *00*, in each event. In the hundreds of imaginal simulations carried out following successful learning, these pairs were always intact. The 2 digits were always within .05 of one another. This is equivalent to saying that one never dreams of people with their eye and ear positions reversed.

In initial simulations, carried out with five digit-pairs (10 digits), there were also no novel or improbable combinations of the digit-pairs in the imaginal phase. A possible reason for this lack of novelty was that 28 of the possible 32 (2^6) response combinations (87.5%) were used in the training set. The probability of a novel response was only 0.125. But in the real world only a small fraction of the possible combinations of features ever occur. Therefore, DREAMIT-BP was retrained in several situations where only 25% of the possible feature combinations were used in the training set, so that the chance probability of a novel event was increased to 0.75.

Under this condition, DREAMIT-BP did produce novel, improbable combinations of features in the imaginal mode, but only following one or more noisy responses. And these noisy responses occurred under the same conditions as in the earlier simulations, at the end of well learned sequences. The improbable combinations generally differed only by one digit-pair from the most similar member in the training sets. For example, DREAMIT-BP might produce the novel response, rounded to *0*s or *1*s, *111111001111*, where the most similar response in the training set was *111111001100*. After producing a novel response, DREAMIT-BP tended to go on to produce good responses in sequence from the original training set rather than to deteriorate into noisy responses.

In conclusion, DREAMIT-BP can simulate the production of a continuous sequence of imaginal events. These events tend to be degraded where the components of the sequence are not well established during perceptual learning. Degraded events tend to be followed by temporal discontinuities in the sequence and by novel events that have improbable combinations of features. In producing an imaginal response to a self-produced imaginal stimulus, DREAMIT-BP is constrained by the similarity of its self-produced stimulus to the stimulus events in its learning history, the relative probability of the alternative responses it has encountered in its perceptual past, and the strength of the learned connections between them.

Although DREAMIT-BP consists of only six feature elements, it can easily be expanded to more complex perceptual events. Furthermore, the elements within each event need not be restricted to the representation of visual features. They may also be used to represent motivational and conceptual contexts.

DREAMIT-S and DREAMIT-BP have been successful in simulating several fundamental characteristics of dream image production. The neural net models upon which the two simulators are based provide investigators with a powerful theoretical tool for the study of dream production processes. It is my hope that future research will obtain the kinds of data that permit the component parts of the model to be clearly specified and tested.

16

REM Sleep and Dream Formation: A Theoretical Integration

STEVEN J. ELLMAN
City College of the City University of New York

LISSA N. WEINSTEIN
Teachers College, Columbia University

REVIEW OF THEORETICAL POSITIONS

In this chapter we examine theories that attempt to explain the function of REM sleep. We also focus on theoretical statements that relate to the issue of dream formation. Although these two types of theories deal with different phenomena, in the history of sleep research the issues they raise have proven to be quite related. Our effort is to synthesize these two types of theoretical statements in order to present the beginning of a unified theory on the function of REM sleep and the mentation associated with this state of consciousness. A reasonable amount of evidence is referred to in the chapter but it is not intended as a review of the literature. Rather, we are presenting some selected positions either in contrast to, or as an attempt to reconcile aspects of our hypothesis, with other positions. Thus, Crick and Mitchison (1983, 1986) are presented as a modern position that attempts to deny the psychological importance of the dream. Positions that stress the function of REM as involving memory consolidation are presented as an alternative position to the one we espouse. The other positions discussed are ones related to our theoretical stance. For example, Ephron and Carrington (1966) and Roffwarg, Muzio, and Dement (1968) have formulated REM sleep in terms of its providing endogenous stimulation to the sleeping organism, and these statements are related to the one we present in the second half of the chapter, where we offer our own theoretical statement. Although we do not exhaustively compare existing theories of the functions of REM sleep, we attempt to look at those aspects of the data that are more or less adequately explained by a given position. Some methodological problems relating to these issues are discussed in Chapter 10.

There are at this point in time a number of findings that any theory of has to explain. For instance, REM sleep occurs in the adults of almost all mammalian species. In addition, REM sleep occurs in sizable percentages of adult members of avian predators (e.g., hawks, eagles). REM sleep occurs in negligible amounts in other types of birds and is not recordable in reptilian species. Thus, in adult animals REM sleep occurs in avian predators and virtually all mammals. If one looks at ontogeny the picture is somewhat different. If a normal adult spends 15 to 20% of his or her night in REM sleep, a human infant might spend anywhere from 50 to 70% of her or his sleep time in REM sleep. We know from intrauterine recording (Jouvet, 1968) that REM sleep occurs in even greater amounts in intrauterine life than in infant life. For all mammals that have been studied across developmental lines there is considerably more REM sleep during infancy than during adulthood. As a mammalian organism ages, both the absolute and relative (or percentage) amounts of REM sleep decrease. The same is the case for birds; even those birds that show negligible amounts of REM sleep in adulthood show greater amounts of REM sleep during infancy. Thus, we can generalize and say that as one records earlier in the life of a given species one will find greater amounts of REM sleep.

A theory of REM sleep would also have to explain the high CNS activity level found during REM sleep. In addition one would have to account for some of the basic findings in sleep mentation studies and studies of REMD that were outlined in the introductory section of the book and detailed in chapters throughout the book.

Crick and Mitchison—Neural Nets

This theory of REM sleep is interesting for several reasons, not the least of which is that a Nobel laureate is attempting a theory in a field outside his original area of interest. Crick and Mitchison's (1983, 1986) reviews have not fully explored the REM sleep literature, but in a general way have included those elements that the authors found useful. Their model of the function of REM sleep emanates from the Hobson and McCarley (1977) activation-synthesis model of dream formation. Hobson and McCarley maintained that the firing of the pontine FTG cells is both the necessary and sufficient cause of REM sleep, and that dreaming is simply a utilization of stored memories to make sense of this random activation. They maintained that the random activation accounts for the bizarreness, discontinuity, and incoherence of dreaming or REM sleep mentation. Thus, the dream is explained in isomorphic terms as a direct, virtually inevitable response to CNS stimulation.

Crick and Mitchison went concluding further when they concluded that REM sleep is a state in which reverse learning (a process "designed to make storage in an associative net more efficient") takes place. In their first paper they stated: "We dream in order to forget." In their second paper they amended slightly and suggested that "we dream to reduce fantasy . . . or to reduce obsession" in the waking state. Thus we dream to reduce the interaction of ideas that might produce fantasy, and as a result "the system becomes less imaginative and more prosaic in its behavior." Reverse learning is an automatic process with no "supervisor"; thus all dream fragments should be forgotten at an equal rate. Recurrent dreams are handled by a subsidiary assumption:

> It is known that certain inputs, even during sleep can awaken the sleeper. . . .
> We have therefore assumed that certain dreams, because of their frightening
> or threatening nature, or whatever, tend to wake the sleeper. Since such
> dreams are likely to demand the attention of the newly awakened person,
> they are more likely to be strengthened in memory, rather than weakened, as
> the ordinary learning process takes over after the sleeper awakes. This we
> would argue would make these dreams more likely to recur in the future.
> (Crick & Mitchison, 1986, p. 237)

Given this brief explanation of recurrent dreams we must assume that the strength of their formulation relates to their position on the biological function of REM sleep. Without question, most, if not all, REM sleep investigators agree that there is an important biological function of REM sleep (see Dement & Mitler, 1973; Dement et al., 1969; Ephron & Carrington, 1966; Roffwarg et al., 1968). Crick and Mitchison, however, dismissed previous attempts at explaining the biological function of REM sleep. The only alternative theory of REM considered was Jouvet's and his hypothesis was handled in brief form:

> Jouvet has suggested that REM dreams help to tune up instinctive behavior
> laid down crudely in epigenesis. . . . This idea seems to us very unlikely

since to do this effectively it would seem essential that there be considerable muscular output in order to receive feedback from the environment. However, there is already a mechanism, highly developed in mammals which seems to perform just this function in the awake animal, "play." (p. 248)

No other theories of REM were mentioned. Crick and Mitchison cited no experimental evidence to support their position. They presented evidence from the USSR that dolphins do not have REM sleep and cited previous reports (Allison & Goff, 1972) that the echidna (spiny anteater) does not have REM sleep. Since the authors considered these reports compatible with their theory, we can conclude that they believed that with greater cortical development there would be less REM sleep. To quote the authors, "The function of REM sleep is to make advanced brains more efficient and, in particular, to allow these brains to have a smaller size than they would otherwise have" (p. 248). Of course, the obvious example is *homo sapiens*, but here the authors stated that "it seemed more reasonable to attribute the size of our brain to our exceptional cognitive ability."

Thus on one hand cortical mass is assumed to be crucial variable in the occurence of REM sleep and when a species does not fit in with this prediction then an alternative hypothesis is presented. There is no way that the authors' hypotheses can account for REM augmentation or for the ontogenetic aspects of REM sleep to be described in the next section. As a final point, if one accepts Crick and Mitchison's position, then the question of dreaming is easily disposed of, since dreaming is considered an epiphenomena and of little importance except that it may be interesting to see "the subject's own interpretation of the dream." The authors implicitly, perhaps explicitly, thought that if the function of REM has important phylogenetic roots, this obviates a psychological function for REM in humans. This is curious evolutionary reasoning, but we touch on this issue when we present our own hypotheses.

Learning-Memory Consolidation Theories of REM Sleep

In recent years the theoretical position linking the function of REM sleep to memory, memory consolidation, learning, and adaptive processes has received the most attention. Various authors have presented versions of this perspective in terms of information processing and/or computer models (e.g., Dewan, 1968, 1970). This position has gained a wide and varied array of adherents, including neurophysiologists, physiological psychologists, and psychoanalysts; thus, we have to be selective in our review of these positions. This selectivity is mitigated by the fact that we have included some discussion of learning-memory consolidation theories in the REMD chapter. In that chapter we were particularly critical of the methodology utilized in REMD studies that involve learning and memory. In this chapter we have the benefit of being able to state the positions without having to rigorously criticize experimental methodology. Moreover, we also have the advantage of 10 years of theory and research with experiments that are not restricted to a REMD paradigm.

Essentially all of these theorists maintain that REM sleep facilitates or is necessary for memory consolidation. One might say that this hypothesis is diametrically opposed to Crick and Mitchison's position, because an extreme form of this position would maintain that without REM no permanent learning could take place, because long-term memory consolidation would be prevented. A milder form of this hypothesis would maintain that, given REMD, learning and memory processes would at least be seriously impaired. The hypothesis presented in this straightforward way is relatively easy to test and one can derive clear predictions from this position. Understandably, the history of sleep research has not reached this degree of clarity. As we have shown in our REMD chapter, the results concerning REMD and learning have been ambiguous at best. In this chapter, we review two types of positions that characterize this perspective. We look at Greenberg and Pearlman's position (Greenberg, 1981, Greenberg & Pearlman, 1974; Greenberg, Pearlman, Schwartz, & Grossman, 1983), which deals with human experience, and at a variety of authors who maintain that some learning experiences lead to increases in REM time or what has been called REM augmentation.

Greenberg and Pearlman maintained that only certain types of learning and memories are affected by REMD; in their view, REM sleep is utilized to process emotional experiences. Thus, the learning of nonsense syllables may not be affected by REMD, but the learning and/or processing of emotional material is affected by REMD. In a recent study, they had 8 subjects view cards that represented latency age experiences. This was done after REMD and after NREM control awakenings. They found that REMD led to subjects' reporting less emotionally laden content in response to the pictures than in response to NREM control awakenings. They concluded that REM sleep normally is involved in making a connection between present affective experiences and emotionally meaningful memories from the past. When REM is disrupted, subjects are not able to make this connection and they respond to emotional material with less relevant emotion. Several other authors (Cohen, 1979; Palumbo, 1976, 1978) presented data to indicate that dreaming involves the processing, matching, and assimilation of childhood and present memories. Some authors, such as Palumbo, felt that their data strongly supported this perspective; other authors waned somewhat in their support of the position. Interestingly, Greenberg and Pearlman viewed their data as contradicting a psychoanalytic drive hypothesis. They stated that a drive hypothesis would lead to a "prediction of increased emotionality" following REMD, but their results contradicted this prediction. Authors writing from a learning memory perspective frequently contrast their position with that offered in a psychoanalytic drive formulation. This does not mean that the authors are not sympathetic to psychoanalytic formulations; rather, they are contradicting this specific aspect of psychoanalytic theory. Later in the chapter we take up this issue more fully.

Pearlman (1979) and other authors (Bloch, Hennevin, & Leconte, 1981) stated that REMD disrupts animal learning when the tasks to be learned are complex and require integrative skills. Some authors maintained that REMD affects memory consolidation if it comes within 3 hours of learning, but REMD after 3 hours does not disrupt consolidation. These findings and many other similar paradigms produced somewhat contradictory results (see Chapter 10). Although there may be a good deal of disagreement about the effects of REMD on learning and memory, there is another paradigm not involving REMD that lends support to the memory consolidation point of view. These experiments involve learning paradigms when REM sleep is augmented. Augmentation is defined as an increase in REM sleep following a given learning task. Thus, if an animal (usually a mouse, cat, or rat) is successful in a newly learned, two-way avoidance task, one might expect an increase in REM sleep so that the animal can consolidate this new learning experience. A variety of experiments reported REM augmentation, and it is perhaps the most powerful experimental evidence for the learning/memory consolidation theoretical perspective. It also lends some credence to the animal/human analogue in which Greenberg and Pearlman suggested that complex learning situations are analogous to what they called emotional situations in the lives of humans. Thus, in the animal paradigms, one might easily understand how a relatively complicated learning situation that is followed by shock is meaningful in the life of a laboratory animal. To paraphrase Bloch et al. (1981): When animals cannot learn, they present no REM augmentation. In addition a simple task, like escape learning, does not produce REM increases, the acquisition of complex tasks, is inevitably followed by an increase of REM time.

There have been a variety of criticisms concerning REM augmentation studies and we have been among the critics, but at this point there have been enough studies to say that at least under some conditions it is possible to augment REM sleep. Without a thorough review of these studies, we can only state that we believe the evidence is convincing from a number of laboratories (Bloch et al., 1981; Fishbein & Gutwein, 1981). There are still a variety of issues that this position has not yet addressed; one we believe crucial is the need for an independent definition of complex learning. Nevertheless it is possible on the basis of existing evidence to conclude that a theory of REM sleep must explain REM augmentation findings.

Although we believe that REM augmentation is a phenomenon to be explained, there are related phenomena that have to be explained as well. For example, we might ask why subjects in a sleep laboratory have reduced REM sleep during the first night in the lab. On the face of it, this question may not seem relevant to the phenomenon of REM augmentation, but we hope to provide a model that shows the relationship between these two phenomena as well as other related phenomena. The question we ask is what is the best explanation of these results and how may one develop a theory that integrates human and animal data from both an ontogenetic and a phylogenetic point of view. Before we attempt to answer this question, we present another perspective that some authors have called the central nervous system (CNS) theories of the function of REM sleep.

CNS Theories of REM Sleep

Two of the earliest theories concerning the function of REM sleep viewed REM as a source of endogenous stimulation that provided stimulation for the CNS. Ephron and Carrington (1966) thought of REM as restoring cortical homeostasis; this restoration is necessary since NREM sleep is seen as a period of deafferentation in which the CNS receives little stimulation. Implicit in their ideas is a notion that optimal, or at least minimal, stimulation is necessary for the cortex to function adequately. REM mechanisms fire periodically to restore cortical homeostasis, and the organism is thus able to sleep without cortical damage or inefficiency. Roffwarg et al. (1966) also saw REM sleep as providing endogenous stimulation to the organism, but their theoretical focus was the large amounts of REM found in the newborn. They drew an analogy between REM mechanisms and the pioneering findings of Hubel and Wiesel (1963), who found that if newborn kittens did not receive enough visual stimulation, certain aspects of the visual system would fail to develop. It was postulated by Roffwarg et al. (1966) that stimulation for the newborn came not only from external sources but also from endogenous or internal sources and that REM sleep is one such endogenous source of stimulation. This would account for the high amounts of REM at birth; endogenous stimulation is being provided to the CNS at a time when the infant finds it hard to process exogenous stimulation. Taken together, these two theoretical positions form one type of explanation of REM mechanisms: during infancy there is a need for endogenous stimulation to provide for CNS maturation, and during later life there is a need for REM sleep during the night to periodically provide the sleeping-deafferented CNS with stimulation to maintain cortical homeostasis. This coupling of theoretical positions is our coupling and not the authors'. In fact, each group of authors has its own version of what happens at other points of the developmental cycle (other than their main emphasis) but in our view we have reasonably stated their theoretical perspectives.

A MOTIVATION HYPOTHESIS

Several other authors (Dement, 1965, 1969; Vogel, 1979) offered this type of hypothesis, but in this chapter we restrict ourselves to the hypothesis that we are proposing. Before we state this point of view, we recount some of Freud's perspectives, since we believe that all the motivational hypotheses are based, at least in part, on Freud's writings. Interestingly, Freud's views on dreams (1990/1953) are not the only, or perhaps even the main, writings that form the basis for this position. Rather, Freud's views on endogenous stimulation or drive have been most crucial. For Freud, drive implied an internal force or source of stimulation. To quote, "They maintain an incessant and unavoidable afflux of stimulation" (Freud, 1915/1953, p. 120). Freud asserted that an essential component in his conception of drive is that, at least periodically, there is an unavoidable amount of internal or endogenous stimulation that will provide some motivational impetus for the organism. Freud assumed that this stimulation could occur in varying intensities ("differences in force," in his terminology) and had a source (biochemical, neurochemical, neurophysiological) about which he could only speculate. While it is true that the concept of drive is virtually taboo in much modern psychoanalytic theorizing (see Ellman & Moskowitz, 1980, for a more complete discussion), it is our contention that Freud's version of drive and the concept of the dream as a "safety valve" led to the first REMD studies. As we have said before (see Chapter 11), it was reasoned that if one eliminated REM sleep (thus eliminating the dream), there would be noteworthy psychological effects. Although the initial reports were striking, very few of the results were replicated (except for REM rebound). Despite this, by 1965 Fisher postulated that REM sleep might be the neurophysiological manifestation of what Freud had called drive. Fisher's ideas were speculative, but they led him to study sexuality in the REM process and to discover the fact that penile erections typically occur during REM sleep.

Although Fisher's work did not form the basis of an empirically testable theory, we believe he was a source that other investigators drew from. When we began our series of studies, the phenomenon of REM rebound had been studied in both human and animal species (Dement et al., 1969; Dement & Mitler, 1973; see Chapter 10). Although REM rebound had become a well established fact, the psychological consequences of REMD remained a puzzle. Given the experimental evidence, the idea of REM as a safety valve was no longer a viable concept. Despite this, we began to think of REM as a source of endogenous stimulation, and in wondering what neurophysiological system could mediate what Freud had called drive, we postulated that the positive reward of the intracranial self-stimulation system (ICSS) could be such a system. Olds had demonstrated that animals will reliably bar-press for brain stimulation to parts of the brain that are primarily located in what Nauta (1958) called the limbic system. Olds (1959) and many investigators after him (Deutsch, 1964) showed that ICSS sites are typically in midbrain areas that are also implicated in such behaviors as eating, drinking, sex, and aggression. We thought that if REM sleep is a source of endogenous stimulation and a system that is involved in drive, it may be that during REM an ICSS neural network is fired. This line of reasoning led us to the following theoretical speculations:

- That during REM sleep an ICSS neural network is fired;
- That this network is fired throughout the 24-hour cycle and not only when the animal is sleeping; thus, these REM mechanisms fire throughout the 24-hour cycle;
- That the firing of this ICSS system is an essential component of the biological function of REM sleep;
- That the ICSS network has sites in the pons and not only in the midbrain (as was thought to be the case in 1968 when we began this research);
- That there can be an experimentally demonstrated reciprocal relationship between the ICSS network and REM sleep.

Our first experiments involved attempts to demonstrate the reciprocal relationship between REM sleep and ICSS. In our first two experiments we demonstrated (a) that REMD lowers ICSS thresholds and raises ICSS response rates and (b) that as little as only 1 1/2 hours of ICSS can reduce 24 hours of REMD by 50%. These findings were subsequently replicated by Cohen, Edelman, Bowen, and Dement (1972). The finding that REMD lowers ICSS thresholds has since then been called into question by some experiments and upheld by others. We can only reiterate that our results have been replicated in experiments that follow guidelines for REMD detailed by ourselves (see Chapter 10) and by Vogel (1975).

There is a further point about the relationship of REM sleep and ICSS that can only be explicated by describing another line of research that our laboratory has pursued. This line of research involves experiments in ICSS that were conducted to substantiate the view that there were ICSS sites in the pons. At the time we began conducting these experiments, most sleep researchers felt that there was substantial evidence that implicated the locus coeruleus (LC) in the initiation and control of REM sleep. Today, one can certainly say that the situation is more complicated, but that, thus far, some experimenters (Hobson & McCarley, 1977) think the role of the LC is to cease firing at the onset of REM and that this in turn triggers cells (FTG cells) that are responsible for at least the phasic activation of REM sleep. Almost all investigators agree that the subcoeruleus is responsible for components of motor inhibition present in REM. It is a matter of dispute as to the role of the LC in activating phasic components of REM sleep. However, it is our position that a reasonable amount of evidence still implicates the LC in triggering aspects of REM phasic activity. While it is clear that the LC is not the central area for the initiation and maintenance of REM sleep as Jouvet (1965, 1968) asserted, it is also clear that the LC plays some central part in the initiation of phasic events in REM sleep (see Jones, 1985; Sakai, 1985). Hobson and McCarley's position has been restated (Hobson, Lydic, & Baghdoyan, 1986), and at this point it is an open question as to the areas in the pons or hind brain that initiate and maintain different aspects of REM sleep. We should also point out that most of the neurophysiological studies attempting to establish "REM centers" have been performed in the cat. There is a continuing assumption that the cat will provide an adequate model for other species. The cat has been the animal of choice in part because of the rich, varied sleep phenomena found in this animal. It is interesting that one of the most studied aspects of REM sleep, the PGO spike, is not found in many other species. We are purposefully vague about how many other species this phenomena is found in, since there is still little agreement on how many species display PGO spikes. As an example, Farber, Marks, and Roffwarg (1980) reported PGO spikes in the albino rat. If that report is correct, then in the rat PGO spikes are recorded exclusively in the LC. Therefore, even if there are PGO spikes in the rat they are manifested in a different manner than is the case in the cat, and it may be that the locus of control for REM sleep is somewhat different in the rat and cat. It should be remembered that our ICSS studies took place in the rat, and although we believe that control of REM phasic events is located in the LC, our assumptions are based on studies done in the cat. However, the Farber et al. (1980) and the Steiner and Ellman (1972) studies suggested that the LC may be as or more important in the rat as in the cat. We include this cautionary note to remind the reader and ourselves that the field is still in need of cross-species research. Nevertheless, the ICSS experiments we performed in rats have elucidated, we think, the relationship between REM and ICSS mechanisms. Essentially, we found that the LC is an ICSS site, and we went on to study the relationship of LC ICSS with midbrain sites (Bodnar, Ellman, Coons, Ackermann, & Steiner, 1979; Bodnar, Steiner, Healey, Halperin, & Ellman, 1978; Ellman, Ackermann, Bodnar, Jackler, & Steiner, 1975; Ellman, Ackermann, Farber, Mattiace, & Steiner, 1974; Ellman, Ackermann, Farber, & Steiner, 1973a, 1973b). Our finding that the LC is an ICSS site was surprising in itself, because investigators to that point had conceived of ICSS as a midbrain phenomenon. The interactions that we found between sites have led us to a model that posits the LC (and areas surrounding it, and perhaps adjoining pathways) as a controlling site for the activation and/or modulation of midbrain and forebrain ICSS sites. Essentially, we found that certain ICSS sites are influenced by and in turn influence the LC, while other ICSS sites are influenced by but do not influence the LC.

To review our interaction data more fully would be beyond the scope of this chapter, but one related experiment will give an indication of our thinking. Based on the interaction studies between the LC and a variety of other sites, we predicted that lesions in the LC should eliminate or reduce ICSS in some areas and facilitate it in other areas. This was a risky prediction because lesions involving ICSS sites had never been successful in previous experiments. ICSS was thought of as a phenomenon that had redundant pathways maintaining this behavior. Our lesion data showed that lesions in the LC virtually eliminated ICSS in several distant midbrain sites (e.g., fields of forel, crux cerebri). These were the sites that were facilitated by but did not facilitate the LC. There were other sites that were facilitated by LC lesions. Thus, we concluded that a function of LC ICSS is to modulate, facilitate, or act as one factor in the control of midbrain (as well as other site) ICSS thresholds. It is important to note that there can be different effects of a lesion on ICSS, depending on the ICSS site being tested. The same is true in terms of reaction to pharmacological interventions, as many laboratories, including our own, have shown. It may be (and we believe it to be the case) that REMD has differential effects on given ICSS sites. Thus, it is important to take into account the ICSS site in determining the effect of REMD on ICSS.

Having established that the LC is an ICSS site, that it interacts in specific ways with midbrain ICSS sites, and that the LC can exert both facilitating and inhibiting influences, we determined to study again the interaction of ICSS and REM sleep. A frequent question we encountered when we presented our research was why we looked at the effect of ICSS on REM rebound rather than the effect of ICSS on the animal's normal sleep cycle. The answer to this question is a complicated one. Simply stated, we considered the REM rebound study the crucial test of our hypothesis; if this experiment had produced negative results, the results would have been conclusive. Since we obtained positive results, we performed a series of related experiments (Spielman, Ellman, & Steiner, 1973). In these experiments, there were essentially two paradigms: (a) animals were allowed varying amounts of ICSS at fixed times of the day, and (b) animals were allowed free access to ICSS. Therefore, the amount of ICSS as well as the time spent in sleep were under the animal's control. In the style (a) experiment, there were several variations: animals were given 2 hours of ICSS every 24-hour period, or 2 hours every 6-hour period (8 hours of ICSS per 24-hour period). In the (a) paradigm animals received lateral hypothalamic ICSS.

If we consider the (a) experiments, a simple, straightforward prediction would be that the more ICSS, the greater the amount of REM reduction. In fact, this is what occurred, but if there is a reciprocal relationship between REM sleep and ICSS, then one should see ICSS completely substitute for REM without a subsequent REM rebound. Following our (a) paradigm, all animals that demonstrated a REM reduction also showed a subsequent REM rebound. When we obtained these results, we considered them to be at least partly negative. At the same time that we were performing these experiments, we were also performing the ICSS studies and we reasoned that ICSS locus might be crucial for determining the extent of reciprocity between REM and ICSS. We decided to change the ICSS site to the LC and at the same time to allow ad-lib ICSS (paradigm (b)). Obviously, by changing both site of locus and access to ICSS, we could not compare the results in (a) and (b) and know which factor accounted for the different results. In paradigm (b) we were concerned with providing what we considered to be a crucial test for our hypothesis. Our results were interesting in several ways:

- Animals chose ICSS for virtually the first 17 hours of the experiment.
- After this 17-hour period, animals had very small amounts of REM sleep.
- In recovery, animals displayed no REM rebound although they were significantly REM-deprived (their REM sleep was reduced by about 90%).

These results strongly supported our position and we are now in the process of studying other sites utilizing the experimental paradigm (b). Our prediction is that other sites will not yield the same results as we obtained with LC ICSS.

Human Studies

Our recent human studies are, to a reasonable extent, based on the animal studies that we have outlined. Weinstein et al. (Chapter 11) have presented some of our recent findings, but in this chapter we wish to integrate these findings more fully into our theoretical model and compare this model with the memory consolidation models that we have briefly reviewed.

While it is true that sleep mentation is not limited to REM sleep, it is also true that the most vivid, most absorbing mentation during sleep occurs in REM sleep, particularly during times of phasic activity (see Chapter 11). While Freud thought that the dream was instigated by the (system) unconscious, we have maintained that dreams are in part influenced by the underlying neurophysiology of REM sleep. During REM sleep, the firing of the ICSS system is one factor involved in the instigation of dreaming. The firing of this reward system is a way of increasing the probability of activating the neurophysiological substratum of drive systems (i.e., neural networks involved with eating, sex, aggression). When these systems fire, there is also an increased probability of activating memories and those ideas that Freud characterized as wishes. This hypothesis does not presume an isomorphic relationship between activating the REM-ICSS network and activating a wish. This lack of a one-to-one relationship could be true for many reasons. To cite one relatively simple example, firing the ICSS system at high intensities is aversive (Steiner, Beer, & Schaffer, 1969). One might say that, if the ICSS system is fired at high rates, this would increase the probability of aversive elements appearing in dream content. It has been reported that on recovery nights following REMD, subjects are awakened by their large

number of frightening dreams. Whether these dreams should be characterized as instigated by "wishes" depends on one's theoretical predilections, but
at least it can be maintained that the intensity of firing increases the probability that dream content is experienced as aversive.

We have hypothesized (following Kripke & Sonnenschein, 1973, Globus,
1970) that REM mechanisms fire throughout the circadian cycle or throughout the 24-hour cycle. In humans, then, REM mechanisms would fire every 70
to 90 minutes throughout the day. Clearly, waking activities will mask or
inhibit this ultradian cycle, but under some circumstances this cycle can be
apparent (Kripke, 1972). We have mentioned that the LC is responsible for the
triggering of a substantial portion of phasic events during REM sleep, and in
our view phasic events (see Chapters 6 and 11) are a compelling form of
endogenous stimulation. More specifically when phasic events are fired during REM, the dreamer will tend to experience the accompanying mentation as
real, absorbing, and occurring in the external world. This would be true even
if one compares points in REM sleep—that is, occasions where there are
many phasic events (REM phasic)—to ones where phasic events are relatively
absent (REM tonic). To test this hypothesis, we developed several scales that
measure aspects of what we have termed a person's *absorption in mentation*
(AIM) (see Chapter 11). We reasoned that a crucial aspect of what makes an
experience absorbing is that during the experience a capacity for observing
one's own activities is temporarily suspended. The scales we developed to
measure such transient suspensions in self-reflection were more successful
than any previous scales at discriminating between mentation reports from
REM phasic awakenings and those from REM tonic awakenings.

To briefly review our findings: After we had developed the AIM scales,
we used them to look at the effect of REMD on mentation. Following some
early findings, (Dement, 1965; Dement et al., 1969), we assumed that REMD
causes some displacement of REM phasic activity into NREM sleep. Thus, we
would expect that NREM mentation following REMD should be experienced
as more absorbing, or, in our terms, more like REM phasic mentation. This
increased absorption should be apparent only on those scales that can discriminate REM phasiT from tonic awakenings. This hypothesis was confirmed, and this result was the first one to demonstrate that REMD has an
effect on mentation. In the same study, we performed a posthoc analysis in
which we divided the subjects into two groups based on a test that measured
the likelihood of their reporting anxiety-producing thoughts.[1] Subjects who
were more willing to report anxiety-producing precepts were considered to

---

[1] The subjects' willingness to report anxiety-producing thoughts was measured by
their responses to the guilt daydreaming scale of the Imaginal Processes Inventory.
An analysis of the responses to the individual items on the scale showed that
subjects who tended to score higher on this scale were more willing to focus on or
report their inner experiences, even if these experiences were not socially acceptable. See Weinstein et al. (Chapter 11) for more detail.

be less anxious about internally generated fantasy material. The REM mentation of these subjects did not change following REMD. This was not a surprising result because, on baseline nights, these subjects demonstrated responses that were virtually at the top of our scales. Thus, REMD for these subjects did not alter REM mentation since they already showed a ceiling effect. The other group of subjects, who tended to avoid thinking about (or perhaps reporting) anxiety-producing thoughts, had significantly less absorbing REM mentation following REMD. Thus, on recovery nights following REMD, these subjects had less absorbing mentation from REM phasic awakenings. That this was not simply a response to stress was shown by their failure to show a similar response during NREM deprivation. That it was specifically a response to the patterning and intensity of REM phasic activation following REMD, was shown by the fact that the effect was only significant with the scales that were good phasic/tonic discriminators.

We expected that subjects whose REM phasic mentation was virtually at the top of all scales during baseline nights would not—indeed, could not—show a REMD effect. We predicted that NREM mentation should become more REM-like following REMD. This prediction was confirmed, and is what one would expect if one assumes that following REMD, REM phasic activity occurs more often in NREM sleep. The result that was not predicted till our post-hoc analysis was that subjects who find fantasy material anxiety-provoking, or at least difficult to admit, show a decrease in absorption in REM mentation following REMD. Our hypothesis is that increased intensity following REMD causes these subjects to attempt to distance themselves from their dream experiences. This characteristic defensive style is intensified by REMD. Before we go on to present our underlying theoretical rationale more fully, we briefly review other findings that are relevant to our theoretical position.

We have already mentioned that REM phasic events can be displaced into NREM sleep—indeed, under some conditions, even into the waking state. Several lines of research relate to these findings. Zarcone, Gulevich, Pivik, Azumi, and Dement (1969) and Gillin and Wyatt (1975) have reported that actively ill schizophrenic patients do not show REM rebound following REMD. Chronic schizophrenic patients do show REM rebound following REMD. On the basis of these studies and pharmacological data, Dement et al. (1969) concluded that actively ill schizophrenic patients are not able to contain phasic events within REM sleep. They maintained that the symptoms of acute schizophrenia are partially related to phasic events intruding directly into the waking state. Despite the fact that some methodological questions remain, these results would be striking if validated. Vogel, in a series of studies (Vogel, McAbee, Barker, et al., 1975; Vogel, Vogel, McAbee, Robert, & Thurmond, 1980), looked at the effect of REMD on depression. Essentially, Vogel found that REMD leads to clinical improvement in endogenous depressives and that this improvement is at least comparable to pharmacological methods of treatment. He related his findings to our ICSS studies and articulated his own version of a REM-drive theoretical model (Vogel, 1979). His findings can be explained by our animal model in that REMD activates reward sites, and it is precisely the type of functions mediated at those reward sites that endogenous depressives have difficulty with. More specifically, endogenous depressives have, as part of their symptom picture, difficulty in eating, sleeping, sexual activities, and a generally low activity level (psychomotor retardation). We maintain that, through the ICSS network, all those functions are activated by REMD.

We have maintained that the ICSS system during REM is part of what is generated by phasic activation during REM sleep. It follows from our hypotheses that intense firing of the REM phasic system may cause dramatic changes in a person's perception of reality. We have implied a model that assumes that individuals, to be appropriately interested in and motivated toward external events, need some optimum level of internally generated stimuli. Too much internally generated stimuli, and the world becomes difficult to perceive; too little, and thresholds for interest in external stimuli are elevated. One may consider acute schizophrenic patients to be pathologically concerned with internally generated events and endogenous depressives to be unmotivated because of a paucity of internally generated events. Thus, REMD helps depressives by increasing internally generated events and making them more receptive to certain stimuli, but acute schizophrenics have such intense internal stimuli that external events are to a large extent obscured. Of course, we are not offering these ideas as anything approaching a complete explanation for either acute schizophrenia or endogenous depression, but we think that some of the factors we have mentioned may be involved in these disorders.

It is possible that individuals may differ in terms of their propensity for displacement. Several authors (Cartwright & Monroe, 1968; Cartwright, Monroe, & Palmer, 1967; Cartwright & Ratzel, 1972; Nakasawa, Kotorii, Kotorii, Tachibana, & Nakano, 1975; Pivik & Foulkes, 1968) suggested this possibility and offered preliminary evidence that this may be the case. We are hypothesizing that there may be characteristic individual differences in how easily people displace phasic events, and also characteristic individual differences in absolute and proportional amounts of REM sleep.[2] This leads us to attempt to explain one more aspect of the REM sleep puzzle, i.e., the developmental course of REM in the sleep cycle.

Developmental Assumptions

Here we refer to the large amounts of REM sleep that one sees in infants (Parmelee, Wenner, & Schutz, 1964; Roffwarg et al., 1968). We agree with

---

[2] By *proportional* we mean the amount of phasic events per unit of REM time.

Roffwarg et al. that REM sleep is a likely candidate to provide endogenous stimuli to the infant at a time when exogenous stimuli are not available. Jouvet has postulated that the large amounts of REM sleep in infants are available for survival mechanisms. What we understand this to mean is that the function of REM sleep in infancy is the facilitation of responses that the infant will need when it begins to ambulate fully and independently. Crick and Mitchison have criticized this notion, claiming that another mechanism exists for this purpose, namely play. It is hard to see how in some species one can invoke play, since for a few hours to many months some mammalian infants are unable to ambulate, much less play. We would hypothesize that total and relative amounts of REM sleep would drop in those species that ambulate more rapidly, because in those species REM would not be needed to the same extent to facilitate survival mechanisms.

Here we are talking about mechanisms that underlie food seeking and aggressive behavior—in short, those activities that are ultimately either life-sustaining or life-threatening. However, in each species, different abilities come into play; in the cat, visual tracking is extremely important for food seeking; in the rat, olfactory mechanisms are essential. We would predict that, in each species, the factors that are used characteristically would be facilitated, providing the animal with built-in mechanisms that enhance survival. Our prediction is that, if animals were not allowed to have REM sleep, then one would see effects similar to the effects Hubel and Wiesel obtained in their pioneering studies on the visual system. Specifically, mechanisms that are used by the animal in drive- or species-specific behavior would be involved in maturational deficits. In the rat, aspects of the olfactory system; in the cat, the visual system; and in both species, aspects of the positive reward system would be impaired. These are, of course, testable predictions that are clearly different from the hypothesis stated by Crick and Mitchison.

How might our views be relevant to the early development of the human infant? To begin, we sketch out our hypotheses about "normal" development. During the first month or first few months of life, REM sleep is not a unified state (Emde & Metcalf, 1970; Petre-Quadens, 1974; Prechtl & Lenard, 1967; Roffwarg et al., 1968). During this period of time, there is neither motor inhibition (or atonia) that is characteristic of REM sleep, nor are phasic events restricted to REM periods. In ontogenetic terms, it appears to be a maturational and perhaps a developmental landmark to fully unite phasic and tonic aspects of REM sleep. Recent research has demonstrated that the infant is capable of learning, but, given the high percentage of time the infant spends in vegetative activities, it is our view that at least in the first month the infant is mostly forming a bond to its caretaker, eating, or sleeping. This view does not exclude other important events in the infant's life; we are only saying that, early on, the infant spends a great deal of time involved in vegetative functions.

We would assume that, when REM mechanisms fire during waking, the infant has far less capacity than the adult to inhibit or supersede this REM firing. In the normal infant, we assume that REM firing would become periodic after a short time and that during waking as well as sleeping one would see phenomena like periodic sucking and erection cycles that are endogenously generated. Most parents will quickly learn that during these cycles the baby is activated and is responsive to only a limited range of stimuli. As the infant develops, there are increasing amounts of what Wolff (1966) described as quiet wakefulness, and at those times the baby will be much more responsive to a wider range of stimuli. Our hypothesis is that, during quiet wakefulness, REM mechanisms are not firing or are firing at low rates. These quiescent times, between feedings or at times when the baby is alert and not extremely active, are the times when considerably more interpersonal learning can take place. The infant can attend more easily to external stimuli because endogenous sources are relatively quiescent. We hypothesize that in the 3-to-4-month-old infant there is an oscillation of quiet and active periods, with increasing amounts of wakefulness that allow the infant to more fully interact with his or her environment. The oscillation of quiet and active periods depends to some extent on the containment of REM phenomena. In support of this notion, there is evidence of major changes in the organization of REM sleep at 3 months, namely the dropping out of undifferentiated REM states (waking, fussing, and drowsy REM) and the coalescing of random eye movements into burst patterns. These changes are temporally correlated with a marked increase in behaviors that demonstrate the infant's enhanced capacity for bonding with the caregiver, namely social smiling, mutual looking, and mutual vocalizing. We hypothesize that, if REM phenomena are not restricted to a unified period in a given infant, then the amount of quiet wakefulness will be curtailed. We then postulate that in the infant (as in the REM-deprived adult), when REM phenomena are not restricted to a single unified period, there is a greater likelihood that internal events will interfere with external perception. Such an infant would have more difficulty perceiving the nurturing object or being able to see satisfaction as originating outside itself (both critical developmental tasks). Thus, we can consider as one important factor in infant development the amount of REM restriction that takes place. Obviously, there may be maturational lags in REM restriction as with any other function, and clearly it is of some importance in this hypothesis when an infant begins to restrict REM phenomena.

A second factor in this developmental picture is the total amount of phasic phenomena that a given infant produces. We are assuming that this is a maturational phenomenon, as is REM restriction, and if a child produces large amounts of phasic phenomena and does not have age-appropriate restriction, then we would assume this will have a larger effect on the infant's development than if the child has the same difficulty with restriction but produces fewer phasic phenomena. In this rudimentary model, we are leaving out the role of the caregiver. It is clear that some parents may be able to gauge their baby's sensitivities quite well and help the infant to overcome these tendencies. We are, however, assuming that a baby who has relatively little quiet wakefulness over a long period of its infancy will be perceived as more difficult by many parents. More specifically, it will be hard for the parent to understand his or her child's restricted range of reactions as well as the infant's relative sensitivity. In this context, let us remind the reader that the greater the firing of the REM-phasic-ICSS system, the lower the threshold for drive behaviors that can include a tendency toward aggression. Thus, the high-phasic-event, poorly restricted infant would have a lowered threshold for certain reactions, a tendency to experience "normal" levels of stimulation as aversive, and at the same time a restricted range of reactions toward the parent.

Although our discussion of the infant may seem to be some distance from even our dream research, conceptually we can bridge the gap in terms of the development of the reflective self-representation (rsr). Our theoretical position is that the child's awareness of itself as a separate entity or object develops originally within the matrix of the parent–child unit and coalesces as the child gradually emerges from that bond. Given either a great deal of exogenous or endogenous stimulation of the child, it is difficult to develop or clearly delineate intrapsychic boundaries between parent and infant. We are certainly aware of other positions that maintain that self-awareness occurs naturally and is something the child is endowed with. Even if one takes this position, the child's ability to self-reflect must develop with age, and there must be some factors that either accelerate or retard this development. From our theoretical position, lack of restriction of REM phasic events is one factor that can retard the development of reflective self-representation. This idea is similar to the conceptualization in our dream research that, given a great deal of activation, it is difficult—at times, impossible—to represent oneself except in terms of action or activity. This would mean that the rsr develops optimally when there is some diminution of both internal and external stimulation. If there is a continuous flow of either or both internal and external stimulation, then it is more difficult to coalesce an accurate and stable representation of the self.

In summary, if the infant is experiencing a great deal of inner stimulation, this reduces thresholds for certain kinds of stimuli, makes other types of stimuli irrelevant, makes the delineation between parent and infant more difficult, and hampers the development of reflective self-representation. This will be particular true if the parent responds to such an infant with a great deal of stimulation. We recognize, of course, that mothers or fathers do not respond to children in terms of stimulation but in terms of actions and meanings, but in this context we are trying to point out the importance of different levels of endogenous stimulation to the infant. Attempting to explicate these ideas further without a fuller developmental framework is, in some sense, meaningless, but for the present purposes we hope that our discussion can give some idea of how our theoretical ideas might be applied within a developmental perspective.

CONCLUDING COMMENTS

The question we should ask at this point is, What does all of this have to do with dreaming? Is dreaming a meaningless event as Crick and Mitchison and Hobson and McCarley maintain? Or is there enough evidence to support a notion that the content of dreams is determined by factors that are psychological as well as physiological? Dividing psychology and physiology seems somewhat strange and artificial to us, but for purposes of this argument we would state that it would be difficult for any purely physiological account of dreaming to predict many of the factors that have been uncovered in modern sleep research. For an example from our own research, we might say that alterations in self-representation during dreaming cannot be explained by any purely physiological theory of dream formation. Accounting for why one subject has a certain type of REM mentation following REMD while another type of subject has a different reaction can, from our perspective, be done only by invoking psychological variables. But one might still ask, why is there mental content at all during REM sleep?

Before we answer this question, we refer back to our animal model. Although we have some evidence for our assertions, we again state that at this point we are putting forth these ideas as theoretical assumptions. Various authors involved in learning research have made a distinction between incentive rewards and consummatory rewards.[3] Incentives are those stimuli that activate the subject toward a particular goal object; consummatory responses are those responses that lead to the consumption of the goal object (i.e., eating food, sexual orgasm, attack) For example, one might distinguish between searching for or gathering food as one type of behavior and consuming food as another type of behavior. In our model, the incentive system continues to be active until the consumption system turns it off and says, in effect, "you can stop pursuing a given goal, we've had enough." The ICSS system that fires during REM sleep is an incentive system. An influence that turns this system off occurs when appropriate consummatory centers fire. If no appropriate consummatory centers fire during REM sleep, the ICSS system will fire at high enough rates so that at some point it will become aversive and arousing to the organism. In Figure 16.1, the X-axis represents

---

[3] The terms *reward* and *response* are used interchangeably, because for each reward some response has been required on the part of the subject.

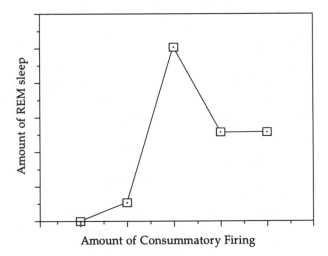

FIGURE 16.1.   REM sleep/consummatory model.

the amount of consummatory firing, the Y-axis the amount of REM sleep. In this illustration, under all conditions there is an assumption that the ICSS-phasic system is firing at the same high rates. Thus, the situation just mentioned (high ICSS with little consummatory firing) will lead to little or no REM sleep. With just enough consummatory firing, we assume there will be a threshold effect with high activation of the ICSS-phasic system and low but just-above-threshold amounts of consummatory firing; under this condition there will be maximum amounts of REM sleep. One can see in Figure 16.1 that, with small amounts of consummatory center firing, at some point there is the maximum amount of REM sleep. When there is a large amount of consummatory firing (normal conditions), there will be a moderate amount of REM sleep. To summarize, when the ICSS-phasic network is firing during REM, whether the animal will have small, large, or moderate amounts of REM will be significantly determined by the amount of firing of these consummatory centers.

We maintain that, under normal conditions in REM, when the phasic-ICSS system fires there will be regular consummatory feedback so that during REM and ICSS system is continuously being attenuated until a given REM period ends. If in the period of wakefulness before the animal sleeps there has been an event or series of events that activates the ICSS system, there will be a tendency toward increased REM only if there is a small amount of consummatory reinforcement (see Fig. 16.1). This furnishes an explanation for the REM augmentation phenomena; during an avoidance paradigm, for example, the animal is put in a situation that is potentially life-threatening. This activates the ICSS incentive system and then the animal is given one reinforcement, which leads to a small amount of consummatory firing. One can see in Figure 16.1 that in this type of situation REM can be maximized. If the animal were given several trials, REM sleep would be diminished. If the reinforcement were withheld, then the animal would have little or no REM sleep. This is a statement of our theorizing with respect to our animal model. But the question that we asked earlier still remains: How does all this apply to dreaming?

As one might ascertain by now, our position is an attempt to reconcile the learning-memory position with a Freudian perspective. We hypothesize that dreams are originally a mental representation of the incentive and consummatory centers firing. Dreams are initially adaptive attempts to represent both an approach to (incentive network) and the consummation (consummatory network) of a sequence of behaviors or thoughts. We assume that infants begin to have this type of mental imagery with the onset of intentional (incentive and consummatory) actions. In adults or older children, recent "drive" behaviors, thoughts, or fantasies are automatically compared with older or past sequences. An attempt is made to reconcile past and present sequences with each dream.

Here, we differ from Freud's account of dreams. Our view is that, while wishes are certainly represented in dreams, it is not theoretically useful to maintain that a wish is the instigator of dreaming. Rather, dreams depict important life-threatening or life-enhancing themes. These themes in the adult frequently (perhaps always) involve some degree of conflict that makes it more difficult to approach a goal or, in psychoanalytic terms, to obtain drive gratification. When the conflict is strong enough, it will be difficult to represent even symbolically a consummatory response. There will then be either anxiety or an awakening from the dream. In our theory, dreams representing traumatic events are an instance of the incentive systems' being mobilized without any consummatory response being possible. Thus, the organism is helpless to respond to an internal signal that is demanding a response. When this sequence is repeated, bringing up former memories is useless because there have been no adequate consummatory responses in the past. As past memories are brought to consciousness, the person is increasingly activated, and is ready to awaken and respond. Put in other terms, the ICSS-phasic system gives the dreamer a powerful feeling of reality, while at the same time there is no dampening of the incentive system by a consummatory response. We can note from this example that the consummatory response has two effects. First, dampening the ICSS-phasic system allows the dream to continue by making the dream slightly less intense and therefore less absorbing. Second, this dampening and diminution of the absorbing qualities of the dream says to the dreamer: "You can continue to sleep, this is only a memory, and you currently are not in danger or in need." To make this last point clearer, we are assuming that if the dreamer is highly aroused when she or he enters sleep and this arousal of the incentive system has not resulted in a satisfactory waking consummatory response (either actually or symbolically), then the dream has an increased probability of being so absorbing as to wake the dreamer or at least create anxiety for him or her. This model would also serve to explain why subjects in the laboratory have reduced REM sleep during the first night in the lab. In this novel situation, the absence of adequate real or symbolic consummatory responses leaves the subjects aroused and with an increased likelihood of having highly absorbing mentation that will disturb their sleep.

From our perspective, dreams in later childhood and adulthood contain wishes and frequently represent conflict. However, the original impetus for a dream is to represent drive behaviors so that they may be facilitated in waking life. Large amounts of REM sleep in the infant enable drive networks to be facilitated before the organism is able to ambulate. When the organism is able to make a range of approach and consummatory responses, REM levels will diminish and muscle atonia will appear. When the animal can ambulate, drive issues begin to be represented mentally, and the manner in which drive-related issues have been handled in the past is reviewed in the dream. In this respect, we agree with the learning-memory position that memories are reviewed in REM sleep. However, we maintain that the types of memories that are reviewed are related to drives or are drive derivatives. Clearly, what an adult may consider life-sustaining or life-threatening may be very far away from the biological roots that we have postulated. Nevertheless, these drive derivatives are the issues that individuals may perceive in their lives as life-sustaining or life-threatening.

It can be discerned from our research that we think the way someone represents himself or herself in a dream is quite important in the process of dream formation. The coalescing of the rsr is, in our view, a developmental achievement. Once this achievement occurs, the dream can be seen as a process of oscillating between relative loss of rsr (absorption in dreaming) and a relatively strong representation of rsr. Unless defensive processes intervene, this oscillation will correspond to the absence or presence of phasic events in the REM period. At times in the dream, the dreamer is the actor; at other times, the dreamer has periods of reflecting on her or his actions and consolidating the implications of these actions. This oscillation will by no means be a perfect correlation with the waxing and waning of phasic activation. We fully expect that, even taking defensive processes into account, individuals will differ as to how they represent themselves and the extent to which they become absorbed in their dream or fantasy life. These differences, we believe, may be important in understanding how individuals process what we have called drive material, or what others have called emotional material.

Clearly, the representation of the self in the dream is a topic that we think important and that in many ways holds some of the answers to the riddle of dream formation. One of the current research issues that we are grappling with is the role of defensive processes in dream formation (as well as in dream reporting) and how to untangle these issues. To attempt to spell out our thinking in this area would bring us to attempt to develop a theory of the self. (Hopefully this will await another publication.) We do think that it is time in dream research to begin to truly integrate a psychological perspective. We are beginning to, from one theoretical viewpoint; Antrobus (Chapter 15) and Fiss (Chapter 9) are beginning to, from other viewpoints. We believe these attempts and others (Bosinelli, Cavallero, & Cicogna, 1982; Cicogna, Cavallero, & Bosinelli, 1986) are exciting new starts in this, the fourth decade of sleep and dream research.

References

Editors' Note: All references printed in the first edition have been included here, even though some text citations were sacrificed in preparing this revision. This merged listing of the references from the two editions offers readers one of the most comprehensive collections of relevant literature that is available for this field.

Aarons, L. (1976). Evoked sleep-talking. *Perceptual and Motor Skills, 31,* 27–40.

Adair, J. G., & Epstein, J. (1967). *Verbal cues in the mediation of experimenter bias.* Paper presented at the meeting of the Midwestern Psychological Association, Chicago.

Adelman, S., & Hartmann, E. (1968). *Psychological effects of amitriptyline-induced dream deprivation.* Paper presented at the meeting of the Association for the Psychophysiological Study of Sleep, Denver.

Adler, A. (1936). On the interpretation of dreams. *International Journal of Individual Psychology, 2,* 3–16.

Adler, A. (1958). *What life should mean to you.* New York: Capricorn.

Agnew, H. W., & Webb, W. B., Jr. (1968). The displacement of stage 4 and REM sleep within a full night of sleep. *Psychophysiology, 5,* 142–148.

Agnew, H. W., Webb, W. B., Jr., & Williams, R. L. (1966). The first night effect: An EEG study of sleep. *Psychophysiology, 2,* 263–266.

Agnew, H. W., Webb, W. B., Jr., & Williams, R. L. (1967). Comparison of stage four and REM sleep deprivation. *Perceptual and Motor Skills, 24,* 851–858.

Alba, J. W., & Hasher, L. (1983). Is memory schematic? *Psychological Bulletin, 93,* 203–231.

Albert, I. B. (1975). REM sleep deprivation. *Biological Psychiatry, 10,* 341–351.

Albert, I., Cicala, G. A., & Siegel, J. (1970). The behavioral effects of REM sleep deprivation in rats. *Psychophysiology, 6,* 550–560.

Alexander, L. (1948). Dreams in Paris. In R. Flores (Ed.), *The psychoanalytic reader* (Vol 1). New York: International Universities Press.

Allan, F. N. (1944). Differential diagnosis of weakness and fatigue. *New England Journal of Medicine, 231,* 414–418.

Allen, C., Kales, A., & Berger, R. J. (1968). An analysis of the effect of glutethimide on REM density. *Psychonomic Science, 12,* 329–330.

Allen, S. (1974). REM sleep and memory. *Proceedings of the Second European Congress on Sleep Research,* Rome, Italy.

Allison, T., & Goff, W. R. (1972). Electrophysiological studies of the Echidna Tachyglossus Aculeatus: 1. Waking and sleeping. *Archives of Italian Biology, 110,* 145–184.

Altschuler, K. Z. (1966). Comment on recent sleep research related to psychoanalytic theory. *Archives of General Psychiatry, 15,* 235–239.

Altschuler, K. Z., Barad, M., & Goldfarb, A. I. (1963). A survey of dreams in the aged, Part II. *Archives of General Psychiatry, 8,* 33–37.

Amadeo, M., & Gomez, E. (1966). Eye movements, attention and dreaming in subjects with lifelong blindness. *Canadian Psychiatric Association Journal, 11,* 501–507.

Anderson, B. F. (1975). *Cognitive psychology: The study of knowing, learning and thinking.* New York: Academic Press.

Anderson, J. R., & Bower, G. H. (1973). *Human associative memory.* New York: Wiley.

Anders, T. F. (1974). An overview of recent sleep and dream research. In L. Goldberger & Rosen (Eds.), *Psychoanalysis and contemporary science* (Vol 3). New York: International Universities Press.

Angeleri, F., Scarpino, O., & Signorino, M. (1984). Information processing and hemispheric specialization: Electrophysiological study during wakefulness, stage 2 and stage REM sleep. *Research Communications in Psychology, Psychiatry, & Behavior, 9,* 121–138.

Antrobus, J. (1977). The dream as metaphor. *Journal of Mental Imagery, 2,* 327–338.

Antrobus, J. (1986). Dreaming: Cortical activation and perceptual thresholds. *The Journal of Mind and Behavior, 7,* 193–212.

Antrobus, J., Ehrlichman, H., & Wiener, M. (1978). EEG asymmetry during REM and NREM: Failure to replicate. *Sleep Research, 7,* 24.

Antrobus, J. S. (1967). Discrimination of two sleep stages by human subjects. *Psychophysiology, 4,* 48–55.

Antrobus, J. S. (1978). Editors' Commentary to Chapter 4. In A. M. Arkin, J. S. Antrobus, & S. J. Ellman (Eds.), *The mind in sleep: Psychology and psychophysiology.* Hillsdale, NJ: Lawrence Erlbaum Associates, 109–110.

Antrobus, J. S. (1983). REM and NREM sleep reports: Comparison of word frequencies by cognitive classes. *Psychophysiology, 20,* 562–568.

Antrobus, J. S., Antrobus, J. S., & Fisher, C. (1965). Discrimination of dreaming and non-dreaming sleep. *Archives of General Psychiatry, 12,* 395–401.

Antrobus, J. S., Antrobus, J. S., & Singer, J. L. (1964). Eye movements accompanying daydreaming, visual imagery, and thought suppression. *Journal of Abnormal and Social Psychology, 69,* 244–252.

Antrobus, J. S., Arkin, A. M., & Ellman, S. J. (1976, September). Dreaming, operant control, and meaning structure. National Institute of Mental Health Grant Proposal.

Antrobus, J. S., Arkin, A. M., & Toth, M. (1972). The effects of REMP deprivation on sleep mentation. *Sleep Research, 1,* 156.

Antrobus, J. S., Arkin, A. M., & Toth, M. F. (1970). The effects of REM period deprivation on sleep mentation. *Psychophysiology, 7,* 332. (Abstract)

Antrobus, J. S., Dement, W., & Fisher, C. (1964). Patterns of dreaming and dream recall: An EEG study. *Journal of Abnormal and Social Psychology, 69,* 341–344.

Antrobus, J. S., Ehrlichman, H., Wiener, M., & Wollman, M. (1983). The REM report and the EEG: Cognitive processes associated with cerebral hemispheres: Their ratios and sums, cross trial contrasts and EEG window duration. In W. P. Koella (Ed.), *Sleep 82* (pp. 49–51). Basel: Karger.

Antrobus, J. S., Ezrachi, O., & Arkin, A. M. (1973). *K-complexes and dreaming in Stage 2 sleep.* Unpublished manuscript.

Antrobus, J. S., Fein, G., Jordan, L. Ellman, S. J., & Arkin, A. M. (1979) Measurement and design in research on sleep reports. In A. M. Arkin, J. S. Antrobus, & S. J. Ellman (Eds.), *The mind in sleep.* Hillsdale, N.J.: Erlbaum Associates. Pp. 19–55.

Antrobus, J. S., Pass, R., Luck, D., Sanders, K., Ellman, S., & Arkin, A. M. (1974). Discrimination of REM/NREM reports. *Sleep Research, 3,* 102. (Abstract)

Antrobus, J. S., Rich, K., Pass, R., Nelson, W. T., & Sanders, K. (1973). Multiple linear regression of mentation reports on REM/NREM sleep. *Sleep Research, 2,* 104.

Antrobus, J. S., & Saul, H. N. (1980). Sleep onset: Subjective, behavioral and electroencephalographic comparisons. *Waking & Sleeping, 4,* 259–270.

Antrobus, J. S., Schnee, R. K., Offer, V., Lynn, & Silverman, S. (1977). *A psycholinguistic scoring manual for mentation reports.* Unpublished test. Princeton, N.J.: Educational Testing Service, ETS Test Test Collection, Set D, 008737.

Antrobus, J. S., Singer, J. L., Goldstein, S., & Fortgang, M. (1970). Mind-wandering and cognitive structure. *Transactions of the New York Academy of Science, 32,* 242–252.

Arkin, A., Antrobus, J., & Ellman, S. (1978). *The mind in sleep.* New York: Lawrence Erlbaum Associates.

Arkin, A. M. (1966). Sleep talking: A review. *Journal of Nervous and Mental Disease, 143,* 101–122.

Arkin, A. M. (1968, April). *The degree of concordance between sleep-talking and mentation recalled in wakefulness.* Paper presented at the meeting of the Association for the Psychophysiological Study of Sleep, Santa Monica, CA, 1967. *Psychophysiology, 4,* 396. (Abstract)

Arkin, A. M. (1970). Qualitative observations on sleep utterance in the laboratory. In M. Bertini (Ed.), *The Atti del Simposio Internazionale sulla psicolifisiologica del sonno e del sogno.* Proceedings of an International Symposium, Rome, 1967. Milan: Editrice Vita e Pensiero Milan.

Arkin, A. M. (1974a). Review of MacNeilage, P. F. & MacNeilage, L. A., Central processes controlling speech production during sleeping and waking. *Sleep Research, 3,* 331–333.

Arkin, A. M. (1974b, May). *Somniloquy as the output of dissociated cognitive subsystems*. Paper presented at the meeting of the Association for the Psychophysiological Study of Sleep, Jackson Hole, WY.

Arkin, A. M., & Antrobus, J. S. (1970). *Sleep mentation as affected by REMP deprivation*. Progress report to National Institute of Mental Health, MH 13866-03.

Arkin, A. M., Antrobus, J. S., Toth, M. F., & Baker, J. (1968, March). *The effects of chemically induced REMP deprivation on sleep vocalization and NREM mentation—An initial exploration*. Paper presented at the meeting of the Association for the Psychophysiological Study of Sleep, Denver. *Psychophysiology, 5,* 217. (Abstract)

Arkin, A. M., Antrobus, J. S., Toth, M. F., Baker, J., & Jackler, F. (1972). A comparison of the content of mentation reports elicited after non-rapid eye movement (NREM) associated sleep utterance and NREM "silent" sleep. *Journal of Nervous and Mental Disease, 155,* 427–435.

Arkin, A. M., & Brown, J. W. (1972, June). *Resemblances between NREM associated sleep speech, drowsy speech, and aphasic and schizophrenic speech*. Paper presented at the Association for the Psychophysiological Study of Sleep, First International Congress, Bruges, Belgium, 1971. *Psychophysiology, 9,* 140. (Abstract)

Arkin, A. M., Farber, J., Antrobus, J. S., Ellman, S. J., & Nelson, W. T. (1973). The effects of repeated sleep interruption and elicited verbalization on sleep speech frequency of chronic sleep talkers: Preliminary observations. *Sleep Research, 2,* 105.

Arkin, A. M., Hastey, J. M., & Reiser, M. F. (1966a, March). *Dialogue between sleeptalkers and the experimenter*. Paper presented at the meeting of the Association for the Psychophysiological Study of Sleep, Gainesville, FL.

Arkin, A. M., Hastey, J. M., & Reiser, M. F. (1966b). Post-hypnotically stimulated sleep-talking. *Journal of Nervous and Mental Disease, 142,* 293–309.

Arkin, A. M., Sanders, K. I., Ellman, S. J., Antrobus, J. S., Farber, J., & Nelson, E. T., Jr. (1975, May). *The rarity of pain sensation in sleep mentation reports*. Paper presented at the meeting of the Association for the Psychophysiological Study of Sleep, Edinburgh, Scotland.

Arkin, A. M., Toth, M. F., Baker, J., & Hastey, J. M. (1970a). The frequency of sleep-talking in the laboratory among chronic sleep-talkers and good dream recallers. *Journal of Nervous and Mental Disease, 151,* 369–374.

Arkin, A. M., Toth, M. F., Baker, J., & Hastey, J. M. (1970b). The degree of concordance between the content of sleep talking and mentation recalled in wakefulness. *Journal of Nervous and Mental Disease, 151,* 375–393.

Arkin, A. M., Toth, M. F., & Ezrachi, O. (1970, March). *Electrographic aspects of sleep-talking*. Paper presented at the meeting of the Association for the Psychophysiological Study of Sleep, Santa Fe, NM. *Psychophysiology, 7,* 354. (Abstract)

Arlow, J. A., & Brenner, C. (1964). *Psychoanalytic concepts and the structural theory*. New York: International Universities Press.

Arseni, C., & Petrovici, I. N. (1971). Epilepsy in temporal lobe tumors. *European Neurology, 5,* 201–214.

Asahina, K. (1962). Paradoxical phase and reverse paradoxical phase in human subjects. *Journal of the Physiology Society of Japan, 24,* 443–450.

Aschoff, J., Gerecke, V., & Wever, R. (1967). Desynchronization of human circadian rhythms. *Japan Journal of Psychology, 17,* 450–457.

Aserinsky, E. (1965a). Brain wave pattern during the rapid eye movement period of sleep. *The Physiologist, 8,* 104. (Abstract)

Aserinsky, E. (1965b). Periodic respiratory pattern occurring in conjunction with eye movements during sleep. *Science, 150,* 763–766.

Aserinsky, E. (1967). Physiological activity associated with segments of the rapid eye movement period. In S. S. Kety, E. V. Evarts, & H. L. Williams (Eds.), *Sleep and altered states of consciousness.* Baltimore: Williams & Wilkins.

Aserinsky, E. (1969a). Drugs and dreams: A synthesis in drugs and dreams. *Experimental Medicine and Surgery, 27,* 237–244.

Aserinsky, E. (1969b). The maximal capacity for sleep: Rapid eye movement density as an index of sleep satiety. *Biological Psychiatry, 1,* 147–159.

Aserinsky, E. (1971). Rapid eye movement density and pattern in the sleep of normal young adults. *Psychophysiology, 8,* 361–375.

Aserinsky, E., & Kleitman, N. (1953). Regularly occurring periods of eye motility and concomitant phenomena during sleep. *Science, 118,* 273–274.

Aserinsky, E., & Kleitman, N. (1955). Two types of ocular motility occurring during sleep. *Journal of Applied Physiology, 8,* 1–10.

Askenasy, J., & Yahr, M. (1985). Reversal of sleep disturbance in Parkinson's disease by anti-Parkinson therapy: A preliminary study. *Neurology, 35,* 527–532.

Atkinson, R. C., & Shiffrin, R. M. (1968). Human memory: A proposed system and its control processes. In K. W. Spence and J. T. Spence (Eds.), *The psychology of learning and motivation: Advances in research and theory* (Vol. 2). New York: Academic Press.

Atsmon, A., Blum, I., Wijsenbeek, H., Maoz, B., Steiner, M., & Ziegelman, G. (1971). The shortterm effects of adrenergic-blocking agents in a small group of psychotic patients. *Psychiatria, Neurologia, Neurochirurgia, 74,* 251-258.

Austin, M. D. (1971). Dream recall and the bias of intellectual ability. *Nature, 231,* 59–60.

Azumi, K., & Ewing, J. A. (1970). *The effects of REM deprivation on GSR during sleep.* Paper presented at the meeting of the Association for the Psychophysiological Study of Sleep, Santa Fe, NM. *Psychophysiology, 7,* 301. (Abstract)

Azumi, K., Takahashi, S., Takahashi, K., Maruyama, N., & Kikuti, S. (1967). The effects of dream deprivation on chronic schizophrenics and normal adults: A comparative study. *Folia Psychiatrica et Neurologica Japonica, 21,* 205–225.

Baekeland, F. (1967). Pentobarbital and dextroamphetamine sulphate: Effects of the sleep cycle in man. *Psychopharmacologia, 11,* 388–396.

Baekeland, F. (1969). Correlates of home dream recall: Reported home sleep characteristics and home dream recall. *Comprehensive Psychiatry, 10,* 482–491.

Baekeland, F. (1970). Correlates of home dream recall: 1. Rem Sleep in the laboratory as a predictor of home dream recall. *Journal of Nervous and Mental Disease, 150,* 209–214.

Baekeland, F. (1971). Effects of pre-sleep procedures and cognitive style on dream content. *Perceptual and Motor Skills, 32,* 63–69.

Baekeland, F., & Lasky, R. (1968). The morning recall of rapid eye movement period reports given earlier in the night. *Journal of Nervous and Mental Disease, 147*, 570–579.

Baekeland, F., Resch, R., & Katz, D. D., (1968). Pre-sleep mentation and dream reports. *Archives of General Psychiatry, 19*, 300–311.

Bakan, P. (1975, May). *Dreaming, REM sleep, and the right hemisphere.* Paper presented at the meeting of the Association for the Psychophysiological Study of Sleep, Edinburgh, Scotland.

Baker, T. L., & Dement, W. C. (1985). Canine narcolepsy-cataplexy syndrome: Evidence for an inherited monoaminergic-cholinergic imbalance. In D. McGinty, R. Drucker–Colin, A. Morrison, & P. L. Parmeggiani (Eds.), *Brain mechanisms of sleep* (pp. 199–234). New York: Raven Press.

Baldridge, B. J. (1966). Physical concomitants of dreaming and the effect of stimulation on dreams. *Ohio State Medical Journal, 62*, 1271–1279.

Baldridge, B. J. (1974). Review of Hauri, P. & Van de Castle, R. L., Psychophysiological parallels in dreams. *Sleep Research, 3*, 312–314.

Baldridge, B. J., Whitman, R. M., & Kramer, M. (1962). *A comparison of variability of some physiological functions during dreaming while telling the dream and during dream playback.* Paper presented at the Association for the Psychophysiological Study of Sleep, Chicago.

Baldridge, B. J., Whitman, R. M., Kramer, M., Ornstein, P. H., & Lansky, L. (1965). *The effect of external physical stimuli on dream content.* Paper presented at the meeting of the Association for the Psychophysiological Study of Sleep, Washington, DC.

Baldridge, B. J., Whitman, R. M., & Ornstein, P. H. (1967). *Smoking and dreams.* Paper presented at the meeting of the Association for the Psychophysiological Study of Sleep, Santa Monica, CA.

Barad, M., Altschuler, K. Z., & Goldfarb, A. I. (1961). A survey of dreams in aged persons. *Archives of General Psychiatry, 4*, 419–424.

Barber, B. (1969). Factors underlying individual differences in rate of dream reporting. *Psychophysiology, 6*, 247–248. (Abstract)

Barber, T., Walker, P., & Hahn, K. (1973). Effects of hypnotic suggestions on nocturnal dreaming. *Journal of Abnormal Psychology, 82*, 414–427.

Barber, T. X. (1960). Letter to the editor, *Science, 132*, 1417–1418.

Barber, T. X., Calverley, D. S., Forgione, A. M., Peaker, J. D., Chaves, J. F., & Bowen, B. (1969). Five attempts to replicate the experimenter bias effect. *Journal of Consulting and Clinical Psychology, 33*, 1–6.

Barber, T. X., Walker, P. C., & Hahn, K. W., Jr. (1973). Effects of hypnotic induction and suggestions on nocturnal dreaming and thinking. *Journal of Abnormal Psychology, 82*, 414–427.

Barnes, R., & Raskind, M. (1980). Strategies for diagnosing and treating agitation in the aging. *Geriatrics, 35*, 111–119.

Barondes, S. H. (1970). Multiple steps in the biology of memory. In F. O. Smith (Ed.), *The neuro-sciences: Second Study program.* New York: Rockefeller University Press.

Barrett, T. R., & Ekstrand, B. R. (1972). Effects of sleep on memory: III. Controlling for time-of-day effects. *Journal of Experimental Psychology, 96,* 321–327.

Barros-Ferreira, M. de, Goldsteinas, L., & Lairy, G. C. (1973). REM sleep deprivation in chronic schizophrenics: Effects on the dynamics of fast sleep. *Electroencephalography and Clinical Neurophysiology, 34,* 561–569.

de Barros–Ferreira, M., & Lairy, G. C. (1976). Ambiguous sleep in narcolepsy. In C. Guilleminault, W. C. Dement, & P. Passouant (Eds.), *Advances in sleep research: Vol. 3, Narcolepsy* (pp. 57–76). New York: Spectrum.

Battle, C., Imber, S., Hoehn–Saric, R., Stone, A., Nash, E., & Frank, J. (1966). Target complaints as criteria of improvement. *American Journal of Psychotherapy, 20,* 184–192.

Baust, W., & Bohnert, B. (1969). The regulation of heart rate during sleep. *Experimental Brain Research, 7,* 169–180.

Baust, W., & Engel, R. (1970). Correlations between heart rate, respiration and dream content. *Pflugers Archives, 319,* 139.

Beck, A. T. (1974). Depressive neurosis. In S. Arieti (Ed.), *American handbook of psychiatry* (2nd Ed.). New York: Basic Books.

Beck, A. T., & Hurvich, M. S. (1959). Psychological correlates of depression. 1. Frequency of "masochistic" dream content in a private practice sample. *Psychosomatic Medicine, 21,* 50–55.

Beck, A. T., & Ward, C. H. (1961). Dreams of depressed patients. *Archives of General Psychiatry, 5,* 462–467.

Belvedere, E., & Foulkes, D. (1971, June). *Telepathy and dreams: A failure to replicate.* Paper presented at the meeting of the Association for the Psychophysiological Study of Sleep, Bruges, Belgium.

Benedek, T., & Rubinstein, B. B. (1939). The correlations between ovarian activity and psychodynamic processes: I. The ovulative phase and II. The menstrual phase. *Psychosomatic Medicine, 1,* 245–270; 446–485.

Bennett, E. L., Diamond, M. C., Krech, D., & Rosenzweig, M. R. (1964). Chemical and anatomical plasiticity of the brain. *Science, 146,* 610–619.

Berger, H. (1969). Hans Berger on the electroencephalogram of man: The fourteen original reports on the human electroencephalogram. In P. Gloor (Ed.), *Electroencephalography and clinical neurophysiology* (Supp. 28).

Berger, M., Lund, R., Bronisch, T., & von Zerssen, D. (1983). REM latency in neurotic and endogenous depression and the cholinergic REM induction test. *Psychiatry Research, 10,* 113–123.

Berger, M., Riemann, D., Weigand, M., Joy, D., & Höchli, D. (1986). Are REM sleep abnormalities in depression more than an epiphenomenon? *8th European Congress of Sleep Research,* Szeged, Hungary, Sept. 1–5, 33 (Abstract).

Berger, R. J. (1963). Experimental modification of dream content by meaningful verbal stimuli. *British Journal of Psychiatry, 109,* 722–740.

Berger, R. J. (1969). Ocularmotor control: A possible function of REM sleep. *Psychological Review, 76,* 144–164.

Berger, R. J. (1969). Physiological characteristics of sleep. In A. Kales (Ed.), *Sleep: Physiology and pathology.* Philadelphia: Lippincott.

Berger, R. J. (1969). Tonus of extrinsic laryngeal muscles during sleep and dreaming. *Science, 134,* 840.

Berger, R. J., Olley, P., & Oswald, I. (1962). The EEG, eye movements, and dreams of the blind. *Quarterly Journal of Experimental Psychology, 14,* 183–186.

Berger, R. J., & Oswald, I. (1962a). Effects of sleep deprivation on behavior, subsequent sleep, and dreaming. *Journal of Mental Science, 108,* 457–465.

Berger, R. J., & Oswald, I. (1962b). Eye movements during active and passive dreams. *Science, 137,* 601.

Berger, R. J., & Scott, T. D. (1971). Increased accuracy of binocular depth perception following REM sleep periods. *Psychophysiology, 8,* 763–768.

Berger, R. J., & Walker, J. M. (1972). Oculomotor coordination following REM and non-REM sleep periods. *Journal of Experimental Psychology, 94,* 216–234.

Berlucchi, G. (1964). Callosal activity in unrestrained, unanesthetized cats. *Archives of Italian Biology, 103,* 623–624.

Berlucchi, G. (1966). Electroencephalographic studies in "split-brain" cats. *Electroencephalography and Clinical Neurophysiology, 20,* 348–356.

Bertini, M. (1968). Procesi de transformazione simbolica nel periodo del dormiveglia e nel sogno (studio sperimentale). Estratta dalla Rivista IKON-Milano, Suppl. al N. 65–66, Aprile–Settembre.

Bertini, M., Bosca, M. A., De Gennaro, L., Perrotta, L., & Solano, L. (1986). Dreamlike mentation in waking and hemispheric activation. *8th European Congress of Sleep Research,* Szeged, Hungary, Sept. 1–5, 34 (Abstract).

Bertini, M., & Pontalti, C. (1971). *Clinical perspectives of a new technique in dream research.* Paper presented at the meeting of the Association for the Psychophysiological Study of Sleep, Bruges, Belgium.

Billard, M., Besset A., & Cadilhac, J. (1983). The clinical and polygraphic development of narcolepsy. In C. Guilleminault & E. Lugaresi (Eds.), *Sleep/wake disorders: natural history of epidemiology, and long term evolution.* New York: Raven Press.

Biondi, M., & delle Chiaie, R. (1982). Verso una psicosomatica del sonno. *Medicina Psicosomatica, 27,* 427–451.

Bizzi, E., & Brooks, O. (1963). Functional connections between pontine rectricular formation and lateral geniculate nucleus during deep sleep. *Archives Italiennes de Biologie, 101,* 648–666.

Blank, H. R. (1958). Dreams of the blind. *Psychoanalytic Quarterly, 27,* 158–174.

Bleuler, E. (1970). *Dementia Praecox,* 1908. Cited by R. L. Williams, The relationship of sleep disturbances to psychopathology. *International Psychiatric Clinics, 7,* 93–111.

Blicher–Toft, M., & Hummer, L. (1977). Serum immunoreactive corticotrophin and response to metapyrone in old age in man. *Gerontology* (Basel), *23,* 236.

Bliss, E. L., Clark, L. D., & West, C. D. (1959). Studies of sleep deprivation-relationship to schizophrenia. *Archives of Neurology and Psychiatry, 81,* 348–359.

Bliwise, D. L., Carey, E., & Dement W. C. (1983). Nightly variation in sleep-related respiratory disturbance in older adults. *Experimental Aging Research, 9*(2), 77–81.

Bliwise, D. L., Carskadon, M., Carey, E., & Dement, W. C. (1984). Longitudinal development of sleep-related respiratory disturbance in adult humans. *Journal of Gerontology, 34,* 290–293.

Bloch, V., Hennevin, E. L., & Leconte, P. (1981). The phenomenon of paradoxical sleep augmentation after learning: Experimental studies of its characteristics and significance. In W. Fishbein (Ed.), *Sleep, dreams and memory.* New York: Spectrum.

Blum, G. A. (1961). *Model of the mind.* New York: Wiley.

Bodnar, R. J., Ellman, S. J., Coons, E. E., Ackermann, R. F., & Steiner, S. S. (1979). Differential locus coeruleus and hypothalamic self stimulation interactions. *Physiological Psychology, 7,* 269–277.

Bodnar, R. J., Steiner, S. S., Healey, J. M., Halperin, J., & Ellman, S. J. (1978). Monophasic pulse pair analysis of intracranial self stimulation loci. *Physiological Psychology, 6,* 48–52.

Bogen, J. E. (1969). The other side of the brain II: An appositional mind. *Bulletin of the Los Angeles Neurological Society, 34,* 135–162.

Bokert, E. (1968). *The effects of thirst and a related verbal stimulus on dream reports.* Doctoral dissertation, New York University.

Bone, R. N. (1968). Extraversion, neuroticism, and dream recall. *Psychological Reports, 23,* 922.

Bone, R. N., & Corlett, F. (1968). Brief report: Frequency of dream recall, creativity, and a control for anxiety. *Psychological reports, 22,* 1355–1356.

Bone, R. N., Nelson, A. E., & McAllister, D. S. (1970). Dream recall and repression-sensitization. *Psychological Reports, 27,* 766.

Bone, R. N., Thomas, T. A., & Kinsolving, D. L. (1972). Relationship of rod-and-frame scores to dream recall. *Psychological Reports, 30,* 58.

Bone, R. W., Hopkins, O. C., Buttermore, G., Jr., Belcher, M. M., McIntyre, C. I., Calef, R. S., & Cowling, L. N. (1973, May). *Sixteen personality correlates of sleep-talkers.* Paper presented at the meeting of the Association for the Psychophysiological Study of Sleep, San Diego, CA.

Bonime, W. (1962). *The clinical use of dreams.* New York: Basic Books.

Bonnet, M. H. (1985). Effect of sleep disruption on sleep, performance, and mood. *Sleep, 8*(1), 11–19.

Bonnet, M. H., & Moore, S. E. (1982). The threshold of sleep: Perception of sleep as a function of time asleep and auditory threshold. *Sleep, 5*(3), 267–276.

Bootzin, R. R. (1973). *Stimulus control of insomnia.* Paper presented at American Psychological Association convention, Montreal.

Bootzin, R. R., & Nicassio, P. M. (1978). Behavioral treatments for insomnia. In M. Hersen, R. M. Eissler, & P. M. Miller (Eds.), *Progress in behavior modification, 6,* 1–45, New York: Academic Press.

Borbily, A. A., & Wirz–Justice, A. (1982). Sleep, sleep deprivation and depression. *Human Neurobiology, 1,* 205–210.

Borowiecki, B., & Sassin, J. (1983). Surgical treatment of sleep apnea. *Archives of Otolaryngology, 109,* 508.

Bosinelli, M., Cavallero, C., & Cicogna, P. (1982). Self-representation in dream experiences during sleep onset and REM sleep. *Sleep, 5,* 290–299.

Bosinelli, M., Cicogna, P., & Molinari, S. (1974). The tonic–phasic model and the feeling of self-participation in different stages of sleep. *Giornale Italiano di Psychologia, 1,* 35–65.

Bosinelli, M., Molinari, S., Bagnaresi, G., & Salzarulo, P. (1978). Caratteristiche dell attitiva psicofsiologica durante il sonno. Un contributo alle techniche di valutazaion. *Ritvista Soerimentale di Freiatria, 2,* 128–150.

Boss, M. (1958). *The analysis of dreams.* New York: Philosophical Library.

Bowe-Anders, C., Herman, J. H., & Roffwarg, H. P. (1974). Effects of goggle-altered color perception on sleep. *Perceptual and Motor Skills, 38,* 191–198.

Box, G. E. P. (1950). Problems in analysis of growth and wear curves. *Biometrics, 6,* 362–389.

Bradley, C., & Meddis, R. (1974). Arousal threshold in dreaming sleep. *Physiological Psychology, 2,* 109–110.

Bransford, J. D., & Franks, J. J. (1971). The abstraction of linguistic ideas. *Cognitive Psychology, 2,* 331–350.

Breger, L. (1967). Function of dreams. *Journal of Abnormal Psychology, 72,* 1–28.

Breger, L. (1969a). Children's dreams and personality development. In J. Fisher & L. Breger (Eds.), *The meaning of dreams: Recent insights from the laboratory.* California Mental Health Research Symposium, No. 3.

Breger, L. (1969b). Dream function: An information processing model. In L. Breger (Ed.), *Clinical-cognitive psychology—models and integrations.* Englewood Cliffs, NJ: Prentice-Hall.

Breger, L., Hunter, I., & Lane, R. W. (1971). *The effect of stress on dreams.* New York: International Universities Press.

Brewer, W. F. (1974). The problem of meaning and the interrelations of the higher mental process. In W. B. Weiner & D. S. Palermo (Eds.), *Cognition and symbolic processes.* Hillsdale, NJ: Erlbaum.

Brooks, O. C. (1967). Localization of the lateral geniculate nucleus monophasic waves associated with paradoxical sleep in the cat. *Electroencephalography and Clinical Neurophysiology, 23,* 123–133.

Brooks, O. C. (1968). Waves associated with eye movement in the awake and sleeping cat. *Electroencephalography and Clinical Neurophysiology, 24,* 532–541.

Broughton, R. (1968). Sleep disorders: Disorders of arousal? *Science, 159,* 1070–1078.

Broughton, R. (1973). Confusional sleep disorders: Inter-relationship with memory consolidation and retrieval in sleep. In T. J. Boag, & D. Campbell (Eds.), *A triune concept of brain and behavior.* Toronto: University of Toronto Press.

Broughton, R. (1975). Biorhythmic variations in consciousness and psychological functions. *Canadian Psychology Review, 16,* 217–239.

Broughton, R., & Ghanem, Q. (1976). The impact of compound narcolepsy on the life of the patient. In C. Guilleminault, W. C. Dement, & P. Passouant (Eds.), *Advances in sleep research, Vol. 3. Narcolepsy* (pp. 201–220). New York: Spectrum.

Broughton, R. J., Poire, R., & Tassinari, C. A. (1965). The electrodermogram (Tarchanoff effect) during sleep. *Electroencephalography and Clinical Neurophysiology, 18,* 691–708.

Brown, C. C. (1979). Toe temperature change: A measure of sleep onset? *Waking & Sleeping, 3,* 353–359.

Brownwell, L. G., West, P., Sweatman, P., Acres, J. C., & Kryger, M. H. (1982). Protryptiline in obstructive sleep apnea. *New England Journal of Medicine, 307,* 1037–1042.

Bruner, J. S. (1957). *On going beyond the information given.* Cambridge, MA: Harvard University Press.

Buguet, A. G. C., Roussel, B. H. E., Watson, W. J., & Radomski, M. W. (1979). Cold-induced diminution of paradoxical sleep in man. *Electroencephalography & Clinical Neurophysiology, 46,* 29–32.

Burch, N. (1965). Data processing of psychophysiological recordings. In L. D. Proctor & W. R. Adey (Eds.), *Symposium on the analysis of central nervous system and cardiovascular data using computer methods.* Washington, DC: National Aeronautics and Space Administration.

Burwell, C. S., Robin, E. D., Whaley, R. D., & Bickelman, A. G. (1956). Extreme obesity associated with alveolar hypoventilation. A Pickwickian syndrome. *American Journal of Medicine, 21,* 811–818.

Butler, R. N., & Lewis, M. I. (1982). *Aging and mental health* (3rd ed.). London: Mosby.

Byrne, D., Barry, J., & Nelson, D. (1963). Relation of the revised Repression-Sensitization scale to measures of self-description. *Psychological Reports, 13,* 323–334.

Calkins, M. W. (1893). Statistics of dreams. *American Journal of Psychology, 5,* 311–343.

Campbell, B. A., & Spear, N. E. (1972). Ontogeny of memory. *Psychological Review, 79,* 215–237.

Campbell, D. T., & Fiske, D. W. (1959). Convergent and discriminant validation by the multitrait multimethod matrix. *Psychological Bulletin, 56,* 82–105.

Campbell, S. S., & Webb, W. B. (1981). The perception of wakefulness within sleep. *Sleep, 4*(2), 177–183.

Carrington, P. (1972). Dreams and schizophrenia. *Archives of General Psychiatry, 26,* 343–350.

Carrol, B., Curtis, G., & Mendels, J. (1976). Neuroendocrine regulation in depression. *Archives of General Psychiatry, 33,* 1039–1044.

Carroll, D., Lewis, S. A., & Oswald, I. (1969). Effect of barbiturates on dream content. *Nature, 223,* 865–866.

Carskadon, M. A., Dement, W. C., Mitler, M. M., Guilleminault, C., Zarcone, V. P., & Spiegel, R. (1976). Self-reports versus sleep laboratory findings in 122 drug-free subjects with complaints of chronic insomnia. *American Journal of Psychiatry, 133,* 1382–1388.

Carskadon, M. A., Seidel, W. F., Greenblatt, D. J., & Dement, W. C. (1982). Daytime carryover of triazolam and flurazepam in elderly insomniacs. *Sleep, 5*(4), 361–371.

Cartwright, R. D. (1966). Dreams and drug-induced fantasy behavior. *Archives of General Psychiatry, 15,* 7–15.

Cartwright, R. D. (1969). Dreams as compared to other forms of fantasy. In M. Kramer, R. M. Whitman, B. J. Baldridge, & P. H. Ornstein (Eds.), *Dream psychology and the new biology of dreaming.* Springfield, IL: Thomas.

Cartwright, R. D. (1970). *The effect of dream opportunity on daytime problem resolution: A preliminary report of a pilot study.* Paper presented at the meeting of the Association for the Psychophysiological Study of Sleep, Santa Fe, NM. *Psychophysiology, 7,* 332. (Abstract)

Cartwright, R. D. (1972). Sleep fantasy in normal and schizophrenic persons. *Journal of Abnormal Psychology, 80,* 275–279.

Cartwright, R. D. (1974a). The influence of a conscious wish on dreams: A methodological study of dream meaning and function. *Journal of Abnormal Psychology, 83,* 387–393.

Cartwright, R. D. (1974b). Problem solving: Waking and dreaming. *Journal of Abnormal Psychology, 83,* 451–455.

Cartwright, R. D. (1983). Rapid eye movement sleep characteristics during and after mood disturbing events. *Archives of General Psychiatry, 40,* 197–201.

Cartwright, R. D., Bernick, N., Borowitz, G., & Kling, A. (1969). Effect of an erotic movie on the sleep and dreams of young men. *Archives of General Psychiatry, 20,* 263–271.

Cartwright, R. D., Lloyd, S., Lilie, J., & Kravitz, H. (1985). Sleep position as training as treatment for sleep apnea syndrome: A preliminary study. *Sleep, 8*(2), 87–94.

Cartwright, R. D., & Monroe, L. J. (1968). The relation of dreaming and REM sleep: The effect of REM deprivation under two conditions. *Journal of Personality and Social Psychology, 10,* 69–74.

Cartwright, R. D., Monroe, L. J., & Palmer, C. (1967). Individual differences in response to REM deprivation. *Archives of General Psychiatry, 16,* 297–303.

Cartwright, R. D., & Ratzel, R. (1970). *Light and deep sleeper differences: Fantasy scores from REM, stage 2 and REM deprivation awakenings.* Paper presented at the meeting of the Association for the Psychophysiological Study of Sleep, Santa Fe, NM.

Cartwright, R. D., & Ratzel, R. W. (1972). Effects of dream loss on waking behaviors. *Archives of General Psychiatry, 27,* 277–280.

Cartwright, R. D., Weiner, L., & Wicklund, J. (1975, May). *Effects of lab training in dream recall on psychotherapy behavior.* Paper presented at the meeting of the Association for the Psychophysiological Study of Sleep, Edinburgh, Scotland.

Cartwright, R., & Monroe, L. (1968). Relation of dreaming and REM sleep: The effects of REM deprivation under two different conditions. *Journal of Personality & Social Psychology, 10,* 69–74.

Cartwright, R., Monroe, L., & Palmer, C. (1967). Individual differences in response to REM deprivation. *Archives of General Psychiatry, 16,* 297–303.

Cartwright, R., & Ratzel, R. (1972). Effects of dream loss on waking behavior. *Archives of General Psychiatry, 16,* 277–280.

Cartwright, R., Tipton, L., & Wicklund, J. (1980). Focusing on dreams. *Archives of General Psychiatry, 37,* 275–277.

Castaldo, V., & Holzman, P. (1967). The effect of hearing one's voice on sleep mentation. *Journal of Nervous and Mental Disease, 144,* 2–13.

Castaldo, V., & Holzman, P. (1969). The effects of hearing one's own voice on dreaming content: A replication. *Journal of Nervous and Mental Disease, 148,* 74–82.

Castaldo, V., & Shevrin, H. (1970). Different effect of auditory stimulus as a function of rapid eye movement and non-rapid eye movement sleep. *Journal of Nervous and Mental Disease, 150,* 195–200.

Cavallero, C. (1987). Dream sources, associative mechanisms and temporal dimension. *Sleep, 10,* 78–83.

Cavallero, C., & Cicogna, P. (1984). Models and strategies of sleep mentation research. In M. Bosinelli & P. Cicogna (Eds.), *Psychology of dreaming* (pp. 65–78). Bologna: CLUEB.

Cavallero, C., Cicogna, P., & Bosinelli, M. (1986). Mnemonic activation in dream production. *8th European Congress of Sleep Research,* Szeged, Hungary, Sept. 1–5, 56 (Abstract).

Charney, D. S., Kales, A., Soldatos, C. R., & Nelson, J. C. (1979). Somnambulistic-like episodes secondary to combined lithium-neuroleptic treatment. *British Journal of Psychiatry, 35,* 418–424.

Chernik, D. A. (1972). Effect of REM sleep deprivation on learning and recall by humans. *Perceptual and Motor Skills, 34,* 283–294.

Cherry, C. (1966). *On human communication* (2d ed.). Cambridge, MA: M. I. T. Press.

Church, J. (1961). *Language and the discovery of reality.* New York: Vintage Books.

Cicogna, P., Cavallero, C., & Bosinelli, M. (1986). Different access to memory traces in the production of mental experience. *International Journal of Psychophysiology, 4,* 209–216.

Cicogna, P., Cavallero, C., Bosinelli, M., Battaglia, D., & Natale, V. (1987). A comparison between single- and multi-unit dream reports. Abstract sent to the Scientific Committee of the *5th International Congress of Sleep Research,* Copenhagen, June 29–July 3.

Clausen, J. (1966). Family structure, socialization and personality. In L. W. Hoffman & M. C. Hoffman (Eds.), *Review of child development research* (Vol. 2). New York: Russell Sage Foundation.

Clemes, S. R., & Dement, W. (1967). Effect of REM sleep deprivation on psychological functioning. *Journal of Nervous and Mental Disease, 144,* 488–491.

Cohen, D. B. (1969). Frequency of dream recall estimated by three methods and related to defense preference and anxiety. *Journal of Consulting and Clinical Psychology, 33,* 661–667.

Cohen, D. B. (1971). Dream recall and short-term memory. *Perceptual and Motor Skills, 33,* 867–871.

Cohen, D. B. (1972). Presleep experience and home dream reporting: An exploratory study. *Journal of Consulting and Clinical Psychology, 38,* 122–128.

Cohen, D. B. (1974). Toward a theory of dream recall. *Psychological Bulletin, 81,* 138–154.

Cohen, D. B. (1977). Changes in REM dream content during the night: Implications for a hypothesis about changes in cerebral dominance across REM periods. *Perceptual & Motor Skills, 44,* 1267–1277.

Cohen, D. B. (1979). *Sleep and dreaming: Origins, nature and function.* New York: Pergamon.

Cohen, D. B., & MacNeilage, P. F. (1973). Dream salience and postsleep interference factors that differentiate frequent and infrequent dream recallers. *Sleep Research, 2,* 111. (Abstract)

Cohen, D. B., & Wolfe, G. (1973). Dream recall and repression: Evidence for an alternative hypothesis. *Journal of Consulting and Clinical Psychology, 41,* 349–355.

Cohen, D., & Cox, C. (1975). Neuroticism in the sleep laboratory: Implications for representational and adaptive properties of dreaming. *Journal of Abnormal Psychology, 84,* 91–108.

Cohen, G. (1975). Hemisphere differences in the affects of cueing in visual recognition tests. *Journal of Experimental Psychology, 1,* 366–373.

Cohen, H. B., & Dement, W. (1968). Electrically induced convulsions in REM deprived mice: Prolongation of the tonic phase. *Psychophysiology, 4,* 381. (Abstract)

Cohen, H. B., Duncan, R., & Dement, W. C. (1967). The effect of electroconvulsive shock in cats deprived of REM sleep. *Science, 156,* 1646–1648.

Cohen, H. B., Edelman, A., & Bowen, R. (1972). Sleep and self-stimulation in the rat. *Sleep Research, 1,* 158.

Cohen, H., & Dement, W. (1965). Changes in threshold to electroconvulsive shock in rats after deprivation of "paradoxical" phase. *Science, 150,* 1318–1319.

Cohen, H., & Dement, W. (1966). Sleep: Suppression of rapid eye movement phase in the cat after electroconvulsive shock. *Science, 154,* 396–398.

Cohen, H. D., & Shapiro, A. (1970). Vaginal blood flow during sleep. *Psychophysiology, 1,* 338. (Abstract)

Cohen, H. D., Shapiro, A., Goodenough, D. R., & Saunders, D. (1965, March). *The EEG during stage 4 sleep-talking.* Paper presented at the meeting of the Association for the Psychophysiological Study of Sleep, Washington, DC.

Cohen, H., Edelman, A., Bowen, R., & Dement, W. (1972). Sleep and self-stimulation in the rat. *Sleep Research, 1,* 158.

Cohen, H., Mitchell, G., & Dement, W. C. (1968). Chlorpromazine and sleep in the cat. *Psychophysiology, 5,* 207. (Abstract)

Cohen, H., Thomas, J., & Dement, W. C. (1970). Sleep stages, REM deprivation, and electroconvulsive threshold in the cat. *Brain Research, 19,* 317–321.

Cohen, J. (1965). Some statistical issues in psychological research. In B. B. Wolman, *Handbook of clinical psychology.* New York: McGraw Hill.

Cohen, J., & Cohen, P. (1975). *Applied multiple regression/correlation analysis for the behavioral sciences.* Hillsdale, NJ: Erlbaum.

Coleman, R. M. (1982). Periodic movements in sleep (nocturnal myoclonus) and restless legs syndrome. In C. Guilleminault (Ed.), *Sleeping and waking disorders: Indications and techniques.* Menlo Park, CA: Addison–Wesley.

Coleman, R. M. (1983). Diagnosis, treatment, and follow-up of about 8,000 sleep/wake disorders patients. In C. Guilleminault & E. Lugaresi (Eds.), *Sleep/wake disorders: Natural history of epidemiology, and long term evolution.* New York: Raven Press.

Coleman, R. M., Roffwarg, H., & Kennedy, S., et al. (1982). Sleep-wake disorders based on a polysomnographic diagnosis: A national cooperative study. *Journal of the American Medical Association, 247,* 997–1003.

Collins, A. M., & Loftus, E. F. (1975). A spreading activation theory of semantic processing. *Psychological Review, 82,* 417–428.

Collins, G., Davison, L., & Breger, L. (1967). *Dream function in adaptation to threat: A preliminary study.* Paper presented at the meeting of the Association for the Psychophysiological Study of Sleep, Santa Monica, CA.

Cooper, J. R. (Ed.). (1977). *Sedative-hypnotic drugs: Risks and benefits.* Rockville, MD: National Institute on Drug Abuse.

Cory, T. L., Ormiston, D. W., Simmel, E., & Dainoff, M. (1975). Predicting the frequency of dream recall. *Journal of Abnormal Psychology, 84,* 261–266.

Crick, C., & Mitchison, G. (1983). The function of dream sleep. *Nature, 304,* 111–114.

Crick, F., & Mitchison, G. (1986). REM sleep and neural nets. *The Journal of Mind and Behavior, 7,* 229–250.

Critchley, M. (1955). *Revue Neurologique, 93,* 101–106.

Critchley, M. (1962). Periodic hypersomnia and megaphagia in adolescent males. *Brain, 85,* 627.

Czaya, J., Kramer, M., & Roth, T. (1973). *Changes in dream quality as a function of time into REM.* Paper presented at the meeting of the Association for the Psychophysiological Study of Sleep, San Diego, CA.

Dallett, J. (1973). Theories of dream function. *Psychological Bulletin, 6,* 408–416.

Dallmeier, Z. K., & Carlini, E. A. (1982). The persistence of hyperresponsiveness to apomorphine in rats following REM sleep deprivation and the influence of housing conditions. *European Journal of Pharmacology, 80,* 90–104.

Davis, K. B. (1929). *Factors in the sex life of twenty-two hundred women.* New York: Harper and Row.

Davison, G. C., Tsujimoto, R. N., & Glaros, A. G. (1973). Attribution and the maintenance of behavior change in falling asleep. *Journal of Abnormal Psychology, , 82,* 124–133.

De Candolle, A. P. (1832). *Physiologie Vegetable* (Vol. 2, pp. 854–862). Paris: Bechet Jeune.

De Koninck, J. M., & Koulack, D. (1975). Dream content and adaptation to a stressful situation. *Journal of Abnormal Psychology, 84,* 250–260.

De la Penl a, A. (1978). Toward a psychophysiologic conceptualization of insomnia. In R. L. Williams & I. Karacan (Eds.), *Sleep disorders. Diagnosis and treatment* (pp. 101–143). New York: Wiley.

Delorme, F., Jeannerod, M., & Jouvet, M. (1965). Effects rémarquables de la reserpine sur l'activité EEG phasique ponto-geniculo-occipitale, *Comptes Rendus des Séances de la Société de Biologie, 159,* 900–903.

de Mairan, J. (1729). Observation botanique. *Histoire de l'Academie Royale des Sciences,* pp. 35–36.

DeMartino, M. R. (1955). A review of the literature on children's dreams. *Psychiatric Quarterly Supplement, 19,* 90–100.

Dement, W. (1964b). Eye movements during sleep. In M. Bender (Ed.), *The oculomotor system.* New York: Harper & Row.

Dement, W. (1965a). An essay on dreams: The role of physiology in understanding their nature. In F. Barron (Ed.), *New directions in psychology* (Vol. II). Fort Worth: Holt, Rinehart & Winston.

Dement, W. (1965d). Studies on the function of rapid eye movement (paradoxical) sleep in human subjects. In M. Jouvet (Ed.) *Aspects anatomofonctionnels de la physiologie du sommeil.* Paris: Centre National de la Récherche Scientifique.

Dement, W. (1978). Cited in Arkin, A., Antrobus, J., Ellman, S., & Farber, J. Sleep mentation as affected by REM deprivation. In A. Arkin, J. Antrobus, & S. Ellman (Eds.), *The mind in sleep: Psychology and psychophysiology.* Hillsdale, NJ: Erlbaum.

Dement, W. C. (1955). Dream recall and eye movements during sleep in schizophrenics and normals. *Journal of Nervous & Mental Disease, 122,* 263–269.

Dement, W. C. (1960a). The effect of dream deprivation. *Science, 131,* 1705–1707.

Dement, W. C. (1964a). Experimental dream studies. In J. H. Masserman (Ed.), *Science and psychoanalysis* (Vol. III). New York: Grune & Stratton.

Dement, W. C. (1965b). Recent studies in the biological role of rapid eye movement sleep. *American Journal of Psychiatry, 122,* 404–408.

Dement, W. C. (1965c). Dreams and dreaming. *International Journal of Neurology, 5,* 168–186.

Dement, W. C. (1966). Psychophysiology of sleep and dreams. In S. Arieti (Ed.), *American handbook of psychiatry* (Vol. 3). New York: Basic Books.

Dement, W. C. (1967). Possible physiological determinants of a possible dream-intensity cycle. *Experimental Neurology Supplement, 4,* 38–55.

Dement, W. C. (1969). The biological role of REM sleep (circa 1968). In A. Kales (Ed.), *Sleep: Physiology and pathology.* Philadelphia: Lippincott.

Dement, W. C. (1972). *Some must watch while some must sleep.* San Francisco: Freeman.

Dement, W. C. (1973). Commentary on "The biological role of REM sleep." In W. B. Webb (Ed.), *Sleep: An active process.* Glenview, IL: Scott, Foresman.

Dement, W. C. (1975). Personal communication to Arkin, A. M.

Dement, W. C., & Fisher, C. (1963). Experimental interference with the sleep cycle. *Canadian Psychiatric Association Journal, 8,* 400–405.

Dement, W. C., Kahn, E., & Roffwarg, H. P. (1965). The influence of the laboratory situation on the dreams of the experimental subject. *Journal of Nervous and Mental Disease, 140,* 119–131.

Dement, W. C., Kahn, E., & Roffwarg, H. P. (1965). The influence of the laboratory situation on the dreams of the experimental subject. *Journal of Nervous and Mental Disease, 140,* 119–131.

Dement, W. C., & Kleitman, N. (1957a). Cyclic variations in EEG during sleep and their relation to eye movements, bodily motility and dreaming. *Electroencephalography and Clinical Neurophysiology, 9,* 673–690.

Dement, W. C., & Kleitman, N. (1957b). The relation of eye movements during sleep to dream activity: An objective method for the study of dreaming. *Journal of Experimental Psychology, 53,* 339–346.

Dement, W. C., Miles, L., Carskadon, M. (1982). "White paper" on sleep and aging. *Journal of the American Geriatrics Society, 30*(1), 25–50.

Dement, W. C., & Mitler, M. M. (1973). New developments in the basic mechanisms of sleep. In G. Usdin (Ed.), *Sleep research and clinical practice*. New York: Brunner-Mazel.

Dement, W., Cohen, H., Ferguson, J., & Zarcone, V. (1970). A sleep researcher's odyssey: The function and clinical significance of REM sleep. In L. Madow & L. H. Snow, *The psychodynamic implications of the physiological studies on dreams*. Springfield, IL: Thomas.

Dement, W. C., Rechtschaffen, A., & Gulevich, G. (1966). The nature of narcoleptic sleep attack. *Neurology, 16,* 18–33.

Dement, W. D. (1965). Recent studies in the biological role of REM sleep. *American Journal of Psychiatry, 122,* 404–408.

Dement, W. D., & Mitler, M. (1973). New developments in the basic mechanisms of sleep. In G. Usdin (Ed.), *Sleep research and clinical practice*. New York: Brunner Mazel.

Dement, W., Ferguson, J., Cohen, H., & Barchas, J. (1969). Nonchemical methods and data using a biochemical model: The REM quanta. In A. Mandell & M. Mandell (Eds.), *Psychochemical research in man. Methods, strategy and theory*. New York: Academic Press.

Dement, W., & Greenberg, S. (1966). Changes in total amount of stage four sleep as a function of partial sleep deprivation. *Electrocephalography and Clinical Neurophysiology, 20* 523–526.

Dement, W., Greenberg, S., & Klein, R. (1966). The effect of partial REM sleep deprivation and delayed recovery. *Journal of Psychiatric Research, 4,* 141–152.

Dement, W., & Wolpert, E. (1958a). Interrelations in the manifest content of dreams occurring on the same night. *Journal of Nervous and Mental Disease, 126,* 568–578.

Dement, W., & Wolpert, E. (1958b). The relation of eye movements, body motility, and external stimuli to dream content. *Journal of Experimental Psychology, 55,* 543–553.

Dement, W., Zarcone, V., Ferguson, J., Cohen, H., Pivik, T., & Barchas, J. (1969). Some parallel findings in schizophrenic patients and serotonin-depleted cats. In D. V. S. Sankar (Ed.), *Schizophrenia: Current concepts and research*. Hicksville, NY: PJD Publications.

Dennenberg, V. H., & Thomas, E. B. (1981). Evidence for a functional role for active (REM) sleep in infancy. *Sleep, 4,* 185–192.

Deutsch, J. A. (1964). Behavioral measurement of the neural refractory period and its application to intracranial self stimulation. *Journal of Comparative and Physiological Psychology, 58,* 1–9.

De Valois, R. L., Abramov, I., & Mead, W. R. (1967). Single cell analysis of wavelength discrimination at the lateral geniculate nucleus in the macaque. *Journal of Neurophysiology, 30,* 415–433.

Dewan, E. M. (1968). The P (programming) hypothesis for REMs. *Psychophysiology, 4,* 365–366.

Dewan, E. M. (1970). The programming (P) hypothesis for REM sleep. In E. Hartmann (Ed.), *Sleep and dreaming*. Boston: Little, Brown.

Dewson, J., Dement, W., & Simmons, F. (1965). Middle ear muscle activity in cats during sleep. *Experimental Neurology, 12*, 1–8.

Dewson, J. H., Dement, W. C., Wagener, T. E., & Nobel, K. (1967). Rapid eye movement sleep deprivation: A central neural change during wakefulness. *Science, 156*, 403–406.

Dewson, J. H., Dement, W. C., Wagener, T. E., & Novel, K. (1967). Rapid eye movement sleep deprivation: A central neural change during wakefulness. *Science, 156*, 403–406.

Dexter, J. D., & Weitzman, E. D. (1970). The relationship of nocturnal headaches to sleep stage patterns. *Neurology, 20*, 513–518.

Dixon, N. F. (1971). *Subliminal perception: The nature of a controversy.* London: McGraw-Hill.

Domhoff, B. (1962). *A quantitative study using an objective indicator of dreaming.* Unpublished doctoral dissertation, University of Miami.

Domhoff, B., & Gerson, A. (1967). Replication and critique of three studies on personality correlates of dream recall. *Journal of Consulting Psychology, 31*, 431.

Domhoff, B., & Kamiya, J. (1964). Problems in dream content study with objective indicators: 1. A comparison of home and laboratory dream reports. *Archives of General Psychiatry, 11*, 519–524.

Dorus, E., Dorus, E., & Rechtschaffen, A. (1971). The incidence of novelty in dreams. *Archives of General Psychiatry, 25*, 364–368.

Doyle, J. C., Ornstein, R., & Galin, D. (1974). Lateral specialization of cognitive mode: EEG frequency analysis. *Psychophysiology, 11*, 567–578.

Duncan, R., II., Henry, P., Karadzic, V., Mitchell, G., Pivik, T., Cohen, H., & Dement, W. (1968). Manipulation of the sleep-wakefulness cycle in the rat: A longitudinal study. *Psychophysiology, 4*, 379. (Abstract)

Duncker, K. (1945). On problem solving. *Psychological Monograph, 58* (No. 5).

Dunleavy, D. L. F., MacLean, A. W., & Oswald, I. (1971). Debrisoquine, guanethidine, propranolol and human sleep. *Psychopharmacologia, 21*, 101–110.

Dunleavy, D. L. F., Oswald, I., Brown, P., & Strong, J. A. (1974). Hyperthyroidism sleep and growth hormone. *Electroencephalography and Clinical Neurophysiology, 36*, 259–263.

Dusan-Peyrethon, D., Peyrethon, J., & Jouvet, M. (1967). Étude quantitative des phénoménes phasiques du sommeil paradoxale pendant et après sa déprivation instrumentale. *Comptes Rendus des Séances de la Société de Biologie, 161*, 2530–2537.

Eagle, E. J. (1974). *An exploratory study of the relationships between cognitive and perceptual styles and drives and defenses in differing states of awareness.* An unpublished study cited by H. A. Witkin, R. D. Dyk, H. F. Faterson, D. R. Goodenough, & S. A. Karp, *Psychological differentiation.* Potomac, MD: Erlbaum. (Original work published 1963).

Eagle, M. (1973). Sherwood on the logic of explanation in psychoanalysis. In B. B. Rubinstein (Ed.), *Psychoanalysis and contemporary science* (Vol 2). New York: Macmillan.

Ehrlichman, H., & Antrobus, J. S. (1974). *Sleep mentation and functional hemispheric asymmetry.* National Institute of Mental Health Grant Proposal.

Ekstrand, B. R. (1967). Effect of sleep on memory. *Journal of Experimental Psychology,* 75, 64–72.

Ekstrand, B., Sullivan, M. J., Parker, D. F., & West, J. (1971). Spontaneous recovery and sleep. *Journal of Experimental Psychology,* 88, 142–144.

Ellman, S. (1970). Unpublished critique of *Tonic and phasic events during sleep: Psychological correlates and implications* by S. Molinari & D. Foulkes.

Ellman, S., Antrobus, J., Arkin, A., Luck, D., Bodnar, R., Sanders, R., & Nelson, W. (1974, May). *Sleep mentation in relation to tonic and phasic events—REM and NREM.* Paper presented at the meeting of the Association for the Psychophysiological Study of Sleep, Jackson, MS.

Ellman, S. J. (1970). *The experimental modification of two aspects of the REM sleep cycle.* Unpublished doctoral dissertation, New York University.

Ellman, S. J. (1976, May). Discussion presented at annual conference of the Center for Research in Cognition and Affect, New York.

Ellman, S. J., Ackermann, D. R., Farber, J., & Steiner, S. S. (1973a). The locus coeruleus as an intracranial self stimulation site: Evidence for a locus coeruleus-limbic system intracranial self stimulation network. *Sleep Research,* 2, 92–95.

Ellman, S. J., Ackermann, R. F., Bodnar, R. J., Jackler, F., & Steiner, S. S. (1975). Comparisons of behavior elicited by electrical brain stimulation in dorsal brainstem and hypothalamus of rats. *Journal of Comparative and Physiological Psychology,* 88, 816–828.

Ellman, S. J., Ackermann, R. F., Farber, J., Mattiace, L., & Steiner, S. S. (1974a). Relation between dorsal brainstem sleep sites and intracranial self-stimulation. *Physiological Psychology,* 2, 31–34.

Ellman, S. J., Antrobus, J. S., Arkin, A. M., Farber, J., Luck, D., Bodnar, R., Sanders, K., & Nelson, W. T. (1974, May). *Sleep mentation in relation to phasic and tonic events—REMP and NREM.* Paper presented at the meeting of the Association for the Psychophysiological Study of Sleep, Jackson Hole, WY.

Ellman, S. J., & Steiner, S. S. (1969a). *The effect of electrical self-stimulation on REM rebound.* Paper presented at the meeting of the Association for the Psychophysiological Study of Sleep, Boston.

Ellman, S. J., & Steiner, S. S. (1969b). *The effect of REM deprivation on intracranial self-stimulation.* Paper presented at the meeting of the Association for the Psychophysiological Study of Sleep, Boston.

Ellman, S. & Moskowitz, M. (1980). An examination of some recent criticisms of psychoanalytic "metapsychology." *Psychoanalytic Quarterly,* 49, 631–662.

Elomaa, E. (1981). The light/dark difference in meal size in the laboratory rat on a standard diet is abolished during REM sleep deprivation, *Physiological Behavior,* 26, 487–493.

Elomaa, E., & Johansson, G. (1980). Daily rhythm of locomotor activity is abolished during REM sleep deprivation in the rat. *Physiological Behavior,* 24, 327–330.

Elomaa, E., & Johansson, G. (1980). REM stage of sleep participates in the generation of the nocturnal meal pattern in the rat, *Physiological Behavior,* 24, 331–336.

Elomaa, E., & Johansson, G. G. (1980b). Daily rhythm of locomotor activity is dropped during REM sleep deprivation in the rat. *Physiology & Behaviour,* 24, 327–330.

Elsenga, S., & Van den Hoofdakker, R. H. (1982/1983). Clinical effects of sleep deprivation and clomipramine in endogenous depression. *Journal of Psychiatric Research, 17,* 361–374.

Emde, R., & Metcalf, D. R. (1970). An electroencephalographic study of behavioral rapid eye movement states in the human newborn. *Journal of Nervous and Mental Disease, 159,* 376–385.

Emerson, R. W. (1884). *Lectures and biographical sketches.* Boston: Houghton Mifflin.

Emmons, W. H., & Simon, C. W. (1956). The non-recall of material presented during sleep. *American Journal of Psychology, 69,* 79–81.

Empson, J. A., & Clarke, P. R. (1970). Rapid eye movements and remembering. *Nature, 227,* 287–288.

Ephron, H. S., & Carrington, P. (1966). Rapid eye movement sleep and cortical homeostasis. *Psychological Review, 75,* 500–526.

Erikson, E. H. (1954). The dream specimen of psychoanalysis. In R. Knight & C. Friedman (Eds.), *Psychoanalytic psychiatry and psychology.* New York: International Universities Press.

Erikson, E. H. (1963). *Childhood and society* (rev. ed.). New York: Norton.

Evans, F. J. (1972). Hypnosis and sleep: Techniques for exploring cognitive activity during sleep. In E. Fromm & R. E. Shor (Eds.), *Hypnosis: Research developments and perspectives.* Chicago: Aldine.

Evans, F. J., Gustafson, L. A., O'Connell, D. N., Orne, M. T., & Shor, R. E. (1966). Response during sleep with intervening waking amnesia. *Science, 152,* 666–667.

Evans, F. J., Gustafson, L. A., O'Connell, D. N., Orne, M. T., & Shor, R. E. (1969). Sleep-induced behavioral response. *Journal of Nervous and Mental Disease, 148,* 467–476.

Evans, F. J., Gustafson, L. A., O'Connell, D. N., Orne, M. T., & Shor, R. E. (1970). Verbally induced behavior responses during sleep. *Journal of Nervous and Mental Disease, 150,* 171–187.

Evans, F. J., & Orchard, W. (1969). Sleep learning: The successful waking recall of material presented during sleep. *Psychophysiology, 6,* 269. (Abstract)

Evans, J. I., Lewis, S. A., Gibb, S. A. M., & Cheetham, M. (1968). Sleep and barbiturates: Some experiments and observations. *British Medical Journal, 4,* 291–293.

Evans, J. I., & Oswald, I. (1966). Some experiments in the chemistry of narcoleptic sleep. *British Journal of Psychiatry, 112,* 401–409.

Fahndrich, E. (1982). Schlafentzug–Behandlung depressive syndrome bei Schizophrenische grunderkrankung. *Nervenarzt, 53,* 279–283.

Fahndrich, E. (1983). Effect of sleep deprivation as a predictor of treatment response to antidepressant medication. *Acta Psychiatrica Scandinavica, 68,* 341–344.

Fahrion, S. L., Davison, L., & Berger, L. (1967, April). *The relationship of heart rate and dream content in heart rate responders.* Paper presented at the meeting of the Association for the Psychophysiological Study of Sleep, Santa Monica, CA.

Farber, J., Arkin, A. M., Ellman, S. J., Antrobus, J. S., & Nelson, W. (1973). *The effects of sleep interruption, deprivation and elicited verbalizations on sleep speech parameters.* Paper presented at the meeting of the Association for the Psychophysiological Study of Sleep, San Diego, CA.

Farber, J., Marks, G. A., Roffwarg, H. P. (1980). Rapid eye movement sleep PGO-type waves are present in the dorsal pons of the albino rat. *Science, 209,* 615–617.

Farber, J., Steiner, S., & Ellman, S. J. (1972). The pons as an electrical self stimulation site. *Psychophysiology, 9,* 150–152.

Feinberg, I. (1969). Recent sleep research: Findings in schizophrenia and some possible implications for the mechanism faction of chlorpromazine and for the neurophysiology of delirium. In S. Sankar (Ed.), *Schizophrenia: Current concepts and research.* New York: Plenum Press, 739–750.

Feinberg, I. (1969). Sleep in organic brain conditions. In A. Kales (Ed.), *Sleep: Physiology and pathology.* Philadelphia: Lippincott.

Feinberg, I., & Evarts, E. V. (1969). Some implications of sleep research for psychiatry. In J. Zubin & C. Shagass (Eds.), *Proceedings of the American Psychopathological Association: Neurobiological aspects of psychopathology.* New York: Grune & Stratton.

Feinberg, I., Hibi, S., Cavness, C., & March, J. (1974). Absence of REM rebound after barbiturate withdrawal. *Science, 185,* 534–535.

Feinberg, I., Koresko, R., Gottlieb, F., & Wender, P. (1964). Sleep encephalographic and eye movement patterns in schizophrenic patients. *Comprehensive Psychiatry, 5,* 44–53.

Fein, G., Floyd, T. C., & Feinberg, I. Computer measures of sleep EEG reliably sort visually stage 2 epochs by NREM period of origin. *Psychophysiology,* 1981, *18,* 686–693.

Feldman, J. A. (1981). A connectionist model of visual imagery. In G. E. Hinton & J. A. Anderson (Eds.), *Parallel models of associative memory* (pp. 49–81). Hillsdale, NJ: Erlbaum.

Feldman, R., & Dement, W. (1968). *Possible relationships between REM sleep and memory consolidation.* Paper presented at the meeting of the Association for the Psychophysiological Study of Sleep, Denver. *Psychophysiology, 5,* 243. (Abstract)

Feldman, R. E. (1969). The effect of deprivation of rapid eye movement sleep on learning and retention in humans. *Dissertation Abstracts* (B), *30,* 4390–4391.

Feldstein, S. (1972). *REM deprivation: The effects on ink blot perception and fantasy processes.* Doctoral dissertation, City University of New York.

Fellman, I., & Strauch, I. (1983). Qualitative and quantitative correlates of sleep onset. *Sleep Research,* 154 (Abstract).

Feltin, M., & Broughton, R. J. (1968). Differential effects of arousal from slow wave sleep versus REM sleep. *Psychophysiology, 5,* 231. (Abstract)

Ferguson, J., Cohen, H., Henriksen, S., McGarr, K., Mitchell, G., Hoyt, G., Barchas, J., & Dement, W. (1969). The effect of chronic administration of PCPA on sleep in the cat. *Psychophysiology, 6,* 220–221. (Abstract)

Ferguson, J., & Dement, W. (1968). Changes in intensity of REM sleep with deprivation. *Psychophysiology, 4,* 380–381. (Abstract)

Ferguson, J., & Dement, W. (1968). The effects of variations in total sleep time on the occurrence of rapid eye movement sleep in cats. *Electroencephalography & Clinical Neurophysiology, 22,* 2–10.

Ferguson, J., & Dement, W. (1969). The behavioral effects of amphetamine on REM deprived rats. *Journal of Psychiatric Research, 7,* 111–118.

Ferguson, J., Henriksen, S., McGarr, K., Belenky, G., Mitchell, G., Gonda, W., Cohen, H., & Dement, W. (1968). Phasic event deprivation in the cat. *Psychophysiology, 5,* 238–239.

Fingl, E., & Woodbury, A. M., (1970). General principles. In L. S. Goodman, & A. Gilman, *The pharmacological basis of therapeutics* (4th ed.). London: Macmillan.

Firth, H. (1972). Eye movements, dreams and drugs. *Sleep Research, 1,* 102.

Firth, H. (1973). Habituation during sleep. *Psychophysiology, 10,* 43–51.

Firth, H. (1974). Sleeping pills and dream content. *British Journal of Psychiatry, 124,* 547–553.

Firth, H., & Oswald, I. (1975). Eye movements and visually active dreams. *Psychophysiology, 12,* 602–605.

Fishbein, W. (1969). *Paradoxical sleep: A periodic mechanism for securing and maintaining information for long-term memory.* Doctoral dissertation, University of Colorado. *Dissertation Abstracts International, 30,* 865B. University Microfilms No. 69-13410.

Fishbein, W. (1970). Interference with conversion of memory from short-term to long-term storage by partial sleep deprivation. *Communications in Behavioral Biology* (A), *5,* 171–175.

Fishbein, W. (1971). Disruptive effects of rapid eye movement sleep deprivation on long-term memory. *Physiology and Behavior, 6,* 279–282.

Fishbein, W., & Gutwein, B. (1977). Paradoxical sleep and memory storage processes. *Behavioral Biology, 19,* 425–464.

Fishbein, W., & Gutwein, B. (1981). Paradoxical sleep and a theory of long term memory. In W. Fishbein (Ed.), *Sleep, dreams, and memory.* New York: Spectrum.

Fishbein, W., McGaugh, J. L., & Schwarz, J. R. (1971). Retrograde amnesia: Electroconvulsive shock effects after termination of rapid eye movement sleep deprivation. *Science, 172,* 80–82.

Fisher, C. (1953). Experimental induction of dreams by direct suggestion. *Journal of the American Psychoanalytic Association, 1,* 222–255.

Fisher, C. (1959). A study of the preliminary stages of the construction of dreams and images. *Journal of the American Psychoanalytic Association, 5,* 5–60.

Fisher, C. (1960). Preconscious stimulation in dreams, associations and images: Classical studies by Otto Pötzl, Rudolf Allers and Jakob Teller. *Psychological Issues, 2,* (Monograph 7).

Fisher, C. (1965). Psychoanalytic implications of recent research on sleep and dreaming. Part I: Empirical findings. Part II: Implications for psychoanalytic theory. *Journal of the American Psychoanalytic Association, 13,* 197–303.

Fisher, C. (1966). Dreaming and sexuality. In R. Lowenstein, L. Newman, M. Schur, & A. Solnit (Eds.), *Psychoanalysis: A general psychology.* New York: International Universities Press.

Fisher, C., Byrne, J., Edwards, A., & Kahn, E. (1970). A psychophysiological study of nightmares. *Journal of the American Psychoanalytic Association, 18,* 747–782.

Fisher, C., & Dement, W. C. (1961). Dreaming and psychosis: Observations on the dream cycle during the course of an acute paranoid psychosis. *Bulletin of the Philadelphia Association for Psychoanalysis, 11,* 130–132.

Fisher, C., & Dement, W. C. (1963). Studies on the psychopathology of sleep and dreams. *American Journal of Psychiatry, 119,* 1160–1168.

Fisher, C., Gross, J., & Zuch, J. (1965). Cycles of penile erection synchronous with dreaming (REM) sleep. *Archives of General Psychiatry, 12,* 29–45.

Fisher, C., Kahn, E., Edwards, A., & Davis, D. (1972). Total suppression of REM sleep with Nardil in a patient with intractable narcolepsy. *Sleep Research, 1,* 159.

Fisher, C., Kahn, E., Edwards, A., & Davis, D. M. (1973a). A psychophysiological study of nightmares and night terrors. I: Physiological aspects of the stage 4 night terrors. *Journal of Nervous and Mental Disease, 157,* 75–98.

Fisher, C., Kahn, E., Edwards, A., & Davis, D. M. (1973b). A psychophysiological study of nightmares and night terrors. II: The suppression of stage 4 night terrors with diazepam. *Archives of General Psychiatry, 28,* 252–259.

Fisher, C., Kahn, E., Edwards, A., Davis, D. M., & Fine, J. (1974). A psychophysiological study of nightmares and night terrors. III. Mental content and recall of stage 4 night terrors. *Journal of Nervous and Mental Disease, 158,* 174–188.

Fisher, C., & Paul, I. (1959). The effect of subliminal visual stimulation on images and dreams: A validation study. *Journal of the American Psychoanalytic Association, 7,* 35–83.

Fisher, J., & Breger, L. (Eds.) (1969). *The meaning of dreams: Recent insights from the laboratory.* Research symposium 3 of the State of California Department of Mental Hygiene.

Fishman, R., & Roffwarg, H. P. (1972). REM sleep inhibited by light in the albino rat. *Experimental Neurology, 36,* 166–178.

Fiss, H. (1969). The need to complete one's dreams. In J. Fisher & L. Berger (Eds.), *The meaning of dreams: Recent insights from the laboratory. Research symposium No. 3.* Bureau of Research, California Department of Mental Hygiene: Sacramento.

Fiss, H. (1980). Dream content and response to withdrawal from alcohol. *Symposium on Perspectives in Dream Research.* Association for the Psychophysiological Study of Sleep, Mexico City, March.

Fiss, H. (1983). Toward a clinically relevant experimental psychology of dreaming. *Hillside Journal of Clinical Psychiatry, 5,* 147–159.

Fiss, H. (1986). An empirical foundation for a self psychology of dreaming. *Journal of Mind & Behavior, 7,* 161–192.

Fiss, H., & Ellman, S. J. (1973). REM sleep interruption: Experimental shortening of REM period duration. *Psychophysiology, 10,* 510–516.

Fiss, H., Ellman, S. J., & Klein, G. S. (1969). Waking fantasies following interrupted and completed REM periods. *Archives of General Psychiatry, 21,* 230–239.

Fiss, H., Klein, G. S., & Bokert, E. (1966). Waking fantasies following interruption of two types of sleep. *Archives of General Psychiatry, 14,* 543–551.

Fiss, H., Klein, G. S., & Schollar, E. (1974). "Dream intensification" as a function of prolonged REM period interruption. In L. Goldberger & V. H. Rosen (Eds.), *Psychoanalysis and contemporary science* (Vol. 3, pp. 399–424). New York: International Universitites Press.

Fiss, H., Klein, G. S., Shollar, E., & Levine, B. (1968). *Changes in dream content as a function of prolonged REM sleep interruption.* Paper presented at the meeting of the Association for the Psychophysiological Study of Sleep, Denver. *Psychophysiology, 5,* 217. (Abstract)

Fiss, H., Klein, M., & Shollar, E. (1974). "Dream intensification" as a function of prolonged REM period interruption. *Psychoanalysis & Contemporary Science, 3,* 399–424.

Fiss, H., Kremer, E., & Litchman, J. (1977). The mnemonic function of dreaming. *Association for the Psychophysiological Study of Sleep.* Houston, April/May.

Fiss, H., & Litchman, J. (1976). "Dream Enhancement": An experimental approach to the adaptive function of dreams. *Association for the Psychophysiological Study of Sleep.* Cincinnati, June.

Fleetham, J., West, P., Mezon, B., Conway, W., Roth, T., & Kryger, M. (1982). Sleep, arousals, and oxygen desaturation in chronic obstructive pulmonary disease. *American Review of Respiratory Disease, 126,* 429–433.

Fleiss, J. (1969). Estimating the magnitude of experimental effects. *Psychological Bulletin, 72,* 273–276.

Fookson, J. E., & Antrobus, J. (1990). DREAMIT: A connectionist simulation of some characteristics of dreaming. In J. Antrobus & M. Bertini (Eds.), *The neuropsychology of dreaming sleep.* Hillsdale, NJ: Erlbaum.

Foote, S. L. (1973). Compensatory changes in REM sleep time of cats during *ad libitum* sleep and following brief REM sleep deprivation. *Brain Research, 54,* 261–276.

Foulkes, D. (1962). Dream reports from different stages of sleep. *Journal of Abnormal and Social Psychology, 65,* 14–25.

Foulkes, D. (1964). Theories of dream formation and recent studies of sleep consciousness. *Psychological Bulletin, 62,* 236–247.

Foulkes, D. (1966). *The psychology of sleep.* New York: Scribners.

Foulkes, D. (1967a). Dreams of the male child: Four case studies. *Journal of Child Psychology and Psychiatry, 8,* 81–97.

Foulkes, D. (1967b). Nonrapid eye movement mentation. *Experimental Neurology, 19* (Supplement 4), 28–38.

Foulkes, D. (1967). Dreams of the male child: Four case studies. *Journal of Child Psychology and Psychiatry, 8,* 81–97.

Foulkes, D. (1970). Review of effects of somatosensory stimulation on dream content. *Sleep Reviews.* Los Angeles: UCLA Brain Information Service.

Foulkes, D. (1971). Longitudinal studies of dreams in children. In J. Masserman (Ed.), *Science and psychoanalysis* (Vol. 19). *Dream dynamics* (pp. 48–71). New York: Grune & Stratton.

Foulkes, D. (1973, May). *What do we know about dreams and how did we learn it?* Paper presented at the meeting of the Association for the Psychophysiological Study of Sleep, San Diego, CA.

Foulkes, D. (1978). *A grammar of dreams.* New York: Basic Books.

Foulkes, D. (1980). How are dreams made? *Symposium on Perspectives in Dream Research.* Association for the Psychophysiological Study of Sleep, Mexico City, March.

Foulkes, D. (1982). *Children's dreams: Longitudinal studies.* New York: Wiley.

Foulkes, D. (1985). *Dreaming: A cognitive-psychological analysis,* Hillsdale, NJ: Lawrence Erlbaum Associates.

Foulkes, D., & Fleisher, S. (1975). Mental activity in relaxed wakefulness. *Journal of Abnormal Psychology, 84,* 66–75.

Foulkes, D., Larson, J. D., Swanson, E. M., & Rardin, M. (1969). Two studies of childhood dreaming. *American Journal of Orthopsychiatry, 39,* 627–643.

Foulkes, D., Pivik, T., Ahrens, J., & Swanson, E. M. (1968). Effects of "dream deprivation" on dream content: An attempted cross-night replication. *Journal of Abnormal Psychology, 73,* 403–415.

Foulkes, D., Pivik, T., Steadman, H. S., Spear, P. S., & Symonds, J. D. (1967). Dreams of the male child: An EEG study. *Journal of Abnormal Psychology, 72,* 457–467.

Foulkes, D., & Pope, R. (1972). PVE and SCE in stage REM: A modest confirmation and an extension. *Sleep Research, 1,* 103.

Foulkes, D., & Pope, R. (1973). Primary visual experience and secondary cognitive elaboration in stage REM: A modest confirmation and an extension. *Perceptual & Motor Skills, 37,* 107–118.

Foulkes, D., & Rechtschaffen, A. (1964). Presleep determinants of dream content: Effects of two films. *Perceptual and Motor Skills, 19,* 983–1005.

Foulkes, D., & Schmidt, M. (1983). Temporal sequence and unit composition in dream reports from different stages of sleep. *Sleep, 6*(3), 265–280.

Foulkes, D., & Scott, E. (1973). An above-zero waking baseline for the incidence of momentarily hallucinatory mentation. *Sleep Research, 2,* 108.

Foulkes, D., & Shepherd, J. (1972). Stimulus incorporation in children's dreams. *Sleep Research, 1,* 119.

Foulkes, D., Shepherd, J., Larson, J. D., Belvedere, E., & Frost, S. (1972). Effects of awakenings in phasic vs. tonic stage REM on children's dream reports. *Sleep Research, 1,* 104.

Foulkes, D., Spear, P. S., & Symonds, J. (1966). Individual differences in mental activity at sleep onset. *Journal of Abnormal Psychology, 71,* 280–286.

Foulkes, D., & Vogel, G. (1965). Mental activity of sleep onset. *Journal of Abnormal Psychology, 70,* 231–243.

Foulkes, D., & Vogel, G. (1974). The current status of laboratory dream research. *Psychiatric Annals, 7,* 7–23.

Fowler, M. J., Sullivan, M. J., & Ekstrand, B. R. (1973). Sleep and memory. *Science, 179,* 302–304.

Fox, R., Kramer, M., Baldridge, B., Whitman, R., & Ornstein, P. (1968). The experimenter variable in dream research. *Diseases of the Nervous System, 29,* 698–701.

Frankel, B. L., Coursey, R. D., Buchbinder, R., & Snyder, F. (1976). Recorded and reported sleep in chronic primary insomnia. *Archives of General Psychiatry, 33,* 615–623.

Freedman, A., Luborsky, A., & Harvey, R. (1970). Dream time (REM) and psychotherapy correlates of REM time with a patient's behavior in psychotherapy. *Archives of General Psychiatry, 22,* 33–39.

Freemon, F. R. (1972). *Sleep research: A critical review.* Springfield, IL: Thomas.

French, T., & Fromm, E. (1964). *Dream interpretation: A new approach.* New York: Basic Books.

Freud, S. (1900/1953). *The interpretation of dreams.* In J. Strachey (Ed. and Trans.), *The standard edition of the complete psychological works of Sigmund Freud* (Vols. 4, 5). London: Hogarth Press. (Original work published 1990).

Freud S. (1915/1953). *Instincts and their vicissitudes.* In J. Strachey (Ed. and Trans.), *The standard edition of the complete psychological works of Sigmund Freud* (Vol 14). London: Hogarth Press. (Original work published 1915).

Freud, S. (1953a/1922). Dreams and telepathy. In J. Strachey (Ed. and Trans.). *The standard edition of the complete psychological works of Sigmund Freud.* (Vol. 28, pp. 195–220). London: Hogarth Press. (Original work published 1922).

Freud, S. (1953b). *Three essays on the theory of sexuality.* London: Hogarth Press. (Original work published 1905)

Freud, S. (1953). Fragment of an analysis of a case of hysteria. In J. Strachey (Ed. and Trans.) *Standard edition of the complete psychological works of Sigmund Freud.* (Vol. 7, pp. 7–122). London: Hogarth Press. (Original work published 1905).

Freud, S. (1953). The interpretation of dreams. In J. Strachey (Ed. and Trans.), *The standard edition of the complete psychological works of Sigmund Freud* (Vols. 4, 5). London: Hogarth.

Freud, S. (1955a/1900). *The interpretation of dreams.* New York: Basic Books. (Original work published 1900).

Freud, S. (1955b/1917). Introduction to psychoanalysis and the war neurosis. In J. Strachey (Ed. and Trans.), *The standard edition of the complete psychological works of Sigmund Freud.* London: Hogarth Press. (Original work published 1917).

Freud, S. (1957). Mourning and melancholia. In J. Strachey (Ed. and trans.), *Standard edition of the complete psychological works of Sigmund Freud.* London: Hogarth Press. (Original work published 1917).

Freud, S. (1964). An outline of psychoanalysis. In J. Strachey (Ed. and trans.), *Standard edition of the complete psychological works of Sigmund Freud* (Vol. 23). London: Hogarth Press.

Fromm, E. (1951). *The forgotten language.* New York: Holt.

Frost, J., & Delucchi, M. (1979). Insomnia in the elderly: Treatment with flurazepam hydrochloride. *Journal of the American Geriatrics Society, 27,* 541.

Fujita, S., Conway, W., Zorick, F., et al. (1981). Surgical correction of anatomic abnormalities in obstructive sleep apnea syndrome: Uvulopalatopharyngoplasty. *Otolaryngology, Head and Neck Surgery, 89,* 923–924. Gaarder, K. (1966). A conceptual model of sleep. *Archives of General Psychiatry, 14,* 253–260.

Gackenbach, J., & LaBerge, S. (1988). *Conscious mind, sleeping brain: Perspectives on lucid dreaming.* New York: Plenum.

Gahagan, L. (1936). Sex differences in recall of stereotyped dreams, sleep-talking and sleep-walking. *Journal of Genetic Psychology, 48,* 227–236.

Gaillard, J. M., Laurian, S., & Le, P. (1984). EEG asymmetry during sleep. *Neuropsychobiology, 11,* 224–226.

Galin, D. (1974). Implications for psychiatry of left and right cerebral specialization. *Archives of General Psychiatry, 31,* 572–583.

Galin, D., & Ornstein, R. (1972). Lateral specialization of cognitive mode: An EEG study. *Psychophysiology, 9,* 412–418.

Gardner, R. A., & Runquist, W. N. (1958). Acquisition and extinction of problem-solving set. *Journal of Experimental Psychology, 55,* 274–277.

Gardner, R., Grossman, W., Roffwarg, H., & Weiner, H. (1975). The relationship of small limb movements during REM sleep to dreamed limb action. *Psychosomatic Medicine, 37,* 147–159.

Gardner, R., Jr., & Grossman, W. I. (1976). Normal motor patterns in sleep in man. In E. D. Weitzman (Ed.), *Advances in sleep research* (Vol. 2). New York: Spectrum.

Gardos, G., Cole, J. O., Volicer, J. L., Orzack, M. H., & Oliff, A. C. (1973). A dose response study of propranolol in chronic schizophrenia. *Current Therapeutic Research, 15,* 314–323.

Garfield, P. (1974). *Creative dreaming.* New York: Simon & Schuster.

Garner, W. R., Hake, H. W., & Eriksen, C. W. (1956). Operationism and the concept of perception. *Psychological Review, 63,* 149–159.

Gassel, M. M., Marchiafava, P. L., & Pompeiano, O. (1964a). Phasic changes in muscular activity during desynchronized sleep in unrestrained cats. An analysis of the pattern and organization of myoclonic twitches. *Archives Italiennes de Biologie, 102,* 449–470.

Gassel, M. M., Marchiafava, P. L., & Pompeiano, O. (1964b). Tonic and phasic inhibition of spinal reflexes during deep desynchronized sleep in unrestrained cats. *Archives Italiennes de Biologie, 102,* 471–499.

Gastaut, H., & Broughton, R. (1965). A clinical polygraphic study of episodic phenomena during sleep—Academic address. In J. Wortis (Ed.), *Recent advances in biological psychiatry* (Vol. 7). New York: Plenum.

Gastaut, H., Tassinari, C. A., & Duron, B. (1965). Étude polygraphique des manifestations épisodiques (hypniques et respiratoires) diurnes et nocturnes, du syndrome de Pickwick. *Review Neurology, 112,* 568–579.

Gelineau, J. (1880). De la narcolepsie. *Gaz. d. Hop.* (Paris), *53,* 626–628.

German, D. C., & Bowden, D. M. (1974). Catecholamine systems as the neutral substrate for intracranial self-stimulation: A hypothesis. *Brain Research, 73,* 381–419.

Getter, H., Mulry, R., Holland, C., & Walker, P. (1967). *Experimenter bias and the WAIS.* Unpublished data, University of Connecticut.

Getzels, J. W., & Jackson, P. W. (1962). *Creativity and intelligence.* New York: Wiley.

Giambra, L. (1975). Daydreaming across the life span: Late adolescent to senior citizen. *Developmental Psychology.*

Giblin, E., Garmon, A., Anderson, S., Kline, N., & DeLancey, D. (1980). Characteristics of sleep and incidence of apnea in patients with chronic obstructive pulmonary disease. *Sleep, 9,* 198.

Gibson, E., Perry, F., Redington, D., & Kamiya, J. (1982). Discrimination of sleep onset stages: Behavioral responses and verbal reports. *Perceptual & Motor Skills, 55,* 1023–1037.

Gillam, P. M. S., & Prichard, B. N. C. (1965). Use of propranolol in angina pectoris. *British Medical Journal, 2,* 337–339.

Gillin, J. C. (1983). The sleep therapies of depression. *Progress in NeuroPsychopharmacology & Biological Psychiatry, 7,* 351–364.

Gillin, J. C., Buchsbaum, M. S., Jacobs, L. S., Fram, D. H., Williams, R. B., Jr., Vaughn, T. B., Jr., Mellon, E., Snyder, F., & Wyatt, R. J. (1974). Partial REM sleep deprivation, schizophrenia and field articulation. *Archives of General Psychiatry, 30,* 653–662.

Gillin, J. C., & Wyatt, R. J. (1975). Schizophrenia: Perchance a dream? *International Review of Neurobiology, 17,* 297–342.

Giora, Z. (1971). REM deprivation: An afterthought. *Comprehensive Psychiatry, 12,* 321–329.

Glaubman, H., Orbach, J., Aviram, O., Frieder, J., Frieman, M., Pelled, O., & Glaubman, R. (1978). REM deprivation and divergent thinking. *Psychophysiology, 15,* 75–79.

Globus, G. G. (1966). Rapid eye movement cycle in real time. Implications for a theory of the D-State. *Archives of General Psychiatry, 15,* 654–659.

Globus, G. G. (1970). Rhythmic functions during sleep. In E. Hartman (Ed.), *Sleep and dreaming.* Boston: Little, Brown. *International Psychiatry Clinics, 7* (2).

Globus, G. G., Knapp, P. H., Skinner, J. C., & Healy, A. B. (1967). *An appraisal of telepathic communication in dreams.* Paper presented at the meeting of the Association for the Psychophysiological Study of Sleep, Los Angeles. (*Psychophysiology,* 1968, *4,* 365. Abstract)

Glovinsky, P., Spielman, A. J., Carroll, P., Weinstein, L., & Ellman, S. J. (1988) Stage 2 & REM sleep analysis: Sleepiness and REM recurrence. *Psychophysiology,* in press.

Goblot, E. (1973). Sur le souvenir des rêves. *Revue Philosophique,* 1896, *42,* 288. Cited by Giora, Z. Dream recall: Facts and perspectives. *Comprehensive Psychiatry, 14,* 159–167.

Goff, W. R., Allison, T., Shapiro, A., & Rosner, B. S. (1966). Cerebral somatosensory responses evoked during sleep in man. *Electroencephalography and Clinical Neurophysiology, 21* 1–9.

Goldstein, L. (1979). Some relationships between quantified hemispheric EEG and behavioral states in man. In J. Gruzelier & P. Flor–Henry (Eds.), *Hemisphere asymmetries of function in psychopathology.* Amsterdam: Elsevier/North Holland.

Goldstein, L., Stoltzfus, N., & Gardocki, J. (1972). Changes in interhemispheric amplitude relations in the EEG during sleep. *Physiology & Behavior, 8,* 811–815.

Goodenough, D. R. (1967). Some recent studies of dream recall. In H. A. Witkin & H. B. Lewis (Eds.), *Experimental studies of dreaming.* New York: Random House.

Goodenough, D. R. (1968). The phenomena of dream recall. In L. E. Abt & B. F. Riess (Eds.), *Progress in clinical psychology* (Vol. 8). New York: Grune & Stratton.

Goodenough, D. R., Lewis, H. B., Shapiro, A., Jaret, L., & Sleser, I. (1965). Dream reporting following abrupt and gradual awakenings from different types of sleep. *Journal of Personality and Social Psychology, 2,* 170–179.

Goodenough, D. R., Lewis, H. B., Shapiro, A., & Sleser, I. (1965). Some correlates of dream reporting following laboratory awakenings. *Journal of Nervous and Mental Disease, 140,* 365–373.

Goodenough, D. R., Sapan, J., Cohen, H., Portnoff, G., & Shapiro, A. (1971). Some experiments concerning the effects of sleep on memory. *Psychophysiology, 8,* 749–762.

Goodenough, D. R., Shapiro, A., Holden, M., & Steinschriber, L. (1959). A comparison of "dreamers" and "nondreamers": Eye movements, electroencephalograms and the recall of dreams. *Journal of Abnormal Psychology, 59,* 295–302.

Goodenough, D. R., Witkin, H. A., Koulack, D., & Cohen, H. (1975). The effects of stress films on dream affect and on respiration and eye-movement during rapid-eye movement sleep. *Psychophysiology, 15,* 313–320.

Goodenough, D. R., Witkin, H. A., Lewis, H. B., Koulack, D., & Cohen, H. (1974). Repression, interference and field dependence as factors in dream forgetting. *Journal of Abnormal Psychology, 83,* 32–44.

Gottschalk, L. A. (1967). Measuring transient psychological states. In *Research in verbal behavior and some neurophysiological implications.* New York: Academic Press.

Gottschalk, L. A., Haer, J. L., & Bates, D. E. (1972). Effect of sensory overload on psychological state. *Archives of General Psychiatry, 27,* 451–457.

Gottschalk, L. A., Stone, W. N., Gleser, G. C., & Iacono, J. M. (1969). Anxiety and plasma free fatty acids (FFA). *Life Sciences, 8,* 61–68.

Gottschalk, L. A., Winget, C. N., & Gleser, G. C. (1969). *Manual of instruction for the Gottschalk-Gleser content analysis scales.* Berkeley: University of California Press.

Gradess, R. S., Stone, J., Steiner, S. S., & Ellman, S. J. (1971). *Conditioned motor responding in sleeping human subjects.* Paper presented at the meeting of the Association for the Psychophysiological Study of Sleep, Bruges, Belgium.

Granda, A. M., & Hammack, J. T. (1961). Operant behavior during sleep. *Science, 133,* 1485–1486.

Graves, E. A. (1936). The effect of sleep upon retention. *Journal of Experimental Psychology, 19,* 316–322.

Greenberg, G., Pearlman, C., Fingar, R., Kantrowitz, J., & Kawliche, S. (1970). The effects of dream deprivation: Implications for a theory of the psychological function of dreaming. *British Journal of Medical Psychology, 43,* 1–11.

Greenberg, G., Pillard, R., & Pearlman, C. (1972). The effect of REM deprivation on adaptation to stress. *Psychosomatic Medicine, 34,* 257–262.

Greenberg, R. (1970). Dreaming and memory. *International Psychiatric Clinics, 7,* 258–267.

Greenberg, R. (1981). Dreams and REM sleep—an integrative approach. In W. Fishbein (Ed.), *Sleep, dreams and memory.* New York: Spectrum.

Greenberg, R., & Leiderman, P. H. (1966). Perceptions, the dream process and memory: An up-to-date version of notes on a mystic writing pad. *Comprehensive Psychiatry, 7,* 517–523.

Greenberg, R., & Pearlman, C. (1967). Delirium tremens and dreaming. *American Journal of Psychiatry, 124,* 133–142.

Greenberg, R., & Pearlman, C. (1973, May). *The source and function of dreams: A study of the psychoanalytic-dream continuum.* Paper presented at the Association for the Psychophysiological Study of Sleep, San Diego, CA.

Greenberg, R., & Pearlman, C. (1974). Cutting the REM nerve: An approach to the adaptive role of REM sleep. *Perspectives in Biology & Medicine, 17,* 513–521.

Greenberg, R., & Pearlman, C. (1975). REM sleep and the analytic process: A psychophysiological bridge. *Psychoanalytic Quarterly, 44,* 392–403.

Greenberg, R., Pearlman, C. A., & Gampel, D. (1972). War neuroses and the adaptive function of REM sleep. *British Journal of Medical Psychology, 45,* 27–33.

Greenberg, R., Pearlman, C., Brooks, R., Mayer, R., & Hartmann, E. (1968). Dreaming and Korsakoff's psychosis. *Archives of General Psychiatry, 18,* 203–209.

Greenberg, R., Pearlman, C., Fingar, R., Kantrowitz, J., & Kawliche, S. (1970). The effects of dream deprivation: Implications for a theory of the psychological function of dreaming. *British Journal of Medical Psychology, 43,* 1–11.

Greenberg, R., Pearlman, C., Schwartz, W. R., & Grossman H. Y. (1983). Memory, emotions and REM sleep. *Journal of Abnormal Psychology, 92,* 378–381.

Greenberg, R., Pillard, R., & Pearlman, C. (1972). The effect of dream (REM) deprivation on stress. *Psychosomatic Medicine, 34,* 257–262.

Greenblatt, D. J., Allen, M. D., & Shader, R. I. (1977). Toxicity of high-dose flurazepam in the elderly. *Clinical Pharmacology and Therapeutics, 21*(3), 355–361.

Greenblatt, D. J., Divoll, M., Abernathy, D. R., & Shader, R. I. (1982). Benzodiazepine hypnotics: Kinetic and therapeutic options. *Sleep, 5,* S18–S27.

Greenblatt, D. J., Divoll, M., MacLaughlin, D. S., Harmatz, J. S., & Shader, R. I. (1981). Kinetics and clinical effects of flurazepam in young and elderly noninsomniacs. *Clinical Pharmacology and Therapeutics, 30,* 475–486.

Greenson, R. (1970). The exceptional position of the dream in psychoanalytic practice. *Psychoanalytic Quarterly, 39,* 519–549.

Grieser, C., Greenberg, R., & Harrison, R. H. (1972). The adaptive function of sleep: The differential effects of sleep and dreaming on recall. *Journal of Abnormal Psychology, 80,* 280–286.

Grob, D., Harvey, A., Langworthy, D., & Lilienthal, J. (1947). The administration of di-isopropyl fluorophosphate (DFP) to man. *Bulletin of Johns Hopkins Hospital, 81,* 257–266.

Grosser, G., & Siegal, A. (1971/1905). Emergence of a tonic-phasic model for sleep and dreaming: Behavioral and physiological observations. *Psychological Bulletin, 75,* 60–72.

Gross, J., Byrne, J., & Fisher, C. (1965). Eye movements during emergent stage 1 EEG in subjects with life-long blindness. *Journal of Nervous & Mental Disease, 141,* 365–370.

Grossman, W., Gardner, R., Roffwarg, H., Fekete, A., Beers, L., & Weiner, H. (1971, June). *Relations of dreamed to actual limb movement.* Paper presented at the meeting of the Association for the Psychophysiological Study of Sleep, Bruges, Belgium.

Gross, M. M., Goodenough, D. R., Hastey, J. M., Rosenblatt, S. M., & Lewis, E. (1971). Sleep disturbances in alcohol intoxication and withdrawal. In N. K. Mello, & J. H. Mendelson (Eds.), *Recent advances in studies of alcoholism.* Washington, DC: U. S. Government Printing Office (Publication No. (HSM) 71-9045).

Gross, M. M., Goodenough, D. R., Nagarajan, M., & Hastey, J. M. (1973). Sleep changes induced by 4 and 6 days of experimental alcoholization and withdrawal in humans. In M. M. Gross (Ed.), *Alcohol intoxication and withdrawal: Experimental studies.* New York: Plenum.

Guilford, J. P. (1967). *The nature of human intelligence.* New York: McGraw-Hill.

Guilleminault, C. (1976). Cataplex. In C. Guilleminault, W. C. Dement, & P. Passouant (Eds.), *Narcolepsy* (pp. 43–56). New York: Spectrum.

Guilleminault, C., & Brusset, B. (1973). Sleep and schizophrenia: Nightmares, insomnia and autonomic discharges. (Study on a young chronic schizophrenic). In U. J. Jovanovic (Ed.), *The nature of sleep.* Stuttgart: Fischer.

Guilleminault, C., & Dement, W. C. (Eds.), (1978). *Sleep apnea syndromes* (Kroc Foundation Series, Vol. 11). New York: Alan R. Liss.

Guilleminault, C. (Ed.). (1982). *Sleeping and waking disorders: Indications and techniques.* Menlo Park, CA: Addison–Wesley.

Gulevich, G., Dement, W., & Johnson, L. (1966). Psychiatric and EEG observations on a case of prolonged (264 hours) wakefulness. *Archives of General Psychiatry, 15,* 29–35.

Hacker, F. (1911). Systematische Traumbeobachtungen mit besonderer Berucksichtigung der Gedanken. *Archiv für die Gesamte Psychologie, 21,* 1–121.

Halberg, F. (1969). Chronobiology. *Annual Review of Physiology, 31,* 675–725.

Hall, C. (1966). A comparison of the dreams of four groups of hospitalized mental patients with each other and with a normal population. *Journal of Nervous & Mental Diseases, 143,* 135–139.

Hall, C. (1966). *The meaning of dreams.* New York: McGraw-Hill.

Hall, C. & Nordby, V. J. (1972). *The individual and his dreams.* New York: New American Library.

Hall, C. S., Van de Castle, R. L., Hess, R., Dertke, M., Daverso, G., Dupont, G., Nordby, V. J., Scott, J., & Clark, S. (1966). *Studies of dreams reported in the laboratory and at home.* Institute of Dream Research Monograph Series, No. 1. Santa Cruz, CA.

Hall, C., & Van de Castle, R. I. (1966). *The content analysis of dreams.* New York: Appleton-Century-Crofts.

Hamilton, M. (1960). A rating scale for depression. *Journal of Neurology, Neurosurgery, and Psychiatry, 23,* 56–62.

Hammond, E. C. (1964). Some preliminary findings on physical complaints from a prospective study of 1,064,004 men and women. *American Journal of Public Health, 54,* 11–23.

Handwerker, M., & Fishbein, W. (1975). Neural excitability after PSD: A replication and further examination. *Physiological Psychology, 3,* 137–140.

Hartmann, E. (1968a). Dauerschlaf: A polygraphic study. *Archives of General Psychiatry, 18,* 99–111.

Hartmann, E. (1968b) The 90-minute sleep dream cycle. *Archives of General Psychiatry, 18,* 280–286.

Hartmann, E. (1970a). A note on the nightmare. In E. Hartmann (Ed.), *Sleep and dreaming.* Boston: Little, Brown.

Hartmann, E. (1973). *The functions of sleep.* New Haven, CT: Yale University Press.

Hartmann, E., Baekeland, F., Zwilling, G., & Hoy, P. (1971). Sleep need: How much sleep and what kind? *American Journal of Psychiatry, 127,* 1001–1008.

Hartmann, E. (Ed.) (1970b). *Sleep and dreaming.* Boston: Little, Brown. *International Psychiatry Clinics, 7*(2).

Hartmann, E., Marcus, J., & Leinoff, A. (1968). The sleep-dream cycle and convulsive threshold. *Psychonomic Science, 13,* 141–142.

Hartmann, E., & Stern, W. C. (1972). Desynchronized sleep deprivation: Learning deficit and its reversal by increased catecholamines. *Physiology and Behavior, 8,* 585–587.

Hartmann, H. (1939). *Ego psychology and the problem of adaptation.* New York: International Universities Press.

Hauri, P. (1970). Evening activity, sleep mentation, and subjective sleep quality. *Journal of Abnormal Psychology, 2,* 270–275.

Hauri, P. (1972). *White noise and dream reporting.* Paper presented at the meeting of the Association for the Psychophysiological Study of Sleep, New York.

Hauri, P. (1974). Review of Arkin, A., Antrobus, J., Toth, M., Baker, J., & Jackler, F. A comparison of the content of mentation reports elicited after nonrapid eye movement (NREM) associated sleep utterance and NREM "silent" sleep. *Sleep Research, 3,* 324.

Hauri, P. (1975). Categorization of sleep mental activity for psychophysiological studies. In G. C. Lairy & P. Slazarulo (Eds.), *The experimental study of human sleep* (pp. 271–282). Amsterdam: Elsevier.

Hauri, P. (1976). Dreams in patients remitted from reactive depression. *Journal of Abnormal Psychology, 85,* 1–10.

Hauri, P. (1981). Treating psychophysiologic insomnia with biofeedback. *Archives of General Psychiatry, 38,* 752–758.

Hauri, P. (1982). *The sleep disorders* (2nd ed.) Kalamazoo, MI: Upjohn.

Hauri, P. (1984). A cluster analysis of insomnia. *Sleep, 6,* 326–338.

Hauri, P., & Hawkins, D. R., (1973). Alpha-delta sleep. *Electroencephalography and Clinical Neurophysiology, 34,* 233–237.

Hauri, P., & Hawkins, D. R. (1973). Phasic REM, depression and the relationship between sleeping and waking. *Archives of General Psychiatry, 25,* 56–63.

Hauri, P., & Rechtschaffen, A. (1963). *An unsuccessful attempt to find physiological correlates of NREM recall.* Paper presented at the meeting of the Association for the Psychophysiological Study of Sleep, New York.

Hauri, P., Sawyer, J., & Rechtschaffen, A. (1967). Dimensions of dreaming: A factored scale for rating dream reports. *Journal of Abnormal Psychology, 72,* 16–22.

Hauri, P., & Van de Castle, R. L. (1970b). Dream content and physiological arousal. *Psychophysiology, 7,* 330–331.

Hauri, P., & Van de Castle, R. L. (1972). Psychophysiological parallelism in dreams. *Psychosomatic Medicine, 35,* 297–308.

Hauri, P., & Van de Castle, R. L. (1973a). Psychophysiological parallels in dreams. In U. J. Jovanovic (Ed.), *The nature of sleep.* Stuttgart: Fischer.

Hauri, P., & Van de Castle, R. L. (1973b). Psychophysiological parallelism in dreams. *Psychosomatic Medicine, 35,* 297–308.

Hawkins, D. R. (1966). A review of psychoanalytic dream theory in the light of recent psychophysiological studies of sleep and dreaming. *British Journal of Medical Psychology, 39*, 85–104.

Hawkins, D. R., Puryear, H. B., Wallace, C. D., Deal, W. B., & Thomas, E. J. (1962). Basal skin resistance during sleep and "dreaming." *Science, 136*, 321–322.

Hays, W. L. (1973). *Statistics for psychologists.* New York: Holt, Rinehart & Winston.

Head, H. (1926). *Aphasia and kindred disorders of speech.* Cambridge, England: Cambridge University Press.

Hebb, D. O. (1949). *The organization of behavior: A neuropsychological theory.* New York: Wiley.

Heine, R. (1914). Über Wiedererkennen und rückwirdende Hemmung. *Zeitschrift für Psychologie und Physiologie der Sinnesorgane, 68*, 161–236.

Hendricks, J. C. , Morrison, A. R., & Mann, G. L. (1980). Behavior during paradoxical sleep differs with lesion site. *Sleep Research, 9*, 31.

Herman, J., Ellman, S., & Roffwarg, H. (1978). The problem of NREM dream recall reexamined. In A. Arkin, J. Antrobus, & S. Ellman (Eds.), *The mind in sleep: Psychology and psychophysiology* (pp. 59–92). Hillsdale, NJ: Erlbaum.

Herman, J., Erman, M., Boys, R., Peiser, L., Taylor, M., & Roffwarg, H. (1984). Evidence for a directional correspondence between eye movements and dream imagery in REM sleep. *Sleep, 7*, 52–63.

Herman, J. H. (1984). Experimental investigations of the psychophysiology of REM sleep including the question of lateralization. *Research Communications in Psychology, Psychiatry, & Behavior, 9*, 53–75.

Herman, J. H., Boys, R., Dunn, D., Peiser, L., Hirshkowitz, M., Homan, R., & Roffwarg, H. P. (1983). EEG asymmetries in the awake state and in sleep. *Sleep Research, 12*, 177.

Herman, J. H., Erman, M., Boys, R., Peiser, L., Taylor, M. E., & Roffwarg, H. P. (1984). Evidence for a directional correspondence between eye movements and dream imagery in REM sleep. *Sleep, 7*, 52–63.

Herman, J. H., Roffwarg, H. P., Rosenmann, C. J., & Tauber, E. S. (1980). Binocular depth perception following REM deprivation or awake state visual deprivation. *Psychophysiology, 17*, 236–242.

Herman, J. H., Tauber, E. S., & Roffwarg, H. P. (1974). Monocular occlusion impairs stereoscopic acuity, but total visual deprivation does not. *Perception & Psychophysics, 16*, 225–228.

Hicks, R. A., & Adams, G. (1976). REM sleep deprivation and exploration in young rats. *Psychological Reports, 38*, 1154.

Hicks, R. A., Hirshfield, C., Humphrey, V., Lauber, A., Giampaoli, J., & Hawkins, J. (1981). REM sleep deprivation and food competition in male rats. *Physiology and Behavior, 26*, 245–247.

Hicks, R. A., & Moore, J. D. (1979). REM sleep deprivation diminishes fear in rats. *Physiology & Behavior, 22*, 689–692.

Hicks, R. A., Moore, J. D., Hayes, C., Phillips, N., & Hawkins, J. (1979). REM sleep deprivation increases aggressiveness in the male rat. *Physiology & Behaviour, 22*, 1097–1100.

Hicks, R., Paulus, M., & Johnson, J. (1973). Effect of REM sleep deprivation on electric shock threshold in rats. *Psychological Reports, 32,* 1242.

Hilakivi, I., Peder, M., Elomaa, E., & Johansson, G. (1984). Validation of the cuff pedestal technique for REM deprivation by electrophysiological recordings. *Physiology and Behavior, 32,* 945–947.

Hildoff, U., Antrobus, J. S., Farber, J., Ellman, S. J., & Arkin, A. M. (1974). Slow eye movements and mental activity at sleep onset. *Sleep Research, 3,* 120.

Hilgard, E. R. (1973). A neodissociationist interpretation of pain reduction in hypnosis. *Psychological Review, 80,* 396–411.

Hinshelwood, R. D. (1969). Hallucinations and propranolol. *British Medical Journal, 2,* 445.

Hinton, G. E., & Anderson, J. A. (Eds.). (1981). *Parallel models of associative memory.* Hillsdale, NJ: Erlbaum.

Hirshkowitz, M., Turner, D., Ware, J., & Karacan, I. (1979). EEG amplitude asymmetry during sleep. *Sleep Research, 8,* 25.

Hirshkowitz, M., Ware, J. C., & Karacan, I. (1980). Integrated EEG amplitude asymmetry during early and late REM and NREM periods. *Sleep Research, 9,* 291.

Hobson, J. A., Goldfrank, F., & Snyder, F. (1965). Respiration and mental activity in sleep. *Journal of Psychiatry Research, 3,* 79–90.

Hobson, J. A., Lydic, R., & Baghdoyan, H. A. (1986). Evolving concepts of sleep cycle generation: From brain centers to neuronal populations. *The Behavioral and Brain Sciences, 9,* 371–448.

Hobson, J. A., & McCarley, R. W. (1975). Sleep cycle oscillation: Reciprocal discharge by two brainstem neuronal groups. *Science, 189,* 55–58.

Hobson, J. A., & McCarley, R. W. (1977). The brain as a dream state generator: An activation-synthesis hypothesis of the dream process. *American Journal of Psychiatry, 134,* 1335–1348.

Hobson, J., & McCarley, R. (1971). *Neuronal activity in sleep: An annotated bibliography.* Los Angeles: University of Southern California at Los Angeles Brain Information Service.

Hockey, G. R. J., Davies, S., & Gray, M. M. (1972). Forgetting as a function of sleep at different times of day. *Quarterly Journal of Experimental Psychology, 24,* 386–393.

Hodes, R., & Dement, W. C. (1964). Depression of electrically induced reflexes ("H"-reflexes) in man during low voltage EEG "sleep." *Electroencephalography and Clinical Neurophysiology, 17,* 617–629.

Holdstock, T. L., & Verschoor, G. J. (1973). Retention of maze learning following paradoxical sleep deprivation in rats. *Physiological Psychology, 1,* 29–32.

Hollingworth, H. L. (1927). *The psychology of thought.* New York: Appleton.

Holmes, M. (1973). REM sleep patterning and dream recall in covergers and divergers: Evidence for different defensive preferences (Occasional Paper No. 16) Edinburgh: University of Edinburgh, Center for Research in the Educational Sciences.

Holt, R. R. (1967). Motives and thought: Psychoanalytic essays in honor of David Rapaport. New York: International Universities Press. *Psychological Issues, 5* (2-3) (Monograph 18–19).

Holt, R. R. (19762). Drive or wish? A reconsideration of the psychoanalytic theory of motivation. New York: International Universities Press. *Psychological Issues, 9* (Monograph 36), 158–197.

Honda, Y., Juji, T., Matsuki, K., Naohara, T., Satake, M., Inoko, H., Someya, T., Harada, S., & Doi, Y. (1986). HLA-DR2 and Ds2 in narcolepsy and in other disorders of excessive somnolence without cataplexy. *Sleep, 9,* 133–142.

Hopfield, J. J., Feinstein, D. I., & Palmer, R. G. (1983). "Unlearning" has a stabilizing effect in collective memories. *Nature, 304,* 158–159.

Horne, J. A. (1977). Factors relating to energy conservation during sleep in mammals. *Physiological Psychology, 5,* 403–408.

Horowitz, M. J. (1972). Modes of representation of thought. *Journal of the American Psychoanalytic Association, 20,* 793–819.

Horowitz, M. J. (1975). Hallucinations: An information processing approach. In R. K. Siegel & L. J. West (Eds.), *Hallucinations: Behavior, experience and theory.* New York: Wiley.

Hospers, J. (1967). *An introduction to philosophical analysis* (2d ed.). Englewood Cliffs, NJ: Prentice-Hall.

Hubel, D. H., & Wiesel, T. N. (1963). Receptive fields and functional architecture of monkey striate cortex. *Journal of Physiology, 195,* 215–243.

Hudson, L. (1966). *Contrary imaginations: A psychological study of the young student.* New York: Shocken.

Humphrey, M. E., & Zangwill, O. C. (1951). Cessation of dreaming after brain injury. *Journal of Neurology, Neurosurgery and Psychiatry, 14,* 322–325.

Ingvar, D. H. (1979). Hyperfrontal distribution of the cerebral grey matter flow in resting wakefulness; on the functional anatomy of the conscious state. *Acta Neurologica Scandinavica, 60,* 12–25.

Institute of Medicine. (1979). *Sleeping pills, insomnia and medical practice* (Publication No. 10M-79-04). Washington DC: National Academy of Sciences.

Jackson, D., & Messick, S. (1967). Response styles and the assessment of psychopathology. In D. Jackson & S. Messick (Eds.), *Problems in human assessment.* Huntington, NY: Kreiger.

Jackson, H. (1958). *Selected writings.* J. Taylor, G. Holmes, & F. Walshe (Eds.). New York: Basic Books.

Jackson, H. quoted by Jones, E. (1961). The relation between dreams and psychoneurotic symptoms. In E. Jones (Ed.), *Papers in psychoanalysis.* Boston: Beacon Press.

Jacobsen, D. (1964). *The self and the object world.* New York: International Universities Press.

Jacobs, L., Feldman, M., & Bender, M. (1971). Eye movements during sleep. I. The pattern in the normal human. *Archives of Neurology, 25,* 151–159.

Jacobs, L., Feldman, M., & Bender, M. (1972). Are the eye movements of dreaming sleep related to the visual images of dreams? *Psychophysiology, 9,* 393–401.

Jacobson, A., Kales, A., Lehmann, D., & Hoedemaker, F. S. (1964). Muscle tonus in human subjects during sleep and dreaming. *Experimental Neurology, 10,* 418–424.

Jacobson, A., Kales, A., Lehmann, D., & Zweizig, J. (1965). Somnambulism: All-night electroencephalographic studies. *Science, 148,* 975–977.

Jacobson, E. (1932). Electrophysiology of mental activities. *American Journal of Psychology, 44,* 677–694.

Jacobson, E., & Kales, A. (1967). Somnambulism: All night EEG and related studies. In S. S. Kety, E. V. Evarts, & H. L. Williams (Eds.), *Sleep and altered stated of consciousness.* Baltimore: Williams & Wilkins.

Jeannerod, M. (1965). *Organisation de l'activité éléctrique phasique de sommeil paradoxal, étude éléctrophysiologique et neuro-pharmacologique.* Thése de Medicine, Lyon.

Jenkins, J. G., & Dallenbach, K. M. (1924). Obliviscence during sleeping and waking. *American Journal of Psychology, 35,* 605–612.

Jenkins, J. J. (1974). Remember that old theory of memory? Well, forget it! *American Psychologist, 29,* 785–796.

Johansson, G., & Elomaa, E. (1986). Effects of partial restriction on nocturnal meal size and feeding speed are counteracted by concurrent REM sleep deprivation in the rat. *Behavioral Brain Research, 20,* 275–280.

Johnson, L. (1974). *The operational consequences of sleep deprivation and sleep deficit.* (AGARDograph No. 193). London: Technical and Editing and Reproduction Ltd.

Johnson, L. C. (1970). A psychophysiology for all states. *Psychology, 6,* 501–516.

Johnson, L. C. (1973). Are stages of sleep related to waking behavior? *American Scientist, 61,* 326–338.

Johnson, L., & Chernik, D. A. (1982). Sedative-hypnotics and human performance. *Psychopharmacology, 76,* 101–113.

Johnson, L. C., & Karpan, W. E. (1968). Autonomic correlates of the spontaneous K-complex. *Psychophysiology, 4,* 444–452.

Johnson, L. C., & Lubin, A. (1966). Spontaneous electrodermal activity during waking and sleeping. *Psychophysiology, 3,* 8–17.

Johnson, L. C., & Lubin, A. (1967). The orienting reflex during waking and sleeping. *Electroencephalography and Clinical Neurophysiology, 22,* 11–21.

Johnson, L. C., Naitoh, P., Moses, J. M., & Lubin, A. (1974). Interaction of REM deprivation and stage 4 deprivation with total sleep loss: Experiment 2. *Psychophysiology, 11,* 147–159.

Johnson, L., Naitoh, P., Lubin, A., & Moses, J. (1972). Sleep stages and performance. In P. Colquhoun (Ed.), *Aspects of human efficiency.* London: English Universities Press.

Jones, B. E. (1985). Neuroanatomical and neurochemical substrates of mechanisms underlying paradoxical sleep. In D. J. McGinty, R. Drucker-Colin, A. Morrison, & P. L. Parmeggianni (Eds.), *Brain mechanisms of sleep* (pp. 139–156). New York: Raven Press.

Jones, E. E., Kanouse, D. E., Kelley, H. H., Nisbett, R. E., Valins, S., & Weiner, B. (1971). *Attribution: Perceiving the causes of behavior.* Morristown, NJ: General Learning Press.

Jones, H. S., & Oswald, I. (1968). Two cases of healthy insomnia. *Electroencephalography and Clinical Neurophysiology, 24,* 378–380.

Jones, R. M. (1970a). The manifest dream, the latent dream, and the dream work. In E. Hartmann (Ed.), *Sleep and dreaming.* Boston: Little, Brown.

Jones, R. M. (1970b). *The new psychology of dreaming.* New York: Grune & Stratton.

Jones, R. M. (1970c). The transformation of the stuff dreams are made of. In E. Hartmann (Ed.), *Sleep and dreaming.* Boston: Little, Brown.

Jouvet, D., Vismont, P., & Delorme, F. (1974). Étude de la privation séléctie de la phase paradoxale de sommeil chez de chat. *Comptes Rendus de Séances de la Société de Biologie, 158,* 576–579.

Jouvet, M. (1962). Récherches sur les structures nerveuses et les mécanismes résponsables des différentes phases du sommeil physiologique. *Archives Italiennes de Biologie, 100,* 125–206.

Jouvet, M. (1965a). Paradoxical sleep. A study of its nature and mechanisms. *Progress in Brain Research, 18,* 20–57.

Jouvet, M. (1965b). Étude de la dualité des états de sommeil at des mécanismes de la phase paradoxale. In *Aspects anatomo-fonctionnels de la physiologie du sommeil.* Actes du Colloque Internationale sur les Aspects Anatomo-fonctionnels de la Physiologie de Sommeil. Lyon, 1963. *Colloques Internationaux du Centre Nationale de la Recherche Scientifique, 127,* 397–449.

Jouvet, M. (1967). Neurophysiology of the status of sleep. *Physiological Reviews, 47,* 117–177.

Jouvet, M. (1969). Paradoxical sleep and the nature–nurture controversy. In P. S. McConnell, G. J. Boer, H. J. Romijn, N. E. van de Poll, & M. A. Corner (Eds.), *Adaptive capabilities of the nervous system* (pp. 331–346). Amsterdam: Elsevier/North Holland.

Jouvet, M. (1974). The role of monoaminergic neurons in the regulation and function of sleep. In O. Petre-Quadens & J. D. Schlag (Eds.), *Basic sleep mechanisms* (pp. 207–236). New York: Academic Press.

Jouvet, M. (1978). Does a genetic programming of the brain occur during paradoxical sleep? In P. A. Buser & A. Rougel–Buser (Eds.), *Cerebral correlates of conscious experience.* Amsterdam: Elsevier.

Jouvet, M., Dechaume, J., & Michel, F. (1960). Étude des méchanismes du sommeil physiologique. *Lyon Medicale, 204,* 479–521.

Jouvet, M., & Delorme, J. (1965). Locus coeruleus et sommeil paradoxal. *Comptes Rendus des Séances de la Société de Biologie, 159,* 895–899.

Jouvet, M., & Jouvet, D. (1965). A study of the neurophysiological mechanisms of dreaming. *Electroencephalography and Clinical Neurophysiology Supplement, 24,* 133–157.

Jouvet, M., & Michel, F. (1959). Correlations electromyographiques du sommeil chez le chat decortique et mesencephalique chronique. *Compte Rendu Sociologie et Biologie* (Paris), *153,* 422–425.

Jouvet–Mounier, D., Astic, L., & Lacote, D. (1970). Ontogenesis of the states of sleep in the rat, cat and guinea pig during the first postnatal month. *Developmental Psychobiology, 2,* 391–399.

Joy, R. M., & Prinz, P. N. (1969). The effect of sleep altering environments upon the acquisition and retention of a conditioned avoidance response in the rat. *Physiology and Behavior, 4,* 809–814.

Jung, C. (1960). On the nature of dreams. In *The structure and dynamics of the Psyche.* New York: Pantheon (original work published 1945).

Jung, C. G. (1933). *Modern man in search of a soul.* New York: Harcourt, Brace, & World.

Jung, C. G. (1939). *The integration of the personality* (translated by S. M. Dell). New York: Farrar and Rinehart.

Jung, C. G. (1944). *The psychology of dementia praecox.* New York: Journal of Nervous and Mental Disease Publishing Company.

Jus, K., & Jus, A. (1972). Experimental studies on memory disturbances in humans in pathological and physiological conditions. *International Journal of Psychobiology, 2,* 205–218.

Jus, K., Kiljan, A., Kubacki, Losieczko, T., Wilczak, H., & Jus, A. (1969). Experimental studies on memory during slow sleep stages and REM stages. *Electroencephalography and Clinical Neurophysiology, 27,* 668.

Kahn, E., Dement, W. C., Fisher, C., & Barmack, J. L. (1962). The incidence of color in immediately recalled dreams. *Science, 137,* 1054.

Kahn, E., Fisher, C., Byrne, J., Edwards, A., & Davis, D. M. (1970). The influence of Valium, Thorazine and Dilantin on stage 4 nightmares. *Psychophysiology, 7,* 350. (Abstract)

Kahn, E., Fisher, C., Edwards, A., & Davis, D. (1973). Mental content of stage 4 night terrors. *Proceedings of the 81st Annual Convention of the American Psychological Association, 8 (Pt. 1),* 499–500.

Kahn, E., Fisher, C., & Lieberman, L. (1969). Dream recall in the normal aged. *Journal of the American Geriatrics Society, 17,* 1121–1126.

Kales, A., Adams, G., Haley, J., Preston, T., & Rickles, W. (1969). Sleep patterns during withdrawal from Tuinal: Effects of Dilantin administration. *Psychophysiology, 6,* 262. (Abstract)

Kales, A., Ansel, R. D., Markham, C. H., Scharf, M. B., & Tan, T. L. (1971). Sleep in patients with Parkinson's disease and normal subjects prior to and following levodopa administration. *Clinical Pharmacology & Therapeutics, 12,* 397–406.

Kales, A., Bixler, E. O., & Kales, J. D. (1974). Role of the sleep research and treatment facility: Diagnosis, treatment and education. In E. D. Weitzman (Ed.), *Advances in sleep research* (Vol. 1). New York: Spectrum.

Kales, A., Caldwell, A. B., Preston, T. A., Healey, S., & Kales, J. D. (1976). Personality and patterns in insomnia. *Archives of General Psychiatry, 33,* 1128–1134.

Kales, A., Heuser, G., Jacobson, A., Kales, J. D., Hanley, J., Zweizig, J. R., Paulson, M. J. (1967). All-night sleep studies in hypothyroid patients, before and after treatment. *Journal of Clinical Endocrinology and Metabolism, 27,* 1593–1599.

Kales, A., Hoedemaker, F., Jacobson, A., Kales, J., Paulson, M., & Wilson, T. (1967). Mentation during sleep: REM and NREM recall reports. *Perceptual and Motor Skills, 24,* 556–560.

Kales, A., Hoedemaker, F. S., Jacobson, A., & Lichtenstein, E. L. (1964). Dream deprivation: An experimental reappraisal. *Nature, 204,* 1337–1338.

Kales, A., & Jacobson, A. (1967). Mental activity during sleep: Recall studies, somnambulism and effects of rapid eye movement deprivation and drugs. *Experimental Neurology, 19* (Suppl. 4), 81–91.

Kales, A., Jacobson, A., Paulson, M. J., Kales, J. D., & Walter, R. D. (1966). Somnambulism: Psychophysiological correlates. I. All night EEG studies. *Archives of General Psychiatry, 14,* 586–596.

Kales, A., & Kales, J. D. (1983). Sleep laboratory studies of hypnotic drugs: Efficacy and withdrawal effects. *Journal of Clinical Psychopharmacology, 3,* 140–150.

Kales, A., Kales, J., Po, J., & Klein, J. (1966). A review of recent sleep and dream studies. *Bulletin of the Los Angeles Neurological Society, 31,* 136–151.

Kales, A., Malmstrom, E. J., Kee, H. K., Kales, J. D., Tan, T. L., Stadel, D., & Hoedemaker, F. S. (1969). Effects of hypnotics on sleep patterns dreaming and mood state: Laboratory and home studies. *Biological Psychiatry, 1,* 235–241.

Kales, A., Malmstrom, E. J., Rickles, W. H., Hanley, J., Ling Tan, T., Stadel, B., & Hoedemaker, F. S. (1968). Sleep patterns of a pentobarbital addict: Before and after withdrawal. *Psychophysiology, 5,* 208. (Abstract)

Kales, A., Malmstrom, E. J., Scharf, M. B., & Rudin, R. T. (1969). Psychophysiological and biochemical changes following use and withdrawal of hypnotics. In A. Kales (Ed.), *Sleep: Physiology and pathology, a symposium.* Philadelphia: Lippincott.

Kales, A., Paulson, M. J., Jacobson, A., & Kales, J. (1966). Somnambulism: Psychophysiological correlates. II Psychiatric interviews, psychological testing, and discussion. *Archives of General Psychiatry, 14,* 595–604.

Kales, A., Preston, T. A., Tan, T., & Allen, C. (1970). Hypnotics and altered sleep—dream patterns I and II. *Archives of General Psychiatry, 23,* 211–225.

Kales, A., Soldatos, C. R., Bixler, E. O., Ladda, R. L., Charney, D. S., Weber, G., & Schweitzer, P. K. (1980). Hereditary factors in sleepwalking and night terrors. *British Journal of Psychiatry, 137,* 111–118.

Kales, A., Soldatos, C. R., Caldwell, A., Kales, J. D., Humphrey, R. J., Charney, D. S., & Schweitzer, P. K. (1980). Somnambulism: Clinical characteristics. *Archives of General Psychiatry, 37,* 1406–1410.

Kales, J. D., Kales, A., Soldatos, C. R., Caldwell, A., Charney, D. S., & Martin, E. D. (1980). Night terrors: Clinical characteristics and personality patterns. *Archives of General Psychiatry, 37,* 1413–1417.

Kales, J. D., Kales, A., Soldatos, C. R., Chamberlin, K., & Martin, E. D. (1979). Sleepwalking and night terrors related to febrile illness. *American Journal of Psychiatry, 136*(9), 1214–1215.

Kamiya, J. (1961). Behavioral, subjective and physiological aspects of drowsiness and sleep. In D. W. Fiske & S. R. Maddi (Eds.), *Functions of varied experience.* Homewood, IL: Dorsey Press.

Kamiya, J., & Fong, S. (1962, March). *Dream reporting from NREM sleep as related to respiration rate.* Paper presented at the meeting of the Association for the Psychophysiological Study of Sleep, Chicago.

Kanzer, M. (1959). The recollection of the forgotten dream. *Journal of the Hillside Hospital, 8,* 74–85.

Kanzow, E., Krause, D., & Kuhnel, H. (1962). The vasomotor behavior of the cerebral cortex in the phases of desynchronized EEG-activity during natural sleep in the cat. *Pflügers Archiv für die Gesamte Physiologie, 274,* 593–607.

Karacan, I., Goodenough, D. R., Shapiro, A., & Starker, S. (1966). Erection cycle during sleep in relation to dream anxiety. *Archives of General Psychiatry, 15,* 183–189.

Karacan, I., Hursch, C. J., Williams, R. L., & Thornby, J. I. (1972). Some characteristics of nocturnal penile tumescence in young adults. *Archives of General Psychiatry, 26,* 351–356.

Karacan, I., & Snyder, F. (1966, March). *Erection cycle during sleep in Macaca mulatta.* Paper presented at the meeting of the Association for the Psychophysiological Study of Sleep, Gainesville, FL.

Karacan, I., Williams, R. L., Bose, J., Hursch, C. J., Warson, S. R. (1972). Insomnia in hemodialytic and kidney transplant patients. *Psychophysiology, 9,* 137.

Karacan, I., Williams, R. L., Littel, R. C., & Salis, P. (1973). Insomniacs: Unpredictable and idiosyndratic sleepers. In P. Levin & W. P. Koella (Eds.), *Sleep physiology, biochemistry, psychology, pharmacology, clinical implications* (pp. 120–132). Basel, Switzerland: S. Karger.

Karacan, I., Williams, R. L., & Raylor, W. J. (1969). Sleep characteristics of patient with angina pectoris. *Psychosomatics, 10,* 204–284.

Karetsky, M., Scoles, V., Fourre, J., & Nahmias, J. (1985). Relief of obstructive sleep apnea utilizing a nasopharyngeal catheter reduces its incidence, morbidity and potential mortality. *Sleep Research, 14,* 176.

Katzman, R. (1986). Alzheimer's disease. *New England Journal of Medicine, 314*(15), 964–973.

Kawamura, H., & Sawyer, C. (1965, March). *Differential temperature changes in the rabbit brain during slow wave and paradoxical sleep.* Paper presented at the meeting of the Association for the Psychophysiological Study of Sleep, Washington, DC.

Keenan, R., & Krippner, S. (1970). Content analysis and visual scanning in dreams. *Psychophysiology, 7,* 302–303.

Keller, H. (1908). *The world I live in.* New York: Century.

Kennedy, J., Cook, P., & Crewer, R. (1968). *An examination of the effects of three selected experimenter variables in verbal conditioning research.* Unpublished manuscript, University of Tennessee.

Kerlinger, F. N., & Pedhazur, E. J. (1973). *Multiple regression in behavioral research.* New York: Holt, Rinehart & Winston.

Kerr, N., Foulkes, D., & Schmidt, B. (1982). The structure of laboratory dream reports in blind and sighted subjects. *Journal of Nervous & Mental Disease, 170,* 286–294.

Kilduff, T. S., Bowersox, S. S., Kaitin, K. I., Baker, T. L., Ciaranello, R. D., & Dement, W. C. (1986). Muscarinic cholinergic receptors and the canine model of narcolepsy. *Sleep, 9*(1), 102–106.

Kirtley, D. D. (1975). *The psychology of blindness.* Chicago: Nelson-Hall.

Klein, G. (1967). Peremptory ideation: Structure and force. In R. R. Holt (Ed.), *Motives and thought.* New York: International Universities Press. *Psychological Issues, 5,* (2-3) (Monograph 18–19).

Klein, G. S. (1969). Freud's two theories of sexuality. In L. Breger (Ed.), *Clinical-cognitive psychology models and integrations.* Englewood Cliffs, NJ: Prentice-Hall.

Klein, G. S., Fiss, H., Shollar, E., Dalbeck, R., Warga, C., & Gwozdz, F. (1970). *Recurrent dream fragments in dreams and fantasies elicited in interrupted and completed REM periods.* Paper presented at the meeting of the Association for the Psychophysiological Study of Sleep, Santa Fe, NM. *Psychophysiology, 7,* 331–332. (Abstract)

Klein, M., Mathieu, P., Gendlin, E., & Kiesler, D. (1970). *The experiencing scale: A research and training manual.* Madison, WI: Wisconsin Psychiatric Institute.

Kleinsmith, L. J., & Kaplan, S. (1963). Paired-associate learning as a function of arousal and interpolated interval. *Journal of Experimental Psychology, 65,* 190–193.

Kleitman, N. (1963). *Sleep and wakefulness* (2d ed.). Chicago: University of Chicago Press.

Kleitman, N. (1970a). Does dreaming have a function? In E. Hartmann (Ed.), *Sleep and dreaming* (pp. 352–353). Boston: Little, Brown.

Kleitman, N. (1970b). Implications for organization of activities. In E. Hartmann (Ed.), *Sleep and dreaming* (pp. 13–14). Boston: Little, Brown.

Kleitman, N. Sleep. *Scientific American,* 1952, *187,* 34–38.

Kling, A., Borowitz, G., & Cartwright, R. (1972). Plasma levels of 17-hydroxy-cortico-steroids during sexual arousal in man. *Journal of Psychosomatic Research, 16,* 215–221.

Klinger, E. (1971). *Structure and functions of fantasy.* New York: Wiley.

Kling, H., Borowitz G., & Cartwright, R. (1972). Plasma levels of 17 hydroxycortico-steroids during sexual arousal in man. *Journal of Psychosomatic Research, 16,* 215–221.

Knapp, P., Greenberg, R., Pearlman, C., Cohen, M., Kantrowitz, J., & Sahsin, J. (1975). Clinical measurement in psychoanalysis: An approach. *Psychoanalytic Quarterly, 44,* 404–430.

Knopf, N. B. (1962). *The study of heart and respiration rates during dreaming.* Unpublished master's thesis, University of Chicago.

Kohler, W. C., Coddington, R., & Agnew, H. W., Jr. (1968). Sleep patterns in 2 year old children. *Journal of Pediatrics, 72,* 228–233.

Kokkoris, C. P., Weitzman, E. D., Pollak, C. P., Spielman, A. J., Czeisler, C. A., & Bradlow, H. (1978). Long-term ambulatory temperature monitoring in a subject with a hypernycthmeral sleep-wake cycle disturbance. *Sleep, 1*(2), 177.

Kopel, B. S., Zarcone, V., De La Pena, A., & Dement, W. C. (1972). Changes in selective attention as measured by the visual average evoked potential following REM deprivation in man. *Electroencephalography & Clinical Neurophysiology, 32,* 322–326.

Kopell, B. S., Zarcone, V., de la Peña, A., & Dement, W. C. (1972). Changes in selective attention as measured by the visual averaged evoked potential following REM deprivation in man. *Electroencephalography and Clinical Neurophysiology, 32,* 322–325.

Koranyi, E. K., & Lehmann, H. E. (1960). Experimental sleep deprivation in schizophrenic patients. *Archives of General Psychiatry, 2,* 534–544.

Koridze, M. G., & Nemsadze, N. D. (1983). Effect of deprivation of paradoxical sleep on the formation and differentiation of conditioned reflexes. *Neuroscience and Behavioral Physiology, 82,* 369–373.

Koukkou, M., & Lehmann, D. (1968). EEG and memory storage in sleep experiments with humans. *Electroencephalography and Clinical Neurophysiology, 25,* 455–462.

Koukkou, M., & Lehmann, D. (1983). The functional state-shift hypothesis, a neuropsychophysiological model. *British Journal of Psychiatry, 142,* 221–231.

Koulack, D. (1968). Dream time and real time. *Psychonomic Science, 11,* 202.

Koulack, D. (1969). Effects of somatosensory stimulation on dream content. *Archives of General Psychiatry, 20,* 718–725.

Koulack, D. (1970). Repression and forgetting of dreams. In M. Bertini (Ed.), *Psicofisiologia del sonno e del sogno.* Proceedings of an international symposium, Rome, 1967. Milan: Editrice Vita e Pensiero.

Koulack, D. (1972). Rapid eye movements and visual imagery during sleep. *Psychological Bulletin, 78,* 155–158.

Koulack, D. (1973). Effect of a hypnogogic type situation and the dull task on subsequent REM rebound: A preliminary report. In M. H. Chase, W. C. Stern, & P. L. Walte (Eds.), *Sleep Research* Vol. 2. Brain Information Service, Brain Research Institute: Los Angeles, p. 167.

Koulack, D., & Goodenough, D. R. (1976). Dream recall and dream recall failure: An arousal-retrieval model. *Psychological Bulletin, 83,* 975–984.

Kovalzon, V. M., & Tsibulsky, V. L. (1980). REM sleep deprivation without stress in rats. In XX Asgian & XX Badiu (Eds.), *Sleep* (1978). Basel: Karger, pp. 411–414.

Kramer, M. (1969). Paradoxical sleep. *Postgraduate Medicine, 45,* 157–161.

Kramer, M. (1970). Manifest dream content in normal and psychopathologic states. *Archives of General Psychiatry, 22,* 149–159.

Kramer, M., Baldridge, B. J., Whitman, R. M., Ornstein, P. H., & Smith, P. C. (1969). An exploration of the manifest dream in schizophrenic and depressed patients. *Diseases of the Nervous System, 30* (Suppl.), 126– 130.

Kramer, M., Czaya, J., Arand, D., & Roth, T. (1974). *The development of psychological content across the REMP.* Paper presented at the meeting of the Association for the Psychophysiological Study of Sleep, Jackson Hole, WY.

Kramer, M., Hlasny, R., Jacobs, G., & Roth, T. (1975). Do dreams have meaning? An empirical inquiry. Paper presented at the meeting of The Association for the Psychophysiological Study of Sleep, Edinburgh.

Kramer, M., & Roth, T. (1973). Comparison of dream content in laboratory dream reports of schizophrenic and depressive patient groups. *Comprehensive Psychiatry, 14,* 325–329.

Kramer, M., Sandler, C., Whitman, R., & Baldridge, B. J. (1970). Hall–Van de Castle scoring of dreams of the depressed. *Psychophysiology, 7,* 327. (Abstract)

Kramer, M., Trinder, J., & Roth, T. (1972). Dream content analysis of male schizophrenic patients. *Canadian Psychiatric Association Journal, 17* (Suppl. 2), 5251–5257.

Kramer, M., Whitman, R., Baldridge, B., & Ornstein, P. (1970). Dream content in male schizophrenic patients. *Diseases of the Nervous System, 31,* 51–58.

Kramer, M., Whitman, R. M., Baldridge, B. J., & Ornstein, P. H. (Eds.) (1969). *Dream psychology and the new biology of dreaming.* Springfield, IL: Thomas.

Kramer, M., Whitman, R. M., Baldridge, B., & Lansky, L. (1965). Depression: Dreams and defenses. *American Journal of Psychiatry, 122,* 411–417.

Kramer, M., Whitman, R. M., Baldridge, B., & Lansky, L. (1966). Dreaming in the depressed. *Canadian Psychiatric Association Journal, 11* (Special Suppl.), 178–192.

Kramer, M., Whitman, R. M., Baldridge, B., & Ornstein, P. H. (1968). Drugs and dreams III: The effects of imipramine on the dreams of depressed patients. *American Journal of Psychiatry, 124,* 1385–1392.

Kramer, M., Whitman, R. M., Baldridge, B., & Ornstein, P. H. (1968). Drugs and dreams III: The effects of imipramine on the dreams of depressed patients. *American Journal of Psychiatry, 124,* 1385–1392.

Kramer, M., Winget, C., & Whitman, R. M. (1971). A city dreams: A survey approach to normative dream content. *American Journal of Psychiatry, 127,* 1350–1356.

Kripke, D. (1972). An ultradian biologic rhythm associated with perceptual deprivation and REM sleep. *Psychosomatic Medicine, 34,* 221–228.

Kripke, D. (1972). An ultradian biologic rhythm associated with perceptual deprivation and REM sleep. *Psychosomatic Medicine, 34,* 221–228.

Kripke, D. F., Simons, R. M., Garfinkel, L., & Hammond, E. C. (1979). Short and long sleep and sleeping pills: Is increased mortality associated? *Archives of General Psychiatry, 36,* 103–116.

Kripke, D., & Sonnenschein, D. (1973). A 90 minute daydream cycle. *Sleep Research, 187.*

Krippner, S., Calvallo, M., & Keenan, R. (1972). Content analysis approach to visual scanning theory in dreams. *Perceptual and Motor Skills, 34,* 41–42.

Krippner, S., & Hughes, W. (1970). Dreams and human potential. *Journal of Humanistic Psychology, 10,* 1–20.

Kris, E. (1952). *Psychoanalytic explorations in art.* New York: International Universities Press.

Kronauer, R. E., Czeisler, C. A., Pilator, S. F., Moore–Ede, M. L., & Weitzman, E. D. (1982). Mathematical model of the human circadian system with two interacting oscillators. *American Journal of Physiology, 242,* R3–R17.

Kubie, L. S. (1962). The concept of dream deprivation: A critical analysis. *Psychosomatic Medicine, 24,* 62–65.

Kueny, S. (1985). *An examination of auditory cuing in REM sleep for the induction of lucid dreams.* Unpublished doctoral dissertation, Pacific Graduate School of Psychology.

Kupfer, D. J. (1984). REM activity and delta wave abnormalities in affective state. *Research Communication in Psychology, Psychiatry, & Behavior, 9,* 149–175.

Kupfer, D. J., Spiker, D. G., Coble, P. A., & Shaw, D. H. (1978). Electroencephalographic sleep recordings and depression in the elderly. *Journal of American Geriatric Society, 26,* 53–57.

Kupfer, D., Wyatt, R., Scott, J., & Snyder, F. (1970). Sleep disturbance in acute schizophrenic patients. *American Journal of Psychiatry, 126,* 1213–1223.

Kupfer, F. J., & Thase, M. E. (1983). The use of the sleep laboratory in the diagnosis of affective disorders. *Psychiatric Clinics of North America 6*(1), 3–24.

Kushida, C., Bergmann, B., Fang, V. S., Leitch, C. A., Obermeyer, W., Refetoff, S., Schoeller, D. A., & Rechtschaffen, A. (1986). Physiological and biochemical effects of paradoxical sleep deprivation in the rat. *Sleep Research, 15,* 219.

Kushniruk, A., Rustenberg, S., & Ogilvie, R. (1985). Electrodermal activity during REM sleep. *Sleep, 8,* 147–154.

LaBerge, S. (1985). *Lucid dreaming.* Los Angeles: Jeremy Tarcher.

Labruzza, A. (1978). The activation-synthesis hypothesis of dreams: A theoretical note. *American Journal of Psychiatry, 135,* 1536–1538.

Lacey, J. I., Bateman, D. E., & Van Lehn, R. (1963). Autonomic response specificity: An experimental study. *Psychosomatic Medicine, 15,* 8–21.

Lachmann, F. M., Lapkin, B., & Handelman, N. S. (1962). The recall of dreams: Its relation to repression and cognitive control. *Journal of Abnormal and Social Psychology, 64,* 160–162.

Ladd, G. (1892). Contributions to the psychology of visual dreams. *Mind, 1,* 299–304.

Langdon, N., Lock, C., Welsh, K., Vergani, D., Dorow, R., Wachtel, H., Palenschat, D., & Parkes, J. D. (1986). Immune factors in narcolepsy. *Sleep, 9*(1), 143–148.

Langer, S. K. (1957). *Philosophy in a new key. A study in the symbolism of reason, rite and act* (3d ed.). Cambridge, MA: Harvard University Press.

Langford, G. W., Meddis, R., & Pearson, A. J. D. (1972). Spontaneous arousals from sleep in human subjects. *Psychonomic Science, 28,* 228–230.

Langs, R. J. (1966). Manifest dreams from three clinical groups. *Archives of General Psychiatry, 14,* 634–643.

Laplanche, J., & Pontalis, J. B. (1973). *The language of psychoanalysis.* New York: Norton.

Larson, J. D. (1971). Hypnogogic mentation of repressors and sensitizers as influenced by hostile and friendly presleep conditions. *Psychophysiology, 7,* 327.

Larson, J. D., & Foulkes, D. (1969). Electromyogram suppression during sleep, dream recall and orientation time. *Psychophysiology, 5,* 548–555.

Lasaga, J. I., & Lasaga, A. M. (1973). Sleep learning and progressive blurring of perception during sleep. *Perceptual and Motor Skills, 37,* 51–62.

Laverty, S. G. (1969). Sleep disorders and delirium associated with the use of ethanol. In T. J. Boag, & D. Campbell (Eds.), *A triune concept of the brain and behavior.* Toronto: University of Toronto Press.

Lavie, P. (1983). Sleep apnea in industrial workers. In C. Guilleminault & E. Lugaresi (Eds.), *Sleep/wake disorders: Natural history of epidemiology and long term evolution* (pp. 127–135). New York: Raven Press.

Lavie, R. J., & Kripke, D. F. (1975). Ultradian rhythms: The 90-minute clock inside us. *Psychology Today, 8,* 54–65.

Lehmann, D., & Koukkou, M. (1973). Learning and EEG during sleep in humans. In W. P. Koella & P. Levin (Eds.), *Sleep: Physiology, biochemistry, psychology, pharmacology, clinical implications*. First European Congress on Sleep Research, Basel, 1972. Basel: Karger.

Lehmann, D., & Koukkou, M. (1981). Dream formation in a psychophysiological model: The state-shift theory. In W. P. Koella (Ed.), *Sleep 1980* (pp. 170–174). Basel, Switzerland: Karger.

Lehmann, D., & Koukkou, M. (1983). Introduction: Information processing during sleep. In W. P. Koella (Ed.), *Sleep 1982* (pp. 46–48). Basel, Switzerland: Karger.

Lehmann, D., Meier, B., Meier, C. A., Mita, T., & Skrandies, W. (1983). Sleep onset mentation related to short epoch EEG spectra. *Sleep Research,* 180 (Abstract).

Leonard, J. P. (1983). Experimental sleep induction: Napping and the role of sleep onset ritual and feedback of sleep success. *Sleep Research,* 158 (Abstract).

Lerner, B. (1966). Rorschach movement and dreams: A validation study using drug-induced dream deprivation. *Journal of Abnormal Psychology, 71,* 75–86.

Lerner, B. (1967). Dream function reconsidered. *Journal of Abnormal Psychology, 72,* 85–100.

Lester, B. K., Chanes, R. E., & Condit, P. T. (1969). A clinical syndrome and EEG-sleep changes associated with amino acid deprivation. *American Journal of Psychiatry, 126,* 815–190.

Levine, M., & Spivak, G. (1964). *The Rorschach index of repressive style.* Springfield, IL: Thomas.

Levitt, R. A. (1967). Paradoxical sleep: Activation by sleep deprivation. *Journal of Comparative and Physiological Psychology, 63,* 505–509.

Lewin, B. D. (1953). The forgetting of dreams. In R. M. Loewenstein (Ed.), *Drives, affects, behavior.* New York: International Universities Press.

Lewin, I. (1980). *The psychology of dreams.* (Hebrew). Tel–Aviv: Dekel Academic Press.

Lewin, I. (1985). *A three-dimensional model for the classification of cognitive processes. Imagination, Cognition & Personality,* 1986–87, 6, 43–54.

Lewin, I., Bergman, I., Glaubman, H., Melamed, S., & Yehuda, S. (1973). The induction of quasi-dreaming mental state by means of flickering photic stimulation. In W. P. Koella & P. Levin (Eds.), *Sleep: Physiology, biochemistry psychology, pharmacology, clinical implications.* Basel, Switzerland: S. Karger.

Lewin, I., & Glaubman, H. (1975). The effect of REM deprivation: Is it detrimental, beneficial or neutral? *Psychophysiology, 12,* 349–353.

Lewin, I., & Gombosh, D. (1973). Increase in REM time as a function of the need for divergent thinking. In W. P. Koella & P. Levin (Eds.), *Sleep, physiology, biochemistry, psychology, pharmacology, clinical implication.* Basel, Switzerland: Separatum.

Lewis, H. B. (1968). Some clinical implications of recent dream research. In L. E. Abt & B. F. Riess (Eds.), *Progress in clinical psychology* (Vol. 8, Dreams and dreaming). New York: Grune & Stratton.

Lewis, H. B., Goodenough, D. R., Shapiro, A., & Sleser, I. (1966). Individual differences in dream recall. *Journal of Abnormal Psychology, 71,* 52–59.

Lewis, H. G. (1970). Effects of sleep and dream research on the handling of dreams in psychoanalytic practice. In E. Hartmann (Ed.), *Sleep and dreaming.* Boston: Little, Brown.

Lewis, S. A. (1968). The quantification of rapid-eye-movement sleep. In A. Herxheimer (Ed.), *A symposium on drugs and sensory functions*. Boston: Little, Brown.

Lewis, S. A., Sloan, J. P., & Jones, S. K. (1978). Paradoxical sleep and depth perception. *Biological Psychology, 6*, 17–25.

Libow, L. S., & Starer, P. (1985). Obscuring urinary incontinence: Diapering of the elderly. *Journal of the American Geriatrics Society, 33*, 467–481.

Liddon, S. C. (1967). Sleep paralysis and hypnogogic hallucinations. *Arch. Gen. Psychiatry, 17*, 88–95.

Linden, E., Bern, D., & Fishbein, W. (1975). Retrograde amnesia: Prolonging the fixation phase of memory consolidation by paradoxical sleep deprivation. *Physiology and Behavior, 14*, 409–412.

Lindsay, P. H., & Norman, D. A. (1972). *Human information processing: An introduction to psychology*. New York: Academic Press.

Ling, G. M., & Usher, D. R. (1969). *Effect of REM and total sleep deprivation on the synthesis and release of ACTH*. Paper presented at the meeting of the Association for the Psychophysiological Study of Sleep, Boston.

Loggan, M. C., & Tredre, B. E. (1967). Diurnal rhythms of renal excretion and body temperature in aged subjects. *Journal of Physiology (London), 188*, 48–49.

Lovatt, D. J., & Warr, P. B. (1968). Recall after sleep. *American Journal of Psychology, 81*, 253–257.

Loveland, N. T., & Singer, M. T. (1959). Projective test assessment of the effects of sleep deprivation. *Journal of Projective Techniques, 23*, 323–334.

Lowenstein, R. J., Weingartner, H., Gillin, J. C., Ebert, M., & Mendelson, W. V. (1982). Disturbances of sleep and cognitive functioning in patients with dementia. *Neurobiology of Aging, 3*, 371–377.

Luborsky, L. (1967). Momentary forgetting during psychotherapy and psychoanalysis: A theory and research method. In R. R. Holt (Ed.), *Motives and thought: Psychoanalytic essays in honor of David Rapaport. Psychological Issues, 5* (2-3) (Monograph 18–19). New York: International Universities Press.

Luby, E. D., Grisell, J. L., Frohman, C. E., Lees, H., Cohen, B. D., & Gottlieb, J. S. (1962). Biochemical, psychological, and behavioral responses to sleep deprivation. *Annals of the New York Academy of Sciences, 96*, 71–78.

Lucero, M. A. (1970). Lengthening of REM sleep duration consecutive to learning in the rat. *Brain Research, 20*, 319–322.

Luchins, A. S. (1942). Mechanization in problem-solving. *Psychological Monographs, 54* (No. 6).

Lugaresi, E., Coccagna, G., & Mantovani, M. (1978). *Hypersomnia with periodic apneas*. New York: Spectrum.

MacNeilage, L. A. (1971). *Activity of the speech apparatus during sleep and its relation to dream reports*. Doctoral dissertation, Columbia University. Ann Arbor, MI: University Microfilms, No. 721355.

MacNeilage, P. F., Cohen, D. B., & MacNeilage, L. A. (1972). *Subjects' estimations of sleep-talking propensity and dream recall frequency are positively related*. Paper presented at the meeting of the Association for the Psychophysiological Study of Sleep, New York.

MacNeilage, P. F., & MacNeilage, L. A. (1973). Central processes controlling speech production during sleep and waking. In F. J. McGuigan & R. A. Schoonover (Eds.), *The psychophysiology of thinking*. New York: Academic Press.

Madow, L., & Snow, L. H. (Eds.) (1970). *The psychodynamic implications of the physiological studies on dreams*. Springfield, IL: Thomas.

Maggs, R., & Neville, B. (1964). Chlordiazepoxide (Librium): A clinical trial of its use in controlling symptoms of anxiety. *British Journal of Psychiatry, 120*, 540–543.

Magnussen, G. (1944). *Studies on respiration during sleep*. London: H. K. Lewis.

Malcolm, L. J., Watson, J. A., & Burke, W. (1970). PGO waves as unitary events. *Brain Research, 24*, 130–133.

Malcolm, N. (1959). *Dreaming*. New York: Humanities Press.

Mandler, G. (1975). *Mind and emotion*. New York: Wiley.

Mark, J., Heiner, L., Mandel, P., & Godin, Y. (1969). Norepinephrine turnover in brain and stress reactions in rats during paradoxical sleep deprivation. *Life Sciences, 8*, 1085–1093.

Marti-Nicolovius, M., Portell-Cortes, I., & Morgado-Bernal, I. (1984). Intracranial Self-Stimulation after paradoxical sleep deprivation induced by the platform method in rats. *Physiology and Behavior, 33*, 166–167.

Martin, R. J., Block, A. J., Cohn, M. A., Conway, W. A., Hudgel, D. W., Powles, A. C. P., Sanders, M. H., & Smith, P. L. (1984). Indications and standards for cardiopulmonary sleep studies. *Sleep, 8*(4), 371–379.

Masling, J. (1965). Differential indoctrination of examiners and Rorschach responses. *Journal of Consulting Psychology, 29*, 198–201.

Matsumoto, J., & Jouvet, M. (1964). Effets de reserpine, DOPA, ex 5 HTP, sur les deux états de sommeils. *Compte Rendu Sociologie et Biologie* (Paris), *158*(2), 137–140.

Maury, A. (1861). *Le sommeil et les rêves*. Paris.

Max, L. W. (1935). An experimental study of the motor theory of consciousness III. Action-current responses in deaf-mutes during sleep, sensory stimulation and dreams. *Journal of Comparative Psychology, 19*, 469–486.

Max, L. W. (1937). An experimental study of the motor theory of consciousness. IV. Action-current responses in the deaf during awakening, kinesthetic imagery and abstract thinking. *Journal of Comparative Psychology, 24*, 301–304.

McCarley, R. (1983). REM dreams, REM sleep and their isomorphisms. In *Sleep disorders: Basic and clinical research* (pp. 363–391). New York: Spectrum.

McCarley, R. W., Hobson, J. A., & Pivik, R. T. (1973, May). *Cortical PGO spikes: Periodicities*. Paper presented at the meeting of the Association for the Psychophysiological Study of Sleep, San Diego, CA.

McClelland, J. L., & Rumelhart, D. E. (Eds.), (1986). *Parallel distributed processing: Explorations in the microstructure of cognition*. 2 vols. Cambridge, MA: MIT Press.

McDonald, D. G., Johnson, L. C., & Hord, D. J. (1964). Habituation of the orienting response in alert and drowsy subjects. *Psychophysiology, 1*, 163–173.

McDonald, D. G., Schicht, W. W., Frazier, R. E., Shallenberger, H. D., & Edwards, D. J. (1975). Studies of information processing in sleep. *Psychophysiology, 12*, 624–629.

McFarland, R. A. (1975). Air travel across time zone. *American Scientist, 63*, 23.

McGaugh, J. L. (1966). Time-dependent processes in memory storage. *Science, 153,* 1351–1358.

McGinty, D. J., & Drucker-Colin, R. (1982). Sleep mechanisms, biology and control of REM sleep. *International Review of Neurobiology Mechanisms, 23,* 391–436.

McGrath, M. J., & Cohen, D. B. (1977). REM sleep facilitation of adaptive waking behavior: A review of the literature. *Psychological Bulletin, 85,* 24–57.

McGuigan, F. J., & Tanner, R. G. (1970). Covert oral behavior during conversational and visual dreams. *Psychophysiology, 7,* 329. (Abstract)

McKellar, P. (1957). *Imagination and thinking.* New York: Basic Books.

Meddis, R. (1977). *The sleep instinct.* London: Routlege & Kegan Paul.

Meddis, R. (1983). The evolution of sleep. In A. Mayes (Ed.), *Sleep mechanisms and functions in humans and animals: An evolutionary perspective.* Berkshire, England: Van Nostrand Reinhold.

Medoff, L., & Foulkes, D. (1972). "Microscopic" studies of mentation in stage REM: A preliminary report. *Psychophysiology, 9,* 114. (Abstract)

Mefford, I. N., Baker, T. L., Boehme, R., Foutz, A. S., Ciaranello, R., Barchas, J. D., & Dement, W. C. (1983). Narcolepsy: Biogenic amine deficits in an animal model. *Science, 220,* 629–632.

Meier, C., Ruef, H., Ziegler, A., & Hall, C. (1968). Forgetting dreams in the laboratory. *Perceptual and Motor Skills, 26,* 551–557.

Mellinger, G. D., Balter, M. B., & Uhlenhuth, E. H. (1985). Insomnia and its treatment: Prevalence and correlates. *Archives of General Psychiatry, 42,* 225–232.

Melstrom, M., & Cartwright, R. (1983). Effects of successful vs. unsuccessful psychotherapy outcome on some dream dimensions. *Psychiatry, 46,* 51–63.

Mendels, J., & Cochrane, C. (1968). The nosology of depression: The endogenous-reactive concept. *American Journal of Psychiatry, 124* (Suppl.), 1–11.

Mendels, J., & Hawkins, D. R. (1967). Sleep and depression: A controlled EEG study. *Archives of General Psychiatry, 16,* 344–354.

Mendelson, J. H., Siger, L., & Solomon, P. (1960). Psychiatric observations on congenital and acquired deafness: Symbolic and perceptual processes in dreams. *American Journal of Psychiatry, 116,* 883–888.

Mendelson, W. B., Gillin, J. C., & Wyatt, R. J. (1977). *Human sleep and its disorders.* New York: Plenum Press.

Mendelson, W., Guthrie, R., Frederick, G., & Wyatt, R. (1973). Should flower pots be used for flowers, pot, or rats? *Sleep Research, 2,* 169.

Mendelson, W., Guthrie, R., Frederick, G., & Wyatt, R. (1974). The flower pot technique of rapid eye movement (REM) sleep deprivation. *Pharmacology, Biochemistry and Behavior, 2,* 553–556.

Messick, S. (1971). The psychology of acquiescence: An interpretation of research evidence. In I. Berg (Ed.), *Response set in personality assessment.* New York: Irvington.

Michel, F., Jeannerod, M., Mouret, J., Rechtschaffen, A., & Jouvet, M. (1964). Sur les mecanismes de l'activité de pointes au niveau du système visuel au cours de la phase paradoxale du sommeil. *Comptes Rendus des Séances de la Société de Biologie, 158,* 103–106.

Mikiten, T., Niebyl, P., & Hendley, C. (1961). EEG desynchronization during behavioral sleep associated with spike discharges from the thalamus of the cat. *Federation Proceedings, 20,* 327. (Abstract)

Miles, L. M., & Dement, W. C. (1980). Sleep and aging. *Sleep, 3,* 119–220.

Miller, J. B. (1969). Dreams during varying stages of depression. *Archives of General Psychiatry, 20,* 560–565.

Miller, L., Drew, W. G., & Schwartz, I. (1971). Effect of REM sleep deprivation on retention of a one-trial passive avoidance response. *Perceptual and Motor Skills, 33,* 118.

Minard, J., Loiselle, R., Ingeldue, E., & Dautlich, C. (1968). Discriminative electro-oculogram deflections (EOGDs) and heart-rate (HR) pauses elicited during maintained sleep by stimulus significance. *Psychophysiology, 5,* 232. (Abstract)

Mirmiran, M., & Uylings, H. B. (1983). The environmental enrichment effect upon cortical growth is neutralized by concomitant pharmacological suppression of active sleep in female rats. *Brain Research, 261,* 331–334.

Mirmiran, M., Uylings, H. B., & Crown, M. A. (1983). Pharmacological suppression of REM sleep prior to weaning counteracts the effectiveness of subsequent environmental enrichment on cortical growth in rats. *Developmental Brain Research, 7,* 102–105.

Mitler, M. M. (1976). Toward an animal model of narcolepsy-cataplexy. In C. Guilleminault, W. C. Dement, & P. Passouant (Eds.), *Narcolepsy* (pp. 387–409). New York: Spectrum.

Mitler, M. M. (1982). The multiple sleep latency test as an evaluation for excessive somnolence. In C. Guilleminault (Ed.), *Sleeping and waking disorders: Indications and techniques* (pp. 145–153). Menlo Park, CA: Addison–Wesley.

Modern, B., Conner, R., Mitchell, G., Dement, W. C., & Levine, S. (1968). Effects of REM sleep deprivation upon shock induced fighting. *Physiology & Behavior, 3,* 425–428.

Moffat, M. C. (1966). Unpublished data, University of British Columbia.

Moffitt, A., Hoffmann, R., Wells, R., Armitage, R., Pigeau, R., & Shearer, J. (1982). Individual differences among pre- and post-awakening EEG correlates of dream reports following arousals from different stages of sleep. *Psychiatric Journal of the University of Ottawa, 7,* 111–125.

Moldofsky, H., Scarisbrick, P., England, R., & Smythe, H. (1975). Musculoskeletal symptoms and non-REM sleep disturbance in patients with "Fibrositis Syndrome" and healthy subjects. *Psychosomatic Medicine, 37,* 4.

Molinari, S., & Foulkes, D. (1969). Tonic and phasic events during sleep: Psychological correlates and implications. *Perceptual & Motor Skills, 29,* 343–368.

Mollenhour, M. N., Voorhees, J. W., & Davis, S. F. (1977). Sleepy and hostile: The effects of REM sleep deprivation on shock-elicited aggression. *Animal Learning & Behavior, 5,* 148–152.

Mondini, S., & Guilleminault, C. (1985). Abnormal breathing patterns during sleep in diabetes. *Annals of Neurology, 17,* 391–395.

Monroe, L. J. (1967). Psychological and physiological differences between good and poor sleepers. *Journal of Abnormal Psychology, 72,* 255.

Monroe, L., Rechtschaffen, A., Foulkes, D., & Jensen, J. (1965). Discriminability of REM and NREM reports. *Journal of Personality and Social Psychology, 2*, 456–460.

Montgomery, D. D., & Bone, R. N. (1962). Dream recall and cognitive style. *Perceptual and Motor Skills, 31*, 386.

Montplaisir, J. (1976). Disturbed nocturnal sleep. In C. Guilleminault, W. C. Dement, P. Passouant (Eds.), *Advances in Sleep Research: Vol 3. Narcolepsy* (pp. 43–56). New York: Spectrum.

Montplaisir, J., Billard, M., Takahashi, S., Bell, I. R., Guilleminault, C., & Dement, W. C. (1978). Twenty-four-hour recording in REM-narcoleptics with special reference to nocturnal sleep disruption. *Biological Psychiatry, 13*(1), 73–89.

Moore, J. D., Hayes, C., & Hicks, R. A. (1979). REM sleep deprivation increases performance for novelty in rats. *Physiology & Behaviour, 23*, 975–976.

Moore, R. (1962). The manifest dream in alcoholism. *Quarterly Journal for Studies of Alcohol, 23*, 583–589.

Moore, S. F., Jr. (1962). Therapy of psychosomatic symptoms in gynecology, an evaluation of chlordiazepoxide. *Current Therapeutic Research, 4*, 249–257.

Morden, B., Conner, R., Mitchell, G., Dement, W., & Levine, S. (1968). Effects of rapid eye movement (REM) sleep deprivation on shock induced fighting. *Physiology and Behavior, 3*, 425–432.

Morden, B., Mitchell, G., & Dement, W. (1967). Selective REM sleep deprivation and compensation phenomena in the rat. *Brain Research, 5*, 339–349.

Morden, B., Mullins, R., Levine, S., Cohen, H., & Dement, W. (1968). Effect of REMs deprivation on the mating behavior of male rats. *Psychophysiology, 5*, 241–242. (Abstract)

Morrison, A. R., & Pompeiano, O. (1970). Vestibular influences during sleep. VI. Vestibular control of autonomic functions during the rapid eye movements of desynchronized sleep. *Archives Italiennes de Biologie, 108*, 154–180.

Morrison, J. D. (1980). Fatigue as a presenting complaint in family practice. *Journal of Family Practice, 10*, 795–801.

Moruzzi, G. (1963). Active processes in the brain stem during sleep. *Harvey Lecture Series, 58*, 233–297.

Moruzzi, G. (1963). General discussion. In *Aspects anatomo-fonctionnels de la physiologie du sommeil. Actes du Colloque International sur les Aspects Anatomo-functionnels de la Physiologie du Sommeil.* Colloques Internationaux du Centre National de la Recherche Scientifique, No. 127.

Moruzzi, G., & Magoun, H. W. (1949). Brain stem reticular formation and activation of the electroencephalogram. *Electrocephalography and Clinical Neurophysiology, 1*, 455–473.

Moskowitz, E., & Berger, R. J. (1969). rapid eye movements and dream imagery: Are they related? *Nature, 224*, 613–614.

Mouret, J., Jeannerod, M., & Jouvet, M. (1963). L'activité éléctrique du systèm visuel au cours de la phase paradoxale du sommeil chez le Chat. *Journal de Physiologie, 55*, 305–306.

Mouret, J., Pujol, J. F., & Kiyuno, S. (1969). Paradoxical sleep rebound in rats: Effects of physical procedures involved in intracranial ingestion. *Brain Research, 15,* 501–506.

Muller, G. E., & Pilzecker, A. (1900). Experimentelle Beitrage zur Lehre vom Gadächtnis. *Zeitschrift für Psychologie,* Supplement No. 1.

Murril, P., Barreca, T., & Gallaminia, H. (1977). Prolactin and somatotropin levels during sleep in the aged. *Chronobiologia, 4,* 135.

Murri, L., Stefanini, A., Bonanni, E., Cei, G., Navona, C., & Denoth, F. (1984). Hemispheric EEG differences during REM sleep in dextrals and sinistrals. *Research Communications in Psychology, Psychiatry, & Behavior, 9,* 109–120.

Muzio, J., Roffwarg, H., Anders, C., & Muzio, L. (1971). *Retention of rote learned meaningful verbal material and alterations in the normal sleep EEG patterns.* Paper presented at the meeting of the Association for the Psychophysiological Study of Sleep, Bruges, Belgium.

Naifeh, K. H., & Kamiya, J. (1981). The nature of respiratory changes associated with sleep onset. *Sleep, 4*(1), 49–59.

Naiman, J., Poitros, R., & Englemann, F. (1972). The effect of chlorpromazine on REM rebound in normal volunteers. *Canadian Psychiatric Association Journal, 17,* 463–469.

Nakasawa, Y., Kotorii, M., Kotorii, T., Tachibana, H., & Nakano, T. (1975). Individual differences in compensatory rebound of REM sleep, with particular reference to their relationship to personality and behavioral characteristics. *Journal of Nervous & Mental Disease, 161,* 18–25.

National Center for Health Statistics. (1978). *The national ambulatory medical care survey: 1975 Summary,* (pp 22–26). Hyattsville, MD.

National Institutes of Health. (1984). Drugs and insomnia: The use of medications to promote sleep. Consensus conference, Office of Medical Applications of Research. *Journal of the American Medical Association, 251*(18), 2410–2414.

Nauta, W. J. H. (1958). Hippocampal projections and related neural pathways to the midbrain in cats. *Brain, 8,* 319–340.

Nebes, R. D. (1974). Hemispheric specialization in commisurotomized man. *Psychological Bulletin, 81,* 1–14.

Newman, E. B. (1939). Forgetting of meaningful material during sleeping and waking. *American Journal of Psychology, 52,* 65–71.

Newman, R., Katz, J., & Rubenstein, R. (1960). The experimental situation as a determinant of hypnotic dreams. *Psychiatry, 23,* 63–73.

Newton, P. (1970). Recalled dream content and the maintenance of body image. *Journal of Abnormal Psychology, 76,* 134–139.

Nocturnal oxygen therapy trial group. (1980). Continuous or nocturnal oxygen therapy in chronic obstructive lung disease. *Annals of Internal Medicine, 93,* 391–398.

Nowlis, V., & Nowlis, H. H. (1956). The description and analysis of mood. *Annals of the New York Academy of Sciences, 65,* 344–355.

Nunberg, H. (1931). The synthetic function of the ego. *International Journal of Psychoanalysis, 12,* 123–140.

Offenkrantz, W., & Rechtschaffen, A. (1963). Clinical studies of sequential dreams. I. A patient in psychotherapy, *Archives of General Psychiatry, 8,* 497–508.

Ogden, C. K., & Richards, I. A. (1945). *The meaning of meaning* (7th ed.). London: Kegan Paul.

Ogilvie, R. D., & Wilkinson, R. T. (1984). The detection of sleep onset: Behavioural and physiological convergence. *Psychophysiology, 21*(5), 510–520.

Ogilvie, R., Hunt, H., Sawicki, C., & Samahalski, J. (1982). Psychological correlates of spontaneous MEMA during sleep. *Sleep, 11,* 11–27.

Ohlmeyer, P., Brilmayer, H., & Hüllstrung, H. (1944). Periodische Vorgänge im Schlaf. *Pflügers Archiv für die Gesamte Physiologie, 248,* 559–560.

Okuma, T., Sunami, Y., Fukuma, E., Takeo, S., & Motoike, M. (1970). Dream content study in chronic schizophrenics and normals by REMP awakening technique. *Folia Psychiatrica et Neurological Japonica, 24,* 151–162.

Okuma, T., Sunami, Y., Fukuma, E., Takeo, S., & Motoike, M. (1970). Dream content study in chronic schizophrenics and normals by REMP-awakening technique. *Folia Psychiatrica et Neurologica Japonica, 24,* 151–162.

Olds, J. (1956). A preliminary mapping of electrical reinforcing effects in the brain. *Journal of Comparative and Physiological Psychology, 49,* 281–285.

Olds, J. (1959). Studies of neuropharmacologicals by electrical and chemical manipulation of the brain in animals with chronically implanted electrodes. In P. B. Bradlye, P. Deniker, & C. Radauco-Thomas (Eds.), *Neuropharmacology (Proceedings of the First International Congress of Neuropharmacology)* (pp. 20–32). Amsterdam: Elsevier.

Olds, J. (1962). Hypothalamic substrates of reward. *Physiological Reviews, 42,* 554–604.

Oniani, T. N. (1984). Does paradoxical sleep deprivation disturb memory trace consolidation? *Physiology and Behavior, 33,* 687–692.

Oppelt, A. W. & Palmer, R. (1972). Cri de coeur: Time out for questions: Therapy. *Emergency Medicine, 4,* 56–73.

Orlinsky, D. (1962). *Psychodynamic and cognitive correlates of dream recall — A study of individual differences.* Unpublished doctoral dissertation, University of Chicago.

Orne, M. T. (1962). On the social psychology of the psychological experiment: With particular reference to demand characteristics and their implications. *American Psychologist, 17,* 776–783.

Orr, W. C., Hall, W. H., Stahl, M. L., Durkin, M. G., & Whitsett, T. L. (1976). Sleep patterns and gastric acid secretion in duodenal ulcer disease. *Annals of Internal Medicine, 136,* 655–660.

Orr, W. J., Dozier, J. E., Green, L., & Cromwell, R. L. (1968). Self-induced waking: Changes in dreams and sleep patterns. *Comprehensive Psychiatry, 9,* 499–506.

Oswald, I. (1962). *Sleeping and waking.* Amsterdam: Elsevier.

Oswald, I. (1969a). Sleep, dreams and drugs. *Proceedings of the Royal Society of Medicine, 62,* 151–153.

Oswald, I. (1969b). Human brain protein, drugs and dreams. *Nature, 223,* 893–897.

Oswald, I. (1973). Drug research and human sleep. In H. W. Elliott, R. Okun, & R. George (Eds.), *Annual review of pharmacology* (Vol. 13). Palo Alto, CA: Annual Reviews.

Oswald, I., Adam, K., Borrow, S., & Idzikowski, C. (1979). The effects of two hypnotics on sleep, subjective feelings and skilled performance. In P. Passouant & I. Oswald (Eds.), *Pharmacology of the states of alertness* (pp. 51–63). Oxford, England: Pergamon Press.

Oswald, I., Berger, R. J., Jaramillo, R. A., Keddie, K. M. G., Olley, P. C., & Plunkett, G. B. (1963). Melancholia and barbiturates: A controlled EEG, body and eye movement study of sleep. *British Journal of Psychiatry, 109*, 66–78.

Oswald, I., Lewis, S. A., Tagney, J., Firth, A., & Haider, I. (1973). Benzodiazepines and human sleep. In S. Garratini, E. Mussini, & L. O. Randall (Eds.), *The benzodiazepines*. New York: Raven Press.

Oswald, I., & Priest, R. (1965). Five weeks to escape the sleeping pill habit. *British Medical Journal, 2*, 1093.

Oswald, I., Taylor, A. M., & Treisman, M. (1960). Discriminative responses to stimulation during human sleep. *Brain, 83*, 440–453.

Oswald, I., Thacore, V. R., Adam, K., Brezinova, V., & Burack, R. (1975). Alpha-adrenergic receptor blockade increases human REM sleep. *British Journal of Clinical Pharmacology, 2*, 107–110.

Othmer, E., Hayden, M. P., & Segelbaum, R. (1969). Encephalic cycles during sleep and wakefulness in humans: A 24-hour pattern. *Science, 164*, 447–449.

Overton, D. A. (1966). State-dependent learning produced by depressant and atropine-like drugs. *Psychopharmacologia, 10*, 6–31.

Overton, D. A. (1973). State-dependent retention of learned responses produced by drugs. Its relevance to sleep learning and recall. In W. P. Koella, & P. Levin (Eds.), *Sleep—Physiology, biochemistry, psychology, pharmacology, clinical implications*. (Proceedings of the First European Congress on Sleep Research, Basel, 1972). Basel, Switzerland: S. Karger.

Owen, M., & Bliss, E. L. (1970). Sleep loss and cerebral excitability. *American Journal of Physiology, 218*, 171–173.

Paivio, A. (1971). *Imagery and verbal processes*. New York: Holt, Rinehart & Winston.

Palmer, J. O. (1963). Alterations in Rorschach's experience balance under conditions of food and sleep deprivation: A construct validation study. *Journal of Projective Techniques, 27*, 208–213.

Palombo, S. R. (1973). The associative memory tree. In B. B. Rubinstein (Ed.), *Psychoanalysis and contemporary science* (Vol. 2). New York: Macmillan.

Palumbo, S. R. (1976). The dream and memory cycle. *International Review of Psychoanalysis, 3*, 65–83.

Palumbo, S. R. (1978). *Dreaming and memory: A new information processing model*. New York: Basic Books.

Parkinson, J. (1817). Essays on the shaking palsy. London, Sherwood, Neely & Jones.

Parmeggiani, P. L. (1977). Interaction between sleep and thermoregulation. *Waking & Sleeping, 1*, 123–132.

Parmeggiani, P. L. (1980). Temperature regulation during sleep: A study in homeostasis. In J. Orem & C. D. Barnes (Eds.), *Physiology in sleep.* New York: Academic Press.

Parmeggiani, P. L., Cianci, T., Calasso, M., Zamboni, G., & Perez, E. (1980). Quantitative analysis of short-term deprivation and recovery of desynchronised sleep in cats. *Electroencephalography & Clinical Neurophysiology, 50,* 293–302.

Parmelee, A., Wenner, W., & Schutz, H. R. (1964). Infant sleep patterns from birth to 16 weeks of age. *Journal of Pediatrics, 65,* 576–582.

Passouant, P., Cadilhac, J., Baldy–Moulinier, M., & Mion, C. H. (1970). Etude du sommeil nocturne chez des uremiques chroniques soumis à une epuration extrarenale. *Electroencephalography and Clinical Neurophysiology, 29,* 441–449.

Patrick, G. T. W., & Gilberg, J. A. (1896). On the effects of sleep loss. *Psychological Review, 3,* 469–483.

Pearlman, C. (1971). Latent learning impaired by REM sleep deprivation. *Psychonometric Science, 25,* 135–136.

Pearlman, C. (1973). REM sleep deprivation impairs latent extinction in rats. *Physiology and Behavior, 11,* 233–237.

Pearlman, C. A. (1979). REM sleep and information processing: Evidence from animal studies. *Neuroscience and Biobehavioral Reviews, 3,* 57–68.

Pearlman, C. A. (1982). Sleep structure variation and performance. In W. Webb (Ed.), *Biological rhythms, sleep and performance.* New York: Wiley.

Pearlman, C., & Becker, M. (1974). REM sleep deprivation impairs barpress acquisition in rats. *Physiology and Behavior, 13,* 813–817.

Pearlman, C., & Becker, M. (1975). Retroactive impairment of cooperative learning by imipramine and chlordiazepoxide in rats. *Psychopharmacologia, 42,* 63–66.

Pearlman, C., & Greenberg, R. (1973). Posttrail REM sleep: A critical period for consolidation of shuttlebox avoidance. *Animal Learning Behavior, 1,* 49–51.

Peder, M., Elomaa, E., & Johansson, G. (1986). Increased aggression after REM sleep deprivation in Wistar Rats is not influenced by reduction of dimensions of enclosure. *Behavioral and Neural Biology, 45,* 287–291.

Perenin, M. T., Maeda, T., & Jeannerod, M. (1972). Are vestibular nuclei responsible for rapid eye movements of paradoxical sleep? *Brain Research, 43,* 617–621.

Pessah, M. A., & Roffwarg, H. P. (1972b). Spontaneous middle ear muscle activity in man: A rapid eye movement phenomenon. *Science, 178,* 773–776.

Pessah, M., & Roffwarg, H. (1972a). Middle ear muscle activity during sleep: An important new phasic phenomenon. *Psychophysiology, 9,* 127–128. (Abstract)

Peterfreund, E., & Franceschini, E. (1973). On information, motivation and meaning. In B. B. Rubinstein (Ed.), *Psychoanalysis and contemporary science* (Vol. 2). New York: Macmillan.

Peterfreund, E., & Schwartz, J. T. (1971). Information, systems and psychoanalysis. An evolutionary biological approach to psychoanalytic theory. *Psychological Issues, 7* (Monograph 1-2), 25–26.

Peterson, L. R., & Peterson, M. J. (1959). Short-term retention of individual verbal items. *Journal of Experimental Psychology, 58,* 193–198.

Petre-Quadens, O. (1974). Sleep in the human newborn. In O. Petre-Quadens & J. Schlag (Eds.), *Basic sleep mechanisms* (pp. 355–380). New York: Academic Press.

Piaget, J. (1951). *Play, dreams and imitation in childhood.* London: Heinemann.

Pittendrigh, C. S., & Daan, S. (1974). Circadian oscillations in rodents: A systematic increase of their frequency with age. *Science, 186,* 548–550.

Pivik, R. T. (1971). *Mental activity and phasic events during sleep.* Doctoral dissertation, Stanford University. (University Microfilms No. 71–19746)

Pivik, R. T., Bylsma, F., Busby, K., & Sawyer, S. (1982). Interhemispheric EEG changes: Relationship to sleep and dreams in gifted adolescents. *Psychiatric Journal of the University of Ottawa, 7,* 56–76.

Pivik, T. (1974). Review of Cartwright, R. D.: Sleep fantasy in normal and schizophrenic persons. *Sleep Research, 3,* 327–328.

Pivik, T., & Dement, W. (1968). Amphetamine, REM deprivation and K-complexes. *Psychophysiology, 5,* 241. (Abstract)

Pivik, T., & Dement, W. C. (1970). Phasic changes in muscular and reflex activity during non-REM sleep. *Experimental Neurology, 27,* 115–124.

Pivik, T., & Foulkes, D. (1966). "Dream deprivation": Effects on dream content. *Science, 153,* 1282–1284.

Pivik, T., & Foulkes, D. (1968). NREM mentation: Relation to personality, orientation time and time of night. *Journal of Consulting & Clinical Psychology, 37,* 144–151.

Pivik, T., Halper, C., & Dement, W. (1969b). NREM phasic EMG suppression in the human. *Psychophysiology, 217.* (Abstract)

Plumer, S., Matthews, L., Tucker, M., & Cook, T. (1974). The water tank technique: Avoidance conditioning as a function of water level and pedestal size. *Physiology and Behavior, 12,* 285–287.

Polanyi, M. (1965). The structure of consciousness. *Brain, 88,* 799–810.

Pompeiano, O. (1966). Muscular afferents and motor control during sleep. In R. Granit (Ed.), *Muscular afferents and motor control.* Stockholm: Almquist and Siksell.

Pompeiano, O. (1967). The neurophysiological mechanism of the postural and motor events during desynchronized sleep. In S. S. Kety, E. V. Evarts, & H. L. Williams (Eds.), *Sleep and altered states of consciousness.* Baltimore: Williams & Wilkins.

Pompeiano, O. (1970). Mechanisms of sensorimotor integration during sleep. In E. Stellar, & J. M. Spraque (Eds.), *Progress in physiological psychology* (Vol. 3). New York: Academic Press.

Pope, R. A. (1973). *Psychological correlates of theta burst activity in sleep onset.* Unpublished master's thesis, University of Wyoming.

Portell–Cortes, M. I., Nicolovius, M. M., & Bernal, I. M. (1983). Relacion entre privacion de suenlo paradojico y autoestimulacion electrica intracanial en ratas. *Qudrens/Caudernon de Psicologia, 7,* 45–54.

Portnoff, G., Baekeland, F., Goodenough, D. R., Karacan, I., & Shapiro, A. (1966). Retention of verbal materials perceived immediately prior to onset of non-REM sleep. *Perceptual and Motor Skills, 22,* 751–758.

Pötzl, O., Allers, R., & Teler, J. (1960). Preconscious stimulation in dreams, associations and images. *Psychological Issues, 7,* 1–40. (Original work published in 1917.)

Prechtl, H. R., & Lenard, G. (1967). A study of eye movements in sleeping newborn infants. *Brain Research, 5,* 477–493.

Pressman, M. P., Spielman, A. J., Korczyn, A. D., Rubenstein, A. E., Pollak, C. P., & Weitzman, E. D. (1984). Patterns of daytime sleepiness in narcoleptics and normals: A pupillometric study. *Electroencephalography and Clinical Neurophysiology, 57,* 129–133.

Prichard, B. N. C., & Gillam, P. M. S. (1964). Use of propranolol (Inderal) in treatment of hypertension. *British Medical Journal, 2,* 725–727.

Prichard, B. N. C., & Gillam, P. M. S. (1969). Treatment of hypertension with propranolol. *British Medical Journal, 1,* 7–16.

Prigot, A., Barnes, A. L., & Barnard, R. D. (1957). Meprobamate therapy. *Harlem Hospital Bulletin, 10,* 63–77.

Prince, M. (1911). The mechanism and interpretation of dreams. *Journal of Abnormal Psychology, 5,* 337–354.

Prinz, P., Blenkarn, D., & Linnoila, M. (1976). Neuroendocrine changes during sleep in elderly males. In M. Chase, P. M. Mitler, & P. L. Walter (Eds.), *Sleep Research* (Vol. 5). Los Angeles: Brain Research Institute.

Prinz, P., Peskind, E. R., Vitiliano, P. P., Raskind, M. A., Eisdorfer, C., & Zemcuznikov, N. (1982). Changes in the sleep and waking EEGs of nondemented and demented elderly subjects. *Journal of the American Geriatrics Society, 30,* 86–93.

Prinz, P., & Raskind, M. (1978). Aging and sleep disorders. In R. Williams & I. Karacan (Eds.), *Sleep disorders: Diagnosis and treatment* (p. 303). New York: Wiley.

Pujol, J. F., Mouret, J., Jouvet, M., & Glowinski, J. (1968). Increased turnover of cerebral norepinephrine during rebound of paradoxical sleep in rats. *Science, 159,* 112–114.

Purcell, S., Mullington, J., Moffit, A., Hoffmann, R., & Pigeau, R. (1986). Dream self-reflectiveness as a learned cognitive skill. *Sleep, 9,* 423–437.

Puryear, H. B. (1963). *Personality characteristics of reporters and non-reporters of dreams.* Doctoral dissertation, University of North Carolina at Chapel Hill. Ann Arbor, MI: University Microfilms, No. 64-1884.

Putkonen, P., & Putkonen, A. (1971). Suppression of paradoxical sleep (PS) following hypothalamic defense reaction in cats during normal conditions and recovery from PS deprivation. *Brain Research, 26,* 333–347.

Quillian, M. R. (1968). *Semantic memory.* Unpublished doctoral dissertation, Carnegie Institute of Technology, 1966. Reprinted in part in M. Minsky (Ed.), *Semantic Information Processing.* Cambridge: MA: M. I. T. Press.

Raffetto, A. (1968). *Experimenter effects on subjects' reported hallucinatory experience under visual and auditory deprivation.* Paper presented at the meeting of the Midwestern Psychological Association, Chicago.

Ramsey, G. V. (1953). Studies of dreaming. *Psychological Bulletin, 50,* 432–455.

Rao, C. R. (1973). *Linear statistical inference and its applications.* New York: Wiley.

Rapaport, D. (1960). The structure of psychoanalytic theory. *Psychological Issues Monograph Series,* Vol. 2. New York: International Universities Press.

Rapaport, D. (1967). States of consciousness: A psychopathological and psychodynamic view. In M. Gill (Ed.), *The collected papers of David Rapaport.* New York: Basic Books. (Original work published 1951)

Rapaport, D., & Gill, M. M. (1959). The points of view and assumptions of metapsychology. *International Journal of Psychoanalysis, 40,* 153–162.

Raynal, D. (1976). Polygraphic aspects of narcolepsy. In C. Guilleminault, W. C. Dement, & P. Passouant (Eds.), *Advances in Sleep Research: Vol 3: Narcolepsy* (pp. 671–684). New York: Spectrum.

Rechtschaffen, A. (1964). Discussion of: Experimental dream studies, by W. C. Dement. In J. H. Masserman (Ed.), *Science and psychoanalysis,* Vol. 1, *Development and research.* New York: Grune & Stratton.

Rechtschaffen, A. (1967). Dream reports and dream experiences. *Experimental Neurology* (Suppl. 4), 4–15.

Rechtschaffen, A. (1973). The psychophysiology of mental activity during sleep. In F. J. McGuigan, & R. A. Schoonover (Eds.), *The psychophysiology of thinking.* New York: Academic Press.

Rechtschaffen, A. (1978). The single-mindedness and isolation of dreams. *Sleep, 1,* 97–109.

Rechtschaffen, A., & Chernik, D. A. (1972). The effect of REM deprivation on periorbital spike activity in NREM sleep. *Psychophysiology, 9,* 128. (Abstract)

Rechtschaffen, A., Cornwell, P., & Zimmerman, W. (1965). *Brain temperature variations with paradoxical sleep in the cat.* Unpublished manuscript.

Rechtschaffen, A., & Dement, W. C. (1969). Narcolepsy and hypersomnia. In A. Kales (Ed.), *Sleep: Physiology and pathology.* Philadelphia: Lippincott.

Rechtschaffen, A., & Foulkes, D. (1965). Effect of visual stimuli on dream content. *Perceptual and Motor Skills, 20,* 1149–1160.

Rechtschaffen, A., Gilliland, M. A., Bergmann, B., & Winter, J. B. (1983). Physiological correlates of prolonged sleep deprivation in rats. *Science, 221,* 182–184.

Rechtschaffen, A., Goodenough, D., & Shapiro, A. (1962). Patterns of sleep talking. *Archives of General Psychiatry, 7,* 418–426.

Rechtschaffen, A., Hauri, P., & Zeitlin, M. (1966). Auditory awakening thresholds in REM and NREM sleep stages. *Perceptual and Motor Skills, 22,* 927–942.

Rechtschaffen, A., & Kales, A. (Eds.). (1968). *A manual of standardized terminology, techniques and scoring system for sleep stages of human subjects* (Publication 204). Public Health Service Publications: U. S. Government Printing Office.

Rechtschaffen, A., & Maron, L. (1964). The effect of amphetamine on the sleep cycle. *Electroencephalography and Clinical Neurophysiology, 16,* 438–445.

Rechtschaffen, A., Michel, F., & Metz, J. T. (1972). Relationship between extraocular and PGO activity in the cat. *Psychophysiology, 9,* 128. (Abstract)

Rechtschaffen, A., Molinari, S., Watson, R., & Wincor, M. (1970). *Extraocular potentials: A possible indicator of PGO activity in the human.* Paper presented at the Association for the Psychophysiological Study of Sleep, Santa Fe, NM. *Psychophysiology, 1,* 336. (Abstract)

Rechtschaffen, A., & Verdone, P. (1964). Amount of dreaming: Effect of incentive, adaptation to laboratory and individual differences. *Perceptual and Motor Skills, 18,* 947–958.

Rechtschaffen, A., Verdone, P., & Wheaton, J. (1963). Reports of mental activity during sleep. *Canadian Psychiatric Association Journal, 8,* 409–414.

Rechtschaffen, A., Vogel, G., & Shaikun, G. (1963). Interrelatedness of mental activity during sleep. *Archives of General Psychiatry, 9,* 536–547.

Rechtschaffen, A., Watson, R., Wincor, M., & Molinari, S. (1971). *Orbital phenomena and mental activity in NREM sleep.* Paper presented at the First International Congress of the Association for the Psychophysiological Study of Sleep, Belgium.

Rechtschaffen, A., Watson, R., Wincor, M. Z., Molinari, S., & Barta, S. G. (1972). The relationship of phasic and tonic periorbital EMG activity to NREM mentation. *Sleep Research, 1,* 114.

Rechtschaffen, A., Wolpert, E. A., Dement, E. C., Mitchell, S. A., & Fisher, C. (1963). Nocturnal sleep of narcoleptics. *Electroencephalography and Clinical Neurophysiology, 15,* 599–609.

Redington, D., Perry, F., Gibson, E., & Kamiya, J. (1981). Discrimination of early sleep stages: Behavioral indicators. *Sleep, 4*(2), 171–176.

Reed, H. (1973). Learning to remember dreams. *Journal of Humanistic Psychology, 13*(3), 33–48.

Reite, M. L., & Pegram, G. U. (1968). Cortical temperature during paradoxical sleep in the monkey. *Electroencephalography and Clinical Neurophysiology, 25,* 36–41.

Richardson, A., & Gough, J. E. (1963). The long range effect of sleep on retention. *Australian Journal of Psychology, 15,* 37–41.

Richardson, G. A., & Moore, R. A. (1963). On the manifest dream in schizophrenia. *Journal of the American Psychoanalytic Association, 11,* 281–302.

Rich, K. D., Antrobus, J. S., Ellman, S. J., & Arkin, A. M. (1975). REM rebound following deprivation as a function of changes in dream mentation fantasy. *Sleep Research, 4,* 244.

Richter, C. P. (1922). A behavioristic study of the activity of the rat. *Comprehensive Psychological Monographs, 1,* 1–55.

Ricoeur, P. (1970). *Freud and philosophy: An essay on interpretation.* New Haven: Yale University Press.

Roffwarg, H. (1975). Inter-model relationships in sleep research. In G. Lairy & P. Salzarulo (Eds.), *The experimental study of human sleep: Methodological problems.* Amsterdam: Elsevier.

Roffwarg, H., Adrien, J., Herman, J., Lamstein, S., Pessah, M., Spiro, R., & Bowe-Anders, C. (1973). The place of the middle ear muscle activity in the neurophysiology and psychophysiology of the REM state. *Sleep Research, 2,* 36.

Roffwarg, H., Bowe-Anders, C., Tauber, E., & Herman, J. (1975). Dream Imagery: The effect of long term perceptual modification. *Sleep Research, 4,* 164. (Abstract)

Roffwarg, H., Dement, W., Muzio, J., & Fisher, C. (1962). Dream imagery: Relationship to rapid eye movements of sleep. *Archives of General Psychiatry, 7,* 235–258.

Roffwarg, H., Herman, J., & Lamstein, S. (1975). The middle ear muscles: Predictability of their phasic activity in REM sleep from dream recall. *Sleep Research, 4,* 165.

Roffwarg, H., Muzio, J. N., & Dement, W. (1968). Ontogenetic development of the human sleep dream cycle. *Science, 152,* 604–619.

Roffwarg, H. P., & Altshuler, K. Z. (1982). The diagnosis of sleep disorders. In M. R. Zales (Ed.), *Eating, sleeping, and sexuality.* New York: Brunner Mazel.

Roffwarg, H. P. (Chairman). (1979). Diagnostic classification of sleep and arousal disorders (1st ed.). *Sleep, 2,* 1–137.

Roffwarg, H. P., Dement, W., & Fisher, C. (1964). Preliminary observations of the sleep-dream pattern in neonates, infants, children and adults. In E. Harms (Ed.), *Problems of sleep and dream in children.* New York: Macmillan Press.

Roffwarg, H. P., Muzio, J., & Dement, W. C. (1966). The ontogenetic development of the human sleep dream cycle. *Science, 152,* 604–618.

Roffwarg, H. P., & Muzio, J. N. (1965). *Sleep onset stage I-A re-evaluation.* Paper presented at the Association for the Psychophysiological Study of Sleep, Washington, DC.

Roffwarg, H. P., Muzio, J. N., & Dement, W. C. (1966). Ontogenetic development of the human sleep-dream cycle. *Science, 152,* 604–619.

Rommetveit, R. (1968). *Words, meanings and messages: Theory and experiments in psycholinguistics.* New York: Academic Press.

Rorschach, H. (1942). *Psychodiagnostics: A diagnostic test based on perception.* Translated by P. Lemkau and B. Kronenburg. Berne: Hans Huber.

Rosch, E. (1975). Reply to Loftus. *Journal of Experimental Psychology: General, 104,* 241–243.

Rosekind, M. R., Coates, T. J., & Zarcone, V. P. (1979). Lateral dominance during wakefulness, NREM stage 2 sleep and REM sleep. *Sleep Research, 8,* 36.

Rosen, J. (1953). *Direct analysis, selected papers.* New York: Grune & Stratton.

Rosenthal, L., Roehrs, T., Sicklesteel, J., Zorick, F., Wittig, R., & Roth, T. (1984). Periodic movements during sleep, sleep fragmentation, and sleep-wake complaints. *Sleep, 7*(4), 326–330.

Rosenthal, R. (1966). *Experimenter effects in behavioral research.* New York: Appleton-Century-Crofts.

Rosenthal, R., & Fode, K. L. (1963). The effect of experimenter bias on the performance of the albino rat. *Behavioral Science, 8,* 183–189.

Rosenthal, R., Friedman, N., & Kurland, D. (1966). Instruction-reading behavior of the experimenter as an unintended determinant of experimental results. *Journal of Experimental Research in Personality, 1,* 221–226.

Rosenthal, R., & Rosnow, R. L. (Eds.) (1969). *Artifact in behavioral research.* New York: Academic Press.

Rosenzweig, M. R., Mollgaard, M. C., & Bennett, E. L. (1972). Negative as well as positive synaptic change may store memory. *Psychological Review, 79,* 93–96.

Rotenberg, V. S. (1984). Search activity in the context of psychosomatic disturbances, of brain monoamines and REM sleep function. *Pavlovian Journal of Biological Science, 19,* 1–15.

Rotenberg, V. S., & Arshavsky, V. V. (1979). REM sleep, stress and search activity. A short critical review and new conception. *Waking & Sleeping, 3,* 235–244.

Rotenberg, V. S., & Biniaurishvili, R. G. (1973). Psychophysiological study of night sleep. *Zhurnal vysshey nervnoy deyatelnosti, 4,* 864–871.

Roth, B. (1978). Narcolepsy and Hypersomnia. In R. L. Williams & I. Karacan (Eds.), *Sleep disorders. Diagnosis and treatment* (pp. 29–59). New York: Wiley.

Roth, B., Bruhova, S., & Lehovsky, M. (1969). REM sleep and NREM sleep in narcolepsy and hypersomnia. *Electroencephalography and Clinical Neurophysiology, 26,* 176–182.

Roth, M., Shaw, J., & Green, J. (1956). The form, voltage distribution and physiological significance of the K-complex. *Electroencephalography and Clinical Neurophysiology, 8,* 385–402.

Roth, T., Hartse, K. M., Saab, P. G., Piccione, P. M., & Kramer, M. (1980). The effects of flurazepam, lorazepam, and triazolam on sleep and memory. *Psychopharmacology, 70,* 231–237.

Roth, T., Kramer, M., & Arand, D. (1976). *Dreams as a reflection of immediate psychological concern.* Paper presented at the meeting of the Association for the Psychophysiological Study of Sleep, Cincinnati, OH.

Routtenberg, A. (1966). Neural mechanisms of sleep: Changing views of reticular formation function. *Psychological Review, 73,* 481–499.

Routtenberg, A. (1968). The two arousal hypothesis: Reticular formation and limbic system. *Psychological Reviews, 75,* 51–80.

Rubin, F. (1968). *Current research in hypnopaedia.* New York: American Elsevier.

Rubinfine, D. (1961). Perception, reality testing and symbolism. *The Psychoanalytic Study of the Child, 16,* 73–89.

Rubinstein, B. B. (1967). Explanation and mere description: A meta scientific examination of certain aspects of the psychoanalytic theory of motivation. In *Psychoanalytic essays in honor of David Rapaport. Psychological Issues, 5* (2-3) (Monograph 18-19, 18-77). New York: International Universities Press.

Rubinstein, B. B. (1973). On the logic of explanation in psychoanalysis. In B. B. Rubinstein (Ed.), *Psychoanalysis and contemporary science* (Vol. 2). New York: Macmillan.

Rubinstein, B. B. (1974). On the role of classificatory processes in mental functioning: Aspects of a psychoanalytic theoretical model. In L. Goldberger & V. H. Rosen (Eds.), *Psychoanalysis and contemporary science* (Vol. 3). New York: International Universities Press.

Rudolf, G. A. E., Schilgen, Y., & Tolle, R. (1977). Antidepressive Behandlung mittels Schlafentzug. *Nervenarzt, 48,* 1–11.

Rumelhart, D. E., Hinton, G. E., & McClelland, J. L. (1986). A general framework for parallel distributed processing. In J. L. McClelland & D. E. Rumelhart (Eds.), *Parallel distributed processing: Explorations in the microstructure of cognition* (Vol. 1, pp. 45–76). Cambridge, MA: MIT Press.

Rumelhart, D. E., Hinton, G. E., & Williams, R. J. (1986). Learning internal representations by error propagation. In J. L. McClelland & D. E. Rumelhart (Eds.), *Parallel distributed processing: Explorations in the microstructure of cognition* (Vol. 1, pp. 318–362). Cambridge, MA: MIT Press.

Rumelhart, D. E., Lindsay, P. H., & Norman, D. A. (1972). *A process model of long-term memory.* New York: Academic Press.

Rumelhart, D. E., & McClelland, J. L. (1986). PDP models and general issues in cognitive science. In J. L. McClelland & D. E. Rumelhart (Eds.), *Parallel distributed processing: Explorations in the microstructure of cognition* (Vol. 1, pp. 110–146). Cambridge, MA: MIT Press.

Rumelhart, D. E., Smolensky, P., McClelland, J. L., & Hinton, G. E. (1986). Schemata and sequential thought processes in PDP models. In J. L. McClelland & D. E. Rumelhart (Eds.), *Parallel distributed processing: Explorations in the microstructure of cognition* (Vol. 2, pp. 7–57). Cambridge, MA: MIT Press.

Rutenfranz, J., Knauth, P., & Colquhoun, W. P. (1976). Hours of work and shiftwork. *Ergonomics, 12,* 331–340.

Safer, D. J. (1970). The effect of LSD on sleep-deprived men. *Psychopharmacologia, 17,* 414–424.

Sagales, T., & Domino, E. (1973). Effects of stress and REM sleep deprivation on the patterns of avoidance learning and brain acetylcholine in the mouse. *Psychopharmacologia, 29,* 307–315.

Sakai, F., Stirling Meyer, J., Karacan, I., Derman, S., & Yamamoto, M. (1980). Normal human sleep: Regional cerebral hemodynamics. *Annals of Neurology, 7,* 471–478.

Sakai, F., Stirling Meyer, J., Karacan, I., Yamaguchi, F., & Yamamoto, M. (1979). Narcolepsy: Regional cerebral blood flow during sleep and wakefulness. *Neurology, 29,* 61–67.

Sakai, K. (1985). Anatomical and physiological basis of paradoxical sleep. In D. J. McGinty, R. Drucker-Colin, A. Morrison, & P. L. Parmeggianni (Eds.), *Brain mechanisms of sleep* (pp. 111–137). New York: Raven Press.

Salzinger, K. (1971). An hypothesis about schizophrenic behavior. *American Journal of Psychotherapy, 25,* 601–614.

Sampson, H. (1965). Deprivation of dreaming sleep by two methods: I. Compensatory REM time. *Archives of General Psychiatry, 13* 79–86.

Sampson, H. (1966). Psychological effects of deprivation of dreaming sleep. *Journal of Nervous and Mental Disease, 143,* 305–317.

Sastre, J. P., & Jouvet, M. (1979). Le comportement onirique du chat. *Physiology & Behaviour, 22,* 979–989.

Satinoff, E., Drucker-Colin, R. R., & Hernandez, P. R. (1971). Paleocortical excitability and sensory filtering during REM sleep deprivation. *Physiology and Behavior, 7,* 103–106.

Saul, L. J., Sheppard, E., Stelby, D., Lhamon, W., Sachs, D., & Master, R. (1954). The quantification of hostility in dreams with reference to essential hypertension. *Science, 119,* 382–383.

Saunders, N. A., & Sullivan, C. E. (Eds.). (1984). *Sleep and breathing.* New York: Dekker.

Schachtel, E. G. (1959). *Metamorphosis: On the development of affect, perception, attention, and memory.* New York: Basic Books.

Schacter, D. L. (1976). The hypnogogic state: A critical review of its literature. *Psychological Bulletin, 83,* 452–481.

Schafer, R. (1968). *Aspects of internalization.* New York: International Universities Press.

Schimek, J. G. (1975). A critical re-examination of Freud's concept of unconscious mental representation. *International Review of Psychoanalysis, 2,* 171–188.

Schjelderup, H. K. (1960). Time relations in dreams. *Scandinavian Journal of Psychology, 1,* 62–64.

Schonbar, R. A. (1959). Some manifest characteristics of recallers and nonrecallers of dreams. *Journal of Consulting Psychology, 23,* 414–418.

Schonbar, R. A. (1965). Differential dream recall frequency as a component of "life style." *Journal of Consulting Psychology, 29,* 468–474.

Schulz, H. (1981). Sleep onset REM episodes in depression. In W. P. Koella (Ed.), *Sleep 1980* (pp. 72–79). Basel, Switzerland: Karger.

Scott, E. (1968). Dreams of alcoholics. *Perceptual & Motor Skills, 26,* 1315–1318.

Scott, J. (1969). Performance after abrupt arousal from sleep: Comparison of a simple motor, a visual-perceptual, and a cognitive task. *Proceedings of the 77th Annual Convention of the American Psychological Association,* 225–226. (Summary)

Seligman, M. E. P. (1970). On the generality of the laws of learning. *Psychological Review, 77,* 406–418.

Selling, L. S. (1955). A clinical study of a new tranquilizing drug. *Journal of the American Medical Association, 157,* 1594–1596.

Serafetinides, A. A. (1966). Speech findings in epilepsy and electrocortical stimulation: An overview. *Cortex, 2,* 463–473.

Shapiro, A. (1967). Dreaming and the physiology of sleep. *Experimental Neurology, 19,* 56–81.

Shapiro, A. (1970). Comments on the 90-minute sleep-dream cycle. In E. Hartmann (Ed.), *Sleep and dreaming.* Boston: Little, Brown.

Shapiro, A., Goodenough, D. R., Biederman, I., & Sleser, I. (1964). Dream recall and the physiology of sleep. *Journal of Applied Physiology, 19,* 778–783.

Shapiro, A., Goodenough, D. R., & Gryler, R. B. (1963). Dream recall as a function of method of awakening. *Psychosomatic Medicine, 25,* 174–180.

Shapiro, A., Goodenough, D. R., Lewis, H. B., & Sleser, I. (1965). Gradual arousal from sleep: A determinant of thinking reports. *Psychosomatic Medicine, 27,* 342–349.

Sharpe, E. F. (1949). *Dream analysis. A practical handbook for psychoanalysis.* London: Hogarth Press.

Sharpless, S. K. (1970). Hypnotics and sedatives. In L. S. Goodman, & A. Gilman (Eds.), *The pharmacological basis of therapeutics* (4th ed.). London: Macmillan.

Sheffield, R. D., Roby, T. B., & Campbell, B. A. (1954). Drive reduction versus consummatory behavior as determinants of reinforcement. *Journal of Comparative and Physiological Psychology, 47,* 349–354.

Sher, A. E., Thorpy, M. J., Shprintzen, R. J., & Spielman, A. J. (1985). Predictive value of Muller maneuver in selection of patients for uvulopalatopharyngoplasty. *Laryngoscope, 95*(12), 1483–1487.

Sherwood, M. (1969). *The logic of explanation in psychoanalysis.* New York: Academic Press.

Sherwood, M. (1973). Another look at the logic of explanation in psychoanalysis. In B. B. Rubinstein (Ed.), *Psychoanalysis and contemporary science* (Vol. 2). New York: Macmillan.

Shevrin, H., & Fisher, C. (1967). Changes in the effects of a waking subliminal stimulus as a function of dreaming and non-dreaming sleep. *Journal of Abnormal Psychology, 72,* 362–368.

Shope, R. K. (1973). Freud's concept of meaning. In B. B. Rubinstein (Ed.), *Psychoanalysis and contemporary science* (Vol. 2). New York: Macmillan.

Sidel, W. F., & Dement, W. C. (1982). Sleepiness in insomnia: Evaluation and treatment. *Sleep, 5,* S182–S190.

Sidowski, J. B. (1966). *Experimental methods and instrumentation in psychology.* New York: McGraw–Hill.

Siegel, J., & Gordon, T. P. (1965). Paradoxical sleep: Deprivation in the cat. *Science, 148,* 978–980.

Simon, C. W., & Emmons, W. H. (1956). Responses to material presented during various levels of sleep. *Journal of Experimental Psychology, 51,* 89–97.

Simpson, R. G. (1969). Nocturnal disorders of medical interest. *The Practitioner, 202,* 259–268.

Singer, J. L. (1966). *Daydreaming: An introduction to the experimental study of inner experience.* New York: Random House.

Singer, J. L. (1968). Research applications of the projective methods. In A. Rabin (Ed.), *Projective techniques in personality assessment.* New York: Springer.

Singer, J. L. (1971). Imagery and daydream techniques in psychotherapy. In C. D. Spielberger (Ed.), *Current topics in clinical and community psychology* (Vol. 3). New York: Academic Press.

Singer, J. L. (1974a). Daydreaming and the stream of thoughts. *America Scientist, 62,* 417–425.

Singer, J. L. (1974b). *Imagery and daydream methods in psychotherapy and behavior modification.* New York: Academic Press.

Singer, J. L. (1975). *The inner world of daydreaming.* New York: Harper & Row.

Singer, J. L. (1976). Review of Foulkes, D., & Fleisher, S. Mental activity in relaxed wakefulness. *Sleep Bulletin.* Los Angeles: Brain Information Service of the University of California at Los Angeles.

Singer, J. L., & Antrobus, J. S. (1963). A factor analysis of daydreaming and conceptually-related cognitive and personality variables. *Perceptual and Motor Skills, 17* (Monograph Supplement), 187–209.

Singer, J. L., & Antrobus, J. S. (1965). Eye movements during fantasies. *Archives of General Psychiatry, 12,* 71–76.

Singer, J. L., & Antrobus, J. S. (1972). Daydreaming, imaginal processes, and personality: A normative study. In P. Sheehan (Ed.), *The function and nature of imagery.* New York: Academic Press.

Singer, J. L., Greenberg, S., & Antrobus, J. S. (1971). Looking with the mind's eye: Experimental studies of ocular motility during daydreaming and mental arithmetic. *Transactions of the New York Academy of Sciences, 33,* 694–709.

Singer, J. L., & Schonbar, R. A. (1961). Correlates of daydreaming: A dimension of self-awareness. *Journal of Consulting Psychology, 25,* 1–6.

Sitaram, N., Wyatt, R. J., Dawson, S., & Gillin, J. C. (1976). REM sleep induction by physostigmine infusion during sleep. *Science, 191,* 1281–1283.

Skinner, B. F. (1953). The operational analysis of psychological terms. In H. Feigl & M. Brodbeck (Eds.), *Readings in the philosophy of science.* New York: Appleton-Century-Crofts.

Skinner, B. F. (1957). *Verbal behavior.* New York: Appleton-Century-Crofts.

Skinner, J. C. (1970). The dream in psychoanalytic practice. In E. Hartmann (Ed.), *Sleep and dreaming.* Boston: Little, Brown.

Slap, J. W. (1977). On dreaming at sleep onset. *Psychoanalytic Quarterly, 46,* 71–81.

Sloan, M. A. (1972). The effects of deprivation of REM sleep on maze learning and aggression in albino rats. *Journal of Psychiatric Research, 9,* 101–111.

Smith, C., & Butler, S. (1982). Paradoxical sleep at selective times following training is necessary for learning. *Physiology and Behavior, 29,* 469–473.

Smith, C., & Young, J. (1980). Reversal of paradoxical sleep deprivation by amygdaloid stimulation during learning. *Physiology and Behavior, 24,* 1035–1039.

Snyder, F. (1960). *Dream recall, respiratory variability and depth of sleep.* Paper presented at the Round Table on Dream Research, Annual Meeting of the American Psychiatric Association, Atlantic City, NJ.

Snyder, F. (1963). The new biology of dreaming. *Archives of General Psychiatry, 8,* 381–391.

Snyder, F. (1965). Sleep and dreaming: Progress in the new biology of dreaming. *American Journal of Psychiatry, 122,* 377–391.

Snyder, F. (1966). Toward an evolutionary theory of dreaming. *American Journal of Psychiatry, 123,* 121–136.

Snyder, F. (1967). In quest of dreaming. In H. A. Witkin & H. B. Lewis (Eds.), *Experimental studies of dreaming.* New York: Random House.

Snyder, F. (1969). Sleep and REM as a biological enigma. In A. Kales (Ed.), *Sleep: Physiology and pathology, a symposium.* London: Lippincott.

Snyder, F., (1970). The phenomenology of dreaming. In H. Madow & L. H. Snow (Eds.), *The psychodynamic implications of the physiological studies on dreams* (pp. 124–151). Springfield, IL: Thomas.

Snyder, F. (1971). Psychophysiology of human sleep. *Clinical Neurosurgery, 18,* 503–536.

Snyder, F., Hobson, J., & Goldfrank. F. (1963). Blood pressure changes during human sleep. *Science, 142,* 1313–1314.

Snyder, F., Hobson, J., Morrison, D., & Goldfrank, F. (1964). Changes in respiration, heart rate, and systolic blood pressure in human sleep. *Journal of Applied Physiology, 19,* 417–422.

Snyder, F., Karacan, I., Thorp, U. R., & Scott, J. (1968). Phenomenology of REM dreaming. *Psychophysiology, 4,* 375. (Abstract)

Snyder, T., & Gackenbach, J. (1988). Individual differences associated with lucid dreaming. In J. Gackenbach and S. LaBerge (Eds.), *Conscious mind, sleeping brain: Perspectives on lucid dreaming.* New York, Plenum.

Solberg, L. (1984). Lassitude: A primary care evaluation. *Journal of the American Medical Association, 251*(24), 3272–3276.

Spence, D. P., & Holland, B. (1962). The restricting effects of awareness: A paradox and an explanation. *Journal of Abnormal and Social Psychology, 64*, 163–174.

Sperry, R. W. (1969). A modified concept of consciousness. *Psychological Review, 76*, 532–536.

Sperry, R. W. (1970). An objective approach to subjective experience: Further explanation of a hypothesis. *Psychological Review, 77*, 585–590.

Spevack, A. A., & Suboski, M. D. (1969). Retrograde effects of electroconvulsive shock on learned responses. *Psychological Bulletin, 72*, 66–76.

Spielman, A. J. (1973). *The effects of varying amounts of intracranial self-stimulation of the "normal" sleep cycle of the rat.* Paper presented at meeting of the Eastern Psychological Association, Philadelphia, PA.

Spielman, A. J. (1984). Sleep and arousal disorders. In *Guides to the evaluation of permanent impairment* (rev. ed., Appendix C, pp. 229–239). Chicago: American Medical Association.

Spielman, A. J. (1986). Assessment of insomnia. *Clinical Psychology Reviews, 6*, 11–25.

Spielman, A. J., Adler, J. A., Glovinsky, P. B., Pressman, M. R., Thorpy, M. J., Ellman, S. J., & Ackerman, K. D. (1986). Dynamics of REM sleep in narcolepsy. *Sleep, 9*(1), 175–182.

Spielman, A. J., Caruso, L., & Glorinsky, P. B. (1987b). A behavioral perspective on insomnia treatment. In: *Psychiatric Clinics of North America*, M. Ermin (Ed.) W. B. Saunders, 541–553.

Spielman, A. J., Davis, L., Marks, G., Halperin, R., Schwartz, D., Halperin, J., Steiner, S. S., & Ellman, S. J. (1974). The effects on sleep of intracranial self-stimulation delivered bilaterally to the locus coeruleus. *Sleep Research, 3*, 25.

Spielman, A. J., Ellman, S., & Steiner, S. S. (1973). The effects of varying amounts of electrical self-stimulation on the "normal" sleep cycle of the rat. *Sleep Research, 2.*

Spielman, A. J., Mattiace, L., Steiner, S. S., Ellman, S. J. (1973). The effects of varying amounts of intracranial self-stimulation of the "normal" sleep cycle of the rat. *Sleep Research, 2*, 38.

Spielman, A. J., Saskin, P., & Thorpy, M. J. (1983). Sleep restriction: A new treatment of insomnia. *Sleep Research, 12*, 285.

Spielman, A. J., Saskin, P., & Thorpy, M. J. (1987a). Treatment of chronic insomnia by restriction of time spent in bed. *Sleep, 10*(1), 45–56.

Spitz, R. A. (1964). The derailment of dialogue: Stimulus overload, action cycles, and the completion gradient. *Journal of the American Psychoanalytic Association, 12*, 752–775.

Stacher, G., Presslich, B., & Starker, H. (1955). Gastric acid secretion and sleep stages during natural night sleep. *Gastroenterology, 68*, 1449–1455.

Stanfield, C. (1961). Clinical experience with chlordiazepoxide (Librium). *Psychosomatics, 2*, 179–183.

Starker, S. (1973). Aspects of inner experience: Autokinesis, daydreaming, dream recall and cognitive style. *Perceptual and Motor Skills, 36*, 663–673.

Starker, S. (1974). Daydreaming styles and nocturnal dreaming. *Journal of Abnormal Psychology, 83,* 52–55.

Stegie, R. (1973). Zur Beziehung Zwischen Traumenhalt und während des Traümens ablaufenden Herz und atmungstätigkeit. Unpublished doctoral dissertation, University of Dusseldorf.

Steiner, S. S., Beer, B., & Schaffer, M. M. (1969). Escape from self produced rates of brain stimulation. *Science, 163,* 98–99.

Steiner, S. S., Bodnar, R. J., Ackerman, R. F., & Ellman, S. J. (1973). Escape from rewarding brain stimulation of dorsal brain stem and hypothalamus. *Physiology and Behavior, 11,* 589–591.

Steiner, S. S., & Ellman, S. J. (1972a). Relation between REM sleep and intracranial self-stimulation. *Science, 177,* 1122–1124.

Steiner, S. S., & Ellman, S. J. (1972). Relation between REM sleep and intracranial self stimulation. *Science, 177,* 1122–1124.

Stekel, W. (1943). *The interpretation of dreams — new developments and techniques.* Translated by E. Paul & C. Paul. New York: Liveright.

Stepanski, E., Lamphere, J., Badia, P., Zorick, F., & Roth, T. (1984). Sleep fragmentation and daytime sleepiness. *Sleep, 7,* 18–26.

Sterman, M. B., & Shouse, M. N. (1985). Sleep centers in the brain: The preoptic basal forebrain revisited. In D. J. McGinty (Ed.), *Brain mechanisms of sleep.* New York: Raven Press.

Stern, W. (1971a). Acquisition impairments following rapid eye movement sleep deprivation on rats. *Physiology and Behavior, 7,* 345–352.

Stern, W. (1971b). Effects of desynchronized sleep deprivation upon startle response habituation in the rat. *Psychonomic Science, 23,* 31–32.

Stern, W. C. (1969). Stress effects of REM sleep deprivation in rats: Adrenal gland hypertrophy. Paper presented at the meeting of the Association for the Psychophysiological Study of Sleep, Boston.

Stokes, J. P. (1973). The effects of rapid eye movement sleep on retention. *The Psychological Record, 23,* 521–532.

Storms, M. D., & Nisbett, R. F. (1970). Insomnia and the attribution process. *Journal of Personality and Social Psychology, 16,* 319–328.

Stoyva, J. (1961). *The effects of suggested dreams on the length of rapid eye movement periods.* Unpublished doctoral dissertation, University of Chicago.

Stoyva, J. (1965b). Posthypnotically suggested dreams and the sleep cycle. *Archives of General Psychiatry, 12,* 287–294.

Stoyva, J., & Kamiya, J. (1968). Electrophysiological studies of dreaming as the prototype of a new strategy in the study of consciousness. *Psychological Review, 75,* 192–205.

Stoyva, J. M. (1965a). Finger electromyographic activity during sleep: Its relation to dreaming in deaf and normal subjects. *Journal of Abnormal Psychology, 70,* 343–349.

Strauch, I. (1969). *Psychological aspects of dream recall.* Paper presented at a symposium on sleep and dreaming, 19th International Congress of Psychology, London.

Sullivan, C. E., Berthon–Jones, M., Issa, F. G., & Eves, L. (1981). Reversal of obstructive sleep apnea by continuous positive airway pressure applied through the nares. *Lancet, 1,* 862–866.

Swanson, E. J., & Foulkes, D. (1968). Dream content and the menstrual cycle. *Journal of Nervous & Mental Disease, 145,* 358–363.

Sweetwood, H. L., Kripke, D. F., Grant, I., Yager, J., & Gerst, M. S. (1976). Sleep disorder and psychobiological symptomatology in male psychiatric outpatients and male nonpatients. *Psychosomatics Medicine, 38,* 373–378.

Szabo, L., & Waitsuk, P. (1971). Contributions to the problem of nocturnal verbal automatisms. *Electroencephalography and Clinical Neurophysiology, 31,* 522. (Summary)

Takeo, S. (1970). Relationship among physiological indices during sleep and characteristics of dreams. *Psychiatria et Neurologia Japonica, 72,* 1–18.

Tani, K., Yoshii, N., Yoshino, I., & Kobayashi, E. (1966). Electroencephalographic study of parasomnia: Sleep-talking enuresis, and bruxism. *Physiology and Behavior, 1,* 241–243.

Tart, C. (1964). A comparison of suggested dreams occurring in hypnosis and sleep. *International Journal of Clinical & Experimental Hypnosis, 12,* 263–289.

Tart, C. (1974). Personal communication.

Tart, C., & Dick, L. (1970). Conscious control of dreaming: I. The posthypnotic dream. *Journal of Abnormal Psychology, 76,* 304–315.

Tart, C. T. (1962). Frequency of dream recall and some personality measures. *Journal of Consulting Psychology, 26,* 467–470.

Tart, C. T. (1964). A comparison of suggested dreams occurring in hypnosis and sleep. *International Journal of Clinical and Experimental Hypnosis, 12,* 263–289.

Tart, C. T. (1965). Toward the experimental control of dreaming: A review of the literature. *Psychological Bulletin, 64,* 81–91.

Tart, C. T. (1979). From spontaneous event to lucidity: A review of attempts to consciously control nocturnal dreaming. In B. Wolman (Ed.), *Handbook of dreams* (pp. 226–268). New York: Van Nostrand Reinhold.

Tatsuoka, M. M. (1971). *Multivariate analysis.* New York: Wiley.

Tauber, E., Roffwarg, H., & Herman, J. (1968). The effects of long-standing perceptual alterations on the hallucinatory content of dreams. *Psychophysiology, 5,* 219. (Abstract)

Tebbs, R. B. (1972). Post-awakening visualization performances as a function of anxiety level, REM or NREM sleep, and time of night. USAF Academy, Colorado. SRL-TR-72-0005. AD-738 630.

Terman, L. M. (1938). *Psychological factors in marital happiness.* New York: McGraw-Hill.

Thomas, J., & Benoit, O. (1967). Individualization of slow wave sleep and phasic activity. *Brain Research, 5,* 221–235.

Thorpy, M. J., Korman, E., Spielman, A. J., & Glovinsky, P. B. (1988). Delayed sleep phase syndrome in adolescents. *Journal of Adolescent Health Care, 9,* 22–27.

Timm, N. H. (1975). *Multivariate analysis.* Monterey, CA: Brooks/Cole.

Tizard, B. (1968). Habituation of EEG and skin potential changes in normal and severely subnormal children. *American Journal of Mental Deficiency, 73,* 34–40.

Toll, N. (1960). Librium as an adjunct to psychotherapy in private practice. *Diseases of the Nervous System, 21,* 264–266.

Tomkins, S. (1962). *Affect, imagery, consciousness* (Vols. I and II). New York: Springer.

Torda, C. (1969). Dreams of subjects with loss of memory for recent events. *Psychophysiology, 6,* 358–365.

Toutain, P., & Ruckebusch, Y. (1972). Secreations nasolabiales au cours du sommeil paradoxal chez les bovins. *Compte Rendu Academie Sciences* (Paris), *274,* 2519–2522.

Townsend, V. E., Johnson, L. C., Naitoh, P., & Muzet, A. F. (1975). Heart rate preceding motility in sleep. *Psychophysiology, 12,* 217–219.

Tracy, R. L., & Tracy, L. N. (1974). Reports of mental activity from sleep stages 2 and 3. *Perceptual and Motor Skills, 38,* 647–648.

Trenholme, I., Cartwright, R., & Gruenberg, G. (1984). Dream dimension during a life change. *Psychiatry Research, 12,* 35–45.

Trinder, J., & Kramer, M. (1971). Dream recall. *American Journal of Psychiatry, 128,* 296–301.

Trosman, H. (1963). Dream research and the psychoanalytic theory of dreams. *Archives of General Psychiatry, 9,* 9–18.

Trosman, H., Rechtschaffen, A., Offenkrantz, W., & Wolpert, E. (1960). Studies in the psychophysiology of dreams, IV. Relations among dreams in sequence. *Archives of General Psychiatry, 3,* 602–607.

Tufik, S. (1981). Changes of response to dopaminergic drugs in rats submitted to REM sleep deprivation. *Psychopharmacology, 72,* 257–260.

Tulving, E. Episodic and Semantic Memory. In E. Tulving & W. Donaldson (Eds.), *Organization of memory.* New York, Academic Press.

Tune, G. (1968). Sleep and wakefulness in 509 normal human adults. *British Medical Journal, 2,* 269.

Tyrer, P. J., & Lader, M. (1973). Effects of beta adrenergic blockade with sotalol in chronic anxiety. *Clinical Pharmacology and Therapeutics, 14,* 418–426.

Ullman, M. (1962). Dreaming, life-style and physiology. A comment on Adler's view of the dream. *Journal of Individual Psychology, 18,* 18–25.

Ullman, M., & Krippner, S. (1974). *Dream studies and telepathy: Experiments in nocturnal ESP.* New York: Penguin Books.

Umbarger, C. (1974). Problems in the psychology of dreaming: A review of the work of Richard Jones. In L. Goldberger & V. H. Rosen (Eds.), *Psychoanalysis and contemporary science* (Vol. 3). New York: International Universities Press.

Valdini, A. F. (1985). Fatigue of unknown aetiology—A review. *Family Practice, 2*(1), 48–53.

Van de Castle, R. L. (1967). *Some problems in applying the methodology of content analysis to dreams.* Paper presented at the Symposium on Dream Psychology and the New Biology of Dreaming, Cincinnati, OH.

Van de Castle, R. L. (1971). *The psychology of dreaming.* New York: General Learning Corp.

Van de Castle, R. L., & Holloway, J. (1970). Dreams of depressed patients, non-depressed patients, and normals. *Psychophysiology, 7,* 326. (Abstract)

van Hulzen, Z. J. M., & Coenen, A. M. L. (1981). Paradoxical sleep deprivation and locomotor activity in rats. *Physiology and Behavior, 27,* 741–744.

van Hulzen, Z. J. M., & Coenen, A. M. L. (1982). Effects of paradoxical sleep deprivation on two-way avoidance acquisition. *Physiology and Behavior, 29,* 581–587.

Van Luijtelaar, E. L. J. M., & Coenen, A. M. L. (1986). Electrophysiological evaluation of three paradoxical sleep deprivation techniques in rats. *Physiology and Behavior, 36,* 603–609.

Van Luijtelaar, E. L. J. M., Kaiser, J., & Coenen, A. M. L., (1982). Deprivation of paradoxical sleep and intracranial self-stimulation in rats. *Sleep, 5,* 284–289.

Van Ormer, E. B. (1932). Retention after intervals of sleep and waking. *Archives of Psychology, 137,* 49.

Van Ormer, E. B. (1933). Sleep and retention. *Psychological Bulletin, 30,* 413–439.

Verdone, P. (1963). *Variables related to the temporal reference of manifest dream content.* Unpublished doctoral dissertation, University of Chicago.

Verdone, P. (1965). Temporal reference of manifest dream content. *Perceptual & Motor Skills, 20,* 1253–1268.

Verdone, P. (1968). Sleep satiation: Extended sleep in normal subjects. *Electroencephalography and Clinical Neurophysiology, 24,* 417–423.

Vermeulen, A. (1976). The hormonal activity of the post-menopausal ovary. *Journal of Clinical Endocrinology and Metabolism, 42,* 247.

Vimont-Vicary, P., Jouvet, D., & Delorme, F. (1966). Effets EEG et comportementaux des privations du sommeil paradoxal chez le chat. *Electroencephalography and Clinical Neurophysiology, 20,* 439–449.

Viscott, D. S. (1968). Chlordiazepoxide and hallucinations. *Archives of General Psychiatry, 19,* 370–376.

Vogel, G. (1973). Review of Wyatt, R., Termini, B. A., & Davis, J. Biochemical and sleep studies of schizophrenia: A review of the literature, 1960–1970. Part II. Sleep studies. *Sleep Research, 2,* 378–379.

Vogel, G. (1978). An alternative view of the neurobiology of dreaming. *American Journal of Psychiatry, 135,* 1531–1535.

Vogel, G. (1979). A motivational theory of REM sleep. In R. Drucker-Colin, M. Shkurovich, & M. B. Sterman (Eds.), *The functions of sleep* (pp. 233–250). New York: Academic Press.

Vogel, G., Barrowclough, B., & Giesler, D. (1972). Limited discriminability of REM and sleep onset reports and its psychiatric implications. *Archives of General Psychiatry, 26,* 449–455.

Vogel, G., Foulkes, D., & Trosman, H. (1966). Ego functions and dreaming during sleep onset. *Archives of General Psychiatry, 14,* 238–248.

Vogel, G. W. (1968). REM deprivation: III. Dreaming and psychosis. *Archives of General Psychiatry, 18,* 312–329.

Vogel, G. W. (1975). A review of REM sleep deprivation. *Archives of General Psychiatry, 32,* 749–761.

Vogel, G. W. (1978). An alternative view of the neurobiology of dreaming. *American Journal of Psychiatry, 135,* 12, 1531–1535.

Vogel, G. W. (1978). Sleep-onset mentation. In A. M. Arkin, J. S. Antrobus, & S. J. Ellman (Eds.), *The mind in sleep: Psychology and psychophysiology* (pp. 97–108). Hillsdale, NJ: Lawrence Erlbaum Associates.

Vogel, G. W. (1979). REM sleep and the prevention of endogenous depression. *Waking & Sleep, 3,* 313–318.

Vogel, G. W. (1983). Evidence for REM sleep deprivation as the mechanism of action of antidepressant drugs. *Progress in Neuro-Psychopharmacology & Biological Psychiatry, 7,* 343–349.

Vogel, G. W., Giesler, D. D., & Barrowclough, B. (1970). *Exercise as a substitute for REM sleep.* Paper presented at the meeting of the Association for the Psychophysiological Study of Sleep, Santa Fe, NM. *Psychophysiology, 7,* 300–301. (Abstract)

Vogel, G. W., McAbee, R., Barker, R., (1975). Endogenous depression improvement and REM pressure. *Archives of General Psychiatry, 32,* 765–777.

Vogel, G. W., Thurmond, A., Gibbons, P., Sloan, K., Boyd, M., & Walker, M. (1975). REM sleep reduction effects on depression syndromes. *Archives of General Psychiatry, 32,* 765–777.

Vogel, G. W., & Traub, A. C. (1968a). Further studies on REM deprivation of depressed patients. *Psychophysiology, 5,* 239. (Abstract)

Vogel, G. W., & Traub, A. C. (1968b). REM deprivation of depressives. *Psychophysiology, 4,* 382. (Abstract)

Vogel, G. W., & Traub, A. C. (1968c). REM deprivation: I. The effect on schizophrenic patients. *Archives of General Psychiatry, 18,* 287–300.

Vogel, G. W., Traub, A. C., Ben-Horin, P., & Meyers, G. (1968). REM deprivation: II. The effect on depressed patients. *Archives of General Psychiatry, 18,* 301–311.

Vogel, G. W., Vogel, F., McAbee, R., Robert, S., & Thurmond, A. J. (1980). Improvement of depression by REM sleep deprivations: New findings and a theory. *Archives of General Psychiatry, 37,* 247–253.

Vogel, G. W., Vogel, F., McAbee, R. S., & Thurmond, A. J. (1980). Improvement of depression by REM sleep deprivation: New findings and a theory. *Archives of General Psychiatry, 37,* 247–253.

Volkan, V. (1962). Sleep (a bibliographical study). *British Journal of Medical Psychology, 35,* 235–244.

Vosberg, H., Wagner, H., & Boeckel, L. (1976). Age dependent changes of hypophysis thyroid regulation. *Aktuel Gerontology, 6,* 279.

Wachtel, P. L. (1977). *Psychoanalysis and behavior therapy: Toward an integration.* New York: Basic Books.

Waelder, R. (1936). The principle of multiple function. *Psychoanalytic Quarterly, 5,* 45–62.

Waldhorn, H. F. (1967). The place of the dream in psychoanalysis. In E. D. Joseph (Ed.), *Monograph Series of the Kris Study Group of the New York Psychoanalytic Institute.* Monograph 2. New York: International Universities Press.

Walker, E. L., & Tarte, R. D. (1963). Memory storage as a function of arousal and time with homogeneous and heterogeneous lists. *Journal of Verbal Learning and Verbal Behavior, 2,* 113–119.

Walker, J. M., & Berger, R. J. (1980). Sleep as an adaptation for energy conservation functionally and physiologically related to hibernation and shallow torpor. *Progress in Brain Research, 53,* 255–278.

Walker, J. M. Glotzbach, S. F., Berger, R. J., & Heller, H. C. (1977). Sleep and hibernation in ground squirrels (citellus spp.): Electrophysiological observations. *American Journal of Physiology, 223,* R213–R221.

Walker, P. C., & Johnson, R. F. Q. (1974). The influence of pre-sleep suggestions on dream content: Evidence and methodological problems. *Psychological Bulletin, 81,* 362–370.

Wallach, H., & Karsh, E. B. (1963). Why the modification of stereoscopic depth perception is so rapid. *American Journal of Psychology, 76,* 413–420.

Wallach, M. A., & Kogan, N. (1965). *Modes of thinking in young children.* New York: Holt, Rinehart & Winston.

Wasserman, M. (1984). Psychoanalytic dream theory and recent neurobiological findings about REM sleep. *Journal of the American Psychoanalytic Association, 32,* 831–846.

Watson, J. B. (1924). *Behaviorism.* New York: People's Institute.

Watson, R. K. (1972). *Mental correlates of periorbital potentials during REM sleep.* Unpublished doctoral dissertation, University of Chicago.

Waugh, N. C., & Norman, D. A. (1965). Primary memory. *Psychological Review, 72,* 89–104.

Webb, W., & Agnew, H. (1965). Effects of a restricted regime. *Science, 150,* 1745–1747.

Webb, W. B. (1969). Partial and differential sleep deprivation. In A. Kales (Ed.), *Sleep: Physiology and pathology.* Philadelphia: Lippincott.

Webb, W. B. (1975). *Sleep: The gentle tyrant.* Englewood Cliffs, NJ: Prentice–Hall.

Webb, W. B. (1979). Theories of sleep functions and some clinical implications. In R. Drucker–Colin, M. Shkurovich, & M. B. Sterman (Eds.), *The functions of sleep.* New York: Academic Press.

Webb, W. B., & Agnew, H. N., Jr. (1979). Sleep onset facilitation by tones. *Sleep, 1*(3), 281–286.

Webb, W. B., & Friel, J. (1971). Sleep stage and personality characteristics of "natural" long and short sleepers. *Science, 171,* 587–588.

Webb, W. B., & Kersey, J. (1967). Recall of dreams and the probability of stage 1—REM sleep. *Perceptual and Motor Skills, 24,* 627–630.

Wehr, T., Wirz–Justice, A., Goodwin, F. K., Duncan, W., & Gillin, J. C. (1979). Phase advance of the circadian sleep–wake cycle as an antidepressant. *Science, 206,* 710–711.

Weinstein, L., Schwartz, D., & Ellman, S. (1988). The development of scales to measure the experience of self-participation in sleep. *Sleep, 11,* 437–447.

Weiss, L. (1967). *Experimenter bias as a function of stimulus ambiguity.* Unpublished manuscript, State University of New York at Buffalo.

Weisz, R. (1972). Phenomenological correlates of discrete events in NREM sleep: The K-complex as a NREM phasic indicator. *Psychophysiology, 9,* 127. (Abstract)

Weisz, R. (1975). Review of Kramer, M., & Roth, T., A comparison of dream content in laboratory dream reports of schizophrenic and depressive patient groups. *Sleep Research, 4,* 371.

Weisz, R., & Foulkes, D. (1970). Home and laboratory dreams collected under uniform sampling conditions. *Psychophysiology, 6,* 588–597.

Weitzman, E. D., Czeisler, C. A., & Coleman, R. A. (1981). Delayed sleep phase syndrome: A chronobiologic disorder with sleep onset insomnia. *Archives of General Psychiatry, 38,* 737–748.

Weitzman, E. D., Moline, M. L., Czeisler, C. A., & Zimmerman, J. C. (1982). Chronobiology of aging: Temperature, sleep-wake rhythms and entrainment. *Neurobiology of Aging, 3,* 299–309.

Weizman, E. D. (1981). Sleep and its disorders. *Annual Review of Neuroscience, 4,* 381–417.

Wessler, R. (1968). Experimenter expectancy effects in psychomotor performance. *Perceptual and Motor Skills, 26,* 911–917.

West, L. T., Janszen, H. H., Lester, B. K., & Cornelison, F. S., Jr. (1962). The psychosis of sleep deprivation. *Annals of the New York Academy of Sciences, 96* 66–70.

Westphal, C. (1877). Eigenthumlick mit einschlafen verbundene anfalle. *Archives Psychiatr Nervenkr, 7,* 631–635.

Whitman, R. (1974). A decade of dreams: A review. *International Journal of Psychoanalytic Psychotherapy, 3,* 217–245.

Whitman, R., Kramer, M., & Baldridge, B. J. (1963). Which dream does the patient tell? *Archives of General Psychiatry, 8,* 277–282.

Whitman, R., Kramer, M., Ornstein, P., & Baldridge, B. (1970). The varying use of the dream in clinical psychiatry. In L. Madow & L. Snow (Eds.), *The psychodynamic implications of physiological studies on dreams* (pp. 24–46). Springfield, IL: Thomas.

Whitman, R. M. (1963). Remembering and forgetting dreams in psychoanalysis. *Journal of the American Psychoanalytic Association, 7,* 752–774.

Whitman, R. M., Pierce, C. M., & Maas, J. W. (1960). Drugs and dreams. In L. Uhr & J. G. Miller (Eds.), *Drugs and behavior,* New York: Wiley.

Whitman, R. M., Pierce, C. M., Maas, J. W., & Baldridge, B. (1961). Drugs and dreams II: Imipramine and prochlorperazine. *Comprehensive Psychiatry, 2,* 219–226.

Whitman, R., Pierce, C., Maas, J., & Baldridge, B. (1962). The dreams of the experimental subject. *Journal of Nervous and Mental Disease, 134,* 431–439.

Williams, H. L. (1973). *Information processing during sleep.* In W. P. Koella & P. Levin (Eds.), *Sleep: Physiology, biochemistry, psychology, pharmacology, clinical implications.* First European Congress on Sleep Research, Basel, 1972. Basel: Karger.

Williams, H. L., Hammack, J. T., Daly, R. L., Dement, W. C., & Lubin, A. (1964). Responses to auditory stimulation, sleep loss and the EEG stages of sleep. *Electroencephalography and Clinical Neurophysiology, 16,* 269–279.

Williams, H. L., Holloway, F. A., and Griffiths, W. J. (1973). Physiological psychology & sleep. *Annual Review of Psychology, 24*, 279–316.

Williams, H. L., Morlock, H. C., Jr., & Morlock, J. V. (1966). Instrumental behavior during sleep. *Psychophysiology, 2*, 208–216.

Williams, R. L., Karacan, I., & Hursch, C. J. (1974). *Electroencephalography (EEG) of human sleep: Clinical applications*. New York: Wiley.

Wilson, W. P., & Zung, W. W. K. (1966). Attention, discrimination, and arousal during sleep. *Archives of General Psychiatry, 15*, 523–528.

Winer, B. S. (1971). *Statistical principles in experimental design*. New York: McGraw-Hill.

Winget, C., & Kapp, F. T. (1972). The relationship of the manifest content of dreams to duration of childbirth in primiparae. *Psychosomatic Medicine, 34*, 313–320.

Winget, C., & Kramer, M. (1974). *Dimensions of dreams*. Gainesville: University of Florida Press.

Winget, C., Kramer, M., & Whitman, R. M. (1972). Dreams and demography. *Canadian Psychiatric Association Journal, 17* (Special Supplement 2), 203–208.

Winick, C. & Holt (1962). Differential recall of the dream and function of audience perception. *Psychoanalysis, 49*, 53–62.

Winograd, C. H., & Jarvik, L. F. (1986). Physician management of the demented patient. *Journal of the American Geriatrics Society, 34*, 295–308.

Witkin, H. A. (1969a). Influencing dream content. In M. Kramer, R. M. Whitman, B. J. Baldridge, & P. H. Ornstein (Eds.), *Dream psychology and the new biology of dreaming*. Springfield, IL: Thomas.

Witkin, H. A. (1969b). Presleep experiences and dreams. In J. Fisher and L. Berger (Eds.), *The meaning of dreams: Recent insights from the laboratory*. California Mental Health Research, *3*, 1–37.

Witkin, H. A. (1970). Individual differences in dreaming. In E. Hartmann (Ed.), *Sleep and dreaming*. Boston: Little, Brown.

Witkin, H. A., Dyk, R. B., Paterson, H. F., Goodenough, D. R., & Karp, S. A. (1962). *Psychological differentiation*. New York: Wiley.

Witkin, H. A., & Lewis, H. (1965). The relation of experimentally induced presleep experiences to dreams: A report on method and preliminary findings. *Journal of the American Psychoanalytic Association, 13*, 819–849.

Witkin, H. A., & Lewis, H. B. (1967). Presleep experiences and dreams. In H. A. Witkin & H. B. Lewis (Eds.), *Experimental studies of dreaming*. New York: Random House.

Witkin, H. A., Lewis, H. B., Hertzman, M., Machover, K., Meisser, P. B., & Wapner, S. (1954). *Personality through perception*. New York: Harper & Row.

Wolff, P. (1966). The causes, controls, and organization of behavior in the neonate. *Psychological Issues Monograph, 5*, 1–104.

Wolin, S. J., & Mello, N. K. (1973). The effects of alcohol on dreams and hallucinations in alcohol addicts. *Annals of the New York Academy of Science, 215*, 266–302.

Wolpert, E. (1960). Studies in psychophysiology of dreams. II. An electromyographic study of dreaming. *Archives of General Psychiatry, 2*, 231–241.

Wolpert, E. A. (1972). Two classes of factors affecting dream recall. *Journal of the American Psychoanalytic Association, 20,* 45–58.

Wolpert, E. A., & Trosman, H. (1958). Studies in psychophysiology of dreams. I: Experimental evocation of sequential dream episodes. *American Association Archives of Neurology and Psychiatry, 79,* 603–606.

Wood, P. (1962). *Dreaming and social isolation.* Unpublished doctoral dissertation. University of North Carolina. Ann Arbor, MI: University Microfilms #6-3571.

Wyatt, R. J., Fram, D. H., Buchbinder, R., & Snyder, F. (1971). Treatment of intractable narcolepsy with a monoamine oxidase inhibitor. *New England Journal of Medicine, 285,* 987–991.

Wyatt, R. J., Fram, D. H., Kupfer, D. J., & Snyder, F. (1971). Total prolonged drug-induced REM sleep suppression in anxious depressed patients. *Archives of General Psychiatry, 24,* 145–155.

Wyatt, R. J., Gillin, J. C., Green, R., Horowitz, D., & Snyder, F. (1972). Measurement of phasic integrated potentials (PIP) during treatment with parachlorophenylalalanine (PCPA). *Psychophysiology, 9,* 127. (Abstract)

Wyatt, R., Termini, B. A., & Davis, J. (1971). Biochemical and sleep studies of schizophrenia: A review of the literature 1960–1970. Part II: Sleep studies. *Schizophrenia Bulletin, 4,* 45–66.

Yaroush, R., Sullivan, M. J., & Ekstrand, B. R. (1971). Effect of sleep on memory. II: Differential effect of the first and second half of the night. *Journal of Experimental Psychology, 88,* 361–366.

Yoss, R., Moyer, N., & Ogle, K. (1969). The pupillogram and narcolepsy: A method to measure decreased levels of wakefulness. *Neurology, 19,* 921–928.

Zarcone, B., Gulevich, G., Pivik, T., Azumi, K., & Dement, W. (1969). REM deprivation and schizophrenia. *Biological Psychiatry, 1,* 179–184.

Zarcone, V., Azumi, D., de la Peña, A., Cartwright, R., & Dement, W. (1969). Individual differences in response to REM deprivation. *Psychophysiology, 6,* 239. (Abstract)

Zarcone, V., Azumi, K., Dement, W., Gulevich, G., Kramer, H., & Pivik, T. (1975). REM phase deprivation and schizophrenia II. *Archives of General Psychiatry, 32,* 1431–1436.

Zarcone, V., De La Pena, A., & Dement, W. C. (1974). Heightened sexual interest and sleep disturbance. *Perceptual & Motor Skills, 39,* 1135–1141.

Zarcone, V., de la Peña, A., Kopell, B., & Dement, W. (1970). *Visual evoked responses following REM deprivation.* Paper presented at the meeting of the Association for the Psychophysiological Study of Sleep, Santa Fe, NM. *Psychophysiology, 7,* 301. (Abstract)

Zarcone, V., Gulevich, G., & Pivik, T. (1968). Partial REM sleep deprivation and schizophrenia. *Archives of General Psychiatry, 18,* 194–202.

Zarcone, V., Gulevich, G., & Pivik, T. (1969). REM deprivation and schizophrenia. *Biological Psychiatry, 1,* 179–184.

Zarcone, V., Gulevich, G., Pivik, T., Azumi, K., & Dement, W. (1969). REM deprivation and schizophrenia. *Biological Psychiatry, 1,* 179–184.

Zarcone, V., Gulevich, G., Pivik, T., & Dement, W. (1968). Partial REM phase deprivation and schizophrenia. *Archives of General Psychiatry, 18,* 194–202.

Zarcone, V., Zukowsky, E., Gulevich, G., Dement, W., & Hodes, E. (1974). Rorschach responses subsequent to REM deprivation in schizophrenic and non-schizophrenic patients. *Journal of Clinical Psychology, 30,* 248–250.

Zepelin, H. (1972). An investigation of age differences in men's dreams. *Sleep Research, 1,* 128.

Zetzel, E. R. (1970). Is the domain of the psychological still floating? In E. Hartmann (Ed.), *Sleep and dreaming.* Boston: Little, Brown.

Zimmerman, J., Stoyva, J., & Metcalf, D., (1970). Distorted visual feedback and augmented REM sleep. *Psychophysiology, 7,* 298.

Zimmerman, W. B. (1967). *Psychological and physiological differences between "light" and "deep" sleepers.* Unpublished doctoral dissertation. University of Chicago.

Zimmerman, W. B. (1970). Sleep mentation and auditory awakening thresholds. *Psychophysiology, 6,* 540–549.

Author Index

565

Subject Index

ECONOMIC
DEVELOPMENT
of the
NORTH ATLANTIC COMMUNITY
Historical Introduction
to Modern Economics

DUDLEY DILLARD
Professor of Economics
University of Maryland

PRENTICE-HALL, INC., ENGLEWOOD CLIFFS, NEW JERSEY

Printed in the United States of America

Library of Congress Catalog Card No. 67-15169

Current Printing (last digit):
10 9 8 7 6 5 4

PRENTICE-HALL INTERNATIONAL, INC., *London*
PRENTICE-HALL OF AUSTRALIA, PTY. LTD., *Sydney*
PRENTICE-HALL OF CANADA, LTD., *Toronto*
PRENTICE-HALL OF INDIA (PRIVATE), LTD., *New Delhi*
PRENTICE-HALL OF JAPAN, INC., *Tokyo*

To Amber and Lorraine

Preface

This book traces the development of the North Atlantic economy from its medieval origins to the present. It covers most of the topics usually treated in conventional economic histories of Europe, on the one hand, and the United States, on the other hand. In two important respects, however, it differs from traditional books in economic history. First, the European and American economies in their evolution are viewed as two closely related phases of a common development. Second, economic analysis is used more extensively than in conventional books on economic history.

Over several centuries the transatlantic mobility of people, technology, capital, and ideas has resulted in so many common institutions that Europe and America have the same general economic system. Among the many institutions which Europe and America have in common are forms of business organization, labor unions, banking practices, and property rights. Clearer insight into these institutional arrangements and into the economic system as a whole is gained by studying the European and American varieties in close association rather than in isolation. Separate economic histories of Europe and the United States will be more fruitful after an introductory study of the type presented in this book.

Some basic concepts of economic analysis have been introduced to facilitate the exposition and to give broader insight into the organization and functioning of the economic system. Prior knowledge of economic theory is not assumed, but a little theory goes a long way. The concept of opportunity cost is introduced to explain the flight of serfs from the manor, and it is used again to explain the high wages of free labor in manufacturing in colonial New England. The classical theory of distribution relating wages, profits, and rent is introduced in order to show the significance of free trade for the continuing industrial leadership of England during the nineteenth century.

The most frequently used theory, however, is modern macroeconomics. In particular, the macroeconomic theory associated with the English economist, John Maynard Keynes, has been employed to explain the behavior of the economic system as a whole. Keynesian concepts of investment, saving, consumption, and aggregate income are central in the present study. The accumulation of capital (investment) under business enterprise has been a dynamic and unstable factor which goes a long way toward explaining the characteristic instability of capitalism. Moreover, the policies associated with Keynes' theories have undoubtedly played a major role in rescuing capitalism from the collapse it suffered during the Great Depression of the 1930's. Atlantic capitalism now

appears to be evolving into a Keynesian-type mixed economy of private and public enterprise, quite different from both classical capitalism and classical socialism. Thus, the student should take away from this book an understanding of some of the basic concepts of economic theory as well as a knowledge of economic development in the Atlantic community.

A "new economic history" has arisen in the United States since World War II. Its special characteristics are the application of economic theory to the study of economic history, and an emphasis on the quantitative testing of hypotheses. New vitality has been infused into historical studies in economics. A number of excellent monographs on particular sectors of the economy have been issued. The work published to date has not stressed general economic theory of a type necessary for a broad synthesis of long-term change in an economic system as a whole, which I believe to be the special contribution which economic history as a separate discipline can make. Understandably, monographic studies must precede a general synthesis, and perhaps we can look forward to this in the future from the "new economic history."

As in any lively and progressive field of scholarship, controversy abounds in economic history. Where appropriate, differences of opinion among scholars have been introduced into the text, but one cannot burden a book of this type with a full rehearsal of all shades of opinion from the most recent journal articles. Bibliographies at the end of chapters contain selections from all sides of disputed issues in scholarship.

The Columbia University Press has kindly granted permission for the use of excerpts from my chapter on "Later Capitalist Theory and Practice" in *Chapters in Western Civilization* (Columbia University Press, 1962). I also thank the Encyclopaedia Britannica, Inc., for permission to use some passages from my article on "Capitalism" in the 1963 and later editions of the *Britannica*.

My interest in economic history was first stimulated by Professor M. M. Knight of the University of California. To Professor Knight I owe the conception of the North Atlantic economy as the appropriate unit for an introductory study of economic history in the West. Special acknowledgment is due Professor E. A. J. Johnson, who read the entire manuscript and made innumerable suggestions for improvements in both substance and style. Professor William N. Parker has also read the manuscript and offered constructive criticisms which have led to marked improvements. My friend Harold R. W. Benjamin has given generously of his time and editorial acuity to improve a number of chapters. I am grateful to my colleague Professor Norton T. Dodge for expert advice on Chapter 33, Russian Economic Development, a subject outside the main orbit of the story but which is so important in the contemporary world that it could not be omitted. Professors W. Paul Strassmann and John P. Henderson of Michigan State University and F. Russell Root of the University of Pennsylvania made helpful comments on parts of earlier drafts of the manuscript.

To my wife, Louisa, I am indebted more than to any other person for substantive suggestions, editorial assistance, and encouragement throughout the period of preparation of the book. She, like the others mentioned above, is responsible for making it a better book, but any shortcomings which remain are my sole responsibility.

DUDLEY DILLARD

Contents

Roots of the Atlantic Economy

PART I

The Dynamics of Capitalism

CHAPTER 1

In 1453 the Turks captured Constantinople. In 1485 the War of the
Roses ended as the last of the Plantagenets fell at Bosworth Field and
Henry Tudor became King of England. In 1492 Columbus landed on
San Salvador in the West Indies. In 1494, in Venice, Lucas Pacioli published a
treatise on double-entry bookkeeping. In 1498 Vasco da Gama reached India.
In 1517 Martin Luther nailed his 95 theses on the church door at Wittenberg.
These are a few events among hundreds that could be selected at random to
mark the beginnings of what is called modern times.

These modern times have now lasted for five centuries. The Europeans
left the Turks in Constantinople and turned out to sea. They brought back
silver from Peru and Mexico, silk and spices from India, and new ideas from
everywhere. At the same time the century of clashing religious views precipitated by Luther and his opponents gave a depth and extent to the new notions
of worldly gain that rode into the European harbors with the ships from
America and India. The western Europeans were off on a new road.

That road, for reasons closely connected with the explorers and the religious reformers, led the Europeans and their colonies to dominate the world
for five hundred years. They did it with the sword in one hand and the cross
in the other, but their greatest instrument of domination was a new economic
system.

This new system has been called capitalism, for want of a better name.
It is a system in which the private owners of the non-personal means of production employ free laborers who cannot employ themselves. The private
owners can do this because they have surplus wealth in the form of money
capital. The free laborers cannot effectively use their productive capacities
because they lack money capital. The people who hold surplus wealth in the
form of money capital are called capitalists.

For half a millennium the West prospered and expanded as capitalism
provided the economic and technological basis for continued superiority. In
the long sweep of history, however, the domination of the West should be
viewed as an abnormal and temporary condition of world history. In the twentieth century the West has been challenged by societies with economic systems
very different from capitalism. The Soviet Union, with an economic system

3

based on collective rather than private ownership of the means of production, has demonstrated its capacity to increase the production of wealth at a high and sustained rate. It has outstripped all the nations of western Europe in the production of steel, planes, and missiles, and speaks with a loud voice in international relations. Today it stands second only to Europe's leading "colony," the United States, as a great industrial nation.

In addition to the external challenge, there are internal changes taking place in capitalism. It is pre-eminently a system in which the decisions that guide economic life are made by businessmen operating their privately owned enterprises for profit. Increasingly, however, the decisions which guide the Western economies are made or are influenced by government officials operating in the public sector rather than by businessmen in the private sector.

Enlargement of the public sector relative to the private sector makes the system less "capitalistic" and gives rise to what may be called a mixed economy of private and public enterprise. As the problems of modern life become increasingly complex, a wider range of decisions are shifted to the public sector because private enterprise is less suited to making them. For example, large investments in pure science and formal education involve costs and benefits that are spread widely over the whole of society. Although the social benefits from these large investments clearly exceed the social costs, they may not justify heavy private expenditures. Competition with the Soviet Union, especially after the launching of the first *Sputnik,* has put pressure on the United States to allocate more resources to the public sector for the education of scientists and engineers.

Whereas the public sector in capitalist economies is growing relative to the private sector, in collectivist (communist) economies the private sector is growing relative to the public sector as the output of consumer goods and services becomes increasingly important. Many signs point toward wider use by communist countries of a market allocation of resources within a framework of national economic planning. Meanwhile, capitalist economies are using general economic planning within the framework of a market economy. With the two systems moving toward each other in broad institutional composition, it is a reasonable inference that insofar as economic forces are important, the conflicts now threatening the existence of the human race will lessen in time. An equilibrium may be reached within the respective systems and between the two systems before the world is destroyed.

APPROACH TO THE PROBLEM

Economics is a study of the employment and allocation of scarce resources. In a well-organized or rational economy, resources are fully employed and efficiently allocated. Because resources are scarce in relation to more or less unlimited wants, choices must be made. These choices are presumably made by comparing the benefits and costs of given resources in alternative uses. What has been called *the* economic principle may be stated as the allocation of scarce resources among alternative uses in such a way as to yield maximum benefit to the economy as a whole. Economizing means satisfying maximum

wants with given resources, or minimizing the resources used (costs) to satisfy given wants.

The allocation and employment of resources take place within a framework of social arrangements or institutions which vary widely from one society to another and which change through time in a given society. Economic development is that branch of economics concerned with cumulative changes in the arrangements or institutions by which social groups earn their livelihood. Development implies progress in the sense that more can be produced with given resources at a later date than at an earlier date. If over a long period an economy were stagnating or retrogressing, development would be an inappropriate term to apply to it. In such circumstances the society would have an economic history but no economic development. Capitalism in the West, however, has been progressive in the sense of yielding long-term increases in per capita output, and therefore its economic history has also been one of development.

We shall attempt in this study to trace the development of modern capitalism from its origins to the present day. Its roots reach back into European feudalism, the decline of which was well under way when Columbus discovered America. Capitalism has changed greatly since it replaced the feudal system in western Europe by the sixteenth century.

In place of the highly controlled economy of medieval Europe, capitalism brought the free market. Adam Smith's *Wealth of Nations* (1776) contains the classic statement of the principles of the free-market system in which decisions made in the self-interest of business enterprises presumably coincide with the public welfare of society at large. A form of free enterprise approximating Smith's principles flourished during the nineteenth century, especially in England and the United States. Evidence of the subsequent retreat from the free market is found in the enlargement of the public sector and the increasing participation of governments in economic decision making.

This tendency for governments to play an increasing role in economic life is perhaps the dominant trend in twentieth-century economic development in all types of economic systems. In socialistic and communistic states the positive role of government is an accepted principle of economic organization. In capitalistic countries such as the United States, the increasing participation of government in economic affairs is viewed as a concession to necessity imposed by emergencies, which significantly have followed one another in continuous succession since 1914. Wars and depressions have been the clearest manifestations of acute crises which have induced governmental intervention, but there is little reason to believe that their absence would reverse the trend toward enlargement of the public sector. One basic reason for enlarging the public sector is to prevent depressions through governmental planning.

More compelling than wars and depressions in the long run are modern science and associated economic technology in the form of mass production, automation, and rapid transportation and communication. Possibly the potential abundance of mass production cannot be channeled successfully through free markets in which profitable prices depend upon the relative scarcity of goods. Commercial crises arising from overproduction did not begin with modern capitalism in the sixteenth century but with the Industrial Revolution at the beginning of the nineteenth century. Depressions may be the conse-

quence of scientific and technological changes which are capable of generating abundance but are frustrated by the malfunctioning of the market system and the distribution of income in the private sector.

Economic factors occupy a fundamental place in the crisis of the twentieth century, a crisis without parallel since the breakup of the feudal system in western Europe five hundred years ago. At the same time it is well to remember that noneconomic forces also help to account for the wars, revolutions, counterrevolutions, terror, and torture which have plagued the twentieth century. Economic factors, though important, are not all-important in determining the affairs of men.

CAPITALISM AND GENERAL ECONOMIC HISTORY

The development of modern capitalism is only one aspect of general economic history. Studies by cultural anthropologists throw considerable light on the economic characteristics of noncapitalistic economies and are useful in placing modern economic evolution in perspective. Anthropology is distinguished from other social sciences in that it involves inquiry into cultures other than our own and projects our own more clearly by indicating similarities and contrasts with other cultures.

One of the impressive findings of anthropological studies is the great diversity of cultures. The special arrangements whereby the life of any society is organized are infinitely varied. Obviously every society must have some kind of economic system of production and distribution, but the particular institutions and their relative importance in relation to the total cultural pattern differ greatly from society to society. This should guard us against designating any particular arrangement or institution as conforming to the requisites of "human nature." For example, findings of social anthropologists seem to lend no support to the notion that the "profit motive," so important in a business enterprise economy, conforms to the requisites of human nature. An outstanding anthropologist concludes that "A characteristic feature of primitive economics is the absence of any desire to make profits from either production or exchange." [1] Another authority says, "Gain, such as is often the stimulus for work in more civilized communities, never acts as an impulse to work under the original native conditions." [2] There is little evidence that human beings are "naturally greedy," "naturally competitive," "naturally lazy," or that there is any "natural propensity to truck, barter and exchange." Strong motivation for individual gain is one of the special characteristics of capitalistic culture and has little to do with "human nature" as such.

Human institutions are, of course, related to the biological nature of human beings. They represent established practices associated with birth, infancy, puberty, marriage, family, death, and burial, but the specific responses to these universal human events are subject to great variation. So malleable

[1] Richard Thurnwald, *Economics in Primitive Communities* (London: Oxford University Press, 1932), p. xiii.
[2] B. Malinowski, *Argonauts of the Western Pacific* (New York: E. P. Dutton and Co., 1932), p. 156.

is the human clay and the human spirit that the most complete knowledge of man's biological nature does not enable one to predict characteristics of a human society. Ruth Benedict, a well-known anthropologist, mentions two traits that are universal among known cultures, namely, animism and exogamous restrictions on marriage. Animism is the basis for spiritual experience and religious institutions. Restrictions on marriage among members of the immediate family appear to be based on the necessity for preserving the integrity of family life.

The activities of human beings are generally directed toward self-expression in relation to their fellow men, but the directions in which activity and self-expression are channeled are as numerous as the cultures themselves. There is no natural or logical or narrowly theoretical explanation for these things. Cultures are necessarily influenced by climate, topography, natural resources, soil fertility, and other aspects of the physical environment.

Despite a diversity of patterns, each particular culture has, in the language of the anthropologist, a general configuration—a dominant theme, idea, motif, *gestalt*. From this general configuration the culture derives its meaning, its dominant motivation, and its social goals and values. Achievements within a culture are judged in relation to the scale of values dictated by the general configuration. Individuals suited to the highest form of self-expression in one culture may lack the endowments necessary for leadership and self-expression in another. Since the culture tends to mold individuals according to its general pattern, the human product well adjusted to one society may be ill at ease in another. Their goals differ and their values are incommensurable.

The findings of anthropologists about other cultures suggest that Western civilization during the past several hundred years and especially during the nineteenth century places far greater emphasis on the material aspect of life than do other forms of society. Western civilization, of which capitalism has been a part, has to a significant degree been dominated by economic motives and institutions. An economic interpretation of culture appears to have more validity in our own civilization than in others of which we have knowledge. The accumulation of possessions is the special vehicle of self-expression in capitalistic society. The rich are honored not necessarily because they are rich but because their wealth is evidence that they are skilled performers in the game to which the civilization attaches prestige. We may justifiably speak of capitalism as a civilization and not just as an economic system.

SOME MAJOR THEMES

Certain themes run throughout this study of the economic development of the North Atlantic community. Among the more important ones are (1) the importance of the concept of an economic system, (2) capitalism as a monetary economy, (3) the accumulation of capital, (4) the changing basis of economic development from medieval art to contemporary science, and (5) the North Atlantic community as the appropriate geographical and cultural unit to study in order to understand the economic development of western Europe and the United States.

Economic system is a basic concept in the present study. By an economic system is meant a complex of institutions, rights, and motives through which a community satisfies its material wants. Capitalism is an economic system in which the material needs of the community are met as a result of the voluntary efforts of private owners of the means of production to increase their money capital through the employment of wage-earners. Capitalism is sufficiently definite as a historical phenomenon to be distinguishable from feudalism, socialism, and communism. England's economy of 1250 was sufficiently different from its economy in 1850 for one to be called feudal and the other capitalist; and the economies of the United States and the Soviet Union are sufficiently unlike today to be classified as two different systems.

Change and continuity are twin characteristics of any economic system. Capitalism has existed continuously for several centuries, yet as an inherently dynamic system it has also experienced turbulent change. On the surface major changes appear to come in clusters during critical transitional periods such as the Industrial Revolution. The putting-out system persisted in England as the dominant form of industrial organization during the sixteenth and seventeenth centuries only to be rather abruptly displaced by the factory system during the Industrial Revolution of the eighteenth century. In one sense the Industrial Revolution did represent a break with the past, but upon closer examination of its origins we see that it depended on a long period of capital accumulation which enabled England to afford to put into use mechanical principles which had been known for some time. Thus change in the economic system is both an evolutionary and a revolutionary process.

Capitalism as a Monetary Economy

In every society, capital represents a form of surplus in excess of the stock used for immediate consumption. The distinguishing characteristic of capitalism is that the social surplus assumes the form of a *money* balance in the possession of individual business enterprises. The saving and investing process related to capital formation involves first of all the accumulation of money capital.

Business enterprise is carried on for the purpose of "making money," and success in business is measured by the ability to convert the real product of hired labor and purchased materials into money sales in excess of money expenses as reflected in a profit and loss statement. Mere physical production (of use values) counts for very little in business; conversion of real output into money is the *sine qua non* of capitalist enterprise. Disposition of the "realized" money surplus is of fundamental importance both to those who own the surplus and to those who, because they have no means of self-employment, are dependent for their income upon others who do possess capital. Elaboration of the term "capital" in its monetary as well as its real forms will be one of the chief tasks of the following chapters.

Consumption and production are closely tied to the earning and spending of money. In this respect, however, capitalism is less unique. Money was used extensively in medieval Europe as well as in earlier times and other places,

and the earning and spending of money by workers in contemporary noncapitalist economies is the prevailing practice. However, the pervading influence of money has no parallel prior to modern times.[3] Nevertheless, in respect
to the close association between effective demand for consumption and capital
formation, capitalism is uniquely a "monetary economy."

Accumulation of Capital

More than any previous economic system, capitalism mobilized the social
surplus for investment in expanded means of production. Social surplus, which
is one of the fundamental concepts in economic development, may be defined
tentatively as production in excess of what is necessary for consumption. In
precapitalist societies the surplus was either small or dissipated in economically
unproductive expenditures such as temples, cathedrals, luxury products, and
wars. Capitalists, on the contrary, plowed back their profits (current surplus)
to enlarge the means of production and thus served as agents for increasing
the wealth of society.

Among important writers on capitalism there has always been a deep
concern with the accumulation of capital. Mercantilists such as Thomas Mun
(1571–1641) believed that the accumulation of "treasure" depended on foreign
trade; Adam Smith (1723–1790) argued that the wealth of nations depended
on the employment of productive labor, which he defined as labor which contributes to the accumulation of capital; and nineteenth-century economists
more or less identified economic progress with the accumulation of private
wealth (capital).

Because of the strategic role of capital formation, capitalism has been
dynamic in a sense not characteristic of other forms of economic society. This
dynamism has contributed to economic instability as well as to growth, especially in the period beginning with the Industrial Revolution. Capitalism cannot stand still; it must either expand or retrogress. This is not characteristic of
either feudalism or socialism. Under advanced capitalism, productive resources
cannot be utilized fully unless more capital is being accumulated, because in
a wealthy capitalist society large savings require large offsetting investment to
generate sufficient demand to maintain prosperity. This argument applies with
more force to the twentieth century than to earlier and poorer centuries.

Thus capitalism has been progressive, but its progress has been unsteady.
Accumulation of capital has proceeded at an uneven rate. Business cycles as
they emerged after the Industrial Revolution are an economic phenomenon
peculiar to capitalist organization. The instability of economic activity associated with alternating periods of prosperity and depression was less evident
during early capitalism when the capacity for accumulation was less; instability
increased during the classical period of the nineteenth and early twentieth
centuries; it became so serious during the Great Depression that public opinion demanded enlargement of the public sector as a means of lessening instability. Some modern economists have made a case for governmental intervention on the grounds that governmental capital formation is needed to fill
the gap created by a deficiency of private capital formation.

[3] See W. C. Mitchell, "The Role of Money in Economic History," *Journal of Economic History* (Tasks) (December, 1944), pp. 61–67.

Perhaps the most important principle which emerges from this study is that economic development in the long run depends on progress in knowledge and its application to economic activity, usually through technology resting on advances in science. In this respect the general concept of capital—not its special meaning with respect to capitalism—refers to an intangible "state of the arts" which inheres in society as a whole and is perpetuated by the transfer of knowledge from generation to generation. Accretions to tangible equipment will increase the output of society and thereby facilitate economic growth, but the largest gains in productivity arise from improvements in knowledge embodied in superior technology. During the medieval period, intangible capital was embodied primarily in the acquired skills of artisans. Since the Industrial Revolution, however, expensive tangible equipment has been required in order to put intangible common knowledge to work. Those who possess the relatively expensive instrumental equipment are potentially able to amass the fruits of the technological efficiency of the community.

Science and technology are the forces shaping the pattern of economic institutions in the modern world. Science is an impersonal and universal phenomenon which is largely independent of economic systems and political rivalries. Differences among national economies are confined to stages of development, rates of change, and forms of political organization employed to guide economic development. In the long run, similarities in science-based technology which influence economic development may override the political and ideological differences which divide people into warring camps. The upshot of the painful process of readjustment to modern scientific and technological developments may be a synthesis of the principles upon which different economies have been based in the past. If these trends are to continue regardless of war or peace and regardless of the outcome of wars that do occur, the futility of war becomes apparent, and in the full realization of this futility lies hope for peace.

The North Atlantic Community
as an Economic Unit

One of the basic themes of our study is that the countries around the North Atlantic basin represent the unit which is appropriate for an introductory study of capitalism. The alternative and traditional approach is to treat western Europe and the United States separately. While Europe and the United States obviously have separate economic histories, a strong case can be made for initially treating them as parts of a single economic unit stemming from common origins and following similar paths of development. For example, the labor unions of Europe, especially England, and the United States have similar origins and stages of development. A clearer insight can be gained into the nature and functioning of labor unions by studying them side by side than by studying either or both in isolation. Likewise, the corporations or joint-stock companies of the United States and Europe have many similarities, and much of significance is lost by discussing them sepa-

rately. Although the economic unity of the North Atlantic community is recog- **11**
nized by all, this study gives fundamental emphasis and not just incidental *THE DYNAMICS*
recognition to transatlantic unity. *OF CAPITALISM*

Transatlantic ties began with Columbus. They increased with the establishment of European colonies in the New World. England became the classic
home of capitalism, and England's colonies in North America became the most
important outposts of Atlantic capitalism. Political independence of the North
American mainland colonies did not sever the economic alliance. People, capital, and technology flowed freely in both directions across the Atlantic, which
has been called a highway which unites, not a barrier which divides. By the
twentieth century, economic leadership itself had crossed the sea from Great
Britain to the United States. After the Second World War steps were taken
toward a formal Atlantic partnership between the United States of America
and an incipient United States of Europe. Whatever the future of this Grand
Design may be, the economic unity of the Atlantic community is a fact of
history, culture, and economic institutions.

GENERAL NOTE ON BIBLIOGRAPHY

Selected bibliographies are listed at the end of most chapters. A comprehensive list of English-language articles published since 1886 will be found under
the "Economic History" classification in the multivolumed *Index of Economic
Journals* published by the American Economic Association. Articles in the 15-
volume *Encyclopaedia of the Social Sciences* (1930–34) are still useful. The
leading English-language economic history journals are *The Economic History
Review* (England) and *The Journal of Economic History* (United States).
Both contain lists of currently published articles and books in economic history
and related subjects. Some articles on economic history and economic development will be found in general economics journals and general history journals.
The important French economic history journals are *Annales* and *Revue
d'histoire économique et sociale*.

The selected bibliography for Chapter 1 contains works of general reference, including selections on method and content. As noted in the Preface, an
important group of economic historians has developed recently a "new" economic history. Articles representative of the method of this school of thought
are listed under the names of Lance E. Davis, Robert W. Fogel, John R. Meyer,
Douglass C. North. Other references to the work of members of this group
are listed in the bibliographies of appropriate chapters.

SELECTED BIBLIOGRAPHY

Method and Content of Economic History
and Development

AITKEN, HUGH G. J., "On the Present State of Economic History," *Canadian Journal
of Economics and Political Science*, XXVI (Feb., 1960), 87–95.

CLAPHAM, JOHN H., *The Study of Economic History.* Cambridge: Cambridge University Press, 1929.

————, HENRI PIRENNE, and N. S. B. GRAS, "Economic History," *Encyclopaedia of the Social Sciences,* V. New York: The Macmillan Co., 1931, 315–30.

DAVIS, LANCE E., J. R. T. HUGHES, and STANLEY REITER, "Aspects of Quantitative Research in Economic History," *Journal of Economic History,* XX (Dec., 1960), 539–47.

FOGEL, ROBERT W., "The Reunification of Economic History with Economic Theory," *American Economic Review,* LV (May, 1965), 92–97.

GAY, EDWIN F., "The Tasks of Economic History," *Journal of Economic History,* I (Dec., 1941), 9–16.

GOODRICH, CARTER, "Economic History: One Field or Two?" *Journal of Economic History,* XX (Dec., 1960), 531–38.

GRAS, N. S. B., "The Present Condition of Economic History," *Quarterly Journal of Economics,* XXXIV (Feb., 1920), 209–24.

HECKSCHER, ELI F., "A Plea for Theory in Economic History," *Economic History,* I (Jan., 1929), 525–34.

————, "Quantitative Measurement in Economic History," *Quarterly Journal of Economics,* LIII (Feb., 1939), 167–93.

KUZNETS, SIMON, "The Integration of Economic Theory and Economic History— Summary of Discussion and Postscript," *Journal of Economic History,* XVII (Dec., 1957), 545–53.

MEYER, JOHN R., and ALFRED H. CONRAD, "Economic Theory, Statistical Inference, and Economic History," *Journal of Economic History,* XVII (Dec., 1957), 524–44.

NORTH, DOUGLASS C., "The State of Economic History," *American Economic Review,* LV (May, 1965), 86–91.

REDLICH, FRITZ, " 'New' and Traditional Approaches to Economic History and Their Interdependence," *Journal of Economic History,* XXV (Dec., 1965), 480–95.

ROSTOW, WALT W., "A Historian's Perspective on Modern Economic Theory," *American Economic Review,* XLII (May, 1952), 16–29.

————, "The Interrelation of Theory and Economic History," *Journal of Economic History,* XVII (Dec., 1957), 509–23.

SCHUMPETER, JOSEPH A., "The Creative Response in Economic History," *Journal of Economic History,* VII (Nov., 1947), 149–59.

SÉE, HENRI, *The Economic Interpretation of History.* New York: Adelphi Co., 1929.

SPIETHOFF, A., "The 'Historical' Character of Economic Theories," *Journal of Economic History,* XII (Spring, 1952), 131–39.

SUPPLE, BARRY E., "Economic History and Economic Growth," *Journal of Economic History,* XX (Dec., 1960), 548–56.

TAWNEY, RICHARD H., "The Study of Economic History," *Economica,* XIII (Feb., 1933), 1–21.

USHER, ABBOTT P., "The Significance of Modern Empiricism for History and Economics," *Journal of Economic History,* IX (Nov., 1949), 137–55.

GENERAL WORKS

CHILDE, V. GORDON, *What Happened in History.* Baltimore: Penguin Books, Inc., 1954. (paperback)

DOBB, MAURICE, *Studies in the Development of Capitalism.* London: Routledge & Kegan Paul, Ltd., 1946.

GRAS, N. S. B., *Business and Capitalism, An Introduction to Business History.* New York, F. S. Crofts & Co., 1939.

HEILBRONER, ROBERT L., *The Making of Economic Society*. Englewood Cliffs, N.J.: Prentice-Hall, Inc., 1962. (paperback)

LANE, FREDERICK C., ed., *Enterprise and Secular Change, Readings in Economic History*. Homewood, Ill.: Richard D. Irwin, Inc., 1953.

ROSTOW, WALT W., *Stages of Economic Growth, A Non-Communist Manifesto*. London: Cambridge University Press, 1960. (paperback)

SUPPLE, BARRY E., *The Experience of Economic Growth, Case Studies in Economic History*. New York: Random House, Inc., 1963.

WEBER, MAX, *General Economic History*. New York: Crowell-Collier & Macmillan, Inc., 1961. (paperback)

EUROPE

BLAND, A. E., P. A. BROWN, and RICHARD H. TAWNEY, eds., *English Economic History, Select Documents*. London: G. Bell & Sons, Ltd., 1914.

BOISSONNADE, P., *Life and Work in Medieval Europe*. New York: Harper and Row, Publishers, 1964. (paperback)

Cambridge Economic History of Europe, Vols. I, II, III, VI. London: Cambridge University Press, 1942–65.

CARUS-WILSON, E. M., ed., *Essays in Economic History*, 3 vols. London: Edward Arnold (Publishers), Ltd., 1954–63.

CLAPHAM, JOHN H., *The Economic History of Modern Britain*, 3 vols. London: Cambridge University Press, 1950–52.

CLOUGH, SHEPARD B., and CHARLES W. COLE, *Economic History of Europe*, 3rd ed. Boston: D. C. Heath and Company, 1952.

———, and CAROL G. MOODIE, eds., *European Economic History: Documents and Readings*. Princeton: D. Van Nostrand Company, Inc., 1965. (paperback)

DEANE, PHYLLIS, and W. A. COLE, *British Economic Growth, 1688–1959; Trends and Structure*. New York: Cambridge University Press, 1962.

HEATON, HERBERT, *Economic History of Europe*, rev. ed. New York: Harper & Row, Publishers, 1948.

LIPSON, E., *The Economic History of England*, 3 vols. 12th ed. of Vol. I, 6th ed. of Vols. II and III. London: Adam & Charles Black, Ltd., 1959, 1956.

———, *The Growth of English Society, A Short Economic History*. New York: Holt, Rinehart & Winston, Inc., 1950.

MITCHELL, B. R., with the collaboration of Phyllis Deane, *Abstract of British Statistics*. New York: Cambridge University Press, 1962.

SÉE, HENRI, *Histoire économique de la France*, 2 vols. Paris: A. Colin, 1948–51.

———, *Modern Capitalism, Its Origins and Evolution*. New York: Adelphi Co., 1928.

SOMBART, WERNER, *Der moderne Kapitalismus*, 3 vols. in 6. Munich: Duncker & Humblot, 1921–28.

UNITED STATES

DAVIS, LANCE E., JONATHAN R. T. HUGHES, and DUNCAN McDOUGALL, *American Economic History*, rev. ed. Homewood, Ill.: Richard D. Irwin, Inc., 1965.

FAULKNER, HAROLD U., *American Economic History*, 8th ed. New York: Harper & Row, publishers, 1960.

JOHNSON, E. A. J., and HERMAN KROOSS, *The American Economy: Its Origins, Development, and Transformation*. Englewood Cliffs, N.J.: Prentice-Hall, Inc., 1960.

KIRKLAND, EDWARD C., *A History of American Economic Life*, 3rd ed. New York: Appleton-Century-Crofts, Inc., 1951.

NASH, GERALD D., ed., *Issues in American Economic History, Selected Readings*. Boston: D. C. Heath and Company, 1964.

NORTH, DOUGLASS C., *Growth and Welfare in the American Past, A New Economic History*. Englewood Cliffs, N.J.: Prentice-Hall, Inc., 1966. (paperback)

ROBERTSON, ROSS M., *History of the American Economy*, 2nd ed. New York: Harcourt, Brace & World, Inc., 1964.

UNITED STATES BUREAU OF THE CENSUS, *Historical Statistics of the United States, Colonial Times to 1957*. Washington, D.C.: Government Printing Office, 1960.

WRIGHT, CHESTER W., *Economic History of the United States*, 2nd ed. New York: McGraw-Hill, Inc., 1949.

Expansion of Commerce
in Late Medieval Europe

CHAPTER **2**

In the evolution of the modern economic system the first important
episode was the transition from feudalism to capitalism. This occurred
in western Europe in a broad band of time centering around 1500. The
strategic external force contributing to the break-up of medieval economic institutions was a growing volume of long-distance trade. Specialized industries
sprang up to serve this expanding trade, and the resulting commercial and
industrial towns exerted pressures which weakened the internal structure of
agriculture based on serfdom, the hallmark of the feudal regime.

Changes in trade, industry, and agriculture were, of course, taking place
simultaneously, and they interacted in a highly complex set of relationships.
It is the theme of this chapter and the two following, however, that long-distance trade set in motion a sequence of cumulative changes which had ramifications throughout the medieval economy and ultimately transformed it into
a new type of economic society. No attempt is made in this discussion to describe the details of medieval economic life; the structure and functioning of
medieval institutions are sketched only insofar as necessary to give the setting
for the transition from feudalism to capitalism.

EXPANSION OF TRADE IN THE MEDITERRANEAN

One thousand years elapsed between the downfall of the western Roman Empire and the downfall of the eastern Roman Empire. During this millenium,
from the fifth century to the fifteenth, the Greek city of Constantinople was
the administrative, cultural, and economic center of Christian civilization. This
thriving city of a million inhabitants served as a gateway for most of the trade
between East and West. Merchants converged on Constantinople from Asia,
Europe, and Africa. Constantinople also specialized in the manufacture of
luxuries such as silk cloth, gold and silver plate, carved ivory, jewelry, and
semiprecious stones, as well as more pedestrian commodities such as linen,
cotton cloth, and armaments. Like other traders, the merchants of western
Europe were attracted by the riches of the great Greek metropolis at the
eastern end of the Mediterranean.

Trade between Constantinople and the West was threatened during

the seventh, eighth and ninth centuries by the vigorous expansion of the Moslem Arabs. The followers of Mohammed swept eastward to India and westward along the southern shore of the Mediterranean, from Egypt to Morocco and into Spain. They captured Sicily, Sardinia, and other important islands in the Mediterranean. By the ninth century the western Mediterranean had become virtually an Arab lake. The Moslems did not succeed, however, in capturing control of the Aegean and Adriatic seas, and in the tenth century a successful counteroffensive was begun in the West. Genoa and Pisa on the west coast of Italy opened an attack on Moslem trade by expeditions against Sardinia (1005–1016), the coast of Africa (1034), Palermo (1062), and Medea (1087). The First Crusade (1096), led by Genoa and Pisa, continued these commercial attacks against the Moslems and expanded Christian territory and commerce.

Although Genoa and Pisa started the counteroffensive against the Moslems, Venice became the greatest center of sea commerce in the West. This remarkable city, built on the marshes of the upper Adriatic, where it escaped conquest by the barbarians as well as by Charlemagne and his successors in the Holy Roman Empire, did not permit religious scruples to interfere with commercial prosperity. Even during the height of Arab control of the Mediterranean and before the First Crusade, Venetian merchants traded regularly with the Moslem world as well as with Christian Constantinople. The merchants of Venice obtained trading concessions with Palermo, Tunis, and Damascus, all of which were under Moslem occupation. By the tenth century Venice enjoyed a thriving commerce. Its ships carried wine, wheat, lumber, and other products to the eastern Mediterranean and returned with cargoes of precious Byzantine fabrics and rich spices from the Far East, as well as raw materials for western craftsmen. Another large export from the West carried by the Venetians was slaves for the workshops and the harems of the Moslem world.

The Fourth Crusade (1202–1204) was turned into a grand commercial conquest by the Venetians. The Crusaders, who traveled in Venetian ships, were employed as raiding armies in the service of Venice. They first captured the Christian port of Zara (modern Zadar) on the eastern shore of the Adriatic. Instead of moving against the infidels in the Holy Land, the Crusaders captured and plundered Constantinople, the bastion of eastern Christendom and Venice's chief rival for power in the Mediterranean world. Genoese merchants were expelled from Constantinople, which became a satellite of Venice. Venetian merchants now had access to the Black Sea, a privilege previously denied to them by the Greeks. The occupation of Constantinople, added to other concessions and monopolies Venice already possessed, made that city supreme in the Mediterranean. As it controlled all the important import-export points along the coasts of what are now Yugoslavia, Albania, Greece, and Turkey, all of eastern Europe and Asia Minor were compelled to buy from and sell to the Venetians.

Ironically the commercial successes scored during the Crusades undermined the religious objectives to which the Crusades were presumably dedicated. When the Venetians sacked Constantinople and subsequently fought the Genoese for the spoils, they weakened the citadel of Christianity in the East and prepared the ground for the capture of Constantinople by the Ottoman Turks in 1453, the famous event which marked the official "fall" of the eastern

part of the "Roman" Empire. In the course of several Crusades the control of Mediterranean commerce had been regained, and economic leadership shifted back to the West by the time America was discovered, but all hope of regaining the Holy Land and of expanding the influence of Christianity in the Middle East was by then a lost cause.

Commercial wars among rival Italian cities became more frequent than the intermittent crusading in the East. It is interesting, for example, that Marco Polo (1254–1324), the son of a Venetian merchant, dictated the account of his famous Asian travels while occupying a prison cell in Genoa after being captured in one of the frequent commercial wars between these two great maritime rivals.

EXPANSION OF TRADE IN NORTHERN EUROPE

Although international and interregional trade in northern Europe dates back to antiquity, it received a major stimulus during the Middle Ages from the Norsemen, or Vikings, whose raids on the coastal regions of the southern Baltic and North seas had a catalytic effect similar to that of the Crusades in the Mediterranean. The Viking raids, extending over three centuries (700–1000), were at their height in the ninth century, after which they were gradually transformed into more conventional types of commercial activity. As one authority has said, "The Vikings, in fact, were pirates, and piracy is the first stage of commerce. So true is this that . . . when their raids ceased, they simply became merchants." (Pirenne) These Scandinavians knew how to build seaworthy ships and learned to navigate in distant waters. Adventure and trade carried them to Iceland, Greenland, and probably to the mainland of North America; eastward they sailed to Russia, thence southward along the Dnieper River, the Black Sea, the Caspian Sea, and the Bosphorus, where they traded with Arab, Jewish, and Byzantine merchants.

The expansion of long-distance trade initiated by the Norsemen accelerated after the beginning of the eleventh century. Perhaps the most important single cause was the growth of population. Heavy settlement in some areas and the eastward frontier movement on the continent of Europe stimulated economic specialization by regions. At an early date, for example, Flanders became so densely populated that the region developed a concentrated cloth industry, importing raw materials (wool and dyes) and food (fish and grain) and exporting finished cloth. Fishing, which provided a basic item in the medieval diet, took place in widely scattered areas, a few of which became centers of production for long-distance trade. The most important medieval fishing ground was the Sound, the waters between the northern peninsula of Denmark and the southern tip of Sweden. Wool growing became a specialty of England early in the Middle Ages, and wool was perhaps the most valuable single item in the medieval trade of northern Europe. Natural resources such as timber, iron, coal, and salt were unevenly distributed geographically. Specialization by region led to interregional trade.

Flanders, in addition to being the center of the medieval cloth trade, became the entrepôt of commerce in northern Europe. Merchants from central and southern Europe came by way of the valleys of the Rhine, the Meuse,

and the Scheldt from the interior onto the coastal plain of Flanders. Merchants with wool from the economically remote and backward British Isles found Flanders a convenient place to dispose of their cargoes. Some trade always came across the Alps from northern Italy to southern Germany and France. German merchants, who gradually supplanted the Scandinavians in the Baltic trade, used Flanders as the entrepôt between east and west. In Flanders the city of Bruges played a role in north European trade comparable to that of Venice in southern Europe, and became known as "the Venice of the North." It was, in fact, a more international city than Venice because the merchants of many lands had depots, counting houses, and ships in Bruges, whereas the Venetians kept tight control over foreigners and only Venetian ships occupied the lagoons of the great Adriatic port.

In one important respect the trade of northern Europe differed from that of southern Europe: Bulky necessities dominated northern commerce, whereas luxuries dominated the Mediterranean trade.[1] Grain, fish, wool, cloth, timber, pitch, tar, salt, and iron were among the most important products in the commerce of northern Europe; spices, silks, brocades and tapestries, sweet wines, fruits, carved ivory, and gold and silver plate were featured in the Mediterranean trade. Since the foodstuffs and raw materials of northern trade were bulky and heavy in relation to their value, they could bear only the cheapest type of transportation, which was usually by water on the Baltic and North seas and along the rivers which penetrated inland from the north. The trade was characteristically interregional rather than intercontinental. Some luxury items did, of course, enter into northern trade to satisfy the wants of nobles, kings, churchmen, and other wealthy consumers. Russian furs and French wines are examples of luxury commodities. Expensive finery and exotic spices percolated north across the Alps and, after 1300, through the Straits of Gibraltar to northern Europe.

In contrast to the bulky primary products of northern European trade, the luxury commodities of the Mediterranean weighed little in relation to their value and could bear the relatively heavy transportation costs from the Far East, Middle East, Near East, and Africa. Just as necessities did not constitute the whole of northern trade, neither did luxuries constitute the whole of southern trade. Foodstuffs and raw materials were also important items in Mediterranean trade. Nevertheless, it was characteristically a luxury trade as opposed to the more pedestrian commerce of the north.

EXPANSION OF TRADE: THE OVERALL PATTERN

The overall pattern of commercial development in continental Europe between 1000 and 1500 can now be indicated. There were two great commercial movements—one on the southern shores of Europe in the Mediterranean and Adriatic seas and another on the northern shores of Europe in the North and Baltic seas. In between lay the land mass of continental Europe, still in the grip of feudalism and economically retarded as compared with its southern

---

[1] For an elaboration of this point, see Michael M. Postan, "The Trade of Medieval Europe: the North," in *The Cambridge Economic History of Europe*, ed. by Michael M. Postan and E. E. Rich (London: Cambridge University Press, 1952), Vol. II, Chap. 4.

and northern coastal areas. Much could be gained by bringing together the two vibrant trading areas. The geography of continental Europe presented no insuperable transportation barriers. Europe's mountains contained passes through which the Romans had built fine roads. There were long rivers reaching far into the interior—especially the Rhine from the north, the Rhone from the south, and the Danube from the east. Since ancient times some merchants had followed the river valleys and mountain passes. Although the Roman roads had deteriorated and there were no major improvements in overland transportation during the thousand years from 500 to 1500, the expansion of commerce on the southern and northern shores of Europe was followed in due course by a swelling volume of transcontinental traffic. During the later Middle Ages new trading centers developed at strategic points. The interior of Europe began to palpitate with commercial activity.

Among the early developments arising from expanded trade between northern and southern Europe were the great international fairs, aptly called "oases of commercialism" on a continent where the vast majority of the populace gained its living by tilling the soil and seldom ventured far beyond the local village. Fairs were centers of long-distance, wholesale trade, as distinct from "markets," which were places of local and mostly retail trade. International fairs met typically for a few weeks each year, whereas local markets operated one or more days each week throughout the year. Local markets existed wherever there was a concentration of population. Military garrisons and church centers were never without local markets. International fairs were a new phenomenon resulting from the expansion of long-distance trade.

A number of significant economic developments arose in conjunction with the medieval fairs. Because merchants came from many regions which used different currencies, money changers were present to convert foreign monies into the standard currency of the fair. To insure uniform and official exchange rates and also the full collection of tax levies, it was customary for the local prince in whose territory the fair was held to send an official exchequer to preside over the exchange. Credit facilities were well developed, debt-clearing arrangements used, and bills of exchange made payable at fairs.

In order to facilitate speedy settlement of the disputes which inevitably arose, medieval merchants developed a separate commercial law and separate courts for the adjudication of disputes. These were known as "pie-powder courts," or "courts of dusty feet," to designate the road-traveling habits of the contesting parties. The body of law practiced at fairs became known as the "law merchant," which forms the basis of modern commercial law, including the law of contracts, negotiable instruments, agency, sale and auction. This was the "private international law of the Middle Ages." Merchants became privileged characters, exempt from the common and canon law of the time.

In the first great surge of north-south trade the most famous fairs were those in the principality of Champagne, to the east and south of Paris. At the high point of development between 1150 and 1300 six large international fairs of an average duration of six weeks each were held annually in this small, neutral territory wherein converged roads from Italy, Flanders, Germany, and France. Here merchants from Venice, Genoa, and Pisa exchanged Oriental perfume, drugs, spices, silks, and velvets for fine Flemish cloth, English wool, German linen, Russian furs, and tar and other naval stores from

Scandinavia. The Counts of Champagne followed an enlightened policy which protected and encouraged trade. Legal disputes were settled speedily and equitably under the simple procedures of the law merchant, and the decisions were strictly enforced.

The Champagne fairs declined after 1300, when annexation of the territory by the French kings created less favorable conditions for trade and when the all-water route from the Mediterranean to the North Sea came into use. Genoese ships first sailed to the North Sea about 1300, and the first regular Venetian galley arrived in Antwerp in 1314. Although the Hundred Years War caused further disruption, the decline of the Champagne fairs was followed by the rise of others. In the fourteenth and fifteenth centuries international fairs took place in every European country. Among the more important were those at Geneva, Lyons, Frankfurt-on-Main, Frankfurt-on-Oder, Strasbourg, and Paris. In England famous fairs were held at Stourbridge (near Cambridge), Winchester, and Westminster. Although some important international fairs continued into the modern period, they were on the decline generally after 1400 in most of western Europe and England because, as the volume of trade expanded, permanent trading centers in towns and cities replaced the intermittent fairs. The fairs were important as a transitional institution which met the needs of wholesale merchants in an age of expanding commerce and were displaced when the volume of trade expanded still further.

RISE OF COMMERCIAL TOWNS

A striking feature of Europe in the later Middle Ages (1000–1500) was the growth of urban centers of population. The swelling volume of long-distance trade after 1000 provided the economic basis of urban life. With the increase in the number of people engaged in trade, the old walled bishoprics and garrisons overflowed. Quarters established outside the old city (bourg, burg) gradually surrounded the old part of the town and became known as the faubourg (fauburg), or outside city. The residents of these new towns were called bourgeoisie (French), burghers (German), or burgesses (English).

Ecclesiastical or lay feudal lords claimed jurisdiction over nearly every town in western Europe. Because the new commercial activity required a type of freedom that was not characteristic of feudal Europe, the towns sought political independence. Usually they were able to purchase a charter which granted freedom from feudal jurisdiction. The freedom of town dwellers presented a marked contrast to the unfree status of the majority of the rural population.

Town charters were granted by kings, bishops, and lay lords. Royal charters from kings were generally preferred, especially in England, where royal power became centralized at a relatively early date. Inevitably towns were drawn into the struggle for power among the church, the feudal lords, and the aspiring kings. Alliances of towns with central governments constituted a sort of town-and-crown club which ultimately broke the power of the church and the feudal lords and established strong national sovereigns. Where national unification was delayed, as in Italy and Germany, economic develop-

ment was also retarded. The important point is that towns received charters which gave legal sanction to a new way of life. The effect of town autonomy was to increase the power and influence of the middle class, the first leaders of which were wealthy merchants.

MERCHANT GILDS

Since medieval society lacked strong central governments, it provided inadequate protection to the life and property of men and goods moving long distances through a multitude of local jurisdictions. Protection was provided through voluntary associations of merchants, known as merchant gilds, which were formed in western Europe in the eleventh century. Members traveled in caravans and pledged themselves to protect the interests of all fellow gildsmen. Gilds also functioned as social and welfare societies. In keeping with this fraternal spirit, no member was supposed to take advantage of any other member of the fraternity.

The discipline of the caravan carried over to activities in trading towns as the sedentary merchant displaced the traveling merchant as the dominant figure in long-distance trade. Foreigners and other nonmembers of a gild were discriminated against even when gilds had no legal right to prevent them from trading in the town. In time merchant gilds acquired legal sanction for what had become in economic fact a commercial monopoly.

Town charters and town politics were important instruments for gaining monopolistic privileges. Since long-distance merchants usually constituted the wealthiest members of urban communities, they were among the most influential citizens in obtaining a town charter from the feudal authorities, who were concerned primarily with collecting revenues in return for granting political autonomy to towns within their jurisdiction. After leading a successful campaign for town independence, this wealthy, well-organized group in the merchant gild were in a strategic position to become the officials who organized and administered municipal governments. Frequently the officers of the merchant gild and the town council were one and the same.

NATIONAL GILDS AND HANSES

A more highly developed type of gild organization arose from the association of the merchant gilds of several towns in regional or national leagues, commonly called hanses. Several of these hanses flourished in the later Middle Ages, and some continued into the modern era. They were more important in northern than in southern Europe. The hanse type of organization prevailed in those areas which lacked strong central governments, e.g., Germany, whereas national gilds tended to be formed in countries with relatively strong national governments, e.g., England. Four important national gilds or hanses were the Flemish hanse of London, the Merchants of the Staple, the Merchant Adventurers, and the Hanseatic League.

The Flemish hanse of London, which flourished around 1200, consisted of an association of Flemish cities, with the Merchant Gild of Bruges providing the nucleus of the organization. These Flemish merchants attempted to regulate

the trade between England and the Low Countries and for a time enjoyed a more or less complete monopoly of this important trade. Its members imported raw wool from England for the great Flemish cloth industry and exported mainly manufactured products to England. Members of the Flemish hanse also traded at the Champagne fairs. Their importance declined during the thirteenth century.

During the fourteenth century a group of English merchants, known as the Merchants of the Staple, gained a quasi-monopoly over the lucrative export trade in raw wool from England. Basic to the "staple" policy of the English government was the concentration of exports at one or a few depots in order to minimize the danger of evasion of export taxes levied on wool. A similar policy was followed for other commodities. A national merchant gild with a monopoly of the wool trade could afford to pay a high tax on wool exports, especially since they were able to pass on the tax to foreign purchasers by raising the price of wool. Moreover, the Merchants of the Staple could not with impunity refuse to advance loans demanded by the Crown for fear of losing their valuable monopoly. For some time the English wool staple moved about from one location to another both in England and across the Channel until in 1363 it finally settled down at Calais, where it remained for some 200 years under English rule garrisoned by English troops.

A monopoly to English merchants which enabled them to raise the price of wool to foreigners proved lucrative in the short run, but in the long run was narrow and self-defeating for the Staplers because the immense differential between the high price of wool abroad and the low price of wool in England stimulated the growth of the domestic woolen cloth industry in England and cut the ground from under the Merchants of the Staple. With further expansion of the cloth industry in England during the early phase of capitalism, the export of wool declined and was finally prohibited by royal edict.

The same process which constricted the export of raw wool stimulated the export of manufactured cloth. A new group of English merchants, known as the Merchant Adventurers, arose to participate in the expanding cloth export business. In return for loans and bribes to the Crown, the Merchant Adventurers received a royal charter which granted them a monopoly of the export of woolen cloth from England. Although by the fifteenth century England had the greatest woolen textile industry in Europe, it had not developed the finishing and dyeing stages as far as the Low Countries and Florence, and the principal export carried by the Merchant Adventurers was unfinished and undyed cloth, most of which went to the Low Countries for further processing. Nevertheless, the simultaneous decline of the Merchants of the Staple, with their monopoly over the export of raw wool, and the rise of the Merchant Adventurers, with their monopoly over the export of woolen cloth, illustrates in a significant way the economic development of England from a country whose foreign trade was primarily in the export of raw materials to a country whose exports consisted primarily of manufactured goods.

Like the Merchants of the Staple, the Merchant Adventurers constituted a national gild, an association of merchants, rather than a league of towns, in which each merchant traded on his own capital and made his own profits or losses. Although entrance into the Merchant Adventurers supposedly remained open to any English merchant complying with specified conditions, new mem-

bership was positively discouraged by such tactics as exorbitant entry fees. Because of their exclusiveness, the Merchant Adventurers encountered political opposition at home and were harassed by "interlopers," who professed a belief in free trade and violated the royal monopoly by engaging in cloth exporting. The Merchant Adventurers in turn contested the privileges granted in England to foreign merchants like the German Hanseatic League.

The Hanseatic League constituted the most famous of all the national gilds or hanses in western Europe during the late medieval and early modern periods. Significantly the Hanseatic League developed in Germany, which was notoriously lacking in strong central government of any type. Germany had strong cities but weak principalities and an even weaker empire, the Holy Roman Empire. The Hanseatic League was an association of German cities which voluntarily entered and remained members only so long as their self-interest was served by membership in the League. There was no sponsorship by a government, other than the municipalities, as there was in England, where the Merchants of the Staple and the Merchant Adventurers both received recognition from the Crown.

Undergoing a number of stages, the Hanseatic League had its roots in the twelfth century, took definite form in the thirteenth century, and attained the height of its power in the fourteenth century, after which there followed a long period of stagnation and then decline, until the Thirty Years War of the seventeenth century finally destroyed it. Lübeck on the Baltic provided dynamic leadership through most of the League's expansion phase; Cologne and Hamburg were usually the second and third most powerful members. At one time or another more than a hundred German towns held membership in the organization, which guaranteed to the merchants of each member town the rights and privileges enjoyed by the League. Although not primarily political in its purposes, the League raised armies and navies and on one important occasion administered a crushing defeat to a troublesome king of Denmark. At its height the Hanseatic League controlled the entire foreign commerce of Denmark, Sweden, and Norway and, more generally, dominated the trade of the Baltic and North seas.

In their role as the middlemen of the east-west trade of northern Europe, the Hansa merchants had the chief outposts of their foreign trade in England (London), Flanders (Bruges), Norway (Bergen), and Russia (Novgorod). Their English headquarters were in the famous London Steelyard, an area on the bank of the Thames granted to the Hansa merchants by the English Crown for the protection of their wares and lives. Like other merchants of the late medieval period, the Hansards gained favors by making loans to financially needy rulers. After the bankruptcy of the Bardi and Peruzzi, the Italian merchant-bankers in England, the Hansa merchants became the chief creditors of Edward III (reigned 1327–1377). The chief imports into England consisted of fine cloth, wax, wine, furs, forest products including naval stores, and in bad harvest years Baltic grain. Exports from England included wool (earlier), cloth (later), tin, and hides. Attempts by English merchants to enter the Baltic trade were largely rebuffed by the German merchants.

To their Flemish headquarters located at Bruges the Hanseatic merchants brought furs from Russia, grain from the Baltic, and forest products from the whole eastern territory; and they took away cloth and a varied assortment of

products which were either produced in northern Europe or brought there from southern Europe. Novgorod in Russia was the eastern outpost where products were gathered for export to the west. Furs were the leading Russian export but timber, leather, wax, and hemp were also exported. Products carried to Russia included cloth from Flanders and wine, beer, salt, and metals. Herring caught in the Sound between the Danish Peninsula and Sweden was probably the commodity of greatest value in the entire Hanseatic trade. Dried and salted herring, and to a lesser extent cod and flounder, constituted staple items in the diet of the great mass of Europeans during the Middle Ages.

Chief among the factors in the decline of the Hanseatic League was the emergence of strong national states which protected and promoted their own merchants at the expense of alien merchants from the German cities. In England, Sweden, and Russia strong rulers began to restrict and finally to expel the Hansards. In Germany the Holy Roman Empire remained very weak, but attempts at political unification within principalities enjoyed some success at the expense of the independent Hanseatic cities. In the fifteenth century a growing number of towns were forced to withdraw from the League and to swear allegiance to the prince of their territory, e.g., in Brandenburg. The decline of the League was well under way before the discovery of America and of the all-water route to India. In the trade revival after the discovery of America it was the Dutch rather than the German cities which dominated the Baltic, and much more.

The great contribution of the Hanseatic League lay in organizing and unifying the trade of northern Europe during the late medieval period. Its functions were both political and economic in an important part of Europe which failed to develop strong central government at an early date. Its membership remained exclusively German, but it served an international purpose in bringing together not only German cities but also the trade of eastern and western Europe.

SELECTED BIBLIOGRAPHY

BLAND, A. E., P. A. BROWN, and RICHARD H. TAWNEY, eds., *English Economic History, Select Documents,* Part I, Sec. VI. London: G. Bell & Sons, Ltd., 1914.

CARUS-WILSON, E. M., and OLIVE COLEMAN, *England's Export Trade, 1275–1547.* Oxford: Clarendon Press, 1963.

DE ROOVER, RAYMOND A., *Money, Banking and Credit in Medieval Bruges.* Cambridge, Mass.: Medieval Academy of America, 1948.

HAVIGHURST, ALFRED F., ed., *The Pirenne Thesis: Analysis, Criticism and Revision.* Boston: D. C. Heath & Company, 1958. (paperback)

LIPSON, E., *The Economic History of England,* I. *The Middle Ages,* 12th ed., chapters 5, 6, 7, and 10. London: Adam & Charles Black, Ltd., 1959.

PIRENNE, HENRI, *Economic and Social History of Medieval Europe.* London: Routledge & Kegan Paul, Ltd., 1949.

―――, *Medieval Cities, Their Origins and the Revival of Trade.* Garden City, N.Y.: Doubleday Anchor Books, 1956. (paperback)

POSTAN, MICHAEL M., and E. E. RICH, eds., *The Cambridge Economic History of Europe*, Vol. II, *Trade and Industry in the Middle Ages*, chapters 3, 4, and 5. London: Cambridge University Press, 1952.

POWER, EILEEN E., *The Wool Trade in English Medieval History*. London: Oxford University Press, 1949.

THOMPSON, J. W., *Economic and Social History of Europe in the Later Middle Ages, 1300–1530*. New York: Appleton-Century-Crofts, 1931.

THRUPP, SYLVIA L., *The Merchant Class of Medieval London*. Ann Arbor: University of Michigan Press, 1962. (paperback)

ARTICLES

BRINKMANN, CARL, "The Hanseatic League," *Journal of Economic and Business History*, II (Aug., 1930), 585–602.

CARUS-WILSON, E. M., "Trends in the Export of English Woolens in the Fourteenth Century," *Economic History Review*, III, No. 2 (1950), 162–79.

CHRISTENSEN, A. E., "Scandinavia and the Advance of the Hanseatics," *Scandinavian Economic History Review*, V, No. 2 (1957), 89–117.

MARCUS, G. J., "The Norse Trade with Iceland," *Economic History Review*, IX (April, 1957), 408–19.

PIRENNE, HENRI, "The Place of the Netherlands in the Economic History of Medieval Europe," *Economic History Review*, II (Jan., 1929), 20–40.

RORIG, FRITZ, "The Hanseatic League," *Encyclopaedia of the Social Sciences*, VII. New York: Macmillan, 1932, 261–67.

Industry in Transition

Two quite distinct types of industry coexisted in Europe during the last few centuries of the Middle Ages. One type produced for local markets, the other for long-distance trade. The former was characteristically small-scale, noncapitalistic production by independent craftsmen and their apprentices and journeymen; the latter required large-scale, capitalistic organization utilizing dependent craftsmen and wage-earners.

The expanding volume of long-distance trade described in the preceding chapter was symptomatic of increasing production. Since only the most primitive type of commerce consists exclusively of the mutual exchange of unprocessed raw materials and agricultural products, much of the increased production took the form of industrial output. Production increased because markets expanded, but it is also true that markets expanded because production increased. The expansion in both markets and production was made possible because of Europe's natural resources, population growth, and improved techniques of production. Europe is richly endowed with natural resources. At the beginning of the Middle Ages it was underpopulated in relation to its natural endowments and existing techniques. Improvements in techniques during the Middle Ages brought about increased production, and a dynamic influence was provided by the growth of population during this period and its expansion into new territory.[1]

Ultimately the capitalistic type of industry triumphed over small-scale organization based on crafts. This took a long time, however, and the process was not uninterrupted. Large-scale industry in the Middle Ages represented islands of capitalism in a precapitalist world. It was often uncertain whether these islands would be submerged completely in the medieval sea or would emerge into whole continents of capitalist activity. The great cloth industries of medieval Flanders and Florence are examples of capitalist-type industries which advanced rapidly for a time only to lapse into stagnation and decay. The significant and permanent breakthrough to industrial capitalism took place in England at the close of the Middle Ages.

Economic progress is not inevitable, nor has it been typical of human societies. Stagnation has, perhaps, been the more normal condition of economic life. Resistance to change is strong in every society, and medieval Europe was

[1] On western Europe's eastward frontier movement, see the next chapter.

no exception. Here the clash between security and progress became intensified because powerful forces acted in both directions. An older generation of economic historians stressed the static, traditionalistic side of economic life in medieval Europe. More recently, emphasis has shifted to the dynamic forces of change. A fair evaluation of the course of events in the transition from medieval to modern times would seem to require a balanced treatment of the resistance to change, on the one hand, and the forces making for change, on the other. In the present chapter emphasis is placed on the changes which occurred in the craft form of industry as a result of expanding markets in which merchants served as the capital-providing, labor-employing, and goods-disposing agents. Preliminary to this, however, we shall attempt to portray the noncapitalistic, handicraft system of industry before the transition.

MEDIEVAL HANDICRAFT INDUSTRY

By industry we mean the transformation of raw materials into finished products. Under the handicraft system of industry, workers convert raw materials into finished products for sale in a market in which the craftsmen act as retail merchants as well as direct producers. Workmen are primarily craftsmen and only incidentally merchants. The existence of a market enables workers to specialize in a single product and to develop the occupational skills that constitute their "craft." This division of labor marks considerable advance over a primitive system of usufacture under which households produce for their own consumption rather than for sale in a market. The manorial village and especially the medieval town were already in this more developed stage of industrial evolution. Even when commerce was at a low ebb in the early Middle Ages, communities required the specialized skills of trained craftsmen. With the growth of commerce, merchants who needed products for exchange seized control of craft production and transformed the system of retail handicraft into one of wholesale handicraft. Under this arrangement the producer sells his products to merchants, thus losing contact with the final product market. With further development in the extent of the market, the producer sells his labor to the merchant, who alone knows the conditions of distant markets and who requires that production be carried on according to his specifications. He puts out to workers raw materials of a desirable quality and collects the finished product. This latter development is known as the putting-out system and is one of the first forms of capitalist industry. It is the chief historic link between the handicraft and the factory system in western Europe.

Characteristics of Handicraft Production

High degree of technical skill The degree of skill required for handicraft production is great, much greater, for example, than that required to operate machinery in modern factories, although machinery presupposes a higher degree of technical knowledge on the part of those who design the machines. Handicraft skills in medieval Europe were acquired through "on-the-job" training, rather than in trade schools, which became common only in relatively recent times and even today are only a partial substitute for the

long apprenticeship required for the mastery of some crafts. Workers in medieval crafts were either apprentices, journeymen, or masters. The length of the apprenticeship varied with circumstances, but there was a tendency to set a uniform period even in the absence of craft gilds. In England in the later phase of the handicraft system, a uniform apprenticeship period of seven years was stipulated under the Statute of Apprentices of 1563. In France the apprenticeship generally ran from three to five years, and in Germany usually three years.

The function of apprenticeship is to transmit from generation to generation society's accumulated technical skill. From an economic point of view it is desirable to make this learning period as short as is consistent with maintaining the quality of workmanship. Under an ideal system the worker passes from apprentice to journeyman to master according to the speed with which he can learn the skills of his craft. In the later phases of the handicraft system in Europe there was a tendency to prolong unduly the period of apprenticeship in order to limit the number of journeymen and masters. Output was thereby restricted and monopoly gains increased. Another abuse of apprenticeship was its use as a device to obtain cheap labor. Apprentices usually received only board and lodging plus a small sum of money upon completion of their apprenticeship. Therefore the longer the period during which workers remained apprentices, the longer the period during which the cost of their labor to the master remained nominal. One indication of the decay of the handicraft system was the difficulty experienced by journeymen in receiving recognition as masters even though they had acquired the requisite technical skills.

After completing his apprenticeship a craftsman served several years as a journeyman. In this intermediate stage of training—what may be called the internship period—he hired himself out to masters for a daily wage. The term "journeyman" derives from the French word "journée" meaning day, a journeyman being literally a "dayman." In parts of Europe, especially Germany, journeymen were expected to travel for a certain period, visiting special works of art and serving under different masters, a practice known as the "Wanderjahr," or travel year.

The fully trained and accredited master craftsman would then establish his own shop, which characteristically was attached to his living quarters because maintenance of both a residence and a workshop was too expensive for his limited means. Shops of a given craft were usually located along a single street, not only because of fraternal ties among men engaged in the same work, but also because under the gilds it was easier to supervise the quality of work that was performed in a concentrated area.

A master became at the same time a self-employed craftsman, a teacher of apprentices, an employer of journeymen, and a retail merchant of the products produced in his shop. Since the high degree of skill needed for handicraft production required some systematic provision for training, this was often formalized within a craft gild. However, handicraft production did not necessarily presuppose a gild system, and perpetuation of the industrial arts often rested with informal customs embedded in the traditions of craftsmen.

Small amount of tangible capital The basis of economic productivity in any community is the accumulated knowledge inherited from past genera-

tions, used in conjunction with tools or equipment. Until quite recently—up to the time of the Industrial Revolution in the eighteenth century—this knowledge could be put into practice with relatively little investment in physical equipment. It was mainly "human investment," that is, the skill of hand and brain, which was the requisite of handicraft production. Little physical or tangible capital was required other than a shop, raw materials, and a few tools, most of which could be made by the craftsman himself. The accumulation in a few hands of large amounts of money capital which could supply many craftsmen with raw materials (the putting-out system) and advances in the technical arts which required costly physical investment in order to put the technical knowledge to work (factory system) were developments which threatened the handicraft system.

No permanent wage-earning class   Because of the small amount of tangible capital required for production and the general accessibility of training through the apprentice-journeyman system, there was no permanent industrial wage-earning class under the medieval craft system. Apprentices normally became journeymen, and journeymen normally became masters. Apprentices learned a trade by actual experience. Journeymen were wage-earners, but unlike factory workers who are rarely factory owners in the making, the journeymen were masters in the making. Apprenticeship and journeymanship constituted stages in the educational or training process rather than a permanent employment status.

Conditions which made it difficult for journeymen to be promoted to independent masters contributed to the breakup of the handicraft system. As will be noted below, this change took the form of differentiation between "big masters" and "little masters." The former became in fact employers of the latter, although both groups retained the nominal status of "master craftsmen." Under these circumstances the "little master" did not differ materially from a journeyman so far as function was concerned. The emergence of a permanent wage-earning class foreshadowed the arrival of the new age of industrial organization.

Integration of the producing and trading function   An essential condition of the medieval handicraft system was that the producing function and the trading function were both performed by the master craftsman. Typically this involved direct contact between the craftsman and the final customers; there was no middleman between the producer and the consumer. Any one of several possible arrangements might exist between a craftsman and his customers. He might produce to fill advance orders either with raw materials provided by customers or with materials he supplied himself; or he might produce goods for chance sale to prospective customers. Theoretically it was possible for craftsmen to sell to wholesalers, but when production reached this stage, craftsmen were in danger of becoming dependent employees of the wholesaler.

Integration of the producing and the trading functions in the hands of a master and in particular the direct contact between producer and consumer could prevail only in the circumstances of a limited, local market. Under production for export trade, the handicraft system, which was typical of local trade, gave way to a quite different form of production organization.

Social homogeneity of craftsmen   Under the handicraft system, men of the same craft formed a homogeneous social group. Masters and journeymen worked in the same shop and often lived under the same roof. Apprentices, journeymen, and masters were of the same socio-economic class differentiated only by degrees of technical skill. As a rule members of the same craft lived on the same street, went to the same social functions, attended the same church, and were buried in the same graveyard. This contrasted sharply with the later factory system under which the owner of the factory and his workers typically live on different sides of the railway tracks, send their children to different schools, attend different churches, and are buried in different cemeteries.

Social control of production   Medieval craftsmen in all their activities were subject to strong social control, which rested fundamentally upon social custom. Social control was often formalized by regulations of municipal governments and frequently, especially in larger towns, administered by a craft gild organization. Whether or not formal gild organization existed in a particular community, the spirit of the age dictated rules of behavior for craftsmen. Production was regulated in the interest of the group and, it should be added, often at the expense of individual initiative.

JUST PRICE

The doctrine of just price reflected the spirit of medieval economic life, especially where production was for a local market under handicraft conditions. A just price was one which would enable a seller to maintain his customary position in society. Of necessity it was also thought of as a price which would preserve equality among members of a particular craft. Each craftsman was thought to have a moral right to receive a reward suitable to his station in life, as well as an obligation not to disturb the stability of his group and of the society in which his craft had a given status. To ask more for his product than was customary would be an unconscionable attempt to rise above the station to which membership in his craft automatically assigned him.

Just price for a particular service or good might move up and down with shifting circumstances, but its guiding principle was always to keep the members of a craft on an equal footing as well as to maintain that craft in its appropriate place in the social hierarchy. Every craftsman enjoyed equality within his group and was morally bound to accept inequality in relation to men in other groups. Medieval society was not only a class system, but a type of caste system as well, for one's station was something to be accepted but not to be improved. Status was the mortar that held together the bricks of the medieval edifice, much as the sanctity of contract holds together the capitalist form of economic society.

If just price was to be something more than an easy generality acceptable to all and hurtful to none, it had to be implemented by concrete rules of behavior and enforced by sanctions against the transgressors of economic justice. Both the rules and the sanctions had their basis in the ethos of medieval society. Communities were small, economic relations personal, and the local market so inelastic that large gains by a few could be made only at the

expense of their fellow townsmen. Therefore the rules of the game required

that none be permitted to take advantage of others. To a ubiquitous moral
authority arising from popular sentiment was added the teachings of the
Church, the regulations of the gild, and the statutes of municipal governments.

The economic teachings of the Church philosophers were not so much
imposed on the community as reflected in its collective conscience. To profiteer
at the expense of a neighbor or charge interest on money lent to a friend in
distress would evoke the odium of fellow citizens. Medieval economic thought
was a branch of religious ethics, and the separation of business from religion
would have seemed as strange as the separation of church and state. Economic
and religious ethics were part of a common code of conduct which subordinated material gain to the salvation of the soul. Such was the medieval
Weltanschauung. This is not to say that medieval men were saints, or that
there were no dissenters from the established moral code. For heretics in religion and in business, medieval society had stronger sanctions.

Specific implementation of just price took several forms. For a few basic
commodities public authorities fixed (assized) the prices. The assizes of bread
and ale set prices according to a scale which varied with the price of grain.
Just prices of other commodities were established by common estimation
within a range considered fair to consumers and just to producers, with due
allowance for fluctuations in supply and demand.

Some pricing practices were specifically outlawed as "unjust." Buying
in order to resell at a profit without adding to the value of the product, a
practice referred to as "regrating," was a form of speculation for which a man
would be "cast forth from God's temple." Another unjust practice was "engrossing," or cornering the market either for the purpose of extracting a high
(unjust) price or to exclude others from possessing a commodity such as a
raw material needed for production. "Forestalling," that is, purchasing an entire
incoming supply of a product before others had an opportunity to buy, constituted a special case of engrossing.

Town and gild authorities supervised in a general way, and often very
specifically, the quality of materials to be used, for example, in making cloth
and shoes. Every craftsman had a right to an equitable share of raw materials,
as the prohibitions against engrossing and forestalling suggest. A craftsman
who obtained special advantages by getting materials not generally available
was required to sell, at a fair price, equal shares to fellow craftsmen. Prescribing the tools that might be used had the effect of controlling costs of production. Control over the volume of output resulted from specifying the number
of apprentices and journeymen who could be employed and by prohibiting
night work. Where gild policy prevailed, one master could not employ another,
and a master was permitted to sell only the products of his own shop, not
those of other masters.

Thus in various and subtle ways, operating through control over prices,
costs, and output, the incomes of craftsmen were limited to amounts just sufficient to permit them to live in their customary manner. With little or no
surplus income out of which to save, capital accumulation was not possible.
Moreover, the incentive to save and reinvest in expanded output was frustrated
by the limitations imposed on production. Insofar as conscious calculation
entered into this behavior, it was less a matter of distaste for capital accumula-

tion as such than fear that capital accumulation by one or a few craftsmen would enable them to outstrip fellow craftsmen, reducing the latter to the status of wage-earners and elevating the accumulators to the position of capitalist employers—which in fact did happen with the development of the putting-out form of industry. Craft-gild policy was oriented toward maintaining the status quo and preserving a way of life which must have seemed to the majority to be the only good life.

Although in the historical long run the medieval philosophy of economic behavior gave way, it did retard the development of capitalism. Nearly everywhere the craft gilds resisted the changes which were to lead to capitalism. Where the craft gilds remained strong, capitalism developed slowly. Thus in most parts of Germany the craft gilds continued strong until the nineteenth century while capitalism remained weak. In England, in contrast, the craft gilds lost their power early and capitalism had an early start. In France the gilds lost some of their strength but not as much as in England, though more than in Germany; as a result the pace of capitalist development in France until the late nineteenth century was more rapid than Germany's but less rapid than England's.

Function and Structure of the Craft Gilds

A craft gild has been defined as "a privileged group of artisans endowed with the exclusive right to practice a certain profession in accordance with the regulations laid down by the public authorities." (Pirenne) Membership in craft gilds appears to have been voluntary at first but subsequently became a necessary condition for the pursuit of a craft in medieval towns. The rule of gild membership as a condition for practicing a craft was given legal sanction by town authorities, who collected taxes as the price of the legal monopoly.

Thus, craft gilds were a form of industrial monopoly. From the point of view of the gilds, the purpose of the monopoly was two-fold: (1) to protect members of the gild against competition among themselves, and (2) to protect the privileged members of this exclusive group against potential and actual competitors outside the gild. Security rated higher than enterprise in the scale of values of medieval handicraftsmen. Craft-gild policy may be described as one of protectionism.

(1) In connection with the desire to protect their members from internal competition, the gilds pursued a brotherhood policy according to which no gildsman would take advantage of a fellow gildsman. The fraternal spirit was strong. "Live and let live" might have served as a motto for the gilds. For example, no master would bid away an apprentice or journeyman who was in the employ of another master, nor would a master bid away a customer from a fellow gildsman. Furthermore, like modern physicians and lawyers, a master was not supposed to advertise. Puffing one's products, which is taken for granted in modern advertising practices, would have seemed quite immoral to a medieval craftsman. All the rules and regulations connected with the administration of just price doctrine were designed to keep competition out of the gild system. Membership was limited usually by the gild itself, subject to control by municipal authority. Craftsmen guilty of violating rules

could be fined for minor infractions and they could be expelled from the gild

for major violations. By virtue of the gild monopoly of the occupation, expulsion was equivalent to denial of the right to practice one's craft.

(2) In pursuit of the policy of protecting members against outside competition, craft gilds employed all economic and political weapons at their disposal. They strove to prevent anyone who was not a gild member from selling at retail in the town. Wholesalers bringing products into town were, as a rule, required to sell at wholesale or not at all. The articles of the gild of London Hatters (1347) provided "that no strange person bringing hats to the said city for sale, shall sell them by retail, but only in gross, and that, to the freemen of the City . . ." In addition, craft gilds attempted to extend their control from the town into the surrounding countryside where rural industry threatened their monopoly. They achieved some success in Germany, but failed in England. Under the English Weavers Act of 1555, an unsuccessful attempt was made to limit a rural weaver to two looms and a rural clothmaker to one loom. This law was designed to prevent the spread of the rural putting-out system. Failure to enforce the Weavers Act was indicative of the strength of industrial capitalism in sixteenth-century England and foreshadowed the early decline of the craft gilds there.

Consumer Protection

Consumers were protected against inferior products under the gild system to an extent probably unequalled in any later exchange economy. Long and rigorous apprenticeship was in itself some guarantee of quality workmanship. All gild ordinances stipulated inspection and provided fines for violating standards. Wardens selected by the gilds and authorized to search the premises of any member were empowered to inspect the products and report under oath to town authorities any defects which they discovered. For example, a London ordinance of 1346 provided for successively larger fines for violations of standards and decreed that on the fourth offense the craftsman "shall forswear the trade for ever."

No matter how well the ideal of sound craftsmanship was upheld, the monopolistic privilege of a relatively small number of producers in any particular craft was enjoyed at the expense of consumers. Gild limitations on the number of craftsmen and on the quantity of output necessarily limited the amount of goods available for consumers and tended to raise prices, or at least prevented prices from falling, as they presumably would have under less restrictive conditions of production. There was a virtual veto on technological progress resulting from minute regulations of production and the gild philosophy that no craftsman should strive to outdo his fellow craftsman. Since the innovation of new techniques by individual craftsmen ran counter to accepted mores, technological progress occurred mainly outside the gild system. It was the Industrial Revolution of later centuries that delivered the final blow to the dying craft-gild system. Industries that arose later and grew up outside the gild system enjoyed a distinct advantage in being able freely to introduce new and more efficient techniques.

In addition to protecting members against internal and external competition and affording protection to consumers, the craft gilds often par-

ticipated in the administration of municipal governments. Craftsmen, like most other townspeople during the later Middle Ages, were free. The important although not entirely valid statement, "town air makes a man free," had meaning in connection with the custom that an escaped serf could not be recalled to the manor after residing a year and a day in a town. As free citizens of towns, craftsmen enjoyed political as well as economic rights. The degree of their participation varied widely, with the right to vote being conditioned upon ownership of a household, and the right to hold office often the special prerogative of wealthier citizens. Here, as elsewhere, political power was roughly proportionate to economic power. Struggles between craftsmen and merchants were often bitter, as were also conflicts between different gilds and between craft gildsmen and the unprivileged workmen associated with production for export trade.

Distinction between the Gild System and the Craft System

The craft, or handicraft, system should be distinguished carefully from the gild system. Handicraft production began long before and lasted long after the gild system. Production based on crafts was present throughout the Middle Ages, whereas the craft gilds appeared relatively late, mainly after 1200. Indirectly, craft gilds resulted from the expansion of long-distance trade, which was also, paradoxically, indirectly responsible for their destruction. Prior to the major expansion of long-distance trade in the second half of the Middle Ages, no serious threat to the handicraft system existed. Activities of craftsmen followed the traditions of their occupations without formalizing them into fixed regulations. When the traditions of the handicraft system were challenged, however, by the growth of industry in the service of long-distance trade, the craft gilds arose as a defense against the encroachments of nascent capitalist organization. Traditional craft practices were now formalized into gild regulations.

Since the formalization of craft practices meant recording rules and regulations in writing, more is known about crafts during the gild period than in earlier times from which few records survive. Professor Postan, the well-known economic historian, has pointed out that the gilds appear to have been more numerous in a defensive period of craft development. Punitive measures were used to hold craftsmen in line, that is, to keep them from going over into the service of capitalist-type activity. Hence craft gilds were more necessary in large cities than in small towns, where the pressures toward breakdown were less. In the long run the craft gilds failed to prevent destruction of the dominant position of handicraft production, but they put up a holding action that lasted for several centuries. Capitalist industry was often forced to operate primarily in rural areas in order to circumvent gild regulations in urban centers.

GROWTH OF EXPORT INDUSTRY

Growth of a large volume of long-distance commerce had a revolutionary effect upon the structure of medieval industry. Industry producing for export proved incompatible with the principles of the handicraft system, a leading character-

istic of which is, as we have noted, the combination of the producing and

selling function in one person, the master craftsman. Such a system was compatible only with relatively small-scale production for local markets. Production for export was highly specialized and necessarily on a much larger scale than industry in the service of local trade.

Craftsmen could not remain primarily craftsmen and also possess the detailed knowledge of distant markets necessary to meet the competition of other large producing centers. While it was theoretically possible, it was unlikely in practice that a craftsman would sell at wholesale and remain an independent worker producing for sale to an export merchant. Generally workers who produced for export became what Professor Gras calls "dependent wholesale" handicraftsmen. In this stage of industrial evolution craftsmen received raw materials from a wholesaler and turned them back as finished goods, being paid for the labor involved in transforming the raw materials into finished products. In western Europe this stage of industrial evolution took the form of the putting-out system. The handicraft system was not immediately displaced, and even in the long run it did not entirely disappear. Handicraft industries exist to some degree in every economy even in the twentieth century. What is significant in the present context, however, is that handicraft ceased to be the typical form of industrial organization. It was replaced by a new, capitalistic form, which became typical in most of western Europe by the sixteenth century.

A sharp contrast existed between medieval craftsmen, producing for a local market, and workers who provided the industrial output for merchants engaged in the export industry. The former were small-scale entrepreneurs, the latter wage-earners. The former—bakers, millers, butchers, cobblers, blacksmiths, hatters—owned their raw materials, tools, and workshops. They also owned the finished product, which they sold directly to consumers. Workers in export industries—weavers, spinners, fullers, dyers—owned neither the raw materials, the goods in process, nor the finished product. They sold their labor rather than the product of their labor. They knew nothing about the distant market in which the products of their labor were sold by their merchant-employer. Craftsman-entrepreneurs were able to control, through their gild or less formal organization, the output and the price of their products and were fairly secure in their customary standard of living. Individual craftsmen could not advance much in wealth or social position, but neither were they likely, under the status system of the medieval town, to descend on the social-economic ladder. Workers in export industries were victimized by every crisis arising from war and other causes that interfered with foreign markets. The relatively free competition of foreign trade offered opportunities for some, but it brought insecurity and poverty to many.

Between these two types of workers there were greater differences in function than in organizational form. Workers in the export industries were usually members of some type of craft organization, often a gild. Export workers included men called "masters" who nominally had apprentices and journeymen under their tutelage. They were, however, masters in name only. They occupied a different economic position from the self-employed master craftsman producing for a protected local market. The changed position of the craftsman may be illustrated by reference to the medieval cloth industry.

Manufacture of woolen cloth constituted by all odds the "great industry" of the Middle Ages. Woolen textiles were produced in widely scattered areas of Europe, but the "great industry" centered in three regions: the Low Countries, Italy, and England. During the last three centuries of the Middle Ages, pre-eminence in the cloth industry passed successively from Flanders in the thirteenth century, to Florence in the fourteenth century, and to England in the fifteenth century. Flanders and Florence failed to solve the problems of an industrial capitalist society, and their industry, after attaining remarkable prosperity, stagnated and decayed on the heels of violent civil strife. The English woolen industry matured more slowly but was able to sustain its development through the later centuries of the Middle Ages and into modern times (after 1500). Success in cloth manufacture was a crucial factor, in a combination of factors, which enabled England to become the classical home of the modern capitalist system. Consequently the cloth industry of Europe has great significance for industrial evolution. It illustrates both the failures and the achievements of medieval capitalism.

Cloth Industry in Flanders During the Thirteenth Century

Under the impetus of trade expansion, population growth, urbanization, and access to English wool, the cloth industry of the Low Countries occupied a pre-eminent position in Europe during the thirteenth century. The industry extended over a considerable area of what is today Belgium and northeastern France, with the greatest concentration in Flanders and Brabant. In Flanders the leading textile centers were Ghent, Ypres, Douai, and Bruges. Brabant lagged behind Flanders during the thirteenth century but gained in importance during the fourteenth century. The leading textile towns in Brabant were Brussels, Louvain, and Antwerp.

At its height during the thirteenth century the Flemish cloth industry was dominated by a class of merchant-manufacturers, who purchased raw wool from England, put it out to artisans, and sold the finished products in distant markets. Local supplies of wool had been important in the early history of the Flemish textile industry, but these supplies soon proved inadequate. Later, when English wool became difficult to obtain, the Low Countries imported Spanish wool. Other than wool, the chief raw material was dyestuffs; some dyes were produced in northern Europe, but the most valuable—red and scarlets, for example—were imported from the Mediterranean.

Processing wool from fiber to finished cloth involved many stages, including initial preparation, combing or carding, spinning, weaving, fulling, drying, shearing, dyeing, and finishing. Each stage in the process was performed by specialized groups of workers. This roundabout method of production required a large investment by merchant-manufacturers in circulating capital in the form of raw materials, goods-in-process, and finished inventories. A few operations were carried on directly in the homes or shops of merchant-manufacturers, but most of the stages were taken care of by putting out materials to "little masters," who in turn employed journeymen to work for them.

By putting out the goods-in-process to "little masters" the merchant-manufacturers economized the use of fixed capital which they would otherwise have had to invest in plant and equipment.

The Champagne fairs provided the chief outlet for Flemish cloth during the twelfth and thirteenth centuries. From Champagne the cloth was distributed into France, Germany, and the Mediterranean region. A considerable quantity of the cloth reaching the Mediterranean was transshipped by Italian merchants to the East. Cloth from northern Europe became an important item in balancing the payments for spices, which were so much in demand in Europe to make over-aged foods less unpalatable.

The career of Jean Boinebroke, a wealthy merchant-manufacturer of thirteenth-century Douai, illustrates the state of affairs in the Flemish cloth industry. Boinebroke imported English wool, employed a large number of small masters to process it, and exported the finished cloth to the Champagne fairs, to England, and to other distant points. He took full advantage of the dependent status of small masters, who in turn paid low wages to their journeymen. When Boinebroke died about 1286, many of the small masters and common workers whom he had exploited so ruthlessly brought claims against his estate. Because Boinebroke's affairs got into the courts, his case is well documented. Undoubtedly there were many other merchant-manufacturers in a similar position in the Flemish cloth industry during its "golden age."

In each Flemish textile center merchant-manufacturers like Boinebroke formed a merchant gild which controlled the industry and commerce of the town. Boinebroke also held office in the town government, which enabled him and fellow merchant-manufacturers to manipulate the law and its administration to their advantage. Through the merchant gild and town government these entrepreneurs exercised minute regulation over the craftsmen, including their wages, hours, and working conditions.

Some craftsmen, such as the highly skilled master dyers and master shearmen, were relatively well off, but the mass of workers were ground down in ruthless fashion by the ruling hierarchy. The large group of poor journeymen at the bottom of the economic ladder were known as the "Blue nails" because of the untidy condition of their hands. Pirenne, the prominent economic historian, describes their existence as follows:

> For the most part these lived in alleys in some room rented by the week and owned nothing but the clothes they wore. They went from town to town hiring themselves out to employers. On Monday morning they were to be met with in the squares and in front of the churches, anxiously waiting for a master to engage them for the week. The working day began at dawn and ended at nightfall . . . Thus the workers in the great industry formed a class apart from the other artisans and bore a pretty close resemblance to the modern proletariat . . . Masters were not afraid to treat them harshly, for they knew that the place of those who had been banished would soon be filled.[2]

Extremes of wealth and poverty in Flanders created dangerous social tensions which exploded into violent class war about 1280. After several decades of preliminary skirmishes involving wage demands, strikes and lockouts,

[2] Henri Pirenne, *Economic and Social History of Medieval Europe* (London: Routledge & Kegan Paul, Ltd., 1936), pp. 189–90.

the "little masters" joined with the journeymen in a general revolution. They sought to destroy the concentration of economic and political power in the hands of their employers and rulers. For more than a century, from approximately 1280 to 1380, the revolution raged between the plebian craftsmen and the patrician merchant-manufacturers. Conflicting feudal claims over Flanders and the Hundred Years War (1337–1453) between France and England, as well as rivalries among the manufacturing cities, impinged upon the class struggles in this most industrialized center of Europe. The oppressed cloth-workers overthrew the ruling oligarchy of merchant-manufacturers and established a "democratic" government in some of the towns. After their triumph, however, factions of the clothworkers fought among themselves for the privilege of carrying out their revolutionary aims. In a successful counterrevolution, the former ruling class crushed the working class.

Virtual destruction of the great Flemish cloth industry was the outcome of the prolonged and violent turmoil. Thousands of skilled clothworkers migrated to Italy and to England, where they assisted in the development of rival cloth industries. The rise of the English woolen industry at first reduced and for a time shut off the most important source of raw wool for Flemish manufacturing. Meanwhile Italian merchants had obtained the exclusive right among foreigners to export English wool and were shipping it to their homeland to provision the Italian industry. The export tax on wool under the "staple system" boosted the price of English wool in Flanders.

Further disruption to the harassed cloth industry arose from disturbances in the chief market outlet for finished cloth when the Champagne fairs fell under the control of the French kings, who attempted to fill their coffers by levying high taxes on the Flemish cloth shipped to Champagne. When the merchants complained, the King cut them off from the market altogether. The decline of the Champagne fairs, which set in toward the end of the thirteenth century, was related to the decline of the Flemish cloth industry. Flanders was caught in the middle of the Hundred Years War. When Flanders tried to protect its source of raw materials by siding with the English, it incurred the wrath of the French King, who wreaked physical devastation even worse than that wrought by the civil wars.

In the end the uprisings of the Flemish clothworkers brought no real improvement in their condition because in the process the whole industry was undermined. Merchant-manufacturers of the Boinebroke type also lost out in the importing and exporting business. In their stead came foreign merchants, mostly Italians and Hansard traders, to dominate the commercial and financial life of the Low Countries during the fourteenth and fifteenth centuries. As the overland outlets to Champagne and points beyond dried up, more cloth was exported by sea, mainly through Bruges, which attained greatness as a shipping center in the fourteenth century.

Another consequence of the stagnation and decay of the Flemish cloth industry was a shift in the center of the industry within the Low Countries from Flanders to neighboring Brabant, which was more prudent than Flanders in managing its economic and political life. Brussels and Louvain became the leading textile cities in the Low Countries. Meanwhile Antwerp, a seaport, became an important outlet for Brabantine cloth.

With the decline of the cloth industry in the Low Countries, northern Italy became the most industrialized region in medieval Europe. The woolen industry in Italy was ancient, but its emergence as a "great industry" organized on a commercial basis sprang from the far-flung trade of enterprising Italian merchants during the later centuries of the Middle Ages. Because of direct contacts in the Mediterranean and the Orient, Italian merchants knew the needs of the market better than other Europeans. Consequently in their trading activities at the Champagne fairs they began purchasing unfinished cloths, which they transported to Italy for finishing and dyeing according to the specifications of their customers. Another advantage favoring the Italian cloth industry was control of the important dye trade by Italian merchants. Special skills and knowledge of finishing and dyeing produced cloth of fine texture and brilliant colors unmatched in other producing areas of Europe.

Among the numerous industrial centers in northern Italy, Florence became by far the most important. It was the greatest industrial city in Europe and perhaps in the entire world during the fourteenth century. Florentine supremacy was still associated with the dyeing and finishing stages of textile manufacture. In the course of the century, however, as Italian merchants took command of the export of English raw wool, ousting the Flemish merchants, Florence expanded its importation of raw wool and made more of its own cloth. Italian wool was of inferior quality, Spanish wool was better, and English wool was best of all for fine cloth.

Ability to pay the costs of importing raw materials from great distances —sometimes back to the area from which the raw material originated—suggests a pattern of trade and industry in Florence not unlike the position attained by western Europe generally during the nineteenth and twentieth centuries. Superior organization and craftsmanship were the secret of Florence's position in the cloth industry. Significantly, the organization was capitalistic. Rich merchants and manufacturers employed great numbers of skilled artisans and common laborers in a highly complex and diverse set of arrangements which were incompatible with a simple handicraft system. The amount of money-capital and knowledge necessary to obtain raw materials, process them, and sell the finished product, far exceeded the means of ordinary artisans.

Although the large-scale industry of Florence was incompatible with a handicraft system, there was a highly organized system of gilds. This was not, however, a genuine gild system in the sense that craft gilds are described above. Heads of large manufacturing firms joined together to form an organization which had more in common with a modern trade association or cartel than with a typical craft gild. The so-called gilds of Florence were really capitalistic trusts, controlled by merchants and manufacturers, who used the organization to keep the masses of artisans and workers submissive. The two great gilds in the cloth industry were the Arte di Calimala and the Arte della Lana. Members of the Calimala imported rough cloth, reprocessed it, dyed it, and finished it. Members of the Lana, the clothmaking gild, imported raw wool

and supervised its manufacture into finished cloth. The Calimala played a larger role in the early period of Florentine greatness, but the Lana surpassed it in importance in the course of the fourteenth century.

Under control of the Lana, raw wool from England and Spain was placed in warehouses from which it was distributed to manufacturing firms in Florence. There were about 200 large firms during the fourteenth century. Manufacturing firms processed the wool in their own large workshops or put it out to subordinate craftsmen, some of whom might employ other workmen to assist them. Spinning and weaving were the operations most commonly performed in the homes of artisans, who worked under contract for entrepreneurs. These "masters" were not independent craftsmen in the full sense. They were either laborers or contractors who undertook to perform an operation for a capitalist by employing the labor of other workers. Cleaning, fulling, dyeing, and finishing were performed in large workshops under the supervision of foremen who were either in the direct employ of manufacturers or of firms which specialized in one or more of these operations. The entire system operated on a fairly free and capitalistic enterprise basis, which allowed for variation in organization. Although the Lana was not a profit-making organization as such, it effectively controlled the cloth industry to the profit of the merchants and manufacturers. Low wages prevailed, and workers were forbidden to organize independently for their economic protection against the powerful group that employed them and dominated the gild.

The differentiation into economic classes associated with the growth of the export industry gave rise to a social unrest which paralleled closely the class warfare that brought down the cloth industry in Flanders a century earlier. The coexistence of the very rich and the very poor in a heavily populated urban community generated seething social unrest. The government of Florence constituted an oligarchy of merchants, manufacturers, and bankers whose political power operated through the gilds. During the tumultuous fourteenth century the latent tensions between the ruling group, on the one hand, and the "little masters" and common workingmen outside the gilds, on the other, broke into open revolution. "Florence, as the most industrialized city in Europe, was the most restless and revolutionary." (Thompson)

The worst violence occurred between 1379 and 1382. A rebellion of the Ciompi, or lowest class of workers, led by Michele Lando, a poor, ragged wool-carder, succeeded in putting across a "democratic" political revolution. Under this regime three new gilds were created: (1) the tailors, shearers and barbers; (2) the wool-combers and dyers; and (3) the Ciompi, or common laborers. Temporarily the common workingmen and lesser gilds held control. However, the artistic gilds maneuvered themselves back into power in 1382 by taking advantage of cleavages among the revolutionaries. More than 150 leaders of the workers' rebellion were executed. The oligarchy of merchants, manufacturers, and bankers ruled Florence until the wealthy Medici family, posing as champions of the common people, seized dictatorial power early in the fifteenth century and held it for three generations until the death of Lorenzo the Magnificent in 1492. Like Flanders in a prior century, Florence had failed to solve the social problem created by the coexistence of the very rich and the very poor in an industrial society, and in consequence its industry declined in the face of civil strife.

By the end of the Middle Ages the English cloth industry was the great-est in Europe. Its pre-eminence in the fifteenth century resembled that of Florence in the fourteenth century and Flanders in the thirteenth century. The significance of the English cloth industry, however, is not that it was similar to those of Flanders and Florence in earlier centuries, but that it was different. For England, and England alone, surmounted the obstacles which brought ruin to the great cloth industries of Flanders and Florence. Consequently the English woolen industry occupies a uniquely important position in the transition from the medieval to the modern economic system. Although it experienced stresses and strains in the course of its long evolution, it did not break on the rocky shores of civil strife as had its Continental predecessors. The great industry of the fifteenth century became a still greater industry in the sixteenth, seventeenth, and eighteenth centuries. It was a crucial factor in the combination of factors which created the modern capitalist *system.*

There are several reasons why England succeeded where Flanders and Florence failed. The English cloth industry, like the others, began in urban centers, but about the time it showed signs of social unrest, it was transformed into a rural system. In a rural environment it enjoyed its greatest strength both at the close of the Middle Ages and in the centuries of early modern capitalism, after 1500.

Ruralization of the English cloth industry was facilitated by a technological event of outstanding importance, namely, the adoption of the fulling mill powered by falling water. Mechanical fulling mills were of necessity located along falling streams, which meant, with few exceptions, in rural areas. The earliest fulling mills were used as adjuncts to urban industry, which brought its cloth into the country to be fulled. Fulling is a process for cleansing and shrinking wool after it has been woven into a web. By the old method the fullers stomped the cloth with their feet under water, using a special type of soil known as "fuller's earth" as a cleansing agent to cut grease from the wool. The essence of the innovation was to replace stomping human feet with wooden hammers propelled by water wheels. The substitution of water power for human labor represented a labor-saving innovation of great magnitude. It displaced many foot fullers, and provoked protests from those adversely affected. According to Professor Carus-Wilson, historian of the woolen industry, the mechanization of fulling in the Middle Ages was as decisive as the mechanization of spinning and weaving in the eighteenth-century Industrial Revolution.[3] Other stages in the processing of cloth followed fulling into the English countryside. Ruralization of the whole cloth industry was strongly under way in the fourteenth century and became the predominant state of affairs in the fifteenth century.

English conditions favored the innovation of mechanical fulling mills while conditions in Flanders and Italy did not. Flanders is a flat country, and the power of falling water from changes in elevation is conspicuous by its

---

[3] See E. M. Carus-Wilson on "The Woolen Industry" in the *Cambridge Economic History of Europe,* Vol. II, Chap. VI, pp. 355–428, for an excellent discussion of the medieval woolen industry.

absence. In Italy some fulling mills were used, for example in the vicinity of Florence, but the climate, if not the topography, of Italy was less well suited to efficient use of water power than England's because Italy's rainfall is highly seasonal. During the rainy winter and spring, streams are frequently raging torrents, whereas during the long dry summer and fall, they may shrink to a trickle. Thus the flat topography of Flanders and the seasonal rainfall of Italy were handicaps inhibiting the use of fulling mills by England's two principal rivals.

Another clear advantage enjoyed by England over all rivals in the cloth industry was the superior quality of English raw wool. In earlier centuries most of England's wool had been exported, and this was still the situation in 1350. By 1450, however, the export of wool cloth far exceeded the export of raw wool. The advantage to the English cloth industry of having a large quantity of high-quality raw wool at relatively low prices was enhanced by the government policy of levying heavy taxes on exports of raw wool. This raised the price of wool abroad without doing so at home, and thereby increased England's natural advantage in the cost of raw wool still further. In contrast to the high export duty on raw wool, cloth was exported free, or, after 1347, with only a moderate duty. Thus the tax structure accentuated the tendency toward use of a larger proportion of the domestic wool clip in domestic cloth production.

There were certain inherent advantages to the system of rural industry, and the one most important at this stage of economic evolution was to provide a more or less automatic solution to the violent social struggles which had led to the ruin of earlier experiments in capitalist industry organized on a large scale. Dispersed as they were under the rural system, English clothworkers could not effectively join together in a revolutionary upsurge, as the "Blue Nails" of Flanders and the Ciompi of Florence had done, to overthrow the ruling classes. Thus England overcame the fundamental social problem of industrial societies, namely, how to prevent the festering sores created by the polarization of wealth and poverty from erupting into a social revolution which impoverishes the rich and pauperizes the poor. Instead of disrupting economic progress as the urban industries of capitalist Flanders and Florence had done, the rural industry of late medieval England broke through the barrier into modern times and became a progressive force in the new system based on free but propertyless workers. This was the contribution of the English cloth industry, and, it may be noted for future reference, the same characteristics carried through to the Industrial Revolution of the eighteenth century, when industry once more became urbanized and the social protest flared anew. But England was able to perpetuate urban capitalism through the nineteenth century. Meanwhile, the English people established a system of political democracy to permit a transition from inequalitarianism to equalitarianism by peaceful means and thus avoid ruin to a great economic empire built up in the course of centuries.

AN ANALYSIS OF THE DECLINE
OF THE HANDICRAFT SYSTEM

The origin of the two groups popularly referred to as "capital" and "labor" may be traced to the disintegration of handicraft as a *system* of industry. The

increase in the extent of the market was the significant factor contributing to the break-up of the handicraft system because it led directly to the separation of the trading function from the producing function, and the accompanying ascendency of traders over producers. From the trading group emerged the capitalists and from the producing groups the laborers.

An analysis of the separation of "capital" from "labor" shows that the application of surplus wealth (capital) was the motive force in the transformation of industrial organization. Surplus wealth (capital) used to employ workers (labor) came from two sources: (1) from merchants outside the craft system and (2) from wealthy master craftsmen within the craft system. Insofar as gilds were involved, the seizure of control of industry by outside capital resulted in the formation of mercantile gilds; and the emergence of wealthy master craftsmen to a position of dominance within the crafts resulted in the formation of livery gilds.

Accumulation of Capital Within Industry

The ideal of medieval craftsmen was economic and social equality. Growth in the extent of markets, in conjunction with an increase in the amount of capital required to produce for expanded markets, differentiated the members of crafts into richer and poorer masters. This changed the internal structure of the crafts. Wealthy "big" masters became in function the employers of the poorer "little" masters, who were reduced to a position more like that of a journeyman than of a truly self-employed master. Separation of the trading and producing functions violated a fundamental principle of handicraft organization. Big masters gave more attention to trading and left production to their hired employees, the little masters and the journeymen.

Rise of Livery Gilds

Directly and indirectly the poor masters were prevented from exercising the rights traditionally associated with a master craftsman. Practices which tended to prevent poorer members of crafts from attaining full status included the following: establishing several types of mastership; patrimony, or the right of the son of a "big" master to become a master without serving an apprenticeship; excessive membership fees and expensive inaugural dinners for masters, which poor journeymen could ill afford; requiring a masterpiece, a special work that might require the labor of an entire year, which was more time than the poor could afford to take; stipulating that no borrowed capital could be employed, which meant that only those who had already accumulated or inherited capital could set themselves up as masters; and expensive regalia, called livery, which only richer masters could afford. It is from the last requirement that the "livery gild'" and "livery company" takes its name. From its original use as a symbol of fraternal solidarity, the livery regalia became the basis of distinction between rich and poor, between "big" and "little" masters. Livery status first developed within the original type of craft gild. Later the livery companies were separately incorporated, usually by royal charter given in return for financial contributions to the Crown. What remained of the original craft gild now became an appendage to the livery gild. Rich

masters became the officers of the livery organization and conducted its affairs in their own interest. In London, livery gildsmen were powerful in the government. Even kings were made honorary members of the livery companies. Thus the former equalitarian craft system was transformed into a totally different kind of organization. Here one may gain a significant insight into how institutions change: The old form is at first modified in response to new conditions and finally, after successive modifications, an entirely new organization is created in recognition of the altered function.

As employer-capitalist masters became organized in livery companies, journeymen and little masters tended to form their own associations, which in England were known as yeomen's gilds, but which may be more clearly recognized for what they were under the name of journeymen's gilds. Their function was to represent the interests of dependent workers in their relations with employers. In some instances journeymen's gilds, which usually began as informal groups, were able to attain a recognized, although subordinate, place in the reformed gild organization. In other instances, journeymen and small masters formed entirely separate groups which operated outside the law in attempting to maintain and improve their working conditions. The latter type of journeymen's gild was similar to the modern labor union, which, unlike the medieval craft gild, does not include employers among its members, but only employees. Sporadic attempts by journeymen to bargain collectively were backed by strikes, which frequently resulted in violence, and brought down upon their organization the hostility of the legal authorities as well as of their employers, since under the common law of England such combinations of workingmen were viewed as conspiracies in restraint of trade. There was little continuity in journeymen's associations and there appears to be no single case in which a modern labor union is descended directly from an early journeymen's gild. The great Scottish economist, Adam Smith, commented in 1776 on the general lack of success of combinations among journeymen: "The workmen, accordingly, very seldom derive any advantage from the violence of those tumultuous combinations, which . . . generally end in nothing, but the punishment or ruin of the ring-leaders." [4] Despite lack of success in attaining their objectives, independent journeymen's combinations were significant in showing how the disintegration of craft gilds into livery gilds, dominated by capitalist-employers, created the need for an independent workingmen's organization to try to offset the power of organized employers.

Amalgamation of Craft Gilds

In addition to the tendency of some masters to gain control over other craftsmen in the same craft, there was a tendency for several crafts in related activities to fall under the domination of other crafts. Significantly, crafts close to the market for final products usually took the initiative in the amalgamation of crafts. In the cloth industry, for example, amalgamation was initiated by finishers and dyers—the crafts nearest the market for the final product, cloth—who absorbed the weavers, spinners, fullers, and shearmen. This may be illustrated in the following manner:

[4] Adam Smith, *Wealth of Nations* (New York: Modern Library edition, 1937), p. 67.

Spinners–Weavers–Fullers–Shearers–Dyers–Finishers $\left.\right\}$ Final
Product
Market

*Amalgamated as Clothmakers
Under Control of Dyers and Finishers.*

In the leather trade similar tendencies toward amalgamation were present. In both London and Paris the saddlers, who were near the product market, were able to gain control over related crafts (joiners, painters, and lorimers) which worked on leather for saddles and other equipment for horses. Being near the market for the final product, the saddlers were able to assume the trading function and dominate the crafts which supplied them with materials from earlier stages of production. A variation within the same general pattern occurred in the leather trade when the leather sellers, a mercantile group not associated with any particular craft, absorbed the glovers, pursers, and pouch-makers in London in the late 1400's and early 1500's. Similar trends were present in the metal crafts (cutlery, bladesmiths, and sheathers) and other allied crafts.

Growth of the market made control of the trading function so strategic that there was constant striving to extend the scope of control over production. Hence crafts struggled against allied crafts for domination. The weavers and fullers of Paris contested with each other during the fifteenth and sixteenth centuries. As one craft sought control over others, various defensive alliances took place for mutual protection against absorption by other crafts. Membership in some crafts was so small as to compel them, in a struggle for survival, to join with other crafts in order to provide substantial protection against more numerous and more powerful crafts. Whatever the special detail in any particular case, the important overall result was separation of the trading and producing functions, with the ascendency of the former as trading capitalists. Where craft gilds existed, they were transformed into trading gilds.

Control of Crafts by Capital Accumulated Outside Industry

Merchants engaged in long-distance trade were not content to accept whatever products craftsmen might make available to them; instead the merchants gradually assumed control over industry producing for export. The tendency for control over a whole industry to begin in the branches nearest the market is illustrated by the Calimala of the great Florentine woolen industry. Here capitalistic cloth manufacture started with dyers and finishers importing semifinished cloth from northern Europe. It was in England, however, that the classic development took place with the rise of mercantile gilds in urban centers.[5]

Whereas the English livery company arose from within the structure of the old craft gild, the mercantile gild had its origins outside production. In

[5] The mercantile gilds were not the same as the old Gild Merchant spoken of in connection with the expansion of medieval trade beginning in the eleventh century. The mercantile gilds were a product of developments in the fourteenth and fifteenth centuries in England.

terms of origin, the livery company is associated with industrial capital used in production, whereas the mercantile gild is associated with capital used in marketing. However, the livery and mercantile companies are to be distinguished more in their origins than in their functions. Both types involved separation of the producing and trading functions. Among the Big Twelve gilds of London in the fifteenth and sixteenth centuries, those which sprang from craft origins were in fact dominated by big traders, who paid only lip service to the traditions and ideals of the craft whose name their company usually bore. The dominance of mercantile capital over industry was characteristic of both the livery and the mercantile companies. On the other hand, there was less than complete harmony among the two groups, which struggled against each other for monopolistic privileges. The strictly merchant group attempted to gain for themselves the exclusive right of being general wholesale traders in merchandise by restricting the gilds of craft origin to selling the product with which they were originally identified. Ordinary craftsmen were usually excluded from general trade, but this restriction was effective mainly against small craftsmen.

Rural Industry and the Domestic System

The livery and mercantile gilds were, like the craft gilds which they displaced, monopolistic organizations. They held charters which gave them exclusive rights to perform their assigned functions within their local territory. A break in this traditional urban monopoly came with the spread of industry into rural areas in the form of the domestic system, usually referred to as the putting-out system.

In several respects conditions in rural areas were favorable for the growth of domestic industry. A large supply of partially unemployed labor was available among the overwhelmingly rural population of the time. After the decline of the manor, and especially in England after the beginnings of the enclosure movement, many rural dwellers possessed insufficient land to keep them fully employed throughout the year. An obvious solution to the increased demand for labor that arose with the expansion of trade was to be found in the rural areas, where industry could be combined with farming to provide more employment for rural families. Moreover, the cost of living was lower in rural areas, which meant that rural workers might earn a higher real wage with the same or an even lower money wage, as compared with urban workers. Even on a small cottage plot, rural dwellers could maintain a garden to supply a large part of their basic provisions, or if they were purchased, they could be bought more cheaply in rural than in urban markets. Hence both employer and employee might be better off under the rural system of industry.

Another condition favoring the spread of industry into rural areas was the freedom enjoyed by rural workers. There was no effective gild control, no restriction on the methods of production, no enforced seven-year apprenticeship, very little supervision, and no right of search of the artisan's domicile as under the urban gild system. Rural artisans enjoyed the status of an apparently independent small master. As urban gilds became closed to new members or to new masters, a journeyman could move to a suburb or into the countryside to ply his craft. He did not enjoy the psychic satisfaction of official

master's status, but this had also become difficult for the poor urban journey-man to attain. It was better to be an independent rural artisan with the appear-ance of mastership than a dependent urban artisan acknowledged only as a journeyman or "small" master. Rural artisans, e.g., weavers, might actually be-come independent in the sense that they acquired their own raw materials and, after processing them, would market the finished product, probably to a middleman or some type of wholesale cloth dealer. In England the presence of a local supply of wool made it possible for country artisans to buy raw mate-rial directly from producers, but the uncertainty of selling, especially when nearby urban markets were restricted to local urban producers, left only long-distance markets available to rural craftsmen, and forced them to receive orders in advance from cloth buyers. Independent retail handicraft was vir-tually impossible under the circumstances, and independent wholesale handi-craft easily gave way to dependent wholesale handicraft, that is, to the putting-out system. Thus the independence of the rural artisan was more apparent than real from the point of view of his actual economic position. As a country dweller and part-time farmer, he did, nevertheless, enjoy a kind of independ-ence which was denied the urban wage-earner.

Rural industry developed under two types of capitalists. Urban traders with market demands which exceeded their available urban sources of supply found that the suburbs and rural districts offered excellent opportunities for expansion because they were outside the jurisdiction of urban monopoly. Where urban craftsmen continued to have a voice, they protested against rural com-petition. Nevertheless, there was a strong tendency for some of the stages of processing like spinning and weaving, and sometimes fulling, to be "put out" to country workers. The more complex stages of dyeing and finishing remained more typically town operations.

A second type of capitalist in rural industry was the "new" man from the country area itself. Although country workers usually remained in a de-pendent status, the more enterprising artisans had a better opportunity to achieve capitalist status in the country than in the towns. For example, a coun-try weaver who accumulated some capital could begin to employ other rural weavers on a putting-out basis. Capitalists of this type often had their origin as country producers and during the period of early capitalism were known as "captains of industry," as distinguished from "merchant princes," who usu-ally sprang from the urban trading class.

Rise of the National State

A famous historian of the craft system has stated: "Thus the handicraft or gild system is associated with the *town economy*, the domestic or commis-sion system with the *national economy*, and the factory system with the *world economy*." (Unwin) The strength of the handicraft system lay in the town economy, and especially in those trades which supplied the local town mar-ket; the national state arose from and created conditions which were incom-patible with a continuation of the handicraft and gild systems. Generally speak-ing, the growth of a national economy, and with it the development of a national state which had no interest in perpetuating local town monopolies, sooner or later eliminated the political and economic environment within

which the craft system could survive. Successful national economic authority seems to have been fatal to gild power even where this was not the intention of statesmen. England's powerful Tudor monarchs attempted to legislate in favor of the small craftsman with results that appear to have been quite the opposite from what was intended. For example, the famous Statute of Apprentices (1563) provided that only one craft could be practiced by any one person, a condition necessary to the existence of a successful handicraft system. The statute also provided that no one could become a master who had not served a seven-year apprenticeship in his craft. Since no attempt was made to enforce the statute in rural areas, it was no handicap to the rural putting-out system, which eventually replaced the handicraft system. By removing the control of industry from gild and town authorities and transferring it to the national government, the Statute did more to destroy than to preserve the craft system. In countries where a strong central government was lacking, the craft and gild systems remained strong, as in Germany until the nineteenth century.

Summary of the Decline of the Handicraft System

Growth in the extent of the market was the primary force in the decline of the medieval handicraft system of industry. A typical handicraftsman produced for a narrow, local, inelastic market. Such markets were usually too small to allow free competition.[6] Since demand in the local market for any particular commodity was relatively inelastic, there was little opportunity or need for individual sellers to expand their sales, or for additional firms to enter the local market. Among medieval craftsmen the typical, and at one time or another almost universal, solution to the threat of competition was to obtain a legal monopoly according to which no new producers were permitted to enter without consent from existing producers; and when admitted, to enter on conditions laid down by the existing group.

Interregional and international trade did not conform to the conditions necessary for maintaining equalitarian group monopoly (or oligopoly) by small producers. In relation to the size of any one producer, these markets were almost unlimited. In order to take advantage of the opportunity offered by long-distance markets, an accumulation of capital was required far beyond the needs of production for local markets. There grew up alongside the system of independent masters a new system of production for export. From two sources there emerged men of large capital to take over control of industry producing for export trade. Rich master craftsmen increased their output by bringing other craftsmen into their employ, reducing the latter to the status of wage-earners. Another type of capitalist organizer came from outside the crafts. They were merchants who had accumulated capital from trading. The former type of capitalist gained control of industry by transforming the craft

---

[6] As the modern theory of monopolistic competition clearly suggests, fierce competition among existing firms for a larger share of the market brings retaliation from the other sellers, whose only alternative to retaliation within a competitive framework is to lose out entirely. Under such circumstances the sensible action for local firms is to shove aside the competitive framework and adopt a policy of live-and-let-live.

organization from its original structure into a new type of organization, which in England was known as the livery company or gild. The other merchant type of capitalist formed mercantile companies or gilds. Old line crafts fought against these usurpers and if they appeared to succeed in urban centers, the new men supplied materials and employment to small masters in rural areas outside the jurisdiction of the craft gilds. Since wealthy merchant capitalists usually controlled the town government, they were able to secure exceptions from the customary controls of the craft organization. But where national states were stronger and town governments subordinate to them, as in England, the urban monopolies were less secure and capitalist industry expanded more rapidly.

Thus we see the handicraft system and, where it existed, the accompanying gild system, undergoing transformation. Changes began as exceptions to customary controls and ended by transforming the entire structure and function of the craft organization. The form often remained long after the function had changed. In time, even the form of gild organization was abandoned, but this was sometimes a matter of centuries. Long before the handicraft forms were obliterated, the small masters, who under the old system had been independent producers owning the materials and the products on which they labored, had become dependent workers employed by "big" masters. The modern system of capital and labor replaced the independent craftsman of the local medieval market.

SELECTED BIBLIOGRAPHY

ASHLEY, WILLIAM J., *An Introduction to English Economic History and Theory*, Vol. I. New York: G. P. Putnam's Sons, 1911.

BLAND, A. E., P. A. BROWN, and RICHARD H. TAWNEY, eds., *English Economic History, Select Documents*, Part I, sections 5 and 6. London: G. Bell and Sons, Ltd., 1914.

BOISSONNADE, P., *Life and Work in Medieval Europe*. New York: Harper and Row, Publishers, 1964. (paperback)

CARUS-WILSON, E. M., "The Woolen Industry," in *Cambridge Economic History of Europe*, ed. Michael M. Postan and E. E. Rich, Vol. II, chapter 6. London: Cambridge University Press, 1952.

LIPSON, E., *The Economic History of England*, Vol. I, 12th ed., chapters 8 and 9. London: Adam & Charles Black, Ltd., 1959.

PIRENNE, HENRI, *Economic and Social History of Medieval Europe*, chapter 6. London: Routledge & Kegan Paul, Ltd., 1936.

POWER, EILEEN E., *Medieval People*. Garden City, N.Y.: Doubleday Anchor Books, 1954. (paperback)

THRUPP, SYLVIA L., "The Gilds," in *Cambridge Economic History of Europe*, eds. Michael M. Postan and E. E. Rich, Vol. III, chapter 5. London: Cambridge University Press, 1963.

UNWIN, GEORGE C., *The Gilds and Companies of London*, 4th ed. London: F. Cass, 1963.

————, *Industrial Organization in the Sixteenth and Seventeenth Centuries*, 2nd ed. London: F. Cass, 1963.

CARUS-WILSON, E. M., "The English Cloth Industry of the Late Twelfth and Early Thirteenth Centuries," *Economic History Review*, XIV, No. 1 (1944), 32–50.

————, "An Industrial Revolution of the Thirteenth Century," *Economic History Review*, XI, No. 1 (1941), 39–60.

DE ROOVER, RAYMOND A., "The Concept of the Just Price: Theory and Economic Policy," *Journal of Economic History*, XVIII (Dec., 1958), 418–34.

THRUPP, SYLVIA L., "Medieval Gilds Reconsidered," *Journal of Economic History*, II (Nov., 1942), 164–73.

————, "Social Control in the Medieval Town," *Journal of Economic History*, I (Dec., 1941), 39–52.

VAN WERVEKE, H., "Industrial Growth in the Middle Ages: The Cloth Industry in Flanders," *Economic History Review*, VI (April, 1954), 237–45.

Decline of the Manorial System

Medieval economic life was overwhelmingly rural. Underlying an infinite variety of physical arrangements and social relations in agricultural organization lay a fundamental division between peasant cultivators, on the one hand, and feudal lords, on the other hand. In the transition from feudalism to capitalism the position of both peasants and feudal lords was basically altered. Cultivators, the majority of whom had been unfree serfs, became free peasants and free wage-earners; feudal lords lost their political, military, and legal sovereignty on a local scale and became rent-receiving landlords and functionaries in the service of sovereign kings.

The following discussion, which seeks to explain the role of agriculture in the transition from feudalism to capitalism, takes up three types of institutions related to medieval agriculture: (1) the open-field system, (2) feudalism, and (3) the manor. As in the two preceding chapters, the structure and function of these medieval institutions are discussed only insofar as necessary to give the setting for the break-up of the manorial system in the latter part of the Middle Ages. No attempt is made to sketch the details of medieval rural economic life.

The Open-Field System

The open-field system was the technical as distinguished from the economic-social (manorial) aspect of medieval rural life. It prevailed even where there were no manors and continued to exist in many parts of Europe long after the feudal and manorial systems had disintegrated. In eastern Europe it persisted into the twentieth century and in England, where feudalism had largely disappeared by the fifteenth century, the open-field system survived in some areas until the nineteenth century. The term "open-field" seems to have come into use during the fifteenth and sixteenth centuries to distinguish the old method of organization from the enclosure system in which lands were fenced or hedged and held in consolidated units rather than in scattered strips.

Village arable lands were usually divided into two or three large fields, although many estates had more than three fields. In a two-field system, one-half of the arable land was cultivated and one-half lay fallow each year. In a three-field system the arable land was divided into three fields, two of which

were cultivated each year and one of which remained fallow. From the point of view of land utilization, the three-field system was more efficient than the two-field system because it utilized for production in any one year two-thirds of the total arable land, as compared with only one-half under a two-field system. In terms of utilization of land and labor the two-field system appears to have been more widely used in the early Middle Ages, but the three-field system seems to have become prevalent by the close of the Middle Ages.

Open-field cultivation is sometimes referred to as "strip farming" because each field was divided into many small strips. Individual tenants would possess a number of strips scattered throughout each of the two or three fields. For example, an individual peasant might hold ten one-acre strips in each of three fields. Between strips there were no fences or other dividing lines except low-lying balks of earth or grass.

The size of strips was probably related to the area which could be plowed in a single day and, although this varied with the type of soil and the technique of plowing, something like one acre appears to have become a standard unit for a day of plowing. In northern Europe the strips were usually long and narrow. The modern term "furlong," designating one-eighth of a mile or 220 yards, is derived from the medieval furrow-long, which was the distance a team of oxen apparently plowed before resting and turning. Such a standard strip 220 yards in length and 22 yards wide would contain 4840 square yards, or 43,560 square feet, thus constituting one acre.

The rectangular shape of the typical strip is interesting because it illustrates how technology (plowing) affects economic organization. The plow is obviously one of the most important tools ever developed. Throughout history most peoples of the world have gained their living by tilling the soil. As Max Weber [1] points out, the plow was in the beginning a hoe-like tool, propelled by human or animal power, which merely scratched the surface of the soil. Where the art of plowing did not progress beyond the primitive hoe-plow stage, it was necessary to plow criss-cross in order to loosen the soil adequately for planting. Even criss-cross scratching did not penetrate the soil deeply. However, in the Mediterranean area, where the soil is light and relatively shallow, the hoe-plow was tolerably satisfactory. In northern Europe, on the other hand, the soil is deep and heavy, and the hoe-plow technique was inadequate. This fact helps to explain why Roman agricultural techniques were not more commonly transferred to trans-Alpine Europe. The Germans and other north European people had to develop a plow better suited to their environment. It was a large, heavy instrument with a knife-like blade which cut deep furrows in the soil and turned it over on a "moldboard," thus putting the humus down where plant roots could feed on it. It did not require criss-cross plowing. Manorial literature suggests that eight oxen were used to draw the huge wheeled plow of the medieval plowman, although there were lighter plows which required fewer oxen. The efficient way to plow with a team of several animals was to do one long furrow and then wheel around and plow back. The result was a standard rectangular strip a furrow long and one day's plowing (an acre) in area. Variations in topography, of course, caused devia-

[1] Max Weber (1864–1920) was a famous German scholar of comparative economic history. See his *General Economic History* (New York: The Free Press of Glencoe, 1950).

tions from the standard strip. The basic unit of cultivation was largely determined by the circumstances of soil and technology.

Of more fundamental economic significance was the method of allotting the arable land of the open-field system to individuals in small parcels scattered throughout the fields. If an individual peasant held a total of thirty acres, why did he not have it in one consolidated thirty-acre farm rather than in thirty one-acre strips? The explanation lies in the cultural mores of village life. In the medieval community there was a strong equalitarian bent within social-economic classes. This was a community in which all people of the same class were supposed to share and share alike. Most families were privileged to share in the cultivation of the best soil and were also obligated to share in the cultivation of the worst soil in use. Land differed in fertility, drainage, distance from the village, and in other respects. Most peasants held some fertile and some infertile soil, some high land and some low land, some land close by and some distant land. The vicissitudes of weather, always so important in farming, were automatically shared under this arrangement. In a year of floods, the crops on low lands would be damaged while the crops on high lands might not be damaged. In dry years opposite conditions would prevail. The strip system guaranteed that families would be affected equally in wet or dry years. Although the disadvantages of strip-farming were obvious, it nevertheless assured each villager from year to year and from generation to generation for the duration of the system that he and his descendants would share more or less equally in resources and yields with their fellow villagers. Scattered holdings also arose with the gradual clearing of land. As population grew, new arable fields were cleared from the forests and doled out to the existing households of the village. Other factors such as inheritance and co-operative plowing may also help account for the system of scattered strip-holdings, but they appear less important than the desire for economic equality and mutual insurance for members of the community as a whole.

The open-field system as described above was the answer of the medieval village to the timeless question of individual initiative versus social security, of freedom versus authority. Compared with the later capitalist era the open-field system was weighted on the side of security and against individual initiative. When the villagers as a group decided to plant wheat in a certain field, each individual strip-holder was required to plant wheat. Deviation from the decision of the group was not permitted. If an individual cultivator had new ideas about the rotation of crops or about improved technology, or if he possessed a special aptitude for raising certain crops, there was little opportunity under this rigid system for him to put his ideas into action except by the dubious method of convincing the group that all should accept the innovation. Since group decisions were based on rigid custom rather than upon rational, forward-looking calculations, the "radicals" who wanted to change the techniques of cultivation were not in a favorable position. All social institutions are resistant to change, but the open-field system was particularly impervious to innovation. Inflexibility in the social process of decision-making resulted in great economic inefficiency. Compared with the later age, technical progress was notoriously slow under medieval husbandry except where special circumstances necessitated departure from tradition. If change were to come, it had to be from the outside since it was not engendered from within the system.

As previously noted, trade and commerce provided the exogenous forces making for change in the medieval economy.

Feudalism

Feudalism refers to a society with no strong central government. Decline of the western part of the old Roman Empire had left western Europe with no organized basis for the protection of life, limb and property. A substitute for the law and order provided by Rome was found in the protection and power of feudal lords. The weak sought the protection of the strong, which the strong provided, at a price. The fief, or feudum, was a hereditary right of land tenure given in exchange for swearing homage to the one who granted the right of tenure. The feudal hierarchy was dominated by military men and by churchmen, whose status ranged all the way from the highest lord, the king, to the lowest noble, the knight. Every lord was the vassal of some other lord; even kings were vassals of other kings. For example, the king of France was at times a vassal of the king of England, and at other times the king of England was a vassal of the king of France. Always the important practical question was how far a lord could go in enforcing his "rights." The inability of princes and kings to enforce their authority over their vassals left to local lords the privilege and the duty of exercising control over local affairs. When a prince was able to enforce his pretended rights down through a long hierarchy of vassals and sub-vassals and over a wide area he became a *de facto* king, and a national state existed. It was the gradual strengthening of central authority, the enforcement of the "king's justice" in local affairs, that accounts for the emergence of the national state and the decline of feudalism. Throughout the medieval period attempts were made to establish central authority in western Europe, but without much success. Charlemagne set up the Holy Roman Empire as a would-be successor of the old Roman Empire, but as Voltaire sagely observed, it was neither holy, nor Roman, nor an empire. In England after the Norman conquest (1066), political and military authority was well centralized, but it was not until after the War of the Roses (1455–1485) that central authority was permanently established. In France, strong central authority was permanently established under the great kings Henry IV (reigned 1589–1610) and Louis XIV (reigned 1643–1715). Germany and Italy lost out as great powers because of their inability to unify principalities into national states until the second half of the nineteenth century.

The Catholic (universal) Church was the nearest substitute for strong central government in the thousand years from the collapse of the Roman Empire in the West to the rise of national states. The Church in the West exerted some influence on lay rulers and lords. Through the Truce of God, for example, the Church attempted to restrict feudal warfare by prohibiting fighting, at first on Sundays, and subsequently from Thursday sundown through Monday sunrise, and during Lent and Church festivals, until only about ninety days a year remained for "legal" warfare. Needless to say, this truce was widely violated but the important point is that the Church paralleled the political strength of the lay lords. Bishops, abbots, and other high Church officials were "spiritual lords" who exercised the power of government in addition to holding land, controlling serfs, and managing enterprises. With the rise of national

states the political and secular power of the Church declined. The long struggle for supremacy between the Church and state ended with the dominance of the state.

The Manorial System

The manor was the basic economic institution of medieval rural life in western Europe. The essential condition of a manor was the coexistence of two classes, the unfree peasant or serf, on the one hand, and the lord of the manor on the other. Corresponding to these two social classes were two types of land, the demesne, or the lord's land, and the land held and worked by serfs for their own sustenance. Most manors had more than one type of tenant. The most important distinction was between the unfree tenant or villein, who had to provide labor service to his lord, and the free tenant, who did not normally render labor services. In between were many degrees of freedom and servitude, depending upon legal privileges as well as economic obligations. In general, free tenants were in the minority when the manorial system was at its height in about the twelfth century. By contrast, one of the signs of the decline of the manorial system was an increase in the number of free tenants.

The entire manorial estate was under the control of the lord or his agent, and it was through the lord that the feudal system was linked with the open-field village. A manor represented the lord's fief, or hereditary grant, which had been conferred upon him by someone of superior military and political power and to whom the lord owed allegiance. The manor was primarily important to the lord because it provided the economic basis by which he and his household were maintained in their accustomed place in society. The privileged position of the lord in relation to the underlying population of the manor was justified, in theory at least, because the lord performed the high functions of protection, supervision, and administration of justice. If the lord was a churchman, the bishop or abbot engaged in religious work required produce from a manor to maintain a cathedral or monastery. In turn, the lord was privileged to live off the labor of his tenants, who tilled his fields and made payments in kind and in money, according to the custom of the manor.

One of the best sources of information concerning the various social classes associated with the medieval manor is the *Domesday Book* of 1086. This famous book contains a census of the lands and people of England. It was compiled for William the Conqueror after he invaded England from Normandy in 1066. At the time of the Norman invasion, England already had a well-developed manorial system, but it attained its highest development in the two centuries following the conquest. The Normans proved to be better organizers and administrators than the Anglo-Saxon lords whose lands they confiscated.

Among the several social classes which constituted the underlying population the largest was the villein class of unfree tenants, who constituted 38 per cent of the total number of tenants recorded in the Domesday survey. The relative size of this class increased under Norman rule. The normal land holding of a villein was called a virgate, which varied in size but was typically about thirty acres, made up perhaps of as many individual one-acre strips. Strips passed from one generation of villeins to the next by right of succession,

which the manorial system recognized in fact, if not by virtue of any secure legal right. In addition to holdings of crop-land, the villein had rights in the common pastures, woods, and wastelands.

The primary characteristic of villein status which marked one as a serf was the obligation to work on the lord's demesne a certain number of days per week. The amount of week-work, as this obligation was called, was related to the amount of land held by the tenant. In general, the number of days increased with the size of the holding. Three days per week appears to have been common for a virgater. In addition to his labor the villein was expected to supply draft animals which were teamed with those of other villeins to constitute a plow-team. These plow-teams not only plowed the peasant strips but demesne land as well. Besides plowing, the villeins were called upon to perform every task associated with the cultivation, harvesting, transporting, and storing of the crops grown on the lord's demesne.

Nor was this all. In addition to rendering a regular number of days of labor on the lord's demesne each week, the villein worked extra or boon days at certain times of year. Boon days came at plantings, harvest, or other busy seasons of the year, such as sheep-shearing time. They were especially onerous to the villein and conversely were highly valued by the lord, who offered free meals and ale as special inducements to get more work done. Rendering labor services on boon days remained after week-work had been commuted into money dues, and even "free" tenants, who owed no week-work, were frequently subject to boon-work.

Besides week-work and boon-work, the villein was obligated to make other contributions to his lord. These took the form of annual levies of grain, chickens, wool, eggs, pigs, honey, ale, malt, sheep, lambs, or other specified commodities. Such payments were customary rather than arbitrary and often represented the price of certain specific "privileges" enjoyed by villeins. For example, capons might be given to the lord as a license fee for the right to take wood from the forest. There were other special fees like the *merchet* and the *heriot*. The *merchet* was a payment to the lord on the occasion of the marriage of a villein's daughter. Additional payment was required in case a daughter married someone on another manor, the presumption behind this extra marriage payment being that the lord was deprived of the labor of the woman and of her future offspring. Payment of *merchet* came to be viewed as the surest test of servile status, and in the period of the decline of serfdom was looked upon as one of the most degrading limitations on the personal liberty of villeins. The *heriot* was a kind of inheritance tax paid by a villein when his land passed to his son. This fee was a recognition by a new tenant of the lord's right in the land which the villein was privileged to use. Villeins were also required to grind their grain into flour at the lord's mill and to pay a toll which was usually a percentage of the flour ground. Similarly, lords established monopolies in sawmills, wine presses, and fulling mills and charged tenants a monopoly price for the "privilege."

On those manors where villeins realized money incomes from the sale of grain, wool, hides, honey, or other produce, they were expected to make payments in money in addition to their payments in kind. Indeed, money rents seem to have been paid by all types of peasants in all parts of western

Europe throughout the manorial period. It is, therefore, a mistake to think of the medieval manor as a self-sufficient entity based on barter.

After giving of his time and of the products of his labor, and after the payment of innumerable dues, fees, rents, and fines, there remained to the peasant and his family very little in excess of bare subsistence. Since villeins had no legal security except that provided by the rather tenuous "custom of the manor," any surplus remaining could be engrossed by the lord, who had the might and the right to take advantage of changes in production and organization.

Viewed through modern eyes there appears to have been much that was unfair in the socio-economic relations between the lord and his serfs. It seems self-evident that the serf was exploited by his lord, when, for example, the serf spent half his working days laboring for the lord, in addition to making numerous contributions of his own produce and even of the little money he might possess. Unquestionably, the concentration of economic and political power in the hands of the lord offered a temptation to tyrannize over his subjects which only the best of men would resist. Whatever economic surplus existed accrued to the lord, who used the surplus in high living, fighting, and building castles, churches, monasteries, and cathedrals.

There were, however, quantitative limitations on the degree of exploitation. The technical inefficiency of production, which severely restricted the amount that could be produced in excess of subsistence, was the primary limitation on exploitation. Agriculture was small-scale, the division of labor was limited, and incentives to technical improvement were weak. Exploitation was further limited because lords were dependent upon the labor of their tenants to keep the manor as a going concern. It was neither profitable nor probable that a lord would abuse his serfs to the point where they became too discontented with their lot. Unlike a wage laborer under capitalism, tenants could not be dismissed because they enjoyed hereditary rights which were rooted in ancient custom. Furthermore, the lord could not count on getting new tenants if his old ones became dissatisfied and ran away, as they frequently did, especially after the rise of new towns.

THE MEDIEVAL EXPANSION OF AGRICULTURE

Along with the expansion of trade and the growth of population in western Europe during the twelfth and thirteenth centuries went a major expansion in arable and pasture land. Forests were cleared, marshes drained, and in the densely populated Low Countries polders were dyked off from the sea. In England, too, the amount of land under cultivation and in pasture increased through reclamation of forests and wastelands and drainage of fens. Even more important was a geographical movement of west Europeans to Europe's land frontier; the Germans led a colonizing drive eastward beyond the Elbe and the Weser rivers into territory only thinly populated by Slavic peoples. Much of this colonizing was organized, financed, and carried out by ecclesiastical groups, especially the Benedictines and Cistercians. Thus more agricultural land came into productive use. These vigorous movements in reclamation

and colonization reflected the need for food and raw materials of an increasing urban and rural population. The growth of population over wider geographic areas was basic to the increase in long-distance trade which was so marked in northern Europe during these centuries (1100–1350).

European agriculture changed in the process of growing. The medieval manor moved in the direction of increasing commercialization in connection with the opportunities offered by expanding markets for agricultural products. Numerous farm commodities were sold for money in nearby urban communities, and some commodities such as wool and grain were among the bulky essentials which constituted an important part of the medieval trade of northern Europe.

The growing market orientation led an increasing number of manorial lords to convert their demesne lands into commercial farms from which they sold the surplus produce for money. They raised grain and sheep and other commercial "crops," sold them in organized markets, accumulated capital, and entered into the new spirit of a new age. Peasants likewise were attracted by the opportunities to sell grain in local markets and strove to produce surpluses in order to earn money which they might use, the lord willing, to substitute for labor services. Lords, however, were reluctant to permit the substitution of money payments for labor services, a process known as commutation —because they wanted as much unpaid labor from their serfs as they could extract. In the ensuing struggle between lords and serfs for command of the serfs' labor, the lords held the upper hand. Legally they were supreme, and consequently demesne farming of the manor entered a kind of golden age. Exploitation of serfs was intensified and commutation slowed down; the (very) long-run trend toward the substitution of money payments for labor services was retarded. Thus the initial impact of the expansion of trade and of the concomitant growth of markets in which products were exchanged against money was to reinforce serfdom. The secular boom in demesne farming lasted two-and-a-half centuries (1100–1350). When the secular expansion was over, however, the manor was weaker, not stronger. The next century (1350–1450) marked the break-up of the manorial system and the general decline of feudalism in western Europe. The kind of market system that was developing, unevenly but persistently, proved incompatible with feudalism and serfdom. To this crucial period of transition we now turn.

THE BREAK-UP OF THE MANORIAL SYSTEM

The decline of the manor in Europe marks a turning point in the history of the Western world. It signals the end of feudalism in the economic sphere and, more than any other economic phenomenon, marks the passing of the Middle Ages and the dawn of modern times. Yet it should be clear that the decline of the manor extended over several centuries; it was a process that proceeded at quite different rates in the several parts of Europe.

General Cause of the Decline of the Manor

The growing volume of long-distance trade and the rise of commercial cities after 1000, and especially after 1100, is one of the well-established facts

of European economic development; and this growth of commerce was the

chief dissolvent of the feudal system and serfdom, despite the fact that feudalism existed side by side with commerce throughout the medieval period. While it is true that the expansion of trade was the essential cause of the decline of the manor, the relation is not a simple one, as is suggested by the foregoing discussion of the golden age of commercialized manors. An analysis of manorial decline must take account of both external and internal forces. The chief external force was trade, the growth of which intensified the internal conflicts inherent in the relations of lords and serfs. But while it accentuated internal conflicts, the growth of trade also moderated the intensity of the conflict by creating alternative opportunities for serfs, who could now flee to towns or to the new frontiers of Europe. In the process of adjusting to market production, the inefficiencies of the manorial organization revealed themselves in various ways: the low productivity of forced labor, the resistance to changes in methods of cultivation, the obstacles to rational management of labor where custom was dominant, and the difficulty of getting rid of unwanted serfs, who had rights as well as obligations to remain on the land and frequently appealed to the "custom of the manor" for protection against changes unfavorable from their point of view.

The transformation of medieval into modern society was attributed by Adam Smith to a growth in the "division of labor." Karl Marx referred to the same phenomenon in terms of new "forces of production," which became inconsistent with the old social relations between lord and serf. Some modern writers have commonly spoken of "economic specialization" as the general cause of the break-up of the manor.[2] There are alternative ways of speaking of the same process. One way is to say that "commercialization" was the general cause of the decline of the manor, the term "commercialization" referring, of course, to the growth of long-distance and local commerce and the innumerable influences associated with it.

The growth of long-distance commerce arising in connection with regional and territorial specialization led to rural-urban specialization. Commercial towns were inhabited by people who required some outside means of providing for their basic needs of food and clothing. Hence greater regional specialization resulted in a greater degree of local rural-urban specialization. Local grain markets, for example, which had existed since antiquity, took on new significance with the rise of extensive long-distance commerce in western Europe in the later Middle Ages. Long-distance commerce initiated a sequence of influences that ramified throughout the medieval economy and ultimately transformed it into a different kind of society.

Specific Causes of the Decline of the Manor

Within the framework of general commercialization the more specific causes of the decline of the manor were the rise of grain markets, commutation of labor services of serfs into money payments, changes in population movements (especially those caused by plagues such as the "Black Death"), alienation (leasing) of the lord's demesne, peasant revolts and general strife, inter-

---

[2] This is clearly explained by M. M. Knight, *Economic History of Europe* (Boston: Houghton Mifflin Company, 1928), pp. 187–97.

national warfare (the Hundred Years War, 1337–1453), and the rise of strong national governments. No one of these factors is fully explained until all the others are related to it because all reacted upon each other in such complex ways as to set in motion a process of cumulative change. More can be said about the relation of the several factors after each has been discussed separately. In order to render the following discussion more specific, particular attention is given to the decline of the manor in England, although in a broad sense, the same general forces were responsible for the decline of the manor elsewhere in western Europe.

Rise of Local Grain Markets

The local market, defined as organized exchange between town and country, began as early as the towns themselves, except where towns had their own fields. Grain was often taken directly to urban markets by producers, but there also arose at an early date a market organization centering around the corn monger who bought and transported manorial grain to local urban markets. In these urban markets consumers were as a rule privileged to buy first. Any surplus remaining could be bought by middlemen for storage and later sale, or for export in some cases. Cities like London, Bristol, and Lynn had corn mongers and other middlemen formally organized in specialized occupations as early as the twelfth century. By this date the proportion of total grain moving into the local and foreign markets was still small, but there was an organized, as distinguished from an occasional, exchange. Existence of markets encouraged peasants and lords to engage in commercial agriculture. Markets were a precondition of commutation since the latter could not take place until peasants had money.

Commutation

Commutation, defined as the substitution of money payments by the serf to the lord in place of labor services performed on the lord's demesne, also began very early in manorial history, long before the manor entered its declining phase. Early in the history of the manor it became customary to place a money value on all produce and services owed by serfs to their lord. By expressing the value of all obligations in terms of a common denominator, the lord could substitute one obligation for another of the same money equivalent. Money served as a unit of account without actually being a medium of exchange. For example, a serf who failed to perform a day of labor-service on the lord's demesne might be required to make up for it by turning over to the lord the equivalent in produce—perhaps a chicken or two dozen eggs or some other type of produce which rated the money equivalent of a day of labor. In addition to establishing a scale of penalties for services not rendered, this system of accounting provided the basis for commutation of labor services into money payments.

The main stimulus to commutation seems to have emanated from a general increase in population, which gave rise to excess tenants. When the services of all tenants were not required by the lord, he chose to receive money rents, as the commutation was called. In the thirteenth century the

total of all money rents paid to lords by villeins exceeded the value of labor

services. Not all money rents represented services commuted in the past, but a considerable proportion may well have arisen in this manner.[3] Moreover the proportion of money payments was higher in areas more distant from centers of population, suggesting that more commercialized manors nearer to markets retained labor services longer than manors in outlying areas where commercialization was retarded by lack of access to markets. Although the trend toward commutation may have slowed down temporarily because of commercialization of the manor, its effect in the long run was to liberate the serf from bondage. Commutation was the most immediate and direct cause of the break-up of the manor. It was the crucial and essential step from compulsory, unfree labor to paid, free labor. As a result of commutation serfs became independent peasants and wage-earners.

Black Death

In the break-up of the medieval manor the critical period occurred from about the middle of the fourteenth to the middle of the fifteenth century (1350–1450). This was the century of the Black Death (1348–49), the peasant revolts in France (1358) and England (1381), and the Hundred Years War between France and England (1337–1453). Each of these events represented a major social catastrophe. In combination and in connection with the more strictly economic phenomena (markets, commutation, money, leasing of the demesne), they transformed the whole complex of economic relations. In 1300 most English countrymen were servile but by 1500 all but a few were free.

Changes in population are one of the important long-run forces in economic development. From 1100 to 1300, marked growth of population took place in Europe. Larger population contributed to general economic growth as older cultivated areas were expanded locally, at the expense of woodland and wasteland, and a general geographical expansion pushed Europe's frontier eastward beyond the Elbe, the Oder, and the Vistula rivers. This period of rural expansion was also marked by urban growth and the expansion of trade, of which the grain and wool trades were important manifestations. Urban and rural population grew simultaneously and not at the expense of each other during the golden age of the manorial system.

The turning point from a golden age to manorial decline coincided with a change from an increasing to a decreasing population. For nearly a century after 1340 the population of western Europe declined sharply, and during the same period there was a cessation in both rural expansion and urban growth. England's population, which was approximately 4,000,000 on the eve of the Black Death, was reduced by about a third during the plague years 1348–49. Recurrent plagues and wars further reduced the population to less than 2,500,000 in the first half of the fifteenth century. England's case was not exceptional. As the great pestilence swept over the Continent the population declined by about a third in nearly every country. France was devastated not

[3] For an interesting discussion of money rents see E. A. Kosminsky, *Studies in the Agrarian History of England in the Thirteenth Century* (Oxford: Basil Blackwell, 1956).

only by plagues but by the Hundred Years War, which was fought entirely on French soil and wreaked great physical destruction.

As a result of the general decline in population, labor became scarce, causing wages to rise. Reapers, for example, who had received two or three pence per day before the Black Death, received five to six pence per day afterwards. Real wages also rose because prices did not increase as much as money wages, and most historians record a decline in prices from 1350 until about 1450. If prices of goods entering into the cost of living of wage earners did in fact fall, then the rise in real wages (goods money wages will buy) was indeed considerable. A doubling of money wages would have meant more than a doubling of real wages.

What is most significant is that there now existed for common people a potential means of livelihood which was more attractive than serfdom. In earlier periods the position of the average serf—say a virgater with thirty acres of land at his disposal—despite all its disadvantages, offered a better alternative than working for wages. Hired laborers had always been at the bottom of the economic ladder. A serf could not as a rule improve his economic situation by running away to become a wage-earner. This was now altered with the scarcity of workers and the large amount of work to be done as a result of the rural and urban expansion of the preceding centuries. If the cost to a serf of being a serf is the income which he sacrifices in the best alternative open to him, it may be said that the cost, the opportunity cost, of serfdom was increased by the labor scarcity and the consequent rise in wages.

In another respect the opportunity cost of serfdom was increased by the Black Death. Servile obligations were usually levied upon families rather than upon individuals. In the case of a family with three able-bodied field hands owing six days of work per week on the lord's demesne, a loss of one of the three would increase the burden on the other two. They would now owe one-half rather than one-third of their time to the lord of the manor. The real cost of serfdom to the family automatically increased with the decrease in the size of family.

The flight of villeins from the manor was provoked by the increase in the burden of serfdom in combination with opportunities for both rural and urban employment at good wages. Mass flights seem to have become common in the second half of the fourteenth century. Traditional immobility of rural tenants was severely disturbed by plague, war, and economic opportunity.

Ruling groups quickly exerted their political power in an attempt to suppress the high wages and new-found economic opportunity of the underlying population. An Ordinance of Labourers was proclaimed by the English King in 1349 and supported by Parliament at its next meeting in 1351 by passage of the Statute of Labourers. The preamble of the Ordinance reads as follows: "Because a great part of the people and specially of the workmen and servants has now died in this plague, some, seeing the necessity of lords and the scarcity of servants, will not serve unless they receive excessive wages. . . ." Under threat of imprisonment all laborers were ordered to work for the wage rates prevailing before the Black Death and were forbidden to run away from their masters. Under threat of fine, employers were ordered to pay wages no higher than those prevailing before the Black Death. Despite zealous attempts at enforcement the wage ceiling failed. As Lipson says, "The Statute

of Labourers failed in fact because two masters were running after one man."

Commutation of labor services, which was common before the Black Death, represented an economic and not a legal change in the status of serfs. Legally the lord had the right to reverse the commutation process and require that serfs who were paying him money dues should once again render their obligations in the form of labor service. Scarcity of tenants and the rise in wages gave manorial lords an incentive to attempt to reverse the commutation process. Without doubt this was their legal right, since commutation brought no basic change in legal status. Serfs remained in a legal sense completely at the command of their lord, but in practice it was not so easy to reverse the commutation process. Families whose services had been commuted were reluctant to go back to their old economic status, and the longer the period in which commutation had been in effect the greater was the resistance because the custom of the manor was always a strong influence.

Commutation as an economic process had undermined serfdom as a legal process. The legal right counted for little if it could not be enforced; hence the appeal to the coercive power of government in the Statute of Labourers to enforce the "rights" of lords and masters. Hence also the "illegal" appeal to force by peasants and workers in the Peasants' Revolt. It is characteristic of revolutionary periods that legalisms are seldom decisive. Individuals and classes who have power do not as a rule surrender it voluntarily. In the absence of concessions based on the recognition that conditions are no longer what they were previously, conflicts of interest like those between serfs and lords in the fourteenth century are resolved by force and violence. Here the underlying conditions upon which serfdom rested had changed. Labor was scarce, wages were high, opportunities existed elsewhere, serfs could and did run away, manorial organization was on the wane. The inflexible system could not adapt itself to the new conditions and so it declined.

Alienation of the Demesne

Alienation of the demesne means that the lord of the manor ceased to exploit his lands directly; instead he leased his demesne land to one or more tenants from whom he received rent. It is obvious that with the renting of his demesne the lord of the manor no longer had any need for the labor services of his serfs. Therefore at this stage commutation followed on a wholesale basis; from serfs who formerly worked on the demesne the lord now received money payments. Commutation had begun as a convenient choice exercised at the option of the manorial lord and ended as the only alternative open to him. He now ceased to be a lord of the manor and became a landlord. Serfs ceased to be serfs in the economic sense and became independent peasants, paying a fixed money fee; or they became wage-earners working for a capitalist farmer, who rented land from the former lord.

There were many reasons why alienation of the demesne, which before the fourteenth century had been exceptional, became the rule in the fifteenth century. Factors already mentioned include the scarcity of tenants, vacant holding, higher wages, the flight of tenants, all of which tended to render demesne farming unprofitable. Another important reason was the absence of many lords from England during the Hundred Years War in France. Also

involved was what may be called the shift from status to contract. Commutation of a serf's obligation was the substitution of a money payment for a customary labor service, but once the commutation fee was recorded on manor rolls it became fixed in amount. A copy of the terms recorded in manorial records was given to the serf-tenant, who then became known as a *copyholder*. When commutation first began, a lord could use the money thus received to employ a wage laborer for a similar amount of money. If the wage labor was more efficient than the forced labor of the serf, there might well have been a mutual gain to both the lord and the commuted serf. However, the arrangement between the lord and the wage-earner differed basically from that between the lord and the serf. The old order of things was based on status, the new scheme of things on contract. The contractual arrangement was subject to change, but the status relation was inflexible. When wages went up and commutation fees did not, the lord's economic position deteriorated. He could no longer buy a day of wage labor with the money he received from his commuted serf.

Leasing demesne land was likewise a contractual agreement, and tenants on the demesne differed from ordinary tenants in this fundamental sense. There was an additional way in which they differed. The demesne holding was usually much larger than an ordinary holding. A demesne holding which was too large to be worked by the tenant and his family would require the employment of wage labor and enlarged the scope of contractual and capitalistic relations. Demesne holdings dispersed among the open fields, of course, could be leased in very small parcels, and in the fifteenth century there were many small leaseholders. The high level of wages in combination with the growth of the woolen cloth trade resulted in many of the English landholders going in for sheep raising rather than grain raising.

By 1500 serfdom as an economic relation had almost entirely disappeared in England, though serfdom as a legal relationship continued to exist. Likewise the English copyholder who prospered during the fifteenth century was to suffer at a later date as a result of his legal insecurity. The era dominated by small-scale landholdings in England was to prove just an interlude between large-scale feudal landholding and large-scale capitalistic landholding. The enclosure movement of the sixteenth and later centuries is discussed in a subsequent chapter.

Peasant Revolts

France   The decline of the manorial system was punctuated from time to time by peasant uprisings. The first great peasant revolt took place in France in the decade following the Black Death of 1348–49. As a result of defeats suffered in the early phase of the Hundred Years War, large areas of France were in political and military turmoil. French and English knights and soldiers robbed, raped, and murdered defenseless peasants, who, provoked by the violence done to them, organized into armed bands and sought vengeance by destroying the castles of feudal barons, robbing their treasuries, and ravaging their women. A contemporary description is paraphrased as follows: ". . . without arms, except staves and knives, they went to a knight's house, and breaking in, slew the knight, his lady, and all his children, and burned the

house. Then they went to a second house, bound the knight to a stake, violated

his wife and daughter before his face, slew the lady, daughter, and all the
other children and then killed the knight. Such crimes continued, and soon
6,000 peasants were on the warpath and the gentlemen were fleeing for safety.
They slew another knight and putting him on a broach, roasted him over a
fire in the sight of his wife and children. Ten or twelve of them ravished the
wife and then forced her to eat of her husband's flesh. Then they killed her
and her children. Wherever these ungracious people went, they destroyed good
houses and strong castles." [4]

This violent uprising of French peasants (known as the Jacquerie) ended
in disaster for the peasants and their leaders, most of whom were hunted down
and massacred by the nobility. The significant aspect of this revolt is the extremely violent nature of the rebellion against feudal authority. Coming as it
did in the midst of the Hundred Years War in which feudalism was also under
challenge, the French civil revolt hurried the process of manorial decay.

England England's most famous peasant revolt occurred in 1381. The
manorial system was, as already indicated, at a critical stage in its decline.
Social unrest was widespread among the less privileged classes. The first phase
of the Hundred Years War, which began in 1337, had just ended unsuccessfully for the English. The French were sacking towns on the south coast of
England, and the Scots were doing the same in the north of England. Tensions engendered by the Black Death had not yet spent themselves. Innumerable complaints were made by serfs against their lords; by "free" peasants
concerning rents; by wage-earners against the Statute of Labourers; by townsmen against their competitors, including foreign merchants. Attempts to enforce a heavy and inequitable poll tax provoked the rebellion, but the main
undercurrent in the movement was resentment against the whole feudal structure where it affected the lives of the common people.

Peasant mobs destroyed records and manor rolls which detailed the customary obligations of serfs or former serfs. If it were necessary to burn a
whole manor house in order to destroy these records, the peasantry did not
shrink from their self-assigned task. After the Black Death, the lords tried to
check the process of commutation. Serfs whose commutation was on a year-to-
year basis could be required legally to meet their obligations by rendering
week-days of labor on the lord's demesne. But peasants who had become accustomed to being free from labor services viewed the annual renewal of
commutation arrangements as a mere formality, and resented the invasion of
their freedom as well as the actual hardship in taking time from their own
fields. They preferred to pay commutation fees (rents or quit-rents) rather
than give of their labor without compensation.

In the county of Kent, where the insurrection began, discontent seems
to have been engendered mainly by the Statute of Labourers. Kent was one
of the freest regions in England; there had been no villeinage for at least a
century before 1381. Officials and lawyers identified with enforcement of the
hated Statute of Labourers were the special objects of vengeance. Wat Tyler,
an artisan tiler from Kent, led a mob of peasants on a march into London in

[4] N. S. B. Gras, *A History of Agriculture in Europe and America* (New York: F. S.
Crofts & Co., 1940), p. 108.

June, 1381. After destroying records and killing some officials the rebels demanded of the king ". . . that you make us free forever, ourselves, our heirs, and our lands, and that we be called no more bond, or so reputed." [5] The king immediately assented and set clerks to work drawing up and affixing the official seals to the documents of manumission.

The peasants soon learned they had been deceived. While meeting alone with the king and his counsellors, Wat Tyler was slain, his head attached to a pole and used to cow the peasants, who were then dispersed. Having broken the organized strength of the revolt, the authorities revoked the concessions which the king had made and hunted down the rebel leaders, who were sentenced and hanged. John Ball, a radical priest who preached that no man should live off the labor of another, was hanged for his participation in the revolt.

This did not, however, put an end to rebellion against manorialism in England. Revolts flared anew in 1385, 1394, and 1426. Although these insurrections did not in themselves destroy the manor, they were significant manifestations of the festering irritations which continued until the system of servile labor was ended.

Germany   One of the bloodiest peasant uprisings in European history cost the lives of about 100,000 persons in Germany in 1524–25. Southern and western Germany, where the revolts centered, were areas of early capitalist development. For two centuries preceding the Peasant War, the common people of the regions had prospered while enjoying increasing freedom from feudal servitude. The revolt broke out at a time when emancipation from feudal restrictions was temporarily halted. Manorial lords were attempting to impose heavier obligations on serfs and to charge higher rents from peasants whose labor services had been commuted.

The demands of the German peasants who revolted were clearly stated in a famous document known as "The Twelve Articles." The religious phraseology of this document suggests the important role of the Protestant Reformation in the uprising. Biblical passages were cited to justify peasant demands. Martin Luther, the leader of the German Protestant Reformation, however, condemned the revolt, saying: "May those wretched peasants be struck down to the ground: The accursed boors are mad, but woe be to their leaders. . . . It is better that all the peasants be killed than that the princes and magistrates perish, because the *rustics* took the sword without divine authority . . . One cannot argue reasonably with a rebel, but one must answer him with the fist so that the blood flows from his nose."

The list of grievances indicates that the substance of the peasant position was not religious; the peasants wanted an end of feudal society. Eight of the articles referred to economic matters:

1. Release from serfdom;
2. Abolition of all tithes except a moderate grain tithe;
3. Right to hunt and fish in flowing water;
4. Right to cut wood in the forests;

[5] J. E. T. Rogers, *Six Centuries of Work and Wealth, The History of English Labour* (London: George Allen & Unwin, Ltd., 1949), p. 258.

5. No extra labor services to the lord except with payment to the peasants;
6. Downward adjustment of excessive rents;
7. Return of common meadows and fields to the community;
8. Abolition of the hated heriot, a kind of inheritance tax.

During the early phase of the revolt the peasants enjoyed successes. They burned castles and monasteries, invaded towns, and destroyed court and manorial records. In the end, however, the rebellion was crushed. Imperial troops of the Holy Roman Emperor returned from a foreign war and slew peasants by the thousands. Especially cruel retribution was meted out to the peasant leaders. In this respect the immediate outcome of the German revolt was similar to the earlier revolts in France and England, although the ultimate triumph over feudalism and manorialism was unfortunately much longer delayed in Germany than in England and France.

Attention is directed to these revolts—called peasant revolts, although they were revolts by all the poorer classes against the feudal masters—because they form part of the process of economic change. Force and violence have been the usual accompaniments of societies in decline. Civil and international wars are often the agents of urgent social change. In retrospect the demands of the peasants seem reasonable and were ultimately realized. But those whose privileges were tied to feudalism resisted blindly and fought furiously to retain the old form of society. Although they won temporary victories, in the longer run all their military might could not stay the course of social change.

The Hundred Years War (1337–1453)

The Hundred Years War was a series of intermittent armed conflicts between England and France lasting from 1337 to 1453. Within this period falls the Black Death (1348–49), the French peasant rebellion (1358), the English Peasants' Revolt (1381), the alienation of the demesne, and wholesale commutation—"the real forces which dissolved the fabric of medieval serfdom." (Lipson) The correspondence in time between the Hundred Years War and the crucial period of manorial break-up is not accidental. This great war forms an integral part of the process of feudal and manorial decay. It acted as both cause and effect, and interacted with the other factors which contributed to the transition from feudal to modern society.

To a degree not true of any previous war in western Europe, the Hundred Years War was a commercial war. At stake was the wool and wine trade of England with the Continent. English wool provided the raw material for the great Flemish cloth industry. English imports were purchased with foreign exchange gained from exporting wool. From Gascony on the Bay of Biscay surrounding Bordeaux the English imported wine. Gascony was also the first important foreign market for the English woolen cloth industry. Taxes on the wool and wine trade provided a major source of revenue to the English Crown. The French king coveted these rich territories in order to control the wool and wine trade. There were, of course, other issues at stake in the Hundred Years War, but the commercial rivalry was very important and illustrates how the increasing flow of trade based on a widening geographical division

of labor was instrumental in causing conflict. The growth of trade, which in the long run undermined the manor, was also a contributory factor to the Hundred Years War, which further undermined the manor.

The Hundred Years War hastened the decline of the manor in numerous ways. It tended to accentuate the rise in wages which was already a disturbing influence. It involved a levy of taxes by the Crown, adding one more cost to the already heavy burdens of manorial lords. It took many lords away from their manors, which hastened alienation of the demesne. The war caused a general dislocation in economic life which, in conjunction with other forces at work especially in England, weakened the manorial structure and strengthened independent peasant agriculture. Demesne farming on a semicommercial basis slumped. There are many indications that the fifteenth century was one of general decline in internal trade. Postan, a careful student of English economic history, characterizes the fifteenth century as a time of commercial retrogression, a century of bad times for lords and of relative prosperity for English peasants and laborers.

In France the physical destruction of war brought economic chaos to all classes. International war frequently brings social revolution in the wake of defeat, as illustrated by the Jacquerie of 1358 as well as by the Russian Revolution of 1917. In France the Hundred Years War disrupted the manor, but the devastation was so great that no new order developed. French economic development remained suspended halfway between the old manorial system and some kind of new system which was struggling to be born. At a later date the destructive Thirty Years War (1618–1648) had a similar effect on German economic development. In England, on the other hand, while there was temporary retrogression, it was not serious enough to prevent wholesale liquidation of the manor by 1500.

Rise of Strong National States

On the political side the decline of feudalism is represented by the rise of strong national states. In the course of the Hundred Years War it was necessary to centralize control of the army, the government, and the collection of taxes. Men who had previously thought of themselves as Normans, Saxons, and Angles became "Englishmen." In France a similar tendency was at work.[6]

On the political as well as the economic side the Hundred Years War brought quicker results to England than to France. The Hundred Years War ended in 1453. Two years later, in 1455, there began in England the famous War of the Roses, which represented a temporary resurgence of feudal strife among contending groups of nobles for control of the Crown. In thirty years of bloody civil war most of the old Norman nobility slaughtered one another. Political feudalism perished with them. England entered upon an age of political absolutism when Henry VII, the first of the powerful Tudor rulers which also included Henry VIII and Elizabeth, ascended the throne in 1485. On the eve of the sixteenth century, political control became securely lodged in the hands of the central government.

Henry VIII broke with the Church in Rome and confiscated the great

[6] George Bernard Shaw in the Preface to *Saint Joan* stresses this point, which forms a significant theme of the play itself.

landed estates of the monasteries, where economic change had lagged behind that of lay estates. This was a direct blow at one of the remaining strong vestiges of manorialism. On the spiritual side, allegiance of the common people was shifted from the Church to the State. The King's army replaced feudal armies and the King's Justice replaced manorial courts. To support its expanding functions the Crown had to have larger revenues, which were raised in part at the expense of manorial dues. Noble lords who once led their own armies into battle now became officers in the King's army.

Summary of Decline of the Manor

The basic facts concerning the decline of the manor may be summarized in this general way. As far as England is concerned, the manor broke up between 1300 and 1500, with the crucial period of decline from about 1350 to 1450. The general cause of this important change was the growth of economic specialization. Specific causes were the rise of grain markets, commutation, decline in population after 1340, peasant revolts, leasing of the lord's demesne, international war, and the rise of strong central governments. All of these specific causes interacted in a cumulative fashion. Economic forces interacted with political and military events. Force and violence in the form of civil and international war were of prime significance. The essence of the decline of the manor may be variously described as a change from servile to free labor, from status to contract, from a natural to a money economy. In general, however, the decline of serfdom as an economic relationship preceded its decline as a legal status. The manor flourished during the early growth of trade and markets, but in the long run the full development of economic specialization created a new environment which was incompatible with economic localism of the manorial type. Commutation existed at an early date, and money rents were extensive from the twelfth century. But commutation in conjunction with population decline, market expansion, and alienation of the demesne was a prime cause of manorial decline. Decay of the manor started earlier in France and other Continental areas than in England, but was in process longer because it was stopped part way by special conditions.

What is most impressive about the decline of the manor is the cumulative nature of the change which brought it about. The individual factors in combination with each other take on quite a different significance than the individual factors in isolation. These several factors acted together and reacted upon each other and upon themselves. The change was cumulative because the factors which caused the change were interrelated. They have their meaning only in relation to the process of decline considered as a whole. Unfortunately, or perhaps fortunately, everything cannot be discussed at the same time. The basic fact, however, is that everything was at work at the same time. Thus a clear view of what actually happened in the break-up of the manor requires that we see the interplay of these factors. It was not trade as such, nor commutation as such, nor the Hundred Years War as such, nor the strong nation states as such that account for the manor's decline. It was these in a special historical relation to each other that provide the explanation to this important process.

The cumulative, interrelated nature of the process may be illustrated

with reference to markets, commutation, and money. Early grain markets provided a place where surplus grain could be sold. The money thus obtained by peasants from selling their surplus could be used to commute their labor services into a money rent to the lord. As the peasants worked more for themselves, they produced a larger surplus, which increased the grain-market activity and brought still more money into manorial relations; thus more commutation, more surplus, a larger market, more money, more commutation, etc., followed in sequence. It is a mistake to attribute too much causal significance to money in the break-up of the manor. It would be nearer the truth to say that money resulted from greater economic specialization than to say that money gave rise to this specialization.

Another example of cumulative change is the sequence beginning with the decline in population, which led to a scarcity of tenants, higher wages, flight of tenants, still fewer tenants, attempted repression, revolt, more flights of tenants, and finally alienation of the demesne and wholesale commutation. A factor which is a cause at one stage may become an effect and a further cause at another stage. This is the meaning of cumulative change.

Granting that change was cumulative, why did it move cumulatively in one direction rather than another? To this question there is perhaps no ultimate answer. As a relation between a landholding lord and a servile tenant, the manor arose out of specific historical circumstances in western Europe in the early Middle Ages. As long as these conditions remained, the manor survived. It was capable of adapting itself to change within limits; but there came a point beyond which it could not adapt itself. The higher degree of economic specialization, the greater division of labor, the new forces of production, or however one may wish to express the underlying change in environment, ultimately rendered obsolete the old relation between serf and lord and brought into existence a new set of social and economic relations.

In economic development there is always change yet there is always continuity. Economic change is gradual, but there are periods of revolutionary change, such as the one between 1350 and 1450 in England. It is the compounding of a number of separate factors, each undergoing gradual, evolutionary change, that leads to explosive, revolutionary change. There are periods of great social crises. As change moves cumulatively in the economic sphere, there arise maladjustments which result in social tensions, which in turn may precipitate the use of force and violence by contending parties. The attempt to enforce legal rights which had become obsolete because of economic changes in the mid-fourteenth century is a case in point. All of this is not without relevance to the twentieth century, which already has experienced several decades of war and revolution since 1914.

SELECTED BIBLIOGRAPHY

BLAND, A. E., P. A. BROWN, and RICHARD H. TAWNEY, eds., *English Economic History, Select Documents,* Part I, sections 1, 2, and 4. London: G. Bell & Sons, Ltd., 1914.

CLAPHAM, J. H., and EILEEN E. POWER, eds., *The Cambridge Economic History of Europe*, Vol. I, *The Agrarian Life of the Middle Ages,* chapters 7 and 8. London: Cambridge University Press, 1942.

KOSMINSKY, E. A., *Studies in the Agrarian History of England in the Thirteenth Century.* Oxford: Basil Blackwell, 1956.

LIPSON, E., *The Economic History of England,* Vol. I, 12th ed., chapters 1–4. London: Adam & Charles Black, Ltd., 1959.

SWEEZY, PAUL M. and others, *The Transition from Feudalism to Capitalism: A Symposium.* New York: Fore Publications, 1954.

VINOGRADOFF, PAUL, *The Growth of the Manor,* 3rd ed. London: George Allen & Unwin, Ltd., 1920.

———, *Villainage in England, Essays in English Medieval History.* London: Oxford University Press, 1927.

ARTICLES

CIPOLLA, CARLO M., ROBERT S. LOPEZ, and HARRY A. MISKIMIN, "Economic Depression of the Renaissance," *Economic History Review,* XVI (April, 1964), 519–29.

HILTON, R. H., "Peasant Movements in England before 1381," *Economic History Review,* II, No. 2 (1949), 117–36.

KOSMINSKY, E. A., "Services and Money Rents in the Thirteenth Century," *Economic History Review,* V (April, 1935), 24–45.

LOPEZ, ROBERT S., and HARRY A. MISKIMIN, "The Economic Depression of the Renaissance," *Economic History Review,* XIV (April, 1962), 408–26.

MISKIMIN, HARRY A., "Monetary Movements and Market Structure—Forces for Contraction in Fourteenth- and Fifteenth-Century England," *Journal of Economic History,* XXIV (Dec., 1964), 470–90.

POSTAN, MICHAEL M., "The Fifteenth Century," *Economic History Review,* IX (May, 1939), 160–67.

———, "Some Social Consequences of the Hundred Years' War," *Economic History Review,* XII, No. 1–2 (1942), 1–12.

TURNER, R. E., "Economic Discontent in Medieval Western Europe," *Journal of Economic History,* VIII, Supplement (1948), 85–100.

Beginnings of Capitalism

Pockets of capitalism developed in several places in medieval Europe. Three principal regions which saw impressive beginnings during the fourteenth and fifteenth centuries were (1) northern Italy, (2) southern Germany, and (3) the Low Countries (present-day Belgium and Holland). Each of these areas lay along or across main trade routes of the later Middle Ages. The city-states of Venice, Pisa, and Genoa were ports through which were channeled goods shipped from the eastern Mediterranean. Southern Germany lay just over the mountains from northern Italy; and across the Brenner and other Alpine passes went the traveling merchants on their way to the outposts of northern Europe. The Low Countries on the North Sea were the centers for the northern trade and later became the entrepôts for Mediterranean galleys coming to northern Europe. In these areas commercial activity of a capitalistic type first began to flourish, and here institutions were created which subsequently became an integral part of the capitalistic matrix.

VENICE IN THE FOURTEENTH AND FIFTEENTH CENTURIES

Venice can perhaps claim to have been the birthplace of modern capitalism. During the later Middle Ages the merchants of Venice engaged in a type of business activity, developed economic institutions, and adopted an attitude toward economic life that were to become typical of European capitalism in the centuries after 1500. Venice was the greatest commercial city in western Europe throughout the second half of the Middle Ages and, with a population of 100,000 in the fourteenth century, was the largest city in the West, with the possible exception of Paris.

Among the important reasons for the commercial supremacy of Venice were its strategic location and the policy and stability of its government. Venice had for centuries traded with the eastern Mediterranean which continued to be the hub of southern European long-distance commerce in the fourteenth and fifteenth centuries. Also, Venice was near the geographical center of Europe. Its location at the upper end of the Adriatic was a convenient distributing point to the hinterland of northern Italy and to northern Europe by overland routes across the nearby Alpine passes to southern Ger-

many, from whence the traffic could continue via the Rhine to the North
Sea.

Venice never became enmeshed with the feudal system. As one writer has stated: "Not a thread of feudal class existed in her social texture." [1] From its beginning Venice was primarily a commercial city, ruled by a mercantile nobility whose main interest was in trade. Venice remained a great city as long as its wealth was invested and re-invested in ships and merchandise rather than in real estate. Although the Venetian republic was ruled by a mercantile oligarchy, there was sufficient economic mobility within the aristocracy to enable men of enterprise to rise to positions of wealth and influence. Even after the nobility became hereditary in 1297, the sons of poorer nobles were given special opportunities to engage in trade on favorable terms.

Venetian commerce rested on an interesting combination of public and private enterprise. The government of Venice built and operated great fleets of ships which had the status of common carriers, that is, they provided transportation to all (qualified) shippers. Space on the galleys was sold to merchants who traded on private account. State-owned galleys were armed with bowmen for protection and, while more expensive than privately owned, unarmed ships, they were safer and faster. Protected transportation was indispensable to a flourishing commerce in this age of constant warfare. The idea behind this policy bears some resemblance to the policy of the merchant gilds, but in the case of Venice protection was provided by a city-nation to all its (qualified) citizens who might wish to engage in trade. The dominant position of public transportation led to considerable government control of business. The Venetian government, for example, acting through the Senate in the fifteenth century, had to specify the use to which limited galley space should be put, and work out means to allocate that space among individual shippers. Private enterprise was in this sense limited by political decisions. However, as Professor F. C. Lane has stated: "Less interference by the Senate would have resulted in less freedom for many individuals." [2] The freedom of the few was restricted in the interest of the group; hence government control was used to prevent private monopoly. The political framework of Venice did not permit permanent coalitions of wealthy merchants to gain control of the transportation system and to use it as the basis for private monopoly. The wealthiest merchants had proportionately more political influence, but the enduring greatness of Venetian commerce appears to have rested on governmental guarantees that prevented a small number of families from monopolizing the protected system of transportation. Venice as a city continued to prosper while the fortunes of individual Venetian families rose and fell.

Although Venice prevented private monopoly among Venetians, its whole policy was consistent with, and in fact was directed toward, the establishment of a monopoly for Venetians against non-Venetians. At times this policy was fairly successful, although not for long periods or in any absolute sense. The Venetians tried to prevent north European merchants from sharing in the Levantine trade, and all German merchants who came to Venice were

---

[1] James Westfall Thompson, *Economic and Social History of Europe in the Later Middle Ages, 1300–1530* (New York: Appleton-Century-Crofts, 1931), p. 244.

[2] Frederick C. Lane, *Andrea Barbarigo, Fifteenth Century Merchant of Venice, 1418–49* (Baltimore: The Johns Hopkins University Press, 1944), p. 84.

placed under close surveillance. They had to reside in special quarters, trade only with Venetians, sell only German or other north European goods, and dispose of all their merchandise before leaving Venice.

Andrea Barbarigo, fifteenth-century merchant of Venice   The economic life of fifteenth-century Venice was exemplified by the activities of Andrea Barbarigo, a typical merchant of the period. He was the son of a once-wealthy Venetian nobleman who by misconduct and bad luck had lost his fortune. As a member of the mercantile nobility, Andrea received a subsidized apprenticeship which permitted him to sail on Venetian galleys, where he associated with experienced merchants and learned at first hand about foreign markets. Starting with 200 ducats at the age of 18, Barbarigo was able to accumulate during his life a modest fortune of between 10,000 and 15,000 ducats. His son, Nicolo, increased the family fortune to about 27,000 ducats by the end of the fifteenth century.

After his early travels as an apprentice, Andrea Barbarigo settled down in Venice as a sedentary or resident merchant. He operated through commission merchants in the Levant, Spain, Bruges, and England. In order to maximize the flexibility of his investments, he avoided long-term commitments. He strongly preferred to invest in inventories of merchandise with a rapid turnover in order to take advantage of short-term market changes. In order to maximize the amount of capital available for investment in merchandise, he lived in a rented residence so as not to tie up any of his capital in a home. Barbarigo bought and sold a great variety of merchandise and avoided specialization in any particular commodities. In 1430 he shipped pepper to Bruges via the Flanders Galley and for the return voyage purchased tinware and cloth in England. In 1431 he purchased gold thread in Constantinople and shipped it overland to northern Europe. In Syria he bought cotton fiber, which was sold in northern Italy and southern Germany, where the cotton was mixed with linen to manufacture fustian cloth. Barbarigo's main objective was to buy cheap and to sell dear. His success in accumulating wealth testifies that he succeeded more often than he failed. He kept detailed records of his profits and losses in a well-developed system of double-entry bookkeeping.

Although never a great industrial city, the far-flung commerce of Venice led to the introduction of several important industries. Most remarkable was the glass industry, the trade secrets of which were jealously guarded from outsiders. Among the glass wares were beads, mirrors, lenses, and hollow ware for general use. The Venetians also specialized in cloth dyeing. In addition to industries, the Venetians had financial institutions for dealing in bills of exchange, writing marine insurance, and carrying on money and credit transactions. But in neither industrial nor financial capitalism were the Venetians the equals of the fourteenth-century Florentines and the fifteenth-century Germans.

In summary, then, the economic life of Venice in the fifteenth century centered in commerce with the Levant, Italy, Germany, Spain, Bruges, and England. The merchants of Venice were primarily engaged in buying and selling in order to make a profit on a rapid turnover. Double-entry accounting was well known and widely practiced in Venice by the beginning of the fifteenth century. By the end of the fifteenth century Venetian commerce had

begun to decline for a variety of reasons including the discovery of all-water routes to the Spice Islands in the Indies. A brief revival of the Mediterranean spice trade in the sixteenth century was followed by a permanent decline. The Portuguese and the Dutch bought the spices at the source, causing the supply in the Levant to dry up. Venice began to lose out to Lisbon and Antwerp. The will of Nicolo Barbarigo, the son of Andrea, reflects the decline of Venetian commerce. In 1496 he advised his heirs to invest in real estate because "commercial activity does not succeed as it used to." [3]

FLORENCE UNDER THE MEDICI

The unique significance of Florence in the history of capitalism lies in the all-around development of its commerce, industry, and finance at a time when Europe as a whole was still predominantly agricultural and feudal. In a preceding chapter, reference has been made to the capitalistic structure of industry in Florence. It was, however, in banking rather than in industry that Florence excelled. Florentine woolen manufacturing had a rival in the great cloth industry of Flanders, but Florentine bankers were the unquestioned leaders of Europe and, in fact, of the entire world during the fourteenth and fifteenth centuries. Yet despite the greatness of Florentine industry and finance, commerce was the heartbeat of its capitalist activity. Industry was organized by merchants, and the bankers were merchant bankers. Florence, like Venice and other important cities, was first of all a commercial city. It was unique in the degree to which its commerce was fed by its own industry and in the degree to which its merchants became the bankers of Europe. Attention will therefore be directed to the combined commerce and finance of Florence, with particular reference to banking institutions.

Northern Italy was the home of capitalistic banking. Among the Italians, the Lombards were the first important bankers. "Lombard Street" in London is a reminder of the important place of the Lombards in banking history. Leadership in banking had passed from Lombardy to Florence (in Tuscany) by the beginning of the fourteenth century. Among dozens of important banking firms in Florence, two of the greatest were the Bardi and the Peruzzi families, both of whom began as merchants and later extended their activity to banking, although remaining important merchants. Both of these family firms were heavily engaged in the English wool trade which supplied Florence with the raw material for its cloth industry. During the Hundred Years War between England and France the Bardi and Peruzzi made loans to the English Crown. They were driven into bankruptcy in 1345–46, when the English King, Edward III, repudiated his debts.

During the fifteenth century Florentine banking attained its zenith under the leadership of the famous Medici family. The Medici were chiefly merchants and bankers with minor interests in industry and mining. The business organization set up by the Medici resembled a modern holding company. It consisted of a number of legally independent firms in which the members of the Medici family held a majority interest and thereby retained effective control over all the branches. There were, in 1458, three branches of the Medici

[3] Frederick C. Lane, *Andrea Barbarigo*, p. 38.

bank in Italy, at Venice, Rome, and Milan; and four branches beyond the Alps, at Geneva (moved to Lyons in 1466), Avignon, Bruges, and London. In addition, the Medici controlled two cloth manufacturing establishments and one silk manufacturing establishment in Florence. Between 1466 and 1478 the Medici operated the papal alum mines near Rome on a monopoly basis. In addition to all this, the Medici acted as fiscal agent for the Pope in collecting revenues and making payments of certain types. In the pursuit of these functions for the Church vast sums of money passed through the hands of the Medici.

Medieval banking of the type in which the Medici engaged consisted mainly in what is now called dealing in foreign exchange. This means transferring claims arising from trading or lending from one place, which uses one kind of money, to another place, which uses another kind of money. For example, the unit of money in Florence was the florin and the unit in Venice was the ducat, so any business transaction between a Florentine and a Venetian involved an exchange of currencies. Banking for the Medici meant exchanging, and exchanging meant buying and selling international bills of exchange.[4]

There was no direct discounting (taking interest in advance) of bills of exchange in the modern sense because this would have been an open violation of the Church prohibition against charging interest. Actually, interest was involved in nearly every purchase and sale of a bill of exchange, but it was hidden in the exchange rates. Since exchange rates were subject to fluctuations, the amount of interest was uncertain and consequently there was some excuse for not applying the usury laws. This was one of numerous accommodations which the Church made to capitalistic types of activity. Capitalists in turn accommodated their business dealings to the doctrines of the Church by camouflaging interest charges. On the surface they appeared to accept the principle that interest was sinful and were scrupulous in avoiding open violations of the official doctrine.

Medici banks also accepted funds from outsiders who were depositors, somewhat in the modern sense, and were not investors in the banks. Interest was paid to these depositors, although again it was camouflaged. There was no written contractual promise to pay any given amount of interest; in fact there was no promise to pay any interest at all. The amount of interest going to depositors depended upon the ability of the bank to pay. As long as the amount of interest was not fixed with certainty in advance, there was some likelihood that the Church would tolerate the practice. Sometimes when the Medici got into financial difficulties, they refused to pay interest to depositors who felt they were entitled to it.

Cosimo de Medici, who was head of the firm from 1434 to 1464, did more than any other member of the family to strengthen the business. Under Cosimo the Medici became the de facto rulers of Florence. In form the government of Florence was a republic, but it had been ruled by a succession of rich mer-

---

[4] Originally a bill of exchange was like a promissory note, drawn by a buyer (importer) promising to pay the seller (exporter) a specified sum of money at a certain time and place. By the time of the Medici the bill of exchange had assumed its modern form, that is, a draft drawn by a seller (exporter) on a buyer (importer) stating that the latter had bought goods of a certain amount and promised to pay a given sum of money at a specified time and place. When a bill of exchange came to be accepted by the one obligated to pay, it became an "acceptance."

chant and banking oligarchs. Some of the civil strife, such as the revolution of 1381, has been described in a preceding chapter. The Medici posed as the champions of the common people, and when the latter drove the oligarchs from power, the Medici stepped into the political vacuum. Cosimo avoided public office for himself and ruled as a political boss, manipulating elections so that only his friends held office. Under his son Piero (ruled 1464 to 1469) and his grandson Lorenzo (ruled 1469 to 1492), political domination of Florence by the Medici continued. Lorenzo the Magnificent, the grandson of Cosimo, was a great patron of the arts and a prominent figure in international politics. However, Lorenzo was a poor businessman, and under his regime the business fortunes of the Medici declined so drastically that the stage was set for collapse two years after his death.

The reasons for the decline of the Medici bank were poor management, large loans to kings and princes, and extravagant living standards by the later Medici. Cosimo had exercised iron control over the far-flung activities of the firm and was particularly careful to keep the branch managers in check. He scrutinized the annual reports demanded of all the branch managers, required periodic personal reports in Florence, and had all managerial personnel appointed from Florence. Lorenzo neglected reports and relaxed control over the branch managers.

It appears to have been Cosimo's policy to avoid political loans. This could not always be done, as the English branch discovered when loans to the Crown were made the condition of renewal of licenses for the export of wool. The London branch was in difficulty at the time of Cosimo's death and collapsed in the course of the English War of the Roses (1455–85) because of royal repudiation and the decimation of other Medici debtors. Under Cosimo, the Bruges branch was forbidden to make loans to princes, but under Lorenzo large loans were advanced to Charles the Bold, ruler of Flanders. When the latter was killed, the Medici were left holding bad debts. In order to bolster the waning fortunes of the family business, Lorenzo took funds from the public treasury of Florence. One by one the branches fell, until the political revolution in Florence in 1494 brought the collapse of the once great Medici business and drove the family from political power. Political loans to feudal princes, which had been the undoing of the Bardi and the Peruzzi, now ruined the Medici. The next great banking family of Europe, the German Fuggers of Augsburg, were to suffer a similar fate.

CAPITALIST ORIGINS IN THE LOW COUNTRIES

After an auspicious beginning, including the golden age of the thirteenth century, capitalism in the Low Countries (Belgium and Holland) fell into a long period of stagnation and decay. Leadership in the great medieval cloth industry passed to Italy in the fourteenth century. For the subsequent history of capitalism, however, this region was more important than Italy because in the Low Countries capitalism never lapsed as it did in Italy. For more than half a millenium cities in the Low Countries remained the leading commodity markets and the financial centers of northern Europe. Bruges, Antwerp, and Amsterdam successively were the leading cities of capitalism. Despite the con-

tinuity of capitalism as a system in England from the fifteenth century, not until the eighteenth century did undisputed leadership pass from the Low Countries to England. By this time the political power and natural resources of a unified national state were necessary to sustain pre-eminence in economic development.

Because of its central location and early capitalist beginnings, the region of the Low Countries experienced significant advances in commercial organization from the time the center of north European trade shifted from the Champagne fairs to Bruges in the latter part of the thirteenth century. Although this shift was influenced by external, noneconomic factors such as the Hundred Years War, unwise fiscal policy by the French kings with respect to Champagne, and the opening of direct sea routes from the Mediterranean to the North Sea, the main reason seems to have been internal developments relating to methods of business organization. In the late thirteenth and early fourteenth centuries accounting was undergoing important changes which were to lead soon to double-entry bookkeeping; it was also the period in which the bill of exchange became the dominant instrument of long-distance trade. Changes in business techniques and organization led to what has been called the "commercial revolution of the thirteenth century," namely, the shift from the traveling merchant to the sedentary merchant as the dominant figure in long-distance trade. Champagne was frequented by traveling merchants, but Bruges was populated by sedentary merchants and the agents of sedentary merchants. The Italian merchants, who first mastered these new business techniques, were the moving spirit in the business life of Bruges during the fourteenth and fifteenth centuries. Bruges replaced Champagne as the central meeting point for the Mediterranean trade of southern Europe and the Baltic trade of northern Europe.

The shift from Champagne to Bruges, which was caused mainly by revolutionary changes in business techniques, brought about a more advanced form of market organization. When Bruges supplanted Champagne, the bourse supplanted the fair as the transactions center for long-distance trade. The following differences between the fair and the bourse indicate the nature of the advance toward a higher stage of market organization: (1) goods were physically present at fairs but they were not physically present at the bourse; (2) exchange transactions in the absence of the actual goods necessitated more standardized items of exchange at the bourse as compared with the fair; (3) since goods were not actually present at the bourse, a much greater concentration of trade was possible; (4) greater concentration of trade at the bourse brought a wider adjustment of supply and demand, which is the chief criterion of a more perfect market.

Bruges has been called the Venice of the North, but this expresses something less well as something more than the full significance of the role of Bruges in northern trade. Venice was in every respect dominated by Venetians, whereas Bruges was an international city, the capitalistic activity of which was dominated by foreigners. In Venice, Germans were the only foreigners who frequented the city and they were carefully chaperoned lest they learn Venetian trade secrets. In contrast, in international Bruges trade and finance were dominated by Italian merchants from Venice, Florence, Genoa, and Milan. Also important in the commercial life of the city were the Hansards,

Teutonic Knights, English, Spanish, Portuguese, Germans, and papal repre-

sentatives. The Hanseatic merchants established headquarters in Bruges in
1336. The native Flemings did not, for the most part, engage in international
trade. They relied largely on foreign merchants to find markets for their
woolen cloth. The Flemings monopolized retail trade and acted as brokers and
money changers in Bruges. But in the vital long-distance trade the domination
of the Italians was so pronounced as to justify calling Bruges an Italian colony.

Banking in Bruges, with the exception of money changing, was also
dominated by Italian merchants, who brought the banking techniques of the
Mediterranean region to northern Europe. The nature of these banking practices has been described in connection with the Medici of Florence, one of
whose most important branches was located in Bruges. The principal banking
activity of late medieval merchant-bankers was buying and selling bills of
exchange, which were important credit instruments. Bills of exchange were
used in long-distance trade as substitutes for money; they reduced considerably
the shipments of gold and silver and increased the efficiency of their utilization. The use of debt as a substitute for money is the essential characteristic
of modern money and banking.

Bruges lost its leadership because of the narrow policy of its municipal
oligarchy, the restrictionist spirit of its gilds, the decline of the Hanseatic
League, and natural catastrophe. During a terrible storm in the winter of
1404–5, the ocean lashed the low-lying coast and silted up the harbor of
Bruges (at Damme) and at the same time moved sandbars out of the Scheldt
River to make a seaport of Antwerp. By the time Columbus discovered America, there were several thousand vacant and deserted houses in Bruges. Bruges
was strictly a medieval city, which time passed by, leaving it *la morte*, a dead
city, an outdoor museum.

Antwerp took over from Bruges the leadership of capitalistic activity in
northern Europe. Antwerp was a modern city without gilds and with complete freedom of trade. The bourse building opened in Antwerp in the early
1500's bore the inscription: "Open to the merchants of all nations." Faced with
the decline of Bruges, merchant capitalists shifted their branches to Antwerp.
During the sixteenth century Antwerp became the greatest commercial and
financial city in Europe. Its position was enhanced by close association with
Spain and the Spanish Netherlands during their golden age in the sixteenth
century. The new cloth industry in the Low Countries came to depend on the
import of Spanish wool and unfinished English cloth. In the seventeenth century, with the decline of Spain and the rise of Holland, Antwerp yielded its
position of capitalistic leadership to another metropolis of the Low Countries,
Amsterdam.

SOUTHERN GERMAN CAPITALISM
IN THE AGE OF THE FUGGERS

At the close of the Middle Ages the most flourishing inland pocket of capitalist
activity was in southern Germany. The chief stimulus to capitalism in this
area was its favorable geographical position in relation to northern Italy, the
original home of modern capitalism. The principal overland trade route be-

tween Italy and northern Europe passed through southern Germany. In addition, there had been since ancient times an important east-west trade route along the Danube to the Black Sea and thence to the Near East. Thriving commercial cities like Regensburg, Augsburg, Nuremberg, and Ulm were located approximately at the crossroads of the north-south and the east-west trade routes. Another important influence in the development of capitalist enterprise in southern Germany was the mineral wealth of the Tyrol and Hungary.

Augsburg became the foremost capitalist city in southern Germany during the fifteenth and sixteenth centuries. It ranks with Venice and Florence in the south and with Bruges and Antwerp in the north as one of the most highly developed centers of economic development in the period of transition from medievalism to capitalism. Jacob Strieder, the historian of the Fugger family, has described Augsburg as "the most progressive town of the time in her business ethics and economic policy." The Renaissance spirit of individualism and rationalism was transplanted from Italy to Augsburg. Anticapitalist doctrines against usury, profits, business speculation, monopolies, and even trade were ignored in the day-to-day activity of Augsburg merchants. An eminent southern German jurist expressed the spirit of Augsburg as follows: "Every merchant is free to sell his wares as dear as he can and chooses. In so doing he does not sin against the canonical law; neither is he guilty of antisocial conduct. For it happens often enough that merchants, to their injury, are forced to sell their wares cheaper than they bought them." [5]

In Augsburg the leading representative of the new spirit and practice of capitalism was Jacob Fugger the Rich (1459–1525). Jacob's grandfather, Hans Fugger, was a country weaver who in about 1380 migrated to Augsburg, where he rose from a craftsman to a putting-out capitalist in the fustian trade. Fustian is a light and durable cloth of linen warp and cotton weft. Cotton had to be imported from the Levant via Venice, where Andrea Barbarigo, for example, had engaged in the trade, probably during the lifetime of Hans Fugger. An underlying tendency everywhere in Europe was for the handicraft system to disintegrate in those cases where the raw material was expensive and had to be imported over long distances. More capital than was available to ordinary craftsmen was required for importing cotton. As a fustian weaver of more than ordinary enterprise, Hans Fugger became a putting-out merchant buying cotton and selling fustian. At his death he left a modest fortune, which was further increased by his son Jacob I. Jacob I was a master in the weavers' gild, but did not actually engage in weaving, which was a typical situation in the transition from handicraft to capitalist enterprise. In the third generation, the two elder sons (Ulrich and George) of Jacob I were both astute businessmen, but the youngest son, Jacob II, later called Jacob the Rich, was the business genius of the family. After the death of his brothers, Jacob II assumed absolute control of the family firm. The Fugger business was organized as a closed family partnership in which no one but a male heir of the Fugger family could become head of the firm. Under the autocratic regime of Jacob II, his nephews were partners with full responsibility but without authority to make entrepreneurial decisions.

[5] Cited in Jacob Strieder, *Jacob Fugger the Rich Merchant and Banker of Augsburg* (New York: Adelphi Co., 1931), pp. 48–49.

Jacob II served his apprenticeship in Venice, where he absorbed the business spirit of the merchants of Venice and acquired an understanding of the significance of double-entry accounting for the conduct of large-scale business. Jacob personified the capitalist spirit. He viewed wealth as the basis for accumulating more wealth. He dedicated his life to the accumulation of capital and laid plans in his will for the continuation of this principle of conduct in succeeding generations of the family. Withdrawals for consumption and for female dowries were to be kept to a minimum. Toward the end of his life Jacob replied to the suggestion that he should retire from business with the statement that he would continue to accumulate more wealth as long as he was able. One of his mottoes was "business is business." Even in dealings with mighty princes, he always demanded security for loans and prompt payment. In a famous letter to Emperor Charles V of the Holy Roman Empire, Jacob used sharp words in calling the debt to the attention of the Emperor and demanding repayment without further delay. On another occasion he wrote to a prince requesting ". . . Your Grace that you bear this debt in mind, and arrange to pay, at the specified time, this sum . . ." [6]

When Jacob the Rich took over as head of the family business, the trade of his grandfather in fustian and cotton had expanded to include woolen cloth, silks, velvets, precious and semiprecious stones, and other products from Italy, the Levant, and the Far East. He continued to trade in these products and expanded, especially into the metal trade. Compared with other German merchants, Jacob did not participate extensively in the new spice trade of Portugal, which had developed with the opening of the all-water route around Africa to the East, but he entered into some Spanish trade in connection with the collection of the Spanish Hapsburg revenues that were pledged as security for the loans advanced to Charles V for his election as Emperor of the Holy Roman Empire. However, the most important expansion of Fugger's merchant activities was in Antwerp, which became the greatest international market in the world during the sixteenth century. Antwerp came into the possession of Spain under King Charles I (later Emperor Charles V), and Fugger, with his excellent Hapsburg connections, was able to operate there effectively. Portuguese spices and Spanish gold and silver were shipped to Antwerp, and Tyrolean copper and silver to Venice. The trade in Antwerp developed rapidly and rivaled Venice in importance for the Fugger business. Jacob Fugger did not trade in France because the ruling French family was the chief rival of the Hapsburgs, whose goodwill he always prized.

The most impressive aspect of Jacob Fugger's activities was the extent to which he became a large-scale industrial capitalist, somewhat of the type which came into prominence for the first time during the English Industrial Revolution of the eighteenth century. In connection with the reconstruction and development of Hungarian mining—mainly copper and silver—Fugger made large direct investments in mines, smelting plants, and rolling mills, and in addition invested in roads and other transportation facilities to move the ores and metals. Fugger's industrial activity in Hungary represented a higher form of capitalist development because it involved investment in fixed capital as contrasted with investment in circulating capital. Only the latter form of

[6] Strieder, *Jacob Fugger the Rich*, p. 214.

capital investment was typical of early or merchant capitalism. Whereas the earlier Fuggers had been exclusively nonspecialized merchants who bought and sold stocks of goods at wholesale and exercised control over production in gaining supplies of goods on a putting-out basis, Jacob made specialized investments in mining plant and equipment of a durable type from which he could not expect as rapid a turnover as from investments in circulating capital. Flexibility was sacrificed and risks were greater, but the rate of return on net worth was correspondingly higher than in the more competitive merchandising field. With a Hungarian partner, who was later displaced, Jacob Fugger organized a separate business firm which gained control of the entire output of Hungarian copper and from which he realized handsome profits.

Fugger's mining enterprise in the Tyrol was less unusual. Here he followed the pattern of other merchants who were granted mineral concessions in return for financial aid to the princes holding legal title to the mineral wealth within their territory. Ore-rich princes were able in this manner to finance their military and political programs, or to defend themselves against the machinations of rival princes. As a reward for making the loan, the capitalist received, in addition to interest, the exclusive right to purchase ore in the territory. Moreover, repayment of the loan was secured by assigning to the creditor the prince's share in mining royalties. Under this arrangement the capitalist played the dual role of banker and merchant, but was not an industrial entrepreneur as Fugger was in Hungarian mining. However, the capitalists frequently made advances to the small mining operator in order to increase the output of minerals available for purchase. The ore might be resold as ore, or refined into metal before sale. Jacob Fugger shipped copper ore purchased from Tyrol miners to his Hungarian smelters. In the later years of his life, Fugger's entangling financial alliances drew him more directly into mining in the Tyrol.

The mining business of the Fuggers has a special interest because it illustrates the tendency for large-scale capitalist activity to lead to cartels and monopolies. In the nature of the case, the sale or lease of exclusive rights tended toward monopoly. Jacob Fugger attempted and came close to succeeding in establishing a complete monopoly of the European copper trade through his direct control of Hungarian mining plus cartel agreements in the Tyrol. Under the terms of these agreements, Hungarian copper was sold only in Antwerp, and Tyrol copper only in Venice and southern Germany. In this way the output of the two adjacent mining areas was prevented from competing in the same market.

Cartel agreements and other monopolistic arrangements of large capitalists like those engaged in by the Fuggers gave rise to vociferous complaints from smaller operators and others who were adversely affected by the resulting high prices and restricted output. These complaints were strong enough to lead to decrees against monopolies and against the large trading companies responsible for them. A "Report on Monopolies" by a Committee of the Diet of Nuremberg in 1522–23 expressed the indignation of an important public body: "While petty robbers and thieves are punished severely, rich companies and their associates who have done more injury to the common good than all the highwaymen and petty thieves taken together, live in extravagant luxury." The Nuremberg committee recommended that "big and financially powerful

companies ought to be dissolved." This represents a kind of sixteenth-century

antitrust policy directed against big business. The Augsburg town Council
took up cudgels in defense of "bigness": "Now if trade is good, it follows that
more trade is better . . . It is to be noted that the big and wealthy merchants,
by attracting artisans and masters, stimulate business in general . . . we have
arrived at the conclusion that any control of the large companies would be
harmful." Thus was "free enterprise" defended against charges of monopoly
in the sixteenth century. Attempts to curb the big companies were ineffective.
Jacob Fugger used his influence with the rulers of the state to avoid legal
steps against his business. In 1523, when charges of monopoly were brought
against the Fuggers, Charles V commanded his subordinates to drop the suit.
Again in 1525, Charles V issued a special order stating that deals entered into
by Jacob Fugger were not to be construed as being in violation of antimonopoly
law.

In addition to being an international merchant and a large-scale industrial capitalist, Jacob Fugger was the greatest banker in Europe. His credit
was so good that the Great Electors who were offered bribes in the election
of Charles V as Emperor of the Holy Roman Empire in 1519 would accept
the pledges of no one but Fugger. Other important bankers in Germany and
Italy attempted to gain influence by offering bribe loans, but the greedy, hard-
boiled Electors refused their pledges. Fugger advanced more than 500,000
Rhenish gold gulden to the credit of Charles to finance his election to the
Emperorship. Many business advantages accrued to Jacob as a result.

In the generation after the fall of the Medici bank, Jacob Fugger became
the most important papal banker in northern and eastern Europe. His firm
served as fiscal agent of the papacy in Germany, Hungary, Poland, and Scandinavia. Loans were advanced to the Pope in the security of papal revenues in
northern Europe. Loans were also advanced for the purchase of bishoprics and
other high Church offices. These offices were of great value to their holders
because they gave control over vast landed estates held in the name of the
Church and the right to sell lesser Church appointments. Trafficking in sacred
offices was common practice in the time of Jacob Fugger, who was a contemporary of the corrupt Medici popes and of protesting Martin Luther. While
no credit redounds to Jacob Fugger for his role in this unsavory business, his
participation was consistent with his motto "business is business" and reflects
the wide gap between the ideals of the Church and the practice of some of its
capitalist members who, like Jacob Fugger, professed to be faithful Catholics.

Jacob Fugger was unquestionably the wealthiest person and the greatest
capitalist of his age. Between 1511 and 1527 the profits of the Fugger firm
averaged 50 per cent per year. Assets of the firm were valued at more than two
million gold gulden at the time of Jacob's death. The value of the assets in the
Fugger firm increased to more than five million gold gulden under Anton
Fugger in 1546 at the height of the family fortune.

Although Jacob Fugger was not a typical capitalist of southern Germany
in the sense in which Andrea Barbarigo was a typical Venetian merchant, he
is historically significant as a representative—the leading representative—of a
class which played the dominant role in the economic development of Germany at the beginning of the capitalist epoch. This class of entrepreneurs conducted its business affairs in accordance with what is called the capitalist

"spirit." Its members attempted to gain wealth through buying and selling instead of by robbing and stealing. Economic gains were based on close comparisons of costs and prices. Members of the new class tended to be farsighted in all business relations. Double-entry accounting was essential to the rational conduct of their activities and to their way of life.

The capitalist way of life was contrary to the ethical precepts of the greater part of society in the Middle Ages and the sixteenth century. The deliberate pursuit of wealth, the taking of interest and speculative profits, the disregard for "just price," were contrary to the Christian doctrines of both Thomas Aquinas and Martin Luther. Jacob Fugger's great wealth brought him great power, but it also created many enemies. The question arises as to why the authorities of Church and State tolerated capitalists like Fugger. The answer is found in the need of Church and State for the financial support which only the great capitalists could provide. Hence the Church tolerated and the State protected the Fuggers and other capitalists like them.

Political support was a source of weakness as well as strength to capitalist families. The Fugger chariot was hitched to the Hapsburg star. When the star fell the chariot came tumbling after it. Despite Jacob Fugger's policy of demanding security for his loans, there was no real protection against the vicissitudes of government bankruptcy and military defeat. The loans lacked one of the fundamental attributes of sound banking practice—liquidity. Jacob Fugger's successors became more and more entangled in the royal finances of the Hapsburgs. The Spanish Hapsburgs declared their government bankrupt in 1557, 1575, and 1607. Each time the Fuggers bore terrific losses estimated at a total of more than 8,000,000 florins. During the seventeenth century the Fuggers sank into relative insignificance. They had gone the way of the Bardi, Peruzzi, Medici, and other illustrious banking families.

The story of south German capitalism may therefore be summarized as follows: Between 1450 and 1550 the economic development of southern Germany attained heights which were not reached again in Germany until the nineteenth century. Discovery of all-water routes to India and to the New World shifted the focus of economic development away from the Mediterranean to the Atlantic Ocean. Although the south German merchants transferred their activities from Venice and Genoa to Lisbon and Antwerp, they were unable to maintain the leadership enjoyed in the time of Jacob Fugger. Discovery of mineral wealth in America reduced the importance of the Hungarian and Tyrol metal trade. The relative inefficiency of overland transportation as compared with water transportation was a serious handicap to landlocked southern Germany. Not until the coming of the railway, the first overland means of mass transportation, did Germany regain first place in European economic development.

FRENCH CAPITALISM IN THE FIFTEENTH CENTURY: JACQUES COEUR

France was less urbanized and less capitalistic in the fourteenth and fifteenth centuries than northern Italy, the Low Countries, and southern Germany. Although Paris was a large city, it was important as a cultural and administra-

tive center rather than as a commercial center of international trade. The Hundred Years War (1337–1453) with England devastated France nearly as much as the Thirty Years War of the seventeenth century devastated Germany. Despite its general economic backwardness, pockets of capitalistic activity developed in France toward the close of the Middle Ages. Economically, the most advanced area in France was the Mediterranean region. In northern France there were important commercial centers influenced by the English woolen trade and the Flemish cloth trade. In the interior important fairs sprang up, first at Champagne and after the Hundred Years War, at Lyons, which ranked next to Antwerp as the financial capital of Europe during the sixteenth century.

Jacques Coeur was the outstanding figure in the rise of French capitalism at the close of the Middle Ages. Coeur (1396–1456) built a mercantile and financial empire extending over much of France and into many foreign lands. The seat of his activities was at Montpellier, which at the time was France's leading Mediterranean port. By unusual organizational ability and skillful diplomatic activity with the King of France, the Pope, and the Sultan of Egypt, Coeur developed a highly profitable sea commerce with the countries of the eastern Mediterranean. His fleet of ships carried nearly all French foreign trade in the Mediterranean, and although French commerce was not large in comparison with the Italian, its concentration in Coeur's hands made him the richest citizen in France, and possibly in Europe, during the fifteenth century. He imported fine cloths, precious stones, and other products and sold them through a chain of retail stores in many French towns. As sidelines he operated a few industrial enterprises, including a silk factory in Florence, a paper mill in Bourges, and mines near Lyons. Coeur's far-flung enterprises became the favorite means for the transfer of funds between points within France and between France and foreign places. Like other great merchants of the period, Coeur became a banker. During the latter phase of the Hundred Years War, Coeur became the chief financial adviser to King Charles VII of France. The great merchant used his business prestige to raise funds from other merchants and bankers. He also placed his personal fortune at the disposal of the King for the mobilization of resources in the war against the English invaders.

The Hundred Years War was more modern than feudal in several respects. Gunpowder and cannon were used almost for the first time in the West. It was a war between nation-states led by kings rather than between city-states of rival feudal lords. The soldiers of France began to think of themselves as Frenchmen rather than as Burgundians, Parisians, etc., and the soldiers of England began to think of themselves as Englishmen rather than as Saxons and Normans. The new techniques of combat and the large-scale military operations made feudal techniques of organization obsolete. The feudal method of mobilizing men for military service on a basis of personal fealty was giving way to mobilization through money expenditures. Prior to the rise of the impersonal money market and systematic public finance, great merchant-bankers like Jacques Coeur were the only medium for raising funds on the scale required for war and other activities of great sovereigns.

After the English were driven from France at the close of the Hundred Years War in 1453, Coeur fell from royal favor. He was accused, falsely, of

poisoning the King's mistress. In a famous trial he was acquitted on this charge only to be accused of other equally preposterous charges. In a further trial he was found guilty of treason and other high crimes. Coeur was imprisoned and his fortune confiscated. He escaped to Rome, where he was warmly received by the Pope, who sent him on an expedition against the infidel Turks, the recent conquerors of Constantinople from Christianity. Although Coeur had plans for rebuilding his shattered economic empire, he died in 1456 while serving on the papal expedition before his plans could materialize.

The shabby treatment accorded Jacques Coeur by his King and country, while not exceptional for the time, does reflect in part a lower state of capitalistic development and thinking in France compared with contemporary Italy and Germany. The need of the King of France for the financial ability and resources of merchant-bankers was as great as the need of any other European sovereign, but he displayed less wisdom in killing the goose that laid the golden eggs. Like other merchant-bankers of his time, Coeur enjoyed great power in the hour of national crisis. After the crisis passed, he appeared dispensable. It was easier for the King and the nobles to dispose of their creditor than to pay their debts. The story of Jacques Coeur is a variation of a theme that runs through the history of early European capitalism. Where merchants and bankers were held in less esteem, as in France compared with Italy and Germany, the accumulations of capitalists were less safe against the ambitions of aspiring monarchs. Not only was capitalism less developed, but its development was subjected to greater discouragement.

ENGLISH CAPITALISM AT THE CLOSE
OF THE MIDDLE AGES

England like France was economically backward at the close of the Middle Ages as compared with Italy, the Low Countries, and Germany. By far the most important commodity in English foreign trade was raw wool, most of which was exported by foreigners. There were, however, trends pointing toward England's later dominant position in capitalistic development. During the fourteenth and fifteenth centuries the growth of England's cloth industry increased the domestic demand for raw wool and reduced the proportion of English wool which was exported. Concurrently, the development of England's commerce reduced the proportion of raw wool exported by foreigners. Flanders began to feel the competition of the English cloth industry during the fourteenth century.

The rate at which English merchants were coming to control foreign trade can be seen from an estimate of an outstanding historian of the medieval English woolen trade who concluded that in the fifteenth century English merchants were exporting four-fifths of England's raw wool, whereas Italian merchants were exporting only one-fifth of the total. This represented a reversal of the situation in the preceding century when the Italian merchants had done most of the exporting. Despite the increasing proportion of trade in the hands of native merchants England still remained capitalistically backward. Its merchant groups were more medieval than modern. English banking did

not begin to match that of Italy or the Low Countries. Professor de Roover describes London as "only a satellite of Bruges" during the fourteenth and fifteenth centuries.[7] During the sixteenth century London was still far behind Antwerp, and during the seventeenth century behind Amsterdam. Not until the eighteenth century did England clearly emerge to a position of leadership in the development of capitalistic institutions.

RELIGION AND CAPITALISM

By the end of the fifteenth century capitalism stood on the threshold of a breakthrough to a dominant position in European economic life. Before a full release of energy could be realized in capitalist enterprise, however, certain subtle changes had to take place in the psychological and spiritual attitudes of society toward the accumulation of wealth. Capitalism needed an ideology which would give it full ethical sanction. Undoubtedly the ethics taught by medieval Catholicism presented obstacles to the development of a capitalist ideology. Hostility toward great accumulation of wealth by private individuals was, of course, not new in medieval Europe. It merely carried forward the teachings of the Christian fathers against mammonism. St. Jerome had said, "A rich man is either a thief or the son of a thief." St. Augustine, who was perhaps the most influential of the Christian fathers, felt that trade was bad because it turned men away from the search for God. Down through the Middle Ages commerce and banking were, at best, looked upon as somewhat dishonorable, as necessary evils. The merchant never quite met the moral standards of medieval Catholicism. Money lending was for a time confined to non-Christians because it was considered unworthy of a Christian. Interest on loans was unlawful under the anti-usury laws of the Church, and of secular authorities. Speculation and profiteering violated the central doctrine of just price.[8]

Catholicism and Capitalism

The expansion of commerce in the later Middle Ages stirred controversies and led to attempts to reconcile theological doctrines with economic realities. Most important were the teachings of St. Thomas Aquinas, a thirteenth-century Dominican and one of the greatest intellects of medieval Europe. St. Thomas Aquinas maintained the traditional opposition to interest, but distinguished between a return on capital by which the lender contracted for the return of principal with a surplus, and a return on capital which involved a risk of loss of principal as well as its return with a surplus. The former type of income was interest, or usury, and was considered unlawful under the anti-usury laws; but the latter type of income was profit, and might legitimately be received by a capitalist since he shared in the risks of the venture. Other means were devised for justifying returns on capital, including interest on loans. One practice (*damnum emergens*) permitted a lender to be compensated for delay in repayment of an otherwise gratuitous loan. By agreeing surreptitiously to

[7] Raymond A. de Roover, *The Medici Bank* (New York: New York University Press, 1948).
[8] See Chapter 3.

delay repayment, this arrangement became an easy subterfuge for regular payments. A still more questionable practice (*lucrum cessens*) permitted money lenders to receive interest on a loan which caused them to forego profitable alternative uses of their money. The common practice of regular money lenders, like the Medici, was to manipulate exchange rates to include a payment for interest.

In Venice, Florence, Augsburg, and Antwerp—all Catholic cities—capitalists found ways and means to violate the spirit and to circumvent the letter of the prohibitions against interest. On the eve of the Reformation, capitalists had by their deeds become indispensable to lay rulers and to a large part of the populace dependent upon them for employment. They were, however, still under the shadow of the sin of avarice. To win their full place in the sun they sought, like other men, ethical sanctions which would justify their way of life in the eyes of the community at large. Catholicism could hardly be expected to provide these positive sanctions. A new ideology which would break cleanly with the ethos of medieval Catholicism was required for the spiritual fulfillment of capitalism.

The Protestant Ethic

The first stage in the Protestant Reformation under Martin Luther (1483–1546) offered little solace to capitalists. Luther proved more hostile to trade, interest, and business activity generally than St. Thomas had been three centuries earlier. Luther was a religious radical but an economic conservative. He denounced the Pope but sanctioned serfdom. His economic outlook was essentially rural. He did not accept the necessity or the desirability of the commercial practices of the emergent urban civilization.

The Protestantism of John Calvin (1509–1564) and his followers, especially the Calvinists in the Netherlands and the Puritans in England, marked the shift to a religious ethic associated with an economic spirit, or outlook, which aided and abetted capitalism. Without in any sense being the "cause" of capitalism, which already existed on a wide and expanding horizon, the Protestant ethic proved a bracing stimulant to the new economic order and not only exonerated capitalists from guilt of the sin of avarice but gave divine sanction to their way of life.[9] They were at once agents of material progress in this world and saints predestined for eternal life in the next world.

According to the Protestant doctrine of the "calling" (life-task), the "good life" could be pursued in any occupation, profession, or trade. All callings were equally noble in God's eyes. The monk in the monastery was no more saintly than the tradesman pursuing his calling in the best and most efficient manner possible. Asceticism was as fundamental to Calvinism as to Catholicism. Whereas Catholic asceticism was an affair for the monk in the monastery to purify his soul for salvation, the Calvinists would have converted the whole world into one great monastery for the glorification of God. In the ordinary conduct of life, worldly asceticism meant hard work, frugality, sobriety, and efficiency in one's calling. Quiet self-reliance would take care of

[9] See Richard H. Tawney, *Religion and the Rise of Capitalism* (New York: Harcourt, Brace & World, 1926), for a masterly account of the historical relations between Protestantism and capitalism.

one's worldly responsibilities. Laziness, slovenliness, and prodigality were un-
forgivable sins leading to poverty. Hence there was no virtue in beggary or
alms-giving, as in the Catholic creed.

For some, if not all, the Protestant creed, applied in a productive environment of expanding trade and industry, led to the accumulation of wealth.
Hard work meant a good income; frugality meant low consumption and high
savings; and savings led to accumulation of wealth used productively to produce more wealth. To become wealthy was never the purpose of a sincere
Protestant but it might well be the unintended result. Hence wealth became a
symbol of Christian virtue, although being wealthy was not itself a virtue. A
complete turn of the wheel had taken place from St. Jerome's pronouncement
that a rich man is either a thief or the son of a thief to the Calvinist notion
that worldly success is a symbol of Christian virtue, and the greater the success the greater the virtue.

Calvin did not justify profiteering or gain from loose practices in business. He did not justify the exploitation of the poor by the rich. He did accept
profits as one of the facts of business life; and what was a greater break with
the medieval Church, he saw nothing wrong with a reasonable rate of interest
on money borrowed by the rich for the purpose of productive (profitable)
investment. Calvin was as stern as earlier theologians in condemning interest
charged on a loan to the destitute, but doubt would be cast on a family which
permitted itself to become distressed and go into debt to relieve its destitu-
tion.

The Spirit of Capitalism

Max Weber contended that the essential elements of the Protestant ethic,
as manifested especially in Puritan worldly asceticism, are the same as the
essential elements of what he called the "spirit of capitalism." [10] The idea of a
capitalist spirit, as developed by Weber, is an historical concept and should
be distinguished carefully from mere greed for gold and gain through plunder,
cheating, and other forms of unrestrained avarice. Weber's capitalist spirit is
the *rational* pursuit of gain, as a way of life, an ethos, which he contended
has existed only in modern times. It is a product of history, not of human
nature as such. Its indispensable elements include rational business calculation and the rational organization of free labor under capitalist control.

The rational calculation of the capitalist spirit manifests itself in double-
entry bookkeeping, which developed in the capitalist environment of northern
Italy in the centuries just prior to the Reformation. Under double-entry bookkeeping all transactions are reduced to abstract value terms (money). Business success is determined by an excess of revenues over costs, both measured
in terms of money values. The activity of the capitalist in the pursuit of abstract gain is unrelated to his material needs, just as the pursuit of a calling is
an end in itself unrelated to man's material wants. There are no absolute limits
to capitalist acquisition since acquisition is an end in itself. The result is a
boundless drive to unceasing activity, to accumulation, which helps to account,
on the one hand, for the remarkable accomplishments of capitalism as a

[10] Max Weber, *The Protestant Ethic and the Spirit of Capitalism* (London: George
Allen and Unwin, Ltd., 1930).

system of production, and, on the other hand, for the unrelenting activity of the capitalist, who drives himself unstintingly and perhaps dies of heart trouble in middle life. Work is a duty, a way of life, an endless quest of an unattainable goal. Clearly this limitless quest for what can never be satisfied is not an inevitable result of human nature. It is, like the Protestant ethic, a type of behavior culturally conditioned by historical factors. Work, which in other historical cultures was a means to satisfy material wants, ceases to be a means and becomes an end in itself.

The other essential element in the capitalist spirit, the systematic organization of *free* labor, also had its roots in the Protestant ethic, according to Weber. By definition, free laborers could not be compelled by force to work hard in the service of others. Moreover, the use of force would have violated the freedom of one's calling. Psychological compulsion enforced through religious belief was the answer. Every occupation was noble in God's eyes; for those with limited talents and to whom no better opportunities were available, Christian conscience demanded unstinting labor even at low wages in the service of God and, incidentally, of employers. It was an easy step to justify inequality of wealth and income, which would hasten the accumulation of wealth by placing it under the guardianship of the most virtuous (most wealthy) and remove temptation from weaker souls who could not withstand the allurements associated with wealth. After all, it did not much matter who had legal title to wealth if wealth was not for enjoyment; it was to be saved and used as the basis for further accumulation. The rich, like the poor, were to live frugally all the days of their lives. Since the wealth of the rich was not to be spent for their enjoyment, the capitalist system found a justification which made it tolerable to the working classes.

Although the capitalist spirit was conjoined with the Protestant ethic at the time of the Reformation, the marriage dissolved into an irreconcilable separation as Calvinism was transplanted from Geneva to other lands, where it was subjected to the strains of political, economic, and religious tensions. In England in the sixteenth century the Puritan divines still claimed spiritual sovereignty over business affairs, but by the seventeenth century the modern view that "trade is one thing, and religion another" had come to prevail. The separation of religion from business, in a regime of growing economic individualism, was accompanied by a moral expediency which tended to justify the Puritan virtues because they were good business. Weber finds this capitalist spirit, minus its religious roots, typified in the utilitarian homilies of Benjamin Franklin: "Time is money." "A penny saved is a penny earned." "Honesty is the best policy [because it pays]."

That the capitalist spirit would break loose from its religious moorings was anticipated by Protestant divines of the post-Calvin era. They lamented the insidious influence of wealth on religion but felt powerless to stem the tide. John Wesley (1703–1791), the founder of Methodism, expressed the paradoxical relation between wealth and religion in the eighteenth century:

> I fear, wherever riches have increased, the essence of religion has decreased in the same proportion. Therefore I do not see how it is possible, in the nature of things, for any revival of true religion to continue long. For religion must necessarily produce both industry and frugality, and these cannot but produce riches. But as riches increase, so will pride, anger and love of the

world in all its branches. How then is it possible that Methodism, that is, a religion of the heart, though it flourishes now as a green bay tree, should continue in this state? For the Methodists in every place grow diligent and frugal; consequently they increase in goods. Hence they proportionately increase in pride, in anger, in desire of the flesh, the desire of the eyes, and the pride of life. So although the form of religion remains, the spirit is swiftly vanishing away. Is there no way to prevent this—this continual decay of pure religion? We ought not to prevent people from being diligent; we must exhort all Christians to gain all they can, and save all they can; that is, in effect, to grow rich.[11]

By the eighteenth century, capitalism had won the sanctions it lacked before the Reformation. Interest was accepted, profit was the heartbeat of the natural economic order, trade was honorable, wealth was a mark of virtue, poverty was caused by deficiencies of individual character rather than by social environment. Capitalism had triumphed and no longer had need for the moral authority of religion. Business was capable of handling its own problems if left free from interference by the church and state.

Psychological Factors in Economic Development

The issue discussed in the preceding paragraphs may now be reduced to its bare essentials. What is involved is the psychological basis for the transition from slow to rapid accumulation of capital in western Europe at the beginning of modern capitalism in the sixteenth and seventeenth centuries. Wealth accumulates because current production exceeds current consumption. Hard work is conducive to production, and frugality is conducive to modest consumption. If the surplus of current production over current consumption is invested productively, the base for further production grows at a compounded rate. The important question for economic development is, What psychological conditions caused so many people to work so hard, produce so much, and consume so little for so long a period of time? The rich might have dissipated their wealth in luxurious consumption or in unproductive expenditures on great cathedrals, but they did neither. The poor might have revolted, as did the plebs of medieval Flanders and Florence, but they did not. Puritan theology provided, in Professor Tawney's phrase, the "new medicine of poverty." Religious sanction of economic virtues in an age when religion was serious business—and the great wars of this period were religious wars—provides a plausible explanation for the necessary but difficult conditions for the rapid accumulation of productive wealth.

Scientific inquiry does not require that hypotheses be proven correct, but only that they not be incorrect. A hypothesis need only be consistent with the data. Weber's hypothesis is not inconsistent with what happened, although there may be other and better hypotheses. In his more modest passages, he contended only that the Protestant ethic was a necessary condition—admittedly it was not a sufficient one—for the full triumph of modern capitalism. If a society is poor, worldly asceticism is a necessary condition for it to become rich. No less important is that the talents of the people be developed and utilized efficiently. Any society which develops the talents of its people, ap-

---

[11] Robert Southey, *The Life of Wesley*, 2nd American ed., Vol. II (New York: Harper & Row, Publishers, 1874), 308.

plies talents industriously, lives frugally, and invests the resulting social sur- plus for further production is well on the high road to economic progress. The broad question concerns psychological attitudes toward work, thrift, and accumulation of wealth, and ultimately the effect of religious outlook on economic development.[12]

SELECTED BIBLIOGRAPHY

Cox, Oliver C., *The Foundations of Capitalism*. New York: Philosophical Library, 1959.

DE Roover, Raymond A., *The Rise and Decline of the Medici Bank, 1397–1494*. Cambridge, Mass.: Harvard University Press, 1963.

Ehrenberg, Richard, *Capital and Finance in the Age of the Renaissance, A Study of the Fuggers and their Connections*. New York: Kelley, 1963.

Hill, Christopher, *Puritanism and Revolution*. London: Secker and Warburg, 1959.

Lane, Frederick C., *Andrea Barbarigo, Merchant of Venice, 1418–1449*. Baltimore: Johns Hopkins University Press, 1944.

————, *Venice and History*. Baltimore: Johns Hopkins University Press, 1966.

Strieder, Jacob, *Jacob Fugger, The Rich Merchant and Banker of Augsburg*. New York: Adelphi Co., 1931.

Tawney, Richard H., *Religion and the Rise of Capitalism*. New York: Mentor Books, 1954. (paperback)

Van der Wee, Hermann, *The Growth of the Antwerp Market and the European Economy*. 3 vols. The Hague: Martinus Nijhoff, 1963.

Weber, Max, *The Protestant Ethic and the Spirit of Capitalism*. New York: Charles Scribner's Sons, 1958. (paperback)

ARTICLES

Cipolla, Carlo M., "The Decline of Italy: The Case of a Fully Matured Economy," *Economic History Review*, V, No. 2 (1952), 178–87.

Fischoff, Ephraim, "The Protestant Ethic and the Spirit of Capitalism," *Social Research*, XI (Feb., 1944), 53–77.

Postan, Michael M., "Medieval Capitalism: Studies in Bibliography, I," *Economic History Review*, IV (April, 1933), 212–27.

Riemersma, J. C., "Calvinism and Capitalism in Holland, 1550–1650," *Explorations in Economic History*, I (March, 1949), 19–22.

Strieder, Jacob, "Origin and Evolution of Early European Capitalism," *Journal of Economic and Business History*, II (Nov., 1929), 1–19.

Walker, P. C. Gordon, "Capitalism and the Reformation," *Economic History Review*, VIII (Nov., 1937), 1–19.

[12] As used in this context, the word "religious" is distinguished from "religion." On this distinction see John Dewey, *A Common Faith* (New Haven: Yale University Press, 1934), Chap. I. Religion usually denotes faith in the supernatural, whereas the adjective "religious" refers to attitudes toward goals and a faith in the realization of those goals. For example, an ardent Communist demonstrates a "religious" zeal or faith in certain goals, while repudiating any belief in supernaturalism (religion).

Founding the Atlantic Economy

PART **II**

The Accumulation of Capital
in Foreign Trade

CHAPTER 6

Capitalism is distinguished from earlier economic systems by its special concern with the accumulation of capital. This accounts for the prodigious rate at which new wealth was accumulated in modern times. It is sometimes referred to as the "profit system." Under capitalism profits are plowed back to increase the quantity of capital available for future production; in this manner the base of production is constantly enlarged, whereas if profits were consumed by the capitalists, there would be no growth of capital. The capitalizing of profits in the sense that surplus is converted into more capital is a justification for using the term "capitalism" to describe this form of economic life. A study of the institutional development of early capitalism as a new system of economic organization should, therefore, focus on the various sources and forms of capital accumulation.

Accumulation in the economic sense means the growth of wealth, either by individuals or by society as a whole. It takes place whenever current production exceeds current consumption. Social accumulation occurs when society at large is increasing the total stock of wealth, and under capitalism this takes the form of enlarging the productive capacity of society. In contrast, the accumulations of earlier societies went largely into unproductive forms such as the pyramids of ancient Egypt, the public works of Rome, and the cathedrals of medieval Europe. Private accumulation under capitalism takes the form of an increasing money balance in the capital account of the business enterprise. Wealth which might be consumed by the individual is saved and employed to make larger profits in subsequent periods. In any society an individual may increase his private wealth without adding to the total social wealth, as when one person robs or steals from another. Under capitalism the accumulation which was significant for economic progress added both to the private and to the social stock of wealth.

In order for accumulation to occur the social product must be large enough to provide a surplus in excess of current consumption in addition to the reproduction of capital used up in the process of production. De-accumulation takes place when the existing social capital is not fully reproduced. War and other social catastrophes may occasion de-accumulation. Reproduction includes the reproduction of the labor supply as well as the material means of production. Thus, in a progressive society the total social product consists of

three parts: current consumption, replacement of the existing means of production (capital and labor), and the surplus, all or part of which is accumulated.

Accumulation of capital on a large scale makes possible, and even requires, changes in the methods of production and organization. More elaborate methods of production can be undertaken when there is a greater stock of capital at the disposal of society. For example, the putting-out system of industry involving a high degree of specialization in the textile industry became possible during early capitalism because of large increases in the quantity of capital available to putting-out capitalists. The techniques were not basically different from those of medieval handicraft, but the organization was much more complex and the ability to produce was greater because of the increase in specialization. Before the Industrial Revolution of the eighteenth century, the most dynamic force in economic development was the accumulation of capital as such, rather than changes in technology. With the onset of the Industrial Revolution technological change became an additional dynamic aspect of capitalist development. Capital continued to accumulate even faster than in the previous period, but the increase in productivity of labor associated with new technology was the more dramatic aspect of the Industrial Revolution, whereas during early capitalism productivity increased mainly from the increasing amount of capital available for production.

Increases in the *capacity to produce* wealth have exceeded many times the actual increase in the tangible *stock* of accumulated physical wealth in modern times. As in precapitalistic societies, the important gains under capitalism have been in intangible capital, which only incidentally becomes embodied in larger amounts of tangible assets. However, the shift in emphasis from a static concept of a stock of tangible wealth to the dynamic concept of an annual flow of production did not take place until the end of early capitalism. Mercantilist writers had stressed the former (accumulated stock) whereas Adam Smith in 1776 stressed the latter (annual flow).[1] Edwin Cannan, the leading interpreter of Adam Smith, suggests that Smith's most important contribution to economic thinking was this shift in the way of looking at the wealth of nations from a stock of wealth to a flow of production. Smith's new emphasis reflected a change which was beginning to take place in economic development at the onset of the Industrial Revolution.

Accumulation of wealth under capitalism is primarily accumulation of capital. This follows from the spirit and structure of business enterprise as well as from the limits to the amount of directly consumable goods that can be stored or preserved. Business organization is designed to increase the net worth of the proprietor. "Making money" is the test of its success or failure as revealed in the periodic statement of profit and loss. Although acquisition in terms of money is the motivating purpose of business enterprise, capital kept in the form of money cannot grow, so it is constantly converted into real capital assets (means of production) which are utilized through the employment of labor to increase further the amount of profit, which in turn is reconverted into still more capital.

---

[1] Adam Smith (1723–1796) is considered by many to be the greatest of the economists. His *Wealth of Nations* (1776) was one of the first treatises to stress competition and free enterprise as the basis of economic progress.

For the realization of maximum profits, the technology used by business enterprise must be the most efficient available. Precapitalist devotion to traditional techniques gave way to a more rational utilization of the lowest-cost methods of production. Complete freedom to choose, unhampered by the traditional outlook of society, was the aspect of capitalism which made it a revolutionary destroyer of medieval institutions and ideas. Individual freedom for the businessman to produce, organize, and sell as he wished became part of the capitalist way of life.

In early capitalism the three important sources of capital accumulations were (1) long-distance trade, (2) the putting-out system of industry, and (3) the enclosure movement in agriculture. English economic development became increasingly important during early capitalism because the accumulation of capital in that island empire prepared the way for the next great advance in the growth of capitalism during the Industrial Revolution. New ways of mobilizing capital as well as the sources of capital accumulation were important in the overall growth of capitalism. New forms of business organization arose for mobilizing capital as well as special institutions for facilitating mobilization of capital for business enterprises. Most important of these were banking and credit institutions.

The discovery of America was an episode in the ferment of European commercial activity that marked the transition from medieval to modern times. The period from the discovery of America to the close of the geographical frontiers about 1900 has been called the "Columbian world," after the discoverer of America. The capitalist system, with roots already well-grounded in Europe, was especially suited to flourish in this expanding economic universe. The growth of long-distance commerce received added impetus from the discovery of the water routes to the East and the New World.

Technical improvements in navigation contributed much to European overseas expansion. Most important was the compass, which was introduced into Europe from China during the twelfth century. With the aid of the compass, crude charts, and observations of the sun, moon, and stars, it was possible for the mariner to locate his position in the open sea. The shift from the Mediterranean to the Atlantic Ocean, which led to the discovery of the new sea routes, was made possible by the work of mariners trained in the school established by Prince Henry the Navigator of Portugal. It was no longer necessary to cling to dangerous and winding coast lines. By 1600 a world map of some accuracy could be drawn.

Ship architecture made possible larger and more seaworthy vessels, which greatly reduced the cost of transportation. Lower transport costs increased the potential geographical division of labor. Whereas previously only items of high value and low bulk could be transported with profit over long distances, it became possible in the sixteenth and seventeenth centuries to carry much heavier and bulkier cargoes between countries and continents. Products such as grain, timber, iron, and coal began to move in greater volume on the Baltic Sea, the North Sea, and even across the Atlantic Ocean. Spices, silks, and precious metals no longer constituted the chief items in the cargoes of long-distance commerce, although these products remained of prime importance for some time in the very long-distance trade, as with the East Indies.

The Indies had a special attraction for the European traders because

the gains from trade were greatest when European products were exchanged for those of the exotic tropics. To European merchants the East and West Indies offered richer prizes, apart from possible gold or silver deposits, than did, for example, the mainland of North America which now constitutes the United States. The latter was good chiefly for settlement rather than for the type of quick exploitation that motivated early colonial empires. More than a hundred years elapsed from the discovery of America by Columbus until the settlement of the mainland colonies which were to become the United States. Long before Jamestown and Plymouth were founded, the Spanish, Portuguese, Dutch, French, and English were swarming into the East Indies and West Indies in search of tropical and semitropical products.

At first the European traders were not concerned with the organization of production in the tropics. Desired products could be obtained cheaply in exchange for inexpensive European trinkets. The Portuguese and the Dutch established little more than trading posts in the East Indies during the sixteenth century. However, the desire for continued and methodical exploitation of native peoples and resources led to the establishment of colonies in which Europeans organized and regulated production. In the West Indies, for example, Europeans employed the forced labor of the native Americans, and after these Indians were largely killed off by hard labor and European diseases, the Europeans began to import African Negroes as slave laborers. The plantation system employing slave labor thus became one of the characteristic institutions of early capitalism.

EAST INDIES TRADE

European traders were interested chiefly in the Moluccas or Spice Islands of the East Indies. The Portuguese were the first to exploit these rich islands, and were followed by the Dutch, who at first welcomed the British as an ally in their fight against the Portuguese. After the Portuguese were driven out, however, the Dutch turned upon the British and drove them from the islands onto the Asiatic mainland. The Dutch took possession of the Moluccas, Java, Sumatra, and other valuable islands, which came to be known as the Netherlands Indies. They gained a monopoly of the pepper trade, the most highly prized article in the commerce with the Far East during the sixteenth and seventeenth centuries. Pepper was important as a preservative of meat and other foods in a period which knew no artificial refrigeration.

Dutch East India Company   The rise of Dutch capitalism at home, the growth of trade with the East, and the desire to break the Portuguese-Spanish monopoly led to the establishment of the Dutch East India Company in 1602. This company occupies an important place in the history of capitalism because it was one of the first and one of the most successful vehicles for the accumulation of capital. It was a symbol of Dutch commercial supremacy during the seventeenth century, and served as a model for other large-scale business enterprises of the early modern period. Some notion of the capital-accumulating capacity of the Dutch East India Company is suggested by the following figures on dividends and profits: During the first five years after it began operating (1605–1609) dividends averaged 35 per cent per year; during

the next five years dividends averaged 28 per cent; by the end of the seventeenth century its original capital had increased tenfold despite the payment
of large dividends; in the approximately two hundred years of its existence
the company paid dividends totalling 3600 per cent, or an average of 18 per
cent per year.

During its first half-century the Dutch East India Company was a loose
type of joint-stock enterprise made up of groups of merchants from six different Dutch cities with a government-controlled Board of Directors exercising central control over the entire operation. Its original capital was raised
by selling shares, which remained a permanent part of the capital of the company. Individual shareholders could sell their securities on an open market, the
forerunner of the later stock exchange. In 1652 the company was reorganized
into a more unified joint-stock company.

British Companies in Foreign Trade

The transition from medieval to modern forms of capital accumulation
may be illustrated with reference to the decline of regulated companies and
the rise of joint-stock companies in British foreign trade during early capitalism. Vacillation between the essentially gild type of regulated company and
the essentially capitalistic joint-stock company indicates that the evolution
toward capitalistic organization was both gradual and somewhat uncertain
during this early period. Older companies such as the medieval Merchant
Adventurers continued to participate in English foreign trade well into the
modern period. These companies were in essence merchant gilds organized
on a national basis and granted a monopoly of certain types of foreign trade.
They were associations of merchants—not of capital—whose ships sailed in
fleets for protection against attack. Certain functions common to all members
were performed by the company, and in this respect they resembled modern
trade associations. Individual merchants traded on their own capital and made
their own profits or losses. Capital was not pooled in a single joint stock
as in a joint-stock company. The individual firms in the regulated company
were typically organized as partnerships, but they might be individual proprietorships, and there existed within the Merchant Adventurers a series of
embryonic joint-stock companies.[2] The regulated companies were not capital-
accumulating organizations, although the members within the federation were.
This type of organization remained in competition with the newer joint-stock
enterprises for a considerable period of time, but it was not well suited to the
needs of long-distance and especially intercontinental trade. Regulated companies disappeared by the eighteenth century.

Russia Company During the second half of the sixteenth century the
regulated companies were still holding their own in competition with the
joint-stock type of organization. Two English trading companies which began
as joint-stock enterprises changed to the regulated form. One was the Russia
Company, chartered in 1555 with a grant of monopoly of the Russia trade by
both the English and Russian governments. The most valuable trade between
Russia and the West at that time was in furs, and for a time the Russia Com-

[2] See E. Lipson, *Economic History of England*, II, 227.

pany prospered. However, the Russian Czar revoked the monopoly, and the Dutch soon took most of the trade from the English. Dissatisfied with the lack of success, which was attributed to the joint-stock principle of organization, the company was converted to a regulated basis in the seventeenth century.

The Levant Company The Levant Company was chartered as a joint-stock enterprise in 1581 by Queen Elizabeth, the Queen herself contributing £40,000 to the capital of the company. When the first charter expired in 1589 there was some debate as to whether the company should continue as a joint-stock or as a regulated company. In urging the joint-stock form the British ambassador to Turkey argued: "If . . . this stock . . . should not be . . . in one joint purse the traders shall lose rather than profit thereby." If the merchants traded on their individual capital the ambassador feared they would be outwitted by "the malicious Turk and crafty Moor and faithless Greek. . . ." [3] The Levant Company was rechartered on a joint-stock basis in 1592, but in 1600, when it was again rechartered, it went over to the regulated basis. Thus at the end of the sixteenth century English merchants still wavered between the joint-stock and the regulated forms of trading companies in long-distance trade.

British East India Company Greatest of all the joint-stock enterprises was the British East India Company, which was founded on December 31, 1600. As was often the case, the first capital put into the East India Company came from profits of earlier trade and plunder. In a famous pirating voyage against the Spanish, Sir Francis Drake returned in 1580, with a cargo worth £600,000 from an original investment of £5000. After "good Queen Bess" and other privileged persons drew their special share of the return, a profit of 4600 per cent upon original investment remained for the ordinary stockholders in Drake's venture. Some of these lush profits were invested in the Levant Company, and when the latter was dissolved as a joint-stock enterprise, some of the capital was used in the first voyage made under the Board of Directors of the East India Company.

Between 1600 and 1657 the British India Company operated with temporary joint stocks that were dissolved at the termination of each voyage or several voyages: In this form it may be referred to as a series of joint-stock *ventures* as distinguished from a true joint-stock company in which the capital is permanently lodged in the control of the enterprise. After each venture the original investment plus the profits would be divided among the investors in proportion to their original investment. Sometimes merchant investors took merchandise in lieu of cash at the time of liquidation. Under the temporary or joint-stock venture arrangement there were often several joint stocks with different sets of investors in operation simultaneously. All ventures, however, had to be approved and carried out under the supervision of a single board of directors.

Like the Dutch East India Company, the British East India Company was an important source for accumulating capital. Because of the system of terminable stocks, the rates of profits are not easily calculated, but it has been

[3] E. Lipson, *Economic History of England,* II, 338.

estimated that the annual rates of profits between 1601 and 1613 averaged
31 per cent. Thereafter the annual rates were generally less, but nevertheless
usually substantial, except in those instances in which ships were lost and
with them the capital as well as the potential profits. The amounts of capital
invested increased. For the First Joint Stock the capital was £418,691 and
for the Second Joint Stock it rose to £1,629,000.

Weaknesses in organization based on individual ventures and temporary
capital led in 1657 to the formation of a permanent joint-stock fund. During
the first twenty-five years under the permanent joint stock, the average annual rate of profit was approximately 18 per cent. In 1682 the shares were
split and in the following ten years profits averaged 20 per cent on the enlarged capital, or 40 per cent per year on the original stock. Meanwhile, by
virtue of its strong financial position, the company was able to borrow outside
capital for as little as 3 per cent, making it highly profitable to the old shareholders to employ borrowed capital rather than to admit new shareholders.
Under these conditions the shares of the company sold at high premiums in
the open market.

In order to pay for an increased volume of imports the East India Company was given special dispensation to export up to £50,000 of gold and
silver bullion per year to offset the unfavorable commodity balance of trade
between India and England. For this special privilege the company was
severely criticized. The export of bullion violated an early mercantilist belief
that gold and silver could be most rapidly accumulated by prohibiting their
export. Thomas Mun, a director of the East India Company and the leading
mercantilist writer of his day, came to the defense of the firm with his famous
general balance of trade theory. Mun accepted the mercantilist principle that
a nation should build up large stores of precious metals. The novelty of his
ideas lay in arguing that in obtaining precious metals what mattered was
not the *particular* balance of trade between England and India but the *general* balance between England and all other countries, including Spain, France,
Italy, Germany, and others. The enlarged quantity of raw materials and other
products brought to England from India by virtue of the export of a relatively
small quantity of bullion would be processed and sold in England and then
re-exported to Spain, France, and other countries. From these enlarged exports, gold and silver flowed into England. The net result, Mun argued, was
a favorable general balance of trade which brought a much greater overall
import of bullion than would have been possible if the export of bullion to
India were absolutely prohibited.

Mun's analysis was substantially correct as far as it went. It was important because it favored freer foreign exchanges and freer international
trade than earlier mercantilists wished to permit. Mun's statement for the advantages of multilateral international trade was a ringing challenge to proponents of bilateral trading and international barter of the type fostered by
mercantilists in the sixteenth and seventeenth centuries and still practiced in
some places in the twentieth century.

Although the British East India Company was the target of much adverse criticism at home, it survived and prospered. Its closest brush with
destiny came at the close of the turbulent, revolutionary days of the seventeenth century. In 1698 a jealous Parliament chartered a new East India

company, but the old company weathered this storm by absorbing the new company.

During the eighteenth century the East India Company became the spearhead of British territorial aggrandizement in India. This joint-stock company trading for private profit was granted territorial sovereignty over India. A group of British merchants interested primarily in their own enrichment became the political rulers of several hundred million people and a vast empire which was exploited as a commercial colony. It is little wonder that the people of India developed a fanatical hatred of British rule. The value of the company's imports, which stood at £500,000 in 1620, rose to £3,000,000 in 1720 and to £10,000,000 in 1800. Directors of the East India Company were among the wealthiest men in England during the seventeenth and eighteenth centuries. For example, Sir Josiah Child, Governor of the company in the latter part of the seventeenth century, was said to be the richest Englishman of his day. Like other wealthy merchants, Child's political influence was more than proportionate to his wealth.

During the seventeenth century the powerful Dutch drove the British East India Company from the Spice Islands to the Asiatic mainland, where India became the center of its activity. This forced withdrawal from the rich Spice Islands proved fortunate to the English in the long run because raw cotton and cotton cloths from India were replacing spices as the most valuable items of European trade with the East. Bright calicoes became fashionable dress in western Europe. Raw cotton from India was used in making fustian.

With the rise of laissez-faire in England after 1800 the East India Company lost most of its exclusive economic and political privileges. In 1813 the monopoly of trade with India was abolished. Similarly the trade with China was thrown open to all in 1833. The East India Company was liquidated and went out of existence in 1858. By this time, however, the Industrial Revolution was well on its way in England, the East India Company having served as one of the great sources of capital.

WEST INDIES TRADE

The West Indies even more than the East Indies was a great source of new European wealth during the period of early capitalism. According to a famous contemporary authority (Davenant), the total trade of Great Britain at the end of the seventeenth century brought a profit of £2,000,000 per year. Of this total the West Indies and southern mainland colonies trade, including re-export, accounted for £720,000, the East India trade £680,000 and the European, African, and Levant trade £600,000. But it was the West Indies that became the hub of the great triangular trade, which involved taking processed goods, including rum, from England to be traded for slaves in Africa, slaves from Africa to the West Indies, and sugar from the West Indies back to Europe.[4] The West Indian trade was adapted to the mercantilistic ideal of

[4] A second triangle was among the North American mainland colonies, the West Indies, and the Slave Coast of Africa. See Chapter 12. There were many variations in triangular trade, which was really multiangular or multilateral.

using colonies as a source of raw materials and as a market for manufactured goods.

The slave trade was one of the most profitable types of colonial enterprise. During the eighteenth century the traffic in slaves from Africa to the various colonies sometimes amounted to 100,000 per year. The British established their superiority in this profitable trade when they took from the French, who had taken from the Portuguese, the monopoly right to transport slaves to the Spanish colonies. The Spaniards did not carry their own slaves for various reasons including lack of capital and lack of Negro colonies. One of the most sought-after prizes in the commercial world was the contract known as the *Asiento,* for carrying slaves to Spanish colonies in the New World.

The slave trade was more profitable than most commercial enterprises because of the great demand and consequent high price which businessmen were willing to pay to hurry along the exploitation of the rich lands and natural resources of the New World. Natural resources are of little value without an adequate supply of human labor to work them, and in relation to its natural resources the human resources of the New World were woefully inadequate. The migration of free laboring men from the Old World was too slow to fill the avaricious demands of the Europeans, so they went to Africa and brought their own labor supply.

Profits in the slave trade were high also because the risks were great. The human cargo was fragile and sometimes difficult to manage. Mutiny, suicide, and epidemics were more common on "slavers" than on other ships. High profits encouraged overloading, but the cargo was too valuable to be unnecessarily abused.

During one decade in the late eighteenth century Liverpool merchants carried about 300,000 slaves valued at £15,000,000 at an estimated average annual profit of 30 per cent on investment. On individual voyages profits of 100 per cent were common, and some trips paid several hundred per cent. The annual gain to Liverpool during the 1780's was estimated at £300,000.[5] A safe and significant conclusion is that the slave trade made an enormous contribution to the accumulation of capitalist wealth.

Although slave labor contributed much to the accumulation of capital, it was not in itself characteristic of capitalist organization, which is based on free labor. Early capitalism created plantation slavery, and later capitalism destroyed it. During the nineteenth century, industrialism became dominant. The powerful planter aristocracy presented an obstacle to the fullest development of industrial capitalism, especially in Great Britain and the United States. British industrialists led the fight for the abolition of slavery in the British Empire in much the same way that industrialists in the Northern states of the United States broke the economic and political power of the planters of the Southern states in the Civil War.

THE PRICE REVOLUTION

The impact of the New World on the rise of European capitalism is clearly revealed in connection with the great flow of American treasure from the

---

[5] For these and other estimates of the profitability of the slave trade, see Eric Williams, *Capitalism and Slavery* (Chapel Hill: University of North Carolina Press, 1944).

mines of Mexico, Peru, Bolivia and elsewhere. The vast increase in Europe's supply of gold and silver raised prices, inflated profits, and speeded the accumulation of capital. The immediate impact of the increase in precious metals was on prices, but the important final effect was on the accumulation of wealth.

The inflationary rise in the general level of prices in western Europe during the sixteenth and seventeenth centuries was so great that it is now referred to as the "Price Revolution." Prices began to rise shortly after the discovery of America and continued to rise for more than a century and a half. Between 1300 and 1450 the production of gold and silver in Europe declined because of the exhaustion of European mines. At the same time there had been growing demands for metallic money to finance a rising volume of trade and to offset the unfavorable commodity balance of trade with the East. By 1450 Europe was confronted with a serious shortage of gold and silver. Some relief came after 1450 when the Portuguese started bringing precious metals from the Gold Coast of Africa and when new mines were opened in Austria and Germany. Increases in the supply of precious metals kept pace with the increase in the volume of trade, and consequently the general level of prices was fairly stable between 1450 and 1500 and even until 1525.

In the sixteenth century, and more particularly after 1545, there began what is probably the greatest inflation *in specie terms* in the history of the world. The relative increase in the supply of metallic money exceeded that of any other recorded period. In accordance with what has come to be known as the quantity theory of money, the increase in the supply of gold and silver led to a corresponding increase in the general level of prices. Although precise relations between increases in the quantity of money and increases in the general level of prices clearly do not hold for short periods, most students of monetary theory and history seem to agree that *in the long run* increases in prices tend to be approximately proportional to increases in the quantity of money if other things remain the same. Since other things never remain the same, especially for a long period of time, the quantitative relations between prices and the quantity of money are not capable of statistical verification. Most difficult is the fact that the meaning of "money" changes as institutional arrangements alter in historic time. Nevertheless, a few statistics may illustrate what happened to the money supply and prices during the Price Revolution, regardless of the causal relations. During the sixteenth century there was perhaps a six-fold increase in Europe's supply of metallic money as compared with a two- or three-fold increase in prices in western Europe as a whole during the same period. The less than proportional change in prices may be accounted for by the rising volume of trade, which required more money to take care of the greater volume of transactions. Furthermore, a considerable part of the gold and silver may have been used in the arts and for other nonmonetary purposes. Also much of the new treasure did not remain in Europe, but was drained off to the East to pay for Europe's chronic unfavorable balance of trade.

Nearly all of the American treasure legally imported into Europe went directly to Spain. Although the Spanish tried to keep the precious metals within their borders, most of the treasure sooner or later found its way to trading centers in the Low Countries, England, and France, especially to

Antwerp, Amsterdam, London, and Rouen. Spanish armies in the Low Countries and in France required large expenditures of gold and silver in these countries. Spain's domestic economy was too retarded to satisfy the wants of its wealthy classes, who spent heavily in foreign countries for goods which were not obtainable from domestic production. Prices rose first and most rapidly in Spain but as the treasure was disseminated prices also rose in other countries. During the sixteenth century prices in Spain increased about four-fold, in the Low Countries perhaps three-fold, in England two-and-one-half fold, in France about two-fold, and in Italy nearly two-fold. Taking western Europe as a whole, there was approximately a two- to three-fold increase in prices in terms of silver from 1500 to 1600. The main impact was felt between 1550 and 1600, but a more gradual rise in prices continued through the seventeenth century in most of the countries of western Europe.

In retrospect it is obvious enough that American treasure was the primary cause of the rise in prices, but among sixteenth- and seventeenth-century contemporaries the reason was not so obvious. In fact hardly anyone grasped what was happening. One man, Jean Bodin, occupies an important place in the history of economic thought because he did correctly analyze the cause of the rise in prices. Bodin was a great political philosopher—a defender of monarchical absolutism. The occasion for his analysis of the Price Revolution was to refute a common fallacy of his day that attributed the rise in prices solely to debasement of the currency. In this period, as in many others, a common practice was to reduce the metal content of the monetary unit. In the beginning monetary units were given names corresponding to their actual weight in silver. Thus the English pound originally was a troy pound (12 ounces) of silver, and the same was true of the French livre and the Italian lira. As sovereigns reduced the metallic content of the money unit without changing the name, the "pound" came to weigh much less than a troy pound and would naturally buy less than 12 ounces of silver. When a sixteenth-century French writer contended that debasement was the cause of the rise in prices and argued that gold and silver would buy as much of other goods as in former times, Bodin, in his *Reply to the Paradox of Monsieur de Malestroit* (1568), refuted this argument with one of the first clear statements of the quantity theory of money. Concerning the cause of the great rise in prices, Bodin wrote: "The principal and almost the only one (to which no one has heretofore referred) is the abundance of gold and silver. . . . The principal cause which raises the price of everything wherever it be is the abundance of . . . gold and silver . . ." Bodin's statement of the quantity theory of money has special significance because it penetrated the basic weakness in mercantilist thought, the failure to see that increases in the supply of gold and silver would tend to raise prices and offset or reverse the favorable balance of trade, which was a keystone in mercantilist policy.

Effects of Price Inflation on Economic Classes

The significance of American treasure in the rise of capitalism lay not in the increase in prices as such, but in the effects which the rise in prices had on the several economic classes. If inflation were to raise all prices and all incomes by exactly the same degree, it would have no important con-

sequences. Everyone would be in exactly the same economic position after the inflation as before. Everyone would have more money income, but prices would be proportionately higher so that no more goods and services could be purchased with the greater money income. However, inflations never happen in this way; they always have important economic and social consequences because different individuals and groups are affected in different degrees, some gaining and some losing wealth and income. In short, the effect of inflation is to redistribute wealth and alter the income pattern of a nation, region, or community. This type of effect may be explored for the Price Revolution of the sixteenth century for the landlord class, the wage-earning class and the capitalist class.

Landlord class Landlords as a class suffered economic losses because money rents did not rise as rapidly as prices. Consequently the real incomes of landlords declined—their incomes, although greater in money terms, would buy less than before. This was an important factor in the general decline of the landowning class during early capitalism. In cases in which rents were fixed by custom in terms of money—as was frequently the case with labor services commuted to money payments—rents could not rise at all, while in other cases rents could rise only slowly and lagged behind prices. Under both circumstances the tenants benefited, while many landlords sank from wealth to poverty. Many landlords sold their lands to prosperous city bourgeoisie, who frequently purchased estates in order to gain the social prestige and political influence attached to ownership of landed property and not to other forms of property.

Some landlords were more fortunate. They broke old customs and substituted short-term leases for long-term leases or perpetual tenure. They were able to raise their rents frequently enough to keep their incomes partly in step with soaring prices. A third type of landowner was the man who farmed his own land. Such farmers tended to gain because they employed wage-earners at relatively low wages and sold their crops at high prices. The Price Revolution provided fuel for the enclosure movement.

Wage-earning class Money wages lagged behind prices during the Price Revolution, and therefore wage-earners were able to buy progressively less with the money received as wages. Money wages did not keep pace with the cost of living, which is to say that real wages fell. The fall in real wages was especially marked in England and France, whereas in Spain real wages, after falling during the greater part of the sixteenth century, caught up with prices by 1600. As Bodin observed: "The haughty and indolent Spaniard sells his effort very dearly." Professor Hamilton, the leading authority on the Price Revolution, gives the following figures on prices, money wages, and real wages in Spain, France, and England for the sixteenth century.[6] Spanish prices in-

---

[6] In a famous article, "American Treasure and the Rise of Capitalism," *Economica*, IX (1929), 338–57, Professor Earl J. Hamilton made rather sweeping claims for the Price Revolution as an important causal factor in the rise of capitalism in western Europe. This thesis has been disputed by numerous critics, including Professor John U. Nef, "Prices and Industrial Capitalism in France and England, 1540–1640," *Economic History Review*, VII (1937), 155–85. Professor Nef challenges the indices of wages and prices used by Professor Hamilton in advancing his thesis. Instead of price-wage relations, Professor Nef stresses changes in technology, especially those associated with the use of coal in a number

creased three-and-a-half times and so did money wages, leaving real wages
approximately the same in 1600 as in 1500. French prices more than doubled,
while money wages increased by about 40 per cent, leaving real wages in
1600 at about 60 per cent of the level in 1500. English prices increased about
two-and-a-half times while money wages increased only about 30 per cent,
leaving real wages in 1600 at about 50 per cent of the level in 1500. These
figures probably exaggerate the extent of the fall in real wages in France and
England. They indicate that in a century of great material progress the standard of living of French and English workers fell by almost one-half. Wage-
earning families that produced some of their own necessities were less affected.
Nevertheless, it may safely be concluded—and this is what matters for capital
accumulation—that the wage-earning class did not share in the fruits of the
great material progress of the period. Certainly there were some unusual
circumstances that render this conclusion feasible. Wages were relatively
high in 1500—the 1400's having been a great century for the common people
of Europe; during early capitalism wage-earners were harassed by severe
laws against group action; the poor laws and the criminal code created a rigid
discipline that left workers with no alternative but to work or starve or be
imprisoned.

Capitalist class   The great beneficiaries of the Price Revolution were
the members of the capitalist class, including merchants, manufacturers and
all who employed wage-labor. The fact that workers received lower real
wages meant that their employers were paying lower real wages. Increases in
prices received for goods sold were greater than the increases in costs of
production (wages and materials). Even if it is assumed that the prices of
raw materials increased as rapidly as the prices of finished goods, a manufacturer or merchant processing or holding stocks of goods for a few months
would gain when he sold at higher prices. The capitalist enjoyed a double
source of gain from the rise in prices: (1) he paid lower real wages and
(2) he received windfall profits on materials.

The process by which prices increase more rapidly than costs of production is known as *profit inflation*. In the economic environment of the sixteenth
century, profit inflation meant not only higher profits but also larger savings
and more rapid accumulation of capital from plowing these back into business.
The latter is the significant point of the Price Revolution for the progress of
capitalism. According to John Maynard Keynes, the famous economist,
". . . the greater part of the fruits of the economic progress and capital ac-

---

of new industries in which England progressed more rapidly than France in the century
(1540–1640) before the English Revolution. Clearly no single causal factor was responsible for the rise of capitalism. What Professor Hamilton seems to have demonstrated is
that the more rapid rise of prices as compared with money wages did contribute to the
formation of capital in England as well as in France but not in Spain. These changes took
place within a general context of an already blossoming industrial capitalism, of technological changes, shifts in outlook toward economic life affected among other things by shifts
in religious doctrines, the impact of overseas discoveries quite apart from American treasure, and others. Since modern economists have tended to stress the incompatibility between
inflation and economic development, Professor Hamilton's work is significant even if it
proves less than he claimed. He seems to have shown that under some circumstances inflation and economic development are compatible. How much more he demonstrated is the
subject of the debate.

cumulation of the Elizabethan and Jacobean age accrued to the profiteer rather than to the wage-earner. . . . Never in the annals of the modern world has there existed so prolonged and so rich an opportunity for the business man, the speculator and the profiteer. In these golden years modern capitalism was born." [7]

The sacrifices of labor (lower real wages) assisted greatly in the accumulation of capital during early capitalism. In later ages after the accumulation of large amounts of capital, real wages could rise and capital could accumulate rapidly at the same time. In a poor economy restricted consumption is a condition of rapid accumulation, and even in wealthy countries the rate of accumulation is potentially greater when consumption is restricted (through low wages). In underdeveloped or backward economic areas sacrifice in the form of curtailed consumption is a factor which may contribute to rapid economic growth. Low real wages are, of course, not a sufficient condition of growth, but they do mean that the sacrifices of workers need not be in vain. English and French workers (involuntarily) sacrificed more than Spanish workers during the sixteenth and seventeenth centuries and the fruits of their sacrifices are reflected in the greater amount of productive wealth (capital) available to future generations of English and French workers and capitalists. Not only were the sacrifices important, but also the incentives offered to entrepreneurs in the form of lush profits. For enterprise, more than sacrifice, has been responsible for the great material achievements of capitalist civilization. To quote Keynes again, "As soon as thrift gets ahead of enterprise, it positively discourages the recovery of enterprise and sets up a vicious circle by its adverse effect on profits . . . if Enterprise is asleep, wealth decays whatever Thrift may be doing . . . Were the Seven Wonders of the World built by Thrift? I deem it doubtful." [8]

Care must be exercised in stating the relation between the influx of precious metals and the progress of real capital accumulation. The Spanish plundered the wealth of the Aztecs and Incas and then put them to work mining more treasure; and Englishmen like Drake pirated the looted treasure of the Spanish. But this was not what mattered for economic progress. Plundering and pirating are as old as human society. Men cannot live nor the world grow rich by plundering each other. Obviously increased hoards of gold and silver can never be the essence of economic progress. Nor did a mere rise in prices during the Price Revolution result directly in the creation of new wealth or real capital. What mattered was that the new wealth fell into the hands of individuals and nations that were most prone to invest it in new and productive enterprise in order to produce more wealth. Money is not real wealth but money is necessary to the acquisition of real wealth in a capitalistic society.

The Price Revolution altered the relations among economic classes in a manner favorable to the rapid accumulation of capital. A major weakness of Spain was that American treasure came into the hands of profligate aristocrats, who were prone to spend rather than to save and invest in productive enter-

---

[7] *Treatise on Money* (London: Macmillan & Co., Ltd., 1930), Vol. II, 158–59. Adapting the statistics of the Price Revolution, Keynes gives comparative figures on the profit inflation (prices rising more rapidly than costs) in England, France, and Spain.

[8] Keynes, *Treatise on Money*, II, 150.

prise. Much of the strength of England, France, and Holland was that American treasure, mostly out of Spain, came into the possession of merchants, who were prone to save and invest rather than to spend.

Profit inflation and wage deflation created a more unequal distribution of income within these countries, and this in turn affected the allocation of economic resources in the direction of relatively more capital goods production and relatively less consumer goods production, corresponding to the relatively greater demand for the former and the relatively smaller demand for the latter. The more unequal distribution of income increased saving and decreased spending for consumption without causing unemployment on a significant scale. Wage-earners got less and capitalists got more of the total product of society than they would have had in the absence of the price and profit inflation. Larger incomes to capitalists meant more savings and more accumulation, and the lesser incomes going to wage-earners meant that a smaller part of economic resources was devoted to producing for current consumption.

Although rich merchants and other capitalists received a legal claim to a larger share of the total national product, they chose to save and invest in new enterprise rather than to consume their larger share. Had the new increments in wealth that accrued to the legal possession of the capitalists gone to the wage-earners, most of it would have been consumed in the form of a rising level of consumption. The working class of the sixteenth century would have been better off, but the future would have inherited less accumulated wealth.

It may be argued that the more unequal distribution of income was less objectionable because the nominal owners of new wealth (capitalists) chose to accumulate rather than to consume it. The capitalist wealth-owners served as the trustees of society's productive wealth. In order for economic inequality to be compatible with economic progress, it is important that the demand for capital goods be such that the decrease in demand for consumers' goods (due to lower real wages) not result in an overall decrease in demand and consequent unemployment. This may be accounted for in terms of the world's being still very poor even though it was rapidly becoming less so. A New World had just been discovered and whole continents lay open for the exploitation of enterprising men. Other ages and richer societies would be less able to make the impoverishment of its working class a condition of economic progress.[9]

[9] *Note on the Price Revolution.* For a variety of viewpoints on the Price Revolution, see the references in the Selected Bibliography under the names of David Felix, Ingrid Hammarström, Y. S. Brenner, J. D. Gould, and J. U. Nef, as well as E. J. Hamilton. Professor Hamilton formulated the modern version of the Price Revolution in his article "American Treasure and the Rise of Capitalism (1500–1700)," in which he made sweeping claims which invited modification. The grounds on which his position has been criticized relate, among others, to (1) why prices rose in England, (2) how much did real wages fall, and (3) whether the quantity theory of money is an appropriate framework for analyzing the causes and consequences of the Price Revolution.

The most serious challenge to Hamilton's thesis is the view that not much New World treasure found its way into England and therefore it could not have caused the sharp rise in prices in that country. An alternative explanation for the price rise is diminishing returns in agriculture in response to a rapid increase in English population; debasement of the English currency is also sometimes given as an important cause of inflation in prices. There is agreement, even by Professor Hamilton, that his original article overstated the

BEVERIDGE, WILLIAM, *Prices and Wages in England from the Twelfth to the Nineteenth Century.* London: Longmans, Green & Co., 1939.

HAMILTON, EARL J., *American Treasure and the Price Revolution in Spain, 1501–1650.* Cambridge, Mass.: Harvard University Press, 1934.

KEYNES, JOHN M., *Treatise on Money,* Vol. II, "Spanish Treasure." London: Macmillan & Co., Ltd., 1930, 148–52.

LIPSON, E., *The Economic History of England* (6th ed.), Vol. II, Chap. 2. London: Adam & Charles Black, Ltd., 1956.

POSTHUMUS, N. W., *Inquiry into the History of Prices in Holland.* Leyden: Brill, 1946.

SCOTT, WILLIAM R., *The Constitution and Finance of English, Scottish, and Irish Joint-stock Companies to 1720,* 3 vols. Cambridge: Cambridge University Press, 1910–12.

WILLIAMS, ERIC, *Capitalism and Slavery.* Chapel Hill: University of North Carolina Press, 1944.

ARTICLES

BRENNER, Y. S., "The Inflation of Prices in Early Sixteenth-Century England," *Economic History Review,* XIV (Dec., 1961), 225–39.

———, "The Inflation of Prices in England, 1551–1650," *Economic History Review,* XV (1962), 266–84.

BROWN, E. H. PHELPS, and S. V. HOPKINS, "Seven Centuries of the Prices of Consumables Compared with Builders' Wage-Rates," *Economica,* XXII (Aug., 1955), 195–206; XXIII (Nov., 1956), 296–314; and XXIV (Nov., 1957), 289–306.

FELIX, DAVID, "Profit Inflation and Industrial Growth: The Historic Record and Contemporary Analogies," *Quarterly Journal of Economics,* LXX (Aug., 1956), 441–63.

GOULD, J. D., "The Price Revolution Reconsidered," *Economic History Review,* XVII (Dec., 1964), 249–66.

---

extent of the fall in real wages during the sixteenth century. An unqualified application of the quantity theory of money, in which all prices and incomes rise proportionately, would be meaningless in this context, as in most others. The issue is what kind of quantity theory. On the significance of price inflation, see J. M. Keynes, "The Consequences to Society of Changes in the Value of Money," *Manchester Guardian, Commercial Reconstruction in Europe* (July 27, 1922), Sect. 5, pp. 321–28.

Important points of agreement on the Price Revolution include (1) that prices did rise sharply in England and western Europe during the sixteenth century, (2) that real wages did fall sharply, especially in England, even if the precise amount cannot be measured, and (3) that agricultural prices rose more than industrial prices. Our analysis in the text has emphasized the effects of disproportionate price and income changes on savings and investment through a redistribution of income. The results indicated would follow irrespective of the reasons for the price rise so long as real wages fell and productivity in the economy rose. Professor Nef has amply documented the latter point with his findings on technological change in England during the period 1540–1640. The issue between Professors Nef and Hamilton is whether technical innovations or capital accumulation is more important in economic progress. A reconciliation of these views may perhaps be found in recent discussions among theoretical economists that most technical change must be embodied in real capital assets, which cost money, so that innovation can occur only with capital accumulation. The views of Hamilton and Nef are more complementary than competing. This issue was, of course, raised a long time ago by Adam Smith in Book I (technical innovation) and Book II (capital accumulation) of the *Wealth of Nations.*

HAMILTON, EARL J., "American Treasure and the Rise of Capitalism (1500–1700)," *Economica,* IX (Nov., 1929), 338–57.

———, "Imports of American Gold and Silver into Spain, 1503–1660," *Quarterly Journal of Economics,* XLIII (May, 1929), 436–72.

HAMMARSTRÖM, INGRID, "The 'Price Revolution' of the Sixteenth Century: Some Swedish Evidence," *Scandinavian Economic History Review,* V, No. 2 (1957), 118–54.

KERRIDGE, ERIC, "The Movement of Rent, 1540–1640," *Economic History Review,* VI, No. 1 (1953), 16–34.

NEF, JOHN U., "Prices and Industrial Capitalism in France and England, 1540–1640," *Economic History Review,* VII (May, 1937), 155–85.

Early Industrial Capitalism

The division of labor is determined by the extent of the market, wrote Adam Smith in 1776. In this brief proposition he summed up the economic development of Europe during the preceding three hundred years. The vast expansion of trade associated with the discovery of the New World, the all-water route to the East, the increase in trade among European nations, and the development of domestic markets within the several European nations provided outlets for products of industrial production on a scale that could not have been supplied by the individualistic handicraft system. The growth of industry during early capitalism was a further development of the export industries of the late medieval period. An important difference was that in the late medieval period capitalistic organization of industrial production was the exception rather than the rule, whereas during early capitalism it became the rule rather than the exception. Handicraft production and marketing survived but sank into insignificance.

Adam Smith wrote before the age of machinery and the factory system. He was, therefore, impressed by the growth of the market and the accumulation of capital as the basis for increases in the wealth of nations. Prior to the Industrial Revolution of the eighteenth century, changes in the techniques of production were less important in raising the productivity of labor than changes in the form of industrial organization brought about by expansion of the market. Industrial capitalism was first of all a method of organization. Changes in technology came for the most part after new methods of organization were developed and expanded. In the process of introducing new technology the organization was subjected to further significant changes. Given the expansion of the market and the accumulation of capital, capitalist entrepreneurs were able to achieve greatly increased output by employing workers to specialize in the separate stages of production, such as cleaning, carding, spinning, weaving, fulling, dyeing, and finishing in the textile industry. Workers pursued simple, routine operations which they repeated thousands of times daily. Production became "mechanical" in the routine sense long before it was mechanized by the application of machinery to repetitive operations.

The hallmark of capitalistic industry was the increasing control of capital over production. Extension of control by capitalists brought changes in social

and economic relations. The late medieval distinction between "big masters"
and "little masters" broadened into a division between capitalist employers
and wage-earning laborers. The increase in the capital of the one was accompanied by the loss of economic independence by the other. A capitalist
system at one pole brought a wage system at the other pole. Unlike the independent craftsman of an earlier age, the worker owned neither the materials
upon which he worked nor the finished product. He sold his labor rather than
the product of his labor. Producers looked to capitalist employers to supply
them with materials. Divorce from ownership of the *raw materials* marked the
advent of the wage system. Divorce from ownership of the *means of production* was a later and important step in completing the capitalistic evolution of
production, but it was subsidiary in principle to the establishment of the
wage system.

THE PUTTING-OUT SYSTEM

Scarcity of capital is the key to the economics of early industrial capitalism.
Western Europe was struggling to build up its stock of capital out of the savings of its own people. There was no other way to get capital since there were
then no more advanced countries from which capital could be borrowed. In
later ages it was possible for the less developed economies to borrow capital
as well as techniques from more advanced economies. Accumulating capital
out of savings meant keeping current consumption below the level of current
production. In the preceding chapter note has been taken of the influence of
the Price Revolution in causing forced saving (involuntary reduction in consumption) on the part of wage-earners.

Economizing the limited supply of capital meant spreading it thinly
among a large number of workers and letting them provide the remainder of
the requisites of production. From the capitalist's point of view it was more
profitable to bring a greater volume of production under partial control than
to bring a smaller amount of production under complete control, and this
seems to have been the most fruitful arrangement from the point of view of the
economy as a whole. Naturally the amount of wage labor and the extent of the
capitalist's control over it increased with the further accumulation of capital,
which went on more or less continuously, interrupted by occasional commercial and financial crises. The result during the first centuries of capitalism
was the spread of the existing and, by later standards, rather primitive methods
of production. Revolutionary change in techniques of production had to await
the Industrial Revolution of the eighteenth century.

Given the great expansion of the market, the older handicraft system
was clearly inadequate; but given the scarcity of capital, a thoroughgoing
capitalistic type of industry was not feasible. The upshot was a compromise
which was partly capitalistic and partly handicraft, with more of the characteristics of the former than of the latter. For the purpose of describing the economic characteristics of the putting-out system a distinction between circulating and fixed capital is useful. Circulating capital was owned by the capitalist;
fixed capital was furnished by the worker. Circulating capital was that part
of the total capital which circulated, more or less literally, from hand to hand,

as, for example, a material like wool which was processed from a raw state into a finished product as it passed through the several stages of production. Fixed capital included tools, machines, buildings, and the like. It remained in the possession of one worker or master and was therefore in some sense fixed or stationary; it did not circulate from hand to hand, from master to master.

By retaining ownership of the product through all the stages of production from raw material to finished good, the capitalist exercised dominant although not complete control over the process of production. He controlled the type of raw material which was used, e.g., the quality of wool, and could specify what type of finished product was desired. The total quantity of work to be done depended upon the total amount of material "put out" by capitalists. Regularity of employment depended on the regularity with which capitalists put out materials to workers. Capitalists in turn were highly sensitive to the demands of the market. In these and other respects the putting-out capitalist was boss. On the other hand, since workmen labored in their cottages away from the physical presence of the capitalist or his representatives, there was an obvious lack of control over the quality of workmanship and therefore lack of control over the quality of the finished product. Lack of quality control in such vital matters was tolerated by capitalists out of necessity imposed by the scarcity of capital in relation to the immense demands of the market. In some instances capitalists preferred to invest more capital per worker in order to bring production together in one large central workshop, but this arrangement was exceptional before the advent of factory machinery.

The putting-out system economized the use of scarce labor as well as scarce capital. Capital is employed to put labor to work and obviously can employ no more labor than is available for working. In predominantly agricultural economies the greater part of the population is scattered in rural areas and is tied to the land by some form of land tenure. The putting-out capitalists were ingenious enough to find ways and means to utilize the surplus labor of rural inhabitants. Being highly seasonal in character, agricultural employment affords surplus labor time during at least part of the year. In addition to the seasonal surplus there was a chronic surplus of labor among rural families such as cottagers and squatters, who held too little land to employ fully all the labor time of the family. Although surplus agricultural labor existed everywhere among the rural Europeans, it was more abundant in England after the enclosure movement began to displace farm tenants from their holdings.[1] Some tenants were totally displaced and some were partially displaced. In either circumstance a mixed system of farming and industry represented a necessity for the family and an economical use of labor for the nation. It helped bridge the gap between a society predominantly rural and agricultural and a society which was to become predominantly urban and industrial. As long as the putting-out system existed, there was no need for displaced persons from agriculture to migrate to urban centers to engage in industrial employment. In fact, for a time the growth of industry was probably accompanied by a relative decline in urban population.

For the most part putting-out industry met the situation in western

[1] On the enclosure movement, see the next chapter.

Europe for some three hundred years. Its tenacity was due in large measure

to the small amount of fixed capital required for efficient production and the availability of increasing numbers of rural workers free from the monopolistic restrictions of urban craft gilds. However, the puttting-out arrangement was not suitable for all types of industry. Industries such as coal mining required amounts of fixed capital in excess of that which individual workers could supply. In such cases the capitalists advanced the fixed as well as the circulating capital. Yet the typical capitalist of this era was reluctant to invest heavily in fixed capital in which the turnover is slower and the risk greater than in circulating capital of an equivalent magnitude.

Changes in financial institutions, in technology, in capitalist mentality, and most of all in the quantity of capital were prerequisites of the factory system. Accumulation of capital during the three hundred years in which the putting-out system was dominant brought gradual changes in the structure of industry. Larger supplies of capital enabled capitalists to extend their control over production. Workers too poor to provide their own looms, for example, were provided with looms by capitalists to whom a rental was paid. This made the worker economically more dependent on the capitalist since the worker now owned neither the materials nor the tools used in production.

English Woolen Industry

The structure and functioning of the putting-out system attained perhaps its most elaborate form in the English woolen industry. Certain other developments which were taking place simultaneously with the development of the English putting-out system may help to place this phase of English economic history in a broader setting. In the realm of politics this was the age of the Tudor monarchs, including Henry VII, Henry VIII, and Elizabeth. The Tudors were succeeded by the weaker Stuart kings, whose struggle with Parliament precipitated the English Revolution, bringing Oliver Cromwell to power for ten years, after which the Stuarts were restored and again dethroned in the bloodless revolution of 1688. The policy of the Tudors was in many respects anticapitalistic, being directed toward protecting the small peasants and small artisans. In these endeavors they were not very successful. They legislated against enclosures, which were being used to promote wool-growing for the woolen industry. Meanwhile the Price Revolution was taking place, inflating profits and deflating real wages. The rapid rise in prices gave added incentive to the enclosure movement. After the Revolution of the seventeenth century the English government, with sovereignty in Parliament, fell into the hands of men under whose rule England rose to a position of unquestioned leadership in economic development.

Clothier as the key figure　The clothier was the key figure in the English woolen industry under the putting-out system. Whether a small operator, as in the Yorkshire area in the north of England, or a large operator, as in other parts of the country, the clothier was the entrepreneur who coordinated the numerous interdependent stages of clothmaking from buying raw wool to processing finished cloth. In woolen manufacture at least ten such stages may be distinguished: cleaning, carding, spinning, weaving, fulling, stretching, burling, shearing, dyeing, and finishing. Some of these stages might be broken

down into additional steps, and in the case of the worsted industry one observer noted forty different processes, each of which constituted a separate trade.[2] These several stages have no special economic significance except to indicate how the technical nature of clothmaking made possible a complex division of labor, which in turn holds the clue to the increase in productivity arising from the application of capital. They also suggest the complexity of the task of the clothier in coordinating the activities of perhaps hundreds of workers engaged in many different tasks.

A large clothier in control of all these stages from the purchase of raw wool to the sale of finished cloth was in one sense primarily a merchant who bought and sold. In another sense he was an industrialist because he placed raw materials in the hands of artisans and arranged the flow of products through the several stages of production. He is sometimes referred to as a merchant-manufacturer. However, he was not a manufacturer in the original and literal sense of working with his hands; nor was he a manufacturer in the modern sense of having a large number of employees working under one roof in a factory. The large clothier was not an artisan, although the small clothier frequently was. The former was sometimes called a "gentleman clothier" to indicate that no social inferiority attached to his association with the cloth industry, and in this respect he was distinguished from the "working clothier," who was an artisan.

In the processing of cloth at least two stages—fulling and finishing—were not well suited to the cottage type of industry because they required large amounts of fixed capital. Clothmaking communities usually had a fulling mill which employed water power to drive mechanical hammers for beating the freshly woven cloth. Except in the most backward areas mechanical fulling had replaced the primitive method of treading under water on the cloth with human feet. Cloth finishing was from medieval times removed from the cottage because it required skills and equipment which the ordinary artisan did not possess. Clothiers without sufficient capital for a finishing mill would sell their cloth unfinished and undyed.

In fact, cloth finishing was a matter of international specialization for centuries. As a latecomer to the textile industry, England continued to export unfinished cloth to countries which specialized in finishing, like the Low Countries and Florence. The use of non-cottage organization for fulling and finishing illustrates that the most general criterion of organization was the most efficient application of capital to production. In this sense the form of organization depended on the state of the industrial arts. Putting-out dominated in most stages of the textile industry because the arts were in a relatively primitive stage at this time.

Defects of the Putting-Out System from the Capitalist's Point of View

From the point of view of the capitalist the great defect of the putting-out system was incomplete control over the physical conditions of produc-

---

[2] Paul Mantoux, *The Industrial Revolution in the Eighteenth Century,* rev. ed. (New York: The Macmillan Company, 1927), p. 91n.

tion. Scattered as they were over the rural countryside, the workers could not

be supervised directly by the capitalist or his representatives. He was in personal contact with his workers only when they came for materials and when they returned finished products. Since the products were already owned by the clothier, he was in no position to refuse to accept them even if he considered the workmanship inferior. The clothier could, of course, refuse to put out any more material to workers whose craftsmanship was unsatisfactory, but in view of the demand for cloth and the scarcity of artisans, this might prove more costly in the long run than inferior products. Certainly it was pointless for the clothier to insist on standards beyond the capacity and skills of ordinary artisans. One virtue of long apprenticeship was to maintain the quality of craftsmanship. However, clothiers were not favorably inclined toward long apprenticeship and other craft gild practices. Finished products of uneven quality might result from causes other than variations in workmanship. Inferior raw materials at an earlier stage of production meant inferior workmanship at later stages, and the finest craftsmanship could not make a silk purse out of a sow's ear.

Lack of actual control over the physical conditions of production made it difficult for the clothier to synchronize the flow of products through the many stages of processing. For example, a failure on the part of spinners to deliver the required amount of yarn to weavers at the required time could delay not only weaving but all subsequent steps in cloth production. Small artisans frequently could not be relied on to meet their promised deliveries. The rather delicate business of operating a household by earning and spending money was an institutional arrangement which had to be learned. It was still new to rural families which had traditionally made their living by planting, growing, harvesting, and storing crops. After payday workers might take extra holidays, perhaps become inebriated, or just loaf until more money was needed for the next meal. Lack of synchronization between stages was self-aggravating. Artisans were not tied to a single employer but usually worked for several clothiers. This both enhanced their bargaining power and protected them against irregular employment. It also tempted workers to accept more work than they could do immediately. When business was brisk, several clothiers would put out materials to the same group of artisans, causing bottlenecks in production all along the line. Clothiers might protect themselves against interruptions in the flow of production by stocking large reserves at every stage, but this tied up extra capital, reduced the speed of its turnover, and lowered the rate of profit below its potential maximum.

Embezzlement of materials by carders, spinners, weavers, and others was another disadvantage of the putting-out system from the point of view of the capitalist. Despite laws against embezzlement, it was a common practice among workers, especially the most poorly paid, to substitute inferior for superior materials and to falsify the weight of material processed by adding moisture to the wool. This was sometimes done by steaming wool over boiling water or otherwise placing wool where it would absorb moisture. This kind of practice is said to have added as much as a pound of weight in twelve.

Inability to exercise rational control over the decentralized process of production led some clothiers to establish large central workshops for cloth production. Workers were assembled under one roof where the embezzlement

of materials could be prevented and where control of the quality and quantity of output was possible.

In the early sixteenth century John Winchcombe of Newbury, known as Jack of Newbury, is said to have employed more than 800 workers in his cloth manufactory. These included 150 sorters, 100 carders, 200 spinners, 50 clippers, 80 dressers, 20 fullers, and 40 dyers, plus miscellaneous types of workers. Winchcombe was a contemporary of King Henry VIII, who is reported to have remarked on seeing a long string of carts loaded with Winchcombe's cloth: "This Jack of Newbury is richer than I." Jack of Newbury was exceptional but by no means the only clothier with a central manufacturing establishment. There is, however, no record of any textile workshop larger than Winchcombe's before the late eighteenth century. Manufacturing establishments in the sense of large, central workshops without machinery never became prevalent. The putting-out system, which was unsatisfactory in so many respects, was tolerated because the quantity of capital at the disposal of clothiers could be more profitably employed in ways other than operating central workshops and paying for the direct supervision of workers. The tenacity of the putting-out system shows that, despite its many faults, it was adapted to the circumstances of the period. Only with the continued progressive accumulation of capital and the perfection of heavy and expensive machinery did centralized production attain a dominant position in industry.

Conditions of Workers under the Putting-Out System

Early industrial capitalism placed workers in the status of permanent wage-earners, whose economic welfare depended on the amount of wages, the length of the working day, the regularity of employment, and their access to means of subsistence other than that purchased with money wages.

Wages During the fifteenth century the real incomes of the common people of western Europe had improved considerably and by 1500, at the dawn of modern times, real incomes probably were higher than ever before. The Price Revolution of the sixteenth century lowered real wages drastically. The nature and significance of the Price Revolution depended on the state of development of the wage system. The larger the proportion of total income derived from money wages, the more easily was the consumption level undermined by the rise in prices. A nation of completely independent and self-supporting peasants would have been affected very little by price inflation because they would not have entered either the commodity market to buy and sell produce or the labor market to buy and sell labor. To an important degree the nonrevolutionary influence of price inflation in Spain, referred to in the preceding chapter, can be accounted for by the lack of industrial development and the absence of a numerous class of Spanish wage-earners. A rise in the price of grain made little difference to a Spanish peasant who raised his own food, whereas a rise in the price of grain from an index of 100 to 300 accompanied by a rise in money wages from an index of 100 to 200 lowered the grain-wage of English workers by one-third. They would be able to buy only two-thirds as much grain as before the rise in price. This is approximately what happened to wage-earners in the developing capitalistic countries of

Europe during the sixteenth century. Real wages fell less rapidly during the
seventeenth century and rose in the latter half of the seventeenth and in most
of the eighteenth century. In England real wages fell because of the marked
rise in the cost of living during the quarter-century from 1790 to 1815, the
years of the French Revolution and the Napoleonic Wars.

The Elizabethan Statute of Artificers (1563) recognized the effects of the
Price Revolution on real wages. It states ". . . wages and allowances limited
in many of the [older] statutes are in divers places too small . . . respecting
the advancement of prices . . . and the said laws cannot conveniently without
the greatest grief and burden of the poor labourer and hired man be put in
due execution." The statute provided that the local authorities, who were
charged with the obligation of fixing money wages, should take into consideration "the plenty and scarcity" of the time in order to give to every worker
"a convenient proportion of wages." Despite apparent good intentions, the
law was a maximum (not a minimum) wage law, under which money wages
obviously failed to keep pace with the increasing cost of living. A later statute
(1603) explicitly acknowledged this fact and empowered local authorities to
fix minimum wages, especially for textile workers, whether piece-wages or
time-wages.

A seventeenth-century English ballad entitled *The Clothier's Delight*
suggests that weavers were paid as little as sixpence per day:

> We will make them to work hard for sixpence a day
> Though a shilling they deserve if they had their just pay.

The statistical objectivity of the ballad is open to question because it was
designed to express the sorrows of downtrodden workers and the delight of
villainous clothiers in exploiting them. Presumably weavers received more
than sixpence a day, but even a wage twice that amount would have been
hardly sufficient to support a family. Evidence suggests that in the eighteenth
century an artisan weaver could earn a shilling and a half to two shillings per
day. Since weavers were paid according to the amount of work they did rather
than on an hourly or daily basis, there were variations in the earnings of individual weavers according to their productivity. However the data be interpreted, real wages appear to have been very low for skilled artisans in terms
of the annual income that would accrue at these daily wages even if employment were steady throughout the year, which characteristically it was not.

If the wages of the relatively skilled weavers were low, those of spinners
were incredibly small. Spinning was not regarded as a craft. Most of it was
done by women and children whose earnings were supplemental to the family's
main source of income either from farming or from industry. There were a few
independent spinners who worked on their own material, but they were always
few in number in modern times and they were virtually nonexistent by the
eighteenth century. Spinners worked on materials put out by clothiers, or
sometimes by master weavers or wool combers. Their wages were scarcely
more than a few pence a day, and were far too low to provide full support for
a family. As some families had no other regular source of income, it may be
supposed they were always on the verge of poor relief.

Length of the working day   The Statute of Artificers (1563), which applied to all wage-earners and not just to putting-out labor, specified that hours

of work should be from five in the morning to seven at night during the spring and summer with two-and-a-half hours out for meals and rest. In the fall and winter the working day was from sunup to sundown. As in other respects, the hours provision of the famous statute was more honored in the breach than in the observance. Actually there was no more regularity of working hours than there had been in former ages, which was to be expected, especially among rural laborers who were free to work when they wished. There was, however, the compulsion of hunger to keep them humping, perhaps on an average of ten to twelve hours a day. As already noted, one of the disadvantages of the putting-out system from the employer's point of view was the lack of discipline over the working time and conditions of his employees. There was nothing in the nature of the putting-out system to effect much change in the traditional working hours of the population. Workers employed in larger workshops and mines and later in factories found themselves subjected to a much more rigorous discipline.

Unemployment   Unemployment was another important defect of early industrial capitalism. What was to become in the nineteenth century the rhythmic pattern of depression and prosperity was present in embryo form as early as the sixteenth century. Industrial crises did not take place with the regularity that characterized later business cycles, but they did occur from time to time and in some instances were severe enough to call forth direct governmental intervention, as in England in 1528, 1586, and 1620–1624.

The Tudor and early Stuart governments tried to protect wage-earners from unemployment because they feared the social unrest which might arise if large numbers of able-bodied men were idle. In addition to legislative attempts to require that workers be employed on a full-year basis, the Tudors and Stuarts ordered employers to retain their workers even though this might involve temporary losses to capitalist employers. That those who employed workers for profit when trade was good must be content to employ them at losses when trade was bad seems to have been the philosophy behind the government's intervention during trade depressions. Possession of the means of production was assumed to involve a social responsibility on the part of the owners for the employment of those without any means of production to which to apply their labor. The notion that the means of production are purely the private property of those who possess the legal title to them and that they are free to use or not to use them as profit or loss dictates did not develop until after the English Civil War of the seventeenth century, when this new philosophy was linked to the development of laissez-faire in government and economics.

Throughout early capitalism unemployment was accentuated by artificial restrictions on the mobility of labor. Under a series of English poor laws permission to settle in a new community was contingent upon being able to demonstrate that new settlers would not become public charges. Migration of poor workers from depressed economic areas was made difficult since those who were most in need of moving, namely the unemployed, would have the greatest difficulty proving to another community that they would not become public charges.

Landholdings and working conditions   For the majority of putting-out

workers who were rural dwellers, their access to land had an important in-
degree of independence. The mixture of rural industry and farming was subject to many possible combinations. Some middle-class artisans were incidentally farmers or gardeners, raising some or much of the family food supply.
Prosperous freeholders retained more independence than poor cottagers. Even
the small freeholder was not likely to be pushed into circumstances in which
he would be forced to sell his labor at unreasonably low wages. He could
refuse to work if the proffered wages were too low. Because he had some
economic reserve he was in a more favorable bargaining position than the
landless worker. His next meal did not depend upon being employed regardless
of the wage offered. In times of trade depression the landholder could direct
more of his effort to farming and after the economic storm had passed and
wages had improved he could re-enter the labor market. Freeholders were not
in danger of having to mortgage their looms as security for distress loans from
clothiers. Ownership of land as well as ownership of simple tools of industrial
production provided defenses against total dependence on capitalist employers. A weaver who owned his loom could try independent production if
conditions in the labor market were too intolerable. All he had to do was to
secure the raw material and find a market for his product, and although both
might involve difficulties, they did provide safety valves against oppression.
The degree of security in small landholdings by various types of English
peasants is discussed in the next chapter on the enclosure movement.

121

EARLY
INDUSTRIAL
CAPITALISM

AN EARLY INDUSTRIAL REVOLUTION

There were two compelling motives for capitalists to make a complete transition to ownership of the tools as well as the materials used in production. The
first was organizational—the desire to rationalize the process of production by
bringing it under complete control and central direction. The second was
technical—the large amounts of fixed as well as circulating capital required
for efficient operation in certain types of industry. The effect of the first motive
is seen in the growth of large central workshops in clothmaking and other industries which did not use expensive machinery and equipment. The second
influence, the technical requirements of large fixed capital, proved the more
compelling in the long run. With the advance of technical knowledge, more
and more industries came to require expensive equipment and machinery in
order to put this knowledge into operation.

The big breaking point came with the Industrial Revolution in the last
third of the eighteenth century. But even during early capitalism there were
a number of industries which fell into this category. Fulling and finishing in
the cloth industry have already been mentioned. Professor Nef has shown
that industries with relatively heavy fixed capital requirements made a striking
advance in England in the period between 1540 and 1640, which was mainly
the age of Elizabeth and the early Stuarts preceding the revolutionary disturbances of the seventeenth century. At the beginning of this period England
was still industrially backward as compared with Continental areas such as
the Low Countries and parts of France, Germany, and Italy.

As a matter of conscious policy the English borrowed from the Continent the technology of a number of strategic industries in which England was deficient. In the process of borrowing and developing these industries in the special circumstances of the English environment some of them were transformed into something quite different from what they had been on the Continent. Consequently, by 1640 English industry was in advance of the Continental economies and went on to achieve its Industrial Revolution, which the Continent as well as overseas areas borrowed from the English during the nineteenth and twentieth centuries. This early period between 1540 and 1640 during which England started in arrears of the Continent and moved into the lead within a hundred years has been called by Professor Nef "An Early Industrial Revolution." [3]

Professor Nef finds in the rise of the British coal industry the strategic factor in the Early Industrial Revolution because most of the new, large-scale industries required coal as a fuel for heating and processing. The shift from vegetable to mineral products opened the way for much greater production of energy. Forests (a vegetable matter) were becoming so scarce in Elizabethan England that wood was too expensive to be used as a fuel in some industries and for some householders. An increased demand for coal rendered surface mining from open pits quite inadequate as a source of supply. Coal was brought up from pits which were sunk deeper and deeper into the earth. Deep-pit mining was expensive for several reasons. In addition to the cost of sinking the pit, heavy outlays were needed for machinery to hoist coal from the mines. Most expensive of all, however, was extracting water from deep mines. This was not only expensive but uncertain as to outcome, and the many failures made coal mining a risky type of enterprise. Aqueducts and tunnels were used to drain water by gravity where feasible. A bolder method was to try to pump water from the mines. In this connection the modern steam engine developed as a device for "lifting water with fire," as Thomas Savary described his early steam engine. Newcomen's engine, invented in 1712, was the first really successful application of steam power to mine pumping. James Watt's steam engine was begun as an attempt to improve upon the Newcomen engine. Such devices were expensive and could be afforded only by capitalists of some means. As a result coal mining became an industry in which the workers owned neither the material they produced (coal) nor the fixed capital used in mining.

Among the important industries which were dependent upon coal and which themselves involved large outlays of fixed capital were cannon foundries, shipbuilding, glass manufacture, soap making, salt processing, breweries, paper, and gunpowder (saltpeter). In 1540 England was dependent on the Continent for cannons, but in 1640 the English had become the best cannon makers in Europe, a fact of some significance in a world of nearly continuous warfare among the power-hungry nations of Europe. Another industry borrowed from the Continent was glassmaking. In the sixteenth century France had a highly developed glass industry, which operated on a rather small scale,

---

[3] Professor John U. Nef has pioneered important research on the Early Industrial Revolution beginning with *The Rise of the British Coal Industry*, 2 vols. (London: Routledge & Kegan Paul, Ltd., 1932). See bibliography at the end of this chapter for other works by Professor Nef on this subject.

employed highly trained artisans, and turned out a luxury product for a relatively small number of rich buyers. When transferred to England, glassmaking
took on a different economic complexion. It was produced in large plants using
relatively unskilled labor. In quality the English glass was not as good as the
French, but it was much cheaper and sold at prices which persons of modest
means could afford to pay. This type of development was characteristic of
what is meant by "An Early Industrial Revolution."

COMMERCIAL VERSUS INDUSTRIAL CAPITAL

From the twelfth to the seventeenth century commerce dominated industry in
western Europe. Initiative and control usually rested with merchants rather
than with industrial producers because commerce expanded in advance of
industry. Beginning in England in the eighteenth century the balance of power
shifted away from commerce to industry. The Industrial Revolution may be
defined as the period of transition from a dominance of commercial over industrial capital to a dominance of industrial over commercial capital. Although
the reversal of the balance of power from commerce to industry was dramatically evident during the decades of the English Industrial Revolution, the
transition was in process for several centuries. Under the putting-out system
of industry merchant capitalism maintained its dominant position, but during
the sixteenth and seventeenth centuries changes were at work in England
which ultimately led to the triumph of industrial capitalism over commercial
capitalism. The forces making for this transformation were complex, and only
a few of many facets can be described here in order to portray the broader
evolutionary forces of early industrial capitalism and to lay a foundation for
a later discussion of the Industrial Revolution.

The dichotomy between commercial and industrial capital in the period
of early capitalism is a further development of the separation of the distribu-
tive (marketing) function from the productive function, which was the fundamental feature of the break-up of the medieval handicraft system. The entering wedge in this break-up occurred when craftsmen were brought under the
control of merchants engaged in long-distance trade. Crafts which had been
independent were amalgamated and fell under the domination of the wealthier
members of one of the crafts, usually the craft nearest the market. In London,
for example, the hatters and cappers fell under the control of the haberdashers.
Where formal industrial organization existed, the decline of the craft gild led
to the formation of the livery company, which usually included a subordinate,
second-class membership known as the yeomenry consisting of small masters
and journeymen.

Widening of the market in the sixteenth and seventeenth centuries was
accompanied by further alterations in the organization of industry and in some
respects a reversal of the earlier changes. Among the yeomen there arose a
new class of industrial capitalists who dominated the producing function, and
at the other pole the mercantile group specialized in trading. Between these
two groups of capitalists there was a struggle to monopolize the expansion
of trade. Merchants based their claims for control of the market on the right
of craftsmen to sell their products to anyone whom they pleased. During the

Elizabethan age the amalgamated companies in London held together despite strained relations between the livery sector, which remained in command, and the yeomen sector, which was struggling to free itself from mercantile domination.

Under the early Stuarts many of the industrial groups broke away from the amalgamated companies to establish separately incorporated companies of producers with royal charters. After a long struggle the feltmakers (hat and cap craftsmen) obtained their freedom from the haberdashers (merchants). In the leather industry a similar struggle took place. The leatherworkers broke away from the Leathersellers' Company to form the Glovers' Company with a royal charter of incorporation. The independence of the Feltmakers' and Glovers' companies represented gains for industrial capital in a contest for emancipation from commercial capital. This was not a struggle between labor and capital, but between two groups of capitalists. Once independence was attained by the industrial group from the commercial, the poorer craftsmen came under the domination of the wealthy industrial capitalists.

In the important cloth industry the separation of groups representing industrial and commercial capital followed a pattern similar to that in the leather and felt industries, with the important difference that the yeomen clothworkers achieved independence as an autonomous group within the nominally still amalgamated Clothmakers' Company. The Clothmakers' Company was the successor to the craft gild in the sense that it included among its members both craftsmen and merchants.

As the export of English cloth grew in importance, the merchant element within the company tended to specialize in purely trading functions and left the management of cloth production to the leading members of the yeomenry. The latter group demanded a voice in the control of production and finally was granted an autonomous position. No separately incorporated company of industrialists was created, but the effect was much the same as in the case of the feltworkers and leatherworkers. Industrial capital achieved relative independence from commercial capital, and the small masters and journeymen in turn became subservient to the industrial capitalists.

In the provincial towns of England industry gained more freedom from commercial capitalists than in London. This is not surprising since London was the mercantile center of the nation and consequently the stronghold of commercial capitalists. Merchant-manufacturers in provincial towns at first welcomed the expansion of industry into the surrounding countryside because they held control of the new industry and also because the competition of rural craftsmen helped place urban craftsmen in a weak bargaining position. However, as rural industry grew and the country clothiers established direct contacts with London merchants, the town clothiers lost control of rural industry. At the same time the old type of town industry was weakened by the migration of craftsmen, especially weavers, into the country. Attempts were made by the town clothiers to limit the expansion of industry into rural communities by appealing to the ancient gild tradition that industry should be carried on exclusively in towns.

Since town governments had no jurisdiction over rural territory, the town clothiers solicited the support of the national government to pass legislation

which would limit the growth of rural industry. A striking illustration of town-
inspired legislation directed against rural industry is the Weavers' Act of 1555.
Under this law provisions were made which, had they been enforced, would
have effectively curbed the growth of the rural cloth industry. The statute
provided that rural clothiers could own or rent out only one loom; that rural
weavers might own or rent out no more than two looms; that rural weavers
should be limited to two apprentices; and that all apprentices should serve
the full seven-year apprenticeship. On the other hand, the Weavers' Act placed
no limitations upon the number of looms or apprentices which an urban
clothier might have in rural areas or elsewhere.

The Weavers' Act was an attempt to invoke the traditions of the craft
gild against the new industrial capitalism, which had migrated into the rural
areas in order to circumvent the monopolistic control of the gilds in urban
areas as well as to utilize the cheaper labor of rural communities. The town
clothiers had no interest in maintaining the craft gilds as such. They flagrantly
disregarded the traditions of the craft gilds when there was an opportunity
to seize control of rural industry, but when they saw rural industry slipping
from their hands, they did not hesitate to invoke these same gild traditions
they had recently violated.

In practice the Weavers' Act was not enforced and had little influence
upon the actual course of English industrial development. The town clothiers,
who were unable to stem the flow of putting-out industry into rural communities, shifted their capital into the finishing and dyeing of cloth, which activities remained as town enterprises because they required too much fixed
capital for cottage industry. In this manner the provincial town capitalist, who
had at first been primarily a merchant putting out materials to country
weavers, now became primarily an industrial capitalist. Thus in the provincial
towns of England the balance of power was shifting away from commercial
toward industrial capital during the sixteenth and seventeenth centuries.

One of the leading issues between industrial and commercial capitalists
in Elizabethan England was whether the nation should continue to export
mainly unfinished cloth or whether it should limit or prohibit the export of
unfinished cloth in order to encourage the development of the finishing and
dyeing stages of the industry. Although the English cloth industry had come
a long way since the days in which the leading English export was raw wool
(its export was prohibited in 1614), it was still not the equal of the Flemish,
Dutch, and Florentine cloth industries. Great export merchants like the Merchant Adventurers favored the status quo with regard to cloth export because
the greatest foreign demand was for unfinished English cloth. They feared
that any drastic change in English policy would disrupt the market for English
goods and would provoke retaliation by foreign countries. The industrial capitalists, especially those engaged in the finishing and dyeing processes and
the artisans who were employed by them, favored special measures to limit
or prevent the export of unfinished cloth. From time to time proposals were
made to prohibit the export of unfinished cloth. Under the first Stuart king,
James I, a grandiose plan was attempted.[4] It proved a disastrous failure which

---

[4] The plan of Alderman Cockayne in 1614.

threw the entire country into a severe depression and soon had to be repealed. It illustrates the type of issue which divided the industrial and commercial capitalists of this period.

Stuart Monopolies and the English Revolution of the Seventeenth Century

Another event of momentous importance in the early transition to industrial capitalism in England was the Revolution of the seventeenth century. Its general import in this connection was to lodge political sovereignty in Parliament, the members of which represented a middle class endowed with some elements of a philosophy of laissez-faire and hostility to autocratic paternalism. Events leading up to the English Revolution developed bitter resentment against monopoly, and industrial capitalists in particular resented the Stuart policy of handing out exclusive privileges for the development of old and new industries to a narrow clique of courtiers and royal favorites. Before the Revolution special groups of capitalists favored those monopolies which were advantageous to themselves, and opposed those which were unfavorable to their interests. Stuart policy convinced the business class that government-sponsored monopoly was an evil, and out of the Revolution there emerged a general antimonopolistic philosophy.

Probably nothing less than a violent revolution could have shaken the historic acceptance of medieval and mercantilistic monopoly as a necessity of social policy. Countries which did not experience a similar revolution did not develop a negative attitude toward monopoly and a positive attitude toward the right of capital alone to determine its status. In this is to be found an important part of the answer to the question why the Industrial Revolution occurred first in England. The freedom of capital to determine its own fate meant, among other things, the freeing of industrial capital from artificial restraints imposed by special interests, including commercial capitalists.

Economic as well as political and religious motives stimulated the English Revolution of the seventeenth century. The immediate struggle between the Crown and Parliament focused on control of the purse strings of government. According to English political tradition, taxes could be raised only with the consent of Parliament. During the Stuart regime of the early seventeenth century Parliament was reluctant to consent to any increase in taxes. In order to circumvent the power of Parliament, James I and Charles I raised revenue by granting monopolies to special groups in return for substantial financial payments to the Crown. Precedent for grants of industrial monopoly had been set in the sixteenth century by Queen Elizabeth, whose moderate and intelligent policy in this connection had been successful in transferring from the Continent to England important industries such as cannon foundries, soap making, glassmaking, and salt processing.

Elizabeth's policy of special grants to foreign, new, and risky industries was perverted under the Stuarts into a purely fiscal device for raising money in face of the opposition of Parliament. Despite the famous Patents of Monopoly Law, passed by Parliament in 1624 limiting grants of individual (not corporation) monopoly to new inventions, Charles I persisted in selling monopolies. He granted a monopoly for making playing cards, which was neither

risky nor in need of foreign skill. He granted monopolies for the manufacture
and distribution of items of common consumption such as salt, soap, tobacco,
and coal transportation. To the Crown an obvious advantage of selling exclusive rights to industries producing for common consumption was the high
premiums they would command; whereas in new and risky industries financial failure might be as likely as financial success.

English capitalists, apart from the favored few who were recipients of
special privileges, vigorously opposed the Stuart policy of exclusive monopoly.
Since the fundamental issue in the Revolution involved raising revenue and
since monopoly was the chief device employed by the Crown for this purpose,
monopoly was a central issue in the violent civil war which ensued. By de-
molishing the spirit of government-sponsored monopoly in the public mind
and by establishing a form of representative government, the Revolution
marked an important turning point in the rise of industrial capitalism.

Continental Versus English Industrial Capitalism

Considerable interest attaches to a comparative study of the growth of
industrial capitalism in England and the growth of industrial capitalism on
the Continent of Europe. On the one hand, Continental commercial capitalism attained a high stage of development before a similar position was
achieved by commercial capitalism in England. On the other hand, the Continental countries did not make the transition from predominantly commercial
to predominantly industrial capitalism until long after England.

There are many reasons for this. Attention here is focused on the more
or less simultaneous emergence in England, and the lack of this condition on
the Continent, of a new class of industrial capitalists without roots in medieval
and mercantilistic monopolies and a new class of proletariat with few if any
claims to tenure of the land. The appearance of the latter class was related to
the English enclosure movement, which was not duplicated on the Continent.
It is not easy to explain why the industrial capitalist class which emerged in
England had no parallel on the Continent, but one important factor was the
aforementioned antimonopolistic aspect of the English Revolution of the seventeenth century and the absence of a similar revolution on the Continent.

In some respects the French Revolution of 1789 possessed these antimonopoly qualities, but it occurred more than a century after the English
Revolution had run its course (1688) and at a time when the French peasants
were given unlimited title to their land, thus eliminating the possibility of a
strong enclosure movement and a consequently large supply of industrial
labor. During the late 1600's Colbert's efforts to stimulate industrial development in France enjoyed success in many individual cases, but clearly France
did not experience a rate of general industrial development comparable to
England's at that time or in the succeeding century. Colbert's industrial subsidies were given mainly for urban rather than rural enterprise.

For this there were two important reasons: (1) in the absence of an
enclosure movement the supply of cheap rural labor for industry was not
available in France as in England, and (2) Colbert leaned heavily on the
gilds, which persisted in the tradition that industry should be an urban and
not a rural activity. Instead of legislation like the English Statute of Artificers,

which ignored the gilds while "nationalizing" some of their practices such as compulsory seven-year apprenticeship, the French put into effect statutory controls which strengthened the gilds by making them the local agents for the administration of national industrial statutes. The putting-out system was opposed everywhere by the craft gilds and wherever the latter were strengthened the progress of industrial capitalism was hindered.

SELECTED BIBLIOGRAPHY

DOBB, MAURICE H., *Studies in the Development of Capitalism*, Chap. 4. London: Routledge & Kegan Paul, Ltd., 1946.

FISHER, F. J., ed., *Essays in the Economic and Social History of Stuart England; in Honor of R. H. Tawney.* Cambridge: Cambridge University Press, 1961.

GRAS, N. S. B., *Industrial Evolution.* Cambridge, Mass.: Harvard University Press, 1930.

LIPSON, E., *The History of the Woolen and Worsted Industries.* New York: Barnes & Noble, Inc., 1965.

NEF, JOHN U., *The Conquest of the Material World*, esp. Part 2. Chicago: University of Chicago Press, 1964.

————, *Industry and Government in France and England, 1540–1640.* Ithaca: Great Seal Books, 1957.

————, *The Rise of the British Coal Industry*, 2 vols. London: Routledge & Kegan Paul, Ltd., 1932.

SINGER, CHARLES J. and others, eds. *A History of Technology*, Vol. III, *From the Renaissance to the Industrial Revolution.* Oxford: Clarendon Press, 1957.

SWEEZY, PAUL M., *Monopoly and Competition in the English Coal Trade, 1550–1850.* Cambridge, Mass.: Harvard University Press, 1938.

TAWNEY, RICHARD H., and EILEEN E. POWER, eds., *Tudor Economic Documents*, 3 vols. New York: Longmans, Green & Co., 1924.

UNWIN, GEORGE C., *Industrial Organization in the Sixteenth and Seventeenth Centuries* (2nd ed.). London: Cass, 1963.

ARTICLES

COLEMAN, D. C., "Industrial Growth and Industrial Revolutions," *Economica*, XXIII (Feb., 1963), 1–22.

HAUSER, HENRI, "The Characteristic Features of French Economic History from the Middle of the Sixteenth to the Middle of the Eighteenth Century," *Economic History Review*, IV (Oct., 1933), 257–72.

NEF, JOHN U., "The Progress of Technology and the Growth of Large-Scale Industry in Great Britain, 1540–1640," *Economic History Review*, V (Oct., 1934), 3–24.

————, "A Comparison of Industrial Growth in France and England from 1540 to 1640," *Journal of Political Economy*, XL (June, 1936), 289–317; (Aug., 1936), 505–33; (Oct., 1936), 643–66.

TAWNEY, RICHARD H., "Studies in Bibliography, II: Modern Capitalism," *Economic History Review*, IV (1933), 336–56.

WILSON, CHARLES, "Cloth Production and International Competition in the Seventeenth Century," *Economic History Review*, XIII (Dec., 1960), 209–21.

Private Property in Land:
English Enclosures and
Capitalistic Agriculture

CHAPTER

8

The decline of the manorial system in western Europe led to a variety of new patterns in agriculture. Over a major part of the Continent the arrested break-up of feudalism resulted in a semimanorial type of land tenure under which the peasants were half-free and half-servile and their masters were partly feudal lords and partly rentiers.[1] In a few centers of vigorous capitalistic development agriculture became thoroughly commercial. In the Low Countries, for example, agriculture enjoyed its earliest and most progressive development under the dual stimulus of demand from a dense urban population and the availability of capital for investment in agricultural improvements. Field crops of clover and turnips provided feed for animals and helped maintain the fertility of the soil. With an improved rotation of crops, land was utilized more intensively by eliminating the wasteful practice of fallowing. Later the English took up many of the advanced practices of the Dutch.

Yet it was in England that agriculture played the most significant role in the general development of capitalism. English landholding evolved from a feudalistic to a capitalistic basis between 1400 and 1800. The medieval open-field system with its scattered strips was replaced by large enclosed fields of compact holdings. There was a relatively brief interval during the fifteenth century when an independent peasantry flourished in England, but this was only a gap between feudal dependence and capitalistic dependence so far as the great majority of the rural population was concerned. Large landholdings resulting from enclosure replaced the large landholdings of feudal England.

A two-fold significance attaches to the enclosure movement in relation to the development of capitalism. (1) It created private property in land. Private ownership of the means of production is an indispensable condition of capitalism, and land is one of the basic means of production. Private property in land did not really exist under feudalism. Feudal land tenure rested on personal, servile relations between overlords and lords and, at the manorial level, between lords and serfs, under which all parties enjoyed customary rights without possessing absolute title to the land. Under capitalism an impersonal, absolute, and individualistic conception of land tenure replaced the personal,

---

[1] A rentier was a person who received a fixed money income from rent of his land.

servile, and social conception of medieval land tenure. (2) The enclosure movement contributed mightily to the industrialization of English society. In the sixteenth century the enclosures supplied the raw material for England's greatest industry, woolen textiles, and also helped to create the labor supply in rural areas for that industry. The later enclosures of the eighteenth century provided food for the rapidly growing industrial population and helped to create an abundant labor supply for the Industrial Revolution.

The term "enclosure" derives from the practice of placing hedges or fences around land which previously had been unenclosed as part of the open-field system. Hedging or fencing was the common but not universal practice when large consolidated fields came under individual control and ownership. Enclosure was viewed as a general remedy for open-field defects, which were numerous: One must plow when his neighbor plowed; plant when and what his neighbor planted; let land lie fallow when his neighbor's was fallow; rotate crops according to the community custom; open one's fields to grazing after the crops were harvested; limit the number of grazing animals according to one's customary "stint"; let a lazy neighbor's neglected field seed one's own field with weeds; and let animals graze and breed with the disease-ridden common herd. The host of customary restrictions were an impediment to the free exercise of initiative in important entrepreneurial matters. An escape from these restrictions was to enclose an area of land and say in effect that it was private property which the owner was free to do with as he chose.

In the broader sense the term enclosure refers to the process of agrarian change which converted land from community control to individual control. With this change went a change in the conception of land tenure as the basis of community sustenance to that of land as an income-yielding investment.

Peasants as well as landlords were aware of the disadvantages of many aspects of open-field agriculture, and peasant initiative and enterprise were responsible for many if not most of the improvements which had taken place with the decline of the manorial system. Consolidation of tenant strips as well as the lord's demesne into compact holdings had been under way on a voluntary basis even before the Black Death of the mid-fourteenth century, and that tragic event had speeded the process. By means of barter and purchase, consolidation took place without altering rights to grazing on the commons. Along with the consolidation of strips into compact parcels had gone the appropriation of wasteland for the use of tenants who enjoyed no legal heritage from the manorial past. All these changes were, however, gradual and attracted little attention. In contrast, the enclosures of the Tudor period were the leading subject of heated controversy in an age which was filled with turmoil and passionate outbursts of social indignation.

ENGLISH ENCLOSURES OF THE SIXTEENTH CENTURY

There were two distinct phases of the enclosure movement in England. The first occurred in the century and a half after the Tudors assumed the throne in 1485; the second took place in the century and a half from about 1700 to 1850. For brevity these may be referred to as the sixteenth- and the eighteenth-century enclosures, respectively. The widely different characteristics of these

two phases of the enclosure movement can be explained only in terms of the seventeenth-century English Revolution, or Civil War, which divided them in time.

Motivation

Motivating factors behind the sixteenth-century enclosures were (1) the demand for wool, (2) the rise in prices, and (3) the strength and stability of the Tudor governments. The increased demand for wool arose from expansion of the woolen textile industry. This circumstance, combined with the presence of potential leaseholders willing to pay higher money rents, tempted landlords to enclose open fields and convert them to pasture even if this meant, as it usually did, displacement of tenants of long standing. The fall in the value of money associated with the Price Revolution and the devaluation of the currency resulted in shrinking real income for landlords whose money rents remained fixed. For the landlord the solution was to displace the customary tenants and lease the land at higher rentals. The third factor—the stability of the Tudor governments—was associated with political unification of the state under absolute monarchy. In former times feudal lords had exercised sovereignty over their local community. Feudal armies were constantly preying upon their neighbors. Consequently there were advantages in having a large number of loyal tenants who, in emergencies, could take up arms in defense of the lands from which they and their lord gained their livelihood. Under the Tudor regime military and political power was effectively concentrated in the hands of the Crown. Transgressors against the King's justice and the King's prerogatives were dealt with in severe fashion. The domestic tranquillity resulting from a strong national government changed the whole political and military environment. Whereas in former times lords had done all in their power to force tenants to remain on their land, they now, in many instances, did all in their power to force them from the land.

Types of Land Tenure

By the beginning of the sixteenth century economic serfdom had almost completely disappeared in England. There were three main types of land tenure at this time, according to a famous inquiry conducted by Cardinal Wolsey in 1517–19. These were freeholds, leaseholds, and copyholds. Freeholders enjoyed permanently secure tenure to their land and were not much affected by enclosure except insofar as they chose to sell their strips to engrossing landlords. Freeholders constituted about 20 per cent of the total of all landholding families. Leaseholders, constituting less than 20 per cent of the total, had temporarily secure tenure but no permanent claim to remain on the land they cultivated. Since the lease was a form of contract, the legal rights of leaseholders were definitely known and established by law. Some leases were for as long as ninety-nine years, some were as short as one year, and some were terminable at the will of the landlord.

The largest number of tillers of the soil in sixteenth-century England were copyholders, or customary tenants, a class which constituted between three-fifths and two-thirds of the total. The impact of enclosure was felt particularly

by this third group. The plight of the copyholder during the enclosure movement is symbolic of the dilemma presented by the fact that the economic collapse of the manorial system was not accompanied by any clear-cut legal abolition of serfdom. Copyholders were not serfs; they were not landowners; they were not leaseholders; they were not wage laborers; they were just customary tenants. The Tudor governments sought to protect all classes of peasantry, including customary tenants, but failed to give them clear title to the land. Since the disappearance of the copyhold more than any other event marks the beginning of private property in land, the legal position of the copyholder calls for further attention. Although a work on economic development must be primarily concerned with economic issues, it is obvious that the legal and economic aspects of a problem cannot always be divorced and that the institution of private property, which is a key institution of capitalism, is as much a legal as an economic institution.

Position of the Copyholder

A copyhold was a right to land tenure based on customs of the manor and recognized by the courts in the period subsequent to the severance of the servile relation of serfs to their masters. Its legal force depended upon the willingness of the community, acting through its legal institutions, to recognize custom as the basis of a legal right. Presumptively the copyholder had some form of documentary evidence which stated in writing his obligations and privileges, but in many cases the copyholders possessed no written evidence of their customary rights. Tenants who had no document to prove their claims were more easily evicted than those who held legally recognized written evidence. Especially easy to evict were the customary tenants who possessed no more than squatters' rights to the land they occupied. They could be evicted without any violation of the law even though long occupancy was assumed by squatters to give them prescriptive rights to their holdings. In the second phase of the enclosure movement during the eighteenth and nineteenth centuries the enclosure acts passed by Parliament gave no weight to copyholds unless claims were supported by documentary evidence, which very few could produce.

Assuming a copyholder held written evidence of his claims, his vulnerability to eviction depended on the specific provisions of his copyhold. Here there were two main considerations: whether the copyhold was held by inheritance, for a single life, or more than one life, or for a specified term of years; and whether the inheritance fee, payable at the time the holding passed from one tenant to another, was fixed or variable in amount. Copyholders by inheritance were relatively secure as long as they met their payments. The annual rent on copyholds was usually a fixed sum of money, which, in view of the Price Revolution, meant that the payment was much less than the true economic rent which could be obtained in a free land market from a leaseholder. The landlord suffered a loss of real income and the copyholder gained an unearned increment as prices rose since his rent remained the same.

Whereas annual rent was usually fixed, the inheritance fee or fine, which was a vestige of the *heriot* of manorial times, was usually variable, more or less at the will of the landlord. Landlords were tempted to increase the fine in

order to make up for the annual loss of real income over a period of years,
and unscrupulous landlords bent on taking the land for enclosure could raise
the inheritance fee to an exorbitant amount which the incoming tenant could
not pay. Less fortunate than the copyholder by inheritance were the tenants
with copyholds for a limited time. At the expiration of this period, be it fixed
in years or for the life of the tenant, or for the life of the tenant, his wife, and
son, the fields reverted automatically to the landlord, who had no legal obligation to renew regardless of how strong the moral compulsion might be to
perpetuate the ancient custom of the manor.

Means of Making Enclosures

Confiscation of monastery lands   In the War of the Roses (1455–1485)
the nobility of England killed each other to such an extent that very few of
the older families remained. The new landlord class was of a more commercial
turn of mind than their medieval predecessors. Henry VIII used the English
Reformation of the early sixteenth century as an excuse to confiscate the vast
monastery lands, which in turn were sold to men who supported the Crown,
to land speculators, and to rich merchants interested in land as a source of
profitable investment.

The resulting redistribution of land disrupted the traditional relations of
tenants and landlords and was often the occasion for wholesale dismissal of
customary tenants and for turning arable land into sheep pasture. Moreover,
the moral example set by the Crown in confiscating land from the Church was
not lost on the landlords, who saw no moral barrier to doing on a small scale
what their King had done on a grand scale. Spurred on by the squeeze of rising prices on their standard of living, the opportunity which beckoned from
the growing demand for wool, the moral bankruptcy of King and courtiers, and
a predisposition toward a capitalistic mentality which resented the inefficiencies
of obsolete methods, the English landlords were psychologically prepared to
crack the whip on their customary tenants whose only claim to the land rested
on the ancient customs of the outmoded manorial system.

Enclosing the demesne   The demesne was the land on the medieval
manor which was reserved especially for the lord. Although worked by his
serfs, the entire produce of the demesne became the property of their master.
As early as the thirteenth century, leasing the demesne betokened the decline
of the manor, and the wholesale alienation of the demesne in the late fourteenth century marked the wholesale break-up of the manorial system. The
earliest large farms sprang from demesne lands which were rented *en bloc* to
enterprising farmers. The large leaseholders of the demesne constituted the
first class of capitalistic farmers in England. They held the demesne in lease
from the landlord and employed wage-earning laborers to till the fields.

Under the medieval manor the demesne lands were frequently dispersed
in small strips just as were the holdings of peasants. With the break-up of this
type of manor the demesne strips were more apt to be rented to numerous
small tenants holding contiguous strips. However, by the sixteenth century
even the demesne which, upon the break-up of the manor, had been divided
among many small tenants had been consolidated into large holdings and
these were, characteristically, leased to one or a few large farmers.

Enclosure of the demesne was the unquestioned legal right of the landlord. If the demesne was in one large block, or in three blocks corresponding to the three fields of the open-field system, there was no serious technical difficulty. On the scattered demesne the claims of the tenants occupying demesne land were not protected by the courts, and they were easily evicted from these strips by enclosing landlords. A serious economic and social problem might arise if, after being enclosed, the demesne were converted from arable land to sheep pasture. Conversion from arable to pasture always decreased the demand for labor and caused former wage laborers on the demesne farm to be thrown out of work.

Enclosing the commons Enclosure of the commons formed a crucial aspect of the struggle between tenants and landlords during the sixteenth century. The most direct way for a lord to increase the amount of grazing land for his sheep was to take over the common pasture, common meadow, and common waste. Moreover, enclosure of the commons often spearheaded a drive to enclose the arable land of the small tenants and in this respect heralded the destruction of the village community.

Common land was a main source of food for peasants as well as their animals. Animal husbandry, fortified by an abundance of good pasture, afforded milk, cheese, butter, meat, eggs, and other human food. It was also a potential source of wool for homespun clothing. A peasant family with even modest rights in the commons was well provided in these things and had the basis of a reasonably comfortable living. The commons was indispensable for feeding beasts of burden used in plowing and general cultivation of arable land. For a given amount of arable land a fairly definite amount of pasture of given quality was necessary. As the ratio of pasture to arable land was reduced, farming became more precarious, and a decrease in pasture below a critical minimum was equivalent to confiscation of beasts of burden without which cultivation was impossible. Robbing the tenant of his rights in the commons was an indirect but effective method of confiscating his arable land.

A landlord who wished to push his tenants from the land might well begin by overstocking the commons. This would put pressure on the tenants, who might object, but there was sufficient doubt concerning the exact nature of the claims of tenants in the commons to camouflage the issue and prevent the landlord's action from having the appearance of an outright violation of the law. Sometimes landlords acted on the theory that the commons belonged exclusively to them, but this claim had no validity in law or custom. There were, however, statutes which gave the lord a residual claim to the commons. According to the Statute of Merton (1235) the lord of the manor might enclose the commons provided he left "sufficient" pasture for his tenants. The meaning of "sufficient" was left to the courts to interpret. Judges were landlord-oriented in their thinking even when their motives were above suspicion, which was by no means always the case.

Residence in the village did not of itself constitute a right to use the commons. Cottagers and other tenants without arable land might have resided in a village for generations, earning a living by working for wages in farming and industry and grazing a few animals in the commons. As long as pasture was abundant there was little incentive to challenge their action, but when

pasture became scarce, their landlords—and sometimes their fellow tenants—

did not hesitate to force them from the commons. Aggrandizement at the expense of this class of tenant was not open to legal challenge.

Successful enclosure had to take place primarily at the expense of the most numerous class, the customary tenants, or copyholders. After overstocking the commons with his animals and ousting the tenants who were without any legal claim to the commons, the lord might erect a hedge around that part of the commons which he wished to appropriate as his own private property. A tenant might find hedges blocking the path along which he drove his animals to pasture. When the landlord bothered at all with legal niceties, he took the position that all the common was his except that which was "necessary" for the legitimate tenants. Customary tenants with arable land had rights in the commons according to "the custom of the manor." The exact meaning of this was sufficiently uncertain and variable from manor to manor to place an illiterate customary tenant who tried to prove his title in an unenviable position before a court of law and in opposition to the landlord's lawyer.

The legal vulnerability of customary tenants to enclosures arose from the historic fact that the decline of the manorial system in England had been mainly economic in nature and did not result in customary tenants receiving clear legal title to the land. Free tenants, by contrast, had clear title to use of the commons, including free access to and from pasture land, but even they could be squeezed by the "necessary" clause of the Statute of Merton. Almost without exception tenants forced from the commons received no compensation for their lost rights.

Enclosing arable open fields What alarmed contemporary critics and government authorities was not so much the enclosure of the demesne and waste or even of the commons but the engrossing of arable open fields into large farms and more particularly their conversion into pasture. The central issue in English agriculture during the sixteenth, seventeenth, and eighteenth centuries was whether to preserve or to destroy the open-field system of cultivation. Taking over the commons was an indirect way of forcing tenants from their arable strips, but there were other and more direct methods for accomplishing this end. Most important was the conversion of a copyhold to a leasehold, considered by Professor Tawney to be the basic legal issue of the sixteenth-century enclosures. A copyhold implied some form of title, vague and fragmentary though it may have been. A leasehold was purely a matter of the contract under which a tenant rented some of the lord's land for a specified period at a specified price. As previously indicated, a legal but ethically questionable device for dispossessing unwanted customary tenants was to raise the flexible inheritance fine so high that the family would have to default and thereby lose its copyhold.

A more ethical method of converting copyholds into leaseholds was to offer the tenant a long lease on favorable terms if he would surrender his claim to the copyhold. Both of these methods required time, and impatient landlords and farmers were frequently unwilling to wait for a copyholder to die of old age or for a long-term lease to expire. Any means were used by landlords to convert copyholds to leaseholds: persuasion, intimidation, destruction of copy rolls, legalistic chicanery, and other devices within and outside

the law. In whatever manner accomplished, the change from copyhold to lease-hold destroyed the semiproprietary claim of the copyholder and made the landlord the unqualified owner of land which his predecessors had once held in fief from an overlord. The disappearance of copyholds is the significant legal indication of the creation of private property in land.

The actual amount of arable land enclosed during the sixteenth century was only a fraction of the total land under cultivation, and some of the arable fields enclosed were not converted to sheep pasture. Only a relatively small number of all peasants were evicted. This statistical point has sometimes been used to minimize the importance of enclosures in the sixteenth century. In the cumulative change of economic institutions, however, what matters is not a statistical figure, but new beginnings and new directions. The predominant facts of one age are not necessarily those which hold the clue to the future. As Professor Tawney has said, "It is a shallow view which has no interest to spare for the rivulet because it is not yet a river." [2]

After a century of freedom, prosperity, and apparent security, English peasants were threatened by a new movement. Lands had been consolidated and enclosed before, but now honest and able tenants were being forced off the land which had been in the possession of their ancestors from time out of mind. If one copyholder could be evicted, no copyholder was secure from a similar fate. This threat was recognized by contemporaries. One indication was social unrest which took the form of peasant uprisings. Most serious was Ket's Rebellion of 1549 in which 3500 rebels were killed, and Robert Ket, the leader, was hanged for treason.

Protests too numerous to ignore came from contemporary statesmen, ministers of the gospel, and social observers. Sir Thomas More (1478–1535) veiled his protest against enclosures only slightly by placing them in his famous *Utopia:* "Your sheep, that used to be so gentle and eat so little. Now they are becoming so greedy and so fierce that they devour the men them-selves . . . The nobility and gentlemen . . . leave no land for cultivation, they enclose all the land for pastures, they destroy houses and demolish towns . . . The tenants are turned out, and by trickery or main force . . . What is left for them to do but steal and so be hanged . . . or to go about begging? And if they beg, they are thrown into prison as idle vagabonds. They would willingly work, but can find no one who will hire them. There is no need for farm labor, to which they have been bred, when there is no arable land left." [3]

Francis Bacon (1561–1625), the famous philosopher and statesman, spoke out strongly against enclosures, protesting that they "bred decay of the people."

Government Policy

Anti-enclosure legislation   The Tudor governments opposed enclosure, which they associated with depopulation and the decay of husbandry. They

[2] The classic work on the sixteenth-century enclosure movement in England is Richard H. Tawney, *The Agrarian Problem in the Sixteenth Century* (New York: Burt Franklin, 1961). The above quotation is from page 403.

[3] Thomas More, *Utopia,* trans. by H. V. S. Ogden (New York: Appleton-Century-Crofts, 1949), pp. 9–10.

feared that enclosure would cause social unrest, which it did, and a weakening of the nation's military and economic manpower. They viewed a sturdy peasantry as a national asset. Typical provisions of the anti-enclosure legislation were: (1) Land should not be converted from arable to pasture, and land recently converted should be reconverted from pasture to arable; (2) peasant houses which had been torn down should be rebuilt and kept in repair to serve as peasant dwellings; (3) the number of sheep owned by any one person should be limited to 2000. (An Act Concerning Farms and Sheep states that some men owned as many as 24,000 sheep.)

Anti-enclosure legislation proved ineffective. At best it served as a warning to enclosers not to go too far or too fast. The state was content to pass legislation and leave its administration in the hands of local justices of the peace, who usually were themselves large landowners. Nominal compliance with the law took the form of plowing a single furrow across the land to keep it in tillage, and repair of one room of an abandoned shack for a shepherd's residence. The Tudors failed to stop enclosures because there was no solution short of giving copyholders full title to their fields. This would have alienated the great landlords, perhaps to the point of civil war, and the Tudors, strong though they were, could not afford to risk that even if they had been genuinely interested in the peasants as an end in themselves rather than as a means of statecraft. One of the characteristics of the Tudor regime, especially under Elizabeth I, was awareness of the limitations of its own strength.

The able-bodied poor Sixteenth-century England was harassed by able-bodied beggars on a scale hitherto unknown in that country. The unique feature of the age was that able-bodied men were free, on the one hand, and propertyless, on the other. Their forefathers had been unfree serfs with rights as well as obligations to till the soil. Now they were dispossessed and thrown onto a labor market which could not absorb their services. Freedom of internal migration would have contributed to a better allocation of labor, but legislation gravely restricted mobility in the parochial interest of keeping down poor rates. This environment produced the able-bodied tramp, the sturdy beggar, the feared and hated vagabond.

The early Tudors dealt brutally with sturdy beggars. Statutes provided that vagabonds and beggars be placed in stocks, branded, whipped, and put to death for repeated offenses of begging without a license. Upon discovering that brutality did not diminish the number of sturdy beggars, the Tudors inaugurated a new poor law policy. Relief was placed on a national and secular basis, whereas historically it had been local and ecclesiastical. Legislation passed under Elizabeth I required that able-bodied unemployed persons be set to work and that the government should provide the materials and instruments required for work. This legislation involved recognition that unemployment was not merely a matter of indolence and improvidence, but an economic condition which obliged the government to provide employment for those willing and able to work but unable to find private employment. The Tudor theory of the social origins of poverty and the social responsibility of property was to be replaced after the Civil War of the seventeenth century by a theory of individual rather than social responsibility for poverty.

The objective test of the existence of private property in land is a market in which land is bought, sold, leased, rented, and otherwise treated as a commodity. Its value is subject to the forces of supply and demand. Land of the medieval manor was clearly not a commodity in this sense. A market in land was the product of historical development between the end of the Middle Ages and the beginning of the Industrial Revolution. The two phases of the English enclosure movement are two stages in the development of the land market. Redistribution of the vast monastic lands at the time of the English Reformation gave impetus to the growth of the land market. Many of the Church estates which were confiscated by Henry VIII found their way into the hands of merchants and commercially minded landlords, the groups which spearheaded the enclosure movement of the sixteenth century. However, this was still a minority movement, though it involved a significant number of landlords and displaced peasants.

Paralleling the displacement of peasants, noble landlords were being displaced by landed gentry—an important change in the make-up of the landlord class. The landed gentry's hour of triumph was the Civil War of the seventeenth century in which the gentry fought in Cromwell's army to overthrow the Crown. They consolidated their power by making the House of Commons, which they controlled, the supreme agent of sovereignty in the English government. The brief restoration of the Stuarts between 1660 and 1688 was but a minor setback in the rise of the gentry.

The landed gentry were large landowners who were not peers of the realm. What distinguished them as an economic group was their attitude toward property in land. Many had made fortunes in commerce or industry and then invested in land. They were bourgeois rather than feudal and resembled merchants more than soldiers. They were more devoted to their estates than to the affairs of state. Members of the landed gentry were among the large purchasers of the lands taken from the monasteries both in the first sale by the Crown and in subsequent sales by Henry's courtiers, who were favored first purchasers. Unlike the landlord class generally, the gentry emerged from the Price Revolution stronger than before, partly because they lived on a more modest scale than the peers and partly because they were more businesslike in the management of their lands and more vigorous in getting rid of unprofitable customary tenants. They avoided getting into debt in order to maintain living standards and they added to their estates both by taking over land from their peasants and by buying land from noble lords.

The landed nobility, in contrast to the gentry, were caught in the squeeze of the Price Revolution. In attempting to maintain traditional living standards in the face of falling real income, many sank into debt. In the two generations prior to the Civil War, which began in 1640, they have been described as "living like a rich beggar, in perpetual want." [4] Harassed by shrinking real income

[4] For an important controversy concerning the relative positions of the nobility and the gentry in the period between the confiscation of the monasteries and the Civil War, see Richard H. Tawney, "The Rise of the Gentry, 1558–1640," *Economic History Review*,

and rising debts, the landed nobility sold parts of their estates to the landed

gentry, thus creating an active land market. Shortly before the Revolution it
was said that the landed gentry occupying the Lower House of Parliament
could "buy the Upper House thrice over." Even by the eve of the Revolution
the transference of land from the peers to the gentry had progressed far, and
in the course of the Revolution confiscation of the lands of the Crown and its
noble supporters accentuated the shift. Oliver Cromwell and the leaders of
his army, which overthrew the monarchy, were members of the landed gentry.
In 1659 the peers, who had once possessed two-thirds of the land in England,
held only one-twelfth.

Landed Property and the Right to Govern

The role of property in relation to political representation was a burning
issue between the members of the landed gentry, who led the revolutionary
army, and the men of small property, who fought under them. The latter
represented the lesser yeomen, freeholders, and copyholders, who were largely
to disappear in the later enclosure movement. Cromwell and his son-in-law,
Ireton, argued in the famous "Army Debates" that voting rights in government should be proportional to property (or taxes, which were mainly on
property). The democrats in his army argued in favor of representation in
proportion to population, that is, one vote per man. Ireton expressed the point
of view of the landed gentry in saying that only those who owned substantial
property should have a voice in the affairs of the nation: [5]

> Government is to preserve property . . . The objection . . . [is] the intro-
> ducing of men into an equality of interest in this government, who have no
> property in this kingdom . . . If a man be an inhabitant upon a rack rent for a
> year, for two years, or twenty years, you cannot think that man hath any fixed
> or permanent interest . . . if you admit any man that hath a breath and being,
> I did show you how this will destroy property . . . Why may not those men
> vote against all property?

One of the men in the army replied to Ireton that it was part of a man's
birthright to participate in governing his country: [6]

> We have engaged in this kingdom and ventured our lives, and it was all for
> this: to recover our birthrights and privileges as Englishmen; and by the argu-
> ments urged there is none. There are many thousands of us soldiers that have
> ventured our lives; we have little propriety in the kingdom as to our estates, yet
> we have had a birthright. But it seems now, except a man hath a fixed estate
> in this kingdom, he hath no right in this kingdom. I wonder we were so much
> deceived. If we had not a right to the kingdom, we were mere mercenary
> soldiers . . . I do think the poor and meaner of this kingdom . . . have been
> the means of the preservation of this kingdom.

XI, No. 1 (1941), 1–38, and H. R. Trevor-Roper, *The Gentry, 1540–1640* (London:
Cambridge University Press, 1953). See also Tawney, "The Rise of the Gentry: A Postscript," *Economic History Review,* VII (Aug., 1954), 91–97.

[5] A. S. P. Woodhouse, ed., *Puritanism and Liberty, Being the Army Debates, 1647–9*
(London: J. M. Dent & Sons, Ltd., 1938), pp. 62–63.

[6] Woodhouse, *Puritanism and Liberty,* pp. 69–70.

Another of the men in the army spoke as follows: [7]

> But I would fain know what the soldier hath fought for all this while? He hath fought to enslave himself, to give power to men of riches, men of estates, to make him a perpetual slave.

Needless to say, the point of view of Cromwell and Ireton prevailed, not because of their superiority in debate about abstract principles, but because they held the power of government in their hands. The reason they held this power was explained by a political philosopher of the revolutionary period, James Harrington (1611–1677).

Harrington's Theory of Property

In an analysis of the role of property in relation to political power, Harrington advanced the thesis that political power depends on economic power and that economic power depends on the distribution of property, especially landed property. A change in the distribution of property must bring a change in the form of government. Applied to the events of his day, Harrington's thesis meant that the redistribution of land to the gentry was the basic force molding the new pattern of society, and that political tranquillity could not be achieved until the framework of political power corresponded to the structure of economic power. More specifically, his argument implied that the political future of England belonged to the House of Commons, representing the interests of the landed gentry, and that the Crown and the House of Lords must inevitably accept a lesser role in the affairs of government. Harrington's analysis is interesting for its theoretical explanation of what was actually to be the future of the English political system. The supremacy of Parliament, and more particularly of the House of Commons, also explains the form taken by the English enclosure movement in the eighteenth century.

Locke's Theory of Property

Even more important than Harrington's theory that property determines the form of government was the theory of John Locke (1632–1704) that the form of government should be appropriate for the security of property. Locke held that absolute monarchy of the Tudor and Stuart type was inconsistent with civil society because it afforded no guarantee of property against intervention by the absolute monarch. Property is a right existing in nature and is therefore anterior to and superior to government. Property, and not government, should be absolute. It is the privilege, indeed the duty, of a people to remove from power any government which does not afford protection to property. "The great and *chief end* therefore, of Mens uniting into Commonwealths, and putting themselves under Government, *is the Preservation of their Property.*" [8] Thus, on the one hand, Locke justified the middle-class revolution against the monarchy and, on the other hand, he placed property above the claims of any future change in government.

---

[7] Woodhouse, *Puritanism and Liberty,* p. 71.

[8] John Locke, *Two Treatises of Government,* ed. by Peter Laslett (London: Cambridge University Press, 1960), Book II, Chap. 9, 368–69.

Property is a natural right, according to Locke, because it originally arises from labor, and every man has a right to the "labor of his body and the work of his hands." A man acquires property in land when "he hath mixed his labor with it." Having gained property rights by working on a piece of land, the individual may justly exclude all others from land which at one time was part of the common property of all other men; no one, not even the government, has any right to invade the privacy of a man's property nor to tell him how he shall use it.

Locke's explanation that property rights derive from labor would seem to limit the amount of property to which one has a natural right to the relatively small quantity which can be personally worked by the owner. It would seem to justify the holdings of peasant proprietors but not of the landed gentry. Locke analyzed the question of the amount of property which an individual might "naturally" acquire in the following manner: No one should have more property than he can use and store; otherwise it would be wasted, and no one has a natural right to waste. Before the introduction of money into society, presumably, large landed estates would not have been justified. However, part of the social compact entered into by organized society is the acceptance of gold and silver as non-perishable wealth. Because money could legitimately be held in excess of immediate need, and therefore unequally, Locke argued that land might be held in excess of what could be personally worked, and therefore unequally: "But since Gold and Silver, being little useful to the Life of man . . . has its *value* only from the consent of Men . . . it is plain, that Men have agreed to a disproportionate and unequal Possession of the Earth, they having by a tacit and voluntary consent found out a way, how a man may fairly possess more land than he himself can use the product of, by receiving in exchange for the overplus Gold and Silver. . . ."[9]

The peculiar logic used by Locke to justify large and unequal ownership of property is less important than the consequences of his ideas. By imparting to private property in land the absolute sanctity of natural law, he seemed to justify unrestrained freedom in the use to which property might be put. His "natural rights" doctrine was consistent with laissez-faire of the type which characterized the outlook of eighteenth-century enclosers. Although an absolute and individualistic right in property seemed to exonerate owners from social responsibility, the champions of laissez-faire contended that the pursuit of self-interest in the use of property must necessarily lead to beneficial consequences for all classes of society; for example, if the conversion of arable land into pasture were inconsistent with the needs of the community, this would be reflected in a rise in the price of grain and a fall in the price of livestock, causing reconversion from pasture to arable land. The price system (and not the good intentions of benevolent monarchs), as Adam Smith was to show later, would take care of the poor as well as of the rich.

LATER ENCLOSURE MOVEMENT

Enclosures in England did not cease after the first major wave in the sixteenth century, but they did slow down during the seventeenth century before once

[9] Locke, *Two Treatises of Government,* Book II, Chap. 5, 319–20.

more gaining momentum in the eighteenth century. Furthermore, a comparison of the earlier and the later phases of the enclosure movement reveals several significant differences. First, the land area and the number of tenants affected were much greater in the eighteenth and nineteenth centuries. Second, the main motive behind the later phase was the brisk increase in demand for food to feed a rapidly growing urban population. The increased demand was for grain rather than for wool. The textile which dominated the Industrial Revolution was cotton, not wool. Cotton, of course, was an imported raw material, the increased demand for which did not directly affect English farming as did the increased demand for wool. Hence the sixteenth-century outcry against the conversion of arable land to pasture was not heard in the later enclosure movement. Third, later enclosures were associated with great advances in agriculture, whereas this had been only a minor feature of the earlier phase. In the eighteenth century progressive landlords and farmers utilized the enclosures to take advantage of the new techniques, which collectively are sometimes referred to as the "Agricultural Revolution." [10] Fourth, in the sixteenth century the government (Tudor monarchy) was hostile to enclosures (which persisted in the face of official opposition and legislative enactments), whereas in the eighteenth century the government (Parliament) actively promoted enclosures. This reversal of government policy is, of course, accounted for by the intervening seventeenth-century Revolution, which shifted political sovereignty from the Crown to Parliament.

Enclosures by Acts of Parliament

By special acts of Parliament between 1700 and 1850 the English enclosure movement was completed. England became again, as it had been in the Middle Ages, a country of large landed estates. In 1850 more than half the total land was held in estates in excess of 1000 acres, and approximately a quarter in estates in excess of 10,000 acres. These were units of ownership, not of production. A typical English landlord leased his land to a number of tenant farmers, who were in effect agricultural capitalists investing capital in farming and hiring wage laborers to work the fields.

Enclosures by special act of Parliament were made in response to petitions from landholders possessing four-fifths or more of the total land in a village community. Since landholdings were already highly concentrated at the beginning of the eighteenth century,[11] the signatures of a few large landlords were usually sufficient to bring the petition for enclosure before Parliament. In that "committee of landlords," passage of an enclosure bill was a formality. Hearings and investigations of local conditions were supposed to be held by Parliament, but these were perfunctory. Commissioners were appointed by Parliament to administer the survey, supervise the exchange of lands, and

---

[10] Some recent scholarship has emphasized the gradual shift to more advanced methods of cultivation in English agriculture and consequently the concept of an eighteenth-century Agricultural Revolution has been de-emphasized. See, for example, G. E. Mingay, "The 'Agricultural Revolution' in English History: A Reconsideration," *Agricultural History,* XXXVII (July, 1963), 123–33.

[11] See the important study by Professor H. J. Habakkuk, "English Landownership, 1680–1740," *Economic History Review,* X (Feb., 1940), 2–17.

see that the enclosures were fenced. Every landholder was supposed to receive back the same quantity and quality of property he gave up, but this was an ideal impossible to realize. Since the commissioners were themselves really agents of the large landholders who promoted the enclosure, the entire procedure placed the interest of the small landholder in jeopardy. For a long period there was no appeal from the decisions of a commission, but after much injustice had been done the General Enclosure Act of 1801 provided certain safeguards to small landowners. The first real reform of enclosure procedure came in 1845 after the movement was virtually completed.

Complaints Against Enclosures

The chief complaints against eighteenth-century enclosures were that they (1) disregarded the economic welfare of the peasants, (2) increased the number of paupers with a consequent increase in the burden of the poor rates, and (3) destroyed peasant villages.

(1) In evaluating the first of these complaints, a distinction should be made between legal right and economic justice based on welfare. Enclosures in the eighteenth century were carried out strictly according to law, but without much attention to economic tradition or the economic needs of the various classes of village dwellers. Squatters' rights were unrecognized, and this poorest class of tenant was pushed from the land. Cottagers might receive an allotment equal to their small holding, but no recognition was given to the practice under the open-field system which permitted cottagers to graze animals on the commons. Since cottagers received no allotment from the commons, their economic position deteriorated under Parliamentary enclosures. Customary tenants without documentary evidence had no legal claim to land and were given little consideration. Leaseholders had no claim to title and no claim to tenure beyond the life of their leases. Freeholders and copyholders with written evidence of title received an allotment equal to their former holdings, with an addition for their share in the commons, the size of which was proportional to the size of their arable holding as compared with the total arable land in the community. In addition to an area equal to their cultivated fields, the great landlords received a large addition based on their proportionately large shares in the old commons.

The quality of land received was as important as the quantity. In a majority of the enclosures the small landholder probably received land inferior in quality to that which he gave up since the administrative advantage was on the side of the great landlords. To say that the enclosures were legal means only that they were performed in accordance with the standards established by the landed gentry in the House of Commons, where the laws were made. Only by a rare exhibit of self-denial could the landed classes have made enclosure laws which conformed to the traditional sentiments of a majority of the community. Despite many fine qualities, the English gentry were not prepared to exercise such self-denial of material interests. Arthur Young, the leading agricultural publicist of the eighteenth century, was much in favor of the principle of enclosures, but he acknowledged the injustices done to the poor by the manner in which enclosures were carried out: ". . . the fact is, that by

nineteen enclosure bills in twenty they [the poor] are injured, in some grossly injured." [12]

(2) Enclosures increased poverty and left the English peasantry worse off as a class than they had been under the open-field system. The fate of squatters and cottagers has already been indicated. They lost economic advantages, meager though these were, and many were driven to seek poor relief. Even as rural wage-earners they may have been on poor relief, because the wages of rural laborers became at times so low in England during the eighteenth century that they were supplemented by poor relief. Other former squatters and cottagers became wage-earners in factories, where their money income probably increased, although there is some reason to doubt that their real incomes were generally higher.

Freeholders and recognized copyholders were in a better position to weather successfully the transformation caused by enclosures. As a group they were economically less secure and generally worse off than before, but probably not many of them sank to pauperism in the first generation. The monetary cost of enclosures was great. Chief among the items of expense were legal fees, surveying costs, and fencing.[13] Commissioners received excessive fees for their services. The total cost might exceed the ability of a small tenant to pay or borrow. Many sold part of their land in order to pay the costs of enclosure on what remained. Others simply sold all their land to large landholders and used the lum-sum of capital to set up as leasehold farmers or to invest in industry. Among the prosperous capitalist farmers were numerous former yeomen, and among the first generation of industrial capitalists in the Industrial Revolution, former yeomen were a prominent group. The children and grandchildren of former yeomen were often among the leaders in professional and intellectual circles. However, for each former peasant who succeeded in regaining economic independence as a prosperous farmer or industrial capitalist, there were others who, like the squatters and cottagers, moved down the economic ladder to become wage-earning laborers in field or factory.

(3) Enclosures of the eighteenth and nineteenth centuries unquestionably changed the face of England. Open-field farming was obliterated, and rural population declined in many communities. Some entire villages were destroyed, but the picture of Sweet Auburn, loveliest village of the plain, painted by Oliver Goldsmith in the *Deserted Village*, was not representative of what actually happened.

The main complaint among contemporaries was not rural depopulation, as it had been in the sixteenth century, but the destruction of "a bold peasantry, their country's pride." The Industrial Revolution and the enclosures caused more than the traditional amount of internal migration, but among the well-informed there was no doubt that England's total population was increasing during the eighteenth century. The first official population census was taken in 1801.

[12] A. E. Bland, P. A. Brown, and Richard H. Tawney, eds., *English Economic History, Select Documents* (London: G. Bell & Sons, Ltd., 1914), p. 537.

[13] For estimates of the costs of enclosure, see W. E. Tate, "The Cost of Parliamentary Enclosure in England," *Economic History Review*, V, No. 2 (1952), 258–65.

The irrefutable argument in favor of enclosures in the eighteenth and nineteenth centuries was that they were accompanied by technical improvements and higher productivity in agriculture. The old argument that enclosures meant the conversion of arable land into pasture had lost its sting by the middle of the eighteenth century, because more and more land was being utilized for raising food for a rapidly growing population. Small holdings were associated with bad farming, as suggested by an English saying that "The poor farmer is always a bad one." The new agricultural techniques required considerable capital as well as land, and small landholders had neither. The introduction of capital into agriculture forced the peasant from the land, on the one hand, and improved the productivity of agriculture, on the other.

Increasing productivity in agriculture resulted from better utilization of resources arising from new knowledge and wider application of existing knowledge. Experimentation with new crop rotations plus the adoption of practices borrowed from the Low Countries led to the elimination of the ancient and wasteful practice of letting one-third of the arable land lie fallow each year. Through the introduction of new crop rotations featuring turnips and clover, most of the arable land could be used each year. This change alone increased the area of land utilization by almost 50 per cent as compared with the three-field system. Animal husbandry was stimulated by the production of artificial grasses like clover and root crops like turnips, both of which provided feed for stock during the winter. Conclusive demonstration of the success of the Agricultural Revolution was the ability of English farmers to feed the additional millions until the end of the eighteenth century. This is particularly remarkable in view of the 40 per cent increase in population in the 50 years from 1750 to 1800.

Jethro Tull, "Turnip" Townshend, Robert Bakewell, and Arthur Young are the names most frequently associated with the English Agricultural Revolution of the eighteenth century. Jethro Tull (1674–1741) invented labor-saving machinery which made it economically feasible to apply the more refined methods of gardening to raising field crops such as turnips. He built a drill plow for planting seeds in rows, as in a garden, in place of the old method of broadcasting the seed. His mechanical sowing was even more efficient than row planting by hand because it spaced the seeds uniformly and placed them at optimum depth for germination and growth. His method of planting not only economized in the use of seed and saved labor by utilizing horse-power, but prepared the planted field for the use of Tull's horse-drawn hoe, which scarified the soil, cut the weeds between the rows, and helped aerate the soil and render the nutrients in it more readily available to the plants. Like other progressive agriculturalists of his day, Tull favored the horse over the ox as beast of burden. Tull wrote a book called *Horse-Hoeing Husbandry*, a title which to him epitomized his system of cultivation.

Lord Townshend (1674–1738) held many high offices in the British government, among them Ambassador to the Netherlands, where "High Farming" had its origin. After retiring from public life, Lord Townshend devoted himself to the development of his estate in Norfolk County, which was to

become famous for its progressive farming. Taking his cue from the Dutch, he drained and reclaimed for productive agriculture large parts of his estate which previously had been worthless waste. He utilized vast deposits of marl to enrich sandy soil, and then experimented with various crop rotations which enabled him to eliminate the uneconomical fallow. Such grains as wheat and barley were used in a standard four-crop rotation along with turnips and clover. Because of the stress he placed on turnips, this gentleman farmer became known as "Turnip" Townshend. About thirty years after Townshend's death, Arthur Young, in his report on farming in Norfolk County, credited the great progress in agriculture there to (1) enclosures, (2) spirited use of marl and clay, (3) good crop rotation, (4) clover and rye grass, (5) long leases, and (6) large farms.

Robert Bakewell (1725–1795) pioneered in the art of stock breeding. In particular he succeeded in developing strains of sheep and cattle which would provide a maximum quantity of mutton and beef. He purposefully selected for breeding through successive generations those types of animals which possessed to a maximum degree the qualities which were desired (a principle of artificial selection which afforded Darwin some of the best and safest clues to his theory of natural selection and evolution). When cattle were valued mainly for draft and sheep as wool producers, long legs for strong pulling and distant grazing were at a premium. On the other hand, the ideal animal for beef and mutton was one with short legs and large body which would supply the maximum quantity of superior quality meat. It is interesting to observe how some of the other developments in agriculture contributed to circumstances which were essential to the success of Bakewell's work. The promiscuous breeding of animals on the old commons stultified efforts to improve the strains of stocks, and therefore enclosure was essential to systematic breeding. Prior to the widespread cultivation of root crops, like turnips, and clover, there was insufficient feed for animals during the winter. The practice was to slaughter all but a few animals at the onset of winter, salt down the meat, and store it for winter fare. The turnips and clover of Tull and Townshend changed all this by making winter feed available for animals. At the same time the growing population and rising standard of living created a demand for more food. Although roast beef was not likely to be seen on the dinner table of factory workers during the Industrial Revolution, there were growing numbers of the middle class who were able to afford a diet consisting of less bread and more fresh meat.

Arthur Young (1741–1820), like Ulysses, was famous for his travels. His contribution to the Agricultural Revolution was the dissemination of information concerning the new methods which were developed by progressive farmers like Tull, Townshend, and Bakewell. Young made extended tours of the counties of England and of Ireland, Wales, France, Italy, and Spain. He believed enclosure was a prerequisite to improved agriculture, although he criticized the way in which English enclosures were carried out and recognized the injustice usually done to small tenants. He believed, however, that substantial capital was required in order to take advantage of the new techniques and therefore thought that men with little capital would enjoy as much income and more leisure as laborers than as small tenants struggling to compete with the highly efficient, large-scale farmer. Young advocated the elimina-

tion of fallowing by the use of proper crop rotation, including artificial grasses
and root crops. He favored manuring and efficient plow teams of horses, although not to the extent of entirely dispensing with oxen. For more than half
a century he was the moving spirit in educating farmers, not only in England
but throughout the Western world. He was in a sense a forerunner of the
modern extension service of colleges of agriculture.

These four men—Tull, Townshend, Bakewell, and Young—were not the
earliest nor the only innovators in English agriculture, but the improvements
associated with their names were the type which made English agriculture
the most advanced in the world at the opening of the nineteenth century.

Summary of Enclosures in England and Comparison with France

Enclosures took place in other European countries, but nowhere were
they as extensive or as significant for capitalist development as in England.
Germany east of the Elbe River became a land of great estates, but the
Junkers who owned them were more feudal than bourgeois, more military
than commercial, in attitudes toward landholding. They kept serfs instead of
wage-earners until the nineteenth century.

In France enclosures took place and were among the conditions which
contributed to the great Revolution of 1789. The famous French school of
economists, the Physiocrats, were staunch advocates of large-scale capitalistic
agriculture of the English type. The Physiocratic program for a single tax on
land was designed to promote commercial agriculture by shifting some of the
burden of taxation from bourgeois and peasant farmers to the tax-exempt
lands of the nobility and the Church. In the Revolution the lands of the Church
and of emigré nobles were confiscated and sold at auction; however, since most
of the land was purchased by the bourgeoisie, there was no important change
in the distribution of landholdings by size, and the course taken by the Revolution checked the growth of capitalism in agriculture.

While street fighting was going on in Paris, the peasants staged uprisings
in the provinces against the feudal legacy. Peasant protests led in 1793 to the
abolition of all feudal obligations, without compensation to the nobility.
French peasants secured absolute title to their small holdings. While consolidation of strips could take place by means of barter and purchase, an enclosure movement of the English type faced insuperable obstacles in France.
Although the Revolution abolished the remnants of feudal property and established private property in land, it was for the most part personal, small-scale
peasant property. Capitalistic private property of the English type is large-
scale and depends on the employment of wage labor for its utilization. Self-
sufficient peasant proprietorship in France perpetuated primitive methods of
cultivation because the peasants lacked the capital and the knowledge required
for progressive agriculture.

Differences in the land tenure systems of England and France affected
the entire pattern of economic development in the two countries. England's
land system facilitated rapid and large-scale industrialization, whereas the
French land system formed a barrier to rapid and large-scale industrialization.
Peasants, who had recently been semi-serfs, became attached to the soil

through the unqualified ownership of their land. Industrialization of the English type did not develop because the French peasant became a landowner whereas the English peasant became a wage-earner. All of this was neither inevitable nor merely fortuitous. Much of it can be accounted for by the differences in the English and French Revolutions. Historical circumstances determined that as a result of the English Revolution, the landed gentry would take command of the state. Likewise, historical circumstances in France at the time of its Revolution led to the dominance of the peasants.

SELECTED BIBLIOGRAPHY

CHAMBERS, J. D., and G. E. MINGAY, *The Agricultural Revolution, 1750–1880*. London: B. T. Botsford, 1966.

FISHER, F. J., ed., *Essays in the Economic and Social History of Tudor and Stuart England*. London: Cambridge University Press, 1961.

GONNER, E. C. K., *Common Land and Inclosure*. London: Macmillan & Co., Ltd., 1962.

HAMMOND, JOHN L. and BARBARA, *The Village Labourer, 1760–1832*. London: Longmans, Green & Co., Ltd., 1932.

JOHNSON, ARTHUR H., *The Disappearance of the Small Landowner*. London: Merlin Press, Ltd., 1963.

MINGAY, G. E., *English Landed Society in the Eighteenth Century*. London: Routledge and Kegan Paul, Ltd., 1963.

PROTHERO, R. E. (LORD ERNLE), *English Farming, Past and Present* (6th ed.). London: William Heinemann, Ltd., 1961.

STONE, LAWRENCE, *The Crisis of the Aristocracy, 1558–1641*. Oxford: Clarendon Press, 1965.

TAWNEY, RICHARD H., *The Agrarian Problem in the Sixteenth Century*. New York: Burt Franklin, reprint of 1912 ed.

——, *Harrington's Interpretation of His Age*. (From the Proceedings of the British Academy, Vol. XXVII). London: Humphrey Milford, 1941.

TREVOR-ROPER, H. R., *The Gentry, 1540–1640*. London: Cambridge University Press for the Economic History Society, 1953.

WOODHOUSE, A. S. P., ed., *Puritanism and Liberty, Being the Army Debates (1647–9) from the Clarke Manuscripts*. London: J. M. Dent & Sons, Ltd., Publishers, 1938.

ARTICLES

FUSSELL, G. E., "Low Countries' Influence on English Farming," *English Historical Review*, LXXIV (Oct., 1959), 611–22.

GAY, EDWIN F., "Inclosures in England in the Sixteenth Century," *Quarterly Journal of Economics*, XVII (Aug., 1903), 576–97.

HABAKKUK, H. J., "English Landownership, 1680–1740," *Economic History Review*, X (Feb., 1940), 2–17.

JONES, E. L., "Agriculture and Economic Growth in England, 1660–1750: Agricultural Change," *Journal of Economic History*, XXV (March, 1965), 1–18.

LAVROVSKY, V. M., "Expropriation of the English Peasantry in the Eighteenth Century," *Economic History Review*, IX (Dec., 1956), 271–82.

MINGAY, G. E., "The 'Agricultural Revolution' in English History: A Reconsideration," *Agricultural History*, XXXVII (July, 1963), 123–33.

————, "The Size of Farms in the Eighteenth Century," *Economic History Review*, XIV (April, 1962), 469–88.

PLUCKNETT, T. F. T., "Bookland and Folkland," *Economic History Review*, VI (Oct., 1935), 64–72.

TAWNEY, RICHARD H., "The Rise of the Gentry, 1558–1640," *Economic History Review*, XI, No. 1 (1941), 1–38; and 2nd series, VII (Aug., 1954), 91–97.

The Mobilization of Money Capital: Banking and Credit

Capitalism is a money economy in a sense which was not true of medieval society and is not true of a thoroughgoing socialist economy. Under capitalism the immediate and significant motivation on the part of those who employ and direct the means of production is to "make money" by increasing the money balance of the capital account. The so-called profit and loss statement of a business enterprise periodically shows whether the objective of "making money" has been realized. A balance sheet of the money value of assets and the money value of liabilities reflects success in money making when the difference between these two sets of values increases the net worth of the business. "Capital" and "surplus" accounts in the balance sheet refer to net proprietorship values that have been or are expected to be realized in terms of money.

Double-entry bookkeeping originated with capitalism as a rationale of the money-making spirit of that system. The revolutionary way of looking upon economic activity, embodied in the capitalist spirit, helps to explain the great enterprise and unprecedented growth of material wealth that dates from the beginning of the capitalist era. A capitalist entrepreneur is not content with making a living, but is driven by the urge to enlarge his net worth (wealth) in money terms. Of course, he must live, and usually lives very well, but he does not as a rule limit his enterprise as soon as his consumption needs are met. His attitude is epitomized by Jacob Fugger's statement, "Let me earn as long as I am able."

The starting point of a business firm or of a particular business transaction lies in obtaining, by one of several means, a sufficient quantity of money capital to carry out the activity in question. Once in hand, the money capital is used to purchase labor, raw materials, machinery, and other means of production, according to the technical requirements of the particular form of business activity. These means of production are coordinated by the entrepreneur to produce a product which is then placed on the market for sale. When the sale takes place, the assets again assume a money form. Ability to sell the product for more money than was laid out for its production is the real test of a business transaction. If the product cannot be sold (for money), the firm has failed in its objective. If inability to convert products into money persists, the entire business enterprise will fail. The purpose of business enter-

prise is to "make money" rather than to make goods. Goods are, of course, produced, but their production is not the real objective of business enterprise. They are produced to be sold and not for the use of the producing firm. Before goods can be enjoyed for their utility, their ownership must be transferred from the business firm to a consumer who has specific need for them as well as the means with which to buy them. This elaboration of the simple and obvious facts of business enterprise is presented in order to show the central importance of money in capitalist production as money capital and in order to provide a setting for the discussion of the institutions by which money capital is mobilized.

Money capital is a stock of surplus wealth which is held in the form of money and which is in excess of that needed for immediate consumption. It may be accumulated out of past income or it may be borrowed. In the former case the money capital is ownership or equity capital; in the latter case it is borrowed capital. In small handicraft industry, workmen may produce tools with their own labor (real saving), or in a small business a wage- or salary-earner may be able to save out of income enough money to finance his own trade or business without calling upon outside funds. These instances, however, are not really typical of capitalism since a considerable amount of money capital is required to start a business; hence self-created or self-earned assets are likely to prove inadequate. Large-scale business enterprise typically relies upon outside or borrowed capital. Professor Joseph Schumpeter viewed borrowed capital as so essential that he defined capitalism as "that form of private property economy in which innovations are carried out by means of borrowed money, which in general, though not by logical necessity, implies credit creation." [1] One need not accept this definition of capitalism as correct or adequate to appreciate the importance of borrowed capital in the functioning of the capitalistic form of economy. It is clear, however, that complex institutional arrangements have arisen for financing commercial, industrial, and agricultural activity. These institutions, which have formed an essential part of the general evolution of capitalism, include banks, joint-stock companies, stock exchanges, and a number of related institutions concerned with the mobilization and creation of money credit and debt.

Before the money or capital market could develop into its modern form, ancient prejudices against the taking of interest had to be dissolved. Borrowing and lending money at interest was almost universally condemned before the era of capitalism. Greek philosophers, Christian fathers, and medieval Churchmen said that interest was sinful and immoral. They argued, for example, that money was barren and could not multiply, and therefore to take interest was to take something which did not really exist. In effect, this meant that interest was an exploitation payment, the existence of which was usually explained in terms of the distress of people forced to borrow in order to live. The chief purpose of the legal and moral condemnation of interest appears to have been the protection of the weak and poor against the rich. Most loans were consumption loans, taken in distress, by persons who lacked the means to repay the principal, to say nothing of a premium in excess of the principal.

To the new class of enterprising men who emerged in the late medieval

---

[1] J. A. Schumpeter, *Business Cycles* (New York: McGraw-Hill, Inc., 1939), II, 223.

period, however, money was barren only if it was locked up in chests. Money in the market place was fruitful because it could be used to buy goods which could be sold at a profit. In this sense money could be used to beget more money. Borrowed money turned into productive channels was a blessing to both borrower and lender. Borrowers would gladly pay lenders some part of the enhanced gains which flowed from the additional money capital at their disposal. This became possible with the development of a new type of market, the money or capital market, in which money capital was bought and sold like a commodity in somewhat the same manner in which land was bought and sold in the newly created land markets.

Banks were the most important form of institutional development for the mobilization of money capital. Banks may serve the general function of middlemen between savers and investors, or of manufacturers or creators of additional means of payment. The function of middleman developed first and satisfied a more obvious need than the second function. The two functions were closely associated, however, and the role of banks in creating new purchasing power grew out of the first function. Since there are many savers who do not engage directly in business enterprise and since there are many businessmen who cannot save enough out of their incomes to meet all their capital needs, capital mobilization involves bringing together the savers with money to invest and the businessmen who want money capital for investment. In a strict sense the problem is one of mobilization rather than one of accumulation of money capital. If the small savings of large numbers of persons are collected, a large and usable sum will be available for entrepreneurs. Banks serve as the agency for channeling money which would otherwise be idle into productive enterprise. The performance of this function for short-term lending is called commercial banking. For long-term lending it is called investment banking. Commercial banking provides money capital for investment in circulating capital, whereas investment banking provides money capital for investment in fixed capital.

ORIGINS OF MODERN BANKING

Modern banking began where early capitalism began, namely in the Mediterranean region, and spread with the growth of capitalism to southern Germany, the Low Countries, and England. The Medici of Florence were the leading bankers of the fourteenth century, and the Fuggers of Augsburg were the leading bankers of the fifteenth and early sixteenth centuries. In the sixteenth and seventeenth centuries, as the main course of capitalistic development shifted to northern Europe, Antwerp and Amsterdam became the financial centers of Europe. In the eighteenth century, the English assumed banking leadership from the Dutch. London remained the most important financial center of the world until the First World War, when New York City began to replace London to an increasing degree. Meanwhile banking spread to smaller centers throughout the capitalist world.

The money-changers and money-lenders of medieval fairs were forerunners of modern banking. Buyers of goods who could not immediately make

payment in specie could go, in the company of the seller, to a money-lender

who would guarantee the promise of the buyer to make payment in specie at
the end of the fair. If at the end of the fair a merchant had bought more
than he had sold and was unable to pay the difference in specie, it was
common practice at the later Champagne and other fairs for a money-lender
to advance a loan to meet the merchant's unpaid balance.

In early commercial centers such as Venice, Genoa, Milan, and Amsterdam, private money-changers lent the specie which had been deposited
with them for safekeeping and for transfer. Bankruptcies frequently resulted
from improperly secured loans, which seem to have been related to the
absence of a satisfactory type of negotiable, short-term commercial paper.
With banking in the hands of private, unregulated money-lenders official exchange rates were lacking, and this added uncertainty concerning the value
of money to the other risks of trade. The need for more security of deposits
and for more stability in the exchange rates led to the establishment of public
banks, which were either directly operated or closely supervised by municipal
governmental authorities. Among the well-known exchange or *giro* banks of
this type were those of Genoa (established 1407), Venice (established 1587),
Milan (established 1593), Amsterdam (established 1609), and Hamburg
(established 1619). In addition to fixing official exchange rates, the public
banks held deposits for safekeeping and facilitated transfers from one depositor to another. These banks were usually specifically forbidden to engage in
credit-creating transactions, although in the Mediterranean region the credit
facilities of the public banks were often available to the city governments and
the collection of municipal revenues.

The Bank of Amsterdam was perhaps the most famous of the early
deposit and transfer banks. It was modeled after the Bank of the Rialto in
Venice and, like the Dutch East India Company, was a symbol of the pre-
eminence of Dutch capitalism during the seventeenth century. Amsterdam,
being a center of commercial capitalism, received coins from all parts of the
trading world. The intrinsic value of the gold and silver coins was usually
less than their nominal or standard value because their weights were reduced
below par by wear, clipping, and sweating. Another major factor in coinage
disorganization was debasement of money by local and national governments.
In these chaotic circumstances merchants were harassed by the shrewd dealings of unscrupulous money-changers, who were able to turn the disorganized
state of the money market to their profit. The municipal government of
Amsterdam established the Bank of Amsterdam as a public institution with
offices in the city hall with the aim of relieving merchants of the hazards of
uncertain, fluctuating, and speculative exchanges. The Bank held a monopoly
of money-changing in Amsterdam.

When the Bank of Amsterdam received deposits in coin, it credited the
account of the depositor with the value of the gold and silver actually contained in the coins. This deposit with the Bank in a standard unit of account
was known as bank money. All large-scale transactions were cleared at the
Bank because bills of exchange of 600 florins or more were required by law to
be payable at the Bank. Consequently, all large merchants were obliged to
have an account at the Bank. Withdrawals of coins or bullion could be made
upon presentation of proper credentials. As a rule, however, withdrawal of

coin from the Bank was uncommon because bank money stood at a premium as compared with the circulating coins of Amsterdam. A florin in the Bank was worth more than a florin in coin because even a newly minted coin, once it got into circulation, was worth little more than a worn coin, from which it could not readily be distinguished. Bank money commanded a further premium because it was secure from fire, robbery, and other accidents. In addition to receiving coins, the Bank of Amsterdam accepted bullion deposits and during the seventeenth and eighteenth centuries became the greatest single warehouse of European bullion.

Although the Bank of Amsterdam performed very important functions in receiving deposits and in transferring funds from the account of one customer to another, it did not discount bills, it did not issue notes, and it did not pay interest on deposits. On the contrary, it charged fees for accepting deposits (for storage of funds) and for making transfers. It could not afford to pay interest because it professed to lend no part of its deposits. Actually the Bank did advance secret loans to the Dutch East India Company and to the city government of Amsterdam. The inability of the sober and religious Dutch to resist the temptation to make some use of the gold and silver lying idle in their vaults illustrates how credit creation was likely to accompany banking even when loans were specifically prohibited. The Bank of Amsterdam continued to serve the merchants of Amsterdam until early in the nineteenth century. When the Dutch East India Company failed, it brought the Bank down with it and in 1819 the latter was abolished. This was long after Dutch capitalism had passed its zenith. Meanwhile, new and more significant developments were taking place elsewhere, especially in England.

GOLDSMITH BANKERS OF ENGLAND

Storing wealth where it would be safe from outlaws and sovereigns—especially the latter—has always been an important problem for men of wealth. Throughout recorded history holders of wealth have tended to hoard their valuables in secret hiding places, a circumstance which poses a major obstacle to the mobilization of money capital and to the establishment of a banking system. In England at the beginning of the seventeenth century a common practice was to deposit gold and silver for safekeeping at the Royal Mint in the Tower of London. On the eve of the Civil War in 1640 Charles I, true to the tradition of kings, seized these deposits at the Mint. Thereafter wealthy Englishmen deposited their money with goldsmiths. As merchant-manufacturers whose raw materials were the precious metals, goldsmiths had strong boxes and strong rooms. They likewise were accustomed to dealing in coins as well as bullion used in the arts. In the environment of the time, these holders of monetary wealth (precious metals) were in a favorable position to expand their activities into a banking business.

For deposits of coin or bullion lodged with them for safekeeping, goldsmiths gave receipts, which could be used to make payment to a third party. If the third party receiving payment had no pressing need for coin, he would leave the coin which had been transferred to him in the care of the goldsmith. He might receive a new receipt or arrange for a transfer on the books of the

to a third party constituted what came to be called a cheque (check). Checks
were in use in England by the latter part of the seventeenth century. With a
considerable number of persons holding and transferring deposits, goldsmiths
were on the way to becoming bankers.

Because many depositors preferred to hold claims against goldsmiths rather than to possess coin or bullion on their own premises, the goldsmiths —or anyone in a similar position—could add a considerable fraction of the deposited money to the capital of their own businesses or lend the idle coin to interest-paying borrowers. They needed in reserve only a fraction of the total claims of depositors. If the loans were for short terms and were made on good security to trustworthy borrowers, the danger of loss was slight and the opportunity for gain considerable. Furthermore, the legality of using or lending money deposited by others had been established by English jurists. Deposited coin of the realm became the property of goldsmiths, who were thus free of any legal obligation to keep on hand the specific coins left with them. According to Professor Abbott P. Usher this seems to have been generally the case in Europe: "There was no period in which it would not have been lawful for a money-changer to accept a deposit of funds which he might employ in trade or lend to others, subject only to the obligation to repay the depositor on demand in coin or equivalent value." [2]

Since deposited money became the property of the goldsmith, the depositor did not have any "money in the bank." What he had was a claim against the goldsmith, who was obligated to pay on demand or according to the terms of the contract. Goldsmiths became debtors to their depositors; depositors became creditors of the goldsmiths. Individuals who borrowed from goldsmiths and took loans in the form of deposits with goldsmiths were both creditors and debtors of the goldsmiths. They were obligated to repay their loan at the end of the specified period, with interest; and the goldsmiths promised to pay on demand to any party designated by the borrowers. By this process banking became what it is today, a business concerned with the creation, transfer, and repayment of debts (credits).

Whereas in the beginning depositors paid the goldsmiths for storing money, much as one pays today for the use of a bank safe deposit box, presently the goldsmiths began paying depositors in order to encourage deposits. During the reign of Charles II (1660–1685), goldsmiths paid 6 per cent per annum on deposits and charged about twice as much for loans.

The payment of a premium on money under what appeared to be relatively safe circumstances tended to bring money out of private hoards into banks where it was available for lending to borrowers willing and able to pay for it. Since borrowed money spent on immediate consumption did nothing to facilitate the accumulation of capital, banking developments did not center around consumption loans, but concentrated on business loans and on loans advanced to governments. The transfer of coined money from savers to investors, although it merely shifted purchasing power from one person to another, greatly assisted in the mobilization of capital. It transferred money capital (which represented command over productive resources) from persons

[2] "The Origins of Banking: The Primitive Bank of Deposit, 1200–1600," *Economic History Review*, IV (April, 1934), 402.

who did not wish to spend immediately to persons who wanted money capital for employing labor, materials, and other resources in business enterprises.

In addition to transferring money capital from savers to investors, the goldsmith-bankers also created additional means of payment. They lent not just other people's money but their own credit, represented by their promises to pay, that is, by money created by the goldsmith-bankers. Money capital was made more readily available in greater quantity than if the banker had been limited to lending the actual sums of money deposited with him. Bankers and businessmen were able to take up the slack in community spending without waiting for the public to learn the virtues of placing its money in the bank. An economy which might otherwise have been retarded because coin was hoarded in old mattresses, stockings, and chests was able to proceed with the important business of financing new enterprises. One may say either that the velocity of circulation of actual money was increased by the use of bank credit or that the total quantity of money, including bank credit as one type, was increased. Bank credit is not money in the legal tender sense or in the bank reserve sense, but as long as it is readily accepted in lieu of money it is nearly the same as money and may be called money or near-money.

There were, and are, dangers in this method of manufacturing new means of payment, and especially in leaving it in the hands of goldsmiths and merchants who had no social responsibility for the possible consequences of their banking practices. One danger is that an excessive increase in the quantity of means of purchase will lead to an inflation of prices. If all, or nearly all, resources in the economy are fully employed before the additional means of payment are created, the additional purchasing power that comes into the market as a result of the creation of bank credit will tend to increase prices. Resources already employed will find others demanding their services and willing to pay more than existing rates of remuneration to lure them into other uses.

The goldsmith-banker of the late seventeenth century created new means of payment in two related ways: (1) by issuing goldsmith notes, or what came to be called banknotes; and (2) by creating additional deposit balances against which checks or drafts could be drawn. Goldsmith notes developed from the deposit vouchers or receipts of goldsmiths and represent the oldest form of banknote in England. The banknote, which was legally only a claim to money, became as readily acceptable as money. Although originally the receipt or voucher arose from actual coin or bullion deposited with the goldsmith, it gradually came to represent the promise of the goldsmith to pay. A borrower who wanted readily negotiable claims would borrow money from a goldsmith and take the proceeds of the loan in the form of goldsmith notes, which represented not specie deposited but a promise of the goldsmith to pay specie or other legal tender money on demand. Such notes circulated in the same way as gold and silver coin, and when deposited with a banker, would be treated as a deposit of actual specie. This was not a deposit in the original meaning of that term, that is, of coin or bullion given by the customer to his banker; but it does illustrate the basic function of modern deposit banking, i.e., making loans in bank credit.

In creating additional balances with which depositors were permitted to make payments to third parties, the goldsmith-banker was creating means

of payment which could be used as money capital. Such balances usually

resulted from borrowing and represented, in the hands of the capitalist, borrowed capital. In an accounting entry in his books the goldsmith-banker credited a deposit to the borrower. This was a clear departure from the original meaning of the term deposit. Literally speaking it was not a deposit at all. It was a debt or claim created by the goldsmith-banker against himself in favor of the borrower in return for compensation in the form of interest and, of course, the promise of the borrower to repay the debt at its expiration. The interest, when earned, represented the banker's income. The advantage to the borrower was in having the means at his disposal for purchasing labor and raw materials which could be used to make a product which he might expect to sell at a profit over and above the interest on the loan. Private borrowers presumably were willing to pay interest because they expected that a profit in excess of the interest would arise from employing the money capital. By enabling entrepreneurs to redirect real resources (labor and materials) into new channels, bank credit provided the basis for innovations and capitalist development.[3]

Not only merchants and landlords but also the government borrowed from the goldsmith-bankers. In the period of the Commonwealth (1650–1660), Oliver Cromwell had been a heavy borrower, and under the restoration of the Stuart kings Charles II continued in the same vein. Most government borrowing was for short periods to cover expenditures during months between the levying of taxes and their collection. A promising start toward a well-organized banking system under the leadership of the goldsmiths was disrupted in 1672 when Charles II stopped repayment of government loans to the goldsmiths, who in turn had to suspend payments to their depositors, forcing many goldsmiths and their depositors into bankruptcy. England's goldsmith-bankers never regained their former importance after Charles' "Stop of the Exchequer." Like many bankers before them, they fell afoul an irresponsible ruler who reneged on his debts.

CENTRAL BANKING

Bank of England

Following the eclipse of the goldsmith-bankers, the English government sought new ways of financing its mounting expenditures. Understandably the credit rating of the Stuart kings suffered irreparably from Charles' Stop of the Exchequer, and only after the Glorious Revolution of 1689 had thrown out the Stuarts and brought Parliament into undisputed sovereignty, did English central banking move forward again. In Stockholm a Bank of Sweden was founded in 1656 and is viewed as the first national central bank of modern times. In England several proposals for a bank which would serve as the government's fiscal agent were considered before the one advanced by William Patterson, a Scotsman, was accepted in 1694. Patterson and a group of wealthy London merchants agreed to advance the government £1,200,000 as a perpetual loan

---

[3] On the role of credit creation in economic development under capitalism, see J. A. Schumpeter, *The Theory of Capitalist Development* (Cambridge, Mass.: Harvard University Press, 1934), Chap. III, "Credit and Capital."

in exchange for annual income of £100,000 in perpetuity, consisting of interest at 8 per cent (£96,000 on £1,200,000) plus £4,000 for the administration of the Bank. From the government's point of view an advantage of the arrangement was that it received more than a million pounds immediately but would have to increase its revenues by only £100,000 annually to service the perpetual loan. From the point of view of Patterson and his associates a major advantage of the arrangement was receipt of a charter for a joint-stock bank, a privilege highly prized. The charter included the right to circulate Bank of England notes (paper money) in an amount equal to the bank's capital (£1,200,000), all of which was offered to the government as a loan.

Modern money is sometimes equated to debt, especially to bank debt. The financial arrangements associated with the founding of the Bank of England illustrate this relation between money and debt. Government borrowing increased the public debt; in turn, the Bank issued paper money to the extent of the increase in the public debt, and thus increased the circulating media by an amount equal to the increase in the public debt. The Bank of England notes, representing debts of the Bank, were lent at interest or spent by the Bank as money and so became in effect the same thing as money. Alternatively to saying that money is debt, it can be said that money is credit, or is based on credit. Credit and debt are two sides of the same coin. Since one man's credit is necessarily another man's debt, credit is always equal to debt, and every change in one involves a change in the other.

By subsequent authorizations Parliament increased the government borrowings from the Bank of England and permitted the Bank to increase the quantity of its notes. A cardinal principle of the bank's operation, however, limited the amount of its notes to the amount of its capital. If the amount of notes issued exceeded the Bank's capital, the shareholders became personally liable for the Bank's debts. Adherence to the principle of limited note issue helps to explain the unbroken success of the Bank of England through a succession of crises in an age in which bank failures were more the rule than the exception.

Although the principal business of the Bank of England was to serve as fiscal agent for the British government, it also engaged in private banking, specializing in dealings with large companies such as the East India Company. Very early it began to accept deposits from other bankers, including the goldsmith-bankers, and gradually in the course of the eighteenth century it became a true central bank, that is, a bankers' bank. Officials of the Bank of England contended into the nineteenth century that it was just like any other bank, all the while being quite unique in the British fiscal system—and only after 1873 did it take clear responsibility for acting as a lender of last resort. The Bank of England remained privately owned (until 1945) but always remained under government control.

Bank of France

While England succeeded in establishing a central bank, France failed. A spectacular but unsuccessful attempt by John Law to found a central bank in France in 1715 delayed until 1800 the establishment of the modern Bank of France.

When Louis XIV, the great Sun King, died in 1715 after decades of
aggressive rule, he left France saddled with a heavy public debt. This situation provided an opening for John Law, a Scotsman with ideas about monetary
reform. Law's general scheme was to retire the public debt of France by
issuing paper money for the debt and to back the paper notes with the land
of the Mississippi territory, which then belonged to France. Law's basic idea
was to back paper money with a productive asset (land), rather than with
gold and silver, which were not productive. In 1716 Law founded a private joint-stock company called the Bank of France, and soon established another joint-stock company, the Mississippi Land Company, which enjoyed the
exclusive right to develop the Mississippi territory. Unfortunately Law's companies became deeply entangled in political intrigue; Law's initial success
generated jealousy of the great power he obtained with the French sovereign.
Notes issued to excess caused an inflationary spiral in prices in France and
led in 1720 to a speculative orgy, followed by a collapse of the so-called
Mississippi Bubble. France's entire financial structure crashed, and Law was
forced to flee to save his handsome head. A similar speculative mania in
England, known as the South Sea Bubble, threatened for a time the solvency
of the Bank of England but did not topple it.

Law's disastrous experiment generated widespread mistrust of joint-
stock banks in France and retarded the development of French banking,
which, in turn, held back the general economic development of France prior
to the Revolution of 1789. Even the modern Bank of France, founded in 1800,
fell prey to a financial hierarchy of speculators and manipulators whose activities inhibited French economic growth during the nineteenth century. In
1945 the Bank of France was nationalized by a socialist government that came
to power at the close of the Second World War.

EXCHANGES AND OTHER FINANCIAL
DEVELOPMENTS OF EARLY CAPITALISM

Specialized exchanges for wholesale trade among merchants developed in
several western European countries between the sixteenth and eighteenth
centuries. These bourses, as they were called, were successors to the medieval
fairs at a more advanced stage of economic development. (See Chapter 5.) An
increasing volume of wholesale trade necessitated year-round meetings where
buyers and sellers could come together in a regular and businesslike manner.
After the decline of Bruges in the fifteenth century, the most important
bourses in Europe were located in Antwerp during the sixteenth century and
in Amsterdam during the seventeenth century.

Exchanges designed primarily for buying and selling commodities were
also used for exchanging financial instruments. At first the predominant financial trade was in bills of exchange, but government bonds (rentes in France,
consols in England) and company shares were also traded. Kings and princes
turned to these exchanges to negotiate public loans from merchants and other
capitalists. The Spanish Hapsburgs sought loans at Antwerp and Augsburg,
and the French kings used the bourse at Lyons as a source of financial assistance for their many wars. The importance of Lyons as a French financial

center arose in part from its geographical proximity to the great banking houses of northern Italy.

True stock exchanges in the modern sense resulted when brokers specializing in joint-stock shares separated from the commodity bourses and set up their own meeting place and organization. Separate stock exchanges were a relatively late development, emerging generally in financial centers such as Amsterdam, London, and Paris during the eighteenth century. Full flowering of stock exchanges awaited the railways and industrial joint-stock companies in the nineteenth century.

In an ideal capital market a stock exchange performs the important social functions of enhancing the mobility of capital and allocating scarce capital resources to their highest uses. By providing an organized market in which long-term investments can be converted readily into money, the stock exchange encourages individual investors to place their surplus funds (savings) at the disposal of others (investors) for fixed investments. Thus mobilization of capital is facilitated.

The allocation of capital resources among alternative uses is guided by the relative rates of return available from different securities. Rates of return presumably reflect the urgency of wants in various lines of economic activity. For example, rising share prices on the stock exchange reflect high profits and therefore the desirability of additional investment in those enterprises with rising share prices. Allocating capital effectively among alternative uses forms an essential part of any rational economy.

Although the social functions of security exchanges are to assist in the mobilization and allocation of scarce resources, stock exchanges are subject to abuses that may contribute to quite opposite results. Speculation in the exchanges can disrupt production and lead to a breakdown of the wealth-creating process they are supposed to promote. Buying and selling in the expectation of realizing a profit from fluctuations in share prices is a process that may be manipulated and subjected to many abuses. False rumors, loud whispers, planted information or misinformation, and all types of chicanery were employed by professional speculators to fleece amateur investors. Professional brokers, divided into optimistic "bulls" and pessimistic "bears," tend to some extent to gain and lose at the expense of each other. Bulls would spread rumors of military victories, large profits, and big dividends in order to increase their gains through a rise in the prices of their holdings. The pessimistic bears, who gained from falling prices, sounded tales of military defeat, business disasters, and impending bankruptcy. If prices go up, the bulls gain at the expense of the bears; and if prices go down, the bears gain at the expense of the bulls. Speculators as a group however were neither richer nor poorer. Price fluctuations either up or down have no direct bearing on the wealth or income of the community as a whole. As among gamblers, wealth may be redistributed but the total wealth of all gamblers and of society is unchanged. However, speculative over-exhilaration frequently led to over-investment in some lines of enterprise, to be followed by a wave of extreme pessimism which contributed to general economic breakdown affecting the general public as well as the professional and amateur speculators. The tulip mania in Holland in 1636 and the Mississippi and South Sea Bubbles of 1720 in France and England, respectively, illustrate how speculative excesses had

a generally depressing effect on current production of wealth and handicapped long-term capital accumulation by creating mistrust of institutions potentially valuable for facilitating the mobilization of capital.

When the South Sea Bubble burst in 1720, the British Parliament passed the so-called "Bubble Act." This law provided that joint-stock companies could be chartered only by special acts of Parliament. The Bubble Act retarded but did not stop the growth of joint-stock companies in England during the eighteenth century. Finally in 1825, after more than a century, the Bubble Act was repealed and the way prepared for more general application of joint-stock companies in industrial and other types of business enterprise. France reacted similarly to the Mississippi Bubble by passing legislation which restricted the incorporation of joint-stock companies in France.

SUMMARY: THEORY AND PRACTICE OF THE CAPITAL MARKET

Capital markets facilitate the mobilization of money capital and thereby hasten the accumulation of productive wealth. Full development of capital markets was not possible until interest as a payment for the use of money capital became generally accepted. Banks have been the most important institution for channeling money capital from savers to investors and for creating additional means of payment in the form of bank credit, which can be used to mobilize real resources. The issuance of negotiable securities in the form of banknotes also assisted in the mobilization of money capital, as did also the issuance of transferable shares in joint-stock companies. These securities were made more attractive to investors by the creation of a ready market (stock exchange) in which individual holders could reconvert their wealth from long-term investments into money. The ability of the individual investor to become liquid through the sale of shares does not result in a withdrawal of capital from the business firm. While resources are better mobilized and allocated under organized markets, the large degree of speculation which inheres in these arrangements has had adverse consequences for the capitalistic economy and has been a source of hostility toward it.

SELECTED BIBLIOGRAPHY

BARBOUR, VIOLET, *Capitalism in Amsterdam in the Seventeenth Century*. Baltimore: Johns Hopkins University Press, 1950.

CASWELL, JOHN, *The South Sea Bubble*. Stanford, Calif.: Stanford University Press, 1960.

CLAPHAM, JOHN H., *The Bank of England, A History, 1694–1914*, 2 vols. New York: The Macmillan Company, 1945.

RICHARDS, R. D., *The Early History of Banking in England*. London: Frank Cass & Co., Ltd., 1965.

SCOTT, WILLIAM R., *The Constitution and Finance of English, Scottish, and Irish*

Joint-stock Companies to 1720, 3 vols. London: Cambridge University Press, 1910–12.

Usher, Abbott P., *Early History of Deposit Banking in Mediterranean Europe.* Cambridge, Mass.: Harvard University Press, 1943.

Van Dillen, J. G., ed., *History of the Principal Public Banks.* The Hague: Martins Nijhoff, 1934.

Wilson, Charles, *Anglo-Dutch Commerce and Finance in the Eighteenth Century.* Cambridge: The University Press, 1941.

ARTICLES

Clapham, John H., "The Private Business of the Bank of England, 1744–1800," *Economic History Review*, XI, No. 1 (1941), 77–89.

de Roover, Raymond A., "New Interpretations of the History of Banking," *Journal of World History*, II (1954), 38–76.

Postan, Michael M., "Credit in Medieval Trade," *Economic History Review*, I (Jan., 1928), 234–61.

Posthumus, N. W., "The Tulip Mania in Holland in the Years 1636 and 1637," *Journal of Economic and Business History*, I (May, 1929), 434–55.

Richards, R. D., "Pioneers of Banking in England," *Economic History*, I (Jan., 1929), 485–502.

———, "Evolution of Paper Money in England," *Quarterly Journal of Economics*, XLI (May, 1927), 361–404.

Supple, Barry E., "Currency and Commerce in the Early Seventeenth Century," *Economic History Review*, X (Dec., 1957), 239–55.

Unwin, George C., "The Merchant Adventurers' Company in the Reign of Elizabeth," *Economic History Review*, I (Jan., 1927), 35–64.

Usher, Abbott P., "The Origins of Banking: The Primitive Bank of Deposit, 1200–1600," *Economic History Review*, IV (April, 1934), 399–428.

Wilson, Charles, "The Economic Decline of the Netherlands," *Economic History Review*, IX (May, 1939), 111–27.

Mercantilism

10

The term "mercantilism" refers to the policies, and to the doctrines underlying the policies, of national governments in western Europe during early capitalism. Mercantilism was preceded by feudalism and followed by laissez-faire; it was dominant in Europe between the Middle Ages and the Industrial Revolution. Mercantilist policy involved extensive government regulation and participation in economic life. It contrasts with earlier medieval policy in which social control over economic life was exercised primarily by *local* authority, including town governments and feudal lords, and it also contrasts with the later policy of laissez-faire according to which national governments were supposed to follow a hands-off policy toward business. Unlike laissez-faire, which presupposed the compatibility of private profit and public welfare, a basic presupposition of mercantilism was the necessity of social control in order to direct profit-seeking enterprise into socially desirable channels.

Mercantilism was not opposed to capitalism. It was, however, much concerned with coordinating and, to some extent, directing private capitalist activity so that the total effect on national economic activity would be maximized. Mercantilism should be distinguished from socialism. The latter is a type of economic system essentially different from capitalism, whereas mercantilism was one type of economic policy under capitalism. Socialism involves government ownership and operation of economic enterprise, whereas mercantilism mainly involved the public regulation of privately owned (capitalistic) enterprises. The re-emergence of extensive government regulation in the twentieth century has sometimes been referred to as neo-mercantilism, that is, a policy similar to mercantilism. However, if the term "mercantilism" is used at all, it seems wise to confine it to its original historical setting.

STATE-BUILDING

Mercantilism has been called state-building. Its problems were those of rising national states under aspiring monarchs struggling for existence at the end of the Middle Ages against feudal anarchy, and later, against the aggressive threats of rival monarchs. War was the accepted instrument of national policy

among mercantilist states. Meanwhile, the threat of civil war was never entirely absent even in the strongest monarchies. Economic policy and economic welfare were subordinated to the incessant struggle for survival against internal and external enemies. Economic advancement was largely a by-product of the struggle for power among nations. It was seldom a result of a conscious desire for economic development as such, or a result of the desire to assist capitalists in the business of profit-making. Generally speaking, the patriotism and loyalty of merchants was suspect by statesmen and monarchs. There was no explicit alliance between government and business. Nevertheless, there were advantages to the monarch which the merchants could provide. They were an important source of funds for extensive military and political activities of government. Private companies could be used as agents of colonial imperialism with the nation accepting the fruits but the government avoiding the responsibility for armed warfare, as the British did in India, where a private company was the unofficial ruler of India's millions for two and one-half centuries. Also there were advantages to merchants which the sovereign could provide: monopolistic concessions in domestic and foreign trade; protection against foreign competition; and legislative acts which would enhance the profits of private groups. So while no formal alliance existed between merchants and sovereigns, there was frequently a tacit agreement to use one another for the advantages to be gained thereby.

Monarch-Bourgeois Struggle

Although in general it was absolute monarchs who wrested power from feudal lords and town authorities, mercantilism did not cease with the passing of absolute monarchs. Even the bourgeoisie who served their monarchs well enjoyed only a precarious existence so long as the latter had absolute authority. A long struggle occurred within the bourgeois-monarch alliance. It ended with the monarchs being stripped of their power by the bourgeoisie, who vested it in their own representatives.

Evolution of the bourgeois struggle for power finds its classic example in England. The War of the Roses (1455–1485) ended the feudal threat to national authority, and brought to the throne the strong Tudor line, which ruled supreme throughout the sixteenth century. In the course of the seventeenth century the middle classes, under the leadership of wealthy merchants and commercial agriculturalists, successfully challenged the power of the monarchy; and in the prolonged Civil War from 1640 to 1689 these bourgeois interests seized power in English national life. With the shift in the structure of internal power, internal controls were relaxed and more attention was turned to foreign trade and to colonies.

A trend toward laissez-faire in internal affairs began during the eighteenth century. The Industrial Revolution brought a further decline of mercantilism and the extension of laissez-faire to external as well as to internal affairs. The victory of the commercial classes was marked by the Bloodless Revolution of 1688, and their fall from power was marked by passage of the Great Reform Bill in 1832. A few years later, in 1846, repeal of the English Corn Laws closed the mercantilist age in England. The relatively early triumph as well as the relatively early fall of mercantilism in England goes a

long way toward explaining England's leadership in economic development **165**
for three hundred years.

MERCANTILISM

INTERNAL ECONOMIC UNIFICATION

Although state-building appropriately describes the overall aim of mercantilist statesmen, the economic significance of mercantilism is more specifically described as economy-building, which may be translated simply as national economic development. For reasons associated with national survival and expansion, it was imperative to develop the productive power of nations. Creation of an internally unified economy included, among other things, the elimination of barriers to internal trade; good transportation and communication facilities; a uniform and generally acceptable currency; uniform weights and measures; uniform commercial laws; and a large and disciplined labor force.

In addition to these several aspects of internal state-building, mercantilist statesmen sought by various measures to increase the power of their nation in relation to the power of rival nations. These external aspects of mercantilism, discussed in the following section, included a powerful army and navy; a strong merchant marine; good harbors; self-sufficiency in agriculture and industry, especially in commodities strategic in war (food, cloth, arms and munitions); extensive foreign markets and sources of cheap raw materials, preferably in areas under political control (colonies); and a large supply of international money(gold and silver).

The classification of items as internal and external is sometimes arbitrary. The general distinction is between the internal economic unification of a single national state, on the one hand, and the strength of one national state relative to other states, on the other hand. National unification is the key to the former; international power is the key to the latter.

Tolls

During the medieval period the flow of trade was greatly hampered by tolls along highways and rivers. One of the chief tasks of mercantilist policy was to eliminate these and to create a free internal trade. Mercantilism is often associated with protectionism. This is accurate so far as *inter*national trade is concerned, but it should be emphasized that mercantilism stood for free *intra*national trade. From the vantage point of the Middle Ages the mercantilists advocated freer trade than had been characteristic of Europe in the past and in this sense deserve to be called freer traders if not free traders.

Success in eliminating tolls was an index of success in achieving internal unification. In this connection a comparison of Germany, France, and England is of interest. In Germany the toll system was disastrous to the development of efficient commerce. Along the Rhine, which was the most important trade route in Germany, a merchant of the late sixteenth century recorded in his diary that he had to pay tolls at thirty-one points between Basle and Cologne, or an average of one toll every ten miles. Inability of German princes to eliminate the toll system was an important cause of Germany's backwardness during the sixteenth, seventeenth, and eighteenth centuries. The most im-

portant reason for this intolerable situation was the inability of German principalities to substitute any other form of revenue for tolls, and of course some form of revenue was indispensable to the conduct of government. Commerce continued to be badly disrupted until the famous Prussian tariff of 1818, and the more famous Zollverein (Customs Union) of 1833, brought significant reforms.

France succeeded more than Germany but less than England in eliminating tolls. During the medieval period almost every landlord levied some form of toll on trade passing within taxing distance. Along the Loire River, between Roanne and Nantes, in the fourteenth century there were 74 toll stations, or an average of one every five miles. Relatively early political unification under Louis XI and other strong monarchs contributed to improvements in France. Colbert, the famous seventeenth-century minister of Louis XIV, put through a tariff reform in 1664 which ranks as one of the boldest attempts at unification ever undertaken by a mercantilist government. Although Colbert and his successors were unable to finish the reforms he proposed, the way was prepared for the completion of this work shortly after the end of the *ancien régime* in 1789.

Two conditions favorable to the elimination of internal tolls in England were its early political centralization under a strong monarchy and its extremely long coast line, which made England less dependent on inland transportation than Continental countries like Germany and France. The English state had the power as well as the foresight to establish relative freedom of domestic trade and uniform customs duties on foreign trade. Early internal economic unification was an important step in preparation for the early triumph of the Industrial Revolution in England.

Transportation

Mere elimination of man-made barriers to trade was not enough to weld isolated communities together into a national economy. Positive steps in the form of improved transportation and communication were needed. By and large the achievement in overland transportation was not great during early capitalism. Roads were not as good as in Roman times, although there were more of them. The only important means of mass transportation was by water. Here the English advantage was great because no point was far from the sea or a connecting water route.

In France Colbert undertook the most ambitious canal-building program of the age. He linked the Atlantic Ocean to the Mediterranean Sea by constructing the Languedoc Canal, which was 180 miles long and 600 feet above sea level at the highest point. The cost of freight over the canal was much less than by land along the same route. It was a boon to commerce in southwestern France, but it did not achieve the expectations of its builders that it would divert the bulk of Mediterranean-Atlantic shipping from the Straits of Gibraltar.

The French were also ambitious in road construction. King Henry IV, who reigned from 1589 to 1610, spent a million livres a year on highways, and Colbert undertook a more modest road-building program. Labor was provided

by requiring able-bodied men to work on roads one month a year as a special tax (*corvée*). Labor of this type was not efficient and was often evaded, but despite disadvantages it helped give France the best road system in Europe in the latter part of the eighteenth century.

England relied on the natural advantages of its coast line and inland waterways, the navigability of which were lengthened and improved during the seventeenth and eighteenth centuries. Drafted labor was used to maintain roads, but the *corvée* was only four to six days per year for each householder.

Coinage

The coinage problem which confronted mercantilist statesmen arose from the medieval practice of farming out coinage rights to feudal princes and from debasement of the currency by princes and sovereigns alike. England and France both achieved a high degree of national unification at an early date, whereas Germany, as in other aspects of internal economic unification, lagged far behind. By the twelfth century in England the king had effectively unified the coinage and in the sixteenth century Elizabeth brought a long sequence of debasements to a halt. Consequently the English pound never departed as far from its original meaning of one pound (12 ounces) of silver as did the French pound (livre), the Italian pound (lira), and other Continental currencies. The stability of the metallic content of the English pound contributed to England's leadership in international finance and banking.

In France the decay of Charlemagne's empire in the ninth century was followed by a confused state of coinage, but by the thirteenth century royal coinage had replaced feudal coinage. In the competition between provincial and royal coins the latter had the dubious merit of being devalued more frequently. In keeping with the monetary principle known as Gresham's law, that bad money drives out good, the royal coins of lesser weight prevailed. While French coinage achieved unification, it lacked the stability which characterized the English monetary system.

In Germany the weakness of the medieval Holy Roman Empire was a factor contributing to the chaos of the currency. The Empire had the right to coin money but this right was frequently farmed out to territorial princes. As feudal princes gained power at the expense of the Empire, their control over coinage increased at the expense of effective control by the Empire. In some of the stronger territorial principalities the Emperor agreed not to coin or to circulate imperial money. Even when the statute books asserted the right of imperial coins to circulate everywhere within the Empire, these coins were often excluded from the stronger principalities. In both France and Germany national money and provincial money were for a time circulated in competition with one another. Whereas in France the royal coins won out in this competition, in Germany the provincial coins tended to drive out the imperial coins. Even the territorial princes in Germany were frequently not successful in gaining a monopoly of coinage against other usurpers of power within their territory. The coinage situation was not merely confused; it was chaotic. This was typical of the failure of German state-building prior to the nineteenth century.

The external aspects of mercantilist state-building may be discussed conveniently under (1) bullionism, (2) balance of trade, (3) protectionism, and (4) the relations among these three aspects. All three aspects are closely related to foreign trade, which was looked upon as the chief source of national wealth by the western European powers during the period of mercantilism. In this period the emphasis in policy and doctrine shifted from bullionism during the sixteenth century to a stress on the favorable balance of trade in the seventeenth century and to protectionism during the eighteenth century. This chronological sequence is, of course, only a rough approximation because the policies and doctrines connnected with each period were entertained simultaneously—necessarily because of their logical interrelations. The change was one of emphasis, which shifted with progress in the economic structure, the advance in statesmanship, and the growing sophistication of economic thinking.

Bullionism

Bullion means uncoined gold and silver, and bullionism refers to a national policy of accumulating large stores of these precious metals. In the absence of domestic gold and silver mines, this objective could be achieved only by discovery, pirating, or foreign trade. All three were utilized, but discovery fell mainly to Spain. The other mercantile states therefore had the alternative of pirating, which was done on an extensive scale, or trading the Spanish out of their treasure, which in the long run was the most effective procedure.

Bullionism has been so much identified with mercantilism that its most famous critic, Adam Smith, accused mercantilist writers of confusing money with wealth. Although this definition of mercantilism was perpetuated by the nineteenth-century economists, it is essentially wrong. Nevertheless, the precious metals did have a special fascination for the mercantilists. (And for whom do they not have a fascination?) The precious metals were then, as they are today, the universally acceptable form of money, that is, international money. The desire for a large supply of international money is understandable, especially in a world of chronic warfare, even though there may have been some illusions about the real advantages of having a large stock of money even of a generally acceptable type.

The strict bullionists advocated an embargo on all export of the precious metals. Others urged control of the foreign exchange rates as a device for encouraging the import and discouraging the export of bullion in the belief that its export was always undesirable. The logic of this position, if it can be called logical, was that the best way to accumulate a large supply of gold and silver was to import as much as possible and not to let go of the metals once they were captured. This so-called bullionist stage of mercantilism terminated between 1575 and 1625. Later writers saw more clearly the connection between imports and exports and tolerated the export of limited quantities of bullion if it could be shown that this would result in imports which, upon being processed and re-exported as finished goods, would bring in an even greater quantity of bullion than that which had been exported originally. This

is still basically a bullionist position, but makes less of a fetish of the precious

metals. As noted below, the stages in bullionist theory and practice are related
to the development of the balance of trade doctrine.

Favorable Balance of Trade

During the seventeenth century one major concern of mercantilist writers
and statesmen was with the favorable balance of foreign trade. A favorable
balance of trade meant exports in excess of imports. In one respect this was
but a further development of the bullionist position, since a surplus of exports
over imports would normally be collected in bullion.

The phenomenal gains to be realized from foreign trade contributed to
the prevailing notion that the chief source of a nation's wealth lay in its foreign
trade, and further that the measure of gain from foreign trade lay in the extent
of the balance of exports over imports. Thomas Mun, England's most famous
mercantilist writer, expressed the prevailing belief of the age in the title to his
book *England's Treasure by Forraign Trade, or The Ballance of our Forraign
Trade is the Rule of Our Treasure* (written in the 1620's and published in
1664). Mun advised: "Wee must ever observe this rule: to sell more to strangers yearly than wee consume of theirs in value. . . . that part of our stock
which is not returned to us in wares must necessarily be brought home in
treasure." [1]

Although mercantilist writers continued to attach great importance to
gold and silver, the most plausible reason for the uniform concern with the
favorable balance of trade seems to have been a preoccupation with wider
markets. Merchant capital had begun to expand into production, and markets
were gaining added significance. If more could be sold abroad than was bought
abroad, a net increase in sales resulted. In view of the limited state of the
domestic markets and the large gains from trade in foreign commerce, there
is every reason to suppose that merchants of the seventeenth century were
eager to expand the volume of business.

There was also concern with buying cheap and selling dear, that is, with
favorable *terms* of trade as contrasted with a favorable *balance* of trade. The
former refers to the *prices* of exports in relation to the prices of imports; the
balance of trade refers to the *quantity* of sales. Mercantilist writers assumed
that the quantity of exports would not be much affected by prices (an inelastic
demand), which was reasonable enough in view of the monopolistic nature
of much of the trade, especially that with colonies subject to coercion by the
metropolitan country. Imperial mercantilism attempted to force colonies to
buy manufactured goods from the parent country and to sell raw materials only
in the parent country. For example, under the English Navigation System
(see below) English colonies were permitted to sell "enumerated" commodities (sugar, tobacco, etc.) only in England, thus depressing the prices of these
raw materials. The prices of English manufactured goods were maintained by
forbidding the colonies to buy them anywhere except in England. Such coercive
measures enabled the metropolitan countries of Europe to maintain favorable
terms of trade with minimum adverse effect on the balance of trade. Mo-

[1] Thomas Mun, *England's Treasure by Forraign Trade* (Oxford: Basil Blackwell,
1949), p. 5.

nopolies against foreigners (and colonists) were always held to be justified even if monopolies in domestic trade and industry were not.

Protectionism

Mercantilist statesmen, with an eye to the warring world around them, advocated policies designed to generate productive power in their nation. Whatever other arguments may have been advanced for protective tariffs— and they were all advanced—they can best be understood in relation to the incessant threat of war. National strength meant self-sufficiency in the essentials of war production. Since nations at the time were largely agricultural, the pressing task which confronted them was the growth of industry. Manufacturing and the export of manufactures were to be encouraged by favorable legislation. Raw material production was also encouraged, but as a rule the import of raw materials was not to be discouraged by protective duties. Export of raw materials was discouraged and sometimes prohibited. As an industrious and skilled labor force was one of the chief national assets in a world of power politics, the skill to be promoted was that of domestic not foreign labor. In England there was widespread criticism of the trade with France because England's balance with France appeared to be unfavorable and imports were mostly of a luxury variety (wine, brandy, and silk). The unfavorable balance was said to enrich France, something that England ought not do.

Industry In all European countries special subsidies and other incentives were offered to encourage new industries. Monopolies were granted to private interests to start new industries. In France Colbert and other ministers of Louis XIV spent large sums during the seventeenth century to stimulate factory production, but these attempts were largely unsuccessful.

Attempts to stimulate new industries were more successful in England than in France. The remarkable growth of English industry during the century 1540 to 1640 was examined in Chapter 7, where the great woolen industry was discussed. Here reference is made only to special protective devices. Early in the sixteenth century an embargo was placed on the export of raw wool from England in order to insure a large, cheap, and stable supply of raw material for cloth manufacture. Sheep could not lawfully be sheared within five miles of the seacoast, and the export of live sheep from England was punishable by mutilation and death. A statute passed during the reign of Elizabeth I provided that on first offense an exporter of sheep was to forfeit all his wealth, be imprisoned for one year, and have his left hand cut off on a market day and nailed up in the market square for all to see. On second offense the statute declared the exporter of sheep to be guilty of a felony punishable by death. The embargo on wool exports limited the market of wool-growers and tended to depress the price received for their wool. Despite the strong penalties against the export of wool and of sheep, smuggling was widespread.

Further protection was afforded the English woolen cloth industry by means of embargoes and tariffs on imports that might compete with domestic woolens. Foreign woolens were excluded, and cotton, silk, and linen discriminated against. In 1700 the importation of the bright and colorful Indian calicoes (cotton) was prohibited, which had the interesting effect of stimulating calico printing in England of unfinished imported cotton cloth. The woolen interests

protested vehemently against the "worthless, scandalous, unprofitable sort of goods embraced by a luxuriant humour among the women, prompted by the art and fraud of the drapers and the [East India] Company, to which alone they are profitable." [2] Street gangs in the service of the woolen industry harassed wearers of calicoes and even tore calico dresses from the backs of the "Calico-madams," as women wearers were called, who were so bold as to venture forth garbed in this apparel. The Government yielded to pressures and prohibited the *use* of calico cloth in the famous Calico Act of 1721. Even the powerful East India Company could not prevent the woolen industry from putting on the statute books almost any law it wanted.

Further protection to industry was afforded by embargoes on the export of English machines and tools and by not allowing craftsmen to emigrate. Conversely, foreign craftsmen were encouraged to settle in England. French Huguenots and other persecuted Protestants, who were among the most skilled and industrious groups in the Continental population, poured into England during the seventeenth and eighteenth centuries and added much skill to the English labor force. Protests by English craftsmen that their jobs were being taken from them by foreigners went unheeded. A large population was considered essential for national power and had the further advantage, from the point of view of mercantilist statesmen and employers, of lowering wages. Keeping down costs, especially labor costs, was openly advocated as a means of increasing the wealth of the country, a doctrine which in Heckscher's words "approximates suspiciously closely to the tendency to keep down the mass of the people by poverty, in order to make them better beasts of burden for the few . . ." [3]

The iron industry was of obvious importance for national defense. Because of a shortage of fuel the English imported much iron from Sweden. One seventeenth-century writer suggested the importance of encouraging iron production by pointing to England's possible embarrassment in wartime: "If there should be occasion for great quantities of guns and bullet and other sorts of iron commodities for a present unexpected war, and the Sound happen to be locked up and so prevent iron coming to us, truly we should then be in a fine case." [4]

Nonessential industries were treated quite differently from the essential ones. Luxury industries were frequently discouraged, especially when they produced mainly for domestic consumption. True virtue, at least for the poor, consisted in hard work and simple living in which there was neither time nor place for "delicacies, superfluities or trifles." (Lipson, III, 89) Luxury production was more permissible if intended for export since it was assumed to be good strategy to let the people of a rival nation indulge their pleasure, live high, and grow soft.

Agriculture A principle of mercantilism was self-sufficiency in food. Bread made from grain, or "corn" as it is called in England, was the staple item in the diet of the bulk of the population. In order to stimulate grain pro-

[2] Cited in E. Lipson, *Economic History of England* (London: Adam & Charles Black, Ltd., 1931), III, 43.

[3] E. F. Heckscher, *Mercantilism* (New York: The Macmillan Company, 1935), II, 166.

[4] Yarrington, *England's Improvement* (1677), p. 63, cited in Lipson, III, 2.

duction up to and beyond self-sufficiency a dual system of tariffs and bounties was developed. Protective tariffs on grain imports served to shield English farmers from foreign competition. Bounties on exports were intended to prevent the price received by English growers from falling, in the face of large crops, to levels which would discourage future production. In years of bad harvests at home, export of grain might be prohibited and the tariff on imported grain lowered or suspended in order that the price not go so high as to prove a hardship to consumers.

Severe criticisms were leveled at the bounties, but there is some basis for believing that they achieved the desired object of stimulating production. Whether the Corn Laws raised or lowered the domestic price of grain in the long run is uncertain, although it is likely that they did raise prices. Increased production in itself tended to lower prices, but the subsidies given to selling abroad and the duties on imported grain tended to reduce the volume of wheat for sale in the domestic market and so to raise the price. In terms of national self-sufficiency in food, the criterion of success was the increase in domestic production rather than a lower domestic price. For a lower domestic price would benefit only the consumers, and mercantilist principles gave very little attention to consumer welfare.

Navigation System A well-known economic historian of English mercantilism lists, as its three pillars, protection to industry, the Corn Laws, and the Navigation System, protecting respectively industry, agriculture, and maritime commerce.[5] The Navigation System will be discussed in connection with the American colonies; here it is sufficient to emphasize that it was an integral part of the overall program for making England strong and self-sufficient. Perhaps more than any other single phenomenon it illustrates external state-building, that is, the attempt to increase one nation's power at the expense of other powers.

The English Navigation Acts (1651 and 1660) were aimed against the Dutch, who were the leading maritime power of the seventeenth century. The general intent of the laws was to keep English foreign trade under English control by preventing the Dutch from trading with any English colonies, by preventing them from bringing goods from the East Indies or any place except Holland for sale in England or in any English colonies. Under this system, for example, the Dutch could no longer lawfully bring supplies of hemp, flax, timber, and other raw materials from the Baltic to England. The Navigation System, by requiring the use of British ships and British sailors, fostered seamanship and so enhanced British naval power as well as British trade. Moreover, encouragement to shipping afforded by the Navigation System gave rise to "invisible exports" (shipping services for which England received payment) to promote a favorable balance of trade.

RELATION OF BULLIONISM, BALANCE OF TRADE, AND PROTECTIONISM

Some obvious relations among bullionism, the balance of trade, and protectionism may now be stated explicitly. If more goods were exported than im-

---

[5] Lipson, *Economic History of England,* III, 1–2.

ported (favorable balance of trade), the surplus balance could be collected in

the form of money (bullion). A leading device for increasing the size of the favorable balance was to discourage imports by means of protective duties on imports. The extent of the favorable balance might be further enhanced by paying bounties or other types of subsidies to encourage exports, as was done in the case of English grain under the Corn Laws.

The mercantilists realized that all nations could not have a favorable balance of trade simultaneously, since total exports of all countries together must be equal to total imports of all countries. This was quite consistent with their general outlook that national gains are always made at the expense of rival nations. One of the main objectives of the state-building policies of mercantilism was to make certain that one's own country did not have the unfavorable balance. However, insofar as a net import of bullion was the objective, an extenuating circumstance of great historical significance was the great influx of American treasure into Europe. Under the circumstances it was quite feasible for all European nations to increase their stocks of bullion simultaneously. Spain was the funnel through which most of the precious metals entered Europe, and Spain was also the sieve through which treasure reached other countries, especially England, France, and Holland. Spain's inability to retain American treasure was viewed by other countries as a lesson in how not to operate an economy. Spain was notably unsuccessful in the task of internal state-building and failed to develop the productive powers of industry and agriculture. At the same time Spain waged innumerable wars in an attempt to protect and preserve the unwieldy empire gained with relative ease. It may be said that Spain's weakness was too many wars and too few wares.

An important mercantilist argument for the favorable balance of trade may be called the "employment argument." Exports involve employment of domestic labor, whereas imports employ only foreign labor. In order to achieve maximum employment of domestic labor, exports should be as large as possible and imports as small as possible. It follows logically that the export of manufactured goods is preferable to the export of raw materials because the former embody more labor. Domestic raw materials should be retained in order that the labor of domestic manufacturing could be added to them before they are exported. Moreover, raw materials should be imported in order to give employment to still more domestic labor; the imported raw materials may be re-exported with domestic labor added.

Another aspect of the employment argument was emphasis on increasing the skills of domestic labor. Improvement in the arts was an essential mercantilist objective which was quite consistent with the general principle of creating the productive capacity of the nation. An industrious and skillful labor force was viewed as a nation's greatest asset by many mercantilist writers. Thomas Mun, "prince of the mercantilists," attributed the greatness of the Dutch to the development of the "artificial" wealth of industry. England's greatness he attributed mainly to "natural" wealth, which contrasted with the "natural" poverty of the Dutch. He recommended that England "add Art to Nature" and become truly rich and prosperous. This is one form of the employment argument. The "export of labor" was a further development of the balance of trade principle. Some writers substituted "balance of labor" for

"balance of trade" in order to emphasize the importance of a skilled labor force in export industries.

The merit of the employment argument depends largely on whether unemployment, underemployment, and underdevelopment were important aspects of mercantilist economies. Unemployment was at least periodically important, being more so during the sixteenth century in England than during the seventeenth and eighteenth centuries. Underemployment was a chronic problem. Underdevelopment is a relative matter, but in terms of future achievements, all the countries of Europe were underdeveloped during the mercantilist period. The encouragement given to domestic manufacturing was a forcing device designed to elevate the average level of skill and productivity of the laboring population. Thus there would seem to have been merit in the employment argument in connection with the need for furthering the economic development of their countries.

Among sovereigns a strong motive for encouraging the importation of bullion was the wish to increase the taxable capacity of their subjects by monetizing the economy. The most important domestic as well as international money was gold and silver. With the passing of the feudal system the concept of labor dues and payments in kind gave way to the notion that taxes levied in money provide the appropriate basis for supporting the activities of government. Revenues in kind were awkward from both the collection and expenditure points of view. Prior to the influx of American treasure there was scarcity of coins, especially in rural communities, where much exchange continued at a barter stage and provided no satisfactory tax base. Administrative convenience, which is a major consideration in any tax system, helps to account for the bullionist fetish in official circles.

BASIC IDEAS OF MERCANTILISM

In retrospect, the historic significance of mercantilism lies in the achievement of the conditions necessary for rapid and cumulative economic change in the countries of western Europe. At the end of the Middle Ages western Europe stood about where many underdeveloped countries stand today, and some appreciation of the nature of the task and the scope of the achievement of mercantilist states may be gained by viewing their basic problem in this perspective. Once an economy has begun to develop, further advancement seems to follow almost automatically. The difficult task is to get the process of development under way. Often nothing less than a social revolution is required. Power must be transferred from reactionary to progressive classes. New energies must be released, often by uprooting the old order. Religious outlook is frequently a barrier to material advancement. An entire framework must be created within which cumulative change can take place. Every old society standing on the threshold of a new one is confronted with a similar range of problems.

Although poor in relation to what they were to become later, the economic systems of Europe were then capable of producing a surplus above the necessities of life. The immediate problem was to direct this social surplus into productive investment. The capitalistic framework was already implanted in

many countries, which meant there was available a powerful apparatus for the productive employment of the social surplus. However, there were many tasks which private capitalists were unable or unwilling to perform. They could hardly be expected to create the environment within which they could operate successfully. This was a collective task in which the initiative rested with governments rather than with private enterprise.

The foregoing discussion suggests that most of the things the mercantilist statesmen tried to do were those which were prerequisite to productive investment of the social surplus and to cumulative economic change. Among the essential conditions of the economic environment were a domestic market free of tolls and other barriers to free trade within nations; a uniform monetary system; a legal code appropriate to capitalistic progress; a skilled and disciplined labor force; domestic tranquillity against internal violence and external aggression; sufficient literacy and education among business classes to use credit instruments, contracts, and the other paraphernalia required in a commercial civilization; basic facilities in transportation, communication, harbor installations; and many other conditions.

Sovereign power as well as great economic resources were necessary for the creation of these conditions. Very few of these undertakings promised returns soon enough to be attractive to private investors. Frequently the social benefits were great but were not capable of being channeled for monetary gain. Construction of a national network of roads illustrates a precondition of national economic development which required large government investment. Canals are another example. Similarly, the development of a great harbor would probably not be profitable for a single merchant, but it might be very advantageous for a country; and after the harbor had been developed the profits of private merchants in general might be greatly increased along with the standard of living of the people as a whole as a result of the increase in trade resulting from the harbor improvements.

Investments of this type represent social overhead capital. They are a form of capital because they contribute to the revenue of the nation. They are overhead because the contribution to productivity is indirect. For the most part such investments yield no final goods and services although they are essential for the production of final goods and services. Because social overhead capital yields nothing that can be sold at a profit, it must normally be made by government and be paid for out of the general revenue of society. This means it falls within the province of public finance and is paid for by taxation and by public loans.

Given the investment in social overhead capital, private capital may be invested profitably in projects which are directly productive in the sense that the investment may be expected to yield a good or service which may be sold for money at a profit. The extent to which private investment is profitable will depend upon the extent of investment in social overhead; for example, the better the network of roads, the larger the number of private investors who can find markets for the products of their investment.

Because of its indirect contribution to output, its often intangible nature (national defense, monetary system, etc.), and its association with government spending, social overhead capital is often not thought of as capital at all. Government expenditures may be viewed as a deduction from the funds avail-

able for capital accumulation, and government expenditure and regulation as likely to discourage rather than promote private investment. The danger always exists that measures taken by government to encourage economic development may overstep the bounds of prudence and have the opposite effect of retarding economic development. Indeed the golden mean between the extremes of too much and too little government participation was seldom realized.

Statesmen and monarchs responsible for making investments in social overhead capital were interested in having these tasks performed because they recognized them as conditions of survival and expansion in a world of national rivalries. They were not consciously thinking of creating conditions which would make for a maximum rate of economic growth. They were probably seldom conscious of the dilemma that government activity, which up to a point is so essential to economic development, may hinder it if carried beyond the optimum point.

Laissez-faire writers later accused mercantilist governments of going much too far in intervening in economic activity. However, laissez-faire thinking was the product of a later age, after the essential beginnings of capitalistic development had already been achieved. Advocates of laissez-faire erred in their wholesale condemnation of mercantilism; they did not understand the extent to which they themselves were creatures of their own environment and did not appreciate that what was appropriate for their age may not have been appropriate for an earlier stage of economic development. They failed to realize that by their time mercantilism had fulfilled its mission, and that the range of government activity could be much restricted. Certainly mercantilist practitioners were not infallible, and they undoubtedly made many mistakes; but this does not mean that their entire conception of economic policy was wrong in the sense that it was an obstacle rather than an agent of progress.

Most of the things the mercantilists tried to do needed to be done, and most of them could have been done only by governments. How well they were done in any particular country at any particular time is an important, but a different, issue. The necessity of investing productively, if indirectly, in social overhead capital was fully consistent with the prevailing doctrine that the accumulation of capital holds the key to economic progress. In this regard, it should be recorded that the nations most successful in mercantilistic policies enjoyed the most rapid economic development. England and, to a lesser extent, France demonstrate the connection between successful mercantilist policy and rapid economic advance. Spain and Germany are examples of countries which did not succeed in carrying out mercantilist policies and they experienced a corresponding lack of economic progress.

In a capitalist society the augmentation of wealth takes the form of capital accumulation, that is, the accumulation of productive wealth. In the early stages of capitalism when the shortage of capital was acute, the passion for accumulation made for the glorification of thrift. Among mercantilist commentators, a corollary of the emphasis on accumulation and the virtue of thrift was a lack of recognition of the importance of consumption. For wage-earners, consumption in excess of subsistence was held to run counter to the national interest, to be a tax upon progress. Hence there was widespread advocacy of low wages. One mercantilist writer argued that an "increase of wages is the

greatest tax on the nation." Mercantilism was not humanitarian; it was pre-
humanitarian. Mercantilist society was not a welfare state; it could not afford
to be. The concern for channeling the surplus into productive use is seen in
the reprimand to luxury consumption. One of the reasons for discouraging imports was that many imports were of a luxury variety.

The later, classical economists, who were also preoccupied with capital
accumulation, looked upon saving as a virtue because it was a means for increasing consumption and welfare in the future. The shift away from the mercantilist outlook is signalized by the ideas of Adam Smith, who was a humanitarian primarily concerned with per capita wealth and income rather than
with aggregate national wealth and income, which might be increased through
increasing population. It was against the background of the mercantilist view
of consumption that Smith wrote, with accent on revelation, "consumption
is the sole end and purpose of all production."

Mercantilist preoccupation with capital accumulation helps to explain
the psychology of bullionism. For example, a plausible sequence of cause and
effect runs as follows: Saving is a virtue; saving is identified with the accumulation of money (precious metals); therefore the accumulation of precious metals
is a virtue. This involves confusion between private saving (accumulating
money) and social saving (accumulating means of production), but such confusion is not surprising in view of the unsophisticated state of economic reasoning.

Max Weber has defined mercantilism as "carrying the point of view of
capitalism into politics." This means that mercantilists regarded the aim of
national policy to be making money, that is, selling (exporting) more than is
bought (imported), and realizing the surplus in the form of money (bullion),
just as capitalists seek to have their sales exceed their costs in order to make a
profit. The analogy between the points of view of capitalist profit-making and
mercantilist trade policy may be illustrated by Thomas Mun's exposure of the
fallacy of an embargo on the export of bullion, which represents a more
sophisticated view of both processes. A nation like a business makes profits
by selling (exporting) more than it buys (imports). It collects the surplus in
money (bullion); but it should use the money to buy more in order to be able
to sell more in the next round of circulation. Money is the real object of
national and capitalist activity, but more money can be made by spending
(exporting) money (bullion). Hoarded money (bullion) is sterile. It must be
used if the advantages of its possession are to be realized. It must be thrown
back into the circular flow again and again so it can return each time with
a profit.

Interestingly the term "balance" as used in "balance of trade" was apparently adopted from the term "balance" as used in business accounting, in
which the balance represents the profit. This lends plausibility to the idea
that mercantilism involved carrying the point of view of business over into
politics. The "illusion" that money is real wealth is fortified by the nature of
business enterprise itself, quite apart from the accounting techniques used to
determine profit and loss. Profits of business enterprise are said to be realized
when goods are sold for money. If goods cannot be converted into money,
the business transaction is a failure and is so recorded in the profit and loss
account. To the merchant with 10,000 yards of cloth to sell, what is important

in judging the success of his activity is the money received from the sale of the cloth. The cloth as such has little if any "real" value to the merchant-owner. If he cannot sell it, it is worthless; he has nothing, or virtually nothing, except some cloth to wrap around his body. Money is the "real" form of wealth to the individual businessman. The reason money is so important is because it is a *socially recognized* form of private wealth. The bullionist fallacy may be said to have involved a confusion between social wealth and a socially recognized form of private wealth.

SELECTED BIBLIOGRAPHY

COLE, CHARLES W., *Colbert and a Century of French Mercantilism* (2nd ed.). 2 vols. Hamden, Conn.: Archon Books, 1964.

————, *French Mercantilism*. New York: Columbia University Press, 1943.

CUNNINGHAM, WILLIAM, *The Growth of English Industry and Commerce in Modern Times* (5th ed.). Vol. II. London: Cambridge University Press, 1910–12.

HECKSCHER, ELI F., *Mercantilism* (rev. ed.). 2 vols. New York: The Macmillan Co., 1955.

JOHNSON, E. A. J., *Predecessors of Adam Smith*. New York: Augustus J. Kelley, Inc., 1960.

KEYNES, JOHN M., *The General Theory of Employment, Interest and Money*, Chap. 23. New York: Harcourt, Brace & World, Inc., 1936.

LIPSON, E., *The Economic History of England* (6th ed.). Vols. II and III. London: Adam & Charles Black, Ltd., 1956.

MUN, THOMAS, *England's Treasure by Forraign Trade*. Oxford: Basil Blackwell, 1949.

SCHMOLLER, GUSTAV, *The Mercantile System and Its Historical Significance*. New York: P. Smith, 1931.

SMITH, ADAM, *An Inquiry into the Nature and Causes of the Wealth of Nations*, Book IV. New York: Modern Library, 1937.

VINER, JACOB, *Studies in the Theory of International Trade*. New York: Harper & Row, Publishers, 1937.

ARTICLES

COLEMAN, D. C., "Eli Heckscher and the Idea of Mercantilism," *Scandinavian Economic History Review*, V, No. 1 (1957), 3–25.

HAMILTON, EARL J., "The Decline of Spain," *Economic History Review*, VIII (May, 1938), 168–79.

HECKSCHER, ELI F., "Mercantilism," *Encyclopaedia of the Social Sciences*, X (New York: The Macmillan Company, 1933), 333–39.

————, "Mercantilism," *Economic History Review*, VII (Nov., 1936), 44–54.

LIPSON, E., "England in the Age of Mercantilism," *Journal of Economic and Business History*, IV (Aug., 1932), 691–707.

WILSON, CHARLES, " 'Mercantilism': Some Vicissitudes of an Idea," *Economic History Review*, X (Dec., 1957), 181–88.

————, "Treasure and Trade Balances: The Mercantilist Problem," *Economic History Review*, II, No. 2 (1949), 152–61; IV, No. 2 (1951), 231–42; XV (Dec., 1962), 364–69.

British Mercantilism and
Colonial Economic Development

CHAPTER **11**

Four factors were of prime significance in the development of the
American economy during the colonial period: (1) The colonies
were the product of a capitalist environment; (2) The colonies were
under English jurisdiction and the people and institutions were primarily English; (3) The colonies were established during the century of the English middle-class revolution; and (4) The colonies were established as a part of an imperial mercantilist regime.

By the seventeenth century the social-economic-political pattern of feudalism had pretty well disappeared in western Europe and especially in England. Capitalism was still in its early stage of development and had not transformed all English economic life, but it was triumphantly in the saddle, and the battle against feudal remnants was in the "mopping up" phase. In political evolution England had passed from the feudal stage, characterized by a weak central government, and was in the later stages of political absolutism under which strong monarchs like the Tudors had been able to carry economic unification a long way toward success. The death of Queen Elizabeth I (1603) brought the strong Tudor line to a close and ushered in the pretentious but weak Stuarts, who were to wage a losing struggle to retain absolute power. The decline of monarchical power was accompanied by the rise to power of representative government under control of the House of Commons.

As a result of England's economic evolution and political revolution, immigrants to the colonies were quite advanced in their ideas about capitalist institutions and political democracy. Yet, perhaps paradoxically, the very breakdown of monarchical power, which created an atmosphere of economic and political liberalism in England, tended to accentuate the mercantilist emphasis on economic exploitation and political subordination of colonies. Englishmen who fought for liberalism at home were equally determined to enjoy the advantages that might accrue from the exploitation of colonies. At the same time, Englishmen who migrated to the colonies knew the meaning of political freedom and were equally determined to enjoy it in the colonies. Herein lay the ideological roots of the American Revolution.

John Cabot, whose voyages provided the basis for English territorial claims in North America, was, like Columbus, a north Italian product of the

early stirrings of European capitalism. His explorations were financed by merchant capitalists of Bristol and London. The territory claimed by the English as a result of Cabot's voyages remained unexplored and undeveloped throughout the sixteenth century. The only exceptions were the abortive attempts of Sir Humphrey Gilbert and Sir Walter Raleigh to establish colonies in the Carolinas. An irony of history is that the territory which was destined to become in the twentieth century the greatest capitalist nation in the world was neglected for more than a century after its discovery. When at last, in the seventeenth century, the English began to show interest in their real estate across the Atlantic, they had advanced sufficiently to use capitalistic techniques in order to forge the link between Europe and America. American economic development from the beginning had a distinctly capitalist flavor.

The colonial period of American history began with the English Revolution and ended with the American Revolution. The English Revolution of the seventeenth century was a prolonged political, religious, and economic struggle led by Puritans against the Stuart kings and their royalist supporters. The first Stuart king, James I, believed in the doctrine of the divine right of kings. Such doctrine was not palatable to the British middle classes, which were eager to control the government in order to protect and promote their political, religious, and economic views and interests.

Although James I avoided open civil war, his son, Charles I, was less fortunate. In 1629 Charles began his personal rule after dispensing with the Long Parliament, which did not meet between 1629 and 1642. Charles attempted to enforce uniformity of religious belief. In 1642 the struggle between the King and Parliament broke into open violence, and the following period until 1647 was the most crucial in the nearly century-long revolution. The King and his armies were beaten by the insurgent middle classes under the leadership of Oliver Cromwell, a devout Puritan and wealthy landowner. Cromwell abolished the monarchy and established the Commonwealth with himself at the head of the government. He attempted to rule with the aid of Parliament, but became impatient with the bickerings of conflicting groups. He dismissed Parliament and ruled as a dictator until his death in 1658. Cromwell's chief supporters were landed gentry of the upper middle class and wealthy merchants.

Having won out in the struggle for control of government, the upper middle classes turned their attention outward toward the consolidation of existing colonies and the conquest of additional ones. The avowed object of the imperial policy was to use colonies for the benefit of England, which meant, in the light of the new power structure of the nation, for the benefit of the upper middle classes. Where imperial mercantilist policy conflicted with the interests of colonists, the colonial interests were subordinated. In the colonies of the North American mainland there were, generally speaking, only minor conflicts in the earlier stages of development of the colonial economy, but in the later period the conflicts grew more intense and finally erupted into violent revolution against English rule. Thus the colonial period began with one revolution and ended with another.

In discussing the motives of colonization a distinction should be drawn between promoters and immigrants. The promoters were usually capitalists seeking outlets for profitable investment. The motives of actual settlers were often partly economic, but were also political and religious. Like all revolutions, the English Civil War of the seventeenth century created conditions from which many persons sought escape. Thousands of families were uprooted from long-established ways of life and went in search of new beginnings. Amid the shifting fortunes of war, nearly every group was subjected to persecution at one time or another: anti-royalists, royalists, Catholics, Puritans, Dissenters. Small yeomen were driven from their ancestral homes by enclosures. The unemployed poor were subjected to harsh treatment under the statutes against idleness and beggary. The seventeenth-century settlers in America were truly the sons and daughters of revolution.

Whatever the ultimate motivation of individual settlers might have been, colonization was a costly process and required considerable capital. The English government gave moral support but no direct financial aid for establishing colonies. In this respect the English differed from the French and Spanish, whose governments took the initiative and provided capital for colonies in the New World; indeed the century of delay in British colonization on the North American mainland probably resulted from the lack of governmental initiative in this connection. The failures of Gilbert and Raleigh in the sixteenth century indicated that colonization was beyond the means of individual capitalists. Raleigh lost about £40,000 in his unsuccessful Carolina colony. Since the Government did not undertake to provide the necessary economic resources and since colonization was beyond the means of individual capitalists, it was the success of joint-stock companies at the beginning of the seventeenth century which gave impetus to English colonization in North America. This may be illustrated with reference to the first colonies at Jamestown and Plymouth, both of which utilized the joint-stock principle for raising capital for settlement.

Jamestown

Jamestown, the first permanent English colony in North America, was established by a joint-stock company under a charter granted by King James I in 1606. The motives for chartering this company were almost exclusively economic. The English East India Company had been in operation only a few years, having first been chartered in 1600, but by 1606 it was already yielding large profits to its investors. With the example of the East India Company before them, a group of wealthy London and Plymouth merchants and gentlemen sought and secured a monopoly of the right to trade and settle in what was then called Virginia, a territory extending from the present state of Maine to the Carolinas. Some of the promoters of the Virginia Company were prominent members of the East India Company, including Sir Thomas Smith and Sir Edwyn Sandys. The charter from the King authorized two incorporated joint-stock organizations: the Virginia Company of London (sometimes called the London Company) with exclusive rights to the southern part of the territory,

and the Virginia Company of Plymouth (sometimes referred to as the Plymouth Company) with exclusive rights in the northern part of the territory. A certain middle area of the total grant might be occupied by either of the two companies, although they were not to settle within 100 miles of each other. The companies had, in addition to the right to explore, settle, and carry on economic projects, the privilege of levying import and export duties on all trade coming into and going out of the colonies. The King was to receive one-fifth of all gold and silver mined in the colonies.

The Virginia Company of London, so called because it was organized by London merchants, undertook as its first project the establishment of a colony at Jamestown. The promoters thought of Jamestown more as a trading post or exploitation colony of the type set up by the East India Company than as a settlement colony. Profits from gold mining and from trade with the Indians were the chief objectives of the London merchants who put up the original capital for Jamestown.

The price of each share of stock in the Jamestown joint-stock venture was £12, 10 shillings, which was the estimated cost of equipping and transporting a settler to Virginia. At the end of seven years a special dividend of 100 acres of Virginia land was to be paid for each share of stock held in the company. Settlers who paid for their own transportation and equipment were given credit for one share of stock and were entitled to the 100-acre dividend at the end of seven years. Those settlers whose expenses were paid by the company were its "servants" and were expected to work for seven years during which the full produce of their labor was placed in a common store from which they were to be given only subsistence. Thus the man without capital was a common laborer obligated to work for the company for seven years.

The Jamestown settlement was controlled by investors in London, but the local administrators under Captain John Smith were granted increasing autonomy in dealing with settlers. A rigid, autocratic discipline designed to increase the returns to investors was established. Despite these efforts, however, the company and the settlement proved a poor financial investment. Between £100,000 and £200,000 were sunk without profit and there was virtually no return of the capital. Jamestown operated as a plantation of the London joint-stock company until 1624, when disagreement with the King caused him to withdraw the charter and convert Virginia to a royal colony.

Jamestown's failure as a financial investment did not detract from its success as a settlement nor from the contribution of capitalist institutions to the subsequent economic development of America. Capital funds accumulated by London merchants had made possible a link between England and North America. This link was never broken, although it came perilously close to snapping on more than one occasion; for example, on one occasion the Jamestown settlers physically abandoned their colony and were moving down the James River when they met a ship with supplies coming up the river.

The achievement of a permanent settlement at Jamestown suggests that business enterprise can be of great social significance even when it fails by its own standard of profit-making. One of the limitations of business enterprise is that it normally does not continue to operate unless the monetary returns exceed the monetary outlays. Fortunately, in this instance the English investors were overly optimistic in estimating the yield from their investment,

and society benefited from their mistaken judgment. The importance of Europe's capitalistic structure is obvious when it is recognized that privately accumulated funds provided the indispensable economic basis for the first permanent colony in what later became the leading capitalist nation.

Plymouth

A joint-stock company also provided the capital for founding the Pilgrim colony at Plymouth, Massachusetts. A grant for establishing a "particular plantation" was secured from the Virginia Company of London (the southern Virginia Company). The accidental landing near Cape Cod was north of the jurisdiction of this company so a new patent was obtained from the Council for New England, the successor to the Virginia Company of Plymouth. The Virginia Company of London had refused to invest in the project of the Pilgrim dissenters, but a capital fund of £7,000 was provided by a separate group of London merchants. Each share in the joint-stock company was worth ten pounds, which, as in the Jamestown case, was the estimated cost of outfitting and transporting a settler from Europe to America. Each Pilgrim was credited with one share in the company. Thus, unlike the Jamestown settlers, every Pilgrim was a stockholder in the company and would share in the profits, if any. They were permitted to subscribe to additional shares if their economic circumstances permitted. For a period of seven years each colonist was to put all he produced into a common stock from which, as in Jamestown, subsistence was to be taken as needed. Produce from colonial labor was to be supplemented by provisions sent from England during the early years. Any surplus above subsistence belonged to the company. At the end of seven years the accumulated surplus, in the form of houses, land, goods and chattels, was to be divided among the English investors and the New England settlers in proportion to the number of shares held.

The London capitalists, who had hoped for large and immediate returns, were disappointed with the investment outlook and refused to continue to send supplies in the quantities needed; whereupon the Pilgrims revised their plan of organization. Families were given individual grants of land on which they could raise their own corn and other crops without having to place the produce into the common store. At the end of the seven-year period the London merchants accepted a settlement of approximately one-quarter of their original £7,000. In the intervening years no dividends had been paid. As in the case of Jamestown, Plymouth proved a poor financial investment to its business promoters, but again the wealth advanced by English capitalists had forged a permanent link in the chain that still binds the North Atlantic region into a relatively homogeneous community.

Massachusetts Bay Company

Jamestown and Plymouth were but two of several early colonies begun as joint-stock organizations. The Dutch West India Company established colonies in New York and Delaware, and a Swedish Trading Company founded a settlement in Delaware. More important in terms of size and permanent influence on American society was the founding of Massachusetts. The Massachusetts Bay Company was chartered in 1629 for commercial purposes by men

who were for the most part Puritan merchants. Shortly thereafter, King Charles I attempted to force all religious groups to conform to the official dogmas of the Church of England. The nonconforming Puritans, among whom were some of the richest men in England, fled in numbers. The Massachusetts Bay Company was reorganized as the "Governor and the Company of Massachusetts Bay" under the control of Puritan leaders domiciled in Massachusetts with John Winthrop as Governor. The corporation became the government of the colony under a type of corporate state. The worsening situation for Puritans in England brought the Great Migration of the 1630's to Massachusetts. Since many of the immigrants were wealthy in their own right, a relative abundance of personal capital was available and the Massachusetts Bay Company ceased to function as a source of newly invested capital. By the time the Puritans won out in the English Civil War, a substantial colony had been planted in Massachusetts. Although the incentive of Puritans to leave England declined after 1649, their colony in America was already too much of a going concern for the settlers to think of abandoning it.

With the roots of American civilization firmly planted in Virginia and Massachusetts, other colonies followed more easily and with less financial risk. Meanwhile, however, the joint-stock companies, which had provided the initial links, became less popular because of the losses suffered by investors in the early ones. Hence another important technique for procuring and investing capital emerged in the form of the proprietary colony, exemplified by Maryland.

Maryland

A mixture of capitalistic and feudalistic institutions was reflected in the business arrangements under which Maryland's first settlers arrived in 1634. The charter granted by King Charles I to the Calvert family made Maryland a proprietary colony, as distinguished from a joint-stock settlement of the type utilized in founding Jamestown and Plymouth. As proprietor of the entire colony of Maryland, Lord Baltimore resembled a feudal lord with the right to create manors, collect quitrents, levy taxes, administer justice, make laws, and perform most of the functions of a medieval sovereign. This charter was as pretentious and unrealistic as the king who gave it, for King Charles I, who wished to win back the power of his predecessors, succeeded only in losing his head. The Calvert family was much more in step with the times and did not mistake the form of its charter for reality. The Calverts were not of the old nobility; rather the first Lord Baltimore (who died in 1632) was one of the new men who had risen through the British bureaucracy and, when forced to resign as Secretary of State because of conversion to the Roman Catholic faith, sought his fortune in real estate development. He was associated with the Plymouth Company and the Council for New England, both of which were commercial enterprises.

The Calverts looked upon Maryland as a capital investment from which they might make money-profits from the disposal and rental of land. They made an initial investment of about £30,000 in the colony. The expectation was that this investment (plus that of other wealthy associates) would make the colony attractive to a first group of settlers whose presence in the colony

would raise the value of all land in the colony. The unoccupied land could then be sold to later settlers at a profit. A free settler was given 100 acres for himself, 100 acres for his wife, 100 acres for each servant, and 50 acres for each child. Under this headright system any person transporting a settler was also granted land. Grants were made as freeholds subject to a small quit-rent. The headright system of land grants was discontinued after the colony became sufficiently populated for land to become scarce enough to command a price.

Actually little attempt was made to establish feudal institutions in Maryland. This is not surprising because by the seventeenth century the decline of feudalism in England was an economic fact even though it was without explicit legal recognition. England had never bothered to abolish feudalism legally. Quitrents were the nearest approximation to feudal practice in the colonies. Just what were these payments? In England quitrents still existed in the seventeenth century as legacies from the commutation of labor services into money payments for the privilege of not having to work for the lord of the manor. In the colonies, where labor services had never been paid, quitrents did not have the same significance. Nor were quitrents a "rent" in the sense of a payment for the use of someone else's property because the proprietor to whom the quitrents were paid did not own the land after it was granted or sold to others. Quitrents were intended by the proprietor to be a permanent source of personal income. However, colonists often demanded that the revenues be used for public purposes, and insofar as this was done quitrents constituted a form of property tax payable to the government of the colony.

Quitrents were more successfully collected in Maryland than in other colonies, but even in Maryland scarcely 50 per cent of those owed were ever paid despite the fact that they were nominal in amount. One of the reasons for nonpayment of quitrents was the competition among colonies for settlers. If quitrents were too high, settlers would turn to other colonies where quitrents were lower or did not exist at all. If punitive action were taken against non-payers, they had the alternative of moving elsewhere. The abundance of land and the scarcity of settlers made the quitrent system difficult to enforce in the colonies. Although they never became a serious burden in any colony, quitrents were nevertheless resented. One reason was that colonists did not really have clear title to their land as long as quitrent claims existed. The resentment against quitrents reflects the conditions which rendered impossible the establishment of feudalism in the colonies. The quitrent system, which existed in all the mainland colonies outside New England, was abolished at the time of the American Revolution.

Even religious toleration had economic advantages for the proprietors of Maryland. As a Roman Catholic, Lord Baltimore wished to provide a haven for fellow Catholics, but it was contrary to the laws of England to make Catholicism the official religion or to discriminate against those who adhered to the official Anglican faith. Since relatively few Catholics came to the colonies, it was important to avoid the charge, or impression, of intolerance of Protestants if settlers were to be attracted to Maryland. Just after the Puritans had won a military victory in the Revolution in England—in fact in the same year in which Charles I was beheaded—Lord Baltimore secured passage of the famous Toleration Act of 1649. Radical Protestants driven from other colonies

like Virginia (which adopted the official Anglican faith) came to Maryland in numbers. In the second half of the seventeenth century Maryland grew rapidly, with less than 10 per cent of the population being Catholics. The increase in population increased land values in the colony. Religious toleration was not only a fundamental principle of personal liberty; it also turned out to be a sound business principle.

TYPES OF ECONOMIC ACTIVITY IN THE COLONIES

Resource utilization is subject to certain principles which may be useful in getting a bird's-eye view of the pattern of economic activity in the American colonies. In any economy the most advantageous type of activity is determined by the relative scarcity and abundance of labor, natural resources, and capital, taken in the context of the state of technical knowledge concerning methods of production and commercial intercourse with other economic areas. The new economy of colonial America had as its two outstanding features a scarcity of labor and an abundance of natural resources. As a consequence labor was relatively dear and natural resources were relatively cheap. "Economizing" involved engaging in types of activity which used relatively small amounts of dear labor and relatively large amounts of abundant natural resources. The third factor of production, capital, was also scarce, but it gradually became available, originally from Europe and subsequently from colonial accumulations.

What the English colonists attempted and what they ultimately achieved was to transplant European technology and European institutions to the New World. The primitive nature of the colonial environment, however, did not make feasible wholesale transplantation of a European type of economy. For one thing, the physical manifestations of social overhead capital in the form of roads, communications, and public utilities were entirely lacking in the colonies; and therefore European techniques did not have the same significance as they had in Europe. The absence of this social overhead capital was a serious handicap to the operation of the economy. It meant that well-trained and able people lifted out of their environment in Europe were, in the beginning, very much less productive. Even if the social overhead capital had been present in the colonies, a population of far less than optimum size would have suffered a correspondingly lower productivity. The special economic problem of the colonies was to adapt the state of the technical arts they knew from European experience to the new environment. The English colonists were an advanced people in an undeveloped country. Natural resources were abundant and the economic potential was great, but time was necessary to develop the potential into an actual wealth-creation process.

An alternative to transplanting European technology and institutions would have been to try to amalgamate the existing native (Indian) economy with European technology and institutions. Something like this happened in Mexico and South America under the Spanish and produced a mixed culture and a mixed population. Amalgamation was much less feasible in the English colonies because of the low state of the Indian culture, which was much more primitive than that of the Aztecs and Incas. In the English colonies, Europeans

had little to learn from the North American aborigines beyond a few points

about survival in the early years of settlement. Moreover, the English colonial policy generally was to avoid mixing with native populations. The English did not, as a rule, intermarry or attempt to civilize or assimilate the natives. They did not even make use of their labor power in North America. All the English wanted from the Indians was their land, and this they could and did take pretty much as they pleased, sometimes by making token payments. The Indians were more an obstacle than an asset to the development of a strictly European type of society, although in the long run they were a relatively minor obstacle because of their inability to resist European power by force. The not infrequent massacres of colonists do indicate, however, that they did sporadically resist.

Thus from the beginning the colonies were outposts of European civilization. They constituted a new Europe, or—as New Holland, New Sweden, and New France lost out—a New England. The colonists were and remained Europeans in a cultural if not in a geographical sense. One of the contemporary European practices which helped to shape the pattern of the colonial economy was mercantilism, which conceived of colonies primarily as sources of raw materials and as markets for manufactured goods. By and large the economic imperatives of the colonial situation fit reasonably well into this pattern. It was economical for the colonists to produce and export raw materials and to import manufactured goods. The colonial economy, however, changed rather rapidly; and the original position of essential harmony between colonial and metropolitan Europe became one of increasing tension under mercantilist policy. In its economic aspect the American Revolution of the late eighteenth century reflected these growing disharmonies in an intense form, especially in the northern colonies, where the resources were such as to make for competing rather than complementary types of economic endeavor.

Given the foregoing circumstances affecting resource utilization, a general economic pattern emerges. Agriculture was the most important, and manufacturing the least important, type of activity in the colonies. Agriculture utilized abundant and cheap land to give maximum returns to scarce and dear labor. Between agriculture and manufacturing lay a wide range of other activities. Next to agriculture the most important commercial industries were those in which the cheapness of raw materials and the limited amount of labor required for processing placed colonial products at a comparative advantage in the North Atlantic economy. Abundant grain led to flour milling; abundant forests to shipbuilding and the extraction of naval stores; abundant furs to hatmaking; abundant seas to fishing; abundant iron ore and coal to iron smelting and rudimentary iron processing. Maritime trading was significant because of excellent harbors, a long coast line, access by sea to European markets, and the encouragement given to some kinds of trade within the Navigation System. In addition, of course, many colonists engaged in local crafts, shopkeeping, and petty industries for meeting community and family needs.

Agriculture

Agiculture was the leading occupation in every colony. Subsistence food crops were grown everywhere, and in the middle colonies, especially Pennsyl-

vania, subsistence crops such as wheat were also the leading export, going chiefly to the West Indies. In the colonies as a whole, corn, or maize, was the principal food for domestic consumption. Unlike wheat, maize could be grown in all the colonies, including the warm southern ones. A high degree of self-sufficiency among colonial farmers limited the extent of their participation in the market. Nevertheless, hardly any colonial farmer was completely independent of the market, and a great majority had some cash crop or other activity for making money with which to purchase basic necessities such as salt, ammunition, and hardware, and to make payments on mortgages and other forms of indebtedness.

Tobacco Commercial agriculture was most highly developed in Virginia and Maryland, which were the leading producers of tobacco, the great staple of the American economy during the seventeenth and eighteenth centuries. Tobacco-growing dovetailed nicely with the mercantilist principle that raw materials should be produced in colonies, processed in the home country, and re-exported to other countries. In order to protect the colonies against competition, the British Government took the unusual step of prohibiting tobacco-growing in England despite strong protests from some English farmers. There were fiscal advantages to the Government, which levied a heavy tax on all tobacco imports. In addition there was some doubt about the quality of English-grown tobacco, and moral disapproval of tobacco was widely expressed, starting with James I, who called it a "contemptible weed." Nevertheless, the ban on English tobacco-growing reflected a genuine desire by British statesmen to help the colonies fit into the mercantilist scheme of things.

Protection of the British market for colonial tobacco was accompanied by certain disadvantages to the colonies. Tobacco was an "enumerated commodity," which meant it could be exported only to England. The tax levied on it in England was several times as great as the price paid for tobacco in the colonies. The heavy tax was justified on mercantilist grounds that tobacco was a luxury the consumption of which should be discouraged in the domestic market. In fact, encouragement to produce a luxury product could scarcely have been justified under mercantilist principles had not a large proportion of the processed tobacco been re-exported from England to European countries to improve the balance of trade. Upon re-export the high sumptuary tax was refunded. In other words, domestic consumption in England was discouraged by high taxes which caused the domestic price to be high, whereas export for foreign consumption was encouraged by rebating the high tax.

The soil of Virginia and Maryland was well suited to tobacco-growing. Land planted to this crop was many times more profitable than the same land planted to wheat or other crops. In Virginia production of tobacco increased from 16,000 pounds at Jamestown in 1616 to 500,000 pounds in 1627. In the colonies as a whole tobacco production was 100,000,000 pounds on the eve of the American Revolution. On the other hand, tobacco-growing exhausted the soil in a few years and forced planters to bring new land under cultivation. This "wasteful" exploitation of soil was possible only because land was abundant and inexpensive. Despite cheap land, tobacco-growing was frequently a marginal undertaking because of the scarcity and low physical productivity of labor, the heavy taxes on tobacco, and the fluctuating price received at the

plantation. Toward the close of the colonial period the soil of much of Virginia

and Maryland was exhausted by the failure to restore what had been taken
from it. Many tobacco planters were kept solvent by supplementary activities
in land speculation, fur trading, and general merchandising.

Rice and Indigo   South of the tobacco provinces lay the rice and indigo
colonies. Rice grew exceedingly well in the humid swamps of South Carolina,
and slave labor was well suited to its cultivation. Since rice could not be
grown in northern Europe, there was a brisk demand for the colonial staple,
which was of major significance during the first half of the eighteenth century.

In the later colonial period indigo tended to replace rice as the chief
export crop of South Carolina; indeed, during the Revolution it was the commodity form of money in the area. Indigo was a valuable dyestuff used in the
great English woolen cloth industry. In 1749 Parliament authorized a bounty
of sixpence per pound on indigo produced and exported to England. Returns
to capital invested in rice and indigo appear to have been quite high, often
ranging from 30 to 50 per cent per year.

Extractive Industries

Fur trade   The virgin forests of America were richly endowed with
animal life providing valuable furs and skins. Obtaining these products from
nearby forests was relatively simple for the early colonists. The Pilgrims paid
off their £1,800 of indebtedness to the British merchants who had financed
their settlement with funds raised mainly from the sale of furs. Beaver skins
used for making hats were the most important animal product in the northern
colonies. Deerskins for domestic clothing and for export were the most valuable
animal product in the southern colonies. Otter, mink, bear and fox were also
important pelts. As the colonies grew and as the land was cleared, fur-bearing
animals became scarcer. Indian hunters and trappers brought in skins and
hides from more remote forest areas. In the struggle for empire between the
French and the English the fur trade became one of the important issues. Wars
were fought over a vast wilderness, the chief value of which lay in the fur
trade.

Naval stores   Another important economic activity based on the rich
natural resources of the colonies was the production of naval stores. These
included tar, pitch, turpentine, masts, hemp (for ropes), and flax (for sail
cloths). Most of these were products of the forest. They were used for building
and maintaining maritime vessels of all types, including men-of-war for the
royal navy. Obviously great importance was attached to these supplies by war-
minded British mercantilists. As early as the reign of Elizabeth I the scarcity
of forests in England was a cause of alarm since Britain was becoming dependent upon the Baltic countries for its supplies of naval stores. In view of
the importance attached to self-sufficiency in mercantilist policy, especially
where anything concerning war was involved, it was logical that the colonies
of North Ameria should be looked to as an important source of supply within
the Empire. Moreover, this was consistent with the mercantilist principle of
directing colonial enterprise toward raw materials and diverting it from manufacturing. Encouragement was given to the production of naval stores in the

colonies by exhortation in the seventeenth century and by monetary bounties in the eighteenth century.

Mere exhortation did not result in a satisfactory flow of naval stores. Consequently, when difficulties with Sweden developed early in the eighteenth century and threatened to cut off the Baltic supplies, monetary bounties were offered to the colonists by the English government. It was anticipated that New England, which was otherwise a more or less worthless colony from a mercantilist point of view, might become the important source of naval stores and thus help to free Great Britain from dependence on foreign nations. New Englanders, however, showed less than the expected enthusiasm. Instead, the Carolinas became the chief colonial supplier of naval stores.[1] Although naval stores never bulked large among colonial exports, they illustrate again the mercantilist principle of giving positive encouragement, including monetary bounties, for certain colonial products.

Shipbuilding   A third extractive industry based on the forest resources of the colonies was shipbuilding. Shipbuilding in England was handicapped by the high price of domestic timber and the high transportation cost of imported timber. Since ships provided their own transportation to England, they were an ideal type of product for distant colonial construction. Under the British Navigation Acts colonial ships were given the same privileges as English-built ships.[2] This policy encouraged shipbuilding in the colonies. New England became the center of a flourishing industry which supplied its own as well as English merchants with ships.

Fisheries   Offshore and deep-sea fishing was another leading extractive industry participated in by the North American colonies. In addition to the fish-infested coastal waters of New England, colonial fishermen competed with the men of other nations in the famous Newfoundland banks, where Europeans had come to fish since very early times—in all probability long before the formal discovery of America by Columbus. Cod was by far the most important type of fish, but many other varieties were caught, including mackerel, halibut, haddock, and herring. Among New England's exports, fish was an important item. Although colonial merchants were not permitted under mercantilist regulations to sell fish in England or in north European markets, they were allowed to trade them in southern Europe. Here they marketed the better quality catch. The poorer quality was sold to the West Indies as food for slaves on sugar plantations.

Whaling was a special type of deep-sea activity in which New Englanders excelled. They started in nearby fisheries, expanded into the Greenland whale fisheries, and as the supply of whales in the North Atlantic diminished, the Yankee whalers fished in the distant waters of the Antarctic. Spermaceti (melted and refined blubber) was used for making candles, and whale oil was used in lamps and as a lubricant for machinery. Fisheries created a demand for ships and gave stimulus to the New England shipbuilding industry.

Iron   Iron production was encouraged in the colonies because the scarcity of domestic timber in England meant a shortage of charcoal with

---

[1] Hence the name "tar-heels" for North Carolinians.
[2] The British Navigation System will be explained in Chapter 12.

which to convert iron ore into pig iron. Technology in the iron industry did

not permit the use of coal for smelting iron ore before 1750. Of Britain's annual
consumption of 40,000 tons of iron in the early eighteenth century, about one-
half was imported from other European countries, mostly from Sweden. When
Sweden levied an additional 25 per cent tax on its iron exports, the British
government turned seriously to the colonies for a substitute source of supply.

Although the colonial iron industry had started shortly after the first
settlements, its rapid expansion dates from about 1720. Given the acute shortage of fuel in England and its superabundance in the colonies, the mercantilistic philosophy called for colonial production of pig iron, and possibly bar
(semi-wrought) iron, with the manufacture of iron wares reserved for British
producers. If pig and bar iron are viewed as raw materials for iron manufacturing, then their production in the colonies and the manufacture of iron
wares from these raw materials in the home country was consistent with mercantilist policy. As a corollary, further processing of iron manufacture in the
colonies was to be discouraged. This was the principle behind the Iron Act
of 1750. It encouraged colonial production of pigs and bars by permitting
them to enter England duty free. The intent was to provide British manufacturers of iron products with an abundant and cheap supply of iron.

The same act attempted to discourage iron manufacturing in the colonies
by prohibiting "the erection of slitting and rolling mills, and plate, forge, and
steel furnaces." Furnaces for making cast iron were not prohibited as this
would have been difficult because of their close connection with smelting iron
ore. The law did not require that iron manufactories already erected in the
colonies be dismantled. Many household utensils and farm implements continued to be made in the colonies for colonial consumption. At the end of the
colonial period iron production reached 30,000 tons annually. Most of this was
pig and bar iron for export to England; in 1764 iron was placed on the
"enumerated" list of commodities which could be exported only to England.
The colonial iron industry concentrated first in Connecticut, Massachusetts,
Maryland, and Virginia and was spreading into Pennsylvania and New Jersey
at the end of the colonial period.

MANUFACTURING AND THE SCARCITY OF LABOR

Commercial manufacturing was of minor significance in colonial America.
There were two reasons for this: mercantilist restrictions and the underlying
economic circumstances of the colonial environment. The latter was much more
important throughout the colonial era. Mercantilist limitations on manufacturing possibly became more important as the colonies developed economically,
but even at the close of the colonial period they were much less important
than the underlying economic conditions.

High Opportunity Cost of Free Labor

Scarcity of labor was the chief economic factor which limited the extent
of commercial manufacturing in the colonies. As compared with other major
types of economic activity, manufacturing requires large quantities of labor.
Labor can be economically allocated to manufacturing only if it is either very

cheap or highly productive. Dearness or cheapness of labor is a relative matter which can be measured only in terms of alternative ways in which the labor might be employed. The concept of "opportunity cost" [3] introduced earlier is useful in this connection. The opportunity cost of any economic activity is the alternative which is sacrificed by employing resources in that use rather than in the best alternative use. If a man works in a factory, he cannot work on a farm at the same time; hence his potential farm produce is the sacrificed alternative.

The opportunity cost of employing manpower in colonial manufacturing was high measured in relation to the alternative opportunities available for employment in agriculture, extractive industries, and commerce. Manufacturers had to pay wages high enough to attract workers out of agriculture, extractive industries, and commerce. Usually it was cheaper to purchase manufactured goods from Europe than to pay the prices necessary to cover the high wage costs of manufacturing in the colonies. The governor of New York put the issue succinctly when he wrote in 1767: "The price of labour is so great in this part of the world that it will always prove the greatest obstacle to any manufacturers attempted to be set up here, and the genius of the People in a Country where everyone can have Land to work upon leads them so naturally into Agriculture that it prevails over every other occupation." [4]

Apart from articles made for self-consumption, the colonies relied mainly on European manufactured goods. Whereas colonial labor was scarce and natural resources almost unlimited, European labor was relatively abundant and natural resources relatively scarce. The relative advantage to both the colonies and the European nations lay, therefore, in trading European manufactures for colonial raw materials and semiprocessed goods. The putting-out system of Europe depended for labor upon rural workers who were not fully employed in agriculture, either because they held too little land or because of the seasonal nature of agriculture or because some members of the family had labor-time which could not be fully used in agriculture. Colonists also spun and wove in their spare time, but mainly for family consumption. There was no lack of natural resources to which to apply their labor. Only in a few instances such as the boot and shoe industry in New England did the capitalist putting-out system of commercial manufacture occupy a significant position in colonial America.

Easy access to natural resources in the colonies was prejudicial to capitalistic activity of all types because free men preferred to work for themselves on farms or elsewhere rather than to labor for the profit of someone else, whether in a factory, a workshop, or on a farm. In any new economy free men tend to work for themselves on the natural resources that are cheap or free for the taking. Consequently the owners of large capital and large estates experience difficulty in procuring the labor of other men necessary for the productive utilization of their factors of production. Free laborers may be induced to work as wage-earners on farms and in other callings if the wages offered are sufficient to offset the advantages of self-employment. Professor

[3] See Chapter 4 on the "Decline of the Manorial System."
[4] *Documents Relative to the Colonial History of New York*, ed. by E. B. O'Callaghan (Albany: 1856–1887), VII, 888–89, cited in E. L. Bogart and C. M. Thompson, *Readings in the Economic History of the United States*, p. 67.

Morris, the historian of labor in the colonies, has pointed out that the main

objective of colonial workmen was security through agriculture rather than employment in industry. Although high wages were necessary to induce men to labor in the service of others, they had the paradoxical effect of shortening the period of time required for the wage-earner to save enough to purchase land for his self-employment.[5]

High wages were the corollary of easy access to natural resources. Writing in the 1770's, Adam Smith observed that wages were higher in the English colonies of North America than anywhere else in the world. Professor Morris records the story of a master who had to sell two oxen in order to pay wages to his servant. When the master told his servant he saw no prospect of being able to continue to pay him wages, the servant suggested he should sell more cattle. "What shall I do when they are gone?" asked the master. "You can serve me and get them back," replied the servant.[6] Such were the obstacles to transplanting from Europe to America the capitalist relation between free labor and owners of the means of production.

Forced Labor: Slavery and Indentured Servants

In view of the great scarcity of free labor, a system of forced labor developed in the colonies. Forced laborers were of two types, slaves and indentured servants. The common basis for both types of forced labor lay in the need of owners of capital equipment for labor of some type. Abundance of means of production and the scarcity of free labor combined to produce forced labor. The pressures making for this type of social relation were suggested by Edward Wakefield, a well-known writer on the theory of colonization: "If all the members of the society are supposed to possess equal portions of capital . . . no man would have a motive for accumulating more capital than he could use with his own hands. This is to some extent the case in new American settlements, where a passion for owning land prevents the existence of a class of laborers for hire."[7] Wakefield observed that slavery had been about the only basis for producing capitalist wealth in a colonial economy with abundant land.

Of the two forms of forced labor, indentured servitude was used earlier and more extensively. As a conservative estimate, one-half of the total white immigrants to the thirteen colonies came as indentured servants. In the first half-century of colonial settlement, the number of immigrant indentured servants far exceeded the number of Negro slaves immigrating to Virginia. Slavery, that is, full servitude, became the dominant form of forced labor in the South only after limited servitude based on indenture proved unequal to the demands of expanding capitalist agriculture utilizing the plantation system of landholding.

An indenture is a formal agreement in which a servant agrees to serve a master for a specified period of time. In the colonies the period was usually

[5] Richard B. Morris, *Government and Labor in Early America* (New York: Columbia University Press, 1946), p. 48.

[6] Morris, *Government and Labor*, p. 45.

[7] Edward G. Wakefield, *England and America* (New York: Harper & Bros., 1834), II, 17.

four or five years for adults and longer for children and convicts. The indenture was attested to by a contract, normally in written form. It differed from an ordinary labor contract in that the master could compel the indentured servant to carry out his contract by specific performance.[8]

A majority of the indentured servants coming to the colonies entered the contractual arrangement voluntarily. They were often people of ambition with insufficient means to transport and establish themselves in the colonies. They hoped to improve their position in the long run by voluntarily submitting to a temporary period of servitude.

Although a majority of indentured servants assumed their status voluntarily, there were large numbers who entered servitude involuntarily. Among the latter were debtors, criminals deported by the courts, paupers on public relief, vagrants, and victims of force and fraud who were kidnapped off the streets of European cities. Upon arrival in the colonies these involuntary "recruits" were sold at good prices by ship captains and agents. Because many such persons resented the plight into which they had fallen against their will and because of the opportunities for economic independence, there was serious difficulty in enforcing indentures. Masters were permitted to punish runaways by whipping and by extending the period of servitude. On the other hand, indentured servants enjoyed more legal rights than slaves and were usually much better off than slaves in the economic as well as in the legal sense.

As a device for increasing the mobility of labor there is, of course, something to be said in favor of indentures. No matter how rich the natural resources of a country may be, enterprise cannot flourish without manpower. Regardless of their economic potential, resources have no economic value unless there is human labor to develop them. This probably explains why, in periods of great and rapid expansion, forced labor in one form or another has been a standard device for meeting the cost and overcoming the inertia to human migration. Impatient men of enterprise have used and abused their fellow men in order to get things done in a hurry. Indenture avoids the degradation of full slavery and is more temporary and flexible than serfdom. It promises advantage to both master and servant if properly administered. On the other hand, indenture is subject to many abuses. It has been unconstitutional in the United States since passage of the Thirteenth Amendment, and has gradually been outlawed throughout the world.

Whatever the defects of forced labor, its importance in the economic development of the American colonies was very great since all Negroes came as slaves and at least one-half of all white immigrants came as indentured servants. While indentured servitude may be used under any form of economic system, it was especially important in the early stage of capitalism because it created the conditions necessary for the employment of capital which owners could not employ with their own labor. Unequal access (in the economic but not necessarily legal sense) to the means of production is a requisite of capitalistic forms of production. In the United States the existence of cheap and abundant land retarded the development of capitalist institutions during the colonial period. Slavery in the South and indentured servants in the North

---

[8] A free laborer who enters a contract to work for someone else cannot be compelled to perform the actual work. He can, of course, be sued for damages resulting from failure to fulfill the terms of the contract, provided the court rules the terms are reasonable.

overcame some of the disadvantages of the abundance of cheap land. Manufacturing did not develop rapidly in the United States until large-scale immigration from Europe began in the second half of the nineteenth century.
Under classical capitalism, legal and political restraints, which marked the
early capitalist period, ceased to be the basis of economic dependence of the
wage-earning classes.

Mercantilist Restrictions on Manufacturing

Insofar as mercantilist legislation was used to curb colonial manufacturing
it tended to operate by limiting the market for colonial products. The Woolen
Act of 1699, which was intended to crush the manufacture of woolen yarn or
cloth in the colonies, prohibited the shipment of yarn and cloth from one
colony to another, or to England, or to any other place outside the colony of
manufacture. It did not prohibit manufacture for sale within the colony where
it was produced. Since capitalistic manufacture requires an extensive market,
for practical purposes limiting the market was almost as effective as prohibition of manufacturing itself. In a similar way the Hat Act of 1732 limited the
market. The cheapness of beaver skins in New England gave rise to commercial hat-making, whereupon the Hat Act prohibited the sale of hats outside the colony in which they were manufactured. Another provision of the
Hat Act required a seven-year apprenticeship, which was much too long for
any colonial resident to tie up his labor in training for a trade.

In summary, it may be said that economic conditions were more important than mercantilist legislation in accounting for the general lack of
manufacturing in the American colonies. The scarcity of labor and the abundance of land rather than legal restrictions of the British government were
the important considerations in explaining the structure of the colonial economy. Moreover, the labor which was available for employment by others,
consisting mainly of slaves and indentured servants, was a type generally
unsuited for manufacturing.

The fact that mercantilistic policy did relatively little harm to colonial
manufacturing suggests mainly that legislation was incapable of influencing
industry one way or the other. However, in the types of economic activity
for which colonial resources were better suited, imperial mercantilism was
capable of doing considerable damage to colonial interests. Colonial merchants
engaged in maritime commerce were at no special economic disadvantage in
competition with English merchants, and they could be injured by the enforcement of discriminatory legislation aimed at colonial commerce. The following
chapter examines the pattern of colonial commerce and the economic forces
leading to the American Revolutionary War.

SELECTED BIBLIOGRAPHY

(Selected Bibliography: See end of Chapter 12.)

The Decline of Mercantilism
and the American Revolution

CHAPTER **12**

COLONIAL COMMERCE

Colonial commerce reflected the internal economic development of
agriculture and industry. Manufactured goods loomed large among total
imports, and exports consisted chiefly of products of agriculture and extractive industries. Foreign trade was more affected than agriculture and manufacturing by the political framework within which the colonies operated as a
part of the British empire. The Acts of Trade and Commerce making up the
Navigation System were the aspects of British mercantilism most important
for colonial commerce.

Navigation System

Although the British Navigation System dated as far back as the Middle
Ages, it was codified and systematized by the Navigation Acts of 1651 and
1660 at a time when the English government came under the influence of the
commercial classes as a result of the English Revolution. This was an important aspect of the shift in British mercantilism from internal to external
state-building. The Navigation Laws sought to make England a stronger
maritime nation, an objective which required more ships and more sailors for
peace and war.

One important tactic used to further mercantilist aims was to place all
colonial trade in the hands of the British and keep it out of the hands of
foreigners, especially the Dutch. Previously the Dutch had traded extensively
with British colonies. Under the Navigation Laws all goods shipped into and
out of the colonies had to be carried in British ships. For the purpose of these
laws colonial ships were treated as British ships. Ships of European nations
were allowed to carry goods from their own country to England and Wales,
but transshipment to the colonies had to be in British (including colonial)
ships. The monopoly of colonial trade was intended to strike at the Dutch
and to encourage British shipbuilding, increase the number of British sailors,
increase revenues of the British government, and increase the profits of commercial classes in the British empire.

A second important device for controlling colonial trade was the list of

"enumerated articles." Commodities on the enumerated list were the important colonial raw materials, which had to be sent to England directly from the colonies and could not be sold anywhere else. The list was revised from time to time, but the important commodities included tobacco, sugar, indigo, cotton, rice, naval stores, beaver and other furs. Control of enumerated commodities assured English manufacturers a good supply of raw materials and buttressed the objectives sought in connection with control over shipping.

Patterns of Colonial Commerce

The mainland colonies south of Pennsylvania carried on a shuttle trade with England. Tobacco, which was always the leading single export from the colonies as a whole, was shipped from Virginia and Maryland directly to England in British ships, which returned with cargoes of manufactured goods. Maryland also exported flour while the Carolinas exported rice, indigo, and naval stores. All of these exports except flour were enumerated commodities. The chief import other than manufactured goods was slaves, which came by way of the West Indies. As a rule trade between the southern colonies and England was fairly well balanced. In some years it favored the colonies and in other years it favored England.

The colonies north of the Mason-Dixon line engaged in a more complex trade than the colonies to the south. Their leading exports were foodstuffs, which were not wanted in England. Pennsylvania and New York exported mostly wheat. Under the Corn Laws England maintained a policy designed to achieve self-sufficiency in grain until the end of the colonial period. New England's leading export was fish, but England had its own fisheries and did not welcome colonial competition. Consequently the northern colonies were in a position of having to buy their manufactured goods from England without being able to sell to England. In order to pay for English manufactured goods the northern colonists had to sell in third markets to get exchange or specie with which to pay for English imports. These circumstances account for the complex nature of the northern trade in contrast with the shuttle trade of the tobacco colonies. Although the northern trade was multilateral in nature, for simplicity in exposition it may be treated as triangular.

On one triangle, for example, the three points were southern Europe, England and the northern colonies. New England merchants carried grain, fish, lumber, and meat to southern Europe, where these products were exchanged for wine and fruit and usually some hard money. Wine and fruits were then carried to England, and sold; next a cargo of manufactured goods would be loaded for shipment to the colonies. Sometimes Yankee skippers sold their ships (built in New England) in England after completing two sides of the triangle. Colonists were not permitted to sell to the Continental countries in northern Europe; English merchants wanted these markets reserved to themselves. It may be noted that the purchase of goods like wine and fruit in southern Europe meant the empire was not living up to the mercantilist ideal of self-sufficiency, and these imports were criticized by some mercantilist writers.

A second triangle might have its three points in the West Indies, England, and the northern colonies. Fish, flour, lumber, and meat were exported

to the West Indies, where they were exchanged for sugar and molasses. These commodities were then taken to England, where they were exchanged for manufactured goods for the colonies. The sugar and molasses imported by England were either consumed or re-exported to the Continent.

A third triangle could have its corners in the West Indies, the Slave Coast of Africa, and the northern colonies. From the sugar plantations of the West Indies molasses was carried to New England, where it was manufactured into rum, which was in turn shipped to the Slave Coast to be exchanged for slaves and gold for shipment to the West Indies. Some slaves might be carried to the mainland colonies on the return trip to New England. The Slave Coast and Gold Coast trade via the West Indies was also a source of specie for the mainland colonies. Rum-making in New England was the only important colonial manufacture involving the use of an imported raw material, and foreshadowed New England's incipient capacity for manufacturing.

Not all northern colonial commerce was in triangles. Some skippers shuttled between New England and the West Indies, taking flour and fish to the islands and bringing back molasses to the mainland. Some Yankee ships carried naval stores and lumber to England and returned with manufactured goods. In general, however, the contrast between the foreign commerce of the southern and the northern states was quite distinct. Southern commerce was primarily a shuttle trade; northern commerce was primarily triangular and multilateral, with direct trade the exception.

ECONOMIC BACKGROUND
OF THE AMERICAN REVOLUTION

As seen through mercantilist eyes a good colony was one which complemented the economic activities of the parent country. Colonies which by geographic location or natural endowment were capable of producing commodities that could not be produced in the parent country were considered most valuable. Colonies which were similar to the parent country were viewed as actual or potential competitors. Sugar-producing Jamaica and Barbados were excellent colonies, and tobacco-producing Virginia and Maryland fitted nicely into the mercantilist scheme. New England fit poorly because its potentialities lay mainly in trade and manufacture, while its exported foodstuffs (fish and wheat) were not welcome in England. In its underdeveloped stage, however, New England was probably more of a nuisance than a threat to imperial Britain.

Besides supplying raw materials, colonies were supposed to provide markets for manufactured products of the parent country. Herein lay one of the basic dilemmas, nay contradictions, of mercantilism. New England could pay for English goods only if permitted to develop trade and manufacturing, but if these activities developed too far they became competitive with the trade and industry of England. The northern colonies were able to pay for English imports with the foreign exchange and specie gained from the flourishing West Indian trade. There were no gold mines in New England nor in the middle colonies. Without the foreign exchange or specie gained in the West

Indies, England could have "collected" its favorable balance of trade with the northern colonies only by investing heavily in them. However, mercantilist policy did not advocate investment in colonies, and even if it had, the northern colonies were the least desirable for British investment because the most advantageous opportunities were in activities directly competitive with British home investments. Imperial capitalists invested much more capital in the West Indies and in the southern mainland colonies than in the northern mainland colonies. At the end of the colonial period, for example, British investments in the several types of American colonies were as follows: West Indies, £60,000,000; southern mainland colonies, £4,000,000; northern mainland colonies, negligible.

West Indies Trade

Because the West Indies occupied so strategic a position in the trade of both England and the northern colonies, a brief description of the economy of these Caribbean islands is necessary in order to understand the commercial rivalries which contributed to the American Revolutionary War. Rivalries were not just between Great Britain and its colonies, but also between groups of colonists, especially between the British West Indian sugar planters and the New England merchants.

The West Indies were the chief source of Europe's sugar supply in the seventeenth and eighteenth centuries. In the seventeenth century the British West Indies produced most of the sugar consumed in Europe, but during the eighteenth century competition was encountered from the French and Dutch West Indies. Nevertheless, sugar continued to be the most important single commodity in the foreign trade of Great Britain during the eighteenth century. In addition to sugar, the West Indies also produced tobacco, cotton, fruits, and other tropical products. So great was the degree of specialization in the West Indies that they were dependent upon outside supplies of foodstuffs as well as manufactured goods. The latter came from Europe; the former came largely from the North American mainland. Flour from Pennsylvania and fish from New England were the important staples. Negro slaves on the island plantations ate third-grade New England fish and second-grade Pennsylvania flour. Many more slaves were used in the West Indies than on the mainland. The slave trade itself was a valuable source of income for New England merchants.

The Spanish, Dutch, and French, as well as the British, possessed islands in the West Indies. The Spanish claim was established through Columbus, but with the decline of Spain as a great power, many Spanish colonies were seized by rival European nations. In the eighteenth century the remaining Spanish islands (Cuba and Puerto Rico) lagged in economic development. The Dutch were mainly interested in developing the carrying trade among all the islands and especially those of Spain. All the West Indies were dependent upon northern mainland British colonies for fish, flour, and lumber. The Navigation Acts legally excluded the Dutch from carrying supplies from the English colonies to Dutch colonies or from carrying sugar and other produce directly to the English colonies.

The French West Indies figured most prominently in a conflict of interest which became a leading source of friction between Great Britain and the northern mainland merchants and was a major factor in the economic background of the American Revolution. Under the principles of mercantilism, New England merchants were supposed to purchase molasses only from the British West Indies (Jamaica and Barbados). They discovered, however, that they could trade on much more favorable terms with the French West Indies (Martinique, Guadeloupe, and Santo Domingo). British molasses was subject to a special export tax which the colonial merchants avoided by purchasing from the French islands. French planters were not permitted to sell rum in Europe because it would compete with French brandy, which was given favored treatment under French mercantilist policies. In addition to these important advantages, the French sugar plantations were more efficient than the British. The British West Indies had dominated the sugar trade during the seventeenth century, but in the eighteenth century the French plantations gained rapidly because they were newer, had better soil, and were better managed than British plantations. French planters were typically residents of the West Indies, whereas the British were more frequently absentee planters residing in England and sitting as members of a powerful sugar bloc in the House of Commons. Others viewed their residence in the West Indies as temporary. Adam Smith attributed the superiority of French plantations especially to the superior management of slaves.

As good merchants, if not as good subjects, the colonists preferred to purchase where the goods were cheapest. The British sugar planters protested against the New Englanders trading with the French and in 1731 just failed to obtain passage through Parliament of a bill which would have forbidden the importation of foreign sugar, rum, or molasses into any part of the British empire, including the colonies. Two years later in 1733 the same objective was achieved by passage of the famous Molasses Act, which placed prohibitive duties on the import of foreign molasses. Had this act been enforced, it would have diverted colonial trade from the French to the British Indies. However, it was not enforced. In the three decades following 1733 smuggling on a grand scale became a cornerstone of New England's commercial capitalism. Massachusetts is said to have smuggled twenty-five times as much molasses as it imported legally. Several dozen rum distilleries flourished in Massachusetts and Rhode Island. The most important use of rum was in the slave trade, but it was also used in the fur trade with the Indians.

While New England's rum distilleries and merchants flourished on the illicit molasses trade, the British West Indian sugar planters suffered from loss of business. In Parliament the sugar bloc was in a position to exert pressure for favorable legislation, but under the British policy of "salutory neglect" before 1763 they were unable to obtain effective enforcement of the Molasses Act against the New England smugglers. The end of the long war between France and England (1756–63), however, provided an opportunity to bring more serious charges against the New England merchants. They were accused of having continued to trade with the "enemy" during the war. This was probably true; they sold supplies to the French as well as to the

British, and this treasonable behavior was used by the British planters to force

the government to tighten the screws on New England's smugglers and traitors.

At the close of the war as part of a general program to enforce the colonial system the Sugar Act of 1764 was passed. It lowered the import duty on foreign molasses and sugar in order to weaken the incentive to smuggle. More important, strong measures were taken to enforce the law and to punish smugglers. Prominent New England merchants, including John Hancock, had their ships seized by British customs officials and were threatened with fines and imprisonment. When Parliament cracked the whip, these wealthy, conservative, peace-loving New England merchants, who had created a bristling capitalism of their own, were prepared to listen to a call for drastic action. They would not passively tolerate having their interests subordinated to those of princely West Indian planters or imperial British capitalists. Under the old colonial system of "salutory neglect," the New England merchants expanded outside the lawful limits of mercantilism. After 1763 strict enforcement by the British led to an inevitable collision between imperial British commercial capitalism and expanding colonial New England capitalism. A small group of New England merchants provided the leadership and wealth which was indispensable for carrying on the ensuing fight for economic and political independence.

Southern Planters and Western Lands

Another major source of conflict between British and American interest arose in connection with the imperial policy toward western lands. Before 1763 the rich Ohio Valley as well as Canada was a French possession. British policy had been to encourage settlement in the west as a means of encroaching on the French, who had only sparsely settled the territory and whose control over it was tenuous at best. When the French were driven from the mainland, the North American fur trade fell into British hands, and the empire builders in London had to decide upon a policy for developing their newly acquired real estate. They decided in accordance with mercantilist ideology in favor of imperial interests and against colonial interests that the lucrative fur trade would be endangered by too rapid settlement of the wild lands of the West. Since too many settlers would spoil the fur trade—when settlers move in, the fur-bearing animals move out—British policy changed from one of encouraging settlement to one of cautious and controlled development.

Colonial capitalists did not take kindly to this new policy toward western lands. They had visions of great profits from the development of this territory. Seaboard farmers, including southern planters, had moved westward since the beginning of the colonial period. They had supplemented tobacco planting and small-scale farming with speculation in western real estate. The interest of George Washington as a young man in surveying is indicative of the concern of planter families with real estate development in the west. By the close of the war with France colonists were moving across the mountains into the valleys beyond. Planters were speculating in lands of present-day West Virginia and Ohio. George Washington wrote of the desirability of shifting the emphasis in Virginia's trade from tobacco to wheat by developing the back

country. Ohio was superior to Virginia for wheat cultivation. Virginians made claims and attempted to obtain control of the entire Ohio territory. Although no one knew just how rich were the natural resources of the American West, land speculators, planters, farmers, and merchants in the eastern colonies knew it was rich enough to be worth fighting for. The western frontier was second only to the trade of the Atlantic as an outlet for expanding American enterprise.

Under mercantilism it was inevitable that British policymakers would decide the conflict of interest between the American and the British in favor of the latter. Beginning with a Royal Proclamation in 1763 and culminating in the Quebec Act of 1774, the American colonists were legally excluded from the West. By the Proclamation of 1763 all land west of the crest of the Appalachian Mountains was placed under the direct control of imperial authority. The right of colonial governors to authorize surveys and to make land grants was forbidden. The attempt by Virginia to dominate the Ohio Valley was dealt a serious blow. In effect the Proclamation of 1763 meant that no colonial frontiersmen, land speculators, or planters could acquire land in the trans-Appalachian West. Squatters who had already ventured into this territory were ordered to withdraw. The British gave as the main justification for their new policy the pacification of the Indians, who, under Pontiac, had risen against the English settlers in 1763 and killed many of them. Whatever the real motives behind the new land policy, the power of colonial governments and the activities of colonial capitalists were curbed by the Royal Proclamation of 1763.

British control of the Ohio territory and the exclusion of colonial opportunity for economic expansion were further extended by the Quebec Act of 1774. By this law the land north of the Ohio River was annexed to the province of Quebec. The effect was to channel the fur trade through Montreal, where British merchants had replaced French merchants after 1763. Philadelphia and New York were bypassed as coastal outlets for the fur trade. While the ostensible purpose behind British policy was still to pacify the Indians and to preserve the territory for fur trading, Professor Nettels has stated, "The restrictive policy applied to the thirteen colonies did not mean, however, that British investors and speculators were being ignored. After 1763 the Crown conferred numerous large tracts upon merchants, army officers, and wealthy landowners (all residents of Britain). . . . Britain created speculative opportunities for her own investors while opposing the schemes of colonial promoters to develop the trans-Allegheny West." [1]

Among the colonial groups affected, the most important for the American Revolution were the southern planters. They, along with others, were alienated as loyal British subjects by a discriminatory and restrictive land policy. The wealthy, conservative plantation owners included the most able leaders in the southern colonies. They first sought an alleviation of their grievances, and failing that, they joined forces with other groups in the colonies seeking to overthrow the existing government.

[1] Curtis P. Nettels, *The Roots of American Civilization* (New York: Appleton-Century-Crofts, 1939), p. 610.

Leadership of the New England merchants and southern planters was essential to the success of the revolutionary movement, but so was widespread popular resistance to British rule. Ready support for radical changes was forthcoming among large numbers of the small farmers, small tradesmen, artisans, and laborers. These underprivileged groups had long-standing grievances against restrictions on their political and economic freedom within the colonies. They sought the right to vote, which on the eve of the Revolution was restricted to men of property of a specified amount. In Philadelphia, the largest city in the colonies, only one man in fifty owned enough property to vote. Back-country farmers sought equal representation for their districts in the colonial legislatures, which were usually dominated by a minority of tidewater merchants and planters. These radical democrats who sought more popular rule in colonial government included among their demands free access to new lands, elimination of quitrents, elimination of entail and primogeniture, and the right of colonies to issue paper money. They welcomed a revolution against British rule as a means of winning their own freedom within the colonies. Their interests often ran directly counter to those of the wealthy merchants and aristocratic planters, but special circumstances united them in an alliance with the privileged colonial classes against a common enemy.

The two principal factors which brought the smouldering discontent of the underprivileged groups to the surface in the dozen years before the Revolution were an economic depression and the repressive measures imposed by the British government upon the colonies. During the years of the French war, 1756–63, the colonies had enjoyed prosperity. This war prosperity was followed by a postwar depression after 1763. Frontier farmers were less affected than most groups, but all the seacoast population felt the decline in the volume of trade and the fall in prices. The depression was not severe by standards of the nineteenth and twentieth centuries, but it was sufficiently felt to engender social unrest and to make the lower middle classes conscious of their inferior status within the colonial society.

Some of the several measures adopted by the British government after 1763 were wide enough in their incidence to be significant in molding public sympathy for strong counteraction. Whereas the Sugar Act affected directly only a few influential New England merchants and the Proclamation Line of 1763 affected only a limited number of planters and frontiersmen, the Currency Act of 1764 forbidding the colonies to issue paper money was felt by debtors generally throughout the colonies.

The Stamp Act (1765) provided a focal point for propaganda in all the colonies even though it was negligible in its effect upon the multitude of colonists and was repealed within twelve months of its imposition as a result of protests from the colonies and from British merchants, who were severely injured by the nonimportation policy of the colonies. The Stamp Act hit directly publishers and lawyers, the two groups most sensitive to incursions on freedom of the press and freedom of speech. Publishers provided the chief media for expressions of public opinion, whereas lawyers were the chief politicians agitating for political action—hence, the inflammatory denuncia-

tions of the law in the press and in the colonial assemblies. Moreover, the Stamp Act, as well as certain other measures passed at about the same time, was an *internal* tax levied *by the British* and as such was contrary to precedent in colonial affairs. Previously internal taxes had been levied only by or with the consent of colonial governments for purposes directly beneficial to individual colonies. Imperial taxes had formerly been confined to import and export duties. Had the Stamp Act been allowed to go unchallenged, it might have become the forerunner of other internal taxes by the Crown and Parliament. Although the Stamp Act was repealed quickly, the principle of the right of the British government to tax was reasserted in the Declaratory Act, which provided "that the said colonies and plantations in America have been, are, and of right ought to be, subordinate unto, and dependent upon the imperial crown and parliament of Great Britain."

Leaders of the radical democrats included Samuel Adams of Massachusetts and Patrick Henry of Virginia. Tom Paine was the foremost pamphleteer of their cause. Fellow travelers included Thomas Jefferson, whose social outlook transcended his personal status as an aristocratic planter, and Benjamin Franklin, who spoke the philosophy of the artisan from whose ranks he had risen to a position of great wealth and influence. These men wanted a social revolution within the colonies and believed it could be carried through if British rule were relaxed or eliminated. The conservatives, on the other hand, feared the revolution not only because it represented treason against the established government, but also because they feared it would mean setting up liberties against privilege within the colonies. In the early phase of the revolution, including the writing of the Declaration of Independence and the formulation of state constitutions, the radicals held the upper hand in colonial politics. By the time the Constitution was adopted in 1789, they had fallen from power.

In proclaiming the inequities of British rule, it was necessary to stress the rights of all the colonists, and not just those of the wealthy and aristocratic minority. Such declarations by conservatives were often but a smoke screen to cloak real motives. If, for example, "taxation without representation" were to be a general principle, it must apply to the right of the poorer colonists who were being taxed but not permitted to vote in colonial elections, as well as to the right of all the colonies to be represented in Parliament if they were to be taxed by Parliament. The necessity of speaking for the liberty of all the colonists, if any at all were to be spoken for, forced the conservatives into the position of seeming to support the claims of the underprivileged within the colonies. This was not consistent with the habits of thought of large property owners, who feared the masses. While this became obvious in the struggle for the Constitution, it did result in a radical upsurge in the first phase of the struggle for independence.

British statesmen and other defenders of the Old Colonial System probably believed quite sincerely that the colonists were well off under the existing economic and political arrangements—that they were indeed fortunate to be a party to the "colonial pact." Certainly there were many advantages which were specifically given or which accrued to the colonists as part of the British empire. Their trading vessels and their seacoast enjoyed the protection of the finest navy in the world. The colonies were protected against Indian

attack by British soldiers. Colonial ships and colonial sailors had the same

privileges as British ships and sailors under the Navigation System. The colonies traded in protected markets in Britain and in other colonies, with tobacco the most conspicuous but by no means the only example. British colonists enjoyed greater freedom than colonists anywhere else in the world. In matters relating to local affairs they were permitted political autonomy. They had colonial legislatures.

Actually, the colonists felt the denial of some political rights more than ordinary Englishmen because they enjoyed more rights than ordinary Englishmen. It was their long experience in local self-government that made success in and after the Revolution possible. Moreover, there could be no doubt of the general economic prosperity of the colonies despite temporary depressions. Wages were higher in the North American colonies than anywhere else in the world, and much higher than in England. The richest Americans were not as wealthy as the richest Britons, but there were many affluent merchants in the colonies. Hence there were good reasons for paternalistic British statesmen to be incensed by the charge that they were oppressing their colonial "children."

Without undertaking to describe all the complexities, an attempt has been made to throw some light on the role of economic factors in the revolutionary movement by indicating the position of two strategic groups—the New England merchants and the southern planters. Despite the favorable economic and political conditions of the colonists, these two normally conservative groups joined in a forceful revolution to overthrow the legally constituted government. The mass support of the lower middle class was conditioned more by political than by economic considerations. It arose from a desire for a revolution within the revolution.

THE AMERICAN REVOLUTIONARY WAR

The Revolutionary War did not change in any fundamental way the course of American economic development. The United States remained an economic colony of Great Britain, importing manufactured goods and exporting raw materials and foodstuffs. After a period of readjustment from the inevitable disruptions of war, United States foreign trade continued to be mainly with England just as it had been during the colonial regime. Manufacturing did not develop rapidly because most manufactured products could be purchased much more cheaply from England than they could be produced in the United States. The close of the American Revolution coincided with the upsurge of England's Industrial Revolution, which increased the relative advantage of England in manufacturing and the relative advantage of the United States in nonmanufactured products. Post-Revolutionary events suggest strongly that mercantile restrictions upon trade and manufacturing were much less important in determining the allocation of resources than were underlying economic conditions, because the elimination of these restrictions was accompanied by relatively little change in the main pattern of economic activity.

Although the Revolution was not a turning point in American economic development, it did, of course, have economic effects. One was the redistribution of wealth, especially landed property confiscated in the Revolution. An-

other economic effect was the readjustment in shipping, which now was forced to operate outside the British Navigation System. A third effect was in the public and private finance associated with the cost of the war and the distribution of its burden in the postwar era, along with the necessity for creating a new monetary system in the independent United States. The first two will be discussed briefly here. The third will be taken up in connection with the financial program of Alexander Hamilton in the next chapter.

Land Redistribution

Many large colonial landholders remained loyal to the British Crown after the outbreak of the Revolution, although thousands of loyalists, including the big landholders, fled to Canada and elsewhere to save their lives. Their property was confiscated by individual states and the land was sold or given to patriots. The loyalists hoped that the Revolution would fail and that with the restoration of law and order they would receive back their lands. At the end of the Revolution five thousand dispossessed loyalists asked the British government to compensate them for their lost property. They received only a fraction of their requests. Land taken from loyalists fell mainly into the hands of men who were already wealthy and were in a position to purchase it or to manipulate a land grant to their advantage. Huge areas of settled land and still greater amounts of unsettled land were gobbled up by promoters who organized land companies and purchased land warrants at low prices. These land warrants, though given as compensation to men who fought in the Revolution, usually found their way into the hands of land speculators. Although landholdings among the mass of the people probably increased somewhat as a result of confiscation of loyalist property, this had no great impact on the development of the new nation. By reopening the West to settlers and speculators, the Revolution renewed the westward expansion which had been temporarily checked by the Proclamation Line of 1763.

Perhaps more important than changes in the distribution of landholdings was the elimination of vestiges of feudalism which had been transplanted from Europe to some of the colonies. Quitrents went unpaid during the Revolution and were legally abolished after it was over. Entails and primogeniture were abolished in most states. These changes in the direction of democratization of the American system did not, however, resolve the internal conflict between the privileged few and the underprivileged many. This struggle continued to be a major issue in American history.

Foreign Trade

After being temporarily disrupted by the American Revolution foreign trade, as previously noted, continued to be mainly with Great Britain. United States merchants, now operating outside the British Navigation System, were free of restrictions but conversely were excluded from the privileges accorded to British subjects. The immediate disadvantages probably outweighed the advantages of this new freedom. American ships no longer enjoyed the protection of the Royal Navy and were set upon by pirates in Caribbean and African waters. They were not allowed to trade with the British West Indies,

which had been the bulwark of colonial commerce. Fish and meat from the United States could not be sold in this market even if carried in British ships. The British would no longer purchase American ships. Bounties on naval stores were removed, and American tobacco lost its exclusive position in the British market, although it could now be sold in other markets.

Yankee merchants, however, were ingenious enough to develop new trade to offset British losses. One of the important new outlets was direct trade with the Orient, where tea, silk, and chinaware were taken in exchange for American furs. The British, being eager to retain the profitable American trade, made some concessions such as keeping down the import duties on several types of American goods. Mercantilism was on the wane in Britain. This helped to ease the difficulties in expanding British trade with the United States far beyond the volume of colonial commerce.

THE RISE OF LAISSEZ-FAIRE

The American Revolutionary War as a protest was a species of a larger genus; it was one important episode in the decline of mercantilism. Adam Smith stated in the *Wealth of Nations* that "Monopoly of one kind or another, indeed, seems to be the sole engine of the mercantile system." (p. 595) [2] In the decline of mercantilism the basic issue was between monopolistic imperialism, on the one hand, and the groups at whose expense these monopolies and privileges were enjoyed, on the other hand. Colonial capitalists were one of the groups victimized by the British merchant capitalists under mercantilism. A second group, which suffered no less acutely than the colonists, was the majority of British capitalists, including nonprivileged merchants and rising industrialists. All groups victimized by the governing mercantilist classes demanded fewer privileges for others and greater freedom for themselves to pursue their own interests. This was the obvious criticism of a system based on restrictive monopoly. In Great Britain the pressure against mercantilist privilege was no less acute than in the colonies.

In the long run the struggles against mercantilism at home and in the colonies were both successful. Triumph came first, however, in the colonies, where the brilliant military and political victory over imperial mercantilism represented a significant blow to the prestige of those in Britain who championed mercantilistic policies. The American Revolution thus bolstered those in Britain who were leading the attack against mercantilism. Final victory over mercantilism at home demanded reform of the British government itself, which was a more difficult task, requiring the maturing of industrial capitalism. The political upshot of the English Industrial Revolution was passage of the Great Reform Bill in 1832, which was followed in 1846 by repeal of the Corn Laws and other remaining mercantilist legislation.

In America the successful revolt against British mercantilism was easier because it required not reform of the British government but merely separation from it. When this happened, the United States was still in the pre-factory stage of economic development. Geographical separation of the

[2] All page references to Smith's *Wealth of Nations* are to the Modern Library edition (New York, 1937).

colonies from the parent country made military resistance more feasible than if they had been situated near England. Moreover, geographical separation made economic exploitation and political domination more glaringly obvious to the colonists. Economic exploitation of colonies was, in fact, a professed principle of mercantilism, at least for home if not for colonial consumption. Exploitation of fellow countrymen by privileged mercantilists was not professed even though it was practiced on a grand scale.

The most complete repudiation of mercantilist theory and policy emanated from Great Britain. David Hume, the great eighteenth-century philosopher, historian and political economist, was one of the leaders in the new thought. But by any measure, the most potent attack on mercantilism came from the pen of Adam Smith. As has often been pointed out, the Declaration of Independence was signed in the same year in which Smith's *Wealth of Nations* was published. These two events were closely related in the currents of history. Smith expressed on the philosophical and theoretical level what the American Revolution expressed in action. Both were aimed at special privilege; both demanded a broader basis for economic opportunity by clearing the decks of mercantilist restrictions on trade. The *Wealth of Nations*, probably the most famous book ever written on economics, was in itself a sufficiently important event to be classed as an epoch in the decline of mercantilism.

Smith held the thesis that the wealth of nations is most rapidly promoted when individuals are allowed to pursue their private interests without government interference. The original French phrase was *laissez-nous faire*, literally "Let us do (it)." Smith recommended free competition as the desirable form of domestic and international economic policy. He repudiated the central mercantilist conception of the "favorable balance of trade." Following Hume on this point, Smith reasoned that if a nation exports more goods than it imports and collects the balance in money, the increased quantity of money will raise the general level of prices at home. With prices higher the nation becomes a less favorable market in which to buy. Foreigners will purchase less, thereby reducing exports. Higher prices will also cause the home population to buy less in the domestic market and to seek to buy more abroad where prices are relatively lower. This will tend to increase imports. The double pressure of decreased exports and increased imports will convert the "favorable" balance of trade into an "unfavorable" balance, that is, one in which imports exceed exports. In the long run the tendency is for exports to equal imports, with the domestic price level rising and falling in response to the influx and outflow of specie. The volume of money will adjust itself to the needs of the nation. Government policy should not try to encourage the import, or to prevent the export, of bullion, or attempt to increase the balance of trade. All mercantilist paraphernalia, such as import duties, export duties, bounties and drawbacks, and lists of enumerated commodities, interfere with the "simple and obvious system of natural liberty." Except as legitimate revenue measures, these various types of levies should be abolished.

Adam Smith advanced two powerful arguments against the mercantilist system as applied to colonies: (1) The monopoly of colonial trade is in itself harmful to the people of the parent country; and (2) the cost of defending the colonies is an added burden on the parent country.

(1) **Monopoly of colonial trade** Smith's first argument is a special application of his general case against monopoly, which he viewed as contrary to the natural system of free trade and free competition. All monopolies divert capital investment from its most advantageous employment and are therefore harmful to society. All monopolies involve an exclusive privilege of some sort. It may benefit the few but is always harmful to the majority. Indeed it "raises the rate of mercantile profit, and thereby augments somewhat the gain of our merchants" (p. 577), but it also limits the total investment of capital and thereby reduces the opportunity for investment and the absolute amount of profit. So even capitalists as a group lose when a few gain by monopolistic restriction. Furthermore, monopoly lowers wages, rents, and the value of land because it limits the amount of capital invested. If more capital were invested, workers would be more productive and would receive higher wages. The same applies to the use of land. Therefore, wage-earners and landlords, along with nonprivileged capitalists, are injured by the monopoly of colonial trade, so that "Every derangement of the natural distribution of stock is necessarily hurtful to the society in which it takes place" (p. 597). The derangement caused by the monopoly of colonial trade was especially hurtful because it involved such a large amount of capital investment (p. 595). Thus the British people were doing harm to themselves by allowing a few merchants and manufacturers to exploit the colonies.

(2) **Cost of defending the colonies** Adam Smith pointed out that in addition to the economic loss suffered as a result of the monopoly of colonial trade, the British people were further burdened by great military expenses for defending this monopoly. He asserted that colonies never had and probably never would contribute enough revenue to the Empire to pay even a part of the cost of defending colonial possessions. Therefore the bulk of the tax burden required to defend colonies must fall on the people of the parent country. He pointed out how the war with France (1756–63) was "altogether a colonial quarrel," and the "Spanish war which began in 1739 was principally a colony quarrel." (p. 581) He concluded, "Under the present system of management, therefore, Great Britain derives nothing but loss from the dominion which she assumes over her colonies." (p. 581) Since the colonies could not be made to bear their full share of the burden of their defense, he believed that Britain should get rid of the colonies. A voluntary separation would have been very advantageous, even though unlikely. Commerce with the colonies could continue on a free trade basis, which would be "more advantageous to the great body of the people, though less so to the merchants, than the monopoly which she at present enjoys." (p. 582) When Smith wrote in 1775 and 1776, fighting had already begun at Lexington and Concord. While he did not expect the British to be sensible enough to grant voluntary independence, his argument pointed to the fruitlessness of the entire political, economic, and military effort.

Adam Smith's ideas are important not so much in themselves but because they appealed to a very numerous class in British society. The immediate popularity of the *Wealth of Nations* is some indication of its appeal to the rising class of manufacturers on the eve of the Industrial Revolution and to the wage-earners and landlords, and to nearly all classes except the few who

had an economic stake in perpetuating the mercantile system. This has significance for the military course of the American Revolution. It portrays clearly the lack of popular support in Britain for the war against the colonies. Any accurate assessment of the military potentials of the British and the Americans must indicate that the British could have easily defeated the colonies if they had had the determination to do so. But the ideas of Adam Smith and others had infiltrated the fabric of British society and had subverted faith in the mercantile system to a point where there was little will to persist in a struggle which, if won, would merely perpetuate an unsound policy and a heavy tax burden. Britons had ceased to believe, or at least had begun to doubt seriously, the value of politically dependent colonies.[3] One of Smith's disciples was William Pitt, the younger, who became prime minister just after the close of the unsuccessful war against the colonies. Pitt used his powerful office to direct the British economy toward a more liberal trade policy.[4] When the political loss of the North American colonies was followed by economic gains in trade, the wisdom of Smith's position seemed demonstrated. The movement toward free trade was well launched. By the middle of the nineteenth century it was complete in England, the classic home of mercantilism.

THE POSITIVE SIDE OF MERCANTILISM AND THE AMERICAN CONSTITUTION

The decline of mercantilism, as outlined above, refers to a weakening of the monopolistic, imperialistic, and colonial aspects of early capitalism. Mercantilism also had its positive aspects, including the elimination of tolls, the unification of coinage, and the creation of a strong system of national public finance. These aspects of internal state-building were retained by the British government in the age of laissez-faire, and in countries where they did not already exist, as in the newly created United States, they had to be instituted as a condition for promoting economic development. The American Constitution of 1789 provided a type of strong central government essential to internal state-building.

The Articles of Confederation and the early state constitutions justified the fears of those who believed that overthrow of British rule would lead to attacks on the privileges and property of the colonial aristocracy. The Articles were made weak because of widespread mistrust of strong government authority. The central government created under the Articles could not regulate commerce among the states or with foreign nations; it could not establish a uniform and stable monetary system; it had no power to tax or otherwise to

---

[3] Josiah Wedgwood, one of England's great industrial capitalists and a leading manufacturer, wrote in a letter in 1778: "I am glad that America is free, and rejoice most sincerely that it is so, and the pleasing idea of a refuge being provided for those who choose rather to flee from, than to submit to, the iron hand of tyranny, has raised much hilarity in my mind." Cited in Paul Mantoux, *The Industrial Revolution in the Eighteenth Century* (New York: The Macmillan Company, 1927), p. 393.

[4] In a speech in the House of Commons, February 12, 1796, Pitt stated: "Look to the instances when interference has shackled industry, and when the best intentions have often produced the most pernicious effects. . . . Trade, industry and barter will always find their own level, and be impeded by regulations which violate their natural operation and derange their proper effect." (Mantoux, p. 403.)

raise the revenues needed for carrying out the functions of a sovereign state;
it could not protect property in land or slaves, or assist traders against the
leveling tendencies of the several states and against the threats of domestic
and foreign aggression. Although a constitution is basically a legal and political document, the general spirit and some particular provisions of the United
States Constitution of 1789 arose from economic conditions and forces of the
post-Revolutionary era and had significant consequences for subsequent economic development.

Military victory in the Revolution swept away the authority of the British
Crown and left nothing in its place. The individual states were sovereign in
theory and in practice. Struggles between radicals and conservatives went on
within individual states for control of the government. Following the radical
Declaration of Independence, most of the states had written new constitutions.
In about one-half the states the radical element, represented mainly by small
farmers, was in the majority, and wrote leveling documents (Pennsylvania,
Rhode Island, Delaware, Connecticut, and North Carolina). In other states
radical uprisings threatened the property and privileges of the well-to-do.
Daniel Shays' rebellion in Massachusetts in 1786 involved back-country farmers
who objected to the property qualifications for voting and holding office. They
threatened violence against courts which ordered foreclosure of their farms on
which they were unable to pay mortgages. Prices had fallen drastically after
the war and the real burden of debt was consequently increased to the disadvantage of the farmers and the advantage of Boston creditors. Shays' men
were subdued by a private militia financed by coastal merchants and capitalists. Shays continued, however, to enjoy popular sympathy.

The movement for the federal Constitution was most actively supported
by men of large property who saw in the existing weak central government a
threat to their fortunes and a danger to the survival of their country. Merchants, planters, slaveowners, land speculators, government creditors, and
men of large capital generally spearheaded the drive. They were a small
minority of the population, but because of wealth and influence they were
powerful out of proportion to their numbers. The Constitution as it was drawn
represents the outlook of this group. John Jay expressed the philosophy of the
men of property when he said: "Those who own the country ought to rule it."
Alexander Hamilton, who was probably more responsible for calling the
Constitutional Convention than any other individual, favored a strong hereditary magistrate approaching a constitutional monarchy. Hamilton's mistrust of
the masses is reflected in his statement: "The people! The people is a great
beast." John Adams, the first vice-president under the Constitution, was
nearly as contemptuous as Hamilton of popular rule.

To James Madison, called the Father of the Constitution, property was
the central institution of economics and politics. In the Federalist papers
Madison advanced the following argument for the Constitution: Men are
naturally endowed with different talents. Corresponding to differences in
talents there arise inequalities in the distribution of property. Men of greater
talent acquire more property; men of lesser talent have less property or none
at all. All societies, Madison believed, are divided into factions according to
the distribution of property. The proper function of government is to protect
and to preserve differences in property which arise, inevitably, from differences

in talents. Tyranny is a potential threat from above and from below. The danger of tyranny from above had been eliminated in the United States by throwing off the yoke of George III and Parliament. The remaining task to be taken care of in the Constitutional Convention was to protect the property of men of greater talent from the tyranny of the masses, from the unreasoning attacks of propertyless men upon whom nature had bestowed little talent.

Madison's economic interpretation of history and politics expressed in philosophical terms the ideology of other members of the Constitutional Convention. Exceptions were Benjamin Franklin of Pennsylvania, who, as noted above, had the outlook of an artisan, and Luther Martin of Maryland, who was sympathetic to debtor classes.

Charles A. Beard in his *Economic Interpretation of the Constitution* points out that nearly all members of the Constitutional Convention held large tracts of land for speculation, that others held federal securities, and that in one way or another they stood to gain from making the Constitution the supreme law of the land. Beard seems to suggest that they were motivated by their pecuniary interests. Undoubtedly men with business interests did largely favor the Constitution as it was drawn up at Philadelphia. It is, however, not necessary to impugn the motives of the Founding Fathers. Motives are necessarily subjective; they are sometimes, even often, unconscious; and if they are thought to be evil, the evil will not be acknowledged by those alleged to hold them. The important consideration is the ideas, not the motives, of the framers of the Constitution. Like all men, they were products of their time. Moreover, they were special products of their time. The late eighteenth century was an Age of Property. John Locke had been a spokesman a century earlier for the English Revolution and had formulated ideas similar to those expressed by the Founding Fathers. Cromwell had held similar ideas, but the common soldiers of Cromwell's army had expressed ideas like those of the radical democrats of the United States a century later. The American Revolution was a restaging of the English Revolution insofar as ideas about property and popular government were concerned. Madison's philosophy of history and politics was similar to that of James Harrington, although Harrington was a more sophisticated scholar than Madison.

What the American Constitution stood for is clear. The good faith of the men who wrote it need not be called into question. They may be assumed to have been men of good will; most of them had fought a bitter struggle for independence. It may be assumed they were genuinely interested in establishing a government that would be best for the new nation as they saw its needs. If what they believed best for the nation was also best for themselves, this does not negate their good intentions. Between ideas and interests there is usually an intimate connection.

Whatever may have been the motives, ideas, and interests of the makers of the Constitution, their essential contribution to the economic development of the United States was a document which increased the power in the hands of the federal government. In mercantilist terms this was a creative act of state-building. Control over interstate commerce eliminated tolls which had been set up between some of the states. The vast domestic market that was to become the distinguishing characteristic of the American economy could not have developed if New York, for example, had continued to levy duties

on firewood from Connecticut and vegetables from New Jersey. The Constitution required the establishment of a uniform national currency in place of the multiform state currencies under the Articles of Confederation. States were denied the right to coin money and to issue paper currency. The greatest defect of the Articles of Confederation was its failure to authorize the national government to levy and collect taxes. This absolutely essential function of effective government was met under the Constitution. In these and other respects the replacement of the Articles by the Constitution created the type of strong national state required for the economic development of the American economy.

SELECTED BIBLIOGRAPHY, CHAPTERS 11 AND 12

ANDREWS, CHARLES M., *The Colonial Period of American History*, 4 vols. New Haven: Yale University Press, 1964.

BAILYN, BERNARD, *The New England Merchants in the Seventeenth Century*. New York: Harper & Row, Publishers, 1964. (paperback)

BAXTER, W. T., *The House of Hancock: Business in Boston, 1724-1775*. Cambridge, Mass.: Harvard University Press, 1945.

BEARD, CHARLES A., *An Economic Interpretation of the Constitution of the United States*. New York: The Free Press of Glencoe, 1965.

BEARD, CHARLES A. and MARY R., *The Rise of American Civilization*, Vol. I, Chapters 1–7. New York: The Macmillan Company, 1927.

BEZANSON, ANN, *Prices and Inflation During the American Revolution, 1770–1790*. Philadelphia: University of Pennsylvania Press, 1951.

BIDWELL, PERCY W., and JOHN I. FALCONER, *History of Agriculture in the Northern United States, 1620–1860*, Parts I and II. Washington, D. C.: Carnegie Institution of Washington, 1925.

BREBNER, J. BARTLETT, *North Atlantic Triangle: The Interplay of Canada, the United States, and Great Britain*. New Haven: Yale University Press, 1945.

BROWN, ROBERT E., *Charles Beard and the Constitution, a Critical Analysis of "An Economic Interpretation of the Constitution."* Princeton, N.J., Princeton University Press, 1956.

BRUCHEY, STUART W., *The Roots of American Economic Growth, 1607–1861*. New York: Harper & Row, Publishers, 1965.

CLARK, VICTOR S., *History of Manufacturing in the United States*, Vol. I. Magnolia, Mass.: Peter Smith, 1949.

DORFMAN, JOSEPH, *The Economic Mind in American Civilization*, Vol. I, Books I and II. New York: Viking Press, 1946.

EAST, ROBERT A., *Business Enterprise in the American Revolutionary Era*. New York: Columbia University Press, 1963.

GIPSON, LAWRENCE H., *The Coming of the American Revolution, 1763–1775*. New York: Harper & Row, Publishers, 1954.

GRAY, LEWIS C., *History of Agriculture in the Southern United States to 1860*, Vol. I. Magnolia, Mass.: Peter Smith, 1958.

HACKER, LOUIS M., *The Triumph of American Capitalism*, Parts I and II. New York: Columbia University Press, 1947.

HARRINGTON, VIRGINIA D., *The New York Merchant on the Eve of the Revolution*. Magnolia, Mass.: Peter Smith, 1964.

HAZARD, BLANCHE, *The Organization of the Boot and Shoe Industry in Massachusetts before 1875*. Cambridge, Mass.: Harvard University Press, 1921.

JOHNSON, E. A. J., *American Economic Thought in the Seventeenth Century*. New York: Russell & Russell, 1961.

JOHNSON, EMORY R. and others, *History of Domestic and Foreign Commerce in the United States*, Vol. I. Washington, D.C.: Carnegie Institution of Washington, 1915.

KNORR, KLAUS E., *British Colonial Theories 1570–1850*. Toronto: University of Toronto Press, 1944.

MORRIS, RICHARD B., *Government and Labor in Early America*. New York: Columbia University Press, 1946.

NETTELS, CURTIS P., *The Money Supply of the American Colonies before 1720*. Madison, Wisc.: University of Wisconsin Press, 1934.

———, *The Roots of American Civilization*. New York: Appleton-Century-Crofts, 1939.

PARRINGTON, VERNON L., *Main Currents in American Thought*, Vol. I, "The Colonial Mind." New York: Harcourt, Brace & World, Inc., 1954. (paperback)

SCHLESINGER, ARTHUR M., *The Colonial Merchants and the American Revolution, 1763–1776*. New York: F. Ungar Publishing Co., 1957.

SCHUYLER, R. L., *The Fall of the Old Colonial System: A Study in British Free Trade, 1770–1870*. New York: Oxford University Press, 1945.

SMITH, ADAM, *An Inquiry into the Nature and Causes of the Wealth of Nations*. New York: Modern Library, 1937.

WAKEFIELD, EDWARD G., *England and America*, 2 vols. New York: Harper & Bros., 1834.

ARTICLES

BAILYN, BERNARD, "Communications and Trade: The Atlantic in the Seventeenth Century," *Journal of Economic History*, XIII (Fall, 1953), 378–87.

GRAY, LEWIS C., "The Market Surplus Problems of Colonial Tobacco," *Agricultural History*, II (Jan., 1928), 1–34.

HAMILTON, EARL J., "The Role of Monopoly in the Overseas Expansion and Colonial Trade of Europe before 1800," *American Economic Review*, XXXVIII (May, 1948), 33–53.

NETTELS, CURTIS P., "British Mercantilism and the Economic Development of the Thirteen Colonies," *Journal of Economic History, XII* (1952), 105–14.

PRICE, JACOB M., "The Economic Growth of the Chesapeake and the European Market, 1697–1775," *Journal of Economic History*, XXIV (Dec., 1964), 496–511.

SACHS, WILLIAM S., "Agricultural Conditions in the Northern Colonies before the Revolution," *Journal of Economic History*, XIII (Summer, 1953), 274–90.

SMITH, ABBOTT EMERSON, "Indentured Servants: New Light on Some of America's 'First' Families," *Journal of Economic History*, II (May, 1942), 40–53.

THOMAS, ROBERT PAUL, "A Quantitative Approach to the Study of the Effects of British Imperial Policy Upon Colonial Welfare: Some Preliminary Findings," *Journal of Economic History*, XXV (Dec., 1965), 615–638.

National Beginnings Under a Political and Economic Union

CHAPTER **13**

Like all wars the American Revolution created serious financial problems. During the war taxes were far from adequate to meet the relatively heavy expenditures of the revolutionary forces. The Continental Congress and the individual colonies resorted to borrowing from the public at home and from private and public sources abroad. The Continental Congress also issued paper currency, which, as suggested by the colloquialism "not worth a Continental," became valueless. After the war little could be done under the Articles of Confederation because of the lack of central control over the fiscal and monetary system. With the adoption of the Constitution, however, Alexander Hamilton, as first Secretary of the Treasury, came forth with a program which established a strong fiscal and monetary system under the direction of the federal government. Hamilton's four proposals related to the (1) public debt, (2) coinage system, (3) First Bank of the United States, and (4) government revenues.

The Public Debt

Hamilton proposed that the federal government should redeem at par the existing debts of both the federal and state governments. Under his plan new federal bonds were to be exchanged directly for the old certificates of debt or sold to raise cash to pay off the holders of old debt. By assuming the obligations of the states as well as the federal government, Hamilton hoped to strengthen the credit standing of the federal government and to enhance its power relative to the states. The federal debt was partly domestic ($42 million) and partly foreign ($11.7 million). In 1790 state debts amounted to an additional $25 million, of which about $18 million was attributed to wartime expenditures.

Since the infant nation was eager to establish its claim as a sovereign country, the wisdom of paying in full the debts owed to foreigners was accepted without much question. Concerning the domestic debt, strong arguments were advanced against full payment, and there were heated debates about the assumption of state debts by the federal Treasury. Many original subscribers to the domestic debt had sold their paper much below par to speculators; if the government were to repay at par, this would reward the

216

NATIONAL
BEGINNINGS
UNDER
A POLITICAL
AND ECONOMIC
UNION

speculators and leave the original patriotic subscribers with heavy losses. With the first rumors of Hamilton's proposals, speculators, taking advantage of the slow communication of news, sent their agents through the country to buy up more certificates of debt before Hamilton's proposal became generally known.

Strong opposition to federal assumption of state debts came from the states with debts which were small in proportion to the burden that would fall on them as payers of federal taxes and hence of federal debts. These were mainly the southern states. A compromise was reached on this issue when the southern states agreed to Hamilton's proposal on condition that the permanent capital of the national government be located on the banks of the Potomac River.

Hamilton's proposals concerning the public debt were accepted by Congress with slight modifications. Instead of paying off the old debts in cash, Hamilton exchanged new securities for the old ones. He believed that a sizable public debt had advantages for the economy. In 1781 he wrote to Robert Morris, "A national debt if it is not excessive will be to us a national blessing; it will be a powerful cement of our union." [1] He also believed that if investors held secure government bonds they would be more willing to venture part of their wealth in risky private enterprises.

The Coinage System

Hamilton demonstrated keen analytical insight in presenting proposals for a coinage system. The main question was whether to establish a gold standard, a silver standard, or a bimetallic (gold and silver) standard for the monetary system. As between gold alone and silver alone, Hamilton preferred gold because it had a more stable value on account of the unlikelihood of great increases in its supply and the high esteem in which gold was generally held throughout the world. He recognized that if both gold and silver were adopted as standards, the market ratio between their values might fall out of alignment with the legally established mint ratio. If this should happen, the metal money which was overvalued at the mint (by reason of government purchase at a fixed price) would drive the metal money that was undervalued at the mint out of circulation. No rational person would bring undervalued metal to the mint for coinage; he would first sell it for the overvalued metal and take that to the mint.

According to the principle known as Gresham's law, the undervalued money would disappear from circulation; the bad money (overvalued at the mint) would drive out of circulation the good money (undervalued at the mint). Hamilton was at considerable pains to examine the prevailing market ratios between the values of equal weights of gold and silver in an attempt to arrive at the ideal ratio. After a detailed analysis in which he recognized the general desirability of a monometallic standard (preferably gold) and the dangers of a bimetallic standard arising from a discrepancy between the fixed mint ratio and the fluctuating market ratio, he nevertheless recommended that both gold and silver be made monetary standards.

[1] *The Papers of Alexander Hamilton,* ed. by H. C. Syrett and J. E. Cook (New York: Columbia University Press, 1961), II, 635.

Hamilton's main reason for recommending a bimetallic standard was to assure a more abundant quantity of circulating media to carry on the large volume of monetary transactions which American economic development was certain to generate. He feared that if gold alone were selected, silver would lose status and would tend to be exported from the United States to countries on the silver standard. The fear of an inadequate quantity of money was conditioned and probably justified by the colonial experience. The colonies had suffered from a chronic shortage of circulating media and had found it necessary to improvise along less than ideal lines; as a result, the colonies had been among the earliest experimenters with paper money. In addition, the underdeveloped status of banking in Hamilton's time meant that bank notes would not be plentiful; they would not become more plentiful and stable in value in the absence of a goodly quantity of precious metals as reserve behind them.

A ratio of 15 to 1 was chosen for the relative values of equal weights of gold and silver under the proposed bimetallic standard. The dollar became the basic monetary unit. It was similar in weight and value to the Spanish dollar which circulated at the time from the West Indies trade and was familiar to most Americans.[2] The decimal system was chosen in preference to the British system of pounds, shillings, and pence.

Once Hamilton's proposals were adopted, the difficulties he analyzed in his report were not long in appearing in the United States. At the mint ratio of 15 to 1, gold was undervalued at the mint and soon disappeared from circulation. Silver dollars also went out of circulation in the United States because they contained less silver than the dollar of the Spanish West Indies, where they were acceptable as a circulating media. As a result, United States silver dollars tended to be drained off to the West Indies. Not many coins were minted, and in 1806 the mint was closed. This left the nation without a metallic money except odds and ends of foreign coins.

In order to attract gold to the mint and keep it in circulation, Congress in 1834 changed the mint ratio to 16 to 1 by reducing the content of the gold dollar. At the new ratio gold was slightly overvalued, that is, the market ratio of equal weights of gold and silver was slightly less than 16 to 1. This situation worsened with the great gold discoveries in California and Australia at midcentury. Silver dollars remained out of circulation until the late 1870's, when discoveries of rich deposits were made in the American West. The increase in the supply of silver reduced its value and caused it to be worth less than one-sixteenth an equal weight of gold. There followed in the 1880's and 1890's a great debate concerning the place of silver in the American monetary system, and the troublesome problem of monetary ratios was not eliminated until 1900, when the gold standard was adopted.

The Bank of the United States

The bank recommended by Hamilton was a central bank—he called it a "public bank"—patterned after the Bank of England. It served as fiscal agent of the central government, became the chief depository of the national specie reserve, issued its own bank notes, was subject to controls by the central gov-

[2] Originally the Spanish got the dollar from the German "thaler" (taler), first coined in Bohemia in 1519.

217

NATIONAL
BEGINNINGS
UNDER
A POLITICAL
AND ECONOMIC
UNION

218

NATIONAL
BEGINNINGS
UNDER
A POLITICAL
AND ECONOMIC
UNION

ernment, exercised control over the creation of credit by other banks, and established several branches which served as clearinghouses in their respective districts. Whereas the Bank of England was entirely under private ownership (until 1945), the Bank of the United States was one-fifth government-owned. By restricting issue within moderate limits, the Bank's notes circulated at par with coin. Other banks, operating under state charters, were held somewhat in check against excessive note issue by the threat that the Bank of the United States might ask for payment of its loans in specie.

As an economic institution the Bank of the United States was successful. It met with political opposition, however, and its charter was not renewed at the end of its twenty-year authorization in 1811. The banking situation deteriorated badly in the next five years, so in 1816 a new twenty-year charter was issued to the Second Bank of the United States. Toward the end of this second twenty-year period the (Second) Bank was again confronted with strong political opposition. President Jackson withdrew federal deposits and rendered the Bank ineffectual several years before its charter expired in 1836. From this date until 1863 the United States experienced an unstable, uncoordinated banking system—sometimes called the period of "wildcat banking"— under state-chartered banks. During the Civil War period stable money and banking became an important issue, and in 1863 the Republican Party established the National Banking System. This, however, did not constitute a central banking system. Not until 1913, when the Federal Reserve System was established, did the United States again enjoy the advantages of central banking. This system set up twelve central banks tied together by the Federal Reserve Board, the members of which were appointed by the President of the United States with the approval of the Senate.

Federal Revenue

Under the Articles of Confederation the national government had no direct power to tax. It was supposed to receive revenue by addressing requests for funds to the separate states. Proceeds from the sale of public lands were also available to the Confederation. Under the Constitution, the public lands continued as a source of revenue, but chief reliance was placed on customs duties and excise taxes. The first law passed by the first Congress was the Tariff Act of 1789. Since the first tariff was intended to raise revenue rather than to afford protection to American business, the rates were sufficiently low not to exclude imports. Obviously tariff rates high enough to exclude all imports would not yield any revenue at all. Hamilton also recommended excise taxes, that is, taxes on specific commodities produced and sold within the United States. An excise on whiskey brought forth bitter protests and direct resistance from frontier farmers who had been accustomed to converting their grain into whiskey before selling it. Grain was too bulky to be shipped economically by the then existing means of overland transportation from the frontier to eastern markets. Consequently grain was first distilled into whiskey, which was of high value in relation to its weight and could bear the cost of transportation. In the "Whiskey Rebellion" of 1794 western farmers defied the federal government by refusing to pay the excise tax on whiskey. Their rebellion was crushed by armed federal troops.

Through these four measures—debt payment, a coinage system, a central bank, and federal revenues—Hamilton succeeded in giving the national government a fairly sound fiscal and monetary foundation. Each measure involved difficult and controversial decisions. The controversial side is illustrated by the debate over federal assumption of state debts, the bitter opposition to the Bank of the United States, and the Whiskey Rebellion arising from excise taxes. More fateful than any of these, however, was the disposal of public lands. Should the public domain be treated primarily as a source of revenue or should it be managed in such a way as to maximize the rate of settlement?

219

NATIONAL
BEGINNINGS
UNDER
A POLITICAL
AND ECONOMIC
UNION

PRIVATE APPROPRIATION OF THE PUBLIC DOMAIN

The Ideal and the Reality

The United States was endowed by nature with physical resources which were probably unmatched by any other nation. At the beginning of the colonial period these resources were unexploited and unclaimed, except by the Indians, whose claims were not a serious obstacle. When the Constitution became the effective law of the new nation, the territory west of the Appalachian Mountains was still in a virgin state. A century later the American frontier was officially closed; nearly all the vast natural resources had passed from the public domain into private ownership. Private appropriation of the public domain was the outstanding economic phenomenon in the economic development of the United States during the nineteenth century. It overshadowed every other development prior to the Civil War, and only the rapid industrialization after the Civil War rivaled its significance in the overall economic development of the nation.

Western Europe and the American West have been the two major influences molding economic institutions, and the pattern of culture, in the United States since its earliest beginnings. Settlement of the American East was an expansion of Europe into America, and settlement of the American West was a continuation of that expansion under somewhat altered political and economic conditions. The physical resources of the West had no economic value so long as they remained inaccessible by economical means of transportation. Roads, canals, rivers, and finally railways gave economic value to the physical resources of the West; therefore the story of transportation is intimately linked with the winning of the West.

A fundamental principle of capitalist society is private ownership of the means of production, including natural resources. Since the vast western territory that was already or was to become territory of the United States was lodged in the possession of the federal government, the great problem was how the public domain should be transferred to private ownership. Almost unanimously the people, including government officials, believed that all land should be made private property as rapidly as possible. The significant political and economic issue was just how this should be done. A widely accepted ideal among the common people was equality of opportunity to share in the private appropriation of the public domain. The reality, however, often departed widely from the ideal. Engrossment of agricultural land, timber, minerals, grazing land, fur trade, and other parts of the public domain frequently over-

220

NATIONAL
BEGINNINGS
UNDER
A POLITICAL
AND ECONOMIC
UNION

shadowed free access to ordinary settlers. Enterprising, greedy, and clever men managed by hook or crook to gain much more than their share of the vast natural assets of the American economy.

Thomas Jefferson probably expressed the democratic ideal of equal access to the public domain better than anyone else. Jefferson believed in agrarian democracy. Above all he wished to avoid in America the degrading influence of great industrial cities and factories like those which were springing up in England during his lifetime (1743–1826). Jefferson did not think political democracy could flourish in a predominantly industrial economy. The Jeffersonian ideal was that every family should possess some means of production so as not to be the employees of others. This goal was to be realized through equal and easy access to the public domain. This belief influenced Jefferson's decision to purchase the vast Louisiana territory from Napoleon. Jefferson once expressed the view that a thousand years would be required for full settlement of all the territory east of the Mississippi River. Throughout this millennium the public domain would pass gradually into private possession and provide the economic basis for agrarian democracy. Jefferson expressed his view as follows:

> Whenever there are in any country uncultivated lands and unemployed poor, it is clear that the laws of property have been so far extended as to violate natural right. The earth is given as a common stock for man to labor and live on. If for the encouragement of industry we allow it to be appropriated, we must take care that other employment be provided to those excluded from the appropriation. If we do not, the fundamental right to labor the earth returns to the unemployed. It is too soon yet in our country to say that every man who cannot find employment, but who can find uncultivated land, shall be at liberty to cultivate it, paying a moderate rent. But it is not too soon to provide by every possible means that as few as possible shall be without a little portion of land. The small landholders are the most precious part of the state.[3]

To a considerable extent the United States did become a nation of small landholders during the nineteenth century and to that extent Jefferson's dream was realized. But in retrospect it is obvious that Jefferson was very wrong in his estimate of the length of time required to settle the West. He was also wrong in supposing that the private appropriation of the public domain would take place on an equitable basis. Land-grabbers, claim-jumpers, railway companies, lumber kings, cattle and sheep barons, and speculators of all types, aided by fraud and corruption, combined to engross a large proportion of the valuable public domain. Public lands were usually sold to large companies dominated by speculators, and later they were given away by the millions of acres to railways. Mineral rights fell mainly into the hands of a few joint-stock companies. Water rights were monopolized by a relatively few. The fur trade was monopolized and the fur-bearing animals soon trapped out. Timber lands were engrossed through fraud by giant lumber companies. Only agricultural farm land was reasonably evenly divided, and much of this only after it had first been bought and resold by large land companies. Against this reality the Jeffersonian ideal persisted and won some important legislative victories, but in general it remained no more than a dream.

[3] Jefferson, *Writings*, XIX (Monticello ed.), 18.

Agricultural Land Policy   **221**

NATIONAL
BEGINNINGS
UNDER
A POLITICAL
AND ECONOMIC
UNION

Early phase   The objective of land sales from the public domain was two-fold: to raise revenue for the federal Treasury and to encourage settlement. To realize the first objective land had to be sold rather than given away; in order to realize the second objective the price had to be low enough to encourage purchase by actual settlers. The early policy was to sell large parcels of land to the highest bidder with a minimum reservation price below which it would not be sold. In 1785 the minimum tract was set at one section, or 640 acres, and the minimum price at $1.00 per acre, with three months to pay. Since settlers with $640 in cash were rare birds and had little need for 640 acres of uncleared land—sometimes ten years were required for a family to clear eighty acres—the original purchases were usually made by land companies and real estate promoters, who resold in smaller lots to settlers. Since one of the purposes of land sales was to reduce the public debt, evidences of federal debt were accepted in payment for federal land. These securities were so depreciated that the equivalent price in hard money was only about 10 cents an acre. These arrangements played directly into the hands of speculators, who were able to purchase vast tracts of land cheaply and to resell them in smaller quantites at a good profit. Robert Morris, the financier of the American Revolution and a member of the Constitutional Convention, was the biggest land speculator of the early post-Revolutionary period. At one time he controlled six million acres of unsettled land situated in several states, mainly from Pennsylvania south to Georgia. Although Morris was the greatest of the land speculators (in the early decades of the nation's history), nearly every man of large means engaged in land speculation.

Partly in an attempt to price speculators out of the market and partly in order to increase Treasury revenue the minimum price of land was raised to $2.00 an acre in 1796, with the minimum parcel unchanged, but with one year to pay the full balance. The higher price shut out the speculator, but it also shut out the settler. A settler now had to have $1,280 to become an original buyer of any part of the public domain. Under frontier conditions if a settler did not have money at the time of purchase, he was unlikely to have it at the end of the first year. Thus the credit provision was of little help. Very little federal land was sold under this law. Several of the eastern states still owned western lands, which were available at lower prices than federal lands.

Beginning about 1800 with the Jeffersonian era new legislation for disposing of the public domain was directed more in the interest of the pioneer farmer and less in the interest of the Treasury, although the latter objective was not dropped until the Civil War. In 1800 the minimum acreage which could be purchased was lowered to half-sections of 320 acres, and in 1804 to quarter-sections of 160 acres. Meanwhile a more liberal credit system was introduced, presumably for the benefit of the settler of small means and aimed at preventing speculation. Actually, however, the credit provisions increased speculation by enabling more people to speculate. Optimistic purchasers expected to be able to meet subsequent payments, but intervening disappointments found them without the necessary cash on payment day. Foreclosures were heavy under the credit system. Consequently, in 1820 credit sales were eliminated and a cash system reintroduced with the price per acre lowered to

222

NATIONAL
BEGINNINGS
UNDER
A POLITICAL
AND ECONOMIC
UNION

$1.25 and the minimum acreage reduced to 80. Direct access to the public domain was now possible for anyone with $100 in cash or its equivalent in acceptable warrants.

Another legislative triumph for democratic forces was recognition of squatters' rights by the Preëmption Act of 1841. Legal title could not be obtained until after land had been surveyed and officially offered for sale. Settlers frequently cleared land, built shelter, and made improvements before land was put on the market. When it was finally placed on the auction block, title to the land and the improvements thereon went to the highest bidder. Since frontier life was not conducive to building up a cash balance, squatters were at an economic and legal disadvantage in bidding against speculators. Actually the "law of the frontier" made it unhealthy for interlopers to try to buy a squatter's land from under him. There was, nevertheless, a legal hazard in the existing arrangements. Under the Preëmption Law squatters received the right to settle on unappropriated public land and the option to buy it at the minimum price when it became available for purchase from the government.

Homestead Law of 1862 The Jeffersonian ideal of easy and equal access to the public domain gained fullest recognition in the Homestead Law of 1862. Under this act any citizen or intended citizen could receive title to 160 acres of land free of charge after filing a claim and living on the land for five years. Free homesteads marked an end to the earlier emphasis on the public domain as a source of federal revenue. Free land in small amounts to actual settlers was a blow to speculators and a strike in favor of men of limited means. Passage of the Homestead Act represented the culmination of popular pressures on a democratic government in a country with great quantities of unsettled land. As the political power of the West grew with an increasing number of western states, and with the secession of the southern states at the outbreak of the Civil War, free land became in a sense inevitable. In the pre-Civil War period the South provided the strongest opposition to free land for actual settlers.

Two types of arguments were advanced for free homesteads. The first was that undeveloped land was worth no more than the cost to the pioneer of clearing and developing it and therefore that it was inequitable to add a monetary price to the labor cost of acquiring it. The other argument was that men have a natural right to as much land as they can use when the land is available. The condition imposed in the Homestead Law that the quantity of free land should be limited suggests the influence of the natural rights philosophy, and implies, perhaps, that a man does not have a right to more than he can make use of with his own labor. This is similar to the argument advanced by John Locke in the seventeenth century. The Homestead Law had its shortcomings and its privileges were abused, but for two generations of Americans after the Civil War it produced the general results intended by its champions.

Federal Land Grants to Railroads

Although the Preëmption and Homestead laws gave actual settlers free access to land, they did not put a stop to large-scale appropriation of the public domain by men of capital. The same legislation of 1841 which gave preëmp-

tion rights to squatters provided land grants for internal improvements and inaugurated one of the great give-away programs in history. Early land grants for internal improvements were made by the federal government to the states, which in turn sold the land to finance roads, canals, bridges, and river improvements, carried on as public enterprises. Much more important, however, were the land grants to privately owned railway companies. Beginning with an Illinois Central grant in 1850, the federal government gave away to the railroads (in a period of twenty-one years) 129 million acres of land, an amount exceeding the combined area of all six New England states plus New York, New Jersey, Pennsylvania, Delaware, Maryland, and West Virginia. The land grants consisted of alternate sections of a specified number of miles on either side of the railroad. The Illinois Central received alternate sections of six miles of land on each side of the road from Chicago to Mobile; the Union Pacific and Central Pacific received alternate sections of twenty miles on each side; and the Northern Pacific, Southern Pacific, Santa Fe, Burlington, and other western roads received generous land grants. These grants were made between 1856 and 1871.

The railways sold the land for cash. Receipts from sales by the Northern Pacific amounted to $136,000,000, which was nearly twice as much as the $70,000,000 cost of building the railroad. The Illinois Central received $30,-000,000, which equalled approximately 85 per cent of the cost of construction. These were the most enormous subsidies ever lavished on private enterprise. Probably no other country could have afforded such generosity with the public domain.

Much criticism has been leveled against railway land grants and much criticism is justified. However, a distinction should be made between the abuses in administering land grants and the economic principle behind the grants. The principle was simple: Railways increase the value of the land through which they run and they should receive some part of the new value which they create. The subsidy will attract capital which would not otherwise be available for railway construction and will therefore speed up the economic development of the region through which the railway passes. Recognition of this principle was embodied in the legislation which doubled the minimum price of the alternate sections that were retained by the government along the railway routes. The incentive of the government in making railway grants was the expectation that a greater total revenue would be received from selling the government-retained land at a higher price per acre. Much of the land given to the railways was in wild, unsettled country which had no economic value before the advent of the railways. The alternative to subsidizing private enterprise to build railways through wild frontier lands would have been for the government to construct them. In most countries railways have been built by government, and in the United States other internal improvements such as canals, wagon roads, and river improvements were carried out as enterprises of state governments. Whether government construction would have been a better alternative in the case of western American railways cannot be answered. The fact is that railways did get built in a relatively short time and settlement and development of the nation's natural resources were hurried along as a consequence. Railways were an essential part of the nation's social overhead capital, the formation of which is a chronic problem in every underdeveloped

223

NATIONAL
BEGINNINGS
UNDER
A POLITICAL
AND ECONOMIC
UNION

224

NATIONAL
BEGINNINGS
UNDER
A POLITICAL
AND ECONOMIC
UNION

country. The abuses were in the administration of the land grants and not in the principle of subsidy to private enterprise for performing a socially desirable task.

Timber Lands

Prior to 1878 there was no specific provision for disposing of public timber lands. Earlier laws applied to agricultural land, and while much of this was forested, it was contrary to the spirit of the agricultural land laws to use them as a subterfuge for appropriating timber land. Nevertheless, this was a common practice. Nominal compliance acceptable to land office officials took the form of clearing a few square rods of land, planting some token crops, and passing this activity off as evidence of honest intention to farm the land. Passage of the Timber and Stone Act in 1878 removed timber land from homesteading but did little to prevent large corporations and timber speculators from grabbing valuable timber land. Under this law an individual could purchase a maximum of 160 acres of timber land at auction, with the minimum price fixed at $2.50 per acre. Large companies fraudulently circumvented the acreage limitation by supplying their employees or others with money to make the original purchase of timber land. Title was then transferred to the company. In one instance a trainload of vacationing schoolteachers were used as dummy buyers. A promoter in the vicinity of Hattiesburg, Mississippi, did not even bother to use human dummies. He took out claims in the names of his oxen in order to secure title to a large tract of pine timber. Another notorious scheme reported by the Land Office involved the use of dummies to acquire 100,000 acres of the most valuable redwood trees in Humboldt County, California. Competitive bidding was conspicuous by its absence. The Commissioner of the General Land Office reported to the Secretary of the Interior in 1885: "Under the timber and stone act timber worth $100 an acre is sold for $2.50." [4] In 1909 the National Conservation Commission reported that in thirty years under the Timber and Stone Act timber worth "at a very conservative estimate" $300,000,000 had been sold for one-tenth that amount. The difference of $270,000,000 or more was in effect taken from the pockets of all the people and placed in the pockets of a few lumber kings and speculators.

Grazing Lands

Grazing land in the West was also subject to abuse by cattle and sheep barons. With the coming of cheap barbed wire (about 1880) vast areas of the public domain were fenced in, often without any pretense of legal right. Two companies in Colorado enclosed a million acres each, and others in Colorado, New Mexico, Nebraska, and Kansas enclosed areas of a quarter of a million acres. Enclosures of 100,000 acres were not uncommon; those of 20,000 to 50,000 very numerous. Professor Hibbard, historian of the U.S. land policies, calls these grazing scandals "the most unmistakable, wholesale, shameless instances of land-grabbing that had yet been practiced in America." [5] Fortu-

---

[4] B. H. Hibbard, A History of the Public Land Policies (Magnolia, Mass.: Peter Smith, 1939), p. 466.
[5] Hibbard, A History of the Public Land Policies, p. 477.

nately most of these enclosures were so flagrantly illegal that the culprits were prosecuted, their fences torn down, and the lands restored to the public domain as free grazing areas.

225

NATIONAL
BEGINNINGS
UNDER
A POLITICAL
AND ECONOMIC
UNION

Mineral Lands

In principle, mineral lands were from the beginning given special handling either by reserving mineral rights to the federal government or by withholding mineral lands from disposition by sale, homesteading, or railway grants. In practice, however, lack of knowledge of the subsurface mineral wealth resulted in most mineral lands in the eastern part of the United States being sold under agricultural land laws. This meant they were disposed of at a fraction of their true value. Mineral lands so alienated from the public domain included lead and zinc mines in Missouri and Wisconsin, copper mines in Michigan, coal mines in West Virginia and the Appalachian area, and most iron ore deposits in Minnesota, Alabama, Michigan, and Wisconsin.[6] In the Far West mineral lands were mildly protected after 1866, but not until the twentieth century were effective measures taken to sell this most valuable type of public land at something approximating its true worth.

Summary of Public Land Policy

The Jeffersonian philosophy that the public domain should be used to enable common people to gain direct access to means of production was realized in a limited way during the nineteenth century in the case of agricultural land, but failed notoriously in the case of timber, mineral, and grazing lands. Agricultural land was at first sold at low prices, but popular pressures for free land in quantities that could actually be used by settlers led to passage of the Homestead Law during the Civil War when southern opposition was no longer possible. Lavish grants to the railways caused a rapid diminution in the land available for free homesteads and, again in response to popular pressure, land grants to railways ceased after 1871. Within a century after Jefferson's Louisiana Purchase practically no good agricultural land remained for homesteading. A poor system of land classification contributed to the rapid, inequitable, and often fraudulent appropriation of timber and mineral lands. Speculation of all types was a persistent menace to more equitable sharing of the public domain. Lack of foresight resulted in great waste of irreplaceable natural resources in timber, minerals, and soil. For lack of better management of the nation's resources, later generations were probably poorer and the distribution of wealth and income somewhat more unequal than they otherwise would have been.

The policy of easy access to the public domain tended to spread the population thinly over the United States for a century. Agriculture became overexpanded relative to other economic activities. Agricultural prices were depressed, food was cheap, and discontent was prevalent among the agricultural population in the last third of the nineteenth century. Although spreading the population thinly over a vast area might have lowered the productivity of agricultural labor under stationary technology, the dynamic effect was to

[6] Hibbard, pp. 516–17.

226

NATIONAL
BEGINNINGS
UNDER
A POLITICAL
AND ECONOMIC
UNION

stimulate the introduction of agricultural machinery and to raise the productivity of agricultural labor in the long run.

Cheap land in the West attracted a significant number of easterners and acted as a brake upon industrial development in the East. What the evidence suggests is not so much that discontented wage-earners migrated westward, as might be supposed, but that farmers and the sons of farmers moved west to take up cheap land. Thus the *potential* supply of labor, if not the actual supply of wage-earners at any given time, was reduced in the East and this tended to keep wages higher than they would have been in the absence of migration. If the West was not a safety valve by which discontented eastern wage-earners let off steam, it was effective in preventing the steam from reaching higher pressures. The average wage-earner was too poor to migrate to the West. Even though land became free, some capital was required to transport a family and equip a farm.

AGRICULTURE TO 1830

The same conditions which determined the allocation of economic resources in the American colonies continued to operate well into the nineteenth century. Abundance of land and scarcity of labor and capital attracted men to extensive farming and to the extractive industries, with commerce continuing as the most advanced type of capitalist activity until approximately the middle of the century. The significant decades for the transition from commercial capitalism to industrial capitalism were between 1830 and 1860. Before 1830 there were factories but no factory *system*. Agriculture changed before 1830 but the agricultural revolution came after 1830. Investments in land, in the fur trade, and in internal and foreign commerce were more profitable than investments in factories until 1830.

Relative decline in the size of the merchant marine began in 1826 and absolute decline after 1860. The new means of transportation necessary to weld the vast geographical expanses of the United States together into a national economy began with completion of the Erie Canal in 1825 and gained force with the railways after 1830. The labor movement cannot be dated before 1827. The emergence of these forces which were to change the pattern of the American economy will be discussed in later chapters. In the rest of the present chapter some of the developments before 1830 are noted.

Southern Agriculture

In the commercial agriculture of the southern states cotton replaced tobacco as the main staple. In the colonial period very little cotton was grown and none was exported. The phenomenal rise of cotton production and export arose from two main factors. England's Industrial Revolution created a tremendous new demand for cotton, and the invention of the cotton gin increased the supply correspondingly. While the American Revolution separated the English and Americans politically, the Industrial Revolution drew them together economically. The cotton gin on one side of the Atlantic and the water frame on the other side achieved more than mercantilism in getting America to produce raw material for English manufacturing. Cotton was the strongest

thread tying the North Atlantic community into an economic unit. Before the
Industrial Revolution England's great industry had been woolen textiles, which
were made from home-grown wool. Raw cotton could not be raised in England for climatic reasons. Moreover, the scale of the Industrial Revolution was
so great that English manpower was leaving agriculture for the new factories.

227

NATIONAL
BEGINNINGS
UNDER
A POLITICAL
AND ECONOMIC
UNION

The cotton gin was an epoch-making invention. Early English cotton
came from India, the Near East, and the Caribbean. In the Caribbean islands
a long-staple type of cotton was raised. This sea-island cotton, as it was called,
was transplanted successfully to the low-lying coastal regions of the southeastern United States in 1786. Not much could be produced because the geographical area suited to its cultivation was limited. Much better suited to the soil
and climate of most of the South was short-staple cotton. Whereas the seeds of
long-staple sea-island cotton could be removed easily, seeds of the short-
staple upland cotton were very difficult to remove. Cleaning the seed from
one pound of upland cotton required a full day of labor. Even with slaves this
was too expensive to permit much labor to be allocated to this type of cotton.
The area under cultivation was small until the cotton gin of the Connecticut
Yankee, Eli Whitney, changed it all.

With Whitney's gin fifty pounds of cotton could be cleaned in a day
when operated by hand and much more when operated with water or other
mechanical power. The cost of producing cotton was correspondingly reduced.
Before Whitney's time cotton cloth had been more expensive than woolen
cloth; now cotton became cheaper than wool. An almost unlimited amount
of this excellent textile fiber could be raised as a field crop using only unskilled labor. Conditions in the American South were ideally suited to the new
cotton culture. Slave labor on large plantations and small farms was well
adapted to cotton cultivation. Slavery, which had been on the wane at the
close of the colonial era, experienced a resurgence. Cotton became the largest
commercial crop and constituted more than three-fifths of all U.S. exports by
1860.

Although cotton rose rapidly to a pre-eminent position in southern agriculture, other money crops were also important. The export value of tobacco
exceeded that of cotton until 1800. Tobacco cultivation spread from Maryland
and Virginia into Kentucky and North Carolina. With the acquisition of Louisiana, sugar cane became an important commercial crop. Rice continued to be
grown commercially, but indigo was abandoned after the Revolution with
the end of British subsidies. The South continued to raise subsistence crops,
the most important of which was corn. With specialization in cotton, large
quantities of salt pork were imported from the Ohio region.

Northern Agriculture

Before 1830 there was no new departure in agriculture in the northeast
and northwest comparable to the rise of cotton in the South. Westward migration between 1780 and 1830 continued the colonial expansion which had been
temporarily interrupted by the Proclamation of 1763. In one major respect the
westward movement beyond the Alleghenies was less important than the
earlier westward movement to the crest of the mountains; the trans-Allegheny
West was shut off economically from the East during this period. Not until

228

NATIONAL
BEGINNINGS
UNDER
A POLITICAL
AND ECONOMIC
UNION

after completion of the Erie Canal in 1825 and the cross-mountain railways in the 1840's did the fertile soils of the Ohio Valley have economic significance for the less fertile lands of the East. When this impact did finally come, however, it was felt more sharply because of what had been building up beyond the Alleghenies for several decades. By the time the Erie Canal and the railways tied the East to the West, the latter was already a well-developd agricultural region.

Until 1830 agriculture of the Ohio Valley was mainly, although by no means exclusively, of the subsistence type. The commercial aspect, which was secondary, was oriented toward southern markets because the only economical transportation was down the Ohio and Mississippi rivers to New Orleans and way points. Wheat, flour, hogs, and salt pork were the main exports from the region. The spread of cotton raising into the "New South" provided a market for Ohio Valley products. Before the Erie Canal, cattle and hogs were driven east over the mountains, but this was a minor item in the total picture. Manufactured products were purchased from the East, but the volume was meager because the westerners had difficulty finding means of paying for eastern goods.

By English standards American agriculture remained quite primitive. The scientific methods developed by Tull, Townshend, and Bakewell a century earlier were resisted in the United States. Land was so cheap and abundant that little concern was felt for soil-saving practices such as crop rotation and fertilization. Another reason for American backwardness was the lack of markets for agricultural surpluses. Self-sufficiency continued to be the watchword in northern agriculture, except in the vicinity of the larger cities. The most important change in the early decades of the nineteenth century was noted in areas adjacent to cities like Boston, New York, Philadelphia, and Baltimore, where urban markets stimulated a shift from subsistence to commercial farming and a corresponding improvement in agricultural organization and techniques. Pennsylvania, which had been the leading wheat-producing colony, retained first place among wheat-producing states until 1840. New York was still the third wheat-producing state in 1830, by which time Ohio had risen to second place.

FOREIGN COMMERCE AND SHIPPING

Foreign Commerce

The general pattern of American foreign commerce underwent no basic change prior to the Civil War. Exports reflected the dominant position of agricultural production, and imports reflected the immaturity of industry. Generally speaking, the total volume of foreign trade increased with the growth of total production and consumption. Per capita foreign trade, on the other hand, was less between 1810 and the Civil War than at any other time in American history. The volume of investment in ships and shipping for foreign commerce offers, perhaps, a better index of the changing structure of the American economy than does the volume of foreign trade itself. The percentage of American foreign trade carried in American ships attained a maximum in the 1820's. The merchant marine declined relatively after 1826 and

absolutely after 1860. This is a bellwether of the transition from commercial to industrial capitalism in the United States during the nineteenth century.

Of total exports about four-fifths were agricultural products before the Civil War. Cotton replaced tobacco as the leading article of export. The significance of cotton in southern agriculture and in linking the English and American economies has already been noted. No cotton was exported during the colonial era; by 1830 it constituted two-fifths and by 1860 nearly three-fifths of total exports.[7] Tobacco, which had been the leading export for nearly two centuries, increased in absolute amount but declined as a percentage of total exports. Rice barely held steady in absolute terms, and indigo disappeared.

From the northwest and northeast the leading exports were grain, flour, and meat products, especially pork. The most important foreign markets were in Europe and the Caribbean islands. Although American ships were excluded under the British Navigation Laws from trading with the British West Indies, American products could be carried there in British ships. Southern Europe continued to provide a steady market for American flour and meat, and after 1846 England became an important outlet for American grains. Fishing and whaling grew in absolute terms but declined relatively in the postcolonial era, as did also products of the forests, including naval stores.

The leading imports continued to consist of English and European manufactures. In the period between the American Revolution and the Civil War, finished and semimanufactured goods constituted approximately two-thirds of total imports by value. Cotton and woolen textiles, metal products, glass, paper, leather, and chinaware were among the leading import items.[8]

Shipping

As outlets for investment the various activities of the sea continued to play an important role in the early decades of the nineteenth century. As the center of population moved westward, however, more investment went into internal improvements, including canals and railways, rather than into maritime activity, and as the American economy was gradually woven into one vast market by inland transportation, domestic manufacturing began to command investment at the expense of ocean shipping. The decline in the percentage of foreign trade carried by the American merchant marine after 1830 meant that more and more of the goods which Americans sold to and bought from foreigners were being carried in foreign ships. This should not be interpreted as an economic weakness. The change arose mainly from a shift in the allocation of resources in response to greater opportunities for investing in railways and factories as compared with the returns from investing in ships and in the shipping business.

Between the Revolutionary and Civil wars the American merchant marine was second only to that of Great Britain. Throughout the era of wooden ships, American shipbuilders enjoyed a significant economic advantage over

[7] See Douglass C. North, *The Economic Growth of the United States, 1790–1860* (Englewood Cliffs, N.J.: Prentice-Hall, Inc., 1961), p. 233.

[8] For a list of leading imports, see Emory R. Johnson, *History of Foreign and Domestic Commerce of the United States* (Washington: The Carnegie Institution, 1915), II, 23.

230

NATIONAL
BEGINNINGS
UNDER
A POLITICAL
AND ECONOMIC
UNION

the British. The cost per ton of constructing shipping capacity was only 50 to 60 per cent of the British cost in 1790. Lumber and masts were close at hand for New England shipbuilders, whereas the British had to import much of their lumber and all of their masts. These they obtained either from the Baltic or from North America. Until repeal of the Navigation Laws in 1849 British shipowners were not permitted to purchase ships from non-British shipbuilders even though this would have been greatly to their advantage, as the experience after repeal indicates. Because wages generally were much higher in the United States, American sailors were better paid than British sailors; Yankee skippers could afford to pay higher wages and still carry freight as cheaply as British shipowners of expensive British ships.

Although the United States enjoyed a steady advantage in building ships, this advantage could not always be translated into the business of shipping goods. American shipping was in the doldrums from the Revolution until adoption of the Constitution, partly because the federal government was without authority under the Articles of Confederation to reach understandings and to make treaties with foreign governments. Under the stronger national government after the adoption of the Constitution, conditions improved. Between 1792 and 1807 the Napoleonic wars in Europe created conditions which resulted in great prosperity for American sea merchants. France and England were locked in a death struggle and sorely needed the shipping tonnage which only the Yankee ships could provide. Although the hazards for American ships were great, so were the profits. Beginning in 1807 with Jefferson's unfortunate —for American merchants—Embargo Act, American shipping fell again upon some evil days. The nadir of depression was reached during the second American war with England, when the powerful British fleet bottled up the American merchant marine so tightly that even tiny sloops in the coastwise trade dared not venture out of port. At the close of the War of 1812 in America and of the Napoleonic wars in Europe, several years of postwar prosperity for American shipping followed. Then followed a dozen years of relative stagnation. The period after 1830 was characterized by more ups and downs between prosperity and depression, with a closing spurt of prosperity between 1847 and 1860.

Coastal shipping, which constitutes domestic rather than foreign commerce, enjoyed a more regular growth than international trade. During the colonial era the coastal trade had not been very important because the colonies were relatively isolated from each other. The peculiar circumstances created by the Napoleonic Wars, in which American ships enjoyed the advantages of "neutrals," perpetuated the emphasis on foreign trade and restricted the coastwise trade. The Embargo Act of 1807 did not apply to coastal trade, which expanded while foreign trade slumped badly. Between 1807 and 1815 the growth of manufacturing in the coastal states stimulated coastal trade, especially in view of the almost complete lack of overland transportation for heavy freight. The trans-Allegheny West was shut off from the East until 1825 but found a commercially significant outlet through New Orleans where transshipment was made for East Coast ports.

In 1818 the federal government created a mercantilistic type of American monopoly by legislating that the coastal trade should be carried only in ships which were American-owned and American-manned. Since the important

231

NATIONAL
BEGINNINGS
UNDER
A POLITICAL
AND ECONOMIC
UNION

route from New Orleans to New York was equal to more than one-half the distance across the Atlantic, and since the later route around South America to the California coast, which was considered coastal trade, was some 12,000 miles, this legislation offered a real stimulus to American shipbuilding and shipping. The tonnage of enrolled and licensed vessels in the coastal trade was only one-third that of the tonnage of registered vessels in foreign trade in 1810; in 1831 for the first time the tonnage in the coastal trade equalled that employed in foreign trade; and by the Civil War the tonnage in coastal trade was much in excess of that in foreign trade. The coastwise trade, as a part of domestic commerce, reflects the increase in domestic trade in relation to foreign trade especially before inland transportation became important. During the 1850's a large amount of traffic was diverted from the sea to the railways connecting the East with the West.

The rise and decline of the American merchant marine is illustrated by an international comparison. Including the tonnage of both foreign and coastal shipping the merchant marine increased from 50 per cent of total British tonnage in 1815 to nearly 100 per cent in the 1850's. This upsurge in American tonnage resulted from the rapid construction of the clipper ships after 1845. In Britain there was considerable concern, and in the United States much boasting. In retrospect, however, the American challenge to British superiority of the seas was more apparent than real. The important innovation of the time was not the beautiful and speedy clipper but the ugly, dirty, iron steamer. Wind and wood proved no match for steam and iron (and later steel). After a final brilliant spurt at the end of the era of wooden ships, the American merchant marine declined drastically. Total tonnage was less in 1907 than in 1807. Whereas 92.5 per cent of American foreign trade was carried in American ships in 1826, less than 10 per cent was carried in American ships at the outbreak of the First World War. The reason was simple. In the United States investments in factories were now much more profitable than investments in ships.

SELECTED BIBLIOGRAPHY

DAGGETT, STUART, *Chapters in the History of the Southern Pacific*. New York: The Ronald Press Co., 1922.

GATES, PAUL W., *Illinois Central Railroad and Its Colonization Work*. Cambridge, Mass.: Harvard University Press, 1934.

HACKER, LOUIS M., *Major Documents in American Economic History*, Vol. I. Princeton: D. Van Nostrand Co., Inc., 1961. (paperback)

HIBBARD, BENJAMIN H., *A History of Public Land Policies*. Madison, Wisc.: University of Wisconsin Press, 1965. (paperback)

JENSEN, MERRILL, *The New Nation*. New York: Alfred A. Knopf, Inc., 1950.

NETTELS, CURTIS P., *The Emergence of a National Economy, 1775–1815*. New York: Holt, Rinehart & Winston, Inc., 1962.

NORTH, DOUGLASS C., *The Economic Growth of the United States, 1790–1860*. Englewood Cliffs, N.J.: Prentice-Hall, Inc., 1961.

232

NATIONAL
BEGINNINGS
UNDER
A POLITICAL
AND ECONOMIC
UNION

ROBBINS, RAY M., *Our Landed Heritage: The Public Domain, 1776–1936*. Princeton: Princeton University Press, 1942.

VEBLEN, THORSTEIN B., *Absentee Ownership and Business Enterprise in Recent Times. The Case of America*, Chap. 7. New York: The Viking Press, Inc., 1923.

ARTICLES

BJORK, GORDON C., "The Weaning of the American Economy: Independence, Market Changes, and Economic Development," *Journal of Economic History*, XXIV (Dec., 1964), 541–60.

BOGUE, ALLAN and MARGARET, "Profits and the Frontier Land Speculator," *Journal of Economic History*, XVII (March, 1957), 1–24.

DOVRING, FOLKE, "European Reactions to the Homestead Act," *Journal of Economic History*, XXII (Dec., 1962), 461–72.

FERGUSON, E. JAMES, "Speculation in the Revolutionary Debt: The Ownership of Public Securities in Maryland, 1790," *Journal of Economic History*, XIV (Winter, 1954), 35–45.

GATES, PAUL W., "The Homestead Act in an Incongruous Land System," *American Historical Review*, XLI (July, 1936), 652–81.

LEE, LAWRENCE B., "The Homestead Act: Vision and Reality," *Utah Historical Quarterly*, XXX (Summer, 1962), 215–34.

SWIERENGA, ROBERT P., "Land Speculator 'Profits' Reconsidered: Central Iowa as a Test Case," *Journal of Economic History*, XXVI (March, 1966), 1–28.

TRESCOTT, PAUL B., "Federal-State Financial Relations, 1790–1860," *Journal of Economic History*, XV (Sept., 1955), 227–45.

Industrializing the Atlantic Economy

PART

The Industrial Revolution

CHAPTER 14

"*The* Industrial Revolution" is a term used to refer to certain economic and technical changes which occurred in England in the latter part of the eighteenth and the early part of the nineteenth centuries. This "Revolution" was a product, at least in part, of modern capitalism after the latter had been in the process of development for two or three centuries. Like any great historical event, the Industrial Revolution could occur only when circumstances were ripe for it. All the changes that have been described in the preceding pages are important as background of the Industrial Revolution. Improvements in agriculture, the growth of commerce, the greater division of labor in industry, together with the accumulation and mobilization of capital, were prerequisites of the Industrial Revolution.

In addition to these strictly economic developments, another factor heretofore mentioned only incidentally impinged directly on the economic sector. This factor, or circumstance, was the advance in science. Scientific discoveries became increasingly the basis for advances in technology. The Industrial Revolution marked the marriage of science with capitalism to produce new wealth on an unprecedented scale. Although the contributions of science were not necessarily the contributions of capitalism, the two were so intimately linked in the historical process that their respective contributions can hardly be separated. Scientific principles were applied to economic production in the West at a time when capitalism was the prevailing economic system. Given the contributions of scientists like Sir Isaac Newton and the practical genius of men like James Watt, capitalist institutions were sufficiently dynamic to convert new ideas into profitable and highly productive undertakings.

WHY THE INDUSTRIAL REVOLUTION BEGAN IN ENGLAND

Circumstances accounting for the priority of England in the Industrial Revolution may be stated in terms of the four-fold classification of the factors of production: (1) labor, (2) capital, (3) natural resources, and (4) organization.

1. Labor A rapid increase in the productivity of English agriculture

during the eighteenth century enabled a smaller proportion of the labor force to produce the necessary food and agricultural raw materials. Consequently a larger proportion of the total labor force became available for industrial employment. Eighteenth-century statistics on the labor force and its distribution are not very good, but some approximations may be made from information now available.[1] The proportion of the English labor force engaged in agriculture and closely related activities decreased from about four-fifths toward the end of the seventeenth century (c. 1688), to three-fifths in 1750, one-third in the early 1800's, one-fifth in 1850, and one-tenth in 1880. The sudden drop from three-fifths to one-third between 1750 and the early 1800's reflects the increasing pace of industrialization associated with the onset of the Industrial Revolution. From the middle of the eighteenth century to the middle of the nineteenth, approximating the span of the Industrial Revolution, the number of workers engaged in agriculture fell from six in ten to two in ten. Thus four in ten additional workers became available for nonagricultural employment within the period of a century.

The Industrial Revolution was accompanied by a rapid increase in England's total population. The rate of growth was relatively low in the first half of the eighteenth century but rose rapidly in the second half of the century. From 1750 to 1820, total population doubled. Yet English farmers were able to grow enough grain to feed this rapidly increasing population—a remarkable achievement. Without this revolutionary change in agricultural productivity, large imports of food would have been required, and the process of industrialization surely would have been impeded. In fact, without the increase in agricultural productivity the Industrial Revolution would not have occurred.

2. Capital   England's progress in commercial and financial capitalism from the sixteenth to the eighteenth century made capital available for investment in industrial enterprise. Many men had accumulated surplus funds of modest proportions, and British financial institutions were probably better prepared for mobilizing money capital than those of any other country except Holland. The great manufacturers of the Industrial Revolution were for the most part "new men" who started with relatively little capital of their own. Consequently an important condition of industrial development was mobility of capital whereby the funds of older merchant capitalists would be transferred to the new class of industrial entrepreneurs. To invest heavily in fixed assets such as ironworks, factory buildings, and machinery required a different outlook from that of the merchant capitalists, who characteristically required a rapid turnover of their capital and were fearful of commitments which would realize a return of capital with profit only over a long period. Probably the most common device used by the new industrialists was the formation of partnerships with men who possessed capital. Industry in this period was seldom organized on a joint-stock or corporate basis. The corporate form of business, although developed in the seventeenth century, did not become characteristic of industrial organization until the age of mass production of the late nineteenth century.

[1] See Phyllis Deane and W. A. Cole, *British Economic Growth, 1688–1959* (London: Cambridge University Press, 1962), Chap. 4; and W. A. Cole and Phyllis Deane, *Cambridge Economic History of Europe*, Vol. VI, Chap. 1, "The Growth of National Incomes" (London: Cambridge University Press, 1965), esp. p. 45.

3. **Natural resources** Steam power derived from coal and used to drive

machinery made of iron is symbolic of the Industrial Revolution. The island of Great Britain had rich deposits of both coal and iron ore. Moreover, in a century which was still without any means of cheap overland mass transportation, the coal and iron resources were fortunately located near each other. A noteworthy fact of economic development is that England was the only country which experienced an industrial revolution prior to the coming of the railway. In the pre-railway era, long overland transportation of either coal or iron in quantities necessary for large-scale industry would have been prohibitively costly.

If one considers the other countries which might conceivably have enjoyed priority in the Industrial Revolution, he can easily see the importance of England's geography of iron and coal resources. Holland was in the seventeenth century the most highly developed capitalist nation in the world, but Holland lacked the natural resources to continue its leadership when industrial capitalism replaced commercial capitalism as the dominant form of economic organization. In another area of early capitalist development, northern Italy, coal was completely lacking, and Italy was therefore severely handicapped. Southern Germany was landlocked and unable to develop industry on a massive scale prior to the coming of railways in the nineteenth century. France possessed both coal and iron, but the deposits were distant from one another, and could not be brought together economically until railways developed.

Even the English climate contributed to the Industrial Revolution. In the Lancashire district, where the cotton industry flourished, the damp climate with a modest range of temperature was ideally suited for spinning fine yarn. The textile industry, of course, spearheaded the Industrial Revolution.

4. **Organization** The political, legal, and religious institutions of England provided a social setting favorable to the Industrial Revolution. These institutions as they developed in England formed a loose cultural texture into which technological and social changes could penetrate easily. Once technological changes had occurred, they set in motion the cumulative process of social change which is a fundamental characteristic of economic development.

The contrasting role of the craft gilds in England and France may serve to illustrate England's advantage in one important respect. In England one feature of the growth of strong central government during the age of mercantilism had been the weakening of the craft gilds. Under the famous Elizabethan Statute of Artificers (1563), apprenticeship and wage controls were transferred from the gilds to the national government. In France, by contrast, the gilds were strengthened because they were made the agents of local administration for the central government. Strengthening of the craft gilds tended to perpetuate the economic localism that had characterized the medieval economy against which modern institutions have struggled. As a rule, wherever the gilds remained powerful, the introduction of new industrial techniques was successfully resisted. Even in England in those industries in which the gilds remained strong, progress was impeded. Consequently, industries which progressed most rapidly were those which grew up outside gild influences; for example, in textiles it was the cotton industry rather than the woolen industry in which the famous spinning and weaving inventions of the eight-

eenth century found ready application. Most of the industries which experienced phenomenal growth during the Industrial Revolution were those whose origins were so recent that they had never been subjected to the gild form of organizational control.

England's middle-class revolution (1640–1689) came earlier than in any other country. This seventeenth-century revolution sealed the triumph of parliamentary government and assured to capitalists a political representation congenial to the growth of private business enterprise. The legal climate was also favorable. The "Law Merchant," which had been developing since the Middle Ages, was further advanced in England than elsewhere. The law of property, resting in no small part on the ideas of John Locke, gave a green light to the pecuniary aims of business enterprise.

Although England retained its class stratification, the movement of individuals between classes was freer than in Continental countries. Wealthy commercial families who purchased landed estates were readily accepted as members of the gentry. Nobles with dwindling resources did not hesitate to marry their daughters to wealthy merchants and industrialists in order to restore the family fortune. Many displaced yeomen rose to positions of wealth as manufacturers and thence progressed to the landed aristocracy.

English economic development was also favored by the military posture of Europe. Geographical isolation prevented the physical destruction which Continental countries suffered during the seventeenth, eighteenth, and nineteenth centuries. Wars increased the demand for goods, both for English armies and navies when England chose to participate in wars on the Continent and also when she remained at peace and merely sold goods to warring factions. The uniform nature of war goods such as guns and ammunition as well as military uniforms stimulated the routine and mechanical methods of production which were to become characteristic of large-scale industrial capitalism. Shortly after England's Industrial Revolution got under way and before it had spread to other countries, England was relatively isolated for a quarter-century (1790–1815) by the French Revolution and the Napoleonic wars. During these years England increased an already considerable lead over its rivals.

TECHNOLOGY OF THE INDUSTRIAL REVOLUTION

Technological progress based on the accumulation of scientific knowledge is the leading factor accounting for the difference between medieval and modern standards of living. Although the accumulation of knowledge bearing on economic technology extends back to ancient times, the phenomenal changes which have revolutionized economic processes date from the eighteenth century and are related in turn to the great scientific advances of the seventeenth century. Alfred North Whitehead, a great philosopher of science, has called the seventeenth century the "century of genius." It was a century in which the discoveries of many minds extending over centuries were consolidated into major scientific advances. In a similar manner, the eighteenth century was one in which scattered economic developments were consolidated into the Industrial Revolution. The technological and economic changes which

began in England during the last third of the eighteenth century represented

something new in human history. These changes marked the transition to the "machine age." Although there had been machines previously, the term machine age can be applied appropriately only to the period beginning with the eighteenth century.

Changes in methods of production stemming from the Industrial Revolution have in turn had a powerful impact upon institutions of all types. No society has escaped its influence. Nations have either adopted the machine technology and risen to positions of great power, or remained subordinate in failing to do so. As machine technology resting on science has become the basis of military power, nations are strong or weak according to the state of their industrial arts. Although the Industrial Revolution involved more than new machines and new chemical processes, these technological changes were an indispensable part of the Industrial Revolution. Consequently attention must be directed to the specific technological changes which marked the beginning of the new machine age.

Innovation rather than invention was the highlight of technological advances in the eighteenth century. Innovation means the actual adoption for the first time of a new technique, as distinguished from an invention, which is the original discovery of a new process or new mechanical contrivance. An invention increases the technological possibilities but remains only a potential improvement unless it is economically practicable or feasible to use in production. In England by the eighteenth century conditions were ripe for the innovation of new techniques, many of which had been known for centuries. Many mechanical inventions were anticipated by Leonardo da Vinci, the famous Italian, who is most noted for his paintings but whose claim to fame rests no less on his talent as an inventor and mechanical engineer. Leonardo (d. 1516) left notebooks containing sketches and drawings of mechanical devices, a mere listing of which would require two pages. A few examples in the textile field include drawings of spinning machines, a power loom for weaving, a flying shuttle, a machine for shearing cloth, a gig mill to raise the nap on woolen cloth or felt hats, a silk doubling and winding apparatus, and a rope-making device. Why were these ideas, which proved practicable later, not adopted as standard techniques until the eighteenth century? The answer is, of course, that the situation was not ripe. Leonardo was ahead of his time in the sense that he anticipated innovations which became important in a later age but which were not practicable during his lifetime.

One aspect of the ripening of the environment may be illustrated by the role of the putting-out system in conditioning English industry for the use of machine technology in textiles. Under the putting-out system manufacture was divided into an increasing number of separate and relatively simple, routine steps or stages. In order to obtain large numbers of workmen to turn out relatively uniform products, early industrial capitalists were led to regularize methods of production. This tended to reduce the task of each individual workman to the level of the least skilled workman. After dividing the work among many laborers each performing specialized tasks that became simple and routine, a logical next step was to look for a mechanical device which would perform the simple, routine task. Even though wages were low, the daily output of a human laborer could not match that of a machine, and the

greater output of the machine would probably result in lower net cost. Substitution of machines for human labor involved, for the same output, more capital and less labor. In brief, the more specialized and routinized the tasks of workmen became, the easier it was to find machines that could duplicate man's power to twist, stretch, form, cut, and weigh. Where the task performed was somewhat complicated, as in the case of setting the flying shuttle in motion, mechanical control was often delayed. This partly explains why nearly a century elapsed between the invention of the flying shuttle and the commercially successful power loom. By the process of division and specialization of human tasks, laborsaving devices are frequently invented. The putting-out system, which was based primarily on hand or *manu*-facture, tended to lead to the mechanization of production.

Textile Machinery

For the nontechnical student of economics perhaps the most meaningful approach to textile technology is to visualize oneself in the position of having to produce cloth from wool still on a sheep's back or from cotton standing in a field. There are two fundamental steps: first, to convert the raw fiber into yarn or thread; and second, to interlace the yarn into a compact piece of cloth. The first involves spinning and the second weaving, which together constitute the two main technical divisions of textile manufacturing. The essential task in spinning is to twist and draw the fibers in such manner as to give length and strength to the yarn, and the essential task in weaving is to make the web tight enough to meet wearing needs.

Of the two main processes in textile manufacture, weaving is basically simpler, and therefore it is not surprising that the first major invention in the age of mechanization was the flying shuttle, which approximately doubled the productivity of weavers. Whereas a single weaver could process the yarn of five spinners before the flying shuttle, now a single weaver could process the yarn of ten spinners. The greater potential saving for labor both before and after the flying shuttle lay in spinning. For centuries the simple spinning wheel had been used. In the hands of skilled artisans it produced a good quality yarn, but it was slow and costly in terms of human labor. Invention of the flying shuttle greatly increased the demand for yarn and set the stage for a remarkable series of spinning inventions.

Many attempts were made to develop a workable multiple spinning wheel which could spin more than one thread at a time. The first important success was the well-known spinning jenny which James Hargreaves developed between 1764 and 1767. This multiple spinning wheel was powered by hand or foot and, being relatively inexpensive, could be operated in the homes of workers. Temporarily it reinvigorated the domestic system of manufacture. Hargreaves' first jenny had eight spindles, and the number soon increased to eighty.

The next important advance in spinning was the water frame introduced by Richard Arkwright. Although Arkwright received a patent on his machine, he was unable to defend the patent when it was challenged in the courts. The water frame was a large, heavy, and expensive piece of equipment requiring mechanical power, which meant it required a special location where mechani-

cal power was available as well as considerable capital. Being unsuited for domestic employment, the water frame led directly to the establishment of factories. In 1771 Arkwright set up a water-powered factory and soon had 600 workers, mostly children, employed in it. More than any other single innovation, the water frame marked the beginning of the factory system associated with England's Industrial Revolution.

Arkwright's commercially successful application of water power stepped up greatly the production of coarse yarn, but the water frame was unsuited to making fine yarn. The cotton fiber was first stretched through a series of parallel rollers (with each succeeding pair of rollers moving at higher speed) and then twisted on a flyer spindle. If the untwisted fibers were too few in number or were drawn too finely they would break under the tension caused by stretching. In contrast, the jenny twisted and stretched the fibers simultaneously. Thus only coarse yarn could be made on the water frame.

The disadvantage of Arkwright's coarse yarn was overcome by the spinning mule invented by Samuel Crompton in 1779. Crompton's machine was called a mule because it was a hybrid between the "jenny" and the water frame, sometimes referred to as a "jack" frame. As with the jenny, the mule represented a form of intermittent spinning in which twisting and stretching occurred simultaneously. Like the water frame, the mule utilized rollers, although for a different purpose than the water frame. Smaller mules could be operated by hand, but larger ones were driven by mechanical power. Even in its further development the mule could not match the quantity of output of continuous spinning machines like the water frame, but it continued to occupy an important place in the textile industry because of the high quality of its product. This remarkable machine could spin finer yarn than any produced by the old hand spinning wheel. It quickly supplanted the spinning jenny and accentuated the movement toward the factory organization begun by the water frame.

With the invention and commercial adoption of the mule, the spinning branch of the textile industry fully extricated itself from the plight into which it had been placed half a century earlier by the great advance in weaving brought about by the flying shuttle. Kay's shuttle was a hand-operated process carried on by hand-loom weavers. In the conversion of spinning to mechanical power the chief technological obstacle lay in perfecting an automatic device which could replace the human hand in manipulating the shuttle. Edmund Cartwright, an English clergyman, patented a power loom in 1787, but it was not a commercial success. Only after 1822, when the machine-building firm of Sharp and Roberts put a power loom into effective use, did weaving cease to be primarily a handicraft. Long after spinning had become a mechanized, factory process, hand weavers remained dominant. In England the hand weavers were finally forced to the wall with the extensive introduction of power looms during the later phase of the depression of 1837–43. In other countries, hand weaving continued dominant into the second half of the nineteenth century.

Iron and Coal

Prior to the English Industrial Revolution wood, in the form of charcoal, was the fuel used to smelt iron ore. Wood had two major disadvantages: (1)

its relative shortage in England, and (2) its inefficiency in attaining high temperatures. Shortages of wood were noted as early as the time of Elizabeth I and became acute by the eighteenth century. For high-quality iron England had become increasingly dependent on Sweden, which enjoyed abundant supplies of wood as well as high-grade iron ore.

Charcoal-burning furnaces required as long as two weeks to reduce iron ore to molten metal. Great quantities of charcoal were consumed in the process. English ironmasters would set up a furnace where wood was abundant and, after consuming the local supply of fuel, would move to another district where the voracious consumption of fuel would be repeated. The long period required for heating limited the output per furnace, five tons per week being a good average output for charcoal furnaces. Total output of iron in England probably declined during the first half of the eighteenth century.

Substituting coal for wood represented the greatest technical advance in iron technology during the eighteenth century. For more than a century Englishmen had experimented with coal for making pig iron without success until Abraham Darby about 1710 converted coal into coke and succeeded where his predecessors had failed. His son, Abraham Darby II, improved the blowing bellows and achieved commercial success in smelting iron ore with coke about the middle of the century. A further advance in ironmaking resulted about 1760 when John Smeaton introduced a compressed air pump which yielded much higher temperatures than were possible with the bellows used by the younger Darby. Smeaton's new blowing, or blasting, apparatus was at first driven by water power and later by steam engines. The smelting furnace became a "blast furnace."

As a result of the discoveries of the Darbys and Smeaton, pig iron and cast iron became relatively cheap. Pig iron was an intermediate product used for making wrought iron at the forge. The iron which came from coke furnaces was much superior for casting to that made with charcoal because it contained fewer impurities and, being heated to a higher temperature, would run freely into the smallest channels of molds. Improvement in the quality of cast iron brought about many new uses for iron in hinges, domestic stoves, rails, bridges, lock-gates for canals, castings for steam engines, and parts for other types of machinery. In some uses the new and superior cast iron replaced the still expensive wrought iron.

Although pig iron and cast iron were now cheap and abundant, there remained innumerable and increasing uses for which pure, or wrought, iron was required. The existing method of producing wrought iron was a tedious process involving alternate heating and hammering of pig iron at the forge. By the use of hand and mechanical hammers the impurities, including carbon, were literally hammered out of the pig iron.

A first major step in improving the process of making wrought iron came with the reverberatory furnace, which kept the flame and fumes of the fuel out of contact with the iron. Then in 1784 Peter Onions and Henry Cort simultaneously developed a new technique known as the "puddling process," by which the molten pig iron in the reverberatory furnace was stirred continuously in order to burn out impurities. About the same time Cort provided a second great innovation, the rolling mill, which replaced hammers for pressing out the impurities and also shaped the metal for further use. Using the pud-

dling process and the rolling mill, fifteen tons of wrought iron could be produced in the time formerly required to produce one ton. Moreover, the rolling mill produced sheet iron, which was indispensable for large steam boilers such as those used in applying the newly developed Watt steam engine to steamboats and locomotives.

Thus in the course of the eighteenth century two major advances had been made in iron technology. Pig iron and cast iron became relatively cheap as a result of the use of coal in place of wood as the fuel in smelting iron ore, and wrought iron became relatively cheap as a result of the puddling process and the rolling mill. Cheap iron was an achievement of the early phase of the Industrial Revolution and the fundamental technological basis of its later phase.

Methods of producing cheap steel did not come into use until the second half of the nineteenth century. The eighteenth century was an age of cheap iron but it was not an age of cheap steel. Nevertheless some progress was made toward producing better quality steel during the eighteenth century. The most important new process was the discovery of crucible steel by Benjamin Huntsman about 1740. Prior to the Huntsman process, steel was made by heating high-grade Swedish bar iron with charcoal to increase its carbon content to the desired amount. (The carbon content of steel is less than that of cast or pig iron but greater than that of bar iron.) Because of swellings on the surface of this product it was called "blister" iron. By hammering and heating small bits of "blister" steel a better grade known as "shear" steel was produced. Huntsman placed "blister" steel in an airtight crucible along with a proper quantity of ground glass. After being subjected to intense heat, the molten contents of the crucible were poured into molds to produce "crucible" or "cast" steel. This high-grade steel was used for watch springs, razors, fine cutlery, and machine-making tools like Wilkinson's cylinder-boring machine, which rendered practicable the improved steam engine of James Watt. Huntsman's contribution was to produce a better quality steel than was formerly available. His process did not result, however, in lowering the price of steel. A price of $250 to $300 per ton was in itself enough to prevent widespread use of steel in industry. Steel for structural purposes was economically out of the question. When the age of cheap steel did finally arrive in the latter half of the nineteenth century, it became the technological basis for a new age, sometimes referred to as the "Age of Steel."

Watt's Steam Engine

James Watt's steam engine was the greatest single technological advance of the eighteenth century. Thinking men had often been impressed with the potential power of expanding steam, and as early as 100 B.C. Hero of Alexander described a model steam engine which performed "magic tricks" for the entertainment of the idle rich. For the mine, the forge, and the factory, however, the steam engine had little significance before the eighteenth century, and even in the eighteenth century its development would have been virtually impossible except in the English environment.

Between 1689 and 1702 Thomas Savery, an Englishman, developed what he called "The Miner's Friend, or an engine to raise water with fire," which,

as the name suggests, was a steam engine used to pump water out of mines. A few years later another Englishman, Thomas Newcomen, patented the steam engine which was the immediate predecessor and for a time a competitor of Watt's engine. The principle of Newcomen's engine was to create a vacuum in a cylinder by first filling it with steam and then condensing the steam by injecting a jet of cold water into the cylinder. (At first Newcomen sprayed the water on the outside of the cylinder.) Atmospheric pressure above the open cylinder forced the piston down and furnished the pulsating power for pumping. It should be noted that steam was not the real source of power in the Newcomen engine; steam served merely to create a vacuum inside the cylinder in order that atmospheric pressure could be utilized.

Like all other men James Watt was a product of his time. He was trained as a "mathematical instrument maker," and being possessed of a superior and disciplined mind, he was familiar with contemporary developments in physical and chemical theory. Both his training and his interest reflected the scientific and technical drift of the age. When a model of a Newcomen engine was presented to him for repair, he was impressed with its great inefficiency, which resulted from alternately heating and cooling the cylinder, since it was first filled with steam and then cooled by an injection of cold water to condense the steam to form the vacuum. Watt's original insight arose in answer to the question: How can steam be condensed without the necessity of cooling the cylinder? His solution was to condense the steam in a separate chamber rather than in the cylinder itself. This notion of a separate condensing chamber represented an insight which started him on the road to an invention that, in terms of its consequences for economic development, was one of the greatest of all times.

Watt was an innovator as well as an inventor. During the thirty years after inventing the separate condensing chamber he added new ideas and supervised their practical application. He abandoned the atmospheric pressure principle of the Newcomen engine for a genuine steam engine in which expanding steam was applied alternately on both sides of the piston. In this double-action engine both ends of the cylinder were closed. The steam engine under the guidance of Watt developed from an attachment for pumping water out of mines into an energy-supplying device of universal application in mechanical industry. The revolutionary implications of the improved steam engine were recognized in Watt's patent application of 1784.

Watt and his partners experienced a long and heartbreaking struggle in the period from the conception of the separate condensing chamber to the commercial success of the finished steam engine. The financial burden was heavy, and Watt's first partner went bankrupt. Watt was fortunate in obtaining as a second partner an enterprising and resourceful capitalist, Matthew Boulton. Even with adequate financial resources and a clear vision of the mechanical principles, there remained the almost insuperable task of building steam engines on a commercial basis with the men and tools available. Contemporary inventors like Smeaton admired Watt's ingenious models, but said they could not be successful commercially because precision parts could not be made. There were no tools for boring cylinders and there were too few skilled mechanics. Fortunately, however, there were other men of mechanical ingenuity in eighteenth-century England. John Wilkinson, for example, in-

vented a boring machine which was indispensable to the ultimate success of
Watt's engine. The earlier cylinders had been hammered into shape and by
this imprecise method eighteen-inch cylinders were sometimes out-of-round
by three-eighths of an inch. But Boulton and Watt had to undertake the training of skilled workmen in order to make a success of their commercial production of steam engines.

Like its predecessors the Watt engine was first employed primarily in
mines. Here some time was required to replace the Newcomen engine, which
in spite of its inefficiency was a fairly suitable machine especially in and near
coal mines where fuel was cheap. The revolutionary significance came, however, after Watt adapted his engine to factory use by converting the back-
and-forth motion of the piston to rotary motion. The early factories were
located along streams and rivers where water power was harnessed by means
of the water wheel. Obviously there were disadvantages in being tied to
streams. Seasonal decreases in water flows often necessitated the use of horses
as a supplementary source of power. Streams were frequently poorly located
in relation to labor supply, markets, and transportation facilities. In contrast,
the steam engine was a highly mobile source of power.

In 1785 the first Watt engine was installed in a cotton spinning mill.
By 1800, when their patent expired, Boulton and Watt had constructed 289
steam engines in England. As these figures suggest, the steam engine wrought
no immediate transformation of industry. Nevertheless the conversion to steam
power continued irresistibly and by the middle of the nineteenth century
water power was almost completely displaced by steam power in England.
On the Continent and in the United States the transition came later, but it
was equally irresistible. The steam engine provided the dynamic ingredient
for cumulative change in socio-economic institutions. The steamboat and the
steam railway locomotive were developed during Watt's lifetime. In less than
a century after Watt's invention, the steam engine had revolutionized both
the industrial system and the transportation systems of the world.

TECHNOLOGY AND ECONOMIC DEVELOPMENT

Technology as such is primarily the concern of engineers, technicians, and
mechanics rather than of economists and historians. However, the direct impact and the ultimate incidence of technological change upon economic institutions is so great that a discussion of economic development must address itself
explicitly to the question of the significance of technology for economic
development.

Technological change is important as an entering wedge by which
economic institutions at first, and social institutions later, are modified and
ultimately transformed. As a rule, technological changes are more readily accepted than changes in religious belief, or in political position, or in property
rights. All parts of a total culture are, however, interdependent. Changes at
one level call for adaptive adjustments at other levels. Therefore, that part
of the total culture in which change is most readily accepted becomes the
initiating point, or entering wedge, for broader changes. Economic institutions
stand in more intimate relation to technical change than do institutions of a

nonmaterial type, and the impact of technical change is usually felt earlier in economic arrangements than in noneconomic institutions. Arkwright's water frame, for example, required factory organization (an economic arrangement), and this change was made long before the chain of related events set in motion by the factory system led to urbanization and a change in the status of the family (a social institution).

Although technology serves as an entering wedge for wide-ranging social change because there is less resistance to technical change as such, this does not mean that technical change has not been resisted. History is replete with instances of opposition to technical change motivated by fear of its social and economic consequences. Medieval gilds opposed technical change because gildsmen feared that new techniques of production would undermine the stability and security of their privileged position in society deriving from their monopoly of occupations. The city council of Danzig, fearing the consequences of unemployment from a ribbon loom invented in the seventeenth century, had the inventor secretly strangled. Arkwright's cotton spinning machine was opposed by a group of poor English spinners in a petition to Parliament. In their petition the spinners represented their plight as "so intolerable as to reduce them to despair, and many thousands assembled in different parts to destroy the causes of their distress [water frame]." From the opposite pole of society, English landlords resented the invention of Arkwright's machine because they feared they would have to pay higher taxes for poor relief for spinners thrown out of work. In the famous Luddite risings in England between 1812 and 1815 armed bands of workmen roamed the countryside smashing machines and burning factories. The real opposition was not against machinery, but against its actual and anticipated social consequences. Although such opposition is irrational for society as a whole, it may be well founded from the point of view of particular groups. The great English economist of the Industrial Revolution, David Ricardo, concluded that the introduction of machinery in industry might be harmful to the wage-earning class.

Although history records many violent attacks against machinery, characteristically these have been directed against the more sensational innovations the economic consequences of which have been obvious to those adversely affected. Seldom have they been attacks on technical change as such. More frequently technical change occurs gradually, and the ultimate consequences are not obvious to any but the most acute observer of social change. Given the capitalist's passion for rational technology and his disregard for traditional methods of production, the resistance to technical change under capitalism was even less than in precapitalist societies. Hence technology, which had always been an entering wedge of social change, became revolutionary under capitalism.

Technological change is interdependent, cumulative, and irreversible. Interdependence may be illustrated by the steam engine, which, in addition to being used in mines and factories, stimulated the invention of the steamboat, the steam locomotive, and the steam turbine. The invention of textile machinery created a new demand for cheap iron, which hastened the development of the steam engine, and the steam engine promoted new developments in the textile, iron, and nearly all other branches of industry requiring

mechanical motive power. Rolling mills provided sheet iron for steam boilers

for steam engines. Wilkinson's boring machine enabled Watt to bore round cylinders for his steam engines. Crucible steel made better machine tools possible for the production of the boring machine. Skilled mechanics trained in all these activities provided a mobile source of highly essential labor for the development of new technology in eighteenth-century England. In the nineteenth century, the sewing machine was a fundamental invention which revolutionized not only the clothing trade but shoemaking, tailoring, hatmaking, and the leather goods industry. Application of steam power to the sewing machine brought together two revolutionary inventions, multiplied the productivity of labor, and delivered a crushing blow to hand trades working without machinery.

Technological change is cumulative because each step forward opens the possibility for several further steps. The accumulation of knowledge which underlies inventions provides a higher and higher springboard from which greater leaps may be made in all directions. Nearly every so-called invention derives from a knowledge of prior inventions. Often what is "new" about an invention is slight and even difficult to determine. In the case of Watt's acknowledged "revolutionary" invention, the start was made from the repair of a Newcomen engine. All the parts were already present, cylinder, piston, steam boiler, valves, etc. Once a certain stage of technology has been attained, further steps become possible. This suggests a fundamental truth that invention is a social process in relation to which the contribution of any single individual, no matter how great his genius, is relatively small. The many cases of simultaneous invention are explicable only in terms of the social and cumulative nature of technological knowledge. Professor Ogburn lists thirteen pages of significant inventions and scientific discoveries made independently by two or more persons almost simultaneously. Among the famous simultaneous inventions are the puddling process by Cort and Onions, the rolling mill by Cort and Huntsman, the reaper by McCormack and Hussey, cheap steel by Bessemer and Kelley, the telephone by Bell and Gray, and the airplane by Wright and Langley.[2]

Technology is also important in general economic development because it imparts to the course of developing economic institutions an irreversibility which no other type of factor is capable of imposing. The joint-stock companies of early capitalism were for the most part based upon special grants of political privilege, which could be, and in fact were, easily withdrawn when the new laissez-faire philosophy demanded the end of such special privilege. On the other hand, the growth of large-scale machine technology during the nineteenth century increased the size of the technologically most efficient unit of production to a point where any form of organization other than the corporate one became impracticable. A retreat from corporate to noncorporate industrial enterprises would require what is technologically impossible, that is, a retreat from large-scale to small-scale production. Technological imperatives not only make economic developments irreversible, but they limit the choices available at any time and thus impart a degree of determinism to the future course of economic development.

[2] See William F. Ogburn, *Social Change* (New York: The Viking Press, 1950), pp. 90–102.

Capitalism was a powerful promoter of technological change because the accumulation of capital under this system made possible the innovation of inventions which society could not otherwise have afforded. In a surplus-saving economy like capitalism new methods of production were given a chance they would not have enjoyed if the social surplus had been invested unproductively or consumed currently. Under capitalism many new techniques failed, but, given the existing state of scientific and technical knowledge, enough succeeded to revolutionize methods of production. Inventive geniuses like James Watt found partners who were able to finance their inventions through years of experimentation and discouragement to ultimate commercial success. Aggressive entrepreneurs like Arkwright found partners who were willing and able to venture their capital in the novel types of industrial organization which were required for the exploitation of new machines. Two or three centuries of capital accumulation were beginning to pay off in a big way in the eighteenth century. Now it was possible to make practical use of the mechanical knowledge which had been accumulating for centuries. Societies other than capitalism had been wealthy, but none had managed its wealth in such a way as to be able to take advantage of the more efficient methods of production which an increasing mastery over nature made physically possible.

The diffusion of improved methods of production was directly fostered by competition among profit-seeking enterprises. An innovator of a superior machine might first exploit his ability to produce more cheaply by selling at the prevailing price and making a larger profit than his rivals or by selling at a lower price and taking business from his rivals. In either case, his more progressive rivals would try to imitate his superior machine in order to increase or retain their own profits. Once the superiority of the new machine process was firmly established, the total output coming on the market was greater than under old methods. Output from more productive equipment could be produced at lower cost and hence could be sold at lower prices. In order to sell profitably at lower prices, other firms were compelled to adopt the more efficient technique. For a while old and new techniques would exist side by side. In the long run, however, firms which failed to install the new methods of production could not survive, and in time the old techniques disappeared. Hand spinning, for example, disappeared early with the prompt adoption of the greatly superior factories utilizing the water frame and the spinning mule. Hand weaving was more tenacious. In some parts of England independent weavers, using hand looms, literally worked themselves to death by laboring too hard and too long in trying to make a living in competition with the tireless efficiency of mechanical looms. The most pathetic working conditions created by the English Industrial Revolution were probably not found in the factories—bad as these often were—but among independent craftsmen in small shops and households where they clung to outmoded methods of production. This was part of the human cost of technological progress under the social and economic conditions of the time.

Patent law as it developed in England was intended to stimulate technological progress by granting to inventors a temporary monopoly of their in-

ventions. James Watt received a patent on his new steam engine and this patent was renewed for twenty years in 1780. Watt was afforded time to develop his idea to commercial success, and he and Matthew Boulton made a modest fortune. Less fortunate were the inventors Kay, Hargreaves, Crompton, Cartwright, and Cort, all of whom died poor. Even if money making was not the prime goal in life of the inventors of this age, probably few of them were indifferent to the prospects of making money from their ideas. In this respect the rational patent law probably served as a tonic for invention. Restricting the inventor's monopoly (patent) to a limited period was consistent with the principle that in the long run the fruits of inventions should be shared by all.

SOCIAL EFFECTS OF THE INDUSTRIAL REVOLUTION

In English society at the time of the Industrial Revolution there were three major socio-economic classes: the landlords, the capitalists, and the wage-earners, receiving respectively rents, profits (and interest), and wages. In this section discussion is confined to the social effects of the Industrial Revolution and the factory system on wage-earners, who were the most numerous of the three classes. The impact of the Industrial Revolution on landlords and factory owners is discussed in the next chapter.

The factory was more than a new place of employment for wage-earners; it involved a new way of life. The common people had always worked long and hard for a living, but prior to factory employment they had lived largely in rural areas where they were close to nature and where they controlled to a considerable extent the time as well as the immediate conditions of their employment. Children worked under the supervision of parents rather than of factory overseers, with long hours, no doubt, but, let us hope, with more tolerant discipline than that which developed in the factories. Industrial workers in the putting-out system usually owned or rented some land and worked out-of-doors tilling the soil. Certainly the domestic system combining industry and farming represented no utopia. The homes of workers were hovels, diets were inadequate, clothes were often rags, and incomes were miserably low. Yet the domestic system was associated with a relatively carefree way of life in comparison with which factory employment was viewed as little better than imprisonment. One reason why the first generation of factory owners experienced difficulty in getting workers was because men accustomed to a rural way of life found the regimented work schedule of the factory quite intolerable. The psychological adjustment to the new way of life was very difficult for the first generation of factory workers. The revulsion felt toward the hated discipline of the factory was one of the psychic costs of machine technology.

The factory was the final stage in the separation of workers from ownership of the means of production. Under the handicraft system workers owned the materials and the tools with which they worked as well as the final product which they produced. Under the putting-out system, workers typically owned the fixed capital, that is, the tools and small machines with which they worked, as well as the premises on which they labored. They did not own the materials on which they worked nor the finished product. They sold their labor rather

than the product of their labor, which gave to the putting-out system its essentially capitalistic character. Under the factory system workers were divided from ownership of the means of production (machinery) as well as from ownership of materials and the product of their labor. They owned nothing but their bodies and their capacity for labor. Thus the separation between capital and labor became complete.

In another sense, also, workers become more dependent under the factory system. Whereas the tools used under the handicraft and putting-out systems were passive and under the full command of the worker, factory machines were not under full control of workers. To a considerable extent the pace at which the machine operated depended on the factory owner or manager. The workers' task was to keep pace with the machine, which was coordinated with dozens or hundreds of other machines and hundreds and thousands of other factory operatives. Discipline and regimentation were imposed by the nature of the technical processes of machines operating from a central source of power in a highly complex and regulated system of production. The machine process was less human, not to mention less humane, than older techniques of production. The clock became symbolic of the regimented working habits of factory employees. A sense of subjection to machines was an inevitable feeling under the new regimentation.

Wages

Wage-earners, on the one hand, attempt to sell their labor at as high a price as possible because their welfare and that of their families depends on the amount of wages received. Employers of labor, on the other hand, have to keep costs of production low in order to remain in business under a system of competitive enterprise. Since wages are usually a major item of expense, employers have a strong incentive to pay low wages to their employees. In a competitive world, benevolence may lead only to bankruptcy. The outcome of the conflicting interest of the worker in high wages and of the employer in low wages is determined by the relative bargaining power of the two parties in the so-called labor market. A wage contract, either oral or written, states the terms of employment. In the bargaining process, which determines the terms of the wage contract, the advantage obviously goes to the stronger party.

In England during the Industrial Revolution of the eighteenth century the reign of "free" competition in the labor market clearly operated to the advantage of employers because their resources and bargaining power were greater than the resources and bargaining power of individual workers. Although low wages were an advantage to the employer because they meant higher net income (profits), they were not necessarily an advantage to society, because wages as well as profits are part of the net income of society as a whole. The relative bargaining power determined the distribution of national income between wage-earners and capitalists but it did not affect the size of the national income.

Efforts on the part of workers to organize in order to bargain collectively, instead of individually, were suppressed in the eighteenth century by employers and by legislative authority. Labor unions were illegal conspiracies

under English common law. The hand of employers was further strengthened

by statutes against combinations of workers. Numerous statutes were passed to prohibit combinations in particular trades, and finally general laws against combinations were passed in 1799 and 1800. The anti-combination laws provided for imprisonment of a worker who tried to persuade another worker to ask for higher wages, shorter hours, or better working conditions, or to quit working unless conditions were improved. The anti-combination law of 1800 made some pretense of impartiality by providing for a fine of twenty pounds against any employer who attempted to promote an employers' agreement to influence wages, hours, and working conditions. Under these laws many workers were imprisoned, but there is no record of any employer being fined. This law, like others, was a weapon in the hands of the rich against the poor: "The Parliament that passed the Combination Laws proclaimed a doctrine of serf labour and low wages. Every working man was either to accept the wages that his employer, with the law behind him, chose to give, or to become a vagrant." [3]

Wage trends   Unfortunately we do not have the data necessary to construct a general index of either money wages or the cost of living during the eighteenth century. Some major facts, however, seem reasonably certain. Money wages in industry were higher than in agriculture; therefore the relative shift of workers from agriculture into industry was accompanied by a higher level of money wages. Wages were lower for women and children than for adult males, a fact which helps to account for the widespread employment of the former in factories. Wages were higher in expanding industries than in contracting ones; for example, they were higher in factories than in domestic employment. There were regional differences in wages; for example, money wages were higher in the great new cotton textile area of Lancashire, because of the brisk demand for workers, than in the centers of the old woolen industry (Yorkshire and the Cotswolds). Wages were influenced by shifts in technology; for example, the early innovation of spinning factories soon drove down the wages of hand spinners and the same development temporarily increased the wages of hand weavers, whose services were more in demand because of the increased output of yarn from spinning mills. As the wages of weavers rose, however, the number of weavers increased in a decade or two, and by the 1790's weavers' wages turned down because of the increased supply of weavers. Power weaving did not have any marked influence on wages in the eighteenth century, but in a few more decades, by 1840, power weaving crushed the hand weavers much as power spinning had extirpated the hand spinners in the 1770's. From weighting these various forces one may hazard the guess that the overall trend in money wages was upward in England during the second half of the eighteenth century, with an important exception in the case of thousands of workers who remained in domestic industry.

Offsetting the rise in money wages was the rise in the prices of goods entering into workers' household budgets. Food prices, especially bread and wheat, rose noticeably after 1750 and sharply in the 1790's. Wheat prices per

[3] John L. and Barbara Hammond, *The Town Labourer, 1760–1832, The New Civilization* (London: Longmans, Green & Company, Ltd., 1932), p. 141.

quarter (of a ton) rose from 31 shillings in 1750 to 46 shillings in 1775, and to 128 shillings in the crisis year 1800. Manufactured goods rose less in price and in some cases fell as output increased under improved methods of production.

We may now combine our guesses about the trends in money wages with our guesses about the trends in cost of living to hazard some guesses as to the effect on real wages. Lower-paid workers, who had to spend most of their meager money income on food, probably experienced a fall in real wages because of the increase in the price of foodstuffs. Better-paid workers, whose budgets included a variety of manufactured goods, probably experienced an increase in real wages because the prices of manufactured goods remained relatively constant. It seems reasonable to conclude that skilled workers outside the domestic system were becoming better off in terms of real income and that the poorest workers were becoming worse off. The sharp rise in the price of wheat and bread in the 1790's probably subjected all workers to a falling real wage during these years. In the worst years, ". . . every penny was needed to keep body and soul together. Some died of sheer hunger . . ." (Ashton, *An Economic History of England: The Eighteenth Century*, p. 235). The most unfortunate victims of the Industrial Revolution were those who continued to be employed (and unemployed) in domestic industry and agriculture. It is probably not possible or meaningful to say whether real wages as a whole rose or fell during the last half of the eighteenth century. One must be satisfied with the somewhat unsatisfactory generalization that some workers were becoming better off and some were becoming worse off in the closing decades of the century, and that the sharp increase in living costs associated with war during the 1790's caused a general decline in real wages in those years.

Whatever may have been the overriding trend of real wages, it is certain that real wages did not increase in proportion to the increase in the productivity of labor. Consequently profits rose in relation to wages, and there was profit inflation similar to that which occurred during the Price Revolution of the sixteenth century, except that reductions in the cost of production associated with increased productivity resulting from the use of machine technology were more important in the eighteenth than in the sixteenth century.[4] Enlarged profits became the source of rapid capital formation in the shape of factory buildings, machinery, steam engines, iron works and other forms of capital goods. In retrospect it can be seen that the sacrifices of the generation of workers who witnessed the onset of the Industrial Revolution provided a basis for the greater accumulation of wealth, which in turn permitted the real wages of their descendants to rise during the nineteenth century. After 1820 the trend of real wages in England seems unquestionably to have been upwards.

Yet perhaps the most striking phenomenon concerning wages during the Industrial Revolution was acceptance of the doctrine that the natural wage is one equal to subsistence. This subsistence theory of wages became a basic

---

[4] Professor Earl J. Hamilton, using London data, which he believes typical of England as a whole, concludes that real wages fell during the eighteenth-century Industrial Revolution. "It seems certain that daily real wages dropped considerably in London during the last five or six decades of the eighteenth century." "Profit Inflation and the Industrial Revolution," in *Enterprise and Secular Change*, ed. F. C. Lane (London: George Allen & Unwin, Ltd., 1953), p. 325.

tenet in the political economy of the classical economists, including Malthus and Ricardo. This wage doctrine was related to what critics of capitalism called the "iron law of wages." The pessimistic prospects for the future of the working class caused economics to be called the "dismal science."

Hours

During the early phase of the Industrial Revolution the working day was probably longer than in any other period of English history. Before the Industrial Revolution the normal working time was from sunup to sundown, which meant a twelve-hour day on the average through the year. When artificial illumination was introduced during the eighteenth century, night work became possible. A significant influence tending to lengthen the working day was the desire on the part of capitalists to utilize fully the costly fixed investment in factory buildings and machinery. By working the equipment more intensively capitalists shortened the time required to get back their investment, that is, they shortened the amortization period, i.e., the turnover period of capital. In the early factories a fourteen-hour day seems to have been typical, a sixteen-hour day not uncommon, and an eighteen-hour day not unknown. Women and children as well as men were subjected to these long hours. Strong protests against long hours began to be heard early in the nineteenth century, but it was not until 1850 that belated factory legislation reduced the normal work day in English factories to ten hours.

Working Conditions

Much has been written about the terrible working conditions of the Industrial Revolution. The conditions most complained about, in addition to low wages and long hours, were the employment of young children in ways which deformed their bodies, stunted their growth, and often led to an early grave; the employment of women under harmful and immoral conditions; and the unhealthy living conditions of towns like Manchester, which grew rapidly without providing facilities for sewers, drinking water, and recreation. The chief sources of information about working conditions in Britain are official government documents by committees of Parliament and special commissions established for the purpose of reporting conditions of employment. There is little reason to question the integrity of these sources, although it should be realized that bad conditions were more likely to be reported than good conditions when the purpose of the investigation was to propose legislation for correcting bad conditions. This suggests that the blue books of the royal commissions may not have been wholly representative of general working conditions. On the other hand, there were undoubtedly many situations equally bad or worse which were not recorded.

In the twentieth century, child labor in factories is so generally acknowledged to be undesirable that it seems strange that in the eighteenth and early nineteenth centuries there were many persons who acclaimed the new machines because they enabled children to be usefully employed at tender ages. A contemporary apologist for the factory system wrote as follows about child labor in factories: "The scene of industry, so far from exciting sad emotions

in my mind, was always exhilarating. It was delightful to observe the nimbleness with which they pieced the broken ends . . . The work of these lively elves seemed to resemble a sport, in which habit gave them a pleasing dexterity." [5] Other contemporaries, however, did not take such an exalted view of child labor. Children and women were often employed in place of, rather than in addition to, men because the former were more docile and would work more cheaply.

A major source of labor supply for the factories in the eighteenth century were pauper children from orphanages and poorhouses. Property owners trying to hold down rates (taxes) were partly responsible for the unfortunate orphans and paupers being bound out to employers through indenture of apprenticeship under arrangements that constituted a form of human slavery. The parish poor came at an early age and were kept imprisoned in factories for years. They were housed and fed, but seldom received any money wage. Conditions of working and living were incredibly bad. They were brutally treated by overseers whose remuneration depended on the quantity of work done. Owing to the fatigue of excessive hours they met with more accidents than was usual in the operation of unguarded machinery; mutilated fingers and crushed limbs were common occurrences. They were very poorly fed and hardly clothed at all, and they lived in filthy and overcrowded quarters. Those who survived apprenticeship came out with bowed legs and crooked backs, as well as warped minds and often vicious characters. Until 1802 there was no law to control the conditions under which the helpless paupers were employed.

British Factory Acts, 1802–1850

Robert Peel, who as a factory owner had employed more than a thousand pauper apprentices, introduced the bill which became the first of a series of important laws regulating the conditions of employment in factories. These laws are known as the Factory Acts.

The Health and Morals Act of 1802 limited the working day for pauper children to 12 hours. Night work was to be abolished gradually; each apprentice was to be given two suits of clothing per year; boys and girls were to sleep in separate rooms, with no more than two children to a bed; and some provision was made for the education and religious salvation of the children. The law proved ineffective, especially under wartime conditions. Moreover, it came too late to do much good because the system of pauper labor was disappearing with the relocation of factories associated with the shift from water power to steam power, which brought factories nearer centers of population. The supply of "free" children (those living with parents) was abundant in population centers. Employment of "free" children had for employers the advantage that the expense of housing and feeding the children fell on their parents, and it was cheaper to pay a small money wage when the "free" children were actually employed than to maintain the paupers throughout their apprenticeship.

The Factory Act of 1819 extended protection to all children employed in

5 Andrew Ure, *The Philosophy of Manufacture,* 3rd ed. (London: H. G. Bohn, 1861), p. 301.

cotton factories. Children under nine years could not be employed at all; children between nine and sixteen could be employed only twelve hours a day; night work was prohibited. As enacted, the 1819 law was a watered-down version of a proposal made by Robert Owen, a famous social reformer and former owner of model factories. Owen testified that children were commonly employed at five and six years and that seven years was the most common age of entry into factory employment for children. Many of these children worked fourteen and fifteen hours a day. Opponents argued that productive labor was a virtue and that enforced idleness would be bad for the morals of children. No effective means was provided for enforcement of the 1819 act, and it had little influence in preventing child labor.

The Factory Act of 1833 was the most famous of several laws of its type. Children were still without legal protection except in cotton mills, and even in cotton mills a master could legally employ a nine-year-old child twelve hours a day. A Select Committee of the House of Commons was appointed in 1832 to investigate child labor in factories. Before the committee there filed "a long procession of workers, men and women, girls and boys. Stunted, diseased, deformed, degraded, each with the tale of a wronged life, they pass across the stage, a living picture of man's cruelty to man, a pitiless indictment of those rulers who in their days of unabated power had abandoned the weak to the rapacity of the strong." [6] The resulting law of 1833 applied to children in all textile mills (cotton, wool, linen, silk). Employment of children under nine was prohibited; children between nine and thirteen were limited to a nine-hour day and a 48-hour week; young people between thirteen and eighteen were limited to a twelve-hour day and a 69-hour week; night labor was prohibited for persons under eighteen years. Children in the age group nine to thirteen were required to attend school. Outside inspectors were authorized to enter a factory at any time in order to render effective enforcement of the law.

The Factory Act of 1844 extended to women the same protection that the 1833 law had given to young people between thirteen and eighteen years of age; hours were limited to twelve and night work was prohibited. The law also required the fencing of dangerous machinery. Neither this act nor any of the earlier factory acts were directly applicable to adult male workers, who were assumed, under the philosophy of individualism, to be able to look out for themselves. Indirectly, however, restrictions on the working day for women and children tended to limit the working day for men also because they all worked together on the same shifts. Between 1844 and 1847 the twelve-hour day became fairly general in British textile mills.

The Ten Hours Act of 1847 climaxed the struggle for a shorter working day in textile mills. The first ten-hour bill introduced into Parliament in 1831 was promptly defeated. Its champions through the years consisted of a strange combination of working-class representatives, outside of Parliament, and Tory reformers. Lord Shaftesbury was the Parliamentary leader among the Tory group. In debates for the ten-hour day, Lord Shaftesbury pleaded: "We ask but a slight relaxation of toil, a time to live, and a time to die; a time for those comforts that sweeten life, and a time for those duties that adorn it; and,

[6] John L. and Barbara Hammond, *The Town Labourer*, p. 171.

therefore, with a fervent prayer to Almighty God that it may please him to turn the hearts of all who hear me to thoughts of justice and mercy, I now finally commit the issue to the judgment of humanity." Opponents of the ten-hour day included John Bright, a leader in the free trade movement and a champion of political democracy. Bright argued that a reduction in working time would result in less production and lower real wages. Workers would be worse off rather than better off. A leading economist, Nassau Senior, argued against the ten-hour day by contending that all profits were made during the last hour of a day's employment. By lopping off the last hour all profits would be wiped out, the factory owners would be pushed into bankruptcy, and workers would find themselves unemployed. The champions of industrial capitalism asserted that repeal of the Corn Laws was the best way to aid the working classes, and it is significant that the ten-hour day did not become law until after the repeal of the Corn Laws in 1846.

In 1850 another factory act was needed to render effective the ten-hour law of 1847. Legislation after 1850 extended the coverage to industries other than textiles.

The significance of the Factory Acts lay in the recognition by society that an unregulated labor market has antisocial consequences. In the "free" labor market the advantage was on the side of industrial capitalists. Factory legislation curbed their otherwise uncontrolled power over individual workers. Some factory owners like Robert Owen and Arkwright had voluntarily established conditions better than those required under factory legislation. Other factory owners were willing to establish better conditions in their factories provided their competitors would do the same. Short of legislation applying to all, there was no way to assure uniform conditions. The necessity for making profits in order to survive led to a disregard, whether intentional or not, of the welfare of the wage-earning class. The Factory Acts marked the initial form of social protest against conditions created by the Industrial Revolution. Later this protest took other forms, including labor unions and political action by working-class groups.

The British Factory Acts illustrate how modern capitalism generated at a relatively early date abuses which called forth government intervention and thereby opened the way for the evolution of laissez-faire into regulated capitalism and ultimately into the welfare state, which constitutes the twentieth-century mixture of private and public economy. This trend toward government intervention has persisted in the face of shifting political representation and alignments. When the Factory Acts were passed, the working class had no representatives in Parliament; they did not yet enjoy the right to vote. Their plight was championed by the landed gentry as a way of expressing political opposition to the new industrial bourgeoisie at a time when the economic power of the landlords was waning but their political power was still dominant.

ASHTON, T. S., *An Economic History of England: The 18th Century.* New York: Barnes & Noble, Inc., 1961.

——, *The Industrial Revolution, 1760–1830.* New York: Oxford University Press, 1962.

——, *Iron and Steel in the Industrial Revolution.* Manchester: The University Press, 1951.

BOWDEN, WITT, *Industrial Society in England Towards the End of the Eighteenth Century,* 2nd ed. New York: Barnes & Noble, Inc., 1965.

BOWDITCH, JOHN, and CLEMENT RAMSLAND, eds., *Voices of the Industrial Revolution, Selected Readings from Liberal Economists and Their Critics.* Ann Arbor: University of Michigan Press, 1962. (paperback)

CLARK, G. N., *The Idea of the Industrial Revolution.* Glasgow: Jackson, 1953.

DEANE, PHYLLIS, *The First Industrial Revolution.* London: Cambridge University Press, 1965.

GILBOY, ELIZABETH W., *Wages in Eighteenth Century England.* Cambridge, Mass.: Harvard University Press, 1934.

HAMMOND, JOHN L. and BARBARA, *The Rise of Modern Industry,* 7th ed. London: Methuen & Company, Ltd., 1947.

——, *The Skilled Labourer, 1760–1832.* New York: Longmans, Green & Co., 1927.

——, *The Town Labourer, 1760–1832, The New Civilization.* New York: Longmans, Green & Co., 1932.

LANDES, DAVID S., "Technological Change and Industrial Development in Western Europe, 1750–1914," *Cambridge Economic History of Europe,* Vol. VI, Chap. 5. London: Cambridge University Press, 1965.

MANTOUX, PAUL, *The Industrial Revolution of the Eighteenth Century.* New York: The Macmillan Company, 1927.

POLANYI, KARL, *The Great Transformation: The Political and Economic Origins of Our Time.* Boston: Beacon Press Inc., 1957. (paperback)

SINGER, CHARLES J. and others, eds., *History of Technology,* Vol. IV, *The Industrial Revolution, 1750–1850.* New York: Oxford University Press, 1956–58.

TOYNBEE, ARNOLD, *Lectures on the Industrial Revolution of the Eighteenth Century in England.* Boston: Beacon Press Inc., 1956. (paperback)

USHER, ABBOTT P., *A History of Mechanical Inventions.* Boston: Beacon Press Inc., 1959. (paperback)

ARTICLES

ASHTON, T. S., "The Industrial Revolution, Studies in Bibliography," *Economic History Review,* V (Oct., 1934), 104–19.

——, "The Standard of Life of Workers in England, 1790–1830," *Journal of Economic History,* IX (Supplement, 1949), 19–38.

CHAMBERS, J. D., "Enclosure and Labour Supply in the Industrial Revolution," *The Economic History Review,* V, No. 3 (1953), 319–43.

DEANE, PHYLLIS, "The Industrial Revolution and Economic Growth, The Evidence of Early British National Income Estimates," *Economic Development and Cultural Change,* V (Jan., 1957), 159–74.

HAMILTON, EARL J., "Profit Inflation and the Industrial Revolution, 1751–1800," *Quarterly Journal of Economics,* LVI (Feb., 1942), 256–73.

HAMMOND, JOHN L., "The Industrial Revolution and Discontent," *Economic History Review,* II (Jan., 1930), 215–28.

HARTWELL, R. M., "The Causes of the Industrial Revolution: An Essay in Methodology," *Economic History Review*, XVII (Aug., 1965), 164–82.

———, "The Standard of Living During the Industrial Revolution," *Economic History Review*, XVI (Aug., 1963), 135–46, and XIII (April, 1961), 397–416.

HOBSBAWN, ERIC J., "The British Standard of Living, 1790–1850," *Economic History Review*, X (Aug., 1957), 46–68, and XVI (Aug., 1963), 119–34.

NEF, JOHN U., "The Industrial Revolution Reconsidered," *Journal of Economic History*, III (May, 1943), 1–31.

British Industrial Leadership
in the Nineteenth Century

CHAPTER **15**

The nineteenth century witnessed the golden age of capitalism, with England as the brightest jewel in this crowning achievement. Britain had been a great nation in the century before Waterloo, but the period from 1815 to 1914 was truly the British century. British hegemony in world affairs rested on industrial supremacy. There developed in this island an economic system unique in world history; from the far corners of the earth, raw materials and foodstuffs flowed in and manufactured goods flowed out; Britain was appropriately called "the workshop of the world."

British capitalism after Waterloo was to experience a century of peace, interrupted only by minor wars; amelioration of the worst evils of the Industrial Revolution and general prosperity, broken by periodic crises; the creation of economic and political liberalism in its classical form in which the middle class ruled in a limited but expanding democracy; an era of pervasive laissez-faire highlighted by repeal of the Corn Laws and the adoption of free trade; a great outflow of British capital which created an economic empire even more far-flung than the vast political Empire.

Only toward the end of the century did British leadership come under challenge by Germany and the United States. A century after defeating Napoleon at Waterloo, the British were again engaged in mortal combat with the leading Continental power. The Kaiser's empire tumbled just as had Napoleon's, but this time the British faced contracting influence and power. In the twentieth century British capitalism became lethargic; laissez-faire declined; free trade and the gold standard were cast aside; socialism and communism began to spread. Much else changed too after the First World War; what it all added up to was the end of the golden age.

THE CORN LAW CONTROVERSY AND THE DEFENSE OF INDUSTRIAL CAPITALISM

The British were rapidly increasing their industrial leadership in 1815. At this time Germany was still a semi-feudal state without political unity and at least half a century short of its industrial revolution. The United States had scarcely entered the formative stage of its industrialization. France showed no

signs of recovering quickly from a quarter-century of violent internal revolution and aggressive international war which had culminated in a decisive
military defeat and domestic reaction. Moreover, the pace of industrial change
in France had been slower than that of England since the sixteenth century.
Clearly there was in 1815 no serious external challenge to British industrial
leadership.

The question which most affected Great Britain's industrial future was
an internal one which could be answered only by the British themselves. The
issue may be variously stated: laissez-faire versus mercantilism, free trade
versus protectionism, manufacturing versus agriculture, factory owners versus
landlords. It was both an economic and a political question. The economic
aspect concerned the allocation of resources between agriculture and industry.
If Great Britain were to remain moderately self-sufficient in agriculture, then
labor and capital would have to be employed to grow more food on land of
inferior quality for a rapidly increasing population. Home-grown food would,
under the circumstances, be increasingly expensive. Industry would be handicapped because the cost of feeding industrial workers with expensive home-
grown food would be high. The advantages which British industry enjoyed
over other nations would be lessened and might in the long run disappear
entirely. If, on the other hand, Great Britain gave up the mercantilist ideal of
national self-sufficiency and permitted the free importation of food and other
agricultural products, more labor and capital would be available to British
industry on favorable terms. Costs of production in industry would be lower,
and Britain's advantages over other nations might continue almost indefinitely.
A policy of protectionism would be favorable to landlords and unfavorable to
factory owners. A free-trade policy would be favorable to factory owners and
unfavorable to landlords. Which policy would be more favorable to the nation
as a whole was the subject of a great debate.

The political aspect of the question concerned the structure of power in
the Parliament, which would decide how resources should be allocated between agriculture and industry. More specifically, the economic problem would
be decided in terms of legislation on the Corn Laws, the laws relating to the
protection of British grains by tariffs or other measures to restrict imports of
food and by subsidies to domestic producers of grain.

Before the Industrial Revolution, England had experienced no special
difficulty in raising enough food to feed its people. A main purpose of the old
Corn Laws had been to keep the price of grain high enough to enable the
farmer to prosper and low enough to enable the poor to live. Import duties
and export duties were flexible in order to operate toward these objectives
from year to year, depending upon whether the harvest was good or poor. The
great increase in population which came with the Industrial Revolution increased the demand for grain relative to the supply and pushed up the price
of bread. During the Napoleonic wars new legislation imposed a sliding scale
of import duties which varied inversely with the price of wheat. As the price
of wheat increased, the import duty was automatically lowered; and as the
price of wheat decreased, the import duty was automatically raised. Prices
rose to unprecedented heights during the war years. The food question was
very much in the public eye as the war with Napoleon drew to a close.

A common purpose of the bills introduced into the landlord-dominated

British Parliament was to maintain or to increase the protection to agriculture.

Opposition inside and outside Parliament was sufficient to defeat the more
extreme measures for maintaining a high price of grain with the existing
sliding scale of import duties. The bill which became law in 1815 was intended
to support the price of wheat at the relatively high fixed price of 80 shillings
per quarter, but this new Corn Law abandoned the sliding scale of import
duties. The 1815 law adopted a new principle under which the import of
wheat was prohibited when the price was less than 80 shillings, and wheat
could be imported free of duty when the price rose above 80 shillings.

The basic decision involved in passage of the Corn Law of 1815 was to
continue protection to agriculture. The degree of protection promised by the
new law was too little to satisfy the protectionists, but it was much too great
to please the opponents of protection. The latter, drawing strength from
industrialists and working-class groups, protested vigorously. Petitions addressed to Parliament objected to the law. Members of Parliament who supported the bill were mobbed and, on occasion, beaten in the streets. The Corn
Law controversy became the featured issue in thirty years of class warfare.

Ricardo Opposes the Corn Laws

The Corn Law controversy has special significance for economics because from it there arose a system of economic analysis which dominated nineteenth-century economic theory and still forms the basis for much modern
economic analysis. David Ricardo, the formulator of this theory of value and
distribution, was a severe critic of the Corn Laws. During the Parliamentary
debates of 1815 he wrote a pamphlet criticizing protection to agriculture
on grounds that it constituted a barrier to England's economic development.
Ricardo's political economy represented a theoretical defense of industrial
capitalism. First in his pamphlet on the effects of a high price of grain on
profits in general, and later in the *Principles of Political Economy and Taxation*
(1817), Ricardo developed an analysis of the conditions for capitalist progress.
That condition was, in brief, free trade. It meant that the Corn Laws should
be repealed. He stated in the pamphlet: "The interest of the landlord is always
contrary to that of every other class in society."

Ricardo began his *Principles* by stating the problem of the distribution
of income: "The produce of the earth—all that is derived from its surface by
the united application of labor, machinery, and capital—is divided among
three classes of the community; namely, the proprietor of the land, the owner
of the stock or capital necessary for its cultivation, and the labourers by whose
industry it is cultivated." According to Ricardo, the amount of produce which
goes to laborers is just sufficient for their subsistence. On the least productive
land under cultivation, the entire produce is divided between laborers and
capitalists. Such land commands no rent and is called marginal land. On
marginal or no-rent land the produce which is not required for the subsistence
of the laborers goes to the capitalist in the form of profits. There is nothing
left over for the landlord from the cultivation of marginal land.

Ricardo argued that as population increases, the increasing demand for
food arising from the larger population will bring under cultivation land
which is less and less productive. This means that from equal applications of

labor and capital, the resulting produce will become less and less. Clearly if the laborer, who shares the total produce from marginal land with the capitalist, receives a constant amount (equal to subsistence) of a diminishing total produce, the capitalist necessarily gets progressively less in profits as the margin of cultivation is extended to less productive soil. A lesser *amount* of profit from a given quantity of capital meant, of course, a lower *rate* of profit. Thus profits must decline on marginal land, and, since Ricardo assumed that capital within a country is mobile, causing the rate of profit to tend to be the same everywhere, profits will decline on all types of investment, whether in marginal land, better than marginal land, industry, trade, or any other investment.

Ricardo's important principle was that anything which brings less productive land into use forces down the rate of profit, impedes the accumulation of profit, and limits the extent of economic progress. This was his theoretical argument against the Corn Laws; by bringing inferior soil under cultivation, they impede industrial development and economic progress generally. Free trade, on the other hand, would bring to English tables inexpensive food grown on the fertile soil of less densely populated countries, would raise profits, and promote economic progress.

According to Ricardo's analysis, the Corn Laws, which lower profits on capital, only tend to raise the rents on land. Rent is defined as the *difference* between the yield—both in produce and in money—from a given piece of land and the yield from marginal land, when the same amount of labor and capital is applied to both pieces of land. As inferior land is brought under cultivation, the difference in produce between the best land and the worst land in use increases; likewise the difference in produce between the next best land and the worst land in use increases; and therefore rents increase all along the line.

The Ricardian theory of rent may be represented in the following diagram:

Figure 15–1. Ricardian Theory of Rent: Two Qualities of Land.

In the diagram it is assumed that equal amounts of labor and capital are applied to both pieces of land. As a result of equal applications of capital and labor, land of the best quality yields 50 bushels of wheat and the land of second quality yields 45 bushels. If laborers require 25 bushels for their subsistence, on the land of second quality there will be 20 bushels left over for profits of the capitalist. Since competition is assumed to equalize profits, there will also be 20 bushels on the land of first quality. The five remaining bushels of the best quality land will be the rent of the landlord. In other words, on the best quality land the total yield is 50 bushels, compared with 45 bushels

on the marginal (no-rent) land, leaving a rent on the best land of five bushels.

Now if population increases and brings under cultivation land of the third quality on which the same amount of capital and labor will yield only 40 bushels, as compared with 50 and 45 respectively on first and second quality land, the rent on the first quality land increases from 5 to 10 bushels, and the rent on the second quality land increases from zero to 5 bushels. The third quality land is now the marginal or no-rent land. The situation is shown in the following diagram:

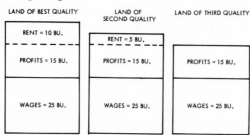

Figure 15–2. Ricardian Theory of Rent: Three Qualities of Land.

A comparison of the two diagrams indicates that increases in rents are at the expense of profits. Rent that goes into the pocket of the land-lord comes out of the pocket of the capitalist. Rent is thus a transfer of in-come from one class to another and does not represent the creation of new wealth. Rent is a windfall gained by landlords because the amount of land of good quality is limited and cannot be increased as a result of an increase in rent. Rent is an unearned income. This was the dim view Ricardo took of the landed interests.

Ricardo's important theoretical generalization was that the long-run trend in the relative shares in the distribution of income is for profits to fall, rents to rise, and wages to remain at a subsistence level. His important practical conclusion was that repeal of the Corn Laws would indefinitely postpone the fall in profits by opening to England the abundant supply of fertile soil else-where in the world. Grain imports could be paid for with manufactured ex-ports on terms which would enrich England. Whereas the law of diminishing returns was characteristic of agriculture, it did not apply to industry. By allocating England's labor and capital to manufacturing and other nonagricul-tural pursuits the fall in the rate of profit would be greatly slowed down, and for the calculable future virtually prevented. A high rate of profit would give capitalists an incentive to accumulate more and more capital. Profit was viewed as the spur to economic development.

The obvious and simple meaning of Ricardo's analysis was that (1) Britain's economic future lay in the direction of industrialization, and (2) the Corn Laws were the greatest barrier to economic progress and should be repealed. These views were well received by industrial capitalists, who be-lieved that under free domestic and international trade and laissez-faire British industry could continue to lead the world for a long time. Ricardo's views were not well received by landlords because they meant that British agricul-ture would have to compete with foreign agriculture and under these cir-

cumstances British agriculture would become progressively less important. Industrial capitalists and those who shared their perspective were willing to make this sacrifice, which, as they saw it, was in the national interest. The landlords, however, and those who shared their perspective, were not prepared to make this sacrifice. Moreover, the landlord class still controlled Parliament.

Malthus Favors the Corn Laws

Opposition to repeal of the Corn Laws did not come only from the landed interests. Other men who had been thinking about economic questions entered the combat. Ricardo's pamphlet on rent and profits was only one of four statements on the theory of distribution provoked by the heated Corn Law controversy in the spring of 1815. Next to Ricardo's, the most important pamphlet was written by the clergyman-economist, Thomas Robert Malthus, who some years before had published the famous essay on population. Malthus, unlike Ricardo, defended the Corn Laws as necessary for preserving the rural way of life in England. Although he accepted free trade in principle, he made an exception in the case of the Corn Laws. Malthus contended that national welfare would be furthered by continuing the Corn Laws, because they would enable Britain to be more nearly self-sufficient in food. He pointed out that other countries such as France, which was the chief source of foreign grain for England, would continue to levy import duties on grain as well as on the industrial products which England hoped to export in order to pay for imported grains in the event the British Corn Laws were repealed. Moreover, France in 1814 enacted legislation which prohibited the export of French grain in years of shortage and high domestic prices. In years of famine or war, where was England to get bread to feed its people?

In contrast with Ricardo, who said "the interest of landlords is always opposed to the interest of every other class in the community," Malthus defended landlords as a class with interests "always associated with the prosperity of the community." Malthus asserted that repeal of the Corn Laws would harm not only landlords but also capitalist farmers and wage-earners. Landlords would be harmed because rents would fall. Capitalist farmers would be harmed by a fall in profits associated with a fall in the price of grain. Workers would be harmed because a depression in agriculture resulting from free trade in grain would lower money wages and, although the price of bread would fall, the prices of other products would not fall. Lower money wages would not be fully compensated for by a fall in the cost of living, causing real wages to be lower under free trade than under protection. Malthus thought the only beneficiaries from repeal of the Corn Laws would be "a small number of capitalists in manufacturing and foreign trade."

Who was right, Ricardo or Malthus? In a sense they were talking about different things: Malthus about the short run and Ricardo about the long run. Ricardo was right in the sense that the course of action he recommended was consistent with the greatest economic development of Great Britain. In retrospect it seems obvious that England's long-term future was brightest as an industrial economy, not as a nation struggling to raise food for a rapidly increasing population. In 1815 the population of the island of Great Britain (England, Scotland, and Wales) was approximately 13,000,000 and was barely

able to grow its own food supply in years of good harvests. In 1914 the population of Great Britain was approximately 40,000,000, living at a standard much higher than their forebears a century earlier and also higher than any other people in Europe. This clearly would not have been possible except in a highly industrialized Britain which exchanged manufactured exports for imports of food and raw materials. The great British navy provided insurance against the danger of the island's being shut off from foreign sources of food supply in time of war.

Repeal of the Corn Laws in 1846

Although Ricardo was right on the Corn Law controversy in the sense that Britain's greatness in the nineteenth century lay in industrialization, this did not alter the political decision in the landlord-dominated Parliament of 1815. In that year the new Corn Law was passed by a wide margin (128 to 21) in the House of Commons. Industrialism translated its economic power into political power only slowly. The Industrial Revolution altered the balance of economic power and in the long run changed the political structure of society, but three decades of fierce conflict elapsed from the passage of the new Corn Law of 1815 until the repeal of the Corn Laws in 1846. Noble, and not so noble, landlords fought to retain the privileges which their class had maintained since feudal times. However, the tide of change rolled irresistibly against them. Their power was eroded by the shift of population to urban centers. Great cities grew up and provided mass support for the claim of industrial capitalists to share in the right to rule.

The height of the political struggle to reform Parliament was reached with passage of the Great Reform Bill in 1832. Three times the reform bill passed in the House of Commons only to be beaten in the House of Lords, whose membership was not, of course, subject to popular election. The obstinacy of the Lords provoked organized demonstrations in industrial centers and in the rural south of England. Reformers and agitators aroused the populace and threatened to lead armed bands in a march on London to coerce recalcitrant members of Parliament. Violent civil war seemed a distinct possibility. Tory reactionaries in the House of Lords seemed determined not to surrender their power voluntarily to the middle classes. Finally, after several governments had failed, the King promised the Whig Prime Minister, Earl Grey, that he would create a sufficient number of new peers to sit in the House of Lords to carry the reform vote if the bill were defeated there again. Confronted with the possibility of having the House of Lords flooded with new peers, a sufficient number of Lords absented themselves to permit the Great Reform Bill to pass.

The new law provided for an extension of suffrage to the middle class and for reapportionment of seats in the House of Commons. The right to vote was, however, still restricted by property qualifications (which excluded the wage-earning classes from the ballot). Shopkeepers and many other members of the urban middle class met the property qualifications for voting. "Rotten boroughs" with less than 2000 population lost their representatives, who were reapportioned to industrial centers like Manchester, Birmingham, Sheffield, and Leeds. The disequilibrium between political and economic power created by

the Industrial Revolution was broken. Under the new regime the representatives of industrial property shared with the representatives of landed property the right to rule. The Tory Party became the Conservative Party, and the Whig Party became the Liberal Party. The balance was fairly equal, but tilted toward the Liberals. These representatives of industrial capitalism were now in a position to repeal the Corn Laws, given favorable immediate circumstances.

In the meantime the Corn Law of 1815 was disappointing to both its friends and its enemies. Its proponents were dissatisfied because the price of wheat was too low much of the time, and its opponents were dissatisfied because the price of wheat was too high much of the time. Contrary to expectations, the law did not stabilize the price of wheat. In 1817 wheat sold as high as 117s and in 1822 it sold as low as 39s. British ports were alternately opened and closed to foreign corn depending on whether the price was above or below 80s. In order to overcome some of the rigidity of the law, a more flexible provision was introduced in 1822. In 1828 the principle of the 1815 law was repealed, and the old sliding-scale principle was reintroduced and remained until 1846.

Under the reformed Parliament, with repeal of the Corn Laws in their grasp, the champions of industrial capitalism organized a vigorous campaign highlighted by the Anti-Corn Law League under the leadership of two brilliant orators and organizers, Richard Cobden and John Bright. Ricardian economics and the general philosophy of laissez-faire and free trade were the underpinnings of the agitation for Corn Law repeal. The Corn Laws were stigmatized as a tax on bread and a tax on the poor.

A combination of special circumstances finally brought repeal of the Corn Laws in the 1840's. A terrible potato famine in Ireland led to Irish pressure to permit free importation of grain to save millions of lives threatened with starvation. Sir Robert Peel, the Conservative Prime Minister who had been elected on a protectionist platform, deserted his party's historic position and voted with the Liberals in 1846 for the outright repeal of the Corn Laws (to become effective in 1850). Significantly, as the son of a great factory owner, Peel was conditioned in his thinking by the needs of industrial capitalism despite his leadership in the landlord-dominated Conservative Party. The ideology of industrial capitalism had infiltrated the historic party of landlords.

Repeal of the Corn Laws marked a turning point in British economic development. It ushered in the era of free trade, gave full rein to industrial capitalism, and enabled Britain to become for a time the "workshop of the world." Economic resources were no longer diverted artificially into agriculture in an uneconomical attempt to raise food for a rapidly rising population on the limited and inferior soil of Great Britain. Ricardo's dictum that labor and capital should be freely allocated to the activity which would be most productive was now given operational significance. Industrial capitalism was liberated from the bonds of mercantilistic-inspired protectionism.

THE INSTABILITY OF INDUSTRIAL CAPITALISM

Another economic issue which engaged the attention of the economists after 1815 was the instability of industrial capitalism. Britain's industrialism, based

on machine technology, was just getting well under way when the wars with
France broke out in the early 1790's. During the Napoleonic wars there was
a great expansion of British industrial capacity without any offsetting physical
destruction, since the wars were fought entirely on the Continent and on the
sea; hence British industrial superiority over other nations increased in this
period. When peace came again in 1815 the British commanded a productive
capacity far greater than the world had even known before; the return of peace
presented Britain with the prospect of the greatest prosperity ever known.
The actual result, however, was quite the opposite. Depression rather than
prosperity followed Waterloo, with England experiencing the most widespread
and severe depression ever recorded. There had been earlier crises such as
the South Sea and Mississippi Bubbles, but these arose from speculative
manias. The post-Napoleonic commercial crises were associated not so much
with speculation as with overproduction of goods.

The course of events was as follows. Business activity reached a peak
in 1815 and fell off rapidly, reaching a trough in 1816. A brief postwar boomlet
reached a peak in 1818 and was followed by a sharp retreat, which led to the
worst phase of the overproduction crisis in 1819. There were numerous business failures. Export industries were hard hit by a bad slump in foreign trade.
The great cotton trade was especially distressed, and the general condition
was one of severe stagnation.

Ricardo versus Malthus on Overproduction

Here indeed was an economic problem worthy of consideration by the
best minds of the day. Ricardo and Malthus again featured in the discussion
and, as in the Corn Law controversy, took different positions on the question
of overproduction crises. Ricardo defended industrial capitalism against the
criticisms of Malthus, who contended that it was inherently unstable. Ricardo
recognized the unmistakable fact that business was depressed and unemployment widespread, but he attributed the difficulties to interference with free
competition and to maladjustments in production. The most important interference with free competition was the Corn Laws. He argued that trade was
depressed because profits were low, profits were low because wages were high,
and wages were high because so much labor was required to grow food on
the inferior soil forced into cultivation by the protective tariffs on grains. Related also to the Corn Laws was the export of capital caused by the low rate
of domestic profit and a consequent shortage of capital with which to employ
labor at home. Labor was unemployed because there was not enough saving
to provide capital for the employment of labor. Another source of trouble was
the misdirection of production, that is, production of the wrong things in the
immediate postwar period. Producers had not yet had time to adjust their
output to the demands of consumers. Some things were overproduced but
other things were underproduced. Ricardo asserted there could be no such
thing as *general* overproduction.

Ricardo believed that unemployment and depression would be only temporary, and that automatic adjustments would iron out the difficulties in the
long run. He reasoned as follows: Overproduction tends to correct itself by

destroying profits in those lines of business suffering from overproduction. Consequently production will be redirected into lines in which the rate of profit is higher. Moreover, if the rate of profit in general falls too low to attract capital, the capitalists will cease to save and will begin to consume a larger proportion of their income. The resultant demand for consumers' goods will result in re-employment of jobless workers. Thus the Corn Laws might, by lowering the rate of profit on capital, discourage accumulation of wealth, but they would not cause unemployment in the long run. The fact that workers received a wage approximately equal to subsistence was no barrier to production because luxury consumption by the rich would fill any deficiencies in effective demand. In brief, Ricardo defended industrial capitalism on grounds that it was self-adjusting in response to changes in the rate of profit. He denied that capitalism had any fundamental flaws such as a tendency to generate chronic unemployment because of a deficiency of demand associated with the low wages of the working classes.

Malthus in support of his view that industrial capitalism was inherently unstable contended that *general* overproduction was possible and that large-scale unemployment might be chronic. Economic stagnation results from a deficiency of effective demand. Too much saving (oversaving) would reduce the demand for consumption to a point at which there would be no need to produce more capital goods. Saving in moderation was desirable, but carried to excess it resulted in depression and distress. He contended that: "If the conversion of revenue into capital [saving] pushed beyond a certain point must, by diminishing the effectual demand for produce, throw the labouring classes out of employment, it is obvious that the adoption of parsimonious habits beyond a certain point may be accompanied by the most distressing effects at first, and by a marked depression of wealth and population afterwards."

Who was right on the overproduction question, Ricardo or Malthus? Malthus was correct in the sense that his analysis of the cause of unemployment appears to have resulted from a more accurate assessment of the characteristics of capitalism. Using Malthus' analysis, one could have predicted that nineteenth-century capitalism would be characterized by periodic crises of overproduction like those of 1816 and 1819. This is precisely what the historical record shows. It was apparently not the Corn Laws or the Napoleonic wars which were responsible for economic instability, because after repeal of the Corn Laws in 1846 and in a century largely free of major wars, overproduction and business cycles continued to recur. Instead of getting better during the century of peace, depressions tended to get worse. Beginning in 1873, and again in the 1890's, Britain experienced its most severe depressions prior to the 1930's. Malthus appears to have been right in his conviction that industrial capitalism, instead of being automatically self-correcting, was inherently unstable. Ironically, however, it was the views of Ricardo, not those of Malthus, which dominated the thinking of the nineteenth century. Only the shattering experience of the great depression of the 1930's caused statesmen and economists in capitalist countries to re-assess the workings of a capitalistic economic system, and in this re-examination they found that Malthus' views on overproduction and unemployment were far more prophetic than those of Ricardo.

LONG-RUN TRENDS IN THE BRITISH ECONOMY,
1790–1914

269

BRITISH
INDUSTRIAL
LEADERSHIP

In the century and a quarter from the beginning of the French Revolution to the outbreak of the First World War, five distinct periods in the development of the capitalist economies of the Western world may be distinguished. The turning points which mark the end of one and the beginning of another phase of economic development were 1815, 1848, 1873, and 1896. Although they vary by a few months or years from one capitalist country to another, there is a remarkable similarity in the timing and in the trends in all of these countries. This similarity between countries lends support to one of the underlying themes of this book, namely, that there has been a distinct unity and coherence in the economic development of the various political units which constitute the North Atlantic community. This fact of observed similarities finds support in the international character of the whole Western economy in which changes in one part were transmitted to other parts through the international market.

The general movement of commodity prices provides the most obvious and measurable trend marking these periods as distinct time units of economic development. From 1790 to 1815 prices moved sharply upward under the impact of the French Revolution and the Napoleonic wars, followed by a prolonged period of falling prices until the late 1840's. Beginning with the discovery of gold in California and Australia in 1848, prices moved upward again for a quarter-century in Europe (until 1865 in the United States), followed by another quarter-century of falling prices. In the late 1890's new gold discoveries in South Africa and Australia started a new price rise, which continued through the First World War.

The economic character of these periods is not determined solely, or even primarily, by price trends. Price changes not only reflect the influence of war and gold discoveries on the quantity of money but also represent reactions to underlying economic forces affecting supply and demand, such as technological innovations, costs of production, types of investment outlays, the division of output between consumers' and producers' goods, and real wages. The broad pattern of economic growth in Great Britain between 1793 and 1912 is indicated by Table 15–1, which gives the annual average percentage rates of change in certain strategic variables in the British economy.

The movement of general prices gives a picture of pulsation in economic growth, rising in the first, third, and fifth periods, and falling in the second and fourth periods. With the exception of the middle period, the figures show real wages moving in the opposite direction from prices. Real wages fell during the Napoleonic period because prices, especially wheat prices, outstripped the increase in money wages; and increases in money wages again failed to keep pace with the rising cost of living in the period after the discovery of gold in South Africa and Alaska.

The overall average rate of increase in industrial production was 2.6 per cent per year, or 1.6 per cent greater than the average annual rate of increase in population. The period of most rapid industrial advance was between 1815 and 1847, when the rate was 3.5 per cent, and the next most rapid industrial growth occurred in the following period, 1847 to 1873. Thus the approximate half-century between 1815 and 1873 were the years of greatest

Trends in the British Economy
Annual Average Percentage Rate of Change, 1793–1912

FOR PERIOD ENDING	PRICES	REAL WAGES	POPULATION UNITED KINGDOM	CONSUMERS' GOODS PRODUCTION	PRODUCERS' GOODS PRODUCTION	TOTAL INDUSTRIAL PRODUCTION
1815	1.8	−0.5	1.4	1.9	2.3	2.1
1847	−1.4	0.7	1.1	3.2	4.4	3.5
1873	0.6	0.6	0.7	2.6	4.1	3.2
1900	−1.5	1.2	0.9	1.3	2.2	1.7
1912	1.5	−0.5	0.9	1.0	1.9	1.5
1793– 1912 (avg)	—	—	1.0	2.2	3.2	2.6

Source: Walt W. Rostow, *British Economy of the Nineteenth Century* (Oxford: Clarendon Press, 1948), p. 8. The rates are five-year moving averages.

industrial progress in Great Britain. Prior to 1815 the French wars were a drain on industrial expansion, and after 1873 the Long Depression was a retarding influence. The rate of growth in total industrial production reached a peak before the middle of the century, after which expansion took place at a declining rate: 3.2 per cent in the period 1847–1873, 1.7 per cent in the period 1873 to 1900, and 1.5 per cent in the period 1910–1912. The decline in the rate of industrial growth in Great Britain after 1847 is attributable in part to an increase in the size of the base on which the computation of the rate of increase is made.

SOME LEADING INDUSTRIES

Thus far we have considered the basic issue of resource allocation between agriculture and industry, the short-run cyclical instability which characterized the nineteenth century, and the long-run trends in economic growth. Each of the foregoing has been concerned with the totality of British economic development. Attention will now be directed to some of the parts of the total picture. Certain industries loomed large in British economic history during the nineteenth century. Selected for special attention because of their key roles are coal and iron, textiles, and railways.

Coal and Iron

The substitution of coke for charcoal in iron smelting was one of the greatest innovations of the Industrial Revolution. With the invention of Watt's steam engine, coal became the great source of power for all types of industry.

In no small degree the industrial leadership of nineteenth-century Britain rested on the exploitation of its rich coal resources. There was a marked move- ment of industry and population toward the coal-producing areas, the "Black Country." When the steam engine was placed on wheels, coal became the chief source of power for transportation, and the railways consumed a sizable portion of total coal production.

Because coal became an all-purpose source of power, the volume of its production is one of the best indexes of industrial progress. Figures for British coal production during the nineteenth century are shown in Table 15–2.

TABLE 15–2

Coal Production in the United Kingdom, 1800–1913

YEAR	OUTPUT (millions of metric tons)	YEAR	OUTPUT (millions of metric tons)
1800	11.0	1860	80.0
1816	15.9	1870	110.4
1820	17.4	1880	146.8
1830	22.4	1890	181.6
1840	33.7	1900	225.2
1850	49.4	1913	287.4

Source: Phyllis Deane and W. A. Cole, *British Economic Growth, 1688–1959* (London: Cambridge University Press, 1962), p. 216.

In the four decades after 1816 British coal output increased four-fold. In the two decades from 1850 to 1870, output more than doubled. Over the entire century after 1816 the output increased approximately eighteen times. The United Kingdom was by far the greatest coal-producing nation in the world until the last decade of the nineteenth century, when the United States suddenly assumed the lead. The wide margin in favor of the United Kingdom in 1860 and its sudden eclipse by the United States by 1900 is shown in Table 15–3 on comparative coal production in the leading industrial nations.

Although the United Kingdom fell behind the United States, it remained ahead of Germany in coal production after Germany had passed the United Kingdom in overall industrial production. This is accounted for by large British coal exports. In 1913 nearly 100 million tons, or one-third, of British-mined coal were sold abroad. This constituted 10 per cent of the value of total exports. As a highly industrialized nation, Great Britain normally did not export raw materials, but coal was an important exception to the general rule. It was used as cargo on outgoing shipments and served to balance the imports of bulky raw materials and foodstuffs. This lowered the cost of imports and improved Great Britain's competitive position in international trade and shipping. While advantageous to the international balance of payments, heavy coal exports were a disturbing portent for the future. British mines were getting deeper, diminishing returns had set in, and in 1865 Stanley Jevons, a well-known economist, made a rather alarming prediction of the exhaustion of coal

Coal Production in the Leading Nations, 1860–1900
(in millions of metric tons)

YEAR	UNITED KINGDOM	UNITED STATES	GERMANY	FRANCE
1860	80.0	15.2	12.3	8.1
1870	117.4*	42.5	29.3	12.9
1880	147.0	64.8	47.0	18.8
1890	181.6	143.1	70.2	25.6
1900	225.2	244.6	109.3	32.7

Source: Encyclopaedia of the Social Sciences, III (New York: The Macmillan Company, 1950), 583.
* Compare figure of 110.4 tons in Table 15–2.

mines in the United Kingdom. Jevons' concern about diminishing returns in coal mining may be compared to Ricardo's concern about diminishing returns in agriculture half a century earlier. Repeal of the Corn Laws had removed Britain's dependence on domestic food supplies, but the key position of coal in an industrial society caused new concern that rising coal costs might jeopardize the superiority of British manufacturing.

Another good index of general industrial progress in Britain and of its leadership as an industrial power during the nineteenth century is the volume of production of pig iron. Table 15–4 gives figures for pig iron production

TABLE 15–4

Production of Pig Iron in Principal Producing Countries, 1740–1930
(in thousands of gross tons)

YEAR	UNITED KINGDOM	UNITED STATES	GERMANY	WORLD TOTAL
1740	20	1	18	160
1790	68	30	30	280
1800	190	40	39	460
1810	250	55	45	620
1820	368	110	89	1,010
1830	677	180	118	1,590
1840	1,396	290	167	2,770
1850	2,249	564	396	4,470
1860	3,890	821	522	7,300
1870	5,964	1,665	1,240	11,840
1880	7,749	3,835	2,429	18,160
1890	7,904*	9,203	4,035	26,750
1900	8,960	13,789	7,429	39,810
1910	10,012	27,304	12,905	64,760
1920	8,035	36,926	6,299	62,850
1930	6,192	31,752	9,542	79,400

Source: Encyclopaedia of the Social Sciences (New York: The Macmillan Company, 1950), VIII, 301.

in the United Kingdom, the United States, Germany, and the world between 1740 and 1930.

As late as 1870 the United Kingdom was still producing more than one-half of the world's total and more than three and a half times as much as the United States. Just twenty years later, in 1890, the United States held a substantial lead, and by 1910 Germany had moved into second position, ahead of the United Kingdom. Although the United Kingdom lost ground relative to the United States and Germany after 1870, substantial increases were registered until 1910. These figures reflect the much swifter pace of industrialization in the United States and Germany, with the British losing ground relatively, but progressing absolutely. The absolute drop in British iron production after the First World War reflects the depressed state of that country in the 1920's and the greater depression in the 1930's. The postwar decline of German iron production reflects in part the loss of Lorraine, the Saar, and Upper Silesia, all important iron-producing areas, under the terms of the Treaty of Versailles in 1919. Great Britain was not as well endowed with iron ore as with coal resources and became a substantial importer of iron in the twentieth century.

Textiles

In textiles Britain's lead over other nations started earlier and lasted longer than in any other industry. Textile manufacturers had pioneered the Industrial Revolution, and textile mills became almost synonymous with the early factory system. Whether measured in terms of value of product or in numbers of workers employed, textiles ranked first among all industries in the United Kingdom during the nineteenth century. The chief demand for textiles derived from the demand for clothing at home and abroad, but with the general advance of industry as a whole textile fibers became important raw materials in other industries.

Of the four textiles, wool, linen, silk, and cotton, it was the last, and newest, branch of the industry which became the special pride and symbol of British supremacy in the nineteenth century. By the close of the Napoleonic Wars cotton spinning was almost completely carried on in factories, but power-loom weaving was still in its infancy. Cartwright's loom of 1784 never enjoyed much practical success. Only during the 1820's, by virtue of new technical improvements, did the power loom begin to reduce the number of hand weavers. In the next two decades the hand weavers fought a desperate rear-guard struggle. By the middle of the century mechanization in factories was virtually complete throughout the cotton industry, the first and at that time the only mechanized industry. The Jacquard loom for weaving complex figured fabrics was introduced from France. Technical changes occurring after 1850 were refinements of techniques already in use. Ring spinning was introduced from the United States but was not well suited to British specialization in finer yarns. The Northrop or completely automatic loom, also from the United States, was likewise better for plain cloth than for the complex designs in which Lancashire specialized.

English cotton textile manufacture was heavily concentrated in a small area around Manchester in the county of Lancashire. Reasons for this con-

centration were partly historical, partly geographical, and partly economic. Cotton spinning had originally grown up there as an adjunct to relatively small woolen and fustian industries.[1] Among the advantages which perpetuated the growth of cotton textiles around Manchester were nearness to the great port of Liverpool (making possible the ready receipt of imported cotton and facilitating export of cloth), the deposits of coal for steam power, a humid climate especially important for finer spinning, and pure water so important for bleaching. An important self-perpetuating advantage arose from supplementary industries, which were attracted by the presence of many cotton mills and in turn attracted other cotton mills; for example, textile machinery was produced nearby, and dye-making was also important. These supplementary industries provided special economies—known as external economies because they existed outside the walls of the textile factory—which were not duplicated anywhere else in the world. As much as any other factor they accounted for the supremacy of Manchester as the textile center of the world.

Alongside the sensational growth of cotton manufacturing in the nineteenth century, its rapid growth in the eighteenth century pales into insignificance. Raw cotton imports increased from 120,000 bales in 1801 to 2,614,000 bales in 1860, or a twenty-two-fold increase. Manufactured textiles constituted Britain's largest single export throughout the nineteenth century. In 1850 yarns and fabrics made up 60 per cent of the total export values of the United Kingdom, and over many years furnished about one-half of the value of all exports. Although textile exports declined as a percentage of the total value of exports after 1850, the absolute value of textile exports increased. Cotton cloth and yarn maintained their position in the world market better than the other textiles, although after 1843 textile machinery was exported freely and found its way to other countries which began to manufacture some of their own fabrics. In the short run, at least, the export of machinery swelled the total of all British exports; in the intermediate run it increased the foreign demand for British yarn because the overseas countries, for technical reasons and because of lack of capital, mechanized weaving before spinning and utilized mostly yarn from the advanced countries; and in the long run, it led the British to concentrate on high-quality fabrics for the export market. The dominant position of the British in the world textile market continued without a major challenge until the First World War. Changes caused by the great conflict disrupted international commerce and led to the entrance of new countries, especially Japan, into the world market, with a resulting challenge to British supremacy.

Railways

As noted earlier, Great Britain enjoys the unique distinction of being the only country in the world which underwent an industrial revolution prior to the railway age. On the European continent and in the United States the railway age was a forerunner of large-scale industrialism. Mass land transportation was less essential to England in part because of the proximity of coal to

---

[1] The main woolen industry in the north of England was located further east in Yorkshire.

iron ore and because of the location of the famous Newcastle coal fields on the

sea with easy water access to London.

English developments in railroading are, nevertheless, very significant because here for the first time railways were operated successfully with steam locomotives. Steam railway transportation was one of the by-products of England's Industrial Revolution. George Stevenson and others succeeded in putting steam engines on wheels and operating them with success by 1815. In 1825 the world's first steam railway line was opened between Stockton and Darlington, and a few years later the more important Liverpool to Manchester railway began operation. For a decade thereafter the relative efficiency of horses and steam locomotives was debated. Opponents of steam granted that there were some short lines operating successfully in the technical sense but they questioned the profitability of the steam lines. Recognized profitability was important because railways were expensive and required subscriptions from the public to joint-stock companies.

By 1835 the superiority of the steam locomotive was acknowledged and a real spurt in domestic railway construction began and continued for the next thirty-five years, with periodic interruptions caused by recurring economic crises. By 1845 Great Britain had 2500 miles of railway, and ten years later more than 8000 miles. A construction boom in the 1860's added more than 5000 miles, to bring the total mileage to 15,537 miles in 1870. With minor exceptions, the "iron veins" of Britain were completed by the onset of the Long Depression in 1873.

In 1850 Great Britain's 6600 miles of railways were twice that of Germany and nearly four times that of France. The traffic density on British railroads continued to be greater than that of any other country. Because it was a smaller country it did not continue to hold the lead in total mileage. Britain's mileage was exceeded by Germany in the early 1870's and by France in the early 1880's. In the United States railway mileage had already surpassed that of any other nation by 1840 (2800 miles), and by 1860 it was three times that of Great Britain (30,000 compared with 10,000 miles), and was equal to one-half the total mileage in the world.

Much of the American mileage was directly significant to Europeans, especially Britons, because it lowered the cost of food and raw materials such as cotton and opened up new markets for British manufactured goods. On five continents the British were building railways before their own network was completed. They provided capital, engineering skill, steel rails, locomotives, and rolling stock for less developed areas all over the world and thereby increased their exports of iron and steel products directly and of other products indirectly. They were also helping to develop these less developed areas, some of which were soon to challenge British leadership. After 1870 railways did more for the industrial efficiency of England's chief rivals than for England.

In shipbuilding the British were not subjected to the limitations of railway building. In fact, the continued supremacy of the "Island Empire" depended much more on its ships than on its railways. The trackless seas and the ports of all continents were open to British ships. The nature of the country's economic development as the workshop of the world required vast increases in shipping tonnage. The tonnage built in 1900 was seven times as great as that built in 1850. The increase was particularly impressive during the

last quarter of the century, which corresponds to the great growth of mass production and world markets.

The position of the United States in shipbuilding presents an interesting contrast with British shipbuilding. Before 1860 the Americans made a strong bid to wrest from the British their leadership in shipbuilding. In the age of wooden ships the British were handicapped by lack of domestic timber. The American clipper ship of wood and sail threatened to dominate international shipping before the Civil War of the 1860's. With the transition to iron and steel ships driven by steam, the British quickly regained a dominant position. Following the Civil War the American merchant marine dwindled to insignificance and was of negligible importance in world commerce at the outbreak of the First World War. In the age of steel and steam the British merchant marine had no close rival up to the middle of the twentieth century. The sensational increase in British shipbuilding suggests an external expansion, whereas the sensational increase in American railway building points to concentration of internal development. While the British were filling the sea lanes of the world with ships, Americans were building railways over their vast land mass. The ocean steamer meant to the new British Empire what the railway meant to the United States of America.

RELATIVE DECLINE IN BRITISH INDUSTRIAL CAPITALISM

Toward the close of the nineteenth century the industrial leadership of the world began to pass from Great Britain to other nations. The British decline was relative rather than absolute, and therefore the full story can be seen only after the rise of Germany and the United States has been described; but a preliminary view of some leading forces at work on the British side should be helpful at this point.

The relative decline of Great Britain is important because it reversed the pattern of industrial power among nations which had existed for two centuries. The numerous advantages the British had enjoyed as the pioneer of the Industrial Revolution did not include the ability to perpetuate its leadership. England became less and less the "workshop of the world." Among the reasons for the relative decline were: (1) the export of industrialism (machines, capital, technical know-how, and skilled workmen); (2) the industrialization of larger and more populous nations with richer natural resources; (3) the disadvantages of having been the first nation to adopt machine technology; and (4) the deficiencies of the British educational system.

(1) Prior to 1843, the British made some effort to prevent the spread of the Industrial Revolution to other nations by prohibiting the export of machinery. With the development of the free-trade philosophy, the law against exporting machinery was repealed. This swelled the total volume of exports in the short run, but it had the effect in the long run of enabling other nations to industrialize more readily and to reduce the relative volume of manufactured goods exported by the British. Textile machinery may be used to illustrate the consequences for British industry and trade of exporting producers' goods.

The immediate or short-run effect was to add machinery to the total existing volume of exports. These new exports increased Britain's ability to purchase imports consisting primarily of foodstuffs for industrial workers and raw materials for factories.

In the next or intermediate stage, the presence of textile machinery in foreign countries reduced their dependence on British textiles and tended to offset the increase in exports caused by selling machinery abroad. New countries which purchased British machinery typically set up weaving sheds for the imported looms and did not at first go in strongly for mechanical spinning. Much of the yarn, especially of finer count, was imported from Lancashire, and this also tended to offset the decrease in the export of British cloth and further reduced the export of British cloth to these industrializing nations.

In the third or long-run stage, the newly industrializing countries went in for spinning as well as weaving, and in addition often began to produce their own textile machinery, and perhaps to export cloth, yarn, and machinery in competition with British exports in world markets. At this stage the British textile producers relied on their greater experience and skilled workers to concentrate on the output of high-quality yarn and cloth for the export market. The overall result was a reduction in the British share of cloth, yarn, and machinery exports, partly compensated for by larger exports of quality yarn and cloth.

In addition to exporting machinery, the British aided their rivals by exporting other ingredients of industrialization. British banking houses exported capital to help finance industrialization and to construct railways, public utilities, and other forms of social overhead capital needed for industrializing the new countries. British technicians and engineers were also sent out to assist with installations of factories, railway construction, and other types of activity requiring skilled personnel. Thus by "living dangerously," that is, by exporting both producers' and consumers' goods in the short run, the British undermined some of their markets for both consumers' and producers' goods in the long run. The results of this policy began to show up by the latter part of the nineteenth century. Of the manufactured goods in world trade, 38 per cent were of British origin in the latter half of the 1870's. Thereafter the percentage fell. Although the relative position of British exports declined, the absolute volume of industrial production and exports continued to increase. The slowing down in the rate of expansion of foreign markets was a major factor in the relative decline of British industry.

(2) Germany and the United States were the two nations which passed the United Kingdom in total industrial production toward the close of the nineteenth century. Both countries had a larger territory and a greater population than the United Kingdom. The United States, especially, had richer natural resources than Great Britain, which except for its coal was not particularly well endowed with natural wealth. It is hardly surprising, therefore, that this small island with mediocre resources should have fallen behind in the race for industrial supremacy. Nor was it any special cause for alarm from the British point of view in a world of peaceful coexistence among industrial nations. In some respects per capita production is a more significant index of economic achievement than total national production, and in per capita output the British remained ahead of other nations with the exception of the United

States and, in some industries, Germany. The standard of life was rising for all classes, including industrial wage-earners. England was still the center of a great metropolitan economy drawing food and raw materials from the hinterlands of the whole world.

(3) Perhaps the most important reason for the relative decline of British industry was associated with technological and business characteristics of machine technology in a capitalistic society. Railways, iron and steel, and electricity may be used to illustrate the nature of these disadvantages.

As noted earlier in this chapter, the network of British railways was completed earlier than elsewhere. Roadbeds, bridges, rails, rolling stock, and locomotives were products of the early railway age. Roadbeds had been constructed for relatively light traffic burdens. Early locomotives were less powerful than later ones. Cheap steel had just begun to affect railroading about the time the British completed their network of iron roads. Iron and wooden cars were small and light in comparison with later steel cars. Railway companies were naturally reluctant—and could not afford—to tear up costly roadbeds and rails in order to replace them with heavier and more costly beds and rails. Old rolling stock was scrapped only as it wore out over time. Countries which entered the railway age at a later date and continued to build networks in the age of cheap steel could adopt the later and superior technology of railroading with less financial disadvantage to investors.

In the iron industry the technology of the blast furnace remained relatively constant during the nineteenth century, but there were significant differences in the adaptations to this basic technology in various countries. Comparisons of the average output per blast furnace in the principal iron-producing nations shows Great Britain falling rapidly behind after 1880, at which time the output per furnace was not radically different in the several countries. Thirty years later, in 1910, the British output per blast furnace was only about one-half that of Germany and less than one-third that of the United States. British blast furnaces were even smaller than in France, which by comparison with other nations had been rather backward in the tendency toward large-scale industrial production. Since the size of blast furnace crews had been fairly constant, the increase in output per furnace reflected an increase in productivity per man, which in turn meant that British productivity increased more slowly than German, American, and French productivity.

The lag in Great Britain can be attributed to technological continuity, that is, the tendency to retain in use the existing plant and equipment, which in this case had been installed in earlier decades and was therefore smaller and less efficient than the newer installations of countries with iron industries of later vintage. Moreover, British firms had more capital tied up in the old models and therefore had more to lose in capital values than did investors in the newer countries. Conservative British capitalists accepted as satisfactory the techniques with which they were familiar. Reluctance to accept new techniques meant that even newly constructed plants were more old-fashioned than in Germany and the United States.

In new industries like electrical and chemical products the British lagged behind the Germans and Americans. A first major use of electricity was for street lighting. For these services the British had a well-established gas lighting system. Wealthy and influential gas companies were able to delay the

installation of electric lighting. In consequence, the entire electric generating
industry and other phases of electrical technology were retarded. This was
rather clearly a phenomenon of the British business community, because
British scientists and inventors included some of the most creative minds of the
new age of electricity. Lord Kelvin and Clerk-Maxwell, for example, did
pioneer work of great importance in the fundamental principles of electricity,
and Sir Charles Parsons invented the steam turbine, which made possible the
efficient transformation of energy from coal into electricity for industrial and
commercial utilization.

(4) Although the British contributed important ideas and inventions to
the age of mass production, as a nation they lacked education in depth for
the widespread and successful application of these ideas and principles to industry. The British were slower to change their school system to the special
demands of scientific technology. While Germany and the United States were
purposefully adapting their schools and universities to the new technology,
the British continued to follow a policy of laissez-faire in education as well
as in other aspects of social control. Compulsory education was not introduced
into England until 1876.

In higher education the United States and Germany established engineering colleges and technical institutes to promote the technology of physics
and chemistry. Americans set up dozens of state universities designed primarily
to apply the principles of natural science to mechanical and agricultural pursuits. Free higher education produced an outpouring of well-trained specialists.
Germany had dozens of state-supported universities turning out a large supply
of well-educated engineers and industrial scientists. In chemistry especially
the Germans made their scientific training felt by developing by 1914 a chemical industry which was by far the best in the world. In the electrical industry
the Americans and Germans enjoyed the advantage of a generous supply of
electrical engineering graduates, whereas the British suffered in comparison.
In summary, the countries which began their industrialization by borrowing
technology from the British were more cognizant of the importance of increasing the capacity of their people through education than were the British, who
had had the intrinsically more difficult function of inaugurating machine technology. At the very time when the paucity of natural resources was limiting
the expansion of their economy, the British were not devoting sufficient attention to the development of their human resources to retain world leadership
in an industrial civilization based increasingly on the technology of physics
and chemistry.[2]

---

[2] In comparing business enterprise in Britain and the United States in the late nineteenth century, Professor H. J. Habakkuk of Oxford stresses the more limited supply of
entrepreneurship in the United Kingdom because of the stronger attractions of the professions, civil service, and other callings which were more prestigious in Britain than in the
United States. This position seems to assume that the supply of general talent among the
population is strictly limited. While this is not an easy proposition to prove one way or the
other, it seems reasonable to assume that among the British people there were many of
great potential achievement who would have flowered in a less restrictive educational system. Although the stock of fundamental ideas available to technologists in the two countries was about the same and the British scientists contributed more than their share to
these fundamental ideas, large numbers of well-educated engineers and scientists were
needed by the late nineteenth century to carry this stock of technological knowledge into
effect. Education in depth, especially higher education, was essential. The British educa-

BRITISH
INDUSTRIAL
LEADERSHIP

BARNES, DONALD G., *A History of the English Corn Laws, from 1660–1846*. London: Routledge & Kegan Paul, Ltd., 1961.

CHECKLAND, S. G., *The Rise of Industrial Society in England, 1815–1885*. New York: St. Martin's Press, Inc., 1964.

CLAPHAM, JOHN H., *An Economic History of Britain*, 3 vols. 2nd ed. London: Cambridge University Press, 1930–38.

DEANE, PHYLLIS, and W. A. COLE, *British Economic Growth, 1688–1959*. London: Cambridge University Press, 1962.

GAYER, ARTHUR D., WALT W. ROSTOW, and ANNA J. SCHWARTZ, *The Growth and Fluctuations of the British Economy, 1790–1850*, 2 vols. New York: Oxford University Press, 1953.

HABAKKUK, H. J., *American and British Technology in the Nineteenth Century*. London: Cambridge University Press, 1962.

HOFFMAN, WALTHER J., *British Industry, 1700–1950*. Oxford: Basil Blackwell, 1955.

KNOWLES, L. C. A., *The Industrial and Commercial Revolutions in Great Britain during the Nineteenth Century*, 4th ed. London: Routledge & Kegan Paul, Ltd., 1950.

MALTHUS, THOMAS ROBERT, *Principles of Political Economy, Considered with a View to their Practical Applications*, 2nd ed. New York: Augustus M. Kelley, Publisher, 1951.

MARSHALL, ALFRED, *Industry and Trade*, rev. ed., Chapters 1–5. London: Macmillan & Co., Ltd., 1923.

RICARDO, DAVID, *On the Principles of Political Economy and Taxation*, 3rd ed. London: Cambridge University Press, 1951.

ROSTOW, WALT W., *British Economy of the Nineteenth Century*. Oxford: Clarendon Press, 1948.

ARTICLES

BLAUG, MARK, "The Poor Law Report Reexamined," *Journal of Economic History*, XXIV (June, 1964), 229–45.

DEANE, PHYLLIS, "Contemporary Estimates of National Income in the First Half of the Nineteenth Century," *Economic History Review*, VIII (April, 1956), 339–54.

———, "Contemporary Estimates of National Income in the Second Half of the Nineteenth Century, *Economic History Review*, IX (April, 1957), 451–61.

HABAKKUK, H. G., "Second Thoughts on American and British Technology in the Nineteenth Century," *Business Archives and History*, III (Aug., 1963), 187–94.

———, "The Historical Experience on the Basic Conditions of Economic Progress," *Indian Economic Journal*, II (Oct., 1954), 103–18.

HOFFMANN, WALTHER G., "The Growth of Industrial Production in Great Britain: A Quantitative Study," *Economic History Review*, II, No. 2 (1949), 162–80.

---

tional system seems to have been very deficient for applying the technology of physics and chemistry, which was promoted so extensively by state universities in the United States and Germany. See H. J. Habakkuk, *American and British Technology in the Nineteenth Century* (London: Cambridge University Press, 1962), Chap. 6. One of the few positive conclusions reached by Professor Charles Kindleberger in his long book comparing British and French economic growth is "the British amateur tradition is excellent for getting an Industrial Revolution started, but not well suited for taking it into the age of electricity, chemistry, and metallurgy." *Economic Growth in France and Britain, 1851–1950* (Cambridge, Mass.: Harvard University Press, 1964), p. 324.

Development of Industrial
Capitalism in France

CHAPTER

16

A century after Louis XIV died at Versailles (1715) Napoleon was defeated at Waterloo (1815), and another century later (1915) France was fighting for survival against Germany, which had replaced France as the aggressor nation of Europe. In two centuries France declined from the heights of the richest, most populous, and militarily most powerful nation in the world to second rank among the great powers. Yet as late as the 1860's Emperor Louis Napoleon (reigned 1851–70) dreamed of duplicating some of the feats, while hoping to avoid the mistakes, of his great uncle. The ambitions of the later and lesser Napoleon turned into a nightmare when France fell in a few months under the heel of Bismarck in the Franco-Prussian War of 1870–71. The difference between the achievements of Napoleon I and Napoleon III represents more than a difference in the personal talents of uncle and nephew.

Between 1815 and 1870 France progressed slowly, while other great nations, especially Germany, the United Kingdom, and the United States, grew rapidly in economic strength. In 1870, 1914, and 1939 the economic and military weakness of France invited the aggression of its powerful neighbor to the east. These unpleasant facts in French history are to no small extent related to the initially slower economic growth of France, as compared with the other powers, after the Revolution of 1789. The fact that France grew is less important to history than the fact that it grew less rapidly than its rivals. This phenomenon of retarded economic growth in France will be examined in this chapter.

TRANSFER OF INDUSTRIAL TECHNIQUES
TO THE CONTINENT

From its origins in England during the eighteenth century, manufacture by machinery spread to the European Continent and to the United States of North America during the nineteenth century. Early efforts by the British to contain the Industrial Revolution within its political boundaries proved futile for numerous reasons. The scientific knowledge upon which much of the

new technology rested was international. British technologists emigrated, often under strong financial inducements from abroad, despite attempts by the British government to keep skilled artisans and engineers at home. Non-Britishers proved hardly less ingenious with technology than the British. Once capitalism matured to the point where other countries could afford expensive machinery, they began to shift from the old *manu*-facturing to the new *machino*-facturing because machines were many times more efficient than hand work.

Not surprisingly, northern France provided a beachhead for the transfer of new industrial techniques from England to the Continent. The provinces along the upper portion of the Channel, including Flanders of the famous medieval cloth industry, had a long and distinguished tradition of industrial development. In earlier centuries the English had learned much from the artisans and businessmen of the Low Countries. Industrial capitalism in the Low Countries never disappeared, but it suffered greatly from destructive warfare among the great powers. The territory known today as Belgium passed successively under the domination of France, Spain, Holland, France, Austria, and Holland, and finally, in 1830, emerged as independent Belgium. When the Industrial Revolution began in England in the eighteenth century, the Belgians were the people best prepared to borrow the new techniques. Aided by emigrant English engineers and mechanics, shops for making the new machinery were established in Belgium in the late eighteenth and early nineteenth centuries. From Belgium machines were shipped to France, to Germany and elsewhere on the Continent. Ironically, English restrictions on the export of machines and on the emigration of mechanics protected the Belgian machine-makers against legal competition, and by the time the English lifted the ban on machine exports in 1842, Belgian machine-makers had no difficulty meeting the competition of their former masters across the Channel.

Early Capitalism in France

When the new technology associated with the Industrial Revolution began to spread outward from England in the eighteenth century, France had already experienced several centuries of capitalist evolution. In addition to the long and continuous development of capitalism in northern France along the Channel, other parts of France had experienced similar early capitalist beginnings. Southern France felt the awakening effects of expansion of trade in the Mediterranean in the later Middle Ages. Europe's greatest capitalist in the fifteenth century was probably the Frenchman, Jacques Coeur. The "Money-man," as Coeur was called, had his headquarters in Montpellier, a few miles from the Mediterranean coast. Up the Rhone 175 miles from the Mediterranean lay Lyons, where the Italian Medici and the German Fuggers had had large branch banks and where an important medieval fair had been located. The greatest medieval fairs had been in Champagne in eastern France. In Gascony on the Atlantic Coast around Bordeaux the wine trade had been another important form of medieval capitalist activity.

Feudalism began to weaken in France about the same time it went into decline in England. Political power became centralized under Francis I, a contemporary of Henry VIII in England, and Henry IV, whose reign in France

overlapped those of Elizabeth I and James I in England. The great seventeenth-century French ministers Sully, Richelieu, and Mazarin achieved a high degree of political unity for France. Colbert, their able successor, reduced, eliminated, and unified road and river tolls within France. Among mercantilist steps toward national economic unification, Colbert's tariff reforms of 1664 and 1667 have been rated second only to the English Statute of Apprentices. Attempts by Colbert to establish large-scale industry through state subsidies and grants of monopoly succeeded less well than his tariff reforms. Minute regulations may have improved the quality of French products, but they impeded free industrial growth. Most of France's royal manufacturers failed when government subsidies were withdrawn. In France, as in other countries of Europe, when capitalism progressed to the point where it was capable of operating independently of government assistance, a reaction set in against mercantilism. Use of the term "laissez-faire" to describe a policy of "hands off business" is a legacy of the French reaction against government regulation in the early eighteenth century.

In the eighteenth century, when the putting-out system was giving way to the factory system in England, the French putting-out system was still battling urban monopolies held by craft gilds. Craft gilds in France remained strong because the Crown used them as instruments of national industrial regulation. "As a result largely of the intervention of the crown in municipal industry, the gilds flourished during the reign of Louis XIV as they had never flourished in the Middle Ages." [1] At a time when craft gilds in England were atrophying, the French government was transforming local gilds into national gilds. Municipal gild authorities consistently attempted to check the growth of rural industry. Only in 1762 did an edict give rural artisans without membership in gilds the right to manufacture all kinds of cloth. Although urban control over rural industry had been circumvented prior to this edict, the new freedom after 1762 stimulated further expansion of rural industry. Some merchant-manufacturers encouraged industry in the countryside in an attempt to weaken the monopolistic power of town gilds. In 1776 Turgot, the famous reform minister, issued an edict which in effect abolished gild monopolies, and, despite the withdrawal of this edict with the early fall of Turgot, the revolutionary government of 1789 effectively abolished the gilds in France fifteen years later.

On the eve of the Revolution of 1789 French industry consisted of a mixture of urban handicraft, rural putting-out, and a few large workshops, mostly without machinery. Urban handicraft on the medieval pattern under gild monopolies was fading and received a *coup de grâce* from the Revolution: the rural putting-out system was dominant and expanding in 1789; while the incipient factory system was just beginning to be felt as Crompton's spinning mule made headway in cotton mills in some areas of France.

The Revolution of 1789 had important, although indirect, significance for France's economic development. By breaking the power of the nobility and solidifying the position of the peasants, the Revolution assisted the middle classes of France in their political and economic ascendancy. The Revolution

[1] John U. Nef, *Industry and Government in France and England 1540–1640* (Ithaca, N.Y.: Cornell University Press, 1957), p. 15.

fixed the course of long-range development toward industrial capitalism by sweeping away the remnants of feudalism, the craft gilds, and an intolerable tax burden on the most enterprising classes of France. In the short run, however, the Revolution and the ensuing Napoleonic wars probably retarded French industrial progress by placing a barrier between England and France for nearly a quarter of a century at a time when the English Industrial Revolution had begun to spread to the Continent.

INFLUENCES RETARDING FRENCH INDUSTRIAL DEVELOPMENT

French industrial development presented a contrast to industrial growth in England, Germany, and the United States during the nineteenth century. At no time did French industry change fast enough to justify the appellation "Industrial Revolution," whereas the term may appropriately be used to refer to developments in England (1760–1840), the United States (1860–1900), and Germany (1871–1913). France did, however, grow more rapidly than other countries, apart from these three leaders. In the course of the nineteenth century, only Germany and the United States caught up with and passed France in industrial production. France had great potentiality for growth and, in her own way, made an important contribution to industrial leadership, in what the great English economist, Alfred Marshall, called "individuality and refinement of production." Among the advantages enjoyed by France were an early start in capitalism, a strong central government, a colonial empire, a fertile soil, a long if too-smooth coast line with some good ports, good roads dating from Roman times, healthful climate, good natural resources (if French coal was poor and limited in quantity, Italy had no coal and Spain very little), abundant iron ore, creative scientists, well-trained engineers, a love of beauty and high standards of workmanship making for quality products of artistic design. These numerous advantages for potential industrialization together with the special nature of France's contribution to quality production should be borne in mind in the following discussion.

Special Nature of the French Industrial Labor Force

An industrial labor supply of the type needed for a factory system depends on high productivity of labor in agriculture. As labor in agriculture becomes more productive, a smaller proportion of the total labor force is required for raising food and fiber and hence a greater proportion becomes available for industrial employment. In the absence of good statistics for output per *worker* in agriculture, data on production per *acre* provide the best available measure of changes in the productivity of French agricultural labor during the nineteenth century. Table 16–1 shows the yield per acre of wheat in France from the end of the Napoleonic wars to the eve of World War I.

Yield per acre of wheat increased slowly but steadily during the century after Waterloo. After 1880 better land utilization and chemical fertilizers stepped up wheat productivity. Yet in 1910, when the French yield stood at

TABLE 16–1

285

DEVELOPMENT
OF
INDUSTRIAL
CAPITALISM
IN FRANCE

Wheat Yields in France, 1815–1910

YEARS	BUSHELS PER ACRE
1815-20	11.0
1821-30	13.0
1831-40	14.0
1841-50	15.0
1851-60	15.5
1861-70	15.8
1871-80	15.8
1881-90	17.3
1891-1900	17.0
1901-1910	19.4

Source: Annuaire Statistique (1913), p. 43.

approximately 20 bushels per acre, Germany and Great Britain had yields of 30 and 32 bushels, respectively. France also lagged behind neighboring European countries in sugar beet yield per acre, in yield of sugar per ton of beets, and in milk production per cow, which was approximately one-half that of England and Germany and only one-third that of Denmark and Switzerland.

In contrast to France, the enclosure movement in England between 1750 and 1850 greatly raised agricultural productivity and, along with rapid population growth, provided an abundance of labor for full-time factory employment. Enclosures broke the tie of the English yeomen with the soil and converted England to a nation of large landed estates. The French Revolution, on the other hand, solidified the tie of French peasants to the soil and created an independent peasantry of small landholdings. Thus at the very time England was entering a new era of industrialization based on factories, historical forces in France brought redistribution of land and an increase in the number of independent peasant proprietors. Moreover, the French adopted egalitarian inheritance, which reinforced the attachment of peasants to the fertile soil of France. In contrast, the British system of primogeniture tended to perpetuate large landholdings in England. Although French peasants were liberated from feudal burdens, the Revolution brought few changes in methods of cultivation and therefore did little to raise productivity. Small holdings prevented adoption of the most efficient farming techniques. These political changes, however, gave the French peasantry great political power. Attempts to reimpose feudal obligations on the peasantry during the Restoration of the French monarchy (1815–30) failed, even though many nobles received back the estates confiscated during the Revolution.

Small landholdings, perpetuated and accentuated by egalitarian inheritance, contributed to widespread underemployment or partial employment of rural labor. At convenient seasons of the year, small landholders would readily accept part-time industrial employment at low wages. But they would not sever their ties with the land to accept full-time industrial employment at the existing wage rates. Low wages and miserable working conditions among the

full-time urban proletariat provided little incentive for them to do so. Rural Frenchmen knew enough about contemporary conditions of labor in English factories to be wary of accepting the English way of life. The rigid discipline of factory employment was repugnant to the French, as in fact it was to rural Englishmen newly introduced to it. Professor Dunham, the historian of French industry, tells of workers who "were intelligent and friendly and reasonably contented in their homes, where they worked in very small groups, usually composed of one or two families. Then came the advent of the factory system, and these same laborers proved obstinate and undisciplined." [2] Rural laborers were abundant and willing to work for low wages, but they were often poorly trained and hence had low productivity in comparison, for example, with full-time English factory workers. Small-scale industrial entrepreneurs in France did not think it worth while to devote the time to and undergo the expense of training workers for specialized tasks. Many workers residing in urban communities supplemented their industrial earnings with part-time employment in farming during the harvest season.

These conditions in the labor market fostered the domestic system, which in France held its own against the factory system during the first half of the nineteenth century. Between 1815 and 1848 about one-fourth of French industrial workers were employed in what may be called large-scale industry. Most of the remaining three-fourths of industrial workers retained a connection with agriculture. Industrial labor remained relatively inefficient. Labor cost per unit of output was high even though (money) wage rates were low. Industrial employment was for many small landholders a second occupation, a source of supplementary income. In the face of these handicaps, the transformation to modern industrial techniques came slowly in comparison with England, Germany, and the United States.

The economists' distinction between the *supply* of labor and the *quantity* of labor is helpful in making clear the relation between industrial retardation and the system of small landholdings. Although the quantity of labor available may have been abundant, the supply was scarce. Supply means the quantity available at a specific price (or at a specific wage rate). To say that French peasants were tied to the soil means they would leave the land only at relatively high industrial wages. The supply of labor for factory employment was inelastic, that is, relatively unresponsive to increases in wage rates. This does not mean, of course, that peasants were totally unresponsive, but only that the response was sufficiently sluggish to retard factory-type industrialization in France.

French urban wages were higher than rural wages but not high enough to attract full-time factory workers in large numbers. Even when the amount of part-time, irregular labor available for employment in industry was plentiful, the number of full-time, year-round workers of the type needed for efficient factory operation was relatively small at prevailing wage rates; and we may assume the number would not have increased much even at higher wage rates. A combination of high wage rates and low efficiency raised the labor cost of production of factory output to a point at which French factory owners

---

[2] Arthur L. Dunham, *The Industrial Revolution in France, 1815–1848* (New York: Exposition Press, 1955), p. 185.

could not easily compete with imported British products in French markets and even less so in foreign markets where French products enjoyed no protective tariffs. Ability to sell in foreign as well as domestic markets was an important condition of rapid industrial expansion, as the British experience illustrates.

The fact that the quantity of labor (irrespective of wage rates) was abundant but the supply (quantity in relation to wage rates) was scarce had meaning in French economic history in this respect: The French peasant had a choice as to how he would make a living. So long as he owned some land, he could choose between remaining a small proprietor or migrating to an urban community. Ownership of land made the supply of labor more inelastic. Given this institutional setting, the reluctance of Frenchmen to leave the land may be attributed partly to temperament. We may assume that by choosing to remain on the land, many French peasants were poorer but happier—poorer, because they could have migrated to higher paying employment in towns. Of course, some did migrate to towns and cities—Paris had its attractions—but among the migrants many preferred to become artisans or to set up small shops in order to retain the individuality of person they valued so highly.[3]

Population Growth

When Napoleon's conquering legions marched across Europe, France was, next to Russia, the most populous nation in Europe. Yet during the nineteenth century France's population grew more slowly than that of other major nations in Europe, and in the second half of the century France fell behind Germany, Great Britain, and Austria-Hungary, as well as the United States. French population increased from 27,500,000 in 1800 to 36,500,000 in 1860; and on reduced territory, from 36,200,000 in 1871 to 39,700,000 in 1913. This represented a growth of 50 per cent during the period from 1800 to 1913. In contrast, the population of Germany rose by 200 per cent and that of Great Britain by 300 per cent during the same period. Still more revealing for industrialization are the statistics on urban population. Between 1850 and 1913 Germany's urban population increased four-fold, from 10,000,000 to 40,000,000, whereas France's urban population grew from 9,000,000 to 18,000,000 during the same years. The extent, if not the rate, of urbanization in Great Britain exceeded that of Germany. At no time in France was there a rapid shift from rural to urban population, which is a further indication of the absence of swift changes that might be called an industrial revolution. Not until after the First World War did the urban population equal the rural. Thus France's slow growth of population, in combination with the relatively equal division of landed property, retarded industrial development by limiting the manpower available for full-time urban employment.

[3] On industrial retardation and agrarian conditions, see Rondo E. Cameron, *France and the Economic Development of Europe, 1800–1914* (Princeton, N.J.: Princeton University Press, 1961), esp. pp. 27, 506. Cameron points out that "In the hundred years following the Revolution the number of agricultural proprietors doubled in France, while the agricultural population remained stationary and the population as a whole increased by less than 50 per cent." See also Charles P. Kindleberger, *Economic Growth in France and Britain, 1851–1950* (Cambridge, Mass.: Harvard University Press, 1964), esp. pp. 225–38.

Among the retarding factors in French industrial development, poor and inadequate coal deposits are frequently mentioned. French coal was generally inferior in quality to British and German coal, and coal deposits were mostly small and inaccessible, with thin and irregular seams. About one-third of the coal consumed in France was imported. While importation was not in itself a major handicap to industrialization, French ports and waterways were poorly located with respect to industrial centers. High-cost transportation was clearly a critical problem in French coal utilization. Often the price of coal at the point of consumption was ten times the cost at the mine. Improvements in waterways in the first half of the nineteenth century eased the situation, and the railway network completed in the second half of the century did much more to relieve the coal "shortage" for industry.

Expensive coal retarded the introduction of steam engines in France. Continued reliance on water power tended to keep French industry widely dispersed. The number and size of steam engines in France increased in the course of the century, but lagged far behind England and, in the second half of the century, Germany. A tariff on imported steam engines after 1818 checked the importation of superior British steam engines and, while stimulating French production of steam engines, raised their price and kept down their size.

Iron and steel, along with coal, provided the sinews of nineteenth-century industry. France had abundant deposits of iron ore, but prior to completion of a railway network in the 1860's French iron production was handicapped by high transport costs. Much French coal was unsuited for coking, and coking coal had to be imported from Germany at high prices. Conversion from coal to coke furnaces in France was delayed by the country's relative abundance of wood. The geographical scatter of both iron ore and wood tended to foster small-scale, charcoal-using furnaces for iron production in many parts of France. As late as 1850 more ore was smelted with charcoal than with coke. Railway construction, beginning in the 1840's, increased greatly the demand for iron and also eased the problem of transporting coal and iron ore.

During the 1860's the Bessemer process for making steel was introduced from England. France was second only to England in attaining during the 1860's an annual production of one million tons of wrought iron and steel. Output remained stationary at about a million tons a year for two decades, and meanwhile Germany's iron and steel output passed that of France. In the Franco-Prussian war (1870–71) France lost to Germany the province of Lorraine, which contained the most extensive iron ore fields in Europe. With the discovery of the basic steel-making process in the late 1870's, the Lorraine ores, previously not usable for steel because they contained phosphorous, enabled Germany to shoot ahead of both England and France in iron and steel output. In the 1890's French steel production leaped forward again, and on the eve of the First World War reached 5 million tons a year. This was two-thirds of British steel production (7.5 million tons), but less than one-third of Germany's (17 million tons). Compared with Italy and Spain, however, France enjoyed great advantages in both coal production and steel-making.

Cotton Spinning jennies appeared early, during the 1770's, and proved popular in France because they fitted in with the existing domestic system. Arkwright's water frame, on the other hand, never became popular in France, probably because it produced coarse yarn and required considerable capital as well as a factory organization, none of which meshed with the French scheme of things. In contrast, the spinning mule proved popular in France because it spun fine, soft yarn and required less capital and organization for its utilization than the water frame. Hand spinning of cotton had largely disappeared from France by the time of Waterloo (1815), but during the Continental blockade imposed by the British against France in the Napoleonic Wars raw cotton had become very scarce, and this political factor delayed the entire cotton textile industry.

The big push in mechanical spinning, as well as improvements in the quality of yarn, came after 1815. Mechanical weaving spread slowly in France and made little headway until the depression which began in 1837. Richard Roberts of the famous English machine-making firm of Sharp and Roberts, which perfected the power loom in England in the 1820's, went in the 1830's to Alsace, where he taught the French how to make and use power looms in cotton weaving. This typifies the direct influence which English technologists, including engineers and mechanics, had on the mechanization of French industry.

Alsace was the one region of France which developed a cotton textile industry comparable to the great industry of England's Lancashire. The closest approximation in France to a real industrial revolution in textiles was experienced around Mulhouse in Alsace between 1815 and 1850, and under the Second Empire (1851–70) this region continued its remarkable progress. Alsatian yarn was the finest in France. In that province, machinery was as good as that found anywhere and superseded hand weaving at a relatively early date. When Germany took Alsace at the end of the Franco-Prussian war, France lost its most valuable textile region. Stagnation characterized French cotton textile production during the 1870's and 1880's, followed by another period of rapid growth from 1890 up to the First World War, at which time France ranked fifth in the number of cotton spindles, behind Great Britain, the United States, Germany, and Russia. Counting the spindles of Alsace-Lorraine, France would have ranked third.

Wool Wool fibers proved less adaptable to mechanization than cotton, and partly for this reason the French achievement in woolen manufacture compared more favorably with the British than did cotton manufacture. In producing fine woolen cloth with artistic designs for women's dress goods, for example, the limited output and relatively high cost of hand weaving constituted no great disadvantage. France achieved an international reputation for beautiful designs and fashionable women's clothes for which there was a strong export demand. More than one-half of the fine worsteds exported from France went to the tariff-free English market.

Improvements in woolen textiles were not confined to luxury products.

Production of lower-priced cloth for the more numerous middle-income classes also expanded rapidly during the nineteenth century. France's wool clip increased in quantity as well as in quality and met the domestic demand until 1835. Although it increased in total quantity until about 1890, after 1835 Australian imports provided an increasing proportion of the raw wool consumed in French manufacture. Costs and prices were more crucial considerations for the non-luxury market, and mechanization was the answer to cheaper products. A notable French contribution to mechanization was Josué Heilmann's remarkable invention for combing short wool in preparation for manufacturing worsteds. Previously, only long wool of the English type could be combed with machines. Mechanical spinning of both combed and carded wool was nearly complete by the middle of the nineteenth century. Power weaving came more slowly in the second half of the nineteenth century, with considerable hand weaving remaining in the luxury trade well into the twentieth century. All things considered, the French performance in woolen textiles was impressive, especially in the first half of the nineteenth century, with the improvement in the quality of domestic wool, the high quality of worsteds of artistic design, and the contribution to the mechanized processing of short wool.

Silk   France was to silk what Great Britain was to cotton textiles during the nineteenth century—the unchallenged leader of the world. Lyons in southeastern France was the center of the industry. Here the mild Mediterranean climate was well suited to growing silkworms which produced the cocoons from which the delicate silk fibers were unravelled. Raw silk production in France increased about six-fold between 1815 and 1848, but the demand for silk increased even more rapidly and the industry enjoyed widespread prosperity. Careless handling of silkworms induced a serious disease which ravaged raw silk production just after mid-century. Raw silk production recovered only partially from this catastrophe, and France became increasingly dependent on raw silk imports from the Far East, French Indo-China, Japan, and China. In the twentieth century the silk industry suffered from Japanese competition and from the introduction of artificial silk, rayon, and other synthetic fibers.

Silk production elicited the special genius of the French people. Its end product was a fine, soft fabric which appealed to the artistic creativity of workmen, who prided themselves on their individuality and craftsmanship, and which gave satisfaction to consumers who sought, and were able to pay for, the most beautiful and stylish fabric available. Special significance may be attached to the fact that the remarkable Jacquard loom was invented by a Frenchman for use in the silk industry. Joseph-Marie Jacquard helped his father in the family weaving shop in Lyons and later became a silk weaver and manufacturer himself. His loom, invented in 1804, answered the long-felt need of French silk weavers for a loom which would weave complex designs in finished fabric inexpensively. Jacquard's loom was all the more remarkable because it was easily adapted to other fibers, including cotton, wool, and linen. It represented France's most important contribution to textile technology.

In other respects, too, silk production typified French industrial develop-

ment during the nineteenth century. Raw silk was produced by large numbers of rural families who also did the initial processing (pulling and reeling) of the raw silk in their homes or in small workshops. The spinning (called "throwing") of reeled silk as well was carried on in rural dwellings and small workshops, and thus the close tie between agriculture and industry was maintained. Weaving took place in towns like Lyons and in smaller communities, including rural villages. Manufacturing establishments were typically small, and competition among producers was intense. Returns to capital were small and wages were low as a consequence. The Lyonese proletariat was among the most revolutionary in revolutionary France. Serious strikes occurred in 1831 and 1834 and were crushed by the bourgeoisie, who controlled both the trade and the town government. Worker reaction against capitalism was strong, perhaps partly because the ideology of rational, large-scale organization never penetrated French society. Forces which retarded economic growth also forestalled a sharp break with the older forms of economic organization.

Railways and the Pace of Industrial Growth

By European standards France is a large country (about the size of Texas), and its economic unification presented difficult obstacles which were overcome only after the railway network had been laid down about 1870. At an early date, between the reigns of Henry IV and Louis XIV, good roads had facilitated political unification. Napoleon's engineers improved French roads for military purposes with some economic side effects. During the restoration (1815–30) much attention was given to waterways, and the earliest railways in France were intended as connecting links between waterways.

As the significance of railways for national military and economic policy became apparent, there ensued a prolonged national debate concerning appropriate methods of construction and operation. The "Organic Law" of 1842 called for close cooperation between government and private enterprise in constructing railways, according to a national plan. With Paris as the hub, rail lines were to radiate like the spokes of a wheel into the French provinces —north, east, south, and west. The government was to acquire the right-of-way and construct roadbeds, bridges, and tunnels. Private companies were to lay rails, provide the rolling stock and station facilities, and operate the lines. Operating rights were granted to private companies for limited time periods, usually about forty years, with the state reserving the right to assume ownership and operation of the entire property at any time upon compensating the private companies. With some important variations in this basic plan, the national trunk lines were completed by about 1860. Since the lines radiating from Paris provided limited access between industrial regions in the provinces, except through Paris, other main roads were subsequently constructed, and by 1870 the French railway system had assumed substantially its modern geographical pattern. Six great companies, operating in recognized regions, made up the national network. These companies were the North, East, Paris–Lyons–Marseilles (P–L–M), Southern, Orleans, and West.

In France the economic effects of railways were similar to those in other large geographical areas—a revolutionary change in the division of labor resulting from major reductions in the cost of transport. Areas and products

which previously had no economic intercourse suddenly became integrated into a common market. Peasants were roused from lethargy bred of self-sufficiency by the bright prospects of distant markets. Speaking of the effect of railways on French agriculture following 1852, Professor Clapham says, ". . . forces were set free vastly more powerful than had ever played upon it, forces capable of doing in decades what under all previous conditions might have taken centuries." [4] Village laborers in search of employment found their mobility enhanced and their opportunities increased. A change, obviously of great importance, resulting from the first form of mass overland transportation took place in the movement of coal. Iron and steel production spurted to more than a million tons per year in the 1860's. The fruits of the railway age were manifest in a stepped-up rate of overall economic growth in France under the Second Empire (1851–70).

Although the gains from railways in France were great, they did not match those of some other countries. Germany (Prussia) surely gained more from railways because of an earlier start and because it had less coastal shipping than France. So did the United States, which had a greater need even than France to bring economic unity to its vast territory. France lost some ground by delaying the start of major railway construction and initiating all major lines at about the same time, thus delaying the completion of all. It would have been more efficient to have built one main line at a time, completing it quickly, in some system of national priorities.

The specifics of railway economies depend on details of geography and cost data concerning production and transportation before and after railway operation begins. Three circumstances may be distinguished. (1) Some railways yield immediate and abundant gains which render them socially desirable as well as profitable to private investors without financial assistance from the state. The North line from Paris to Belgium and the Channel was a clear example of this type. Baron James de Rothschild, France's leading financier, offered in 1843 to construct this railway entirely with private capital, only to be rebuffed by the French government, which wanted to impose conditions which would have given the state a share in the financial returns. The Paris–Lyons–Marseilles line seemed likely to prove profitable after an initial period of operating losses. (2) For other railways neither the private nor the social gains are sufficient to justify the allocation of resources required for their construction and operation. The second line between Paris and Versailles, one along the right bank of the Seine and the other along the left bank, in the late 1830's was an obvious example of this second type. One line between Paris and Versailles would have been sufficient and perhaps profitable, but given the uneconomical duplication, neither proved financially successful. The number of socially uneconomical lines in France was limited because of the timidity of capitalists and because France soon developed a coordinated national plan for railway construction. In Great Britain, where railways developed without an overall plan, the number of failures was much greater and the number of lines abandoned before completion was considerable. (3) A third type of railway is that which yields social returns in excess of social costs

---

[4] John H. Clapham, *The Economic Development of France and Germany, 1815–1914,* 4th ed. (London: Cambridge University Press, 1951), p. 158.

but with returns so widely dispersed as to be unprofitable to private investors bearing the full cost of construction and operation. Here the case for government subsidy to a private operator or for government ownership and operation is clearest. Railways constitute part of the social overhead capital of an economic system and cannot safely be left to the sole test of private profitability.

When returns cannot be narrowly channeled into private accounts but the projects are socially desirable according to other economic criteria, governments have a responsibility to assist or carry through such projects directly. Government construction and operation can disperse the costs to correspond to the widely scattered returns. France's Western Railway line probably fell into this category. As a private enterprise, even with government subsidy, it was in constant financial difficulty although it seems to have justified itself in terms of its contribution to the economic development of the territory which it served. Finally in 1908 the central government exercised its right to nationalize its operation, and the Western became the first major state-owned railway in France. In 1936 all French railways became nationalized property.

Tariffs

When the restored monarchy took over from Napoleon in 1815, it buttressed an established policy of ultra-protectionism for French industry and agriculture. High tariffs were maintained until the Second Empire, when Napoleon III for a brief period gave France its lowest tariffs in modern times. But Napoleon's low-tariff policy, embodied in the Cobden Treaty of 1860 and similar treaties with other countries, was followed by a protectionist reaction which raised tariffs in several steps beginning in 1881 and culminating in the ultra-protectionist Méline tariff of 1892. The high-low-high tariff history of France in the course of the nineteenth century offers some opportunity to observe the effects of tariffs on economic growth, although the difficulty of separating the effects of tariff changes from other factors makes a definitive judgment difficult. Nevertheless, some tentative conclusions may be drawn, especially with respect to individual industries and products.

Manufacturers and agriculturalists clamored for protection and most of the time the government responded affirmatively to their demands. The split between free-trade industry and protectionist agriculture, which dominated British tariff history in the first half of the nineteenth century, or the split between protectionist industry and free-trade agriculture (cotton), which characterized the United States before the Civil War, was not part of the French scene. At one time or another nearly all industrial and agricultural products in France received protection against foreign competition either by tariff duties or by prohibitions against importation. A 30 per cent duty was imposed on coal imports in 1816. Coal was the material resource most vital for rapid industrialization. The demand for coal increased so rapidly that domestic producers could not expand fast enough to meet the needs, and large amounts continued to be imported from Britain, Belgium, and Germany despite the tariff. The general effect of the duty was to increase the price of coal to domestic users and to place them at a competitive disadvantage with British, Belgian, and German manufacturers. Duties on coking coal raised the price of coke to about twice that in England and Germany. For this reason and

because of the relative abundance of wood for charcoal, the transition from charcoal to coke in the French iron and steel industry was delayed. Among the supporters of the tariff on coking coal were large landlords, including the central government itself, who owned timber and wanted to continue to sell it at high prices to ironmasters. Improvements in French metallurgy were also delayed by a tariff of 120 per cent on English iron. Tariffs on coal and iron clearly worked to the disadvantage of French economic growth. Some recognition of the adverse effects came in 1836 with a reduction in the duty on coal. The duty on imported iron continued at a high level.

Tariffs were more justified in cotton textiles than in the woolen and silk branches of the industry. At the beginning of the nineteenth century France's cotton textiles qualified as an "infant" industry in danger of being smothered by the mighty English cotton factories. There was, however, no reason for a duty on raw cotton, since France produced none and had no prospects of doing so. A ban on the import of cotton yarn seems to have enabled French spinners to realize great profits while providing French weavers with inferior and expensive yarn. The prohibition on fine British yarn was so unrealistic that it led to large-scale smuggling, and in 1834 a duty replaced the prohibition on fine yarn. Imported cotton cloth continued to be banned although a modest import duty would have served the nation's welfare better. By the second half of the century France's cotton industry should have outgrown its infancy and have been able to meet foreign competition, and the protective tariffs of the last two decades of the nineteenth century seem hardly justified on economic grounds. Protective duties on woolen yarn and cloth probably retarded rather than promoted economic growth in this ancient and well-established branch of the textile industry. The transition from hand to machine weaving was delayed by the protective tariff. Protection to woolen cloth also sustained the domestic system of manufacture and impeded the transfer of manpower out of agriculture into full-time industrial employment, which was one of the primary needs for French industrial progress. France needed no protective duties on silk cloth, and their main effect was to induce other countries to levy retaliatory duties on French silk and thus handicap the expansion of much-needed exports in an industry in which France enjoyed an absolute as well as a comparative advantage over all other countries during the nineteenth century.

The effects of agricultural tariffs on economic growth may be illustrated by the duties levied on wheat during the strong protectionist revival in the last two decades of the nineteenth century. As in other European countries, farmers in France suffered from the competition of more efficient American and Australian grain growers, the fierce competition in agriculture having precipitated the Long Depression beginning in 1873. When the duty on wheat was raised to three francs in 1885, to five francs in 1887, and to seven francs in 1894, the price of wheat became substantially higher in France than in the world market. This meant that wages had to be substantially higher than in free-trade England, for example, in order for French workers to meet the higher cost of living.

French farmers received protection from foreign competition at the expense of French industry. High agricultural tariffs impeded the shift in resources from agriculture to full-time urban industry, a movement consistent

with general economic development. Undoubtedly the pace of industrialization in France was slowed down by the high tariff on agricultural products.
High tariffs on wheat and other foodstuffs continued well into the twentieth
century and retarded the growth of the entire French economy. Admittedly
the agricultural tariff did maintain an equilibrium between industry and
agriculture in France, an equilibrium that was lost in some other countries
such as England and Germany, which moved ahead more rapidly toward
industrialization.

Concerning the central query of this chapter—France's slower economic
growth relative to the other great powers during the nineteenth century—
tariffs did play a role. In some respects they stimulated but in more ways
they retarded France's economy, with an overall influence toward retardation.
During the low-tariff period of the Second Empire the rate of economic growth
was higher than it was earlier in the century, although growth was more rapid
in the 1850's, before the major reduction in tariffs, than in the 1860's, after the
low tariffs came into effect. Economic stagnation set in before tariffs were
raised again in the 1880's, and the period after 1892, when the high Méline
tariff became effective, saw the most rapid rate of industrial advance in
France. This growth may well have been in spite of rather than because of the
high tariffs, although this would be difficult to prove. We have it on the
authority of Professor Dunham that "The tariff was probably not the chief
cause of French industrial backwardness, but it was certainly one of the
causes. It is clear that in almost every case its influence was unfortunate, if not
definitely harmful."[5] This conclusion is drawn from the period 1815–1848,
but would probably apply to the period after 1848 as well.

Of interest are the comparative effects of tariffs, on the one hand, and
improvements in transportation, on the other. Lower transport costs unquestionably stimulated France's economic development during the nineteenth
century perhaps more than any other influence. Natural barriers to trade and
exchange were reduced by cheapening the cost of transport. Tariffs, on the
contrary, created artificial barriers to free trade and exchange. In part, tariff
walls were raised, especially after 1880, because transportation (ocean and
rail) reduced natural barriers to trade. French wheat growers, fearing competition from the virgin lands of America and Australia, sought and received
protection behind tariff walls. Higher tariffs in the 1880's and 1890's undoubtedly tended to cancel some of the potential gains made possible by the
French railway network. Some protectionist-minded French producers protested a cut in rail rates in the 1890's because they offset the advantages (to
them) gained from higher duties introduced by the 1892 tariff.

To protest reductions in rail rates may seem more illogical than to advocate higher tariffs, but the economic effects run in the same direction. The
French protesters were logically consistent, and their distaste for lower rail
rates illuminates the economic case against protective tariffs. Frederick Bastiat,
a mid-nineteenth-century French economist, presented a most revealing ex-
pose of protectionism in a parable concerning candle manufacturers. Bastiat
satirically suggested that protectionist-minded legislators who imposed protective tariffs against foreign competition of inexpensive coal, iron, and wheat

[5] Dunham, *The Industrial Revolution in France*, p. 399.

should also require that all sunlight be shut out from houses and other buildings in order to protect candle manufacturers of France from competition with the sun.

Political Instability as a Retarding Influence

Protective tariffs are but one example of the way in which government affects economic development. Frequent political revolutions in France (1789, 1830, 1848, and 1871) created an economic environment which retarded the growth of private enterprise. Capital investment, which is the key to economic growth, was held back by lack of confidence on the part of businessmen in the future stability and security of their investments. Consequently many Frenchmen preferred to hoard rather than to invest, or to invest in foreign securities rather than in domestic securities.

Yet French governments were not necessarily unfriendly to business interests. The so-called July Monarchy of Louis Philippe (reigned 1830–48), for example, was notoriously pro-bourgeoisie. That government supplanted the old landed aristocracy in 1830 with a new aristocracy of bankers, industrialists, and merchants. The new king, formerly the Duke of Orleans, had been a businessman, and his close friends were leaders of French finance and industry. When the banker Lafitte helped crown the Duke as King Louis Philippe he is reported to have said, "From now on the bankers will rule." The great French historian de Tocqueville characterized the July Monarchy as follows: "Master of everything in a way no other aristocracy had ever been, the middle class, once in control of the government, took on the character of private industry . . . Posterity will perhaps never know to what degree the government of that time was a capitalist enterprise in which all action is taken for the purpose of profit for its members." [6] Close connections between business and government led to excesses of speculation in the bourse, abuses in chartering joint-stock companies, and other practices which created a strong reaction among the people and contributed to the popular revolt which culminated in the overthrow of the July Monarchy in the Revolution of 1848. No matter how friendly a government might be to business, investors could never be certain how long it would remain in power in politically unstable France. Even after the Third Republic emerged in 1871, it remained in grave danger of being overthrown for two decades; and within the political framework of the Republic, political instability manifested itself in frequent changes of prime ministers and their cabinets.

Entrepreneurship as a Retarding Influence

In examining the forces which retarded economic growth in France, the role of entrepreneurship cannot be ignored, even though generalizations on this subject are more treacherous than most. Certainly there was no deficiency of individual talent among the great French entrepreneurs and capitalists. In foreign countries and in colonies Frenchmen initiated new industries and achieved great feats. French business leaders, for example, made important

---

[6] *De la classe moyen et du peuple,* a pamphlet published in 1847.

contributions to German industries before 1870, when the ground was being prepared for Germany to skyrocket to its position of eminence.

For reasons peculiar to France's cultural environment, however, economic development was retarded by the relatively low prestige enjoyed by French businessmen. Perhaps because great entrepreneurs express their individualism by subjugating the individualism of those who serve under them, too few Frenchmen were willing to become pawns in the kingmaking process of large business adventures.

Both the clergy and the nobility of France were more hostile to commercial pursuits than the same classes in England. France's leading money makers (entrepreneurs and capitalists) were Protestants in disproportionate numbers. It has not been uncommon historically for those excluded by religious prejudice from honorific callings to find consolation in making money. Protestants were especially prevalent among the most successful French businessmen. The more numerous class of smaller French entrepreneurs often lacked the business qualities which command admiration; they valued security more highly than risky business ventures and preferred protection to free competition. Small businesses in France were likely to be family affairs, and family firms are traditionally conservative and cautious in outlook. Many of the best minds among Frenchmen pursued careers in science, art, letters, medicine, law, and government, and many Frenchmen who succeeded in business subsequently transferred to public service or to other activities rated higher on the prestige scale than business.

Another serious obstacle to entrepreneurship was the underdeveloped state of the capital market. New capital for business came typically from reinvestment of profits, which contributed more to perpetuating existing firms than to inaugurating new ones. Joint-stock companies (corporations) were rare in France compared with Germany and the United States. Thus men of talent and ambition had difficulty getting money to match their ideas. Inventions made by ingenious Frenchmen frequently were developed by business concerns outside France.

Defective Capital Market and Slow Capital Formation

A slow rate of capital formation also retarded economic growth of France. Capital equipment per employed worker remained less than in the United Kingdom and the United States and, toward the end of the nineteenth century, less than in Germany as well. Since the French are notably frugal and industrious and their country is favorably endowed with natural resources, the low rate of capital formation cannot be explained simply. A substantial proportion of domestic savings were channeled into foreign investments during the nineteenth century; France ranked second only to the United Kingdom as a source of capital for export overseas and elsewhere in Europe. Frugal Frenchmen, seeking the safest type of personal investment, subscribed heavily to the securities of foreign governments only to discover repeatedly that these bonds were very risky outlets for their hard-won savings. More important from the viewpoint of French economic growth, savings channeled into foreign bonds did not contribute to domestic capital formation.

The export of capital, however, was not in itself large enough to account for the failure of Frenchmen to invest more heavily in domestic industry. A basic weakness was the backward state of financial institutions for channeling savings into domestic investment. Individual savings can be realized as social savings only if they find outlets in real investment (capital formation). Individual Frenchmen were frugal, but not much came of this frugality because weak entrepreneurship limited the outlets for savings. Low capital formation kept real incomes low and, despite a strong *propensity* to save out of given income, absolute *amounts* of savings remained low because income grew slowly. The retarded development of the process by which savings are channeled into capital formation was related to the national character of France, which in turn was influenced by its historical experience with monetary and financial institutions. Two examples of conditioning influences were John Law's Mississippi Bubble and the vicious system of tax collection through tax farmers.

As one of the first centers of modern capitalism, France developed banking facilities for mobilizing loanable funds at an early date. In the sixteenth century the Price Revolution concentrated incomes in the hands of capitalist groups at the expense of wage-earners, whose real incomes fell under the impact of rising prices. Despite profligate spending by Louis XIV, by 1750 France probably had accumulated as much wealth as England or any other nation in the world, despite banking facilities inferior to those of England and Holland. John Law's unfortunate Mississippi Bubble episode between 1715 and 1720 set back central banking and discouraged the formation of joint-stock companies. A statute similar to England's Bubble Act limited the chartering of joint-stock companies. Family firms continued to be the chief form of business organization in France. Partnerships with transferable shares (*société en commandite par actions*) enjoyed popularity among larger business undertakings but were more appropriate to the earlier phase of capitalism than to the nineteenth century, when massive amounts of capital became necessary for the most efficient techniques of mass production.

Prior to the Revolution of 1789 the accumulation of capital in France was retarded by a vicious tax system. Lands of the Church and nobles were exempt from direct taxation, which caused a heavier burden to fall on the nonprivileged, productive classes. De Tocqueville noted that in the eighteenth century the only exemptions from taxation in England were enjoyed by the poor, whereas in France the only exemptions were for the rich. In France the *gabelle*, or salt tax, was particularly offensive and oppressive to the peasants, as was the *taille*, which raised money to support the armed forces.

Worst of all, however, was the method of collection of land taxes. Instead of employing public tax collectors, the French government used mainly "tax farmers," who paid a lump sum to the government treasury in exchange for the "privilege" of collecting taxes. Collections in excess of the lump sum were pocketed by the tax farmer. This lucrative form of enterprise attracted many talented entrepreneurs who found they could make more money by taking it away from other people than by producing and selling goods. Since the government treasury remained in chronic difficulty, advances were made by tax farmers at high rates of interest. Adam Smith, who had traveled widely in France and was acquainted with its customs, said of the tax farmers: ". . . [they] are generally the most opulent people. Their wealth would alone

excite the public indignation, and the vanity which almost always accompanies such upstart fortunes, the foolish ostentation with which they commonly display that wealth, excites that indignation still more." [7] Inequitable taxes and the oppressive methods used to collect them retarded real capital formation and created an understandable reluctance by Frenchmen to place their savings at the disposal of capital-mobilizing institutions.

The catastrophic failure of John Law's Banque Royale (1720) so shocked the public that France had to get along without a central bank until Napoleon founded the present Bank of France in 1800. Law's fiasco also bred suspicion of paper money and credit instruments such as the check, which did not become negotiable in France until 1869. In the absence of checks and related clearing operations, domestic bills of exchange and bank notes assumed major importance as means of payment in France. The Bank of France obtained a monopoly of issue of bank notes, but these notes were accepted with reluctance at first, and only after 1848 were they accepted throughout France. Business transactions were carried on by means of domestic bills of exchange which the Bank of France was required to discount, that is, to redeem for bank notes.

Deficiencies in the French banking system became apparent in the crisis of 1847–48 during which the Bank of France suspended all discounts and other payments, which led to the ruin of many businesses. These deficiencies were recognized by Louis Napoleon (1851–70), who remedied some of the defects by establishing banks for industrial development, such as the Crédit Mobilier (1852), Crédit Industriel et Commercial (1859), and the Crédit Lyonnais (1863). The Crédit Mobilier was primarily an industrial-development bank designed to raise money capital for industrial joint-stock companies. It functioned well for a few years but failed because of illiquidity of its assets. The other banks proved more successful, but mainly by becoming commercial banks specializing in short-term loans rather than as industrial banks assisting in the formation of new industrial enterprises. Failure of the Crédit Mobilier once again caused the French public to lose confidence in banks and slowed industrial development by impeding the mobilization of capital for industrial expansion. French financial institutions functioned well enough for moderate economic growth but not well enough to enable France to keep pace with the other great industrial nations, Britain, Germany, and the United States.

SPECIAL CONTRIBUTION OF FRANCE TO INDUSTRIAL DEVELOPMENT

Having accounted for the relative retardation of France's industrial development during the nineteenth century, we may look more closely at the special, positive contribution of the French to industrial development. High-quality products of artistic design have been a distinguishing characteristic of French industry. In their own peculiar way the French have been leaders in industry, especially in "individuality and refinement of production." French products have appealed to the tastes of consumers who place a premium on variety and novelty in design. This has been noted in the superiority of French silks, the unexcelled quality of its best woolen and cotton cloth, and leadership in

[7] *Wealth of Nations* (Modern Library Edition, 1937), p. 854.

feminine fashions; also in fine wines and liquors, French perfume, and articles of refined craftsmanship, including metal products. The Jacquard loom is representative of French ingenuity in the industrial arts. Mechanical looms and steam engines made their way into French industry without destroying the traditions of craftsmanship inherited from the pre-machine age. This was a remarkable achievement.

The individualistic and artistic bent of French industry stems from a way of life, a whole scheme of cultural values, which defies explanation in purely economic terms. These cultural values have their origin in French history and have been conditioned by political, military, and social forces. Prior to 1789 the wealth of France was highly concentrated in the governing and owning classes, a fact which gave rise to a large demand for luxuries. Dissipation of wealth in war and in extravagances of the French court led to oppressive tax burdens on the peasants and working classes. The unequal distribution of disposable income yielded a market structure which demanded artistic and expensive products such as silks, jewelry, wines, fashionable clothing, and the like. The underlying population of France was too poor to have much impact on national markets. In the absence of a mass demand for ordinary products by prosperous artisans and yeomen, as in England, industry catered to the luxury demands of the rich.

Werner Sombart, one of the historians of capitalism, maintains there has been an underdevelopment of capitalist tendencies in the French people, and he associates this with their positive ideals of artistic individualism. In the pre-machine period of capitalist production, Sombart found this anticapitalist outlook reflected in a disdain for commerce and trade, in a "supercilious, almost insulting attitude towards commercial and industrial avocations, and the contemptuous utterances concerning their social value, which even as late as the eighteenth century were found broadcase nowhere else (if we except Spain) so much as in France." [8]

French preoccupation with artistic individualism in production did not arise because of incapacity for mechanical invention or lack of technical aptitude for large-scale output. One of the inspirations for mass production methods in the United States came from France via Thomas Jefferson, who reported from France in the 1790's on a project whereby guns (muskets) were to be produced by making every part so alike that it could be interchanged with any comparable part in any other musket. France led the world in establishing excellent engineering schools. Early textbooks used at the U. S. Military Academy (the first American engineering school) were translations from French texts. Many early American internal improvements were engineered directly by Frenchmen or by Americans who learned from French engineers. The Suez Canal was built by the French, and the Panama Canal was begun by them. Frenchmen pioneered in many great inventions including the watch, bicycle, automobile, submarine, and aeroplane. The French can, when they choose, carry on large-scale mass production, as illustrated by some of their iron and steel works and automobile plants.

According to a French publicist, André Siegfried, the upshot of this characteristic of French economic life, this refusal to sacrifice cultural values to

[8] Werner Sombart, *The Quintessence of Capitalism,* translated and edited by M. Epstein (New York: E. P. Dutton & Co., 1915), p. 140.

routine mechanization, has been to make the French "a happy people"—an achievement of no mean significance if true. M. Siegfried has criticized the American way of life for its emphasis on technical and scientific subjects at the expense of the humanities; in this respect the Americans are "the true successors of the Germans," and the United States is also similar to Communist Russia, an "adorer of the technical." Another distinguished interpreter of French culture, M. François Mauriac, has also criticized the United States and the Soviet Union for placing faith in mechanization and for tending to standardize men after the model of their machines. "It is not what separates the United States and the Soviet Union that should frighten us, but what they have in common. Their ideological oppositions are perhaps less to be feared than their agreement regarding the scale of human values. Those technocrats that think themselves antagonists are dragging humanity in the same direction of dehumanization." [9] Whatever one may think of M. Mauriac's comparison of the Soviet Union and the United States, his view and M. Siegfried's typify the philosophy which has conditioned France's psychological adaptation to industrialization during the machine age.

Although what appears as a slow pace of industrialization was hardly a matter of conscious choice by the French, their distaste for routine production on a massive scale cost them dearly in national prestige and military defeat. By failing to grow as fast as their national rivals in a world of warring nations, they fell easy prey to Prussia in 1870, had to be rescued by allies in the First World War, and suffered crushing defeat at the hands of Germany in 1940. With their great talent for science and engineering the French could have done much better in achieving economic growth and military power had their statesmen chosen to lead the nation in that direction.

France seems to be one of those cases in which statesmen learned something from history, if we are to judge by the period after World War II. France's humiliating defeat by Germany in 1940 created a sense of national crisis and instilled a sense of unity and determination to overcome national weakness whatever might be the cost. As early as possible after the war, France put into effect the Monnet Plan for transforming France into a modern economy. Major innovations and heavy capital investments were made under an imaginative system of general national planning. The birth rate increased. French statesmen assumed the lead in forming new international organizations looking toward a united Europe. By the mid-1950's results began to show up in the form of a high rate of economic growth. Frenchmen could again think of their nation as important economically.

SELECTED BIBLIOGRAPHY

CAMERON, RONDO E., *France and the Economic Development of Europe, 1800–1914.* Princeton: Princeton University Press, 1961.

CLOUGH, SHEPARD B., *France: 1789–1939. A Study in National Economics.* New York: Charles Scribner's Sons, 1939.

[9] *New York Times* (February 21, 1950), p. 11.

COLE, CHARLES W., *Colbert and a Century of French Mercantilism*, 2 vols., 2nd ed. Garden City, N. Y.: Doubleday Anchor Books, 1964.

DUNHAM, ARTHUR L., *The Industrial Revolution in France, 1815–1848*. New York: Exposition Press, 1955.

GERSCHENKRON, ALEXANDER, *Economic Backwardness in Historical Perspective*. Cambridge, Mass.: Harvard University Press, 1962.

GOLOB, EUGENE O., *The Méline Tariff, French Agriculture and Nationalist Economic Policy*. New York: Columbia University Press, 1944.

HOSELITZ, BERT F., "Entrepreneurship and Capital Formation in France and Britain since 1700," in National Bureau of Economic Research, *Capital Formation and Economic Growth*. Princeton: Princeton University Press, 1956.

KINDLEBERGER, CHARLES P., *Economic Growth in France and Britain, 1851–1950*. Cambridge, Mass.: Harvard University Press, 1964.

———, "The Postwar Resurgence of the French Economy," in *In Search of France* by Stanley Hoffman and others. Cambridge, Mass.: Harvard University Press, 1963.

LABROUSSE, CAMILLE ERNEST, *La crise de l'économie française à la fin de l'ancien régime et au début de la révolution*. Paris: Presses Universitaires, 1944.

MARSHALL, ALFRED, *Industry and Trade*, 2nd ed., Chap. 6, "The industrial leadership of France: Individuality and refinement in production." London: Macmillan and Co., Ltd., 1923.

SAWYER, JOHN E., "The Entrepreneur and the Social Order: France and the United States," in William Miller, ed., *Men in Business*. Cambridge, Mass.: Harvard University Press, 1952.

———, "Strains in the Structure of Modern France," in Edward M. Earle, ed., *Modern France*. Princeton: Princeton University Press, 1951.

SÉE, HENRI, *Histoire économique de la France*, 2 vols. Paris: A. Colin, 1948–51.

———, *Economic and Social Conditions in France in the Eighteenth Century*. New York: Alfred A. Knopf, Inc., 1927.

SIEGFRIED, ANDRÉ, *France, A Study in Nationality*. New Haven: Yale University Press, 1930.

ARTICLES

CAMERON, RONDO E., "The Crédit Mobilier and the Economic Development of Europe," *Journal of Political Economy*, LXI (Dec., 1953), 461–88.

———, "Economic Growth and Stagnation in France, 1815–1914)," *Journal of Modern History*, XXX (March, 1958), 1–15.

CLOUGH, SHEPARD B., "Retardative Factors in French Economic Development," *Journal of Economic History*, VI (Supplement, 1946), 91–102.

DUNHAM, ARTHUR L., "How the First French Railways were Planned," *Journal of Economic History*, I (May, 1941), 12–25.

GERSCHENKRON, ALEXANDER, "Social Attitudes, Entrepreneurship and Economic Development," *Exploration in Entrepreneurial History*, VI (Oct., 1953), 1–19.

HAUSER, HENRI, "The Characteristic Features of French Economic History from the Middle of the Sixteenth to the Middle of the Eighteenth Century," *Economic History Review*, IV (Oct., 1933), 257–72.

KINDLEBERGER, CHARLES P., "Foreign Trade and Economic Growth: Lessons from Britain and France, 1850–1913," *Economic History Review*, II (Dec., 1961), 289–305.

LANDES, DAVID S., "French Business and the Businessmen in Social and Cultural Analysis," in *Modern France*, Edward M. Earle, ed. Princeton: Princeton University Press, 1951.

————, "French Entrepreneurship and Industrial Growth in the Nineteenth Century," *Journal of Economic History*, IX (May, 1949), 45–61.

MARCZEWSKI, JAN, "Some Aspects of the Economic Growth of France, 1660–1958," *Economic Development and Cultural Change*, IX (April, 1961), 369–86.

SAWYER, JOHN E., "France's New Horizons," *Yale Review*, XLVIII (Winter, 1959), 161–73.

SÉE, HENRI, "The Economic and Social Origins of the French Revolution," *Economic History Review*, III (Jan., 1931), 1–15.

German Industrial Development During the Nineteenth Century

CHAPTER **17**

In southern Germany during the age of the Fuggers in the fifteenth and sixteenth centuries, financial and industrial capitalism was more highly developed than anywhere else in Europe. With the opening of all-water trade routes to the East Indies and to America, the center of economic gravity shifted to the Atlantic seaboard—to Portugal, Spain, Holland, England, and France—leaving Germany isolated from the main stream of activity. During the seventeenth and eighteenth centuries Austria and Prussia continued to be major powers among European nations but their importance was more political and military than economic.

In northern Germany the shift of activity to the Atlantic seaboard also dimmed the lights of the cities which had shone so brilliantly in the late medieval and early modern period as members of the Hanseatic League. These cities of northern Germany suffered a geographical disadvantage compared with the Atlantic ports and, more important, the absence in Germany of a strong central government meant there was no agency to provide financial and political support for long overseas ventures.

Nominally German provinces enjoyed political unity as members of the Holy Roman Empire, but this shadow empire was always weak and became weaker as a result of the Protestant Reformation of the sixteenth century and the ensuing religious strife which culminated in the devastating Thirty Years War (1618–1648)). Martin Luther's break with the Roman Catholic Church divided Germany into rival camps, with the Austrian Hapsburgs remaining loyal Catholics while most of the north German provinces followed Luther in his revolt against Rome.

Among German states, the incipient nationalism of sixteenth-century Europe took a peculiar turn because Austria, as leader of the Holy Roman Empire, overreached itself in attempting to bring non-German states under its rule. Emperors Charles V (d. 1558) and Philip II (d. 1598) reigned for a time over most of the New World as well as central Europe, Spain, and Portugal. While the Hapsburgs attempted to rule half the world, political erosion took place at home, and when this pretentious political organization splintered, Germany became more divided than before. The Thirty Years War, sometimes called the last of Europe's religious wars, decimated German manpower, devastated material wealth, and reimposed on Germany a medieval

political and economic status. While France and England were moving forward toward political unification, Germany moved backward toward political feudalism. To France and England overseas trade brought economic expansion, capital accumulation, and new forms of business organization under the guiding hand of mercantilist statesmen. In Germany, on the other hand, neither geography nor transportation nor historical conditions favored political unification and economic development. After the ruinous Thirty Years War of the seventeenth century, the Holy Roman Empire remained in a state of complete demoralization until Napoleon liquidated it in the early nineteenth century.

At the opening of the nineteenth century there was nothing that could legitimately be called a German economy. In northern Germany, Prussia had extended its borders, and under Frederick the Great (d. 1786) it became a power in Europe. In the south, Austria under the Hapsburgs continued to play a major role in the military and political affairs of Europe. Bavaria, Saxony, and other smaller German states feared the military power of Prussia and Austria, and Germany remained politically and economically disunified. Defeats administered by Napoleon at Jena and elsewhere forced the proud Prussians to realize that military and economic power could be achieved only by eliminating feudal institutions. Edicts of 1807 and 1808 emancipated Prussian serfs, although no adequate provision was made for giving land to the newly liberated peasants. In eastern Prussia on the large estates of Junker landlords, German peasants remained in virtual servitude well into the nineteenth century.

Emancipation of the serfs was only a first and a faltering step toward modernization of German society. Craft gilds persisted in the towns, and as late as the revolution of 1848 supported the conservative landlords in thwarting the establishment of a middle-class, liberal government. Legal restrictions on the movement of peasants lent a medieval air which perpetuated a "society of estates not of economic classes." (Clapham) Industry progressed most in Saxony, where trades were learned in trade schools rather than by the medieval apprenticeship system. During the first half of the nineteenth century German manufacture remained a mixture of handicraft and putting-out elements with only scattered factories.

Lack of political and economic unity was at the root of German weakness. Aspirations toward national unification formed the dominant ideology of German statesmen, historians, philosophers, and economists during the nineteenth century. Just after the close of the Napoleonic Wars in 1815 English goods flooded German markets and drove thousands of small, inefficient industrial firms into bankruptcy. A first step in the direction of national union was taken with the moderate, well-fashioned tariff of 1818, which in turn was the forerunner of the much more important Zollverein, or Customs Union, of 1833.

Under Prussian leadership the Zollverein brought all German states, except Austria, together in a common market. By eliminating interstate barriers to trade, the Zollverein stimulated German economic development. By keeping the external tariffs low at the borders of the union, goods came into Zollverein territory and enabled member states to collect as much revenue as they had previously realized from higher tariffs. Saxony, the most industrial-

ized German state at the time, showed reluctance to accept membership in the Zollverein until the king of Saxony became convinced that in the sharing of revenues he could make himself financially independent of his Parliament.

At the time of its formation the economy encompassed by the Zollverein was more commercial and agricultural than industrial, and a low-tariff policy seemed consistent with the prevailing interests of member states. As the territory became more industrialized, duties were raised on competing manufactured imports such as English pig iron and cotton yarn.

Friedrich List (1789-1846), German economist, called the Zollverein and the railways the Siamese twins of German economic development. The former eliminated the artificial barriers to trade, and the latter reduced the natural barriers. In no other country of western Europe did railways have the revolutionary impact which they had in Germany. The railways enabled Germany to re-enter the world stage from which it had departed with the discovery of America. From a stagnant economy with poor roads and sleepy rural villages, Germany leaped forward toward economic integration and urbanization. By the time the network of German railways reached completion in the 1870's Germany had become the greatest Continental power and was on the march toward dominating the whole of Europe. After unification Germany stood at the geographical center of all Europe, with access to markets and raw materials in all directions, while the other great powers—Britain, France, Italy, Spain, and Russia—stood on the periphery of the European continent. Geographical location proved a momentous advantage in Germany's economic growth after 1871.

Germany's first railway was opened in 1835 in Bavaria, but Berlin, in Brandenburg, soon became the hub of the national system, much as Paris became the hub of the French railway system. Early German railways provided a good supplement to the existing waterways. Both private and public ownership existed in early railway construction and operation, but after the formation of the German Empire in 1871, the railways were taken over by individual state governments, including Prussia, and unified into a national network by Bismarck. They were laid out and were operated with an eye to military as well as economic advantages. At the close of the First World War all German railways were transferred to the national government. The growth of German railways is shown in Table 17–1.

Revolution of 1848 in Germany

The Revolution of 1848, which rocked the capitals of Europe from Paris to Budapest, demonstrated two things about Germany. (1) Capitalism in Germany had not yet evolved far enough for a middle-class, liberal government to come to power; and (2) Prussia was still not strong enough to wrest control of the other German states from Austria. Momentarily in 1848 liberals in Germany seized control of Prussian and other German governments and proclaimed the "Fundamental Rights of the German People." This called for the establishment of parliamentary government along British lines. Reaction soon asserted itself, however, and found support among the peasants, who mistrusted urban liberals even more than they mistrusted conservative landlords, and among

TABLE 17-1

307

GERMAN
INDUSTRIAL
DEVELOPMENT

Growth of German Railroads, 1845–1910

YEAR	KILOMETERS	YEAR	KILOMETERS
1845	2,131	1880	33,865
1850	5,822	1885	37,572
1855	7,781	1890	41,818
1860	11,026	1895	45,203
1865	13,821	1900	49,878
1870	18,560	1905	54,680
1875	27,795	1910	59,031

Source: Werner Sombart, *Die deutsche Volkswirtschaft im neunzehnten Jahrhundert* (Berlin, 1912), p. 493.

craftsmen, who still preferred gild controls which restricted the right to practice trades. Not only was there no place for proletarian radicalism, but conditions in Germany were not even ripe for bourgeois liberalism. After the successful counter-revolution against liberalism, Austria remained sufficiently powerful
to force Prussia to accept Austrian leadership under the German Confederation.

Conditions portrayed by the revolution and counter-revolution of 1848–
49 were soon to change drastically. In 1867 Prussia, now under the leadership
of Bismarck, crushed the once-powerful Austrian armies in seven weeks. A
German Empire excluding Austria was formed under Prussian domination in
1871, after France had also been given a licking in a test of arms with Prussia.
German nationalism was on the march. Unfortunately for the future of Europe
and the world at large, the powerful economic energies unleashed by the
formation of the Empire remained under the political and military control of
a dynastic state, which continued to utilize the genius and productiveness of
the German people for primarily nationalistic and warlike purposes.

Preparation for the Industrial Revolution, 1850–70

In the two decades between 1850 and 1870 the ground was prepared for
Germany's industrial revolution. The trend toward urbanization, characteristic
of industrialization, accelerated gently at first and then more rapidly. Rural
population, which constituted 73.5 per cent of total population in 1816, had
fallen only to 71.5 per cent by 1852; but in the next two decades, the percentage
of rural population fell 7.5 points, to 64 per cent of total population. The other
side of these figures showed up in the growth of cities of substantial size.
Forces pushing Germany toward industrialization included the railway system,
the Zollverein, the growth in basic industries like coal mining and iron production, the formation of joint-stock banks geared to rapid industrialization, and an
aspiration for national greatness which would give Germany its rightful "place
in the sun." In this setting Bismarck realized his ambition of a Prussianized
German Empire by humiliating, in successive military defeats, Denmark,
Austria, and France. Bismarck's sinews of war were in coal and iron output,
which exceeded that of France by 1870, when France was crushed at Sedan.

What is the explanation for the remarkably rapid industrial progress of Germany in the four or five decades before the First World War, the period of Germany's industrial revolution? Humiliated by Austria in 1850, the Prussians were able to turn the tables on Austria by 1866, defeat mighty France with ease in 1870, and shoot ahead of indomitable Britain by the end of the nineteenth century. Not even the United States, with its sensational industrial push after the Civil War, moved as rapidly as Germany, although by virtue of superior natural resources, larger territory, population, and markets, and an earlier start with modern mechanical industry, the United States remained ahead of Germany in absolute industrial production, sometimes by a narrow margin. In view of its limited natural resources and its economic backwardness until 1850, Germany's industrialization was the most remarkable economic achievement of the nineteenth century. Nothing so dramatic had ever happened before in economic development.

Science in the Service of Industry

"Science in the service of industry" was the phrase used by Alfred Marshall to describe the special contributions of Germany to industrial leadership. Startling success in applying science to industry arose from the fact that the Germans were the best-schooled people in the world in the nineteenth century. Under Frederick the Great, the "Enlightened Despot," Prussia instituted a system of compulsory general education more than a century before Great Britain, France, or the United States. Education was strengthened under the reforms which swept Prussia in the wake of military defeats at the hands of Napoleon. Moreover, at an early date Prussia transferred control of education from the church to the state, which shifted the curriculum from a religious to a secular emphasis and provided a foundation for teaching science. Universities and advanced technical schools also came under state control and included in their curricula a strong emphasis on science. Universal education for the common people provided a massive flow of literate and alert workers, and the universities and advanced technical schools supplied the leadership for applying science to industry. Its large number of educated people, especially scientifically trained people, proved a resource of incalculable value to Germany.

Chemical Industries

Synthetic dyestuffs illustrate the special contribution of Germany to industry. For centuries dyestuffs had been garnered from vegetable and animal substances scattered around the world. Modern dyestuffs from coal tar awaited the developments of the science of chemistry in the nineteenth century. In 1856 a young English scientist discovered, quite accidentally, how to produce one of the synthetic dyes (mauve) from coal tar and set up a plant for its manufacture. For a short while the British dominated the dyestuff industry, but in the early 1870's leadership in dyes shifted suddenly to Germany. Only university professors possessed the theoretical knowledge upon

which the technology of the industry must be based, and among British bankers and industrialists at the time "the words academic and theoretical were sarcastic epithets connoting inefficiency." (T. J. Kreps) A laissez-faire government such as Britain's was disinclined to subsidize research for developing new industries. In Germany the esteem for education and the prestige of professors brought quite different results.

Close working relations were established between industry and the universities, the real innovators in synthetic industries being chemistry professors. The German government poured large sums of money for chemical research and training into the universities and technical schools. Synthetic indigo, for example, was produced in 1880 from coal tar after nearly two decades of research subsidized by the equivalent of several million dollars in government research funds. Thousands of well-trained chemists constituted a sort of intellectual proletariat working for modest salaries. A British mission which visited Germany in 1872 found more students studying chemistry in one German university (Munich) than in all the universities and colleges of England combined.

Germans surpassed their untrained competitors. Approximately 80 per cent of the total production of German synthetic dyestuffs was exported in 1913. In the same year Germany produced 88 per cent of the world's total output of synthetic dyestuffs, as compared with only 3 per cent by Great Britain. The remainder of the world's production was as follows: Switzerland, 6 per cent; United States, 2 per cent; France, 1 per cent.

Under the impact of this chemical revolution, dyestuffs fell sharply in price and displaced natural dyestuffs. Millions of acres of land in India, where indigo had previously been grown, were doomed by German coal mines. The economics of chemistry had arrived, with Germany far in the lead among nations. The influence of science, and chemistry in particular, pervaded German industries.

Success in dyestuffs opened the door to the whole modern organic chemical industry. Many joint-products and by-products emerged from the chemical processes of dye-making. Among the more important were pharmaceuticals (e.g., aspirin), flavoring extracts (e.g., wintergreen), perfume bases, photographic chemicals, high explosives, plastics, and synthetic fibers. Picric acid, for example, can be used either as a dye or antiseptic or in high explosives. The first of the sulfa drugs (sulfanilamide) was initially prepared in Germany in 1908 as an intermediate dyestuff and later was found to be a powerful antibiotic. Phenol (carbolic acid) can be used either for dyestuffs or plastics or as a disinfectant. By the time the German chemists got through with coal it yielded more than a thousand different dyes and thousands of other products.

Another offshoot of modern chemistry is the fertilizer industry. Justus von Liebig (1803–1873), a German chemistry professor, revolutionized agriculture through the discovery that inorganic (artificial) fertilizers, as well as organic material such as animal manure, can sustain the productivity of soil. Inorganic minerals—mainly phosphates, nitrates, and potash (a potassium compound)—placed in the soil were found capable of nourishing plants. Liebig discovered that *all* the required elements must be present for the soil to be productive. The lack of any one nutrient would cause plants to

fail. Following through on Liebig's theoretical discoveries, German industry took the lead in developing the chemistry of the fertilizer industry. German farmers were soon using more fertilizer per square acre than any other country, except Holland, and this compensated for a natural deficiency of minerals in German soil. Agriculture throughout the civilized world has become dependent upon artificial fertilizers. One of the first steps in programs for underdeveloped areas is to set up fertilizer plants in order to increase agricultural productivity. Liebig's chemistry inaugurated developments which have probably contributed as much as any other factor to put aside, or at least to postpone, man's reckoning with the evil specter of mass starvation portrayed so gloomily by Malthus.

Coal, Iron, and Steel

Coal If the application of science to industry by a well-schooled working force constituted Germany's greatest human resource, coal was its most important natural resource. Even more than with Great Britain earlier, the industrial leadership attained by Germany under the Empire was made possible by rich mineral resources. In addition to its value in the chemical industry, coal was highly important in powering the steam engine, as the fuel for the railways, as coke for smelting and refining iron, and as a raw material for numerous industries.

Germany made only slight use of coal before the nineteenth century. Not surprisingly, the railways increased both the demand for coal and the supplies available in districts which previously could not afford to pay freight from mines. After 1840 coal production increased very rapidly and prepared the way for the great commercial upsurge under the Empire. In 1871 German coal production was already double that of France and by 1913 it was nearly five times that of France, or if German lignite is included, seven times that of France. When the Empire was formed, Germany's coal output was only one-fourth that of Great Britain (31 tons as against 120 million tons); by 1913 it had risen to two-thirds that of Great Britain (190 tons as against 290 million), or if German lignite is included, 95 per cent of Britain's in 1913 (280 million tons as against 290 million). Since Great Britain exported one-third of its coal before the First World War, including a substantial amount to Germany, the consumption of coal, including lignite, in Germany exceeded Britain's at the beginning of the First World War. Coal consumption is a better index than coal production of the extent of industrialization. Because of a late start, German mining firms operated efficiently on a large scale, averaging more than 800 employees per concern at the turn of the century.

In Germany the horsepower generated for industry by steam engines remained negligible before 1840 and was only 62,000 in 1855. During the next twenty years it increased nearly ten-fold (to 600,000 horsepower), and before the First World War again increased ten-fold (to 6,000,000 horsepower). In addition to this rapid growth in the use of steam power, new forms of energy were introduced, including hydroelectric power, gas from coke ovens, and gasoline for internal combustion engines.

Iron Next to coal the primary mineral of the industrial revolution was iron, with which Germany was much less richly endowed. Germany had an

ancient iron industry, and through the first half of the nineteenth century it
consisted mainly of small, scattered plants utilizing charcoal for fuel. Fortunately, Ruhr coal had excellent coking qualities. Conversion to coke came
rapidly after 1860, and by 1870 Germany had passed France in iron and steel
production. The transfer of Lorraine to Germany in 1871 had far-reaching
consequences, although at the time the economic significance of the transfer
was largely unanticipated. This territory, which produced only 4 per cent of
Europe's pig iron in 1869, produced nearly one-half of a much larger European total in 1913.

Lorraine's phosphoric ores became valuable largely as a result of the
discovery in 1878 of the so-called basic (non-acid) process by the English
chemist Thomas. Germany purchased rights to use the Thomas process in
1881 and thus laid the foundation for its leadership in European iron and
steel production. Beginning in 1880 German steel output doubled each decade up to the First World War; in millions of tons the figures were: 1880,
1.5; 1890, 3.1; 1900, 7.3; and 1910, 13.1. Pig iron production increased at
nearly the same rate. During the 1890's Germany passed Great Britain in
steel production and became the largest producer in Europe, ranking second
only to the continent-spanning United States.

Steel Since steel-making is a branch of metallurgy which in turn is a
major division of chemical engineering, German excellence in chemistry was
reflected in technical achievements in the steel industry. The Kaiser Wilhelm
Gesellschaft was established to conduct and sponsor research in the chemistry
and physics of iron, steel, and coal. Industrial laboratories sprang up for research and development of iron and steel alloys. Krupp, one of the older steel
firms, helped create the Empire by producing superior artillery with which
Prussia defeated France in 1870. German research helped to discover stainless
steel, an alloy using chromium and nickel. Late development of the German
iron and steel industry proved beneficial in constructing modern plants of
massive size. Individual German blast furnaces exceeded British furnaces in
output by 1890, and larger output per furnace meant lower unit costs of
producing iron and steel.

Perhaps most symptomatic of the new age was the manner in which
chemical processes drew iron and steel together with coal mining, coking,
and chemical by-product utilization into single, integrated operating units.
Coking, which is intermediary between coal mining and iron production,
yields by-products which provide the raw material for innumerable other
industries. Gas for heating and illumination is the most important by-product
from cokeries. In addition to servicing the internal operations of the plant
where it is generated, coke ovens also provided surplus gas for generating
light and power, for distribution through a network of pipelines to other
industrial concerns and domestic households over a wide geographical area.
Other by-products from coke ovens included ammonia, used mainly for nitrogen fertilizer; and coal tar and the thousands of derivatives from coal tar
as well as many other chemical substances which are formed along with coal
tar in the distillation of coking coal.

Another "waste" product turned to good account was slag from the
Thomas steel converter. The phosphorus in the iron ores of Lorraine, which

made the ore unusable before the invention of the Thomas process, was absorbed in the non-acid lining of the converter. By this process the Germans quite literally converted a liability (phosphorus in iron ore) into an asset in the form of phosphorate fertilizer, which was produced in huge quantities for both domestic and foreign agriculture. Instead of being piled in mountainous heaps around steel mills, this "waste" slag from the Thomas converter was utilized for making cement for road construction and for other productive uses as well as fertilizer.

Electrical Industry

The economics of physics found its most challenging opportunity in the electrical industry, which, next to the chemical industries, offered the greatest outlet for the scientific and organizational bent of the Germans. Progress in the science of electricity provided the starting point. Beginning with basic discoveries by physicists, the electrical industry was cradled and nurtured in research and development laboratories. The German electrical manufacturing industry, which is to be distinguished from the generation and sale of electric power, became concentrated in two great firms, a circumstance arising from control of inventions and patent rights. One of these firms owed its success to the genius of Werner Siemens (1816–92), who invented the dynamo (1867), developed the first electric railway (1879), and contributed numerous other innovations. The second and still larger firm was formed in the 1880's to exploit Thomas Edison's incandescent lamp, and became the German General Electric Company (*Allgemeine Elektrizitäts-Gesellschaft*, or *A.E.G.*). Its leading figure was the organization genius, Emil Rathenau, and later his son, Walther Rathenau. An unusual capacity for large-scale business organization, so vividly displayed in electrical manufacturing, characterized German industry generally and ranks, along with the talent for science, among the factors accounting for Germany's remarkable industrial success in recent times. In fact, the two activities have something in common, as is suggested by the phrase "scientific management," a term coined in the United States but a practice in which Germans excelled.

German electrical manufacturing grew rapidly with applications to communication (telegraph and telephone), transportation (tramways), illumination (lamp bulbs), metallurgy (steel-making), electro-chemical processes (nitrogen fixation from the atmosphere), and innumerable machines and appliances utilizing electric motors. By 1913 Germany led the world in the manufacture of electrical products and equipment, closely followed by the United States, but in the export of electrical products and equipment Germany had no close rival. Professor Clapham, an authority on comparative economic development, has said of electrical manufacturing, "Beyond question, the creation of this industry was the greatest single industrial achievement of modern Germany." [1]

[1] John H. Clapham, *The Economic Development of France and Germany (1815–1914)* (London: Cambridge University Press, 1951), 4th ed., p. 308. Clapham's book contains an excellent general treatment of German economic development in the century from the end of the Napoleonic Wars to the beginning of the First World War.

Whereas coal was even more important, textiles were much less important to Germany than to Great Britain. One would have expected a higher percentage of manpower to be allocated to heavy industries based on coal and steel and a smaller percentage to textiles during the German industrial revolution because a century of technological progress separated the English and German industrial revolutions. Textiles also loomed relatively less important for Germany than for France because of the latter's earlier start toward industrialization. Nevertheless, German textiles developed from a primitive to an advanced stage in the course of the nineteenth century and became a respectable component of the total German industrial complex.

Cotton Apart from minor beginnings, cotton textiles did not recapitulate the hand spinning stage of England and France. Because of a late start, cotton yarn in Germany's industrial age was spun in factories or imported from England. Until 1850 cotton manufacture advanced slowly and in output lagged far behind France, as well as Great Britain, up to 1871. The big event of the century was the acquisition of Alsace, which in 1870 spun and wove more cotton than all Germany at the time. Thus in statistical terms, Germany's output of cotton manufactures more than doubled as a result of this empire-building territorial aggrandizement, although German cotton producers did not welcome the new domestic competition.

Wool In German woolen manufacture the putting-out system based on household spinning and weaving remained dominant as long as German sheep provided the main source of raw wool. This condition continued until about 1850. In the second half of the nineteenth century Germany became increasingly dependent on imported wool, and this change undercut the putting-out system and converted woolen manufacturing to a factory system. Worsted cloth manufactured from imported combed wool made the most rapid progress and in the early twentieth century constituted Germany's most valuable textile export, a position normally occupied by cotton cloth in European countries at the time.

Linen In earlier centuries linen clothed a majority of German rural dwellers, but in the nineteenth century this ancient industry declined. Linen manufacture utilized local crops of flax and operated as a domestic usufacture and manufacture. With the advance of mechanical spinning and weaving in other countries, German hand spinners and weavers struggled valiantly but in the end were overwhelmed by foreign competition. They delayed too long their bid to meet this competition with machinery of their own.

Silk In silk production Germany ranked second only to France, and ahead of Switzerland and Great Britain, during the nineteenth century. German advances were associated with mechanization in the manufacture of silk, which is the strongest of the natural textile fibers and therefore lends itself to machine processes. Another characteristic of silk which worked to the advantage of Germany is its suitability for rich and refined dyeing, and the Germans excelled in applying as well as in producing dyes.

GERMANY'S SPECIAL CONTRIBUTION
TO INDUSTRIALIZATION

Germany's phenomenal rise to industrial leadership cannot be explained in terms of natural resources. Apart from coal and potash, Germany was not richly endowed with mineral and other natural resources. Before Lorraine became German territory in 1871, iron ore was deficient. Nonferrous metals were sparse in relation to the needs of modern industrialism. German soil is of no more than average fertility, and is less fertile than French soil. In relation to the voracious demands of large-scale industry, all natural resources may be said to be scarce and their use subject, other things being equal, to diminishing returns beginning at an early stage of industrialization. Nevertheless there are relative degrees of scarcity. The United States is more richly endowed with the natural resources useful for modern industry than any comparable geographical area. By comparison Germany may be said to be poor in natural resources. Consequently its achievement in industrialization was all the more remarkable. To a significant degree Germany's emphasis on science was motivated by a paucity of natural resources.

Germany's rapid industrial advance has frequently been attributed to skillful borrowing of technology from more advanced countries, especially from England. Like other countries embarking on the transition from a rural, handicraft economy to modern mechanical industry, Germans stood on the shoulders of their English cousins, who first worked out the difficult initial stage during their Industrial Revolution of the eighteenth century. Germany was, however, more systematic about the borrowing process. In 1821 the Prussian government established in Berlin the Gewerbe Institut (Institute of Trades), which imported British machines, constructed working models, and assisted German manufacturers in trying out in their factories the promising machines. By starting from scratch, German firms could begin production with the most modern and efficient plant and equipment known to the technological world. In contrast British firms still carried on their books and operated in their factories much obsolete and semi-obsolete equipment. Germany started with the advantage of eliminating error from the trial-and-error method which had brought the British to a high state of the industrial arts by the middle of the nineteenth century. A late start represented in this respect a significant advantage to Germany, and in contrast, its early lead represented a disadvantage to the British.

Admittedly the Germans proved skillful borrowers, and adeptness at borrowing is a quality not to be belittled. Other countries had equal opportunity to borrow from the English, but with the possible exception of Japan, none did it as well as the Germans. Ability to borrow was sharpened by the general scientific outlook which pervaded German industry. A first step in the scientific approach to any problem is to search out and test the already existing knowledge bearing upon its solution. German leaders were sufficiently alert to comprehend readily the advantages of the new technology; they had the initiative to organize the borrowing process systematically; and the German people were sufficiently well schooled to be able to absorb the new ideas and organize the new technology into a comprehensive, coordinated system of operation. In brief, Germany had more capacity for borrowing than other countries.

These circumstances—the advanced state of English mechanization and Germany's aptitude for borrowing—were prerequisite to Germany's great forward leap in the second half of the nineteenth century.

Germany did more, however, than just borrow British technology. Its special contribution—the application of science to industry through a well-trained population—opened the way to a new phase of the industrial process, a phase which has been aptly described as the technology of chemistry and physics.[2] Chemical processes had been used prior to the nineteenth century, but they were largely the outcome of commonsense observations by experienced artisans with practical insight who operated by rule-of-thumb.

The systematic application of chemistry to the problems of industry in the nineteenth century operated on quite a different level. It grew out of fundamental scientific research leading to the discovery of new principles of cause and effect in chemical relations. University professors of chemistry working in laboratories discovered new phenomena which were beyond the comprehension of even the most intelligent layman. A working relation between university laboratories and industrial plants was required because only scientists with long training in the classroom and laboratory could participate creatively in these complex chemical discoveries and operations.

Moreover, the right degree of understanding of the relation of theory to practice was important in the industrial outcome. The theory must not be too general, and practice must not be too empirical. France is said to be the mother country of modern chemistry (Lavoisier), and Englishmen often broke new ground, as in the case of coal tar for synthetic dyes (Perkin), but it was Germany which exploited and developed in detail the application of science to industry. French and English scientists operated on a high general level isolated from the industrial applications of their discoveries. They contributed about as much to the world at large as to their native lands, but Germans contributed in a way which was most useful for German industrial development. After 1870 Germany came quickly to excel in both light and heavy chemical industries as well as in other industries which utilized, in greater or lesser degree, the principles of chemistry for the solution of practical problems. Chemistry is, of course, a basic science which can be applied ubiquitously in industry and agriculture. Hence its impact was felt throughout the economy.

Rigid discipline acquired from training in school, at home, and in compulsory military service constituted a fundamental quality of German behavior which helped to account for the special nature of Germany's contribution to industry. This was not necessarily the kind of training which developed maximum creativity, but it was an effective discipline for accomplishing the painstaking, systematic exploration of innumerable possibilities leading to a workable solution of problems. More successfully than any other people, the Germans organized industrial groups or teams under an experienced leader who assigned detailed tasks to his less experienced helpers. Team captains with insight and ingenuity, assisted by technically competent helpers, enabled Germany to reap the rich rewards which science is capable of yielding.

The only resource existing in unlimited reserve and not subject to dimin-

[2] See Thorstein B. Veblen, *Absentee Ownership and Business Enterprise in Recent Times* (New York: The Viking Press, 1923), Chapter 10, "The Technology of Physics and Chemistry."

ishing return is the ingenuity of the human mind. By definition, this resource is potentially available to the people of any country in any age. It does, however, like other resources, require investment in order to convert its potentiality into an actuality. Investment in human resources, undoubtedly the most important basis for the wealth of nations, is "education" in the broadest sense. Germany's long tradition of investment in education in the form of compulsory elementary schooling, excellent technical high schools, and the best university system in the world yielded increasing returns as soon as universal science had advanced far enough for men to unlock the secrets of nature and turn them to the creation of material wealth.

Investment in human capital through formal education has become progressively more important with the accumulation of scientific knowledge and the related advancing levels of industrial technology. By the late eighteenth century the Germans were probably already the best-schooled people in Europe; yet this did not lead them to initiate the Industrial Revolution, a role which fell, for reasons explained elsewhere in this volume, to the British. By the late nineteenth century academic education, including universal literacy, had become a strategic factor in industrial leadership. England's Industrial Revolution differed from earlier industrial systems in requiring a much greater quantity of tangible equipment in order to exploit the intangible know-how which is the accumulated heritage of the human race from all preceding generations. The new era of physics and chemistry, while still requiring much tangible equipment, placed the emphasis once again on the intangibles of human skill and dexterity, but with a shift from art to science, from handicraftmanship acquired through apprenticeship to chemistry and physics learned through academic education in classrooms and laboratories.

If investment in human capital was strategic for industrial leadership in the late nineteenth century, it became indispensable for industrial leadership in the second half of the twentieth century. The remarkably rapid advances of the Russian economy after the Second World War were accompanied by tremendous investment in education, especially in mathematics, science, and technical education. The appreciation of education shown by the despotic Hohenzollerns reappeared in the educational policies of the Soviet Commissars for catching up with and passing their democratic rivals in the struggle for world leadership. Underdeveloped countries in the twentieth century are confronted with the choice of borrowing less than the best technology of advanced countries or of investing heavily, perhaps beyond their means, in human capital in order to raise their capacity for borrowing at the more advanced level. A secular rise in the level of investment in human capital (education) has been a fundamental feature of economic development over the past two centuries.

BOWDEN, WITT, MICHAEL KARPOVICH, and ABBOTT P. USHER, *An Economic History of Europe Since 1750*, Chap. 24. New York: American Book Company, 1937.

BOWEN, RALPH H., *German Theories of the Corporate State with Special Reference to the Period 1870–1919*. New York: McGraw-Hill, Inc., 1947.

DAWSON, WILLIAM H., *The Evolution of Modern Germany*, 2nd ed. New York: Charles Scribner's Sons, 1919.

GERSCHENKRON, ALEXANDER, *Bread and Democracy in Germany*. Berkeley, Calif.: University of California Press, 1943.

HENDERSON, WILLIAM O., *The Industrial Revolution in Europe, 1815–1914*. Chicago: Quadrangle Books, 1961. (paperback)

———, *Studies in the Economic Policy of Frederick the Great*. London: Frank Cass & Co., Ltd., 1963.

———, *The Zollverein*. New York: Cambridge University Press, 1939.

HOFFMAN, ROSS J. S., *Great Britain and the German Trade Rivalry, 1875–1914*. New York: Russell & Russell, Inc., 1964.

MARSHALL, ALFRED, *Industry and Trade*, 2nd ed. Chap. 7, "The Industrial Leadership of Germany: Science in the Service of Industry." London: Macmillan & Co., Ltd., 1923.

PARKER, WILLIAM N., "National States and National Development: French and German Ore Mining in the Late Nineteenth Century," in *The State and Economic Growth*, Hugh G. J. Aitken, ed. New York: Social Science Research Council, 1959.

SARTORIUS VON WALTERSHAUSEN, AUGUST, *Deutsche Wirtschaftsgeschichte, 1815–1914*. Jena: G. Fischer, 1923.

SOMBART, WERNER, *Die deutsche Volkswirtschaft im neunzehnten Jahrhundert*. Berlin: Georg Bondi, 1912.

STOLPER, GUSTAV, *German Economy, 1870–1940*. New York: Reynal & Company, Inc., 1940.

TOWNSEND, MARY E., *The Rise and Fall of Germany's Colonial Empire, 1884–1918*. New York: The Macmillan Company, 1930.

VEBLEN, THORSTEIN B., *Imperial Germany and the Industrial Revolution*. New York: Augustus J. Kelley, Inc., 1964.

ARTICLES

BOWEN, RALPH H., "The Role of Government and Private Enterprise in German Industrial Growth, 1870–1914," *Journal of Economic History*, X (Supplement, 1950), 68–81.

BRADY, ROBERT A., "The Economic Impact of Imperial Germany: Industrial Policy," *Journal of Economic History* (Supplement, Dec., 1943), 108–23.

BRINKMANN, CARL, "The Place of Germany in the Economic History of the Nineteenth Century," *Economic History Review*, IV (April, 1933), 129–46.

HENDERSON, WILLIAM O., "The Genesis of the Industrial Revolution in France and Germany in the 18th Century," *Kyklos:* IX (Fasc. 2, 1956), 190–206.

———, "Germany's Trade with Her Colonies, 1884–1914," *Economic History Review*, IX (Nov., 1938), 1–16.

KREPS, THEODORE J., "Dye Industry," *Encyclopaedia of the Social Sciences*, V. New York: The Macmillan Company, 1931, 301–305.

PARKER, WILLIAM N., "Entrepreneurship, Industrial Organization, and Economic Growth: A German Example," *Journal of Economic History*, XIV, No. 4 (1954), 380–400.

The Take-off Period in American Capitalism

CHAPTER 18

A transformation of the American economy took place after 1830 as a consequence of a coalescence of historical forces. Agricultural machinery, new modes of transportation, expanded domestic markets, the westward movement, and the growth of industry coalesced to reshape the American scene. Laborsaving machinery greatly increased the productivity of agricultural labor and enabled a limited, though growing, population to spread itself thinly over a wide geographical area without dissipating industrial development. This vast territory was integrated into a single market economy for the first time by the trans-Appalachian railways in the 1850's. Textile manufacture in New England manifested an emerging factory system, and elsewhere between 1830 and 1860 other industries developed along lines which enhanced the productivity of labor in industrial employments.

The transformation of the American economy in the nineteenth century involved regional differences and regional conflicts. In the South the area and volume of cotton production increased rapidly, but no basic change occurred in the productivity of agricultural labor nor was there any notable trend toward industrialization. Slavery, which appeared to be the greatest strength of the South, turned out to be its greatest weakness. Dynamic growth in the North and West shifted economic and political power toward these regions and laid the groundwork for the sectional conflict that erupted into violent civil war in the 1860's. This armed conflict temporarily disrupted existing trends toward industrialization in the North and greatly delayed industrialization in the South.

AGRICULTURAL MACHINERY

Laborsaving techniques have contributed significantly to the high productivity in American agriculture since the beginning of the nineteenth century. During the colonial period American agriculture remained relatively backward; the type of improvements featured in the English agricultural revolution of the eighteenth century (Chapter 8), especially crop rotation and other land-saving improvements, were less significant in a new country with abundance of fertile soil than in an old country like England. Moreover, until extensive markets developed from improved transportation, farmers lacked the incentive to pro-

duce large surpluses of any one crop. American farmers ate well, but they
consumed a limited variety of goods. At the opening of the nineteenth century
farmers used animal power for plowing, harrowing, and hauling, but for little
else. Grains were reaped with the cradle and threshed with a flail or by treading.

Plow   Improvements in the plow led the way in raising the productivity of American farmers. In the first quarter of the nineteenth century a more scientific design for the moldboard produced a plow which cut a more even furrow, turned over and pulverized the soil, and reduced the manpower and animal power required for plowing. Further improvement occurred when metal replaced wood for the moldboard. Cast iron was first introduced and worked well in the eastern states, but the sticky soil of the western prairie clogged on cast iron. In order to avoid clogging and to break the tough prairie soil, John Deere introduced in the 1830's a highly polished steel moldboard on a relatively light plow which could be operated with less manpower and animal power.

Formerly, plows had been the handiwork of village blacksmiths, but during the 1830's they were produced in factories by the thousands and later by the tens of thousands. Quantity production lowered the cost of plows and thereby facilitated the wide use of superior implements. At the London Exposition of 1851 American plows proved superior to European plows, and became models throughout much of the world.

Reaper   Probably the most revolutionary innovation in agricultural machinery ever made in the United States was the mechanical, horse-drawn reaper. Through the ages farm labor had been scarcest at harvest time. This bottleneck in agricultural production discouraged large-scale grain farming, since there was little point in raising a larger crop than could be harvested in time to prevent its destruction by the elements. Although the need for a mechanical reaper to replace the scythe, and later the cradle, had long been felt, the great shortage of labor in the United States and the vast potentialities for marketing grain at home and abroad encouraged inventors to make financial sacrifices to develop an economically workable machine.

Reapers were patented almost simultaneously by Obed Hussey (1833) and Cyrus McCormick (1834). Hussey began to manufacture his machine in Baltimore in 1838 and at first held an advantage over McCormick since Baltimore, including Ellicott Mills, was then the leading flour milling center of the United States. Technical improvements were made in 1845 and 1847 in McCormick's machine, and he showed business acumen in transferring his operations to Chicago at a time when the railways were just beginning to penetrate the wheat lands of the West. After his death McCormick's firm merged with four others to form the International Harvester Company.

Improvements continued to be made and other reapers entered the market. At the Paris Exposition of 1855 an American reaper accomplished in 22 minutes an amount of work which an English machine required 66 minutes to perform and a French (Algerian) machine 71 minutes. The United States won renown for its superior agricultural machinery.

In 1852 a test showed a saving of the labor of five men in fourteen required to reap fifteen acres of wheat in one day by using a mechanical har-

vester in place of a hand cradle. Although the cradle was still widely used where wheat was grown on a small scale, in the important wheat-growing areas the reaper had supplanted the cradle by 1860 and with each improvement the advantage of the harvester increased.

In addition to plows and reapers many other laborsaving machines were in use by 1860. These included threshing machines, hay mowers, horse-drawn wheeled rakes, seed drills, corn planters, cultivators, and harrows. The mechanical thresher complemented the mechanical reaper for harvesting grain. A mechanical thresher (Pitt's) had been invented by 1836 and was being widely used in the important grain-growing areas of the United States by 1860. Among other laborsaving machines, the corn-planter was perhaps the most important because the amount of corn a farmer could raise was determined primarily by the acreage he could plant and cultivate, just as the amount of wheat he could raise was determined by the amount he could harvest.

Bidwell and Falconer estimated that in 1860 a typical (Ohio) farmer who used the available methods of production could produce his crops with only two-thirds of the labor required in 1840.[1] Of course, not all farmers took the trouble to inform themselves of the latest technology, and some of those who did could not afford the relatively expensive machinery. Yet there was strong incentive to adopt the new machinery whenever the market price for farm products was good because the machines soon paid for themselves out of increased productivity. At an early date, manufacturers of farm machinery began selling to farmers on an installment basis. The resale value of farm machinery protected sellers against defaulting buyers. This was an early example of installment selling, a financial practice which was of considerable importance in the nineteenth century.

Increased agricultural productivity by means of laborsaving devices made possible the rapid industrialization of the United States. A smaller proportion of the population was employed in agriculture and a larger proportion became available for industry. Put in another way, farmers using machinery produced larger surpluses above their own family needs. These farm surpluses supported men working in nonagricultural pursuits. The surpluses were large enough not only to provide food and raw materials for American industries but also to provide an export surplus to pay for the imported capital goods needed for industrial development. A principle of general applicability in economic experience is that increased agricultural productivity is a prerequisite for large-scale industrialization. The parallel should be noted between the American experience of the nineteenth century and the British exprience of the eighteenth century, in which an agricultural revolution accompanied the English Industrial Revolution. While it is conceivable that a nation might industrialize without raising the productivity of agriculture, examples would be hard to find. The splendid American performance in agriculture provided food for thought as well as for bodily nourishment because it flew in the face of the dire predictions of Malthus that population would outrun food supply and thereby keep the great mass of humanity always at a subsistence level. Malthus died in 1832, the year before Hussey patented his reaper.

---

[1] Percy W. Bidwell and John I. Falconer, *History of Agriculture in the Northern United States, 1620–1860* (Washington, D.C.: The Carnegie Institution, 1925), p. 305.

A geographic fact of great significance for the economic development of the United States is the mountain range which runs north-south within a hundred to three hundred miles of the Atlantic Coast. In the absence of cheap mass overland transportation, the Appalachian range presented a topographical barrier to the integration of the new territory west of the mountains with the old territory east of the mountains. Before the Erie Canal and the trans-mountain railways, the area west of the Appalachians was either crudely self-sufficient or commercially oriented to the South via the Ohio and Mississippi rivers. General economic unification and rapid industrialization of the United States awaited the completion of the Erie Canal in 1825 and, more important, of the trans-Appalachian railways by 1855.

During the colonial period the roads were so inferior as to have limited economic significance. Most inter-colonial trade as well as travel was by sea and by rivers. Early settlement and economic development followed the seacoast and the rivers that penetrated inland—the Hudson, Delaware, Susquehanna, Patuxent, Potomac, James, and others. After 1790 internal transportation in the United States began to improve. Following the British lead, numerous turnpikes were built. One of the early turnpikes was the excellent Philadelphia to Lancaster road constructed during the 1790's. However, the most significant road-building achievement of the early period was the Cumberland Road, also called the National Road, which linked the Atlantic Coast with the Ohio Valley via Cumberland, Maryland, and Wheeling, West Virginia. It reached Wheeling on the Ohio River by 1818 and subsequently was extended to Columbus, Ohio, in 1833, and finally to Vandalia, Illinois, in the 1850's.

Despite Constitutional misgivings and sectional jealousies, federal funds were used to construct the National Road. It was a broad, well-engineered highway which greatly reduced the time and cost of passenger and freight traffic across the Appalachian Mountains into the Ohio Valley. It was heavily trafficked by Conestoga wagons, stagecoaches, private carriages, horseback riders, pedestrians, and drovers with large herds of cattle and hogs moving from the Ohio Valley to eastern markets. Baltimore, because of its location at the eastern terminus of the Cumberland Road, gained a special advantage over other East Coast cities. Although the Cumberland Road represented a major advance over earlier transportation facilities, it did not provide an economical means for moving heavy and bulky traffic between East and West. Products such as wheat and flour could not bear the cost of long-distance shipment across the mountains to eastern centers of population.

Whereas the United States imitated Europe in road building, Americans pioneered in river steamboat transportation. In Europe a canal-building era preceded the river steamboat era, but in the United States the river steamers preceded the canals. Shortly after the development of James Watt's steam engine, the idea of putting one of these engines on a boat was tried out by numerous individuals. James Rumsey of Virginia made a trial run on the Potomac in 1784–85, and John Fitch carried passengers on the Delaware River for several months during 1790. Oliver Evans and John Stevens in the United States and William Symington in Great Britain were other early innovators

in building and operating steamboats. None of these ventures attained commercial success, and credit for the first commercially successful steamboat must be given to Robert Fulton's *Clermont* on the Hudson River between New York City and Albany beginning in 1807. This trip could be made in eight to ten hours, which was faster, and also cheaper, than the journey could be made by stagecoach.

America's western rivers were not so easily conquered by steamboats as the Hudson. A few years after his initial success in the East, Fulton projected a grand master plan for steamboat service between Pittsburgh and New Orleans on the Ohio and Mississippi rivers. In 1811 Nicholas Roosevelt made a successful trip from Pittsburgh to New Orleans, but his boat could not ascend the river system all the way. Fulton, who had obtained a monopoly of the right to operate steamboats on the rivers of New York state, received a similar grant for Louisiana, but a groundswell of indignation against exclusive privileges curbed the extension of monopoly to other western states, and in the famous case of Gibbons v. Ogden (1824) the United States Supreme Court invalidated grants by states of monopoly on rivers on grounds that river transportation is interstate commerce and therefore, under the Constitution, can be regulated only by Congress.

Fulton's boats operated successfully on the lower Mississippi, but the development of western river transport fell to others. In 1817 a steamboat built and commanded by intrepid Captain Henry Shreve successfully ascended the Mississippi as far as Louisville in twenty-five days. After the Fulton monopoly on the lower Mississippi was broken, the volume of traffic on the Ohio and the Mississippi increased rapidly. It was, in fact, on the rivers of western America that the steamboat enjoyed its greatest commercial success.[2]

Commercial shipping on western rivers was not a force which unified the American economy; indeed, the effect was quite the opposite. The success of steamboat transportation on western rivers oriented the economy of the Ohio Valley toward the South rather than toward the East. Some trade flowed through New Orleans to the East Coast of the United States, but in volume this traffic was but a trickle compared with the total river traffic. The distance from Cincinnati to New York via New Orleans by water is equal to the distance from New York to Liverpool and proportionately much more expensive for carrying freight. In the economic development of the American West the river steamer was very important, but its effect was not to unify the East and West as a basis for industrialization of the former, nor did the steamboat link the American West with Europe. Its main effect was to link the West with the South, which had even less industrial potential at this stage of American development than did the West.

Canal building started later in the United States than in Europe and had less significance for general economic development. American canals got off to a good start, but within less than two decades they were overtaken by the railways, which supplanted them as the main agency of mass transportation. Although canals were of limited importance in the United States, the Erie Canal was an exception because it was the first transportation route to carry

---

[2] For a definitive and fascinating account of the economics of western steamboats, see Louis C. Hunter, "Invention of the Western Steamboat," *The Journal of Economic History,* III (Nov., 1943), 201–20. See also Professor Hunter's book on the same subject.

heavy commerce between the East and West at rates low enough to affect the sectional division of labor.

Since colonial times settlers moving to the Great Lakes and Ohio country had ascended the Hudson River Valley to Albany and thence had gone west along the Mohawk Valley to Lake Erie. The Mohawk Valley was the one low passage to the West through the long Appalachian barrier. The Erie Canal, which was begun in 1817 and completed in 1825, followed this route. It covered 363 miles from Albany on the Hudson River to Buffalo on Lake Erie.

By significantly reducing the cost and increasing the volume of freight between the East Coast and the Ohio Valley–Great Lakes region, the Erie Canal stimulated eastern industry by providing western markets and stimulated western agriculture by providing eastern markets. Agriculture in New England suffered a relative decline but industry there was stimulated. The impact on trade is indicated by the fact that the Erie Canal, more than any other factor, made New York the greatest port and the largest city in the United States. Before 1825 Boston and Philadelphia successively had been the largest cities in the country. A comparison of freight costs by the Erie Canal and by the National Road, which previously had been the cheapest route to the West, reveals the extent of the superiority of the canal over the road as a means of transportation. On the Erie Canal the cost of freight was one-half cent to three cents per ton-mile as compared with twenty-five to fifty cents per ton-mile by the National Road.

Railways   Whereas the Erie Canal inaugurated the preparatory period of American industrialization, the completion of the trans-Appalachian railway during the 1850's catapulted the United States into the status of an industrial nation. The Atlantic Coast economy meshed with the Ohio Valley–Great Lakes complex to form an integrated American economy. This period of the "transportation revolution" coincides with Professor W. W. Rostow's dating of the "take-off" of the United States economy between 1843 and 1860. Moreover, the American experience illustrates the general proposition that industrial revolutions did not occur, except in England, prior to the coming of the railways.

At first American railways served as feeders and connecting links for water transport facilities. As the fuller potentialities of railways became apparent, businessmen in eastern seaboard cities saw them as competitors with the canals for cheap transportation to the West. Baltimore, Philadelphia, and Charleston turned eagerly to railways as a rival to the advantages which the Erie Canal had conferred on New York City after 1825. When officials of the Chesapeake and Ohio Canal decided to start from Georgetown on the Potomac rather than from Baltimore, the merchants of the latter community made plans for a trans-mountain railway with an eastern terminus at Baltimore. Ground was broken for the Baltimore and Ohio Railroad and the ill-fated Chesapeake and Ohio Canal on the same day, July 4, 1828, with an appropriate mixture of patriotic zeal and business optimism. The railway reached Cumberland, Maryland, in 1842 and was extended to Wheeling on the Ohio River by 1853.

Meanwhile progress was slow for the Chesapeake and Ohio Canal, which reached Cumberland in 1850, eight years behind the railway. The ambitious plan to extend the canal to the Ohio Valley was never fulfilled. Within Maryland it carried considerable freight, especially coal, but did not succeed as a

profit-making venture. Success of the Baltimore and Ohio Railroad and failure of the Chesapeake and Ohio Canal marks the date at which railways took the lead over canals.

Running west from Philadelphia, the Pennsylvania Railroad reached Pittsburgh in 1852. Meanwhile New York City and New York state were building railways to the Great Lakes to reinforce the advantages already provided by the Erie Canal. In 1850 a number of short rail lines, later to be consolidated as the New York Central, made direct connections with the Great Lakes. In 1851 the Erie Railroad, serving the southern counties of New York state, reached Lake Erie at Dunkirk. During the 1850's these four great rail lines—the Baltimore and Ohio, the Pennsylvania, the New York Central, and the Erie Railroad—provided connecting service with Chicago, which soon became the transportation gateway between the East and the trans-Mississippi West. During the 1850's the total mileage of railways in the United States more than tripled; New England was covered with a network of short lines; the Mississippi River was reached and crossed; and agitation began for transcontinental railways to the Pacific Coast.

The impact of railway building on general economic development is demonstrated by the phenomenal growth of Chicago during the 1850's. At the opening of this decade, Chicago was still a small village. By 1853 the first through rail connections with the Atlantic seaboard were made. From 1852 to 1853 Chicago's population increased from less than 40,000 to more than 60,000. Most of the new residents poured in by rail. By 1855 the population had reached 80,000, which represented a seven-fold increase in ten years. In 1860 the official census placed Chicago's population at 109,260. The rapid growth of population created a building boom and caused land values to skyrocket. Within a few decades the agglomeration effect of Chicago's basic industry, railways, lifted it to second position among the nation's great cities. Stockyards, meat packing, farm machinery, grain trade, iron and steel plants, banking, and general trade and manufacturing were all attracted to this metropolis of the Middle West. Analogous developments took place at St. Louis and, to a lesser degree, at Cincinnati and Cleveland.

The tendency of railways to polarize trade and industry at the western terminals was matched by a similar tendency at East Coast terminals—New York, Philadelphia, Baltimore, Boston. Along the right-of-way, population density and economic activity also increased, but they did not fan out in the manner characteristic of terminal cities. The initial cost of constructing a railroad is very great, but the potential for carrying traffic is tremendous. Consequently costs per unit of traffic decrease with increases in traffic density, that is, railroads are very economical provided they operate on a massive scale. This fundamental characteristic of railroads introduced external economies to the terminal communities and generated giant metropolitan communities in contrast to the village communities associated with inland areas in the pre-railway age.

With New England and the Middle Atlantic states now linked to the Great Lakes region by iron and steam for the first time, a massive interregional division of labor became economically feasible. The essentially colonial status of the American economy, reaching back more than two hundred years, was at last drawing to a close on the eve of the Civil War.

INDUSTRIAL DEVELOPMENT OF THE UNITED STATES
BEFORE THE CIVIL WAR

325

THE TAKE-OFF
PERIOD
IN AMERICAN
CAPITALISM

Given increased productivity in agriculture, the revolutionary impact of railways, and the resulting extension of markets and regional specialization, the United States was prepared for a rapid march into industrialization. Although the major sweep of industrialization occurred after the Civil War, a lively preparatory development of industry took place in the decades just preceding 1860. In comparison with British industry, the United States remained backward in most respects, but among the other great nations, only France could lay claim to being more advanced during the first-half of the nineteenth century. By virtue of institutions nurtured in a British environment, the United States enjoyed a heritage favorable to industrial capitalism.

To the coalescence of historical forces, discussed earlier in this chapter, was added rich natural resources, an ingenious native population, and continuing large-scale immigration of Europeans. For the textile industry the United States enjoyed a superabundant supply of raw cotton and a reasonably good supply of raw wool. For the iron industry the country was endowed with excellent reserves of coal and iron ore. To the native American pool of manpower, there was added in the course of the nineteenth century millions of Europeans who responded to the lure of enlarged economic opportunity in the New World. For example, an early influx of Irish immigrants replaced New England farm girls in textile mills in the 1840's and 1850's. Although Britain attempted to retain exclusive knowledge of its newly invented machines and processes, this information was readily transferred by emigrating British technicians and American business leaders who saw British factories in operation. Americans exercised ingenuity in adapting European technology to special American conditions. Labor remained the scarcest factor, just as it had been during the colonial era. Fortunately the machine technology of the Industrial Revolution was capable of high productivity with relatively unskilled operatives. In resource-rich America a system of industry depending on highly skilled labor requiring long apprenticeship would have been slow to develop. Like American agriculture, American industry placed great stress on raising the productivity of labor through mechanization.

The labor-economizing adaptations of American industry merit special attention in the following discussion of some leading industries. The textile industry, which developed first, utilized the labor of New England farm girls. The iron industry reversed the order of technical change in England because, as Professor Louis Hunter has pointed out, "Whereas in England the original impulse to change was given by scarcity of timber, in this country the primary factor was scarcity of labor." [3] Flour milling exemplified an early American trend toward automated processing, and meat packing used assembly lines before the Civil War. Small arms production introduced the principle of manufacture by interchangeable parts, a principle upon which the subsequent age of mass production was based. Each of these industries in its own special way illustrates the adaptations made in the United States in the course of general

[3] "Heavy Industries before 1860," in *The Growth of the American Economy*, ed. by H. F. Williamson (Englewood Cliffs, N.J.: Prentice-Hall, Inc., 1944), p. 213.

industrial evolution. Together these industries give a representative picture of American industrialism up to 1860. After the Civil War the United States became progressively industrialized and within three decades after Appomattox became the leading industrial nation of the world. Obviously this sensational growth had its roots in the pre-Civil War period.

Textiles

The beginnings of the cotton textile industry in the United States were associated with the transfer of technology from Europe, the transfer of capital from commercial to industrial enterprises within the United States, the utilization of natural resources especially water power, and the recruitment of a labor force from rural areas for employment in urban factories. This great industry concentrated in New England, where it utilized the ingenuity, capital, resources, and labor of New Englanders. Only after they were well launched in Massachusetts, Rhode Island, Connecticut, and New Hampshire did textile factories spread to other parts of the United States, and only in the twentieth century did other regions offer serious competition to New England's manufacturers.

The strategic missing link in America for textile manufacturing was technology comparable in efficiency to that of Europe. America had capital, labor, and natural resources which might be diverted to manufacturing if the state of the industrial arts could justify factory production. Although the transfer of technology to the United States took place within a few decades after its development in England, its coming was by no means automatic or without special obstacles. Until 1843 British law forbade the export of machinery and the emigration of skilled artisans. However, a few individuals surmounted the obstacles to transference of technology to the United States.

Samuel Slater, a talented, trained mechanic who had worked in an Arkwright factory in England, is probably the best known pioneer in the American textile industry in this respect. In response to special bounties offered for models of new textile machines in the United States, Slater left England secretly for America and set up an Arkwright cotton spinning mill at Pawtucket, Rhode Island, in 1791. Slater's success led to the erection of other spinning mills, and Rhode Island became the first center of cotton textile manufacture in the United States.

Although Slater built a mill he did not create a factory system; he could not have done so because conditions in the United States were not yet ripe for a factory system. The business organization within which his mill operated clearly indicates the immaturity of industrial capitalism at the time. Slater's mill spun a coarse yarn which was woven into cloth under a putting-out system in which the labor was performed in the homes of the rural families of the children who did most of the work in the mill. Wages of the child operatives were paid in "truck" from the store of the merchant capitalists, Brown and Almy, who financed Slater. Agriculture was still too attractive even in New England for a full-fledged factory, not to mention a factory *system*.

Waltham-Lowell System While the Rhode Island textile industry fluttered, spurted, and flickered, a further advance involving genuine factories, but still short of the factory *system*, was made in Massachusetts beginning at

Waltham in 1816. Francis Cabot Lowell, the innovator of the new advance, was
a wealthy Boston merchant who, like other American merchants at the time,
found foreign commerce very dull just before and during the War of 1812.
Jefferson's Embargo Act and the ensuing war meant that the quantities of imported manufactures to which the country was accustomed were not available.
This stimulated the demand for domestic manufacture.

While temporarily residing in England, Lowell visited the great cotton
factories of Lancashire, and while residing in Scotland near New Lanark, he
probably visited Robert Owen's factories, which, in contrast with other British
factories, provided model working and living conditions for employees. When
Lowell returned to Massachusetts, he built at Waltham a large plant which
embodied machinery as much like British machinery as he could remember.
Since there was much that Lowell could not reproduce from memory, his mechanics had to rely on native ingenuity to carry through the project. One important innovation was the integration of spinning and weaving in a single
plant. Cotton entered in the raw state and emerged as finished cloth.

Lowell's factory at Waltham, the largest ever built in America up to that
time, required a great deal of capital. Fortunately for the success of the enterprise other wealthy Boston merchants had been forced by the depression in
foreign commerce to reduce their normal trading activity and found themselves with idle capital for which they sought profitable outlets. They refused
to invest in war bonds because they bitterly opposed what they called "Mr.
Madison's War." Lowell was able to raise $300,000, of which the initial $100,000
came from his close Boston associates.

Among the Boston merchants who invested in the Waltham factory,
special interest attaches to Nathan Appleton, who later became the greatest
of New England's mill magnates. Appleton was a successful, self-made merchant with an interest in finance. At the onset of the trade depression, brought
on by the War of 1812, he dissolved his mercantile partnership and contemplated retirement to a life of study and leisure on the modest income from
a $200,000 fortune. In 1812 he wrote to his brother: "I know of nothing to lay
out money in with any profit or advantage." (Hannah Josephson, *The Golden
Threads*, 126) Shortly thereafter Lowell and associates induced Appleton to
invest in the Boston Manufacturing Company, a corporation which had lately
been formed to carry through the projected textile factory at Waltham. He
was asked to invest $10,000 but decided to risk only $5,000. He appears to
have had little confidence in a manufacturing venture which involved a large
investment in fixed plant, machinery, housing, and other facilities for an
entire industrial community. Like other merchant capitalists, Appleton was
not accustomed to making large investments in fixed capital with a relatively
low turnover, as compared to merchant capital with its rapid turnover. Once
his $5,000 was committed, Appleton expressed anxiety lest the Waltham plant
be unable to begin operating before an end to the war with Great Britain
should bring a flood of imported goods.

Although the sale of Waltham cloth did not begin until eight months
after the end of the war, the new firm proved efficient enough to meet the most
formidable foreign competition. Lowell had decided wisely to specialize in the
manufacture of coarse, unbleached cotton sheeting that was much in demand
in pioneering, agricultural America. He did not attempt to compete with the

finer British fabrics. Other American textile mills which had sprung up during the embargo and War of 1812 proved vulnerable to British competition, and such mills failed by the hundreds. These failures led Congress to pass the protective tariff of 1816 with approval from all sections of the country. However, the old-line New England merchants, of the type which Lowell and Appleton had formerly been, opposed the tariff because they feared it would hurt foreign commerce. Francis Cabot Lowell, merchant turned industrialist, journeyed to Washington to lobby effectively for the tariff on cotton textiles. His firm did not need protection in order to survive but it was in a position to benefit from the tariff.

When the Waltham enterprise proved even more successful than Lowell had anticipated, Nathan Appleton's attitude toward industrial investment changed. He increased his investment in the Waltham company to $26,000, and after Lowell's death in 1817 at the age of 42, Appleton became the prime mover in the next major undertaking of the Boston merchants at Lowell, Massachusetts. He subscribed to $180,000 worth of stock in the new company and induced his brothers to make additional subscriptions to the total capitalization of $600,000. Until his death in 1861 at the age of 82, Nathan Appleton remained America's "Lord of the Loom."

The Boston Associates, a small group of industrial capitalists associated with Appleton in New England textiles, operated through corporations which they retained in their control while utilizing the capital of other investors. These were among the first industrial corporations in the United States. By 1833 the capital invested in the Lowell mills alone amounted to more than $6,000,000. Dividends were liberal but earnings were even better, and much of the addition to capital came from plowing back profits. In 1844 after the water power in Lowell had been fully utilized, the Boston Associates created a new mill city named Lawrence, after Abbott Lawrence, who ranked next to Nathan Appleton as the leading industrial capitalist of New England. Textile mills were built in many other New England towns. The highly rationalized factories of the Boston Associates proved very lucrative business ventures. They by no means constituted the entire cotton textile industry, but they were clearly in the vanguard of American industrial capitalism between 1820 and 1850.

Labor force   The shortage of labor for manufacturing formed the basis for the most unique feature of the Massachusetts textile industry during its first three decades. First at Waltham, again at Lowell, and later in other factories of the Boston Associates the main labor force was drawn from New England farm girls who, while in the employ of the textile magnates, lived in well-chaperoned dormitories and maintained a social status entirely unlike that associated with an industrial proletariat. In advance of opening his textile plant at Waltham, Lowell seems to have had the idea of recruiting a labor force from among the girls of the New England countryside. His inspiration for creating the idyllic conditions in which these "ladies of the loom" toiled and lived probably came from his visit to Robert Owen's spinning mills at New Lanark, Scotland. Owen had demonstrated that good wages and good working conditions were fully consistent with the profitable operation of factories.

Typically, New England farmers were poor and they and their daughters welcomed an opportunity to accumulate a small nest egg of hard cash. But these families of good old Puritan stock valued their honor and virtue more than money; therefore the atmosphere of the mill town which would attract them had to be impeccable. Nothing must be allowed to cast any doubt on the respectability and the dignity of the girls. Lowell and his associates built dormitories, provided chaperones, made church attendance compulsory, and encouraged educational and intellectual pursuits for their employees. In this genteel atmosphere the mill magnates had little difficulty in recruiting mill hands. Among 5000 operatives in Lowell in 1834, 3800 were young New England farm girls. As the textile empire of Appleton and Lawrence grew, the number of mill girls increased. Visitors from all over the world came to Lowell to marvel at the "ladies of the loom," who read the best literature, studied music, and wrote poetry.

While the mill girls toiled in factories without being stigmatized by inferior social status and without jeopardizing their chances of marriage to young New England farmers upon returning home, their working conditions were somewhat short of a heaven on earth. They labored long hours at low wages for autocratic employers. They received about $2 a week plus board for toiling 72 hours a week. Girls who complained or who took action to improve working conditions were summarily dismissed, and their names were placed on a blacklist which circulated among factories to prevent their being employed elsewhere. When the girls supported a movement for the ten-hour working day during the 1840's, they were defeated by their masters, who had the Massachusetts legislature well in hand.

After the ten-hour movement was beaten, the girls who had participated in strikes and other acts which were unconscionable in the eyes of their employers were dismissed. Others quit voluntarily. The system vanished as suddenly as it had appeared. The entire episode is significant because it indicates not the ripeness of the United States for industrial capitalism, but quite the opposite. It reflects the immaturity of industrial capitalism which had to resort to artificial measures to recruit a labor supply. By the late 1840's conditions had changed. The Yankee farm girls were replaced by immigrant Irish girls, who were more docile in accepting low wages and long hours. These Irish constituted a landless proletariat with no farm to which to return. The rise of a permanent wage-earning class to replace the Yankee farm girls marks the approach of a full-fledged industrial capitalism in the United States.

In 1860 New England produced three-quarters of all cotton cloth in the United States. Among all nations the United Kingdom was, of course, far in the lead with an output of cloth six times that of the United States. The latter was, however, the second largest producer of cotton textiles, being slightly ahead of France in the amount of cloth produced, although slightly behind France in the number of spindles. American textile production stressed quantity rather than quality. It specialized in rough types of cloth suitable to the pioneer demands of a large proportion of the people, just as F. C. Lowell had in 1816, when he began specializing in rough sheeting. The finer cloths were imported. An important contribution to quantity production was made by the invention in 1831 of the ring spindle. This continuous type of spinning permitted a

factory operative to attend a greater number of spindles as compared with the spinning mule, which produced less yarn but of a superior quality.

Woolen textiles Woolen textile production in factories increased more slowly than cotton textiles. The United States lacked a good grade of domestic wool. As in the case of cotton textile machinery, the technology for woolens was borrowed from England and there was a lag in the development of machinery adapted to spinning and weaving wool. The chief agents of transfer of technology in the woolen industry were John and Arthur Scholfield. These Yorkshiremen immigrated to New England, where they set up the first improved woolen textile machinery a few years after Samuel Slater had brought the first Arkwright cotton mill to America.

Not until after 1830 was woolen textile manufacturing in factories firmly established, and it was even later before the output from factories exceeded household production. As in the case of cotton cloth, American woolen producers specialized in coarser fabrics, including blankets, flannels, felts, and carpets. Finer woolens and worsteds were imported. Woolen mills were generally smaller and more scattered than cotton mills and in 1860 there were twice as many woolen mills as cotton mills with an aggregate output only one-half as great. Domestic producers received substantial protection against foreign competition on most types of woolen cloth from a high duty (25 per cent ad valorem) imposed by the tariff of 1816.

Iron and Coal

Iron had been an industry of some importance in colonial America. Vast forests provided abundant fuel for use in smelting iron ore into pig iron for domestic use and for export to timber-scarce England. In England the shortage of timber provided the main stimulus for the discovery and adoption of coke in place of charcoal for smelting iron ore. By contrast, in the United States the abundance of timber, which was the main basis of strength during the colonial era, proved a source of delay in progressing from the charcoal to the coke stage in the evolution of the industry. The United States lagged a full century behind England in the use of coke; not until the Civil War did coke surpass charcoal as the main smelting fuel in the United States.

As long as iron production remained in the charcoal stage, it was a scattered, rural type of industry unable to catch up with the rapidly increasing demand for iron products. As late as 1850, 60 per cent of the iron needs of the United States were imported, mainly from England. In the decade 1850 to 1860 British pig iron production increased more than American production, both relatively and absolutely. Nevertheless, in the three decades 1830 to 1860 the foundation was laid for the sensational rise of iron production after the Civil War. During the 1880's the United States passed the United Kingdom in pig iron output to become the world's leading producer.

Before the Civil War the most important technical changes in the American iron industry took place in processing pig iron into wrought iron rather than in smelting iron ore into pig iron. While pig iron production remained a small-scale and largely rural industry, the puddling process and rolling mills, invented by Cort in England in 1783, were widely adopted in the United States to convert pig iron into wrought iron. Prior to the rolling mill and pud-

dling process, wrought iron was made by the labor-consuming process of

heating the pig iron and hammering out the impurities. Even with the aid of
large trip-hammers and mechanical bellows, this was very costly in terms of
labor, and because of the scarcity of labor in the United States, especially of
the skilled type required in iron forging, there was strong incentive to adopt
the laborsaving rolling mill and puddling process. First came the rolling mill,
which expelled impurities and shaped the iron slabs by pressing rather than
by hammering them. Since rolling mills were technically most efficient when
operated on a large scale, the puddling process soon replaced the forge as the
method for producing the wrought iron slabs because greater quantities could
be processed by puddling than by forging. The puddling process utilized the
reverberatory furnace, which kept the metal out of direct contact with the
fuel and thereby permitted the use of coal in place of charcoal. Although wood
remained cheap in America, coal was cheaper than charcoal and more efficient
because of its concentrated heat energy. A rolling mill could process fifteen
times as much puddled metal as a forge in the same amount of time. Hence
the saving in labor was very great.

Since coal mines were less widely dispersed than timber, adoption of the
puddling furnace and the rolling mill tended to concentrate this phase of iron
production in a few urban centers near coal mines or, prior to the railway age,
at points where coal could be transported by water. Centers of wrought iron
production included Philadelphia, Scranton, Baltimore, and Pittsburgh. The
latter city, located at the center of vast deposits of excellent coking coal, became the seat of the American iron industry.

Geographical concentration of pig iron production developed more
slowly and ultimately depended, as did concentration of wrought iron production, upon the use of coal in place of wood as fuel. An American contribution
to iron technology was the use of hard (anthracite) coal for smelting iron
ore. British coal used for coking was soft (bituminous) coal. In the anthracite
regions of eastern Pennsylvania coke was important after 1840, although the
output of anthracite iron did not exceed charcoal iron until 1860. To the west,
including western Pennsylvania, where coal was of the soft type, the use of
coke was delayed by the abundance of timber and also by the nature of the
market for iron products. Wrought iron made from charcoal-smelted pig
iron differed in quality from that made from coke-smelted pig iron. Charcoal
iron was better adapted to the agricultural uses of the West, where blacksmiths
and farmers purchased iron bars from country stores to make miscellaneous
articles needed in rural communities—for example, nails, agricultural tools, and
hardware.

The huge demand for iron associated with railways, especially iron
rails, gave impetus to the use of (bituminous) coke in the West, and on the
eve of the Civil War coke was widely used in blast furnaces for iron smelting.
In addition to creating a huge demand for iron, railways also provided cheaper
transportation, which made possible a greater division of labor in manufacturing iron and iron products. Heavy and bulky iron products could now be
transported cheaply over long distances. Iron fabrication shifted from the
blacksmith shop to factories, and wrought iron bars became less important
merchandise in country stores. Thus did the coming of the railways merge
with the expansion of the market to create a factory system.

Food processing led all other American industries, measured in terms of gross value of product. It was the type of economic activity that befitted the American economy in which scarcity of labor and abundance of fertile land were dominant characteristics. Technical change, new methods of transportation, and growth of markets affected the development and location of these industries.

Flour milling   Flour milling is a semi-manufacturing activity which yields a valuable product with relatively little labor added to the raw material. The United States was well situated to produce flour for domestic needs and to export a considerable surplus to countries less favored for wheat growing. Economy in the use of labor in flour milling advanced significantly under the guiding genius of the great American inventor and mechanical engineer, Oliver Evans, who devised a method for mechanizing the entire process from receipt of grain at the mill to barreling the processed flour. Labor was needed in the Evans mill only to operate machinery.

Evans' flour mill saved labor, but it necessitated more capital for expensive plant and machinery. Consequently its adoption limited entry to more capitalistic firms and, although smaller and less efficient mills continued to produce for local markets, production for the populous centers and for export became concentrated in the hands of capitalistic millers in commercial centers favored by water power and good transportation for receiving grain and for shipping flour.

During the colonial era flour milling had been widely dispersed, but the producers for export to the West Indies and elsewhere were found principally along streams in the vicinity of Philadelphia. With the use of Evans' equipment, leadership shifted to Baltimore, which for several decades remained the leading flour-producing community in the United States. To its excellent water transport Baltimore added the first link of the Baltimore and Ohio Railway between Ellicott Mills and Baltimore in 1830. Other large milling centers before the Civil War were Richmond and Rochester. After 1825 the latter city enjoyed the advantages provided by the Erie Canal for receiving grain from the Ohio Valley and shipping flour to New York City and other eastern ports. Eastern cities retained leadership until the Civil War, after which the leading milling cities were located in the West, successively at St. Louis and Minneapolis.

Meat packing   Meat packing was a second important industry which, like flour milling, showed a marked tendency toward large-scale processing on a capitalistic basis in strategically located centers. Although there was no revolutionary technological change comparable to Evans' mechanization of flour milling, processing of meat was subjected to extensive division of labor as a result of improvements in means of transportation and growth of markets. Meat packing in the United States is distinguished among all industries for having been the first to adopt the principle of the assembly line, which was to become a dominant feature of American mass production and was to be adopted to some degree in all industrial nations. Carcasses of slaughtered ani-

mals moved continuously along a conveyor while being "disassembled" by the cleavers and knives of hand operatives.

By the 1820's the trans-Allegheny country was sufficiently settled and developed to take over from the East a dominant position in meat packing. From 1825 to the Civil War Cincinnati was the leading hog, cattle, and sheep market and the center of the nation's meat-packing industry. Pork was such an important product that Cincinnati was called "the most hoggish place in the world," and was nicknamed "Porkopolis." Barrels of salt pork, hogsheads of bacon, and other salted and smoked meats were sufficiently well preserved to be shipped anywhere in the world. Southern slaves were the largest but by no means the exclusive consumers of Cincinnati products. The Ohio and Mississippi rivers served as avenues to markets all over the world. With the coming of the trans-Allegheny railways much of the river traffic to the South was diverted by rail to the East. After increasing steadily until the early 1850's, shipments of salt pork and bacon from Cincinnati down the Ohio River declined by more than 50 per cent between the beginning and the end of that decade. This is but a single illustration of a general tendency for the railways to reshape the general structure of the American economy and to weld the regions east and west of the Allegheny Mountains into a single economy. With the extension of railways to the great plains and the accompanying westward shift of the corn belt, leadership in meat packing moved to Chicago, which had superlative railway facilities to the West, East, and South.

Meat packing demonstrates how growth in the size of the market as a result of improved means of transportation leads to large-scale production. Despite the fact that hand labor still predominated, a high degree of specialization characterized by assembly-line technique developed in meat packing. As the size of operations increased in centers like Cincinnati and Chicago, supplementary industries and facilities entered these communities to reinforce their advantages. For example, Cincinnati developed a barrel-making industry which employed 1,500 workmen in 1849. Banking facilities were also important to large, capitalistic enterprises such as those engaged in meat packing. By virtue of the minute division of labor and the external economies like cooperage and banking in the meat-packing centers, large-scale processing became progressively more efficient than small-scale processing. Of course, farmers still retained their smokehouses and salting pots, and small-scale packinghouses served the local village trade. But as in the late medieval period, the growth alongside small-scale producers of large-scale industry in the service of long-distance trade furnished the potential for a new type of economic society.

Small Arms

Small arms merit special mention because the principle of interchangeable parts was first used in the manufacture of muskets by Eli Whitney (1765–1825) and Simeon North (1765–1852). Whitney won fame but no great fortune from his invention of the cotton gin in 1792. His patent was infringed and the lawsuits by which he attempted to protect his patent were prohibitively expensive. Consequently Whitney turned his talents to other tasks, including

the manufacture of small arms. Under government contract he produced muskets by first making a separate machine tool for each part. After "tooling up" Whitney produced on a mass scale by making thousands of identical parts of each type required for a musket. He then assembled the finished musket from the supply of identical, interchangeable parts.

Unlike firearms made by gunsmiths, Whitney's muskets could be assembled without special fitting of one part to another because each individual part was made with sufficient precision to be used interchangeably. A disadvantage of this method was that no final product could be produced until the entire tooling up process was completed, and this preparation required several years of Whitney's time and effort. However, once the machine tools were ready, the muskets could be turned out very rapidly at relatively low cost per unit, providing a large number were produced. This was not an operation to be employed profitably for a small order or a small market or by a producer with small capital. Whitney's "capital" took the form of a government contract, with advance payments which were, in effect, a form of credit or loans.

In 1813 Simeon North, another Connecticut Yankee, received a government contract which specified that pistols were to be manufactured with interchangeable parts. Over a long lifetime North advanced the new method of manufacture beyond its use by Whitney and did much to overcome an initial prejudice against the interchangeable principle for small arms production. Yet another Connecticut Yankee, Samuel Colt (1814–1862), produced revolving pistols on government contract during the Mexican War, but he did a still larger business for sale to private consumers. The Colt revolver became the stock-in-trade of gun carriers in the American West during the nineteenth century. Colt's influence made itself felt in the Old World as well as on the frontier of the New World. At mid-century he set up in England a factory to make small arms by means of interchangeable parts and seems to have startled the English with the superiority of the American method of manufacturing small arms. In most forms of industry the British led the United States, but in light manufacturing where interchangeable parts were used, the Americans were far ahead of the British.

Clock-making

During the first half of the nineteenth century American clock-makers gained world superiority by applying the principle of interchangeable parts to their industry. Here the famous pioneers were Eli Terry (1772–1852), Seth Thomas, and Chauncey Jerome (1793–1868), all of Connecticut. Terry's wooden clocks sold for about $40 each. Jerome replaced wood with brass clock movements and sold his superior clocks for about $5 apiece. Although Connecticut clocks lacked precision as time-keepers, they were low enough in price to find a wide market and became the first American manufactured product to be exported on a large scale. American clocks invaded the English market and drove from business British clock-makers, who clung to the old concept of the clock as a work of craftsmanship in contrast to the American practice of replacing costly handwork with machinery. Production for an inter-

national market lowered still further the cost per clock and brought down the

price within the reach of ordinary families.

By the eve of the Civil War the United States had already developed a distinct system of manufacturing which excelled that of any other country, including England, in turning out light products such as firearms, clocks, watches, locks, farm machinery, sewing machines, hand tools, mechanical toys, and many other articles of everyday use. Eli Whitney's method of manufacturing muskets embodied the principles upon which this American system of manufacture rested: interchangeable parts, standardized products, labor-saving jigs and machine tools, and ingenious general organization for squeezing the most from small capital and scarce labor.

What American manufactures lacked in artistic elegance that appealed to European aristocrats, they more than made up in utility and rough-and-ready serviceability that, in keeping with the times, appealed to mechanics, farmers, and the host of other energetic, dynamic Americans who were preoccupied with their material welfare. Ordinary people in other countries also appreciated better plows, sewing machines, and inexpensive clocks. The system which had developed by 1850 had an orientation that was to usher in the American system of mass production in the second half of the nineteenth century and adumbrate the fearful but irresistible automation of the second half of the twentieth century.[4]

TARIFFS AND INDUSTRIALIZATION

In 1816 protective tariffs became part of the American pattern for industrial development, but tariffs appear to have been a more important feature of political than of economic history in the United States before the Civil War. Alexander Hamilton argued persuasively for protectionism in his well-known "Report on Manufactures" issued in 1791, but this paper had a limited circulation and does not seem to have had much direct influence on policy. Protection for American manufacturers against foreign competition began with the tariff of 1816, when the post-Napoleonic flood of English goods swept into the United States and sent many firms into bankruptcy. The trend in tariff duties was upward from 1816 to 1828, when the notorious "tariff of abominations" slipped through Congress. Lower tariff rates in 1832 began a downward trend in American duties that continued until the Civil War.

Protective duties probably helped most between 1816 and 1830, when the textile and iron industries were truly in their infancy. Although Lowell and his Boston Associates did not need the duties provided by the tariff of 1816, they nevertheless benefited from them through higher prices. Other cotton textile producers with less capital and less efficient machinery than the Boston Associates may have been able to survive their infancy because of protection against foreign competition afforded by tariffs. Iron producers in

[4] See chapter 20 for a more detailed discussion of the American system of mass production. On the pre-Civil War developments along these lines, see John E. Sawyer, "The Social Basis of the American System of Manufacturing," *Journal of Economic History*, XIV, No. 4, 1954, 361–79.

the eastern United States were also aided during the formative years. Iron producers in the trans-Allegheny region enjoyed sufficient natural protection by virtue of high transport costs before 1850 to have been much affected by tariff duties. At the same time, the American iron industry may have remained in its backward state longer as a result of the artificial protection afforded by import duties. If during the years 1816 to 1832 American industrialization correlated with rising protective walls, between 1832 and 1860 the much more rapid tempo of industrial growth occurred with declining protectionism. Other forces such as those described earlier in this chapter were more significant in the rise of American industry. Import duties were more important as the chief source of revenue for the federal government than as the basis for industrial development.

SELECTED BIBLIOGRAPHY

BIDWELL, PERCY W., and JOHN I. FALCONER, *History of Agriculture in the Northern United States, 1620–1860,* Parts III and IV. Washington, D.C.: Carnegie Institution of Washington, 1925.

CLARK, VICTOR S., *History of Manufactures in the United States,* Vol. II. Magnolia, Mass.: Peter Smith, 1949.

COLE, ARTHUR H., *The American Wool Manufacture,* 2 vols. Cambridge, Mass.: Harvard University Press, 1926.

DORFMAN, JOSEPH, *The Economic Mind in American Civilization,* Vol. II, Book II. New York: The Viking Press, 1946.

FISHLOW, ALBERT, *American Railroads and the Transformation of the Ante-Bellum Economy.* Cambridge, Mass.: Harvard University Press, 1966.

FOGEL, ROBERT W., *Railroads and American Economic Growth: Essays in Econometric History.* Baltimore: The Johns Hopkins University Press, 1964.

GOODRICH, CARTER, JULIUS RUBIN, and HARVEY H. SEGAL, *Canals and American Economic Development.* New York: Columbia University Press, 1961.

HILL, FOREST G., *Roads, Rails and Waterways: The Army Engineers and Early Transportation.* Norman, Okla.: University of Oklahoma Press, 1957.

HUNTER, LOUIS C., *Steamboats on the Western Rivers.* Cambridge, Mass.: Harvard University Press, 1949.

JOHNSON, EMORY R., et al., *History of Domestic and Foreign Commerce in the United States,* 2 vols. Vol I, Parts II and III. Washington, D.C.: Carnegie Institution of Washington, 1915.

JOSEPHSON, HANNAH, *The Golden Threads, New England's Mill Girls and Magnates.* New York: Duell, Sloan & Pearce, 1949.

KIRKLAND, E. C., *Men, Cities, and Transportation,* 2 vols. Cambridge, Mass.: Harvard University Press, 1948.

MACGILL, CAROLINE E., and others, *History of Transportation in the United States Before 1860.* Washington, D.C.: The Carnegie Institution of Washington, 1917.

MIRSKY, JEANNETTE, and ALLAN NEVINS, *The World of Eli Whitney.* New York: The Macmillan Company, 1952.

NORTH, DOUGLASS C., *The Economic Growth of the United States, 1790–1860.* Englewood Cliffs, N.J.: Prentice-Hall, Inc., 1961.

PARRINGTON, VERNON L., *Main Currents in American Thought,* Vol. II, "The Ro-

mantic Revolution in America, 1800–1860." New York: Harcourt, Brace &

World, Inc., 1954. (paperback)

ROGIN, LEO, *Introduction of Farm Machinery in Its Relation to the Productivity of Labor in Agriculture of the United States During the Nineteenth Century.* Berkeley: University of California Press, 1931.

TAUSSIG, FRANK W., *The Tariff History of the United States,* 8th ed. New York: G. P. Putnam's Sons, Capricorn Books, 1964. (paperback)

TAYLOR, GEORGE ROGERS, *The Transportation Revolution, 1815–1860.* New York: Holt, Rinehart and Winston, 1951.

WARE, CAROLINE F., *The Early New England Cotton Manufacture: A Study in Industrial Beginnings.* Boston: Houghton Mifflin Company, 1931.

ARTICLES

COOTNER, PAUL H., "The Role of the Railroads in United States Economic Growth," *Journal of Economic History,* XXIII (Dec., 1963), 477–521.

DAVIS, LANCE E., "New England Textile Mills and the Capital Markets: A Study of Industrial Borrowing, 1840–1860," *Journal of Economic History,* XX (March, 1960), 1–21.

HUNTER, LOUIS C., "The Invention of the Western Steamboat," *Journal of Economic History,* III (Nov., 1943), 201–20.

JENKS, LELAND H., "Railroads as an Economic Force in American Development," *Journal of Economic History,* IV (May, 1944), 1–20.

MURPHY, JOHN J., "Entrepreneurship in the Establishment of the American Clock Industry," *Journal of Economic History,* XXVI (June, 1966), 169–86.

SAWYER, JOHN E., "The Social Basis of the American System of Manufacturing," *Journal of Economic History,* XIV, No. 4 (1954), 361–79.

TAYLOR, GEORGE ROGERS, "American Economic Growth Before 1840: An Exploratory Essay," *Journal of Economic History,* XXIV (Dec., 1964), 427–44.

TEMIN, PETER, "Steam and Waterpower in the Early Nineteenth Century," *Journal of Economic History,* XXVI (June, 1966), 187–205.

————, "Labor Scarcity and the Problem of American Industrial Efficiency in the 1850's," *Journal of Economic History,* XXVI (Sept., 1966), 277–98.

ZEVIN, ROBERT B., "The Growth of Manufacturing in Early Nineteenth-Century New England," *Journal of Economic History,* XXV (Dec., 1965), 680–82.

Planter vs. Industrial Capitalism
and the American Civil War

CHAPTER **19**

In American economic development the Civil War has been viewed traditionally as the watershed between an agricultural and an industrial society. Several decades of preparatory development had brought the United States to the threshold of massive industrial output by 1860. A basic framework for an industrial economy had been laid. The social and economic overhead capital included a network of railways and other efficient means of transportation, rationalized factory organization like the New England textile industry, an advanced iron industry, factories making farm machinery, an army of skilled mechanics to produce and maintain industrial and agricultural machinery, and experience with interchangeable parts in small arms manufacture, complete mechanization in flour milling, and assembly-line techniques in meat packing.

During the war years the technology of mass production proved well adapted to meet, with a lag, the standardized demands for war production, including in addition to soldiers' "uniforms," ammunition, guns, shoes, tents, and other items. In terms of quantity of industrial output, however, the direct impact of the war was mixed, some industries being retarded while others were accelerated, with an overall deceleration of the rate of growth in manufacturing as compared with the decades just preceding 1860.

The significant economic effect of the Civil War, however, did not lie in the statistics of output of the 1860's but in a basic shift in the power structure of the nation. Control of the federal government shifted conclusively to groups interested in promoting industrial capitalism. The role of the American Civil War in this respect is analogous to Great Britain's Great Reform Bill, which brought belated political power to match the greater wealth and economic power of industrial groups as compared with a landholding aristocracy.

The rise and triumph of American industrial capitalism was accompanied by the decline and fall of a special form of commercial capitalism in the South, planter capitalism. The leaders of this system had prevailed in the South since the beginning of the colonial period. Toward the end of the colonial era, planter capitalism began to lose ground, only to experience a vigorous revival based on cotton growing for the factories of the Industrial Revolution. Cotton culture became the basis for a rapid westward movement in the southern United States during the first half of the nineteenth century. Cotton dominated

the nation's export trade. But even as cotton planting expanded into the Southwest, the struggle for national political power was being won by proponents of northern industrialism and western free farming. The South sought to secede from the federal union as a means of retaining control of its destiny. The ensuing Civil War resolved the economic, political, and social antagonisms between the South and the North in favor of industrial capitalism and released the energies of American industrialism. Within a few decades after the Civil War the United States became the world's leading industrial nation. The present chapter describes the characteristics of planter capitalism and the role of the Civil War in the maturing of industrial capitalism in the United States.

ECONOMICS OF SLAVERY

Planter capitalism in the American South was based on slave labor. From an economic point of view the distinguishing characteristic of slavery under capitalism is that the laborer is part of the fixed capital of the slave owner. By contrast, free workers as such constitute no part of the employers' capital, either fixed or circulating. By definition a free laborer is the property of no one. Unlike slaves, free laborers do not appear in the balance sheet, which lists the assets and liabilities of an enterprise. Payment of wages to free laborers takes the form of an outlay of cash (or kind). Thus the free wage-laborer is reflected in the capitalist's balance sheet only very indirectly through the cash account, some part of which will be used to pay wages. This outlay of cash for wages is paid from circulating capital and is one of the expenses appearing in the statement of profit and loss. Under both slavery and the wage system labor is an important item of cost, but the slave owner buys his labor all at once whereas the employer of free labor buys labor a little bit at a time. Consequently the slave owner has a large fixed investment in his labor supply. This special characteristic of the relation of capital to labor was important for the functioning of planter capitalism in the American South before the Civil War.

In addition to the large fixed investment in slaves the planter also had a large fixed investment in land. Circulating capital was relatively small in relation to total capital. The large fixed investment meant a slow turnover of total capital, that is, a long period of time from the conversion of money capital into assets and their reconversion into money capital again. A slow turnover tied up capital for extended periods and introduced inflexibility into planter capitalism. Once the planter's investments were sunk in slaves and land, he was committed to continue in this type of operation for a considerable time. In the absence of special offsetting advantages, capitalists normally tend to avoid tying up capital in investments which turn over slowly because, among other things, slow turnover increases the risk of loss from changes in market conditions between the time of original investment and the conversion of the final product into money. During early capitalism merchants like Andrea Barbarigo placed a premium on rapid turnover.[1] Maximum flexibility was part of the

[1] See Chapter 5.

capitalists' creed. They systematically avoided investments which could not easily and quickly be converted into cash in the normal course of business. A major obstacle to starting the factory system, for example, was the large amount of fixed capital tied up in expensive buildings and machinery. The degree of planning and foresight required for successful management increases as the proportion of durable fixed capital rises. Slavery was in this sense less desirable than free labor because the former absorbed relatively more capital than the latter.

The historic reason for the growth of slave labor (either under a plantation system or a small slave-holding enterprise system) was not its economic superiority over wage labor, but the fact that free workers were not available for employment and a labor force could not be mobilized in any other way for arduous labor in tropical and semitropical latitudes. Slavery was a special aberration of capitalism during its early phase in colonial areas and then persisted because there was no easy way to get rid of it. Its presence usually prevented the growth of a substantial class of free wage-earners. Where free labor was available at reasonable (low) wages, it was preferable to slave labor. Free workers were responsible for the maintenance of their own families whereas masters were responsible for the maintenance of their slaves. Nowhere did slave labor survive the triumph of industrial capitalism.

CRISIS OF PLANTER CAPITALISM IN RELATION TO THE ECONOMICS OF SLAVERY

Planter capitalism in the South was in a state of crisis about 1860. The pressures which caused this crisis arose in connection with the following: (1) the high price of slaves; (2) the low and unstable price of cotton; (3) soil exhaustion associated with the system of cultivation; (4) dependence on outside credit; (5) lack of direct trade with Europe; and (6) inability to diversify the southern economy. Measures to relieve these pressures were suggested from time to time and represented the general program of southerners for solving their economic problems. An increasing awareness of the economic inferiority of the South in comparison with the North and a strong desire by southerners to do something about it form a significant part of the background of the Civil War.

1. High price of slaves   A sharp rise in the price of slaves between 1800 and 1860 reflected conditions of demand and supply. The demand for slaves grew steadily with the increase in the demand for cotton by the factories of England, Continental Europe and New England. The supply of slaves did not keep pace with the demand. By Constitutional provision (Article I, Section 9) no more slaves were to be imported into the United States after 1808. Although smuggling was common, the estimated 250,000 immigrant slaves between 1808 and 1860 were too small a number to exert significant influence on the total supply or the price of slaves. The natural increase from the excess of births over deaths was more important than smuggling in increasing the slave population. Within the United States slaves were sold from places of lesser demand to places of greater demand, that is, from border states like Delaware, Maryland, Virginia, and Kentucky to the "New South" in Alabama, Mississippi,

Louisiana, and Texas. The domestic slave market redistributed the limited
number of slaves in a manner which increased cotton production, but it did
not alleviate the basic shortage of labor. Since the great increase in the demand
for slaves could not be met by increasing the number available to a corresponding extent, the price of slaves rose sharply.

At the beginning of the great era of cotton growing around 1800 the
price of a prime field hand between the ages of 18 and 30 was $300–$450.
By 1860 the price had risen to $1800–$2000. Prime females between the same
ages sold consistently for about 25 per cent less than prime males. Special
qualities affected the prices of individual slaves, who were typically sold at
auction. Intelligent domestic slaves were worth more than those lately brought
from Africa. Skilled artisans were at a premium, and unusually attractive
females might bring two or three times the price of ordinary female field
hands. Slaves beyond the age of useful labor were of no value in the slave
market. Infants were valued at $7 to $10 per pound in 1859.[2] The domestic
slave trade tended to equalize the level of prices of slaves throughout the
South, although complete uniformity was never attained.

High prices for slaves affected both large and small planters, but they
were most acutely felt by small planters who possessed only male slaves. Large
planters who owned both male and female slaves could replace retired and
deceased slaves with young slaves born and reared on the plantation. Since
on the average and in the long run there was an excess of births over deaths
among slaves, the large planters could not only replace but gradually increase
their supply of slave labor without having to pay high market prices. The
small slave owner, on the other hand, possessed only a few male field hands
and could replace a retired or deceased slave only by purchasing a replacement in the open market.[3] Consequently the owners of small numbers of slaves
felt more keenly the rising price of slaves. Small planters seem to have been
among the most bitter critics of the Constitutional embargo against the importation of slaves and were leaders in a movement to reopen the African slave
trade. Agitation for reopening the external slave trade persisted despite widespread doubt concerning the wisdom of pushing the issue because of fear that
it might solidify opinion in the free states against slavery. At a convention held
in Vicksburg in 1859 a resolution was passed to the effect that "All laws, State
or Federal, prohibiting the African slave trade ought to be repealed." The cost
of importing a slave from Africa at this time was estimated at $50, which con-
trasted sharply with the price of $1500 to $2000 for slaves in the internal
market.

[2] For an excellent discussion of the price of slaves and other economic aspects of
slavery, see L. C. Gray, *History of Agriculture in the Southern United States to 1860*
(Washington, D.C.: Carnegie Foundation, 1933), 2 vols.

[3] In connection with small and large slave holders attention should be called to the
"plantation legend." This refers to the fact that, contrary to common opinion, there were
relatively few plantations with large numbers of slaves. The census of 1860 lists only one
plantation with more than a thousand slaves; only 14 with more than 500 slaves; only 88
with more than 300 slaves; only 312 with more than 200 slaves, and fewer than 2300 with
as many as 100 slaves. In 1850 the average number of slaves owned per slave holder was
9.2; and by 1860 this had risen to only 10.2. The "legend" probably stems from the fact
that the best records were kept on larger plantations and consequently historians know more
about them.

2. Price of cotton Whereas the price of slaves went up, the price of cotton went down. Falling prices and rising labor costs exerted a double downward pressure on the rate of return on capital and eliminated profits entirely in some parts of the "Old South." At the opening of the nineteenth century when cotton was just becoming a major crop in the South, the price was 15¢ per pound.[4] It rose during the early years of the century, fell during the embargo and non-intercourse years, and reached a peak at the close of the Napoleonic Wars. In 1817 the average monthly price was 30¢ per pound. By decades the average prices were as follows:

1810's	20¢
1820's	12½¢
1830's	11½¢
1840's	7½¢
1850's	10¢

The most critical decade was the 1840's. The lowest year was 1844, when the price fell to 5½¢ per pound. There was considerable recovery in the 1850's, and during the last half of this decade the average price was 11½¢ per pound. This recovery was sufficient to restore confidence among southerners that "cotton was king."

The downward trend of prices after 1815 and the rising trend after the mid-forties correspond to the trend of the price level in general. Special characteristics of the plantation system, however, made cotton more subject to downward pressures than commodities in general. Slave labor was to the planter a fixed or overhead cost once the slaves were acquired; slaves had to be fed, clothed, and otherwise supported whether they were used or not used in production. Consequently, it was unprofitable to have them idle even when the price of cotton was extremely low. Slave labor was "free" to the planter in the sense that no *additional* labor cost was incurred by having them work in the cotton fields. If the planter had employed wage-laborers, he could have laid them off when the market price for cotton was too low to make a profit after paying wages and other additional costs incurred in actual production. As a slave owner he had paid for his labor all at once and in the face of falling prices had no alternative in the short run but to keep on producing cotton. In the long run he could sell his slaves and retire from planting, but there was a reluctance to give up a well-established way of life.

3. Soil exhaustion under planter capitalism Planter capitalism as a system of cultivation followed the principle of maximum yield per laborer rather than maximum yield per acre. Labor, the scarce and limiting factor of production, was spread over as much land as could be planted, cultivated, and harvested. To the individual planter this combination of factors of production was dictated by the high price of slaves and the relatively low price of land; for the economy as a whole it was the economical way to combine in

---

[4] The price referred to is that of short staple cotton at New Orleans for the cotton year, which runs from September to August. The figures are from L. C. Gray, *History of Agriculture in the Southern United States to 1860,* II, 696–700, 1027.

optimum proportions scarce labor and abundant land. Maximum yield per laborer was pursued mainly by gaining access to more fertile land on which the output per worker would be higher. Another way to raise the productivity of labor would have been to introduce laborsaving machinery, the method so prominently featured in northern agriculture. Although technical progress was by no means absent in cotton cultivation, the possibilities of employing labor-saving machinery were limited by the lack of individual responsibility on the part of slaves and the gang system of cultivation. Moreover, a chief bottleneck in cotton production was in harvesting, and satisfactory cotton-picking machines were intrinsically difficult to devise, so hard in fact that no workable solution was found until the end of the first quarter of the twentieth century.

In considering the number of acres of cotton a field hand could cultivate, account must be taken of the general practice of having slaves raise their own subsistence. Corn, which provided the chief basis of subsistence, was consumed directly in the form of corn bread and indirectly in the form of pork, especially bacon. When slaves worked in the corn field they were in a sense working for themselves and their families. Time devoted to growing cotton was time at the disposal of their masters. Corn was the subsistence crop; cotton was the cash crop. About six acres in corn per field hand were needed for subsistence of slaves and work stock, but the acreage was smaller where the soil was more fertile and larger where it was less fertile. A double advantage of more fertile soil was that it permitted a slave to work less time for himself raising corn and more time for his master raising cotton. This advantage was reflected in a higher rate of return on capital invested in the rich, alluvial land of the Southwest. In addition to six acres of corn, ten acres of cotton per hand could be grown on level, stumpless land. In hilly, stumpy country the areas in cotton might be as little as three acres per field hand. In some areas of the South corn could be purchased more cheaply than it could be raised, in the sense that it proved more profitable to have slaves devote full time to growing the cash crop (cotton) and using some of the proceeds from the sale of cotton to purchase corn and bacon. In this circumstance as much as twenty acres per hand might be cultivated in cotton.

Cotton cultivation as practiced in the South quickly exhausted the soil. Conditions such as poor plowing, lack of capital for fertilizer, and ignorance contributed to soil exhaustion, but the basic cause of exploitative methods was the relative abundance of land and the scarcity of labor. Crop rotation for restoring exhausted elements to the soil was not feasible under the one-crop system. Successive plantings of the same crop reduced the annual yields to a point where scarce labor could be more profitably applied to fresh lands; consequently, from South Carolina and Georgia the center of cotton planting moved westward to Alabama, Mississippi, Louisiana, Arkansas, and Texas. Yields per acre and per slave were greater on the fertile, alluvial soils of the West than they had ever been in the East. As masters and slaves emigrated to the West, they left the older regions in a state of protracted stagnation. Slavery and the plantation system first destroyed its competitors, the independent farmers, and then sapped the economic strength of the region over which it passed like a scourge. In vampire fashion it sucked life from the soil and moved on to afflict new victims with its curse.

4. Dependence on outside credit Dependence on outside credit was another characteristic of planter capitalism. This was a corollary of the South's position as a debtor region, which in turn followed from the pressing need for capital to finance rapid expansion of the plantation system and from the immaturity of southern financial and banking institutions. In this respect the position of the American West was similar to that of the South. Both sections were dependent upon the Northeast for credit and consequently were heavily in debt to that area. The entire United States was a debtor nation relying heavily on European capital for financing rapid expansion and the movement of exports and imports. Within the United States by 1860 financial institutions were most highly developed in New York City, which became the focal point for mobilizing domestic and foreign capital for use in agriculture, commerce, and industry. Like typical debtors, the southerners and westerners felt that interest and other financial charges of New York bankers and middlemen were excessive, a complaint not without justification.

Since colonial times, agents known as factors had been important middlemen between agricultural producers and English importers. In the period after independence the cotton factors acted as selling agents for planters in disposing of their cotton and also served as bankers for planters. Factors advanced both long-term and short-term loans. Long-term loans for purchase of land and slaves were an important basis for expansion of the plantation system before the Civil War. These long-term loans were secured by mortgages on land and slaves. Short-term loans for the purchase of supplies were secured by the planter's crops.

The factor-planter credit system was subject to abuses. Conditions which the factor, as creditor, imposed to protect his interests were frequently disadvantageous to the planter. Interest rates were high, ranging from 8 to 12½ per cent per year. Short-term loans to planters usually took the form of purchases of supplies on credit through or from the factor. In the one case the factor charged a commission for his services as purchasing agent, and in the other case the prices paid for credit-purchases were higher than cash prices. The difference between credit and cash prices represented hidden interest paid to the factor by the planter because of the latter's debtor status. A factor who furnished credit was given the exclusive right to sell the borrowing planter's entire cotton crop. Under this arrangement the money income of the planter flowed through the hands of his creditor (factor), who deducted what was owed to him and paid the planter only the remaining balance, if any.

By another typical arrangement the factor protected the amount of his commissions as selling agent. As a condition of receiving loans the planter contracted not only to sell his entire crop through the factor but also guaranteed a minimum number of bales of cotton, with the further stipulation that the factor would receive a commission on at least the minimum number even if a smaller number were delivered. These financial provisions, in addition to tying planters to particular factors, tended to bind them to the one-crop system of cotton production. As a result of their debtor status, planters were under strong pressure to sell their crops quickly in order to liquidate their debts. With most planters in a similar position the market price at the time of sale tended to be unfavorable to the planter. Factors also paid freight, drayage, storage, insurance and other handling charges for planters, who in turn were supposed to

be billed at cost. In fact, many of these charges assumed conventional values and became a source of profit to factors and of irritation to planters.

While the factor was the local banker for the planter, he was only the first of several links in a long chain of credit relations extending from the cotton fields of the South to the textile factories of Europe and New England. Planters sold their cotton through factors to the southern representatives of English and northern buyers. In payment the planter received a draft or bill payable in two to four months in New York. The planter discounted (sold) his draft or bill with a southern bank or merchant, who sent the bill or draft to New York to pay for manufactured goods bought from northern merchants. Southern merchants, who bought both domestic and imported goods in northern cities, were short on liquid capital and usually bought their merchandise on long credits (12 to 18 months) extended to them by northern merchants. For this credit they naturally paid interest. In international trade northern merchants and importers were typically in debt to English merchants and banking houses, such as the famous Baring Brothers. What southerners resented in this arrangement was the payment of interest and commissions to New York houses engaged in financing the export of cotton.

Resentment was heightened by financial crises which interrupted the flow of credit in one direction and therefore the flow of goods in the other. During the crisis of 1857, for example, the New York money market was so strained that southern planters could not discount their drafts and bills except at heavy losses to themselves. The prices received for exported cotton fell drastically because of the collapse in the New York money market and the unfavorable exchange rates associated with the panic.

This panic resulted mainly from speculative overexpansion in the West, but the impact fell heavily on innocent victims in the South. Quite naturally such experiences strengthened the belief that direct trade and direct financial relations with Europe would relieve the South of this type of pressure. The New York bottleneck would be broken. Economic vassalage to northern bankers and merchants would be eliminated. Separation from the Union was looked upon as one way, perhaps the best way, to achieve financial independence.

5. Lack of direct trade   In buying imports as well as in selling exports the South suffered a disadvantage. There was little direct trade between Europe and the South. Southern imports from Europe came by way of North Atlantic ports, especially New York, which in the decades before 1860 became the great entrepôt of American commerce. Contributing to the rise of New York as the nation's greatest port were many influences including a fine harbor, the Erie Canal hinterland, and enterprising merchants. In 1860 when cotton constituted two-thirds of the total national exports, New York handled more than two-thirds of total imports. Boston, Philadelphia, and Baltimore led any southern port in terms of shares of total imports.

Imports coming from Europe to New York were redistributed to southern ports; thus Charleston, Savannah, Mobile, and New Orleans received most of their imports as part of the coastwise trade from North Atlantic ports. Goods manufactured in the North as well as those imported from Europe were taken south in northern ships, financed by northern bankers, and dis-

tributed by northern middlemen. New York's import business was aided by the shipment of cotton from southern ports to New York, where it provided an important part of the return cargo to Europe. Much cotton was also shipped directly from southern ports to Europe, but even in these circumstances the return voyage was to a northern port, where freight and immigrants were unloaded. Completion of the "cotton triangle" to southern ports was made with relatively light cargo.

Southerners viewed the dependence on New York for indirect import trade as a major source of regional exploitation. They felt that goods which were imported in exchange for cotton exports should come directly from Europe to the South; costs and prices would be lower and the profits would accrue to southern merchants and middlemen rather than to New York Yankees. Undoubtedly direct trade would have benefited the South, especially if tariffs on imports had been eliminated as proposed by free-trade southerners.

Unfortunately for the South the lack of direct trade was related to its underlying economic weaknesses, especially to its rural structure and its undeveloped financial institutions. In the absence of adequate credit facilities, trade is difficult to attract. Moreover, without trade, credit facilities are difficult to develop—a vicious circle which confronts all underdeveloped regions. There was a strong inclination to blame the federal government and to look for a political solution to this essentially economic problem. By 1860, on the questions of direct trade as well as on the other economic problems, southerners were becoming convinced that political independence would divert the bulk of imports directly to southern ports, bypassing northern merchants, bankers, and brokers who were growing rich at the expense of the South. At the numerous commercial conventions, direct trade with Europe was one of the main planks in the southern program.

6. Inability to diversify Pressures on planter capitalism have been shown to have arisen in connection with the high price of slaves, low and fluctuating prices of cotton, soil exhaustion, financial dependence, and lack of direct trade with Europe. The crisis associated with these pressures was long term in nature. Conditions were at their worst during the 1840's because of the very low price of cotton. Pressure was eased by higher prices in the 1850's. The crisis was much worse in the eastern than in the western states of the South.

As with all human relations, the course of economic development does not run smoothly all the time. Western competition was keenly felt by agriculture in the North Atlantic as well as in the South Atlantic states. Ohio soil was more fertile than New England soil had ever been, just as Mississippi delta soil was more fertile than that of South Carolina. But the reaction and adjustment in the North Atlantic states to these geographical factors were fundamentally different than in the South Atlantic states. Although New England's agriculture was depressed by western competition, New England's economy was not depressed because it began quickly to transform itself from a rural to an urban and from an agricultural to an industrial society. Whereas western competition stimulated economic development in the North Atlantic states, it resulted in protracted stagnation for the economy of the South Atlantic

states. The economic inferiority of the South as a whole before the Civil War arose from its inability to adapt to changing circumstances.[5]

Slavery was the root cause of the inability of the southern economy to diversify. Raw materials (especially cotton) were available, and water power as well as coal and iron ore were at hand. The barrier to diversification in general and to industrialization in particular was the labor supply. Although slave labor on plantations was efficient in raising cotton, it was not a system which could be adapted easily to other types of economic activity. Moreover, the existence of slavery was a barrier to the formation of a free labor supply, and sentiment in the South for abolition was negligible.

American slaves were not well suited to factory or other forms of industrial employment as practiced in the nineteenth century. They were unskilled and illiterate, not because of any inherent incapacity as people but because the whites in the South did not think it a good idea for slaves to be educated. In five states there were laws against teaching Negroes to read, and where there were no statutory prohibitions, traditional prejudice against Negro education was strong. Thus, so long as it lasted, slavery doomed the human resources of the South to perpetual underdevelopment and compounded the economic inferiority of the region. Little use could be made of slaves except as field hands, as menial servants, and in lumber camps. In a few instances they were used in factories, but this practice showed little promise of developing into a factory system.

Even if it had been otherwise feasible to employ slaves in factories, it would not have been economically desirable in any significant number because slaves were too scarce and too valuable to be used except in agriculture as long as an abundant supply of fertile soil remained. Westward expansion continued to make available rich, virgin land for cotton. Slaves and masters migrated westward leaving eastern areas in a state of depression. Diversification within agriculture was also limited because slave labor was more efficient working as field hands in large gangs under overseers.

Free wage-labor was lacking in the South because immigrants avoided the South and because poor white farmers in the South either migrated westward or were unresponsive to the labor market. To Europeans, slavery was morally degrading and they wanted no part of it. Irish and German immigrants who poured into northern ports in the 1840's and 1850's either remained in the East as factory operatives or went west to take up independent farming. A large stream of European immigrants would hardly have been welcomed in the South because their hostility to slavery would have threatened the existing order. Climate also influenced Europeans to avoid the South.

The numerous class of southerners who were neither planters nor slaves

[5] Alfred H. Conrad and John R. Meyer, in an interesting study in econometric history in which the main theme is that slavery in the South was profitable, contend that slavery was an economically viable institution. They cite a few cases in which slaves were used in nonagricultural employments. It is highly implausible, however, that a society in which the labor force could not read, and in which there were laws against teaching slaves to read, could develop into a modern industrial society. See *The Economics of Slavery* (Chicago: Aldine Publishing Co., 1964), esp. pp. 80, 83, 224, 231. For an account of what happened to slavery in industry and other urban pursuits, see Richard C. Wade, *Slavery in the Cities, The South 1820–1860* (New York: Oxford University Press, 1964). Professor Wade's theme is that "By 1860 slavery was disintegrating in Southern cities . . . wherever it touched urban conditions it was in deep trouble." (p. 3)

were not attracted to the wage-labor market. Small farmers found difficulty competing with the large plantations. As one writer has said: "Slavery eats out the life of free yeomenry." (Gray) Small farmers migrated westward or into the back country where they carried on self-sufficient farming. As a class they were stubbornly independent with a proud arrogance equalled only by the servility of slaves. Although great numbers of poorer whites lived in abject poverty, they were unresponsive to the demands of the labor market. As in slave societies generally, an odium was attached to labor for hire and a strong impetus would have been needed to cause the poorer whites to give up their poverty-stricken independence to enter the employment of others. So long as the South could neither attract a substantial force of wage-laborers from outside nor generate it from within, an essential requisite for economic diversification was absent.

The lack of capital as well as the shortage of labor was an obstacle to economic diversification in the South. The capacity for capital accumulation was small, and the institutional arrangements for mobilizing capital were inadequate. Planters strained to get enough capital for agriculture, which, despite its depressed condition over wide areas, was the most profitable outlet for new investment.

Only in a few ports were indigenous mercantile and financial institutions beginning to develop strength by 1860. The railways of the 1850's dissolved some of the rural isolation, but the potentialities of railway building were limited in the absence of prospects for industrial growth. The volume of traffic would be too small in a purely agricultural economy to justify a network of rail lines. Moreover, railways were themselves great absorbers of capital. Subsidies and direct construction by state governments helped to allay the shortage of capital for railways, but scattered lines rather than a network of railways were built. Capital accumulation was further limited in the South because part of the social surplus was drained into luxury consumption by the wealthy, aristocratic planters. Unlike the Puritan capitalists of the North, the wealthy class of the South was not noted for frugality. The inability of the southern economy to generate its own capital was, of course, the reason why its indebtedness to outside areas continually increased.

Slavery was at once the strength and the weakness of the South: the strength because the overwhelmingly important cotton crop was produced largely by slave labor; the weakness because the socio-economic rigidities resulting from slavery precluded adaptation to new methods and new types of economic activity which were essential for economic progress. With its human resources underdeveloped the South could not hope to match the accumulation of wealth that was taking place in the North. The South could neither get along with slavery nor could it afford to get rid of it. This was the dilemma about 1860.

Of the eight million whites in the South in 1860, fewer than 400,000, or less than 5 per cent, owned slaves. However, this minority constituted the ruling class, and for political as well as social and economic reasons it was not in their interest to abolish slavery. Political and social domination rested on the ownership of plantations. Freeing the slaves would have left the plantations without labor, and without labor to work them the great estates would have lost their value as plantations. Social ostentation also influenced the

desire to retain the plantation system. Slaves were valuable property in a monetary sense, but they were in addition necessary for preserving the institutions in which the privileges of the ruling classes were involved.

Although the non-slave-owning whites had no direct economic interest in the preservation of slavery, they were hardly less opposed to its abolition than the slave owners. Poor whites feared the consequences to themselves as small farmers and as wage-earners of the potential economic competition of four million freed slaves. Hence, in the foreseeable future there was little to indicate that slavery would disappear as a result of forces operating within the South. Yet in the long sweep of history this system based on institutions that were morally repugnant, economically static, and politically aristocratic could not stand against the forces unleashed by the Industrial Revolution. Man's love of freedom in Western civilization, the dynamics of machine technology, and the pressures toward democratic equalitarianism would in due time override the unfree, static, and aristocratic institutions of the South. Being unable to face the hopeless dilemma presented by slavery, southern leaders attributed their growing economic inferiority to political abuses of the federal system rather than to weaknesses inherent in their own culture.

EFFECT OF CIVIL WAR ON INDUSTRY

The differing responses of the North and the South to the economic requirements of the Civil War followed from their economic characteristics on the eve of the struggle. In the North, where the basis for large-scale output had been prepared over several decades, the response was in terms of meeting the economic needs of war by mass production techniques. In the South, where specialization had been in large-scale agriculture and industrial needs before the war had been met by importing, the response was in terms of attempting to stimulate a primitive type of domestic industry. The dissimilar responses of the North and South were analogous to those of Germany and France, respectively, in the Franco-Prussian War of 1870–71. Prussia easily outstripped France in war production and won an easy military victory in eighteen months. France was, of course, much further advanced than the American South and in some respects even further advanced than Prussia, but French emphasis on artistic production based on handicraft was not adaptable to large-scale war production. Prussian industrial production, which had been more like that of the North, made an easy transition to large-scale war production. Perhaps a closer analogy to the plight of the South can be found in the case of Austria, which also suffered defeat on the battlefield in the Seven Weeks War against Prussia in 1866. The experience of the American South, of France, and of Austria gave conclusive evidence that weakness in industry meant weakness in war. The day had passed when gallant knights in shining armor could turn the tide of military battle with heroic feats of personal valor.

In view of the North's great industrial superiority, the military strength and tenacity of the South may seem surprising. The four long years required to crush the armies of the South reflect another characteristic of the industrial society which was coming of age in the North. Except for small-arms production, northern industry had been developed with no concern for military out-

put. Much time elapsed, therefore, before industry could be converted from civilian to military production. Once tooling up for war production was completed, however, final products poured out in a flood tide, and superiority in the factory was translated into victories on the battlefield. Prussia's lightning war against Austria in seven weeks in 1866 and Prussia's quick victory over France in eighteen months in 1870–71 reflected a military orientation of Prussian industry prior to the declaration of war. Prussia's military orientation of industry in turn reflected the dynastic, warlike character of a society which only recently had emerged from feudalism. In contrast, the American North lacked the military propensities of dynastic Prussia. Although the ultimate military potential of the North was very great, much time was required to bring this potential to the battlefield. Time was the North's best ally. After Gettysburg (1863) the outcome became merely a question of how long the South could withstand the superior military-industrial power of the North.

Northern industries stimulated by war demands included woolen textiles, shoe and boot manufacture, iron, and farm machinery. Woolen textile mills operated around the clock to turn out the cloth for soldiers' uniforms and army blankets for the Union forces, although cotton textile output declined sharply during the war because of shortages of raw cotton from the South. The recently invented sewing machine was utilized to produce ready-made civilian clothing as well as military uniforms, and was also adapted to shoe manufacture. Traditionally shoes were produced by artisan shoemakers on a handicraft, putting-out basis, but a few years before the Civil War the sewing machine was adapted to sewing soles to shoe tops, and under the stimulus of standardized military purchasing, shoe manufacturing became a mass production industry. In iron production the wartime increases in total output were modest, but the war stimulated the transition from charcoal to coke as a result of centralization and integration in a few centers in western and eastern Pennsylvania. In response to a growing shortage of farm labor, the demand for farm machinery increased dramatically. A greater number of harvesters were produced during the Civil War than during the thirty years since the invention of the harvester.

Despite these examples of sensational increases, the Civil War was a major disrupting influence to American life and retarded perhaps as many economic activities as it stimulated. It was not a total war in the sense of either World War I or World War II and did not have a comparably exhilarating influence on the economy.

Southern industry during the war   Although the South felt the need for industrial production as much as did the North, it responded in a quite different manner. Instead of catapulting forward into methods of mass production, there was a reversion to the domestic system to meet many needs. A few factories, of course, did exist in the South before the war and more factories were built during the war, but with the tight blockade imposed by northern ships, the usual sources of outside manufactures were not available, and even normal needs could not be met. Moreover, the South lacked machinery to install in factories, it lacked mechanics to build machines, and it lacked facilities for training mechanics. Heroic efforts were put forth in the South to make

up for deficiencies, but hand looms and spinning wheels operating in homes could not hope to compete with the tireless efficiency of power-driven machinery operating in rationalized factories in the North.

ECONOMIC SIGNIFICANCE OF THE CIVIL WAR

In the long-term economic development of the United States the Civil War marks the critical phase in the transition from the dominance of commercial capitalism to the dominance of industrial capitalism. Such a transition formed part of the normal process of capitalist evolution and was not peculiar to the American scene. Its British counterpart, for example, lay in the struggle between the landlords and factory owners in the years from 1815 to 1846, with the turning point toward industrialism coming with the Great Reform Bill of 1832. Behind the Great Reform Bill lay the English Industrial Revolution, which had brought into existence a class of wealthy industrialists and a numerous class of urban factory workers. The Napoleonic Wars delayed the struggle between landlords and factory owners, but it broke into the open after 1815 and was the leading issue in British politics during the first half of the nineteenth century. Behind the American Civil War lay the development, during the early nineteenth century, of industries which likewise created a class of wealthy industrialists and a numerous class of urban wage-earners. These new classes in both countries aspired to political power more nearly proportionate to their wealth and to their numbers. Both the British Reform Bill and the Civil War broke the political power of a landed aristocracy whose general position had been undermined by the increased importance of industrial wealth in relation to large landed property. In both countries the landed aristocracy sought to retain political power for its own sake as well as to bolster its waning economic power. The British and American aristocracy fought passionately to preserve the institutions with which their privileges were associated. Finally, the landed aristocracy was overwhelmed by the economic power of the industrial capitalists and by the force of numbers of the working class. In both countries the defeat of the landed aristocracy was accompanied by an extension of political democracy, and in both countries these events brought to a close an early phase of capitalism and signalled the beginning of a new phase, dominated by industrialism in both economics and politics.

There were, of course, important differences between the American and the British transition from predominantly commercial to predominantly industrial capitalism. In Britain the political revolution of 1832 took place peacefully through Parliament reforming itself. This reform did not come easily, and at times England teetered on the brink of violent flare-up. In the United States the transition was marked by bloodshed. The American situation was peculiar because political-economic conflict was also a sectional and constitutional issue further aggravated by the slavery question. Even the specific economic issues were different in the two countries.

Free trade versus protection was an important economic issue in both cases, but in Great Britain the industrialists favored free trade and the landlords favored protection, whereas in the United States the industrialists favored

protection and the planters favored free trade. British industrialists and southern planters did not need protective tariffs on the products they produced because of an overwhelming economic superiority over potential competitors in other countries. American industrialists and British landlords did need protection because they were at an economic disadvantage in free international competition. In the United States free farmers of the North and West joined forces with the industrial capitalists and wage-earners, whereas in England the farmer-capitalists were closer to the landlords in demanding protection for agricultural products.

Despite these differences, however, the issue in both countries focused on growing industrialism as the basis for a shift in the balance of economic and political power. As surely as the industrialists gained the upper hand in wealth and property, so was their economic superiority translated sooner or later into political power. If the powerful landed aristocracy in the United States had been geographically interspersed with the industrial regions, as in Great Britain, military violence might have been avoided. The military struggle was one aspect of the underlying political-economic transition. The political-economic struggle, not the armed conflict, was "irrepressible" and the victory of industrialism was in a sense "inevitable" in the forward march of economic evolution.

Carrying Out the North's Program

The ascendancy of American industrialism took the concrete form of a program which was put into action during and after the Civil War. Political measures were closely linked with this program because its implementation required control by the federal government. A new political party, the Republican Party, sympathetic to industrial capitalism, was formed in 1856 and won its first presidential election in 1860. From 1860 to 1912 it remained in power in all but eight years. Judged by their economic consequences the following measures taken during and after the Civil War contributed to the ascendancy of industrial capitalism in the United States: (1) the abolition of slavery, (2) high protective tariffs, (3) large-scale immigration, (4) transcontinental railways, and (5) the Homestead Law.

1. Abolition of slavery The abolition of slavery dealt a fatal blow to planter capitalism, which was the chief obstacle to the full development of American industrialism. Slavery was the most hotly debated issue and the source of greatest emotional antagonism between the North and South. In 1860 when the Republican majority still hoped to avoid an open break with the South, it confined its platform to the assertion that "the normal condition of all the territory of the United States is that of freedom." The Republicans demanded only that slavery not spread to new territory and to newly admitted states. After the start of open hostility and especially after the Emancipation Proclamation of 1863, the Republicans actively opposed slavery. Their platform of 1864 stated: "Slavery was the cause, and now constitutes the strength, of the rebellion. [We] . . . demand its utter and complete extirpation. . . ."

Opposition to slavery was moral and ideological as well as economic.

Industrial wage-earners in the North were probably more strongly opposed to slavery than were their employers. Some influential northern industrialists did not oppose slavery; the Boston Associates, for example, were sympathetic to the South and to slavery during the 1830's and 1840's. But the general incompatibility of industrial capitalism and slavery is illustrated by the British experience. Slavery was abolished in the British Empire in the year following passage of the Great Reform Bill of 1832. No great modern industrial nation has ever been built with slave labor.

2. Protectionism   High tariffs were imposed during the Civil War and retained after the war. During the war fiscal needs led to a sharp increase in excise taxes on domestic products and, to offset these internal taxes and thus ensure that the level of customs protection would not be reduced, increased duties were also imposed on imported products. The general tariff duty rose from 20 per cent in 1860 to 47 per cent at the end of the war.

After the war the excise taxes were largely eliminated, but the higher import duties were largely retained. Consequently domestic manufacturing automatically received stronger protection against foreign competition. A reduction of 10 per cent in import duties passed in 1872 lasted only three years. Protective walls were raised still higher by the tariff laws of 1890 and 1897. By the latter tariff the average duty rose to 57 per cent and the degree of protection became the highest in the nation's history up to that time.

Meanwhile the tariff became a strong political issue between the Republican and Democratic Parties. The issue, however, was not between free trade and protection, but between high tariffs favored by the Democrats and very high tariffs favored by the Republicans. Democratic President Cleveland in his tariff message of 1887 stated: "The question of free trade is absolutely irrelevant, and the persistent claim made in certain quarters that all the efforts to relieve the people from unjust and unnecessary taxation are schemes of so-called free traders is mischievous and far removed from any consideration for the public good . . ." The Republican platform of 1896 contained the following plank: "The ruling and uncompromising principle is the protection and development of American labor and industries." Thus did the devotion to protection of American industry dominate the economic thinking of both major political parties after the Civil War.

3. Immigration   Since colonial times a scarcity of labor had been a handicap to industry in America. Under slavery the South was unattractive to immigrants, who, though poor, were free and had no desire to work in competition with slaves. Opposition to immigration was sufficient to cause Republicans to include a plank in the 1860 Platform against liberalization of naturalization and immigration laws. The platform of 1864 was more favorable to immigration: "Resolved that foreign immigration, which in the past has added so much to the wealth, development of resources, and increase of power to this nation, the asylum of the oppressed of all nations, should be fostered and encouraged by a liberal and just policy." Between 1860 and 1890 more than ten million immigrants came to the United States, and between 1895 and 1915 the rate was more than a million per year. Both President Taft (Republican) and President Wilson (Democrat) vetoed laws providing literacy tests for immi-

grants. Taft forwarded as part of his veto message a statement from his Secretary of Commerce which read as follows: "The measure . . . is defended purely upon the ground of practical policy, the final purpose being to reduce the quantity of cheap labor in this country. I can not accept this argument. . . . We need labor in this country, and the natives are unwilling to do the work which the aliens come over to do."

An important effect of large-scale immigration was to retard the growth of a strong movement of organized labor in the United States. Immigrants were accustomed to lower wages than native-born workers and saw less need for unions as a weapon for raising wages. Membership in early American labor unions was confined mainly to native-born, skilled workers. Related to immigration also was the system of contracting for foreign labor for projects like the construction of western railways. Chinese were widely used for this purpose.

4. Transcontinental railways Before the Civil War both Democrats and Republicans favored a transcontinental railway, but differences of opinion concerning its location prevented federal chartering of such a project. With southern opposition out of the way during the war, a charter granted by the Union government in 1862 authorized the Union Pacific–Central Pacific line, and a second charter granted in 1864 authorized the Northern Pacific line. The Union Pacific was to extend west from Omaha to join the Central Pacific, which was to be built east from the San Francisco area. The Northern Pacific was to be constructed from Lake Superior to the Pacific Northwest. Rights-of-way were guaranteed to these companies and lavish land grants made to them.

In 1869 the first transcontinental railway was completed when the Union Pacific and the Central Pacific met at Promontory, Utah. Eastern industries now had access to markets across the continent and were able to draw raw materials from the same vast area. The drain of labor from East to West was a disadvantage, but the advantages of the continental market more than offset the disadvantages. A coast-to-coast telegraph line spanned the country as early as 1862, and with the completion of coast-to-coast railways the grand design of welding a continent together with rapid and inexpensive transportation and communication had at last been realized.

5. Homestead Law Another important factor in opening the West was the Homestead Law of 1862.[6] Such a law had been promised by the Republicans in their platform of 1860. Its advocacy and enactment were motivated by a desire to bind westerners into a loyal union with the East. Cheap land had been one of the chief needs for expanding cotton cultivation before the Civil War, but this had to be in large tracts in states which permitted slavery. Clearly, the free grant of homesteads limited to 160 acres was made in response to the demands of free farmers and not of slave owners. As in the case of transcontinental railways, there was a potential danger that the labor supply in the East would be drained off by the Homestead Law, but the actual consequences of the free land legislation were more favorable than unfavorable to the development of American industrialism.

[6] See Chapter 13.

**THE UNITED STATES TAKES WORLD
INDUSTRIAL LEADERSHIP**

355

PLANTER
VS.
INDUSTRIAL
CAPITALISM

Statistics tell the story of the industrialization of the United States more clearly than mere words. Rising ratios of urban to rural population, nonagricultural to agricultural workers, and value of manufacturing to value of agricultural output all indicated a strong trend toward urbanization and industrialization in the post-Civil War period. Half a century before the urban population exceeded the rural population in absolute numbers, the decennial addition to urban population exceeded the decennial addition to the rural population. This began in the decade of the 1860's and after a temporary relapse in the 1870's, caused in part by the Long Depression, urban population increased more than rural population in every subsequent decade. The figures, beginning with the 1840's, are shown in Table 19–1.

TABLE 19–1

Changes in U.S. Rural-Urban Population Increments by Decades, 1840's to 1940's
(in millions of persons)

DECADE	ADDITION TO URBAN	ADDITION TO RURAL	DECADE	ADDITION TO URBAN	ADDITION TO RURAL
1840's	1.7	4.4	1900's	11.8	4.1
1850's	2.7	5.6	1910's	12.2	1.6
1860's	3.7	3.4	1920's	14.8	2.3
1870's	4.2	7.8	1930's	5.5	3.4
1880's	8.0	4.8	1940's	14.5	4.5
1890's	8.1	5.0			

Source: U. S. Bureau of the Census, *Historical Statistics of the United States, Colonial Times to 1957* (Washington, D.C., 1960), p. 14.

Division of the labor force between agricultural and nonagricultural pursuits is another index of the trend away from farming toward industrial activity. The percentage of gainfully employed persons in nonagricultural pursuits exceeded those in agricultural pursuits for the first time in the late 1870's. Between 1860 and 1910 the percentage of the labor force engaged in agriculture fell from approximately 60 to approximately 30 per cent. This change is illustrated in Figure 19–1.

Additions to the nonagricultural labor force exceeded additions to the agricultural labor force for the first time in the 1850's, and the increment to the former was five times as great by 1900.

The average annual value of *manufacturing* alone exceeded that of agriculture for the first time during the decade of the 1880's, and by the decade following the First World War the annual value of manufacturing was more than double that of agriculture. Manufacturing as a percentage of total na-

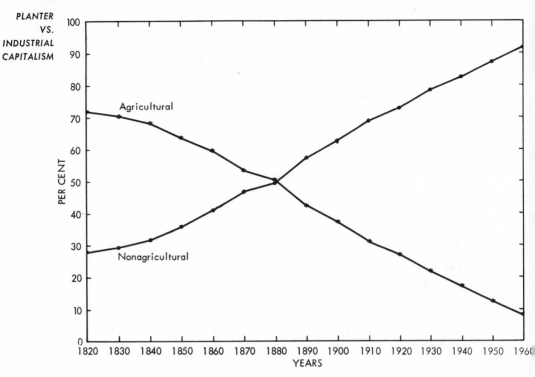

Figure 19–1. Agricultural and Nonagricultural Labor
Force in the U.S. 1820–1960.

tional product began to decline during the 1920's, indicating a still higher
stage of development in the American economy (Colin Clark). This tertiary
stage of economic development is characterized by a greater stress on services
than on physical product of the agricultural and manufactured type.

The general growth in manufacturing between 1859 and 1954 is shown
in Table 19–2 from the Census of Manufacturing.

Perhaps the best index of increase in manufacturing is the data on value
added in the last column of Table 19–2. This value increased seven-fold from
the eve of the Civil War to the end of the nineteenth century, and seven-fold
again during the first three decades of the twentieth century.

These statistical indicators support the proposition that the Civil War
marked the turning point from an agricultural to an industrial society. Before
1860 the United States was predominantly agricultural. Within a few decades
after the Civil War industrialism was in the saddle. When used in international comparisons the statistics also show that the United States outstripped
every other nation in industrial production during these same decades. A British century ended in 1900, and an American century began in 1901.

Some Leading Manufacturing Industries

Textiles   Cotton cloth resumed the leadership in textiles which was
temporarily lost during the Civil War. The bales of cotton consumed in Amer-

TABLE 19–2

357

PLANTER
VS.
INDUSTRIAL
CAPITALISM

Growth of Manufacturing in the United States, 1859–1954

	NUMBER OF ESTABLISHMENTS	NUMBER OF WAGE-EARNERS	VALUE ADDED BY MANUFACTURE ($1,000)
1849	123,025	957,059	463,983
1859	140,433	1,311,246	854,257
1869	252,148	2,053,996	1,395,119
1879	253,852	2,732,595	1,972,756
1889	353,864	4,129,355	4,102,301
1899	509,490	5,097,562	5,474,892
1899*	204,754	4,501,919	4,646,981
1909	264,810	6,261,736	8,160,075
1919	270,231	8,464,916	23,841,624
1929	206,663	8,369,705	30,591,435
1939	173,802	7,808,205	24,487,304
1947	240,807	11,917,884	74,290,475
1954	286,817	12,373,030	116,912,526

* Figures before 1899 include hand and neighborhood industries as well as factories; data after 1899 exclude hand and neighborhood industries.
Source: U. S. Bureau of the Census, *Historical Statistics of the United States* (Washington, D.C. 1960), p. 409.

ican cotton mills increased seven-fold from 1860 to 1914. Despite this large absolute increase, cotton cloth fell in rank, measured by value of product, from second place among all American industries in 1860 to sixth place in 1914. Woolen textiles increased in absolute terms but declined relative to cotton textiles after the Civil War. Scarcity of domestic raw wool was a handicap. During this period several important American inventions were made in cotton textile technology. The ring spinner and the Northrop loom, for example, increased the output per worker and were therefore especially adapted to the historic American need to economize in the use of scarce labor. American woolen manufacturers were less progressive in inventing new techniques and were able to compete with superior British woolens and worsteds only behind the high walls of the protective tariff.

Regional shifts occurred in the cotton textile industry, away from New England toward the South, after 1880. Nearness to raw material, low wages, and abundant water and hydroelectric power enabled the southern states to assume the lead in textile manufacture by 1920. The ring spindle and the Northrop loom facilitated the growth of textile manufacture in the South by enabling relatively unskilled workers to operate machinery of increasing productiveness.

New England suffered in the short run from the out-migration of textile manufacturing. However, the resiliency which had marked its earlier transformation from agriculture to textiles enabled the area to shift to other and higher forms of industry, such as machine tools, watches, clocks, and similar

precision products, which required well-educated and highly skilled workers. Not least important in the adaptability of New England's economy was an excellent system of general education plus technical high schools, especially in Connecticut, which consistently ranked near the top among the states in per capita income.

Food processing Measured by value of product, food processing continued to hold first place in American manufacturing through 1914. Meat packing, flour milling, canning, and baking were carried on less and less by individual families in small villages and more and more in slaughterhouses, mills, canneries, and bakeries in medium-sized towns and large cities. Food processing, especially meat packing, became concentrated in the hands of a few large firms. Mechanical refrigeration revolutionized meat packing in the 1870's. From Cincinnati, where it had been concentrated before 1860, meat packing moved west to Chicago, Omaha, St. Louis, Kansas City, and Denver.

Heavy industries Food and clothing are so basic to the life of any community that food processing and textile production are always major economic activities. However, in the more advanced stage of economic development which the United States reached toward the close of the nineteenth century, the heavy industries such as machinery, iron and steel, and chemicals began to supplant food and clothing as the leading industries. Measured in terms of value added by manufacture, the machinery and iron and steel industries ranked higher than food processing and textiles in 1914.

In assessing the importance of industries, the value added by manufacturing is a better index than the value of the final product because the former takes into account only what happens in manufacturing whereas final value of product includes the value of the raw materials with which an industry begins its manufacturing. These raw materials constitute a relatively high percentage of the final value of food processing and textile products, or what is a corollary, the value added in food processing and textiles is a relatively low percentage of the value of the final product. In meat packing, for example, value added is characteristically less than 10 per cent of the gross value of the final product. In the heavy industries value added is characteristically a much higher percentage of the value of the final product. In iron and steel, machinery, and chemicals value added constitutes more than 50 per cent of the total value of the product.[7] The increasing importance of steel, machinery, and chemicals betokens the age of mass production.

Pig iron production may serve as an indicator of American industrial growth during the nineteenth century. Table 15–4 shows no decade before 1860 in which American pig iron production more than doubled, whereas in each of the three decades beginning in 1860 pig iron production in the United States more than doubled. As an index of comparative industrial production among the three leading industrial nations of the later nineteenth century, pig iron production in Table 15–4 [8] shows America's rise to first position. As late as 1880 British iron ore production was more than twice that of the United

---

[7] The ratio of value added to value of product will, of course, vary widely depending on the classification of industries and the degree of integration of those industries.
[8] See Chapter 15, p. 269.

States, but in the decade of the 1880's the United States passed the British and held a comfortable lead in 1890.

FACTORS IN AMERICAN INDUSTRIAL SUPREMACY

Admittedly the performance of the American economy between the Civil War and World War I was phenomenal. For rapidity of development nothing quite like it had ever happened before. The closest approximation was the performance of contemporary Germany between the formation of the Empire in 1871 and the outbreak of the war in 1914. In France industrial development followed a more moderate pace. English industrial development of the eighteenth century was much less rapid because the English were breaking new ground in introducing machine technology to industry. There were up until the end of the nineteenth century no other major industrial nations, although Japan and Italy were beginning to move in that direction. China, India, and Russia were large in population and territory but still lacked the social overhead capital for rapid industrialization.

Since colonial times the level of living in the United States had been the highest in the world. This was clearly a result of the rich endowment of natural resources in the control of an economically advanced people. These same natural resources had brought no comparable result to the American Indians, and lesser resources in the control of the more advanced English economy did not yield as high a level of living as in the colonies of mainland North America. Thus a high level of living was not novel to Americans. Such was the setting and the nature of the American achievement. The question remains why the United States was able to attain world leadership in industrial production so easily and so quickly.

The United States was favorably situated with respect to all factors of production—land, labor, capital, and enterprise. None of the major natural resources required for mechanical industry were lacking. Coal, iron ore, water power, and other raw materials were present in great abundance. Shortage of labor remained the chief disadvantage for manufacturing, but the shortage was partly overcome by a large influx of European immigrants to work in mines, foundries, and factories and by Chinese laborers to construct western railways. More important, however, was the fact that the scarcity of labor provided the stimulus for greater strength. Laborsaving devices, assembly-line techniques, and interchangeable parts were adopted early in flour milling, meat packing, and small-arms manufacture. These characteristics carried over into the post-Civil War era and became the basis of American superiority. They were also widely adopted in other countries.

Capital was not abundant in the United States at any time before the twentieth century, but institutions were devised for borrowing it from abroad, mobilizing it at home, and accumulating it in commerce and industry. Commercial banking was patterned after the superior British system for advancing short-term loans to commerce and industry. Corporations were quickly adapted to industry when the occasion demanded in the second half of the nineteenth century. New York became an important satellite of the London money market in the late nineteenth and early twentieth centuries.

The United States possessed the basis for the social and economic overhead capital requisite for rapid industrial expansion. Government provided the most important social overhead capital through an excellent system of general public education, first at the elementary level, then at the secondary level, and finally at the college level through the land-grant colleges. In any economy investment in human capital is the surest road to economic growth, but the United States invested more to develop this potential than other countries. Government contributed heavily to the economic overhead capital by building roads and canals and subsidizing railroads through land grants; generally speaking, it intervened in economic activity sufficiently to provide what could not be provided by private enterprise but not enough to undermine the belief of businessmen that the economic system was under their command. One of the by-products of the educational, social, and cultural milieu was a large number of small entrepreneurs in every community across the land and a sizable class of large entrepreneurs who became internationally famous for their unbounded energy in pursuit of great fortune and vast enterprise.

However, the superiority of American industry lay not in any single factor, but in a special combination of circumstances involving historical timing, institutional developments, and physical resources. The special circumstances which distinguish the American case and account for its phenomenal performance may be stated as follows: Machine technology of the English Industrial Revolution was available for the rapid exploitation of the fabulously rich natural resources of the American continent, which was welded into a single economy for delivering raw materials and distributing products by a revolutionary new form of transportation, the railway, itself a product of the new technology. The most dynamic, that is, the historically most significant element was technology. This technology gave control over nature, including natural resources and distance. Adaptation of the British technology to labor-scarce America yielded a marvelously efficient system of mass production for a mass market serviced by means of mass transportation. Mass production resulted from adaptation of the new technology to the scarcity of labor and the abundance of raw materials. The mass market was in part a consequence of fortunate political circumstances, which integrated a large geographical territory into a single political unit with a constitution which forbade artificial barriers to commerce such as handicapped Europe and hindered the free flow of trade in much of the world. Mass transportation took the form of a network of railways which drew raw materials into factories and carried the manufactured goods from the factories to the rapidly increasing population. The large population in a rapidly growing economy provided the demand for the things produced by this same population. For the most part, the supply of goods and services created its own demand, and potential deficiencies in demand were taken care of by spending out of incomes arising from the rapid growth. Market demand was limited only by the technical capacity to produce, which brings the analysis back again to the single, most strategic factor, technology.

Something significantly new had been created by the English Industrial Revolution of the late eighteenth century. By the early nineteenth century this technology was available to all who were capable of borrowing and adapting

it. In the United States the best combination of circumstances awaited the utilization of the new technology for the rapid conversion of nature's treasure, hoarded for geologic ages, into a higher level and standard of living than heretofore achieved by any people.

SELECTED BIBLIOGRAPHY

ANDREANO, RALPH, ed., *The Economic Impact of the American Civil War.* Cambridge, Mass.: Schenkman Publishing Co., Inc., 1962.

BEARD, CHARLES A. and MARY R., *The Rise of American Civilization,* Vol. I, Chapters 13–16; Vol. II, Chapters 17–20. New York: The Macmillan Company, 1927.

CAIRNES, JOHN E., *The Slave Power,* 2nd ed. New York: Carleton, 1862.

COMMAGER, HENRY STEELE, ed., *Documents of American History,* 4th ed. 2 vols. New York: Appleton-Century-Crofts, Inc., 1948.

CONRAD, ALFRED H., and JOHN R. MEYER, *The Economics of Slavery and Other Studies in Econometric History.* Chicago: Aldine Publishing Co., 1964.

DORFMAN, JOSEPH, *The Economic Mind in American Civilization,* Vol. II, Book III. New York: The Viking Press, 1946.

FOGEL, ROBERT W., *The Union Pacific: A Case of Premature Enterprise.* Baltimore: The Johns Hopkins University Press, 1960.

GATES, PAUL W., *Agriculture and the Civil War.* New York: Alfred A. Knopf, Inc., 1965.

———, *The Farmer's Age: Agriculture 1815–60.* New York: Holt, Rinehart & Winston, Inc., 1960.

GENOVESE, EUGENE D., *The Political Economy of Slavery, Studies in the Economy and the Society of the Slave South.* New York: Random House, Inc., 1966.

GILCHRIST, D. T., and W. D. LEWIS, eds., *Economic Change in the Civil War Era.* Greenville, Del.: Eleutherian Mills-Hagley Foundation, 1964.

GRAY, LEWIS C., *History of Agriculture in the Southern United States to 1860,* Vol. II. Magnolia, Mass.: Peter Smith, 1958.

HACKER, LOUIS M., *The Triumph of American Capitalism,* Part III. New York: Columbia University Press, 1947.

NORTH, DOUGLASS C., *Growth and Welfare in the American Past,* Chapters 6–8. Englewood Cliffs, N.J.: Prentice-Hall, Inc., 1966.

PHILLIPS, ULRICH B., *American Negro Slavery.* Magnolia, Mass.: Peter Smith, 1959.

———, *Life and Labor in the Old South.* Boston: Little, Brown & Co., 1957.

RAMSDELL, CHARLES, *Behind the Lines in the Southern Confederacy.* Baton Rouge: Louisiana State University Press, 1944.

SMITH, ALFRED G., *Economic Readjustment of an Old Cotton State, South Carolina, 1820–1860.* Columbia, S.C.: University of South Carolina Press, 1958.

STAMPP, KENNETH M., *The Peculiar Institution: Slavery in the Ante-Bellum South.* New York: Alfred A. Knopf, 1956.

TEMIN, PETER, *Iron and Steel in Nineteenth-Century America: An Economic Inquiry.* Cambridge, Mass.: M. I. T. Press, 1964.

UNITED STATES BUREAU OF THE CENSUS, *Historical Statistics of the United States, Colonial Times to 1957.* Washington, D.C.: Government Printing Office, 1960.

WADE, RICHARD C., *Slavery in the Cities, The South 1820–1860.* New York: Oxford University Press, 1964.

BONNER, JAMES C., "Advancing Trends in Southern Agriculture, 1840–1860," *Agricultural History*, XXII (Oct., 1948), 248–59.

COCHRAN, THOMAS C., "Did the Civil War Retard Industrialization?" *Mississippi Valley Historical Review*, XLVIII (Sept., 1961), 197–210.

CONRAD, ALFRED H., and JOHN R. MEYER, "The Economics of Slavery in the Ante-Bellum South," *Journal of Political Economy*, LXVI (April, 1958), 95–130; and LXVI (Oct., 1958), 442–43.

GENOVESE, EUGENE D., "The Significance of the Slave Plantation for Southern Economic Development," *Journal of Southern History*, XXVIII (Nov., 1962), 422–37.

GOVAN, THOMAS P., "Was Plantation Slavery Profitable?" *Journal of Southern History*, VIII (Nov., 1942), 513–35.

PHILLIPS, ULRICH B., "The Economic Cost of Slaveholding in the Cotton Belt," *Political Science Quarterly*, XX (June, 1905), 257–75.

SMITH, ROBERT W., "Was Slavery Unprofitable in the Ante-Bellum South?" *Agricultural History*, XX (Jan., 1946), 62–64.

TEMIN, PETER, "The Composition of Iron and Steel Products, 1869–1909," *Journal of Economic History*, XXIII (Dec., 1963), 447–71.

The Age of Mass Production

CHAPTER 20

Competitive capitalism reached the high point of its development about the middle of the nineteenth century. Repeal of the British Corn Laws in 1846 symbolized the beginning of this golden age of capitalism, and the crisis of 1873, which inaugurated the Long Depression (1873–96), marked the beginning of the end of the golden age. Prior to 1846 the prevailing movement was away from the highly controlled economic life of the middle ages and of mercantilism. The years between 1846 and 1873 most nearly approximate the conditions which were presupposed in the classical theory of the functioning of free market capitalism.

Although competition began to decline after 1873, the free market remained dominant until the First World War. That great holocaust laid bare the nature of the forces which had been at work for several decades to change the economic system of the West. The economic significance of the First World War and the postwar period will be considered in later chapters. This and the immediately succeeding chapters are concerned with the nature of the forces which lay beneath the surface and erupted during and after World War I.

The conscious application of science to industrial technology was the root cause of fundamental changes in the structure and functioning of the North Atlantic economy. Science had played a role in earlier economic changes, such as the English Industrial Revolution of the eighteenth century, but it was now applied systematically on a greatly enlarged scale to existing industries, including iron and textiles, and became the basis of new industries, including chemical and electrical products. The new situation has been described as "the technology of physics and chemistry."[1]

For efficient operation the technology of chemistry and physics required large-scale corporate enterprise, which in turn undermined the conditions necessary for effective price competition of the free market variety. Price competition among large-scale rivals proved mutually destructive to profits, and after a brief period of cutthroat competition, business enterprise turned to cartels, trusts, and other monopolistic forms of organization designed to reduce or eliminate price competition. Working-class groups began to form combinations,

---

[1] For a provocative discussion of science and technology in this period, see Thorstein Veblen, "The Technology of Physics and Chemistry," in *Absentee Ownership* (New York: The Viking Press, 1923), pp. 251–83.

or unions, on an enlarged scale in order to take labor out of the competitive market. Farmers also felt the impact of mass production, even though the application of large-scale production was less notable in agriculture. Farmers were more the victims than the active agents in the destruction of the free market, except insofar as they exerted political pressures for tariff protection on agricultural products (France and Germany) or for price and income supports under government subsidy (the United States). Businessmen, wage-earners, and farmers became the mutual victims of the free market economy under conditions of mass production; and in reacting against their plight they became the mutual destroyers of the free-market system.

TECHNOLOGY OF MASS PRODUCTION

Large-scale production and organization sprang from two related developments. (1) Advances in technology as such, which increased the size of the technologically most efficient plant, and (2) growth in the extent of the market, associated especially with revolutionary changes in transportation and communication. Since changes in technology, especially the steam engine and cheap steel, were primarily responsible for the transportation revolution, it is reasonable to attribute the development of large-scale production in the late nineteenth century to technological changes, which rested upon advances in science. The generalization that science has been the most potent factor in modern economic development is again borne out.

Cheap Steel

Three inventions within less than a quarter of a century revolutionized the technology of steel-making: the Bessemer converter (1856), the Siemens-Martin open hearth (1865), and the Thomas-Gilchrist basic process (1878). Sir Henry Bessemer produced steel in large quantities at low cost for the first time by injecting air through holes in the bottom of a converter containing molten metal. He was able to convert pig iron directly into steel, thus eliminating the puddling process. The cost of producing steel fell to about one-seventh its former level.

A major weakness of Bessemer steel was its uneven quality. This difficulty was overcome by the open-hearth process, which was first developed in the 1860's by William Siemens, a British subject of German origin, and the Martin brothers, metallurgists of France. Like Bessemer, Siemens was a professional inventor and a master of applied science. In place of the closed Bessemer converter, the Siemens-Martin process used a large, shallow pan in which the molten metal was processed slowly and remained under precise control at all times. It permitted large-scale production of uniformly high-quality steel. The open-hearth process came into commercial use after 1865 and gradually surpassed the Bessemer process in total output.

Both the Bessemer and Siemens-Martin processes were unsatisfactory in one very important respect. Neither could utilize iron from ore containing phosphorus, a type prevalent in both Europe and America. In 1878 the world greeted enthusiastically the announcement of a new process by which steel could be made from phosphoric iron. This new Thomas-Gilchrist method in-

volved lining a Bessemer converter or an open hearth with a basic substance

which would combine chemically with phosphorus. One of the inventors, Percy
Gilchrist, was a professional chemist, and his cousin, Gilchrist Thomas, was
thoroughly trained in metallurgy. Thus all three of the great inventions in
steel were by men who understood science and its application to technology.
The importance of science to technology is illustrated in a negative way by
the experience of William Kelly, an ironmaster of Kentucky, who discovered
a process for making steel similar to the Bessemer process. Kelly was, however,
unable to bring his process into successful operation because of his lack of
understanding of chemistry, and he failed in business largely because of his
lack of scientific knowledge. This weakness was characteristic of American
iron and steel technology before the Civil War.

Machine Tools and Interchangeable Parts

The new steel-making processes provided low-cost, high-quality steel,
but the use of steel for making machines depended also on effective means of
shaping steel bars, rods, sheets, plates, castings, and forgings into machine
parts of accurate dimensions. This function came to be performed by machine
tools, which attained advanced development in the second half of the nineteenth century. Machine tools are mechanically operated machines for cutting
and finishing metals. Some important machine tools were invented during the
Industrial Revolution of the eighteenth century; one of the most important was
Wilkinson's cylinder-boring machine, which contributed so much to the practical development of Watt's steam engine. The most significant developments
in machine tools, however, occurred during the nineteenth century and were
a prerequisite for mass production based on the principle of interchangeable
parts, precision manufacture, and the assembly line.

Several basic types of general machine tools were developed early in the
nineteenth century, mostly by British engineers and toolmakers. These general-
utility machine tools included metal planers, metal grinders, metal borers, and
several types of lathes. They were used in England for making steam engines,
textile machinery, locomotives, and mining machinery.

General machine tools were also used to produce specialized machine
tools, which in turn produced accurate, interchangeable parts. This was a
fundamental step toward true mass production. American inventors and innovators took the lead in the development of manufacturing based on interchangeable parts. The role of small arms in the development of the principle
of interchangeable parts has already been noted (Chapter 18). Eli Whitney
is usually credited with being the pioneer in the use of interchangeable parts,
in connection with a government contract under which he produced thousands
of sets of identical parts which he then assembled by selecting a part from
each set of identical items. Many important innovations in machine tools and
interchangeable parts were made in government arsenals. Under this system
the United States soon led the world in small-arms production and nearly all
European nations purchased American machinery for their armories. Manufacture based on interchangeable parts was applied in the United States to
many products, and by the beginning of the second half of the nineteenth

century Europeans referred to this practice as "The American System of Manufacture."

Precision Manufacture

Accuracy was the key to interchangeability. Whitney made use of metal patterns called jigs, to guide the cutting tool along exactly the same path each time a part was made. The parts were necessarily duplicates and could be interchanged in assembly or repair. Progress in the techniques of measurement came through improved calipers and micrometers. Measurement had to be inexpensive as well as accurate. For this purpose various types of gauges were devised, with upper and lower limits of tolerance for acceptable size. This satisfied the criterion of interchangeability without having actually to measure the absolute size of the parts. With the growth of interchangeability, measurements themselves had to be standardized. Carl Johansson of Sweden worked for ten years to produce simple blocks of steel accurate to one four-millionth of an inch. These so-called "jo blocks" became the standard against which calipers, micrometers, and gauges were compared. Precise uniformity within single plants was necessary; but *standardized* precision between factories using each other's products was also essential because otherwise parts used in one plant would not fit perfectly with parts made in another plant.

The Moving Assembly

A further development toward the technology of mass production was the moving assembly line, which was also an American innovation. It was first used effectively in meat packing in Cincinnati during the 1830's. Slaughtered animals were butchered by operatives as the carcass moved along a continuous conveyor. The "disassembly line" of the slaughterhouse was a relatively crude beginning unrelated to the manufacture of interchangeable parts. For one thing, the animal carcass was not a standardized product and butchers were required to exercise judgment in deciding just where to wield their cleavers. Just as the assembly line did not require interchangeable parts, so interchangeable parts did not require a moving assembly line. Whitney, for example, did not use a moving assembly line. Nevertheless, the moving assembly was a logical complement to the more fundamental principle of interchangeability.

The assembly line and interchangeable parts were used in combination about the time when steel was becoming cheap. One of the earliest, if not the first, combination was in making carriages in Connecticut just before the Civil War. The Newhall Company turned out finished carriages at a rate of one per hour. Other items assembled along a moving conveyor from interchangeable parts were brass clocks, watches, agricultural equipment, sewing machines, typewriters, and bicycles. It reached maturity in 1913 when Henry Ford applied the moving assembly line to automobiles consisting of several thousand parts.

Moving assemblies of interchangeable parts were widely applied in the United States after the First World War to mass-produced items such as washing machines, radios, and refrigerators. In addition many products which do not require assembly or disassembly in the regular meaning of that term are

routed through factories from machine to machine in a continuous progression from raw material to finished product. For example, dishes, glass, shoes, stockings, iron pipe, and wire are produced in plants in which the materials flow from station to station in a highly rationalized manner. In the period after the Second World War a higher stage of automatic mass production was attained with the widespread use of automation, a process by which machines regulate themselves by continuously feeding back information about themselves.

Electricity and Increasing Automaticity

Automaticity grew with the increased use of machine tools and was accelerated by the industrial use of electricity beginning in the last decades of the nineteenth century. Electricity made other fundamental contributions to the technology of mass production. Electric power eliminated noisy, dangerous, and not always dependable belts and shafts which previously had cluttered factories. It permitted industrial engineers to apply power exactly where it was needed. Machine tools were redesigned with built-in electric motors. Machines with individual motors could be arranged more effectively for routing the flow of materials and products along assembly lines. Single machines and groups of machines could be operated by remote control. The speed, accuracy, and quality of production was increased, and machines became more automatic with the use of electrical devices like the photoelectric cell. The growing automaticity of machine operation heralded the age of automation.

Interrelatedness of Technological Change

The interrelatedness of technology can be observed in the various elements of mass production. As metal-working tools became power driven and more and more automatic, they became genuine machines; the stage had been reached where machines were used to make machines; and the use of general machine tools to make special machine tools illustrates the further stage at which machines are used to make machines to make machines. Interchangeable parts are the product of machine tools; and assembly lines are the economical manner of putting together interchangeable parts. Production tasks are simplified and routinized, with the result that machines are more easily substituted for human labor. New forms of power—steam and electricity—render the machines more powerful and more automatic. Progress in steel-making permitted high-quality cutting tools, which were more durable and capable of being operated at higher speeds. Precision, durability, high speed, and automaticity all contributed to efficiency of operation, lowering of unit costs, and capacity to produce on a massive scale. The several factors reinforced each other and together they cumulatively accelerated the mechanization of economic activity.

TRANSPORT REVOLUTION AND WORLD MARKETS

Although railways and steamships predated the age of mass production, transportation was much changed by cheap steel and the related technological developments in the last third of the nineteenth century; and, in turn, im-

provements in transportation cheapened the cost of overcoming distance and thereby did much to promote the growth of mass production. Large-scale production arising from the economies of interchangeable parts and assembly-line manufacture required extensive markets and would have utilized existing transportation facilities more intensively even if the latter had not improved. Fuller utilization of the social overhead capital invested in railways lowered the unit costs of transportation by spreading the cost over a greater number of units (ton-miles). But in addition the intrinsic superiority of steel rails, steel locomotives, and steel cars, as well as the cheapness of steel produced by new processes and the relative cheapness of locomotives made by inter-changeable parts, contributed to a cumulative fall in the unit costs of trans-portation. Better transportation enlarged the geographical division of labor and thus extended the markets for large producers. Steel plants, for example, would not have been economical on a large scale except in combination with inexpensive methods of transporting steel far beyond the local area of production.

Steel rails replaced iron rails, "steel horses" replaced "iron horses," and steel cars replaced wooden cars, as a direct consequence of the Bessemer, open-hearth, and basic processes. The earliest rails were made of wood covered with iron strips. During the 1850's and 1860's, rails were made of solid iron and constituted a substantial part of the total demand for iron. Steel rails replaced iron rails within a fairly short period between 1873 and 1877. Although steel was more expensive than iron, rail for rail, it was more durable and could sustain much heavier loads, which made possible the use of larger and more powerful steel locomotives, cars, and cargoes. Some early machine tools were designed for making locomotives, and in the United States the system of inter-changeable parts was applied to locomotives by the Baldwin Locomotive Works in 1860. Railway cars and cargoes became much heavier. Costs per ton-mile of traffic fell sharply and, consequently, so did freight rates during the last third of the nineteenth century.

In ocean transportation cheap steel made a significant contribution. The modern era of steel ships followed that of wooden ships so closely that iron dominated the construction of new tonnage for only about thirty years. Iron ships had been built before 1855, but they were not common until after that date. Bessemer steel was used in building a number of ships in the years 1863–1865, but objections from insurance companies (Lloyds) and from the British Admiralty to its uneven and uncertain quality halted steel shipbuilding for a decade. Then, in about 1876, steel assumed the lead in new ship con-struction and after the mid-eighties, when the Thomas-Gilchrist method began furnishing steel quite inexpensively, the relatively brief age of iron ships came to an end.

British ships and American railways, both made of steel and powered by steam, created world markets for a number of basic commodities in the last quarter of the nineteenth century. The transport revolution thus greatly enhanced the international division of labor. A typical British textile worker ate bread made with wheat from the American Middle West and processed cotton raised in the American South. In 1850 only one loaf of bread in four consumed in Great Britain was made from imported grain, as contrasted with two of every three in 1885. Frozen meat transported in refrigerated ships was first imported into France from Argentina in 1877, and into Great Britain

from Australia in 1880. Refrigerated railway cars supplemented refrigerated ships.

England, which in an earlier age had been one of the great exporters of raw wool, began to import large quantities of wool from Australia and other overseas areas. Completion of the first transcontinental railroads across the United States and the opening of the Suez Canal occurred in the same year (1869) and created world markets for other basic commodities. Western Europe became more than ever before an exporter of manufactured products and an importer of food and raw materials. As a corollary, other parts of the world became more than ever importers of European manufactured goods and exporters of foodstuffs and raw materials. This was the grand design of Europe's economy between 1870 and 1914. Neither before nor since has there been such a high degree of geographical concentration of industrial activity. Europe's share of total world manufacturing fell from 68 per cent in 1870 to 42 per cent in 1925–29 and to 25 per cent in 1948.

SPREAD OF CORPORATE BUSINESS ORGANIZATION

Changes in technology and increases in the size of markets led to much larger business units in the age of mass production than in previous periods of economic development when single proprietorships, family firms, and partnerships had been the predominant forms of business organization. Small-scale industrial plants required relatively little fixed capital, a requirement that was not changed markedly even by the English Industrial Revolution of the eighteenth century. Adam Smith, writing in 1776, viewed joint-stock or corporate forms of business organization as creatures of mercantilistic monopoly operating under special privileges from government. Smith felt the privilege of an incorporated joint-stock company should be restricted to three types of economic activity: banking, insurance, and certain public utilities such as canals and turnpikes. John Stuart Mill, writing in the middle of the nineteenth century, saw no particular need for extensive use of joint-stock companies. Smith and Mill underestimated the corporation, probably because they lived before the age of mass production and did not forsee its coming. Joint-stock companies, however, became indispensable for industrial enterprise because of the need for mobilizing great quantities of money capital to provide the plant, machinery, and equipment required for large-scale production and marketing.

The terms "joint-stock company" and "corporation" have similar but not identical meanings. "Joint stock," the term used in Europe, is primarily an economic concept, whereas "corporation," the term used in the United States, is primarily a legal concept. The economic and legal characteristics are usually embodied in the same business organization, but there may be unincorporated joint-stock firms as well as corporations which are not true joint stocks. A joint-stock enterprise is one in which several, or many, persons pool their capital in one common business enterprise, usually one with transferable shares and a board of directors. An unincorporated joint-stock enterprise is not clearly distinct from a partnership in the purely economic sense, although usually the latter does not have transferable shares or a board of directors. Through incorporation a joint-stock enterprise ceases to be just an association

of individuals and becomes recognized at law as a single unit; the organization is united as a body (corpora). As a single body—called a "legal person" in the United States—an incorporated joint-stock company can sue and be sued independently of its members. Individual investors are not agents of the company nor are they free to avail themselves of the company's property.

Evolution of the Corporation

Before joint-stock companies could come into general use as the typical form of industrial organization, restrictions hampering their formation had to be removed. Under Anglo-Saxon common law the privilege of limited liability always accompanied incorporation of a joint-stock company. The famous British Bubble Act of 1720 required that charters for joint-stock companies be granted only by special act of Parliament. This procedure was expensive and, in view of the reaction against joint-stock companies after the speculative manias that had led to the Bubble Acts of England and France, the privilege was not easily obtained from Parliament. In the century following passage of the Bubble Act, numerous joint-stock enterprises were formed without charters, that is, they were unincorporated. As unincorporated enterprises they were handicapped in several respects. All investors were subject to unlimited liability. The firm could not sue or be sued as a company but only in the names of its individual members. Preference for the unincorporated joint-stock enterprise over the partnership lay in the greater capital-mobilizing potential of the former arising from its transferable shares, greater continuity of existence, and centralized control in a board of directors. But even these economic and administrative differences were blurred in France and Germany. In France the *société en commandite sur actions* is a partnership with transferable shares and limited liability for partners who do not participate directly in the management (sleeping partners). In Germany the *Kommanditgesellschaft auf Aktien* is a similar arrangement. Most of the states in the United States, beginning with New York and Connecticut in 1822, borrowed from Continental Europe the device of limited partnership, but attempts to legalize it in Great Britain did not succeed until 1907.[2] Unincorporated joint-stock enterprises exist today in the United States, where they are viewed as a form of partnership, but they have no great economic significance.

In Great Britain during the eighteenth and nineteenth centuries the idea persisted that joint-stock companies were identified with monopoly. This formed the basis of Adam Smith's opposition to them. Most of the chartered companies were large trading enterprises holding exclusive rights to a certain type of trade or to all trade in a certain territory. The British East India Company, for example, held a monopoly of the trade with India, which meant that no other British company or individual could legally engage in the lucrative India trade. Limited liability was also unpopular because of a strongly held belief in the virtues of individual enterprise and responsibility. A student of the joint-stock company has written of the Bubble Act: ". . . the one hundred and fifty years following the statute of 1720 is the story of an

---

[2] For a comparison of American and English corporation law, see L. C. B. Gower, "Corporation Law in England and America," University of Chicago, *Law School Record*, Vol. 4, No. 3 (Spring, 1955).

economic necessity forcing its way slowly and painfully to legal recognition against strong commercial prejudice in favor of 'individual' enterprise . . ." [3]

When the British Bubble Act was repealed in 1825, statutory provision was made for chartering joint-stock companies with unlimited liability, which as previously noted, was not possible under common law. Beginning in the 1830's changes were made which gradually (1) liberalized the conditions for forming joint-stock companies, and (2) extended the privilege of limited liability. As the philosophy concerning joint-stock companies changed, the procedures for their establishment also changed. Incorporation of joint-stock companies had formerly been looked upon as a privilege granted by legislative generosity; in the age of mass production it came to be viewed as a right open to any group complying with certain minimum conditions intended to protect creditors and shareholders. Charters were granted by administrative procedure rather than by special legislative action. Limited liability became an accepted privilege of incorporated joint-stock companies, on the condition that "Ltd." be placed after the name of the firm and that the company publish its financial statements. The disadvantage of limited liability to creditors was offset by the provision that the original capital should not be impaired by the payment of dividends in excess of current earnings and accumulated surplus. Limited liability stimulated the mobilization of capital from numerous investors of small and large means. It is a notable coincidence that incorporation with limited liability by a simple process of registration became effective in the same year (1856) in which the Bessemer process was invented.

During the nineteenth century France, Germany, and the United States followed Britain in easing the legal procedures for incorporating joint-stock companies and for extending the privilege of limited liability. Although the conception of the corporation as a creature of government remained, the extent of state control was gradually relaxed during the nineteenth century, especially in the United States, where competition among the several states to attract chartering in order to gain revenue led to a lower standard of control over the activities of share companies. In New Jersey and Delaware, corporations could receive charters which permitted them to do very much as they pleased, and since a corporation engaged in interstate commerce was not subject to the control of other states, freedom of corporate enterprise became almost unlimited.

One of the early industrial enterprises to be organized as a corporation was the Boston Manufacturing Company, the first of the large New England textile firms, established in 1813 with capital stock of $300,000. The capital stock was soon enlarged to $1,000,000, and within a few years the Boston Associates formed several other million-dollar corporations. This was an exceptional group, however, both for America and Europe. These establishments were referred to as "The Corporations" to distinguish them from numerous unincorporated mills engaged in textile manufacture in New England.

Among railway companies in America and Europe, the corporation soon became a necessity because of the huge amounts of capital required for railroad construction. In manufacturing the main growth came rapidly in the latter part of the nineteenth century, and by the close of that century two-

---

[3] Bishop C. Hunt, *The Development of the Business Corporation in England, 1800–1867* (Cambridge, Mass.: Harvard University Press, 1936), p. 13.

thirds of all products manufactured in the United States were made by corporations. In the twentieth century the corporate form continued to grow in importance while other forms of industrial organization dwindled in importance.

Not only did the corporation take over in industry, but a small number of giant corporations dominated many industries, especially in the important heavy industries. In the United States by 1929, the 200 largest nonfinancial corporations owned 45 per cent of the nation's total industrial assets; in 1953 this had increased to slightly more than 50 per cent of the total industrial assets. In Germany and Japan the extent of concentration was perhaps greater in 1929 than in the United States; in Great Britain and France it was undoubtedly less than in the United States. But in all major capitalist nations, one main conclusion holds: a significant proportion of total industry is owned by a relatively small number of very large corporations or joint-stock companies.

The Modern Corporation

Thus the technological and financial advantages of large-scale business led to domination by a few giant corporations, often with thousands and even hundreds of thousands of shareholders. The giant corporation has become one of the key institutions of modern business life. Two important consequences have been (1) a change in the meaning of private property in the means of production, mainly by separating ownership from control; and (2) the rise of the stock exchange as the barometer of the economic climate of capitalist society.

The modern corporation and private property   The functional theory of private property handed down by John Locke [4] taught that one acquired property in a means of production like land by mixing his labor with the land. Property rights were based upon active, functional participation in the creation and management of the object owned. Under this personal form of private property, ownership and control were inseparable. In the giant, quasi-public joint-stock company or corporation of the twentieth century, ownership and control have been separated more and more. Just as the factory separated the worker from ownership of the instruments of production, so the modern corporation has separated its owners from control of their property. Ownership has become passive. The more widely scattered the absentee owners, the more easily can effective control be maintained by a minority interest, and in extreme cases a small oligarchy of self-perpetuating managers can dictate the use of vast amounts of property to which they have little or no legal title.

This, on the one hand, is perhaps the greatest shortcoming (in a democracy) of the corporate system of business enterprise. On the other hand, by spreading ownership among large numbers of small shareholders there is a broad participation in ownership of productive property and the income which accrues from it. Through organized security markets small investors can use their savings to purchase part ownership in business enterprises. Millions of "little people" who could not hope to go into business for themselves

---

[4] See Chapter 8.

are able to become small capitalists and feel they have some stake in the system. Stockholding also serves as a hedge against creeping inflation.

Whether the giant corporation has done more to promote economic democracy or its opposite is a question that is difficult to evaluate. Functional rather than passive ownership would appear to be essential for the democratic argument. This condition might be realized if workers owned significant amounts of stock in the enterprise which employed them, especially if arrangements were made for worker representatives to share in control of the company. Employees are often encouraged to purchase stock in the company which employs them, but worker participation in policy-making has been actively opposed. Representatives of management characteristically maintain that participation by worker groups is contrary to the principles of business enterprise, and frequently worker groups are not interested in sharing the burdens of management. In any event, it would be impracticable for the workers and the owners to consist of the same individuals.

In the total picture of modern corporate development, the most striking feature is disenfranchisement of shareholders at one pole and the great concentration of power in the hands of management at the other, through the separation of ownership from control. The great mass of shareholders are owners in name only and, in economic fact, are mere suppliers of capital. They have no guaranteed return, as in the case of bondholders; the payments to common stockholders often depend on the caprice of an autonomous, non-owning, self-perpetuating management.

The significant conclusion is that the joint-stock or corporate method of organizing business enterprise has revolutionized the basic capitalist institution of private property. Owners are often not managers, and managers are often not owners. Corporate property is collective or joint property. In its more advanced stage it represents an extreme form of collective ownership which is difficult to reconcile with an equally extreme theory of economic individualism which carries over from the age of Locke.

Corporations and the stock exchange   The stock exchange was no newcomer to capitalism in the age of mass production, but with the spread of corporations to industry the extent and significance of the stock market expanded greatly until it became the heart throb of the capitalist system. Early stock exchanges dealt mainly in government securities, but industrial and railway bonds and stocks dominated trading on the exchanges by the end of the nineteenth century. Millions of middle-class investors avidly read share quotations in the daily press around the world, and the stock exchange became well known to the general public as the avenue for participation in the serious business of investing money for income and for capital gains. All this provided a stimulus to saving and investing.

The special function of the stock exchange was to make financial investments liquid, in the sense of providing a market in which any holder of securities could readily convert them into money. While the stock exchange did not mobilize capital directly for industrialists—since what one man invested another man disinvested on each exchange transaction—the existence of a market where securities could be converted easily into cash if the exigencies of personal or business finance so dictated made the original subscribers, including investment bankers, more willing to advance money capi-

tal for enterprise. Moreover, the state of the market for securities already outstanding influenced the decisions of promoters with respect to floating new securities.

Stock exchanges had always been centers of speculation. A share of stock is a perfectly standardized product with no intrinsic value, and as such is a perfect object of speculation concerning the future value which it may realize for its holder. In the past, this type of speculation had usually been confined to professional investors. Occasionally, as in the South Sea and Mississippi Bubbles of the eighteenth century, a wider public was drawn into "get-rich" schemes, but this was never common practice. In the new age of corporate industry the professionals continued to operate in the exchanges, but in sheer volume of holdings they were outranked by the amateurs. At best, amateur investors were only superficially informed about the real activity of the firms in which they invested; at worst, they were completely ignorant, easily misled, and more often wrong than right in their judgment concerning the market. In addition there was the hard truth that the future earning power of any company was highly conjectural because the trend of economic development and the course of cyclical fluctuations in business activity were highly uncertain. Not even the professional investor or speculator could know the future. If to this uncertainty be added the basic principles upon which the securities market is organized, the principle of liquidity for the individual investor but lack of liquidity for investors as a whole, the precarious nature of the value of securities becomes distressingly evident. Summing up these attributes of the economic environment—separation of ownership from control, wide participation by the general public, general ignorance of real factors in company activity, the uncertainty of the future, and the passion for liquidity —the total result is a market basically unstable and subject to wide and erratic fluctuations; in brief, a highly speculative market.

The stock exchanges in London, New York, Paris, Berlin, Vienna, and Tokyo have differed in detail according to the national characteristics of their respective countries. The London market, for example, has been less volatile than New York's because Englishmen have been prone to invest for income, whereas Americans have shown a stronger propensity to speculate for capital gains. National differences notwithstanding, the history of every stock exchange is pretty much the same: upswings based on overoptimism, followed by collapse and prolonged periods of overpessimism. The international character of the capital market has tended to keep the various exchanges in line with each other. While the stock exchange can hardly be blamed for the instability of capitalism, i.e., for the business cycle, it undoubtedly has been a major factor accentuating the instability.[5]

SELECTED BIBLIOGRAPHY

See end of Chapter 21.

[5] More attention will be given to the stock exchanges in connection with the great bull market boom of the late 1920's and the subsequent collapse in the Great Depression following 1929.

Money and the Mobilization
of Capital in the
Age of Mass Production

CHAPTER 21

International markets and large corporate enterprises generated new monetary systems and complex banking institutions during the nineteenth century. Paralleling the growth of world markets for commodities there arose a world-wide market for channeling money capital to the metropolitan centers of industry and commerce. The mobilization of money capital on an international scale was aided by the establishment, toward the end of the nineteenth century, of an international monetary system based on gold. The international gold standard tied together the money markets and commodity markets of the world into a fairly uniform system, the like of which had not previously existed. Domestic gold standards and domestic banking systems were prerequisites for the achievement of an international monetary and banking system. Although domestic and international finance involved many highly specialized institutions and technical practices, the key developments were, in addition to the gold standard, central banks, commercial banks, and investment banks.

SPREAD OF THE GOLD STANDARD

Europe

As in so many economic developments, Great Britain pioneered in establishing the gold standard, which by the end of the nineteenth century became the dominant monetary standard of the world. The British had been on a *de facto* gold standard for some time before adopting it officially in stages after the Napoleonic Wars. The final step occurred in 1821 when notes of the Bank of England became freely convertible into gold. The British pound sterling was defined as containing a specific weight of gold. Anyone holding silver, bank notes, silver coins, or other claims to British pounds, at home or abroad, could, if they wished, receive payment in gold.

Steps toward an international money system were taken by France, Belgium, Italy, and Switzerland with the formation of the Latin Monetary Union in 1865. With the franc as a common unit, standard coins of uniform weight and fineness were minted in all four countries and circulated freely among them. Other countries were invited to join the Union, which was viewed by its founders as the beginning of a world currency system. Several states

375

took initial steps toward affiliating, but only Greece actually joined. Other nations were deterred by the Union's adherence to a bimetallic standard for some time after the conviction had spread that bimetallism was unworkable. During the 1870's the Latin Monetary Union bowed to the trend of the times and adopted the gold standard. The Union was badly shaken by World War I and was formally abandoned in 1927. This experiment provides an interesting example of the movement toward an international monetary system in the age of world markets.

Germany achieved a uniform monetary system during the nineteenth century by adopting the gold standard. The states which had joined the Zollverein agreed to a common monetary unit in 1838, and this proved a preliminary step toward the gold standard, which was adopted shortly after formation of the German Empire in 1871. By 1914 Russia, Austria-Hungary, Holland, Scandinavia, Japan, the United States, and other important nations, except China, had all gone onto the gold standard.

The United States

In the United States a long and bitter struggle over the place of silver in the monetary system preceded the official adoption of the gold standard. Throughout the nineteenth century the bimetallic standard worked poorly, with first one metal and then the other falling out of circulation in accordance with Gresham's law that money overvalued at the mint drives out money undervalued at the mint.

The discovery of gold in California in 1848 drove silver coins from circulation, leaving gold as the sole metallic money in the United States. During the Civil War the federal government issued great quantities of inconvertible paper currency (greenbacks) in order to finance military expenditures. Commodity prices rose sharply in a characteristic wartime inflation. Following the Civil War prices declined for thirty years and placed debtors at a disadvantage in relation to creditors.

Meanwhile the discovery of rich silver mines in the American West during the 1870's lowered the value of silver in relation to gold. Still more silver poured onto the American market and further depressed its price about the time European countries abandoned the silver and bimetallic standards in favor of the gold standard. Silver now became the "cheap" money in the United States, and restive debtors demanded that it be coined in unlimited quantities. A coinage act of 1873, which failed to provide for the minting of silver because at the time silver had been out of circulation for many years and was too valuable to be brought to the mint, was denounced as the "Crime of '73." This derogatory label was intended to elicit sympathy for silver coinage. It was a battle cry against the growing support given to gold as the standard money. Beginning in 1879 the previously inconvertible greenbacks were made convertible into gold at parity, and the United States was on a *de facto* gold standard. The champions of silver, however, were by no means prepared to concede defeat.

Under political pressure from western farmers and other debtor groups, a limited coinage of silver was begun under the Bland-Allison Act (1879) and

was increased under the Sherman Silver Purchase Act (1890). Large purchases of silver under the latter act threatened to drain the federal treasury of its entire gold reserve during the panic of 1893. In order to avert departure from the *de facto* gold standard the Silver Purchase Act was repealed. The battle of gold vs. silver rose to fever pitch. It was the great national issue in the presidential election of 1896. William Jennings Bryan, the colorful Democratic nominee, demanded free and unlimited coinage of silver at a ratio of 16 to 1. Bryan and his supporters believed that a 16:1 ratio would end the long post-Civil War deflation and thus bring relief to debtors as a class. In his famous "cross of gold" speech Bryan denounced the gold standard as a symbol of class oppression, declaiming with religious fervor, "You shall not press down upon the brow of labor this crown of thorns; you shall not crucify mankind upon a cross of gold." Despite hard campaigning and brilliant oratory Bryan lost the presidential election to William McKinley. The conservatives who came into office ended the stormy career of bimetallism by passing the Gold Standard Act of 1900. This law defined the dollar exclusively in terms of a fixed weight of gold and provided that other forms of United States money (silver and paper) were convertible into gold. This remained the basic law until 1934.

In the United States the gold standard proved less oppressive than the free silverites had predicted, largely because new discoveries of gold in South Africa and Alaska reversed the falling price level about 1897. Prices rose steadily until 1914, when the First World War forced suspension of the gold standard in all European countries (but not in the United States). It was widely restored in the 1920's, but was abandoned during the Great Depression of the 1930's.

Between 1870 and 1914 the almost universal trend toward the gold standard may be interpreted as reflecting the needs of an incipient world economy for a world currency. In these few decades prior to World War I, the world achieved, under the guidance of the (relatively) free market, the most highly unified system of international trade and exchange in the history of capitalism. Capital funds and commodities flowed easily from one center to another according to the conditions of demand and supply, abetted of course by cheap transportation and rapid communication.

CENTRAL BANKING

Although gold became the standard upon which money was based, it did not constitute the chief medium of exchange in advanced economies. Instead, gold became a reserve money, lodged in the custody of central banks, while bank notes and bank deposits served as the chief media of circulation. Paper currency had often tempted statesmen, but yielding to the temptation had usually resulted in excessive issue, price inflation, business speculation, and economic upheaval. John Law's Mississippi Bubble and the assignats of the French Revolution are two notorious cases. Bank deposit money had been used for centuries, but only in the nineteenth century did it become the chief means of payment, and then only in more advanced countries.

Progress in the art of central banking during the nineteenth century did much to overcome the dangers and limitations of bank notes and bank deposits. The British experience best illustrates the development of central banking in response to demands placed upon the economy for greatly increased media of circulation and upon the money market by the necessity of mobilizing capital for massive enterprise in the age of mass production.

During the Napoleonic Wars the British government ordered the Bank of England to suspend payment of gold for notes of the Bank lest the nation's gold reserve be exhausted if all the increased notes issued to finance the war were presented for redemption. In 1825, shortly after convertibility was resumed, a commercial crisis again strained the reserves of the Bank and renewed the threat of suspension. In the famous Bank Charter Act of 1844 an attempt was made to eliminate the threat of inconvertibility in the future by adopting the "currency principle," which provided that Bank notes could be increased in quantity only to the extent that bullion reserves increased. The Bank of England was separated into the Issue Department, which was responsible for the issue of paper currency, and the Banking Department, which carried on general banking activities. The Issue Department received a monopoly of the future issue of bank notes in England. Existing banks which already had notes in circulation were not permitted to expand their issue, and as these banks failed or changed their status in any way their right of issue was to be transferred to the Bank of England. Apart from a fixed initial quantity (14 million pounds) of Bank notes backed by government securities and the rights which might be transferred from other banks, every note issued by the Bank had to be backed in full by bullion (silver never to constitute more than one-fifth, and in fact it was not used) in the vault of the Issue Department. Thus the quantity of Bank notes was strictly limited in accordance with the principle that the way to assure a sound paper currency is to require any increase in its quantity to be backed pound for pound by increases in bullion reserves held by the central bank.

Flexibility was sacrificed for security in the Bank Act of 1844. By creating an inelastic supply of currency the act limited the ability of the Bank of England to come to the aid of hard-pressed businessmen and bankers in periods of emergency. In the crises of 1847, 1857, and 1866 the Bank was authorized by the government, in the form of a letter from the Chancellor of the Exchequer to the Bank, to break the law by issuing, if necessary, notes not backed in accordance with the law of 1844. In the severe crisis of 1857 the Bank actually issued two million pounds of "illegal" notes. Obviously there was something wrong with a law which had to be violated in order to work successfully. What was unsatisfactory was the inability of the Bank to draw down its reserves in emergencies.

There was, however, a more fundamental limitation to the conception of banking implied in the Bank Act of 1844. It presumed that control of the quantity of bank notes, and the reserves behind them, was the chief function of central banking. Actually British banking was passing into a new phase in which the checking system replaced the bank note as the important media of circulation. The focus of central bank functions was presently to be on the

Banking Department rather than on the Issue Department of the Bank of

England. The quantity of Bank notes expanded hardly at all in the half-century
after 1844; the very great increase in total transactions was financed by
transfers drawn on checking deposits. No doubt the absence of restrictions on
the Banking Department, in combination with the rigid restrictions imposed
on the Issue Department, stimulated the growth of the checking system; but
there were other and more important reasons for its growth. It was much
better adapted to the needs of large-scale industry and commerce.

In the new circumstances the most important function of the Bank of
England was as the holder of the central reserves supporting the checking
system and as the lender of last resort in emergencies. These were not new
functions, but they now had to be performed in a manner consistent with a
different type of banking system. The men in the Bank who proposed the
Bank Act of 1844, and the men in Parliament who had most to do with its
passage, insisted that the Banking Department of the Bank of England was
"just like any other bank." Later events proved them wrong; the Banking
Department was not "just like any other bank." First, the reserves held by the
Banking Department were much larger, in relation to its liabilities, than the
reserves of other banks. Since the Banking Department kept a reserve of 30
to 50 per cent in hard cash and legal-tender notes while the commercial banks
kept very small reserves because reserves represent non-earning assets, the
earning capacity of the Bank of England's Banking Department was relatively
less than for ordinary banks. The Directors of the Bank of England thus found
themselves primarily in the role of trustees of the public and the nation and
only secondarily servants of the Bank's shareholders (owners), who naturally
appreciated high dividends. Second, as custodian of centralized reserves of
the entire banking system, the Bank of England was looked to in emergencies
as the ultimate source of credit. It was not a commercial bank for ordinary
businessmen and investors, but a bankers' bank and the government's bank.
It had to stand ready to lend its reserves freely in critical credit situations;
for mere reluctance on its part would make credit even tighter and precipitate
a crisis or make an existing crisis worse. Joint-stock banks, private bankers, and
bill brokers, whose customers clamored for legal-tender money (Bank notes),
had to have access to the reserves of the central bank when they needed it.
The Bank of England could make the bankers and bill brokers pay for new
money by raising the rate of interest (Bank rate), but it could hardly refuse
to lend, provided the borrowers had good securities to sell or pledge against
their loans. So the Banking Department was different because ultimately the
credit of all banks rested on the liquidity of the central bank. It was the lender
of last resort.

Under the gold standard the Bank of England was obligated to maintain the national reserves of gold against foreign drains. As in the domestic
market, the international gold standard required payment on demand to
depositors; and since Bank notes were not legal tender in international exchange, gold had to be exported if demanded by foreign claimants. Increases
in the rate of interest brought about by increases in the Bank rate were used
to attract money to London and to prevent a drain of English reserves.

In this manner the Bank of England initiated the basic functions of
central banks as the lender of last resort. Its directors learned to resist the

temptation of maximizing earnings; instead they maintained larger reserves than other banks; they held the central gold reserves for the entire banking system. Their unused lending power in normal times was available for use in emergencies arising in connection with commercial crises, bad harvests, and other causes. As lender of last resort, the Bank was protected by its reserve of Bank notes and of gold. Behind this was the support of the government, and the confidence in the central bank became identified with confidence in the government. As Walter Bagehot, the great historian of the London money market, wrote, "Neither the Bank (of England) nor the Banking Department have ever had an idea of being put 'into liquidation'; most men would think as soon of 'winding up' the English nation." Thus even in a society which was presumed to represent the high achievement of the principles of laissez-faire, the ultimate value of money depended upon the power, and the wisdom, of the state.

Bank of France

Among central banks of the world the Bank of France ranked next in importance to the Bank of England during the nineteenth century. It was formed by Napoleon in 1800 in order to establish credit for his newly formed government, which had risen from the flames of the French Revolution of 1789. In this respect the Bank of France bore an interesting parallel to the Bank of England, which also had been formed in order to finance the military expenditures of a new government emanating from the Revolution of 1689. Although privately owned (until 1945), the Bank of France always remained under close government control.

The Bank of France possessed varying degrees of monopoly over the issue of bank notes until 1848, when it received a complete monopoly for all of France. Bank note issue was not as strictly limited as in England under its Bank Act of 1844. In France a ceiling was placed on the total quantity of notes that might be issued, but the ceiling was raised from time to time according to the needs of trade. The metallic reserve behind notes remained prudently high, ranging from 50 to 80 per cent most of the time. In the British crisis of 1825 the Bank of France advanced two million pounds to the Bank of England.

One important reason for the high reserve ratio arose in connection with the obligation of the Bank of France to discount bills of exchange. Since the checking system did not develop in France as it did in England, business was typically transacted by drawing bills of exchange, which sellers took to their bank for discounting, that is, to receive cash in the form of coin or bank notes. As the exclusive issuer of bank notes, the Bank of France became the ultimate discounter of all transactions. It established numerous branches in order to widen its discount facilities. It discounted not only for small traders and large merchants, but also for other banks. Ordinary banks maintained a minimum of notes and coin for their customers' discounts, and rediscounted bills at the Bank of France when they needed additional cash. Thus the Bank of France became, like other central banks, the custodian of the nation's monetary reserves. Relative to the needs of the French economy, the Bank of France was at least as central as was the Bank of England in the English economy.

In Germany the modern phase of central banking began with the conversion of the Bank of Prussia (established in 1846) into the Reichsbank in 1875, four years after unification of Germany under the Empire. The Reichsbank gradually absorbed the bank notes of other banks in a manner similar to the Bank of England after 1844. Despite the existence of a large number of banks of issue in the numerous German political units before the Empire, centralization of note issue was substantially achieved by the First World War. A maximum figure was fixed for the quantity of notes which could be issued by the Reichsbank without metallic backing, with some flexibility introduced by permitting this maximum to be exceeded upon payment of a penalty of 5 per cent per annum on the excess issue. As with the central banks of England and France, the Reichsbank became the chief custodian of the cash reserve of the Empire.

In order to provide banking facilities all over Germany, the Reichsbank set up nearly 100 branches and 4000 sub-branches. One of the obligations of the Reichsbank and its branches was to transfer cash at a low cost from one part of Germany to another for any person who might request it. This was the German substitute for the checking system of the British, and later the American, type. Like the Bank of France, the Reichsbank discounted bills of exchange of both small and large amounts.

The Federal Reserve Banking System in the United States

As with the gold standard, the United States lagged behind European countries in establishing a full-fledged central banking system. Some of the functions of central banking were necessarily performed in the absence of a formal organization. Bank note issue was controlled to a degree under the National Banking system. Checking and clearing facilities existed through private correspondence banks, and bank reserves tended to concentrate in a few large private banks in New York City.

Inflexibility of the total supply of reserves was probably the most unsatisfactory feature of American banking before 1913. The reserves of country banks held by New York banks were lent "on call" to security dealers in the stock market. When interior banks needed additional cash, they drew on their New York balances, which forced the New York banks to recall money from security dealers. Emergency withdrawals could precipitate a crisis in the stock market, which in turn might set off or reinforce a business depression. The money supply was inelastic because no bank or banks had the power to create new reserves to meet such emergencies. There was no lender of last resort.

Following a series of paralyzing financial crises in 1873, 1893, 1903, and 1907 the Federal Reserve System was established in 1913. It set up not one but twelve central banks operating semi-autonomously in their respective geographical districts. Each Federal Reserve Bank had its Board of Directors, and in addition a federal authority, known as the Federal Reserve Board, advised and supervised the system as a whole. The large geographical area of the United States and the country's traditional mistrust of centralized finan-

cial power, dating back to the Jeffersonian and Jacksonian opposition to the First and Second Banks of the United States, lay behind this unique system of decentralized central banking.

For the most part the principles of operation of the Federal Reserve System resembled those of other central banks. Gold reserves behind central bank notes and central bank deposit liabilities were held initially by the Reserve Banks, and subsequently by the United States Treasury. Bank notes could be issued by each of the twelve Reserve Banks (Federal Reserve *Bank* notes) and by the system as a whole (Federal Reserve notes), the latter always being more important. A monopoly of note issue came slowly with the elimination of National Bank notes and was not achieved until the depression of the 1930's. The Reserve Banks were obligated to rediscount the eligible financial assets of member banks to enable the latter to increase their reserves. By raising their rediscount rate the Reserve Banks could discourage borrowing (rediscounting) by member banks and by lowering their rediscount rate they could encourage it.

In due course the Federal Reserve authorities assumed more initiative in controlling credit conditions by purchasing and selling government securities in the open market. A purchase of government bonds by the Federal Reserve, paid for by a check drawn on the central bank, increased the reserves outstanding in the banking system and tended to ease conditions for borrowing. A sale of government bonds by the Federal Reserve resulted in payment to it and reduced the member bank reserves, thereby tending to tighten conditions for borrowing. The Federal Reserve System was a vast improvement over the archaic financial system which preceded it. It did not, however, prevent a financial panic during the world-wide crisis of 1931–33, when thousands of banks in the United States failed. Subsequent changes, including federal insurance on bank deposits, added to the stability of the American banking system.

COMMERCIAL AND INVESTMENT BANKING

A central bank is a banker's bank; it performs functions for the banking system as a whole, such as issuing paper currency, holding and creating reserves, clearing interbank balances, and acting as the fiscal agent of the national government. Banks which serve commerce and industry directly are called commercial and industrial, or investment, banks.

Early central banks like the Bank of England also functioned as commercial and industrial banks. Not until the nineteenth century was a clear distinction made between the essential functions of central banks and other banking functions which might be performed incidentally by central banks or alternatively by non-central banks. Likewise it was not until the nineteenth century that a clear distinction was drawn between commercial and investment banking. As the terms are commonly used, commercial banking is concerned primarily with *short-term* loans to business enterprises, including industrial, commercial, and agricultural firms.

Investment banking, which is synonymous with industrial banking, is concerned primarily with long-term credit, as represented by stocks and

bonds. Investment banks arose in order to facilitate the mobilization of money capital to provide plant and equipment for large industrial firms, railways, and other enterprises requiring heavy fixed investment. Hence the rise of investment banking is correlated historically with the spread of joint-stock companies with transferable shares, a phenomenon closely associated with the age of mass production.

Commercial Banking

Commercial banks themselves became joint-stock enterprises in the course of the nineteenth century. In England, after many failures by private banks in the crisis of 1825, joint-stock banks quickly came to the fore in commercial banking. Although not permitted to issue bank notes—the Bank of England held this exclusive right among English *joint-stock* banks even before the Bank Charter Act of 1844—the commercial joint-stock banks found a wide scope of activity in deposit banking. Most of these newly chartered joint-stock banks either failed or were absorbed as branches by a few giants. As Bagehot observed, "A large bank always tends to become larger and a small one tends to become smaller. People naturally choose for their banker the banker who has most present credit. The one who has most money in hand is the one who possesses such credit."

In all major European nations there was a tendency toward concentration in commercial banking. British commercial joint-stock banking soon was dominated by the "Big Five" (Barclays, Lloyds, Midland, National Provincial, and Westminister), each of which had more than a thousand branches in the twentieth century. Together they held approximately five-sixths of the total deposits of all English commercial banks. In France there was a similar concentration in four great commercial banking firms (Crédit Lyonnais, Comptoir Nationale d'Escompte, Société Générale, and Crédit Industriel), with many branches scattered throughout France. Because the Bank of France continued to engage in commercial as well as central bank functions, the French joint-stock banks were more a supplement than a complement to the Bank of France. Their main business was discounting bills of exchange, which could be rediscounted at the Bank of France. They also held deposits, made commercial loans, and acted as retail brokers in the disposal of industrial and commercial bonds. In Germany the concentration of banking was even greater than in England and France. The famous Big Four "D" banks (Deutsche, Dresdner, Discontogesellschaft, and Darmstädter) were reduced to only two through mergers by 1931.

Commercial banking in the United States developed along lines similar to the United Kingdom so far as functions were concerned, but it was not characterized by the high degree of concentration of European banking. Branch banking was subject to strict limitations under both state and federal laws. Some commercial banks were chartered by states and some by the federal government. State banks did not issue notes, but the national banks were permitted to issue their notes until the 1930's. In the absence of branch banking, clearing facilities were awkward until after the formation of the Federal Reserve System in 1913. The essential function of American commercial banks was to provide working capital for industrial, commercial, and agricultural

enterprises, which they did mainly by creating deposits against which checks could be drawn by the borrowers.

Investment Banking and Mixed Banking

The immediate antecedents of modern investment banking for industry are found in the great family banking firms of western Europe. These private banking houses, such as the Rothschilds of Frankfurt, Germany, initially engaged primarily in financing government loans in war and peace. The Rothschilds became prominent during the Napoleonic wars, in which they financed Britain and its allies against Napoleon. The activities of the firm were international in scope, with one of five brothers operating, respectively, in Frankfurt, London, Paris, Vienna, and Naples. In the century of peace, 1815–1914, the Rothschilds and other international bankers played a leading role in diplomacy as well as finance. They were an integrating and unifying force among national political units operating in an international economy which lacked an international political authority. Their power lay in their supranational character.

With the coming of railways, promoters turned to the international bankers for assistance in marketing stocks and bonds in order to raise money for construction. Sometimes the bankers purchased securities outright, but more typically they acted as middlemen, underwriting new issues of stocks and bonds, and disposing of them to smaller banks and ultimate investors.

Crédit Mobilier

In France the Crédit Mobilier was an interesting example of a type of investment bank set up to promote general economic development. In spirit it was somewhat similar to the "economic development corporations" of under-developed countries of the twentieth century. The Crédit Mobilier was sanctioned by Emperor Napoleon III, who was dissastified with the financing which private bankers like the House of Rothschild were providing for French industrial development. In theoretical terms, the Crédit Mobilier was a device for mobilizing money capital and channeling it into new enterprises. It did this by selling its own securities; the money thus raised was used to finance new joint-stock enterprises, and after an enterprise was launched the Crédit Mobilier would sell the securities of the new enterprise to investors. If all went well, it now had liquid funds with which to launch more enterprises. During its brief but hectic career (1852–71) the Crédit Mobilier caused quite a stir. It promoted and launched railways, public utilities, and industrial enterprises. It met a real need because France was a country of strong savings habits but was short on large-scale enterprise.

The Crédit Mobilier suffered, however, from a weakness which is fatal to banking organizations, lack of liquidity. In good times its earnings were high, but in crises its assets were not easily converted into cash. It was too dependent on favorable conditions in the stock exchange. The Crédit Mobilier was bankrupt in 1867 and was liquidated in 1871. Its main significance lay in stimulating the formation of similar organizations, the most important of which was the Credit-Anstalt of the Rothschilds in Austria, and as an inspiration for the great mixed industrial-commercial banks of Germany.

A mixed system of investment and commercial banking was carried on by the great German joint-stock banks, the Big Four "D" banks previously mentioned. Because of the degree of backwardness in the German economy when the Empire was founded in 1871, rapid economic development was possible only by harnessing industry directly to banking. The mixed banks sold their own shares and used the proceeds, along with some customer deposits, to purchase and to underwrite the securities of industrial enterprises. Like any investment bank, they would then sell some of these industrial securities and keep some of them in their portfolio, depending on their salability at the moment and other strategic considerations.

In addition to raising long-term capital, the mixed banks supplied industrial firms under their wing with short-term commercial credit, thus serving the functions of both investment and commercial banker. Representatives of the great banks sat on the boards of directors of their sponsored industrial firms. Bank control over industry was enhanced by the practice of small investors leaving their shares in the care of their banker, who had authority to vote these shares by proxy. Particular banks were allied with particular industries, which facilitated the formation of industry-wide cartels for fixing prices and setting output quotas. It has been said of the German mixed banks that they "accompanied industrial enterprises from the cradle to the grave, from establishment to liquidation."

Mixed banking was by no means an ideal arrangement because the long-term credits were not easily liquidated. Yet it was better fortified against illiquidity than the French Crédit Mobilier because the mixed banks held short-term loans which could be converted into cash by discounting at the Reichsbank. An important clue to Germany's rapid industrialization is found in the German banking system, which was dominated by the note-issuing, discounting Reichsbank and the small group of powerful mixed, joint-stock banks.

Investment Banking

Investment banking in the United States was retarded by dependence on imported capital and government loans for financing railways and public utilities. Toward the close of the nineteenth century, American financiers with strong European connections rose to great power and influence in connection with railway reorganization and the trust movement. Among the important investment banking houses were J. P. Morgan and Co., with English background, and Kuhn, Loeb and Co., with central European connections. The House of Morgan extended its activities into nearly every type of business enterprise, including railways, public utilities, industrials and government, whereas Kuhn, Loeb specialized in railway finance.

In each of the several countries banking institutions adapted themselves to the special requirements of the economy. Where appropriate types of banks did not exist, as they usually did not, they were invented. The contrast between the relations of banking to industry in England and in Germany may serve to illustrate the point. Industrialization began early in England, and by

the time the age of mass production dawned, considerable capital had been accumulated for industrial enterprises. Therefore industry was less dependent upon banks for long-term credit. The chief English development came in commercial banking, which provided short-term credit to industry and commerce. In Germany, on the contrary, industry was retarded, and relatively little capital for industry had accumulated at the beginning of the age of mass production. In order to meet the situation a close marriage between industry and finance, resulting in the peculiar system of mixed banking, characterized the German scene.

Large-scale banking, which came into existence primarily to serve the needs of large-scale business, became in turn an active force promoting large-scale business enterprise. Since banks found it more profitable to deal in the securities of larger and better known enterprises, there was a tendency for investment bankers to promote the sales of these securities rather than those of smaller and less well-known companies. Hence small business did not enjoy equal advantage in the money market. During periods of business boom it was especially profitable for investment banking houses to float securities merely for the purpose of enriching the promoters. The larger volume of shares fed speculation in the stock exchanges and extended the scope of commercial crises.

The London Bill Market

As the London money market evolved, other financial institutions developed to perform special functions. Of particular interest were the London discount houses, also known as bill brokers, which discounted bills of exchange originating in international trade. By close attention to experience with the drawers and drawees of international bills of exchange, the bill brokers of London assessed the credit ratings of importers and exporters around the world. Not only English imports and exports but also international trade between two non-English countries came to be financed via London. For example, a transaction between a Japanese exporter and an American importer would involve financing through a London discount house, even though the shipment of goods went directly from Japan to the United States. The Japanese exporter would draw a bill of exchange on the American importer and the bill would be "accepted" by the London discount house, to become a banker's acceptance.

Bill brokers obtained funds largely from the English commercial joint-stock banks (the Big Five). The bill brokers' profit consisted of the difference between the rate of discount they received on the bankers' acceptances and the rate of interest they paid to the joint-stock bank. The rate of interest paid to the joint-stock banks was in turn closely related to the Bank rate charged by the Bank of England because bill brokers could borrow directly from the Bank of England at the official Bank rate if, for any reason, they did not borrow from the joint-stock banks. The Bank of England's discount rate (Bank rate) became in effect a ceiling on London interest rates, with the rate of interest charged by the joint-stock banks somewhat below the Bank of England's rate.

If money became tight in the London money market, the bill brokers would discount their acceptances at the Bank of England, and in the process

additional credits (deposits) would become available to the public. Central banks act as money factories. If gold reserves in the Bank of England fell below a safe level, the Bank rate could be increased in order to attract funds to London from other countries. Thus the London bill market played a critical role both in world trade and in the world money market.

CONCLUSION

One of the truly striking developments of the nineteenth century was the money market, especially the London money market. Money markets had existed since the beginnings of modern capitalism, but only in the nineteenth century did they become an indispensable part of private capitalism. The railways and later the industrial joint-stock companies mobilized money capital for their giant enterprises through investment bankers who operated in the money markets of the world. Railway promoters from all corners of the world came to London to raise capital for their joint-stock companies. They usually achieved this objective by selling their securities to investment bankers, who in turn sold them to the investing public. Bagehot described the London money market as a great "floating loan-fund which can be lent to any one or for any purpose." To a much greater extent than on the Continent, Englishmen kept their money in banks, where it became "borrowable" money. With some lag, but subsequently on an even greater scale, the United States followed the lead of England rather than the Continent.

The London money market was different from others in that it was especially oriented toward international rather than domestic financial needs. Britain attained a dominant position in world commerce before the industrial joint-stock company became important. To a certain degree British domestic industrial enterprise suffered because it played second fiddle to international demands. What really distinguished the pre-1914 London money market from others was its higher stage of development. Paris, Berlin, Rome, Vienna, New York, and other markets were satellites revolving around London. In every country, money markets served both domestic and international functions. There was, however, a sense in which London served world needs for the simple reason that money was cheaper and easier to get in the "main office" than anywhere else. "The money market is always, as it were, the headquarters of the capitalist system." [1]

When the First World War rudely interrupted the century of peace, 1815–1914, the international money market proved a delicate and fragile thing. The long-held dream of a world economy based on an international gold standard, free exchanges, liberal trade policies, and capitalist private property was shattered in the face of resurgent economic nationalism and social revolution. The gold standard was suspended and then abandoned. Exchange controls and trade barriers multiplied rapidly in the 1920's and 1930's.

In the interwar years London was forced to share its leadership with New York, and after the Second World War New York, with the immense

[1] Joseph A. Schumpeter, *The Theory of Economic Development* (Cambridge, Mass.: Harvard University Press, 1934), p. 126.

wealth and prestige of the American economy behind it, dominated the international capital market as surely as London had dominated the pre-World War I capital market. New York's only rival was Washington with its many federal agencies for dispensing the American taxpayers' dollars for reconstruction of war-torn Europe and for developing underdeveloped countries around the world. The power and influence of central banks grew tremendously, and on a broader front, the International Monetary Fund filled part of the vacuum created by the disappearance of the gold standard and held some promise of developing, in time, into a genuine international central bank.

SELECTED BIBLIOGRAPHY

BAGEHOT, WALTER, *Lombard Street, A Description of the Money Market.* Homewood, Ill.: Richard D. Irwin, Inc., 1962.

BURN, DUNCAN L., *The Economic History of Steelmaking, 1867–1939.* London: Cambridge University Press, 1961.

CLAPHAM, JOHN H., *The Bank of England, A History, 1694–1914,* Vol. II. New York: The Macmillan Company, 1945.

CLARK, JOHN MAURICE, *Studies in the Economics of Overhead Costs.* Chicago: University of Chicago Press, 1957.

DAVIS, JOSEPH S., *Essays in the Earlier History of American Corporations.* Cambridge, Mass.: Harvard University Press, 1917.

EMDEN, PAUL H., *Money Powers of Europe in the Nineteenth and Twentieth Centuries.* New York: Appleton-Century-Crofts, Inc., 1938.

EVANS, GEORGE HEBERTON, *British Corporation Finance, 1775–1850.* Baltimore: The Johns Hopkins University Press, 1936.

FEIS, HERBERT, *Europe: The World's Banker, 1870–1914.* New York: Augustus J. Kelley, Inc., 1964.

FISHER, DOUGLAS ALAN, *Steel: From the Iron Age to the Space Age.* New York: Harper & Row, Publishers, 1966.

FRIEDMAN, MILTON, and ANNA J. SCHWARTZ, *A Monetary History of the United States, 1867–1960.* Princeton: Princeton University Press, 1963.

HARRIS, SEYMOUR E., *Twenty Years of Federal Reserve Policy.* Cambridge, Mass.: Harvard University Press, 1933.

HAWTREY, RALPH G., *A Century of Bank Rate.* New York: Longmans, Green & Co., Inc., 1938.

HIDY, RALPH W., *The House of Baring in American Trade and Finance.* Cambridge, Mass.: Harvard University Press, 1949.

HUNT, BISHOP C., *The Development of the Business Corporation in England, 1800–67.* Cambridge, Mass.: Harvard University Press, 1936.

LAVINGTON, FREDERICK, *The English Capital Market.* London: Methuen & Co., Ltd., 1929.

ROLT, L. T. C., *A Short History of Machine Tools.* Cambridge, Mass.: M.I.T. Press, 1965.

SINGER, CHARLES J. and others, eds., *History of Technology,* Vol. V, *The Late Nineteenth Century.* New York: Oxford University Press, 1956–58.

TEMIN, PETER, *Iron and Steel in Nineteenth-Century America: An Economic Inquiry.* Cambridge, Mass.: M.I.T. Press, 1964.

VEBLEN, THORSTEIN, "The Technology of Physics and Chemistry," Chap. 10 in
Absentee Ownership and Business Enterprise in Recent Times. New York:
Augustus J. Kelley, 1964.

WHALE, P. BARRETT, Joint-Stock Banking in Germany. London: Macmillan & Co.,
Ltd., 1930.

ARTICLES

CLARK, JOHN MAURICE, "Some Social Aspects of Overhead Costs," American Economic Review, XIII (March, 1923), 50–59.

DAVIS, LANCE E., "The Investment Market, 1870–1914: The Evolution of a National Market," Journal of Economic History, XXV (Sept., 1965), 355–400.

HAMMOND, BRAY, "Banking in the Early West: Monopoly, Prohibition, and Laissez-Faire," Journal of Economic History, VIII (May, 1948), 1–25.

HANDLIN, OSCAR and MARY F., "Origins of the American Business Corporation," Journal of Economic History, V (May, 1945), 1–23.

NORTH, DOUGLASS C., "International Capital Flows and the Development of the American West," Journal of Economic History, XVI (Dec., 1956), 493–505.

———, "Ocean Freight Rates and Economic Development, 1750–1913," Journal of Economic History, XVIII (Dec., 1958), 537–55.

POSTAN, MICHAEL M., "Recent Trends in the Accumulation of Capital," Economic History Review, VI (Oct., 1935), 1–12.

POTTER, J., "Atlantic Economy, 1815–60: The U.S.A. and the Industrial Revolution in Britain," in Studies in the Industrial Revolution, L. S. Pressnell, ed. London: Athlone Press, 1960.

ROSENBERG, NATHAN, "Technological Change in the Machine Tool Industry, 1840–1910," Journal of Economic History, XXIII (Dec., 1963), 414–43.

SHANNON, HERBERT A., "The Coming of General Limited Liability," Economic History, II (Jan., 1931), 267–91.

Growth of Organized Business
in Germany and England

Large-Scale Enterprise and Destructive Competition **22**

Mass production, cheap transportation, rapid communication,
world markets, joint-stock companies, and the organized money market contributed to the development of big business after 1870 in western Europe and
the United States. The techniques of mass production required large amounts
of investment in fixed plant and equipment before any finished output could
be produced. But once such investment had been made, a million units could
be produced at a small fraction of the average unit cost of a few thousand
units. Firms with large investments sought to expand their markets and spread
their fixed (or overhead) costs over as many units as possible in order to
lower the average unit cost of production. The result was a massive output of
goods which could only be sold, if at all, at lower prices—a tendency which
contributed to the long period of falling prices between 1873 and 1896. In these
circumstances, price competition proved to be destructive in the sense that
firms could not survive in the long run if they did not get back their fixed
investment in plant and equipment.

Since business firms cannot survive in the long run by selling at prices
which do not cover the total cost of production, the inclination was to abandon
price competition in favor of monopolistic-type agreements, conforming to
the philosophy of "live and let live." Large-scale production thus undermined
the basis of workable price competition; it greatly weakened the foundation
of the self-regulating market which presupposed many small firms freely entering and leaving an industry. Prior to the age of mass production, markets had
grown more rapidly than productive capacity and there was constant pressure
to expand supply to meet demand. Now the capacity to produce grew more
rapidly than markets, and there was pressure to adjust supply downwards to
demand with declining attention to price flexibility because price cutting became mutually unprofitable when several large-scale producers engaged in it
simultaneously.

The destructive nature of price competition under conditions of large-
scale production is illustrated by the condition in which the best price avail-

able to a firm is less than sufficient to cover the total unit cost of production.[1]

391

GROWTH OF
ORGANIZED
BUSINESS
IN GERMANY
AND
ENGLAND

Under circumstances which were typical of mass production situations, price competition became "destructive" or "cutthroat." No matter how much consumers might benefit from low prices, this type of competition was intolerable from the point of view of business enterprise because it eliminated profits. Any sensible businessman caught in this web of circumstances would seek to extricate himself by one means or another. Obviously profits disappeared because the selling price was too low, and just as obviously the solution lay in raising the price. One businessman could benefit by raising his price, however, only if fellow businessmen all did the same, assuming the products of the several firms were equally satisfactory to the buyers. The obstacle to higher prices and profits was competition. In the nature of the case the solution was to agree, at some point in the destructive process, that the price should be maintained by all sellers at a higher level. This was the primrose path to monopolistic-type agreements.

Tendency Toward Monopoly

Under mass production, competition proved to be the death of enterprise and not, as is sometimes said, the life of trade. This result is hardly surprising. Under any circumstances competition tends to be profit-destroying. It is monopoly which is profit-preserving. Hence there is nothing abnormal or unnatural about monopolies in business enterprises geared to profit-making; on the contrary, monopoly is to be expected in the absence of unusual conditions which prevent it. To some degree these unusual conditions existed in the time of Adam Smith and for a century or so thereafter. The presupposition underlying Smith's "natural" economic order is that effective competition among many small enterprises will reconcile the apparent contradiction between the private pursuit of personal profit and the social goal of maximum general welfare. It was in terms of this presupposition that Smith identified "natural" price with "competitive" price. Smith believed that monopolies were the creatures of government policy and therefore "artificial." He also believed that in the absence of special privileges such as exclusive charters to joint-

---

[1] Assume a situation in which one of several large firms has invested $10,000,000 in fixed plant and equipment with a normal life of 10 years and a capacity output of 100,000 units per year of a homogeneous product. The fixed cost per unit at capacity is then $10. Assume further that the direct cost is $5.00 per unit, making a total unit cost of $15 per unit. Starting from a higher price, successive price reductions forced by competition from rival firms of similar structure may lower the price to $12 per unit, at which the firm sustains a loss of $3.00 per unit, or a total loss of $300,000 per year on 100,000 units. At any price higher than $12 the loss would be greater than $300,000 because the firm would lose sales to its rivals. If the price were set below $12 per unit, presumably rivals would retaliate and a greater loss would result. Hence $12 is the best available under the circumstances even though it is less than sufficient to cover the full cost of production ($15). The firm would continue to operate until its plant and equipment wore out because if it were to shut down entirely, it would recover none of its fixed investment; at a price of $12 it is recovering $7 of fixed costs on each unit sold, or $700,000 per year on 100,000 units. Naturally it is preferable to recover $7,000,000 of a $10,000,000 investment over its life than to recover nothing at all. So the firm goes on operating at a loss in order to prevent still greater losses. It could go on having losses for ten years and then retire from this line of business. It would surely not reinvest on the same terms and prospects. The probability is, however, that long before the plant wore out, the folly of price competition would be discovered, and a price-fixing agreement, involving restriction of output, would be reached.

392

GROWTH OF
ORGANIZED
BUSINESS
IN GERMANY
AND
ENGLAND

stock companies and protective legislation, monopolies could not persist. Smith thought sellers would constantly *attempt* to form monopolies but that they would be frustrated by competition with many rival sellers. The reasonableness of Smith's supposition is suggested by the growth of effective competition following the repeal of mercantilist legislation. The golden age of capitalism occurred during the decades after these artificial forms of monopoly were abolished and before small-scale production gave way to mass production. Competition was to a considerable degree a historical fact during the early part of the nineteenth century.

In more recent times, and especially since the 1870's, there has been a tendency in capitalist countries for business enterprises to form combinations of more or less monopolistic character. In this context the term combination means a transfer of some or all decision-making power from several hitherto competing enterprises to a group authority which constitutes a significant proportion of the total output of the industry. Business combinations have taken many forms, but all have as a common objective the increase or preservation of profits. Business combinations sought to increase profits in two ways: either by increasing prices or by lowering costs. Increases in prices tend to reduce the amount of product sold. A monopolist is always faced with weighing the advantages of increases in prices against the disadvantages of smaller (physical) sales. By virtue of economies of scale, business combinations frequently lowered costs of production, although by the logic of profit-making they could not be expected to pass on to consumers the full benefit of the reduction in unit cost.

There were very few, if any, complete monopolies in the sense that a single firm dominated an entire industry, but all combinations tended toward monopoly in the sense that they reduced the number of autonomous firms and thereby lessened the degree of competition. Pure competition is defined as a market condition in which there are many small sellers of a homogeneous product, with freedom to enter or leave the industry. Each firm is so small in relation to the total size of the market that it cannot appreciably influence the price at which it sells its product. Competitive prices are determined impersonally by the market. A monopolistic firm, on the other hand, has the power to influence, and within limits to determine, the price at which it sells its product. Monopoly is essentially control over supply. Even complete monopolies cannot determine demand.

Since the conditions of pure monopoly and pure competition are rare, referring only to limiting cases, other terms are necessary to describe the in-between situations which actually developed. Following usage that has become accepted among economists, an industry or market situation with a small number of sellers of large size is called an "oligopoly," and an industry or market situation with a large number of firms selling similar but not identical products is called "monopolistic competition." Mass production industries were among the most important type which developed oligopolies, that is, a small number of sellers of a product, either homogeneous or differentiated, in an industry. A leading characteristic of oligopoly situations is reluctance to compete in terms of price because destructive retaliation by rivals is part of the normal expectations of a firm initiating price cuts. The existence of destructive

competition, and later the mere threat of it, led to explicit or tacit agreement not to compete price-wise. Tacit agreements became especially important in the United States where combinations were driven "underground" by anti-combination legislation. Anti-combination laws changed the form of explicit agreements and resulted in greater reliance on tacit agreements. The important principle of oligopolistic behavior is recognition of the potential retaliatory effects of price changes, especially price reductions. Neither oral nor written agreements of an explicit type are required for rival enterprises to behave oligopolistically. Where rivalry among firms continued to be an important condition of the market, stress was on non-price competition in the form of advertising and other selling expenditures.

393

GROWTH OF
ORGANIZED
BUSINESS
IN GERMANY
AND
ENGLAND

Types of Combinations

The numerous business combinations which arose in capitalist countries may be classified into three general types: (1) combinations by agreement among firms which remain autonomous (cartels, pools), (2) combinations through financial control, usually involving the manipulation of the voting shares of several joint-stock companies by a separate financial concern (trust, holding company), and (3) direct merging or fusion of the assets of several previously independent firms (mergers, consolidations, amalgamations). Combination by agreement is a loose form and is typified by the European cartel and the American pool. Formation of a cartel or pool does not add to or subtract from the number of business firms. For example, if ten firms came together into a cartel, they remain ten separate firms. They retain their former independence except for the agreement to sell at a certain price and (usually) to produce a certain quota. Financial combinations such as the holding company and the American trust leave less freedom of action to individual members of the combine than does the looser cartel or pool. Unlike a cartel, a holding company is a business enterprise. If ten operating firms form a holding company, there will then be eleven firms, the original ten plus the holding company. The trust was employed extensively in the United States after pools proved unsatisfactory because of their legal vulnerability under Anglo-American common law. Holding companies in turn replaced the trust, which was outlawed by statute. The direct merging of assets is the most complete form of combination. It has been widely used in Great Britain, under the name amalgamation, and also in the United States after anti-trust legislation outlawed the trust and cast a shadow of legal doubt over the holding company. When ten firms merge or amalgamate, the result is a single business enterprise.

Combinations are also classified as either vertical or horizontal. A vertical combination integrates a number of firms operating at successive stages of production. A horizontal combination brings together a number of firms operating at the same stage of production. An example of a vertical combination would be one which included coal mining, coking plants, blast furnaces, steel ingot production, and steel rail manufacture under unitary control. An example of a horizontal combination would be an association of steel rail producers. Neither vertical nor horizontal combinations are necessarily monopolistic in intent or result, but horizontal combinations are a more direct approach to

394

GROWTH OF
ORGANIZED
BUSINESS
IN GERMANY
AND
ENGLAND

monopolistic control over the market. Cartels are usually combinations of the horizontal variety. Vertical integration would approach a monopolistic position only if it dominated one or more of the stages of production included in the combination. Horizontal combinations make for control over the market whereas vertical combinations make for independence of the market.

The remainder of this chapter is devoted to a discussion of the combination movements in Germany and Great Britain and brief observations on business combinations in France. The combination movement in the United States is the subject of the following chapter.

BUSINESS COMBINATIONS IN GERMANY AND GREAT BRITAIN

Although there was a tendency everywhere for business combinations to develop, the extent and form of the movement as well as the attitude of public authorities and businessmen toward combinations differed widely in the several countries of Europe and America. German and British attitudes provide an interesting contrast. These were the two leading nations in Europe after 1870, and their combination movements illustrate significant differences as well as similarities in the growth of organized business in the age of mass production.

In Britain, by virtue of the long period of capitalist evolution and general acceptance of the free market as a rational guide to economic behavior, the underlying public attitudes and legal traditions were hostile toward monopolies generally and to cartels in particular. Under British common law, agreements in restraint of trade were illegal in the sense that anyone who was injured by an agreement could sue in the courts with a reasonable expectation of receiving favorable treatment if he could prove damages. Furthermore any contract for the purpose of establishing an agreement in restraint of trade was unenforceable in courts of law. Parties to such contracts were said to come into court with "unclean hands."

In Germany, on the other hand, where capitalism rose abruptly out of a mixed medieval and mercantilist environment and where there existed no long tradition of a market-determined allocation of resources, business combinations, including cartels, were accepted as desirable and even necessary in the social interest. The gild attitude of mutual protection to producers and consumers through a monopoly regulated in the public interest led to an acceptance of capitalistic monopolies subject to governmental control. The medieval notion of social responsibility to the community was carried over from the early nineteenth-century gild system to the late nineteenth-century capitalist system.

In both Germany and Britain the optimum social performance of private industry was the ultimate objective of national economic policy toward combinations. In Britain social performance was assumed to be maximized by the free play of market forces, whereas in Germany no such tradition existed. These contrasting views are reflected in the respective attitudes toward mercantilism. After Adam Smith (1776) nearly all British opinion was hostile to mercantilism, but in Germany mercantilism was sympathetically interpreted by such outstanding latter-day social theorists as Gustav Schmoller (1838–1917).

*GROWTH OF
ORGANIZED
BUSINESS
IN GERMANY
AND
ENGLAND*

Among European nations, monopolies and combinations were most widespread in Germany. Combinations of the cartel type had been a feature of German "Big Business" as far back as the age of the Fuggers in the fifteenth and sixteenth centuries, but the failure of Germany to keep pace with countries along the Atlantic seacoast tended to render insignificant the German monopoly problem as a factor in economic development. With Germany's economic renascence in the nineteenth century, private monopoly again sprang into prominence. Underlying tendencies toward monopoly associated with mass production, destructive competition, and legal sanctions were reinforced by the formation of the Empire in 1871, the onset of the Long Depression in 1873, and the return to protection in 1879. Although the mere number of cartel agreements is not necessarily an accurate index of the growth of monopoly and combinations in Germany, the figures do suggest the rapidity of that movement. According to estimates, there were approximately 16 cartel agreements in 1879, 35 in 1885, 300 in 1900, 600 in 1911, 1000 in 1922, 1500 in 1925, and 2100 in 1930.

Legal and Economic Justification of Cartels in Germany The legal and economic justification of business combinations in Germany was stated in a basic court decision of 1897. An association of wood pulp manufacturers had formed a cartel in 1893. One of the members subsequently withdrew from the cartel (and selling syndicate) and proceeded to sell its product independently. The remaining members of the cartel brought suit against the deviating firm on grounds that it had violated the agreement, as it obviously had. The court held that the cartel agreement was legally valid and therefore enforceable and binding against members who violated its provisions.

Interestingly this court decision held that cartel agreements are consistent with freedom of trade (Gewerbefreiheit), which in Anglo-Saxon law was the fundamental grounds for refusing to enforce cartel-type agreements. The German court maintained that businessmen are free to enter contracts fixing prices and setting quotas and, having voluntarily entered such contracts, are bound by their provisions, unless it be shown that the agreement runs counter to the public interest. In brief, freedom to make a contract carries with it responsibility to abide by the terms of the contract.

In economic terms, the crux of the matter was whether the agreement was consistent with the public interest. The court recognized that competition might drive prices so low that the firms would be forced out of business, a condition which it held was not in the best interests of the public. The legal justification of cartels therefore really rested on their economic and social consequences. Since ruinous competition is not in the best interest of the public, agreements to prevent ruinous competition are socially desirable and legally enforceable. The court stated its position as follows:

> If in a certain trade the prices of products decline too much, such as to make the prosperous pursuit of the trade impossible or to endanger it, the ensuing crisis is ruinous not only to the individual, but also to the economy as a whole, and therefore it is in the interest of the community that immoderately low prices should not exist permanently in any trade . . . Therefore it cannot be considered simply and generally against the interest of the community if the

396

GROWTH OF
ORGANIZED
BUSINESS
IN GERMANY
AND
ENGLAND

entrepreneurs of a certain trade associate in order to prevent mutual underselling and the resulting fall in prices. Instead their association may be considered a measure serving the community interests, constituting at the same time a rightful exercise of the drive for self-preservation, provided that otherwise prices would continue so low as to threaten economic ruin to entrepreneurs. Indeed the formation of syndicates and cartels of the kind considered here, if applied properly, has repeatedly been considered a device especially useful for the economy as a whole, since they can prevent uneconomic overproduction and ensuing catastrophe.

The last sentence just quoted justifies cartels on grounds that they help prevent economic crises and depressions, which are held to be caused by overproduction. This view was widely held by German economists until 1929. It is of special interest because it contrasts with the views of economists in the English-speaking countries where cartels and other forms of business combinations were held to be strong contributory factors to economic instability. The logic of the latter position is in terms of the inability to sell mass-produced products except at prices which are lowered presumably to competitive levels. Only at lower prices can enough products be sold to maintain a high level of employment. If prices are artificially maintained, firms and industries must curtail output, lay off workers, and further reduce the effective demand for the products of industry. In this way monopoly prices contribute to depression. This would seem to be one of the strongest arguments against monopolistic combinations. The German position that monopoly contributes to the stability of capitalism does not appear justified by the experience after 1929.[2]

German coal cartel The most remarkable of all European cartel syndicates has been the one that grew up among the coal producers of the Ruhr valley, probably the most concentrated industrial area in the world. In the Ruhr, coal is the basis of industrial life. Coal producers began to experiment with loose agreements during the 1870's and during the severe depression of 1893 formed the famous cartel and syndicate, officially known as the Rhenish-Westphalian Coal Syndicate. Conditions which stimulated the producers to form a monopolistic union were fierce competition, overcapacity in relation to the market, price cutting and generally unprofitable operations, especially during depressions.

The avowed objectives of the Rhenish-Westphalian Coal Syndicate were to (1) end price competition; (2) establish profitable prices; (3) regulate production; and (4) minimize fluctuations in output. The first three of these aims were achieved with remarkable success. Prices were fixed at levels profitable to members of the cartel by limiting the output of coal for the group as a whole. In areas where no competition existed, the syndicate would charge high prices, and, where competition did exist, the coal syndicate lowered its prices in order to meet the competition of outside groups. The price of Ruhr coal in Mannheim, which was near the Saar coal mining district, was lower than in Hanover, which was nearer the Ruhr but farther from any other coal producing area. Price discrimination of this sort was common among cartels.

Each member of the syndicate was assigned a quota in the total output.

---

[2] See the article written in 1928 by a German-American economist, Professor Joseph A. Schumpeter, "The Instability of Capitalism," *Economic Journal*, XXXVIII (Sept., 1928), 361–86.

397

GROWTH OF
ORGANIZED
BUSINESS
IN GERMANY
AND
ENGLAND

Because the quotas were transferable, larger firms bought out smaller ones within the cartel in order to increase their share in the total output. Higher cost mines were bought up and withdrawn from production. The syndicate also attempted to eliminate potential competition by buying up unworked areas. In this way high prices had less tendency to bring new capacity into the market. The German government sanctioned the coal cartel and on occasions when there was a possibility that the agreement might lapse, the government threatened to force the participating firms to continue the cartel.

The fourth objective—to minimize fluctuations in output—was more difficult to achieve within the framework of any single industry because the demand for coal fluctuated with the general level of economic activity. However, it was a common contention among German economists and businessmen that cartels are a force for overall economic stability.

The Ruhr coal cartel was well administered, the provisions were strictly enforced, and from the producers' point of view it was remarkably successful. Strict enforcement of the provisions avoided suspicion on the part of participating members and prevented the kind of trouble which frequently led to a breakdown of pooling agreements in the United States and Great Britain, where the common law made enforcement of similar agreements impossible. The Rhenish-Westphalian Coal Syndicate is another illustration of a successful attempt on the part of businessmen to establish a monopoly in order to avoid the fluctuation in prices and the other insecurities that arise in a freely competitive market, especially as it operates under conditions of large-scale production.

German Steelworks Union   Second only to the Ruhr coal cartel was the German Steelwork Union (Stahlwerksverband) formed in 1904. The general purpose of the steel cartel was similar to that of the coal syndicate, namely, to maintain profits by keeping up prices through limitation of output in the domestic market. Cartel control is easier in the case of minerals like coal and other raw materials, which are easily standardized, than in manufactured products like steel. However, steel industries in all countries have tended toward monopolistic combinations because of certain economic characteristics, especially in the basic steel products for which standardization is more easily established. Standardization is important because the product which is to be controlled must be carefully defined. Cartels in ladies' hats are most uncommon.

Of all modern industries, except perhaps railways, steel involves the greatest capital investment for efficient production. Because of its relatively late start the German steel industry employed the newest and most efficient methods of production, which meant enormously expensive plant, heavy fixed costs, and a large spread between total costs and the direct costs involved in the output of specific units (prime costs). Consequently it was an industry in which destructive price competition always presented a potential threat to the large amounts of invested capital. Given these basic economic characteristics, the incentive to cartelize was especially strong. Other conditions favorable to cartelization were the small number of basic steel producers, a high protective tariff on steel, and a close tie between steel enterprises and the great German banks. The latter had been indispensable in raising the large amounts of money capital required to finance great steel plants.

398

GROWTH OF
ORGANIZED
BUSINESS
IN GERMANY
AND
ENGLAND

The Stahlwerksverband was a union of a number of existing cartels among steel firms; it was a combination of combinations similar to the United States Steel Corporation, which was formed only three years earlier in 1901. All the organizing genius characteristic of German leaders was necessary to operate successfully the vast cartel of cartels in German steel. A high protective tariff on iron and steel imports was responsible for certain special characteristics of the German steel industry. Although tariffs are not essential for cartels, as seen in the case of coal, on which Germany had no tariff, protective tariffs are a powerful factor in the establishment and enforcement of cartel discipline. Tariffs are walls that shield domestic producers from outside competition. No quotas were placed on the amount of steel that could be exported. This led to the practice of dumping steel in excess of domestic quotas on foreign markets. The export price was characteristically less than the price charged domestic buyers. International price discrimination of this type was inherent in mass production; it was an outcome of the economics of overhead costs as it operated in international trade. It was profitable to sell at lower prices in foreign markets as long as these prices were sufficient to cover the additional or direct costs of producing and transporting the additional units of steel. The tariff made it impossible to undermine the high cartel-enforced domestic price by buying German steel in foreign markets to export back into Germany for sale at low prices.

Price discrimination tended to cause vertical integration, that is, a combination of plants at successive stages of production. German steel producers operating only a single stage, say the manufacture of tin plate, were severely handicapped in trying to compete with integrated firms. The former had to buy in the open market at the cartel-established prices, while to the integrated firms the cost of steel for tin plate was the actual cost of producing it themselves.

Foreign dumping, which was by no means confined to German cartels, is another phase of cutthroat competition, the domestic aspect of which has already been observed as one of the fundamental consequences of mass production. Control of international price cutting required international cartels of the type formed in Europe in 1926, when the steel producers of Germany, France, Belgium, and Luxembourg came together in the European Steel Cartel. An international cartel was possible only after strong domestic cartels had already been established.

Mixed cartels   High prices and limited quotas on coal and steel in Germany led to the formation of mixed coal and steel firms at the expense of pure coal mines and pure steel mills. Because steel production requires large quantities of coal, many steel companies own coal mines. Coal mined by steel companies for their own use was exempt from the quotas established by the Rhenish-Westphalian Coal Syndicate. Since the actual cost of mining coal was significantly less than the market price, pure steel mills, which bought coal in the market, were at a disadvantage compared with mixed companies and thus had an incentive to acquire their own coal mines. Furthermore, coal mining companies had an incentive to align themselves with steel mills in order to gain exemption from the quota on part of their coal production. This meant that a steel company owning coal mines or a coal company owning steel mills enjoyed

advantages over pure coal mines and pure steel mills. The growth of large
mixed companies simultaneously increasing their quotas in both the coal syndicate and the steel union brought closer ties between the two giant industrial
combinations and an increasing concentration of economic power in German
heavy industry.

Other and later German cartels   The German potash cartel was one
of the strongest and most unusual business combinations in the world. Before
the First World War Germany enjoyed a monopoly of the world's supply of
commercial potash. Unregulated competition among German producers contributed to the formation of a potash cartel in the 1870's. High prices attracted
new German producers and finally led in 1910 to compulsory membership in
the selling syndicate associated with the producers' cartel. The loss of Alsace
after the First World War broke the German monopoly, but French and German producers soon got together to establish prices and quotas in the world
market.

Germany's great new electrical and chemical industries were characterized by a high degree of concentration of control. An initial period of fierce
competition in the electrical industry was followed at the turn of the century
by effective curbs on competition. Soon the industry was dominated by two
giant concerns, the Allgemeine Elektrizitäts-Gesellschaft (A.E.G.) and the
Siemens-Halske group. These two dominant organizations in turn made agreements between themselves concerning prices, product specialization, spheres
of influence, and other monopolistic arrangements.

In the chemical industry a combination movement of a quarter of a century culminated in the formation of the vast I. G. Farbenindustrie A.G. in 1926.
Like the Steelworks Union, I. G. Farben represented a combination of combinations. It not only dominated the German chemical and dye industry but
was the moving force in bringing the great chemical companies of the United
States and Great Britain into international cartel agreements. As a great research organization, I. G. Farben enjoyed a monopoly of many chemical for-
mulae, which it exchanged for market privileges around the world.

The success of cartelization in German industry was strongly influenced
by the concentration of German banks and the close association of these banks
with industry.[3] Especially in the steel, chemical, electrical, engineering, and
other heavy industries the great German banks provided the investment capital, with particular banks associating with particular industries. The parent
banks were intolerant of ruinous competition among their progeny; they would
not permit the "wastes of competition" to erode the profits upon which the
payment of interest and principal must in the long run depend. Control was
exercised mainly by having bank representatives serve on the boards of directors of industrial firms, often as chairman and vice-chairman. The Dresdner
Bank was most active in the steel industry, being closely associated with the
Krupp interests. The Deutsche Bank's special sphere of influence was in foreign trade and shipping. The Darmstädter Bank and the Diskontogesellschaft
were deeply entrenched in various manufacturing industries, including chemical and metal production. After 1900, when these infant industries "came of
age," they exercised reciprocal influence on the banking community, but they

[3] See Chapter 21.

400

GROWTH OF
ORGANIZED
BUSINESS
IN GERMANY
AND
ENGLAND

did not separate themselves from their parent banks. In Clapham's words, "The Kartell movement was to a great extent the work of the banks."[4]

The German economy was honeycombed with cartels and syndicates. Cartelization was not confined to mass production industries with a small number of firms. By its nature as a loose combination which preserves the autonomy of its members (except in price and output determination), the cartel is an effective device by which small firms can shield themselves against ruinous competition. Cartels are good regulators of competition as well as destroyers of it. Smaller firms seeking self-preservation against competition were assisted by protective tariffs, which effectively shut out or limited foreign sources of supply and facilitated the formation of national cartels. Depressions stimulated the cartel movement, but it also flourished during prosperity. Nearly all raw and semi-manufactured goods, where grading was usually possible, and a large part of finished industrial goods were produced under cartel or other monopolistic-type agreements.

In order to limit the coercive power of cartels against their members the Weimar government of Germany passed a law against "the abuse of economic power" in 1923. This law made it easier to withdraw from cartels, provided a member had good cause, which meant any unfair restriction on its economic freedom, especially with respect to production, marketing, or price fixing. Moreover, sanctions agreed to as a condition of cartel membership (boycotts by the group or forfeiture of bonds pledged by dissenting members) could be effected only with the consent of the Cartel Court, a special judiciary body established under the law for cartel litigation. The 1923 cartel law was well intended and probably had some liberalizing effect on the behavior of cartels, but it did not curb the growth of cartels or reduce the concentration of economic power in Germany's economy. Whatever liberalizing tendency it had was eliminated forthwith as soon as Hitler came to power in 1933. By one statute the Nazis removed the protection of dissenting members against boycotts by the group, and a second statute decreed compulsory membership in cartels. Thus cartels proved a convenient tool in the hands of the totalitarian Nazi government. After the Second World War, a cornerstone of American policy in Western Germany was to eliminate cartels and set up a system in accordance with American anti-trust policy; this anti-trust philosophy was incorporated into the treaty establishing the Common Market.

Business Combinations in Great Britain

British hostility toward business combinations in restraint of trade extends back to the age of mercantilism, when there was strong public reaction against widespread grants of monopoly by the Crown and Parliament. "Patents of Monopoly" granted by the Stuart kings were a leading issue in the English Revolution of the seventeenth century. The Stuarts granted monopolies in domestic trade in return for revenues which enabled these sovereigns to bypass Parliament in the historic struggle for control of the purse strings of government.

With the coming of laissez-faire, monopolies based on government grants

[4] John H. Clapham, *The Economic Development of France and Germany, 1815–1914* (London: Cambridge University Press, 1951), p. 394.

were abolished, although a few which did not rely upon government sanction persisted into the nineteenth century. The most famous was the Newcastle Vend, a cartel arrangement based on control of ocean transport of coal from Newcastle to London. The Newcastle Vend existed, with a few interruptions, from 1585 until 1844, when the coming of the railways provided an inexpensive alternative for transporting coal to the London market. After 1873 attempts were made to re-establish group control, but without success. Coal-producing areas and coal-mining firms were too numerous and the individualistic tradition too strong to make a coal cartel of the Ruhr type feasible in Britain. Joint action in coal mining with government sanction was attempted during and after the First World War, but the results were not significant. Not until nationalization in 1946 did combinations in coal mining make notable progress, and then within an entirely different framework than that which characterized the capitalistic form of enterprise under discussion here.

Combinations in the British steel industry were more successful than in coal, although there was nothing comparable to the German Steelworks Union. The new steel processes of the second half of the nineteenth century increased the size and reduced the number of producers to a degree that made combination feasible. Some heavy steel products like ship and boiler plate were effectively monopolized. However, free trade was a major obstacle to the control of steel prices and output. Foreign steel could be shipped into Great Britain duty free until 1932. The supply of steel on the domestic market was at the mercy of conditions beyond the control of British producers. Actually conditions for monopoly in steel were not too unfavorable in the decade preceding the First World War. This was a period of general economic expansion, especially in Germany, where the armament drive left little steel for export to Britain. A loose group authority for disciplining the market was provided by the British Steel Association.

Amalgamation, which along with association ranks as the most important form of British combination, is an actual merging of the assets of several previously competing firms into a single business enterprise under one management, with one balance sheet and one profit and loss statement. Amalgamations occurred early among British railways, which were consolidated into four main companies. British joint-stock banks began to amalgamate in the nineteenth century, and on the eve of the First World War the Big Five commercial banks were well along toward the domination they finally achieved after the war.

One of the most successful British amalgamations occurred in cotton sewing thread. J. and P. Coats merged with four of its rivals in 1896 to form a virtual monopoly of the domestic market and expanded its foreign activities until it dominated cotton sewing thread markets throughout the civilized world. Factories were built inside tariff walls in the United States, Canada, Russia, Germany, and Austria-Hungary. The success of this remarkable firm was primarily a result of its efficiency, especially in marketing. Because of the immense value of its trademark and the inelastic demand (that is, a sales volume insensitive to price changes) for thread of high quality, Coats was able to prevent rivals from undercutting on prices by refusing to sell to dealers who sold other brands at lower prices. Annual profits of 20 per cent or more were earned regularly by Coats.

Perhaps the greatest of all British combinations was formed in the soap

402

GROWTH OF
ORGANIZED
BUSINESS
IN GERMANY
AND
ENGLAND

industry by means of both amalgamation and association. W. H. Lever began a successful soap business in the late 1880's, when vegetable oils were just beginning to be used for making soap. By the end of the century Lever Brothers were operating copra mills in Australia, cotton seed mills in the United States, and soap works in Germany and Switzerland. In 1906 Lever attempted a cartel-type agreement with ten other British soap firms, but the arrangement was abandoned after three weeks in favor of a giant amalgamation. In 1914 a soap manufacturers' association under the domination of Lever Brothers was established.

Virtual domestic monopolies were created by combinations in wallpaper and salt production. The Wallpaper Manufacturers combination brought together 98 per cent of the wallpaper sales to gain a nearly complete monopoly. This proved an efficient and profitable combination. The Salt Union of 1888 combined sixty-four firms which controlled approximately 90 per cent of the total salt production of the United Kingdom. In two years the Union raised the price of salt nearly 70 per cent. This predatory use of monopolistic power to exploit consumers backfired on the Salt Union, and it was forced to lower its prices in order to keep out domestic rivals and to maintain export markets.

British capital played an important role in many international combinations. As a large consumer of petroleum and its products, British nationals engaged in the transportation of oil. An early oceanic shipper was the Shell Transport and Trading Company, which brought oil to the British Isles from the Netherlands Indies, the United States and Russia. Strong competition led to a merger with the Royal Dutch Company by stages in 1902, 1903, and 1907, until Royal Dutch Shell became one of the largest business combinations in the world. Another important firm in the petroleum industry was the Anglo-Persian Oil Company launched in 1909. The Nobel Dynamite Trust Company of 1886 was perhaps the first instance of a true holding company designed to eliminate competition. British and German users of the Nobel patents had engaged in severe competition before the holding company was formed, but afterwards competition was suppressed and profits increased.

Control of rubber prices and production was the object of a famous British cartel, the Stevenson Plan, during the 1920's. As with most raw materials, the price of rubber is highly volatile in the free market. The price had risen during the First World War and fallen sharply in the postwar depression of 1920–21. Under government sponsorship and at the urging of Winston Churchill, then Secretary of State for Colonies, the British rubber producers of Ceylon and Malaya set up a cartel to stabilize (raise) the price of rubber. In order to raise the price it was necessary to restrict production; this was arranged in good cartel fashion by establishing quotas for each rubber grower, most of whom were large plantation owners. When this scheme began to operate in 1922, the price of raw rubber was 13 cents a pound. It skyrocketed to $1.25 per pound in 1925. This exorbitant price brought vigorous complaints from consumer nations, especially the United States, which was then in the midst of a rapid expansion of the automobile industry and was the leading consumer of rubber.

The dizzy heights of 1925 were not long maintained. Rubber growers in the Netherlands Indies, who were not members of the cartel, rapidly increased

their exports in order to reap the lush profits afforded by high world prices. **403**

GROWTH OF
ORGANIZED
BUSINESS
IN GERMANY
AND
ENGLAND
The price of rubber fell to 40 cents in 1927 and continued to fall. In 1928 the
Stevenson Plan was abandoned. The price reached 20 cents in 1929 but this
was not the end. About this time the new plantings made by the Dutch in the
early and middle 1920's under the stimulus of high prices began to come into
full bearing to flood the market at a time when the Great Depression had
carried all prices, especially raw materials, to record lows. The price of rubber
dropped to 4 cents a pound in 1932, or approximately $1/30$ of the 1925 level,
which proved disastrous for Dutch as well as British rubber producers. In 1934
the two groups got together to establish the International Rubber Restriction
Committee, a plan which remained in effect until the Japanese invasion of
Southeast Asia in 1942. Under the new plan the price of rubber rose to 20
cents during the Depression.

The breakdown of the Stevenson Plan illustrates the basic difficulty in
controlling prices through restrictionist schemes. If a significant proportion of
the producers remain outside the cartel and are in a position to increase their
output, the cartel is in a vulnerable position. Non-members gain the advantage
of high prices without the disadvantage of restricted output. Slavish adherence
to high prices may well mean economic suicide to members of the cartel. Such
schemes often do not last long, unless they are successful in bringing all producers into the fold and preventing new producers from entering the market.
In one important respect raw materials lend themselves to cartelization: they
are reasonably homogeneous products and therefore quotas are more easily
quantified than in the case of less homogeneous manufactured products. Ease
of entry of new producers is the Achilles heel of most raw materials cartels,
unlike mass production industries where new entry is made difficult by the
large amount of capital required to set up the fixed plant and equipment
necessary to begin operation. The small number of firms in a mass production
industry requires each producer to take into account the effect of his policies
upon his rivals, and thus to accept controlled prices and restricted production
even in the absence of formal agreements covering prices and output. This
is the fundamental principle of oligopolistic rivalry.

BUSINESS COMBINATIONS IN FRANCE

As compared with Germany and Britain, the combination movement was relatively weak in France because of the less developed state of mass production
and the traditional French emphasis on quality production. Combinations are
more difficult to organize when there are many small firms, and they are
scarcely practicable where the emphasis is on quality rather than quantity
production. France never quite achieved full capitalistic status and therefore
did not manifest the same degree of capitalistic combination and monopoly.
Some influence against combinations stemmed from the *Le Chapelier* law of
1791, which attempted to abolish all vestiges of gild organization and in so
doing also prohibited trade unions and business combines. This law was mitigated in 1884 with respect to both unions and employers' organizations. Large-
scale combinations did emerge in the heavy industries: iron and steel, electric

404

GROWTH OF
ORGANIZED
BUSINESS
IN GERMANY
AND
ENGLAND

power, machinery, and chemicals. The French steel industry was sufficiently well organized in 1926 to become a responsible member of the European Steel Cartel.

Steel, however, represented an exception to the general state of business combinations in France. More characteristic and more important for the state of competition was the trade association type of employer organization. Nearly every industry organized a syndicate in which membership was voluntary but nearly universal. The French syndicates were primarily information-gathering bureaus, but they also took on policy-making functions including the price-fixing activities performed by cartels in other Continental countries. Free competition of the classical conception in which price and output respond freely to the market forces of supply and demand was not characteristic of the French economy despite the undeveloped state of mass production and the persistence of small-scale enterprise.

SELECTED BIBLIOGRAPHY

CLAPHAM, JOHN H., *The Economic Development of France and Germany, 1815–1914*, 4th ed. Chapters 3, 4, 10, and 11. London: Cambridge University Press, 1951. (paperback)

——, *An Economic History of Modern Britain*, Vol. II, Chap. 4; Vol. III, Chap. 4. London: Cambridge University Press, 1932.

EHRMANN, HENRY W., *Organized Business in France*. Princeton: Princeton University Press, 1957.

LEVY, HERMANN, *The New Industrial System: A Study of the Origin, Forms, Finance and Prospects of Concentration of Industry*. London: Routledge & Kegan Paul, 1936.

LIEFMANN, ROBERT, *Cartels, Concerns, and Trusts*. New York: E. P. Dutton & Co., Inc., 1932.

MARSHALL, ALFRED, *Industry and Trade*, rev. ed. London: Macmillan & Co., Ltd., 1923.

STOCKING, GEORGE W., *The Potash Industry, A Study in State Control*. Peterborough, N. H.: The Richard R. Smith Co. Inc., 1931.

UNITED STATES INDUSTRIAL COMMISSION, *Report on Industrial Combinations in Europe*. Washington, D.C.: Government Printing Office, 1901.

ARTICLES

ABRAMS, MARK A., "The French Copper Syndicate, 1887–1889," *Journal of Economic and Business History*, IV (May, 1932), 409–28.

BRADY, ROBERT A., "Modernized Cameralism in the Third Reich: The Case of the National Industry Group," *Journal of Political Economy*, L (Feb., 1942), 65–97.

——, "The Role of Cartels in the Current Cultural Crisis," *American Economic Review*, XXXV (May, 1945), 312–20.

GRAS, N. S. B., "The Rise of Big Business," *Journal of Economic and Business History*, IV (May, 1932), 381–408.

Lewis, Ben W., "Development of Large-Scale Organization: Economic Implications," *Journal of Economic History*, XII (Fall, 1952), 425–37.

Liefmann, Robert, "German Industrial Organization Since the World War," *Quarterly Journal of Economics*, XL (Nov., 1925), 82–110.

Schweitzer, Arthur, "Big Business and the Nazi Party in Germany," *Journal of Business*, XIX (Jan., 1946), 1–24.

———, "Business Power under the Nazi Regime," *Zeitschrift für Nationalökonomie*, XX (Oct., 1960), 414–42.

Walker, Francis, "The German Steel Syndicate," in W. Z. Ripley, ed., *Trusts, Pools and Corporations*, 2nd ed. Boston: Ginn and Company, 1916.

See also Selected Bibliography at end of Chapter 23.

405

GROWTH OF
ORGANIZED
BUSINESS
IN GERMANY
AND
ENGLAND

The Growth of Organized Business
in the United States

In the United States after 1870, as in Germany and Great Britain, a brief period of destructive competition was followed by a combination movement aimed at limiting and suppressing competition in business. Unlike Germany and Great Britain, the combination movement in the United States provoked a determined attempt to prevent monopoly and to preserve competition through state and federal legislation. In order to escape the meshes of the law the business community changed the forms of business combinations. Consequently the anti-combination movement, or anti-trust movement as it has been called, became an integral part of the combination movement itself and made it more complex than the combination movements in other countries.

The four main forms of business combinations in the United States have been the pool, trust, holding company, and merger. The first was ineffectual under Anglo-American common law; the trust was specifically outlawed by anti-trust legislation in 1890; but the holding company and merger have survived and remain important forms of business combination in the United States in the second half of the twentieth century.

POOLS

A pool is a loose form of combination in which a number of rival firms agree to some arrangement which will lessen competition and maintain the profits of the group. In one form or another the agreement usually affects the selling price. As in a cartel, each member of a pool maintains its independence as a proprietary enterprise and no new business organization is established. In its loosest form a pool is simply an unwritten gentlemen's agreement. Other forms include agreements to share markets, divide revenues, apportion territory, pool patents, or otherwise to limit competition.

Several important pools appeared in the railway field as a device to stop rate wars during the 1870's and 1880's. In one of these famous rate wars between Cornelius Vanderbilt of the New York Central and Jay Gould and Jim Fisk of the Erie, the freight charge for shipping cattle from Chicago to New York was slashed to $1.00 per carload. If long continued, such rates would

407

THE GROWTH
OF ORGANIZED
BUSINESS
IN THE
UNITED STATES

have driven all the railways involved into bankruptcy. In 1877, the year following this rate war, the four main railways connecting the Ohio Valley with the East Coast entered a pooling agreement to share westbound traffic as follows: New York Central, 33 per cent; Erie, 33 per cent; Pennsylvania Railroad, 25 per cent; and Baltimore and Ohio, 9 per cent. In another railway pool, which lasted fourteen years (1870–84), three railways agreed to share all through traffic between Chicago and Omaha.

Railroads had a strong incentive to form pools because high overhead costs meant that rate cutting could go to fantastic lengths, as illustrated by the case cited above. Once a pool had been formed, the capital structure of the railway industry protected members of the pool against interlopers. High monopolistic rates and excess profits did not attract newcomers into the industry because the requisite capital outlays and other obstacles to starting a railroad were very great. Between some points railroads did have to contend with the competition of water transport carriers. In this situation a favorite device was to charge lower rail rates between points where competition was offered by water carriers and to charge higher rates to landlocked destinations, even though the latter points involved shorter hauls. This was known as long-and-short-haul discrimination, as it discriminated against shippers at intermediate (shorter) points.

Less successful than most of the railway pools was the Wire-Nail Association of 1895–96. This pool arose because of cutthroat competition and failed because high prices attracted new firms. One of the promoters of the wire-nail pool gave the following justification for it: "There is nail machinery enough in this country to produce four times as many nails as can be sold. When there is no pool the makers simply cut each other's throats. . . . There is only one way to make any money in a business like the nail business, and that is to have a pool." [1]

Important pools existed in cast iron pipes, meat packing, tobacco, wallpaper, and electrical equipment. The last-named was a patent pool between the General Electric Company and Westinghouse, the two companies which produced 90 per cent of the electrical equipment in the United States.

The fatal weakness of the pool under Anglo-American law was the inability to enforce its terms against members who might violate the agreement. The courts considered pooling agreements combinations in restraint of trade and therefore void and unenforceable. On the other hand, pooling agreements were not necessarily illegal in the sense that membership in one was a criminal or civil offense. Courts did not initiate action to dissolve pools. It was, however, difficult for members of a pool to be certain that other members were not violating the agreement sub rosa, and such suspicions weakened the ties holding the group together. Persons outside the pool who were harmed by it could bring action in court for damages and, if they could prove injury from the combination, the court might award damages against members of the pool.

A wave of protest against pools, railway discrimination, and industrial combinations generally spread over the United States during the 1870's and 1880's and resulted in state laws designed to protect farmers, shippers, and the

---

[1] Quoted in William Z. Ripley, *Trusts, Pools and Corporations* (Boston: Ginn & Co., 1905), pp. 70–71.

408

THE GROWTH
OF ORGANIZED
BUSINESS
IN THE
UNITED STATES

general public against business combinations. These state laws were called Granger laws because their main support came from farmers organized in granges. The right of states to regulate rates and prices in intrastate business was upheld, and the Granger laws had some salutary effects. The major problems, however, especially those involving railways, were in interstate commerce over which the states had no authority.

The first important federal law directed against monopoly in the United States was the Interstate Commerce Act of 1887. Although this law applied only to transportation agencies, the railways were at the time of its enactment the most troublesome source of monopoly practices. Railways not only engaged in discriminatory practices against shippers, but they conspired with large customers like the Standard Oil Trust against small producers and shippers. Advantage in transportation had long been one of the most effective devices for the promotion of industrial monopolies.

The Interstate Commerce Act was hailed as a triumph for farmers and small businessmen over giant industrial and transportation enterprises, but enthusiasm for this apparent victory faded with the early interpretation of the law by the courts and the administration by the Interstate Commerce Commission. As Charles Beard, the eminent American historian, remarked, "At the end of twenty years the act was hardly more than a scarecrow." [2] After a shaky start, however, the power of the Interstate Commerce Commission was increased, and it has proved a rather substantial instrument for safeguarding the public interest in transportation.

TRUSTS AND THE SHERMAN ANTI-TRUST LAW

Inherent weaknesses in the pool led American businessmen to search for more effective forms of combination. A device in vogue during the 1880's was the trust. The trust was formed by an exchange of non-voting trust certificates for the voting stock of a number of potentially competing business firms. Trust certificates were evidence of ownership of stock in the operating companies and constituted the basis for claims to dividends from the earnings of these companies. The trustees did not own the shares of stock; they merely held them in "trust." The trust did, of course, have control of the several companies and therefore could make all important decisions concerning prices, output, and related policies. There would have been little point in this except to convert a competitive situation into a monopolistic one. Use of the trust to suppress competition was an obvious perversion of the time-honored fiduciary relation under Anglo-American law by which one person acts as the trustee of another, who is the beneficiary. In its legitimate use, the trust is commonly employed to protect the property of minors or of insane persons, and to assure continuance of a family fortune.

The first and most notorious of the trusts was the Standard Oil Company, which became a trust in 1882. Other trusts created during the 1880's included the sugar trust, the whiskey trust, the lead trust, the linseed oil trust, the cotton oil trust, and the cordage trust. Overshadowing all of these, how-

---

[2] Charles A. and Mary R. Beard, *The Rise of American Civilization*, new edition (New York: The Macmillan Company, 1947), II, 341.

ever, was the oil trust, which occupied a major role in the growth of big **409**

THE GROWTH
OF ORGANIZED
BUSINESS
IN THE
UNITED STATES
business and the attempts to combat monopoly in the United States.

The Standard Oil Trust

The oil industry dates from the discovery of petroleum in western Pennsylvania in 1859. It attained the status of a great industry because of the demand for kerosene for illumination in the days before electric lighting and before there was a demand for gasoline for automobiles. The early years of the industry were characterized by severe, unrestricted competition in both crude oil production and refining. The creators of Standard Oil, who were in their formative years during the late 1860's and 1870's, at first accepted the traditional belief in the virtues of competition, but they soon discovered that this was not the way to make money. Like many of their contemporaries they turned to the suppression of competition through business combinations in one form or another. They found that combination (cooperation) worked in the sense that they made money; among them were some of the wealthiest men in the world. Some of the circumstances which set them apart from American businessmen of the preceding generation were the presence of the railways, the technology of large-scale refining, the availability of the corporation as a business device in industry, and the Long Depression (1873–96). Out of these new conditions came a period of destructive competition followed by business combination to restrict competition and establish monopolistic control. So much criticism and scorn have been heaped upon John D. Rockefeller and his associates in Standard Oil that it is important to view them in this historical perspective as men responding to circumstances which they did not create and over which they had little control. The founders of Standard Oil, like all men, were products of their time. Their motives and ethical behavior, whatever may be thought of them in retrospect, were neither much better nor much worse than those of their contemporaries in the business world. What is important is the consequence of their behavior for the evolution of the system of business enterprise.

Under the guiding genius of John D. Rockefeller the chaotic oil industry was "stabilized." The history of Standard Oil illustrates, perhaps better than any other, how advantages in transportation may be used to promote monopolistic control over a great industry. Rockefeller entered the oil industry through the refining branch, with plants located in Cleveland, Ohio. Crude oil was obtained from the oil regions of western Pennsylvania, and the principal markets were in the East. Hence transportation was a major expense. In 1870 Standard Oil was producing about 10 per cent of the country's output of refined oil. This quickly increased to 20 per cent by an ingenious and notorious scheme involving the South Improvement Company in 1872. Refiners associated with the South Improvement Company were to receive rebates, presumably for acting as "eveners" in the oil traffic pool formed at the same time among the Pennsylvania, New York Central, and Erie Railroads. The open rate on crude oil by rail from the oil regions in western Pennsylvania to Cleveland was to be 80 cents per barrel, and the open rate on refined products from Cleveland to New York City was two dollars ($2.00) per barrel. Thus the combined open rate was $2.80. The open rate was the same to all shippers, but

410

THE GROWTH
OF ORGANIZED
BUSINESS
IN THE
UNITED STATES

the members of the South Improvement Company were to receive a secret rebate of 90 cents (40 cents on crude and 50 cents on refined products). In addition to a rebate on all their own shipments, members of the South Improvement Company were also to receive the same rebate on all petroleum shipped by their competitors. Thus the harder their competitors worked, the more money Rockefeller and associates would make. Other rates such as those on crude petroleum shipped from the oil regions direct to New York were rigged so that no one could gain an advantage over Standard's effective (net) rates. Nor did the conspiracy stop here. Members of the South Improvement Company were to receive copies of their competitors' waybills, which contained all data relating to shipper, buyer, product, price, and terms of payment. Thus the South Improvement Company scheme provided Rockefeller and his associates with rebates on all their own shipments, rebates on all shipments by their competitors, and in addition a complete spy system on their competitors.

Armed with this contract, Standard representatives bought out most of their competitors. Within three months twenty-one of twenty-six Cleveland refiners went out of business. Their plants were either junked or put into use by Standard Oil producers. Although the agreement was signed between the railways and the South Improvement Company the scheme never actually went into operation so far as railway rates were concerned. Yet it was fully effective in achieving its purpose: the elimination of competition. A sympathetic biographer of John D. Rockefeller has said: "Of all the devices for the extinction of competition, this was the cruelest and most deadly yet conceived by any group of American industrialists." [3]

Although the notorious South Improvement Company scheme did not actually go into effect, there were numerous rebate arrangements which did. According to the United States Commissioner of Corporations, "unquestionably, the most important single element in this early extension of the company's power was the railroad rebate." By 1879 the Standard Oil alliance controlled 90 to 95 per cent of the country's refined petroleum output, as contrasted with the 10 per cent before the South Improvement scheme seven years earlier.

The Standard Oil Trust was formed in 1882. It gave a tighter and more systematic control over the *de facto* combination already in operation. Forty-one firms engaged in various phases of the oil business were brought together into an organization which could be manipulated secretly. Concealment from public scrutiny was one of the cardinal principles of the Standard Oil Company under Rockefeller's leadership.[4] The Trust continued to concentrate on the refining stage of the industry while still holding a whip hand over its few remaining rivals by advantages in transportation. When pipelines replaced railroads for transporting crude oil, the Trust gained control of the new transportation agency and used it with the same telling effect against actual and potential competitors. Profits on the trust certificates and capital stock averaged 19 per cent between 1882 and 1897.

Although profits were very good, the Trust was headed for legal diffi-

[3] Allan Nevins, *John D. Rockefeller: The Heroic Age* (New York: Charles Scribner's Sons, 1940), I, 325.

[4] On this and other characteristics of the Standard Oil Trust, see Ralph W. and Muriel E. Hidy, *Pioneering in Big Business, 1882–1911, History of Standard Oil Company (New Jersey)* (New York: Harper and Row, Publishers, 1955).

culties. The state of Ohio went to court to demand that the Trust return all the shares of the Standard Oil Company of Ohio, which was the original Rockefeller company, chartered in Ohio. The Ohio attorney-general contended that the Standard Oil Company of Ohio had violated the public interest through association with the Trust, which was a monopoly. The decision went against the Standard Oil Trust. The court made the significant point that the real offense was the threat to the public interest from the possession of power by Standard Oil and not the actual evils resulting from the abuse of power.

> Much has been said in favor of the objects of the Standard Oil Trust, and what it has accomplished. It may be true that it has improved the quality and cheapened the costs of petroleum and its products to the consumer. But such is not one of the usual or general results of a monopoly; and it is the policy of the law to regard, not what may, but what usually happens. Experience shows that it is not wise to trust human cupidity where it has the opportunity to aggrandize itself at the expense of others.[5]

Trouble was brewing elsewhere. The attorney-general of New York state was preparing to bring suit against the Standard Oil Company incorporated in New York. Most important, the federal Sherman Anti-Trust Act had been passed. The usefulness of the Standard Oil Trust was at an end.

The Sherman Anti-Trust Act of 1890

What is usually called the Sherman Anti-Trust Act of 1890 is formally titled "An act to protect trade and commerce against unlawful restraints and monopolies." The important provision of the act states that "*every* contract, combination in the form of trust or otherwise, or conspiracy, in restraint of trade or commerce . . . is hereby declared to be illegal . . ." Another provision is that "every person attempting to monopolize or conspiring to monopolize is guilty of a criminal offense." Clearly this was legislation designed to outlaw monopolistic combinations and to preserve competition. It left no doubt about the illegality of trusts in the technical sense of the Standard Oil Trust. But it went much further and said *every* combination in restraint of trade is illegal. It reads like a statute to outlaw *all types* of business combinations which might endanger competition in trade and commerce.

Hence the term "anti-trust" must be interpreted broadly, in a generic sense, and not in the narrow technical sense in which the Standard Oil organization of 1882, for example, was a trust. Hereafter "voting trust" will be used to designate a trust in the technical sense defined above, and when used without a modifying adjective, trust and anti-trust are used in the generic sense.

The Sherman Act of 1890 remains today the basic American law against business combinations. All federal anti-trust history since 1890 turns on the issue whether given forms of business organization are lawful under the Sherman law as interpreted in the courts. The American business community was much too resilient to be stopped even by what appeared to be a sweeping prohibition against combinations.

---

[5] *Ohio State v. Standard Oil Co.* 49 Ohio, 137 (1892).

Judicial interpretations of anti-trust legislation have limited its scope and jurisdiction much more than proponents of the anti-trust philosophy believe desirable. A major setback came in the first case before the United States Supreme
Court under the Sherman law, the E. C. Knight, or sugar trust, case (1895).
The American Sugar Refining Company brought under its control 98 per cent
of the sugar refining capacity of the country. Although the Court conceded
that this constituted virtually a complete monopoly, it ruled that sugar refining was "manufacturing," not commerce, and therefore the federal government
had no jurisdiction over the case. The regulation of manufacturing was a function of the states and not of the federal government. The federal anti-trust laws
were greatly weakened by the decision in the Knight case. Whatever the legal
merit of the tightrope walk between commerce and manufacturing, the economic effect of the decision was to pave the way for the greatest outburst of
business combinations in the nation's history in the years between 1897 and
1904. With voting trusts outlawed and pools legally unsatisfactory, the combinations of the period took the form of corporate holding companies and
mergers.

The holding company was not much more than a modification of the
illegal voting trust. Shares of stock in the holding company were exchanged
for shares in operating companies, instead of exchanging trust certificates for
shares in operating companies. The holding company became legal owner of
shares in operating companies, whereas the voting trust merely held these
shares "in trust" for the owners; and a board of directors was substituted for a
board of trustees. These differences had no economic significance. The distinction between the holding company and the voting trust was slight even in the
legal sense. Interestingly, when the voting trust was first used in 1882, the
holding company was more clearly illegal than the voting trust. Under common law one corporation could not hold stock in another corporation unless
granted special authority by a legislature to do so. This limitation on holding
companies was part of the long tradition of Anglo-American common law
which looked with grave suspicion on corporations in general; the idea that
one suspicious character should hold shares in another suspicious character was
repugnant to public morality until the close of the nineteenth century. During
the early 1880's the preference for the voting trust over the holding company
was a preference for something which business might get away with over a
device which was clearly beyond the pale.

As events turned out, however, these bedfellows changed places. The
voting trust became definitely illegal, first by judicial and then by legislative
action, and the holding company achieved dubious legality as a form of business combination. The bar against holding companies was let down by New
Jersey, partly in 1889 and fully in 1893, by legislation which permitted any
corporation chartered in New Jersey to hold the securities of any other corporation. Several other states, not wishing to be outdone by New Jersey in collecting incorporation fees and taxes, quickly followed suit. In 1891 the old sugar
trust reorganized temporarily as a holding company. When the Standard Oil
trust was formally dissolved by its own hand in 1892, the Standard Oil Company (New Jersey) assumed holding company status vis-à-vis some of its many

associated branches, and the entire Standard Oil empire was reorganized in 1898 with Jersey Standard as the parent holding company.

413

THE GROWTH
OF ORGANIZED
BUSINESS
IN THE
UNITED STATES

Formation of the United States Steel Corporation (1901)

Andrew Carnegie, who was the dominant figure in the American steel industry between the Civil War and 1900, believed in rugged individualism and unlimited competition based on maximum technological and organizational efficiency. No major combination was possible in the steel industry without Carnegie, yet he was not disposed to join his plants with those of less efficient producers. There were few successful combinations in the steel industry until the great combination drive began in the late 1890's. Between 1898 and 1900 monopolistic combinations of the horizontal type were formed among the manufacturers of tin plate, sheet steel, steel wire, steel rods, steel tubes, and seamless pipes. These divisions of the steel industry are usually referred to as the secondary group, as distinguished from the primary group, which produces steel ingots, semifinished steel, and heavier finished products such as rails and structural "shapes." Carnegie belonged to the latter group and was not directly affected by the horizontal combinations among secondary producers.

Some of the secondary producers now initiated steps to expand their facilities to include basic steel plants. A large producer of wire rods, for example, announced plans to become a primary producer. This move toward vertical integration by secondary producers was, of course a threat to primary producers like Carnegie, who depended on the secondary group as outlets for their heavy steel. As a countermove, Carnegie intimated he would build a large wire rod plant and followed with an announcement of plans for the largest steel tube plant in the world. Both sides were capable of carrying through their plans for expansion into each other's domains. The secondary producers were closely allied with J. P. Morgan and Company, the great investment banking house. Carnegie enjoyed great financial strength, and no one doubted his ability to make good his threat of aggressive retaliation against the secondary group. A battle of the giants seemed imminent.

If all the announced plans had been carried out, the enormous expansion of productive capacity would have greatly exceeded the normal consuming power of the nation for years to come. The newly formed combinations among secondary producers would have lost their recently acquired monopolistic and quasi-monopolistic positions. A knock-down, drag-out price war in steel was in prospect. Carnegie's rivals and potential rivals, however, chose not to do battle with him. Although the House of Morgan had great financial resources, it also had far-flung interests which benefited from the then flourishing state of the stock market. A price war in steel would surely have depressed the prices of steel securities and have jeopardized Morgan's position in other lines of business, especially railroads. Carnegie, on the other hand, operated independently of the financial markets, and while he would have suffered losses from a drastic price war, the basic stability of his firm was not endangered. A realistic assessment of the facts suggested that Carnegie would win out in any prolonged competitive struggle.

414

THE GROWTH
OF ORGANIZED
BUSINESS
IN THE
UNITED STATES

Rather than submit to an indefinite period of destructive competition the Morgan group approached Carnegie for a settlement. Andrew Carnegie was a man of unusual qualities, who saw life as much more than making money and beating down his rivals. He had made known his desire to retire from active business in order to have more time to plan the use of his great fortune for human betterment. He was willing to sell and he was in a position to set his own price. Carnegie sold out for $213,000,000 in 5 per cent gold bonds, and J. P. Morgan formed the United States Steel Corporation in April, 1901. The underwriting syndicate headed by Morgan received an extravagant fee of $62,500,000 for promoting the combination. This first billion-dollar combination was a holding company established for the purpose of restricting or eliminating competition in the steel industry.

The Steel Corporation issued securities capitalized at approximately $1.4 billion, in exchange for tangible property in plant and equipment which the United States Commissioner of Corporations valued at approximately $700 million. In accounting terms this meant that on the right side of the balance sheet, securities were listed totalling approximately $1.4 billion. Since a balance sheet must balance, the book value of the assets was arbitrarily increased by $700 million above their actual value. As the saying goes, one-half of the stock was "water," that is, it had no tangible property behind it. Another way to describe the situation is to say that the Steel Corporation was grossly overcapitalized. In a competitive situation there would have been no justification for this mark-up of asset values. Earnings would have gone first to pay 5 per cent interest to bondholders and what was left would have paid part of the 7 per cent due to preferred shareholders. The owners of common shares would have received nothing on stock that was worth nothing. Any value the common stock might have rested on the anticipation of excess earnings arising from monopolistic pricing in the steel industry. This expectation proved well founded. In subsequent years the prices of steel were "stabilized" at high levels, with the Steel Corporation in the role of price leader, setting prices which other firms in the industry followed. At these prices, profits were good, and the common shareholders were handsomely rewarded for the "risk" they took that the monopolistic advantage might not actually materialize.

When the Steel Corporation was formed in 1901 it controlled two-thirds of the steel ingot capacity and three-fifths of the total steel business of the United States. It retained its position as the giant of the industry but did not maintain the same relative share in the industry. There are several possible explanations for this loss of relative position. In view of the great amount of watered stock with which it started its career, the Steel Corporation may have preferred high prices and high profits in order to strengthen its financial position even if high prices caused other firms to expand their capacity more rapidly than U.S. Steel expanded its capacity. The failure of U.S. Steel to maintain its proportionate share also suggests that the economies of large-scale integration, so much talked about as justification for the combination, were grossly exaggerated. Steel companies much smaller than the mammoth U.S. Steel Corporation were able to produce steel as cheaply. In fact, U.S. Steel was not the low-cost producer in its industry. The combination of combinations, as it was called, created domination of the market rather than technological superiority.

Holding companies received a severe setback in the Northern Securities decision of 1904. The two great transcontinental railways, the Northern Pacific and the Great Northern, had been competing lines between Lake Superior and the Pacific Northwest. In 1901 the two lines were brought under common control through the formation of a holding company known as the Northern Securities Company. A majority of the stock of both railways was exchanged for stock of the holding company. With the backing of President Theodore Roosevelt, sometimes referred to as the "trust-buster," the government instituted proceedings against the Northern Securities Company. In 1904, by a 5 to 4 vote, the United States Supreme Court rendered a decision that the Northern Securities Company was an illegal combination in restraint of interstate commerce and therefore in violation of the Sherman Anti-Trust Act. The court ordered the Northern Securities Company dissolved. The same groups who controlled the two railways under the holding company continued to control them after its dissolution so the decision had limited economic significance. Legally, however, it was a very significant decision.

The Northern Securities case was the first important court victory against business combinations under the anti-trust law. It encouraged anti-trust authorities to institute proceedings against other combinations. The decision also discouraged the formation of new holding companies and even caused some combinations which had organized as holding companies to abandon them in favor of other business forms. The tobacco trust, for example, changed from a holding company to an asset-owning, or merger, type of combination in 1904. Paradoxically, success in enforcing the anti-trust laws against holding companies, voting trusts, and pools probably strengthened the monopoly movement by driving business enterprises away from the looser forms into the tighter, stronger, and legally safer merger.[6] Mergers were not immune from anti-trust prosecution, but they were less vulnerable to the charge of being agreements in restraint of trade.

MERGERS

A merger is the most complete form of business combination. Like the holding company it is a corporate form of combination, which cartels, pools, and voting trusts are not. A merger is a property-owning corporation, whereas a holding company is a security-holding corporation. A merger is an operating company as distinguished from a holding company. Whenever the central corporation of a group of companies is an operating company, the combination is called a merger even though the central corporation may also, incidentally, own securities in other companies. A merger unites the operating property of an entire combination under one concern.

[6] On this important point see, for example, Willard Thorp in Temporary National Economic Committee, 75th Congress, 3rd session, Hearings, Part I, *Economic Prologue* (Washington, D.C.: Government Printing Office, 1939), p. 112. In 1899 (Addyston Pipe case) the Supreme Court held that a loose association (pool) among rival manufacturers of cast iron pipe was an unlawful conspiracy in restraint of trade. This added impetus to the corporate form of combination, especially the merger.

416

THE GROWTH
OF ORGANIZED
BUSINESS
IN THE
UNITED STATES

As compared with other forms of combination, the corporate structure of the merger is simpler and the concentration of managerial control is more direct. Despite the fact that mergers are more difficult to form, because of legislative and statutory regulations, a large proportion of American combinations since 1890 have been of this type. The most notable exceptions were the Standard Oil Company (1899) and the United States Steel Corporation (1901), to which reference has already been made.

Among the leading mergers during the great combination movement between 1898 and 1904 were the following: International Harvester, E. I. du Pont de Nemours, United Shoe Machinery Company, Bethlehem Steel, Republic Iron and Steel, Allis-Chalmers, Eastman Kodak, American Tobacco, United Fruit, Pullman, American Can, Corn Products, and National Steel.

American Tobacco Company

Mr. James B. Duke, who consciously patterned his career in the tobacco industry after the career of John D. Rockefeller in the oil industry, used similar means to attain a monopolistic position in tobacco manufacturing in the United States. He started in the cigarette branch of the industry in the 1880's when machines were just beginning to be used to make cigarettes. He purposely precipitated a vicious trade war in order to force other cigarette manufacturers to join him in forming the American Tobacco Company in 1890. This company, which combined five of the leading manufacturers, produced 95 per cent of the total output of cigarettes in the United States. During the 1890's the American Tobacco Company maintained a near-monopoly in cigarette production by gaining exclusive control of cigarette-making machinery and by buying out strong competitors.

Next Duke moved to gain control of plug tobacco by resorting to heavy advertising, selling below cost, and even having agents distribute free samples of "Battle Ax" plugs to every man encountered on the streets in territory where rival brands were popular. After succeeding in plug tobacco, Duke and his associates gained control of smoking tobacco and then conquered the snuff business after a vigorous competitive war. By 1900 Duke and his associates produced more than nine-tenths of the cigarettes, about five-eighths of the plug and smoking tobacco, and four-fifths of the snuff in the United States. His group tried to dominate cigar making but was unsuccessful, mainly because cigars were still made mostly by hand by many small producers. In 1901 the several branches of the tobacco industry under Duke's control were brought more closely together by the formation of a holding company, Consolidated Tobacco Company. After the Northern Securities decision in 1904 the tobacco combination was reorganized as a merger in the hope of avoiding prosecution under the anti-trust laws, with the American Tobacco Company as the central corporation.

SUMMARY OF PERIOD 1897–1903

The greatest wave of business combinations in American history occurred between 1897 and 1904. There are several reasons for the timing and magnitude of this wave. In the Long Depression from 1873 to 1896, mass production

came of age and businessmen learned from bitter experience that price competition can be destructive of profits. This generated a mentality of "live and let live," which provided the psychological basis for the combination movement. Since noncorporate combinations such as cartels, pools, and voting trusts were outlawed by common or statutory law in the United States, it was necessary to await business conditions favorable to the formation of corporate combinations. The favorable time to float corporate securities is, of course, during prosperity when securities markets are buoyant. The years immediately following 1897 brought this opportunity for the first time after the onset of mass production.

417

THE GROWTH
OF ORGANIZED
BUSINESS
IN THE
UNITED STATES

Characteristically, American combinations have come in waves during prosperity accompanied by a bullish stock market. In contrast, the formation of cartels in Germany characteristically was most active in depression, though not curbed in prosperity. By 1897 investment banking had also come of age in the United States, and with railway reorganization fairly well disposed of, investment bankers could turn their attention to financial reorganization in industry. Further stimulus was provided by the Spanish-American War, a war of ideal magnitude, that is, big enough to stimulate the economy but not so large as to disrupt business as usual.

By 1903 most American industries suited to large-scale combination had been reorganized. The stock market panic of 1903, which was partly caused by reckless combinations recently completed, dimmed the prospects for promoters' profits. Following the decision in the Northern Securities case in 1904 a few combinations, like tobacco, scurried from the vulnerable holding company to what was hoped would be the safer ground of mergers. By 1904 public sentiment was running strongly against the "trusts." Muckraking books appeared on best-seller lists. This sentiment against big business ramified into the political arena. "Trust-buster" Teddy Roosevelt was sitting in the White House girding for re-election in 1904.[7]

The magnitude of the combination movement between 1897 and 1904 may be measured in various ways. Approximately 200 combinations capitalized at $1 million or more had been formed, with aggregate capitalization in excess of $5 billion. Approximately 40 per cent of the nation's total capital in manufacturing was controlled by these combinations. Single combinations produced all of the aluminum ingot (Aluminum Company of America), nine-tenths of the petroleum products (Standard Oil Company), nine-tenths of the tobacco (American Tobacco Company), nine-tenths of the cane sugar (American Sugar Refining Company), between eight- and nine-tenths of the farm machinery (International Harvester Company), nearly all shoe-making machinery (United Shoe Machinery Company), and two-thirds of the steel (United States Steel Company).

More important than any statistical measurement, however, was the transformation in the structure of American industry which was to set the pattern for the twentieth century. Complete monopolies, although not unknown, were rare, but in many of the basic industries one business dinosaur dominated the market situation, became the price leader, and made its power

---

[7] In popular literature Theodore Roosevelt probably has more of a reputation than he deserves for "trust-busting." Mr. Dooley characterized Roosevelt's position as follows: "On wan hand I wud stamp thim undher fut; on th' other hand not so fast."

418

THE GROWTH
OF ORGANIZED
BUSINESS
IN THE
UNITED STATES

felt by independents, who had learned by this time that price competition was not healthy. In other basic industries a few giant firms produced more than one-half the total product of their industry. These oligopolists respected each other and cowed smaller independents by their mere existence. The historic significance of this was that the ideal of the self-regulating market, idealized by classical economics, was now an anachronism.

THE RULE OF REASON

In 1911 the Supreme Court ruled that the Standard Oil Company and the American Tobacco Company were combinations in unreasonable restraint of trade and ordered them dissolved. Decisions against these two giants of the combination movement represent a high mark in the application of the anti-trust laws. Ironically, however, in the hour of greatest triumph, the starch was taken out of the anti-trust laws by a new principle laid down in the Standard Oil case and reiterated in the American Tobacco case—the "rule of reason."

The rule of reason involved a distinction between combinations in reasonable restraint of trade and those in unreasonable restraint of trade, with the Court asserting that only combinations in unreasonable restraint of trade were illegal under the Sherman law. In effect, the Court distinguished between "good trusts" and "bad trusts."

This interpretation limited severely the applicability of the anti-trust laws. The Sherman Act states that *every* combination in restraint of trade is illegal. By invoking the rule of reason the Court interpreted the Sherman law to mean only that every combination in *unreasonable* restraint of trade is illegal. The corollary, of course, is that some combinations in restraint of trade, or competition, are not illegal because they are reasonable restraints. The Court thus imposed upon itself the obligation to decide how much restraint of competition is consistent with the public interest. It must decide how much injury to the public a combination may inflict and still stay within the law. It concluded that Standard Oil and the American Tobacco Company had gone over the lawful hill into the valley of badness and therefore must be dissolved.

The wording and title of the Sherman Act ("an act to protect trade and commerce against unlawful restraints and monopolies") seem to suggest that it was the intention of Congress to direct it against all efforts to restrict freedom of competion in national markets. The 1911 ruling was a novel interpretation, inconsistent with the earlier findings of the majority of the Supreme Court in anti-trust cases. The Court had explicitly rejected the "rule of reason" in several earlier decisions (the Trans-Missouri Freight Association case, 1897, the Joint Traffic Association case, 1898, and the Northern Securities case, 1904). Congress had also explicitly rejected a proposal to modify the Sherman law as it was in effect amended, by judicial legislation, in the 1911 cases.

As in the Northern Securities case, the legal dissolution of the Standard Oil holding company did not mean an economic break-up of the community of interests. The holding company distributed to its shareholders the stock it held in subsidiaries. The Court did nothing to prevent a single individual or family from holding large blocks of shares in several of the Standard com-

panies. The Rockefeller family and allied groups remained the dominant force in the several Standard companies and perpetuated their control through directorships as well as ownership. Standard Oil interests were temporarily disturbed but not disrupted by the Court's decision.

419

THE GROWTH
OF ORGANIZED
BUSINESS
IN THE
UNITED STATES

One notable change which came over the oil industry in the years following the dissolution of the trust in 1911 was a rapid overall expansion resulting from the growth of the automobile industry. Gasoline, which had previously been of minor significance, quickly became the leading petroleum product. In the expansion several new firms entered the oil industry and converted the market situation from a near-monopoly to an oligopoly. Cooperation rather than competition continued as the characteristic pattern of the industry. Except for sporadic outbreaks in local territory, price competition in gasoline has not prevailed. In most areas of the United States, Standard Oil companies nave set the price and other firms have been content to follow their lead.

The rule of reason in the 1911 cases was both a *non-sequitur* and an *obiter dictum*. It did not follow from the common law rule of reason nor the Sherman law nor Congressional intent. It had no direct bearing on the outcome of either of the two 1911 decisions, which would have been decided in the same way with or without the rule of reason. Justice Harlan, who dissented vigorously on the rule of reason, voted with the majority in the unanimous decision to dissolve the Standard Oil Company. The significance of the 1911 rule of reason was as a portent of things to come. It was, for example, decisive in the United States Steel Corporation case. Proceedings in this case were instituted in 1911 but because of the First World War the decision was delayed until 1920.

U.S. Steel Case (1920)

In a 4 to 3 decision the Supreme Court found the United States Steel Corporation was a "good trust" and refused to order its dissolution.[8] The Court said, "the law does not make mere size an offense or the existence of unexerted power an offense." Thus big business is not per se bad business. Moreover, the Court refused to give weight to admittedly illegal methods which had been employed by the Steel Corporation in order to exert influence arising from its great size and power: "Whatever there was of evil effect was discontinued before the suit was brought and this, we think, determines the decrees." In other words, culprits must be caught in acts of oppression in order to be in violation of the anti-trust laws. The Sherman law ceased to be a law to preserve competition; it ceased to be a law against the power to oppress. It became a law to prevent the use of overt acts of oppression currently in use. It applied "only to the abuse of power, not to the power to abuse." [9]

[8] This was a 4 to 3 decision, as two justices did not participate in the case. One had been Attorney-General during an earlier phase of the proceedings against the Steel Corporation, and a second had expressed the opinion that it was illegal and uneconomical. The decision of the Court, therefore, probably did not represent the opinion of the majority of its members.

[9] For an excellent discussion of all phases of the trust and anti-trust movement see George W. Stocking and Myron W. Watkins, *Monopoly and Free Enterprise* (New York: Twentieth Century Fund, 1951).

420

THE GROWTH
OF ORGANIZED
BUSINESS
IN THE
UNITED STATES

Some insight into practices which the Court tolerated may be indicated by referring to the "Gary dinners" and "Pittsburgh Plus." Judge Elbert Gary, as president of the Steel Corporation, entertained representatives of other steel companies at an annual banquet. As host and speaker he conveyed to the industry the prices which his company planned to set for the coming year. Working committees and subcommittees were organized to supplement the banquet committee. While the Steel Corporation had no legal basis for imposing its price structure on the steel industry as a whole, it did have the potential economic power to threaten and to keep in line wayward firms. There were no important wayward firms, however, because the steel industry had learned that price competition does not pay. They followed, willingly or not, the lead of the giant of their industry. This illustrates the "live and let live" philosophy associated with mass production.

"Pittsburgh Plus" refers to the single basing point system used to fix the prices of steel and steel products. It greatly facilitated and strongly reinforced the price leadership of the Steel Corporation and was still in effect when the case was decided in 1920. Under "Pittsburgh Plus" the price of all steel was calculated in terms of a base price at Pittsburgh plus the railway freight from Pittsburgh to the point of destination. All steel firms followed the same method of pricing. The only prices quoted were delivered prices; customers did not have the choice of paying the price at the plant and assuming the freight charge. Pittsburgh was chosen as the basing point because it was the center of the steel industry, and United States Steel had most of its large plants there. A customer in a given location paid the same price for steel regardless of where it was manufactured. It was not possible to buy more cheaply from a nearby plant than from a distant plant. The price and freight charges were always based on Pittsburgh. For example, a customer in Denver who purchased steel produced in nearby Pueblo, Colorado, would pay the Pittsburgh base price plus freight charges by rail from Pittsburgh to Denver despite the fact that his steel came from Pueblo and not from Pittsburgh. Obviously the customer in this instance would be charged for more freight than the steel firm paid to the railroad for shipping it to him. The charge for freight which never actually existed became known as "phantom freight." If the base price of a certain type of steel were $100 per ton, the freight from Pittsburgh to Denver $10 per ton, and the freight from Pueblo to Denver $2 per ton, then the "phantom freight" would be $8 per ton. On steel shipped from Pueblo to Denver the customer in Denver would pay the base price of $100 plus freight from Pittsburgh of $10, making a total delivered price of $110 in Denver.

The advantage of the basing point system of pricing to a producer with a few large plants concentrated in Pittsburgh was to place the firm on at least equal terms with steel plants located anywhere in the country. In the example just cited the customer in Denver would pay the same price ($110) for steel whether it came from Pueblo, Pittsburgh, or anywhere else. Consequently the producer in Pittsburgh suffered no disadvantage in meeting the price of rivals even though the actual freight costs from Pittsburgh to Denver were higher than from Pueblo to Denver. Actually the net price received on a Pittsburgh shipment, after paying freight, was less than the net price on steel shipped from Pueblo. Since cost per ton of producing steel normally decreases

as the volume increases, large plants enjoy an advantage under the basing point system. The average cost of production per ton is lower if the large plant has access to a wide market without the handicap of high prices caused by high freight costs. This is a social as well as a private advantage associated with the economics of large overhead costs.

421

THE GROWTH
OF ORGANIZED
BUSINESS
IN THE
UNITED STATES

A social disadvantage of the basing point system is the great amount of "cross-hauling," that is, excess transportation induced by the failure to give customers the option of paying a mill price and assuming the transport shipping cost from mill to final destination. It is a form of price discrimination in the sense that prices do not reflect large differences in costs. The Supreme Court in 1920, however, did not find the basing point system a violation of the anti-trust laws. The single basing point system (Pittsburgh Plus) was replaced by a multiple basing point system in 1924 as a result of action by the Federal Trade Commission. In 1945 the Supreme Court finally ruled the basing point system to be a violation of the anti-trust laws and ordered it discontinued as the exclusive system of price quotation.

In summary, it may be said that the Sherman Anti-Trust Act as modified by the rule of reason and as interpreted in the United States Steel case was still a law against pure monopoly; but the United States Steel Corporation was not a monopoly and, in fact, no industrial monopolies of the pure type existed in American industry. The Sherman Act was still a law against guerrilla warfare of the type engaged in by the old Standard Oil and American Tobacco Companies; the business community, however, had outgrown such jungle warfare tactics. The Sherman Act was no longer a law to maintain competition, but a law to prevent overt acts of collusion. What the Court had done in effect was to sanction a market situation which technology and a new business ethos had already created. This meant that the Court accepted oligopoly, even of the one-sided type in the steel industry in which a single giant dominated the other firms. In brief, the Supreme Court was against what the business community had already outgrown, namely predatory price policy. Under the circumstances there was not much for the anti-trust authorities to do.

CLAYTON ACT OF 1914 AND THE FEDERAL TRADE COMMISSION ACT

When Democratic President Woodrow Wilson entered the White House in 1913, his "New Freedom" program included a determined effort to strengthen the anti-trust laws against business combinations and to render competition more effective than preceding Republican administrations had been able to do. These objectives were embodied in the Clayton Act of 1914, which sought mainly to clarify by making more specific the broad, but unenforceable, aims of the Sherman Act. The chief substantive provisions of the Clayton Act were the following:

(1) *Holding companies.* Corporations were prohibited from holding stock in other corporations where the effect was to lessen competition substantially. A company could still own stock in another for investment and was still free to purchase the assets of other com-

422

THE GROWTH
OF ORGANIZED
BUSINESS
IN THE
UNITED STATES

panies. The test "to lessen competition substantially" was indefinite and perhaps more severe than under the Sherman Act.

(2) *Interlocking directorates.* The Clayton Act made it unlawful for any person to serve simultaneously on the board of directors of two or more corporations which were or had been competitors if any one of the corporations had capital, surplus, and undivided profits in excess of $1,000,000. This prohibition was easily circumvented by dummy directors, who served nominally in place of the real directors. No limitation was placed on interlocking officers, nor upon common ownership of stock in competing companies.

(3) *Price discrimination.* This section was directed against local price cutting and personal discrimination. A favorite device of the trusts was to cut prices in a local area in order to drive out a smaller competitor or to bring a recalcitrant one into line. Personal discrimination was one form of unfair competition which the Clayton Act and the Federal Trade Commission Act tried to correct.

(4) *Tying agreements and exclusive dealing contracts.* The intent here was to prevent a seller from requiring as a condition of sale that the purchaser buy other articles exclusively from the seller, and to prevent a manufacturer from requiring that his wholesale and retail distributors not handle products of rival manufacturers. Both applied only where the effect would be to lessen competition substantially.

(5) *Labor unions.* The Clayton Act specifically stated that the anti-trust laws were not to be used against labor unions. In part this was based on the principle that "the labor of a human being is not a commodity or article of commerce." Labor unions are organized for mutual help and do not have capital stock and are not conducted for profit. Although Congress had not intended that the Sherman Act should apply to labor unions, it had been interpreted by the courts in such a way as to make it a weapon against labor organizations. In the notorious Danbury Hatters case a trade union which had engaged in a boycott against an employer was held to be a conspiracy in restraint of trade. Workers in the union were ordered by the court to pay triple damages to the employer, in accordance with one of the special provisions of the Sherman Act. Some union members were forced to sell their homes in order to pay the damages assessed against them. In view of this background the provision in the Clayton Act declaring that the anti-trust laws were not applicable to unions was hailed by Samuel Gompers, long-time president of the American Federation of Labor, as "labor's magna carta." Subsequent application of the anti-trust laws in labor cases proved that Gompers had been overoptimistic. The courts continued to hold that certain practices of unions were violations of the anti-trust laws. The willingness of the courts to apply anti-trust laws against labor unions and the reluctance to apply them effectively against business combinations reflected the generally conservative orientation of the judiciary in the United States at the time.

The Federal Trade Commission was established to supplement the punitive anti-trust laws with a preventive approach to monopolistic practices.

423

THE GROWTH
OF ORGANIZED
BUSINESS
IN THE
UNITED STATES

By 1914 experience had demonstrated the inadequacy of relying solely on trust-busting to maintain free and fair competition. By eradicating certain devices it was supposed that incipient monopolies could be plucked before they ripened. The Federal Trade Commission was authorized to administer the substantive provisions of the Clayton Act and to issue cease-and-desist orders against unfair methods of competition. Its effectiveness has varied in accordance with the support given to it by the judicial and executive branches of the government.

ANTI-TRUST POLICY SINCE 1920

Inactivity was the main characteristic of anti-trust policy in the decade of the 1920's during which the Harding, Coolidge, and Hoover administrations viewed with complacency a merger movement second only to the one at the turn of the century. Under the New Deal of Franklin D. Roosevelt anti-trust policy passed through two quite distinct phases. In the first stage the National Industrial Recovery Act played directly into the hands of business combinations of the trade association type. This tended to weaken competition and place the anti-trust laws in cold storage. After this ill-fated attempt at industrial recovery the Roosevelt administration embarked upon a policy of vigorous enforcement of the anti-trust laws under the leadership of Thurman Arnold, head of the anti-trust division. Some progress was made. The Temporary National Economic Committee (TNEC) conducted the most exhaustive investigation of monopoly that has ever been made in any country. The Committee's most notable recommendation was that national business corporations should be chartered by the national (federal) government.

During the Second World War anti-trust policy entered another period of quiescence. Many important cases brought by Thurman Arnold were suspended when companies engaged in war production complained they could not put forth their best production effort when harassed by anti-trust proceedings. In those cases which were concluded after the war, conditions had changed so fundamentally that prewar evidence seemed an unsatisfactory basis for making postwar decisions. In the very important case against the Aluminum Company of America the court of final jurisdiction reached a decision in 1945 requiring that the Aluminum Company be dissolved. Once again, as in the Standard Oil case, the difficulty of dissolving a major company was demonstrated. Alcoa's monopoly was broken by requiring that government-owned plant constructed during the war be turned over to rival concerns. This case has been put down as a legal triumph and an economic defeat for the anti-trust laws.[10]

Another significant postwar decision was in a new tobacco case in 1946. The big three cigarette producers were found *jointly* to hold a monopoly of the market and were fined for restraining the market even though there was no demonstrated collusion among the three companies. They were behaving like monopolists because self-interest dictated they should take account of the

[10] See Walter Adams, "The Aluminum Case: Legal Victory—Economic Defeat," *American Economic Review*, XLI (Dec., 1951), 915–22.

424

THE GROWTH
OF ORGANIZED
BUSINESS
IN THE
UNITED STATES

probable reactions of each other, according to the principle of oligopolistic rivalry. If the courts were to apply this approach consistently it would probably revolutionize anti-trust policy. Even in the tobacco case, however, action was limited to assessing fines against the guilty companies. Other postwar decisions suggest that too much significance should not be attached to the decisions in the aluminum and tobacco cases.

Du Pont–General Motors case (1949–1962)   In the biggest anti-trust case in its history the United States Supreme Court ordered E. I. du Pont de Nemours & Company to dispose of 63,000,000 shares of General Motors Corporation stock valued at $3 billion. The Court upheld the view of the anti-trust division that Du Pont's ownership in General Motors, constituting 23 per cent of its common stock, violated the Clayton Act because the ownership relation tended to create a monopoly. After acquiring these shares General Motors purchased two-thirds of its paint and one-half of its fabrics from the Du Pont Company. The Court saw no safeguard against the tendency toward monopoly of General Motors business except to divest Du Pont of its General Motors stock. Furthermore, the court settlement required that the Du Pont family and those close to Du Pont management divest themselves of all General Motors stock coming to them from the Du Pont Company in the divestiture. The Court also prohibited any interlocking directorates between General Motors and Du Pont for ten years.

Electrical Products Conspiracy Case, 1961   In the biggest criminal conspiracy case in anti-trust history seven business executives in the electrical products firms went to prison and their companies paid fines of nearly $2 million. General Electric, Westinghouse, Allis Chalmers and twenty-six other firms pleaded guilty or accepted consent decrees to charges of price fixing, bid rigging, and market sharing brought against them in a grand jury investigation. Numerous products were involved, but significantly the most flagrant violations occurred in heavy equipment in which chronic excess capacity plagued the producers and where cutthroat competition threatened chronic losses. Some defendants in the case described collusion as a way of life in their industry. This case was the most sensational but not the only one in the electrical products industry. General Electric was cited in 39 anti-trust violations between 1911 and 1961.

Two General Electric executives at the $127,000 and $135,000 per year level were among those imprisoned. A $200,000-a-year executive was indicted but charges were dropped because evidence for conviction in court did not seem conclusive. Executives above this level were not indicted, although the judge in the case clearly indicated his belief in the guilt of those at the very top when he said: "One would be most naive indeed to believe that these violations of the law, so long persisted in, affecting so large a segment of the industry and finally involving so many millions upon millions of dollars were facts unknown to those responsible for the corporation and its conduct. . . ." In the words of Robert A. Bicks, head of the anti-trust division: "These men and companies have in a true sense mocked the image of that economic system which we profess to the world." The President of General Electric resigned, supposedly because of "poor health."

425

*THE GROWTH
OF ORGANIZED
BUSINESS
IN THE
UNITED STATES*

The significance of this sensational case was not primarily in the revelation that cartel-like collusion pervaded the electrical products industry, but rather in the penalties used to deter this practice in the future. Among wealthy men and firms, fines or the threat of fines have proven ineffectual deterrents, but imprisonment of company officials found guilty of conspiring may carry a real sting.

CONCLUSIONS ON ANTI-TRUST POLICY IN THE UNITED STATES

Since 1890 the United States government has been attempting to legislate and to administer laws which are supposed to preserve a competitive economic order. Even a superficial glance at the American economy today indicates a dominant and growing position for big business, great concentration of economic power, and an unchecked merger movement. While complete monopolies are absent, industrial oligopolies predominate in the heavy industries. So far as price policy is concerned, oligopolists behave much more like monopolists than competitors. If these facts be granted—and they seem impossible to deny—it follows that the anti-trust movement has failed in its major purpose of maintaining an effective form of price competition.

The reason for this is not difficult to discover. If the foregoing analysis is correct, large-scale production destroys the basis of free and effective price competition and renders futile laws which are supposed to enforce competition after its foundations have been swept away. The failure of the anti-trust laws was the failure of a philosophy, not of a tactic. Within narrow limits the anti-trust laws have produced positive results. The Standard Oil Company was dissolved in 1911. Industrial monopolies have been prevented. Failure in the broad purpose of maintaining price as the effective instrument for the allocation and employment of resources does not mean that anti-trust laws should be abolished. It means that too much may be expected of them by those who accept trust-busting as a philosophy. Anti-trust laws should be kept and enforced because they undoubtedly prevent some actions by businessmen which would not be in the interest of the general welfare.

Early trust-busting was essentially a protest by small businessmen, farmers, and consumers against "big business." Today, however, to oppose "big business" is to oppose business enterprise itself. The basis of mass production is large-scale technology, and no sensible person would suggest that the economies of large-scale production should be sacrificed merely to create conditions under which free competition can function successfully. Even if a return to a simpler technology were in any sense possible, such a policy would acknowledge failure to devise a socio-economic organization appropriate to modern science and technology. It would say in effect that we do not know how to deal with abundance so we must destroy our machines in order to return to an age of competition. In any event, this alternative is closed because technology is an irreversible process. How to preserve the virtues of competition in the presence of conditions which defy competition is a dilemma which confronts the American economy in the second half of the twentieth century.

426

THE GROWTH
OF ORGANIZED
BUSINESS
IN THE
UNITED STATES

COMPARISON OF COMBINATION MOVEMENTS IN GERMANY, GREAT BRITAIN, AND THE UNITED STATES

The combination movement, a phenomenon common to all capitalist countries, especially Germany, Great Britain, and the United States, was a product of the age of mass production which began around 1870. The destructiveness of price competition among large-scale producers engendered business combinations as a defense against the free market.

The greater strength of the combination movement in Germany and the United States than in Great Britain may be attributed to the emergence of industrialism in the former countries at a time when large-scale production was essential to the most efficient scale of output. Other factors contributing to stronger combinations in Germany and the United States were protective tariffs and the prominent role of investment banks. In Great Britain the persistence of free trade undoubtedly checked the growth of monopolistic combinations. In this respect Great Britain was more faithful to the professed ideal of free enterprise than the United States since competition in international as well as in domestic trade is an essential aspect of freedom of enterprise. High protective tariffs were adopted by the United States during the Civil War and by Germany in 1879.

In legal terms the contrast in combination movements is between the United States and Great Britain, on the one hand, and Germany on the other hand. Whereas Anglo-American law rejects monopolistic combinations, German law has accepted them. The differences are, however, not absolute and even in Germany the criterion for determining the legality of a business combination is its relation to freedom of trade (Gewerbefreiheit), which is analogous, although not identical, to the Anglo-American criterion of freedom from restraint of trade. The difference is in the meaning of "freedom of trade." In German law it includes freedom to make a contract, including a monopolistic cartel agreement, and to have it enforced in a court of law. A German cartel contract which might be consistent with "freedom of trade" would be judged in "restraint of trade" in Anglo-American courts and would not be enforceable. Nor would all such contracts be upheld in German courts; the agreement must not be contrary to public welfare, and even if the cartel is deemed legitimate in the legal sense, it is subject to government control and regulation. In German law the business combination has been accepted more readily, but it can hardly be contended that German policy has been more callous with respect to the public than has Anglo-American policy. The economic consequences as well as the legal formalities must be considered in comparing the respective merits of the two views.

Legal differences spawned different forms of business combination. In Germany, where nonproprietary confederations among business competitors (cartels) were accepted and enforceable at law, they became the most widely used type of combination. Since this form of combination was illegal under Anglo-Saxon common law, combinations tended to be either the very loose, informal type of the trade association or corporate combinations like holding companies and mergers (amalgamations).

While British law, like American, was antipathetic toward monopolistic

combines, the American practice in interstate business has been to rely on statutory legislation rather than the common law to combat monopoly. Anti-trust legislation is the distinguishing characteristic of the American combination movement. Since pools, cartels, and trusts were clearly illegal in the United States, recourse was to the corporate forms of combination. These are the most solid and durable types of monopolistic combination. American corporation officials enjoy much more complete control over their combination than German cartel officials, who decide only price and output policy and are not much concerned with the internal organization and operation of the firms constituting the cartel. In this respect the American anti-trust movement tended to strengthen monopolistic combinations by forcing them into the most secure and durable form. Even in the exceptional instances when combinations have been legally dissolved, economic control has not been eliminated from the combination. Contrary to what is probably the common belief, the German cartel is more consistent with the maintenance of independent enterprise than the American system of corporate combinations, which tend toward greater concentration of control and giant quasi-public corporations with wide public ownership of capital. The German economy was not without marked concentration in some areas such as the electrical, chemical, and steel industries, but the concentration of ownership in industry as a whole was less in Germany than in the United States.

The economic repercussions of legal differences are significant. Cartels are clearly monopolistic; otherwise their existence would hardly be justified. Corporate combinations, on the other hand, are not necessarily monopolistic; the motivation may be primarily greater operating efficiency. On the one hand, American anti-trust laws have largely eliminated complete monopolies in industry and, on the other hand, they have not preserved pure competition. American conditions have encouraged a high degree of concentration in important sectors of the economy. Since the 1920's it is estimated that two hundred largest manufacturing firms have produced more than one-half of total industrial output. In numerous industries a few firms produce more than one-half the total output of that industry.

When industries are reduced to a small number of giant firms, cartels of the formal type are really not necessary. Firms in such industries behave as they would if they were members of a monopolistic cartel without being formally or legally bound to such behavior. Under oligopolistic conditions they maintain prices and restrict output to the amount which can be sold at these fixed prices. It is, of course, impossible for corporation officials to acknowledge that they behave monopolistically (or oligopolistically, which here means the same thing) because they would then be subject to prosecution under the anti-trust laws. But from the point of view of economic analysis this is how they do in fact behave with respect to price. They take into account the basic lesson of early attempts to engage in price competition under conditions of large-scale production; they anticipate retaliation which would wreak mutual destruction. Ironically, confident giants such as General Motors are inhibited from lowering their prices or using their entire strength to gain a larger share of the market because they might be penalized under the anti-trust laws if they were to succeed too well.

Fierce rivalry persists among firms in many American industries, but

428

THE GROWTH
OF ORGANIZED
BUSINESS
IN THE
UNITED STATES

characteristically such rivalry takes the form of advertising and salesmanship rather than price competition. Sporadic outbreaks of price cutting do occur and sometimes drive competitors into price-fixing arrangements, as witness the electrical products industry, but usually business rivals take their stand on the safer ground of advertising and salesmanship. Customers are subjected to high-pressure salesmanship to buy from one firm and shun its rivals. Since the rivals have little choice but to retaliate in kind, selling costs are increased and the price paid by the consumer includes heavy selling costs. The businessman's preference for high selling costs rather than lower prices is rational for the individual firm but not for the economy because it results in a poorer allocation of resources. The benefits of price competition acclaimed by Adam Smith do not carry over to non-price "competition."

A legalistic bias can be detected in the American reliance on the anti-trust laws to enforce competition and in the antics of the Supreme Court under the "rule of reason." This bias is similar to one noted earlier in the American predilection for the legal term "corporation" instead of the economic term "joint-stock company." Lawyers rather than economists have played the leading role in administering the anti-trust laws. As a consequence of the legalistic bias American policy has become more concerned with technical violations of specific legal tenets than with attempts to formulate and enforce market conditions which would make for the best performance of the economic system. If business combinations do not admit a monopolistic-type behavior—which they cannot—and if such behavior cannot be proved—which is very difficult in a court of law—the real economic facts tend to become veiled. The illusion that competition still dominates the American economy and that the price system operates in the classical manner persists in the face of a preponderance of evidence to the contrary. The legalistic bias may help to account for the paradox that a policy designed to maintain competition has contributed to the concentration of market control by large-scale enterprise.

SELECTED BIBLIOGRAPHY

BERGLUND, ABRAHAM, *The United States Steel Corporation*. New York: Columbia University Press, 1907.

BRADY, ROBERT A., *Business As a System of Power*. New York: Columbia University Press, 1943.

BRANDEIS, LOUIS D., *Other People's Money, and How the Bankers Use It*. New York: Frederick A. Stokes Co., 1934.

BURNS, ARTHUR R., *The Decline of Competition, A Study in the Evolution of American Industry*. New York: McGraw-Hill, Inc., 1936.

CARNEGIE, ANDREW, *The Gospel of Wealth*, ed. by Edward C. Kirkland. Cambridge, Mass.: Belknap Press of Harvard University Press, 1962.

CLARK, JOHN BATES, and JOHN MAURICE CLARK, *The Control of the Trusts*. New York: The Macmillan Company, 1912.

CLARK, JOHN MAURICE, *Competition As a Dynamic Process*. Washington, D.C.: The Brookings Institution, 1961.

Cochran, Thomas C., and William Miller, *The Age of Enterprise*. New York: Harper Torchbook, Harper & Row, Publishers, 1961. (paperback)

Dorfman, Joseph, *The Economic Mind in American Civilization*, Vol. III, Parts II, III, IV. New York: The Viking Press, 1949.

Edwards, Corwin D., *Big Business and the Policy of Competition*. Cleveland: Western Reserve University Press, 1957.

Faulkner, Harold U., *The Decline of Laissez-Faire, 1897–1917*. New York: Holt, Rinehart & Winston, 1951.

Fuller, John G., *The Gentlemen Conspirators, The Story of Price-Fixers in the Electrical Industry*. New York: Grove Press, Inc., 1962. (paperback)

Galbraith, J. K., *American Capitalism, The Concept of Countervailing Power*. Boston: Houghton Mifflin Company, 1956. (paperback)

Hidy, Ralph W. and Muriel E., *Pioneering in Big Business, 1882–1911. History of the Standard Oil Company (New Jersey)*. New York: Harper, 1955

Jones, Eliot, *The Trust Problem in the United States*. New York: The Macmillan Company, 1929.

Josephson, Matthew, *The Robber Barons; The Great American Capitalists, 1861–1901*. New York: Harcourt, Brace & World, Inc., 1962. (paperback)

Kirkland, Edward C., *Industry Comes of Age, Business Labor, and Public Policy, 1860–1897*. New York: Holt, Rinehart & Winston, 1961.

Mansfield, Edwin, ed., *Monopoly Power and Economic Performance*. New York: W. W. Norton & Co., Inc., 1964. (paperback)

Mason, Edward S., ed., *The Corporation in Modern Society*. Cambridge, Mass.: Harvard University Press, 1959. (paperback)

Mason, Edward S., *Economic Concentration and the Monopoly Problem*. Cambridge, Mass.: Harvard University Press, 1957.

Moody, John, *The Truth About Trusts; Description and Analysis of the American Trust Movement*. New York: Moody Publishing Co., 1904.

National Bureau of Economic Research, *Trends in the American Economy in the Nineteenth Century, Studies in Income and Wealth*, Vol. XXIV. Princeton: Princeton University Press, 1960.

Nevins, Allan, *Ford, The Times, The Man, The Company*. New York: Charles Scribner's Sons, 1954.

————, *Study in Power, John D. Rockefeller, Industrialist and Philanthropist*, 2 vols. New York: Charles Scribner's Sons, 1953.

Seager, Henry R., and Charles A. Gulick, *Trust and Corporation Problems*. New York: Harper & Row, Publishers, 1929.

Stocking, George W., and Myron W. Watkins, *Cartels or Competition*. New York: Twentieth Century Fund, 1948.

————, *Monopoly and Free Enterprise*. New York: Twentieth Century Fund, 1951.

Tarbell, Ida M., *The History of the Standard Oil Company*, 2 vols. New York: The Macmillan Company, 1937.

————, *The Nationalizing of Business, 1878–1898*. New York: The Macmillan Company, 1936.

Temporary National Economic Committee, *Investigation of Concentration of Economic Power*. Hearings, Monographs, and *Final Report and Recommendations*. Washington, D.C.: Government Printing Office, 1939–41.

United States Industrial Commission, *Report on Trusts and Industrial Combinations*, 2 vols. (Commission Reports, Vols. 1 and 13.) Washington, D.C.: Government Printing Office, 1900–01.

United States Senate, Subcommittee on Antitrust and Monopoly of the Committee on the Judiciary, *Hearings on Economic Concentration*, Parts I to IV. Washington, D.C.: Government Printing Office, 1964–65.

429

THE GROWTH
OF ORGANIZED
BUSINESS
IN THE
UNITED STATES

430

THE GROWTH
OF ORGANIZED
BUSINESS
IN THE
UNITED STATES

WILCOX, CLAIR, *Public Policies Toward Business*, rev. ed. Homewood, Ill.: Richard D. Irwin, Inc., 1960.

ARTICLES

ADELMAN, MORRIS A., "The Antimerger Act, 1950–60," *American Economic Review*, LI (May, 1961), 236–44.

CLARK, JOHN MAURICE, "The Orientation of Antitrust Policy," *American Economic Review*, XL (May, 1950), 93–99.

———, "Toward a Concept of Workable Competition," *American Economic Review*, XXX (June, 1940), 241–56.

DESTLER, CHESTER McARTHUR, "Entrepreneurial Leadership Among the 'Robber Barons': A Trial Balance," *Journal of Economic History*, VI (Supplement, 1946), 28–49.

DEWEY, DONALD, "Mergers and Cartels: Some Reservations About Policy," *American Economic Review*, LI (May, 1961), 255–62.

HANDLIN, OSCAR and MARY F., "Origins of the American Business Corporation," *Journal of Economic History*, V (May, 1945), 1–23.

HEFLEBOWER, RICHARD B., "Corporate Mergers: Policy and Economic Analysis," *Quarterly Journal of Economics*, LXXVII (Nov., 1963), 537–58.

JONES, ELIOT, "Is Competition in Industry Ruinous?" *Quarterly Journal of Economics*, XXXIV (May, 1920), 473–519.

KAYSEN, CARL, "The Social Significance of the Modern Corporation," *American Economic Review*, XLVII (May, 1957), 311–19.

KIRKLAND, EDWARD C., "The Robber Barons Revisited," *American Historical Review*, LXVI (Oct., 1960), 68–73.

MASON, EDWARD S., "Market Power and Business Conduct: Some Comments," *American Economic Review*, XLVI (May, 1956), 471–81.

The Growth of Organized Labor
in Europe

24

Labor unions arose as a protest by the wage-earning classes against the capitalist system. In terms of the challenge-and-response thesis of the famous historian Arnold Toynbee, capitalism is the challenge to which the labor movement is the response. Labor unions are, in other words, a product of modern capitalism.

Although the craft gilds of the precapitalistic era bear some outward similarities to labor unions, their function was quite different from that of the union. Craft gilds included in their membership the employer-master as well as the employee-journeyman and the employee-apprentices, whereas a labor union is an association of employees only; it would cease to be a labor union if it included employers as regular members. During early capitalism (1500–1750) there were sporadic organizations of workingmen in journey-men's associations, but these were neither very successful nor continuous in their development. The modern labor movement based on a permanent organization of trade unions dates from the Industrial Revolution in England and from the nineteenth century in other capitalist countries of the Western world. Even in England the labor movement did not take definite shape until the second half of the nineteenth century. Hence it is a relatively recent development even among capitalistic institutions.

The essential condition of a labor movement is the existence of a large body of workers who have ceased to be independent producers and have become conscious of their status as wage-earners. Since they do not own the requisite instruments of production for self-employment, they must sell their labor services to the capitalist owners of these instruments. This is, of course, the crux of the capital-labor relationship. Not only are wage-earners property-less in the capitalistic sense, but they are also free men who, upon recognition of their dependent economic status, can voluntarily assume the initiative in organizing to protect and advance their interests. The individual bargaining power of workers is weak because as individuals they are dispensable to the owners of the instruments of production, but as members of an organized union they possess great bargaining power because their collective services are indispensable to the owners of capital. In union there is strength.

Diversity as well as unity has been characteristic of the development of the labor movement in different countries at different stages of economic

development. Labor's protest has varied with the special conditions of each country. Important influences have been the legal status of worker organizations, the state of technology, types of unions, degree of political activity of unions, alternative forms of social protest, the extent of business combinations, business cycles, and the degree of racial and religious homogeneity in the country.

THE BRITISH LABOR MOVEMENT

The development of the labor movement in Great Britain may be divided into three main periods: the formative period, the craft union period, and the industrial union period. The formative period of the British labor movement began in 1824 with repeal of the Combination Acts, which prohibited the organization of both workers and employers but were used effectively only against workers. The second period began about 1851 with the formation of "New Model" unionism by the Amalgamated Society of Engineers. Transition from the second to the third stage occurred during the 1880's and 1890's, the most significant event in this transition being the famous Dockers' Strike of 1889.

The Formative Stage

Under common law, worker organizations designed to raise wages and shorten hours were criminal conspiracies in restraint of trade. From time to time the common law was reinforced by statutes prohibiting labor organizations in specific trades, and in 1799 and 1800 the Combination Acts provided a blanket statutory prohibition against combinations. In 1824 these laws were repealed, not because members of Parliament believed in the desirability of unions but because they believed unions could perform no significant function, either good or bad, and if tried would fall apart because of their impotency.

The law of 1824, amended in 1825, established the basic right of collective bargaining, that is, the right of wage-earners to act in concert to control the sale of their labor and to withhold it collectively (to strike) from the market. During the next ten years extensive attempts to organize unions culminated in formation of the Grand National Consolidated Trades Union (GNCTU) under the leadership of Robert Owen, the factory owner turned reformer. As the name implies, the GNCTU was a national organization which brought together in one big union all workers who wanted to join. Its sensational rise is partly explained by the bitter disappointment felt by working-class groups with the Great Reform Act of 1832.[1] Middle-class industrialists had solicited the aid of the working class in reforming Parliament only to exclude workers from the ballot by placing income requirements on the right to vote. Disappointment among working-class leaders was now channeled into a working-class movement. The GNCTU was the first important attempt to bring together working-class groups, trade unions, cooperatives, friendly societies, and agricultural workers. The purpose of the GNCTU was "nothing

[1] See Chapter 15.

less than the entire supersession of capitalism and of the system of competition by a cooperative system of worker control. It aimed not only at controlling industry, but at superseding Parliament and the local governing bodies, and of becoming the actual government of the country." [2]

This revolutionary activity was met by vicious retaliation on the part of employers and government. Workers known to be affiliated with the GNCTU were locked out from their place of employment. Employers resorted widely to what was called the "documents," a sworn statement by workers that they were not and would not become members of a labor organization.[3] Some working-class leaders were arrested for administering "illegal oaths" under the reactionary "Six Acts" legislation of 1819. Under these body blows the GNCTU collapsed like a house of cards. Its organization was too weak even to begin to carry out its grandiose aims. It lacked the power to win economic and legal struggles against employers and the government.

After the GNCTU collapsed in 1834, the social protest against the status quo swung back to political reform where the emphasis had been before the disappointing Reform Act of 1832. Unrest among working-class groups was aggravated by the new Poor Law of 1834, which viewed labor as a commodity properly subject to the free market laws of supply and demand. Working-class aspirations found expression in the Chartist movement. Chartism was fundamentally an economic movement, but its means were purely political. It offered a People's Charter, the *magna charta* of the working class, with six demands: (1) universal manhood suffrage; (2) vote by ballot; (3) annual Parliaments; (4) no property qualifications for Members of Parliament; (5) compensation for Members of Parliament; (6) and equal electoral districts.

Once universal suffrage and other political reforms were accepted, the Chartists expected the populous working class to elect to Parliament representatives who would vote into law the economic program demanded by the working class. Parliament rejected the Charter in 1839. Chartism remained active during the 1840's until the movement was crushed by troops under the old Duke of Wellington in 1848, the year in which a revolutionary movement threatened to upset the status quo in western Europe but faded as rapidly as it had bloomed.

The Craft Union Stage

After the failure of the Grand National Consolidated Trades Union in 1834 and the collapse of the Chartist movement in 1848, the British working class launched a small but cohesive labor movement in 1851, when several unions in the metal trades formed a federation called the Amalgamated Society of Engineers. These unions were organized on craft lines and their membership consisted mainly of better-paid skilled workmen. These aristocrats of the working class formed a homogeneous group under able leadership with limited goals. They consciously avoided the mistakes of Owen's "one big union" with its heterogeneous membership and revolutionary goals that had aroused the fears and hostility of employers, government, and the middle

---

[2] G. D. H. Cole, *A Short History of the British Working-Class Movement* (London: George Allen & Unwin, 1948), p. 85.

[3] This is similar to what is called the "yellow-dog contract" in the United States.

class. The craft unions stood on solid ground. They accepted the capitalist order and devoted their energies primarily to getting higher wages and better working conditions for themselves. Skilled labor was a scarce commodity for which a high price could be demanded if the workers acted in unison rather than as individuals.

One important function of the craft union was to provide sickness, unemployment, and disability benefits for its members. Since they were able to provide a reasonable measure of security for themselves through their union organization, these skilled workers felt little concern for social security through government. They were more concerned with the safety of the large sums of money which accumulated in their treasuries. Parliament enacted legislation which seemed to protect union funds against embezzlement by union officials and, more important, against claims that might be made against unions in the pursuit of legitimate activities such as strikes.

Apart from the extension of suffrage to urban male wage-earners under the reform bill of 1867, the most important gain of the working class in the third quarter of the nineteenth century was the passage of legislation strengthening the legal position of trade unions. Parliamentary legislation in 1871 and 1875 gave full legal status to trade unions. The right to strike was guaranteed by the provision that no act done by a combination of workers was punishable unless the same act by an individual was a criminal offense. Peaceful picketing was expressly legalized. The weapons required for successful collective bargaining were now guaranteed by statutory law.

Industrial Unionism and Political Representation

The British labor movement entered a new phase of development during the 1880's and 1890's. The old unionism with its conservative outlook, its narrow membership among skilled workers, and its essentially laissez-faire point of view failed to meet the needs of the growing masses of unskilled, semi-skilled and white-collar workers. Even the workers in the metal trades, who had made up the bulk of membership in the aristocratic Amalgamated Society of Engineers, found themselves affected by the new methods of automatic machinery, by assembly-line production and by other mass production techniques. Furthermore, the old unions had been weakened by the Long Depression of the 1870's. As unemployment spread, leaders of the old unions contented themselves with paying unemployment benefits and maintaining wage rates for their employed members.

Among the groups which were most important in the growth of industrial unionism were the dock workers, gas workers, transport workers, woolen textile workers, miners and white-collar workers. Leaders of the new unionism took a broader view of the labor movement than their predecessors. To the new leaders unionism meant more than benefit payments for old age and unemployment. They saw in the trade union an instrument for molding a better form of society. Whereas the craft unions preferred to provide their own social insurance, the lower-paid, less skilled workers in the new unions looked to government for protection against the hazards of industrial society. Since these workers lacked economic bargaining power, they sought to

achieve their goals through direct political action. Their philosophy was basically equalitarian; ultimately it became socialistic along the lines of the Fabians, a society of middle-class intellectuals who developed the "gradualist" philosophy and played a prominent role in the labor movement and in the Labour Party. Although the ultimate aims of the new unionism were socialistic, its immediate goal was to improve the position of the entire working class under capitalism.

The crucial years of the transition from the old to the new unionism were from 1888 to 1893. The most important single event in this transition was probably the famous Dockers' Strike of 1889. Without previous formal organization a great army of unskilled dock workers won a notable triumph in a strike that lasted four weeks. By their model conduct the strikers gained widespread public sympathy and financial support. Success in the Dockers' Strike sparked a trade union boom that increased total union membership from about three-quarters of a million to more than one-and-a-half million in 1892. This doubling of trade union membership was accompanied by substantial increases in wages.

The link between the unions and political action was provided by the Trades Union Congress, the central organization in which representatives from nearly all British trade unions came together in an annual "Parliament of Labour." After gaining control of the Trades Union Congress, the new labor leaders attempted to use it to promote favorable government legislation. Labor representation in Parliament now became a major objective in the British labor movement.

The Independent Labour Party, under the leadership of Keir Hardie, was organized in 1893 with the blessing if not the official backing of the Trades Union Congress. In the constitution of the Independent Labour Party the stated objective was "to secure the collective ownership of all means of production, distribution and exchange." Despite this avowed socialist goal, the term "socialist" was explicitly rejected in choosing a name for the new party. This arose not from a desire to conceal the ultimate ends, but from a greater preoccupation with immediate gains to the laboring classes. "Gradualism" became the keynote of the socialist labor movement in Great Britain.

An official link was forged between the unions and political action in 1900, when the Trades Union Congress established the Labour Representation Committee, with Ramsay MacDonald as its first secretary. The step from the Labour Representation Committee to the full-fledged Labour Party of 1906 was stimulated by the Taff Vale decision of 1901.

The Taff Vale Railway Company of Wales brought a civil suit against the railway union for damages resulting from loss of business during the strike. There was no legal question of physical damage to the property of the railway company or of any other form of criminal action on the part of the workers or the union. Nevertheless, a court decision, which was upheld in the House of Lords, awarded the Taff Vale Company £23,000 in damages against the union to be paid from the union treasury.

The Taff Vale decision was a crippling blow to the whole labor movement. Gains which appeared to have been won in the 1870's now seemed lost. Each time a union engaged in an organized strike, its funds, including those held for old age and other security benefits, were endangered. Therefore the

Taff Vale decision virtually ruled out the right to strike as a weapon in labor disputes. Trade unionists had assumed that under the legislation of the 1870's a labor union, as an unincorporated association of individuals, although subject to all the laws of criminal action and destruction of property, could not be sued for damages caused by organized union support of strike actions on the part of the union and its members. However, the law of 1875 applied to criminal liability and this was a civil suit.

Alarm spread among the trade unions. The Labour Representation Committee pushed its activities and gained widespread support from the ranks of all unions. The older, more conservative unions feared they might lose their large security benefit funds. Between 1901 and 1906 the size of the vote for labor candidates grew rapidly. In the election of 1906, forty-four working class representatives and a dozen "Lib-Labs" (Liberal-Labor candidates) won seats in Parliament. The Liberal Government of 1906 worked closely with labor's representatives. One of the first acts of the new government was to pass the famous Trade Disputes Act of 1906, which removed the danger of another Taff Vale decision. This act provided that courts should not hear any action brought against trade unions for the recovery of damages resulting from the action of a union or its members. By this remarkable law trade union funds became exempt from liability for civil damages.

By the end of 1913 membership in British trade unions had grown to four million. By 1920 it was in excess of eight million. In the general election of 1923 the Labour Party returned 191 Members of Parliament and in 1929 the number jumped to 287. On the eve of the Great Depression, Labour had displaced the Liberals as one of the two great political parties.

In the general election at the close of the Second World War the Labour Party won a thumping victory with nearly twelve million popular votes and an overwhelming majority of the seats in the House of Commons. In less than half a century an entirely new political party had arisen out of the trade union movement to first place in a great democracy. The Labour Party immediately began to put into law its long-standing program to socialize the means of production in basic industries (coal, transportation, communication, the Bank of England, public utilities, iron and steel) as part of a planned economy which would realize its long-sought goal: to remove labor from the private capitalist market.

THE GERMAN LABOR MOVEMENT

Like industrial capitalism, the labor movement emerged later but developed more rapidly in Germany than in England. By the First World War the labor movements in these two leading capitalist nations of western Europe stood in approximately the same position. In both cases there was a close alliance between organized labor and a political party having socialist goals which it sought to attain by gradual, parliamentary methods. However, in Britain it was the trade unions which had generated a socialist party whereas in Germany the socialist movement had generated the trade unions.

Ferdinand Lassalle, a brilliant lawyer and orator, established the first political party of German workers in 1863 and did much to stimulate the labor

movement even though he was not essentially a believer in labor unions as a method of improving the conditions of workers. About ten years after Lassalle was killed in a duel, his workers' party merged with a Marxist party to form the present German Social Democratic Party in 1875. The Social Democrats accepted the general principles of Marxian socialism, including its revolutionary slogans, and believed that significant gains for workers would come only with the abolition of capitalism. They were, however, tolerant of labor unions, if only as recruiting agencies for socialism and as "political schools of socialism."

The political orientation of German unionism proved a handicap under the ultra-conservative regime of Chancellor Bismarck. When the Social Democratic Party began to receive a large popular vote, Bismarck put through anti-socialist laws banning all socialist parties and all trade unions sympathetic to socialism. Since most of the German unions were political in nature, the anti-socialist laws virtually banned labor unions. Only small, nonpolitical unions were permitted to exist during the period of the anti-socialist laws (1878–1890).

With the end of the anti-socialist laws in 1890, there was a great upsurge of union and socialist activity in Germany. The free trade unions—those associated with the Social Democratic Party—were brought together in the General Commission of German Trade Unions, an organization analogous to the British Trades Union Congress. Union leaders, however, strove to elevate their organizations, and by 1906 unions had attained co-equal status with the Social Democratic Party as twin forces in the struggle to improve the conditions of labor.

One important effect of the increased voice of trade unionists in the labor movement was to modify orthodox Marxism, which had heretofore been the official doctrine of the Social Democrats. Rank-and-file workers in Germany, like those of Great Britain, were interested in getting higher wages and better working conditions immediately, leaving to the future the attainment of socialism. This philosophy involved more compromise with the existing capitalist order than was consistent with strict Marxist doctrine that very little improvement can take place as long as capitalism survives. Under the intellectual leadership of Eduard Bernstein there developed within the Social Democratic Party a revisionist movement which conformed closely with the gradualist philosophy of the German trade unionists. "Revisionism" was the German counterpart of British Fabianism. This is what is meant by the statement that the German social movement and the British social movement had reached approximately the same position with respect to social philosophy and political power by 1914. Both, though socialist in their ultimate aims, were preoccupied with improving day-to-day working conditions. In both countries the working class formed the core of a significant minority party which was growing in strength and was destined to occupy a larger place in postwar political life.

The issue of craft versus industrial unionism was discussed but never became a divisive force in the German labor movement. Mass production followed close on the heels of German feudalism, and before unions became ensconced rapid technological change blurred the boundaries between crafts and led to the amalgamation of independent unions of similar types. Working-

class solidarity, which was associated with the traditional caste system of feudalism, prevented an intermediate stage of aristocratic unionism of the British "New Model" type.

There were, however, non-socialist unions in Germany. One result of the adoption of Marxist principles in the political labor movement was the alienation of certain groups of German workers. Many Catholics would not join an organization with philosophical doctrines critical of their religious beliefs. Another group, the highly skilled workers in craft unions, formed the Hirsch-Dunker Unions. This latter group, which was of the type that had been dominant in Britain for nearly forty years, always remained a small minority element in the total German labor movement. Mass production, industrial unionism, and political action along socialist lines left little room for the growth of aristocratic unions in Germany.

Amalgamation of unions led to concentration of membership in a few giant unions. On the eve of the First World War, about 20 per cent of the two and one-half million members in German trade unions were in the metal workers' union, and two-thirds of the total membership was contained in the five largest unions (metal, building, transportation, woodworking, and general factory workers). Mass unionism contributed to the political power of the labor unions operating through the Social Democratic Party.

In 1914 German patriotism proved stronger than socialist pacifism; the unions and a majority of Social Democrats supported Germany's war effort, although the Party continued its policy of non-participation in government Cabinets. During the short-lived revolution which followed military defeat and overthrow of the Kaiser in 1918, the Social Democrats emerged as the only major German political party not discredited by participation in the pre-war and wartime governments. Consequently the Social Democrats and the labor unions held a commanding position in the formation and administration of the Weimar Republic. The first Chancellor after the Kaiser's Empire collapsed and the first President of the Weimar Republic was the head of the Social Democratic Party, Friedrich Ebert (1870–1925).

In this favorable political climate the German labor movement grew rapidly. Union membership skyrocketed to nearly nine million in 1921. Because of the split in the ranks of the Social Democrats during and after the war, the unions declared themselves politically neutral, but they remained close allies of socialism and pledged themselves to class solidarity. In the aftermath of the disastrous inflation of 1922–23 and in the face of a determined anti-union drive by powerful employer groups, union membership fell.

During the 1920's the Social Democrats were usually the largest single party but they did not have majority control and did not attempt to legislate a socialist economy into being. They were in the strange position of being socialists charged with responsibility for administering a capitalist society. After the great inflation of the early 'twenties and the great deflation of 1929, the Social Democrats were somewhat discredited. They were confronted by a strong upsurge of Communist strength from the left and of Nazi strength from the right. The Social Democrats and Communists were unable to work together, whereas the representatives of big business embraced the Nazis and paved the way for Adolf Hitler's rise to power. Once in office, Hitler destroyed the labor movement, confiscated union funds and property, abolished

the Social Democratic as well as the Communist Party, and placed many labor leaders and socialists in prison and concentration camps. The greatest labor movement in history up to that time sank into oblivion under the heel of Nazism.

One of General Eisenhower's promises to the German people as the Allied armies approached in 1945 was that workers would again be free to organize labor unions in the new Germany. Under the four-power occupation, trade union movements developed rapidly. In Eastern Germany unions were subordinated to the Communist program to establish a socialist regime. In Western Germany 40 per cent of the total labor force was included in unions by 1949, and by 1952 membership in unions was larger than ever before. The German Federation of Labor was formed as the central agency of organized labor in the western zones in 1949. Officially the Federation was politically neutral, as were all the member unions, but since its social and economic objectives were attainable mainly through political action, the so-called neutrality in politics must be understood in a limited sense. On most domestic issues the Social Democratic Party and the German Federation of Labor took similar stands; on some questions of foreign policy such as the Schuman Plan for integrating the French and German iron and coal industries, the trade unionists initially stood closer to the conservative German government of Chancellor Adenauer than to the Social Democratic opposition.

Perhaps the most important demand of the German trade unions in the early postwar era was "co-determination," that is, participation by the representatives of labor in the policy-making decisions of the business enterprises by which they are employed. This policy was consistent with long-standing demands of the German labor movement for economic as well as political democracy. Co-determination was achieved first in the coal and steel industries. Unions were to be equally represented with stockholders on the boards of directors of coal and steel companies. In some respects, co-determination is a substitute for socialization of industry, which was until recently a fundamental principle of the Social Democratic Party. Understandably German employers resisted co-determination.

To some degree cooperation between management and labor was forced upon the Germans by the occupation authorities. The right to strike was virtually banned in Western Germany, and consequently a policy of cooperation was essential to protect the rights of both labor and management. Even after the end of the official occupation, German unions called very few strikes. Real wages remained low, especially in relation to the rapid rise in the productivity of postwar German industry. Heavy reconstruction costs were more easily met as a consequence of the low level of consumption associated with the low incomes of German workers. With the end of the reconstruction period, the great political and potential economic strength of German labor under a democratic regime asserted itself in a demand for a greater share of the total product of industry.

THE FRENCH LABOR MOVEMENT

The French labor movement reflects the revolutionary tradition, the intense individualism, and the political instability of France. Although the French

Revolution of 1789 was a middle-class phenomenon, it symbolized to the working classes the power of one group to overthrow the existing order with a single revolutionary blow. The working classes drew inspiration from the Great Revolution as the model to be followed some day in casting aside their bourgeois masters and establishing a new order patterned after the workers' conception of the good society.

The French revolution of 1830 was a mild affair between contending middle-class elements, but the revolution of 1848 promised briefly to usher in a worker-led government. These hopes were quickly dashed in June, 1848, when 3000 workers were shot down in the streets of Paris for protesting discontinuance of public works on which they had been given employment as appeasement against revolution. Violent class war flared again in 1871, when 20,000 members of the Paris commune were executed in one of the most brutal repressions in history. These bloody episodes embittered French workers and reinforced their predisposition to believe that compromise was not one of the virtues of bourgeois governments. The anarchistic-syndicalistic belief that salvation lay in class war by direct action became deeply embedded in French working-class tradition.

Labor unions were tolerated but not legalized prior to 1884. Many local and national unions were formed during the ensuing decade and in 1895 French unions were brought together in the *Confédération Générale du Travail*, the CGT (General Confederation of Labor), which ever since has been the leading French labor organization. The CGT has passed through three main periods:

1895–1914, the period of revolutionary syndicalism;
1914–1945, the period under reformist, mostly socialist, leadership;
1945–   the period of Communist domination.

In organizational structure the CGT resembled the British Trades Union Congress, but its social philosophy differed sharply from the gradualist views of the Fabians, except in the middle period when the CGT was under reformist rather than revolutionary leadership. The syndicalists who dominated the CGT during its first two decades advocated violent overthrow of capitalism by direct action. Through sabotage and the general strike, workers were to prepare for the great day on which they would take over and operate for themselves the factories and the fields. Syndicalists refused to cooperate with any political party in or out of office. They were scornful of the French socialists, who, like other socialists, believed capitalism could be transformed into socialism by parliamentary methods. French socialists disagreed among themselves, but in 1905 the contending groups merged into a unified socialist party to form a substantial force in French political life.

Germany's invasion in 1914 showed that French unionists were not as revolutionary as they fancied themselves to be. Hard-bitten syndicalists, who had been taught to condemn all wars between capitalist nations as imperialistic ventures, rallied to the colors and marched off to war in full support of flag and country. Syndicalist romanticism never again dominated French labor, although its strain by no means disappeared and a substantial part of the revolutionary phraseology remained.

From the beginning of the First World War to the end of the Second World War the unions of the CGT were led by reformers who sought immediate improvements in the conditions of the laboring classes. Among the important gains were a comprehensive social security law in 1928 and a 1933 law requiring the payment of family allowances. The ultimate goal of the labor movement was socialism, but the here-and-now was always clearly in view. Thus the dominant group in the French labor movement adopted a position not substantially different from British Fabianism and German Revisionism.

During the early 1920's the more radical elements in the French labor movement broke away from the CGT to establish their own labor federation and affiliate with the Communist Party. In the mid-1930's during the Popular Front period the Communist unions reunited with the CGT. With a government sympathetic to labor and with employer groups intimidated by sit-down strikes, the neglected art of collective bargaining made progress under the Popular Front.

At the end of the Second World War the old ruling classes of France—the financial and industrial leaders, the politicians of the right and center parties, the upper bureaucracy, much of the ecclesiastical hierarchy, and the military—were in low public esteem because they supported the puppet Vichy government and collaborated with the Nazis. Labor groups, on the other hand, had led the underground movement against German occupation and emerged with more public prestige than any other class in France. The Communists in particular had distinguished themselves by opposing the Vichy government from the beginning and the Nazis after 1941, for which they suffered severe persecution and heavy loss of life. Assisted by this hard-won prestige among the rank-and-file workers, the efficient Communist organization took control of the CGT after the liberation of France, and despite the cold war and their opposition to the Marshall Plan the Communists maintained control of France's largest group of organized laborers.

One reason why a majority of organized French workers maintained membership in the Communist CGT unions and voted the Communist ticket in public elections was the same reason why an earlier generation of French workers supported syndicalism: It reflected the revolutionary tradition of France and expressed a deep mistrust of parliamentary government, which on the surface appeared justified by the characteristic instability of French governments and the slow progress of the French economy relative to its potentialities. In the early postwar period the CGT members and their families constituted the main support which enabled the Communist Party to elect a larger number of deputies than any other political party in France. In the 1955 election, for example, 150 Communists were elected to the Chamber of Deputies, as compared with 98 Socialists, the second largest party representation in a total of 576 seats. Many Frenchmen voted the Communist ticket as a protest against the status quo rather than from any conviction that Communism offered the positive answer to the nation's economic and social evils. Despite the plurality of representatives in the Chamber of Deputies, the Communists were not included in postwar cabinets, perhaps mainly because other parties did not wish to risk cooperation with Communist Cabinet members, but also because the Communist deputies themselves shunned the responsibilities of office, preferring to be in opposition to the government.

Under the strong presidency of General de Gaulle, the French labor unions and their affiliated political parties, as well as other independent political groups, were submerged. Yet insofar as a potential opposition to de Gaulle existed, it centered in labor and left-wing groups. In 1964, for example, a wage freeze designed to help maintain price stability brought a nationwide, 24-hour strike by labor groups. In the presidential election of December, 1965, the left-wing candidate, François Mitterand, showed unexpected strength in forcing de Gaulle into a run-off election and received 45 per cent of the popular vote in the final election.

The weaknesses which were apparent in the French labor movement, in contrast to the British and German movements, had close parallels in the Italian labor movement. In both France and Italy, collective bargaining did not develop very fully, partly because the earlier syndicalism and later Communisim of French and Italian unions permitted little common ground for collective bargaining between employers and their workers. Both the French and Italian labor movements were intensely class conscious and anticapitalistic and showed hostility for the existing governments in their respective countries.

The characteristics of union development in France and Italy are related to the fact that labor unions have been primarily a product of industrialism. Where industrialism was relatively retarded, as in France and Italy compared with England and Germany, the labor movement was likely to be relatively weak. The maturing of French and Italian industrialism may bring changes in the structure and functioning of their labor movements.

SELECTED BIBLIOGRAPHY

CLAPHAM, JOHN H., *An Economic History of Modern Britain,* Vol. II, Chap. 11; Vol. III, Chap. 8. London: Cambridge University Press, 1932.

COLE, G. D. H., *Attempts at General Union, 1818–1834.* London: Macmillan & Co., Ltd., 1953.

———, *A History of Socialist Thought,* 5 vols. London: St. Martin's Press, Ltd., 1953–60.

———, *A Short History of the British Working Class Movement, 1789–1947,* rev. ed. London: George Allen & Unwin, Ltd., 1948.

COLE, MARGARET, *The Story of Fabian Socialism.* London: William Heinemann, Ltd., 1961.

DAWSON, WILLIAM H., *Social Insurance in Germany, 1883–1911.* New York: Charles Scribner's Sons, 1912.

EHRMANN, HENRY W., *French Labor from the Popular Front to Liberation.* New York: Oxford University Press, 1947.

GALENSON, WALTER, *Trade Union Democracy in Western Europe.* Berkeley: University of California Press, 1961. (paperback)

HAMMOND, JOHN L. and BARBARA, *The Bleak Age.* New York: Penguin Books, 1934. (paperback)

———, *The Age of the Chartists, 1832–1854, A Study of Discontent.* New York: Longmans, Green & Co., Inc., 1930.

KUCZYNSKI, JÜRGEN, *Labour Conditions in Western Europe, 1820 to 1935.* London: Lawrence & Wishart, 1937.

LORWIN, VAL R., *The French Labor Movement*. Cambridge, Mass.: Harvard University Press, 1955.

SAPOSS, DAVID J., *The Labor Movement in Post-War France*. New York: Columbia University Press, 1931.

SOMBART, WERNER, *Socialism and the Social Movement*, trans. from 6th German ed. New York: E. P. Dutton & Co., Inc., 1909.

STURMTHAL, ADOLF F., *The Tragedy of European Labor, 1918–1939*. New York: Columbia University Press, 1943.

TAWNEY, RICHARD H., *The British Labour Movement*. New Haven: Yale University Press, 1925.

———, *The Radical Tradition*. London: George Allen & Unwin, Ltd., 1964.

THOMPSON, E. P., *The Making of the English Working Class*. London: Victor Gollancz, 1963.

WEBB, SIDNEY and BEATRICE, *The History of Trade Unionism*, rev. ed. New York: Longmans, Green & Co., Inc., 1935.

WUNDERLICH, FRIEDA, *Labor Under German Democracy; Arbitration 1918–1933*. New York: New School for Social Research, 1940.

ARTICLES

DUFFY, A. E. P., "New Unionism in Britain, 1889–1890: A Reappraisal," *Economic History Review*, XIV (Dec., 1961), 306–19.

GRAY, JOHN H., "The German Act Against Socialism," *Quarterly Journal of Economics*, IV (April, 1890), 320–25.

HOBSBAWM, ERIC J., "General Labor Unions in Britain, 1889–1914." *Economic History Review*, I, No. 2, 3 (1949), 123–42.

MARSHALL, ALFRED, "The Social Possibilities of Economic Chivalry," *Economic Journal*, XVII (March, 1907), 7–29.

OLIVER, W. H., "The Consolidated Trades' Union of 1834," *Economic History Review*, XVII (Aug., 1964), 77–95.

PELLING, HENRY, "The American Economy and the Foundation of the British Labour Party," *Economic History Review*, VIII (Aug., 1955), 1–17.

TAUSSIG, FRANK W., "Workman's Insurance in Germany," *Quarterly Journal of Economics*, II (Oct., 1887), 111–34; II (Jan., 1888), 215–18; and XXIV (Nov., 1909), 191–94.

The American Labor Movement

CHAPTER **25**

The stages of development in the American labor movement have followed closely those in the British labor movement, with a time lag of three or four decades. The formative stage in the United States closed with the collapse of the Knights of Labor at the end of the 1880's; it was followed by the unquestioned hegemony of the craft unions within the American Federation of Labor; and the third stage since 1936 has been marked by the ascendancy of industrial unionism.

Formative Stage

Local labor unions were present in larger American cities like Philadelphia, Boston, and New York as early as the 1790's, but the historian of American unionism, John R. Commons, dates the beginning of the labor *movement* from 1827, when several unions in Philadelphia combined into an association of city locals. This was followed in the 1830's by some combinations of local chapters into national unions. A primary stimulus to these early national unions was the completion of a national system of transportation and national markets, beginning with the completion of the Erie Canal and culminating in the network of railways. The early national unions led a precarious existence and did not stay organized continuously.

The legality of labor unions in the United States was in doubt until 1842, when the case of *Commonwealth v. Hunt* was settled in favor of the right to organize. At issue was the question whether a labor union constituted a criminal conspiracy, as that legal doctrine had come down through English common law since the labor disturbances of the fourteenth century.[1] Several members of a bootmakers' union in Boston had been convicted by a lower court for organizing a strike against an employer for hiring a journeyman bootmaker who was not a member of the union. The Massachusetts Supreme Court reversed the conviction of the lower court. Speaking for the State Supreme Court, Chief Justice Shaw ruled that what was charged as criminal conspiracy against members of the union was merely an attempt to induce all workers engaged in the same trade to become members of their organization. This, he held, was not an unlawful objective; workers are free to join together for the purpose

[1] On the Statute of Laborers, see Chapter 4.

of improving their level of living. After this important decision, the common

law doctrine of criminal conspiracy was seldom used against unions. The decision did not, of course, legalize any action which a union might take, but the existence of a union as such was no longer illegal, following Judge Shaw's reasoning. *Commonwealth v. Hunt* is a landmark in legal recognition of unions in American labor history somewhat analogous to repeal of the British Combination Acts (1824) in British labor history.

The national labor unions which had been organized during the 1830's were broken by the panic of 1837, and during the 1840's the labor movement gave way to a variety of schemes for uplifting workers through land reform, bank reform, communist communities, wealth redistribution, and producers' and consumers' cooperatives. After this interlude of "utopianism," the national craft unions came back stronger during the 1850's than before. This was the decade in which the United States achieved economic unity through the trans-Appalachian railways, which in turn developed east-west trade and national markets for the first time. The early national labor unions were mainly of the craft type, including printers, stonecutters, hat-finishers, machinists, molders, blacksmiths, and cigar-makers.

By the end of the Civil War the elements were at hand to forge a national organization for labor as a whole: local unions were affiliated in city trades' councils and also with other locals of the same craft in national unions. For two decades attempts were made to achieve an overall national labor organization. The first attempt was the short-lived National Labor Union, founded in Baltimore in 1866 and abandoned in 1872. It brought together in a loose federation the city trades' councils, local unions, national unions, and miscellaneous reform organizations. Control of the National Labor Union fell into the hands of social and political reformers who embraced greenbackism and an independent labor party. It sought to assist dependent wage-earners to become independent, self-employed producers. Although the national craft unions were affiliated, their interest in collective bargaining, union recognition, and better wages was subordinated to political activity and they withdrew their support.

The drive toward a national labor organization was next taken over by the Knights of Labor, which was founded in 1869, assumed national scope in the late 'seventies, and dominated the labor movement through the 'eighties. In structure the Knights of Labor was one big union, in which membership was direct rather than through affiliated unions. Its place in the American labor movement is similar to that of Robert Owen's Grand National Consolidated Trades Union in the British labor movement. Everyone was eligible for membership regardless of craft, skill, religion, sex or color, except for bankers, stockbrokers, lawyers, gamblers, bartenders and liquor manufacturers. The opening sentence of the preamble of the Constitution of the Knights indicates the scope of its objectives, including an antimonopoly attitude toward big business and the monied interests:

> The recent alarming development and aggregation of wealth, which, unless checked, will invariably lead to the pauperization and hopeless degradation of the toiling masses, render it imperative, if we desire to enjoy the blessings of life, that a check should be placed upon its power and upon unjust accumulation, and a system adopted which will secure to the laborer the fruits of his

toil; and as this much-desired object can only be accomplished by the thorough unification of labor, and the united efforts of those who obey the divine injunction that 'In the sweat of thy brow shalt thou eat bread,' we have formed the * * * * * with a view of securing the organization and direction, by co-operative effort, of the power of the industrial classes.

In its activities the Knights of Labor was like the man who mounted his horse and rode off in all directions. Its polyglot membership had many and conflicting objectives, a situation typical of the formative stage of labor movements. Like the English Chartists, the Knights of Labor vacillated between middle-class reform and a genuine working-class movement. The bulk of its membership consisted of unskilled workers, artisans displaced from their crafts by factory machinery, and semi-skilled operatives in the young mass production industries. These workers were in revolt against an economic system which they felt was victimizing them, but they were more inclined to look backwards to an idealistic world of independent artisans and farmers than forward to the realities of mass production. They opposed bankers and monopolists, but not the capitalist system as such, that is, they were petty bourgeois rather than socialist in outlook. They did not quite accept for themselves the status of permanent wage-workers.

Political and social reform rather than hardheaded business unionism guided the Knights' activities and objectives. Among the measures they advocated were producers' cooperatives, elimination of private banks, antimonopoly legislation, and land reform. These essentially lower-middle-class reforms reflected the opportunity open to American workers and militated against a genuine working-class consciousness. The impetus and preparation for a genuine working-class movement were present in the United States after the Civil War, but the Knights of Labor lacked the organizational structure and leadership to fulfill this historic mission. Some temporary successes were scored in strikes (even though the leaders did not believe in strikes), mostly against railways during the 1880's, and advocacy of the eight-hour day attracted many members; but soon the Knights fell apart from sheer lack of cohesiveness. Thus ended the first stage of the American labor movement.

Craft Union Stage—The American Federation of Labor

The second, or craft-union, stage of the American labor movement matured with the founding of the American Federation of Labor in 1886.[2] In organization and outlook the American Federation of Labor paralleled the "New Model" unionism which began in Great Britain in 1851; it focused on skilled crafts and was not much concerned with common and semi-skilled laborers, who had been so important in the philosophy of the Knights of Labor. The AFL unions were craft-conscious rather than class-conscious; they ac-

[2] Its forerunner, the Federation of Organized Trades and Labor Unions (1881), had a basically different function from the later American Federation of Labor. The earlier organization was primarily *political* in function, whereas the 1886 organization was primarily *economic*. The 1881 organization was similar to the British Trades Union Congress and comparable in purpose to the state federations of the American Federation of Labor. The continuity was mainly in the men who founded the 1881 and 1886 organizations, Gompers and Strasser being leading lights in both.

cepted the capitalist system and devoted their efforts to getting more out of it in the form of higher wages, shorter hours, and improved working conditions through collective bargaining, trade agreements, and strikes. Whereas the Knights of Labor stressed the solidarity of all labor, the AFL stressed the autonomy of skilled labor.

The AFL was primarily a loose confederation of autonomous craft unions. In contrast to the Knights of Labor, individuals as such did not hold membership in the AFL; individuals were members of sovereign unions, which sent delegates to national conventions of the Federation. The Federation itself, of course, was not a labor union. In order to make certain that the sovereign power of the national craft unions was not submerged under the mass voting power of less skilled groups such as had threatened them in the Knights of Labor, the men who organized the AFL created an organization of limited central authority, albeit an important authority.

Perhaps the most important function performed by the central authority in the AFL was to protect the principle of craft autonomy by guaranteeing to each national union a definite and exclusive jurisdiction in its charter. In this manner rival or dual unionism was prevented. Jurisdiction was usually granted on a craft basis. The carpenters in the steel industry fell under the jurisdiction of the carpenters' union; machinists in the automobile industry fell under the jurisdiction of the machinists' union. By granting charters on a craft (horizontal) basis, industrial (vertical) unions were excluded, except by special permission of the craft unions, because their claims to organize workers would overlap and violate the principle of exclusive craft jurisdiction. Any union violating its jurisdiction would be expelled forthwith without mercy from the Federation. Charters were sometimes granted to industrial unions, but grounds were easily found for rejecting them. Of 106 national unions in the AFL in 1924, only fifteen were industrial unions. The proprietary right to organize was not exercised among skilled workers in mass production industries, and unskilled workers in mass production were out in the cold with no union claiming jurisdiction because no industrial charter existed. The dog-in-the-manger attitude of the craft unions helped to keep total membership in organized labor in the United States lower than in any other major industrial nation. In 1924 German industrial labor was 75 per cent organized, British 65 per cent organized, and American only 15 per cent organized.

Trade agreements arrived at through collective bargaining with employers were the chief means used by the unions of the AFL to pursue their businesslike ends (higher wages, shorter hours, and better working conditions). Strikes, picketing, and boycotts were the chief weapons used to reinforce the bargaining power of the unions. The AFL has been described as representing "pure and simple unionism" with no ultimate aims, only immediate aims in the form of more for union members *now*. Measured in these terms a remarkable degree of success was attained. Wages of skilled, union workers were sometimes six or seven times as high as the wages of unskilled unorganized workers, whereas in European countries the wages of skilled workers were seldom more than two or three times those of the unskilled. Hours of work were as low as thirty-five per week in organized crafts, as compared with twice that number in unorganized industries; for example, the regular work week in the unorganized steel industry was seventy-two as recently

as 1924. High wages and short hours were attained by limiting the supply of labor in the skilled crafts.

Union security was, of course, a prerequisite of successful collective bargaining. Union security means protecting the union against loss of jobs; it is achieved by limiting the absolute control of employers over hiring and firing workers. One form of union security, the "closed shop," is used to prevent anti-union employers from undermining the union by hiring non-union members. A "union shop" means that no one may continue to work in the shop without becoming a member of the union. An "open shop" means theoretically that both union and non-union members may be employed in the same shop; however, with anti-union employers doing the hiring, the "open shop" typically becomes a non-union shop, that is, one in which union members are not employed, by preference of the employer. It is "closed" to members of unions.

Another policy of the AFL has been to avoid permanent affiliation with existing political parties and to eschew a labor party. Its policy has been to "reward labor's friends and punish its enemies." The Federation consistently opposed legislation for social security, minimum wages, and maximum hours. The strong craft unions dominating the AFL preferred to make social gains through their own economic strength and to remain independent of government intervention.

A surprising aspect of the hard-boiled business unionism of the AFL is that its two main founders were socialists. Samuel Gompers from England and Adolph Strasser from Germany first attempted to transplant a European-style labor movement to the United States. The preamble of the Federation's Constitution reads like something directly out of Karl Marx: "Whereas a struggle is going on in all the nations of the civilized world between the oppressors and the oppressed of all countries, a struggle between the capitalist and the laborers, which grows in intensity from year to year. . . ." This radical language remained in the Constitution until the AFL merged with the CIO in 1955. Gompers and Strasser wanted above all, however, a labor organization which would endure, and they discovered by trial and error that in America it was better to bargain with capitalism than to try to supplant it. Through most of the nineteenth century, inchoate labor movements had sailed along for several years on waves of prosperity only to be shattered on the rocks of depression, as in 1837, 1857, and 1873. Heterogeneous conglomerates usually fell apart over politics and social reform in periods of depression. Survival required a resilient, homogeneous, nonpolitical labor organization. Gompers and Strasser, on the one hand, had no illusions about turning society back to lower-middle-class self-employment schemes like greenbackism, free land, and cooperation; and, on the other hand, they were fully cognizant of the limitations of a genuine labor movement in the American environment.

In the first decade after its formation in 1886 the AFL grew slowly while the Knights of Labor collapsed. The AFL survived the double depression of 1893 and 1896 and thus demonstrated a degree of stability which no earlier American labor organization had exhibited. Membership increased more rapidly during the prosperity of 1897–1902, then lapsed into slower growth, and spurted again during the First World War. In 1920 total membership exceeded 4,000,000. This fell sharply during the prosperous 'twenties and by 1932 had decreased to 2,500,000 paid-up members. Such was the plight of the leading

body of organized labor in the United States at the end of the craft union stage.

Industrial Union Stage

The third stage of the American labor movement has been marked by the rapid growth of industrial unionism and the development of vigorous political action by organized labor. These changes were precipitated during the Great Depression of the 1930's by the friendly attitude toward organized labor of Franklin D. Roosevelt's New Deal. A major struggle between craft unionism and industrial unionism split the American labor movement during the early phase of the third stage, but after twenty years of division the labor movement closed ranks to form a unified labor front.

Since industrial unionism is the obvious counterpart of mass production, the retarded development of industrial unions as a central force in the American labor movement is surprising in view of the country's long tradition of mass production. The latent forces of industrial unionism were manifest in numerous ways before the Great Depression. The AFL included a few industrial unions and compromised with the industrial principle by permitting amalgamated, as contrasted with pure, craft unions in greater number. Moreover, the AFL created as part of its structure four "Departments" (metal workers, railway employees, mine workers, and building trades workers), which were a step toward industrial unionism.

Outstanding industrial unions existed, outside the AFL, in the needle trades. In 1905 the Industrial Workers of the World (IWW) was founded to promote industrial unions, especially for unskilled and semi-skilled workers, who were excluded from the unions of the AFL. The IWW was violently anti-capitalistic, however, and always stood outside the mainstream of the American labor movement. The retardation of industrial unionism despite its latent power arose from the resolute opposition of the conservative, complacent, craft-minded AFL, on the one hand, and the militant anti-unionism of powerful American industrialists in the mass production industries, on the other hand.

Both these restraints were swept away by the Great Depression, which rocked the capitalist system to its foundations. The traditional conservatism of the United States was relaxed. Industrialists fell from grace in the eyes of the public because their leadership had resulted in economic disaster, and the heads of the craft unions had proven themselves incapable of leadership in the eyes of workers. When the New Deal gave the green light to organized labor, the field was wide open for new leadership and new types of union organization. Section 7a of the National Industrial Recovery Act guaranteed wage-workers the right to bargain collectively through representatives of their own choosing. After the NIRA was declared unconstitutional, section 7a was reaffirmed in the National Labor Relations Act, or Wagner Act.

The craft unionists at the head of the AFL were immediately confronted with a dilemma: How to take advantage of the new opportunity for expanding membership in organized labor and at the same time protect the rights of craft unions chartered under the principle of exclusive jurisdiction? They pretended to compromise, but actually balked at surrendering their jurisdictional privileges. When a group of leaders of industrial unions within the AFL

set up a Committee for Industrial Organization (CIO) and began to organize mass production industries, they were charged with violating the jurisdictional rights of craft unions and with fomenting insurrection in the AFL. Their unions were summarily expelled from the AFL. The expelled unions then formed the Congress of Industrial Organizations, a federation of unions entirely independent of the AFL. The principle of exclusive jurisdiction, which had been a bulwark of strength in the early history of the AFL, had become a fetter on the growth of organized labor and precipitated open revolt by proponents of industrial unionism against the domination of craft unionism.

The CIO moved rapidly from one striking success to another in the mass production industries. Hard-shelled and traditionally anti-union companies capitulated with surprisingly little resistance. The big breakthrough came when two industrial giants, the United States Steel Corporation and General Motors, recognized CIO unions as collective bargaining agents. No strike was necessary to arrive at the "Big Steel" agreement. General Motors came to terms with the United Automobile Workers after sit-down strikes in the Detroit area. Henry Ford, who had threatened a permanent shut-down of his plants rather than recognize a labor union, signed a collective bargaining contract in 1941. Other major industries which fell into line were rubber, aluminum, and electrical products. At times the combined membership of unions affiliated with the CIO exceeded the total membership of the AFL unions. In self-defense, the AFL was forced to liberalize its policies toward industrial unions. Membership in craft unions also increased as trades became more completely organized, but for the labor movement as a whole industrial unionism was in the ascendancy.

Statistics for the period show a phenomenal growth in membership of organized labor in the United States. Between 1933 and 1936 total membership in all unions doubled, from 3 to 6 million; it doubled again by 1943 to 12 million; and in 1953 after two decades it had increased more than five-fold to 17 million. In the latter year, 50 per cent of the total membership was in AFL unions, 30 per cent in CIO unions, and the remaining 20 per cent in the railway brotherhoods and other independent unions.

Apart from the industrial structure of its unions, the most important characteristic of the CIO was active participation in politics. A Political Action Committee was formed and played an important role in the nomination and election of presidential, congressional, state, and local candidates. Unlike industrial unionism in nearly every other country, however, the CIO did not attempt to form a labor party. Instead it worked through the Democratic Party and wielded great influence in its liberal wing. In the New Deal it found a political movement receptive to the ideas of the progressive, but not radical, leaders of industrial unions.

The split between the AFL and CIO continued for two decades until 1955, when the two groups merged to form the AFL-CIO. A major influence drawing the labor movement together was the Taft-Hartley Act of 1947, passed by a Republican Congress over the veto of President Truman. Like the British Taff Vale decision of 1901, the Taft-Hartley Act limited the right to strike (for which reason labor groups referred to it as the "slave labor act") and tended to solidify the labor movement in opposition. The Taft-Hartley Act proved less of a threat in practice than on paper, but nevertheless organized labor carried on a strong campaign against it. With the rise of industrial

unionism, the labor movement became a potent force in the American political scene.

RETARDING INFLUENCES IN THE AMERICAN LABOR MOVEMENT

Although the labor movement in the United States has followed the same general pattern as the labor movements of other industrial nations, it has developed more slowly. There are certain basic characteristics of American life which account for the retardation of the labor movement: (a) large-scale immigration, which has stratified the labor force; (b) the middle-class outlook, or lack of working-class consciousness; (c) greater economic opportunity, associated with the frontier and the progressive advance of American capitalism; (d) the conservative attitude toward private property as reflected in the courts as well as in general public opinion.

a. Immigration In the late nineteenth and early twentieth centuries great waves of immigrants poured into the United States. Language barriers, national rivalries, and religious differences tended to stratify the labor force into native and foreign-born workers and created obstacles to solidarity of the wage-earning class. The "new immigration," which came after 1890 from southern and eastern Europe, was especially resented by native workers because these immigrants were accustomed to extremely low standards of living and were willing to work for low wages. They were more easily intimidated than workers reared in countries where wage-earners enjoyed the right to vote and other democratic privileges, including the right to organize unions. American unionists saw immigration as a threat to their jobs and sought protection by excluding immigrants from unions while gaining union control over hiring and firing. Negro workers, as a culturally nonassimilated group, occupied a position similar to immigrants. Membership in American unions tended to be restricted to native-born, white, skilled workers. The cleavage between elite workers and other workers was sometimes sharper than between wage-earners and their employers.

It should be pointed out, however, that some immigrants made significant positive contributions to the American labor movement. Class-conscious immigrants like Gompers and Strasser from countries with advanced labor movements provided much-needed leadership in the American labor movement. Two models of American unionism have been the Amalgamated Clothing Workers and the strong International Ladies Garment Workers Union, both organized with a majority of foreign-born workers.

b. Middle-class outlook The tenacity of lower-middle-class reform schemes in the American labor movement reflects an aspiration on the part of wage-workers to rise to the status of self-employed. The lingering appeal of these schemes accounts for the long duration of the formative stage of the American labor movement. An unending parade of antimonopoly schemes, including land reform, cheap credit, producers' cooperatives, greenbackism, populism, grangerism, and all the rest of the plans for ending the special privileges which were thought to have prevented propertyless wage-earners

from rising to self-employment status, afflicted the labor movement through the Knights of Labor period. American wage-earners identified themselves with small farmers, small businessmen, and the lower middle class. The tradition of equality stemming from the Declaration of Independence plus the early attainment of universal manhood suffrage, together with innumerable examples of successful upgrading of wage-earners into the employing class, nourished middle-class consciousness. Since an essential condition of a mature labor movement is consciousness of the separateness of the interests of wage-earners from those of their employers, the persistence of the myth that everyone could rise to the status of self-employment was an obstacle to stable American unionism.

In contrast, the British labor movement enjoyed "built-in" solidarity because of the acknowledged class system and the long struggle for universal manhood suffrage. Likewise, the definitely "lower-class" status of German wage-earners provided fertile soil for a class-conscious labor movement. In view of the strength of middle-class ideology in the United States, one may well question, not why the labor movement was retarded, but how any mature labor movement was able to develop at all. Part of the answer is provided by the European immigrants, Gompers and Strasser, who had no illusions about the permanent wage-earning status of the vast majority of American workers.

c. Greater economic opportunity   Behind the persistence of middle-class ideology has been the greater economic opportunity for the "common man" in the United States than elsewhere. As noted earlier,[3] the frontier contributed indirectly, if not directly, to higher wages and less labor unrest in the United States. The Homestead Act of 1862 further eased the access to the means of production. One may read significance into the fact that a genuine labor movement came into being in the United States about 1890, the year in which the geographical frontier officially closed. Not in agriculture alone, however, but in urban occupations as well America offered greater opportunities for advancement than did Europe and other "old countries." Large-scale employers were long able to forestall unions by meeting the demand of workers for material gains out of increases in productivity. Employers often used the tactic of promoting to higher positions energetic employees with organizing ability which otherwise would be turned to union activity, thus draining from the labor movement the cream of potential leadership.

d. Conservative attitude toward property   Since a labor movement, to the extent that it succeeds, must inevitably encroach upon some of the prerogatives previously enjoyed by property owners, the progress of the labor movement is influenced by attitudes toward private property. In this respect the American community has been extremely conservative, and therefore the labor movement has been held back by the traditional sanctions of private property. Nowhere is this better illustrated than in the courts, which are the special agencies for review and evaluation of legislative and administrative performance in the American system of government.

The Fifth and Fourteenth Amendments to the federal Constitution provide that property may not be taken without "due process of law." As inter-

[3] See Chapter 13, section on "Summary of Public Land Policy."

preted by the courts, the due process clause has proved an obstacle to the

labor movement. Just when the American labor movement was getting into full
swing after 1890, the courts began to issue injunctions against strikes, boycotts,
and picketing on grounds that these actions deprived the employer of his property without due process of law. Union leaders who failed to abide by injunctions were held in contempt of court and subjected to fines and imprisonment. In practice injunctions were easily obtained and were an effective
limitation on the right to strike. For several decades the AFL concentrated its
legislative fire on the injunction and finally succeeded in 1932 in obtaining
federal legislation limiting its use in labor disputes (the Norris-La Guardia
Act). Use of the injunction was restored by the Taft-Hartley Act of 1947.

By its nature the labor movement is "radical" in the sense that it represents an innovation of recent times. In their restraining role, the courts not
only acted unfavorably toward the weapons of labor, but at the same time
acted favorably toward weapons of employers. The so-called "yellow-dog"
contract, which requires an employee to sign a statement that he is not a
member of a union, was used extensively until the 1930's as an anti-union
device. Another employer weapon tolerated by the courts has been the use
of strikebreakers. Although it would seem that workers have property rights
in their jobs in the same sense that employers have property rights in their
business, the courts did not follow this logic.

The use of strikebreakers frequently led to violence in the labor movement. A widespread practice was for large, anti-union employers to enlist the
services of armies of private detectives to act as strikebreakers, not because
they were good workers, but because they were trained in the use of arms and
ammunition. Many industrial plants kept large supplies of firearms to be used,
if necessary, against striking workers. Until recent times employers also had
at their disposal in labor disputes the police, state militia, national guard,
and regular army troops. American workers reared in the tradition of equality
have been vigorous in literally fighting for their rights. The upshot has been
more violence in the American labor movement than in that of any other
country. Although employers frequently initiated the violence, the blame for it
in the public press and in public opinion was typically placed at the door of
labor, with the result that the community at large viewed union organizers as
bomb-throwing anarchists and communists. The fall of the Knights of Labor,
for example, was precipitated by the notorious bombing in Chicago's Hay-
market Square in 1886, although the Knights had no connection with this outbreak of violence. The conservative attitude of the American community lent
encouragement to the militant anti-unionism of American industrialists. This
traditional conservatism was broken by the Great Depression, and since the
1930's the labor movement has received the stamp of community approval in
the United States.

COMPARATIVE ANALYSIS OF LABOR MOVEMENTS

In precapitalist economic systems propertyless men were typically slaves or
serfs and were not legally free to express their hostility toward the economic
system. Slaves and serfs rebelled sporadically and their cause was sometimes

championed by free men, but there was no legal and systematic challenge to the economic system. In classical Greece, for example, there were individuals who opposed slavery, but there was no anti-slavery movement as such. Even during early capitalism the right to organize labor unions did not exist. Under Anglo-American common law labor unions were at first viewed as criminal conspiracies. Legislative enactments and judicial interpretations have given to labor unions in all democratic nations the recognized legal status which is a prerequisite for the full development of the labor movement. In a well-structured form, the labor movement did not begin even in Great Britain until the second half of the nineteenth century and is therefore so recent that its full implications as a force for social and economic change are not yet fully apparent. Although the right to organize is sometimes still challenged, labor unions have become so much a part of democratic societies that their elimination seems improbable except in a totalitarian state. In a very basic sense the labor movement is a product of the rights of free speech and assembly.

Private Property and the Labor Movement

The labor movement is always a challenge to the institution of private property, a cornerstone of capitalism; this accounts for the strong opposition of capitalist employers to the labor movement. Labor's challenge takes many forms, ranging from a demand for immediate and outright confiscation of private property in the means of production to a demand for shop rules which will enable the union rather than the employer to control job opportunities, with the employer retaining legal title to the means of production and bearing the risks of profit and loss. Under the AFL type of trade agreement, for example, the union strives to control apprenticeship, the introduction and use of machinery, work sharing during layoffs, the admission of new members to the union, and other working rules involving general control of hiring and firing. A union shop always implies some control by the union over the working conditions of its members. Thus the socialistic aims of the European labor movements and the acceptance of capitalism by the American labor movement reflect not absolute differences, but positions on a continuum ranging from fully private to fully collectivized ownership of the means of production. Private property is, of course, challenged from other directions such as the replacement of private proprietorships by giant quasi-public corporations and the various forms of business combination. The labor movement is usually considered a radical challenge, whereas the merger movement is considered a conservative challenge.

In the early stage of the labor movement the majority of wage-earners had recent antecedents in agriculture and in small-scale manufacturing, and they did not accept as historically definitive their divorce from ownership of the means of production. As a result the formative period of the labor movement, especially in Great Britain and the United States, was characterized by numerous schemes for enabling workers to escape the status of wage-workers. These schemes included producers' cooperatives, cheap credit and other forms of bank reform, and various types of land reform. They may be characterized generally as antimonopoly programs which rested on the premise that given

equal access to capital and to land, the great majority of workers would rise from the ranks of wage-earners to become self-employed. In Great Britain these elements were strong in the Grand National Consolidated Trades Union and in the Chartist Movement. In the United States the antimonopoly view pervaded the Knights of Labor and other early labor organizations. French syndicalism is another approach to worker control of factories and fields. In a chronological sense these are reactionary schemes which fail to reckon with the onward march of large-scale production and the increasing division of labor arising from revolutionary changes in transportation and communication.

The more mature unionism of Great Britain after 1850 and of the American Federation of Labor proved durable because it regarded as permanent the wage-earning status of the great majority of workers under capitalism and sought to gain more control over working conditions and to get more of the group product of industry. Business unionism accepts the reality that under capitalism the product of industry is divided into two main parts, wages for workers and profits for owners and managers. Like all unionism, it rejects the doctrine that the interests of workers and employers are the same. The aristocratic business unions of the craft stage also rejected the assumption that the interests of all workers are identical, that "an injury to one is an injury to all," as the Knights of Labor stated in their preamble. By artificially restricting the supply of skilled workers in their craft or by preventing technological innovations that would lessen the premium on their skills, craft unions can gain at the expense of other groups of workers. Group selfishness rather than class solidarity was the basis for the policies pursued by the aristocratic craft unions in the intermediate period of the labor movement.

The more recent prevalence of mass production has tended to lessen the distinctions between labor groups and to bring about a return to the psychology of solidarity in the labor movement. But by this time no basis exists for the utopianism of the formative stage; small-scale self-employment having become technologically unrealistic. A labor movement either accepts capitalism and with it the conflict over sharing the joint product of industry, or it aims ultimately to resolve the conflict by substituting for the wage system some form of socialism under which the product is, in theory at least, the common property of all.

The Free Market and the Labor Movement

Labor's challenge to capitalism may also be expressed in terms of its meaning for the market. The organization of wage-earners into unions has always been motivated by a desire to eliminate competition from the labor market. England's Industrial Revolution demonstrated the degrading effect of a free market in labor upon the propertyless wage-earning classes. Labor's protest was moral as well as economic. The view implicit in the free market that labor is a commodity like grain and potatoes, with a price to be determined by the laws of supply and demand, was repugnant to the dignity of free men. It is interesting and significant that the first national labor organization, the British Grand National Consolidated Trades Union, was formed in the same year (1834) in which the "supply-and-demand" poor law replaced

the old poor law, which had maintained a layer of paternalistic protection for wage-earners against the play of market forces. In the United States, Congress expressed a moral protest when it declared in the Clayton Act that "labor is not a commodity." Organized labor, no less than organized business, was a protest against the destructive forces of the free market; and the growth of organized labor, no less than the growth of organized business, is a chapter in the decline of the free market system.

Since the full removal of competition from the labor market can be achieved only by the elimination of capitalism, the labor movement pushed to its logical limit becomes anticapitalistic. Among well-disciplined labor groups in Europe the upshot of the trade union movement has been a socialistic philosophy. In Britain and Germany the labor movement looks in the long run to the elimination of the competitive labor market, while in the short run it is primarily concerned with improving the conditions of workers within the market system. In France, Italy, and Spain the anticapitalism of the labor movement first assumed the form of syndicalism, but with a strong cohesive socialist group, especially in France, following the lead of British and German labor groups.

In the United States, with minor and sporadic exceptions, the labor movement has not aimed at eliminating the labor market (socialism), but has been content to limit competition in various ways. Labor movements everywhere are torn between displacing capitalism and bargaining with it. Special historical circumstances have placed the American labor movement definitely in the latter camp of reforming rather than displacing capitalism.

Influence of Technological Change on the Labor Movement

Like every other economic institution, trade unionism has been significantly affected by changes in technology. In every country the labor movement arose in conjunction with the modern type of industrialization based on machine technology. In the early stage of the labor movement, the formation of the "one-big-union" with members drawn from all types of workers reflected the uprooting of agricultural and handicraft workers by the onward sweep of machinery and the higher division of labor connected with the transition from agrarianism to industrialism. In the next stage, the remaining skilled craftsmen withdrew from the heterogeneous mass and set themselves above and apart from the unskilled and semi-skilled factory workers. This, however, proved a transitory phase in trade union structure. As the labor movement grew in general strength, it invaded mass production industries in which the appropriate form was inevitably the industrial union. Meanwhile further mechanization displaced more craftsmen with machine operations. Some crafts resisted both mechanization and industrial unionism, but in the total labor movement unions organized on a craft basis lost ground to those organized on an industrial basis. Craft unions were still important, especially in the building trades, but they became relatively less important in the total picture. In recent times, then, the influence of technology on the labor movement has been felt in the strong drift toward industrial unionism.

With the surging strength of industrial unionism, political action in the labor movement becomes potentially important both because there are so many voters in these unions and because their needs are of a type which can be reasonably, and perhaps exclusively, provided by government, through such provisions as social security, minimum wages, and guaranteed employment. Industrial workers engaged in mass production tend to concentrate in urban and suburban areas where the members can exert strategic influence on the election of political candidates. The extent to which labor's potential political power is translated into actual power depends on whether the politics of union members are mainly determined by their economic interests and whether they feel these interests are sufficiently involved in the choice of political party and candidates. Clearly, any political party in a democratic, industrial nation is asking for trouble if it openly defies the rights and privileges which union members feel are legitimately theirs. No political party can long survive unless it can convince a reasonable proportion of union members that their interests will be best served through that party. At the same time labor leaders are aware that in a free, democratic country no labor organization can dictate the vote of its members. It can only appeal to their common interests and provide real leadership in their attainment. The Taff Vale decision, which led to the formation of the British Labour Party, is a classic example of provoking labor unions into political action to defend themselves when their basic rights are threatened. The effect of the Taft-Hartley Act of 1947 on the surprise election of President Truman in 1948 is probably another example of labor's power at the polls when it feels its interests are threatened by unfavorable governmental action by an unsympathetic party. The Taft-Hartley Act, which placed restrictions on the political activities of labor unions, actually had the effect of increasing the political activity of union members.

In class-conscious societies in which workers enjoy the ballot, industrial unionism has led to a labor or a socialist party. Both the British and German labor movements have been closely associated with political parties—the Labour Party and the Social Democratic Party respectively—which hold as their ultimate goal the transformation of capitalism into socialism by parliamentary means. The French labor movement has a non-political tradition stemming from syndicalist advocacy of direct action to take over factories and fields, and even the Communist unions are not officially connected with the Communist Party, although in practice the relationship is quite close. Likewise, the French Socialist and Catholic unions, while nominally non-political, are in fact closely tied to political parties.

The American labor movement has not developed its own political party nor has it enunciated socialism as its ultimate goal. Americans tend to be less ideological in a self-conscious sense than Europeans, perhaps because feudalism never existed to set up tight class distinctions which have been handed down in varying forms in European countries. Of course, the absence of a labor party in the United States may be merely an aspect of the lag in the American labor movement, but it appears to reflect different basic conditions. More rapid increases in real wages and the more dynamic nature of American capitalism have undoubtedly been factors militating against a labor party.

Industrial unionism in the United States has carried on the tradition of craft unions of accepting capitalism and striving to get more out of it—and there has been more to get out of American capitalism than out of any other economic system. The threat of a labor party remains in the background if labor groups feel their vital interests are threatened. For example, on the day following the merger of the AFL and CIO in 1955, President Meany replied to criticism by the National Association of Manufacturers of union political activity with the warning: "If the N.A.M. philosophy to disenfranchise unions is to prevail, then the answer is clear. If we can't act as unions to defend our rights, then there is no answer but to start a labor party." [4] Meanwhile, given the acceptance by labor of the existing economic and political system, the American labor movement exercises a powerful influence on politics and government by the traditional policy of "Reward labor's friends and punish its enemies." Whether in the form of a labor party or, as seems more likely in the United States, by continuing the policy of endorsing some candidates and opposing others, labor cannot be kept out of politics any more than business can be kept out of politics. Business has more money to contribute to influencing the results of elections but labor has more votes. In an enlightened democracy the latter presumably has the greater power in the long run. Trends since the Great Depression point to an increase in political action by organized labor in the United States. Thus the principle that the ascendancy of industrial unionism brings increased political action by labor is valid for the United States as well as for European countries.

SOCIAL LEGISLATION AND THE RIGHT TO WORK

The labor movement was the most important but not the only form of protest against the evils of industrial capitalism. Even before labor unions had become important, governments enacted legislation designed to ameliorate the conditions of employment. The British Factory Acts of the first half of the nineteenth century attempted to limit the hours and improve the conditions of child and female labor in factories and mines. [5]

Another very important innovation in social legislation was social insurance, which was introduced first in Germany under Bismarck. Labor unions substituted collective bargaining for individual bargaining, but they did not eliminate the insecurity of unemployment, the risks of accident and sickness, and the infirmity of old age. Only a small percentage of workers belonged to trade unions which provided security benefits, and such benefits were generally inadequate. Fundamentally, the insecurity of wage- and salary-earners under capitalism stemmed from their complete detachment, except through the market, from any means of production, that is, it stemmed from their economic dependence on the sale of their labor in the market. Slaves and serfs enjoyed more economic security, though less freedom, than wage-earners under capitalism. Factory workers who became unemployed, incapacitated, ill or too old had no place to turn except to the degrading poorhouse. They had

---

[4] *New York Times* (December 10, 1955), p. 1.
[5] See Chapter 14.

no land on which to grow their own potatoes; they probably owned no home; and their wage-earning children were not able to support them.

Under the factory system the family ceased to function as an economic unit. In theory, perhaps, workers were supposed to save enough while employed to take care of contingencies arising from lack of employment. For the multitude this was hardly feasible in the face of low wages, lengthening periods of unemployment, the high incidence of accidents in mechanized industry, and the increasing difficulty of finding employment after middle age. To provide security on an individual basis against these multiplying hazards was impossible for any but the most able, frugal, and fortunate worker. Compulsory social insurance on a national scale was the method adopted to meet this situation.

The social insurance laws effected by Bismarck were an attempt to appease the German workers, who resented his antisocialist laws. The Sickness Insurance Act of 1883 provided compulsory health insurance for industrial workers, with contributions paid by both employers and employees. The compulsory provision of this law distinguished it from earlier voluntary schemes of health insurance. The Accident Insurance Act of 1884 provided compensation to workers who were incapacitated by injuries. By defining "accident" broadly the law rendered employers responsible for all injuries incurred by workers during employment and removed the necessity of litigation to prove employer responsibility.

The Old Age and Invalidity Act of 1888 provided for contributions from both employer and worker. Benefit payments for old age began at seventy. Protection against premature incapacity to work was also provided under this law. Social security measures of the type instituted by Bismarck subsequently spread to nearly all modern nations. One important type of social security which Bismarck did not attempt was unemployment insurance. It was left to the British to pioneer in this field in the years just prior to the First World War.

At first the Social Democrats did not take kindly to Bismarck's paternalism, but the social insurance measures were so popular with the rank and file of industrial workers that union and socialist leaders eventually reconciled social security under capitalism with their "gradualist" philosophy.

In the United States social security lagged far behind European countries. Among the important reasons were the hegemony of the craft union philosophy of the American Federation of Labor, which was opposed to government social security legislation until the 1930's, and also the lingering belief on the part of politicians that rugged individualism would take care of the insecurity of industrial workers. When the Great Depression of the 1930's showed that nearly everyone is economically insecure under industrial capitalism, a national social security law was enacted by the Roosevelt administration. This provided for old-age (retirement) annuities, old-age pensions, and unemployment benefits. Compulsory health insurance was delayed mainly by the effective lobbying of the medical profession, which has castigated sickness insurance as "socialized medicine." Thirty years after the initial 1936 Social Security legislation, government-sponsored medical care for persons over 65 went into effect under the Medicare program.

While nearly all elements in the British labor movement accepted social

insurance as an important forward step for the working class, the more militant and the more socialist-minded members viewed it as merely a palliative. In the period just before the First World War, when unemployment insurance measures were before Parliament, the Labour Party's own approach to unemployment was a Right to Work Bill. The "right to work" issue had appeared sporadically throughout modern history. It played a prominent role in the French revolution of 1848, in which Louis Blanc and his followers championed a constitutional guarantee of the right to work. The basic idea behind this right is that it is the duty of society, acting through its representative, the government, to find employment for all able-bodied workers and, failing that, to provide adequate maintenance. The right to work, if achieved, would have removed, or gone far toward removing, the commodity status of labor. It is a doctrine which denies the purely private nature of the means of production and is thus in conflict with a fundamental principle of capitalist society.

Attempts have been made at a partial solution to the "right to work" question within the framework of collective bargaining agreements. The "guaranteed annual wage," advocated most strongly in the United States by the automobile workers union, was accepted reluctantly by automobile manufacturers in agreements signed in 1955. Right-to-work and guaranteed income plans under private auspices can provide no more than a very limited solution to the unemployment question, unless capitalism is stabilized and average unemployment reduced to low levels, in which case the need for such plans is greatly reduced. Unemployment is a disease of the economy as a whole, and private employers, no matter how wealthy, cannot reasonably be expected to bear the brunt of this social cost. High employment and full employment acts by legislation represent a step in this direction, but they are really statements of intent rather than concrete guarantees of employment. In 1966 a presidential commission recommended guaranteed employment by means of public service programs in which the government would serve as employer of last resort.[6]

SELECTED BIBLIOGRAPHY

ADAMIC, LOUIS, *Dynamite, The Story of Class Violence in America,* rev. ed. New York: The Viking Press, 1934.

BEARD, MARY R., *A Short History of the American Labor Movement,* New York: The Macmillan Company, 1927.

BOWEN, WILLIAM G., ed., *Labor and the National Economy.* New York: W. W. Norton & Co., Inc., 1965.

BRISSENDEN, PAUL F., *The I.W.W., A Study of American Syndicalism,* 2nd ed. New York: Columbia University Press, 1920.

COMMONS, JOHN R. and others, eds., *A Documentary History of American Industrial Society,* 10 vols. New York: Russell & Russell, Inc., 1958.

[6] See Chapter 38 for a discussion of this and related proposals.

DULLES, FOSTER RHEA, *Labor in America*. New York: Thomas Y. Crowell Company, 1955.

DESTLER, CHESTER MCARTHUR, *American Radicalism, 1865–1901*. New London, Conn.: Connecticut College, 1946.

FAULKNER, HAROLD U., *Labor in America*. New York: Harper & Row, Publishers, 1944.

GALENSON, WALTER, *The CIO Challenge to the AFL: A History of the American Labor Movement, 1935–1941*. Cambridge, Mass.: Harvard University Press, 1960.

———, ed. *Comparative Labor Movements*. Englewood Cliffs, N. J.: Prentice-Hall, Inc., 1952.

GOMPERS, SAMUEL, *Seventy Years of Life and Labor, An Autobiography*, 2 vols. New York: E. P. Dutton & Co., Inc., 1925.

GREGORY, CHARLES O., *Labor and the Law*. New York: W. W. Norton & Co., Inc., 1946.

LONG, CLARENCE D., *Wages and Earnings in the United States, 1860–1890*. Princeton, N. J.: Princeton University Press, 1960.

LORWIN, LEWIS L., *The American Federation of Labor: History, Politics, and Prospects*. Washington, D.C.: The Brookings Institution, 1933.

MILLIS, HARRY A., and EMILY CLARK BROWN, *From the Wagner Act to Taft-Hartley: A Study of National Labor Policy and Labor Relations*. Chicago: University of Chicago Press, 1950.

PERLMAN, SELIG, *A History of Trade Unionism in the United States*. New York: The Macmillan Company, 1929.

———, *A Theory of the Labor Movement*. New York: Augustus J. Kelley, Inc., 1949.

POWDERLY, TERRANCE V., *Thirty Years of Labor, 1859 to 1889*. Columbus: Excelsior Publishing Co., 1890.

———, *The Path I Trod: An Autobiography*, H. J. Carman and others, eds. New York: Columbia University Press, 1940.

ROSS, ARTHUR M., and P. T. HARTMAN, *Changing Patterns of Industrial Conflict*. New York: John Wiley & Sons, Inc., 1960.

TAFT, PHILIP, *Organized Labor in America*. New York: Harper & Row, Publishers, 1964.

ULMAN, LLOYD, *The Rise of the National Trade Union*. Cambridge, Mass.: Harvard University Press, 1955.

WARE, NORMAN J., *The Labor Movement in the United States, 1860–1865*. New York: Appleton-Century-Crofts, Inc., 1929.

ARTICLES

DANHOF, CLARENCE H., "Economic Validity of the Safety-Valve Doctrine," *Journal of Economic History*, I (Supplement, Dec., 1941), 96–106.

GROB, GERALD N., "The Knights of Labor and the Trade Unions, 1878–1886," *Journal of Economic History*, XVIII (June, 1958), 176–82.

———, "Reform Unionism: The National Labor Union," *Journal of Economic History*, XIV (Spring, 1954), 126–42.

Industrial and Labor Relations Review, "The AFL–CIO Merger," Special Issue, IX (April, 1956), 347–467.

LORWIN, VAL R., "Reflections on the History of the French and American Labor Movements," *Journal of Economic History*, XVII (March, 1957), 25–44.

MURPHY, GEORGE G. S., and ARNOLD ZELLNER, "Sequential Growth, the Labor-Safety-Valve Doctrine and the Development of American Unionism," *Journal of Economic History*, XIX (Sept., 1959), 402–21.

SHANNON, FRED A., "A Post Mortem on the Labor-Safety-Valve Theory," *Agricultural History*, XIX (Jan., 1945), 31–37.

TAUSSIG, FRANK W., "The Homestead Strike," *Economic Journal*, III (June, 1893), 307–18.

VEBLEN, THORSTEIN B., "Farm Labor and the I.W.W.," *Essays in Our Changing Order*. New York: Viking Press, 1943. Reprinted from *The Journal of Political Economy*, XL (Dec., 1932), 797–807.

Agriculture in the Age
of Mass Production

CHAPTER

26

In agriculture as in industry the new technology of mass production brought fundamental changes. Within agriculture itself as well as between industry and agriculture the division of labor was greatly extended. Overall, there was greater economy in the use of resources. More wants were satisfied with the superior utilization of given resources. Levels and standards of living consequently rose, although not uniformly for everyone or for every country. The uneven distribution of gains among individuals and countries constituted the essence of the "agrarian problem" in the new era. Western European farmers, especially the British, suffered the most, but even American farmers suffered prolonged depression between 1873 and 1896 and again between 1920 and 1940.

Within the North Atlantic Community an important shift occurred in the geographical distribution of agricultural activity as the transportation revolution in railways and steamships lowered the cost of transport. Agriculture declined in England because wheat, for example, could be grown in the American Midwest and transported by rail and ship to England to be sold at prices which were below the cost of production in England. Agriculture also declined, to a slightly lesser degree, in other countries of western Europe. Germany was more subject to overland competition from Russia and eastern Europe than from overseas. Canadian, Australian, and Argentinian products also flooded into European markets. A new international division of labor was hurting European farmers and providing overseas farmers with worldwide markets.

In another sense, agriculture also declined in the United States—that is, the proportion of the labor force engaged in it fell. According to a principle known as Engel's law, the proportion of total income spent on food declines as incomes rise for individual families and for society at large. This principle is modified in degree and timing by the international division of labor. For example, the proportion of the English labor force in agriculture fell to one-tenth by 1880, a figure not reached in the United States until after the Second World War. The contrast was between a more rapid decline in England and a less rapid decline in the United States. Falling agricultural employment reflected, of course, the falling relative demand for agricultural products.

Great Britain

Initial prosperity under free trade For nearly three decades after the Corn Laws were repealed in 1846 British agriculture enjoyed unprecedented prosperity. This prosperous state of affairs ran counter to the dire predictions of the protectionists, and even the free traders expected the landlords to suffer economic losses under free trade.

For the longer run the prophets of gloom were correct, but until the Age of Mass Production began in the 1870's British agriculture prospered for several reasons. (1) British farming was in the forefront of scientific progress in the middle of the nineteenth century. The enclosure movement, which came to an end about the time of Corn Law repeal, left a system of very large landholdings. A special study of 1871–73, sometimes referred to as "The New Domesday Book," showed that a quarter of the arable land was owned by 1200 persons, and about one-half by 7400 persons, in estates which averaged 7300 acres each. These large holdings and the capitalistic methods of operating them contributed to the success of mechanized farming and scientific methods in general. Machinery such as harvesters found ready adoption in Britain. (2) Overseas competition even under free trade was not a serious factor before 1870. Although direct rail traffic between Chicago and New York began in the 1850's, the feeder lines from the wheat-growing districts of the Midwest were some time in being completed. Steel rails and steel locomotives were introduced in the 1870's, and steel ships in the 1880's. Consequently the drastic fall in transport costs and rates was not felt until the 1870's. (3) Although repeal of the Corn Laws brought stronger competition for bread grains, expansion in the urban demand for fresh meat tended to compensate the English farmer. Only in the 1880's did refrigerated ships carrying large cargoes of frozen meat to Europe from Australia, New Zealand, and the American continents come into operation, facing the English farmer with a new type of competition. (4) Moreover, the impact of foreign competition in grains was delayed in the 1850's by the Crimean War, which checked the import of Russian grains into Europe, and in the 1860's by the American Civil War, which limited imports from the United States. (5) Finally, the years between 1850 and 1873 yielded good harvests in England. These several factors prolonged the prosperity of British agriculture for three decades after the repeal of the Corn Laws.

Depression in British Agriculture after 1874 British agriculture fell on evil days after 1874. The Long Depression which affected general economic conditions in the Western world between 1873 and 1896 was primarily an agricultural phenomenon. In western Europe a fundamental cause of this agricultural depression was overseas competition from North America and competition from eastern Europe, especially Russia and Rumania. As previously noted, in the 1880's the British imported four out of every five loaves of bread consumed, as against only one out of three in 1850. English workers were leaving farms for factories, where they produced textiles and machinery to be exported in exchange for wheat. This represented a higher stage in the division of labor, and it helps to explain why British standards of living were

the highest in Europe. The price of bread in England fell approximately 25 per cent between the 1850's and the 1880's.

Britain was a democratic country in the 1880's—much more so than it had been in 1815 or in 1846. In addition to the Great Reform Bill of 1832, which had increased the political power of the industrial capitalists, another reform bill in 1867 gave the ballot to industrial workers, and a third reform bill passed in 1883 gave the ballot to agricultural workers. In their role of consumers, British voters preferred higher living standards to protection for landlords and capitalist farmers. Increased importation of foodstuffs placed more British exchange in the hands of foreigners and enabled them to buy more manufactured goods from British factories; it also enabled British investors to collect interest and dividends on their foreign investments. Importation of agricultural products was a logical sequel to Britain's position as the workshop of the world.

For the British landlord and farmer this great experiment in international free enterprise was hard to take. Between 1875 and 1896 total arable land declined by one-half; wheat acreage by one-half; the number of farm laborers by 40 per cent; land values fell sharply and landlords lowered rents in order to hold their old tenants or to attract new ones. In general, the gloomy prophecies of the protectionists, who had opposed repeal of the Corn Laws, were realized with a vengeance. To make matters worse, the period was one of bad crop weather and poor harvests.

Readjustment of British Agriculture   Although British agriculture generally and cereal production in particular were adversely affected by overseas competition, the new circumstances did present favorable opportunities for alert farmers. Urban dwellers required more fresh vegetables, fresh fruits, fresh milk, and other foods which could not be imported economically. Agriculture began to take on a new look. An upturn of the general price level after 1896 aided the adjustment, and by the beginning of the First World War in 1914 British agriculture was fairly well adjusted to the changed facts of economic life. During the war years 1914–18 there was a partial reversal of the adjustment process, but fortunately for the British the Royal Navy was able to keep the sea lanes open and to enable the 45 million people on the little islands to survive the great war, including the submarine warfare of Hindenburg and Ludendorff.

In the postwar period British agriculture again slumped badly because of the general lack of prosperity in Great Britain. During the Great Depression beginning in 1929 a new agricultural policy was adopted. Subsidies were given to encourage agricultural production. The Second World War brought another food crisis, which again was met successfully with the cooperation of the British Navy and overseas allies. Following the war the new policy begun in the Great Depression was continued. It was stimulated by the difficulty of paying for imported food, especially from the dollar area. A hint of the new development could be gleaned from the dismissal of a junior minister of the British Labour Government for making such critical statements as "No other nation featherbeds its agriculture like Britain." [1] The country of classical free

[1] *New York Times*, April 17, 1950, p. 1.

trade had finally succumbed. British official policy no longer deemed the free market an appropriate regulator of agriculture.

France

The great French Revolution of 1789 did not change substantially the distribution of landholdings or the techniques of cultivation. It did halt an incipient French enclosure movement and, under a system of equalitarian inheritance, gave the peasants full legal title to their small holdings. The small holdings and accompanying lack of capital by peasant-owners acted as a brake on progress in mechanization and scientific agriculture of the type which dominated farming in England during the nineteenth century. It doomed France to small-scale agriculture.

Beginning in the 1850's the railway age produced significant changes in French agriculture. Low-cost transportation widened the market and provided an incentive for specialized production. During the 1860's and 1870's wheat acreage was greatly increased by the availability of rail transportation from outlying farm regions to the industrial towns and cities. Wheat yields per acre increased by 50 per cent between 1818 and 1889. The other great staple crop of France, vineyard grapes, also increased rapidly during the early railway age.

When the "invasion" of cheap overseas products hit France in the Age of Mass Production, the reaction was quite different from Britain's. Instead of letting their farmers sink or swim in the free world market, French governments protected them by raising tariff walls against foreign commodities. A law of 1885 imposed a tariff of three francs per hectoliter of wheat; this was raised to five francs in 1887 and to seven francs in 1897. The price of wheat at the time was between twenty and twenty-five francs per hectoliter. Wheat imports into France became negligible toward the close of the nineteenth century. Among European nations, France remained second only to Russia in wheat production. With the assimilation of North Africa into the French tariff system, the workers of Paris benefited from the wheat fields of Tunisia and Algeria, which had fed the Roman mobs in the days of the old Roman Empire.

The French wine industry experienced a severe depression during the last quarter of the nineteenth century because of heavy losses of vines from an insect pest, the phylloxera. France, which had been a great wine-exporting country, had to import wine on a considerable scale. Wine growers abandoned their traditional free trade views in favor of a protectionist position.

During the protracted fall in prices after 1873 protectionist psychology spread, and under the well-known Méline Tariff of 1892 nearly all important agricultural products in France were placed under partial or complete protection from foreign competition. Unlike other western European nations, France attained self-sufficiency in food production, for which France naturally paid a price. The relatively high cost of food was a limiting factor in industrial progress. Restricted imports necessarily limited exports, since in the long run a nation which does not buy from other nations cannot sell to them. The main purpose of agricultural tariffs—protection of French farmers from the perils of the world market—seems to have been substantially achieved. While there

was some lack of agricultural prosperity during the 1870's and 1880's, France experienced no such depression as that suffered by British farmers. The differing reactions of Britain and France to the overseas "invasion" of agricultural products is related to the differing political structure of the two countries. Both were democratic, but in Britain landlords were few, while in France they were legion. France enjoyed universal manhood suffrage, and peasants were the most numerous group.

When the fertile fields of France became the chief battle ground of the First World War, agriculture suffered tremendous losses in equipment, manpower, and improvements. Constructive measures restored the prewar level of agricultural production by 1925. When the Great Depression hit in 1929, the French answer was still higher protective tariffs. In 1931 the price of wheat in France was three times higher than in England, which still enjoyed free trade. France persisted in keeping down the real wages of its industrial workers for the benefit of its peasant farmers. In Britain the wheat farmer had long since been sacrificed for the benefit of industrial workers.

Germany

German agriculture was more heterogeneous than either the typically large-scale British or the typically small-scale French agriculture. In southern and western Germany small-scale landholdings were common. They were smaller in the south, especially in Bavaria, where the peasant dominated, than in the north and west along the lower Rhine. East of the Elbe, on the other hand, great feudal-type landholdings remained intact even after the nominal liberation of the serfs in the first decade of the nineteenth century. These Junker landlords remained a powerful influence in German economic, political, and military life throughout the nineteenth century and into the twentieth century until their estates were broken up by Russian occupation after the Second World War.

As in France, the spread of an internal network of railways marked the significant beginnings of unfreezing a backward, self-sufficient German agriculture. Economical access to urban markets stimulated improvements and led to commercialization and specialization. In the middle of the nineteenth century Germany became a significant exporter of grain, wool, and other farm commodities. The import duty on grain was dropped by the Zollverein in 1865 because, in the absence of grain imports, it had no practical significance.

The crucial change in German agriculture came in the 1870's. This decade marked the beginning of accelerated industrialization under the newly formed Empire and almost simultaneously the "invasion" of foreign agricultural commodities. Railways linking Germany with eastern European countries brought in cheap grains. Russian rye lowered the price of this staple from which two-thirds of Germany's bread was made. Other grains came from Russia, Rumania, Hungary, and overseas. Wool from Australia and meat from the New World undermined the profitability of these branches of German agriculture. Prices went down in the domestic market, and foreign sales vanished. Germany changed quickly from a food-exporting to a food-importing nation.

German farmers, large and small, now appealed for protection against

"destructive" foreign competition. They were joined by German industrialists, who sought protection against the still superior industries of Great Britain. Bismarck, the dictator, was neither a free trader nor a protectionist, but he listened sympathetically to the appeals of the several groups, and especially to his fellow Junkers, who were most severely hit by the Russian grain "invasion." Bismarck's motives in effecting the famous tariff of 1879, which ended Germany's brief tenure in the free-trade camp, differed from those of the agriculturalists and industrialists. He was first of all an empire builder, and by virtue of the Empire's political and constitutional structure it was dependent for revenue on indirect taxation such as import duties. The new import taxes were only moderately protective since tariffs that are so high as to exclude imports bring in no revenue at all.

It is interesting to note how the reaction of Great Britain, France, and Germany to the "invasion" of foreign agricultural commodities differed according to the political situation in each of these countries. The political climate in Great Britain was conditioned by the long, historic struggle to repeal the Corn Laws and by the suffrage laws of 1867 and 1883, which extended the ballot to the working classes, who were in no mood to tolerate a renewed "tax on bread." British industrialists had little to fear from foreign competition. The handful of British landlords and their farmer tenants who sided with them were hopelessly outnumbered in the political struggle to gain protection against overseas competition. British agriculture was consequently left exposed to the hazards of the world market. In France the peasants constituted the most numerous and influential political element. When overseas competition threatened their economic prosperity, they entrenched themselves behind high tariff walls. France continued to be self-sufficient in food production. Germany was a dictatorship under a new Empire, which was rather loosely formed and in need of revenue from indirect taxation. Bismarck, the dictator and empire builder, used the complaints of the German peasants, Junker landlords, and Ruhr industrialists as an excuse for imposing a tariff which would bring moderate protection to the complainants and also yield much-needed revenues to the government of the Empire. Germany stood midway between Britain and France on protection for farm products: The British gave no protection and became heavily dependent on imported food; the French gave such complete protection as to maintain self-sufficiency in food production; Germany followed a middle course between British dependent free trade and French protective self-sufficiency.

Germany's sensational rise to industrial supremacy in Europe after 1871 had a powerful impact on German agriculture. While foreign competition was driving down the prices of agricultural commodities, the demand for labor in urban industry was causing rural depopulation, a shortage of agricultural labor, and higher wage costs. Chiefly affected by the rise in rural wages were the big capitalist farmers of the East. They met their labor shortage partly by employing migratory labor from neighboring countries, especially Poland, during the harvest season.

The main solution to the double squeeze on agricultural profits (lower prices and higher wage costs), however, was increased productivity through scientific and mechanical improvements. German agriculture made steady progress throughout the Age of Mass Production, with the large-scale farmers

being more progressive than the small-scale peasants and farmers. From their internationally famous countryman, Justus von Liebig (see Chapter 17), German farmers learned to use chemical fertilizers. In sugar beet production, they increased both the yield of beets per acre and the sugar content of the beets. Germans became the world's greatest potato producers. They utilized the lowly spud for alcohol, animal feed, and human consumption. Agricultural colleges and schools were established for the dissemination of the practical knowledge of husbandry to its practitioners. German success in applying science to agriculture was surpassed only in the United States.

During the First World War the high degree of self-sufficiency in food stood Germany in good stead. By the end of the war, however, the Germans were hungry. Considering the loss of manpower from agriculture, the under-maintenance of farm equipment, and the underfertilization of the soil, the wartime performance was a remarkable tribute to the progress of German agriculture during the preceding seventy years.

The peace treaty which followed the First World War took important arable lands from Germany and made the nation more dependent than before on foreign food. In the late 1920's Germany's concerted national effort to increase its overall productivity through rationalization was extended to agriculture. Big commercial farmers went heavily into debt in order to finance improvements. When prices tumbled in the Great Depression of 1929, they faced bankruptcy.

Under the Nazis (1933–45) the economic policy was to make Germany as self-sufficient as possible. In pursuit of this objective a semi-feudal status was imposed on agricultural labor. At first farm workers were not permitted to leave the land, and peasants were not permitted to sell their land. The drain on manpower for industrial recovery and rearmament led in a few years to a relaxation of restrictions on the mobility of farm workers. In the period since the end of the Second World War, the division of Germany has created special problems because of the limited trade between surplus-food-producing eastern Germany and food-importing western Germany.

Denmark, The Food Factory

Agriculture in Denmark made a remarkably successful adaptation to the new role of European agriculture resulting from the American "invasion" of grain markets. For a short time after repeal of the British Corn Laws in 1846, the Danes increased their specialization in grain growing, but by the 1860's their yields per acre were falling. In the following decade the American "invasion" began to be felt strongly and the price of grain fell drastically. Meanwhile, in 1864 Denmark lost its rights to the agriculturally important duchies of Schleswig-Holstein as a result of the aggressive war of Bismarck. Confronted with a national crisis, the Danes deliberately shifted from cereal culture to animal production. Difficulties were overcome through general education, hard work, scientific research, and cooperative processing and marketing of farm commodities.

Soon there emerged a new pattern which is best expressed in the description of Denmark as a "food factory." With dairy cattle, hogs, and chickens the Danes specialized in producing butter, bacon, and eggs for the export

market. Applying the recently invented cream separators (Nielson, 1878, and Laval, 1879), they utilized cream for making butter, skim milk for making cheese, and buttermilk for feeding hogs. The hogs were processed into high-quality bacon and ham, and as a complementary commodity the Danes raised poultry for eggs. The result was another "invasion," the capture of the British breakfast table. Danish bacon and eggs and Danish butter on rolls made from American wheat became standard fare at a British breakfast. Denmark became part of the metropolitan British economy. Like the British they operated their agriculture without protective tariffs, but they were more progressive than the British in adopting new techniques and were able to prosper. Denmark became virtually a food factory, importing raw materials (feed and fertilizer) and exporting finished products (butter, bacon, and eggs). The model of the economy was in many respects similar to that of Great Britain except that the Danes exported food products whereas the British exported mostly textiles and other industrial products.

U.S. AGRICULTURE IN THE AGE OF MASS PRODUCTION

The story of American agriculture in the Age of Mass Production may be summed up as follows:

(1) Agricultural productivity has risen continuously through the application of farm machinery, science, and education.

(2) Rising productivity has produced large surpluses which in earlier decades were exported to pay for the industrialization of the nation, including capital equipment and interest on borrowed capital.

(3) After foreign markets diminished following the First World War, the surpluses represented general overproduction of the commodities formerly exported.

(4) Overproduction of farm products was not easily adjusted through the market process.

(5) Non-market adjustments have failed to eliminate overproduction but have socialized it by transferring costs from farmers to taxpayers and urban consumers.

(6) The overall result is that the adjustment of agriculture to a position of declining importance has been difficult within the market process and, like business and labor, solutions have been sought outside the market process. It is another aspect of the retreat from the free market of the past several decades.

1. Increased Productivity Through Farm Machinery, Science, and Education

Agricultural productivity in the United States has risen continuously throughout the nineteenth and twentieth centuries. As noted previously,[2] the 1830's saw the invention of revolutionary new machines. Although much of

---

[2] See Chapter 18.

the later farm machinery was invented before the Civil War, it came into

general use only after 1870 during the age of mass production.

One measure of productivity is the number of persons supported by one farm worker. In 1860, one farm worker supported five persons; by 1920 this had risen to ten persons; and by 1950, to fifteen persons. In other words, productivity doubled in the sixty years after 1860 and tripled in the ninety years after 1860. This is an overall figure. In some crops and in some activities the increase was much greater; on the other hand, there are still farmers who work under conditions no more efficient than their great-grandfathers'.

Another measure of productivity is the number of man-hours required to produce crops. For wheat production in the United States the Department of Agriculture figures are as follows:

YEAR	HOURS PER ACRE	HOURS PER BUSHEL	BUSHELS PER ACRE
1830—U. S. average	57.70	2.88	20
1896—Central Wheat Belt	8.80	0.44	20
1930—Great Plains	3.30	0.16	20
1949—Great Plains	1.82	0.09	20

In 1830, on the eve of the epoch-making invention of the mechanical reaper, 57.7 man-hours were required to plow, plant, and harvest an acre of wheat land by means of a horse-drawn walking plow, broadcast seeding, hand sickle, flail, wagon and winnowing. In 1949 by using a five-plow tractor, grain drill, and self-propelled combine, this was reduced to 1.82 man-hours, or only 3 per cent of the man-hours of 1830. Note that the yield per acre has remained unchanged in the United States. The improvements have been labor-saving rather than land-saving. Land being relatively abundant there has been little pressure to economize its use in agriculture. Labor has been the scarce factor to be economized. Since the yield per acre has been constant, the increase in output per man-hour is easily calculated at thirty-fold between 1830 and 1949. Other field crops such as corn and cotton have shown large increases in labor productivity.

The most sensational gains in productivity have been associated with farm machinery. Using wheat as an example, the development of the reaper with a twine binder about 1878 was a major innovation. At the same time the threshing machine, which had been invented several decades earlier, was being perfected. A spectacular advance was realized in the wheat combine, which brought together harvesting and threshing in a single machine. Factory production of large combines began in California during the 1880's, but not until the First World War did combines come into general use on the Great Plains. In 1935 a one-man combine was perfected and used in all sections of the nation. One-man combines were a boon to the family-size farm and rendered obsolete the colorful threshing crews of earlier decades.

The tractor Replacement of men and animals by mechanical power has unquestionably been the most important contribution of mass production

techniques to agricultural productivity. Steam engines were used successfully for gang plowing, harvesting, and other farm activities beginning about 1876. The real revolution came, however, with gasoline traction engines, commonly known as "tractors." The tractor is a by-product of internal combustion engines for automobiles. On a national scale the tractor dates only from the First World War. The number of horses and mules in the United States attained a maximum in 1924 and decreased during the following twenty-five years by two-thirds, from 23 million in 1924 to 7.5 million in 1949. A collateral saving of land and labor has resulted from a reduction in forage crops for draft animals. The mechanized farmer spends less time working for his draft animals and more time for himself. As an all-purpose source of power for plowing, harrowing, seeding, cultivating, transporting, and harvesting, the tractor, more than any other innovation, accounts for greater output with fewer farm workers.

Science The contribution of science to productivity is more indirect and therefore more difficult to measure than the contribution of farm machinery. Perhaps the most important thing to be said is that the United States has had a *policy* of systematic application of scientific principles to research in agriculture. This policy has been implemented mainly through state experiment stations financed by the federal and state governments. Experiment stations became an integral part of land-grant colleges (see next section on Education), which were designed to discover and disseminate knowledge in the practical arts of husbandry and mechanics. The basic premise was that no task of the farm or factory is too humble for scientific experimentation and improvement. Among the important contributions of science to agriculture have been control of insects and diseases of plants and animals, new varieties of plants and improvements in existing varieties, scientific animal breeding, improved seeds and fertilizers, and soil analysis.

Education Under the Morrill Act of 1862, the federal government gave public land to each state. Proceeds from the sale of the land were to be used by the several states to found a college which would teach, among other subjects, the agricultural and mechanical arts. These schools represented an innovation in higher education and were not welcomed by leaders of the existing universities.[3] They represent perhaps a unique contribution of American higher education, having been responsible in no small degree for American leadership in agriculture and industry. The idea of the land-grant college gave recognition at the level of higher education to the principle that investment in human capital is a main source of the wealth of nations.

In order to render the practical results of scientific research available to practicing farmers, extension services were instituted by the land-grant colleges and universities. County agents working in the rural districts of every state constituted the applied productivity "faculty" of American agriculture.

[3] A bill similar to the one which later became the Morrill Act was passed by Congress but was vetoed by President Buchanan on the advice of the Presidents of Harvard and Yale, who said that the proposed colleges would supplant the existing colleges and universities and lower the quality of higher education in America. Needless to say, these fears have not been realized even though the land-grant colleges have become a dominant influence in American higher education.

2. Rising Productivity Produced Large Farm Surpluses Which Were Exported to Help Pay for Industrialization of the United States

473

AGRICULTURE IN THE AGE OF MASS PRODUCTION

In conjunction with cheap rail and ocean transportation, the rising productivity of American agriculture resulted in enormous farm exports. What Europeans saw as the American "invasion" was from the American side a huge export surplus in excess of domestic consumption. American farm surpluses rose rapidly during the closing three decades of the nineteenth century and attained a peak around the turn of the century. Corn exports reached a maximum in 1897 and wheat in 1901, when two-fifths of the domestic wheat crop was exported. Foodstuffs and cotton constituted the bulk of all American exports at this time. The exported farm surpluses made a major contribution to American industrialization by helping to pay for imported capital goods and to pay interest on the foreign capital borrowed for the construction of industrial, transportation, and public utility facilities. As imports into western Europe, especially Great Britain, American farm surpluses furnished food and fiber to Europe's industrial workers, many of whom would otherwise have had to be employed in agriculture on unproductive soil. Thus the industrialization of both America and Europe was accelerated by the prodigious performance of American farmers.

3. Foreign Markets Diminished After the First World War and the Former Export Surpluses Were Converted to General Overproduction of Farm Commodities

After the close of the frontier around the turn of the century the quantity of new land coming under cultivation slowed down, and the United States became more industrialized and urbanized. Farm surpluses fell off relatively and absolutely. Throughout the nineteenth century American agriculture had characteristically expanded at the extensive margin (use of more land) rather than at the intensive margin (use of more capital and labor on a given amount of land).

Falling prices, which harassed American farmers during the Long Depression (1873–96) and converted them to greenbackism, free silver, and other radical agrarian movements, came to an end in 1897. For nearly a quarter of a century thereafter, American farmers enjoyed prosperity. Population grew faster than cereal output, so that production was more nearly absorbed in domestic markets. The increase in farm prices was relatively greater than the increase in nonfarm prices. Although American farmers relied more on the domestic market, the foreign market remained an important outlet. The United States was still a debtor nation, and its international balance of payments required a surplus of commodity exports over commodity imports.

World War I greatly stimulated agricultural expansion. Much new land was brought under cultivation in response to government exhortation and high prices for farm commodities. Land under cultivation reached an all-time high in 1920. In order to purchase more land, farmers assumed heavy mortgage obligations, and in order to work the land with diminished manpower

they went further into debt for tractors and other expensive farm equipment. Productive capacity once again far exceeded the normal requirements of domestic consumption.

Shortly after the First World War American agriculture slumped into a severe depression from which it did not emerge until the beginning of the Second World War. For the American economy generally the 1920's was a decade of prosperity, but farming was an important exception. After 1929 conditions in agriculture went from bad to worse. Thus the agricultural crisis, which was so apparent during the first phase of the Age of Mass Production (1873–96) and then seemed to disappear for nearly a quarter of a century (1897–1920), returned with a vengeance during the interwar period. The excess of production over consumption, which in 1900 constituted an exportable surplus, now meant overproduction.

The role of the First World War in the subsequent farm depression should not be overestimated. General mechanization of farming was already under way, and the war merely hurried it along. In a sense agricultural surpluses had completed the task of providing foreign exchange to pay for the outside assistance required to industrialize the American economy. The job being over, the farmers were left literally holding the sack.

Apart from a rise in productive capacity, the major element in the overproduction of farm commodities was the loss of foreign markets for the domestic surplus. Why had these markets, which had absorbed farm surpluses previously, vanished? The important reasons were: (1) competition from new areas for the European market; (2) the change in the status of the United States from prewar debtor to postwar creditor; and (3) high protective tariffs, which restricted imports and therefore exports.

(1) The new competition for European markets came from areas which were less developed than the United States and had responded more slowly to the potential fall in the cost of long-distance transportation. Typically, these countries borrowed farm machinery after it had been perfected in the United States. In the wheat market the chief competitors were Canada, Australia, and Argentina. The severity of competition corresponded closely to the completion of railway networks connecting seaports with the wheat-growing interiors of these countries. In cotton less serious competition came from Brazil, Egypt, and India.

(2) The change from debtor to creditor status was precipitated by the large loans made by the American government to its wartime allies. The ability of the United States to make these loans reflected its industrial maturity and a capacity for exporting capital. Foreigners experienced difficulty in finding dollars with which to pay for American exports. The dollars which foreigners earned by exporting goods to the United States were now needed, in whole or in part, to meet payments of interest and principal on debts owed to the United States. Moreover, industrial America ceased to be the large importer of manufactured goods it had been during the nineteenth century. Instead, the United States now produced an industrial as well as an agricultural surplus. Industrial Europe found it easier to finance its trade with Argentina, Australia, Canada, Brazil, Egypt, and India than with the United States because these less developed economies were large purchasers of Europe's industrial products as well as Europe's debtors.

(3) American tariffs had been high since the onset of the Civil War,

with temporary reductions during the Democratic administrations of Presidents Cleveland and Wilson. During the 1920's new legislation boosted tariff barriers to trade to the highest level in American history. Traditionally American farmers, except in the South, had given their political support to tariffs for industry. They now paid an economic price for their political folly because the tariffs which kept industrial goods from coming in also kept agricultural commodities from going out of the country. Like potential exporters in any country, American farmers learned that a nation which does not buy from other countries cannot expect to sell to them.

4. Overproduction of Farm Surpluses Was Not Easily Adjusted Through the Market

In the face of shrinking demand, caused by loss of foreign markets and other factors, the production of agricultural commodities remained high. The consequences were overproduction followed by a fall in farm prices. According to the rationale of market allocation of resources, the fall in prices should have gradually eliminated overproduction by (1) reducing the quantity produced and (2) increasing consumption (more consumed at lower than at higher prices). For various reasons these market forces did not eliminate farm surpluses, and agricultural overproduction became chronic in the United States.

Supply and demand factors influencing overproduction On the supply side the main cause of chronic overproduction of farm commodities was too many farmers. According to the theory of market adjustment the least efficient farmers would suffer losses and leave agriculture for other occupations, thus reducing the total farm output. During the 1920's farmers did leave agriculture, but not rapidly enough. With productivity rising rapidly, fewer farmers could produce as much or more than before. Since farming is a way of life as well as a business, farmers are reluctant to pick up stakes and move to urban centers, especially when alternative opportunities are limited, as they were throughout the interwar period. Agriculture suffered from overemployment in the sense that too many people were employed in it for a proper economic balance.

When demand falls, as it did in 1920 and again in 1929, farmers are reluctant to reduce the amounts they produce. Frequently, when prices fall in response to a fall in demand, farmers try to produce more rather than less in order to maintain their cash income and to meet fixed charges such as taxes, interest, mortgage principal, and living expenses. Many remain in farming as long as they earn barely enough income to subsist. The level of living of farmers on the average fell during the decade of the 1920's while the nonfarm sector of the economy enjoyed rising levels of living.

Many agricultural products satisfy basic wants like food and clothing. Fulfillment of these wants is not very sensitive to changes in prices, that is, the demand for farm products is relatively inelastic. When supply is short, prices rise sharply if uncontrolled; and when supply increases, prices tend to fall sharply without amounts purchased being much increased. As the prices of farm products go down, consumers can satisfy their needs with less money ex-

penditure and have money left over to spend on other things. The corollary of this is that as prices go down and consumers spend less for food and clothing, farm incomes fall relative to other incomes. This characteristic of demand helps to account for the fall in farm incomes during the prosperous 1920's.

The stability of farm output and the flexibility of farm prices may be illustrated with reference to wheat production and prices between 1919 and 1932, shown in Table 26–1.

TABLE 26–1

Prices and Production of Wheat in the U.S., 1919–1932

YEAR	PRODUCTION (millions of bushels)	PRICE (season average)	TOTAL REVENUE Price × Production) (millions)
1919	952	$2.16	$2,056
1920	843	1.83	1,543
1921	819	1.03	844
1922	847	0.97	822
1923	759	0.93	706
1924	842	1.25	1,052
1925	669	1.44	963
1926	832	1.22	1,015
1927	875	1.19	1,041
1928	914	1.00	914
1929	824	1.04	857
1930	887	0.67	594
1931	942	0.39	367
1932	756	0.38	287

Source: U. S. Bureau of the Census, *Historical Statistics of the United States, Colonial Times to 1957* (Washington, D.C.: Government Printing Office, 1960), pp. 296-97.

The price of wheat per bushel declined from $2.16 in 1919 to $1.03 in 1921, or more than 50 per cent. Meanwhile production fell from 952,000,000 bushels in 1919 to 819,000,000 bushels in 1921, or only 14 per cent. From 1929 to 1931 the price of wheat decreased from $1.04 to $.39, or nearly two-thirds; while the production of wheat actually increased from 824,000,000 to 942,000,000 bushels. Production in 1931 was approximately the same as in 1919, but the price was only about one-sixth that of 1919. The last column in the table indicates the effect of price movements on the money income received from wheat production. In 1932 it was only one-seventh the gross income of 1919.

Why did farmers do nothing about their low and falling incomes? There was little that individual farmers could do about their plight because they were at the mercy of the market over which they as individuals had no control. Because the production of any one farmer is very small in relation to the total output of all farmers, a change in his production cannot influence the market price. Individual farmers behaved quite rationally when they re-

sponded to falling farm prices by working harder to produce more in order to maintain their cash income. Each farmer who did not respond in this manner became worse off as a result. Yet the aggregate result of rational behavior for individual farmers was irrational for farmers as a whole; their increased production reduced prices and total money receipts. In heavy industries, as noted above,[4] cutthroat competition led to cartels and other forms of business combinations to curtail output and maintain prices and profits. Farmers as individuals had no such easy escape; private cartels involving so many producers were hardly feasible. The only way in which farmers could lift themselves out of a chronic state of ruinous competition was to have the government act as their agent to curtail production and create scarcity. The policies subsequently used to enable American farmers to escape from the free market were of this nature. They brought results gradually, although wastefully and incompletely.

The fact that nonfarm prices and production behaved differently from farm prices and production was a crucial consideration in the plight of the farmers. If the prices of the things farmers purchased had fallen by the same amount as the prices of things farmers sold, there would have been no fall in real income because with fewer dollars farmers could have purchased as much as before. The fall in farm income would have been nominal rather than real.[5] Unfortunately for farmers this was far from the actual situation. As noted in the earlier chapter on organized business, industrial prices tend to be rigid because of the ability of large, monopolistic firms to control the prices of their products and, if necessary, to cut back on production when confronted with falling demand. Prices of farm machinery, for example, remained fixed between 1929 and 1932, while the prices of farm products fell more than 50 per cent. At the same time the output of farm machinery was curtailed drastically, whereas the output of farm products remained relatively stable. Thus, industry was characterized by inflexible prices and unstable output, whereas agriculture was characterized by flexible prices and stable output. The resulting disparity between the prices received by farmers and the prices paid by farmers meant that farmers did not receive what their spokesmen called a "fair share" of the national income. Farmers were being "exploited" by non-farmers.

5. Non-market Adjustments to Achieve Parity of Farm Prices Failed to Eliminate Overproduction of Farm Commodities in the United States

With the failure of the market to eliminate overproduction of farm commodities, adjustments were attempted outside the market, mainly through special legislation promoted by the politically powerful "farm bloc" in the national Congress. The solution attained in agriculture was analogous to that achieved earlier by businessmen through combinations and by laborers through unions. All three represented a retreat from the free market. Relief

[4] Chapter 22.

[5] However, interest and mortgage payments incurred when prices were high during the First World War would have remained fixed in money terms and therefore, as a debtor class, farmers would have been worse off than a non-debtor class.

for farmers from the intolerable results of the free market, however, depended primarily on government legislation, and effective measures awaited a change in political philosophy, which meant that matters had to get much worse before they could get better. The Great Depression discredited laissez-faire sufficiently to give sanctions to programs under which the government acted as the agent of farmers to do what industry had learned to do for itself early in the Age of Mass Production, namely, to restrict output in order to maintain prices higher than those which would prevail in the free market. Schemes to solve the farm problem outside the market were not notably successful in eliminating over-production of farm commodities, but after a number of failures, the cost of the surpluses was shifted from farmers to taxpayers and consumers.

Non-market adjustments included (1) the tariff, (2) plans for dumping surpluses abroad while maintaining high domestic prices and (3) crop restriction plans accompanied by price supports and government purchases of surpluses.

Tariffs on farm products　Ironically, attempts were made to use tariffs to protect American agriculture in much the same manner that tariffs had been used by the French and Germans to protect their farmers from American competition. There was, of course, little point in placing tariffs on commodities which American farmers produced much more cheaply than foreigners and which the United States normally exported. Some agricultural commodities, notably sugar, did benefit from tariffs. In the case of sugar not only was there a departure from the free market in terms of the tariff, but import quotas were also imposed as a second line of protection to domestic sugar beet and sugar cane growers. On farm products generally, however, American farmers were not in a position to benefit from protective tariffs.

Proposals to dump surpluses abroad　During the 1920's the farm bloc supported the McNary-Haugen bills, which incorporated the cartel principle of raising prices by restricting the amounts offered for sale in the domestic market. These bills proposed to separate domestic requirements from exportable surpluses. Surpluses in excess of the quantities which could be sold in the domestic market at fixed prices were to be dumped on foreign markets. The McNary-Haugen bills passed both houses of Congress on two occasions. Only presidential vetoes prevented them from becoming law.

Dumping surpluses on the federal government (Federal Farm Board, 1929–32)　Just prior to the big crash in 1929 President Hoover called a special session of Congress to deal with the farm problem through voluntary cooperation among farmers under governmental auspices. The resulting legistion was the Agricultural Marketing Act, which, among other things, established the Federal Farm Board and authorized governmental stabilization corporations to withdraw surplus crops from the market. Stabilization corporations were set up for two basic commodities, wheat and cotton. Large surpluses were purchased by these government corporations with the expectation that the reduced volume available in the open market would sell at higher prices. Presumably the surpluses held by the government would be sold later when the open market was better able to absorb them. The plan was better designed to stabilize than to raise prices. No provision was made for curtail-

ment of production, but as surpluses increased the Farm Board exhorted farmers to reduce their acreage, using the motto, "Grow less, get more." The Federal Farm Board, which was never intended to meet the catastrophic situation brought on by the Great Depression, was abandoned in 1932. One important lesson learned from this experience was that a successful plan for raising farm prices and incomes would have to strike at the root of the farm problem, overproduction.

Paying farmers more to produce less When Franklin Roosevelt assumed the Presidency in 1933 the situation in American agriculture was desperate. To the earlier loss of foreign markets had now been added a drastic shrinkage in the domestic market arising from the severe depression in the industrial sector of the economy. Prices of farm products had fallen by 56 per cent between 1929 and 1932, whereas the prices paid by farmers, including interest, taxes, and wages had fallen by only 30 per cent; for example, mortgages contracted in earlier years when prices were high had not fallen at all in money terms. Millions of farmers were confronted with immediate foreclosure.

Determined efforts were made under the New Deal to solve the farm problem. Much stress was placed on the lack of balance between the farm and the nonfarm sectors of the economy. The disparities between farm and nonfarm prices were attacked through the parity program. Parity prices for agriculture were defined as prices which would give to farmers the same relative purchasing power which they had enjoyed in the base period 1909–14. Parity prices as calculated by the United States Department of Agriculture are shown in Table 26–2.

Achieving parity for farmers meant raising the prices of farm products relative to nonfarm products. In order to raise prices it was necessary to reduce production and to keep surpluses off the market. Various devices were used for this purpose, but the general principle was to pay farmers more for producing less. In 1933 under an emergency plan incentive payments were made to farmers who plowed under every third row of cotton and to hog farmers who slaughtered little pigs and pregnant sows. During 1934 and 1935 other crop-restriction plans were placed in operation.

At first participation in crop-restriction plans was purely voluntary on the part of the individual farmers. Of course, those who refused to restrict production did not receive benefit payments from the government. Insofar as the program was successful, however, the non-cooperators gained from higher prices while remaining free to produce as much as they wanted. The system which finally evolved provided that acreage restriction would apply to all farmers of a given crop in a given state if farmers with two-thirds of the acreage of the crop voted in favor of restriction. Like business cartels, price supports in agriculture could not operate successfully without some control over the total production coming onto the market.

Price supports took the form of non-recourse loans to farmers on a "Heads I win, tails you lose" basis. The amount of a loan advanced to an individual farmer was based on parity. If the market price of the commodity fell below the amount advanced, the loan was cancelled and the government took title to the commodity. If the price rose above the loan-price, farmers

Parity Ratio of U.S. Farm Prices* 1910–1965
(1910-14 = 100)

YEAR	PARITY RATIO	YEAR	PARITY RATIO	YEAR	PARITY RATIO
1910	107	1929	92	1948	110
1911	96	1930	83	1949	100
1912	98	1931	67	1950	101
1913	101	1932	58	1951	107
1914	98	1933	64	1952	100
1915	94	1934	75	1953	92
1916	103	1935	88	1954	89
1917	120	1936	92	1955	84
1918	119	1937	93	1956	83
1919	110	1938	78	1957	82
1920	99	1939	77	1958	85
1921	80	1940	81	1959	82
1922	87	1941	93	1960	80
1923	89	1942	105	1961	79
1924	89	1943	113	1962	80
1925	95	1944	108	1963	78
1926	91	1945	109	1964	76
1927	88	1946	113	1965	77
1928	91	1947	115	1966	80

* Parity is the ratio of prices received by farmers to prices paid by farmers, including interest, taxes, and wage rates.
Source: U. S. Bureau of the Census, *Historical Statistics of the United States, Colonial Times to 1957,* p. 283; *Economic Report of the President* (January, 1966), p. 295.

could pay off the loan and sell the produce at a profit. Although restricted acreage was a condition for price supports (through guaranteed loans at parity prices), there was no comparable restriction on increased production through increased yields per acre. Higher prices provided an incentive to increase yields per acre through more intensive use of fertilizer and the application of technical improvements developed by scientists and farm experts of the United States Department of Agriculture. To this extent the program was self-defeating.

A price support program was utilized during the Second World War as an incentive to farmers to increase production to meet added war needs for agricultural commodities arising from military and foreign demand. Actually farm prices rose above parity during the war and price supports were mainly important as insurance against the danger that prices might suddenly collapse as they had after the First World War. In the postwar period, however, price supports became the focal point of a great debate over the cause of continuing farm overproduction (surpluses). Perhaps the most interesting point about this debate is that no major political group questioned price sup-

ports as such. The debate centered around the extent of support (the per cent of parity) and whether the supports should be rigid or flexible, that is, whether they could be changed by legislative authority alone or whether the Secretary of Agriculture should have the power to vary the level of support. This meant that the nation had accepted a policy of subsidies to farmers as a class. Overproduction as such was not eliminated, but its cost was transferred from farmers to taxpayers in the form of taxes (to buy surpluses) and to consumers in the form of higher prices.

The Agricultural Adjustment Acts under which the farm programs operated after 1933 were severely criticized. Many of these criticisms were thoroughly justified. One point which should not escape the attention of critics, however, is that the AAA was designed to rescue private enterprise in agriculture from a desperate situation which had persisted for at least a dozen years. Farmers could not individually afford to restrict output because there was, in the absence of an overall program, no reason to believe that farmers in general would restrict their output. What was needed was a government-sponsored program for creating artificial scarcity which would parallel the restrictionist policies pursued by industry through administered prices and business combinations. The agricultural program did achieve a balance between industry and agriculture in the sense that it introduced into the latter some of the major characteristics of the former. Clearly, this was not the best of all possible solutions, but the alternative would have been much more radical.

6. General Significance of the Agricultural Problem in the United States

The foregoing discussion of American agriculture may be summed up as follows: The adjustment of agriculture to a position of declining importance has been difficult within the market process and, as with business and labor, solutions have been sought outside the market process. In brief, the retreat from the free market, a dominant characteristic of industry and labor during the age of mass production, has also been the dominant trend in agriculture.

Retreat from the free market in agriculture does not imply that the free market, if permitted to operate, could not or would not have eliminated agricultural overproduction in the United States. While it is true that farmers are not easily eliminated by the market process—partly because they can escape the market process by supplying their own subsistence if necessary—and while most American farmers managed to weather the hard times of the 1920's, the Great Depression would probably have knocked out the surplus producers if the New Deal had not come to their rescue. By 1932 millions of hard-working, honest farmers were faced with bankruptcy. They would have been foreclosed and forced out of production simply by doing nothing about their situation. This would have been the rugged individualist, free market solution to agricultural overproduction in the United States. This, however, was not permitted to happen. Society acting through duly elected government officials did not permit the free market process to reach its logical culmination. Presumably farmers were rescued from the free market because their elimination seemed morally repugnant to those who held the power to act in their

behalf. Forcing farmers off the land by wholesale foreclosure in a major depression was politically unacceptable. Economic institutions must operate within a framework which is morally acceptable to controlling groups, which in a political democracy means ultimately the population at large.

COMPARATIVE ANALYSIS

Every country discussed above experienced a crisis in agriculture during the age of mass production. Underlying these crises was a single cause of a two-fold nature: (1) the "invasion" of western European countries by agricultural commodities from the New World and from eastern Europe; and (2) the general decline of agriculture relative to total economic activity. In England and western Europe the decline of agriculture set in earlier because the American "invasion" shifted specialization in agricultural staples, especially cereal production, across the Atlantic. The decline of agriculture came quite as definitely to the United States, however, in response to greater specialization between farm and nonfarm activity, that is, from a higher stage in the division of labor.

The response to the American "invasion" in each European country was different. In England the farmers, who were politically weak, were left exposed to overseas competition until the Great Depression of the 1930's, when protective measures, especially subsidies, were instituted. France, where the agriculturalists were politically strong, very early provided high protective tariffs against imported agricultural commodities. These tariffs enabled France to remain self-sufficient in food production. Among the effects of protection were high prices for food, lower real incomes for urban wage-earners, and a retardation of industrial development. In Germany moderate protection was instituted by Bismarck, partly as a fiscal measure. Later, under the Nazis, self-sufficiency was attempted by Germany. In Denmark a rapid transition from cereal culture to animal production enabled the Danes to convert their economy into an efficient "food factory"—a remarkable example of planned adjustment to an altered market situation. The Danes were in no position to delay facing the facts of the new overseas competition. They could not afford a lengthy period of costly subsidies from the nonfarm to the farm population, such as characterized attempts to solve the American farm problem.

Although the United States was able for a while to dispose of its farm commodities in European markets, it did not escape an agricultural crisis. The basic American farm problem was one common to all progressive economies sooner or later—adjustment of farming to a position of declining relative and, in some instances, absolute importance. The most important source of demand for farm commodities arises from human consumption of food and clothing. As economies progress to higher levels of productivity and living, a relatively smaller part of family and national budgets (expenditures) are spent for these basic necessities.

After the First World War the American farm problem was made more acute by loss of foreign markets. With the laborsaving devices which characterized American agricultural development, a smaller number of farm workers could supply the needs of an increasing population. Since agriculture is a way

of life as well as a business, there is an inertia against migrating to nonfarm activity and a consequent tendency for surplus population to accumulate in agriculture and to produce agricultural surpluses. In 1939, at the end of the Great Depression and before the start of the Second World War, it was estimated there were three million surplus workers in agriculture in the United States. As in any economy with progressive technology and limited foreign markets, the most economical solution to the American farm problem is fewer farmers.

The adjustment of agriculture to a position of diminishing importance is rendered more difficult by the restrictionist tendencies of industry under mass production. Monopolistic policies in industry limit opportunities for surplus farmers to enter nonfarm occupations. At the same time inflexible, monopolistic prices for industrial products, in combination with flexible farm prices, set up a disparity between farm and nonfarm prices and incomes. This chronic disparity, accentuated by the Great Depression, finally drove the federal government of the United States to intervene strongly in the market for farm commodities in the interest of "equality for agriculture" under the parity programs. Various devices were proposed and several were utilized; all had as a general objective the elimination of surplus commodities from the market in order to increase farm prices and incomes. The destruction of farm commodities and payments to farmers for *not* producing were severely criticized as contrary to common sense. However, they should be understood, if not accepted, as means of giving to competitive agriculture the characteristics of monopolistic industry, that is, induced scarcity in order to maintain prices at levels profitable to private enterprise.

Since the beginning of the age of mass production in the 1870's, agriculture in both western Europe and the United States has suffered more years of depression than it has enjoyed years of prosperity. The Long Depression (1873–96) was more an agricultural than a general economic depression, but at the time farming was so important that depressed agriculture had a major influence on the total economy and set the tone of economic thinking. During the 1920's agriculture again suffered from acute depression in a period of industrial expansion, but by that time had declined to a point where it no longer served as a bellwether for the whole economy.

Although such things as weather and fertility of the soil enter into the details of every farm situation, the crises in agriculture have not been caused by famine, drought, or scarcity. Nor have they arisen from diminishing returns, so much feared by Ricardo and Malthus early in the nineteenth century. Like those in industry, they have been crises of abundance, complicated by an uneven distribution of gains among countries and between industry and agriculture. Agricultural development in every country has shown steady and impressive improvements in productivity. While it is, of course, a sad commentary on collective social intelligence that abundance should be permitted to become a curse, like the curse of Midas, the fact that crises arise from abundance imparts a basically optimistic note because it suggests that the faults lie not in nature but in economic and social arrangements for conducting business and that future crises may be eliminated by altering economic and social arrangements.

The last few chapters have surveyed the dominant trends in industry,

labor, and agriculture during the age of mass production. The most important single conclusion is that all three of these major sectors of modern economies have followed similar patterns in the sense that they have all come to depend less on the free market as the chief guide for the allocation and employment of resources. The ideals of laissez-faire and free competition have given way to business combinations, labor unions, and government-sponsored monopolies in agriculture. Free markets persisted longest in agriculture, especially in Great Britain and the United States, but the disparities created by operating in the free market after business and labor had withdrawn gave rise to intolerable conditions for farmers. They felt, and in a real sense were justified in feeling, that they were being exploited by nonfarm groups in the economy. Societies acting through their governments have supported widespread intervention and subsidies on behalf of farmers. The trend in the foreseeable future is for more rather than less government intervention as a means of easing the position of agriculture as a declining sector of the total economy. The market system has not been abandoned in the countries analyzed, but it has been subjected to major modifications. It gives additional support to the generalization that mass production is moving economic life further and further from laissez-faire toward a system of economic planning under governmental auspices.

SELECTED BIBLIOGRAPHY

BARGER, HAROLD, *American Agriculture, 1899–1939: A Study of Output, Employment and Productivity.* New York: National Bureau of Economic Research, 1942.

BENEDICT, MURRAY K., *Can We Solve the Farm Problem? An Analysis of Federal Aid to Agriculture.* New York: Twentieth Century Fund, 1955.

————, *Farm Policies of the United States, 1790–1950: A Study of Their Origins and Development.* New York: Twentieth Century Fund, 1955.

COCHRANE, WILLARD W., *Farm Prices: Myth and Reality.* Minneapolis: University of Minnesota Press, 1958.

DOVRING, FOLKE, "The Transformation of European Agriculture," in *The Cambridge Economic History of Europe,* Vol. VI, Part II, Chap. 6, pp. 604–72. London: Cambridge University Press, 1965.

EDWARDS, EVERETT E., "American Agriculture—The First 300 Years," in *U. S. Dept. of Agriculture Yearbook, 1940.* Washington, D.C.: Government Printing Office, 1940.

GERSCHENKRON, ALEXANDER, *Bread and Democracy in Germany.* Berkeley: University of California Press, 1943.

GRAS, N. S. B., *A History of Agriculture in Europe and America.* New York: The Meredith Publishing Co., 1940.

HATHAWAY, DALE E., *Government and Agriculture: Public Policy in a Democratic Society.* New York: The Macmillan Company, 1963.

HERTEL, HANS, *A Short History of Agriculture in Denmark.* Copenhagen: Bianco Luno, 1925.

HICKS, JOHN D., *The Populist Revolt. A History of the Farmers' Alliance and the People's Party.* Lincoln: University of Nebraska Press, 1961.

ORWIN, CHRISTABEL S., and EDITH H. WHETHAM, *History of British Agriculture, 1846–1914*. London: Longmans, Green & Co., Ltd., 1964.

POLLACK, NORMAN, *The Populist Response to Industrial America; Midwestern Populist Thought*. Cambridge, Mass.: Harvard University Press, 1962.

PROTHERO, R. E. (LORD ERNLE), *English Farming, Past and Present*, 6th ed. London: William Heinemann, Ltd., 1961.

ROGIN, LEO, *Introduction of Farm Machinery in Its Relation to the Productivity of Labor in Agriculture of the United States During the Nineteenth Century*. Berkeley: University of California Press, 1931.

SCHULTZ, THEODORE W., *The Economic Organization of Agriculture*. New York: McGraw-Hill, Inc., 1953.

SPRING, DAVID, *English Landed Estate in the Nineteenth Century*. Baltimore: The Johns Hopkins University Press, 1963.

THOMPSON, F. M. L., *English Landed Society in the Nineteenth Century*. London: Routledge and Kegan Paul, Ltd., 1963.

ARTICLES

BLACK, JOHN D., "Agriculture in the Nation's Economy," *American Economic Review*, XLVI (March, 1956), 1–43.

BONNEN, JAMES T., "The First Hundred Years of the Department of Agriculture-Land-Grant College System: Some Observations on the Organizational Nature of a Great Technological Payoff," *Journal of Farm Economics*, XLIV (Dec., 1962), 1279–94.

BOWMAN, MARY JEAN, "The Land-Grant Colleges and Universities in Human-Resource Development," *Journal of Economic History*, XXII (Dec., 1962), 523–46.

FAIRLIE, S., "The Nineteenth-Century Corn Law Reconsidered," *Economic History Review*, XVIII (Dec., 1965), 562–75.

FLETCHER, T. W., "The Great Depression of English Agriculture, 1873–1896," *Economic History Review*, XIII (April, 1961), 417–32.

RASMUSSEN, WAYNE D., "Forty Years of Agricultural History," *Agricultural History*, XXXIII (Oct., 1959), 177–84.

——, "The Impact of Technological Change on American Agriculture, 1862–1962," *Journal of Economic History*, XXII (Dec., 1962), 578–91.

SALOUTOS, THEODORE, "The Agricultural Problem and Nineteenth Century Industrialism," *Agricultural History*, XXII (July, 1948), 156–74.

SCHMIDT, LOUIS B., "The Agricultural Revolution in the Prairies and the Great Plains of the United States," *Agricultural History*, VIII (Oct., 1934), 169–95.

SHANNON, FRED A., "The Status of the Mid-western Farmer in 1900," *Mississippi Valley Historical Review*, XXXVII (Dec., 1950), 491–510.

SIMON, MATTHEW, and DAVID E. NOVACK, "Some Dimensions of the American Commercial Invasion of Europe, 1871–1914: An Introductory Essay," *Journal of Economic History*, XXIV (Dec., 1964), 591–605.

WILCOX, WALTER W., "The Farm Policy Dilemma," *Journal of Farm Economics*, XL (Aug., 1958), 563–71.

Economic Imperialism and the
Development of Backward Areas

CHAPTER **27**

One consequence of the Age of Mass Production was the new economic imperialism: "new" because it differed in important respects
from the "old" capitalist imperialism of the mercantilist period;
"economic" because it had its genesis in forces which were peculiarly economic,
especially in the export of capital from the advanced to the underdeveloped
areas of the world; "imperialism" because it involved control, in varying degrees, over weak and unstable governments in economically backward areas.
The purpose of the control was to protect the economic interests, both private
and public, of the advanced capitalist countries.

The American Revolution and the Industrial Revolution lessened the interest of Europeans in colonies in the old, mercantilist sense. An increased
volume of trade between Great Britain and the United States after the latter's
independence indicated that political possession was not necessary for close
international economic relations between more advanced and less advanced
areas. Great Britain permitted its remaining Europeanized colonies—Canada,
Australia, and New Zealand—to develop virtual political independence within
the framework of the British Commonwealth of Nations, but retained close
economic ties with them. The Industrial Revolution increased the demand for
domestic capital in Great Britain, and railway construction reinforced for a
time the domestic demand for capital. Anti-colonialism meshed with the philosophy of laissez-faire and the doctrine of free trade, which flourished among
western European nations during the first half of the nineteenth century.

Export of Capital

Capital accumulation on an expanding scale tended to lower the rate of
return on domestic investments and made foreign investments more attractive.
Great Britain, as the leading capitalist nation in the nineteenth century, was
also the greatest exporter of capital. Before other economies had attained a
sufficient degree of maturity to produce surplus capital for export, British
funds flowed into transportation, public utilities, and manufacturing industries in the politically stable, independent nations of western Europe and the
United States. In this manner the British helped to develop the economic
potential of their future rivals. British funds, British engineering, and British

locomotives were used in France, Germany, Italy and elsewhere on the Continent as well as in the United States.

With the advent of mass production, Britain's rivals matured capitalistically to the point where they generated their own surplus capital for export and confronted the British with international rivalry in overseas investment. Now the main outlets for capital exports were in the less developed areas in Africa, Asia, South America, and eastern Europe. In the context of intense national rivalry, which characterized the period between 1870 and 1914, the Great Powers tried to outdo each other in staking out claims to raw materials and markets. Promoters and investors took advantage of the political weakness of underdeveloped areas in order to gain concessions in mining, oil wells, plantations, transportation, and public utilities in the knowledge that their governments would support their actions and protect their private interests. Even statesmen who were in principle opposed to imperialism neverthless sanctioned imperialistic behavior on the grounds that resources, territory, and markets would fall under the control of a rival power if they did not encourage and support their own nationals. Behind the sudden overseas expansion of the Great Powers in the decades preceding World War I was the rapid growth of mass production at home.

Mass Production and Economic Imperialism

We have already discussed the main characteristics and some of the important consequences of mass production.[1] An essential aspect of the development of mass production was cheap transportation and rapid communication, which greatly enlarged the geographical division of labor. Whereas in earlier times only the coastal fringes of overseas territories had been accessible to the European countries in any economically significant sense, railways now enabled them to penetrate the interior of whole continents. This happened first in Europe itself, then in North America, and finally in Asia, Africa, Australia, and South America.

The export of capital was a two-fold process, which corresponded to the dual manner in which mass production affected the domestic economy. Mass production created a larger output of goods (and services) and, in accounting terms, created a larger national income. The larger national income generated larger savings, which were available as loanable funds to finance capital formation. As rates of return on domestic loans fell, capitalists turned to foreign loans on which the rate of return was higher. The selling and buying of foreign bonds and securities of enterprises operating overseas were facilitated by the international money market and the international capital market. Funds made available by European lenders were used to finance overseas enterprises; they were used, for example, to purchase steel rails, steam locomotives, mining machinery and other types of capital goods required for overseas economic development.

The same mass production process which turned out more goods also generated larger income and, out of that enlarged income, a larger demand for domestic goods. However, the increase in domestic demand was less than the potential output of goods. The resulting gap between increased income

[1] See Chapter 20.

and increased domestic demand was filled partly by increased overseas (investment) demand. In other words, potential overproduction (in relation to aggregate effective demand) at home was offset in part by the export of goods and the export of money capital with which to purchase goods. Aggregate domestic and foreign demand were not always sufficient to maintain full employment and production, as the Long Depression of 1873–96 illustrates; [2] but the tendency to compensate for deficient domestic demand by exporting money capital and capital goods was a logical outcome of the process of mass production operating in the context of the private enterprise system. Pressures to seek more profitable outlets by foreign investment had always been present. The significance of the new mass production system in this connection is that it greatly intensified these pressures.

While the logic of the investment and saving process was not basically different in domestic and foreign markets, the political consequences were quite different. Large-scale export of capital was bound to have an impact on the weak and unstable governments of the underdeveloped countries. Various devices were employed by representatives of the advanced countries to promote their economic interests and to protect their investments in the backward areas. The results included the partition of Africa, spheres of influence in Asia, and intensified national rivalries among the Great Powers which eventually led to the First World War.

THE PARTITION OF AFRICA

In 1800 Europeans knew only the coastal areas of Africa. By 1900 this great continent had been partitioned among the European powers in the most sensational land-grabbing, empire-building episode in history. In 1913 European nations controlled 93 per cent of African territory, or more than ten million square miles. The French held approximately 40 per cent, the British 30 per cent, and Germany, Belgium, Portugal, and Spain the remaining 30 per cent. Much of the French territory was the barren Sahara Desert. In terms of population and resources the British had the richest holdings.

The British in Egypt

Britain's interest in Egypt dates from the building of the Suez Canal by the French in the 1860's, and more specifically from Disraeli's purchase of a controlling share in the Suez Canal Company in 1875.[3] At this time Egypt was nominally part of the Ottoman (Turkish) Empire, but that "sick man of Europe" was too weak to prevent encroachments by stronger powers in the West. The ambitious Khedive (viceroy) of Egypt went heavily into debt to western

---

[2] This analysis follows the modern Keynesian position that supply does not automatically create its own demand to produce full employment; output adjusts itself to the volume of effective demand; and aggregate effective demand consists of domestic consumption, domestic investment, government purchases, and net foreign investment (excess of exports over imports).

[3] Disraeli secretly borrowed money from the Rothschilds in order to purchase from the financially embarrassed Egyptian government a sufficient number of shares in the Canal Company to wrest control from the French. Although Disraeli's action was unconstitutional, it was given ex post facto ratification by the British Parliament.

European capitalists. Within a dozen years he borrowed the equivalent of approximately half a billion dollars and was hard pressed to meet the interest payments, which led to further borrowing. Bondholders became concerned about the safety of their investments and urged the British and French governments to take charge of Egyptian finances.

British reluctance to intervene in Egypt was overcome by the fear that the French would gain exclusive control of Egypt's public finances. Great Britain and France agreed to participate in the "dual control" of Egypt, a situation which prevailed between 1879 and 1882. In the latter year an Anglo-French fleet was sent into Egyptian waters to strengthen the position of the Khedive. This sword-rattling fomented latent Egyptian unrest. The French ships departed, but British troops landed and within a few weeks Egypt was pacified and under British control.

Gladstone, the anti-imperialist British Prime Minister at the time of his country's intervention in Egypt, pledged that supervision of Egyptian affairs was to be only temporary. Gladstone's sincerity is hardly open to question, but the fact is that he was unable to honor his pledge. The British had a bear by the tail, so to speak, and could not let go. They remained in control of Egypt for nearly three-quarters of a century.

Financial administration proved the key to British control of Egypt. Major Baring, later Lord Cromer, of the famous banking family became British consul general and high commissioner and *de facto* ruler of Egypt for a quarter of a century (1883–1907). He achieved remarkable success in restoring financial stability and eradicating corruption in the Egyptian government. Among the achievements of his administration was the building of the Aswan Dam [4] across the Nile for flood control and irrigation. He abolished forced labor, built railways, and established a school system.

During the First World War the British prevented Egypt, still nominally a Turkish province, from entering the war on Turkey's side by making Egypt a British protectorate. In 1922 Egypt was declared "an independent sovereign state," but Britain retained the rights deemed essential to protect British interests, including the right to use Egyptian territory to defend the Suez Canal and to control the Anglo-Egyptian Sudan to the South. Only after the Second World War did the British surrender control over Egypt.

The British in South Africa

Cecil Rhodes was the dominant figure in British territorial aggrandizement in South Africa during the last three decades of the nineteenth century. Rhodes went to Africa for his health in 1870 at the age of 17. At 19 he was a millionaire. Diamond mining and gold mining were the source of his personal fortune and also the chief basis for the rapid development of the South African economy. Rhodes amassed his great fortune not by gathering diamonds in the dust nor by prospecting for gold, but by using the capitalistic technique of joint-stock companies to build a great business empire which monopolized diamond mining and controlled much of the gold production of South Africa.

[4] Not to be confused with the Aswan High Dam, which was engineered by the Soviet Union after Nasser's negotiations for its construction with Western powers broke down, precipitating the Suez crisis in 1956.

Rhodes began by buying up the claims of discouraged fortune-seekers and over a period of years gained control of the famous De Beers Diamond Mining Company.[5] He then secretly bought a controlling interest in the only important remaining rival company and forced it into an amalgamation as De Beers Consolidated Mines (1888). This company gained a monopoly of South African diamonds, and mined 90 per cent of the world's total output. The supply was deliberately restricted in order to keep the price of diamonds high all over the world.

Rhodes enjoyed similar success in gold mining. Through the Consolidated Gold Fields of South Africa Company he approached a monopoly position in a region which became the leading gold-production area in the world. At the height of his prosperity in the 1890's Rhodes' personal income is estimated to have been about $5 million annually.

From the point of view of British imperialism the important joint-stock company in South Africa was the British South Africa Company. It was chartered in London in 1889 as a profit-making enterprise with authority to "make treaties, promulgate laws, preserve the peace, maintain a police force, and acquire new concessions." It could construct railroads, harbors, and public works; engage in mining and banking and make land grants. In brief, it could do virtually anything it chose to do. The northern limit of the company's jurisdiction was left undefined because one of its objectives, as envisaged by Rhodes, was to push British control as far north as possible, and ultimately to join the British expansion southward along the upper Nile in the Anglo-Egyptian Sudan. Rhodes contributed to the Liberal Party in England on condition that it "not scuttle out of Egypt."

The South Africa Company illustrates how the British utilized a private joint-stock company to extend the Empire at the expense of backward peoples. As with the East India Company of an earlier age, the British government was able to garner the fruits of empire without direct responsibility for the acts of its agents. A joint-stock company organized for profit was the economic and political ruler of a vast territory and millions of people. The British government was represented by a Secretary of State with limited supervisory powers, but only occasionally did the London government exercise a restraining hand to protect the often abused natives.

Rhodes controlled the South Africa Company through his complex of holding companies and his great personal wealth. The De Beers Diamond Company, which he controlled, purchased a large block of shares; Rhodes' gold mining companies bought another large block; and Rhodes personally held enough additional shares in the South Africa Company to control it legally and to dominate its policies and make it an instrument of his ambitions for the British Empire.

Actually the only legal power of the South Africa Company over the territory where it operated arose from agreements with the native tribes, who granted rights for mining and other economic concessions. The Company was in fact sovereign as soon as the military resistance of the natives was broken. A typical pattern was as follows: A treaty or agreement was made with a native tribe. The natives would violate the treaty, or would be accused of doing

[5] De Beers was a Boer farmer on whose land the famous diamond mine was dug.

so. The British would assemble an army of troopers to chastise the natives and take over control of their territory. Between 1879 and 1887, before the South Africa Company was formed, a war against the Zulus had converted Zululand, a large area north of Cape Colony, into a British possession. In similar fashion a protectorate was proclaimed over Bechuanaland (1885), another large area north of Cape Colony. In 1893 Rhodes and his lieutenant, Dr. Jameson, picked a quarrel with King Lo Bengula and then invaded and took control of his lands.[6]

A greater obstacle than the power of the natives to British consolidation of South Africa was imposed by the presence of the two Dutch republics, the Orange Free State and the Transvaal Republic. Cape Colony had been settled originally by the Dutch as a supply station in the mid-seventeenth century in the period when Holland almost ruled the seven seas. In 1806, during the Napoleonic Wars, a British fleet seized Cape Colony, and the descendants of the Dutch settlers (Boers) migrated northward and settled along the Orange River and across the Vaal River.

The most unsavory episode in the history of the British South Africa Company occurred when Dr. Jameson, acting as an agent of Rhodes, invaded the Transvaal Republic with the avowed intention of overthrowing the Boer government and making the Republic part of the British Empire. Jameson's raid failed miserably, and Jameson was captured and ransomed. Relations between the Boers and the British in South Africa were embittered and relations between Germany and Great Britain became strained when the Kaiser sent a congratulatory telegram to President Kruger of the Transvaal for putting down the British raid.

Rhodes' political career was broken by the ill-fated Jameson raid. He was forced to resign as prime minister of Cape Colony, a position he had held from 1890 to 1896. His career as an empire builder was not over, however. This many-sided individual, the "King" of the diamond city of Kimberley, bachelor and woman-hater, monopolist and millionaire capitalist, patriotic imperialist, philosopher and dreamer who believed the salvation of the world lay in the domination of the English-speaking people, and founder of the Rhodes scholarships, moved north to what is now called Rhodesia to busy himself with the extension of the British Empire.

The Jameson Raid was a prelude to the Boer War (1899–1902), which accomplished, at much greater cost, what the Jameson Raid was intended to do. The Dutch republics were crushed, and Britain was supreme in South Africa. The British gave the Boers full political equality, and in democratic elections (among whites) the Boers won political control of the government. In 1910 the Union of South Africa was given dominion status within the British Empire.

South Africa continued to be first and foremost a mining region. British capital came in and built an efficient system of railways. Manufacturing grew rapidly, although most of it was for local consumption. The great unsettled problem has remained that of the Negro natives, who constitute the bulk of the population but hold only a minute fraction of the land and are kept in the status of an unwilling proletariat at discriminatorily low wages.

[6] See the pathetic letter of Lo Bengula to Queen Victoria explaining how he had been tricked into signing a paper containing provisions of which he was unaware.

French possessions in Africa were concentrated in the north and west, consisting of Algeria, Tunisia, Morocco, French West Africa, and French Equatorial Africa. The first step in rebuilding the French colonial empire, which had been shattered by the British in 1763, was the conquest of Algeria in 1830. Algeria became France's jumping-off point for new imperialist ventures in the late nineteenth century. In 1881 a French army invaded Tunisia from Algeria and in less than three weeks "pacified" the entire country. Tunisia was ruled by the weak and irresponsible Bey of Tunis, who had borrowed heavily from French capitalists and financiers. Heavy taxes levied to meet these obligations constituted one of the causes of rebellion, which the French army came in to quell in 1881. Jules Ferry, the Prime Minister of France when Tunisia was seized, was an acknowledged imperialist who championed the new French empire on economic grounds. In response to criticism in the Chamber of Deputies, Ferry replied that France needed Tunisia as "an outlet for our manufacturers" and as "a lucrative means of investing capital" . . . "You must admit that the capitalists and companies which undertake the establishment out there of railways, banks, mortgages, and similar undertakings are collaborators in the economic conquest, and not cut-purses who deserve the anger and contempt of Parliament." Ferry's leading critic was a young Radical, Georges Clemenceau, who announced in the Chamber of Deputies: "In all these enterprises . . . I see only persons . . . who wish to do business and make money on the Bourse. . . . In short, it is to satisfy such 'interests' that you have made war, violated the Constitution, and have placed Parliament face to face with an accomplished fact." The whole affair was, in brief, a *coup de bourse*, as the French would say. Although Ferry was turned out of office for the quasi-scandal caused by the seizure of Tunisia, France nevertheless retained the fruits of the *coup de bourse*. In taking possession of Tunisia, France gained the enmity of Italy, which also had designs on the Carthage (Tunis) of old. Indignation over France's seizure of Tunisia was a major factor causing Italy to join the Triple Alliance with Germany and Austria—an alliance against France, Russia, and later Great Britain.

France experienced more difficulty in gaining control over Morocco because of stern opposition from Germany. The political independence of Morocco was pledged by the Great Powers in 1880, but under a weak and profligate Sultan, who became heavily indebted to foreigners, Morocco was vulnerable to economic penetration and political domination. It became a happy hunting ground for political intrigue by those in pursuit of economic concessions. Great Britain agreed to give France a free hand in Morocco in exchange for a French pledge to give the British a free hand in Egypt (1904). France purchased Italian support by giving a green light to Italy in Libya and Cyrenaica.

Germany, on the other hand, provided persistent opposition. France had pledged an "open door" policy on the economic front, and Germany agreed to French political hegemony if given economic equality. France, however, used its political advantage to discriminate against German trade and investment. On one occasion (1911) Germany sent a warship into Moroccan coastal

waters in order to intimidate the French, who were on the verge of seizing complete control of Morocco. Germany was bought off when France ceded 100,000 square miles of French Equatorial Africa to Germany (1912).[7] France became firmly implanted in Morocco.

The Morocco question, however, had aroused national animosities in all the capitals of Europe and in particular deepened the cleavage between Germany, on the one hand, and France and Great Britain, on the other. It was one of a series of similar issues which contributed to the First World War. After the war the anti-imperialist phase began in Morocco with costly fighting between native groups and Europeans, and culminated in the French being driven from Morocco after the Second World War. Independence for Tunisia followed almost immediately, and within a decade France was forced to surrender all claims to Algeria.

The Belgian Congo

In 1879 the British-born American journalist, Henry Morton Stanley, who had found Dr. Livingstone in central Africa, was employed by the Belgian king, Leopold II, to return to Africa on a "scientific" expedition for the International Association for the Exploration and Civilization of Central Africa. This fancy name was a front for a private company, organized and headed by Leopold, for the purpose of exploiting African natural and human resources for the private profit of Leopold and his associates. Stanley set up trading posts, made "treaties" with native chiefs, and laid plans for road construction. After Leopold gained international recognition for his organization, he changed its title to the Congo Free State, with himself individually, not as King of the Belgians, as the "sovereign" ruler of a personal empire of 900,000 square miles—seventy-five times the area of European Belgium.

Leopold proceeded to exploit his personal empire for private gain in a ruthless fashion. Rubber and ivory were the potentially valuable exports of the Congo. Rubber had to be gathered from wild rubber trees and ivory from elephants roaming the jungles. In order to realize the potential value of these and other resources, labor power was necessary. This type of labor was not for white men. The only available supply was the African natives; but the Africans were untutored in the ways of the voluntary wage system. Furthermore they had no strong incentive to become interested in it so long as they had their huts, their cultivated fields, and the forests and streams for hunting and fishing.

The institutional arrangements of the two civilizations clashed head-on at this point. The outcome was a system of forced labor under which economic, legal, and physical coercion was used to bring the natives into the service of Europeans, which is to say that the technologically inferior culture was subordinated to the technologically superior one. Leopold's new "government" began by declaring that all "vacant" land should become the property of the state. "Vacant" land included the forests, from whence came the rubber and ivory, and other lands not directly occupied and cultivated by natives. Rubber

---

[7] France took back this territory at the end of the First World War.

and ivory production was declared a state monopoly under an arrangement by which these products could be sold only to agents of the government. This was a first step toward coercing natives to work for whites, but it was not adequate to meet the demand for labor.

A tax system under which each village was required to provide certain quantities of ivory and rubber was introduced. Other taxes were payable in labor services in lieu of money payments. Labor was recruited in gangs on a basis of contracts with native chieftains who held despotic power over members of their tribes. Individual natives often did not understand why they worked, but their chiefs soon learned it was profitable to recruit labor for white men. When Leopold's government gave concessions to private companies, he often authorized them to employ police power to levy and collect taxes. Leopold held shares in these concessionary enterprises and also established a Crown Company for his exclusive profit. From his vast holdings Leopold added immense profits to his private fortune.

The brutal methods employed against native labor in the Congo Free State became an international scandal. Charges were made that in the ruthless exploitation of labor, atrocities were committed to force obedience. There were denials, but the burden of evidence indicates that recalcitrant native laborers had their fingers and hands cut off, that their women were held as hostages until the men delivered their quotas of rubber and ivory, and that in some instances workers were executed. Leopold was forced by pressure from other nations to transfer his personal kingdom to the control of the Belgian state.

Under governmental administration, conditions improved. The scandalous rubber gathering of the Congo lost out in the twentieth century to the cultivated rubber plantations of Indonesia and Malaya. As rubber exports declined from 87 per cent to 1 per cent of total exports between 1901 and 1928, copper exports rose in the latter year to 50 per cent of the total. Diamond and uranium mining also produced important exports. Large-scale copper mining brought railroads, which in turn encouraged plantation agriculture. Cotton plantations provided raw material for Congo textile mills. Palm oil, palm kernels, and coconuts for soap, candles, and margarine were developed.

Although capital from other sources was permitted to enter the Congo, most economic development remained under strict Belgian control. The Congo's nearest equivalent to a Royal Niger Company or a South African Company was the *Union Minière du Haut Katanga* (founded 1906), a mining concern with great political influence as well as economic power. At the end of World War II, the Congo ranked after South Africa and Egypt as the most advanced industrial and mining region in Africa.

In the mid-1950's the Belgian Congo appeared outwardly to be one of the few remaining stable centers of European imperialism, but appearances proved deceiving. Belgium granted Congolese demands for political independence, and the country became the Republic of the Congo (1960). Terrible vengeance was wreaked on whites, as if to repay them in short order for the atrocities of earlier decades, and the Congo became the focal point of an international political and military crisis. In this revolutionary crisis, the Congo economy sagged badly. It suffered especially from a lack of educated native leaders. Although the level of technical training for native workers had been

among the highest in Africa, there was an almost complete lack of natives educated at advanced levels. For example, the first Congolese to be graduated from a university received his degree in 1956 from Louvain University in Belgium. The failure to develop human resources was one of the major shortcomings of European imperialism.

IMPERIALISM IN ASIA

At the opening of the nineteenth century, the continent of Asia was only slightly better known to Europeans than was Africa. The British had long held a foothold in India through the East India Company but did not thoroughly penetrate the interior until the railway age began in India in 1857. Some trade was carried on by Europeans at a limited number of Chinese ports, but the Chinese had by their own preference isolated themselves from what they considered the inferior Western civilization. As the outward thrust of Western capitalism gained momentum during the nineteenth century, Asia was subjected to economic penetration followed by political domination.

What happened in Asia was in many respects what happened in Africa: economic penetration followed by European intervention and control. There was, however, a vast difference between Asia and Africa. Asian countries were centers of ancient and advanced civilizations which, on the one hand, greatly enhanced their ability to resist the Europeans and, on the other hand, made it easier for them to borrow techniques from the West. Asia was penetrated and controlled, but it was not partitioned after the fashion of Africa. Asian countries were capable of becoming powerful in their own right, as illustrated by Japan's ability to adapt and its sudden rise to the status of a Great Power. China and India were slower than Japan but much in advance of any African state in attaining the status of a Great Power. Asia was able to assert its independence from European control earlier than Africa.

India

In 1857 the British began to construct a network of Indian railways designed to facilitate military and economic objectives. Hope was expressed that cotton raised in India might become the main source of supply for the mills of Lancashire. The transportation revolution on land and sea, in combination with the Suez Canal (1869), brought the interior of India into an economic relation with England comparable to the position of the American Midwest after the completion of trans-Appalachian railways in the United States. British capital had poured into American railways and now it poured into Indian railways. The capital which British investors placed in India, however, enjoyed advantages over British investments in American railways by virtue of Britain's political domination over India. A minimum return of 5 per cent was guaranteed on Indian railway securities by a provision that the earnings from operations could be supplemented with tax revenues levied on the Indian population. The contrast between American and Indian railway finance illustrates clearly the difference between the mere export of capital, on the one hand, and economic imperialism, on the other hand. The guaranteed profit on Indian

railway securities was achieved through political control over Indian taxpayers for the advantage of the British investors.[8]

China

China was virtually closed to Europeans until the nineteenth century. A limited indirect trade was carried on between foreign merchants and special firms designated by the Chinese government. As Western capitalism expanded in all dimensions on the eve of the age of mass production, Western traders stepped up their demands that China open its ports and trade directly with Western merchants. The Chinese made it quite clear that they wanted no traffic with foreigners and for a time successfully resisted the aggressive moves of Westerners.

The opening wedge of European imperialism in China was the Opium War, which arose from the insistence of British traders that they be permitted to bring opium from India to China despite a Chinese prohibition on the import of opium. The treaty ending the Opium War (1842) provided that five Chinese ports should be open to British merchants and ceded the island city of Hongkong to Great Britain. Once the Europeans got their foot in the China door they were able to push it wide open by force and threats of force (the treaties of Tientsin, 1858, and Peking, 1860).

The vulnerability of China to European guns, merchants, concessionaires, investors, and missionaries became apparent once the door was forced open. In the ensuing clash between occidental and oriental civilizations, one incident provoked another in an unending series of conflicts in which the Chinese proved no match for the gun power of the Europeans. As in Africa, a technologically inferior culture was subordinated to a technologically superior one. In a series of aggressions, the French carved Indo-China from the Chinese dragon by 1884. Subsequent treaties granted France advantages in the south China trade and guaranteed participation in railway construction. The British gained control of the strategic Malay peninsula; they invaded Burma, deposed the king, and forced China to cede its claims on Burma to them. Russia took territory in the north. The opium-peddling Europeans, who thus robbed China of its territory, protested that the Chinese violated the maxims of business morality and called upon their governments to force the Chinese to respect the opium trade and to accept the blessings of Christianity.

A partition of Asia similar to that of Africa might have followed had not the European powers become frightened that the mad scramble for territory would lead to war among themselves. Outright partition by European powers was also discouraged by the sudden rise of Japan. Like China, Japan had been opened by Western countries in the second half of the nineteenth century, but the Japanese reacted quickly to the threat of Western domination by adopting the technological, military, and economic system of the West in order to protect itself against Western imperialism. Having transformed itself into a Western-style nation, the Japanese proceeded to participate in the spoil of China. In a war on China in 1894–95, Japan seized Formosa and Korea.

[8] "India is at our mercy; we can charge her what we wish." Sir Charles Trevelyan (1873) quoted in Leland Jenks, *The Migration of British Capital to 1875* (New York: Alfred A. Knopf, 1938), p. 193.

In place of political partition the imperial powers set up economic "spheres of influence" within which they sought and gained concessions from the weak Chinese government. France operated mainly in the southern provinces of China, the British in the rich Yangtze basin, Germany in the Shantung Peninsula, Russia in Manchuria, and Japan in Formosa, Korea, and after the Russo-Japanese war, in southern Manchuria. In their respective spheres of influence, the Great Powers obtained concessions for railway building and for exploiting mineral resources. Large loans were made to the Chinese government for railway construction and other internal improvements. In order to guarantee payment of the interest and principal on these loans, the imperial powers took control of the main source of taxation, the customs. Seizure of the customs was perhaps the surest indication that China's sovereignty was being violated, because no sovereign government voluntarily surrenders control of its main source of revenue.

Imperialism evoked outbursts of violent anti-imperialism but these proved ineffective in China. In the Boxer Rebellion (1900) the "righteous league of patriotic fists" ("Boxers") led an uprising against foreign residents and their property. In retaliation the imperialist powers, including Great Britain, Russia, France, Germany, the United States, Italy, and Japan, organized an international military expedition which marched on the capital at Peking, crushed the rebellion, and levied a heavy indemnity upon China.

A turning point in the clash between East and West came when Japan astonished the world by defeating Russia in a war over Manchuria and Korea (1904). For the first time in modern history an oriental nation had administered a licking to a Western power. The penetration of Asia by Europeanism was transforming oriental nations and held out promise that they might regain their political autonomy if they were willing to sacrifice their cultural heritage to Western-type institutions. In 1911, Dr. Sun Yat-sen, who was educated in the United States, led a Western-style revolution which brought an end to the decadent Chinese Empire. A leading plank in Dr. Sun's revolutionary program was expulsion of the imperialists from China.

During the First World War Japan took advantage of the preoccupation of the other Great Powers in Europe to make aggressive advances on China but was checked by stern warnings from the United States. During the 1920's China strove to reorganize its government and to unify the nation, but beginning in 1931 China again fell victim to Japanese aggression, which continued through the 1930's and reached a peak during the Second World War. After the defeat of Japan in 1945, the ferment in China led to a second revolution, the Communist Revolution of 1949–50, which carried the most populous nation in the world into the Communist camp. At the same time it brought national unification and the status of a Great Power to China.

CONSEQUENCES OF IMPERIALISM

1. Backward Areas Became Appendages to Metropolitan Capitalist Economies

Under the new economic imperialism the backward areas of the world became appendages to the advanced capitalist nations. They became pro-

ducers of raw materials for capitalist factories in a process which was controlled from beginning to end by the advanced peoples. Even when the behavior of capitalists was modeled after their own ethical standards, which it by no means always was, economic development in the backward areas was oriented to the values and institutions of capitalist civilization. It would hardly have occurred to investors and concessionaires to give paramount consideration to the mores and welfare of the peoples of the economically less advanced countries. European investments were made according to the conventions of modern business practices; they had to be made in this manner or not at all. Subordination of the values and institutions of the peoples of backward areas was probably a more or less inevitable consequence of the contact between technologically superior and technologically inferior cultures. This involved more than a question of force, although force was often used and the potential use of force may have been the ultimate and compelling weapon in the hands of the imperialists. It involved the ability to impose alien institutions on a technologically inferior culture without having to be much concerned, in the short run at least, with the cost of manipulating the inferior culture to serve the purposes of Europeans. From the point of view of the backward peoples the behavior of the Europeans involved an arrogance which was deeply resented in the short run and actively opposed by force, violence, and all other means at their disposal in the long run. The imperialism which preceded the First World War found its answer in the anti-imperialism which followed that war.

2. Backward Areas Became Specialized Producers of Raw Materials

As the backward areas became integrated into the world economy under the domination of the metropolitan capitalist countries, they assumed the role of specialized producers of primary products, especially mineral and agricultural commodities. As producers of raw materials they were in a vulnerable position because the ups and downs of the capitalist business cycle magnify the instability of the prices of primary products. Except in time of war, colonial products were subject to unfavorable terms of trade in exchange for manufactured products from the advanced countries.

Even after the underdeveloped areas won political independence, they remained at a disadvantage because their welfare continued to depend on the export of a few primary products. They could escape the status of an economic colony only by diversification of economic activity, including industrialization. Their progress toward industrialization was handicapped because the capital goods needed for industrialization had to be purchased with foreign exchange mainly obtained by selling primary products. The unstable prices of the latter constituted an obstacle to long-range planning of capital imports.

As producers of primary products the backward areas occupy a position analogous to farmers within industrial nations. They are victims of the free market in the sense that their primary products are sensitive to changes in supply and demand, whereas the prices of products they purchase are strongly influenced by monopolistic practices.

European concessionaires and planters pumped out oil, depleted the soil, and extracted the mineral resources of backward areas by methods designed to yield quick returns on their invested capital. In oil and mineral extraction there was less incentive and less compulsion than usual to apply principles of rational conservation of natural resources. Plantation agriculture in the tropics was more destructive than one-crop agriculture elsewhere because the heavy tropical rainfall leached from the soil the organic matter. Thus economic imperialism resulted in the exploitation of the natural wealth of colonial territories.

4. Failure to Develop Human Resources

Perhaps the most significant factor accounting for the scant economic development of the backward areas was the failure to develop their human resources. Natives were employed as common laborers in mining, road building and agriculture. To have employed them otherwise would have required investment in literacy, education, science, technology, and other forms of intangible social overhead capital. This type of investment does not yield quick returns and generally cannot be justified in terms of private profit calculations. Since government expenditures were mainly for military purposes, there existed no solid foundation for development of the human resources. A few Asiatics and Africans were educated in Western universities, but their numbers were insignificant except as potential leaders of political revolt against their European masters.

In some respects the European overlordship was positively harmful to the people of the backward areas. Diets which were adequate for the native way of life proved inadequate to sustain the population at hard labor in mining, in road building, and on plantations. Africa lacked the protective foods required for adequate nourishment. Poor diets caused adverse physical effects and a high incidence of disease and death. Forced labor was another manifestation of exploitation of human resources. When white and native workers engaged in similar labor, wage rates were discriminatory against the latter.

5. Some Economic Development Did Take Place

Despite the burden of social disorganization and exploitation which fell upon the peoples of the underdeveloped countries under the regime of economic imperialism, the activities of European capitalists and promoters had some consequences which were to prove significant for the future development of the backward areas. Tangible social overhead capital was provided and became the basis for later development. Railways held the key in the development process. Their construction was economically justified by large-scale mining activity, and after interior areas were penetrated by railways, plantation agriculture could be expanded and mining activity intensified. Since railways are very expensive and the capital invested is locked up in them for a long time, the peoples of Africa and Asia would have been able to construct them from their scant resources only over many decades.

The question of how much economic development took place should be distinguished from a similar question: Did colonies pay? This question can be answered only in specific terms. Pay whom? A few individuals like Cecil Rhodes and Leopold II profited richly from imperialistic activity. So did the shareholders of some of the joint-stock companies in mining, oil, and plantations, and the holders of tax-guaranteed securities in Indian railways.

For European nations as a whole, however, colonies were dubious investments from a profit-and-loss point of view. The cost of maintaining armies and navies laid a heavy burden on European taxpayers. If the cost of actual wars is included in the profit-and-loss calculation, the deficits from colonialism were quite large. It is difficult to see what was gained from the colonies that could not have been gained without political control, which constitutes the essence of the imperialistic relation.

The British experience shows that trade with the Dominions, which were not under British political control, increased more rapidly than trade with those parts of the Empire which were closely controlled. France had some success in channeling the trade of North Africa to France, but this might have come to pass anyway because of the geographical propinquity of these colonies to Mediterranean France. Italy's colonies were very costly and the returns small; Germany's colonies were not much better. The Dutch experience with the Netherlands Indies suggests that a free-trade policy between colonies and the metropolitan country may pay better than controlled trade. Overall, the balance sheet of imperialism suggests that economic development financed by advanced countries cannot be expected to yield surpluses to private investors except at the expense of the taxpayers in the advanced countries. Only in terms of long-run, enlightened self-interest can the export of capital be said to have been "profitable" for advanced countries.

6. Colonial Wars

Rival imperialism of the great European powers led directly to a number of minor wars and near-wars. The Boer War in South Africa was the most costly of the period. It is estimated to have cost the British $45 for every acre of land that was added to British territory by the defeat of the Dutch republics in South Africa. At the time, this land was selling for considerably less than $1.00 per acre. The British and the French nearly went to war over the Fashoda incident on the upper Nile in 1898. France and Germany nearly became embroiled in the war over Morocco in 1911, and this was but one of three instances in which the "Morocco Question" threatened the peace of Europe and the world. Italy went to war against Turkey in 1911 in order to gain Libya from the crumbling Ottoman Empire. Italy and France fell out over the latter's annexation of Tunisia. Japan defeated China and took Formosa in 1894. Japan and Russia fought a war over conflicting claims in Manchuria in 1904. Hostility arose between Germany and Britain over islands in the Pacific, between Britain and Russia in Persia and Afghanistan; and between Germany and both Britain and France over German attempts to gain influence through economic penetration into the Middle East, notably over the Berlin-to-Baghdad Railway. In the Western Hemisphere the Spanish-American War of 1898 involved a

clash between the waning colonial empire of Spain and the rising overseas interests of the United States. For twenty years before 1914 rival colonial claims and jealousies were a constant source of conflict among the Great Powers. Only their desire to avoid a major showdown prevented the First World War from coming earlier than it did.

7. Economic Imperialism a Contributing Factor to the First World War

In 1912 war broke out in the Balkans while Italy was taking Libya from Turkey by aggression against the "sick man of Europe." The shot in the Balkans which ignited the First World War in 1914 had as its background these and many similar small wars. Some authorities contend that economic imperialism was the main cause of the First World War. Even assuming a healthy skepticism about cause-and-effect sequences in historical events, one may still concede that economic imperialism was an important factor contributing to the outbreak of this great military conflict. There were, of course, other factors, one of the most important of which was Germany's rise to a position of industrial pre-eminence in Europe—a subject to be discussed in the following chapter.

CONCLUSION

Whatever may have been the cause or causes of the First World War, it marked a turning point in the course of European imperialism. Under the covenant of the League of Nations the colonial peoples were declared to be "the sacred trust of civilization." Imperialism, at least in its cruder forms, was acknowledged to have failed. Attempts by more highly developed countries to give economic aid to less developed countries were in the future carried on in a new spirit and with different objectives.

After the First World War, the former colonial areas developed strong independence movements which bore fruit after the Second World War. Former colonies and protectorates like India, Egypt, Ghana, Tunisia, Morocco, Malaya, and Indo-China gained political independence. The economic relations between advanced and underdeveloped countries, however, was not solved by the political independence of the latter. In the second half of the twentieth century this remains a most perplexing question.

Paradoxically the peoples of backward areas who fought European imperialism tended in the long run to accept European institutions, as witness, for example, the adoption of Parliamentary government in India and other former colonies. Imperialism became a powerful device for the spread of Europeanism to geographically non-European areas; and in the Western Hemisphere it involved a spread of North Americanism to the Latin peoples of Central and South America and to the island areas in adjacent waters. Since Americanism is but a variety of Europeanism, the entire process of cultural diffusion may be described as a phase of the Europeanization of the world. Its spread to nearly every part of the globe has been perhaps the most striking phenomenon of the second millennium of the Christian era.

ECONOMIC
IMPERIALISM

FEIS, HERBERT, *Europe: The World's Banker, 1870–1914.* New York: Augustus J. Kelley, Inc., 1964.

GREGORY, THEODORE E., *Ernest Oppenheimer and the Economic Development of South Africa.* New York: Oxford University Press, 1962.

GULL, E. M., *British Economic Interests in the Far East.* New York: Oxford University Press, 1943.

HALÉVY, ÉLIE, *A History of the English People in the Nineteenth Century,* Vol. V, *Imperialism and the Rise of Labor.* New York: Barnes & Noble, Inc., 1961. (paperback)

HOBSON, JOHN A., *Imperialism,* with a new introduction by Philip Siegelman. Ann Arbor: University of Michigan Press, 1965.

JENKS, LELAND H., *The Migration of British Capital to 1875.* New York: Alfred A. Knopf, Inc., 1938.

KNAPLAND, PAUL, *The British Empire, 1815–1939.* New York: Harper & Row, Publishers, 1941.

———, *Gladstone and Britain's Imperial Policy.* London: George Allen & Unwin, Ltd., 1927.

KNIGHT, MELVIN M., *The Americans in Santo Domingo. Studies in American Imperialism.* New York: Vanguard Press, Inc., 1928.

KNOWLES, L. C. A., *The Economic Development of the British Overseas Empire.* Vol. III, *The Union of South Africa.* London: Routledge & Kegan Paul, Ltd., 1936.

LANDES, DAVID S., *Bankers and Pashas—International Finance and Economic Imperialism in Egypt.* Cambridge, Mass.: Harvard University Press, 1958.

LAVINGTON, FREDERICK, *The English Capital Market,* 2nd ed. London: Methuen & Co., Ltd., 1929.

MOON, PARKER T., *Imperialism and World Politics.* New York: The Macmillan Company, 1926.

NADEL, GEORGE H., and PERRY CURTIS, eds., *Imperialism and Colonialism.* New York: The Macmillan Company, 1964. (paperback)

NEARING, SCOTT, and JOSEPH FREEMAN, *Dollar Diplomacy: A Study in American Imperialism.* New York: The Viking Press, 1925.

ROBEQUAIN, CHARLES, *The Economic Development of French Indo-China.* New York: Oxford University Press, 1944.

SCHUMPETER, JOSEPH A., *Imperialism and Social Classes.* Cleveland, O.: Meridian Books. (paperback)

TINLEY, JAMES M., *The Native Labor Problem of South Africa.* Chapel Hill: University of North Carolina Press, 1942.

TOWNSEND, MARY E., *The Rise and Fall of Germany's Colonial Empire, 1884–1918.* New York: The Macmillan Company, 1930.

WILBUR, MARGUERITE EYER, *The East India Company and the British Empire in the Far East.* Peterborough, N. H.: The Richard R. Smith Co., Inc., 1945.

WILLIAMS, BASIL, *Cecil Rhodes.* New York: Holt, Rinehart & Winston, Inc., 1921.

WOOLF, LEONARD S., *Economic Imperialism.* New York: Harcourt, Brace & World, 1920. (paperback)

WRIGHT, HARRISON M., *The "New Imperialism," Analysis of Late Nineteenth-Century Expansion.* Boston: D. C. Heath & Company, 1961.

DALTON, JOHN H., "Colony and Metropolis: Some Aspects of British Rule in Gold Coast and Their Implications for an Understanding of Ghana Today," *Journal of Economic History*, XXI (Dec., 1961), 552–65.

FIELDHOUSE, DAVID K., " 'Imperialism': An Historiographical Revision," *Economic History Review*, XIV (Dec., 1961), 187–209.

HEIMANN, EDUARD, "Schumpeter and the Problem of Imperialism," *Social Research*, XIX (June, 1952), 177–97.

HENDERSON, WILLIAM O., "British Economic Activity in the German Colonies, 1884–1914," *Economic History Review*, XV, No. 1–2 (1945), 56–66.

———, "German Economic Penetration in the Middle East, 1870–1914," *Economic History Review*, XVIII, No. 1–2 (1948), 54–64.

———, "Germany's Trade with Her Colonies, 1884–1914," *Economic History Review*, IX (Nov., 1938), 1–16.

HOVDE, B. J., "Socialistic Theories of Imperialism Prior to the Great War," *Journal of Political Economy*, XXXVI (Oct., 1928), 569–91.

JENKS, LELAND H., "British Experience with Foreign Investments," *Journal of Economic History*, IV (Dec., 1944), 68–79.

LANDES, DAVID S., "Some Thoughts on the Nature of Economic Imperialism," *Journal of Economic History*, XXI (Dec., 1961), 496–512.

NEISSER, HANS, "Economic Imperialism Reconsidered," *Social Research*, XXVII (April, 1960), 63–82.

NICHOLS, JEANNETTE P., "The United States Congress and Imperialism, 1861–1897," *Journal of Economic History*, XXI (Dec., 1961), 526–38.

SAUL, S. B., "The Economic Significance of 'Constructive Imperialism,' " *Journal of Economic History*, XVII (June, 1957), 173–92.

STALEY, EUGENE, "Mannesmann Mining Interests and the Franco-German Conflict Over Morocco," *Journal of Political Economy*, XL (Feb., 1932), 52–72.

THORNER, DANIEL, "Great Britain and the Development of India's Railways," *Journal of Economic History*, XI (Fall, 1951), 389–416.

USHER, ABBOTT P., "The Role of Monopoly in Colonial Trade and in the Expansion of Europe Subsequent to 1800," *American Economic Review*, XXXVIII (May, 1948), 54–62.

WINSLOW, EARLE M., "Marxian, Liberal, and Sociological Theories of Imperialism," *Journal of Political Economy*, XXXIX (Dec., 1931), 713–58.

ZIMMERMAN, LOUIS, and F. GRUMBACH, "Saving, Investment and Imperialism: A Reconsideration," *Weltwirtschaftliches Archiv*, LXXI (Hft. 1, 1953), 1–19.

Integrating the Atlantic Economy

PART **IV**

Economic Consequences
of the First World War

CHAPTER **28**

The First World War marked a turning point in the development of capitalism in general and of European capitalism in particular. In the decades prior to the war European capitalism exercised vigorous leadership in the international economic community. World markets expanded, the gold standard became almost universal, Europe served as the world's banker, Africa became a European colony, Asia was divided into spheres of influence under the domination of European powers, and despite rising tariff barriers in much of the world, Europe remained the center of a growing volume of international trade.

After World War I these trends were reversed. International markets shrank, the gold standard collapsed, banking hegemony passed to the United States, African and Asian peoples began successful revolts against European imperialism, and trade barriers multiplied. Western Europe as an entity declined and capitalism in western Europe began to disintegrate. Leadership among capitalist nations crossed the Atlantic to the United States. The Russian Revolution, a child of the war, uprooted in a vast area not only the institution of private property in the means of production but also the class structure, traditional forms of government, and established religion. Moreover, the juggernaut unleashed by the Russian Revolution was destined to challenge the historic superiority of capitalist organization within less than half a century. Meanwhile, the inner structure of western European economies was tending away from the traditional forms of capitalism.

Another important change wrought by World War I was in the relation of the state to economic life. Laissez-faire had been the accepted policy of the nineteenth century. Although not complete nor universal, the absence of government intervention was the ideal to be striven for. The war, however, had disclosed the great productive potential of modern technology operating under extensive state controls. Faith in the superiority of an automatically functioning market system was severely shaken. Recognition that conscious calculation on an economy-wide basis could be used for peacetime as well as wartime objectives marked the beginning of a transition from laissez-faire to economic planning.

Among the economic forces related to the origin of the war the two which merit special attention are economic imperialism and the rise of Germany as the leading industrial nation in Europe. The first has been discussed in Chapter 27, where it was shown that imperialism contributed to numerous colonial conflicts and in turn to alliances and incidents which erupted in a full-scale war in 1914.

Germany's rapid rise to industrial supremacy between 1870 and 1914 (see Chapter 17) disturbed the balance of political and military power among European nations. At least from the time of Louis XIV to Napoleon I, France had been the most powerful nation in Europe. Against both Louis XIV and Napoleon, Great Britain held the balance of power over France. By siding in political and military conflicts with Prussia, Austria, and other Continental rivals of France, the British were able to hold France in check. By the opening of the twentieth century Germany had replaced France as the strongest Continental nation. In order to maintain the balance of power in Europe, the British now allied themselves with France against Germany. There was no assurance, however, that Great Britain and France could match Germany's industrial and military might in an ultimate test of arms. The facts of industrial life raised serious doubt on this important point. Steel capacity, which may be taken as a rough index of war potential among industrial nations in the early twentieth century, stood as follows on the eve of World War I:

Germany	17 million tons
United Kingdom	7 million tons
France	5 million tons

Thus Germany's steel capacity was more than twice that of the United Kingdom and more than three times that of France. It was nearly 50 per cent greater than the combined steel capacity of the United Kingdom and France. Although no one could be certain how steel output would influence a nation's performance on the battlefield, the German figures were sufficiently impressive to place in jeopardy Britain's historic balance of power. The possibility that Germany might be able to overwhelm France and Britain at the same time made any existing balance of power a precarious one. Britain's greatest reserve lay in the filial allegiance of its former colony, the United States, which had a steel capacity of 31 million tons in 1913.

The rapid rise of Germany to a position of industrial superiority had taken place under circumstances which contributed to the dangers of war. Germany's political unification had been achieved under the domination of Prussia, a state with a long military tradition and strong military propensities. Bismarck had deliberately used war as an instrument of national unification in successive aggressions against Denmark, Austria, and France. Having attained national unification tardily, Germany's rulers were eager to make up for lost time by extending German power within the family of nations. The social surplus derived from an efficient machine technology was directed in the Prussianized Empire to elevating Germany to its "place in the sun."

Under Kaiser Wilhelm II (Emperor 1888–1918), Germany continued the

policy of glorification of the ruling classes which Bismarck had developed for Wilhelm I. According to Thorstein Veblen, the American economist: ". . . the dynastic spirit of the Prussian State had permeated the federated people . . ." [1] Industrialization had occurred so rapidly under the Empire that Germany acquired the technology of capitalistic mass production while the military and political mores of German society were still dominated by a feudal heritage. Warlike aspirations of the Prussian leaders found support in the romantic loyalty, militant patriotism, and overweening sense of pride of the whole German people in their recent achievements. These propensities were probably not inherent nor are they enduring aspects of German culture, but in 1914 they were strategic factors in the historical configuration which helped to plunge Europe and the world into a holocaust.

Unlike the Germans, the English-speaking peoples in 1914 had long since ceased to be dominated by a dynastic and warlike spirit. English feudalism had disappeared by a long and gradual process, and the remnants were still further challenged by the political revolution of the seventeenth century. English industrialization in the eighteenth and nineteenth centuries was accompanied by a gradual extension of political democracy. Although the Crown endured in Great Britain, it became more a symbol than a significant institution. British industrial power was not dedicated to the glorification of a royal dynasty.

In Germany the mobilization of the economic surplus for warlike ends became apparent in many ways. Railways were constructed with an eye to military strategy. A rapidly growing merchant marine was designed for quick conversion to war use. After the turn of the century German governments voted record budgets for a navy which loomed as a challenge to Britain's Royal Navy. German steel masters such as the Krupps and others excelled in applying industrial technology to the arts of war.

Although Germany obtained a few overseas colonies in Africa and the Pacific Ocean, its chief imperial thrust was southeastward through the Balkans in the direction of the strategic Middle East. A projected railway from Berlin to Baghdad highlighted the imperialistic drive to the East. In the Balkans, Germany trod on the sensitive toes of the Russians, who viewed themselves as protectors of the Slavic peoples. Germany's presence in the Middle East threatened British and French interests. In the ever dangerous game of power politics the great new fact of life in the early twentieth century was Germany's industrial superiority over its European neighbors. This above all upset the historic balance of power and ramified into international diplomacy, foreign investments, colonial rivalries, domestic affairs, and every aspect of political life.

IMPACT OF THE WAR ON MARKET CAPITALISM

In all belligerent countries the war brought massive governmental intervention in economic activity. To a marked degree governmental controls replaced the free market in allocating resources, determining prices, and rationing con-

[1] Thorstein Veblen, *Imperial Germany and the Industrial Revolution* (New York: Viking Press, 1946), p. 249.

510

ECONOMIC
CONSEQUENCES
OF THE
FIRST WORLD
WAR

sumers' goods and services. The impact of the war on traditional economic institutions may be gauged by what happened to the gold standard, the security markets, and the commodity markets.

The era of the classical gold standard, which began shortly after the end of the Napoleonic Wars, came to a close shortly after World War I. During the nineteenth century, nation after nation adopted the gold standard, which gradually assumed its classical, semi-automatic characteristics. Paper currency and bank credit could be converted to gold coin within domestic economies, and gold coin or gold bullion could be freely exported from gold-standard countries. When Europe was plunged into war in 1914, the belligerents suspended the privilege of gold exports in order to prevent the flight of gold. Moreover, the enormous increases in the quantity of paper currency and bank credit made impossible their free convertibility into gold. Only the United States, which entered the war late and which had large gold reserves, was able to remain on the gold standard throughout the war. In the postwar period, European nations attempted to return to the gold standard, but after scattered and temporary successes, the revived gold-standard system collapsed completely during the Great Depression.

Another early casualty of the war was the stock exchange. In London, Paris, Vienna, and New York, the stock markets closed with the outbreak of military conflict in Europe. Security markets are highly sensitive to changing views about the future. In normal times security prices move with reasonable orderliness from day to day by accepting the convention that what has been happening in the recent past will probably continue in the near future. A catastrophe like war throws the market into near panic because the usual conventions no longer hold. Precarious as judging the economic future is in peacetime, it becomes totally unpredictable at the outbreak of a major war among well-matched antagonists. Of the major stock exchanges, only the Berlin bourse, which was never so highly developed as the others, remained open but subject to rigid governmental control. The New York stock market closed in 1914 because of heavy selling caused by the uncertainty of future events even though the United States was not directly involved in the war at that time. Security markets reopened after the initial shock of war. Unlike the gold standard, the stock market as an institution was not permanently shaken by war, as the performance of the New York Stock Exchange during the 1920's attested. The crash of 1929, however, impaired confidence in stock exchanges as reliable guides to the trend of economic activity.

Priorities, price controls, and administrative rationing   In order to allocate scarce materials and other resources into the uses most essential for the conduct of war, belligerent governments established "priority" systems. The price system, which normally controls priorities automatically, was not permitted in wartime to perform this important function. Priority systems were government regulations requiring that scarce materials go first into the most essential use, then into the next most essential use, and so on according to an administratively determined hierarchy of uses. War uses took precedence over civilian uses, and essential civilian uses over nonessential civilian uses. In brief, the important economic function of resource allocation was determined by administrative decisions rather than by the price system.

Civilian goods and services were in short supply in relation to demand. In order to prevent an inflationary rise in prices which would otherwise occur under such circumstances, ceilings were imposed on prices. Price ceilings, in turn, necessitated administrative rationing in order to assure an equitable distribution of scarce goods. Ration cards, coupon books, and similar paraphernalia were used to implement administrative rationing.[2] Despite these attempts to suppress inflation, prices rose in all belligerent countries. On the whole, the cost of living increased two- to three-fold in European countries between 1914 and 1920.

511

ECONOMIC
CONSEQUENCES
OF THE
FIRST WORLD
WAR

ECONOMIC CONSEQUENCES OF THE FIRST WORLD WAR

The most direct economic consequences of World War I were associated with national shifts in the ownership of coal and iron resources, German inflation, reparations and war debts. Equally important, although less direct, were increased class conflict and social instability leading to the rise of communism, fascism, nazism, and other manifestations of social discontent.

Coal and Iron Shifts Resulting from Territorial Changes

Although basic economic relations are not determined by political boundaries, the territorial changes stipulated in the Versailles Peace Treaty of 1919 had important economic consequences. Germany lost approximately one-third of its coal resources, the important areas being the Saar and Upper Silesia. France took over the Saar in order to have coal for producing steel from the iron ore of recaptured Lorraine.[3] The loss of coal mines in Upper Silesia was a severe blow to industry in eastern Germany. In addition to the loss of approximately one-third of its coal resources, Germany was obligated under the Treaty to supply from its diminished resources sufficient coal to France to compensate for the war damage to coal mines in northeastern France. Germany was also to ship, as part of general reparations, millions of tons of coal to France, Italy, Belgium, and Luxembourg. The coal which remained after meeting these obligations was insufficient to supply Germany's postwar industry. The central European countries carved from prewar Austria-Hungary had been large importers of coal before the war; they now found themselves with no adequate source of supply.

Approximately three-fourths of Germany's prewar production of iron ore had come from the province of Lorraine, which had been taken from France by Germany in 1871 but which was ceded back to France by the Versailles Treaty. The ore of Lorraine had gone mainly to Germany's Ruhr before the war. Even after the war France possessed insufficient coal to utilize all of its

[2] For a fuller discussion of price controls and administrative rationing, see Chapter 36.
[3] The Versailles Treaty provided that a plebiscite should be held in the Saar fifteen years later to determine whether the territory should be permanently attached to France or to Germany. In 1936 the plebiscite resulted in the return of the Saar to Germany. It had been attached to Germany for a thousand years before the war and was German in language, custom, and religion.

512

ECONOMIC
CONSEQUENCES
OF THE
FIRST WORLD
WAR

output of iron ore, so Lorraine ore continued to be shipped to the Ruhr. Nevertheless, the new political boundaries interfered with the well-integrated prewar structure of Germany's iron and steel industry and brought disorganization and loss of efficiency to the European steel industry as a result of German losses of coal and iron.

German Inflation

One of the great disasters of the postwar decade was Germany's hyperinflation of 1921–23. This was the most extreme inflation in the history of a major industrial nation. At the end of the inflation, prices in paper marks attained fantastic heights one trillion times the prewar price level.

Among the causes of this startling inflation were (1) the fiscal and monetary policy of Germany, (2) the large deficit in Germany's balance of payments, (3) speculation, and (4) reparations.

Fiscal and monetary policy   During the war years 1914–18, the amount of price inflation in Germany was less than in France and only slightly greater than in Great Britain. Money in circulation in Germany at the end of the war was five times the prewar quantity, and prices were two and one-half times the prewar level. This represented substantial inflation, but it was not unusual in view of Germany's wartime fiscal policy of financing government expenditures largely by borrowing rather than by taxing. Only 6 per cent of Germany's war costs were financed by taxation. In the postwar years the German government's expenditures continued to exceed its tax receipts by substantial amounts. The German Empire had not been a truly centralized state, and the sources of taxation available to it were quite limited. Under the Weimar Republic fiscal reforms brought the budget approximately into balance by 1922, but it was already too late to restore confidence in the faltering German mark. The government deficit, which began as an initiating cause of inflation, was increased in the later stages by inflation because government expenditures at inflationary prices increased more rapidly than did tax revenues and other receipts. For example, taxes per package of cigarettes or per pint of liquor did not rise with inflation except by special administrative acts.

Deficits in the government's budget were financed by borrowing. At first substantial amounts of government securities were purchased by the German public, but as inflation continued the government was forced to issue Treasury bills and discount (sell) them at the central bank (Reichsbank). In payment for these bills, the central bank issued paper currency to the government. This led to a continuous increase in the quantity of money and a continuous increase in prices. In the later stages of inflation the Reichsbank had to keep its printing presses running day and night in order to meet the demand for its bank notes. As prices rose, there appeared to be a scarcity of money to take care of transactions, and demands were made for further issues of paper money. The inflation had reached a stage where it fed on itself. Each increase in prices caused prices to increase still more.

In addition to accommodating the government with tremendous issues of bank notes, the Reichsbank responded to the demands of the business community for more and more money. Beginning in the summer of 1922, the Reichs-

bank discounted the commercial bills of industrialists and merchants. The official discount rate remained fixed at 5 per cent from 1915 until July, 1922, and thereafter it was raised by stages up to 18 per cent. Increases in the rediscount rate came too late to have any repressive influence. Thus, in addition to providing inflationary financing to the government, the Reichsbank fed inflation with a great expansion of bank credit for the business community. Increasing quantities of money caused prices to rise, which depreciated the value of the currency and in turn caused it to be spent more rapidly. From the combined force of larger quantities of money being spent faster and faster came a cumulative rise in prices.

Deficit in the balance of payments   The ultimate destruction of the German mark came in the foreign exchange market. At the end of the war Germany was defeated, its people starving, and its great productive machine badly disorganized. Germany needed more imports than could be paid for with its current exports. Germany's accumulated foreign assets had been either confiscated or frozen. The great German merchant marine, which had been an important source of prewar foreign exchange earnings, was taken over by the Allied nations. Germany's commercial relations, broken by the wartime blockade, could not be quickly re-established. To the deficit of exports in relation to imports were added the early postwar reparations payments, the servicing of private debts owed to foreigners, and miscellaneous costs associated with the peace treaty.

Despite many difficulties, by 1922 Germany managed to attain a temporary equilibrium in its balance of payments; but this balance came too late to save the mark from external depreciation. Heavy speculation in the foreign exchange market turned strongly against the mark.

Speculation in the mark   Germany's excess of imports over exports prior to 1922 had been financed principally by the sale of marks to foreign speculators, who assumed, quite wrongly, that the depreciation of the mark had reached its limit and would improve rather than deteriorate further. Confidence by foreign speculators reflected faith in the great productive potential of the German economy to produce goods for export once the economy got back on its feet. The demand for the mark by foreigners checked its depreciation in terms of foreign currencies for some time. Meanwhile many Germans were speculating against the mark, expecting (and in some cases hoping) that it would depreciate further. When events proved the latter group to be correct, the foreign speculators ceased to buy marks and dumped those already purchased on the foreign exchange market. With virtually no buyers and many heavy sellers of German marks in the foreign exchange market, the value of Germany's currency plummeted until it became practically worthless. Although speculation was not an independent or initiating cause of German inflation, in the context of continual budget deficits, large issues of paper money and bank credit, deficits in the balance of payments, and political uncertainty it operated to accelerate the fall in the value of the mark.

Reparations   Another significant factor in Germany's hyperinflation was reparations. Under the "war guilt" clause of the Versailles Treaty, Germany was obligated to pay reparations, the amount of which was to be determined

514

ECONOMIC
CONSEQUENCES
OF THE
FIRST WORLD
WAR

by a Reparations Commission. In May, 1921, a staggering reparations bill of 132 billion gold marks (approximately $32 billion) was handed to the German government with an ultimatum to begin cash payments at once. Whether or not Germany had the economic ability to pay these huge reparations is discussed later in this chapter; the important fact for the great inflation was that the Germans had no will to pay them. The French in particular insisted that Germany be made to pay for all damage done to civilians during the war. Civilian damages were interpreted by the French to include the cost of post-war pensions for Allied soldiers, a point of dubious legality under the peace treaty.

In September and November, 1921 Germany paid 1.5 billion gold marks in reparations. Lacking gold and foreign exchange and being unable to float a foreign loan, the German government had to raise a substantial part of the reparations payments by selling paper marks on the foreign exchange market. The effect was to depreciate the external value of the mark. Germany then announced it could not meet future reparations, including coal shipments to France and other countries. In retaliation for Germany's default, French and Belgian troops occupied the Ruhr in January, 1923. The outraged Germans responded with passive resistance in the Ruhr. Workers refused to produce under the bayonets of an army of occupation. The Ruhr strike sharply reduced the output of coal and industrial goods. Meanwhile, the German government supported the Ruhr workers and industrialists with monetary payments, which further increased government expenditures and increased the government deficit. At this point total chaos enveloped Germany's monetary system. It ceased to be a system at all. Domestic prices rose to astronomical heights. If the payment of reparations in late 1921 had an adverse effect on the mark, the inability or unwillingness to pay future reparations in 1923 delivered the *coup de grâce* to the German mark.

The course of inflation   Economic life had to go on in Germany whether or not the mark had any value. Consumers rushed to spend basketfuls of paper currency before it became worthless. The velocity of circulation accelerated sharply. A circular process now ground the mark to nothing. The circle began with depreciation of the mark in the foreign exchange market; internal prices rose, with a lag, as the external value of the mark sank; more paper money was issued to meet expenditures of the government and the demand of the public for more money for transactions; and the increase in the quantity of money once again depreciated the mark in the foreign exchange, causing domestic prices to rise still more; and so the vicious process continued leading ultimately to monetary chaos.

Since the paper mark ceased to have value, a new unit was invented to replace it. By what seemed to many a miracle, domestic prices were stabilized when a new unit of money, the *rentenmark*, was introduced. One rentenmark was declared equivalent in value to one trillion old paper marks and to one gold mark (approximately $.24 U.S.). Pretense was made at giving the rentenmark convertibility. On demand, 500 rentenmarks would be converted into a bond having a nominal value of 500 gold marks. The bonds carried interest at 5 per cent per annum and were backed by agricultural land and industrial property. Actually the rentenmark, was inconvertible, but it was accepted at

face value, that is, as equivalent to one trillion old, depreciated marks. An
important condition of the rentenmark's stability was a strict limitation on
the quantity which could be issued. In 1924 the rentenmark was replaced by
the *reichsmark*, with one reichsmark = one rentenmark = 1,000,000,000,000
paper marks = 24 U.S. cents.

Social Consequences of Germany's Hyperinflation

The social consequences of Germany's inflation may be analyzed in terms
of the following groups: (1) landowners, (2) businessmen including industrialists and merchants, (3) wage-earners, and (4) middle-class investors
and salaried and fixed-income groups. Landowners and businessmen gained,
wage-earners lost to some extent, but the severest blow was dealt the lower
middle class. The overall effect of inflation may be characterized as a massive
redistribution of wealth away from the lower middle class to the advantage of
capitalist groups.

(1) **Landowners** Landowners with mortgages on their property
gained from the inflation because their debts were wiped out by domestic
inflation. A substantial debt incurred before the inflation could be paid off
after inflation with a postage stamp. Among farm owners, the large landowners of eastern Germany gained the most because their indebtedness was
greatest. Middle-sized landowners and peasants gained from inflation insofar
as they were in debt. They also were in a position to gain by selling produce
at inflated prices and reinvesting the proceeds in their income-earning property.

(2) **Industrialists, merchants, and other businessmen** Businessmen
who understood the process of inflation profiteered at the expense of their less
sophisticated victims. Great private fortunes and huge concentrations of capital were amassed during the years 1919–23. Generally it was big businessmen
who profited at the expense of smaller businessmen, investors, workers, and
creditors. Businessmen borrowed heavily from banks and repaid their loans
in depreciated currency. They profited by buying labor and raw materials at
lower prices and selling the finished product a week or month later at inflated
prices. After a sale they would immediately reinvest the proceeds before the
marks depreciated further. Cautious shareholders, deluded by the apparently
high price of shares, were induced by speculators to sell their shares, only to
learn by subsequent events that they had in effect been swindled.

Fortunes were amassed not by producing wealth but by taking it from
others. The most notorious empire builder during the inflation was Hugo
Stinnes, a ruthless speculator, who manipulated shares and mergers until he
controlled businesses employing approximately a million workers. His conglomerate industrial empire included coal, iron and steel, petroleum, electrical
products, shipyards, ocean and inland shipping, forests, paper manufacture,
and newspapers. This combination proved unsound after the inflation and subsequently collapsed.

Merchants and industrialists who exported German goods received
foreign currency which they would hold as a foreign balance for a while and
then buy quantities of paper marks, which in turn they employed to buy prop-

516

ECONOMIC
CONSEQUENCES
OF THE
FIRST WORLD
WAR

erty. In this manner they could realize huge speculative gains because the internal price level did not rise as rapidly as the mark depreciated in the foreign exchange market. Thus did the "inflation profiteers" manage to strip their fellow countrymen of much of their worldly goods.

(3) **Wage-earners**   During early phases of the postwar inflation in Germany money wage rates rose less rapidly than the cost of living and thus brought a fall in the real wages of workers. On the other hand, employment increased in Germany as a whole, so that the total real incomes of some workers may have actually increased during the inflation. This is all the more remarkable in view of the unemployment experienced in other countries during the deep primary postwar depression of 1920–22. In the last phases of Germany's hyperinflation (1923), wage agreements tied money-wage rates to the cost of living in a manner designed to avoid a fall in real wages. These were forerunners of the escalator clauses in modern wage contracts. Although the fall in real wages between 1919 and 1922 probably resulted in a net loss to wage-earning groups, the deterioration in their economic position as a result of the inflation was not great.

(4) **Middle-class investors, salaried workers, and fixed-income groups** The chief victims who lost their wealth to the speculators, big businessmen, and landowners, as a result of the processes of inflation, were middle-class investors, salaried workers, and pensioners. Individuals who had their wealth invested in bonds, mortgages, bank deposits, and insurance policies were cleaned out by the rise in prices. During the war the German middle classes responded to patriotic appeals to purchase large amounts of government securities. Inflation rendered these securities worthless.

Salaried workers whose money incomes did not keep pace with the cost of living, as most of them did not, suffered a decline in real income. Many older persons and those on fixed money incomes were reduced to abject poverty by the inflation. All persons with incomes fixed in terms of money were victimized. Thus the German middle classes had their economic underpinnings knocked from under them. Herein lay the significance of Germany's hyperinflation, for it was the disillusionment of the middle classes with the existing social order which made possible their subsequent conversion to Adolf Hitler's Nazi Party.

Overall Balance Sheet of Germany's Inflation

Employment and production remained high, although much output was lost through export, and production for domestic use may have been inefficiently directed. Rapid depreciation of money removed all incentives to save through financial institutions, and gave an advantage to those with opportunity to invest in their own business. The incentive to work does not appear to have been substantially lowered by the inflation. The chief social consequence of Germany's hyperinflation was a massive redistribution of wealth. Some Germans gained great fortunes at the expense of their countrymen. In general the transfer was from lower income groups to higher income groups; from the lower middle class to wealthy capitalists and landowners. One reason the inflation persisted as long as it did was because powerful and influential speculators and industrialists had much to gain from continuing the inflation.

But by converting businessmen into profiteering speculators, the inflation undermined the faith of a generation of ordinary Germans in the capitalist system.

517

ECONOMIC
CONSEQUENCES
OF THE
FIRST WORLD
WAR

Bitter seeds were sown among the lower middle classes by this arbitrary usurpation of wealth. The middle-class victims of the inflation blamed the Social Democratic Party, consisting largely of working-class membership, which was at the helm of the Weimar government, for their inability to deal with the situation. The middle classes also developed a hatred of speculators, profiteers, and financiers. During the closing stages of the hyperinflation Hitler led an unsuccessful "beer-hall *putsch*" in Munich, posing as the people's champion against the hated speculators, profiteers, and financiers. Mass support for his movement sprang up subsequently during the Great Depression from the German lower middle classes to whom the great inflation of 1919–23 remained a traumatic experience. Certainly the rise of the Nazi Party in Germany cannot be understood except in terms of the social impact of the hyperinflation of the early 1920's.

REPARATIONS AND WAR DEBTS

Massive financial entanglements arising from the war plagued international economic and political relations for a decade. The legal structure of debits and credits inherited from the war proved economically unworkable, and the entire system of reparations and war debts collapsed during the Great Depression beginning in 1929. In addition to the huge $32 billion reparations bill handed by the victorious Allies to vanquished Germany in 1921, the Allied powers were debtors and creditors among themselves. During the war the nations with greater economic resources gave financial assistance to their Allies. Great Britain made large loans to Belgium, Russia, France, and Italy. France assisted Italy and Russia; and after the United States entered the war, it gave large-scale financial assistance to all its Allies, including Great Britain. In total, Britain lent about twice as much as it borrowed; France borrowed three times as much as it lent; the United States was a lender only, to the extent of about $10 billion; and the other Allies were borrowers only. The amounts of reparations and war debts were so large that they could be paid, if at all, only in installments extending over many decades.

Apart from the inability of nations to pay their obligations, an important question was whether the Allies would benefit from receiving reparations from Germany and whether the United States, the net creditor, would benefit from receiving payment of war debts from its Allies. An analysis of the economic implications of the payment of reparations and war debts suggests strongly that the statesmen who insisted upon full payment must have been either stupid or insincere. Take first the case of reparations. In order to meet these immense obligations, Germany would have had to (1) build up tremendously its industrial productive capacity; (2) have exports in excess of imports by at least the amount of reparations; (3) dispose of the huge export surplus either directly to the Allies or sell in competitive world markets; (4) keep domestic consumption far below domestic production for several generations by means of heavy taxation. Let us examine these four possibilities.

(1) A major postwar build-up of German industrial capacity meant

518

ECONOMIC
CONSEQUENCES
OF THE
FIRST WORLD
WAR

reproducing on an enlarged scale one of the prime factors which contributed to the outbreak of war in 1914. German capacity sufficient to meet the reparations demands would have greatly exceeded that of 1914 and would have been much in excess of the postwar industrial capacities of Britain, France, Italy, and other European allies. One doubts that Allied statesmen really wanted to force upon Germany a program the success of which required that Germany become again an industrial giant, especially in a world in which industrial strength and military potential were so closely linked.

(2) Even a tremendous increase in productive capacity would not have enabled Germany automatically to pay its reparations. In order to acquire sufficient claims to pounds, francs, lira, and other foreign currencies in which reparations had to be paid, a great excess of exports over imports would have been necessary. Prior to the war Germany's commodity imports had exceeded commodity exports. Income from the merchant marine and foreign investments had yielded a small surplus in the annual prewar balance of payments. At the end of the war Germany was stripped of its merchant marine and its foreign investments, not to mention much of its territory containing important raw materials and industrial capacity. The postwar prospect of exporting barely enough to pay for imports was dim; the possibility of an export balance sufficiently large to meet reparations was nil.

(3) Even if by some miracle Germany had been able to produce enough for export, in what foreign markets was the surplus to be sold? This question Allied statesmen never answered. It was probably unanswerable. The markets did not then exist and probably could not have been created in the foreseeable future. There was reluctance even to face this issue because special interests in the Allied countries would have suffered from the competition of larger German exports. French industrialists used their influence to curb the payment of reparations in goods which would have competed with their own. British coal firms complained that German coal shipped to Italy as reparations cut into British coal exports to Italy and that the Italians even exported German coal in competition with British coal. Throughout the 1920's the stagnant British economy suffered from inadequate markets for all kinds of products at home and abroad. The effect of massive German exports directly into British or into competitive world markets would have been to depress the British economy still further.

(4) Reparations involved internal German finance as well as an export surplus. Since it was the German government which owed reparations, the claims on foreign currencies acquired from the export surplus had to be transferred to the government. This required a large budget surplus above normal expenditures. Sources of revenue included loans and profits from government-owned enterprises such as railways, but in the long run taxation must have become the chief source of internal finance. Germany's internal tax structure would in the long run determine the distribution of the burden of reparations on individual German citizens. Obviously this represented a major potential source of conflict among groups of Germans. Any German government which would have increased taxes enough to meet reparations was in grave danger of being turned out of office. In whatever manner the budget surplus was realized, it required sharp curbs on consumption in relation to production.

Just a little insight into history and economics should have warned

Allied statesmen that Germans would not long be willing to produce great
surplus wealth for the benefit of their victorious enemies while the German
people struggled at or near subsistence. Even if the war generation of Germans had accepted as true the war-guilt clause and had been duly repentant
—and there is little evidence that they did accept it or repent—future
generations of Germans, who had nothing to do with the war, were not
likely to feel the same way; and even if they also accepted the war-guilt
clause as historical truth, they were not likely to pay willingly for the sins of
their fathers and their fathers' fathers. Hence, the Allied statesmen were unwise, if not unjust, in assessing these immense burdens on present and future
generations of Germans.

519

ECONOMIC
CONSEQUENCES
OF THE
FIRST WORLD
WAR

What one might have expected to occur did in fact happen. After Germany's economic capacity was built up during the 1920's, highlighted by the
rationalization of industry, Hitler in the 1930's repudiated all reparations,
defied the ban against German armaments, and proceeded to use Germany's
industrial might to build a still more terrible war machine, which was then
used to devastate France, Belgium, Britain, and other former reparations
seekers. Surely the reparations imbroglio after World War I had few prece-
dents for lack of wisdom and foresight.

Inter-Allied War Debts

The United States did not seek any reparations from Germany but insisted that its Allies repay in full the financial aid which had been advanced
during the war. Although the American position on inter-Allied war debts may
have been legally correct, it was offensive to the moral sentiments of its wartime Allies and inconsistent with their ability to pay. John Maynard Keynes,
who was the official draftsman in the British Treasury for all financial agreements with the European Allies and with the United States, indicated that
these wartime agreements were drawn up in the form of loans rather than
subsidies in order to preserve a greater sense of responsibility and economy
in spending the money. Keynes took the position that the American policy of
viewing wartime advances as regular investments to be repaid in full with
interest violated the spoken professions of Americans when they entered the
war and afterwards. During the war the British lent much more to their Continental Allies than they received from the United States, but the British were
prepared to cancel all war debts at considerable expense to themselves.

Britain earlier and the United States later in the war gave financial aid
because they were unable to send soldiers to utilize all the munitions and
materials produced in Britain and America. As a consequence the French, for
example, sacrificed more lives and the United States more dollars. When the
United States provided a gun for a French soldier, the French were supposed
to pay for the gun, but when the United States provided a gun plus an American soldier, no repayment was expected. In brief, when the French sacrifice
was greater, repayment was expected. When the French sacrifice was less, no
repayment was expected. This seemed illogical as well as immoral to the European Allies. Nevertheless, after victory was won in this life-and-death struggle against a common enemy, the United States wanted its dollars repaid in

520

ECONOMIC
CONSEQUENCES
OF THE
FIRST WORLD
WAR

full with interest. The French, on the other hand, could present no claim for the life of the French soldier lost fighting with American guns.

Quite apart from the legal and moral issues, there were sound economic reasons why the United States should not have insisted upon payment of war debts. Insofar as European Allies were required to use scarce dollars to repay war debts, they would have fewer dollars with which to buy American goods. American farmers whose prosperity depended on large exports would suffer especially from the loss of foreign markets for cotton, wheat, and other agricultural products. American manufacturers would also have been adversely affected by the dollar shortage resulting from the use of dollars for war debts.

To add insult to injury, American policy-makers raised tariff barriers against foreign goods. The Fordney-McCumber Tariff of 1922 and the Smoot-Hawley Tariff of 1930 boosted American protectionism to the highest level it had ever been, before or since. High tariffs meant obviously that the United States did not welcome payment of war debts in goods. Payment in gold would have been acceptable but there was not enough monetary gold outside the United States for payment of the debts.

Although the United States government recognized no connection between the payment of reparations by Germany to the Allies and the payment of war debts by the Allies to the United States, a strong economic connection was obvious. If the Allies could have collected reparations from Germany, they could have used the proceeds to pay war debts to the United States. One reason the European Allies persisted in demanding reparations was American insistence on payment of war debts.

During the 1920's two special reparations commissions were appointed and worked out improved arrangements known as the Dawes Plan (1924) and the Young Plan (1929). Meanwhile the United States made concessions to its Allies by lowering the rate of interest at which the war debts accumulated. Between 1924 and 1929 all seemed to go quite well. Germany was able to make reparations payments and the Allies to make war debt payments according to schedule.

The apparent solution was, however, illusory. It rested on the fact that American private investors were making large dollar loans to Germany. The borrowed dollars were used by Germany to pay reparations, and the Allies in turn used the dollars to pay war debts. In effect the United States was paying itself.[4]

This ring-around-the-rosy in international finance was disrupted suddenly by the Great Depression of 1929. American loans to Germany ceased, German reparations to the Allies ceased, and war debt payments to the United States ceased. By this time the United States Treasury had recovered approximately $2.5 billion in war debts, but private American investors had lent and lost a much larger sum. German industry had been reconstructed and strengthened, but democratic government in Germany had been undermined, partly over the reparations issue. International relations among wartime Allies as well as between Germany and the Allies had become embittered. By nearly

---

[4] The new loans were made by private American investors under the inducement of high interest rates. The war debts were paid to the United States government. Thus American capitalists were helping to reduce the size of the United States public debt.

any test the attempts to collect reparations and war debts had proved a **521**

ECONOMIC
CONSEQUENCES
OF THE
FIRST WORLD
WAR
colossal failure.[5]

The lesson of reparations and war debts was so painfully obvious that the mistakes connected with them were avoided during and after World War II. "Lend-Lease" agreements replaced war loans as the device for advancing financial aid from the United States to its Allies. The reparations assessed against defeated Germany were very light compared with those after the First World War.

SELECTED BIBLIOGRAPHY

ALPERT, PAUL, *Twentieth Century Economic History of Europe*. New York: Henry Schuman, 1951.

ANGELL, JAMES W., *The Recovery of Germany*. New Haven: Yale University Press, 1929.

BOWDEN, WITT, MICHAEL KARPOVICH, and ABBOTT P. USHER, *An Economic History of Europe Since 1750*, Chapters 35, 36. New York: American Book Co., 1937.

BRESCIANI-TURRONI, COSTANTINO, *The Economics of Inflation*. London: George Allen & Unwin, Ltd., 1937.

CLARK, JOHN MAURICE, *The Costs of the World War to the American People*. New Haven: Yale University Press, 1931.

DAY, JOHN P., *Introduction to World Economic History Since the Great War*. London: Macmillan & Co., Ltd., 1939.

GRAHAM, FRANK D., *Exchange, Prices and Production in Hyper-Inflation: Germany, 1920–1923*. Princeton: Princeton University Press, 1930.

HOFFMAN, ROSS J. S., *Great Britain and the German Trade Rivalry, 1875–1914*. New York: Russell & Russell, Inc., 1964.

KEYNES, JOHN M., *The Economic Consequences of the Peace*. London: Macmillan & Co., Ltd., 1920.

———, *A Revision of the Treaty*. London: Macmillan & Co., Ltd., 1922.

KULISCHER, EUGENE M., *Europe on the Move: War and Population Changes, 1917–1947*. New York: Columbia University Press, 1948.

MANTOUX, ÉTIENNE, *The Carthaginian Peace*. New York: Charles Scribner's Sons, 1952.

OHLIN, BERTIL, *International and Interregional Trade*. Cambridge, Mass.: Harvard University Press, 1935.

SCHACHT, HJALMAR, *The Stabilization of the Mark*. New York: Adelphi, 1927.

VEBLEN, THORSTEIN B., *Imperial Germany and the Industrial Revolution*. New York: Augustus J. Kelley, Inc., 1964.

[5] Our conclusion concerning the lack of wisdom of trying to collect the debts of World War I from our Allies is supported by the American economist, John Maurice Clark, who questioned whether the debts could be ". . . paid in a way that will enrich the American producing-and-consuming economy, as distinct from filling the federal Treasury and relieving taxpayers of some monetary burdens? . . . It is the writer's conviction that these debts are not fully collectible assets: that if we receive fiscal payment in full, our national economy will not gain that much real wealth, and might conceivably even lose rather than gain . . . And even granting fiscal repayment as practicable, it is far from certain that we can collect these sums in a form which will mean a net addition to the wealth our nation would otherwise be producing and consuming." *The Costs of the World War to the American People* (New Haven: Yale University Press, 1931), pp. 95–96, 280.

522

ECONOMIC
CONSEQUENCES
OF THE
FIRST WORLD
WAR

————, *An Inquiry into the Nature of the Peace and the Terms of Its Perpetuation.* New York: Augustus J. Kelley, Inc., 1964.

WEBB, SIDNEY and BEATRICE, *The Decay of Capitalist Civilisation.* New York: Harcourt, Brace & World, Inc., 1923.

ARTICLES

ANGELL, JAMES W., "The Reparations Settlement and the International Flow of Capital," *American Economic Review,* XX (March, 1930), 80–88.

BRADY, ROBERT A., "The Economic Impact of Imperial Germany: Industrial Policy," *Journal of Economic History* (Supplement, Dec., 1943), 108–23.

BRESCIANI-TURRONI, COSTANTINO, "The Movement of Wages in Germany During the Depreciation of the Mark and After Stabilization," *Journal of the Royal Statistical Society,* XCII (Pt. 3, 1929), 374–414.

CLAPHAM, JOHN H., "Europe After the Great Wars, 1816 and 1920." *Economic Journal,* XXX (Dec., 1920), 423–35.

CLARK, JOHN BATES, "The Economic Costs of War," *American Economic Review,* VI (March, 1916), 85–93.

GRAHAM, FRANK D., "Germany's Capacity to Pay and the Reparation Plan," *American Economic Review,* XV (June, 1925), 209–27.

HARTSOUGH, MILDRED L., "The Rise and Fall of the Stinnes Combine," *Journal of Economic and Business History,* III (Feb., 1931), 272–95.

KEYNES, JOHN M., "The City of London and the Bank of England, August, 1914." *Quarterly Journal of Economics,* XXIX (Nov., 1914), 48–71.

————, "The Economics of War in Germany," *Economic Journal,* XXV (Sept., 1915), 443–52.

————, "The German Transfer Problem," *Economic Journal,* XXXIX (March, 1929), 1–7.

————, "War and the Financial System, August, 1914," *Economic Journal,* XXIV (Sept., 1914), 460–86.

OHLIN, BERTIL, "The Reparations Problem: A Discussion (followed by a rejoinder by J. M. Keynes), *Economic Journal,* XXXIX (June, 1929), 172–82.

PEDERSEN, J., and K. LAURSEN, *The German Inflation, 1918–1923.* Amsterdam: North Holland Publishing Co., 1965.

PIGOU, ARTHUR C., "The Burden of War and Future Generations," *Quarterly Journal of Economics,* XXXIII (Feb., 1919), 242–55.

————, "Government Control in War and Peace," *Economic Journal,* XXVIII (Dec., 1918), 363–73.

SELIGMAN, E. R. A., "The Cost of the War and How It Was Met," *American Economic Review,* IX (Dec., 1919), 739–70.

————, "The Economic Influence of the War on the United States," *Economic Journal,* XXVI (June, 1916), 145–60.

TAUSSIG, FRANK W., "Germany's Reparation Payments," *American Economic Review,* X (March, 1920), 33–49.

————, "The Tariff Act of 1930," *Quarterly Journal of Economics,* XLV (Nov., 1930), 1–21.

VINER, JACOB, "Who Paid for the War?" *Journal of Political Economy,* XXVIII (Jan., 1920), 46–76.

YOUNG, ALLYN A., "Economics and War," *American Economic Review,* XVI (March, 1926), 1–13.

Interwar Europe I: Growth and Stagnation in Industry

CHAPTER 29

Stagnation rather than growth characterized Europe's economy in the period between the First and the Second World Wars, thereby demonstrating the principle that capitalism must expand rapidly or slump into depression. It cannot stand still and enjoy the fruits of its past achievements. European capitalism had expanded rapidly before World War I, but its altered position in the world economy after the war led to a marked slowing down in its rate of growth.

Failing to recognize this change, Europeans misdirected their efforts toward a "return to normalcy" during most of the 1920's. What was needed for more rapid growth and prosperity was a transformation of the European economy to adapt to its new and reduced role. This new role was related to the progressive industrialization of non-European countries—a trend which predated the war, was accelerated by the war, and became acute following the war.

Free market institutions which had guided capitalism in its expanding phase proved inadequate to meet the problems of transformation; consequently, there arose in all countries increasing resort to government intervention to grapple with fundamental problems of readjustment. Belatedly and haltingly, the transformation of Europe's economy got under way toward the end of the interwar period. By the middle of the 1930's, Great Britain had moved some distance toward adapting its economic activities and institutions to the country's altered position in the international economy.

Economic Transformation

"Transformation," as used here, refers to reallocation of productive resources associated with long-term economic growth. It encompasses new end-products (i.e., new industries), the reallocation of labor from low to high productivity industries (i.e., increase in output and income per worker), new forms of capital formation (i.e., innovations, with the resulting obsolescence of old capital equipment), and the progressive substitution of capital for labor. Economic growth, defined as increased income per capita, necessarily involves transformation because as incomes rise, consumer budgets are distributed in different proportions. (For example, as mentioned in connection

with the agricultural depression in the age of mass production, consumers spend a smaller proportion of their incomes on food as those incomes rise.) As national economic growth continues, textiles decline in the sense that a smaller proportion of the total labor force is employed in their production; and at some further point of development all manufacturing employs a smaller part of the labor force.

In addition to the inevitable problems of transformation arising from growth, interwar Europe had to adjust to lesser demands for exports which were goods now being produced in newly industrialized non-European countries. Cotton textiles were the leading example of a major export for which demand decreased. Consequently the cotton textile industry, which might have been expected to decline relatively in any case, suffered an absolute decline in Great Britain. Economic transformation required a transfer of productive resources out of textiles into new export industries of a type which would permit the British to take advantage of their long tradition and accumulated skills of industrialization, and which would meet less competition from the newly industrializing areas of the world.

Interwar Plight of Industry Similar to That of Agriculture in 1870's

The plight of European industry during the interwar years paralleled that experienced by European agriculture after 1870. Overseas competition in grain and certain other basic commodities had pushed European farmers into a depression from which recovery through readjustment took place very slowly and acted as a drag on the entire economy. In fact, European agriculture had never been really prosperous after the American "invasion" of the 1870's. Adjustments had, however, been made away from grain to dairy products, fresh fruits and vegetables, and other commodities in which Europe enjoyed a comparative advantage in the European market over non-European competitors. In addition tariff walls were raised to protect farmers from foreign competition—usually at the expense of consumers. The main exceptions were Great Britain, where farmers suffered severely, and Denmark, where a rapid shift from grain farming to protein farming took place. To seek protection against overseas industrial competition through tariffs was more difficult because such competition involved an invasion of European markets overseas rather than in Europe. European countries could refuse to buy (agricultural) imports, but they could not insist upon selling (manufactured) exports to unwilling buyers.

General Features of Interwar Capitalism

Capitalism in the interwar period was characterized by relatively slow growth, rapid increase in productivity, high unemployment of labor, and chronic excess plant capacity.

Real income per capita of the total European labor force increased by only 0.6 per cent per year in the period 1913–40, as compared with an increase of about 2 per cent in the period 1880–1913 (Svennilson). Some coun-

tries progressed more rapidly than the average (Finland, Sweden, and the Netherlands) and some more slowly (Italy, Poland, and Belgium), with the big countries (the United Kingdom, France, and Germany) near the average rate of growth. The rate of growth in industry was more rapid than in agriculture. Working hours fell from an average of 57 per week in 1913 to 47 at the end of the interwar period. Hence, an important gain was realized in the form of increased leisure.

Total output per worker rose at the same time that working hours declined because of a relatively rapid increase in productivity as measured by output per man-hour. This rise in productivity reflected continued progress in science and technology. The application of scientific methods was extended beyond the engineering phase to all aspects of management of individual firms and even to whole industries. This phase of "scientific management"—pioneered in the United States before the First World War—became known as the "rationalization movement" and constituted one of the leading economic developments of the period. The term "rationalization" first became popular in Germany, where it was applied to the widespread economic reorganization necessitated by the disorganization arising from war, revolution, and inflation.

High Interwar Unemployment

High unemployment of labor constituted a major weakness in all capitalist countries not only during the Great Depression of the 1930's, when it rose to massive proportions, but also during the relatively prosperous twenties. In Great Britain unemployment averaged 12 per cent during the 1920's, and 18.5 per cent in the years 1930–35. In Germany unemployment was low only during the great inflation and in the feverish years of war preparation after 1936; during the prosperity of 1924–29 unemployment averaged 11.5 per cent. With the onset of the Depression it rose to 22.2 per cent in 1930, 33.7 per cent in 1931, and 43.7 per cent in 1932. In the United States during the worst depression years one-third of the labor force was unemployed; 13 million were out of work and seeking employment in 1932. These figures refer to wholly unemployed males in urban occupations. If account is taken of females seeking employment, surplus farm population, and others unemployed, underemployed or working in sub-standard occupations, the figures are considerably higher. They suggest a tremendous loss of potential wealth-creation as a result of underutilized manpower; perhaps as much as one-fourth of European manpower was wasted through idleness and inefficient use during the interwar period.[1]

Mass unemployment of such persistence was unknown in the pre-1914 era of capitalism. Among the big four capitalist countries (the United Kingdom, Germany, the United States, and France) only France escaped chronic, large-scale unemployment. As a result of the great loss of life during the war and the low birth rate long characteristic of France, labor was so scarce in France during the 1920's that needs were met only by attracting immigrant labor.

[1] Ingvar Svennilson, *Growth and Stagnation in the European Economy* (Geneva: United Nations, 1954), p. 32. This is a brilliant study of the interwar European economy.

Co-existing with unemployed labor was excess capacity of plant and equipment. Estimates of capacity, and of excess capacity, are difficult to obtain because statistical studies are lacking and also because of uncertainty as to how to measure excess capacity. The best study of excess capacity for the interwar years was made for the United States by the Brookings Institution. In the peak interwar year, 1929, the Brookings study shows that the American economy operated at 80 per cent of capacity, with liberal allowances for stand-by equipment, shutdowns, vacations, and the like. On a basis of 80 per cent in 1929, the American economy operated at only 50 per cent of capacity in 1932. In Great Britain excess capacity was greater than in the United States during the 1920's but less during the 1930's. Germany also had excess capacity probably equal to the United States except during the war preparation years of the late 1930's. France operated more nearly at capacity during the 1920's but had sizable excess capacity during the 1930's.

Monopolistic restriction had much to do with the large amount of excess capacity, which surely must have been greater in the interwar years than in any previous period of capitalism. A whole literature grew up to explain excess capacity.[2] The restrictive tendencies of monopolies led to cutbacks in output in order to maintain prices at higher levels than would have prevailed if capacity had been fully utilized.

Cyclical Pattern of the Interwar Period

Within the longer-run trends of the interwar period cyclical fluctuations occurred. After a brief postwar boomlet and inflation (1919–20), a primary postwar depression of considerable severity but short duration took place (1921–22). Ironically, the prolongation of inflation in Germany through these years prevented the primary postwar depression from appearing there. Following the primary postwar depression came a period of postwar prosperity of the middle and later 1920's. Between 1929 and 1932 the contraction phase of the Great Depression carried economic activity to the lowest level of the interwar years. The expansion phase of the Great Depression began in 1933, with the earliest recovery in Great Britain, which had not shared in the prosperity of the 1920's. In France economic activity fell off less after 1929 but recovery was slow and incomplete. Germany experienced rapid recovery after 1933 and attained full employment by 1936. In the United States the level of economic activity in 1932 was very low and recovery relatively rapid after 1933 but full recovery was not attained during the 1930's.

INDUSTRIAL DEVELOPMENT

The slow growth of the European economy during the interwar period was associated with the sluggish performance and gradual reorganization of key industries such as coal mining, steel, textiles, and shipbuilding. Some newer

---

[2] See E. H. Chamberlin, *Theory of Monopolistic Competition* (Cambridge, Mass.: 1933) and J. M. Clark, *Studies in the Economics of Overhead Costs* (Chicago: University of Chicago Press, 1923).

industries such as chemicals, automobiles, and electrical products demonstrated enough vitality to grow relatively rapidly in spite of the general condition of stagnation. All major industries, whether the sluggish old ones or the vigorous new ones, tended away from competitive behavior toward dependence on industry-wide decisions implemented through cartels or government intervention. Technological progress moved steadily forward in all industries, as reflected in rising output per man-hour, with the rationalization movement providing the special means by which higher efficiency was realized. Major difficulties arose in the contraction of industries like coal and textiles, for which there was an absolute decrease in demand.

Coal Mining

From the invention of the steam engine until the First World War the demand for coal increased continuously, but after the war coal mining became a "sick industry" in the major capitalist countries. The demand for coal declined for numerous reasons including competition from substitute fuels such as petroleum products, generation of electricity from water power, and more efficient utilization of coal. Meanwhile, the capacity for producing coal increased through improvements such as mechanical cutting in place of hand cutting of coal in mines and other mechanized techniques. The coal industry in the United Kingdom, Germany, Poland, and the United States experienced chronic excess capacity. During the 1920's capacity exceeded actual output by approximately one-third in the United Kingdom and one-quarter in Germany and Poland.

United Kingdom   Coal mining was most depressed in the United Kingdom, which was Europe's largest producer and a major exporter of coal. A special British advantage had been the use of coal as marketable ballast on outgoing cargoes of manufactured goods. This had lowered freight rates and assisted British shipping and the British balance of payments. Hard hit by loss of markets during the war and by coal reparations from Germany to former British export markets after the war, Britain's coal industry went into the doldrums in 1919 and failed to recover at any time during the interwar period. The general slump in the rest of the British economy reinforced the distress in coal mining.

The situation in coal mining provoked much agitation and public investigation in Britain. Following serious labor trouble in 1919, a National Coal Commission, headed by a distinguished jurist, Sir John Sankey, recommended nationalization of the coal mines, but the government, contrary to its pledge, ignored the Commission's recommendations. Instead, voluntary cartelization was advocated. British coal owners were obstinately individualistic and opposed cooperative programs for meeting industry-wide problems. Since coal mines operate with a high proportion of fixed investment and are subject to flooding and caving when shut down, owners have a double incentive to keep them open even when operating at a loss, on the principle that it is better to lose something than to lose everything.

British coal mines needed modernization. In 1929 only 28 per cent of British coal was cut by machines, as compared with 91 per cent in Germany,

72 per cent in France, 89 per cent in Belgium, and 78 per cent in the United States. In order to modernize mines, however, large amounts of new investment were required, and the low profits associated with depressed conditions were not conducive to attracting new capital into coal mining. After voluntary cartelization failed, legislation calling for compulsory cartelization on a regional basis was passed in the Coal Mines Act of 1930 and reinforced by additional legislation in 1938. Companies within designated regions were required to amalgamate their operations, withdraw the least efficient mines from production, regulate prices, and fix quotas. By 1935 the number of British coal mines had been reduced from 3000 to 2000. The 1938 legislation socialized mine royalties, the private receipt of which had long been a sore point with the powerful miners' union, which advocated outright nationalization. The evolution of policy with respect to British coal mining began with unregulated competition at the beginning of the interwar period and passed by stages to voluntary cartelization, compulsory cartelization, and finally, in 1946, to full government ownership and operation.

Germany   Coal was as vital to Germany as to any other nation. Heavy industry in the Ruhr was quite literally built on coal. The coal question in Germany arose in connection with disorganized conditions resulting from the war, the Versailles Treaty in respect to territorial changes and reparations, and postwar occupation of the Ruhr by French and Belgian troops during the Great Inflation. In the postwar reorganization of its coal industry Germany held an advantage over Britain in that the tradition of unregulated competition did not stand in the way of coordinated action of the whole industry to put mining on a more efficient basis. Immediately following the war the Weimar government slated coal mining for socialization, but a legislative compromise fell back on the cartel tradition by placing the privately owned and operated mining industry under close supervision of the federal government, with ten regional cartels authorized to regulate production and sale of coal under coordinated direction and control. Between 1924 and 1929 the industry underwent thorough reorganization, including further concentration of production and ownership; closing of high-cost mines; standardization of tools, machines and equipment; mechanization of cutting, transporting and loading; fuller utilization of by-products such as gas and chemicals; systematic selling through distributing syndicates, and a general rationalization of the whole industry. From negligible mechanization in 1913 the industry had advanced to nearly complete mechanization by 1929. Productivity as measured by output per man-shift doubled during the period of vigorous rationalization from 1924 to 1929, whereas British output per man-shift in 1929 was barely above that of 1913.

Increased productivity, however, did not answer all problems. Excess capacity placed coal mining in a generally unsatisfactory state even in 1929. Cartelization of this basic industry under government regulation was a halfway measure between unregulated competition and fully planned coordination in relation to the rest of the economic system. As in other industries, rationalization in coal mining was technically efficient and increased greatly the capacity to produce but it did nothing to fulfill the promise of abundance be-

cause a deficiency in effective demand left much of the capacity unused and many miners without employment.

The Steel Industry

The steel industry, which formed the technological basis of the mass production era, experienced its most rapid growth between 1880 and 1914. After the First World War the rate of growth in the consumption of steel declined while capacity continued to increase almost at the pre-1914 rate. Consequently, there developed in steel, as in coal, a capacity for production much in excess of actual consumption. Failure of the economy to grow fast enough to create sufficient demand to utilize available capacity led to intensified competition and contributed to the breakdown of competition in both domestic and international markets.

United Kingdom   Britain's steel industry illustrates the "disadvantage of taking the lead" in industrial development under capitalism. In 1914 the British steel industry was obsolete by the standards of Germany and the United States. Since it was the oldest steel industry, it was the first to need technological and managerial reorganization, but since it was growing at a slower rate than steel industries in other countries, there was less incentive to add new and more modern capacity. Moreover, there were too many small producers who were unwilling or financially unable to install the latest techniques of production.

Amalgamation in the British steel industry did, however, take place during the interwar period. By 1926 concentration had proceeded to a point at which twelve concerns possessed 60 per cent of the nation's steel capacity, as compared with 70 per cent control by the three largest concerns in Germany and 55 per cent by the two largest producers in the United States. Capacity in Britain increased, and in the late 1920's was 50 per cent above the prewar level. The industry operated at about two-thirds of capacity during the interwar years. Large excess capacity reflected a low level of economic activity in the stagnating domestic market and a loss of export markets. Under free trade the British domestic market was open to invasion by the surplus capacity of other steel-producing countries. Despite foreign competition, however, prices were fairly well maintained until the outbreak of the world crisis after 1929. In this desperate situation England's departure from free trade included a 33⅓ per cent tariff on imported iron and steel products. British recovery after 1933 brought improved conditions to British steel companies but this was mainly at the expense of steel users, including ultimately the consuming public.

Germany   Germany's steel industry suffered from the same basic difficulty that afflicted Britain's steel producers—failure of demand to grow as rapidly as productive capacity. The Versailles Treaty prohibited Germany from having an armaments industry and thus removed one of the main sources of demand for steel. Some German steel firms like the famous Krupp works were oriented almost entirely toward armaments and had to redirect their entire production during the 1920's. Those provisions of the peace treaty involving territorial changes disrupted Germany's steel industry. In particular,

the transfer of Lorraine back to France removed the chief source of iron ore and necessitated the import of ore for more than 80 per cent of Germany's pig iron output during the 1920's as compared with about 40 per cent before the war.

As in other German industries, after 1924 the difficulties in steel were attacked vigorously as part of the rationalization movement. Technically obsolete plants were shut down and sometimes scrapped entirely. Plant specialization by products was carried out extensively in order to gain economies of scale. Individual blast furnaces increased to an average size twice the capacity of British blast furnaces and approximated the large size of American blast furnaces. Steel production became concentrated in a small number of large concerns operating under cartel agreements to stabilize price and limit output for sale in the domestic market. High tariffs protected the domestic market from foreign competition after 1925 while surplus steel was dumped onto the world market at whatever price it would bring.

European steel cartel   By 1927 western Europe's major steel-producing countries had increased productive capacity by 50 per cent and output by only 25 per cent over 1913. Because of the large capacity in excess of domestic demand steel producers depended heavily on international markets as an outlet for surplus production. In the late twenties, in order to operate at full capacity, Belgium and Luxembourg had to export 75 per cent of total steel output, France about 50 per cent, Germany and Great Britain between 20 and 35 per cent, and the United States 25 per cent. This did not necessarily indicate maladjustment in the distribution of the world's steel capacity because steel is a heavy industry requiring coal and iron ore and its production is often uneconomical for such small countries and backward areas as southeastern Europe, Asia, South America, and Africa were at that time.

When Germany began dumping steel onto the international market about 1925, producers in France, Belgium, and Luxembourg became alarmed because they were so largely dependent on foreign markets. Out of this situation grew the European steel cartel with Germany, France, Belgium, and Luxembourg as charter members; subsequently they were joined by Czechoslovakia, Austria, Hungary, and Poland. The purpose of the cartel was to limit output to demand. Production quotas were fixed, and members were to be fined for exceeding the quotas.

A successful international cartel presupposes strong national cartels in the participating countries reinforced by high tariffs. An additional factor favoring a cartel in steel is the fact that the demand for steel is inelastic, that is, when its price is raised the total revenue will increase because the higher price will more than offset the smaller (physical) quantity sold. Consequently, sellers who are protected against domestic and foreign competition by cartels, tariffs, and the great amount of capital needed to enter the industry may profitably increase prices. Contrariwise, they are reluctant to reduce prices because lower prices will result in less total revenue; the (physical) quantity sold at lower prices will not increase enough to offset the reduction in price.

Since two large steel exporters, the United Kingdom and the United States, remained outside the European steel cartel, it could not prevent international steel prices from falling. Members of the cartel agreed not to invade

each other's domestic markets, an agreement reinforced by high tariffs except
in the case of Belgium and Luxembourg, whose foreign sales were so large a
proportion of the total output that they had little to gain by trying to sell more
dearly at home than abroad. Cartel members other than Belgium and Luxembourg were able to maintain domestic steel prices much above the international, free market prices. In France, for example, domestic steel prices were
50 per cent above free market prices. A similar differential existed between
German domestic steel prices and international market prices.

The European steel cartel functioned satisfactorily for the member countries until the onset of the Great Depression in 1929, after which domestic
demand for steel, and everything else, fell drastically and led to desperate
attempts to dispose of surplus steel in the world market. Steel prices were well
maintained in the protected markets, but the free international market price
fell precipitously. British prices, which had been fairly well maintained during
the twenties despite the absence of a protective tariff, collapsed under the
pressure of large imports. At this point, behind a newly built tariff wall and
with the full backing of the government, a nation-wide steel cartel, the British
Iron and Steel Institute, was formed.

Meanwhile with the worst of the crisis over, the European steel cartel,
which had broken up by 1931, re-formed on a strong basis in 1933. The British
steel industry, now strongly cartelized, joined in 1935. In 1938 the European
cartel became a world cartel with admission of the United States, the remaining large exporter of steel. Quotas were fixed based on steel production in
1927–29 and the first half of 1932. A change in quota could be obtained only
by bargaining within the cartel. The free market in steel had now been thoroughly demolished in both domestic and international spheres. The nearly
complete retreat of this vital industry from the free market provides another
illustration of the abandonment of laissez-faire capitalism. The world steel
cartel, of course, dissolved during the Second World War, after which private
interests were supplanted by governments in establishing the European Coal
and Steel Community. (See Chapter 35.)

Textiles

The British cotton textile industry is a classic example of the pains of
adjustment resulting from Europe's altered position in the world market. Prior
to World War I, the textile industry in Great Britain had experienced almost
uninterrupted expansion. After the war it suffered absolute as well as relative
contraction. Using an index of 100 for 1913, the production of cotton cloth in
the United Kingdom declined to 41 in 1927 and rose a point to 42 in 1937.
Meanwhile, the index of exports fell from 100 in 1913 to 36 in 1927 and 29 in
1937. Thus exports declined more rapidly and more persistently than production. Exports in physical terms declined more rapidly than exports in value
terms, because the British lost more sales of coarse cloth than of fine cloth,
causing the average value per yard to rise. Nevertheless, by any measure the
decline in British cotton cloth production and export was severe and left the
industry in a desperate condition.

Furthermore, British textile exports declined relative to competitor countries. Just prior to World War I, the British exported 58 per cent of the value

of the world's cotton textiles, and more than five times the value exported by its nearest rival, Germany. By 1929 the British still held a slight lead over its closest rival (then Japan), but its proportion of world exports had fallen drastically. While the value and physical volume of British exports were falling, Japan's were rising, and by 1933 the yardage of Japanese cloth exports exceeded that of Great Britain for the first time. India, which had been one of the largest importers of British textiles before World War I, became a major exporter and competitor during the interwar period, and by 1950 India's cotton textile exports exceeded those of all countries except Japan. The tonnage of raw cotton consumed in British textile factories in 1950 was only one-half what it had been in the period immediately preceding World War I.

The decline in the British cotton industry can be attributed to several factors, including the substitution of synthetic fibers, especially rayon, for cotton. However, the chief cause of the distress in the British cotton industry was a structural change in the world market. Again one finds an illustration of the "disadvantage of taking the lead" in industrial capitalism; the British cotton industry suffered from obsolescence of capital equipment, rigidity in business organization, and anachronistic attitudes toward fundamental changes in the international economy.

During the First World War Japan, which was already well advanced industrially, took advantage of the temporary withdrawal of European products from the world market to supply outlets formerly dominated by European exporters. Less industrialized areas like India, Australia, South Africa, China, and South America were stimulated by the shortage or unavailability of European textiles to promote industry at home during the war and to protect their infant industries with tariffs after it was over. Industrialization of these areas was not caused by the war inasmuch as they would have industrialized sooner or later anyway, just as the war of 1812 was not the cause of the industrialization of the United States; but the First World War did accelerate industrialization much as the war of 1812 launched the industrial revolution in the United States. European predominance in staple manufactures like textiles was certain to decline sooner or later because these industries usually lead the industrial development of new economies.

The plight of the British textile industry during the interwar period reflects not so much the abandonment of the free market as its operation in a declining sector of a stagnant economy. British textiles epitomized the laissez-faire tradition. Fierce competition for survival among British producers resulted in low profits, low wages, high unemployment, large excess capacity, and protracted and painful readjustments. Combination movements, leading to monopolistic control of the market in other industries, made virtually no headway in textiles. Attempts at combination on a voluntary basis usually failed. Capital for large-scale reorganization was lacking, as in the British coal industry, because of low earnings and general distress. Finally during the world crisis free competition began to give way. Textiles were included under the 10 per cent tariff of 1932, although the impact was negligible because Britain did not import textiles. After the failure of voluntary cartels, the Cotton Spindles Act of 1936 provided a means for buying out surplus spindles. In two years some 4,500,000 spindles of an estimated 10,000,000 were bought out and

scrapped with funds raised by a special tax on the industry. Further legislation (the Cotton Industries Act) was enacted on the eve of the Second World
War but its application was postponed by the war. During the war many
cotton factories were converted to other uses essential for military purposes.

Chemical Industry

Europe was the original home of the chemical industry and up to the
First World War retained undisputed leadership, producing in 1913 about 60
per cent of world output in chemicals and exporting 85 per cent of world
exports. Chemical industries flourished especially in Germany, which led the
world in applying the science of chemistry to industrial technology. In addition to a large output of numerous heavy inorganic chemicals, Germany held
a virtual monopoly of the valuable synthetic dyestuffs and most pharmaceutical
chemicals. This monopoly was broken during World War I, when Germany's
patent rights were abrogated and taken over by other countries. Germany
came back strongly, however, and retained its world leadership in chemical
technology. Under the domination of the giant combination, the Community
of Interest of the Dye Industry (I.G. Farben Industrie), German chemical
industries were streamlined into highly efficient operations. Patents were
pooled, obsolete plants closed down, products standardized, production specialized by plants, research concentrated and intensified in well-equipped
laboratories, by-products utilized, and markets pooled.

In several other countries including Great Britain, Switzerland, Italy, and
Scandinavia, the chemical industry grew rapidly during the interwar years. It
was a progressive rather than a stagnant industry. Chemical industries depend
more upon human than upon natural resources, which helps to account for
their extensive national development in countries with high educational standards and other progressive characteristics. One result of the spread of chemical
industries to numerous countries was a decline in the proportion of production
entering international trade which dropped from one-third in 1913, to one-sixth
during the interwar period, to one-tenth after World War II.

Price competition has never been strong in the chemical industry, as the
demand for most chemicals is relatively inelastic and hence sellers have only
slight incentive to lower prices. Strong national and international cartels centered around patent and market pooling. In Britain the industry became concentrated under the Imperial Chemical Industries, Ltd., formed in 1926.
Imperial Chemical worked closely with I.G. Farben through agreements concerning patents and markets. Numerous international sharing and exclusion
agreements were made between these two giants of the European industry
and the big chemical concerns in other countries, including E. I. du Pont de
Nemours and Allied Chemical and Dye in the United States. Some of these
agreements among private business interests for their private advantage had
grave consequences for the national security of their countries. For example,
one much criticized agreement between Standard Oil and I.G. Farben left the
United States with no synthetic rubber industry at the outbreak of the Second
World War; the war was more than half over before the synthetic rubber
problem was licked in the United States.

Another industry moving against the stagnant tide of the European economy during the interwar period was automobile manufacturing. World automobile production was concentrated in the United States and in three countries of western Europe, the United Kingdom, Germany, and France, with Italy as a minor producer. At the beginning of the interwar period European automobile manufacturers had not yet adopted the mass production techniques introduced into the industry by Henry Ford before the First World War. In the course of the 1920's rapid gains were made in output and efficiency by the rationalization of the industry along American lines. The rate of growth in Europe's auto output considerably exceeded the rate of growth in output in the United States, although the absolute numbers of autos turned out in the United States remained higher. As a result of the adoption of assembly-line techniques automobile production in Europe became concentrated in fewer and larger plants. In each country the industry was dominated by a few firms. In France the Big Three produced 68 per cent of the total output in 1928; in the United Kingdom the Big Six produced 90 per cent of the total in 1938; and in Germany the three largest firms produced 74 per cent and the five largest 90 per cent of the total output in 1937.

The increased efficiency and lowered costs associated with rationalization of European automobile production led not only to larger domestic sales but also brought major gains in exports at the expense of the United States. European automobile exports rose during the 1920's and continued to increase during the Great Depression in the face of a general contraction of international trade. The same trend in exports continued after the Second World War. The growth of European exports and the decline of United States exports are indicated by the following figures:

	NO. OF EUROPEAN AUTOMOBILES EXPORTED	NO. OF UNITED STATES AUTOMOBILES EXPORTED
1929	122,000	536,000
1938	205,000	278,000
1950	766,000	252,000

As the tabulation indicates, in 1929 the United States exported four times as many automobiles as Europe; in 1950 Europe exported three times as many as the United States. Europe's share in total world exports of automobiles rose from 15 per cent in 1929, to 40 per cent in 1938, to 75 per cent in 1950. In the 1960's Germany replaced the United States as the leading exporter of automobiles, although the United States remained by far the largest producer.

Summary: Departure from the Free Market

The foregoing survey of some leading European industries indicates, on the one hand, a tendency toward stagnation or retrogression in older industries (coal, steel, textiles) and, on the other hand, some counter-trends in younger, more vigorous industries (chemicals and automobiles). Other examples of both types could be cited; shipbuilding and the agricultural sector stagnated,

while the electrical and cement industries grew rapidly. Overall, the interwar trend was one of slow growth, so slow that Europe suffered a major setback in the Great Depression, an experience common to all capitalist countries during the interwar years, and declined relative to newer industrialized nations. Related to this decline was western Europe's inability to transform its economic structure fast enough to adjust to the spread of industrialization of new areas and to the rapid development of the United States during the 1920's and of the Soviet Union during the 1930's.

In all European industries, whether stagnating or growing, there was a marked trend away from the free market. In the coal industry German cartels became stronger and in the United Kingdom, after voluntary cartelization failed, legislation imposed compulsory cartels, which were replaced by nationalization of coal mines at the end of the Second World War. In steel the large-scale nature of production inherent in the technology of the industry had long militated against free competition and tended toward monopolistic control of prices and output. Strong domestic cartels led first to the European and then to the world cartel among the leading steel-exporting nations. Inability of private enterprise to solve the transformation problem in British cotton textiles finally resulted in government intervention to eliminate excess capacity, a method falling outside the traditional free market procedure. The chemical industries of Germany and Britain came under the domination of giant combinations, I.G. Farben and Imperial Chemical respectively, and these monopolistic combinations in turn entered into international cartel agreements for pooling patents and sharing markets. As a result of the concentration of automobile production in the hands of a few firms, price competition declined and was replaced by non-price rivalry.

The rapid spread of industrialization to the rest of the world necessarily meant that Europe would have to transform the structure of its industry. Some transformation did take place during the interwar period, but it was slow and unplanned. This was perhaps inherent in the nature of capitalist industry with its substantial vested interests and dependence on the market as an indicator of long-run trends. The scope of conscious calculation was too limited to plan for the transformation of a whole national economy and for entire industries within national economies. In any event, private enterprise proved inadequate to transform the stagnating and declining industries. Hence, governments intervened to speed transformation and reorganization, as in coal, steel, and textiles. Characteristically government intervention was conceived in a spirit of protecting the existing interests against losses rather than increasing overall economic efficiency and thereby raising the real national income. Lady Barbara Wootton described the British situation as "a community more planned against than planning." In Germany, where the tradition of free competition was weak, private enterprise carried out rationalization on its own initiative, although it could depend on government support whenever needed. As in Britain, however, German interwar rationalization was typically half-hearted and failed to accomplish full transformation. As practiced in Germany rationalization became known as the art of cutting costs while raising prices. Rationalization was a necessary but not a sufficient condition of transformation. It was technically efficient but under the auspices of business firms and industry cartels, it contributed to excess capacity and unemployment.

Thus the wide departure from a rational pricing system such as that envisaged by a properly functioning free market did not carry all the way to a system of rational economic planning. Europe was caught midway between the old and the new. The transitional nature of economic policy in this period accounts for the generally unsatisfactory performance of Europe's economy. As a leading student of interwar European economic development has stated: "The functioning of the European economic system in the inter-war period cannot be understood if one does not take into account that this was a transitional period between economic liberalism and national economic planning." [3]

SELECTED BIBLIOGRAPHY

ALLEN, GEORGE C., *British Industries and Their Organization.* London: Longmans, Green & Co., Ltd., 1935.

ARNDT, H. W., *The Economic Lessons of the Nineteen Thirties.* London: Frank Cass & Co., Ltd., 1963.

BRADY, ROBERT A., *The Rationalization Movement in German Industry, A Study in the Evolution of Economic Planning.* Berkeley: University of California Press, 1933.

CLARK, JOHN MAURICE, *Studies in the Economics of Overhead Costs.* Chicago: University of Chicago Press, 1957.

HEXNER, ERVIN, *International Cartels.* Chapel Hill: University of North Carolina Press, 1946.

———, *The International Steel Cartel.* Chapel Hill: University of North Carolina Press, 1943.

HUTCHISON, KEITH, *The Decline and Fall of British Capitalism.* New York: Charles Scribner's Sons, 1950.

KAHN, ALFRED E., *Great Britain in the World Economy.* New York: Columbia University Press, 1946.

KEYNES, JOHN M., *The End of Laissez-Faire.* London: Leonard & Virginia Woolf, 1927.

MADDISON, ANGUS, *Economic Growth in the West, Comparative Experience in Europe and North America.* New York: Twentieth Century Fund, 1964.

OGBURN, WILLIAM F., and WILLIAM JAFFE, *The Economic Development of Post-War France. A Survey of Production.* New York: Columbia University Press, 1929.

PIGOU, ARTHUR C., *Aspects of British Economic History, 1918–1925.* New York: The Macmillan Company, 1947.

SVENNILSON, INGVAR, *Growth and Stagnation in the European Economy.* Geneva: United Nations Economic Commission for Europe, 1954.

ARTICLES

BRADY, ROBERT A., "The Meaning of Rationalization: An Analysis of the Literature," *Quarterly Journal of Economics,* XLVI (May, 1932), 526–40.

[3] Ingvar Svennilson, *Growth and Stagnation in the European Economy,* p. 36.

GREGORY, THEODORE E., "Rationalization and Technological Unemployment," *Economic Journal*, XL (Dec., 1930), 551–67.

KESSLER, WILLIAM C., "German Cartel Regulation Under the Decree of 1923," *Quarterly Journal of Economics*, L (August, 1936), 680–93.

LUCAS, ARTHUR F., "A British Experiment in the Control of Competition: The Coal Mines Act of 1930," *Quarterly Journal of Economics*, XLVIII (May, 1934), 418–41.

———, "British Experiments in the Reduction of Excess Industrial Capacity," *Harvard Business Review*, XII (July, 1934), 389–97.

———, "The British Movement for Industrial Reconstruction and the Control of Competitive Activity," *Quarterly Journal of Economics*, XLIX (Feb., 1935), 206–35.

MACGREGOR, DAVID H., "The Coal Bill and the Cartel," *Economic Journal*, XL (March, 1930), 35–44.

———, "Rationalization of Industry," *Economic Journal*, XXXVII (Dec., 1927), 521–50.

MARTIN, GERMAIN, "The Industrial Reconstruction of France Since the War," *Harvard Business Review*, V (April, 1927), 257–68.

SAUNDERS, CHRISTOPHER T., "Recent Trends in the Lancashire Cotton Industry," *Economic Journal*, XLVII (March, 1937), 70–76.

SCHUMPETER, JOSEPH A., "The Instability of Capitalism," *Economic Journal*, XXXVIII (Sept., 1928), 361–86.

SHELDON, OLIVER, "The Development of Scientific Management in England," *Harvard Business Review*, III (Jan., 1925), 129–40.

SIEGFRIED, ANDRÉ, "French Industry and Mass Production," *Harvard Business Review*, VI (Oct., 1927), 1–10.

TAWNEY, RICHARD H., "The British Coal Industry and the Question of Nationalization," *Quarterly Journal of Economics*, XXXV (Nov., 1920), 61–107.

Interwar Europe II: Crisis in International Trade and Changing National Economic Systems

During World War I the gold standard had to be abandoned except
in the United States and a few minor countries. Statesmen, bankers, businessmen, publicists, and most economists accepted restoration of the gold standard
as a desirable objective to be attained as soon as possible after the end of the
war. Between 1923 and 1928 more than thirty nations restored the gold standard in more or less modified fashion. The most interesting and revealing case
was that of Great Britain, which returned to gold in 1924 and was forced to
abandon it again in 1931.

Great Britain At what level to fix the standard was a more debatable
issue in the 1920's than the decision whether to restore the gold standard. For
Great Britain the question was whether the pound sterling should be fixed in
value at its prewar gold content (113 grains of gold) or at the existing postwar value in relation to other currencies. In 1924 Winston Churchill, then
Chancellor of the Exchequer, announced that Britain would return to the gold
standard at the prewar level by permitting free export of gold bullion after
April 1, 1925. When this announcement to return to gold was made in 1924,
the pound sterling was about 10 per cent below its prewar value in relation
to the United States dollar (23.2 grains of gold), the strong currency of the
world. The prewar value of the pound was $4.87 (the ratio of the gold content
of the standard pound and the standard dollar); the current value in 1924 was
around $4.40. To return to gold at the prewar parity meant to appreciate the
pound by 10 per cent above its current (1924) value. To restore the par ratio
(4.87) between the dollar and the pound meant either that prices must rise
in the United States or fall in the United Kingdom. Since prices in the United
States were quite stable during the 1920's, this meant that Britain would have
to deflate its price level in order to make the gold standard workable. In other
words, the appreciation of the pound, which was prerequisite to re-establishing
the British gold standard at the prewar parity, forced the United Kingdom into
deflation. This proved poor medicine.

The effect of appreciating the pound 10 per cent may be illustrated with
respect to the British coal industry, an important export trade. The world price

of coal was more or less independent of the value placed by the British on gold. Let it be assumed that the world price of a given amount of coal was $4.87. When the pound sterling was worth $4.40 a British exporter received 1.1 pounds for this amount of coal. When the pound was raised to $4.87, the British coal exporter received the world price of $4.87 as before, but translated into British money this meant a price of only 1.0 pound, a ten cent reduction in the export price to British exporters. The price of imports in terms of the revalued pound was also lowered by 10 per cent, but this had only a negligible effect on the cost of producing coal. Coal exporters and coal mine owners had to reduce costs of production by 10 per cent in order to retain the same relative position in the export market. Since wages formed the most important element in the cost of producing coal, coal miners were pressured to accept a cut in money-wage rates. Quite understandably the miners resisted wage cuts. When mine operators announced a reduction in wages, the miners struck. The coal strike led in turn to the General Strike of 1926, the most bitter class conflict and the major economic catastrophe in Great Britain between the two wars. Forcing a return to the gold standard at the prewar parity had brought on a policy of deflation and had led to disastrous results.

Since a British pound sterling would now buy 10 per cent more abroad than before and very little more at home, Britishers were encouraged to increase imports. The combination of decreased exports, illustrated by the coal industry, and increased imports meant an adverse balance of trade for Great Britain. To meet the adverse balance by permitting gold to be exported was undesirable because gold reserves were precariously low. Hence, the Bank of England increased the bank rate in order to attract loans to Britain to cover the deficit in the balance of payments. A high rate at the Bank of England meant high domestic interest rates for Britain generally, and high interest rates tended to choke off business investment and place a brake on industrial investment. Deficient investment was probably the main cause of the low level of general economic activity and the high level of unemployment prevailing in the United Kingdom during the 1920's.

High interest rates and the resultant restraints on credit are weapons normally used to curb a boom; in order to save the gold standard they were being used to aggravate a depression. This policy of deflation proved the wrong medicine for business as well as for labor. If any group stood to gain, it was the international banking houses whose shaken financial prestige might be restored by rebuilding the financial supremacy of London's money market.

In the minds of British statesmen, however, the issue was not one of class advantage; the overriding consideration was national honor—to restore the pound to the same value at which large deposits had been accepted from foreigners. What price honor? It included beating down miners' wages, the bitter general strike, outraging social justice, and aggravating unemployment. As events were to prove, even these grave sacrifices could not rescue the gold standard in the long run.

France   Meanwhile France also struggled back to the gold standard. The sobering economic fact confronting France at the end of the war was the tremendous devastation wrought by the war to industry and agriculture in eastern France, where the major land battles of the war had been fought.

Reconstruction was undertaken with vigor. The French government compensated property owners for the war damage and financed these payments with large-scale borrowing. Between 1921 and 1925 the public debt, already swollen by the war, doubled in size, and currency in circulation increased by nearly 50 per cent. The French government hoped to repay the reconstruction debt out of German reparations; this made France sensitive about reparations and led to occupation of the Ruhr when the Germans defaulted on reparations in 1922, a move which proved very costly to France and increased further an already large budgetary deficit. As a consequence of these several factors, France experienced a major postwar inflation, with the exchange value of the franc falling from nine cents in 1919 to a low of two and one-half cents in 1926. Although the basic economic situation was sound, the political uncertainty and instability so characteristic of France led to a flight of capital from the country and exaggerated the fall in the external value of the franc. The situation became desperate, but was stabilized under the premiership of Poincaré, a conservative statesman. In 1928 France officially restored the gold standard at a value of four cents to the franc, which was equivalent to one-fifth of its prewar gold value.[1]

Devaluation of the franc at this level proved a realistic step which enabled France to come out of the postwar monetary tangle better than Britain, which had insisted on returning to gold at prewar parity with dire consequences to domestic and foreign economic relations. France avoided the sacrifices of deflation, wrote down its internal debt by four-fifths (to the relief of the French taxpayer and at the expense of the French rentier bondholder), and became, next to the United States, the strongest nation financially for a decade after 1927.

By 1928 the gold standard had been restored in all the major nations except China, which remained on a silver standard, and the Soviet Union, which lay outside the capitalist camp. A decade after the war the capitalist world had regained the financial basis for an integrated international economy. The great virtue of the gold standard lay in stabilizing foreign exchange rates. Stability of the value of one money in terms of other moneys greatly reduced the risks of buying and selling goods in foreign countries and in this respect increased the volume of international trade. The international gold standard presupposed that flexibility in domestic price levels would permit adjustments for differences in rates of growth in productivity, output, employment, imports, and exports. Unfortunately for the future of the gold standard, the world had changed a great deal since 1914. Upward flexibility of prices presented no insuperable problem, but flexibility downward of domestic price levels imposed deflationary conditions, as proved by the experience of Great Britain when gold was restored at a high international price and as reinforced by the Great Depression after 1929. Instead of being a boon to domestic and international economic activity, the gold standard proved a straitjacket.

---

[1] John Maynard Keynes wrote in 1924 and reiterated in 1926, "The level of the franc is going to be settled in the long run, not by speculation or the balance of trade, or even the outcome of the Ruhr adventure, but by the proportion of his earned income which the French taxpayer will permit to be taken from him to pay the claims of the French rentier." *Essays in Persuasion* (New York: Harcourt, Brace and World, Inc., 1932), p. 105.

Before the First World War western Europe, and especially Great Britain, had served as the world's banker for long-term capital movements for economic development. London was the center of a world-wide trading system financed mainly through London's money market. During the 1920's, Europe was unable to function as the world's banker. With imports increasing relative to exports, the European nations experienced balance-of-payments difficulties. Increasing amounts of income from overseas investments went to pay for imports and left little income out of which to advance capital loans to borrowing countries. The United States stepped into the breach with long-term loans to international borrowers and replaced Europe as the world's banker. Attention has already been directed to the large American loans to Germany during the 1920's. Other countries also borrowed in the millions. An unusually heavy debt structure was built up in countries borrowing for reconstruction and development.

Unfortunately for world trade and the international gold standard, the United States did not qualify as a good world banker. Its banks eagerly lent large sums, but American economic policy placed major obstacles in the way of repayment of loans. As a major creditor nation the United States should logically have increased its imports in order to enable foreigners to earn dollars with which to service their debts to the United States. An important step toward increasing imports would have been to lower tariffs. Instead, the United States did just the opposite; it increased tariffs in 1922 and again in 1930 to the highest levels in its history. Foreigners paid the interest on their debts temporarily out of further loans rather than from increased productivity associated with foreign loans and shifts in world production.

For the proper functioning of the international gold standard the flow of gold into the United States should have raised domestic American prices. Higher prices would have made the United States a less favorable place for foreigners and Americans to buy, with a resultant increase of imports and a decrease of exports. Moreover, a rise in United States prices would have permitted adjustment in the international value of the British pound without the agonizing deflation which kept the United Kingdom in a straitjacket between 1924 and 1931. On price policy as on tariff policy the United States sabotaged the rules of the international gold standard. The Federal Reserve System oriented its program toward stable domestic prices rather than toward stable international exchange rates and thus jeopardized the long-term future of the gold standard. A failure of United States prices to rise prevented necessary shifts in world production.

During the 1920's the state of international trade, especially after the return to the gold standard, depended on a large and continuing volume of long-term loans from the United States. Although a heavy international debt structure was built up, the adjustments in underlying economic conditions needed to liquidate these debts did not develop. Beginning in 1928 the volume of new long-term loans available from the United States began to dwindle and after the New York stock exchange crash in 1929 virtually ceased altogether. The early victims were the countries producing primary products (foodstuffs

and raw materials), the prices of which fell precipitously between 1929 and 1932.

In order to meet their balance-of-payments deficits the agricultural countries threw wave after wave of products on the world market for whatever price they could get. They cut down on imports wherever possible and pushed their exports into tumbling world markets, each time causing further declines. The real burden of debts increased enormously in consequence of the fall in prices. In addition to the severe blow to international trade from the Hawley-Smoot Tariff of 1930, the dollar shortage was accentuated because a sharp fall in incomes in the United States reduced imports of commodities and kept American would-be tourists to Europe and elsewhere at home.

With the drying up of long-term American credits and the shrinkage of international trade, desperate debtor nations borrowed on short term at high interest rates in order to cover deficits in their balance of payments. For example, the depressed agricultural countries of central Europe, confronted with collapsing prices for exports, got short-term credits from Vienna and Berlin (which in turn had borrowed from London) to pay for debt services and essential imports. Short-term credits were essential to rescue the situation and might have been justified if the depression had abated. Unfortunately, the underlying economic conditions deteriorated progressively. The fury of the international economic storm intensified.

Panic broke out in the world money markets in May, 1931, when the largest bank in Austria, the Credit-Anstalt, crashed, a victim of the default on loans made to depressed central Europe. Coming in the midst of a critical financial situation and in the wake of deepening depression, the failure in Vienna caused a complete collapse of confidence. Money markets fell like a row of tenpins. From Vienna to Berlin to London and to New York the debacle spread.

German banks were sensitive to the Austrian money market because they had re-lent large sums borrowed on short term from England. Germany's financial position was already precarious because of the cut-off in the flow of long-term capital at the onset of the depression, the severity of the depression in German industry, and the notorious illiquidity of German banks. Short-term withdrawals came fast and furious. During the early months of 1931 the Reichsbank lost nine-tenths of its gold reserve. Several leading German banks failed, the Berlin bourse closed, and the discount rate rose from 7 to 10 and finally to 15 per cent. In July, 1931, all foreign payments by Germans were suspended, with ten billion Reichsmarks of short-term credit still owed to foreign creditors, mostly in London.

At this point most countries would have formally abandoned the gold standard and permitted the currency to reach its own level in international exchanges. Devaluation in Germany, however, was politically impossible because of the still nightmarish memories of rampant inflation less than a decade earlier. Instead of formally abandoning the gold standard, Germany suspended all foreign payments and imposed rigid exchange controls.

The financial panic which began in Vienna and spread to Berlin now moved to London. British banks had large short-term loans outstanding in Germany and elsewhere in central Europe. Suspension of payments by Ger-

many meant that British credits were frozen and could not be collected. Many foreigners, including the central banks of countries operating on a gold-exchange standard, held large short-term deposits in London. These depositors became alarmed and withdrew heavily from England. The Bank of England raised the rate of interest from 2½ to 3½ to 4½ per cent during July, 1931, but gold flowed out in a mighty torrent. The Bank of England lost more than £200 million within two months after the German "freeze" in July. Between Wednesday and Saturday in the third week of September, £43 million of gold were lost. With the "gold rush" at its height, a political crisis developed and led to formation of a national government to try to save the gold standard. By September 20, 1931, gold reserves became dangerously low, and the Bank of England suspended gold payments. The United Kingdom went off the gold standard.

The frenzied demand for gold during the financial panic of 1931–32 illustrated a significant characteristic of the capitalist system. Capitalism as a distinct system of economic life ultimately rests on the systematic accumulation of money balances. The system operates toward this end by converting raw materials and labor into finished products which in turn realize a value to the producer only when exchanged for money. In prosperous times money has the appearance of a mere medium of exchange, as the "great wheel of circulation," which facilitates the flow of output from producers to consumers. In prosperous times confidence abounds in the operation of the economy, and money is replaced by credit, which is easily created by the stroke of a banker's pen. As soon as products realize their value by being sold for money or its equivalent, the proceeds are thrown back into circulation to make more money. Only a miser would keep his wealth in a money form in which it can earn no premium. In a severe depression, and particularly in a financial crisis, however, money takes on a different meaning.

In the depression after 1929 the terms on which goods could be converted into money became less and less favorable. Losses replaced profits, meaning that at the end of a turnover of capital the producers had less money than at the start of the turnover period. The motive force of the economic system, making money, began to operate in reverse. The object was to conserve rather than to expand wealth. Goods which could not be converted into money became worthless from the point of view of the capitalist producer, who could not eat a million bushels of wheat nor wear a million pairs of shoes. As the depression worsened, panic broke out among capitalist producers and investors. To salvage from the economic ruins what money balance they could became the object of their money-making accounting.

Thus the daily preoccupation of businessmen everywhere to convert goods into money in order to realize their value became a classic drama played on a world stage. Gold was the international money, the real incarnation of socially recognized wealth all over the capitalist world. Nothing else really mattered. Credit ceased to be a satisfactory substitute for money in the crisis. It evaporated like snow in a blast furnace. Massive quantities of wheat and shoes were sacrificed at the altar of gold. This was a crisis growing out of abundance rather than scarcity of "real" goods. The fear of productive capacity meant the idling of thousands of factories and millions of workers all over the world.

Their employment could but add to the losses of money-making employers. An entire business civilization stood on the brink of collapse. Such was the deeper meaning of the "gold rush" of 1931–32.

Aftermath of Britain's Departure from the Gold Standard

Immediately after Great Britain suspended gold payments the pound sterling fell in relation to currencies still on the gold standard; from $4.87 it went down to $3.20 and then returned to an equilibrium at approximately $3.50. British international trade improved immediately upon release from the burden imposed by an overvalued currency. With the pound at $3.50 British goods became a bargain while Britishers found foreign goods expensive in terms of a pound worth only $3.50. Consequently British exports increased and imports decreased. The deflationary pressures which had intensified unemployment and business losses and kept domestic investment at a low level now gave way to mild domestic inflation, increased employment and rising business expectations. Great Britain breathed easier after release from the golden straitjacket of 1924–31.

Many countries quickly followed Great Britain off the gold standard: Scandinavia, Portugal, Egypt, Latvia, most of Latin America, Japan, and all British territories and dominions except South Africa. By the end of 1932 thirty-five countries had suspended gold payments. Only France and the United States among the large nations and Switzerland, Belgium, and the Netherlands among the smaller states remained on gold for the time being.

France and the United States, which held most of the world's surplus gold reserves, suffered the fate of Midas. French and American exporters found virtually no buyers for their goods because francs and dollars were costly in terms of the money of other countries. France and the United States further sealed themselves off from world markets by erecting high tariff barriers and import quotas. They imposed on themselves continuing deflation of domestic prices to the accompaniment of rising unemployment and still deeper depression.

But even these citadels of gold were not impregnable to the forces eroding the gold standard. In the fiscal year ending in June, 1932, the United States lost nearly $2 billion in gold. Foreign withdrawals plus increasing domestic demand for gold caused by shrinking credit led to a gold crisis. More than five thousand banks failed in the United States between 1930 and 1932. Runs on banks grew progressively worse as the weakness of the banking system became more apparent to depositors. Hoarding of gold and currency marked a liquidity crisis. After the temporary closing of all banks in March, 1933, gold payments were suspended, and in 1934 the gold content of the dollar was reduced by 41 per cent (from 23.2 to 13.7 grains). The United States, too, had been forced off the gold standard.

Belgium went off the gold standard in 1935, followed by France, Switzerland, and the Netherlands in 1936. Thus an international financial structure carefully and laboriously erected over the course of a century prior to 1914 collapsed like a house of cards within a decade after its restoration in the 1920's. The faith of an age and the symbol of world economic solidarity per-

ished with the abandonment of the international gold standard. International solutions to economic problems gave way to national solutions. The free market system received a *coup de grâce* with the snapping, one by one, of links in the golden chain that had joined national economies into an international system.

World Trade During the 1930's

Although abandonment of the gold standard relaxed pressures on international and domestic economic relations, it constituted the removal of a restraint rather than a positive solution as such. With all countries seeking to protect themselves against an unfavorable balance of payments, all were led to act in the same way, as a result of which they merely reinforced the unfavorable conditions. Beggar-thy-neighbor policies became the rule. Some statesmen realized the hopelessnes of these policies, but even the most enlightened had to act within a framework which they could control. Since no international or European-wide authority existed, there could be no international or European approach to the depression. Economic nationalism was in the saddle and riding hard. Nationalistic solutions aggravated the depression. Month by month between January, 1929, and June, 1933, the volume of world trade declined.

Abandonment of the gold standard, which was in itself a major step toward economic nationalism, set in motion other nationalistic policies involving restrictions on the free movement of international goods and capital. Among these restrictionist and interventionist policies were (1) protective tariffs, (2) import quotas, and (3) exchange controls.

(1) **Great Britain's departure from free trade** In the long-term perspective probably the most radical change precipitated by the Great Depression was Great Britain's departure from its historic free trade policy following abandonment of the gold standard in 1931. Ever since repeal of the Corn Laws in 1846, England had been the bastion of free trade; it had resisted the return to protectionism which began with the age of mass production in the 1870's. By virtue of its free trade policy between 1929 and 1931 Great Britain had played the role of a vacuum into which foreign goods were drawn for sale at whatever money values could be realized. This had advantages for British consumers—it lowered the cost of living—but had disadvantages for British producers competing with imported goods. Tariff legislation of 1931 authorized duties as high as 100 per cent on imports, but the duties actually imposed were generally 10 per cent, with selected industries protected at higher rates. The duties on iron and steel products were fixed at 33 per cent. Some foodstuffs and raw materials (wheat, fish, raw cotton, and raw wool) remained on the free list. British tariff rates remained low in comparison with those of most other countries including the United States, France, and Germany. Nevertheless, with Britain's departure from free trade the last of the capitalist countries succumbed to growing economic nationalism.

Along with British protectionism came a policy of Imperial Preference, that is, a policy of charging lower duties on goods imported from British overseas territories than from non-British sources. The British Dominions had for

a long time imposed higher duties on non-British than on British imports. Under free trade the United Kingdom could not reciprocate, but with the abandonment of free trade in 1931, the overseas territories demanded and received preferential treatment.

(2) **Import quotas** Tariffs were not always effective in keeping out the flood of goods which streamed into Europe during the world crisis. Sellers willing to take a sufficiently low return could always surmount the tariff walls. More effective than tariffs in keeping out imports was the quota system, which fixed maximum limits to the quantities of imports. Although tariffs interfere with the free international price system and the optimum allocation of resources among nations, they do not involve complete abandonment of prices as regulators of the international distribution of commodities. The quota system, on the other hand, does abandon the price system in favor of administrative rationing of imports in the sense that absolute prohibitions are placed on the international flow of commodities.

Nearly all countries made use of quotas in one form or another during the 1930's. They were used most extensively by France. After stabilizing the franc at one-fifth of its prewar value in 1928, France occupied a strong international financial position. During the Great Depression, however, and especially after Great Britain and its financial fellow-travelling countries devalued their currencies in 1931 and 1932, French exports declined drastically and the tourist trade fell sharply. Meanwhile, in spite of tariffs, imports flooded into France from countries eager to convert goods into French gold. Because the franc was overvalued in relation to non-gold currencies France tended to have an adverse trade balance—more imports than exports—and quotas were contrived to reduce the imports. France imposed quotas on hundreds of commodities constituting perhaps two-thirds of total French imports just prior to further devaluation of the franc in June, 1936. After devaluation many of the quota restrictions were suspended because depreciation of the franc provided encouragement to exports and discouragement to imports and thereby assisted in the trade balance.

(3) **Exchange control** Exchange controls were another technique contrived to regulate international trade and capital movements. Governments, often through central banks, assumed control of foreign exchange by requiring exporters to surrender the foreign money received from sales abroad and by requiring importers to purchase foreign exchange from authorized banks. The prices at which exporters could sell and importers could buy exchange was fixed arbitrarily by the government. Moreover, the amount of foreign exchange which could be obtained and the purposes for which it might be used were subject to government regulation. Exchange controls were designed to check the flight of capital abroad, to restrict the quantity of imports, and to control the purposes for which foreign exchange might be used. It might be restricted to paying interest on foreign debt, for vital imports such as food and essential raw materials, and, conversely, might not be allowed for luxury imports or other nonessentials. Under the international gold standard exporters could do as they wished with foreign exchange acquired from sales, and importers could acquire as much foreign exchange as they could afford with the domestic money at their command. After 1929, and more particularly after the financial

panic of 1931, debtor nations experienced great difficulty in obtaining sufficient
foreign exchange to meet their international obligations. As repudiation and
bankruptcy threatened, investors rushed to transfer their funds to safer countries such as France, Switzerland, and, except during 1932–33, the United
States. By limiting the quantity of foreign exchange available, governments
could control the flight of capital abroad.

Exchange controls directed toward limiting imports tended to foster
bilateral, or barter-like, arrangements in foreign trade. An importing country
would permit countries from which it bought to spend the exchange only in
the importing country; "If we buy from you, you must agree to buy from us,"
became a motto of international economic relations. Imports were purchased
not where prices were lowest but where funds were available to pay for imports. Such bilateral arrangements violated a classical principle of international trade, that goods should be purchased where the price, taking account
of quality, is lowest. Bilateral trading is uneconomical in terms of the most
efficient allocation of resources. Normal trade is seldom bilateral; it is multilateral, or many-sided. Shifts from multilateral to bilateral trade made the
world poorer than it need have been in terms of the pre-existing division of
labor. In other words, the wealth of nations was reduced by limitations imposed on the international division of labor. Bilateral arrangements resulted
from the breakdown of international financial organization and manifested the
flight toward economic nationalism.

Nearly all European countries used exchange controls and bilateral agreements, but Germany utilized them most extensively. Although the gold reserves
of the Reichsbank fell from three billion marks in mid-1930 to less than one
billion marks at the end of 1932, the Weimar government refused officially
to give up the gold standard and devalue the mark to a level more nearly
equal to its international purchasing power. Nor did the Nazis, who came into
power in 1933, formally devalue the mark. They could hardly have done so in
view of their allegations against the democratic parties regarding responsibility for the traumatic inflation of 1923. Refusal to devalue the mark necessitated complicated controls and manipulations including export subsidies to
German exporters to enable them to sell in world markets on competitive terms
with countries which had devalued their currencies. The Nazis kept the official
value of the Reichsmark at the old rate (23.8 cents before and 40 cents after
dollar devaluation) and made skillful and ruthless use of exchange controls
which they imposed on a system of international financial machinations to
support their war-oriented economy.

Under the Schacht Plan of 1934, every transaction involving foreign trade
and exchange had to be cleared through the German government. As the Nazi
war economy moved into high gear, foreign exchange was granted very spar-
ingly for imports from countries with strong currencies and strong economic
bargaining power. Increasing stress was placed on special agreements with
countries with surplus foodstuffs and raw materials needed by Germany. By
1938 Germany had bilateral agreements with some forty countries involving
two-thirds of Germany's total foreign trade. Countries with which agreements
were made included several in Latin America: Brazil (cotton, coffee), Columbia (coffee), Chile (copper) and Argentina (wool).

The most telling agreements, however, were with the agricultural coun-

tries of central and southeastern Europe, including Hungary, Rumania, Yugoslavia, Greece, Bulgaria, and Turkey. These Balkan countries had fallen into desperate financial and economic straits as a result of the world depression and financial crisis of the early 1930's. They needed manufactured goods, and Germany needed food and raw materials. Moreover, the Balkan countries constituted a relatively secure source of supply of food and raw materials in wartime. For the primary products purchased, Germany paid high prices in terms of the local currencies. Payment was made, however, in "blocked marks," that is, marks which could be spent only in Germany. The omnivorous Nazi war economy absorbed huge quantities of imports and built up large debts to the Balkan countries. Some crops were grown on special order under long-term contracts at guaranteed prices, thus reducing the agrarian countries to economic colonies of the imperialist Nazi system.

To their chagrin the Balkan countries discovered that Germany had little to export of the things they wanted. Having been ensnared in the Nazi trap, they dared not protest too vigorously lest the Nazis repudiate their debts and discontinue buying the crops for which there was no alternative market. It was ironical that these poor peasant countries, which were chronic debtors and in need of capital, should have supplied large credits to Germany, thus occupying a position during the 1930's similar to that of the United States during the 1920's. Militarily and politically the agrarian countries were intimidated by the burgeoning Nazi war machine, which soon became the most powerful in the world. In the long run the shabby treatment accorded by the Nazis to their trading partners would probably have backfired and led to disruption of the bilateral arrangements or to absorption of the agrarian states into the Nazi political system. But the long run did not have time to work out because Germany was preparing for war at a feverish pace, and by the time the primary producers fully realized how short their end of the deals would be, the Nazis had plunged Europe into the Second World War. The future of the Balkans now hung on the outcome of a vast military conflict.

Some Generalizations about International Economic Relations During the Interwar Period

Europe's economic troubles in the 1920's were quite different from those of the 1930's. In the first interwar decade the major assumption of policy-makers seemed to be that prewar trends represented the normal path of economic development and that Europe would resume this normal path as soon as certain war-generated problems were solved: physical war destruction, new boundary lines, war debts and reparations, domestic monetary instability, disrupted international trade relations, unbalanced budgets, unstable foreign exchange rates, and deficits in balances of payments. A world economic conference held in Geneva in 1927 to liquidate dislocations still present from the First World War issued optimistic pronouncements about future economic developments. Conditions in 1928 and 1929 lent some plausibility to the optimism of Geneva. Prewar levels of per capita income had been restored or exceeded in Europe, and the volume of international trade was approximately 25 per cent (in real terms) above the level of 1914. Europe's task was to gain back its share of the rising volume of international trade.

In the second interwar decade the shock of the Great Depression forced a change in European policies. In view of the collapse of international trade and the breakdown of international financial organization, the major assumption was that future trends would differ fundamentally from pre-1914 trends because Europe's position in the world economy had undergone basic changes, and indeed the world itself had changed drastically. Whereas in an expanding world market Europe's transformation could have relied primarily on modernizing stagnant industries and developing new export industries, in view of the depression in world trade, transformation took the form of redirecting resources toward production for internal domestic markets. This was the meaning of the shift from the economic internationalism which had prevailed before 1914 to the economic nationalism of the interwar period.

Two long-term trends were behind the fall in demand for Europe's staple exports: (1) the general tendency for foreign trade as a proportion of national product to decline, and (2) the changing composition of demand for European exports. Defining economic development as increasing income per capita, a country's international trade declines relative to its national product because at high incomes physical commodities decline in importance relative to services, and services are consumed where they are produced and do not enter foreign trade. Statistical evidence verifies the tendency for international trade to decline as a proportion of national product, with minor exceptions for some small countries like the Netherlands. For example, United States merchandise exports declined from 15 per cent of national product in 1870 to 3 per cent in 1960. The change in Great Britain has been in the same direction but less pronounced.[2]

The second factor behind the transformation in European export industries—the changing commodity composition of demand—reinforced the decline in old-line staple exports such as textiles, basic steel and coal. Most staples could be easily produced within newly industrialized areas. Cotton cloth is the prime example of the type of product manufactured in the first stages of industrialization, but interwar developments also involved new forms of power which displaced coal, and the construction of new steel capacity in the more advanced of the newly industrialized nations (Japan, Russia, Australia).

Europe's *optimum* transformation would have involved the reallocation of resources from the staple exports (textiles, steel, coal) toward commodities which overseas countries were not prepared to supply for themselves (machinery, electrical equipment, chemicals, automobiles). These were industries in which Europe's long tradition of industrialization including highly trained scientists, engineers, managers, and skilled labor, gave its producers a strong comparative advantage over newly industrialized nations. The stagnation suffered by Great Britain during the 1920's was not an inevitable result of new competition from Japan and India; it arose from the ossification of British capitalism, which was too inflexible to transform itself to meet the changed conditions.

Transformation was delayed throughout the twenties by the expectation that a return to prewar normalcy would bring renewed expansion in

[2] See C. P. Kindleberger, *The Terms of Trade* (New York: John Wiley and Sons, 1956), p. 301.

overseas demand for prewar staple exports. As an understanding of the principles of economic growth should have made clear, this renewal never arrived. In the nature of the case it never could have; the loss of cotton yard-goods markets to Japan and India was beyond recall. The real trouble was that Britain and most of western Europe simply were not producing the new products that overseas markets wanted. Delay in the necessary transformation fostered stagnation, and stagnation fostered depression, which in turn converted stagnation into a debacle. World trade collapsed, and economic nationalism displaced economic internationalism with a vengeance.

The nationalistic transformation which the Great Depression imposed on Europe had its counterpart among Europe's former trading partners. The drastic fall in the prices of primary products (foodstuffs and raw materials) caused panic in the underdeveloped countries by (1) creating balance-of-payments difficulties and (2) turning the terms of trade against them, that is, increasing the quantities of primary products they had to exchange for a given quantity of manufactured imports. Primary producers responded to these unfavorable conditions by encouraging the domestic production of goods formerly imported and then protecting their new industries by means of tariffs, import quotas, exchange controls, and other restrictions. In order to carry through their industrialization the new countries needed textile machinery and other capital goods. They experienced difficulties paying for them out of depleted foreign exchange funds and imposed further restrictions on "nonessential" imports. European exports were bolstered somewhat during the 1930's by a shift to the class of goods with rising total world exports, e.g., machinery, and away from goods with falling total world exports, e.g., cotton cloth. This was a bright spot in the progress of European transformation.

Given the massive contraction in world trade caused by the Great Depression, however, the new exports did not offset the fall in old exports. Europe's next best alternative would have been to create a common European market to take advantage of mass demand and diversity of resources, including the high level of technical skill. This solution unfortunately was barred by intense nationalism, which was moving Europe toward war rather than economic cooperation. Production became more inner-directed on a nationalistic basis.

Expansion in Great Britain after 1932 and in Germany after 1934 took place primarily in domestic markets, including, of course, the rapidly expanding armaments industry. Between 1929 and 1938 British output for foreign markets fell by 20 per cent while output for domestic markets increased by 40 per cent. Protective tariffs, subsidies to agriculture and industry, exchange controls, and all the other paraphernalia of economic intervention and autarky were used to bolster internal markets. In spite of a few bright spots on the international horizon, the depression in world trade slowed down and redirected Europe's transformation and at the end of the interwar period it had been only partially achieved.

CHANGING NATIONAL ECONOMIC SYSTEMS

The failure of private enterprise to cope with transformation problems in stagnating and declining industries led to increasing governmental interven-

tion even in countries in which tradition strongly opposed state control of

private business. Intervention of the British government in the coal, textile, steel and shipbuilding industries illustrates this trend. In countries where laissez-faire had never been strong, governmental intervention burgeoned with less political opposition. Classical laissez-faire, both as a policy and as a faith, was clearly ended. As a policy, laissez-faire in the strict sense may never have prevailed in Europe, but as a faith it dominated the nineteenth century. This faith was shaken by the First World War and abandoned after the 1929 crash and the ensuing financial panic of 1931–32. A repudiation of the philosophical foundations of laissez-faire was expressed in 1926 by John Maynard Keynes in the following passage:

> Let us clear from the ground the metaphysical or general principles upon which, from time to time, *laissez-faire* has been founded. It is *not* true that individuals possess a prescriptive "natural liberty" in their economic activities. There is *no* "compact" conferring perpetual rights on those who Have or on those who Acquire. The world is *not* so governed from above that private and social interest always coincide. It is *not* so managed here below that in practice they coincide. It is *not* a correct deduction from the Principles of Economics that enlightened self-interest always operates in the public interest. Nor is it true that self-interest generally *is* enlightened; more often individuals acting separately to promote their own ends are too ignorant or too weak to attain even these. Experience does *not* show that individuals, when they make up a social unit, are always less clear-sighted than when they act separately.[3]

The interwar period witnessed not only the end of laissez-faire capitalism but also the emergence of strong anticapitalist movements from both the left and the right. The most sudden shift took place in Russia, where the Revolution of 1917 instituted a Communist government committed to nationalization and overall economic planning. Socialist strength in Italy provoked a counter-revolution in the form of totalitarian fascism under Benito Mussolini beginning in 1922. Germany, England, and France all had socialist governments at some time during the interwar period, but they were never strong enough to inaugurate socialist policies such as nationalization or general economic planning. In Germany, as in Italy, the surge of socialism and communism provoked a counter-revolution and a totalitarian form of capitalism under Hitler's Nazis.

Britain's attempted return to normalcy led to economic stagnation and during the Great Depression to abandonment of the cornerstones of laissez-faire, the gold standard and free trade. Two interwar Labour (socialist) governments held office in 1924 and again in 1929. France's socialist-oriented "Popular Front" under Leon Blum took office in 1936 but failed to solve France's economic problems. In 1939 the totalitarian fascist regimes in Germany and Italy plunged Europe into the Second World War against the liberal democracies and Communist Russia. Mussolini and Hitler met inglorious ends at the conclusion of the war while the Soviet Union emerged stronger than before. At the end of the war Britain's socialist Labour Party was elected to office and nationalized the basic industries, including coal mining, transportation, public utilities, and the Bank of England, establishing a semi-socialist economy. Only the United States among Western democracies was without a strong socialist movement, and even American capitalism re-

[3] *Essays in Persuasion*, p. 312.

ceived shock therapy from the New Deal during the Great Depression and experienced further modifications during the Second World War. Hence this great bastion of capitalist strength also found itself breaking with laissez-faire and moving in the direction of positive government.

Thus three types of economic systems may be distinguished during the interwar period: capitalism, fascism, and socialism. Fascism arose as a counter-revolutionary movement in countries where socialism threatened to replace capitalism, emerging as an anti-democratic, totalitarian form of capitalism, in contrast to the traditional democratic capitalism. One distinction between capitalism and socialism relates to the ownership of the means of production; in the former the means of production are privately owned and in the latter they are socially (governmentally) owned. By this test fascism was a type of capitalism because it retained private ownership of the means of production, and income from ownership remained an important share of the national income. In this sense it may be convenient to distinguish democratic and totalitarian (fascist) capitalism on the one hand, and democratic and totalitarian (Communist) socialism, on the other hand.

The following discussion is concerned with the interwar experiments under fascist governments. Changes in democratic capitalist countries will be discussed in the next two chapters on the United States, and interwar socialism in the chapter on the economic development of the Soviet Union.

Italy's Corporate State

In the course of the First World War Italy repudiated its prewar alliance with the central powers (Germany and Austria-Hungary) and entered the conflict on the side of the Western allies only to be disappointed with the Versailles Treaty. National disillusionment with the outcome of the war was accompanied by political and economic instability. During the early postwar years the spectre of revolution hung over Italy. Left-wing parties made large gains in the parliamentary elections of 1919. Trade union membership increased rapidly. The political and economic strength of the working-class movement was used to promote social legislation and to extract favorable wage bargains from employers. In 1920 during a wage dispute in the machinery industry in northern Italy, half a million workers under socialist leadership staged a stay-in strike in six hundred factories. They stayed in the factories after employers had threatened a lockout. With bold leadership the working class might have seized political power and established a socialist regime in Italy. The stay-in strike failed, however, when socialist leaders delayed and disputed among themselves over the course of action to be taken.

Although the threat of social revolution from the left fizzled, it threw a sufficient scare into the middle and upper classes to set in motion strong currents of counter-revolution. Benito Mussolini, who had organized the National Fascist Party in 1919, opportunistically seized this situation to pose as the champion of law and order and to become the leader of the counter-revolution. He gained political support among the middle classes, who feared a working-class revolution, and financial support from industrialists and large landowners, who feared loss of their factories and estates. In October, 1922, Mussolini's illegal army of Blackshirts marched on Rome and, while the King and the

regular army stood aside, seized the reins of government. Within a few years

Mussolini had routed political opposition by eliminating all other political parties, and had merged his Fascist Party with the government and established himself as dictator of a totalitarian state. Italy's brief experience with political democracy came abruptly to an end.

Mussolini's counter-revolution ended the threat of revolutionary changes in the economic and social structure of Italy. Factories continued under private ownership, landed estates remained the property of large landowners, and much-needed land reform in southern Italy failed to materialize. The distribution of income did not change substantially: the rich remained rich and the poor remained poor. Through cruel repression the Fascists smashed the labor and socialist movements. Strikes were outlawed. Unemployment was reduced through a slow although not particularly productive public works program. A high level of economic activity resulted from orienting the nation toward imperialistic expansion.

Despite seven years of Fascist control prior to 1929, Italy's experience in the Great Depression was similar to that of other capitalist countries. Industrial production fell to one-half the 1929 level, imports and exports dropped to one-third the former value, unemployment rose sharply, and prices dropped by 35 per cent. Attempts were made to absorb the unemployed in public works, by reductions in the length of the work week, and by increasing military expenditures. By 1935 Italy had become a war economy, and in that year Ethiopia was attacked amidst the bravado of restoring to Italy the grandeur of the ancient Roman Empire. When the League of Nations applied economic sanctions against Italy for its aggression in Ethiopia, fifty-five nations ceased buying Italian goods. One of the consequences of the sanctions was to push Italy further in the direction of self-sufficiency, but in other respects sanctions seem to have had only a minor effect.

Economic self-sufficiency had been a major goal of Mussolini's policy beginning in 1925 with the so-called "Battle of Wheat," which was designed to stimulate Italy's grain production to the point of self-sufficiency. A protective duty of ninety cents a bushel reduced wheat imports to a trickle by the early thirties. Domestic wheat production rose substantially; in 1931–32 it was 40 per cent above the average level of 1921 to 1925.

Winning the "Battle of Wheat" was, however, costly to Italian consumers for whom bread provided a major portion of the total diet. The price of wheat in Italy increased to more than twice the price in world markets. In 1939 the price of hard wheat was $2.06 per bushel in Italy as compared with $0.73 in Liverpool. Some inferior grains replaced wheat in the cereal diet of Italians, but the prices of these substitutes also rose under the protectionist policy. Italy had more to gain than most other countries from an international division of labor. The "Battle of Wheat" and similar self-sufficiency measures were better suited to satisfying Il Duce's appetite for grandiose nationalistic schemes than for feeding forty million Italians. Italy's drive for self-sufficiency was carried much further than could be justified on economic grounds. The whole economic program, geared as it was to imperialistic ventures and spectacular public works, was more appropriate for full employment than for full enjoyment. Under Mussolini's regime the purchasing power of hourly daily wages of industrial workers appears to have declined by more than 20 per cent.

Mussolini's most pretentious idea was the principle of the corporate state, a modern version of the medieval craft gild in which both workers (journeymen) and employers (masters) in a given industry or trade were members of a common association. Within this institutional framework the Fascists sought to substitute class collaboration for class conflict. Compulsory arbitration replaced free collective bargaining in deciding disputes between labor and capital; strikes and boycotts were prohibited. The Italian Corporations were not actually formed until 1933, when twenty-two of them were set up for the entire Italian economy, each headed by a Council consisting of representatives of employers, employees, and the government. Employers' delegates typically came from large, monopolistic business firms; the employees' delegates were mostly professional persons "safe" from the Fascist Party point of view and included very few rank-and-file workers. All members of the Corporation Councils were appointed either directly or indirectly by the Fascist Party. Resemblance to medieval craft gilds was more one of form than of substance because the real power dictating fundamental policies and decisions was the coercive force of a strong totalitarian state.

The Italian corporate state was a form of controlled capitalism operating within the framework of a self-acknowledged totalitarian state. Fascism rejected both socialism and political democracy. Although laissez-faire was totally rejected, private property in the means of production was retained. The Charter of Labor (1927) stated: "The Corporate State considers private enterprise in the sphere of production to be the most effective and useful instrument in the interest of the nation." Profits as an important share of the national dividend were preserved but the profit motive as the coordinating principle of the economic system was replaced by comprehensive controls over prices, wages, foreign trade, and all other important phases of economic life. Fascism succeeded in preventing revolution, but it led directly to imperialism and national disaster for Italy in the Second World War. Mussolini came to an inglorious end in April, 1945, when, in attempting to flee Italy in the disguise of a German soldier, he was shot by Italian partisans and his body hung upside down beside that of his mistress in a public square.

Socialism and Fascism in Germany During the Interwar Period

Capitalism survived in Germany between the First and Second World Wars under unusual circumstances. From 1918 to 1932 it was administered by socialists, who did not believe in capitalism, and after 1933 it was administered by the Nazis, who disguised their acceptance of capitalism under a heavily regimented system of state control oriented toward war. The leading events in Germany's economic development during the interwar years were revolution in 1918, inflation in 1923, rationalization and relative prosperity from 1924 to 1929, severe depression accompanied by Hitler's rise to power from 1929 to 1933, rapid economic recovery based on public works and armaments from 1934 to 1939, and finally the invasion of Poland in September, 1939.

Revolution came to Germany in 1918 in the wake of military defeat and collapse of the Empire which the Hohenzollerns had established in 1871. The events of 1918 discredited the old ruling classes, including the military group

which had been the senior party in a political alliance with German capitalists
since the German industrial revolution began in the 1870's. For historical reasons Germany had no strong middle-class political party and therefore, with
the fall from grace of the old ruling hierarchy, leadership fell to the working-
class party, the Social Democrats. Although Marxist in doctrine, the Social
Democrats were gradualists in practice. Consequently, the German Revolution
of 1918 turned out to be a relatively mild affair. Although carried out by
socialists, it was not a socialist revolution; in a sense it was no revolution at
all because there was no rupture of class structure, no redistribution of wealth
and income, no challenge to established religion, no break-up of large Junker
estates, no nationalization of industrial property.

At the armistice in 1918 the Social Democrats collaborated with the
German army to put down incipient attempts at a fundamental revolution
similar to the one which had occurred in Russia the previous year. On the
day preceding the armistice that ended the war, the Social Democratic leader
and first president of the Weimar Republic, Ferdinand Ebert, made a secret
agreement with Marshal von Hindenburg, the chief surviving war leader still
in Germany, for steering a course of revolution along "safe" lines. Ebert is
reported to have said of his understanding with von Hindenburg, "We allied
ourselves in order to fight Bolshevism." [4]

In the ensuing years the Social Democrats assumed nominal leadership
of the Weimar Republic. They were in office much of the time but never
really in power. They administered German capitalism, thus assuming responsibility for its faults, but they could not bring themselves to convert it to a
socialist society. The Great Inflation and the Great Depression were shocks
to German economic life which the socialists were in no position to control
but for which they could plausibly be held responsible. This is a clue to the
subsequent fall of German political democracy and the rise to power of Hitler.

After passing rapidly from military defeat to revolution and inflation,
Germany entered a relaxed and prosperous "Indian Summer" between 1924
and 1929. By 1928, within new and smaller boundaries, German industrial
production exceeded that of the larger Germany of 1913. Under the spur of
rationalization, productivity per worker increased by 25 per cent between 1924
and 1929. Real wages rose and profits rose even more. Reparations settled into
an orderly routine after 1924, with the burden being met with borrowed
capital. Meanwhile a disarmed Germany was free from the burden of re-
armaments. Heavy industry was advancing with rapid strides to place Germany in the vanguard of European industrial nations.

Yet, as with many placid streams, swifter and more dangerous currents
lurked beneath the surface. The war had settled few issues and had raised
many others. Political democracy was a new experience for the German people.
The Social Democrats had championed political democracy since their formation as a political party in the nineteenth century, but they had never experienced an opportunity to practice it in national politics. In principle the
Social Democrats were committed to a socialist commonwealth, but they
believed in attaining it gradually by persuasion through the instruments of
parliamentary government. They rejected violent revolution as inconsistent

[4] For a discussion of the 1918 revolution and the Weimar Republic, see Franz L.
Neumann, *Behemoth* (New York: Oxford University Press, 1944), Chapter 1.

with political democracy. Socialism remained their ultimate goal but they refused to press for speedy nationalization of industry. The other powerful party of the left, the Communists, favored decisive action, pointing to the success of the revolution in Russia in 1917 in the wake of military defeat in an international war. The Social Democrats and Communists were unable to join ranks at any time during the 1920's, a split which was in the end to prove fatal for both groups as well as for Germany as a nation.

The power groups of the old Germany—Junker landlords and army generals, monopoly capitalists, the civil service, and the judiciary—were frankly suspicious of political democracy and doubly so when it arrived under the tutelage of socialism. They might tolerate political democracy but not socialism, which would destroy their special privileges. Industrialists in the heavy industries gained wealth and prestige as they guided Germany's economy back to predominance among European nations in the late 1920's. Their position was reinforced by general acceptance, even among the trade unionists, of the illusion that cartels could stabilize capitalism. Although the Social Democrats were the strongest group in the legislature, the civil service bureaucracy remained under the control of conservatives. German courts were strongly counter-revolutionary. The German general staff, temporarily discredited by failure in the field, waited in the wings for an opportune time to re-enter the national stage. What the conservative and reactionary groups lacked was mass support. When the crisis came, this was provided by the embittered middle class in the Nazi Party under Adolph Hitler.

The Nazis remained a relatively insignificant party prior to the Great Depression. In the election of 1928 Hitler's party polled 810,000 votes, the largest number it had ever received. Early in 1928 conferences between Hitler and the large industrialists resulted in financial aid for the purpose of developing popular support for the Nazi Party. After the economic collapse of 1929, the left became more radical and the right more reactionary. Communist strength increased to 6 million votes in the elections of 1932. Most of the Communist gains were at the expense of the Social Democrats, whose moderateness in the face of harsh events caused the more radical workers to lose faith in Social Democratic leadership. The success of Russia's first five-year plan contrasted with the world-wide breakdown of capitalism (which the Communists had predicted at the height of capitalist prosperity) bolstered Communist prestige and political strength. The combined popular vote of the Communists and Social Democrats continued to represent a majority of the total vote until after Hitler's seizure of power. If the two left groups had found some way to cooperate, they could have defeated Hitler's bid for power. Time was on the side of the left. They seemed destined to win if they stuck together and if the right did not crush the democratic machinery of the Weimar Republic.

For the forces of the right, time was short. This helps to account for the willingness of wealthy groups to advance generous financial support to the Nazis. Business groups which contributed funds to Hitler included the National Chamber of Commerce, the National Federal German Employers' Association, and the National Federation of German Industry, along with the Junker Herrenklub. Hitler appealed for votes against the Communist threat, the injustice of Versailles, and mass unemployment, which reached 7 million in 1932. The Nazi popular vote rose from less than a million in 1928 to

6,406,000 in 1930 (107 Reichstag seats), to 13,733,000 in July, 1932. At this

point it began to decline, falling two million to 11,737,000 in November, 1932. The sum of the Social Democratic and Communist popular vote exceeded 13 million. At this point in the political crisis the Social Democrats decided to seek support from the center parties rather than from the far left. The leaders of the Catholic Centre Party were the conservative Brüning and the reactionary von Papen.

Marshal von Hindenburg was re-elected President in 1932 with the support of the Social Democrats and the Centre Party. He was basically anti-democratic but had disappointed his monarchical supporters during his first term from 1925 to 1932. Shortly after re-election in 1932 he became frightened by proposals to break up large landed estates in his native East Prussia and dismissed Brüning from the chancellorship and appointed von Papen, the reactionary aristocrat, who had left the Centre Party to join the ultra-conservative Nationalist Party. Von Papen's ministry got nowhere with the hostile majority in the Reichstag. He resigned after the election of November, 1932, in which the Nazi popular vote fell by two million and their Reichstag seats by 34. Hindenburg then appointed von Schleicher, another conservative, to the chancellorship. Meanwhile the Junkers and industrial leaders, who had been paying debts of the Nazi Party, became convinced that their cause could be rescued only by collaboration with Hitler's Nazis. A Cologne banker, Baron von Schröder, arranged a conference between Hitler and von Papen which led Hindenburg to appoint Hitler chancellor in January, 1933.

Thus the forces of organized business, supported by the landowners, the bureaucracy, and the military, embraced Hitler to save Germany from socialism. In Germany, as in Italy under Mussolini, the counter-revolution triumphed. Industrial Germany had passed through a brief democratic phase only to return to the path of imperialistic expansion. Socialism by means of parliamentary gradualism had failed, and political democracy perished with it.

Once in office, Hitler destroyed his political opposition. The Social Democratic and Communist Parties were liquidated, labor unions were destroyed and their funds confiscated, and many of the political and labor leaders were killed or placed in concentration camps. Whether Hitler's dictatorship was a hollow victory for organized business and large landowners depends on how one assesses the alternative. Certainly the conservatives underestimated Hitler as a force *sui generis*.

After assuming power Hitler was not very circumspect about the way he treated those who had given him financial and political support on the road to power. The wealth of some former supporters like Fritz Thyssen, the Ruhr industrialist, was expropriated.[5] The passionate aim of the Nazis to remain in power required no genuine revolution. Private property in the means of production remained, and in some instances socialized property was converted to private ownership. The inequalities of income and wealth characteristic of capitalism remained. As in Mussolini's Italy, the rich remained rich, except for the Jews, and the poor remained poor. Unemployed workers were given employment. Compulsory cartelization strengthened industrial mo-

---

[5] See Fritz Thyssen, *I Paid Hitler* (New York: Hodder & Stoughton, 1941), for an interesting account of an industrialist's support and subsequent maltreatment by Hitler.

nopolies. Dividends were limited to 6 per cent, but there was no limit placed on corporate earnings retained in a company.

Although private property and income inequalities remained, the right to control privately owned property was severely limited by state interference and regimentation. Nazi economic policy continued and expanded the public works and pump-priming policies as stimulants to private enterprise. War preparation and then war became the dominant fact of economic life, and state controls were rapidly extended and tightened. A leading student of the Nazi movement, Franz Neumann, summed up the position of capitalism in Nazi Germany in the following manner: "The German economy today (1942) has two broad and striking characteristics. It is a monopolistic economy—*and* a command economy. It is a private capitalistic economy, regimented by the totalitarian state. We suggest as a name best to describe it, 'Totalitarian Monopoly Capitalism.' . . . the automatism of free capitalism, precarious even under a democratic monopoly capitalism, has been severely restricted. But capitalism remains." [6]

Among European industrial nations Germany suffered the greatest decline in employment and national income during the Great Depression. Manufacturing decreased by more than 40 per cent between 1928 and 1932. Unemployment stood at 7,000,000 when Hitler took office in January, 1933. The unemployed were absorbed rapidly and by the end of the first Four-Year Plan in 1936 the problem was substantially licked. Public works took the form of road building (autobahns), canal building, public buildings, some public housing, land reclamation and drainage. The government also undertook some industrial expansion, including construction of the huge Hermann Goering Works for utilizing low-grade iron ores and an immense automobile plant to turn out a *Volkswagen*, or "people's car." Married women initially were encouraged to withdraw from employment in order to make jobs available for unemployed males. Later, as a manpower shortage appeared, the policy was dropped and women were encouraged to accept employment.

Under the second Four-Year Plan, beginning in 1937, rearmament became the chief objective of national economic policy in Germany. In order to minimize dependence on imported raw materials a vast program to manufacture synthetic materials got under way. The one raw material which Germany had in abundance was coal, and it was used to manufacture synthetic rubber and oil, two essentials for a mechanized military force. German chemists produced ersatz textile fibers as substitutes for wool and cotton. Ingenious German scientists performed miracles in producing many other substitute products. These synthetic products were usually inferior to and frequently more costly than products from natural raw materials, but they were within the control of German labor and materials and therefore valuable contributions to Germany's war program.

By 1938 Germany's industrial production had more than doubled the 1932 output. Using 1928 as 100, manufacturing output was 58 in 1932 and 126 in 1938. Agricultural output also increased, but much more slowly than industry. Again taking 1928 as 100, agricultural output was 106 in 1932 and 115 in 1938. Although most of the increased output after 1936 went into military

[6] Franz L. Neumann, *Behemoth*, pp. 261, 361.

production, aggregate and per capita consumption seem to have risen as well, not only above the low depression level of 1932 but also above the relatively high levels of 1928 and 1929.

For six years during the Second World War the German economy supported a vast military machine without substantially undermining the standard of living of German civilians. This was truly a remarkable economic performance. At crucial points during the war, circumstances would not have had to be greatly different for the Germans to have won the war. What this would have meant for the postwar German economy, and for all of Europe and the world, is an interesting but hardly a fruitful speculation.

As a socio-economic experiment the Nazi regime must be judged a failure at the bar of history. It did not survive, and survival is one, although not the only, criterion of success. Hitler proclaimed that he was building a system which would last a thousand years. His prediction missed by 987 years. In the unlucky thirteenth year of Hitler's reign the Nazi regime collapsed amidst the holocaust of war. As the Russian armies marched into Berlin in May, 1945, Hitler with his bride and a few other intimate associates destroyed themselves much as they had destroyed their country—and their bodies were consumed in the flames of a burning bunker. Thus ended in violence a system which exalted war as the supreme test of national strength and valor. By its own test it failed and by its own means it perished.

SELECTED BIBLIOGRAPHY

BENHAM, FREDERIC C., *Great Britain Under Protection*. New York: The Macmillan Company, 1941.

BONN, MORITZ J., *The Crumbling of Empire: The Disintegration of World Economy*. London: George Allen & Unwin, Ltd., 1938.

BOWDEN, WITT, MICHAEL KARPOVICH, and ABBOTT P. USHER, *An Economic History of Europe Since 1750*. Chapters 39, 40, 41. New York: American Book Company, 1937.

BRADY, ROBERT A., *Business as a System of Power*. New York: Columbia University Press, 1943.

———, *The Spirit and Structure of German Fascism*. New York: The Viking Press, 1937.

GREGORY, THEODORE E., *The Gold Standard and Its Future*, 3rd ed. New York: E. P. Dutton & Co., Inc., 1935.

———, *Gold, Unemployment and Capitalism*. London: P. S. King & Son, 1933.

GUILLEBAUD, CLAUDE W., *The Economic Recovery of Germany, from 1933 to the Incorporation of Austria in March, 1938*. London: Macmillan & Co., Ltd., 1939.

———, *The Social Policy of Nazi Germany*. London: Cambridge University Press, 1941.

HOOVER, CALVIN B., *Germany Enters the Third Reich*. New York: The Macmillan Company, 1933.

———, *Memoirs of Capitalism, Communism, and Nazism*. Durham, N. C.: Duke University Press, 1965.

KEYNES, JOHN M., *The Economic Consequences of Mr. Churchill*. London: Leonard and Virginia Woolf, 1925.

KEYNES, JOHN M., with H. D. HENDERSON, *Can Lloyd George Do It? An Examination of the Liberal Pledge.* London: Nation & Athenaeum, 1929.

LASKI, HAROLD J., *Reflections on the Revolution of Our Time.* New York: The Viking Press, 1943.

LEAGUE OF NATIONS, *The Network of World Trade.* Geneva: League of Nations, 1942.

LEAGUE OF NATIONS, *World Economic Survey.* Geneva: League of Nations, annual 1932 to 1944.

NEARING, SCOTT, *The British General Strike: An Interpretation of Its Background and Its Significance.* New York: Vanguard Press, Inc., 1927.

NEUMANN, FRANZ L., *Behemoth, The Structure and Practice of National Socialism, 1933–1944.* New York: Oxford University Press, 1944.

POOLE, KENYON E., *German Financial Policies, 1932–1939.* Cambridge, Mass.: Harvard University Press, 1939.

REVEILLE, THOMAS, *The Spoil of Europe: The Nazi Technique in Political and Economic Conquest.* New York: W. W. Norton & Company, Inc., 1941.

SCHWEITZER, ARTHUR, *Big Business in the Third Reich.* Bloomington, Ind.: Indiana University Press, 1964.

WOLFE, MARTIN, *The French Franc between the Wars, 1919–1939.* New York: Columbia University Press, 1951.

YEAGER, LELAND B., *International Monetary Relations, Theory, History, and Policy,* Part II. New York: Harper & Row, Publishers, 1966.

ARTICLES

BALOGH, THOMAS, "The National Economy of Germany," *Economic Journal,* XLVIII (Sept., 1938), 461–97.

CLOUGH, SHEPARD B., "The Evolution of Fascist Economic Practice and Theory, 1926–1930." *Harvard Business Review,* X (April, 1932), 302–10.

GALBRAITH, JOHN K., "Hereditary Land in the Third Reich," *Quarterly Journal of Economics,* LIII (May, 1939), 465–76.

GREGORY, THEODORE E., "The Economic Significance of 'Gold Maldistribution,'" *Manchester School of Economics and Social Studies,* II, No. 2 (1931), 77–85.

GUILLEBAUD, CLAUDE W., "Hitler's New Economic Order for Europe," *Economic Journal,* L (Dec., 1940), 449–60.

HALLGARTEN, GEORGE W. F., "Adolph Hitler and German Heavy Industry, 1931–33," *Journal of Economic History,* XII (Summer, 1952), 222–46.

KESSLER, WILLIAM C., "The New German Cartel Legislation: July 15, 1933," *American Economic Review,* XXIV (Sept., 1934), 477–82.

————, "The German Corporation Law of 1937," *American Economic Review,* XXVIII (Dec., 1938), 653–62.

KEYNES, JOHN M., "The French Stabilization Law," *Economic Journal,* XXXVIII (Sept., 1928), 490–94.

LEDERER, EMIL, "Who Pays for German Armament?" *Social Research,* V (Feb., 1938), 70–83.

LIEFMANN, ROBERT, "German Industrial Reorganization Since the World War," *Quarterly Journal of Economics,* XL (Nov., 1925), 82–110.

ROBERTSON, DENNIS H., "A Narrative of the General Strike of 1926," *Economic Journal,* XXXVI (Sept., 1926), 375–93.

SCHWEITZER, ARTHUR, "Big Business and Private Property Under the Nazis," *Journal of Business,* XIX (Apr., 1946), 99–126.

————, "The Role of Foreign Trade in the Nazi War Economy," *Journal of Political Economy,* LI (Aug., 1943), 322–37.

SMITH, LAWRENCE, "England's Return to the Gold Standard in 1925," *Journal of Economic and Business History*, IV (Feb., 1932), 228–58.

WILLIAMS, DAVID, "London and the 1931 Financial Crisis," *Economic History Review*, XV (April, 1963), 512–28.

WUNDERLICH, FRIEDA, "Germany's Defense Economy and the Decay of Capitalism," *Quarterly Journal of Economics*, LII (May, 1938), 401–30.

Interwar Growth and Stagnation in the American Economy: The 1920's, Prosperity Decade

CHAPTER 31

A decade of stagnation followed a decade of growth in the American economy between the First and Second World Wars. The rate of growth during the 1920's was one of the most rapid while the stagnation of the 1930's was the most severe in United States history. Accordingly, the interwar period has been aptly described as one of "boom and bust." The cyclical pattern in the American economy between the two World Wars resembled that of Europe, but the fluctuations were more extreme. The American prosperity of the twenties reached greater heights and the depression of the thirties greater depths than in Europe.

In the total economic landscape, pulsation in the rate of capital formation was the strategic factor accounting for the flow and ebb of economic activity in the interwar decades. A high rate of capital formation was the primary cause of the expansion in the twenties and a negligible rate of capital formation was the primary factor leading to the depression of the thirties.

Further insight into the boom-and-bust experience is gained by recognition of the two-fold process involved in capital formation, or (real) investment. Capital formation, on the one hand, increases present capacity to consume by disbursing income into the hands of consumers; and, on the other hand, it increases future capacity to produce by enlarging productive plant. Under capitalism there exists no mechanism for maintaining a balance between capacity to consume and capacity to produce. Through the 1920's the building of new factories created the additional incomes required to buy the products of factories already built. However, in order to keep the increasing number of factories running a capitalistic society must always be building more new factories. Toward the end of the 1920's difficulties arose because the capacity to produce outran the capacity to consume and reduced the demand for new productive capacity (capital formation), which in turn lowered further the capacity to consume. Once new factories ceased to be built, the demand for the output of the existing factories slumped off and led to idle plant and unemployed workers. Consequently, much of the new capacity built during the boom of the 1920's was not utilized during the 1930's. Factories as well as men were unemployed on a massive scale. The interwar experience illustrates dramatically that a capitalist economy cannot stand still and enjoy prosperity. It must either grow or stagnate. American capitalism grew during the twenties and stagnated during the thirties.

IMPACT OF THE FIRST WORLD WAR
ON THE AMERICAN ECONOMY

563

INTERWAR
GROWTH AND
STAGNATION
IN THE
AMERICAN
ECONOMY

Any lingering doubts concerning the superior productivity of the American economy were removed by its tremendous performance during the First World War. Once the American economy got tooled up for war production, Allied victory became assured. Germany's leaders did not underestimate the productive capacity of the United States so much as they overestimated the ability of German submarines to prevent delivery from American factories to European shores. Although American fighting men contributed to the Allied victory, the decisive factor which sealed Germany's defeat was the ability of the United States to deliver food, arms, and other products of an inordinately productive economic machine.

One manifestation of the changed role in the world economy of the United States was its shift from a debtor to a creditor nation. Prior to World War I foreigners, mostly Europeans, had more capital invested in the United States than American nationals had invested in foreign countries. Foreigners each year received more income from investments in the United States than Americans received from investments in foreign countries. After the war positions were reversed, with Americans having more capital invested in foreign countries and receiving more income from these investments than foreigners had investments in, and income from, the United States.

Although the shift from debtor to creditor status was precipitated by the war, the change would have occurred anyway, perhaps during the 1920's, even if there had been no war. During the age of mass production the rapid increase in national income generated massive savings seeking investment outlets, and while opportunities for investment within the United States were still great, the large-scale export of capital was a normal consequence of enlarged savings. Only in the sense that the $11 billion war debt owed to the United States tipped the balance can it be said that the war was responsible for the shift from debtor to creditor status. In any event, the new position of the United States in the world economy meant that the traditional economic and political isolationism which still dominated American foreign policy could not be maintained without serious consequences for the United States and, more particularly, for the rest of the world.

Unfortunately, American policy became more rather than less isolationist in the postwar years. Isolationism was manifest in higher tariffs, war debt policy, new immigration laws, and failure to join the League of Nations. The Fordney-McCumber Tariff of 1922 raised American protectionism to the highest level in the country's history up to that time. The narrow view toward war debts, discussed previously, showed a disregard for the plight of Europe and was totally inconsistent with the elevation of tariff barriers, since repayment of war debts could only be made by importing more goods and not by keeping foreign goods out with high tariff walls. Legislation in 1921 and 1924 reduced the permissible number of immigrants and reversed a policy of liberal immigration for the downtrodden and persecuted masses of Europe. Through a system of country-by-country quotas based ultimately on the national origins of the United States population, the new immigration policy cut drastically the numbers eligible to come from southern and eastern Europe.

564

*INTERWAR
GROWTH AND
STAGNATION
IN THE
AMERICAN
ECONOMY*

Restrictions on emigration from these overpopulated areas rendered Europe's adjustment to postwar conditions more difficult.[1] Failure of the United States to join the League of Nations was perhaps not of great direct economic significance, although regular membership would have increased the influence of the League and of the United States in the international organizations associated with the League such as the International Labour Office in Geneva.

Primary Postwar Depression, 1920–21

After a slight dip in business activity immediately following the armistice in November, 1918, a boomlet got under way and carried through to the middle of 1920. A major initiating factor in this postwar expansion was a large federal deficit resulting from expenditures after the armistice on ships and other construction plus a large export surplus of food and other materials to war-devastated Europe. For the fiscal year ending June, 1919, federal government expenditures exceeded federal revenues by $13.4 billion, by far the largest deficit experienced in the United States prior to the Second World War. Large deficit spending in the midst of nearly full employment set off an inflationary price spiral. Inflation attained such a strong upward movement that it became self-reinforcing in the sense that prices rose because prices rose as businessmen hastened to restock inventories before prices climbed still higher. Business inventories increased during 1920 by more than $6 billion, two-thirds of which represented an increase in the physical volume of goods and one-third an increase in prices. In setting off the inflationary spiral, speculation in business inventories was a more potent force than consumer demand.

The postwar boomlet collapsed in mid-1920 and was followed by a depression which, while not protracted, was both very sharp and very deep. On business cycle charts the 1920 fall-off in economic activity is the most rapid ever recorded. Among the important causes of the depression were (1) a rapid shift from a stimulating government deficit to a deflating government surplus; (2) a large decline in the United States export surplus as European nations exhausted their supply of gold and dollars; and (3) the collapse of the inflationary price spiral, which had been motivated and prolonged by speculative activity.

Government fiscal policy was influenced by the prevailing ideology that sound finance required an early budget surplus in order to begin paying off the large public debt accumulated during the war. The decline in the export surplus lowered farm prices and rudely reversed the war-born prosperity enjoyed by American farmers between 1915 and 1920. Wheat prices slid from $2.50 to less than $1.00 per bushel in 1921; corn prices fell from $1.88 in 1919 to $.42 per bushel in 1921; cotton prices from $.36 to $.14 a pound. Nearly half a million farmers lost their farms in this early postwar debacle. Most of the victims had responded during the war to patriotic and pecuniary incentives to expand production, which they had financed with mortgage money at a time when prices and interest rates were high.

Businessmen as well as farmers fared badly after the speculative bubble burst in mid-1920. The wholesale price index of manufactured goods fell from

---

[1] On this point, see Ingvar Svennilson, *Growth and Stagnation in the European Economy* (Geneva: United Nations, 1954), Chapter 4.

240 in 1920 (1913 = 100) to 155 in 1922, a decline of 35 per cent in one year.
The transition from rising to falling prices set off a crisis of liquidation of inventories in the second half of 1920. Bank credit reached the limits of expansion under the gold standard. Interest rates shot up, and bank loans secured
by high-priced inventories could not be renewed. Businessmen, caught with
excessive inventories purchased at speculative prices, tried to get out from
under by unloading their goods for cash as quickly as possible. In the process
more than 100,000 business firms went bankrupt.

*INTERWAR
GROWTH AND
STAGNATION
IN THE
AMERICAN
ECONOMY*

The real as distinguished from the monetary factor in this first postwar
business cycle was fluctuations in investment. Gross investment declined $10.5
billion (from $22 to $11.5 billion) between 1920 and 1921, with 70 per cent
of this being made up of decline in investment in inventories. National income
fell from $79 billion to $64 billion between 1920 and 1921. Unemployment in
1921 reached approximately 5 million or more than 10 per cent of the labor
force. This was a severe primary postwar depression.

NEW ERA PROSPERITY

The primary postwar depression was severe while it lasted but it did not last
very long. Contraction continued through the first half of 1921, but by the fall
of that year revival got under way and 1922 saw the return to prosperity.
Apart from minor recessions in 1924 and 1927, the years from 1922 to 1929
represented a period of unprecedented prosperity. From these ebullient years
the decade of the 1920's has become known as the "Prosperity Decade," the
"Golden Twenties," the "New Era."

Two crucial factors which explain the New Era prosperity of the United
States during the 1920's were the rapid increase in consumer expenditures for
durable goods and the high level of capital formation in residential construction and new industries such as automobiles, household appliances, chemicals,
and certain other growth industries. Prosperity requires a high level of total
spending out of the components of national income. It requires spending by
consumers for goods and services, by businessmen for capital formation, and
by government for government purchases. Government spending in the United
States was relatively small during the 1920's, so the burden of maintaining
prosperity rested on the willingness and ability of consumers and businessmen
to spend.

An examination of the statistics of national income and consumption for
the United States during the 1920's reveals that consumption increased more
or less proportionately to increases in income, a crucial fact in explaining the
long duration of prosperity. A closer look at the facts shows further that consumer expenditures on durable goods increased twice as rapidly as expenditures on non-durables (e.g., food) and semi-durables (e.g., clothes). The output of food increased scarcely more than population; food production rose
1.6 per cent per year and population 1.4 per cent per year on the average between 1922 and 1929. Semi-durable goods (mostly clothes) increased slightly
more rapidly than food; textile output increased 2.2 per cent as compared
with 1.6 per cent for food. Another semi-durable, boots and shoes, actually
decreased, caused perhaps by the substitution of automobile travel for walking!

566

*INTERWAR
GROWTH AND
STAGNATION
IN THE
AMERICAN
ECONOMY*

All non-durables and semi-durables combined increased at an annual rate of 2.8 per cent in the period 1922–29. Among non-durables the average was raised by a high rate of increase in gasoline consumption, and among semi-durables by a high rate of increase in rubber tires, both of which were auxiliary to automobiles, the leading consumer durable good. Between 1914 and 1929 the proportion of total consumption going for food and clothing declined from 59 per cent to 44 per cent.

In contrast to the 2.8 per cent annual increase in non-durable and semi-durable goods, was a 5.6 per cent annual increase in the output of durable goods. This rate of growth in consumer durables resembled more nearly the growth in capital equipment, at 6.4 per cent, than the increase in other consumption goods. The per capita consumption of perishable and semi-durable goods had reached a plateau in the average family budget, and most of the increases in the standard of living were going into durable goods—goods which would yield their utilities slowly over a period of time.[2] This meant that current production was in excess of current (actual) consumption of the utilities stored up in the consumer durables. This process continued for the greater part of a decade and led to a vast accumulation of potential utilities in the possession of consumers but not yet realized. It helped to sustain prosperity during the 1920's, but it also meant that consumers might subsequently consume currently more utilities than they purchased currently, in which event demand would decline and the prosperity would be endangered. The increasing proportion of durable goods production in total production undoubtedly increased the potential instability of production in the American economy, especially toward the end of the decade.

Construction

During the war years a pressing demand for manpower and building materials in war uses led to restrictions on residential construction. In the 1920's the brisk demand for housing arose from (1) the backlog from the war, (2) a growing population, and (3) the general and widening prosperity which enabled many families to afford better housing than they had previously enjoyed. Between 1920 and 1924 the annual value of residential construction increased nearly three-fold, from $1.8 billion to $4.8 billion. Single-family dwellings reached a peak in 1925 and multi-family apartments in 1926, after which residential construction declined. By 1929 residential construction was 45 per cent below the 1925 volume. A significant new stimulus to housing during the 1920's was the movement of population toward the suburbs. Breadwinners with steady jobs could afford a home in the suburbs and commute to work by automobile. The ubiquity of automobiles permitted factories to be located away from centers of population. The reciprocal demand for automobiles and suburban housing was a significant new development in the American economy during the New Era.

Non-residential private construction also increased rapidly during the 1920's. Commercial construction, including office buildings, stores, and ware-

---

[2] A durable good is defined here as one with a useful life in excess of two years. Most of the statistics in this discussion are drawn from F. C. Mills, *Economic Tendencies in the United States* (New York: National Bureau of Economic Research, 1932), esp. Chapter 6.

houses, reached a peak in 1927, declined in 1928, but came back strongly in 1929, although the 1927 peak was not again equaled. Industrial plant was the only major type of construction to attain a peak as late as 1929. Private construction, residential and non-residential combined, reached a peak in 1928; the housing decline after 1925 was offset by non-residential increases. A sharp fall in residential construction between 1926 and 1929 was quantitatively the most important cause of the decline in total construction after 1928.

The upsurge in private construction to 1925 met the accumulated deficiencies inherited from the First World War. After the mid-twenties the continuation of construction at a high level for several years appears to have been more than sufficient to meet the needs of the period. In a sense the building boom was feeding on itself, providing more facilities than the overall rate of growth in the economy required, and in this sense creating capacity which would be justified, if at all, only in terms of sustained future growth. The rest of the economy would have to grow up to this "excess" capacity. As will be seen, when construction declined, growth ceased, and facilities were much in excess of the current demand for them. This became strikingly evident in the large amount of vacant housing and idle plant and office space during the depression of the 1930's.

With the coming of age of the automobile during the Golden Twenties, a vast national network of improved highways was constructed. The burden of building and maintaining streets and highways fell mainly on local and state governments, but the federal government entered the field as coordinator of a national network of highways and also made financial contributions to the construction and maintenance of the federal highway system. Improved roads got farmers out of the mud and enabled urban dwellers to enjoy the beauties and the billboards of the countryside. Other forms of public construction also boomed during the twenties as a consequence of population growth and rising incomes. School construction was stimulated by the increasing proportion of young people attending high schools. A by-product of rising family incomes was a demand for an improved type of school construction. Increased use of automobiles, including school busses, and improved roads tended to displace the rural schoolhouse with larger and better equipped urban and suburban schools. Total public construction, including federal, state and local, in the late twenties exceeded total public construction in any year of the New Deal; during the thirties a drastic curtailment of state and local projects more than offset increases in federal public works.

Automobiles

The most dynamic single growth factor in the American economy during the 1920's was the automobile industry. Although European inventors developed most of the early mechanical models, the significant commercial development of the automobile was peculiarly an American phenomenon. For this there were several reasons, two of the most important being the higher level of per capita income widely dispersed among American consumers and the advanced stage of mass production already developed in the United States. Henry Ford applied mass production, mass assembly, and mass marketing techniques to automobiles prior to the First World War. By concentrating on

568

INTERWAR
GROWTH AND
STAGNATION
IN THE
AMERICAN
ECONOMY

a single model, the popular Model T, Ford took advantage of economies of scale and was able to produce automobiles at progressively lower costs and sell at lower prices, thus tapping a larger and larger market. He converted the automobile from a luxury to a necessity. The standardization of the Model T is illustrated by Henry Ford's quip in 1909 that a customer could have a Ford painted any color he wanted so long as it was black.

Although the automobile industry got off to a vigorous start before the First World War, it did not come of age until the 1920's. At the beginning of the war the annual production of passenger cars had reached the half-million mark; the one-million mark was passed in 1916; the two-million mark in 1922; the three-million mark in 1923; and the four-million mark in 1929. Including trucks, the four-million mark was exceeded in 1928 and the five-million mark in 1929. By the late twenties the replacement demand alone was about three million automobiles per year.

The motor vehicle industry ranked first in value of product among American manufacturing industries in 1928. Automobiles also ranked first in value of exports. The United States produced 83 per cent of the world's total automobile output in 1928 and approximately twenty times as many automobiles as the second largest producing nation (Canada). Nearly half a million workers were directly employed in the automobile industry, and, including all the satellite industries, motor vehicles directly and indirectly provided employment for four million workers in a civilian labor force of less than 48 million in 1929.

The enormous size and rapid growth of the automobile industry stimulated an impressive group of satellite industries, including petroleum, rubber, plate glass, service garages and filling stations. Auto output and operation affected numerous other industries including iron and steel, leather upholstery, copper, aluminum, lead, tin and hardwood. It gave rise to motels, billboards, hot dog and cold drink stands, the motor truck industry, and during the prohibition era, bootleggers and hijackers. The relationship of motor vehicles to road construction and to suburbanization and factory plant dispersal has already been noted. Automobiles imparted to America the characteristics which distinguished it from other nations during the 1920's, the mass consumption of durable consumer goods. The auto symbolized a new era of higher living standards. Not least in importance was the revolution wrought by motor transportation on the manners and morals of the nation.

Electrical Appliances

Apart from automobiles, the most important consumer durables were household appliances, and in particular electrical appliances, which, like automobiles, dated from the prewar period, but came of age during the Golden Twenties. Electric lighting and telephones were standard household equipment in urban America before the First World War, but the big expansion in electrical manufacturing came after the war. Radios were a brand new commercial product in 1920; by 1925 the industry had become a $500-million-a-year giant; and by 1929 annual sales were pushing toward the billion-dollar mark. Electric washing machines became a common household item during the twenties and did much to lighten a burden which had fallen heavily on

housewives from the beginning of civilization. Cleanliness was further fostered by the vacuum cleaner, another laborsaving device common to middle- and upper-income families. The iceman remained a familiar figure in American communities during the 1920's, but his trade began to melt away as refrigerators replaced the icebox in several million households. Annual sales rose from 315,000 to 1,680,000 refrigerators between 1926 and 1929. Electric stoves, heaters, toasters, and flat irons were among other household appliances operated through the magic of electricity.

569

INTERWAR
GROWTH AND
STAGNATION
IN THE
AMERICAN
ECONOMY

Other Growth Industries

Three other growth industries of the twenties may be noted briefly: chemicals, motion pictures, and commercial aviation. Most branches of the chemical industry dated from several decades before the First World War, but like automobiles and electrical appliances, they came of age during the 1920's. The leadership which Germany had enjoyed in chemistry was badly shaken by the war, and American chemical industries moved into the lead during the 1920's. The motion picture industry also had prewar origins but became a giant and the leading form of commercial entertainment in the United States during the twenties. A major stimulus was the "talkie," or sound picture, introduced in 1928. Total capital invested in the motion picture industry increased during the decade 1921–30 from $75,000,000 to $850,000,000, and the value of annual output of motion picture equipment manufactured also rose several fold during the decade.

Commercial aviation was, like radio, a brand new industry in the postwar era. It expanded very rapidly, especially after 1926, with mail, passengers, and some freight moving by air. Large outlays were made on airfields, weather stations, lighted airways, and in signal and direction-finding apparatus. Interestingly, the aviation industry grew up quite independently of the automobile industry despite many common technological and commercial problems. As compared with automobiles and other new industries discussed above, the aviation industry was still an infant during the New Era, although a rapidly growing one.

Consumer Credit

The proliferation of consumer durables during the 1920's led to a rapid extension of consumer credit in the form of installment selling. Installment buying was by no means new, having been used not only for the purchase of houses, at least since Roman times, but also for expensive goods such as jewelry, encyclopaedias, sewing machines, pianos and other musical instruments, reapers, binders, and other expensive farm machinery. However, except for farm equipment, which is really not a consumer good, the sales of these durables represented a small proportion of total consumer purchases, and the enormous increase in consumer durables during the 1920's did usher in a new and much enlarged use of consumer credit. Actually installment buying represented nothing more than an adaptation of the pay-as-you-consume principle to more durable types of goods. A loaf of bread is paid for today and consumed today; an automobile is paid for over a year or two and consumed over a somewhat

570

*INTERWAR
GROWTH AND
STAGNATION
IN THE
AMERICAN
ECONOMY*

longer period. An automobile is to its owner a kind of investment in future services, and might as logically be financed by consumer credit as a business investment in inventory might be financed by credit from a commercial bank. The analogy is by no means complete, but it is relevant.

Presumably the volume of consumer durables that could have been sold would have been substantially less if only cash sales had been permitted. Since durable goods are usually produced by mass production methods, that is, under conditions involving heavy fixed costs, the pressures to expand sales in order to lower the unit costs led to heavy advertising outlays and other forms of high pressure salesmanship in which one of the inducements to buy was the relatively small periodic payment by the purchaser. That the total cost might be considerably greater was often not apparent, and perhaps not important, to consumers. Although automobiles involved the largest amount of consumer credit in the 1920's, the practice became prevalent for other durables including radios, electric refrigerators, washing machines, and household appliances generally. Installment buying represented an adaptation on the part of sellers to the fundamental phenomenon of a larger proportion of total sales taking the form of durable goods.

SHADOWS OVER THE GOLDEN AGE

Agriculture

All sectors of the American economy did not share in the prosperity of the 1920's, agriculture being the most notable case. Agriculture was still a large but declining sector of the economy; 30 per cent of the population lived on farms in 1920 and 25 per cent in 1930. The number of farmers declined by more than one million during the decade. Depressed conditions in agriculture reflected the painful process by which the market system operates to squeeze out excess producers from a declining sector of an economy.

Collapse of farm prices in 1920 ushered in a depression in agriculture from which there was no significant relief, and farmers were plummeted into even deeper depression by the greater-than-average fall in farm prices after 1929. Farm prices were highly competitive whereas industrial prices tended to become administrative and monopolistic, as will be seen. Consequently, resources which could find no outlet in industry tended to remain in agriculture. Although there was a substantial migration from rural to urban areas, the movement was less rapid than required for a proper balance between industry and agriculture. Farm population became redundant and farm production excessive. Aggravating the American farmers' plight was the loss of world markets, especially for wheat, cotton, and other staples.

Sick Industries

Coal mining   In addition to the agricultural sector generally, there were a number of "sick" industries which remained chronically depressed during the 1920's. Notable among these was bituminous coal. The total demand for coal declined because each ton was utilized with increasing efficiency and because

of growing competition from petroleum products, natural gas, and hydroelec-

tric power. Coal mining, like agriculture, suffered from excess capacity and over-competition. The demand for coal was not very elastic, perhaps inelastic; hence, competitive pressures brought prices down without increasing very much the total quantity of coal sold. Total employment in coal mining declined through the decade. About 25 per cent of the coal miners were chronically unemployed, and even when employed, they worked less than the normal complement of days during the year. Coal miners in America, as elsewhere, were the step children of capitalist civilization; they lived in isolated communities under deplorable conditions and their efforts to improve living conditions were often rebuffed. Industrial warfare flared; violence erupted in disputes between mine owners and workers who attempted to organize labor unions in non-organized territory.

Textiles Another older industry which experienced less than full prosperity during the 1920's was textiles. The cotton and woolen branches of this great industry suffered because they were mature industries, because they were highly competitive within themselves, and because of new competition from synthetic fibers like rayon. One feature in textiles was the geographical shift from New England toward the South.

The decline of textile manufacture in New England and its rapid growth in the South offer an interesting parallel to the decline of textile manufacture in (old) England and its rapid growth in Japan and India during the interwar period. Although American textiles, unlike the British, were protected by high tariffs against world competition, within the boundaries of the United States they operated within a free-trade area. What was needed in New England, as in old England, was a more rapid transformation to industries of higher productivity like metallurgy, machinery, and machine tools, which demand the talents of a skilled labor force and mature managerial skills, which are to be found only in mature industrial regions. Textile manufacture is one of the first manufacturing industries to take hold in newly industrialized areas, where it can utilize semi-skilled workers fresh from rural occupations. Because of generally lower labor productivity, wages in the South were 25 to 60 per cent lower than for comparable tasks in New England. Northern trade unions may have played some role in driving textile manufacturing firms from New England to the South, but wage differentials reflected mainly real differences in regional productivity.

Railroads Rail transport was another sick industry during the prosperity decade. After a great spurt in railroad mileage for more than half a century before the First World War, expansion slowed down and attained a maximum just prior to 1920. An early postwar attempt to consolidate the railroads into a more efficient system proved unsuccessful. Meanwhile competition from other transportation agencies cut into both the passenger and freight revenues of railways. Motor trucks operating on the rapidly expanding network of improved highways provided more flexible service, with special advantages on short hauls for all but the heaviest cargoes. Motor busses and private passenger automobiles cut deeply into rail passenger travel. Although commercial air transportation made its debut during the 1920's, it did not become a serious rival in this decade.

INTERWAR
GROWTH AND
STAGNATION
IN THE
AMERICAN
ECONOMY

Unemployment persisted as a serious problem throughout the 1920's despite general prosperity in all but a few sectors of the economy. For this period there are no official figures on unemployment; the nearest approach was a contemporary estimate by a President's Conference on Unemployment of which Herbert Hoover was nominal chairman (the actual research was directed by Professor Wesley C. Mitchell of Columbia University). The findings showed annual average unemployment of 2,307,000, or a rate of 7.8 per cent among the nonfarm labor force for the years 1920 through 1927; the range was from a low of 1,401,000, or 5.1 per cent, in 1920 to a high of 4,270,000, or 15.3 per cent, in 1921. These figures relate only to nonfarm unemployed and the nonfarm labor force because of the difficulty of estimating agricultural unemployment. There was, however, a large surplus of farm population which was partially unemployed and would have added to the total. In a summary of findings, Professor Mitchell stressed that the statistics on unemployment were minimum figures that "minimize the seriousness of unemployment." [3]

Since World War II an attempt has been made to construct a series of unemployment data back to 1900 on a basis comparable to recent unemployment statistics. Table 31–1 shows these figures for the decade 1920 through

TABLE 31–1

Unemployment in the U.S. During the 1920's

YEAR	NUMBER OF UNEMPLOYED (thousands)	PER CENT OF CIVILIAN LABOR FORCE
1920	1,670	4.0
1921	5,010	11.9
1922	3,220	7.6
1923	1,380	3.2
1924	2,440	5.5
1925	1,800	4.0
1926	880	1.9
1927	1,890	4.1
1928	2,080	4.4
1929	1,550	3.2
Averages:	2,192	5.0

Source: U. S. Bureau of the Census, *Historical Statistics of the United States* (Washington, D.C.: Government Printing Office, 1960), p. 73.

1929, during which period the average annual rate of unemployment was 5 per cent of the total civilian labor force. The rates ranged from a low of 1.9 per

[3] Report of the Committee on Recent Social Changes of the President's Conference on Unemployment (Herbert Hoover, Chairman), *Recent Economic Changes*, II (New York: McGraw-Hill, Inc., 1929), 487, 879.

cent in 1926 to a high of 11.9 per cent in 1921. These are among the lowest estimates of unemployment for the 1920's, and 5 per cent is a substantial amount. For a comparable decade after World War II (1947–56) the annual average rate of unemployment was 3.8 per cent of the civilian labor force. Whatever figures are chosen, unemployment was impressively high in the 1920's for a prosperity decade. They are, of course, low compared with the disastrous decade of the 1930's, when unemployment averaged 18.2 per cent of the civilian labor force.[4]

What was the explanation of this seeming paradox of substantial unemployment in a period of high prosperity? The growth in output, although more rapid than in preceding decades, was not rapid enough to absorb the increasing size of the labor force. Increased output was achieved primarily through higher productivity, measured in terms of output per man-hour of employed labor. In manufacturing, for example, the output which required 100 workers in 1919 could be produced with only 70 workers in 1929. The total number of workers employed in manufacturing industries in the United States remained approximately constant during the 1920's despite a very substantial rise in the total value of output of manufactured goods. The rate at which workers were displaced from their jobs through technological changes became very much higher than it had been in earlier decades. To hold a job in industry became more difficult; the security of employment declined. Absorption into new and expanding industries took place, but not necessarily of the same workers or in a short period of time. Older workers displaced from factories were especially victimized because their chances of reabsorption were poorer than those of younger recruits in the labor force who might be expected to adapt more easily to new types of employment.

Since total employment in agriculture decreased and total employment in manufacturing did not increase, the growing labor force had to find employment in other sectors or remain unemployed. Some were absorbed in the service trades and a substantial number remained unemployed. The paucity of employment opportunities in urban pursuits caused many workers no longer needed in agriculture to remain on the farm. Consequently, the United States developed both a surplus farm population and a surplus urban population.

Since the United States had no system of social security in the 1920's, the unemployed and their families had to subsist on their savings, which were usually small, or submit to the humiliation of accepting charity, or just go hungry, as countless families did because the stigma of acknowledged poverty

---

[4] The relatively high unemployment of the 1920's in the United States seems to have been inadequately comprehended by many writers despite evidence from some leading authorities. Professor Joseph A. Schumpeter speaks repeatedly about the "supernormal" unemployment of the 1920's. See *Business Cycles*, II (New York: McGraw-Hill, Inc., 1939), 509–19 and 803–6. Professor Simon Kuznets shows a difference of 4.5 million between the labor force of 45.1 million and the employed of 40.6 million for the period 1919–28, or 10 per cent unemployment for the decade as a whole. An estimate by the U.S. Bureau of Labor Statistics for 1927 placed unemployment for 1927 at 4,000,000, a figure considerably higher than the one (2,055,000) given by the President's Conference on Unemployment, cited above. Another estimate, by David Weintraub, takes account of the partially as well as the fully employed labor by relating the man-years of unemployed wage-earners to the man-years available by wage-earners. Weintraub's unemployment figures are 25 and 22 per cent respectively for 1921 and 1922; 11 to 13 per cent between 1923 through 1928; and a low of 10 per cent in 1929.

574

INTERWAR
GROWTH AND
STAGNATION
IN THE
AMERICAN
ECONOMY

and unemployment was strong in the mores of the nation. During a golden age in this wealthiest of nations there existed the disconcerting paradox of poverty in the midst of potential plenty.

Although security of employment declined, the wages of employed workers increased both in money and in real terms on both an hourly and a weekly basis. The cost of living remained remarkably stable, rising moderately during the early years of the New Era and declining moderately in the later years. Low farm prices were a major factor holding down the cost of living, but many manufactured products also had stable or declining prices. Hours of labor declined generally with wide differences among industries and occupations. The steel industry abandoned the 84-hour week in 1924, and by 1926 the average had dropped to 54 hours in steel. Factory workers averaged about 50 hours per week in the mid-twenties, and building tradesmen now had Saturday afternoon off after working 44 hours during a 5½-day week.

Despite the reduction in the length of the work week and work year, the annual earnings of employed workers rose. Taking 1920 as a base of 100, the annual real wages of nonfarm workers rose to 115 in 1923, 116 in 1926, and 124 in 1929.[5]

Concentration of Economic Power

Another shadow looming darkly across the horizon in the twenties was increasing concentration of ownership and control in American business enterprise. A new wave of mergers swept the economy, especially toward the end of the decade. Anti-trust enforcement was weakened by the Supreme Court dictum in the 1920 U.S. Steel decision that mere size of a business firm is not a violation of the Sherman Anti-Trust Act. The pro-business administrations of Presidents Harding, Coolidge, and Hoover remained complacent toward business concentration and in this attitude probably reflected the prevailing mood of the public during the New Era, when leaders of big business enjoyed great prestige.

Although few firms approached a monopoly—the Aluminum Company of America and the United Shoe Machinery Company being notable exceptions—oligopolies advanced with giant strides. By the end of the New Era the automobile industry was dominated by three firms—General Motors, Ford, and Chrysler. The farm machinery industry was dominated by International Harvester, which produced about 50 per cent of the total output of the industry. Iron and steel output remained heavily concentrated in U.S. Steel and a few other firms. The three largest cigarette firms sold 70 per cent of the total for the whole industry. The two largest meat packers (Armour and Swift) shipped half of the total meat in interstate commerce. In public utilities the holding company was used to concentrate control in a few hands, the most notorious case of the 1920's being the Insull empire with total assets of $2½ billion largely under the control of one man. Banking also became subject to growing concentration of control. Chain stores began to crowd out independent grocers on a nation-wide scale. Hardly any phase of business enterprise escaped the

---

[5] See W. S. Woytinsky and Associates, *Employment and Wages in the United States* (New York: Twentieth Century Fund, 1953), esp. p. 51.

trend toward large firms and higher degrees of concentration of control. Among **575**

INTERWAR
GROWTH AND
STAGNATION
IN THE
AMERICAN
ECONOMY the reasons for the relatively more rapid growth of large concerns were technological efficiencies, higher earnings rates and the plowing back of profits into
plant expansion, advantages in financing expansion with outside funds garnered
in the ebullient capital market, and mergers with other firms. Business enterprise was not uniformly profitable during the prosperous 1920's, but giant
corporations were seldom among those which failed.

The extent and significance of business concentration were revealed in a
famous study by Berle and Means, *The Modern Corporation and Private Property*.[6] They found that the 200 largest nonfinancial corporations owned 22
per cent of the total national wealth, 38 per cent of all business wealth, and
50 per cent of all corporate wealth in the United States. Control was much
more highly concentrated than ownership and less susceptible to exact measurement. They found that concentration had increased rapidly during the
1920's and would, they predicted, continue to increase.

For the performance of the economy the most important consequence of
the growing concentration of economic power lay in the decline in the free
market as a vehicle for automatic adjustment. In industries dominated by a few
large firms, prices were set by one or a few of the sellers and there was reluctance to change these prices, especially in a downward direction. Firms
bold enough to deviate from the price leadership ran the risk of price wars
from powerful rivals. Such "administered" prices contrasted sharply with free
market prices, which fluctuate readily in response to changes in supply and
demand. Concentration of production in a few firms did not always result in
administered prices (copper), but usually it did. A characteristic of giant firms
operating with administered prices was to respond to a fall in demand for their
product by reducing the amount produced rather than by selling at lower
prices. In a business recession this type of behavior leads to worsening conditions by cutting back on employment and therefore the demand for output in
general. Administered prices robbed the market economy of much-needed
flexibility, made for wasteful allocation of resources, led to maladjustments
with the competitive sector (especially agriculture), contributed to unemployment, and slowed down the rate of economic growth in the economy as a
whole.

COLLAPSE OF THE NEW ERA

Paradoxically, the conditions which generated the New Era prosperity of the
1920's contributed to its collapse by creating conditions incompatible with the
perpetuation of prosperity. A high rate of capital formation disbursed income
to consumers and enlarged the demand for consumers' goods. Consumer spending out of income derived from capital formation supplemented consumer
spending out of income derived from the production of consumers' goods.
Stated in slightly different terms, some of the income derived from the production of consumers' goods was saved, thus leaving a gap between the value of
consumers' goods produced and the amount of spending for consumers' goods.

[6] Adolf A. Berle and Gardiner C. Means, *The Modern Corporation and Private Property* (New York: The Macmillan Company, 1933).

576

INTERWAR
GROWTH AND
STAGNATION
IN THE
AMERICAN
ECONOMY

The gap in consumer demand created by saving was filled by spending on consumers' goods out of income derived from capital formation. Thus capital formation was a stimulant to prosperity in the short run.

In the long run, however, the increase in productive capacity arising from capital formation tended to outrun the capacity to consume and thus destroyed the *raison d'être* of enlarged productive capacity. The ultimate reason for the expansion of plant capacity is to meet the demand for increased consumption. In other words, the increase in demand for capital goods rests ultimately on the demand for consumption goods.

Accordingly, capital formation serves two important functions: It enlarges income and therefore consumer demand, which is derived from income; and it increases productive capacity. A point is reached, however, where no further increase in productive capacity is needed for some time: Capacity becomes excessive when consumer demand can be met from existing plant and equipment. Hence it follows that the higher the rate of capital formation, the higher the level of prosperity in the short run and the greater the probable depression in the longer run: the bigger the preceding boom, the bigger the subsequent bust. Thus plant capacity can be built up to a point where no more of it needs to be built for some time.

In the laissez-faire environment of the 1920's there were no appropriate governmental or other policies to prevent a major boom from degenerating into a major depression. Uneven rates of capital formation have led to successive booms and depressions at least since the Industrial Revolution, and what happened in the 1920's and 1930's represented a continuation of the business cycle pattern. The collapse of prosperity in 1929, although not inevitable, had a long historical precedent and deep roots in the existing institutional structure of the American economy.

In the late 1920's the decline in capital formation in construction, automobiles, and the household appliances industry led to the collapse of the New Era prosperity and the beginning of the Great Depression. Many other forces were operating, including the stock exchange and price rigidities, but the dynamic growth of these three important sectors (discussed earlier in this chapter) holds the clue to the rapid expansion of the twenties, and their contraction to the collapse of that prosperity.

Leveling Off of Capital Formation in the Growth Industries

Construction The most important single component of total construction, residential building, reached a peak as early as 1925. The number of new dwelling units started each year during the 1920's is shown in Table 31–2. The decrease from 937,000 dwelling units in 1925 to 509,000 in 1929 represents a 45 per cent decline. The steady fall after 1925 suggests that the war-created backlog had been made up by the mid-twenties and that thereafter the housing market gradually became saturated in the sense that families that could afford modern housing had obtained it by the end of the twenties. The nation possessed a large volume of recently completed dwellings which would continue to be utilized for several decades. Except for public housing projects,

relatively few new dwellings were constructed until after the Second World War.

The early decline in residential building was offset for a while by the continued rise in non-residential construction. As noted previously, total construction reached a peak in 1928 and fell off substantially in 1929. This was the first major factor in the decline in capital formation prior to the collapse of prosperity in 1929.

TABLE 31–2

Urban Residential Construction, 1920–29

YEAR	DWELLING UNITS	YEAR	DWELLING UNITS
1920	247,000	1925	937,000
1921	449,000	1926	849,000
1922	716,000	1927	810,000
1923	871,000	1928	753,000
1924	893,000	1929	509,000

Source: U. S. Bureau of the Census, *Historical Statistics of the United States* (Washington, D.C.: Government Printing Office, 1960), p. 393.

TABLE 31–3

U.S. Passenger Automobile Registration, 1920–1930

YEAR	TOTAL REGISTRATION (thousands)	ANNUAL INCREASE (thousands)
1920	8,132	
1921	9,212	1,080
1922	10,704	1,492
1923	13,253	2,549*
1924	15,436	2,183
1925	17,481	2,045
1926	19,268	1,787
1927	20,193	925
1928	21,362	1,169
1929	23,121	1,759
1930	23,035	−86

* Point of highest annual increase.

Source: U. S. Bureau of the Census, *Historical Statistics of the United States* (Washington, D.C.: Government Printing Office, 1960), p. 462.

Automobiles   Table 31–3 shows the total number (stock) of passenger cars registered in the United States for each year between 1920 and 1930 and the annual increase in registrations. Of special interest is the fact that the

578

INTERWAR
GROWTH AND
STAGNATION
IN THE
AMERICAN
ECONOMY

largest annual increase in the stock of automobiles occurred as early as 1923. One may reasonably assume, with qualifications for such factors as seasonal variations, that in a growing industry of this type, plant will be fully utilized during the growth period and that in order to produce more automobiles additional plant capacity will be required. The amount of increase in plant capacity—the capital formation—in any one year will be roughly proportional to the amount of increase in the total stock.

Up to and including 1923 more automobile plant and equipment had to be built in each succeeding year, but after 1923 fewer additions to plant and equipment were needed than in each preceding year. Consequently 1923 marked the high point in required capital formation for auto production. Net additions to total plant and equipment were needed between 1924 and 1929, but in decreasing annual amounts through 1927. In 1928 and 1929 the requirements for capital formation rose temporarily but remained far short of the 1923 figure. In 1930 the total number of registered automobiles showed an absolute decrease, which meant that the existing plant and equipment did not even have to be fully replaced; in other words, no *net* capital formation was needed for production of automobiles in 1930; net capital formation might have been negative and still have met the demand for current production; net *dis*investment is indicated for 1930. In summary, the table indicates that the need for net capital formation in automobiles began to decline in 1924 and by 1930 could have fallen to zero and still have been more than adequate to take care of automobile output for that year. Excess plant capacity became characteristic of the industry after 1929. The decline in the expansion of this dynamic industry weakened the forces of economic growth fairly early in the decade. The full impact was not felt until later in the decade because of model changes and the large amount of annual replacement of equipment associated with annual changes in style.

There is no mystery about the slowing down in the expansion of the automobile industry. Nearly every industry is characterized by an early period of rapid growth followed by a period of less rapid growth and perhaps a levelling off in annual production. The auto industry was no exception. The lower registration figure for 1927 than for the two subsequent years was accounted for by the shutdown in Ford production for the change-over from the Model T to the Model A. The basic design of the Model T had not changed since the First World War and it was becoming technologically obsolete. The change-over to the Model A gave a fillip to the industry, but it did not change the basic pattern of growth in the industry. For the economy as a whole what was needed to offset the slowing down in the rate of growth of automobiles was not a new model but the rise of another giant industry to carry the economy forward with a high rate of capital formation. No such industry came along.

Electrical appliances   A third pillar of New Era prosperity, the household appliances industries, also slackened the pace of expansion in the late twenties and thus contributed to the 1929 collapse. Electrical appliances, next to automobiles, were outstanding in the trend toward more consumer durables in the 1920's. In radios, for example, the rate of expansion was phenomenal during the first half of the decade, but expansion slowed down greatly in the

second half; between 1921 and 1925 annual dollar sales of radios increased

86-fold, whereas between 1925 and 1929 dollar sales increased only two-fold.
The decline in the rate of expansion during the latter 'twenties was sufficient to
cause an absolute fall in capital formation for the industry. Although the dollar sales of radios was small compared with automobile sales, the combined
volume of household appliances, including refrigerators, washing machines,
vacuum cleaners, flat irons, heaters, fans, and other gadgets had considerable
impact. The capital formation required for their expansion during the twenties
was large in the aggregate.

An examination of the three chief growth industries of the New Era
prosperity reveals a decline in the amount of capital formation required for
their (lower) rates of expansion beginning about the middle of the decade.
This represents a first step in the direction of weakening the underpinnings of
prosperity. What still must be explained, however, are the cumulative forces
of decline which led not merely to a levelling off of the New Era prosperity
but to its total collapse.

As long as many workers were employed on construction projects and in
building new automobile and appliance factories, they could afford to live
in better type dwelling units and to purchase automobiles and appliances. A
fall in capital formation lowered the incomes of these workers and others associated with construction and capital formation generally; and a lowering of
their incomes tended to create vacancies in existing apartments and houses
and to reduce the sales of autos and appliances. In order for existing dwelling
units to be occupied, it was necessary to keep building more dwelling units
and other capital assets, since capital formation generates income most of
which is spent for consumption. One important form of consumption, of course,
is housing; however, the income derived from construction is spent on all
kinds of consumption, including food, transportation, and recreation. Thus the
effect of a decline in construction has ramifications throughout the consumers'
goods industries. The same is true of a decline in other forms of capital formation. A decrease in capital formation in automobile plants means that less
income is disbursed to those who build new automobile plant and equipment
and, because of this reduction in income, there is a decrease in the demand for
all consumers' goods. Lessened capital formation in other industries would
have a similar effect. After 1929 the fall in consumer expenditure became
cumulative with less spending resulting in less income, and less income resulting in less spending. For the houses and factories already built to be fully
utilized, it is necessary always to be building new houses and new factories.

So far the following points have been established. First, the growth
industries (construction, automobiles, household appliances) began to grow
at a slower rate in the mid-twenties, which meant a decline in annual capital
formation in these growth industries. Second, the lessening of annual capital
formation in the growth industries reduced the incomes of workers and others
engaged, or previously engaged, in building houses and auto factories, which
in turn reduced the demand for consumers' goods in general. A third cumulative effect now came into operation. A lower demand for consumers' goods
in general lessened capital formation in those industries which had previously
been swept along by the higher incomes generated by housing, autos, and

580

INTERWAR
GROWTH AND
STAGNATION
IN THE
AMERICAN
ECONOMY

other growth industries. The fall in this type of capital formation (induced disinvestment) had a contracting effect on incomes and consumption similar to that initiated by the decline in housing and factories.

An additional factor contributing to the cumulative decline which characterized the collapse of New Era prosperity was installment buying. When consumer incomes were rising, installment buying enabled consumers to increase their purchases more rapidly than their incomes increased and thus gave a cumulative push to expansion. In contraction, the reverse relation came into play. When consumer incomes were falling, consumer purchases fell off more rapidly than consumer incomes. Durable goods already purchased still had to be paid for even if incomes were reduced. The alternative was to have sellers repossess durable goods. Although it had some reinforcing effect, installment selling was probably of minor significance in the total picture of collapsing prosperity.

Stock Market Crash of 1929

The decline of capital formation in housing, automobiles, and other growth industries as early as the middle of the 1920's raises the question: Why did the New Era prosperity last as long as it did, until 1929, if these industries were the underpinnings of the prosperity? The answer is to be found in the momentum built up during the early twenties and the spread of prosperity to other sectors of the economy. An important aspect of the cumulative process is the fact that capital formation in durable assets depends on profits which are expected in the more or less distant future. In other words, capital formation is a present activity which rests on the *expectation* of future returns. Whether or not the expectation turns out to be justified in the long run, current capital formation will continue to generate prosperity in the present.

Durable capital assets are a bridge between present and future economic activity. Since knowledge about the future is vague and uncertain, the decisions which link present expectations with future realization of profits are necessarily precarious. One might wonder why businessmen are willing to invest at all in fixed assets which will yield a return, if at all, only in the distant future.

Since business expectations about the uncertain future rest on nothing very substantial, they are largely determined by the belief that business conditions will be much the same in the future as they are in the present and have been in the recent past. For reasons which are deeply rooted in historical tradition, the United States is a nation with a strong predisposition toward business optimism. Accordingly, the longer the prosperity of the 1920's lasted, the stronger became the conviction that it would endure indefinitely. Belief that prosperity had come to stay was so firmly held that the boom persisted in the face of adverse developments, which were sloughed off as temporary and accidental deviations from normal.[7] Confidence in the future fed capital formation, and capital formation fed current prosperity. Indicators which in retrospect seem like certain signs that prosperity had passed its peak were ignored. Certainly by the late spring of 1929 the turning point in the business cycle had been reached. The illusion of permanent prosperity was

[7] For an excellent discussion of the American tradition of business optimism, see Eli Ginzberg, *The Illusion of Economic Stability* (New York: Harper & Row, Publishers, 1939).

strong enough, however, to sustain business optimism through the summer

of 1929. When actual events such as lower profits and a general deficiency of demand finally became clear, the illusory expectations collapsed suddenly and violently.

The most dramatic manifestation of expectations prolonging the boom beyond its allotted time, only to collapse suddenly, is seen in the behavior of the stock exchange in the late 1920's. The stock market was already under severe strain in 1927. There were many skeptics who doubted the ability of the market to push much above the existing high levels of 1927. At this point, however, the market entered its most sensational phase. As stock prices soared, the skeptics capitulated to the optimistic view that the market had not spent itself—that in the New Era there would be no more serious depressions. In the daily press, reports of the booming market moved from the financial section to page one. The attention of the general public was increasingly directed to rising stock quotations, and few could resist the temptation to get rich quickly and easily. Even those of small means could become rich, according to the financial experts. John Jacob Raskob, a leading financier and Chairman of the Democratic National Committee, wrote an article entitled "Everybody Ought to be Rich" for the widely circulated *Ladies' Home Journal.* He pointed out that a saving of $15 per month invested in common stock, if dividends were permitted to accumulate, would amount in twenty years to $80,000, which would yield a perpetual income of $400 per month. What need was there for social security in a land which promised abundance from a little work and modest savings?

Moreover, the opportunity to get rich was enhanced by "buying on the margin." With 10 per cent cash plus a broker's loan for the balance an investor could purchase ten times as many shares as his savings alone would permit. Buying ten shares instead of one meant ten times as much profit when the securities rose in price. The loan could then be repaid and the process begun again on an enlarged basis. By encouraging additional purchases, brokers' loans contributed to the rise in security prices. Brokers borrowed money from banks and pledged their customers' securities as collateral. Banks in turn attracted funds from corporations and other sources by offering high interest rates to depositors. Loanable funds flowed to New York's money market in a mighty torrent during 1928 and 1929. The little people of America became as entangled in the golden web of credit as did Gulliver in the bonds of the Lilliputians.

During 1928 and 1929 the United States experienced the greatest stock market boom in history. Security prices soared higher and higher each month, with occasional relapses followed by quick recovery. The value of all securities listed on the New York stock market increased from $27 billion in 1925 to $90 billion in September, 1929. In the eighteen months from March 3, 1928, to September 3, 1929, Montgomery Ward registered gains from 133 to 466, General Electric from 129 to 396, and Radio Corporation of America from 94 to 505 (or after a 5 to 1 split of shares, from 19 to 101). If General Electric could go to 400, what was to prevent it from going ot 500 or even to 1000?

On September 3, 1929, security prices on the New York stock exchange reached their lofty peak. They tossed about uneasily on the currents of frenzied

582

INTERWAR
GROWTH AND
STAGNATION
IN THE
AMERICAN
ECONOMY

finance for six weeks, until the crash in late October. On Thursday, October 24th, nearly 13 million shares changed hands at a time when 5 million shares was considered a prodigious volume. The dangers of buying on margin were revealed to the thousands sold out by their brokers when their equity was wiped out by sharp declines in share prices. Temporarily the market was saved from a complete rout when a few big Wall Street bankers formed a pool in order to buy strategic stocks to blunt the fall in prices arising from panic by fear-ridden investors.

The respite from ruin was brief. Even the gods of Wall Street could not stay the storm that broke loose on Black Tuesday, October 29, one of the tragic days in American history. In the first half-hour of trading 3 million shares were dumped on the market; after two hours, 8 million shares had changed hands at plummeting prices; and for the day, 16½ million shares were recorded as sold and other millions were sold without being recorded. In all perhaps 20 to 25 million shares changed hands on Black Tuesday. Nothing like this had ever happened before. Millionaires and their servants alike were wiped out in the crash. The market declined day after day. When it hit bottom toward mid-November, more than $25 billion in values had disappeared into thin air over the dark Manhattan skies. The Wall Street crash brought to a violent end the Golden Twenties, the New Era, the Prosperity Decade.

This fantastic episode in financial history can be understood only in terms of the expectations concerning the future generated by the over-optimism of the New Era. Given the ideology that capitalist America was destined for perpetual prosperity, very high prices for corporate securities were justified. Even if current yields were low in relation to current quotations, the expectation of higher yields in the future would support these prices, and every elevation in the expectations about future yields would lead to still higher security prices. "Discounting the future" is the daily business of the security exchanges. It has been suggested that in 1929 investors were also discounting the hereafter.

Moreover, a point was reached in the speculative mania of 1929 where one's "true" beliefs about the future yield of assets became less important to profitable speculation than what one thought other people thought about the future. If a professional speculator, who might be skeptical about the New Era optimism, thought that other people thought the price of a security were going to rise, his most profitable action was to purchase that security in anticipation of its rise, being certain, of course, to get rid of it before "real" events proved the optimism unjustified. Social psychology became more important than investment analysis. As John Maynard Keynes observed a few years after the 1929 crash, "Speculators may do no harm as bubbles on a steady stream of enterprise. But the position is serious when enterprise becomes a bubble on a whirlpool of speculation. When the capital development of a country becomes a by-product of the activities of a casino, the job is likely to be ill-done." [8]

Summary of relation of the stock market to real capital formation The relation of the stock market crash of 1929 to the collapse of prosperity and

[8] *The General Theory of Employment, Interest and Money* (New York: Harcourt, Brace and World, 1936), p. 159.

583

INTERWAR
GROWTH AND
STAGNATION
IN THE
AMERICAN
ECONOMY

the onset of depression may be summarized as follows. The stock market crash was not the cause of the Great Depression any more than the stock market boom was the cause of the New Era prosperity. Insofar as one factor can be singled out, the key to both prosperity and depression was the rate of real capital formation in durable assets. However, the behavior of the stock market did influence the extent and the duration of the business boom and the timing and intensity of the depression. In the late twenties real capital formation was carried forward by business optimism after the underpinnings of prosperity (real capital formation) had weakened. An unrealistic optimism manifested in the behavior of the stock market heightened and prolonged prosperity. The disillusionment which followed the stock market crash deepened and prolonged the depression. The stock market crash marked a turning point from over-optimism to over-pessimism. Whether or not durable capital assets will be produced depends on their expected profitability. As a major barometer of these long-term expectations of future profitability, the stock market occupies an important position in the business decisions which lead to capital formation and thus to prosperity or depression. When the optimistic belief in economic stability and permanent prosperity turned out to be a grand illusion, the boom collapsed.

SUMMARY

The overall performance of the American economy during the 1920's may be summarized in the following manner. Backlogs (housing) from the war plus new industries (automobiles, electrical appliances) and population growth led to a higher than long-term average rate of capital formation during the early and middle twenties. The momentum of these growth industries and backlogs stimulated other industries and generated widespread prosperity. The level of per capita consumption increased, and the composition of consumption changed. Other industries expanded to meet the new levels and new directions of consumer demand. The American tradition of business optimism expressed itself through the stock market and carried security prices to unprecedented, and unrealistic, heights. By 1929, however, the pillars of prosperity were crumbling. Backlogs had been used, growth industries were leveling off, and no new growth industries came along to sustain prosperity. In the fall of 1929 the stock market crash burst the optimistic bubble. Capital formation, already slowed down, collapsed in the ensuing months. Gloom engulfed the business community, and the Great Depression descended like a huge dark cloud over the American economy.

SELECTED BIBLIOGRAPHY

ALLEN, FREDERICK LEWIS, *Only Yesterday*. New York: Bantam Books, 1957. (paperback)

BERLE, ADOLF A., JR., and GARDINER C. MEANS, *The Modern Corporation and Private Property*. New York: The Macmillan Company, 1933.

584

*INTERWAR
GROWTH AND
STAGNATION
IN THE
AMERICAN
ECONOMY*

CLARK, VICTOR S., *History of Manufacturing in the United States,* Vol. III. Magnolia, Mass.: Peter Smith, 1949.

DOUGLAS, PAUL H., *Real Wages in the United States 1890–1926.* Boston: Houghton Mifflin Company, 1930.

FABRICANT, SOLOMON, *The Output of Manufacturing Industries, 1899–1937.* New York: National Bureau of Economic Research, 1940.

GALBRAITH, JOHN K., *The Great Crash, 1929,* 2nd ed. Boston: Houghton Mifflin Company, 1961. (paperback)

GINZBERG, ELI, *The Illusion of Economic Stability.* New York: Harper & Row, Publishers, 1939.

LEUCHTENBURG, WILLIAM E., *The Perils of Prosperity 1914–1932.* Chicago: University of Chicago Press. (paperback)

MILLS, FREDERICK C., *Economic Tendencies in the United States.* New York: National Bureau of Economic Research, 1932.

MITCHELL, WESLEY C., *Business Cycles: The Problem and Its Setting.* New York: National Bureau of Economic Research, 1930.

NOURSE, EDWIN G. and ASSOCIATES, *America's Capacity to Produce.* Washington, D.C.: The Brookings Institution, 1934.

PRESIDENT'S CONFERENCE ON UNEMPLOYMENT, Committee on Recent Social Changes, *Recent Economic Changes,* 2 vols. New York: McGraw-Hill, Inc., 1929.

PRESIDENT'S RESEARCH COMMITTEE ON SOCIAL TRENDS, *Recent Social Trends in the United States,* Foreword by Herbert Hoover. 2 vols. New York: McGraw-Hill, Inc., 1933.

SCHLESINGER, ARTHUR M., *The Age of Roosevelt: The Crisis of the Old Order, 1919–1933.* Boston: Houghton Mifflin Company, 1957.

SCHUMPETER, JOSEPH A., *Business Cycles, A Theoretical, Historical and Statistical Analysis of the Capitalist Process,* abridged ed. New York: McGraw-Hill, Inc., 1964. (paperback)

SOULE, GEORGE, *Prosperity Decade: From War to Depression, 1917–1929.* New York: Holt, Rinehart & Winston, Inc., 1947.

ARTICLES

BLACK, JOHN D., "The McNary-Haugen Movement," *American Economic Review,* XVIII (Sept., 1928), 405–27.

BURNS, ARTHUR R., "The Process of Industrial Concentration," *Quarterly Journal of Economics,* XLVII (Feb., 1933), 277–311.

DAVIS, JOSEPH S., "The Export Debenture Plan for Aid to Agriculture," *Quarterly Journal of Economics,* XLIII (Feb., 1929), 250–77.

———, "The Program of the Federal Farm Board," *American Economic Review,* XXI (March, 1931), 104–13.

KNIGHT, FRANK H., "Historical and Theoretical Issues in the Problem of Modern Capitalism," *Journal of Economic and Business History,* I (Nov., 1928), 119–36.

MEANS, GARDINER C., "The Growth in the Relative Importance of the Large Corporation in American Economic Life," *American Economic Review,* XXI (March, 1931), 10–42.

———, "The Separation of Ownership and Control in American Industry," *Quarterly Journal of Economics,* XLVI (Nov., 1931), 68–100.

SCHMOOKLER, JACOB, "The Changing Efficiency of the American Economy, 1869–1938," *Review of Economic Statistics,* XXXIV (Aug., 1952), 214–31.

Interwar Growth and Stagnation:
The Great Depression

Between Black Tuesday in October, 1929, and inauguration day in March, 1933, the United States experienced the worst peacetime crisis in its history. The stock market panic was the first but not the worst in a series of disasters which culminated in a contagion of fear and frustration. Mass unemployment accounted for the greatest amount of human suffering, but business and farm communities were also demoralized by bankruptcies, foreclosures, and bank closings. Even after the bottom was reached in the winter of 1932–33, expansion came slowly and fell far short of full recovery. In the United States even more than in western Europe, the 1930's was a period of severe economic stagnation. The Great Depression and the accompanying mass unemployment were not finally liquidated until 1940, when World War II rescued the economy from what appeared to be chronic stagnation.

Understandably a crisis of this magnitude also had wide-ranging effects outside the economic sphere. Marriage and birth rates fell sharply. Suicides and mental illness increased. Political convictions and ideological beliefs changed. Republicans were turned out of political office and replaced by Democrats, marking a new era of predominantly Democratic national administrations.

From the point of view of long-term economic development, the most important change flowing from the Great Depression was in economic policy. Prior to 1929 the federal government played a negative or neutral role in economic affairs, but in the course of the depression it assumed responsibility for the performance of the economy as a whole. The rugged individualism associated with President Herbert Hoover was supplanted by the interventionism of President Franklin Roosevelt. Much more than personalities and individual preconceptions were involved in this change. The new economic policy, though it emanated from economic breakdown, was in fact a response to changes in technology, corporate institutions, working-class aspirations, the declining position of agriculture, and all the other circumstances underlying economic development. Under these pressures there could probably be no retreat in a mass democracy from such policies as public works relief in periods of depression, social security, government sponsorship of labor unions, control over banking and the stock exchanges, and perhaps most significant of all,

586

*INTERWAR
GROWTH AND
STAGNATION:
THE GREAT
DEPRESSION*

a new type of fiscal policy whereby positive governmental action could no longer be frustrated in periods of depression by adherence to the principle of annually balanced federal budgets. The most important legacy of the Great Depression to political economy was then the assumption of positive responsibility on the part of the federal government for the economic welfare of the nation. Business, labor, and farm leaders still had large responsibilities, but only the federal government was in a position to exercise overall responsibility.

DESCENT INTO THE GREAT DEPRESSION

The contraction of business activity began in the second quarter of 1929 and increased rapidly after the stock market crash in the fall of that fateful year. Although business and political leaders were stunned by the crash, they stubbornly resisted the notion that it might be a portent of general business depression. President Hoover, for example, stated in the midst of the 1929 crash: "The fundamental business of the country, that is, production and distribution of commodities, is on a sound and prosperous basis." Andrew Mellon, a business leader as well as the Secretary of the Treasury, said at the close of 1929: "I see nothing in the present situation that is either menacing or warrants pessimism."

The business forecasts for 1930 were uniformly optimistic despite the historical experience that major stock market crises had been followed by major business depressions. The forecasters got some satisfaction when business activity and security prices showed a brief upturn in the first few months of 1930. On May 1, 1930, President Hoover told a group of business and farm leaders assembled at the White House to discuss ways out of what was then referred to as the "slump" of 1930: "I am convinced we have now passed the worst and with continued unity of effort we shall recover rapidly." How the nation's leaders could have so misjudged what lay ahead is astonishing in retrospect, but their views at the time were surely shared by politicians, businessmen, and the public generally.

Events in the second half of 1930 belied President Hoover's confidence in the future. Unemployment rose to three times the 1929 level. Security prices sagged badly, much below the early post-crash levels. Business confidence was shaken when the promised upturn failed to materialize. The "slump" of 1930 deepened into a genuine business depression by the close of 1930. Yet faith in the old order died hard. When a few rays of hope broke through the darkened sky in the early months of 1931, President Hoover promptly asserted that "Prosperity is just around the corner"—a statement famous for its inaccuracy. Shortly thereafter, in the summer of 1931, a truly catastrophic and unprecedented phase of economic collapse began. In May, 1931, a wave of European financial disasters began in Austria and spread quickly to Germany and England, causing a collapse of the international gold standard.[1]

The second and more drastic phase of economic contraction threatened the whole financial structure of European and American capitalism. A banking panic highlighted this second phase of the downswing, much as the stock market crash had featured the first phase. The proximate cause of the first

[1] See Chapter 30.

phase originated in the United States, the second phase in Europe. The two
were interrelated in the sense that the severe and prolonged security deflation
of the first phase induced the financial liquidation of the second. Presumably
the second phase would not have occurred without the first. Collapse in Wall
Street cut off United States loans to Europe and undermined the shaky European financial structure inherited from the First World War.

In the summer of 1931 the world-wide repercussions of the depression were doubling back on the United States. Collapse of the international gold standard initiated a severe secondary deflation. Great Britain's departure from the gold standard in September, 1931, and the accompanying devaluation of the pound reversed the outflow of gold from the Bank of England and shifted the pressures for liquidation directly to the American dollar. Most of the reverse flow of gold to London after September, 1931, came from the Federal Reserve Bank of New York. British commodity exports now moved more easily in world markets, but American exports were shut out because of the high value of the American gold dollar in terms of devalued foreign currencies.

For the time being, the United States remained on the gold standard, but only by subjecting its financial structure to terrific strains in the form of extreme liquidation and deflation in the domestic economy and the undermining of the entire financial and monetary structure of the nation. Wage rates, which had held up well during the first two years of the depression, now yielded to the growing pressure of liquidation, and substantial wage cuts occurred. Commodity prices, especially of farm products and raw materials, cascaded. Heavy industry responded to the fall in demand for its products with cutbacks in production instead of price reductions and thus distorted the relative price structure. Cutbacks in output accentuated unemployment. Inventory liquidations reached extreme limits in so-called hand-to-mouth buying. Farm foreclosures and business bankruptcies were several times more numerous than during the first two years of the depression.

The magnitude of the descent is attested by the following grim facts. National income in current dollars fell from $88 billion in 1929 to $40 billion in 1933; wholesale commodity prices fell by approximately one-third; the index of industrial production fell by one-half, from 110 in 1929 to 57 in 1932 (1935–39 = 100); gross capital formation, an index of dynamic activity, fell from $16 billion to less than $1 billion between 1929 and 1932, and in net terms (after deducting depreciation) was negative in 1931, 1932, and 1933, meaning that the nation was consuming capital more rapidly than it was being replaced. Consequently real national wealth declined in absolute terms.

Stock prices, which had already been hit hard in the crash of 1929, suffered further declines. Table 32–1 is illustrative. In total dollar value, the stocks listed on the New York Stock Exchange fell from $90 billion at the peak of the market in 1929 to $15 billion at the low in 1932, a shrinkage of $75 billion in the value of claims to real wealth, or five-sixths of the 1929 value.

Unemployment

Unemployment was of most concern to the public as an index of business conditions. No very good statistics on unemployment were available,

588 **TABLE 32–1**

INTERWAR
GROWTH AND
STAGNATION:
THE GREAT
DEPRESSION

Prices of Ten Leading Securities on the New York Stock Exchange, 1929–1932

COMPANY	September 3, 1929 HIGH	November 13, 1929 LOW	1932 LOW
American Telephone & Telegraph	304	208¼	70¼
Bethlehem Steel	140⅜	85	7¼
Chrysler Corporation	73	30	5
General Electric	396¼	193	8½
General Motors	72¾	40	7⅝
New York Central	256⅜	171	8¾
Radio Corporation of America	101	31	2½
Standard Oil (N.J.)	71⅞	57½	19⅞
U. S. Rubber	41½	25⅜	1¼
U. S. Steel	261¾	159½	21¼

Source: New York Times, Sept. 4, 1929; Nov. 14, 1929; and Jan. 1, 1933. All prices are for common stock.

and the tendency of the national administration was to understate the figures. Conservative estimates indicate that unemployment increased from 4 million in 1930 to 8 million in 1931 and to 13 million in 1932. At the depth of the depression, in the winter of 1932–33, the total may have reached 16 million, or one-third of the total labor force. Other millions were employed only part-time. Unemployment on so vast a scale had never occurred before in the United States. The sheer waste of human resources was unmatched in the annals of history. That greatest folly of mankind, war, can be understood, if not excused, but chronic mass unemployment defies rational explanation. The material wealth lost through unemployment between 1929 and 1938 has been estimated at more than $200 billion—enough to have built every family in the United States a new five-room house with up-to-date appliances.

More important, however, than the loss in material wealth was the destructive effect of long-term unemployment on the human spirit. In a democratic society, which prides itself on upholding the dignity of the individual, there is no more effective means of undermining that dignity than chronic mass unemployment. It erodes the self-respect of the unemployed breadwinner, and degrades him in the eyes of his victimized family. Long-term unemployment subjects the family of the unemployed to malnutrition and even to slow starvation. During the Great Depression millions of American children inserted cardboard into their worn-out shoes before going off to school without a lunch, returning home at noon, not to eat—there was no food at home—but because they were ashamed to have their classmates know they had no lunch to eat. Americans had been proud of their self-sufficiency and they did not take easily to charity even when it was available.

Joblessness had other unfortunate effects. As Sir William Beveridge pointed out, chronic unemployment breeds prejudices and discrimination against minority racial and religious groups whose members are rivals for employment. By the standards of any good society, chronic mass unemploy-

ment is both immoral and intolerable. The Great Depression was a national disgrace, which later generations might ignore, but which the victims of the 1930's could not forget.

Farm Distress under Hoover

Farmers as a group did not share in the prosperity of the 1920's and for them the downturn in 1929 meant a change from bad to worse. Farm prices fell to less than one-half the 1929 level, whereas industrial prices declined much less and mortgage obligations declined not at all in money terms (and so increased in real terms). Consequently the disparity between the prices received by farmers for their crops and the prices they paid for machinery and consumers' goods increased. The price of corn fell to 15 cents a bushel, cotton to 5 cents a pound, hogs to 3 cents a pound, and beef to 2.5 cents a pound. Farmers were faced with current operating losses and eventually loss of their farms. Tens of thousands of farms were foreclosed for nonpayment of taxes and mortgage liabilities. Indignation ran so high in some communities that farmers took the law into their own hands and threatened with violence the representatives of banks and insurance companies who came into their communities to buy up property placed on forced sale. Some states passed laws declaring moratoria on mortgages for six months to three years. If the free market brought farmers to their knees in the 1920's, it put them flat on their backs in the early 1930's. There was mounting pressure on Washington to do something about the farm crisis.

Banking Crisis under Hoover

Ultimately the secondary deflation dealt a shattering blow to the banking system of the United States. In the 1920's it was widely believed that the United States could not have any more serious depressions inasmuch as the Federal Reserve System had so improved the banking system that financial debacles like those of 1857, 1873, 1890, and 1907 were no longer possible. In fact, however, during the Great Depression the banking system proved one of the weakest links in the national economy. In part this may have been a result of mistaken policies by Federal Reserve authorities, but a more basic weakness lay in the structure of the banking system itself, and particularly in the large number of small, independent banks with limited resources. While the weakness of the American banking system must not be minimized in explaining the severity of the Great Depression, its weakness became critical only after the depression had been in process for some time—in 1931 and 1932 rather than in 1929.

Deepening depression engendered successive waves of panic which led the public to convert non-cash assets into cash and in time created a liquidity crisis. The first wave occurred toward the end of 1930 when the slump deepened into a real depression and brought a large number of bank failures but not a panic. A second rush to liquidity occurred in 1931 after the breakdown of the international gold standard.[2] Banking legislation in February, 1932, the first

---

[2] In the six weeks following England's departure from the gold standard in September, 1931, the United States lost $700,000,000 in gold. This set up a domestic rush to liquidity and resulted in an increase of domestic cash holdings (hoarding).

590

INTERWAR
GROWTH AND
STAGNATION:
THE GREAT
DEPRESSION

Glass-Steagall Act, gave more flexibility to the money supply by authorizing Federal Reserve banks to use government securities as partial backing for Federal Reserve notes, the chief form of money in circulation. Prior to this legislation the Federal Reserve could increase the supply of money in circulation only by discounting its dwindling supply of commercial paper of member banks as a means of increasing the volume of Federal Reserve notes in circulation. Now the Federal Reserve embarked on a huge open-market operation involving the purchase of billions of dollars worth of government securities in a few months. By absorbing securities and paying out currency the thirst of the public for cash was temporarily satisfied. In addition member banks were subjected to less pressure to rediscount (liquidate) their earning assets in the form of commercial paper. Momentarily the public appetite for liquidity was appeased. Some money returned to the banking system when the public discovered they could have money if they wanted it.

The third and most intense wave of liquidation, beginning in the second half of 1932, brought the banking system and the whole economy to the brink of collapse. By this time the whole capitalistic world economy was in a state of panic. When belief in the possibility of liquidity became seriously threatened on an international scale, panic ensued in runs on central banks for gold and on domestic banks for money. No other form of asset was satisfactory to the overwhelming majority of wealth holders in a community which had lost faith in the economic future. Since cash is a non-earning asset, the pursuit of gain normally leads to a fairly quick conversion of cash into earning assets, but the depression became so deep and pessimism so widespread that the only secure form of surplus wealth was cash.

Like other panics, this one fed on itself. The Federal Reserve could not issue notes fast enough to meet the raging demand for cash. Nevada's banks were closed for a brief holiday in October, 1932. At the turn of the new year the panic gained momentum. Michigan, which had been among the hardest hit by the depression because of its dependence on automobile production for employment, was in serious financial trouble. In mid-February the governor of Michigan proclaimed a state-wide closing of all banks. Several other states were forced to declare bank holidays in February. Member banks withdrew $1,700,000,000 from the Federal Reserve banks in the three weeks between February 8 and March 3. Excess gold reserves declined from $1.5 billion to less than $0.4 billion in February. Out-of-town banks drew heavily on New York banks to meet customer demands. Meanwhile United States gold was being drained abroad, with a third of a billion dollars exported on March 3 alone. By inauguration day on March 4, 1933, most banks in the United States had locked their doors. Conditions could hardly have been worse. A great nation was in the grip of economic paralysis. This was a difficult but dramatic moment in history for a new president to assume the responsibilities of office.

THE NEW DEAL

President Franklin D. Roosevelt proved equal to the grave challenge presented by the national economic crisis. In a stirring inaugural address he told an anxious America, "The only thing we have to fear is fear itself."

Bold words accompanied by swift action broke the psychological deadlock. **591**

INTERWAR
GROWTH AND
STAGNATION:
THE GREAT
DEPRESSION
This was the first essential step on the road to recovery. After nearly four years
of progressive descent, the Great Depression had reached bottom. The worst
was behind, but a long uphill climb lay ahead.

At the time he proclaimed a national banking holiday, President Roosevelt asked that individual banks be reopened as rapidly as they could be certified as sound. In this may be found a clue to the course which the New Deal
would follow. In this hour of decision the new President might have requested
nationalization of the banking system. He probably could have carried a nationalization program through Congress because his prestige and power were
immense, and the public's confidence in private bankers was at a low ebb.
Roosevelt chose instead to preserve private banking and the capitalist system
generally by repairing their worst defects.

The President appraised the situation in these words: "A frank examination of the profit system in the spring of 1933 showed it to be in collapse; but
substantially everybody in the United States, in public office and out of public
office, from the very rich to the very poor, was as determined as was my
Administration to save it."

This statement reveals an awareness of the perilous condition of the
profit system when Roosevelt took office and suggests a conscious choice of
government intervention over socialism.

Although the President chose to preserve the private enterprise system,
the gravity of the crisis called for a departure in economic policy. The limping
laissez-faire of preceding administrations was to be replaced with a "New Deal"
in which the federal government would play a positive role in the management
of economic life. Use of federal authority for relief, recovery, and reform
permeated New Deal policy. Here was a turning point in the history of American economic policy.

Concrete evidence of the shift from a negative to a positive state was to
be found in (1) the substitution of managed currency for the semi-automatic
gold standard; (2) direct federal work relief for the unemployed plus favorable labor legislation; (3) the National Industrial Recovery Act; (4) the Agricultural Adjustment Act; (5) Social Security; (6) the Tennessee Valley Authority; (7) federal control over the securities market; and (8) most important of all, a new type of fiscal policy—planned deficit financing. Each of these
will be discussed, not in detail, but as components of an economic policy which
differed sharply from that of the preceding Hoover administration.

From the Gold Standard to a Managed Currency

The Roosevelt New Deal replaced the gold standard with a managed
currency. As the monetary counterpart of laissez-faire, with its assumption of
automatic adjustments, the gold standard had long been accepted as the most
desirable form of monetary system. In an earlier chapter we discussed the
restoration of the gold standard by European nations forced off gold during
the First World War and the disastrous consequences of the return to gold.[3]
The collapse of the international gold standard in 1931 apparently did nothing
to shake the confidence of the Hoover administration in its desirability.

[3] See Chapter 30.

592

INTERWAR
GROWTH AND
STAGNATION:
THE GREAT
DEPRESSION

Roosevelt's chief reason for wanting a managed currency in place of the gold standard was to restore (reflate) domestic prices to the level which had prevailed prior to the depression in 1929. This was assumed to be a necessary, although not a sufficient, condition for recovery, and a reflation of prices became a major aim of New Deal policies in the early years of the first term. Naturally monetary policy was the chief weapon for achieving higher prices. It was designed in frankly nationalistic terms, rather than in an international setting, and it was this view of domestic recovery which led Roosevelt to torpedo the World Economic Conference in May, 1933.

In proclaiming the Bank Holiday on March 4, 1933, President Roosevelt prohibited the export of gold and also the redemption in gold of paper currency and silver coins. Subsequently the public was ordered by law to surrender all gold coin and gold certificates to banks, and banks were ordered to deliver all gold and gold certificates to the Federal Reserve Banks. All monetary gold was nationalized, with the federal government as the sole legal owner. Private ownership of monetary gold was outlawed. Gold coins were melted down. Gold bullion could be exported only under certain conditions. The President requested legislation abrogating gold clauses in contracts—provisions that payments should be made in gold or its equivalent—and he was supported by Congress and upheld by the Supreme Court.

With the nation's vast gold supply securely lodged in Treasury vaults, the President began monetary manipulations by which he hoped to raise the domestic price level. The government began to purchase gold at prices which for a time changed frequently. Finally, by the Gold Reserve Act of January, 1934, the price was fixed at $35 an ounce. At this point the President formally devalued the dollar from the old content of 23.22 grains of fine gold to 13.71 grains, a devaluation to 59 per cent of the old weight of the dollar. Roosevelt seemed to have accepted the theory that the domestic price level depends on the value of gold in the unit of currency, so that when the content of the dollar is lowered the domestic price level will rise more or less proportionately. Although prices did rise during the period of monetary manipulation, the direct relation between the price level and changes in the gold content of the dollar was not demonstrated.

In the field of banking the New Deal passed legislation designed to impart greater stability to the banking system. The Federal Reserve Board was given more power over the twelve Federal Reserve Banks and the member banks. More banks were brought into the system. A major step toward restoring confidence in banks was the establishment of the Federal Deposit Insurance Corporation, an agency which insured bank deposits up to $5000 (later raised to $10,000)—a measure which met determined opposition from the American Bankers Association, the trade association of private bankers in the United States. The new philosophy behind banking legislation was expressed by Marriner Eccles, the Chairman of the Federal Reserve Board: "Laissez-faire in banking and the attainment of business stability are incompatible."

Federal Relief for the Unemployed

Unemployment constituted the essence as well as the chief measure of the Great Depression. The Hoover administration consistently refused to as-

593

INTERWAR
GROWTH AND
STAGNATION:
THE GREAT
DEPRESSION

sume responsibility for the direct employment of unemployed workers. Responsibility for the unemployed, insofar as it was a government responsibility at all, fell on local and state governments in the form of either direct relief to the distressed unemployed or state and local works projects. Private philanthropy also figured prominently as a source of relief for the needy, whether unemployed or unemployable. Time and again President Hoover reiterated his belief that a "dole" from the federal government would degrade the recipients and bankrupt the nation.

Within limits the Hoover administration was willing to step up the public construction program of the federal government through the usual channels of letting contracts to private construction firms. The workers thus absorbed were employed by private construction companies rather than directly by government. In the early months of the depression Hoover urged expansion of public works as an anti-depression measure and started such projects as Hoover Dam on the Colorado River. He soon discovered, however, that expansion of public works would add to the already mounting budget deficits caused by falling federal revenues. He therefore withdrew support for even this type of public construction as a concession to balancing the federal budget. At all times and with complete consistency Hoover refused to sponsor direct federal employment on work relief projects.[4]

From the beginning the Roosevelt administration reversed Hoover's policy and accepted responsibility for providing work for the unemployed. President Roosevelt justified this policy on grounds that the depression was a nation-wide phenomenon and the national government should therefore accept responsibility for its consequences, including unemployment. In a message to Congress in 1935, Roosevelt provided the following rationale: "This group [the unemployed] was the victim of a nationwide depression caused by conditions which were not local, but national. The Federal government is the only governmental agency with sufficient power and credit to meet this situation. We have assumed this task and we shall not shrink from it in the future."

In November, 1933, when it became apparent that Secretary of Interior Ickes' Public Works Administration (PWA) could not meet the need for work relief, a new agency, the Civil Works Administration (CWA), was created and by January, 1934, some four and one half million persons were employed on improvised projects of various kinds. In 1935 another federal agency, the Works Progress Administration (WPA), was set up to carry on the work relief program and became one of the best-known governmental agencies of the Great Depression. By 1940, 8,000,000 individuals, or one-fifth of the U.S. labor force, had been employed by the WPA on 250,000 projects ranging from highway construction to theatre stage production. Peak employment on WPA at any one time was 3¼ million in the fall of 1938. Total WPA expenditures were $13 billion. Despite the constraint on the WPA to avoid what was being done by private employment many useful things were accomplished, but the most important achievement lay in salvaging the human capital that would otherwise have gone to waste.

---

[4] The Hoover administration was also opposed to direct relief (without work), although in the depth of the depression it did make advances, through the Reconstruction Finance Corporation, to the nearly bankrupt states for direct relief. The New Deal for two years did give direct relief because of the extreme urgency but it rejected in principle direct relief to unemployables and returned this responsibility to the states after 1935.

594

INTERWAR
GROWTH AND
STAGNATION:
THE GREAT
DEPRESSION

Other federal agencies providing direct employment included the Civilian Conservation Corps (CCC) for forest conservation and afforestation, road building, and other outdoor projects; the National Youth Administration (NYA), which provided funds to enable high school and college students to remain in school and out of the regular labor market; and the Resettlement Administration, later the Farm Security Administration (FSA), established for the purpose of aiding lower-income farmers and tenants who did not benefit from the Agricultural Adjustment Administration.

The National Recovery Administration (NRA)

The boldest and most ill-fated experiment of the New Deal in extending the authority and responsibility of the federal government over the national economy was the National Recovery Administration (NRA), established under the National Industrial Recovery Act (NIRA). In signing the bill into law, President Roosevelt asserted: "History probably will record the NIRA as the most important and far-reaching legislation ever enacted by the American Congress." Certainly the NIRA became the focal point of recovery efforts between 1933 and 1935. Industrial production stood at an index of 57 in 1932, down from 110 in 1929. Since the economy was operating at approximately 80 per cent of capacity in 1929, it was at less than 50 per cent of capacity when the New Deal launched the NIRA in May, 1933. The bulk of the 15,000,000 unemployed were from industry and trade. If recovery were to be achieved at all, the key indicator would be expansion in industry and trade.

The central idea in the NIRA was self-regulation of industry operating under so-called codes of fair competition promulgated by trade associations and subject to approval by the federal government. Constructive cooperation was to replace destructive competition. Relations among employers, workers, and government resembled in some respects the medieval craft gilds, and the notion that industry should regulate its own members under government supervision bore similarities to European cartels. Once a code was approved by the federal government, it became binding on all firms in the industry. Clearly the arrangements under the NRA represented a break with American anti-trust tradition and the policy of laissez-faire. Opposition in Congress came mainly from the champions of anti-trust philosophy.

Codes of regulated competition promulgated by trade associations had their roots in the War Industries Board of the First World War. Several key figures in the NRA, including the chief drafter and first administrator, General Hugh S. Johnson, had served on the War Industries Board under Bernard Baruch. During the 1920's a number of business leaders had advocated self-government for industry in peacetime. Gerard Swope, president of the General Electric Company, propounded a plan which found wide support in the business community and received the endorsement of the United States Chamber of Commerce. The Swope Plan was a direct antecedent of the NRA. When the immensity of the Great Depression made it evident that something must be radically wrong with American industrial organization, a growing number of influential leaders in business, labor, and government were prepared to accept some type of national economic planning. Business leaders, discredited as a group in the eyes of the general public by the depression,

were in no position to dictate all the terms of industrial coordination. New
Deal leaders insisted on guarantees to organized labor on collective bargaining, regulation of wages and hours, and the abolition of child labor. The NRA
stipulated that every code must contain provisions relating to these items.

595

*INTERWAR
GROWTH AND
STAGNATION:
THE GREAT
DEPRESSION*

The many conflicting interests and administrative obstacles, including
the sheer bulk of work involved in formulating codes, could not, of course, be
taken care of quickly enough to make a significant contribution to short-term
recovery. Actually the NRA might better have been called the National Reform Administration because it is difficult to see what the codes could have
contributed to short-term recovery. Apparently the framers had some notion
about increasing purchasing power by raising wages and employment, along
with the idea that all employers might benefit if *all* raised wages at the same
time, whereas a single employer could not afford to raise wages if his rivals
failed to do so. The latter part of this proposition seems valid, but not the first
part which held that all would gain if they raised wages simultaneously. If all
wage rates rose simultaneously, costs would rise more or less proportionately,
so that in the absence of higher prices, employers would make less profit (or
suffer more loss) than before wages rose. If prices were raised proportionately
to the rise in costs, the two would tend to neutralize each other and contribute
nothing significant to increased employment.

Perhaps a distinction between direct labor costs and overhead costs
would suggest that overhead cost per unit would fall if output increased; the
fall in overhead per unit would offset the rise in direct labor costs per unit so
that total cost would not rise when wages (and purchasing power) increased.
Consequently more purchasing power from higher wages might be self-justify-
ing if all employers raised wages at the same time. Even this, however, seems
a precarious argument of doubtful validity for relating the codes to economic
recovery.

The recovery aspect of the National Industrial Recovery Act lay in Part
II, which called for the establishment of the Public Works Administration
(PWA), more than in Part I, which authorized the National Recovery Administration. In the minds of those who drafted the NIRA, the two agencies
were closely related and both were deemed essential to recovery. Unfortunately they were placed under separate administrators and were not coordinated in a manner conducive to successful recovery. Consequently the
argument might be made in defense of the conception of the NIRA that it was
never given a fair chance to succeed. Part II authorizing the PWA was placed
under Secretary of Interior Harold Ickes, who moved so cautiously in planning projects and authorizing expenditures that the big push needed to
initiate recovery was not forthcoming. The index of industrial production,
which had risen rapidly during the spring and early summer of 1933 in
anticipation of higher wages and other costs when the NRA codes did come
into effect, slumped badly in the second half of 1933. From 59 in March, the
index rose to 100 in July, and then fell each month until it stood at 72 in
November, 1933. The winter of 1933–34 threatened to be as bad as the preceding one under the Hoover administration. In view of this alarming prospect,
other relief and public works measures (CWA) were rushed into the breach.

Even under the most favorable circumstances, the NRA was a dubious
route to economic recovery. In the prevailing conditions it was plagued from

596

*INTERWAR
GROWTH AND
STAGNATION:
THE GREAT
DEPRESSION*

its inception by contradictions in objectives and by conflicts among contending groups. Self-regulation of industry meant regulation in the interest of private industry primarily and of the public welfare incidentally. The codes gave legal sanction and coercive force to practices followed by trade associations in the 1920's which had contributed to the downfall of the economy in the depression. In authorizing the leaders of trade associations to draft codes, the NRA authorities placed the initiative in the hands of a group more interested in restricting production than in expanding it, in raising prices than in lowering them, in fighting organized labor than in cooperating with it. Code makers tended to view all competition as destructive and therefore undesirable. Consumer interests were ignored. General Hugh Johnson, the NRA Administrator, tried to be "tough" in forcing code makers to hew to the line, but inevitably concessions crept into the codes.

The inability of organized labor to realize the rights presumed to have been accorded under Section 7a of the NIRA provoked numerous strikes. Small businessmen complained bitterly of maltreatment at the hands of big businessmen under the codes. Consumers stood by quite helpless for want of organization. Squabbles and delays created general bedlam in the hurried and harried atmosphere of Washington in 1933.

In order to bring more firms quickly under the act, General Johnson promulgated a blanket code providing for voluntary compliance until regular codes could be formulated industry by industry. Each signer of the blanket code was permitted to display a large blue eagle as a symbol of cooperation with NRA authorities in spreading employment and renouncing unfair competitive practices. Among other things, the voluntary code pledged the bearer of the blue eagle to purchase only from fellow signers. Temporarily the voluntary blanket code rescued the NRA from collapse in mid-1933. However, the contradictions and cleavages inherent in the program multiplied with the passage of time and it was breaking under its own weight when in 1935 the Supreme Court administered the *coup de grâce* to the Blue Eagle on grounds that the NRA involved an unconstitutional delegation of legislative authority to the executive branch and because most of what was to be regulated was deemed by the Court not to be interstate commerce. The verdict of history appears to be that the NRA as a recovery measure was ill-advised.

Despite the failure of the NRA to contribute significantly to recovery, its by-products had a lasting imprint on the American economy. The most important of these was Section 7a, which guaranteed workers the right "to bargain collectively through representatives of their own choosing." Sponsorship of collective bargaining through federal legislation was a milestone in American labor history and introduced a new era in the labor movement. When the NIRA was declared unconstitutional in 1935, the collective bargaining guarantees were re-enacted in the National Labor Relations Act (NLRA), known as the Wagner Act. A labor movement which had faltered through the prosperous 1920's, and had become thoroughly demoralized between 1929 and 1932, spurted forward in this friendly atmosphere after 1933. Union recognition was extracted from recalcitrant employers in traditionally anti-union industries, with correspondingly large gains in union membership and in wages and working conditions. By sanctioning the right of workers to organize with-

out employer interference and to bargain collectively through independent representatives, the New Deal had given organized labor its Magna Carta.

Another important by-product of the NRA was a quick solution to an old struggle to eliminate child labor from industry and trade. The NRA also marked the start of federal minimum wage and maximum hour legislation. Although the NRA did not solve, it did grapple with the immense problem of coordinating American industry. This experience proved valuable during the Second World War, when many former NRA administrative officials assumed positions of leadership in the War Production Board to mobilize American industry for a new and greater struggle.

Agricultural Adjustment Administration (AAA)

The New Deal program in agriculture was less radical and more successful than the National Recovery Administration. The Agricultural Adjustment Administration (AAA) represented a further development of agricultural programs of the 1920's. Farmers experienced such hard times after the postwar depression of 1920 that schemes to solve the farm crisis kept coming before Congress every year. The McNary-Haugen equalization fee bills passed both houses of Congress on two occasions in the late 1920's only to be vetoed by President Coolidge. The Hoover administration enacted the Agricultural Marketing Act, setting up the Federal Farm Board, under which agricultural surpluses were purchased by government corporations in order to keep them off the market. Except through exhortation, however, no attempt was made to limit farm production. Under the Hoover administration attempts to maintain prices led to an increase rather than a decrease in farm surpluses.

In the contraction phase of the Great Depression (1929–32) the farm situation became truly desperate, as farm prices fell by 50 per cent. The New Deal innovation was to move quickly toward a bold plan of production control. The first year (1933), with the cotton crop already planted, an unusual step was taken in paying farmers to plow under some 10,000,000 acres of growing cotton. Again in order to get the program of planned scarcity under way without delay, some 6,000,000 hogs were slaughtered for the purpose of raising the price of pork. The AAA program brought the desired results. Cotton prices doubled in four years following 1932. Hog prices rose from $3.83 per hundredweight in 1932 to $9.89 in 1936. A similar crop control program contemplated for wheat proved unnecessary when nature came to the rescue with unfavorable weather. Wheat prices nearly doubled from 1933 to 1934 and more than doubled from 1933 to 1935. Parity prices for all farm products increased from an index of 58 in 1932 to 75 in 1934 and to 92 in 1936. Net farm income increased 133 per cent between 1932 and 1935.

The economics of scarcity, highlighted by plowing under cotton and slaughtering little pigs, shocked the sensibilities of the general public. It was equally repugnant to Secretary of Agriculture Henry Wallace, who said of the plowing under of cotton: "I hope we shall never have to resort to it again. To destroy a standing crop goes against the soundest instincts of human nature." Secretary Wallace defended planned scarcity in the only way possible, as a method of preserving the private profit system in agriculture. He pointed out

598

INTERWAR
GROWTH AND
STAGNATION:
THE GREAT
DEPRESSION

that restriction of production was a more common though less obvious practice in industry. "How could anyone who granted industry the right to control its production deny the same right to agriculture . . . We must play with the cards we are dealt. Agriculture cannot survive in a capitalistic society as a philanthropic enterprise." He was fully aware that the United States had both the largest food surpluses and the longest breadlines. Farmers cannot afford to grow crops for Americans without money to buy them any more than General Motors can afford to produce Cadillacs for the millions of Americans who cannot pay for them. The defect which led to planned destruction of wealth was by no means restricted to agriculture. To profess astonishment and incredulity was to be ignorant of the operation of the price system in a capitalistic economy. Nowhere can a better illustration be found than in agriculture for the proposition that the depression was a crisis of abundance rather than of poverty.

Social Security

Social security was another New Deal innovation in which the federal government assumed positive responsibility for the economic welfare of the nation. Although other industrial nations had adopted social security systems beginning in the 1880's in Germany under Bismarck, the United States had made virtually no progress in this direction prior to the Great Depression. Neither major political party nor organized labor had advocated statutory social security. The masses of unskilled and semi-skilled workers, those most in need of social security, were largely unorganized and therefore had few channels through which to express their views on the question. Aside from Wisconsin, a progressive state which had instituted unemployment compensation prior to the depression, inaction on the part of state governments had left a vacuum to be filled by the federal government in social security as in other fields. President Hoover did not favor government-sponsored social security and most of all not at the federal level.

Belatedly, the Social Security Act of 1935 recognized the need for protection to workers against the hazards of industrial society. After much debate, a law was drafted which put irresistible pressure on the states to cooperate with the federal government in establishing a federal system of unemployment compensation and of old-age annuities for approximately one-half of the labor force. Sickness and hospital insurance was excluded. In the election campaign of 1936 the Republican Party opposed social security legislation, but after a crushing defeat changed its position and vied with the Democrats in claiming credit for giving wider coverage. From its modest beginnings in 1935 the system has been extended to cover nearly all gainfully employed workers. The switch from an almost complete absence to an overwhelming acceptance of social security represents one of the striking achievements of the New Deal in anticipating the trend toward the welfare state. This much-needed reform quickly became entrenched as a part of the American way of life. Nevertheless, the next major advance was delayed thirty years until 1966, when medical care for older persons became part of the social security system of the United States.

From a long-term point of view perhaps the most audacious undertaking of the early New Deal was a measure designed to develop the whole region of the Tennessee River watershed falling in the seven states of Tennessee, Alabama, Mississippi, Georgia, North Carolina, Kentucky, and Virginia. The Tennessee Valley Authority had its genesis in the First World War when a hydroelectric plant for making nitrates for explosives was developed on the Tennessee River at a power site at Muscle Shoals in Alabama. In peacetime nitrates can be used for fertilizer, but under the conservative Republican regimes of the 1920's Muscle Shoals remained moribund. In the presidential campaign of 1932 candidates Hoover and Roosevelt took diametrically opposite positions on the issue of public power. Roosevelt pledged his administration to large-scale development of public power in four major river basins—the St. Lawrence, Tennessee, Colorado, and Columbia—while Hoover asserted that public power ran counter to the whole spirit of American private enterprise.

After his inauguration Roosevelt moved quickly to establish the TVA. Power generation was only one of the TVA's multiple purposes, and in official pronouncements not the most important. Other purposes included flood control of the troublesome Tennessee River system, soil conservation, afforestation, navigation of the Tennessee River, and fertilizer production. Opposition from private utilities, however, made public power the most controversial aspect of the TVA's multiple operations. Charges of unfair competition were lodged against this government corporation, which sold power at rates much below those prevailing in the region when the TVA began to operate. After the constitutionality of the TVA became established by court decisions, the private utilities, unable to meet the competition, sold out to the TVA. Stimulated by low rates, electric power consumption increased rapidly throughout the region, especially in the rural areas not previously served with electric power. In 1933 only 4 per cent of the farms in the region had electricity, contrasted with 88 per cent twenty years later.

One principle heralded by the New Deal was to use TVA power rates as a yardstick for comparing the rates charged by private utilities. The private utilities objected to the TVA as a yardstick on grounds that less than the full costs of producing power were allocated to power costs in the multiple-purpose TVA. The yardstick principle is fraught with difficulties in the case of power generated from river dams which also serve for flood control and river navigation. In fact there is no uniquely correct cost allocation in a joint-cost project of this type, and it is therefore impossible to determine whether power costs are understated by the TVA. Obviously, social gains are possible through the use of dams for multiple purposes.

Since private enterprise cannot afford to engage in flood control and normally does not invest in river improvements for water navigation, it suffers an inherent disadvantage in competition with a multiple-purpose public project. The objections of the private utilities should be addressed to the whole concept of a government-built, government-owned, and government-operated system of power, navigation, flood control, and fertilizer production. Does the

600

INTERWAR
GROWTH AND
STAGNATION:
THE GREAT
DEPRESSION

inability of private enterprise to undertake an organic system of general social and economic planning mean that such enterprises should not be operated at all? The TVA was alleged to be socialistic, and it was probably the closest approximation to socialism among the numerous experiments of the New Deal, if by socialism is meant government ownership and operation, the usual definition. It differed fundamentally from the NRA, which experimented in self-regulation of business, and from the Securities and Exchange Commission, which cast government in the role of a policeman protecting the interests of the public against avaricious practices by private groups. Even if TVA was socialistic, the New Deal as a whole was not.

Securities and Exchange Commission (SEC)

Another New Deal innovation brought the stock exchanges under federal control. The Securities and Exchange Act of 1934 constituted the most important legislation of this type. It represented a reform rather than a recovery measure. What is surprising, perhaps, is that reform legislation did not come earlier, under the Hoover administration, as a reaction to the great crash of 1929, especially since President Hoover initially attributed the depression to overspeculation in the New York stock exchange. Public reaction may be gauged by the burst of applause which greeted the statement in Roosevelt's inaugural address: "The money changers have fled from their high seats in the temple of our civilization." Inaction by Hoover and strong measures by Roosevelt illustrate again the shift in policy orientation represented by the New Deal.

A series of shocking disclosures before the Senate Banking and Currency Committee between 1932 and 1934 provided the immediate background of regulatory legislation. This inquiry into stock-broker and stock-market operations revealed how Wall Street insiders manipulated the sale and purchase of securities for their own enrichment, often at the expense of the public for whom they were presumed to act as trusted advisers. Investment bankers such as the powerful House of J. P. Morgan had "preferred lists" of customers who were permitted to purchase securities below market value. Rich bankers and brokers avoided payment of income taxes by selling stocks at a loss to relatives and then repurchasing them. J. P. Morgan, one of the richest men in the world, paid no federal income taxes for 1930, 1931, and 1932. Rings of speculators ran up the prices of certain securities in order to dump them on an unsuspecting public during the bull market of the 1920's. On occasion speculators would form pools to force prices down artificially in order to buy back securities to cover short sales.[5] Some of the manipulators were indicted and a few went to jail, but most of their corrupt practices did not violate any law. A humor magazine of the time put the matter thus: "And it's our opinion that banking in this country will never be safe until somebody invents a burglar alarm that will ring every time the directors are in session." The general public, already disillusioned with the "money changers," were incensed by the revelations of the Senate Banking and Currency Committee.

[5] In a short sale securities are sold for later delivery by sellers who do not own the securities at the time of sale but plan to acquire them in time for delivery.

601

INTERWAR
GROWTH AND
STAGNATION:
THE GREAT
DEPRESSION

The financial community struck back at the New Deal with bitter denunciation of proposed reforms. Richard Whitney, President of the New York Stock Exchange, predicted that if the Securities Exchange bill were passed, "The security markets of the Nation will dry up." He said that the stock exchange was fully capable of controlling itself. Despite dire predictions from financiers, the bill passed both houses of Congress by an overwhelming majority, reflecting the general indignation of the country with the behavior of investment bankers and the feeling that stock exchanges should be subject to close scrutiny by a public agency.

The Securities and Exchange Commission was charged with responsibility for protecting the investing public against misrepresentation, dishonesty, and manipulation. Corporations wishing to issue new securities were required to disclose to the Commission all pertinent facts bearing on the value of securities. The Commission was empowered to revoke the trading privileges of brokers and bankers found guilty of shady dealings. Civil and criminal penalties were provided. The Commission was also charged with responsibility for policing the stock exchanges. The Securities Exchange Act gave the Federal Reserve the authority to raise or lower margin requirements in purchases of securities. Public utilities were brought under the jurisdiction of the Securities and Exchange Commission by the Public Utility Holding Company Act of 1935, a law designed to correct the flagrant abuses in this field by promoters and speculators such as Samuel Insull.

A New Fiscal Policy

In the presidential campaign of 1932 Roosevelt criticized President Hoover for failing to balance the federal budget. In a speech in Pittsburgh Roosevelt recommended a 25 per cent cut in governmental expenditures. He used the common, but misleading, analogy between the income and expenditures of a government and a family, and predicted the same tragic consequences for a government with chronic deficits as for a spendthrift family which persists in living beyond its means. Under the Economy Act of 1933 President Roosevelt cut the salaries of government workers and the pensions of veterans. The following year Congress restored these cuts over a presidential veto. In 1935 tax rates were increased on personal and corporate incomes and other taxes, with maximum tax rates on personal income going from 59 to 75 per cent.

A balanced budget remained Roosevelt's goal throughout his first term. He differed from Hoover, however, in not allowing the ideal of a balanced budget to stand in the way of a vigorous, positive program of governmental action designed to overcome the depression. Expenditures increased rapidly under the New Deal, and although national income, and therefore tax yields, were rising, expenditures rose still more rapidly, causing deficits to increase in each succeeding year during the first term. Thus, when Roosevelt came into office and throughout his first term as president, his ideas on fiscal policy were quite orthodox. In practice, however, his willingness to experiment with new and often bold federal programs continually enlarged the federal deficits which had begun in the Hoover administration in the fiscal year 1930–31. This is shown in Table 32–2.

602 TABLE 32-2

INTERWAR
GROWTH AND
STAGNATION:
THE GREAT
DEPRESSION

Receipts and Expenditures of the Federal Government, 1930–1943
(millions of dollars)

YEAR ENDING JUNE 30	RECEIPTS	EXPENDITURES	SURPLUS OR DEFICIT
1930	4,178	3,440	738
1931	3,116	3,577	— 461
1932	1,924	4,659	— 2,735
1933	2,021	4,623	— 2,602
1934	3,064	6,694	— 3,630
1935	3,730	6,521	— 2,791
1936	4,069	8,493	— 4,424
1937	4,979	7,756	— 2,777
1938	5,615	6,792	— 1,177
1939	4,996	8,858	— 3,862
1940	5,144	9,062	— 3,918
1941	7,103	13,262	— 6,159
1942	12,555	34,046	—21,491
1943	21,987	79,407	—57,420

Source: U. S. Bureau of the Census, *Historical Statistics of the United States, Colonial Times to 1957.* Washington, D.C.: Government Printing Office, 1960, p. 711.

At the start of Roosevelt's second term in January, 1937, recovery had gained momentum and was rolling along at a good pace. The index of industrial production in May, 1937, stood at 118 which was slightly above the 1929 level. National income had increased from $40 billion in 1933 to $72 billion in 1937. Meanwhile unemployment had fallen, and the outlays required for works projects and relief were considerably diminished. With rising revenues and falling expenditures a balanced budget loomed as a possibility. The budget deficit fell from $4.4 billion in fiscal 1936 to $2.8 billion in fiscal 1937. Taking social security payments into account, total *cash* receipts exceeded total cash outlays of the federal government in the first nine months of 1937. The pump-priming of the first term seemed to have paid off at long last by stimulating the private sector of the economy to gain the momentum needed to continue under its own power. There were even signs that business expansion might overreach itself and turn into an inflationary trend of commodity prices. Rising prices contributed to heavy inventory accumulation.

Just as the federal budget was on the threshold of attaining balance, the economy went into a tailspin. Inventory accumulation became inventory deaccumulation and the economy plunged back into deep depression. The index of industrial production fell precipitously between May, 1937, and May, 1938. Unemployment increased by three to five million in the same interval. Most of the hard-won gains of the past four years were lost in a few months. The sharp reversal from apparent recovery to actual depression occurred during the very same months in which the cash budget was temporarily in balance.

Fiscal policy was at the crossroads in the spring of 1938. Should the
New Deal press for a balanced budget by reducing expenditures and raising
tax rates in keeping with the traditional conservatism of administration leaders
like Secretary of the Treasury Morgenthau and Vice President Garner? Or
should budget deficits be tolerated, and even fostered, as recommended by a
new point of view which included among its advocates Marriner Eccles, Chairman of the Board of Governors of the Federal Reserve System? After some
soul-searching, President Roosevelt decided to accept deficit finance. In a
special message to Congress on April 14, 1938, he recommended a resumption
of large-scale spending. Fiscal policy had now come to the top of New Deal
recovery measures. According to Rexford G. Tugwell, a New Deal participant
and historian, "This was the first time—after four years—that he appears to
have accepted, not only theoretically but as a matter of positive governmental
virtue, the management of income and outgo as a regulator of the economy." [6]

Among the New Dealers, Eccles was the chief architect of planned
deficit financing. From his experience as a Utah banker and businessman he
arrived independently at ideas similar to those espoused by Keynes, who for
some years had advocated "loan expenditure," that is, "deficit spending," as a
means of increasing the aggregate demand for goods and services as the way
out of depression toward prosperity. Keynes held that unemployment and
depression result from a deficiency of total demand because of inadequate
spending, especially for private capital formation. Public spending should
compensate for the deficiency in private spending and should be financed in a
way that does not reduce private spending. Increased public spending financed
through higher tax rates is therefore inappropriate during depressions because the additional taxation takes money away from those who spend most
of their income anyway. To raise governmental expenditures, with tax rates
unchanged, would, of course, create a deficit in the federal budget. But what
had been considered a necessary evil in the first term of the New Deal became
a virtue in the new perspective presented by Eccles and Keynes. Eccles
favored balancing the budget not by raising tax rates or by retrenching on
expenditures but by raising the level of national income through expansionary
measures. Under the tax rates existing in the late thirties, he estimated that
the federal budget would come into balance when national income reached
$80 billion. This was substantially below the full-employment level of national
income. What Eccles in effect advocated was that the federal government
should act as the compensatory agent in the economy, unbalancing its budget
in depression and creating a budget surplus in periods of high employment.

For maximum benefit to employment the federal borrowing during
depressions should be from banks rather than from the public because borrowing from banks results in the creation of new money (bank credit). The
expenditure of newly created money represents a net addition to the total
spending stream and directly increases demand, employment, and real national income. Although loan financing leaves a deficit in the governmental
budget, it helps to eliminate the much larger and more serious deficit in the
national economy. Idle men and idle machines are put to work producing real

[6] Rexford G. Tugwell, *The Democratic Roosevelt* (Garden City, N. Y.: Doubleday &
Company, Inc., 1957), p. 449.

604

*INTERWAR
GROWTH AND
STAGNATION:
THE GREAT
DEPRESSION*

goods and services, and if carried out on a sufficiently large scale, deficit spending can be expected to result in full employment.

The case for deficit spending was reinforced by the notion that it would increase national income not only by the amount of the deficit but by some multiple of it. Keynes estimated the size of the multiplier to be somewhere between two and three in the United States. Thus each billion dollars in deficit spending might result in two to three billion dollars of additional real national product of goods and services.

In the new theory of fiscal policy, deficit spending was not to be viewed as pump-priming in the sense of being a temporary measure to be withdrawn with impunity at an early date. Expenditures would have to continue as long as private demand remained deficient; national income and employment could be expected to drop when deficit spending dropped, unless for other reasons private spending, especially for capital formation, increased enough to offset the decline in government spending.

Because deficit finance of the income-generating type advocated by Eccles and Keynes operated through increases in the supply of money, only the federal government could successfully engage in long-term, planned deficit spending. Only the federal government possesses the constitutional authority to create money. Herein was another argument for transferring responsibility for national well-being, including work projects, from state and local governments to the national government.

In President Roosevelt's second term, fiscal policy became the chief weapon against depression. The NRA was gladly forgotten. Other measures such as the AAA, the SEC, and the TVA continued to alleviate distress in particular sectors of the economy, but the general weapon, the key to recovery, lay in fiscal policy. It enjoyed the advange of being a general weapon which could be used within the framework of a private enterprise economy and its constitutionality was beyond question. Large deficit spending continued through the thirties without apologies of the type offered during Roosevelt's first term. By the end of the decade the national debt had risen to $40 billion, a figure more than double the national debt in 1929 and 60 per cent higher than the previous peak at the end of the First World War. Full recovery was not achieved, however, until the immensely increased expenditures for World War II rescued the nation from the Great Depression.

The New Social Philosophy

The chief characteristic of Franklin Roosevelt's New Deal was its experimental character. It did not represent a preconceived ideology or a consistent evolution toward a fixed goal. Roosevelt sensed correctly that the American people were dissatisfied with the inadequate measures taken reluctantly by the Hoover administration. Roosevelt's attitude was to try one thing and, if it did not work, to try something else; but above all to do something. To do nothing he considered the worst possible course. In other words, the President and his chief advisers regarded as axiomatic the bankruptcy of laissez-faire policy—all too obvious during the Great Depression—and the necessity of positive action by the federal government in the direction of a welfare state.

605

INTERWAR
GROWTH AND
STAGNATION:
THE GREAT
DEPRESSION

The contrast, however, between the Hoover and Roosevelt administrations was not simply a difference between passivism and activism, between laissez-faire and intervention. Hoover's activities as Secretary of Commerce under Coolidge showed him to be in advance of his party in economic matters. As President, Hoover did not remain oblivious to the need to do something about the depression. He opposed the extreme laissez-faire policy of letting nature take its course, of putting the economy through the wringer of liquidation.

The measures he advocated were not too different from some New Deal policies: (1) Hoover favored the maintenance of wage rates and, while not asking for legislative authority to maintain wages, he exhorted employers not to cut wages. (2) He called a White House conference to coordinate public and private relief programs at the local and state level. (3) His administration created the Federal Farm Board, which supported farm prices by purchasing crop surpluses until nearly a half-billion dollar fund was exhausted. (4) In the early phase of the depression, Hoover supported an expansion of public construction, of which Hoover Dam was an outstanding example. Federal outlays on construction increased in 1930, 1931, and 1932, although not by enough to offset declines in state and local governmental construction. (5) In 1932 the Hoover administration set up the Reconstruction Finance Corporation (RFC) to advance loans to banks and railways which were financially embarrassed. This type of financial assistance to big business became known as the "trickle down theory," meaning that if money were lent to businessmen at the top of the economic pyramid some would trickle down to workers and farmers. (6) Hoover sponsored large open-market purchases by the Federal Reserve authorities as a means of easing the credit position of banks which would then be able to make loans to businessmen and other investors.

Although all of these measures by the Hoover administration were consistent with economic expansion, they suffered from two fatal defects. Either they relied on exhortations to others, including businessmen, state and local governments, and community leaders outside government, to take action when these groups did not have the financial ability, as in the case of state and local governments, or the incentive to do very much of what was urged upon them by the national administration, as in the case of businessmen; or the Hoover policies involved large federal expenditures and therefore ran headlong into a principle which President Hoover came to consider most fundamental of all, an annually balanced federal budget.

After a flurry of activity early in the depression, President Hoover lost enthusiasm for measures such as public works and farm price supports because, to be at all effective, they had to be on a scale which would place the budget beyond all hope of balance. Again and again Hoover pledged himself to a balanced budget. It became an obsession with him. In vetoing a public works bill in 1932 he sent the following message to Congress: "Never before has so dangerous a suggestion been seriously made to our country." He asserted further, "The primary duty of the Government is to hold expenditures within our income." Hoover not only demanded retrenchment of expenditures, but in a desperate attempt to achieve balance he pushed through Congress, with the aid of a Democratic House of Representatives, a major increase in tax rates in 1932. Strive as he might, however, Hoover was unable to achieve a

606

INTERWAR
GROWTH AND
STAGNATION:
THE GREAT
DEPRESSION

balanced budget because national income kept falling so rapidly that even with higher tax rates, total tax revenues declined faster than expenditures could be slashed.

Thus after initially endorsing expansionist plans, President Hoover retreated to a position that was closer to laissez-faire, not because he really believed in laissez-faire but because of his dedication to the type of "sound finance" associated with a balanced budget. Expansion through positive governmental action faded into the background as the depression deepened. As economic conditions worsened, the President became more and more unpopular. The unemployed mocked him by giving the label "Hooverville" to the shanty communities where the jobless and homeless gathered on the outskirts of towns and cities. President Hoover became a brooding and unhappy man. The defeat of his earlier hopeful program is written between the lines of his pronouncement: "Economic depression cannot be cured by legislative action or executive pronouncements. Economic wounds must be healed by the action of the cells of the economic body—the producers and consumers themselves."

When Franklin Roosevelt became President his ideas were, as we have noted, not so very different from those of Hoover at the onset of the depression. Roosevelt accepted at that time the principle of the balanced budget, but he did not permit it to become a straitjacket, and in his second term he at last surmounted orthodox finance and embraced planned deficit spending. Whereas Hoover moved back toward laissez-faire, Roosevelt moved away from it. The critical difference between them lay in Hoover's reiterated devotion to a balanced budget and Roosevelt's willingness to cast aside this ancient maxim of fiscal policy.

The road to planned deficit finance under the New Deal was by no means direct. Within a general trial-and-error framework of experimental thinking, Roosevelt had general ideas about the direction in which he wanted to move and he gathered around him advisers whose ideas on economic policy were similar to his own. In the first term his leading advisers—the "brain trust"—were three professors from Columbia University: Raymond Moley, a professor of political science; Rexford G. Tugwell, a professor of economics; and Adolph A. Berle, a professor of law who had worked in economics as well as in law.

Tugwell and Berle, and especially the former, were the President's closest advisers on economic affairs in the early days of the New Deal. Both men were liberal-progressives, but not in the orthodox American tradition of trust-busting and enforced free competition. Tugwell and Berle consciously acknowledged that the highly integrated, collectivistic nature of American industry was here to stay and they proposed action consistent with its collective nature. Their approach to economics emphasized the cooperative rather than the competitive elements in the American economy. They advocated economic planning rather than laissez-faire and anti-trust policies. They saw the task of industrial reform as one of social management, that is, the operation of giant, quasi-public corporations in the interest of the general public rather than for the benefit of shareholders and private managers.

The NRA was the leading manifestation of this collective approach to economic reform. Tugwell favored the principle of the NRA although, as he conceived it, the federal government should have been the senior partner in a

607

INTERWAR
GROWTH AND
STAGNATION:
THE GREAT
DEPRESSION

position to curb the anti-social proclivities of business in the form of price increases and output restrictions. Tugwell warned Roosevelt that the code-making process was getting out of hand under General Johnson. The TVA was another example of the positive, direct government type of project endorsed by Tugwell. Since TVA was a wholly government-owned and government-managed enterprise, it was automatically protected against the restrictive tendencies which wrecked the NRA. The AAA was yet another form of economic planning. It achieved administrative success, although it did not avoid the restrictionist tendencies of the price system under private enterprise.

The early planning approach of the New Deal achieved some lasting success, as in the case of the TVA, but more generally the passing of the NRA symbolized the failure of planning in the all-important industrial sector of the economy. By 1935 President Roosevelt had begun to revert to orthodox American progressivism which places the blame for economic evils on big business, monopoly, and concentration of economic power. The distinction between the collectivist progressivism of Tugwell and Berle and the orthodox variety of American progressivism is illustrated by the difference between the government-business partnership philosophy behind the NRA and the policeman philosophy of the SEC. The SEC was, however, limited to policing financiers and did not directly challenge big business generally. This latter challenge came during Roosevelt's second term, when the most vigorous anti-trust enforcement campaign in history got under way with Thurman Arnold of the Justice Department in the driver's seat. Simultaneously the Temporary National Economic Committee (TNEC) launched a massive investigation into the concentration of economic power. Undue concentration of economic power presumably would be broken up by reducing the size of business units to a point at which competition would become workable. The TNEC and the anti-trust policies can be reconciled with earlier New Deal policy mainly in terms of the experimental attitude of the President. Having tried the planning-partnership approach and failed, he would now try a different approach even if it meant having to break up some of the concentration put together by the NRA. Instead of encouraging businessmen to get together, as under the NRA codes, they would be denied the right to do so under anti-trust enforcement.

The ideology of the later New Deal stemmed directly from Supreme Court Justice Louis D. Brandeis through Felix Frankfurter, a professor of law at Harvard and later a member of the Supreme Court. The Brandeis-Frankfurter school was ably represented in the New Deal at the legislative-drafting level in the personages of Thomas G. Corcoran, affectionately known as "Tommy the Cork," and Benjamin V. Cohen, both graduates of the Harvard Law School. These brilliant young men replaced Tugwell and Berle in the high counsels of the later New Deal. The switch to a second New Deal seemed vindicated by the sweeping Democratic victory at the polls in the presidential election of November, 1936.

The two parts of the later New Deal puzzle may now be put together. If a distinction is made between the micro and the macro aspects of the total economy, it may be said that later New Deal policy accepted free enterprise, policed by vigorous anti-trust enforcement, in the micro sphere, but rejected it in the macro sphere in favor of deficit financing as a means of maintaining

608

INTERWAR
GROWTH AND
STAGNATION:
THE GREAT
DEPRESSION

an aggregate level of demand consistent with high-level employment. The new policy asserted, in effect, that with proper policing, free private enterprise could allocate efficiently the resources it employed, but it could not guarantee a satisfactory level of employment of those resources. Fiscal policy, accompanied by appropriate monetary policy, was supposed to provide overall stability through (a) deliberate deficits in time of depression and (b) surpluses in periods of full employment. Not much was said about surpluses because in the conditions prevailing in the 1930's budget surpluses were considered neither possible nor desirable. In this two-fold policy, the micro part was not new. It was part of the legacy of nineteenth-century populism. Conscious use of fiscal policy, and in particular of planned deficits, in depression, survived as the unique contribution of the New Deal to American economic policy. Within this policy framework, private enterprise retained a wide latitude while the federal government remained free to pursue the positive measures demanded in the public sector of the welfare state.

Evaluation of the New Deal

No simple answer can be given to the question whether the New Deal succeeded or failed. With brave words and bold deeds President Roosevelt broke the psychological deadlock which gripped the economy in the winter of 1932–33 and launched the longest period of cyclical expansion in American history up to that time, some 50 months of sustained recovery from March, 1933 to May, 1937. During this long upswing several million workers returned to private employment and millions of others received public employment. Meanwhile, under the reforms of the New Deal some of the worst evils of American capitalism were remedied through legislation relating to social security, child labor, control of the stock exchange, wages and hours of employment, banking practices, including bank deposit insurance, and farm distress.

On the other hand, the American economy under the New Deal failed to achieve anything approaching full recovery during eight years from 1933 through 1940. The long period of expansion from 1933 to 1937 may be accounted for by the fact that the economy had fallen to unprecedented depths between 1929 and 1932. Even at the peak of the expansion phase in May, 1937, 7,500,000 workers remained unemployed, and while unemployment did not again go as high as the 15,000,000 of 1933, it was nevertheless 11,000,000 in 1938 and still 10,000,000 when the war in Europe began in 1939. Thus the New Deal coincided with the most prolonged period of stagnation and mass unemployment in American experience. At no time during the 1930's was the level of national income or industrial output of 1929 attained despite an increase in productivity of 3 to 4 per cent per year.

Economic stagnation resulted from the failure of capital formation to return to the levels which prevailed during the 1920's. Representatives of business and finance frequently alleged that the nature of the New Deal itself—large spending and chronically unbalanced budgets—created a lack of confidence which discouraged capital formation in fixed plant and equipment. Certainly the business community showed timidity in making such investment during the 1930's.

Lack of business confidence may have been a factor, but other more **609**

INTERWAR
GROWTH AND
STAGNATION:
THE GREAT
DEPRESSION tangible influences were also at work in limiting investment. So much plant and equipment built in the 1920's was still available for use during the 1930's that there was limited need for more capital formation. Much of the plant and equipment remained idle, which reduced the incentive to produce more of the same. Another factor helping to account for the small volume of capital formation was the absence of important new industries to spearhead expansion on a broad front in the way the automobile industry had done during the twenties. Residential construction boomed in the twenties but stagnated during the thirties. As people lost jobs and could not pay rent or mortgage premiums, they moved in with relatives or friends. Where ties with the land had not been broken, the unemployed families moved back to the farm where they could at least grow their own potatoes. Birth rates and marriage rates were low during the depression years, and the number of family units increased slowly compared with earlier and subsequent decades. Simultaneously foreign investments sank to a low level. Hence the volume of spending on private capital formation remained abnormally low throughout the decade from 1929 to 1939.

President Roosevelt seems to have been fully aware of the precarious state of capitalism when he took office in 1933. An avowed purpose of his administration was to save the private enterprise system from the sorry plight into which it had fallen. He possessed the power and the prestige to swing Congress behind him had he decided to nationalize the banks, railways, and some sectors of heavy industry. Such measures would have facilitated the national planning program which he then had in mind. As events turned out, his planning approach failed, but the profit system survived. In this respect the New Deal may be said to have achieved one of its chief objectives. It saved private enterprise even if it did not succeed in making it work satisfactorily. It discovered a formula (fiscal policy) which it believed would make the system work, but could not apply this formula successfully in peacetime.

In summary, it may be concluded that the New Deal achieved certain important goals but failed to achieve the main economic objectives of any sound economic system, namely, full and efficient utilization of the available resources. Put slightly differently, the New Deal, despite the long distance it brought the economy along the uphill road to recovery, left a huge gap between the actual and the potential level of living of its citizens. More than a decade after the stock market crashed in 1929, the Great Depression remained unliquidated. Moreover, there were few indications that it would be liquidated in the foreseeable future. People were eating regularly and the private enterprise system had been preserved, but the performance remained unsatisfactory. Only the threat of war, and later the actuality of war, lifted the American economy from its moribund state.

In wartime it became possible to do what apparently was not possible in peacetime, namely, for the government to spend enough to create full employment. The deficit for one war year was more than double the sum of the federal deficits for the entire decade 1931–40. (See Table 32–2.) The threat of inflation replaced the evil of unemployment. Although the United States did not enter the war until 1941, American policy from the beginning was clearly sympathetic toward the western allies and by the spring of 1940, when

610

*INTERWAR
GROWTH AND
STAGNATION:
THE GREAT
DEPRESSION*

President Roosevelt announced the bold program of building 50,000 airplanes per year, a small boom was already under way. Thereafter hot and cold war generated demand in such volume that the stagnating tendencies of the 1930's did not reappear. The long war should not, however, obscure the question: What would have happened in the absence of war? No clear answer can be given from actual experience, although the fiscal policies forged during the Great Depression represented a movement in the direction of a viable economic system.

SELECTED BIBLIOGRAPHY

BAKER, GLADYS L., WAYNE D. RASMUSSEN, and others, *Century of Service, The First Hundred Years of the United States Department of Agriculture.* Washington, D.C.: Government Printing Office, 1963.

BEARD, CHARLES A. and MARY R., *America in Mid-Passage.* New York: The Macmillan Company, 1939.

DOUGLAS, PAUL H., *Social Security in the United States: An Analysis and Appraisal of the Federal Social Security Act.* New York: McGraw-Hill, Inc., 1939.

ECCLES, MARRINER S., *Beckoning Frontiers.* New York: Alfred A. Knopf, Inc., 1951.

FUSFIELD, DANIEL R., *The Economic Thought of Franklin D. Roosevelt and the Origins of the New Deal.* New York: Columbia University Press, 1956.

GALBRAITH, JOHN K., *The Great Crash.* Boston: Houghton Mifflin Company, 1955.

HOPKINS, HARRY, *Spending to Save, The Complete Story of Relief.* New York: W. W. Norton & Co., Inc., 1936.

KUZNETS, SIMON, *National Income and Its Composition, 1919–1938,* 2 vols. New York: National Bureau of Economic Research, 1954.

MILLS, FREDERICK C., *Prices in Recession and Recovery.* New York: National Bureau of Economic Research, 1936.

MITCHELL, BROADUS, *Depression Decade, from New Era Through New Deal, 1929–1941.* New York: Holt, Rinehart & Winston, Inc., 1947.

PECORA, FERDINAND, *Wall Street Under Oath, The Story of Modern Money Changers.* New York: Simon & Schuster, Inc., 1939.

ROOSEVELT, FRANKLIN D., *The Public Papers and Addresses of Franklin D. Roosevelt,* 4 vols., ed. by S. I. Rosenman. New York: Harper & Row, Publishers, 1941–45.

SCHLESINGER, ARTHUR M., *The Age of Roosevelt.* Vol. II, *The Coming of the New Deal.* Boston: Houghton Mifflin Company, 1957.

SCHUMPETER, JOSEPH A., *Capitalism, Socialism and Democracy.* New York: Harper & Row, Publishers, 1942. (paperback)

SHANNON, DAVID A., ed. *The Great Depression.* Englewood Cliffs, N.J.: Prentice-Hall, Inc., 1960. (paperback)

TUGWELL, REXFORD G., *The Democratic Roosevelt.* Garden City, N.Y.: Doubleday & Co., Inc., 1957.

WALLACE, HENRY A., *New Frontiers.* New York: Reynal & Hitchcock, 1934.

———, *Sixty Million Jobs.* New York: William Morrow & Co., Inc., 1945.

WECHTER, DIXON, *The Age of the Great Depression, 1929–1941.* New York: The Macmillan Company, 1948.

WRIGHT, QUINCY, ed., *Unemployment as a World Problem.* Chicago: University of Chicago Press, 1931.

BLACK, JOHN D., and JOHN K. GALBRAITH, "The Maintenance of Agricultural Production During Depression: The Explanations Reviewed," *Journal of Political Economy*, XLVI (June, 1938), 305–23.

CLARK, JOHN MAURICE, "Economics and the National Recovery Administration," *American Economic Review*, XXIV (March, 1934), 11–25.

CRUM, WILLIAM L., "Concentration of Corporate Control," *Journal of Business*, VIII (July, 1935), 269–83.

DAVIS, JOSEPH S., "AAA as a Force in Recovery," *Journal of Farm Economics*, XVII (Feb., 1935), 1–14.

GRAY, HORACE M., "The Allocation of Joint Costs in Multiple-Purpose Hydro-Electric Projects," *American Economic Review*, XXV (June, 1935), 224–35.

GREGORY, THEODORE E., "The American Experiment," *Manchester School of Economics and Social Studies*, V, No. 1 (1934), 1–18.

HANSEN, ALVIN H., "Economic Progress and Declining Population Growth," *American Economic Review*, XXIX (March, 1939), 1–15.

HOOVER, CALVIN B., "The 'New Deal' in the United States, Pt. I, The Agricultural Adjustment Act: Principles, Practices and Problems," *Economic Journal*, XLIV (Dec., 1934), 567–90.

PRIBRAM, KARL, "Controlled Competition and the Organization of American Industry," *Quarterly Journal of Economics*, XLIX (May, 1935), 371–93.

SCHUMPETER, JOSEPH A., "The Present World Depression: A Tentative Diagnosis," *American Economic Review*, XXI (March, 1931), 179–82.

TUGWELL, REXFORD G., "The Principles of Planning and the Institution of Laissez-faire," *American Economic Review*, XXII (March, 1932), 75–92.

Russian Economic Development

CHAPTER 33

Two turning points in the long-term economic development of
Russia were the emancipation of the serfs in 1861 and the Russian
Revolution in 1917. Russia remained predominantly feudal until
1861. In that year the liberation of 40,000,000 serfs and crown peasants put
an end to feudalism as a system although important feudal elements persisted
through the First World War. Capitalism, which made inroads before emancipation, never became very strong in Russia but achieved some success in the
period between 1861 and 1917. In the Revolution of 1917 Russia became a
socialist economy in the sense that the means of production, including land,
factories and banks, were nationalized and the employment of wage-labor by
private capitalists was abolished. After temporary concessions to private ownership and private enterprise during the 1920's, the Soviet Union launched a
series of gigantic Five-Year Plans in 1928. Following the Second World War
the Soviet Union made rapid strides in economic development and attained
levels of industrial production second only to the United States.

RUSSIA BEFORE THE REVOLUTION OF 1917

The belated survival of medievalism accounts for much that is otherwise in-
comprehensible in eastern Europe in the twentieth century. Feudalism
emerged there at about the time it was declining in western Europe, and
what in the West is considered modern times, i.e., since 1500, has been characterized in eastern Europe until recently by feudal institutions. The Russian
soldiers who pursued Napoleon's bedraggled armies from Moscow into western
Europe in 1812 brought back ideas of a better world. A movement against
the absolutism of the Russian Czars and in favor of constitutional monarchy
took root among young army officers, liberal nobles, peasant leaders, and the
intelligentsia, including some of Russia's greatest literary figures. When Czar
Alexander I died childless in 1824, an uprising aimed at establishing constitutional government met with bloody repression from the newly enthroned Czar
Nicholas I. Social unrest among serfs and periodic uprisings under Nicholas I
increased pressures for liberation.

Russia's defeat in the Crimean War (1857) convinced the new Czar,

Alexander II, and his advisers that the nation could not be a great power in a
world of rapid industrial and agricultural change while dependent on unfree
labor. Liberation of 20,000,000 serfs and an equal number of crown peasants
followed in 1861, just two years before President Lincoln issued the Emancipation Proclamation which freed the slaves in the United States. The liberated
serfs were given access to land, a provision not made for serfs liberated in
western Europe or for the liberated American slaves.

Unfortunately, the distribution of land to Russian peasants did not end
agrarian unrest. Landlords demanded full compensation for the land surrendered for use by the newly liberated serfs. Since the serfs were too poor to
pay the lords for the land, the government paid the lords. In turn the government was supposed to collect from the peasants, over about half a century,
with interest at 6 per cent. As might have been anticipated, many peasants
were unable to meet their obligations. The so-called "redemption payments"
owed by peasants to the government became a new source of peasant unrest.
The financial burden on the protesting peasants was lightened from time to
time—for example, by 27 per cent in 1881—and finally during the revolutionary
turmoil of 1905 redemption payments were abolished altogether.

Land hunger remained a troublesome problem in Russia up to the Revolution of 1917. The amount of land held by most peasant families was inadequate
for their support, but large landholders opposed further redistribution of
land because they needed the cheap labor of small peasants and landless rural
dwellers as cultivators on their large states. Many less able and less thrifty
peasants fell deeply into debt and lost their land, often to the hated village
kulaks, the rich peasants who made money at the expense of poorer peasants.
Productivity among Russian peasants remained very low by western European standards. Consequently famine continued to be a constant threat in
peace as well as in war. After the Revolution of 1905, land reforms were introduced by the famous minister, Stolypin, which benefited the abler and
richer peasants who could afford capital outlays for improvements. Among
poorer peasants, however, the agrarian problem was still unsolved at the onset
of the First World War.

Against a background of military defeat in the war, the Russian tradition
of revolutionary discontent erupted in a world-shaking event, the Russian
Revolution of 1917. The Czarist regime, which was autocratic, cruel, corrupt,
inept, and entirely lacking in popular support even against its external enemies,
collapsed of its own weight in February of that year. First, the reins of government fell to the liberal regime in which Alexander Kerensky was the dominant
figure. Kerensky's government attempted moderate domestic reforms while
continuing the war against Germany. Little was done by the government to
satisfy the land hunger of the peasants or to meet the need for modern
military equipment by disgruntled soldiers at the front.

Between February and December, 1917, in the midst of virtual anarchy,
the landlord class was deposed by the peasants in the first of two twentieth-
century agrarian revolutions in Russia. Like many oppressed groups, Russian
peasants had from time to time indulged in violent uprisings only to meet
with violent repression. In 1917, with the collapse of any semblance of effective
government, the masses took things into their own hands on a wide scale.
The revolutionary feeling which gripped Russia is vividly suggested in the

following account: "One September day in the fateful year 1917, by a roadside in the south central *stepp,* a man climbed a telephone pole and cut the minute thread of communication which joined a manor-house on the northern horizon with the towns, the police-offices, and barracks along the railway line to the southward. In one sense this manor-house now stood quite alone, but not really so, for within sight of its groves there were several peasant villages . . . and within a few hours the estate had been looted, the mansion was in flames, and somewhere within the fiery circle the master of the house lay dead." [1]

Meanwhile the situation ripened for a revolutionary seizure of power by the Bolshevik (Communist) party under the leadership of Vladimir I. Lenin (1870–1924), who returned to Russia from exile in Switzerland in April, 1917. Kerensky's regime, which refused to sanction withdrawal from the war and confiscation of land by peasants, lost control of the situation. Under Lenin's adroit leadership the Bolsheviks seized control of the government and retained power by responding sympathetically to the demands of the masses of people, promising land to peasants, peace to soldiers, and bread for hungry urban workers. "Land, bread and peace" proved an effective slogan in putting across the first major socialist revolution in modern times.

WAR COMMUNISM

Although Lenin, in the tradition of Marx, believed in the technical superiority of large-scale agriculture, he was in no position to press for collectivized agriculture at the time of the Revolution in 1917. Instead, the Bolsheviks made the most of the situation to gain peasant support by giving legal sanction to peasant seizures of land previously owned by private landlords. In November, 1917, the government decreed that the land belonged to all the people, which nominally meant socialization of land, but under the circumstances this merely gave the government a chance to guide the redistribution process. Equality of landholdings was encouraged as far as possible. Within local villages land was distributed equally to households, but between different areas equality was not feasible without major shifts in population. Where large estates had been numerous, there was considerable land to divide, and the average peasant's holding was considerably enlarged over the pre-revolutionary holdings. Where there had been only a few large estates, however, individual acreage increased hardly at all. More than one-half of the villages received no significant increase in average holding. When, in addition, those who had migrated from the towns to the country during the early years of the Revolution were given land, the average holding increased from about five or six acres to about six or seven acres.

"The Fundamental Law of Land Socialization" (November, 1918) decreed that "the right to the use of the land belongs to him who cultivates it with his own labor." Private employment of wage-labor was forbidden, in keeping with the basic principle of Marxian doctrine that laborers employed by private employers for wages are exploited because of the power advantages enjoyed by employers. Small-scale family cultivation, however, proved a poor

[1] G. T. Robinson, *Rural Russia Under the Old Régime* (New York: The Macmillan Company, 1949), p. 64.

compromise between large-scale capitalist agriculture and large-scale socialist

agriculture because it reduced the amount of marketable surplus available for the urban population. Russian peasants on small farms using only family labor had seldom produced more than enough for their own consumption and seed; and in years of poor harvests they did not always produce enough for seed.

During the years of War Communism (1917–21) the most critical economic problems arose from an inability and unwillingness of peasants to produce food for urban workers and Red Army soldiers. Industry virtually collapsed in the midst of war and revolution, and the output of industrial consumers' goods fell far below the already inadequate level. Peasants who did have surplus grain could get very little in exchange for it, and they had still less incentive to sell produce and hold paper money which was depreciating rapidly as a result of great increases in the quantity.

Faced with these desperate circumstances the government resorted to compulsory requisitioning of surplus grain from peasant farmers. This led to arbitrary and forcible seizure of surplus produce to feed the nonagricultural population. "Food armies" consisting of soldiers, city dwellers, and the poorest peasants swarmed over the countryside in search of provisions. A virtual war broke out between town and country dwellers. Apart from more obvious forms of resistance such as hiding supplies of food and seed, the peasants responded by reducing the area sown to crops. Nature compounded the horrors of civil strife with poor rainfall, which further reduced the yields on the already reduced acreage. In 1921 the worst famine in modern Russian history resulted in the starvation of millions, left other millions of peasants with no seed grain, and further reduced the scanty food rations of tens of millions of Russians. Late in 1921 the limits of human endurance had been reached, and the Revolution stood on the threshold of collapse.

THE NEW ECONOMIC POLICY, 1921–1928

Lenin recognized that continued compulsory requisitioning of grain would alienate the peasants and that ubiquitous food shortages would turn industrial workers against his revolutionary government. With characteristic political acumen he announced in March, 1921, a New Economic Policy (NEP) which greatly increased the extent of private enterprise permitted in agriculture, trade, and industry. Private employers were permitted to hire wage-labor in agriculture and elsewhere. Arbitrary grain requisitioning was replaced with a definite tax which gave peasants an incentive to produce as much as they could in order to sell their surplus produce (above the tax) at whatever price they could get in the open market. Money, which had fallen into desuetude under War Communism, was restored to its conventional role as a medium of exchange. Numerous state-owned factories were leased to private entrepreneurs. Nearly all retail and much wholesale trade returned to private enterprise, and concessions were made to foreign capitalists. The new group of Russian capitalists and entrepreneurs who came to the fore were called NEPmen.

A hostile outside world hailed Russia's New Economic Policy as admis-

sion by the Bolsheviks that collectivism had failed as a workable economic system. Lenin, however, viewed the NEP only as a "strategic retreat," as "taking one step backward in order to take two steps forward." The NEP proved a tribute to Lenin's genius as a political strategist rather than a testimonial to his lack of faith in collectivism. Despite the leeway given to private enterprise under the NEP, the Soviet government retained a firm hold on the economy. All heavy industry, including transportation, the banking system, foreign trade, mineral resources, and all sources of fuel including electric power, remained solidly in the socialist sector. Whatever the interpretation placed on the New Economic Policy, it temporarily solved the food crisis and induced the peasants to support the new regime as a bulwark against possible return to the old order. Farm produce flowed back into market channels, and industrial production increased to prewar levels.

The success of the New Economic Policy during the 1920's afforded the Soviet leaders time to survey the existing situation and to debate the future course of political and economic policy. Bolsheviks agreed that the road to security for the socialist state they had created lay in the direction of industrialization. Open to debate among Bolsheviks were questions of the speed and the means by which they should proceed toward an industrial society. The nub of the political question lay in the relations between peasant agriculture and the resources from agriculture needed for industrial capital formation. Conservative Bolsheviks contended that the NEP had proved a workable policy and should be continued more or less indefinitely. As peasant farmers supplied more raw materials and more food for industrial workers and for export to buy capital equipment, socialist industry could be expanded gradually. This view stressed that the Revolution had been won in 1917 and rescued in 1921 at the end of War Communism by the political acquiescence of the peasants; and that to alienate the peasants by a radical reorganization of agriculture would endanger the revolution again.

The opposite view of the radical or left-wing Bolsheviks regarded the NEP as a breathing space preparatory to plunging into large-scale industrialization. Otherwise, it was argued, the Revolution would gradually dwindle to nought, as rich kulak farmers and prosperous NEPmen became stronger and could spearhead a capitalist counter-revolution against socialism. The radicals pointed to the increase in peasant households from 18 million in 1914 to approximately 25 million in 1925 to show that the trend from urban to rural population was just the reverse of that required for industrialization. They favored collective agriculture over individual peasant farming.

Although agricultural production had been restored to the prewar level by 1925, the surplus produce being marketed was substantially less than before the war. A smaller surplus from equal or larger production was attributable to the increase in small holdings and the decrease in large estates over the prewar era. As a result of the land redistribution which accompanied the Revolution and continued under the New Economic Policy, many peasants were eating better but marketing less of their produce. Another factor contributing to the reduced marketing was a continued shortage of manufactured goods. Farm prices were low, by prewar standards, compared with manufactured goods (the so-called scissors effect). As grain collections decreased

in 1928 and again in 1929, Russia's ability to export grain also fell and forced
a curtailment in the import of capital equipment for industry.

Productivity in Russian agriculture increased slowly during the 1920's, at about 2 per cent a year, at which rate several decades would have been required for any substantial transition to an industrial society. Millions of peasant holdings averaging less than twenty-five acres were too small for efficient use of farm machinery. Moreover, Russian topography, consisting of great level steppes, was eminently suited to the use of tractors, combines, and other types of farm machinery. These factors indicated that too many workers were already engaged in agriculture, and that the large rural population, so characteristic of underdeveloped countries, was increasing.

The decision in the great debate of the 1920's called for all-out industrialization in the form of overall economic planning combined with a movement toward collective farming. Stalin, who rose to leadership of the Communist Party after the death of Lenin in 1924, was largely responsible for this momentous decision. In order to step up long-term agricultural productivity to a rate consistent with rapid industrialization, Stalin and his associates believed collective farming was imperative. Political control of the peasants would also be facilitated by collectivization of agriculture. At the start, however, the move toward collective farming was to be gradual, with one-fourth of the peasant households and 15 per cent of the cultivated area planned for collectivization at the end of the First Five-Year Plan. Meanwhile, the bulk of increased market surplus was to come from huge state farms (grain factories) of several thousand acres on new lands to be worked with tractors and combines. Surplus grain and other farm products would be sold in world markets and the foreign exchange thus obtained used to purchase agricultural machinery and capital equipment for industrial construction. Such was the final resolution of the long debate within the Communist Party during the period of the New Economic Policy. The actual course of events was to run somewhat differently, especially with respect to the pace of collectivization of agriculture.

PLANNING BEFORE THE SECOND WORLD WAR

In 1928 the Soviet Union abandoned the New Economic Policy and launched the "Plan Era," which was a novel experiment in the history of the world. In a series of Five-Year Plans the Russians undertook a consciously planned industrial revolution. Within a decade, after completion of the first two plans, the industrial revolution was substantially completed. Within twenty years (1928–48) the Soviet Union rose to a position second only to the United States in industrial and agricultural production. Within three decades (1928–58) the Soviets had exploded atomic and hydrogen bombs, launched the first man-made satellite, and begun seriously to challenge the scientific, economic, and ideological leadership of the United States.

The Soviet plans were comprehensive schedules of production and investment in industry, agriculture, and other sectors of the economy over five-year periods. The prewar plan periods were as follows:

First Five-Year Plan   —October 1, 1928, to December 31, 1932 (4¼ yrs)
Second Five-Year Plan—January 1, 1933, to December 31, 1937
Third Five-Year Plan   —January 1, 1938, to December 31, 1942
(Disrupted by war)

In industry the plans called for an approximate doubling of total production during each successive five-year period, which if realized, would have meant an eight-fold increase in fifteen years. In agriculture the goals were less ambitious in terms of increased total output and also less completely realized because of special difficulties arising from the rapid, forced collectivization of agriculture during the First Five-Year Plan. The third plan was washed out by the outbreak of the Second World War in 1939 and the German invasion of Russia in 1941.

Industrial Growth under the Early Plans

During the ten years 1928–37 Soviet industry grew at the high rate of 16 per cent per year (cumulative), which was sufficient to double industrial production in the First Five-Year Plan and to redouble it again during the Second Five-Year Plan, for a four-fold increase in a decade. This rate of growth exceeded that achieved in the United States during any decade and exceeded the growth in any comparable period by any country. The existence of advanced technology in capitalist countries played an important role in the high rate of growth in Soviet industry. Many engineers and technologists from the United States and western Europe accepted employment in Russia during the 1930's, when so many were unemployed in the capitalist world because of the Great Depression. Very little foreign capital was available to Russia, however, because of the opposition to the revolutionary, anti-capitalist Soviet system. Ability to borrow advanced technology therefore required an exceptionally high rate of domestic saving. Soviet saving averaged approximately 25 per cent of the gross national product throughout the 1930's.

Stress on heavy industry   A high proportion of gross capital formation was directed into heavy industry, including iron and steel, coal mining, machinery, electric power, and other industries which provided the means of production for producing further means of production (machines to produce more machines). Soviet steel output increased from 4 to 6 million tons during the First Five-Year Plan, 35 per cent below the quota which had been set. Failure to meet the goal of the first plan arose from delays in getting new plants into operation on schedule. In a complex system of interrelated production each stage must be coordinated with all preceding and succeeding stages; a lag in any one stage can retard production all along the line.

Soviet coal production rose from 35 million tons in 1928 to 64 million tons in 1932, which was 10 million tons short of the goal for 1932. During the Second Five-Year Plan coal output doubled to 128 million tons, but this was short of the ambitious goal of 152 million tons. The output of electric power increased seven-fold over the decade of the first two five-year plans.

Production of machinery made sensational gains according to official Soviet statistics. Unlike steel, coal, and electricity, machinery is not a single product and therefore its output cannot be measured in simple physical units

like tons and kilowatt-hours. Consequently the statistics of machine production
are subject to varying interpretations depending on the weights in index
numbers and the values placed on new machinery not produced in the base
year. According to Soviet data, the output of machinery increased four-fold
during the First Five-Year Plan and three-fold on an enlarged base during the
Second Five-Year Plan, both of which outputs were in excess of planned
increases. During the 1930's the Soviet Union became the world's second
largest producer of tractors, harvester combines, freight cars, and railway
locomotives.[2] These, of course, were years of the Great Depression, when production of farm machinery and other heavy equipment fell much below normal
in countries outside Russia. Nevertheless, the figures, like other Soviet data on
increases in production, are impressive.

Light industries Light industries performed less well than heavy industries in meeting goals which were, to begin with, less ambitious. In textiles,
for example, production was less in the last year of the First Five-Year Plan
than in the year preceding the start of the plan. Woolen textiles suffered from
a shortage of raw wool resulting from the slaughter of sheep by recalcitrant
peasants who were forced into collective farms. Cotton textiles also suffered
from a shortage of raw material, resulting from cutbacks in the import of
raw cotton in the face of deteriorating terms of trade for Russian exports.
In the world crisis of the early 1930's, the price of grain decreased more than
the prices of industrial products. In order to maintain the imports of machinery
and construction materials for heavy industry, the Soviets cut back on other
planned imports, including raw cotton. Meanwhile, an ambitious program
for the expansion of domestic cotton production had not progressed very far.

In contrast with textiles, the output of leather goods rose sharply. Boots
and shoes increased three-fold during the first plan and two-fold on an enlarged base during the second plan. Total output of industrial consumers'
goods increased during both the first and second plans, but by much less than
the increases in heavy industrial products. Although the first plan contemplated a rise in total industrial and agricultural consumers' goods, the actual
course of events led to a fall in the real earnings of Soviet workers because of
the poor results in agriculture and concentration on producers' goods. Concessions were made to consumers' goods in the second plan, and toward its
end real wages began to rise. This upward trend in real wages was reversed
a few years later by the great sacrifices imposed by the Second World War.
Substantial increases in Soviet living standards did not begin until the Fifth
Five-Year Plan (1951–55). Thereafter improvements in standards of living
were steady and substantial.

Agriculture and Collectivization

Although industrialization was the prime objective of the Five-Year
Plans, a change in the structure of agriculture was a necessary corollary, as a
prerequisite of industrialization on a wide scale and because of its ideological
impact on the population. In 1929 after a decade of socialism, the Soviet Union

[2] For some years Soviet officials claimed the largest output in the world of tractors,
combines, and locomotives.

remained primarily a nation of peasant households, some 25 million of them, constituting more than four-fifths of the total population. Productivity in agriculture had to be raised before sufficient labor could become available for industrialization on the vast scale encompassed by the Five-Year Plans. A marketable surplus of food and fiber from agriculture was needed to feed nonfarm workers and to supply raw materials for factories.

Since peasants seemed unlikely to become sufficiently productive under small-scale cultivation to support large-scale industrialization, and since the Communist leaders feared that large-scale agriculture on a private enterprise basis would strengthen the opposition to socialism, the Soviet government launched a program of collectivizing agriculture and liquidating the "kulaks as a class." Some Soviet leaders believed that as long as the peasants constituted a majority of the total population, there would be more potential capitalists than socialists. Hence ideological and economic purposes were closely linked in the decision to push ahead at all speed toward an industrial society. In the drive against the wealthy kulaks, Communist Party and government officials got support from the poorer peasants, who had more to gain than to lose by entering collective farms.

Collective farms (kolkhozy) Although the decision by any family to enter a collective farm was supposed to be voluntary, the policy of liquidating the kulaks as a class meant that a rich or even moderately prosperous peasant family really had little choice but to enter a collective or face deportation to Siberia or some worse fate. The number of households in collectives increased rapidly from 5 million to 14 million within a few months in 1929–30. Kulaks fought back by slaughtering their animals, hoarding grain, even burning and murdering in a give-and-take struggle between rich and poor peasants. This second Russian agrarian revolution—the first had been the liquidation of landlords in 1917–1918—went forward with such fury that Stalin felt compelled in March of 1930 to issue his famous "Dizziness from Success," warning to return to voluntary measures of inducing peasants to join collectives. Stalin's letter temporarily reversed the wave of collectivization, but the tide soon surged forward again. By the end of the First Five-Year Plan in 1932, two-thirds of the sown area of Russia was under collective farming. Approximately 14 million families consisting of 70 million people were living on 211,000 collective farms averaging about 1,000 acres in size and 65 to 70 households per farm.

Collective farming at first took several forms, but the *artel* became the leading type and received the official sponsorship of the government. Under the *artel*, individual families on collective farms possessed their own dwellings and a small plot of land for a garden, small livestock (usually a cow and poultry), and small farm tools. The main croplands, farm buildings, and larger farm implements, apart from those rented from machine tractor stations, were held in common, and each family member of the *artel* shared in the distribution of the surplus remaining after payment of fees to machine tractor stations, taxes, and other obligations to the government. Private enterprise could be based only on personal (family) labor. Employment of the labor of others by private individuals was again strictly forbidden as it had been before the NEP, on the grounds that such "wage" labor necessarily resulted in exploitation of the employed by the employer.

State farms (sovkhozy)   A second type of socialist agriculture was the huge state farm directly owned and operated as a government enterprise with hired workers similar to the wage-earners employed in socialized factories. The largest of the state farms were called "grain factories" and were used to bring under cultivation virgin soil in semi-arid areas with marginal rainfall. They required deep plowing and quick harvesting of a type which could best be done with tractors and combines. Nine-tenths of the workers employed on state farms were machine operators and mechanics. Some grain farms of the early thirties contained as many as 500,000 acres and averaged about 6,000 acres. This early experiment in state farms proved disappointing, and state farms declined rapidly in importance after the mid-thirties only to experience a revival in the 1950's under Khrushchev.

Machine tractor stations (MTS)   The amalgamation of small, individual holdings into collective farms required as a complement the use of tractors, combines, and other modern farm machinery in order to realize the potential economies of large-scale cultivation. At the start of the First Five-Year Plan farm machinery was very scarce. To utilize scarce equipment more intensively machines were not placed directly with collective farms but with special government units known as machine tractor stations, which serviced several collectives in surrounding areas on a contractual basis. Contracts took the form of payments in produce, such as grain, as compensation for plowing, harvesting, and other services rendered to the collective farm by machine tractor stations. Along with other methods, the machine tractor station became a device for exercising control over the activities of collectives and for extracting surplus produce from them.

Economical use of farm machinery became all the more necessary after the peasants slaughtered draft animals in their resistance to collectivization. Although the government plan called for imports of farm machinery and for construction of huge tractor plants, the severe loss of draft animals more than offset the increased mechanical horsepower through the end of the First Five-Year Plan. A further advantage of the machine tractor stations lay in placing farm machinery in the hands of skilled operators and expert mechanics at a time when Russian peasants were still untutored in the use of complex machinery. Machine tractor stations remained a keystone in Soviet agrarian collectivisim until the late 1950's, when the merger of collective farms into giant farm units and the disadvantages of dual control of farm management by both collectives and machine tractor stations led to their elimination. Farm machinery was placed directly under the operation and control of collective farms.

Output performance in agriculture   Compared with the sensational increases in industrial production, the results in Soviet agriculture under the Five-Year Plans were distinctly disappointing. Livestock production suffered most of all from the violence of the collectivization drive. The number of cattle fell by almost one-half between 1928 and 1933 and recovered very slowly thereafter. By 1933 the number of sheep and goats dropped to approximately one-third the 1929 total. The number of pigs declined to less than one-half the 1928 total, but recovered more rapidly. The number of draft horses declined to less than one-half the 1928 total and never rose again to the pre-plan total.

In field crops, yields per acre, which were scheduled to increase by some

35 per cent during the First Five-Year Plan, did not increase at all, and, in fact, declined during 1931 and 1932 owing to bad harvests. Compared with the 1928 crop, the total grain harvest fell slightly in 1929, rose in 1930, and fell in 1931 and 1932. Beginning in 1933 total grain production recovered and attained new, all-time highs for Russia, as did domestic cotton production.

More impressive than the increases in total production of field crops was the rise in marketable "surpluses." Economic surplus is defined as an excess over what is necessary for subsistence, but subsistence is a somewhat variable concept in physical terms. Insofar as the consumption of collective farmers fell below the consumption of independent peasant households in the 1920's, some of the so-called surplus represented a decrease in subsistence forcibly imposed by the system of collective farming. "Surpluses" took the form of deliveries to the government from the collectives. Surpluses of grain and other foodstuffs constituted a kind of "wages fund" for feeding nonfarm workers, and surplus cotton, wool, and flax a kind of raw materials fund for textile production. From the viewpoint of industrialization, surpluses delivered to the government were more important than the absolute level of farm production. Compared with 1926–27, deliveries to the government of grain increased two-fold by 1932–33 and four-fold by 1937–38. The marketable surplus of cotton rose two-fold by 1932–33 and five-fold by 1937–38 as compared with the pre-plan period. Marketable surpluses also increased for potatoes, flax, and wool. In short, the "wages fund" for industry registered sharp increases.

Following the disruption resulting from collectivization, the trend in gross agricultural output was upward after 1933 (broken by the war years), while the number of farmers, individual and collective, decreased, which indicates a rise in the productivity of labor in agriculture. Between the census years 1926 and 1939 the agricultural labor force of the Soviet Union decreased by 16.7 million workers (from 71.7 million to 55 million). Expressed as a percentage of the total labor force this represented a decrease from 85 to 61 per cent.[3] Seasonal and partial unemployment, so characteristic and costly in primitive agrarian economies, was reduced substantially with corresponding gains in the nonagricultural labor force. The Soviet census of 1926 listed 8.5 million wage and salary workers in nonagricultural occupations. By the end of the First Five-Year Plan this more than doubled, to 20 million, and in the 1939 census the number stood at 28.8 million, more than triple the number in the 1926 census (Eason, p. 86). The increase of approximately 20 million wage and salary workers in nonagricultural occupations was drawn primarily from the 16.7 million decrease in the agricultural labor force during corresponding years. These figures illustrate dramatically the contribution of large-scale mechanized farming to the sensational growth of Soviet industry during the decade of the thirties. England's eighteenth-century enclosure movement made a similar but much less sudden contribution to the English Industrial Revolution.

End of rationing Increased agricultural production after 1933 was a major factor leading to the abolition of rationing of consumers' goods in 1935.

---

[3] See Warren W. Eason, Chapter II, "Labor Force," in *Economic Trends in the Soviet Union*, ed. by Abram Bergson and Simon Kuznets (Cambridge: Harvard University Press, 1963), p. 77.

Agricultural produce as well as industrial consumers' goods continued to be insufficient to meet the effective demand of consumers, but the increasing output narrowed the gap between the amounts produced and the amounts demanded. Even after rationing ended, prices continued to be controlled by Soviet planners, although consumers were now free to buy as much as they wanted within the limits of their incomes and the availability of goods, many of which were still in short supply. The division of aggregate national product between consumers' goods and capital formation was determined by the central planners, and corresponded to the difference between the aggregate of high prices charged for consumers' goods purchased by urban and rural consumers, on the one hand, and the low wages paid to wage-earners and the low prices paid to farmers, on the other hand. Included in the prices paid for goods was a turnover tax designed to mop up excess purchasing power and to maintain monetary equilibrium. Another factor contributing to the abolition of rationing in the mid-thirties was the reduction in agricultural exports resulting from the diminished need to import machinery and construction materials as the productive capacity of Soviet industry increased.

Third Five-Year Plan and the Second World War

In basic design the projected Third Five-Year Plan continued the pattern of economic development of the First and Second Five-Year Plans. As was to be expected, because of the greatly enlarged industrial base, the magnitudes of projected growth were much greater but the planned *rate* of industrial growth was slightly less. Whereas the first two plans had called for more than doubling total industrial production within five-year periods, the third plan aimed at something less than doubling in five years. Industrial output was scheduled to increase 14 per cent per year as compared with 16 per cent realized growth in the previous ten years.

Priority to heavy industry remained the key to Soviet grand strategy for war and peace. Among the heavy industries scheduled to more than double their output by 1942 (1937 = 100) were: aluminum (346%), chemicals (237%), machine-building and metal-working (229%), electrical-energy production (206%), and cement (202%). Steel, which had increased from 4 to 6 million tons in the first plan and from 6 to 18 in the second plan, was to increase from 18 to 28 in the third plan.[4] Railway construction, which had been relatively neglected during the first ten years of planning, received much more attention in order to meet the rising volume of traffic. Railroad rather than highway transportation has been stressed throughout Soviet development.

Less rapid increases were again projected for light industries and consumer goods production, although these planned increases were impressive by other than Soviet standards. Textiles, the output of which had been disappointing in the previous plans, set relatively modest increases of 42 and 67 per cent for cotton and woolen fabrics, respectively, during the Third Five-Year Plan. Shortage of supply of raw materials rather than inadequate plant capacity constituted the chief limitation on textile production despite the fact that cotton growing registered impressive relative gains. Failure of the sheep

[4] See Alexander Baykov, *The Development of the Soviet Economic System* (London: Cambridge University Press, 1946), p. 289.

population to increase sufficiently to offset their liquidation during collectivization still limited the production of woolen textiles.

In the early years of collective farming the emphasis had been on increasing the marketable surplus of grain and other field crops. An important innovation of the Third Five-Year Plan was improvement of livestock breeding as part of collective farming. Most livestock was owned privately by farmers on their personal homesteads, which constituted an important part of the *artel* type of collective farm, and by other individual peasants. In 1938 collective farms as such owned only a quarter to a third of the cattle, pigs, sheep, and goats of the Soviet Union. The new program was designed to encourage large-scale livestock breeding on collective farms. It called for compulsory meat deliveries by collective farms in proportion to the amount of land owned by the collective in place of the previous levies according to the number of animals owned by a collective farm. This incentive plan had hardly begun to operate when Hitler's armies invaded Russia in the summer of 1941.

From its inception, in 1938, the Third Five-Year Plan was conditioned by gathering war clouds. The continued stress on heavy industry was consistent with armament production, but new plants were of smaller size in order to shorten the interval between the start of construction and the commencement of output from these plants. Plans to locate more plants east of the Urals were accelerated by the threat of war from the west, and plants in western Russia were fashioned in such a manner that they could be dismantled and moved to safer locations eastward. A slight relaxation in favor of consumers' goods, noticeable in the Second Five-Year Plan, disappeared in the third plan.

During the first three years, the Third Five-Year Plan proceeded more or less according to schedule, but when Hitler invaded Russia in June, 1941, in the fourth year of the plan, the need for immediate mobilization and defense against massive attack by land and air removed all meaning from the long-range projections begun in 1938. Again, as in the period of War Communism, the Soviet system was fighting for survival. In sharp contrast with the sorry performance of Czarist Russia in the First World War, the Soviet performance in the Second World War was magnificent. The abstinence from consumption which the five-year plans had imposed in order to build up heavy industries at full speed now provided Soviet armies with armaments with which to blunt the fury of the German army and air force and thereby to stave off the fall of Moscow and Leningrad.

At the outset of the war, the Soviet economy was undoubtedly still weaker than Germany's, and the acquisition of rich Russian industrial and agricultural territory early in the war further increased German economic superiority. Nevertheless; after blunting the massive attacks of 1941 and 1942, the Soviets remained strong enough to mount a counter-offensive along a 2000-mile eastern front by the summer of 1943, by which time the Soviet output of tanks and airplanes appeared to have exceeded that of Germany. The tide turned with the heroic stand in the winter of 1942–43 at Stalingrad, where a million German soldiers were killed, wounded or captured. After Stalingrad the Red armies took the offensive and routed the Nazi invaders.

The war left deep scars on the Russian economy. Most serious, of course, was the loss of approximately 20 million human lives, mostly adults, who were

missing from the postwar labor force and whose unborn children were not available for the labor force a generation later in the 1960's and 1970's. In occupied western Russia, the scorched-earth policy obliterated industrial plants and agricultural capital. The devastated Ukraine alone contained one-half of the prewar iron and steel capacity and the richest agricultural soil in the Soviet Union. Seven million horses and seventeen million cattle were taken from Russia into Germany during the war. The ability of the Soviet people to wage and win a war against the powerful German military forces on the eastern front and against these odds is the highest tribute to the success of the three prewar five-year plans.

Summary and Conclusions Concerning
Prewar Planning

The Five-Year Plans had as their primary purpose the rapid industrialization of Russia. Industrialization was conceived as necessary in order to preserve the Revolution and to strengthen the Soviet Union against its foreign and domestic enemies. In the eyes of Soviet leaders industrialization represented not only the road to a higher level of economic development but also ideological insurance against successful counter-revolution from within. Industrialization necessarily involved an increase in the proportion of urban workers, who were assumed to be ideologically more receptive to socialism than peasants. The purpose of industrialization was also social and military—to strengthen the Soviet Union as a nation which could protect itself against external counter-revolution and also to carry the socialist revolution to other countries. A policy of world revolution had been strongly advocated by Trotsky in the twenties, but Stalin adopted the policy of building socialism in a single country (the Soviet Union) while holding in abeyance international expansion of the Soviet system.

In Soviet planning there has characteristically been closer approximation to goals in heavy industry, such as steel, than in the lighter consumers' goods industries, such as textiles. This outcome is not fortuitous but lies at the base of Soviet planning strategy. Soviet goals have been very ambitious; as they have not been capable of being fully met, high priority has been assigned to heavy industry. When something in the plan has had to be sacrificed because of shortages, labor or materials have been withdrawn from the lower priority consumer industries and reassigned to heavy industry. Of course, resources are not always sufficiently interchangeable to satisfy the needs of heavy goods industries, and sometimes achievements have fallen short of goals even in this sector. The rationale behind high priority to fulfillment of goals for heavy industry is the same as the rationale for setting more ambitious goals for these industries in the first place. If a house, a shoe factory, or a sausage factory is not completed this year, it will mean only that the population will be less well housed, less well shod, and less well fed next year than if the plants were completed on schedule. A steel furnace not completed this year may mean that steel capacity will be unavailable to increase steel capacity next year and thereafter. The direction of Soviet investment toward producing means of production with which to produce more means of production accounts for both

the high rate of increase in industrial output and the low level of consumption by the Soviet citizenry.

Productive investment of the social surplus has been the basis for economic development throughout history. Modern capitalism has achieved a revolutionary role in history because it was the first economic system whose institutions were oriented specifically to productive use of the social surplus, that is, to capital formation—hence the name "capitalism." Soviet Russia became the first noncapitalist economy to dedicate itself to productive use of the social surplus. Prior to the Revolution of 1917 Russia's social surplus was relatively small and most of it was dissipated in unproductive consumption by the leisure classes, the nobility, the clergy, and the military. Russia's social surplus was not large in 1928, and the First Five-Year Plan succeeded only because an already low level of consumption was lowered still further in order that a larger share of the social product might be allocated to capital formation. In poor countries rapid economic development can take place only with great sacrifices in the form of hard work and reduced consumption.

In Russia each successive five-year plan increased the size of the social surplus in something like geometric progression. The Soviet drive toward forced industrialization was absolutely unrelenting, with each succeeding plan plowing back nearly 100 per cent of the social surplus into further means of production. For five years, for ten years, for half a generation, the revolutionary transformation of a backward peasant society into a modern industrial order continued at breakneck speed. The social and economic structure of agriculture and industry were completely transformed as old centers were enlarged many times over and vast stretches of the Urals and Siberia were converted to centers of modern industry and farming. The great human and material sacrifices inherent in such rapid transformation were not always—and not usually—accepted voluntarily despite the great sense of "becoming" that was engendered in the people by the Communist faith. Only a highly motivated people would have borne such great human and material sacrifices for such small immediate rewards. A task of such magnitude might have been impossible in a democratic society, because the governing party would have been thrown out of office long before the plans were completed. The achievements of the Five-Year Plans were enormous, but so were the costs. As in Pandora's box, which loosed so many evils upon the human race, about the only thing that remained was hope, hope that some time in the future the sacrifices would be rewarded with a standard of living commensurate with the productive power residing in the greatly enlarged means of production. A cruel and costly war intervened in the course of the Third Five-Year Plan, followed thereafter by the Cold War.

During the 1930's the two outstanding economic developments in the world were (1) the Great Depression in the capitalist world and (2) the rapid industrialization of the Soviet Union under the Five-Year Plans. As a result of the former, the industrial output of the United States fell by nearly one-half between 1929 and 1932. As a result of the latter, Soviet industrial output nearly doubled between 1928 and 1933. Both events were somewhat incredible. That the American economy would perform so badly could not have been predicted on the basis of past experience. That the Soviet Union was capable of such a great forward leap seemed equally unpredictable in terms of past

experience. The psychological impact of these simultaneous performances of

capitalist and socialist economies was such as to discredit the former and give prestige to the latter. At that time the Soviet leaders set a goal of catching up with and passing the United States in economic performance.

The Great Depression gave way to the Second World War, which wreaked physical devastation on the Soviet Union and set back its timetable for development by at least a decade, whereas the American economy showed great powers of expansion under the stimulus of war production. In the postwar decade the American economy did not return to the depressed condition of the prewar decade. Instead it performed remarkably well. Meanwhile, the Soviet Union made a sensational recovery from the war setback and grew at a pace two or three times as fast as the American economy. The campaign to catch up and pass the United States continued to be an important motif of Soviet production, and by the decade of the sixties Soviet coal production, once a leading index of industrialism, had passed American coal output, and other indexes were approaching their American counterparts. In steel the American capacity was more than double that of the Soviet Union, but the former sometimes operated at only 50 per cent of capacity whereas the Soviet steel output was consistently at full capacity. Consequently, there were some months during the latter half of 1960, for example, in which actual Soviet steel output exceeded the actual United States steel output.

POSTWAR SOVIET DEVELOPMENT

Like the legendary phoenix of Egyptian mythology, the Soviet Union rose in youthful vigor from the smoking ruins of the Second World War. With great energy derived from dedication to national purpose and under the lash of the Communist Party, reconstruction moved forward rapidly. By the end of the Fourth Five-Year Plan in 1950, war damages had been largely repaired and the Soviet economy entered a sustained period of rapid and steady growth. The last years under Stalin (died 1953) and the early years under Khrushchev marked the first "normal" period in the brief history of the Soviet Union, a nation founded in war and revolution in 1917. The Fifth Five-Year Plan (1951–55) met its ambitious goals, which resembled the prewar pattern of concentrating on heavy industries with lower priorities assigned to agriculture and light industries.

After three years the Sixth Five-Year Plan (1956–60) was scrapped and a new Seven-Year Plan (1959–65) begun. Impossibility of fulfillment seems to have motivated the switch in plans. The goals of the Sixth Five-Year Plan were extremely ambitious. The goals of the final year, 1960, became approximately the goals of 1961 or 1962 in the substitute Seven-Year Plan. Over its life the Seven-Year Plan called for a 62 per cent (7 per cent per year cumulative) increase in gross national product, which is formidable by most standards but lower than for any preceding Soviet planning period.

Agriculture Under Khrushchev

During the early 1950's under Khrushchev's leadership, some of the advantages anticipated at the beginning of socialized agriculture began to be

realized. Agricultural productivity increased, incomes of collective farmers rose rapidly, farm management became more efficient, and collective farming became for the first time more than just an efficient device for extracting a surplus from inefficient peasants. Despite these improvements, however, agriculture remained the weakest link in the Soviet economy.

Soviet farms, which were already large by American standards, increased still further in size. Mergers of existing collective farms increased the average size of collectives to 4300 acres by 1960; in the United States, by contrast, only 2 per cent of farms exceed 500 acres. Meanwhile state farms, which had been important for a brief period at the beginning of the plan era, experienced a renascence during the 1950's. Some new state farms resulted from conversion of collectives, but by far the greater acreage derived from virgin land opened in eastern sections of Russia. During the three years from 1954 through 1956, new arable land brought under the plow totalled 90,000,000 acres, an area equal to the combined arable land of France, Western Germany, and the United Kingdom. State farms averaged a gigantic 20,000 acres and some contained 50,000 acres in sown area. Bringing new lands under cultivation was tied to a corn (maize) program aimed at improving the Soviet diet with more meat production.

Another major Khrushchev reform eliminated machine tractor stations in 1958. Several considerations led to this important action, but two developments seem to have been strategic in the light of the dual control which the machine tractor stations imposed on collectives: (1) more and more mergers of collectives created farms sufficiently large to utilize fully the machinery allocated to them by a machine tractor station, and their integration followed as a logical development; (2) prosperity on collectives resulting from higher productivity and higher prices generated a surplus which needed to be diverted from demand for industrial consumers' goods to investment. Machinery was available, and collective farms could afford to invest in it at a time when consumers' goods remained in short supply.

Rapid increases took place during the 1950's in grain, milk, meat, and other farm products and led Khrushchev to promise a relative abundance of agricultural output during the 1960's. In the early sixties, however, the picture changed rather abruptly. After a few good crops, the "new lands" opened by Khrushchev petered out and yielded poor harvests. In 1963 the Soviet Union entered the world market to buy grain to feed its growing population. Khrushchev's ouster from office in October, 1964, stemmed in part from the big discrepancy between his promises and the performance in agriculture. His successors Kosygin and Brezhnev proposed further agricultural reforms which recognized the still urgent need for greater capital investment in fertilizers, machinery, and research to raise agricultural productivity. They emphasized higher yields per acre rather than enlargement of the area under cultivation. The Five-Year Plan for 1966–70 promised collective farmers a guaranteed annual wage as a further step toward improving the condition of this large and relatively neglected group.

Pricing changes to improve incentives   In the heroic period of Soviet industrialization, collective farms were a device for extracting maximum resources from agriculture to finance industry. In this important function collec-

tive farming proved helpful to industry, but it was harmful to incentives and efficiency in agriculture. Under Khrushchev's reforms the prices paid by the government for farm products procured from collectives increased substantially. Moreover, prices paid to farmers were proportioned to costs of production, something which had not been done previously because the government did not want to reveal the extent to which prices fell below the costs of production of collective farmers. Largely because of higher prices, the incomes of collective farms tripled between 1952 and 1958. Farmers who formerly shunned collective tasks as much as possible in order to work on their own small plots now had more incentive to apply themselves to socialized farming.

As material incentives were thus restored, some of the direct controls, including those imposed by machine tractor stations, were removed, and farm managers began to compare costs and prices in a more rational determination of how much of what crops to produce. Since collective farmers are residual sharers in the production of their farm, after paying their share to the government, they would seem to have more incentive to improve agricultural efficiency than farm wage-earners. Nevertheless, the productivity of state farms remained above that of collective farms.

High Growth Rate in Soviet Industrial Output

By any measure the performance of Soviet industry since the Second World War is impressive. The major emphasis continued to be on heavy industry, with steel, coal, electricity, and machine tools leading the way. By contrast with other economies at a similar stage of development, the Soviet output of automobiles, other consumer durable goods, housing, and transportation facilities remained insignificant. Soviet leaders have been much less concerned with increasing consumer durable goods than with enlarging the Soviet industrial base, initially in order to further enlarge the industrial base (steel mills to build more steel mills) and ultimately for whatever purpose seems most important—be it to conquer the world through military or economic might or the universe through space travel, or to enrich beyond all previous Russian standards the level of living of Soviet citizens.

During the 1950's Soviet industrial production increased approximately 10 per cent a year, and in the United States the comparable growth rate was about 4 per cent. In other words, Soviet industrial production was increasing two to three times as rapidly as that of the United States.[5] The Soviet Union increased by 7 per cent and the United States by 3 per cent their gross national products during the 1950's. If these rates had continued through the 1960's, the gross national product of the Soviet Union would have exceeded that of the United States in 1970.[6]

In the early 1960's, however, the growth rate of the Soviet economy slowed down while that of the United States increased. Although the Soviet rate remained higher, the difference was not substantial. The reasons for the Soviet slowdown were, apparently, lower ratios of added output to added

[5] See Robert W. Campbell, *Soviet Economic Growth* (Boston: Houghton Mifflin Company, 1960), p. 49.
[6] See Edmund S. Phelps, ed., *The Goal of Economic Growth* (New York: W. W. Norton & Company, Inc., 1962), p. xiii.

current investment, difficulties with consumers' goods, and the persistent farm problem.

Despite the slowdown, growth in Soviet heavy industries continued to be impressive. A comparison of steel output in the United States and the Soviet Union in 1955 and 1965 illustrates continued Soviet gains in this strategic sector. As shown in Table 33–1, the Soviet steel output doubled from 50 to

TABLE 33–1

U.S.–U.S.S.R. Steel Output, 1955 and 1965
(millions of tons)

	1955	1965	% INCREASE	ABSOLUTE INCREASE
United States	117.0	131.5	12	14.5
Soviet Union	49.8	100.0	101	50.2

Source: Business Week, June 4, 1966, pp. 58-59.

100 million tons, a 100 per cent increase, while steel output in the United States increased from 117 to 131.5 million tons, an increase of only 14.5 per cent during this 10-year period. A Soviet Twenty-Year Plan for 1961–80 projected an increase of 9 to 10 per cent annually in total industrial production, but this seemed unrealistic in view of the experience of the early sixties.

Reasons for the High Soviet Industrial Growth Rate

Factors accounting for the high rate of Soviet industrial growth may conveniently be discussed under the following headings: (1) borrowing advanced technology from other industrial nations; (2) high rate of savings and capital formation; (3) directing investment into enlargement of the industrial base of the economy, i.e., in heavy industry; (4) a large reservoir of manpower diverted into industry from agriculture; and (5) advances in knowledge and skills through high rates of investment in human capital.

(1) **Borrowing technology from more advanced industrial nations** The Soviets have been able to borrow technology from more advanced economies, especially the United States and western Europe. As the earlier German and Japanese experience illustrates, technology can be transplanted easily when conditions are ripe for it. By training engineers, scientists, and managers on a massive scale, the Soviets prepared themselves for successful borrowing. Through an alert system of monitoring technological progress throughout the world, in a manner resembling the activity of Germany's *Gewerbe Institut* of the nineteenth century, the Soviet Union equipped itself to capitalize on innovations elsewhere. In the course of catching up, the backlog of known but unexploited technology has diminished, but not sufficiently to have a noticeable effect on the growth rate in Soviet industry. The diffusion of technology

throughout the length and breadth of the country still offers a wide field for increasing the average level of productivity in the Soviet economy.

(2) **High rate of savings** Successful borrowing of industrial technology requires adequate saving and capital formation. Aggregate saving in the Soviet Union has been at a very high rate since the beginning of the plan era. Saving is enforced by the plan and is by the government primarily rather than by individuals. It constituted a quarter to a third of the gross national product, as compared with approximately one-sixth to one-fifth in the United States. A relatively low level of consumption is the other side of high Soviet savings and capital formation. Although the definition of Communism as a system of producing more and eating less is an exaggeration, it has thus far contained an important element of truth. In 1960 Soviet production was about 45 per cent of United States production, while Soviet consumption was only about 30 per cent of United States consumption on an aggregate basis, and less on a per capita basis, since the Soviet population is larger than the American. Consumption in the Soviet Union has been mostly what the classical economists called productive consumption, that is, consumption which is essential for subsistence of producers.

(3) **Directing investment into an enlarged industrial base** Not only the amount but the direction of capital formation has contributed to the high rate of Soviet economic growth. By concentrating investment on heavy industry, the industrial base has been expanded rapidly. Steel mills used to build more steel mills expand an economy more rapidly than steel mills used to build automobile factories or to produce consumers' goods directly. For example, Soviet coal production slightly exceeded and Soviet machine tool production greatly exceeded that of the United States, while steel output was not far short of United States steel production in 1958. By contrast, output of Soviet automobiles, washing machines and refrigerators was only a small fraction of output in the United States.

Low ratios of capital investment to increases in output have enabled the Soviets to get the greatest mileage out of their capital formation. In industry, where Soviet capital formation has been concentrated, the amount of capital required for a given increase in final production is low as compared with the amount of capital required for housing and for transportation. For example, in order to increase national income by one ruble, only four rubles may be needed in industry as compared with ten rubles in transportation or twenty rubles in housing. By investing heavily in industry and lightly in transportation and housing, the rate of growth in national income was higher than it would otherwise have been. For some years after World War II the square feet of housing space per dweller in the Soviet Union declined, and investment in transportation was restrained through more intensive utilization of railways. The costly capital needs for highways have been held down by the limited production and use of automobiles and trucks. When housing began to increase fairly rapidly in the late fifties, the high investment-output ratio in this sector contributed to the slowdown in the Soviet growth rate.

(4) **Reservoir of rural labor power** By reason of the rise in agricultural productivity, beginning in the 1950's the Soviets were able to divert increasing

numbers of farm workers to industrial production. According to the Soviet census of 1959, 46 per cent of the labor force was engaged in agriculture. In the United States less than 6 per cent of the labor force was engaged in agriculture in 1965. Assuming the Soviet farm worker might some day approach the efficiency of American farm workers, there remained an untapped potential reservoir of 40 per cent of the Soviet labor force for nonagricultural employment. In any case there is a great potential labor supply for more industrial expansion through further enhancement of productivity among agricultural workers.

Unquestionably diversion of labor from rural to urban occupations has in the past and will in the future contribute to rapid industrial growth as well as to the growth of gross national product. Since the measured (value) productivity of workers in industry, especially in heavy industries, is typically higher than the productivity of workers in agriculture, a shift from agricultural to industrial employments raises the average productivity of all workers and thus contributes to an increase in gross national product. In slightly different terms, the low level of efficiency of Soviet agriculture has been and should continue to be an important basis for a high rate of growth in industry and in the economy as a whole. However, an economy cannot go on forever diverting labor from farms to factories, and after a time there are too few workers left in agriculture to be shifted elsewhere. In the United States the less than 6 per cent of the labor force engaged in agriculture must, of necessity, be of relatively high efficiency. It cannot therefore contribute much to economic growth by further reallocation from high-productivity agriculture to high-productivity industry. Of course, inefficiency in agriculture, or anywhere else, is no guarantee of improvement, but in the Soviet case there is reasonable expectation that agricultural inefficiency will decline, and as it does, it will ultimately cease to be a factor contributing to still further improvement. But for several decades the elimination of inefficiency on farms can serve as a source of rapid overall economic growth. In an economy on the move from the old to the new, previous weakness can provide a basis for future improvement.

(5) **High rates of investment in human capital**   In the period just prior to firing the first sputnik in 1959 the Soviet Union was investing 6.5 per cent of its gross national product in education, as compared with only 3.7 per cent by the United States.[7] This is probably the clue to rapid Soviet strides in economic development as well as science. Within a generation millions of unskilled, illiterate peasants were trained to be skilled, literate farmers, factory workers, managers, scientists, and engineers. A strong positive correlation exists between levels of education and levels of economic productivity. Compulsory, universal education, which played such a notable role in the German industrial revolution of the late nineteenth century (see Chapter 17), has been equally important in Russian industrial progress. Soviet advances have taken place all along the line, from common laborers to managers and scientists. Among Soviet managers in industry the proportion of college graduates is higher than among American managers, and more of the "Red" managers are graduates in engineering than are their American counterparts.

[7] Nicholas DeWitt, "Basic Comparative Data on Soviet and American Education," *Comparative Education Review* (June, 1958), pp. 9–11.

In science and engineering Soviet achievements have been phenomenal.

By 1960 the Soviet Union was graduating twice as many engineers and scientists as the United States. Apart from sputniks, few sensational innovations have been reported from the Soviet Union, but the massive output of trained engineers and scientists provides a solid basis for future Soviet economic development. Large investment in human capital is probably the best, and perhaps the only, guarantee against diminishing returns in the long run. The creativity of engineers and scientists depends, of course, on more than a college education, and although it may be contended that creativity can better flourish in a capitalistic society, which provides greater freedom, this is a position more easily asserted than proven. Soviet firsts in sputniks, moonshots, and astronauts, as well as a long tradition of great Russian mathematicians and scientists, suggest that the Russians may be able to capitalize on their investments in human and material resources. To be sure, basic science and, to a lesser degree, technology are international, and, if the Soviets take the lead, other countries should be able to borrow their ideas in the same way the Russians have borrowed ideas from others. Germany's greatest economic gains were made by borrowing British and American technology, not by taking the lead in scientific creativity.

Steady Growth

Not only has the Soviet economy grown at a high rate, but the growth has been continuous because of full employment of labor and capital equipment. Apart from random fluctuations caused by natural vicissitudes, like weather, and social catastrophes, like war and revolution, the Soviet economy has experienced a high degree of stability in employment and output. Nothing resembling the recurrent pattern of prosperity and depression, so characteristic of capitalism since the maturing of the Industrial Revolution, has marked Soviet economic development. Under capitalism, instability of employment and production is closely linked to variations in the rate of capital formation, which in turn is based on fluctuating expectations concerning the profitability of new investments. When the rate of capital formation is high, prosperity prevails under capitalism; and when capital formation flags, recession and depression set in. Capitalist instability is compounded because fluctuations in capital formation generate cycles in the demand for consumers' goods, so that in recession and depression both capital formation and consumption fall below the normal levels associated with high employment.

Under the Soviet economy there is no basis in experience or in economic logic to expect a deficiency of demand because the socialist planning authorities would simply fill the gap with new capital formation or other non-consumer expenditures. The Soviet problem has not been lack of effective demand but rather excessive demand resulting in inflationary pressures, leading in turn to administrative rationing and other devices for restricting consumer expenditures below the level Soviet citizens would voluntarily spend if given free choice. Moreover, it should be noted that Soviet citizens are not only guaranteed the right to employment but are expected to work. In a non-business economy like the Soviet Union, however great its other faults, business cycles are not to be expected.

Clearly, the Soviet economy has been successful in utilizing fully its resources and in achieving a high growth rate. A further criterion of economic performance is the efficiency with which the resources have been employed. Rationality of resource allocation is an especially important issue in the Soviet Union, partly because Western economists had contended, before the advent of socialism in Russia, that rational allocation was impossible except under a market system, based on private ownership of the means of production. In the Soviet Union central economic planning has replaced the market system, and social ownership has replaced private ownership of the means of production. Unlike capitalist entrepreneurs, Soviet planners do not make decisions in terms of private profit calculations but in terms of a national plan for the whole economy. Soviet policy-makers first decide how total national product shall be divided for consumption, capital formation, and military production. Setting national goals of rapid economic growth and maintaining a powerful military establishment have resulted in a relatively small allocation of resources to consumption. Given the arbitrary decision that limits total consumption, the planners must attempt to produce more or less what consumers want as efficiently as possible. Prices of consumers' goods are fixed by the planning authorities and change, if at all, rather sluggishly. Surpluses of particular goods indicate that too much has been supplied at the fixed price, and shortages indicate that too little has been produced at the fixed price. When such surpluses or shortages appear, production and prices can be modified until an equilibrium of supply, demand, and price is attained.

Over time, as tastes and methods of production change, adjustments in price and output are required to maintain balanced production. For consumers' goods and services, the trial-and-error method of adjusting supply and price to consumer demand is not so very different in socialist and in capitalist economies. Socialist planners may be expected to offer fewer brands and models of a product than competing private enterprises under capitalism, and, by producing only a few standard varieties, they may achieve economies of large-scale production not realized under private enterprise. Whether consumer welfare is reduced by the smaller range of choice depends on the quality of products, the intrinsic merit of the choices, and the extent of the economies of scale. In the prevailing seller's market, quality has tended to be low.

Resource allocation in a Soviet-type economy differs most sharply from that occurring in capitalist economies particularly in the non-consumer sector, because the means of production are owned by the government and consequently no market of the usual type exists for producers' goods.[8] The necessity for resource allocation arises from scarcity, which is a fact of economic life regardless of the form of economic organization. Soviet planners cannot escape decisions which direct scarce resources into one use at the cost of alternative uses. Rational allocation of scarce resources means choosing the "best" among several alternatives, so that what is sacrificed is less valuable than what is chosen. This gives rise to the important economic problem of value.[9] In a

---

[8] Sale of machinery to collective farms is a partial but not important exception.

[9] For a significant discussion of the problem of value under socialism, see *Value and Plan, Economic Calculation and Organization in Eastern Europe*, ed. by Gregory Grossman (Berkeley and Los Angeles: University of California Press, 1960).

private ownership economy the price system is the mechanism used to allocate resources among alternative uses, and thereby to determine relative values. In the Soviet economy, in which the means of production are not bought and sold among private owners, no analogous market exists. The allocation of producers' goods among alternative uses depends on conscious calculations by the planning authorities. Prices, therefore, are purely accounting devices, and are not subject to the external checks of a market system.

Most resources have many alternative uses, and the problem of rational decision is infinitely complex. Under capitalism, competition among business firms is supposed to lead to a rational allocation of resources by establishing market prices which just cover the costs of production in the optimum use of the scarce resource. Needless to say, the market does not always function in such a way as to produce the ideal result, but it is usually assumed to be tolerably rational in terms of consumer preferences. While rational allocation is logically possible with non-profit ownership of the means of production, there is no guarantee that rationality will prevail in practice. What in fact has been the Soviet experience concerning the degree of rationality in resource allocation?

The cost accounting upon which prices, either market or accounting, are based should include all the sacrifices (inputs) involved in producing a given product (output). Soviet accounting includes costs of labor and materials, but it has not always given appropriate recognition to the interest cost of capital. Yet capital is a scarce resource with obvious alternative uses. In the generation of electricity, for example, Soviet planners for a long time showed a decided preference for hydro plants over thermal plants. Whereas the operating costs of thermal plants using coal for fuel are substantially higher than the operating costs of hydroelectric stations using falling water as a source of power, the capital required for thermal plants is typically much less than for hydro installations. Soviet planners appear to have underestimated the true cost of generating electricity from hydro plants by omitting the interest cost on the larger capital.[10] Beginning with the postwar period, however, and especially during the Khrushchev era, recognition was given to the interest cost of capital. Consequently, some major hydroelectric projects initially scheduled for the First Seven-Year Plan (1959–65) were excluded from the actual plan. These projects were not cancelled but indefinitely postponed because the "pay-out" period was too long and because they led to the foregoing of numerous other, more pressing, capital needs. This recognition of a "pay-out period" represents a roundabout acknowledgment of interest as a cost of capital. In this respect the Soviet planners moved toward a more rational allocation of resources.

Capital allocation is only one aspect of resource allocation, and, except for some very lavish capital-using projects like hydroelectric power plants, may not have resulted in any serious misallocation of resources. One American student of the Soviet economy (Granick) found that technological policy in the industries he investigated has been rational, that is, based on economic calculation in the sense that relatively abundant resources (e.g. labor) have

---

[10] Some critics have attributed the omission of interest as a cost to Soviet adherence to Karl Marx's labor theory of value, which asserted that all value is produced by labor.

been substituted for relatively scarce factors (e.g. capital) where technically possible, in deciding the proportions between labor and machinery for particular types of production.

Misallocation of scarce resources based on wrong principles are not so obvious and may be called "invisible" inefficiencies. There have been great "visible" inefficiencies as well, but Soviet planners have tried hard to eliminate them. One important visible inefficiency in the 1920's arose from lack of adequate incentives to laborers and managers to perform up to their capabilities. Since then monetary incentives have been used in the Soviet Union to attract labor into desired (planners' choice) occupations and industries and to induce workers to work harder. Wage differentials between unskilled and skilled workers are greater than in the United States. Incomes paid to teachers, scientists, and engineers are larger multiples of the earnings of factory workers in the Soviet Union than in capitalist countries, and thus the attraction of people to these occupations requiring long training is enhanced. Managers in industry enjoy income and prestige in the Soviet system, although not to the same extent as in capitalist countries such as the United States. Industrial managers are, however, given strong monetary incentives to meet their output quotas. Money bonuses to managers are paid monthly, and are quickly reduced or withdrawn if performance falters. Thus Soviet managers have a more immediate monetary incentive to succeed than do American managers, whose bonuses typically are paid annually.

Conclusion on resource allocation   Although resource allocation in the Soviet Union has been far from perfect, it has been tolerably rational in relation to the end goals of Soviet society. The earlier view of Western economists that rational allocation of resources is impossible without private ownership of the means of production has not been proven. The potentialities for making mistakes may be greater in a socialist planned economy than in a private enterprise economy in that losses are absorbed by the economy as a whole. Soviet firms do not go out of business because of decreased efficiency, whereas a private producer who miscalculates badly will go bankrupt simply because there is a definite limit to his ability to force others to absorb the losses resulting from his miscalculations. Moreover, it is probably more difficult to check on errors in a planned socialist economy because the planners can hide mistakes in complex accounting procedures if they wish to do so.

Yet, whereas the central planning of the Soviet system seems to represent a complete departure from the market system of capitalism, in one sense a market can be said to exist even under socialist planning. If a market is defined as a mechanism for deciding among alternative uses for scarce resources, clearly these decisions must be made whether the means of production are privately or publicly owned.[11]

Alternatively, one can accept the more common, and limited, definition of a market, and say the Soviets decide allocation problems without a market mechanism. In either case, planning practices in the Soviet Union have improved over the years. The immense complexity of consciously deciding among countless alternatives, in which every decision affects every other decision,

[11] See Oskar Lange, *On the Economic Theory of Socialism* (Minneapolis: University of Minnesota Press, 1938), for a discussion of this definition of a market.

lends itself to the use of input-output techniques and linear programming, implemented by high-speed electronic computers. The free market of classical capitalism may find its counterpart in an electronic market of socialist planning.

SELECTED BIBLIOGRAPHY

AMES, EDWARD, *Soviet Economic Processes*. Homewood, Ill.: Richard D. Irwin, Inc., 1965.

BAYKOV, ALEXANDER, *The Development of the Soviet Economic System*. London: Cambridge University Press, 1946.

BERGSON, ABRAM, *The Economics of Soviet Planning*. New Haven: Yale University Press, 1964. (paperback)

———, *Soviet Economic Growth: Conditions and Perspectives*. New York: Harper & Row, Publishers, 1953.

———, and SIMON KUZNETS, eds. *Economic Trends in the Soviet Union*. Cambridge, Mass.: Harvard University Press, 1963.

CAMPBELL, ROBERT W., *Soviet Economic Power. Its Organization, Growth, and Challenge*. Boston: Houghton Mifflin Company, 1966. (paperback)

CHAPMAN, JANET G., *Real Wages in Soviet Russia Since 1928*. Cambridge, Mass.: Harvard University Press, 1963.

DOBB, MAURICE R., *Soviet Economic Development Since 1917*. London: Routledge & Kegan Paul, Ltd., 1948.

DODGE, NORTON T., *Women in the Soviet Economy*. Baltimore: The Johns Hopkins University Press, 1966.

GRANICK, DAVID, *Red Executive: A Study of the Organization Man in Russian Industry*. Garden City, N. Y.: Doubleday & Co., Inc., 1960. (paperback)

GROSSMANN, GREGORY, ed., *Value and Plan: Economic Calculation and Organization in Eastern Europe*. Berkeley: University of California Press, 1960.

GRUCHY, ALLAN G., *Comparative Economic Systems, Competing Ways to Stability and Growth*, Part IV. Boston: Houghton Mifflin Company, 1966.

HARDT, JOHN P., and C. D. STOLZENBACK, *The Cold War Economic Gap*. New York: Frederick A. Praeger, Inc., 1961.

JASNY, NAUM, *The Socialized Agriculture of the USSR*. Palo Alto: Stanford University Press, 1949.

JOINT ECONOMIC COMMITTEE, *Dimensions of Soviet Economic Power*, 87th Congress, 2nd Session. Washington, D.C.: Government Printing Office, 1962.

NOVE, ALEC, *Soviet Economy, An Introduction*. New York: Frederick A. Praeger, Inc., 1961. (paperback)

ROBINSON, GEROLD T., *Rural Russia under the Old Regime: A History of the Landlord-Peasant Revolution of 1917*. New York: The Macmillan Company, 1949.

ROSTOW, WALT W., *The Dynamics of Soviet Society*. New York: New American Library Mentor Book, 1954. (paperback)

SCHWARTZ, HARRY, *Russia's Soviet Economy*, 2nd ed. Englewood Cliffs, N.J.: Prentice-Hall, Inc., 1954.

———, *The Soviet Economy Since Stalin*. Philadelphia: J. B. Lippincott Co., 1965.

SPULBER, NICOLAS, *Soviet Strategy for Economic Growth*. Bloomington: Indiana University Press, 1964.

STATE PLANNING COMMISSION OF THE U.S.S.R., *The Second Five-Year Plan (1933–37)*. New York: International Publishers, 1936.

WEBB, SIDNEY and BEATRICE, *Soviet Communism: A New Civilization?* 2 vols. New York: Charles Scribner's Sons, 1936.

ARTICLES

BALASSA, BELA, "The Dynamic Efficiency of the Soviet Economy," *American Economic Review*, LIV (May, 1964), 490–502.

BORNSTEIN, MORRIS, "The Soviet Price System," *American Economic Review*, LII (March, 1962), 64–103.

CLARK, M. GARDNER, "The Soviet Steel Industry," *Journal of Economic History*, XII (Fall, 1952), 396–410.

GERSCHENKRON, ALEXANDER, "The Rate of Industrial Growth in Russia Since 1885," *Journal of Economic History*, VII (Supplement, 1947), 144–74.

GOLDSMITH, RAYMOND, "The Economic Growth of Tsarist Russia, 1860–1913," *Economic Development and Cultural Change*, IX (April, 1961), 441–75.

GRANICK, DAVID, "On Patterns of Technological Choice in Soviet Industry," *American Economic Review*, LII (May, 1962), 149–57.

GROSSMAN, GREGORY, "Industrial Prices in the USSR," *American Economic Review*, XLIX (May, 1959), 50–64.

HOLZMAN, FRANKLYN D., "Soviet Inflationary Pressures, 1928–1957: Causes and Cures," *Quarterly Journal of Economics*, LXXIV (May, 1960), 167–88.

LERNER, ABBA P., "Statics and Dynamics in Socialist Economics," *Economic Journal*, XLVII (June, 1937), 253–70.

LEVINE, HERBERT S., "Input-Output Analysis and Soviet Planning," *American Economic Review*, LII (May, 1962), 127–37.

LIBERMAN, EVSEI G., "Planning Production and Standards of Long-Term Operation," *Problems of Economics*, V (Dec., 1962), 16–20.

NOVE, ALEC, "The Industrial Planning System—Reforms in Prospect," *Soviet Studies*, XIV (July, 1962), 1–15.

——, "Prospects for Economic Growth in the U.S.S.R.," *American Economic Review*, LIII (May, 1963), 541–54.

TIMOSHENKO, VLADIMIR P., "The New Agricultural Policy of Soviet Russia," *Journal of Farm Economics*, XIII (April, 1931), 280–304.

VOLIN, LAZAR, "Soviet Agriculture Under Khrushchev," *American Economic Review*, XLIX (May, 1959), 15–32.

Postwar Recovery and the
Balance-of-Payments Crisis
in Europe

CHAPTER **34**

A deep-seated economic crisis of a two-fold nature confronted Europe at the close of the Second World War. First was the problem of recovery from the devastation and dislocation arising directly from the war itself, and second, the need for structural reforms which would rescue Europe from the malaise which had plagued it during most of the interwar period from 1918 to 1939. Economic difficulties were compounded by a military occupation and political division which disrupted the historic pattern of economic interdependence between industrial western Europe and agricultural eastern Europe. This division increased the dependence of western Europe on overseas trade for food and raw materials, while eastern Europe became part of the Communist bloc led by the Soviet Union.

Recovery came more quickly and reforms met with less resistance than after World War I. Prewar levels of production were substantially attained by 1950 in both western and eastern Europe. Long-range reforms were well under way by 1960. Economic integration on a larger geographical basis than hitherto became the key to reform. In eastern Europe industry was nationalized and agriculture collectivized, and the former national economies integrated their agriculture and industry with the Soviet bloc. Capitalism, which had never advanced very far in eastern Europe, was wiped out under Communist governments. In the West also postwar conditions changed radically from those of the prewar period. The unhappy experience of the interwar period precluded any illusion of a "return to normalcy," such as had blocked needed reforms after the First World War. Popular demands for full employment and welfare programs led to far-reaching changes in the structure of western Europe's economies, and some of the countries became more socialist than capitalist. Economic welfare measured in per capita income advanced more rapidly than at any other period in European history. Economic integration in western Europe featured the creation in 1958 of the European Economic Community, otherwise known as the Common Market, which was without doubt the most important institutional change in western Europe during the twentieth century. These changes evolved within a framework of national and international economic planning.

Extent of War Losses and Damages

Although the Second World War is often described as the most costly and destructive in history, in some respects it was less costly to western Europe than the First World War. Great Britain lost only one-third as many lives and France only one-sixth as many as in World War I. Between the British retreat from Dunkirk in 1940 and the invasion of the Continent on D-Day in May, 1944, no large-scale land fighting took place in western Europe. During this four-year interval, heavy combat was confined in Europe to the eastern front, where there was extensive physical damage in wide areas. Because of its early surrender to Germany in 1940, France did not become a major battlefield until 1944, whereas France had been the main battlefield throughout the First World War.

In another respect World War II was less costly. In the years preceding the war western Europe suffered from mass unemployment and unused plant capacity. War activity increased employment and production far above prewar levels. Consequently the alternatives sacrificed in consumption and capital formation, although substantial, were much less than if Europe had enjoyed high prosperity during the 1930's.

In contrast to Britain and France, in Germany fatalities and damage to industrial plant and equipment, including bombing out of whole cities, was much greater in the Second World War than in the first. Only the Soviet Union suffered greater loss of human life than Germany in the Second World War.[1] Approximately 10,000,000 civilians in Europe were displaced from their country of origin at the end of the war.

Recovery of Production

Actually Europe's industrial capacity at the end of the war exceeded its capacity at the beginning, which means that economic expansion for war purposes during the war exceeded losses caused by war destruction. Considering the extent of bombing, artillery damage, and sabotage inflicted on Europe during the war, this is a remarkable fact. Part of the explanation is that bombing, especially mass bombing of civilian populations, seems to have raised civilian morale and led to greater output of effort by workers. Even more, however, it is a tribute to the prodigious productivity of modern technology and illustrates again the principle that the most important form of capital is the intangible assets, the knowledge and habits of the work force of a community. These cannot be destroyed by bombs and artillery unless nearly the whole population perishes. Productive power in the form of "know-how" is more important than accumulated physical wealth. Damage to plant, equipment, railways, bridges, and highways impaired Europe's capacity to produce only temporarily. A postwar inquiry reported that the damage to productive capacity from bombing was by no means as great as was assumed during the

---

[1] For the principal belligerents military personnel killed and missing totaled: the Soviet Union, 7,500,000; Germany, 2,850,000; China, 2,200,000; Japan, 1,506,000; the United Kingdom, 397,762; Italy, 300,000; the United States, 292,000; and France, 210,671.

war. Machinery and machine tools were much less damaged than the build-

ings that housed them, and the machines and machine tools were currently
repaired.[2]

At the close of the war, production fell sharply for numerous reasons, including the relocation of 10,000,000 displaced persons and the redirection of
production from war to peace needs. Nevertheless, economic recovery took
place more rapidly than after World War I. Industrial output climbed to the
prewar (1938) level in three years (by 1948), as compared with seven years
(by 1925) after World War I. Five years after World War II (1950), industrial production stood about 25 per cent above the prewar level. Recovery
varied greatly from country to country as shown in Table 34–1, which gives an
index of industrial recovery for selected countries of western Europe to 1950
in relation to the prewar level.

TABLE 34–1

Industrial Recovery in Western Europe
(Selected countries to 1950)

COUNTRY	1938	1947	1948	1949	1950
Belgium	100	106	114	116	120
France	100	92	108	118	121
Germany, West	100	33	50	75	96
Italy	100	86	91	96	109
Netherlands	100	95	113	127	139
United Kingdom	100	115	128	137	150
Average	100	88	101	111	122

Source: Economic Commission for Europe, *Economic Survey of Europe in 1950* (Geneva: United Nations
Publication, 1951), p. 30.

Agriculture recovered more slowly than industry because of the great
losses of draft animals and other livestock, but by 1950 agriculture in western
Europe, except Germany, attained its prewar level. German agricultural and
industrial recovery represented a special case for several reasons, including
heavy losses from fighting on German soil in the closing months of the war,
the shattering effect on morale of military defeat, military occupation, and
reparations, and the monetary chaos prior to the German currency reform of
1948. But in 1949 Germany began a rapid recovery and reached the prewar
level of output by 1951.

In the postwar period, capital-intensive investments such as transportation, housing, and commercial buildings took longest to restore because the
normal ratio of annual output to total capital in these durable assets is much
lower than for less durable assets. An early return to prewar levels of production was followed by rapid rates of growth during the 1950's for western

[2] See the United States Strategic Bombing Survey, *The Effects of Strategic Bombing
on the German War Economy*, and also the *Overall Report* (Washington, D.C.: Government
Printing Office, 1945).

Europe, with marked differences in the rates of growth from country to country. During the 1950's the slow-growth countries were the United Kingdom and Belgium, whereas Germany, Italy, and France grew rapidly in total output of goods and services.

According to official statistics, the countries of eastern Europe attained prewar industrial levels more rapidly and agricultural levels less rapidly than the countries of western Europe. Europe's postwar recovery in production was carried out largely by Europeans. Outside assistance from the United States, Canada, and other nations was of secondary importance with respect to production up to 1948. Eastern European nations, except Yugoslavia, received virtually no outside aid after the expiration of the United Nations Relief and Rehabilitation program in 1947, but these countries managed to recover prewar levels as rapidly as the western European nations. With the possible exception of Germany, war damage in Russia was greater than in any other country. In the highly developed western European economies, temporary outside assistance was probably more helpful to recovery than it would have been to the less developed countries of eastern Europe.

EVOLUTION OF POLICY TOWARD ECONOMIC PLANNING

Government planning played a major role in both the recovery and the longer-term economic development of postwar Europe. Eastern European countries in the Soviet orbit (Bulgaria, Czechoslovakia, Eastern Germany, Hungary, Poland, Rumania, and Yugoslavia) experienced economic and political revolutions which brought central economic planning of the Soviet type. In western Europe economic planning evolved in a less revolutionary and less obvious manner. Yet the most striking long-term feature that emerged from the war and postwar experience has been the movement toward general economic planning. As used here, planning implies conscious decisions in the interest of the community as a whole, in contrast with business decisions which are guided primarily by the accounting criteria of a private business enterprise, or in some cases by a monopolistic combination in an industry. Under economic planning the scope of conscious calculation is broader than under business decision-making, and by its very nature, community-wide (social) accounting tends to relate to national income rather than to the income of a business firm or a single industry.

When the war in Europe ended in May, 1945, there was a strong surge of idealism—to cleanse society of collaborators, to create a fairer distribution of wealth, to reform the tax system, and in general to build a better society. Depression and war had brought disillusionment with the old order, and businessmen and officials who had collaborated with the right-wing Nazi and Fascist movements were discredited in the eyes of their fellow citizens. The wartime resistance, or underground, movements had been led mainly by leftists, including many Communists. Radical, anticapitalistic leaders enjoyed strong moral and political influence at the end of World War II. In the early postwar period, socialist premiers headed the governments of Belgium, Czechoslovakia, Italy, Norway, Sweden, and the United Kingdom. Following

the fall of Hitler, socialists were probably the largest political group in de-

feated Germany and in occupied Austria. During 1945 and 1946 the reconstruction of nearly all of Europe seemed destined to be carried out on a
planned, socialist basis. Never in modern history had the prospects for the
future of capitalism been at such a low ebb. In the sense that interwar fascism
had been a counter-revolutionary movement against left-wing tendencies, the
Second World War could, in 1945, have been aptly labeled "a war to make
Europe safe for socialism."

In the United Kingdom, Winston Churchill, the wartime leader, was
voted out of office less than three months after Germany surrendered. The
British Labour Party won an overwhelming victory in an election fought
chiefly on socialist issues. In fulfillment of campaign pledges the Labour Government nationalized the Bank of England, the coal mines, inland transportation, communications, electric power utilities, and insurance, and took initial
steps toward nationalization of the iron and steel industry. Heavy progressive
taxation leveled incomes to a degree which went far toward eliminating the
economic privileges formerly enjoyed by the rich. Administrative rationing
and price controls were maintained long after the war in order to insure
equal sharing of the limited supplies of available consumers' goods. A government health program made medical and dental care available without cost
(except through taxes) to all residents of the United Kingdom. According to
Professor Schumpeter, these measures of social equalitarianism did more to
make Britain genuinely socialist than the nationalization of heavy industry.[3]

In France at the time of liberation (August, 1944) economic planning
was widely accepted. The National Council of Resistance drew up a postwar
program in which planning and nationalization were featured. The first post-
liberation government, which included several Communist ministers, was
committed to a planning program, and the constitution of the Fourth French
Republic adopted in 1946 contained the principle of nationalization. Extensive nationalization began in 1945 with the Bank of France and the four
largest commercial banking chains. Also nationalized were the coal mines,
electricity, gas, insurance, air and sea transportation (railroads had been
nationalized in 1936), and a few manufacturing firms (e.g., the Renault automobile firm). A change in political atmosphere precluded further nationalization, but it did not impede economic planning. Under the Monnet Plan heavy
investments were made in selected key sectors of the economy, not only
in the nationalized sector but also in privately owned industries such as steel
and petroleum refining. French policy-makers tolerated inflation in allocating
scarce resources to heavy investments, which provided the basis for a remarkable improvement in France's traditional slow-growth economy. In 1947
France inaugurated a series of four-year plans (changed to five years for
1966–70), which constituted perhaps the most interesting experiment in postwar Europe in planning a market economy.[4] The French system has been
called "indicative" planning to distinguish it from the "imperative" planning
of the Soviet and East European type.

[3] See Joseph A. Schumpeter, *Capitalism, Socialism and Democracy* (New York:
Harper & Row, Publishers, 1950).

[4] On French planning, see the book by John and Anne-Marie Hackett, *Economic
Planning in France* (Cambridge, Mass.: Harvard University Press, 1963).

As the realities of European reconstruction came to the fore, attention focused on shorter-range problems, and nationalization faded into the background.[5] The relative success in restoring prewar levels was accompanied by an underestimation of the magnitude of the task of balancing international payments. After a false start toward currency convertibility by the British based on an American-Canadian loan, the need for dollar aid on a far greater scale than previously contemplated became apparent. National production and trade goals designed to achieve a balance of international payments for each of several small countries threatened momentarily to return western Europe to a state of interwar autarky, compounded by the postwar division between eastern and western Europe resulting from the cold war beginning about 1947. Massive American aid under the Marshall Plan proved the vehicle which galvanized European countries into regional planning. National plans had to be coordinated into regional plans to avoid wasteful resource allocation and to reconcile discrepancies arising from plans by individual countries to sell to one another while refusing to buy from each other.

Western European planning generated two types of international organizations: (1) the consultative type represented by the Organization for European Economic Cooperation, and (2) the directive type represented first by the European Coal and Steel Community and later by the European Economic Community. By the end of the fifties a new economic order had emerged: a system of national and regional planning devoted to closer economic integration of western Europe. The traditional concept of economic planning, still dominant at the end of the war, as a by-product of socialism resting on nationalization of the means of production, gave way to the new type of planning. For this was essentially economic planning in private ownership economies, abetted, it is true, by doses of nationalization inherited from the prewar or early postwar years. Nationalization, however, ceased to be an important issue, and even the socialists began to abandon nationalization as a key issue. Under the aegis of this planning system western Europe experienced its highest rate of sustained growth and reversed the stagnation of the inter-

[5] One reason why nationalization diminished in importance in the early postwar period was the anti-socialist influence of the United States in its role as an occupying power and as Europe's chief creditor. The United Kingdom and France had their early rounds of nationalization, and West Germany probably would have had also except for American influence. Initially the United Kingdom, with a Labour Government in office, was the occupying power in the zone which included the Ruhr. In 1946 British Foreign Minister Ernest Bevin announced that the giant coal and steel industries in the Ruhr would be socialized in accordance with the wishes of the workers employed in the area. However, in the fall of 1947 Britain's foreign balances were at a desperately low level, and the Labour Government announced it could not continue to carry the full burden of its occupation costs. In the ensuing negotiations in which the United States was asked to assume a share of the expense of the British zone, the U.S. representative is reported by the *New York Times* to have insisted, as a condition of American assistance, that the question of socialization of Ruhr industries be postponed for three to five years (*New York Times,* September 11, 1947). The agreement became known as the "dominant voice formula" under which the United States received a controlling voice in the British zone in return for assuming financial responsibility.

Subsequently the West German states of Rhine-Westphalia (which includes the Ruhr) and Hesse adopted constitutions calling for socialization of heavy industry, but these constitutional provisions were ignored on two grounds: (1) only the Federal German government should decide the question of socialization, and (2) socialization would violate Law 75 of the Federal German Constitution (inserted as an American type anti-trust measure) against excessive concentration of economic power (*New York Times,* June 20, 1950). Thus American influence blunted socialization moves in West Germany.

war period. For example, ten countries of western Europe for which the an-

nual rate of growth in real output per capita had been 1.5 per cent from 1870 to 1913, and had fallen to 1.0 per cent from 1913 to 1950, rose to 3.5 per cent during the decade of the 1950's. During these same periods, the United States experienced growth in real output per capita of 2.2 per cent, 1.7 per cent, and 1.6 per cent, respectively. The figures are shown in Table 34–2.

TABLE 34–2

Per Capita Rate of Growth of Real Output, 1870–1960
Ten European Countries and the United States

COUNTRY	PER CENT PER YEAR		
	1870-1913	1913-50	1950-60
Belgium	1.7	0.7	2.3
Denmark	2.1	1.1	2.6
France	1.4	0.7	3.5
Germany	1.8	0.4	6.5
Italy	0.7	0.6	5.3
Netherlands	0.8*	0.7	3.6
Norway	1.4	1.9	2.6
Sweden	2.3	1.6	2.6
Switzerland	1.3†	1.5	3.7
United Kingdom	1.3	1.3	2.2
Average	1.5	1.0	3.5
United States	2.2	1.7	1.6

* 1900-1913.
† 1890-1913.
Source: Angus Maddison, *Economic Growth in the West* (New York: Twentieth Century Fund, 1964), p. 30.

WESTERN EUROPE'S BALANCE-OF-PAYMENTS CRISIS

Europe's postwar balance-of-payments crisis arose from a breakdown in the world's payments system. For centuries western Europe had been dependent on external markets for exports and on foreign sources of supply for food and raw materials. The payments system based on the international gold standard had functioned reasonably well before 1914, but it was badly shaken by the First World War and collapsed during the Great Depression of the 1930's. World War II caused further disruptions in Europe's traditional position in international trade.

Toward the end of the war, in anticipation of some of these difficulties, the allied nations set up the International Monetary Fund for dealing with international exchange rates and temporary fluctuations in the balance of payments, but the Fund could not begin to operate effectively until the fundamental disequilibrium inherited from the past and accentuated by the war had been corrected. Nor was a return to the pre-1914 gold standard feasible.

Even so, some adherents of the gold standard and of the related classical economic theory of international trade rejected as illusory the whole idea of a dollar shortage, contending that prices should be permitted to rise in surplus countries such as the United States and to fall in deficit countries such as Europe until an equilibrium of exports and imports was reached. If this classical medicine had been relied on, the patient (European capitalism) probably would not have survived. Domestic prices and international adjustments required time to work themselves out. Given sufficient time, there was reason to expect that dollars would become plentiful and that American gold would flow to Europe, and to the rest of the world, to restore healthier conditions of international trade.[6] In the short run, however, strong measures of a different type were needed for survival.

Before World War II Europe had balance-of-payments problems, but they were disguised by innumerable exchange and price controls and by a low level of economic activity in the form of the Great Depression. International payments can always be balanced provided trade falls to a sufficiently low level, and the existence of an actual deficit in the international balance of payments depends on the availability of gold or credit to finance the deficit. In the absence of some means with which to finance a deficit, it disappears, that is, it exists only as a virtual or potential deficit. A decline in trade, however, means sacrificing the advantages of the international division of labor, which especially in countries like those of Western Europe means lowering the level of living.

American Aid

During the Second World War the United States used its great productive capacity to aid its Allies through lend-lease, an agreement under which weapons, food, and equipment were transferred to Europe without any arrangement for payment. Under reverse lend-lease, the United States received some goods and substantial services from European governments; for example, American military personnel traveled many thousands of miles on British railways during the war. At the close of the war lend-lease grants valued at about $50 billion were largely canceled, usually with small payments from the wartime Allies. By this arrangement the troublesome war debt problem, which menaced international relations after the First World War, was avoided. Between 1943 and 1947 several billion dollars in economic aid poured into Europe and other war-torn areas through the United Nations Relief and Rehabilitation Administration (UNRRA). Although UNRRA was an international agency and gave relief to eastern as well as to western Europe, most of its funds came from the Treasury of the United States. UNRRA was more a relief than a recovery agency, distributing food and other emergency aid to save millions of persons from destitution.

When the war ended, there was little conception on either side of the Atlantic of the magnitude of the task which lay ahead before Europe could

---

[6] John Maynard Keynes, in an article published posthumously, pointed out this long-term tendency for the dollar shortage to right itself. "The Balance of Payments of the United States," *Economic Journal*, LVI (June, 1946), 172–87.

become a viable part of the international economy. The abrupt cancellation of lend-lease at the end of the war led the British to ask for a $6 billion gift from the United States government in order to help rebuild the world financial and trading structure. The United States responded with a $3.75 billion low-interest loan and attached a condition that the United Kingdom should restore convertibility of the pound sterling within one year. When the British in good faith attempted convertibility in 1947, it proved disastrous. Contributing to this result was the terrible European winter of 1947 followed by floods which threatened to wipe out all the crop gains of 1946 and presented the prospect of using precious dollars to buy grain from the United States and Canada. Meanwhile, the termination of price controls in the United States was followed by inflation, which greatly reduced the purchasing power of the British loan. At this desperate juncture in postwar history, there began the preliminary thinking which led to the Marshall Plan for systematic and massive United States aid to Europe.

Reasons for Europe's Dollar Shortage

Europe's dependence for recovery on dollar sources of supply arose from a combination of American strength and European weakness.

(1) Among major industrial nations only the United States economy escaped direct war damage, and therefore supplies were available in the United States which could not be obtained from other sources. The war induced great increases in American economic capacity, which was much larger at the war's end than ever before. As a proportion of the world total, industrial production in the United States was higher between 1945 and 1950 than it has ever been before or since, and there were also agricultural surpluses of unprecedented size.

(2) European countries liquidated most of their foreign investments early in the war in order to pay for supplies, food, and equipment. For example, in 1939, the British held in the United States $4.5 billion in investments, short-term balances, and gold. These assets were expended rapidly during 1939–40, when American policy was to sell war goods only on a cash-and-carry basis, a policy which was reversed in 1941 under lend-lease legislation. In the prewar era income from foreign investments had been used by the British and other western European nations to pay for the excess value of imported goods over exported goods. Other receipts from "invisibles" such as shipping revenues were lost during the war.

(3) War-induced changes had cut off one of Europe's chief sources of prewar dollar supply in southeast Asia. Before the war, British and Dutch colonies in southeast Asia sold rubber, tin, tea, copra, and cocoa to the United States, and used the dollar revenue to pay for their traditional dollar imports. Britain, Holland, and other European nations earned these dollars by exporting manufactured goods to their colonies. Japanese occupation of southeast Asia during the war cut off these supplies, and much of the trade with the United States was not restored after the war. Synthetic rubber developed during the war, for example, reduced United States dependence on Malayan rubber, and tin supplies from Bolivia replaced those of Malaya. Moreover,

even if there had been no other changes, western Europe was largely unable to supply the manufacturing needs of southeast Asia immediately following the war.

(4) Industrial development in underdeveloped areas shifted their type of imports from consumers' to producers' goods. Europe could not export these products at the end of the war, whereas the United States export trade was more attuned to producers' goods.

(5) Increases in population in underdeveloped regions reduced the food supplies available for export to Europe, and incipient industrialization reduced the raw materials available for export to Europe.

(6) Another factor accounting for the huge deficit in Europe's balance of payments was the rise during the early postwar years of the prices of the (primary) products imported relative to the prices of the (manufactured) goods exported. Europe had to exchange a larger physical quantity of exports for a given physical quantity of imports. For example, in 1948 western Europe's terms of trade were about 10 per cent worse than in 1947, a development which added one billion dollars to Europe's international payments deficit in 1948. Worsening terms of trade for Europe temporarily reversed a trend which for more than a century contributed to the improvement of Europe's standard of living. In 1938, just prior to the Second World War, Europe's terms of trade were about 50 per cent more favorable than in 1913, which in turn were about 20 per cent more favorable than in 1865. In 1938 Europe's terms of trade were probably more favorable than they had been at any time since 1820. Hence, the worsening of terms of trade in the 1940's came as a rude shock to Europeans and aggravated Europe's dollar deficit. Fortunately for Europe the terms of trade improved in the 1950's as world food and other primary production regained and then surpassed prewar levels of output.

(7) Economic ties of long historical standing between eastern and western Europe were severed by the Cold War. Eastern Europe had been an important source of food and raw material for industrial centers in western Europe. A comparison of western European imports by areas of origin before and immediately after the Second World War shows that the sharpest drop in imports from eastern Europe corresponded with the largest increase in imports from the dollar area.[7]

The Marshall Plan for European Recovery

When at last the magnitude of the change in Europe's trade and finance became generally apparent, the American Secretary of State, George C. Marshall, acting on the advice of his technical economic and political staff, came forward with a bold proposal to restore Europe's equilibrium in international payments through massive American financing and intra-European planning. European statesmen led by British Foreign Secretary Ernest Bevin quickly followed up Marshall's proposal of June, 1947, by calling a conference in Paris to which all European nations except Germany and Spain were invited. Western Europe responded enthusiastically, but the countries of eastern

[7] See Economic Commission for Europe, *Economic Survey of Europe Since the War* (Geneva: United Nations, 1953), p. 86.

Europe, taking their cue from the Soviet Union, boycotted the conference and subsequently refused to join the plan which was adopted. Thus from its inception the Marshall Plan became a western European Recovery Plan (ERP) to coordinate the recovery efforts of seventeen countries and finance their dollar needs.[8]

The United States Congress passed the Economic Cooperation Act in April, 1948, to begin operations immediately and to run until the end of 1952, with projected outlays of $17 billion. To administer the Marshall Plan from the American side, the act created the Economic Cooperation Administration (ECA), and Paul Hoffman, a former automobile executive, became chief administrator. The actual Marshall Plan outlays from the United States were about $12.5 billion, as compared with the original projection of $17 billion, and the actual time of operation was somewhat less than four years.[9]

Organization for European Economic Cooperation (OEEC) On the European side, the Organization for European Economic Cooperation (OEEC) was responsible for a reasonable and workable program for achieving a balance of international payments within the four years of borrowed time under the Marshall Plan. The general alternatives were to export more or to import less. National planners of individual countries were more likely to recommend the latter because a domestic industry for producing import substitutes is more within the control of the planners than is the volume of exports some other countries are expected to buy. One of the tasks of the OEEC was to combat the tendency toward nationalistic autarky and to promote increased economic interdependence within Western Europe.

European Payments Union (EPU) One international organization created by OEEC to liberalize intra-European trade was the Economic Payments Union (EPU) for multilateral clearing of payments among its members. Credits earned by selling to one European member of the EPU could offset debits incurred in buying from some other member. Each member country had only a single net credit or debit with the EPU; and only net credits or net debits against all other members needed to be settled with the EPU. Among the EPU members bilateral trading and bilateral payments, which are inconsistent with an economical allocation of resources, were suppressed.

The ECA contributed $350 million to be used as working capital in the EPU to cushion the debts of members accumulating large deficits in the clearing union. The EPU provided an intermediate step toward currency convertibility; European currencies were freely convertible within Europe for intra-European trade, but they were not convertible into dollars. Hence trade could be multilateral within western Europe although not yet for the whole world. As long as the dollar shortage persisted, the intra-European clearing arrangement fostered European-wide trade, but it did not eliminate dis-

[8] The seventeen participating countries included two geographically eastern European nations, Greece and Turkey, which previously had been recipients of general American aid under the so-called Truman Doctrine, designed to save these countries from Communist domination.

[9] For a definitive study of the finances of the Marshall Plan, see W. A. Brown and Redvers Opie, *American Foreign Assistance* (Washington, D.C.: The Brookings Institution, 1953).

crimination against trade with the United States and other countries of the dollar area. The EPU operated with remarkable success, although not without some difficulties, as a transitional arrangement pending the restoration of full convertibility in the late 1950's. During the EPU's eight and one-half years of life (1950–58) it settled $46 billion of transactions with a working capital of only $350 million.

Solving Europe's Dollar Crisis in the 1950's

European countries had three ways to reduce their dollar deficit: (1) to export more goods and services to the United States or to third areas where dollars could be earned; (2) to import less from the dollar area by diverting purchases to non-dollar areas; [10] and (3) to receive loans, investments, and gifts of dollars from the United States.

(1) **Exporting more to the dollar area**   The most direct approach to earning more dollars was for European countries to export more to the United States. Among important European exports to the United States were textiles, machinery, and whisky from the United Kingdom, wines and specialty articles from France, watches from Switzerland, diamonds from Belgium, tobacco from Greece and Turkey, pulp and paper from Sweden, cork from Portugal, and special foodstuffs such as cheese and processed meats suited to the tastes of European immigrants living in the United States. Invisible exports included maritime transport, migrant remittances, and tourist expenditures by Americans visiting Europe.

European countries made special efforts to push their goods in the American market. Salesmanship was improved and foreign departments were set up in European stores where only Americans could buy. Special fairs were held to display European goods in American markets. In the spring of 1950, for example, the British staged a special automobile show in New York City in an attempt to promote the sale of British cars in the United States. Success in the latter venture and associated efforts was attested by the fact that within a decade European small cars were to be seen everywhere on American highways.

Numerous obstacles confronted Europeans attempting to invade American markets. United States producers were then the most efficient in the world in many of the manufactured items Europeans had for export. United States tariffs were barriers to other European products, and American businessmen protested staunchly any lower tariffs on their products. In processing goods through United States customs there were troublesome delays and regulations. Requirements for special packaging and the "Buy American" law of 1933, according to which the federal government had to give preference to American sellers, created problems.

A European currency devaluation in 1949 effected a 30 per cent reduc-

---

[10] The so-called dollar area refers to the United States and its neighbors, including Canada, Mexico, Central America, Venezuela, Colombia, and the Caribbean republics, except Cuba. These countries derive most of their foreign receipts from the United States. The rest of the world constitutes the non-dollar area. In the present discussion the dollar area refers specifically to the United States except where the broader reference is essential to meaningful analysis.

tion in European prices (in terms of dollars) and probably increased European dollar exports to the United States. The British pound sterling was devaluated from $4.03 to $2.80, which meant that a suit priced at ten pounds cost $40.30 before and $28.00 after devaluation. In order to earn more dollars, however, the British had to increase their (physical) sales by more than the 30 per cent devaluation in the pound.

(2) **Importing less from the dollar area** Western Europe reduced its dollar deficit by importing less from the dollar area. With varying degrees of success, but increasingly with time, western Europe shifted its purchases of grain, cotton, petroleum, machinery, and other products from the United States to non-dollar sources of supply. Algerian and Australian grains received preference over American grain; Egyptian and Indian cotton received preference over American cotton; oil from the Middle East displaced American petroleum.

To develop non-dollar sources of food and raw materials required not only time but also large investments. Insofar as United States investments developed these resources, e.g., oil in the Middle East, indirect dollar aid was available to Europe when it was able to supply machinery and equipment for these investments. However, United States loans which specified that the proceeds could be spent only in the United States—so-called "tied loans"—automatically shut out the Europeans and precluded their earning dollars. Tied loans rested on the notion that they would increase American exports, whereas in fact such loans merely redirected foreign purchases to American producers supplying the equipment needed for investment. If the American loans to non-Europeans could have been spent directly in Europe for capital goods, Europeans would then have had dollars with which to buy American exports. Hence there was no obvious gain to the United States economy as a whole in tied loans, although there were undoubted advantages to special American interests, at the expense of other American interests.

(3) **Loans, grants, and investments from the United States** To export more required strengthening Europe's productive capacity, and to import from non-dollar areas required enlargement of productive capacity in these areas. Both required time, and it was the Marshall Plan which provided that time. It filled the dollar gap temporarily, and enabled Europe to continue to import from the United States while exporting relatively little to the United States. Marshall aid was grant aid and not a loan, which would have required the payment of interest and the subsequent repayment of principal from Europe to the United States. These arrangements were possible only as a government operation since private capitalists cannot afford to make free grants. Yet the burden fell on the American taxpayers who, with some grumbling, shouldered the burden as part of the cost of reconstruction and of the price of saving western Europe from communism.

Private investors as well as governments were free to advance loans to Europe and help meet the dollar shortage. Unfortunately, most private American investments in Europe came after the postwar crisis was over, when Europe's dollar shortage had turned into a dollar surplus, and consequently added to the difficulties of the United States in its period of deficits in international payments. This does not mean that American private investments

abroad are undesirable, but it does mean that their timing was unfavorable both from the point of view of Europe in the early postwar years and of the United States in the later postwar years. But private American investment, especially when the Common Market entered the picture, contributed mightily to the flow of dollars from the United States to western Europe.

SELECTED BIBLIOGRAPHY

(See end of Chapter 35)

European Integration Under the Common Market

Although the Marshall Plan was conceived primarily as a recovery effort, by the end of its second year of operation Paul G. Hoffman, ECA administrator, shifted emphasis to the long-range goal of ". . . nothing less than an integration of the Western European Economy." By integration Hoffman meant ". . . the formation of a single large market within which quantitative restrictions on the movements of goods, monetary barriers to the flow of payments and, eventually, all tariffs are permanently swept away." [1] Hoffman envisioned benefits to Europe from a free-trade market of 275,000,000 customers similar to the gains which had accrued to the United States from a vast unfettered domestic market. Production on a massive scale would raise the productivity of labor and enable western Europeans to enjoy higher wages and higher standards of living.

Unification of Europe has long been the objective of some statesmen and military leaders. Since the feudal period a general trend toward regional economic and political unification has been evident. The rise of national states during the sixteenth and seventeenth centuries manifested this tendency. Napoleon Bonaparte strove unsuccessfully to unify Europe. During the nineteenth century the unification of Italy and Germany represented movements toward larger geographical units. Railways brought some international as well as greater national economic unification.

Political and economic unification interact with one another and the failure of one limits the development of the other. In the twentieth century political integration in Europe failed to keep pace with the new technology of mass production, and frustrated the potential economic gains inhering in mass production. In the interwar period economic nationalism, reinforced by the Great Depression, pushed Europe backwards toward economic autarky rather than forward toward economic integration. Meanwhile, the relative and, in some instances, absolute loss of overseas markets rendered the archaic nature of Europe's fragmented economy more evident and more critical than ever. After the Second World War, however, Europe freed itself from this impasse and, with American persuasion and pressure, moved toward economic integration.

[1] Speech of November 1, 1949.

The most important forerunner of the European Common Market was the European Coal and Steel Community (ECSC), which was established in 1952 by six countries: France, Germany, Italy, Belgium, the Netherlands, and Luxembourg.[2] France took the initiative. Robert Schuman, the Foreign Minister of France, and Jean Monnet, the head of France's postwar planning commission, fathered the idea and worked out the plans for organization. "The most rational distribution of production at the highest possible level of productivity" was the objective set forth in the statutes. Free trade in coal and steel within the Community was facilitated by abolishing all customs and other trade barriers among the six countries. As in all customs unions, tariffs at the borders of the pooled areas were made uniform. Ownership of facilities in the participating nations could be either private or public. In order to ease the transition, a five-year period was provided for high-cost producers to adapt to free trade within the Community. Most vulnerable to free competition were steel companies in Italy and coal mines in Belgium.

Mitigation of the historic rivalry between France and Germany was probably more important in the formation of the ECSC than the purely economic gains likely to be derived from the union. The Community gave France some control over German steel, which in the past had been used to forge military weapons against the French; it also assured France access to Ruhr coal for French steel production. From Germany's point of view the ECSC seemed preferable to internationalization of the Ruhr and to similar proposals current in the early postwar period. A remarkable feature of the Community was the surrender by the six participating countries of a significant degree of national sovereignty over these key industries. A supra-national agency called the High Authority held administrative and legislative power over the coal and steel industries of the member nations.

In the United Kingdom in 1952 both the Labour Party and the Conservative Party opposed British membership in the European Coal and Steel Community. Leaders in the United States looked upon the ECSC as a step toward European integration, and some Senators tried to pressure the British into joining by threatening to slash by one-half Britain's appropriation for Marshall Plan aid if the United Kingdom failed to join the ECSC.

During the five-year transitional period (1952–57) attempts to raise the efficiency of south Belgian coal mines proved unsuccessful. Inefficient mines previously subsidized by the Belgian government lost eligibility for further subsidies at the end of the transition period. Hardships created for coal miners in declining regions were typical adjustments associated with long-term gains in efficiency under competitive conditions. Under the ECSC, as well as the Common Market later, a social fund was set up to assist in retraining and relocating displaced workers. Since the First World War coal mining generally had been a stagnant industry in western Europe, and the ECSC did not alter this condition. Increases in productivity were limited by diminishing returns —with mines getting deeper—and coal met increasing competition from rival fuels, especially petroleum and natural gas. The proportion of total power

[2] Belgium and Luxembourg had formed a customs union in 1921; during the Second World War they agreed to join with the Netherlands to form Benelux.

needs supplied by coal in the Community fell from 74 per cent in 1950 to 43 per cent in 1964 and was projected for about 30 per cent in 1970. Coal output per man-shift in the ECSC countries was projected to increase by one-third (from 1.5 to 2.0 tons) between 1956 and 1975, and total production to increase by 16 per cent (from 246 to 285 million tons) during the same period. French coal mines showed the largest increases in output per man-shift in the early postwar period, owing mainly to large capital investments in modernization under the Monnet reconstruction plan.

655

EUROPEAN
INTEGRATION
UNDER THE
COMMON
MARKET

During the early years of the ECSC no major shifts took place in the location of steel production in western Europe. Steel, like coal, enjoys considerable geographical protection in the sense that freight costs are relatively high in relation to value of product. The most vulnerable country, Italy, expanded steel output at a good rate even after the elimination of protective tariffs at the end of the five-year transitional period in February, 1958. This was possible because Italy built large new plants utilizing the latest and most efficient technology. In a generally expanding domestic and foreign market, such as characterized postwar Europe, steel producers in other countries were not eager to absorb freight in order to invade the Italian market. Nevertheless, expansion of the Italian steel industry in the teeth of free-trade Common Market rivalry proved that a country lacking domestic supplies of iron ore and coal can be competitive in the steel industry. Apart from Italian steel, the costs and efficiency of the various national steel industries within the ECSC were reasonably comparable. In fact, the coal and steel industries of Western Germany, eastern France, Belgium, Luxembourg, and the Netherlands cover a relatively small geographical area, and placing them in a single economic union represented an elementary exercise in economic logic, although the lesson had been learned slowly and at the cost of bitter experience in peace and war.

In one respect the ECSC probably contributed to increased average efficiency in steel production—through economies of large-scale output arising from greater concentration stimulated by the formation of the Community. The early postwar movement toward deconcentration of industry in western Europe—much influenced by American anti-trust philosophy—was reversed under the ECSC, despite the fact that its statutes pay lip service to anti-trust and anti-monopoly principles. Under the ECSC the threat of stronger competition stimulated combinations, and the High Authority embraced them as contributions to efficiency. An obvious contradiction existed between the avowed belief in free competition, on the one hand, and the sanction of concentration, on the other, since concentration leads away from competition toward oligopolistic and monopolistic market structures. As one leading study of the ECSC concluded, "The free price mechanism in steel . . . does not operate in the ECSC, though it is part of the official dogma of the High Authority, because the individual governments have tacitly rejected it . . . The ECSC thus suffers from a divergence between theory and practice and a fragmentation of authority." [3]

Even if the ECSC did believe firmly in anti-trust policy, circumstances could arise in which Europe's heavy industries could challenge and dilute

[3] Louis Lister, *Europe's Coal and Steel Community* (New York: Twentieth Century Fund, 1960), p. 404.

656

EUROPEAN
INTEGRATION
UNDER THE
COMMON
MARKET

its authority. By 1966 steel cartels were back in Europe as a result of general over-capacity, a condition characteristic of capitalist countries throughout the world. Thirty-one German steel producers grouped themselves into four marketing cartels, thus eliminating competition among the member companies of each cartel. At the same time, in France, twelve steel producers secretly grouped into two giant regional cartels for the purpose of eliminating competition. Subsequently the French government sponsored the cartels and agreed to keep ECSC informed, but did not ask permission or advice concerning the legality or illegality of the cartels. A cartel-like movement also developed in Italy in the sixties. The German and French cartels set output quotas, fixed domestic and export prices, and imposed severe penalties on members for violating the cartel agreement. The reasons for forming these cartels were the same that had driven heavy industries to form cartels in the past—declining sales, falling prices, and shrinking profits associated with over-capacity.[4]

THE EUROPEAN COMMON MARKET

With the formation in 1958 of the European Economic Community (EEC), known as the Common Market, a giant step was taken toward the integration of western Europe. Through a treaty signed in Rome in 1957 the six countries which earlier had formed the European Coal and Steel Community became charter members of the European Economic Community. The new Community paralleled in many respects the earlier one in coal and steel but was much broader in scope, more gradual in transition and somewhat less supra-national.

The main purposes of the EEC were: (1) elimination of all customs duties and quantitative restrictions on imports and exports among the six member states; (2) a common external tariff against the outside world; (3) the free movement of factors of production within the six countries; and (4) closer general economic integration through common policies in agriculture, transportation, competition, employment, and fiscal and monetary matters including taxation and balance of payments. The first two steps constitute a customs union; the third and fourth an economic union; and, not stated in the Treaty of Rome but clearly in keeping with the spirit of the founding fathers, possibly an eventual political union in the form of a United States of Europe.

Elimination of Customs Duties Among the Member States

The transition to a free-trade customs union was divided into three stages of four years each, with provision for extending the total period from twelve to fifteen years in exceptional circumstances. Reductions in internal tariffs proceeded ahead of schedule, reaching 50 per cent of the pre-Common Market level in mid-1962, on the way to complete elimination of internal tariffs several years in advance of the 1970 target set up in the Rome Treaty.

[4] See "Cartels Fence in European Steel" in *Business Week* (September 3, 1966), pp. 94–98.

657

EUROPEAN
INTEGRATION
UNDER THE
COMMON
MARKET

All quantitative restrictions (quotas) on trade among the member countries were abolished by the beginning of 1962, eight years before the time required by the Treaty. One reason for accelerating the timetable on internal barriers was the rapid increase in trade which accompanied the initial steps in that direction. Trade among the six countries increased by 19 per cent between 1958 and 1959 and by 28 per cent between 1959 and 1960. Between 1958 and 1963 trade among the Common Market countries grew at a compound rate of 18.3 per cent annually. Intra-Community trade increased 300 per cent between 1958 and 1966.

A Common External Tariff

The second objective of the Common Market, to establish a single tariff around the free internal market, is a condition essential to any customs union. At the outset French and Italian tariffs were above average for the six countries and had to be lowered, and German and Benelux tariffs were below average and had to be raised toward countries outside the Common Market. Serious objections arose because of the inevitable discrimination against non-member countries, including those which were fellow members of the OEEC (later OECD), NATO, and the Atlantic Alliance. After the common external tariff went into effect, British exports to Germany, for example, were confronted with higher customs than before while French exports to Germany enjoyed lower duties and eventually none.

From a world point of view the net economic advantages of a regional customs union such as the European Economic Community are open to question. Since the customs union discriminates against all nonmember countries, it tends to divert some trade from nonmember to member nations, causing gains to members but losses to nonmembers unless aggregate trade increases sufficiently to offset losses to nonmembers. The analysis is usually stated in terms of trade diversion versus trade creation. If the losses from trade diversion exceed the gains from trade creation, the overall effect is that gains to members are at the expense of nonmembers, with a net loss to the world as a whole.

Suppose, for example, that the woolen cloth used in a man's suit can be produced in England and delivered to Germany for $20 and that it can be produced in France and delivered to Germany for $26. If before the formation of the Common Market the German customs duty on this item was $10, the English could sell in Germany for $30 and the French for $36. The French, because of higher costs of production, are not able to compete with the English in the German market. After the Common Market is formed, however, the French may be able to take over the trade in Germany, depending on the height of the common external tariff. If the duty remains at $10, France, as a member of the Common Market paying no tariff, can sell in Germany for $26, but England as a non-member, must continue to pay the $10 duty and sell for $30. Trade will be created for the French but only by diverting it from the English. The world as a whole will be worse off because production has been shifted from the low-cost producer (England at $20) to a higher-cost producer (France, at $26).

Now suppose the Common Market sets an external tariff 50 per cent

658

EUROPEAN
INTEGRATION
UNDER THE
COMMON
MARKET

below the former German tariff, or $5 as compared with the former $10. The English will hold their advantage over the French, since they will be able to deliver cloth, pay the duty of $5, and sell for $25; whereas the French will still have costs of $26 and will be unable to meet English competition, although they may be close enough to try to compete. The price of suits should come down in Germany and lead to greater sales and the creation of more trade. From the examples, it should be clear that nonmembers of a customs union have a strong interest either to join it or to negotiate for low external customs duties in order to minimize discrimination against themselves. The founders of the European Common Market talked in terms of an external tariff equal to the average of the member countries, or lower. If the Common Market does in fact lower tariffs against outsiders it will behave differently from customs unions in the past.

A more optimistic view suggests that the creation of a free-trade area such as the Common Market will enlarge trade in that area and result in a rapid growth of income and living standards so that the volume of imports demanded from outside the customs union will bring a net gain to the outside as well as the inside countries. One basis for this belief is that a very large free-trade area will bring the European Economic Community the benefits of mass production already enjoyed by the United States. While the mass-market argument is not without merit, it should not be pushed too far because it assumes that existing plants (not firms or industries) in Europe were of less than optimum size and that economies of scale would result from building larger plants. In Germany, France, and Italy, however, the domestic markets were quite large enough to justify plants of optimum scale of output in nearly all industries, and in the small Benelux countries the customs duties were quite low when they entered the Common Market so they already enjoyed most of the advantages of low-cost international trade from the mass production countries abroad.

For the European Common Market the factors are too numerous and complex to yield any clear answer whether trade creation more than offsets trade diversion, but the sensational success of the early years suggests that this may well have been the case. In addition to the 18.3 per cent per year cumulative increase cited above in the trade among the member countries, imports to the Common Market from the United States increased cumulatively between 1958 and 1963 at a rate of 12.4 per cent per year and exports to the United States from the Common Market at a rate of 9.0 per cent per year cumulatively. Imports from the United Kingdom rose 15.3 per cent per year as compared with an 8.3 per cent rise in exports from the Common Market to the United Kingdom, and imports from Canada, Japan, and the Soviet Union also rose more rapidly than exports from the Common Market to these countries. Consequently, it would appear that the high rate of growth in the Common Market assisted the growth of nonmember countries.[5] Nevertheless, the great issues between the Common Market countries and outside nations turned on the discrimination against nonmembers. The United Kingdom's behavior toward entry into the Common Market and the United States' drive for lower external tariffs on a world-wide basis are cases in point.

[5] See John M. Letiche, "European Integration: An American View," *Lloyd's Bank Review,* No. 75 (January, 1965), especially pp. 11–15.

The United Kingdom could have been one of the charter members of the Common Market, but chose initially not to affiliate because of special ties with the Commonwealth, reluctance to make direct commitments to Continental Europe which might infringe British sovereignty, and the special conditions of British agricultural policy. In order to prevent discrimination by the Common Market against other western European nations, the British proposed a wider free-trade area in which all seventeen nation members of the OEEC would eliminate trade barriers among themselves but would allow member nations to maintain their individual tariffs and quotas against countries outside the OEEC group. When the six Common Market countries rejected this offer, the British joined with Sweden, Norway, Denmark, Switzerland, Austria, and Portugal (joined later by Finland) to form the European Free Trade Association (EFTA), initially known as the "Outer Seven," in contrast with the "Inner Six" members of the Common Market. In attempting to mediate differences between the EEC and the EFTA, the United States seemed to favor the Common Market because it promised eventual political as well as economic integration in western Europe, something which most members of the EFTA wished to avoid. By 1967 the EFTA countries had eliminated all tariffs and quotas on industrial goods traded among its members.

In 1961, after success of the Common Market seemed clearly established, the United Kingdom applied for membership. In reaching a decision to throw their lot with the European Economic Community, the British negotiators broke with a long tradition of relative isolation from the Continent and also acknowledged the basic wisdom and necessity of European economic integration. Norway and Denmark followed suit and applied for full membership in the Common Market, and the political neutrals (Sweden, Switzerland, and Austria) sought non-political association. A unified western Europe with a population greater than that of the United States or the Soviet Union seemed about to be realized.

After prolonged negotiation, however, the British application for membership in the Common Market was vetoed in January, 1963, by President de Gaulle of France. He described Britain as "too insular and maritime" to become integrated with Continental Europe. De Gaulle's veto came at a time of resurgent French nationalism, with de Gaulle aspiring to win back France's place in the sun by exercising leadership in Europe and around the world. He wished to remain independent of the United States and seemed to view with suspicion Great Britain's close ties to other Anglo-Saxon peoples. A Common Market which included the United Kingdom would certainly have reduced the relative influence of France within the group, although it would certainly have increased the influence of the group as a whole.

In 1962, before the French veto of British entry into the Common Market, President Kennedy moved boldly to expand global trade and to reduce discrimination against United States trade by extracting from the Congress authority to negotiate major reductions in United States external tariffs in exchange for major reductions in Common Market external tariffs. Success in this venture would have alleviated the Common Market's major disadvantage, discrimination against nonmembers. Something approaching a free-trade area between Europe and the United States and much of the rest of the world was Kennedy's objective. This Grand Design was intended to

659

EUROPEAN
INTEGRATION
UNDER THE
COMMON
MARKET

660

EUROPEAN
INTEGRATION
UNDER THE
COMMON
MARKET

create an Atlantic partnership in which western Europe and the United States would reinforce one another in jointly offering aid to underdeveloped nations and confronting the Soviet Union with unprecedented economic and political power. De Gaulle's veto excluding Britain from the Common Market also derailed the Grand Design and led to a more modest approach to unity in the Atlantic Community.[6]

The Free Movement of Factors of Production

In addition to being a customs union aimed at trade liberation, the European Economic Community was designed to be an economic union. Perhaps the most important economic objective set out in the Treaty of Rome is the free movement of factors of production (labor, capital, and enterprise) across the national boundary lines of the Common Market countries. Restrictions were to be removed by the end of the twelve- to fifteen-year transition period. Workers may seek and accept employment anywhere without discrimination on grounds of nationality. This does not, however, include the right of surplus or unemployed laborers to go to another country where there is no employment available. One of the initial steps giving substance to the free mobility of labor was to permit workers to enjoy social security benefits in any country of the Community regardless of where the original contributions were made.

The Rome Treaty also provides that all restrictions on the movements of capital within the Common Market shall be removed during the transition period. Capital may be freely transferred from one country to another, and the earnings may likewise be transferred without restrictions. A firm with headquarters in one country may establish subsidiaries or branches anywhere in the Common Market. A United States firm located in the Common Market would be free to establish a branch plant anywhere within the Community and to hire skilled laborers and professionals within the Common Market without regard to their nationality. Mergers across national boundary lines are as free as mergers within individual countries. By facilitating the mobility of labor, capital, and enterprise the Common Market provides the basis for a more rational allocation of resources than usually exists among nations.

Closer General Economic Integration Within the Common Market

Other important aspects of economic union besides the free movement of the factors of production relate to common policies in agriculture, transportation, competition, employment, and fiscal and monetary policies.

Agriculture   The integration of agriculture was one of the most difficult tasks confronting the European Economic Community. The Rome Treaty called for a common agricultural policy but not necessarily, as in the case of nonfarm production, for the elimination of all barriers to free trade within the Common Market. Neither did it call for reduced agricultural protection against the rest of the world. Uniform price levels were, however, essential conditions for a common agricultural policy. When the Common Market was

---

[6] See Chapter 37 on the "Kennedy Round" under the Trade Expansion Act.

formed, each of the member countries had different price levels for farm
products because of widely divergent costs of production, price supports, import duties, and quota restrictions. In 1958, for example, Italian and German
wheat prices stood 45 per cent above French wheat prices. French and Dutch
farm prices were the lowest, but all had price levels for farm produce in
excess of competitive world prices, including British farm prices.

661

EUROPEAN
INTEGRATION
UNDER THE
COMMON
MARKET

Through high prices, the Continental countries had attained a surprising
degree of self-sufficiency in agriculture. The other side of the coin reflected
high costs of production and low productivity in relation to more favored
agricultural regions of the world. One-half of the farms in the six countries
contained fewer than twenty-five acres in 1960. With only one-tenth as much
land under cultivation as the United States, the Common Market countries
had twice as many farmers. Far-reaching structural changes were essential
for a long-term adjustment to a common price level approximating the world
price level in agricultural products, and the adjustment was estimated to
require the displacement of 8,000,000 to 10,000,000 European farmers to nonfarm occupations.

Europeans had much to gain in living standards through liberal agricultural trade policies with the outside world, but short of that they also had
much to gain by adjustments within the Common Market. Agreement on
policies, however, came slowly. Four years after signing the Treaty of Rome
only the barest outlines of a common agricultural policy were reached, and
thereafter agreement on particulars such as common price levels were slow
in coming. In wheat, for example, French prices were lowest in 1964 (about
$2.50 per bushel), and German prices were highest (about $3.25 per bushel).
Germany was reluctant to agree to a single wheat price because it would mean
lowering the support price to German farmers, while the French wanted a
single price for wheat in order to gain access to the markets of the other Common Market countries. After long negotiations the price of wheat was set at
$3.00 per bushel; this represented a concession by Germany and threatened to
drive thousands of high-cost German farmers out of wheat production, while
it provided an incentive for lower-cost French farmers to expand greatly the
production of wheat to be sold in Germany and other Common Market countries. At the same time the farm program operated to prevent overseas wheat,
which could be produced for one-half the $3.00 price, from being sold in the
Common Market below the fixed price. In agriculture generally, France was
a lower-cost producer than its Community partners, but a higher-cost producer
than overseas countries.

Transportation Discriminatory transportation charges may have effects
similar to tariffs in restricting the free movement of goods and services. Establishing a common transport policy within the Common Market means, among
other things, abolishing discrimination in freight rates and in frontier levies
against shippers because of their country of origin. It also prohibits preferential
freight rates as a method of subsidizing a domestic industry by permitting it
to enjoy lower freight charges than those paid by foreigners. In transport the
task of arriving at a common policy was simplified because the major transportation facilities of Europe are owned and operated as governmental enterprises. Nevertheless, there were many different practices in the six countries

662

EUROPEAN
INTEGRATION
UNDER THE
COMMON
MARKET

and the objective was to create consistent and uniform policies during the transition period.

Anti-trust policy Founders of the Common Market followed the lead of the European Coal and Steel Community in embracing anti-trust measures to reduce monopolistic barriers and to strengthen competition in European market structures. Actually the anti-trust provisions and their implementation by the separate member governments and by the Common Market are very weak. The chief requirement is that merger and cartel-type agreements shall be registered, and even this modest requirement ran into strong opposition. In the Economic and Social Committee of the EEC Commission many representatives of business voted against the Commission's proposal to require that inter-company agreements be registered in advance with the Commission.

The formation of the Common Market stimulated waves of mergers, which have been accepted and even applauded by the Common Market authorities. The feeling has been expressed that European firms are at a competitive disadvantage because they are much smaller than many American firms, and that it is desirable for European firms to grow larger. For example, in 1963 the annual sales of General Motors exceeded the combined sales of Germany's thirteen largest companies; annual sales of the twenty largest American business firms equalled the entire gross national product of Germany; and the annual sales of the five largest business firms in the United States equalled Italy's gross national product.

While cartel-type agreements to fix prices, limit output, and share markets seem to be illegal under the Treaty of Rome, the emphasis is on the results of the agreements rather than on the agreements as such. The burden of proof rests upon the governmental and Common Market authorities, and the investigatory and enforcement staffs are inadequate to be effective against business combinations.

Hope has been expressed that anti-trust measures will be accepted, however reluctantly, as part of the medicine needed to obtain the salutary effects of trade liberalization. Although the outcome in Europe is still pending, American experience suggests that anti-trust measures are of dubious significance even when the philosophy behind them forms part of the ethos of a community. In view of historic beliefs and practices which fostered cartel-type agreements in Continental countries, especially in Germany but hardly less so in the other nations, the anti-trust phase of Common Market efforts would appear unlikely to enjoy much success in stemming monopolistic and oligopolistic practices in business, especially with the full flowering of mass production in Europe.

Fiscal and monetary policy Europe generally has enjoyed high-level employment during most of the postwar period, and its maintenance is one of the objectives of the Common Market employment policy. Unemployment rates in the Netherlands, France, and Germany have been consistently below 2.5 per cent since the formation of the Common Market. Among the Six, Italy has suffered the greatest unemployment, mainly because of the slowness of absorbing unskilled workers from southern Italy into the industrial labor force. Yet even in Italy the unemployment trend was steadily downward. These low levels of unemployment in Europe contrast with higher rates in the United

States during the postwar period, and they contrast even more sharply with
the high levels of the interwar period, when unemployment rates of 10 per
cent and more were common in most of western Europe, especially during the
early 1930's.

663

EUROPEAN
INTEGRATION
UNDER THE
COMMON
MARKET

Because unemployment rates have been low, the employment policy
of the Common Market countries has been directed toward occupational training and geographical mobility of workers. Europe's rapid rate of technological
change has resulted in the displacement of large numbers of workers; consequently retraining programs and mobility have been necessary to keep down
the rate of unemployment. Europe's experience illustrates the principle that
when the general demand for labor is brisk, workers have strong incentives
to upgrade themselves to qualify for well-paying jobs. One specific provision
of the Treaty of Rome calls for a Common Market Social Fund from which
the governments of member countries may be reimbursed for one-half the
cost of occupational retraining or geographical resettlement of workers displaced by conversion of their enterprise to other production. Since the Common Market was formed, the real wages of European workers have risen,
working hours have declined, and social security benefits have been improved.
This improvement in the welfare of wage-earners has not, of course, been
confined to Common Market countries, although by stimulating the rate of
growth, the Common Market has made an important independent contribution to the rising standards of living.

Although the Treaty of Rome goes far toward economic integration, it
leaves in the shadow zone some important conditions for full economic union.
Monetary and fiscal policies of the six countries are coordinated through committees, including a committee of central bankers, but the EEC does not have
authority to issue money, levy taxes, or control major governmental expenditures. Autonomy in monetary and fiscal affairs is close to the heart of national
sovereignty, and its surrender by member states to the supra-national Common Market authorities is not called for in the Treaty of Rome. If, however,
the member states wished to, they could create a central monetary authority
(central bank), have a common currency, and a common balance of payments
against the outside world. Leaders in the European movement such as Jean
Monnet of France have suggested the possibility of a common European currency in the future, but so far this is only a vision of what may come to pass.
From its beginning the Common Market has operated with a common unit of
account, which is equivalent to the gold content of the United States dollar of
1958 (.888 grams = 13.7 grains of fine gold). For example, subscriptions to
the European Investment Bank, a Common Market creation, are stated in
terms of the dollar-equivalent unit. The dollar was chosen in preference to
any other unit because it most nearly approximated international money when
the Common Market was formed.

An all-European employment policy would be superior to national employment policies because it would avoid many of the beggar-thy-neighbor
practices that plagued Europe in the interwar years, but in the absence of all-
European monetary and fiscal autonomy, an all-European employment policy
is hardly feasible. Yet national employment policies are rendered more difficult by partial economic integration because the customs union increases
dependence of individual countries on foreign trade and also erodes national

664

EUROPEAN
INTEGRATION
UNDER THE
COMMON
MARKET

authority over worker migration and capital movements. Moreover, a balance-of-payments equilibrium often conflicts with full-employment policies, which require low domestic interest rates and large-scale deficit financing at some phases of the business cycle. The British Labour Party in 1958 opposed entrance of the United Kingdom into the Common Market because of a conviction that control over a nation's employment policy cannot be wisely handled multilaterally. Thus, on the one hand, Europe's economic integration stops short of the monetary and fiscal controls needed for effective employment policy while, on the other hand, it blunts the effectiveness of national employment policies.

During its formative years the Common Market enjoyed rapid economic expansion and low unemployment and did not have to face the dilemma of part-way integration of monetary-fiscal policies. In a severe crisis concerning inflation, balance of payments, or unemployment, the member countries would be forced to choose between strong national or strong supra-national action. In the early 1960's several years of price inflation in the Common Market countries induced a flood of imports and deterioration of the current external balances of the Six and led to a balance-of-payments crisis in Italy in 1964. The Governor of Italy's central bank scurried to Washington for United States financial aid to meet his country's crisis, much to the chagrin of other members of EEC, who felt they should have been the first to be consulted. This incident led to an agreement to consult first within the EEC in future crises. However, this incident, as well as what came out of it, manifests the absence of a common monetary policy. An unemployment crisis would place much stronger strains on EEC than an inflationary crisis. If the dynamics of creating the Common Market can sustain its prosperity long enough, it may gain the authority to cope successfully with major crises. For this to happen, however, close political integration would have to develop among the members of the EEC.

POLITICAL INTEGRATION

Although the Treaty of Rome does not specifically provide for political integration, it did create certain essentially political institutions for implementing its economic policies. These institutions are a Commission, which proposes policies and has day-to-day administrative authority; a Council of Ministers, which decides Community policy and acts as the final executive authority; an Assembly, which serves as a limited Parliament; and a Court of Justice to pass judgment on legal matters arising from the Treaty and the actions of the Community. At Community headquarters in Brussels, "European" civil servants (Eurocrats) carry out the bureaucratic functions of a "European" government. Members of the Assembly were initially chosen from existing national Parliaments, but provision is made in the Rome Treaty to elect them directly by universal suffrage sometime in the future.

While the Rome Treaty says nothing about a United States of Europe, clearly this goal stood high in the long-term aspirations of some of the founders of the Common Market. Jean Monnet, who might be called the Father of the EEC, spoke of building a "second America in the West." The vision of a po-

litically integrated Europe was perhaps the most compelling force behind the **665**

EUROPEAN
INTEGRATION
UNDER THE
COMMON
MARKET
formation of the Common Market. Sustained United States support for the
Common Market stemmed from a belief that it would greatly strengthen west-
ern Europe as a political and military partner in the struggle with the Soviet
Union and its satellites. The United States did not waver in its support despite
the obvious increased economic competition and discrimination which the
Common Market imposes on American exports to Europe.

In view of the all-pervading influence of the Communist issue in world
politics after the Second World War, United States support of the political
integration of Europe is not surprising. Clearly, the small nation states of
western Europe represented an anachronism in the power structure of the postwar world. Yet they were only slightly less anachronistic in the first half of the
twentieth century when autarky rather than economic integration set the tone
of political economy. The decisive new force which made the difference was
the greatly enhanced political, military, and economic power of the Communist
bloc and the reaction which this generated in the political thinking of anti-
Communist communities. Against this background the major setback to the
Common Market in 1963, when Britain's application was rejected, falls into
place, for it coincides with a lessening of the Communist threat to western
Europe as a result of the growing split between the Soviet Union and Commu-
nist China, on the one hand, and the reduced tensions between the United
States and the Soviet Union following the resolution of the missile crisis in
Cuba in 1962, on the other hand.

Another major crisis arose in 1965 as a result of President de Gaulle's
disapproval of supra-national tendencies within the European Economic Community. The Executive Commission of the EEC took the initiative in suggesting to the Council of Ministers a plan whereby revenues from farm tariffs on
goods from outside countries would be channeled to the EEC under the jurisdiction of the European Parliament in Strasbourg, whose powers up to that
time had been largely consultative. The Commission's plan would have placed
large sums of money at the disposal of the supra-national group and thereby
enhanced its powers. President de Gaulle, who opposed increasing the EEC's
supra-national power, wanted the revenues to flow directly to the treasuries
of the six member nations. Moreover, the French President wanted proposals
such as those for agricultural financing to be initiated by representatives of
member nations and not by the supra-national Commission. When the six
nations failed to reach agreement by a self-imposed deadline (June 30, 1965),
France boycotted for seven months all activities to advance the progress of
the Common Market, including further steps toward economic union. This
not only halted progress toward the long-term goals of the Common Market,
but it stymied the Kennedy Round of tariff negotiations in Geneva, where the
six EEC nations constituted a single bargaining party and occupied a central
position in the negotiations.

An innovation as far-reaching as the Common Market could hardly take
place without encountering crises. As in the American Constitutional Convention of 1787, compromises were essential to attain agreement on fundamental
issues involving conflicts of interest. Continued progress toward economic
cooperation in the EEC depends on political agreements which set the framework within which economic decisions can be made. The compelling advan-

666

EUROPEAN
INTEGRATION
UNDER THE
COMMON
MARKET

tages of economic cooperation must be strong enough to override political obstacles such as the surrender of some degree of national sovereignty.

CONCLUSIONS ON THE SIGNIFICANCE OF THE COMMON MARKET

In order to interpret correctly the significance of the Common Market, the long-term development of western Europe should be viewed in perspective. During the 1950's most countries of western Europe enjoyed general prosperity marked by rapid growth, large increases in productivity, and rising standards of living which narrowed the gap between the American and European standards. This forward momentum was propelled by western Europe's emergence into the age of high mass consumption, characterized by rapid increases in consumer durable goods, including automobiles and household appliances. A parallel stage of high mass consumption reached the United States during the 1920's in the so-called "New Era" prosperity of that gilded decade. The Common Market is a rational adaptation to the age of high mass consumption, which arrived quite independently but, because of the Common Market, developed more quickly, more extensively, and more efficiently than it would have otherwise.

To suggest that the Common Market is more of an accommodation than a causal force in the forward momentum of western Europe in no sense belittles its overall importance. Perhaps its most important mission is, on the economic side, not so much creating a more affluent society but furthering the evolution of economic planning by joining the institutions of the market with extensive governmental decision-making; and, on the political side, restoring to western Europe the influential political status it enjoyed before the Second World War. Given political unity and stable economic growth, western Europe can take its place alongside the United States, the Soviet Union, and China as one of the great powers of the twentieth century.

SELECTED BIBLIOGRAPHY

BALASSA, BELA, *The Theory of Economic Integration*. Homewood, Ill.: Richard D. Irwin, Inc., 1961.

BEVERIDGE, WILLIAM H., *Full Employment in a Free Society*. New York: W. W. Norton & Co., Inc., 1945.

BRADY, ROBERT A., *Crisis in Britain*. Berkeley: University of California Press, 1950.

BROOKS, JOHN, *The European Common Market*. Buffalo, N. Y.: Smith, Keynes and Marshall, Inc., 1963. (paperback)

BROWN, WILLIAM A., JR., and REDVERS OPIE, *American Foreign Assistance*. Washington, D.C.: The Brookings Institution, 1953.

COLE, G. D. H., *Postwar Condition of Britain*. London: Routledge & Kegan Paul, Ltd., 1956.

DOBB, MAURICE R., *Capitalism Yesterday and Today*. New York: Monthly Review Press, 1962. (paperback)

DOVRING, FOLKE, *Land and Labour in Europe.* The Hague: Martins Nijhoff, 1956.

ECONOMIC COMMISSION FOR EUROPE, *Economic Survey of Europe.* Geneva: Economic Commission for Europe, annual since 1948.

EINAUDI, M., M. BYE, and E. ROSSI, *Nationalization in France and Italy.* Ithaca, N. Y.: Cornell University Press, 1955.

HACKETT, JOHN and ANNE-MARIE, *Economic Planning in France.* Cambridge, Mass.: Harvard University Press, 1963.

HARROD, ROY F., *The British Economy.* New York: McGraw-Hill, Inc., 1963.

HENDERSON, WILLIAM O., *Genesis of the Common Market.* Chicago: Quadrangle Books, 1962. (paperback)

HUMPHREY, DON D., *The United States and the Common Market.* New York: Frederick A. Praeger, Inc., 1962. (paperback)

JOINT ECONOMIC COMMITTEE, *A Description and Analysis of Certain European Capital Markets,* 88th Congress, 2nd Session, Joint Committee Print. Washington, D.C.: Government Printing Office, 1964.

LEWIS, BEN W., *British Planning and Nationalization.* New York: Twentieth Century Fund, 1952.

LUTZ, VERA, *French Planning.* Washington: American Enterprise Institute, 1965. (paperback)

KEYNES, JOHN M., *How to Pay for the War: A Radical Plan for the Chancellor of the Exchequer.* New York: Harcourt, Brace & World, Inc., 1940.

MAYNE, RICHARD, *The Community of Europe.* New York: W. W. Norton & Co., Inc., 1962. (paperback)

MYRDAL, GUNNAR, *An International Economy.* New York: Harcourt, Brace & World, Inc., 1956.

ROGOW, A. A., *The Labour Government and British Industry.* Oxford: Basil Blackwell, 1955.

ROSTAS, LASZLO, *Comparative Productivity in British and American Industry.* New York: Cambridge University Press, 1948.

SHONFIELD, ANDREW, *Modern Capitalism, The Changing Balance of Public and Private Power.* New York: Oxford University Press, 1965.

UNITED STATES SENATE, SUBCOMMITTEE ON ANTITRUST AND MONOPOLY OF THE COMMITTEE ON THE JUDICIARY, *Antitrust Developments in the European Common Market, Report.* Washington, D.C.: Government Printing Office, 1964.

WALLICH, HENRY C., *Mainsprings of the German Revival.* New Haven: Yale University Press, 1955.

WILCOX, CLAIR, *A Charter for World Trade.* New York: The Macmillan Company, 1949.

WILSON, THOMAS, *Modern Capitalism and Economic Progress.* London: Macmillan & Co., Ltd., 1950.

WOOTTON, BARBARA, *Freedom Under Planning.* Chapel Hill: University of North Carolina Press, 1945.

668

EUROPEAN
INTEGRATION
UNDER THE
COMMON
MARKET

KLEIN, BURTON, "Germany's Preparation for War: A Reconsideration," *American Economic Review,* XXXVIII (March, 1948), 56–77.

KRAUSE, LAWRENCE B., "European Economic Integration and the United States," *American Economic Review,* LIII (May, 1963), 185–96.

LETICHE, JOHN M., "European Integration: An American View," *Lloyds Bank Review* (Jan., 1965), pp. 1–22.

LEWIS, BEN W., "British Nationalization and American Private Enterprise: Some Parallels and Contrasts," *American Economic Review,* LV (May, 1965), 50–64.

MADDISON, ANGUS, "How Fast Can Britain Grow?" *Lloyds Bank Review* (Jan., 1966), pp. 1–14.

ROBINSON, JOAN, "Beyond Full Employment," *Annals of Collective Economy,* XXXII (April–June, 1961), 159–67.

SHEPHERD, WILLIAM G., "British Nationalized Industry: Performance and Policy," *Yale Economic Essays,* IV (Spring, 1964), 183–222.

SVENNILSON, INGVAR, "Planning in a Market Economy," *Weltwirtschaftliches Archiv,* XCV (Dec., 1965), 184–201.

WELLS, S. J., "The EEC and Trade with Developing Countries," *Journal of Common Market Studies,* IV (Dec., 1965), 150–67.

EFTA Bulletin, published monthly by Information Department of the European Free Trade Association, Geneva, Switzerland.

European Community, bulletin published monthly by European Community Information Service, Brussels, Belgium.

The United States Economy in the Early Postwar Period

CHAPTER **36**

On the eve of the Second World War the United States had suffered a full decade of severe depression. In 1939 nine and a half million workers, or more than one-sixth of the labor force, remained unemployed, and national income was substantially below the level of 1929 despite an increase in the labor force and a marked rise in output per man-hour of employment. The American economy had pulled out of the worst depths of the depression of 1929–32 but had been unable to achieve anything approaching full recovery. In 1937–38 it ran afoul of a major recession within the Great Depression.

President Franklin Roosevelt's numerous New Deal programs for recovery and reform failed to restore national prosperity, and after this decade of depression and stagnation there was little evidence to suggest that American capitalism would return to the comparative prosperity of the pre-1929 era. Traditionally Americans had been perennial optimists looking forward to steadily rising living standards, but the experience of the 1930's profoundly shook their confidence in the future. A changed outlook during the 1930's was reflected in the fall in the birth rate to the lowest level in American history. Just to have a steady job was the new, diminished dimension of the American dream for millions of workers. Full employment was a national aspiration but hardly anyone had faith in its fulfillment. American capitalism was in desperate straits in 1939, and how it would have recovered, if at all, from the Great Depression in the absence of war must remain one of the intriguing but unanswered questions of history.

In Europe by the late 1930's the political and military crises which had been nurtured by the Great Depression reached a climax. Statesmen of Great Britain and France capitulated to Adolf Hitler at Munich in the fall of 1938, and thus allowed Hitler to dismember Czechoslovakia in the spring of 1939. But when Hitler's legions invaded Poland on September 1, 1939, the British and the French declared war on Germany. Six years of war left Europe in a critical economic condition in 1945, but after 1950 a new era of prosperity dawned. In the United States the war quickly restored economic prosperity, which, in contrast to what happened after the Civil War and World War I, projected itself into the postwar period.

THE
UNITED STATES
ECONOMY
IN THE EARLY
POSTWAR
PERIOD

Above all else the Second World War demonstrated beyond any doubt the tremendous productive potential of the American economy. By confirming the huge gap between the actual and potential production of the peacetime economy of the 1930's, the wartime performance held promise for higher living standards after the war. Moreover, the war experience seemed to confirm the view of those who had contended during the Great Depression that a sharp increase in aggregate effective demand was the chief requisite for high-level employment and output.

Not only did total production increase during the war, as was to be expected, but, surprisingly, aggregate civilian consumption also increased. The latter was indeed remarkable in view of the fact that war needs in some years absorbed nearly one-half of total output of United States goods and services and that these were years during which twelve million men and women in prime working years served in the armed forces and the American economy supplied not only its own military needs but also war matériel in great quantities to Allies around the world.

Despite the increase in aggregate consumption, severe shortages of nearly all consumers' goods developed during the war, whereas shortages had not been apparent during the preceding decade. What accounts for the apparent paradox that goods became scarcer just at a time when there was more of them? The answer is, of course, that consumer demand depends on consumer income, and incomes were low before the war but high during the war. Consumers' goods were scarce *relative to the demand* during the war because such a large proportion of total output went into war production rather than into civilian consumer output. Consumer demand increased faster than consumer output.

Strong inflationary pressures resulting from the increase in consumer demand led to a number of anti-inflationary measures. Taxes were increased, especially personal income taxes, which took from income earners some of their excess purchasing power. Purchases of war bonds were encouraged as a means of diverting demand from consumers' goods and services. However, increased taxation plus increased voluntary saving failed to mop up the excess purchasing power in the hands of consumers. Consequently, other, more direct controls were imposed. The Office of Price Administration was created to combat inflation by placing ceilings on prices of civilian goods.

Price controls led, in turn, to another problem, namely, that stocks of goods might be depleted before all people who wished to purchase, and had the means, could satisfy their demands, leaving nothing for those who came to buy later. Since this would have worked gross inequities and would have hit hardest those families too busily engaged in war work to take time to stand in line to buy the limited supply of goods, scarce items had to be rationed by special administrative devices. Coupon books authorizing the purchase of limited amounts of many types of food, gasoline, and other scarce necessities were issued to all consumer units in the country. Price controls and administrative rationing replaced the peacetime "law" of supply and demand in the consumer market out of fairness to all consumers. Without price controls poorer consumers could have been priced out of the market through inflation,

and without administrative rationing rich and poor alike could have been left

in the position of Old Mother Hubbard. In normal peacetime conditions, the function of price is to ration limited supplies among those able and willing to buy. What was novel about the wartime situation was not rationing *per se,* but the replacement of price rationing by administrative rationing.

One consequence of price controls and administrative rationing was a more equal distribution of consumption. High-income groups were forced to consume less and lower-income groups were able to consume as much or more than before the war. For example, between 1942 and 1946 fresh meat was rationed according to rules which applied equally to the rich and the poor. Rich families accustomed to all the beefsteak they wanted before the war were obliged to cut back on their consumption during the war, whereas families whose breadwinners were unemployed in the prewar depression were able to purchase more beefsteak during the war despite the constraints imposed by administrative rationing. The amount of steak which could be purchased for home consumption depended more on the number of coupons in ration books than on the amount of money in pocketbooks. Or, taking another example, automobiles were not produced for civilian consumption after February, 1942, and a family accustomed in peacetime to a new car every year could not maintain its standard; whereas the family accustomed to keeping its automobile for ten years was able to continue its peacetime standard, or possibly to improve it by purchasing a better, used automobile out of higher wartime income. Under wartime controls a significant redistribution of consumption took place, with some families consuming less and others consuming more than before the war, and with a slight increase in aggregate national civilian consumption.

One of the troublesome side effects of price controls was the "Black Market," in which transactions were made without ration cards at prices in excess of legal ceilings. Unspent funds remaining in the hands of consumers after paying taxes and buying limited supplies of rationed goods at ceiling prices presented a temptation to obtain more of the rationed goods outside legal channels. Although troublesome during the war, black markets became a more serious problem as soon as the war ended because the patriotic sanction of winning the war could not be invoked to induce consumers to buy war bonds and to submit to unpopular controls.

Closely related to price controls was the even more difficult problem of wage controls. In order to administer price controls effectively, costs had to be controlled, and wages were in most cases the largest element in costs. Business leaders complained that workers, especially organized labor, kept pressing for wage increases, which forced them to increase prices in the much-discussed wage-price spiral. Wage-earning groups, on the other hand, contended that if wages were controlled, profits should also be controlled. Direct control over profits presented an even more difficult problem than direct control over wages. In order to stop the wage-price spiral the Roosevelt administration adopted the so-called "Little Steel Formula," which forbade further wage increases after May, 1942, except in special cases which required some increase to offset other increases which had occurred before May, 1942. A Wage Stabilization Board, with regional offices throughout the country, was set up to administer wage controls. This apparatus worked with less than complete harmony, but on the

672

THE
UNITED STATES
ECONOMY
IN THE EARLY
POSTWAR
PERIOD

whole wage controls were more successful than might have been expected in a nation unaccustomed to direct regulation of wages, prices, and profits. Inflation was not prevented but it was suppressed during the war. Price levels rose more in a few years just after the war than during the war itself.

The fact that the United States maintained, and even increased somewhat, aggregate civilian consumption during the war meant that no net contribution to war production came from a decrease in civilian consumption. Increases in total production and decreases in civilian capital formation provided the real "fund" which "paid" for the war. By employing millions of workers who had been idle before the war and by increasing the productivity of those who had previously been employed, seven-tenths of the increase in war output was met. The remaining three-tenths came from decreases in nonwar capital formation. The latter had two variants: the depreciation of existing capital assets such as undermaintaining the railways for the duration of the war, and curtailing new investment not essential to the war, such as civilian housing and office buildings.[1]

While price inflation and relative changes in wages and profits affected the distribution of income among individuals and groups and therefore affected the manner in which the burden of the war was borne by individuals, it was an increase in real production rather than a redistribution of income from which the war was paid. Stated in another way, this meant that the economic cost of the Second World War to the American people was small because war production for American and allied military forces was achieved by harnessing resources which had not been utilized before the war and which were brought into use by the stimulus arising from the war itself.

POSTWAR EXPANSION

In the long-term perspective of history the most important characteristic of the United States economy after the Second World War was the movement toward a mixed economy, combining private enterprise with governmental responsibility for a satisfactory performance of the economy as a whole. The public (governmental) commitment to economic welfare was primarily in terms of stability of prices and employment, through monetary and fiscal policy, and the most general legislative recognition of this commitment was the Employment Act of 1946, although a whole maze of economic legislation was directed toward its fulfillment. Statements and actions of postwar presidents abound in acknowledging this commitment, whereas it was virtually nonexistent under Presidents Harding, Coolidge, and Hoover.

President Franklin Roosevelt's New Deal was in this sense the transitional stage, and the Great Depression of the 1930's the occasion for the new departure in national economic policy. The New Deal fell far short of fulfilling its commitment, primarily because it inherited from the preceding administration the worst depression in modern history, but the institutional framework to which it aspired and which it partly succeeded in creating proved appropriate for a much better economic performance after the war. Whether the

---

[1] See Simon Kuznets, *National Product in Wartime* (New York: National Bureau of Economic Research, 1945), pp. 64–66, for reference to estimates of the U.S. Department of Commerce.

postwar performance would have been even better without the New Deal trappings is a question that can be raised but not answered.

THE
UNITED STATES
ECONOMY
IN THE EARLY
POSTWAR
PERIOD

With the stimulus imparted by the Second World War, the American postwar economy took off from a high level and maintained a momentum which the peacetime New Deal never generated. The postwar performance was far from ideal: business recessions occurred, but they were minor ones similar to those of 1924 and 1927; inflation followed the war, but it was contained within tolerable limits; unemployment proved the most persistent problem and grew worse after the war-induced momentum weakened but did not attain the fantastic rates of the 1930's. The significance of the mixed economy was in the avoidance of an economic breakdown comparable to that which began in 1929. America's mixed economy involved governmental activity far short of classical socialism, but it did entail a substantial increase in direct governmental activity in the public sector in addition to the commitment to maintain a satisfactory performance of the private sector. Countries of western Europe followed a similar path after the war, but with larger doses of socialism than the United States experienced. Clearly a relapse to the conditions of the prewar Great Depression would have proven fatal to continued American leadership, especially in view of the rapid economic advances of the Soviet Union under an altogether different economic system.

As a result of its surprisingly good performance after the Second World War, the United States retained by a wide margin the world economic, financial, and technological leadership which it had developed in the early decades of the twentieth century. At the end of the war the United States produced 60 per cent of the world's industrial output with only 6 per cent of the world's population. American economic superiority had never been so great before and probably will never be as great again as in the half-decade immediately following the Second World War. After 1950 it continued to make impressive absolute gains—the standard of living of the American people rose—but it lost ground relative to the Soviet Union, western Europe, and Japan, all of which grew at substantially higher rates than the United States. Like Great Britain in the nineteenth century, the United States suffered the disadvantage of taking the lead. Other nations could borrow more from the United States than it could borrow from them.

The American performance was inferior in another important respect. After the initial postwar spurt, the gap between its potential and actual performance grew wider and was relatively greater than in other leading industrial nations. Unemployment became substantially higher and plant utilization considerably lower after the recession of 1957–58, with unemployment ranging persistently between 5 and 7½ per cent of the labor force in the late fifties and early sixties. Thus the overall picture for the American economy in the postwar period was one of great economic superiority at the end of the war, followed by continued absolute growth but relative decline, attributable in part to a significant gap between potential and actual economic performance.

Backlog of Demand

Having come through the early reconversion period without any major catastrophe, the American economy headed into a bright postwar period of

674

THE
UNITED STATES
ECONOMY
IN THE EARLY
POSTWAR
PERIOD

prosperity and expansion, broken only at intervals by minor recessions. Prosperity rested on a high level of effective demand typical of other postwar periods, and the expansion arose from continued technological progress leading to increased productivity, which has always been a feature of American economic development. Increased savings for capital accumulation enabled the business community to embody technological changes in new capital assets and provide the basis for long-term growth, which resumed a rate of approximately 3 per cent per year after having lapsed almost entirely between 1929 and 1939 because of lack of demand to call forth the potentialities of the economy.

Increases in aggregate supply provide a ceiling above which growth cannot go, but aggregate demand has been the strategic factor in determining economic conditions, being either deficient or excessive. The First World War generated a large volume of effective demand, causing inflation during and just after the war and creating conditions which made for strong demand and prosperity for a decade. During the 1930's the economy performed very poorly not because workers lost their skills or because of natural catastrophe but because the volume of effective demand remained deficient. During the 1940's the Second World War generated excessive demand which was constrained fairly well during the war but caused inflation after price and wage controls were removed in mid-1946. Through most of the 1950's a strong backlog of needs accumulated from the war generated strong demand, which gradually diminished so that after 1958 chronic unemployment and plant underutilization threatened the economy.

This great backlog of demand from the war was the critical element in the economic history of the United States for a full decade after World War II. The components of effective demand may be classified as (1) personal consumption expenditures, especially for durable goods; (2) gross private domestic investment, including outlays for residential construction; (3) governmental expenditures, including federal, state and local; and (4) net foreign investment.

(1) **Personal consumption** At the end of the war American consumers had, on the one hand, large surpluses of liquid assets (cash and securities), while on the other hand, they had major deficiencies in the supply of consumers' goods. As soon as controls were relaxed, goods-hungry consumers rushed into markets to exchange liquid assets for goods and to reestablish an equilibrium position in their total asset holdings. A rise in personal consumption by $20 billion between the first quarters of 1945 and 1946 was autonomous, that is, the amount of consumption out of given levels of income rose. Consumer durable goods in particular had been very scarce during the war and in some instances were not available for purchase at all.

Automobiles played a role almost as important as after the First World War. Demand for cars remained strong throughout the recession of 1948–49, weakened temporarily in the recession of 1953–54, and then spearheaded recovery from that recession. In 1955 automobile production broke all previous records with an output in excess of seven million, which was not surpassed until 1963. Refrigerators, washing machines, vacuum cleaners, radios, and

other durables common to prewar households were joined by two newcomers, television sets and air conditioners. Television became a major industry by 1949, and room air conditioners by the summer of 1953.

675

THE
UNITED STATES
ECONOMY
IN THE EARLY
POSTWAR
PERIOD

(2) **Gross private domestic investment** Although Americans in peacetime spend on the average more than 90 per cent of their disposable (after taxes) income, investment demand is the strategic variable determining the level of national income. Investment demand is more unstable and less predictable than consumer demand, which tends to vary with income. If investment is low, income and therefore consumption expenditure tend to be low; and if investment is high, income and therefore consumption tend to be high. Businessmen make investments if they expect the rate of return on capital assets to exceed the cost of the funds to be invested. Investment opportunities at the end of the war were very favorable, and liquid funds for investing were abundant. No large-scale construction of plant and equipment for producing consumers' goods had taken place since the 1920's—the 1930's were characterized by low business investment and during the war (the early 1940's) most of the plant construction was made by the federal government for war purposes. Meanwhile technological progress rendered old factories and equipment obsolete.

After the war, although many war plants were sold to private enterprises and converted to civilian consumption, they represented only a fraction of the total needed to produce the expanding consumer demands of a population growing rapidly in numbers and affluence. Hence, across the broad front of American industries, there was need for a great volume of business investment, including plant and equipment for automobiles, steel, petroleum, electrical machinery, industrial chemicals, construction materials, communications, public utilities, and many others. Technological progress during the thirties and forties created a great stock of new opportunities for improved equipment and methods of production. Population growth had a broad impact on the demand for all consumers' goods and, because of the high ratio of capital needs to annual output, the influence was particularly felt in construction for electricity, gas, and telephone services. Public utility investment grew more than at any previous period in American history. Fixed business investment averaged 12 per cent of gross national product in the early postwar years, 1947 and 1948; it was 10 to 11 per cent from 1949 through 1957, which were years of rapid growth and expansion, and dropped to an average of 9 per cent in the next five years of lagging growth.

A huge backlog of demand for dwelling units existed at the end of the Second World War, and filling this backlog constituted one of the major sources of sustained postwar expansion and prosperity. From 1929 through the war household formation exceeded the construction of new housing units even though the former was held down by the depression and by the mobilization of marriageable-aged men during the war. When servicemen returned after the war, household formation proceeded at a merry pace, and despite a major housing boom in the late forties, the size of the backlog increased until the early fifties. A movement to the suburbs stimulated massive housing projects while contributing to the abandonment of dwelling units in many cities and farms. The value of residental construction increased more rapidly than the

676

THE
UNITED STATES
ECONOMY
IN THE EARLY
POSTWAR
PERIOD

number of new dwelling units because of rising construction costs and up-graded housing standards associated with higher income levels of the average family.

After the depression-induced and war-induced backlog of housing was filled in the middle to late fifties, the transition to normal demands took place smoothly, whereas, by contrast, the decline in residential construction after 1925 had been an important contributor to the economic collapse of 1929. As one of the most durable of assets, residential construction has been subject to strong cyclical bunching and has in the past constituted a de-stabilizing force in total economic activity. During the post-World War II period, however, residential construction moderated the downturns of 1948–49 and 1953–54 and then leveled out into a more stable pattern than it had followed in earlier decades. Government-guaranteed and government-insured loans for dwelling units helped to stabilize the demand for housing and to limit mortgage fore-closures in periods of postwar financial stringency. The entrance of govern-ment regulations into the housing loan market illustrates one type of policy pursued in the mixed economy to avoid major depressions.

(3) **Governmental expenditures**   Although military spending fell dras-tically at the end of the Second World War, total governmental expenditures remained high compared with prewar levels and constituted an important ex-pansionary force in the American economy. In both international relations and domestic affairs the new responsibilities thrust upon the federal government were reflected in mounting peacetime budgets. Federal expenditures for goods and services averaged ten times as large a proportion of gross national prod-uct in the 1950's as in the 1920's, and two-and-a-half times as large as in the 1930's.

After 1948 national defense expenditures associated with the Cold War with the Soviet Union accounted in large part for the increases over prewar budgets, and when fighting broke out in Korea in the summer of 1950, military spending shot up rapidly and led to an inflationary rise in prices. Following the Korean truce in the summer of 1953, military spending fell sharply and was the strategic factor in the mild recession of 1953–54. In the late fifties fluctuations in spending abated, but the trend in total outlays continued up-ward—for national defense, foreign aid, agricultural price supports, and in response to the space challenge hurled by the Russian sputniks after 1957. A $100 billion federal budget was reached in 1965–66. In most years, federal expenditures exceeded federal revenues, and the resulting deficits stimulated economic activity. By reducing private disposable income, taxes curb private spending, whereas governmental deficits, especially when financed by bank loans, add to the existing stream of demand. If unemployment is high, an addi-tion to total demand will put unemployed resources to work; if unemployment is already low, additional demand tends to create inflationary pressures on wages and prices.

In American society some major public needs such as schools and roads fall primarily within the jurisdiction of state and local governments, and in the postwar period non-federal governmental expenditures increased steadily in response to these needs. State and local government expenditures increased during the cyclical downswings as well as in the upswings of postwar business

cycles and thus added both an expansionary and a stabilizing force to the total demand. Sharp increases in birth rates in the forties and fifties brought, with a five- or six-year lag, unprecedented demands for school facilities for the booming school-aged population, sweeping like a tidal wave from kindergarten in the late forties to university graduate schools in the late sixties. A burgeoning automobile population created a need for more and better roads, and by the late fifties a national network of highways, throughways and byways was under construction.

Because a major part of the nation's taxing power lay with the federal government, demands were made for federal aid for highways and schools. During President Eisenhower's administration (1953–61) a program of federal financing of highways was inaugurated, stimulated partly as a means of recovery from the recession of 1957. Federal aid for schools roused a great national debate, and Congress responded slowly to requests for federal funds for state and local schools. Not until President Johnson's administration did a general school aid bill pass Congress and become law.

(4) **Foreign investment** Another expansionary force operating in the American economy during the postwar years was a high volume of foreign aid, starting with assistance for the reconstruction of western Europe and continuing with grants and loans to underdeveloped nations. In terms of its immediate effect on demand, foreign aid acted in much the same way as domestic investment—it resulted in employment to produce output which did not become available for current domestic consumption. Like domestic investment, therefore, foreign aid enabled the American economy to operate at a higher level without glutting the domestic markets with more consumers' goods and services than could be sold profitably.

Foreign aid differed from domestic investment in that it did not add to the future productive capacity of the American economy; the idea behind foreign aid was to add to the productive capacity of other economies, and in this it was generally successful. Most successful was the Marshall Plan giving aid to western Europe in the early postwar period. Foreign aid to less developed nations necessarily continued for a long time and yielded results less certain and less apparent than the Marshall Plan. American foreign aid averaged about $5 billion annually in the first twenty postwar years and, although small in relation to the gross national product of the United States, it had a considerable expansionary impact at home and, at times in the early postwar years when the economy was near full employment, may have had inflationary effects.

POSTWAR INFLATION

The high level of effective demand which brought rapid expansion in employment and output in the postwar years also exerted a strong upward pressure on prices. Measured in terms of the consumer price index, the cost of living rose by more than 40 per cent in the first decade after the war. Most of this increase came in two spurts, in 1946–48, when price controls established during the war were suddenly discarded, and in 1950–51, largely as a consequence of the outbreak of fighting in Korea. Between 1948 and 1950 the consumer price index fell slightly, and then remained remarkably stable from 1952

678

THE
UNITED STATES
ECONOMY
IN THE EARLY
POSTWAR
PERIOD

through 1955. In 1956 retail prices began to rise again, this time more slowly than in the two previous postwar spurts, but inflation now persisted in the face of a general contraction in economic activity and rising unemployment during the recession of 1957–58. Large expenditures for the Vietnam war renewed the threat of inflation beginning in 1966.

De-control Inflation, 1946–48

The most serious postwar inflation started with the removal of price controls during the second half of 1946 and continued through the first half of 1948. During the two years from June, 1946, to June, 1948, the consumer price index rose 25 per cent. The tremendous inflationary pressures built up during the war had been suppressed by direct controls over prices and wages. From mid-1942 to mid-1946 consumer prices rose less than 20 per cent. In the early postwar period the Truman administration advocated that direct controls over prices remain in effect until the economic transition from war to peace could be completed. From the business community, however, came pressures to end controls as soon as the fighting stopped. One contention was that abolishing price controls would lead to a rapid increase in production and cause prices to fall. Whatever the merit of this argument as a long-run effect, it misrepresented or misjudged the short-run situation in which the public was loaded with liquid assets and was short of nearly every type of durable good. However, a war-weary public was impatient with wartime restrictions, especially rationing controls.

Meat producers withheld supplies from the market in order to increase the political pressures for repeal of price controls and rationing. Black marketeering, that is, selling above ceiling prices and outside legal rationing channels, became increasingly widespread. Without public acceptance, such controls could not function satisfactorily. As the situation deteriorated, many advocates of continued price controls became discouraged. In 1946, when Congress presented President Truman with a weak-as-water price control bill, he vetoed it in favor of no controls.

Thereafter the consumer price index, which had risen only 3 per cent in the first twelve months after victory in Europe, began to rise rapidly. Not since the skyrocketing postwar inflation of 1919–20 had prices shot up so rapidly in the United States. The consumer price index (1935–39 = 100) stood at 133 in June, 1946; at 157 in June, 1947; and at 172 in June, 1948.

Excess demand affected the labor market as well as the product market. Unemployment remained at less than 4 per cent during 1947 and 1948 despite continuing reconversion problems in some industries. From 1946 to 1949 there were three rounds of wage increases, each successive round being started by key collective bargaining agreements in the steel and automobile industries. As wages rose, costs and prices also increased, and higher costs of living led in turn to new wage demands in the cumulative wage-price spiral. Given time for productivity to rise, higher wage rates do not necessitate higher prices or lower profits, but in a situation such as 1946–48, the chief restraints are the intermittent nature of wage bargains—once a year or once in two years—and the self-imposed restrictions by sellers in setting prices below the level which

would prevail with the free play of supply and demand. For example, in the early postwar years new automobiles were sold at prices substantially below their free market value.

679

THE
UNITED STATES
ECONOMY
IN THE EARLY
POSTWAR
PERIOD

A recession followed the sharp inflation of 1946–48. In 1949 unemployment rose to 6.8 per cent of the civilian labor force, while retail prices fell from 175 in September, 1948, to 167 at the close of 1949. With more care and patience in relaxing wartime controls, both the serious inflation and the consequent recession could have been moderated and perhaps avoided. Since the inflation resulted from an excess of demand and the recession from a deficiency of demand, a continuation of some price and rationing restraints a year or two longer could have curbed the inflation and, by releasing pent-up demand when the recession threatened, unemployment could have been checked.

Korean Inflation, 1950–51

Sparked by the outbreak of fighting in Korea in the summer of 1950, the next postwar inflationary wave occurred during 1950–51. Panic buying by civilians was provoked by fears that the Korean conflict might spread into a general war and lead to shortages similar to those still fresh remembered from the Second World War. Retail prices increased by approximately 10 per cent from mid-1950 to the end of 1951. As in 1946–48 this new inflation was a clear case of strong demand pulling up prices, and not of wages and other costs pushing up prices. Unemployment rates fell and remained around 3 per cent from the beginning of 1951 through the first half of 1953. Military spending helped prolong the economic expansion which began late in 1949 and continued into 1953.

The potentially serious economic strain of the Korean conflict led to the establishment of the Office of Price Stabilization, patterned after the wartime Office of Price Administration. Price and wage ceilings went into effect in January, 1951, two months after China's entry into the conflict caused American forces to retreat from the Yalu River. Priorities were instituted for strategic materials, but administrative rationing of consumers' goods proved unnecessary. After the initial upsurge, prices fell back and many remained below the legal ceilings. Following the Korean truce in early 1953, the Eisenhower administration dismantled and laid to rest the Office of Price Stabilization.

Creeping Inflation, 1956–58

The first genuine peacetime inflation after World War II began in 1956, by which time war-generated backlogs and excess liquidity had run their course. Normally price inflation occurs when economic activity is expanding, but the unusual aspect of the 1956-58 price inflation was its persistence in the face of the deepest of the first three postwar recessions, a recession in which industrial production fell by 14 per cent from peak to trough of the business cycle. In the *downswing* of the cycle from July, 1957, through April, 1958, retail prices *rose* 3 per cent while unemployment increased from 4 to 7½ per cent of the civilian labor force. In three years after January, 1956, retail prices

680

*THE
UNITED STATES
ECONOMY
IN THE EARLY
POSTWAR
PERIOD*

rose by 8 per cent, which was the mildest of the three postwar inflationary waves. This creeping inflation, however, is of special significance because it illustrates the forces making for inflation in peacetime, independent of wartime influences and repercussions. It merits some further analysis.

Between 1955 and 1957 an expansion of unusual magnitude took place in plant and equipment and generated a demand which led to sharp price increases in construction, steel, machinery, and other heavy durable goods. Collective bargaining agreements in key industries such as steel and automobiles contained liberal settlements, including productivity and escalator clauses for automatic wage increases extending over a three-year period. These generous wage agreements set the pattern for other industries in which market demand and profits were high during 1956 and 1957. Other sectors of the economy in which market and profit conditions were not favorable found their costs rising also. As the price of steel, for example, increased, it raised the costs of production in the numerous steel-using industries and led to further price increases to meet higher costs of production. Workers in less prosperous industries were influenced by wage agreements in the key industries and were reluctant to be left out of the drive for higher standards of living. Although the investment boom ended in 1956, workers in key industries continued to receive productivity and cost-of-living increases under their three-year collective bargaining agreements of 1956.

Despite a sharp rise in unemployment and a 14 per cent fall in industrial production from the peak to the trough of the 1957–58 recession, the resistance to downward adjustments of prices and wages remained very strong. Consequently the price level continued to rise throughout the recession and beyond. Given downward inflexibilities in prices and wages generally, in combination with sharp increases in prices in some sectors, the average price level rose in a sort of creeping inflation after 1955. This has been called structural inflation, or demand-shift inflation, because a strong shift in demand to a few sectors (e.g., steel, machines, construction) will raise prices in these sectors and push up the general price level in the absence of offsetting decreases of prices in other sectors.

An increase in aggregate demand is not essential to set in motion structural adjustments which lead to general price increases under these conditions. The downward inflexibility is related to the oligopolistic structure of industry in which giant firms with the power to influence the market may choose to maintain or even to raise their prices when the demand for their product falls. Such prices are referred to as administered prices. The so-called ratchet effect by which prices and wages rise but do not fall has imparted a long-run inflationary bias to the American economy.

Conclusions on Inflation

By comparison with earlier historical periods, prices in the United States were relatively stable after 1945. If the two war-related inflations of 1946–48 and 1950–51 are eliminated, prices rose only moderately in the postwar period. A comparison of the sixteen peacetime years 1897–1913 with the sixteen years from 1948–64 indicates that wholesale prices increased by 50 per cent in the

earlier period and by less than 25 per cent in the latter period. The latter period includes a 10 per cent increase during the Korean War.

Nevertheless prices in the post-World War II period showed an inflationary bias, best illustrated by the creeping inflation following 1956. The bias is more apparent in retail than in wholesale prices because the index for the former includes a higher proportion of services, which have risen more than commodity prices over the long run. Services such as medical care, haircuts, auto repairs, and dry cleaning contain a larger proportion of wages and salaries and are subject to smaller increases in measured productivity than physical goods.

A consideration of perhaps greater importance is the inability of index numbers of prices to reflect accurately changes in the quality of the items priced. Assuming that most quality changes represent improvements, index numbers have a built-in upward bias that cannot be measured but which should be taken into consideration in evaluating the significance of inflation measured by index numbers, especially of consumers' goods. For example, if the overall quality of automobiles improves by 2 per cent in a year in which prices of automobiles also rise by 2 per cent, it can reasonably be contended that there has been no increase in price for value received. Unfortunately, to quantify improvements in quality is difficult in any particular case as well as in principle, and consequently it may be preferable to treat price changes independently of quality changes and to say merely that the consumer pays higher prices for better products. Nevertheless, improved quality clearly moderates the social significance of the secular upward drift in prices and may more than offset a price rise of one or 2 per cent per year.

In part, the long-term upward trend of prices after World War II reflected the absence of any offsetting downward trend during recessions. The capitalist era has generally been marked by alternating long-term upswings and downswings in prices, with the overriding tendency for prices to rise from century to century. During the nineteenth century prices fell from 1815 to 1848, rose from 1848 to 1873, and fell again from 1873 to 1896. The periods of falling prices were marked by major depressions, such as the post-Napoleonic crises and the depressions of the 1870's and 1890's. Likewise, the Great Depression of the 1930's brought large reductions in prices. Large contractions in demand such as occur in major depressions cause deflation of prices as well as contraction of employment and output.

The absence of a major depression in the post-World War II period undoubtedly was a major factor accounting for the absence of price declines. Insofar as public policies in a mixed economy have succeeded in avoiding major depressions, there may also have been removed the occasion for falling price levels. This might be judged to represent a net gain in the sense that, while deflation and inflation are both inequitable, deflation is worse because in addition it wastes real wealth through unemployment. In any case, secular inflation may be part of the price paid for conquering major depressions. Since inflation has always outrun deflation over historic epochs anyway, the case for a depression-proof economy is reinforced. At best, depressions are an expensive form of price control, and society should be able to find a better way.

THE
UNITED STATES
ECONOMY
IN THE EARLY
POSTWAR
PERIOD

ABRAMOVITZ, MOSES, *Resource and Output Trends in the United States Since 1870.* Occasional Paper 52. New York: National Bureau of Economic Research, 1956.

BERLE, ADOLF A., JR., *The 20th Century Capitalist Revolution.* New York: Harcourt Brace & World, Inc., 1954.

BURNS, ARTHUR F., *Prosperity Without Inflation.* Buffalo, N. Y.: Smith, Keynes & Marshall, Inc., 1958.

CHANDLER, LESTER V., *Inflation in the United States, 1940–1948.* New York: Harper & Row, Publishers, 1951.

COMMISSION ON MONEY AND CREDIT, *Report, Money and Credit; Their Influence on Jobs, Prices, and Growth.* Englewood Cliffs, N.J.: Prentice-Hall, Inc., 1961. (paperback)

COUNCIL OF ECONOMIC ADVISERS, *Annual Report.* Washington, D.C.: Government Printing Office, 1946–.

DEWHURST, J. FREDERICK, *America's Needs and Resources: A New Survey.* New York: Twentieth Century Fund, 1955.

DOWD, DOUGLAS F., *Modern Economic Problems in Historical Perspective.* Boston: D. C. Heath & Co., 1962. (paperback)

DUNLOP, JOHN T., ed., *Automation and Technological Change.* Englewood Cliffs, N.J.: Prentice-Hall, Inc., 1962. (paperback)

FRIEDMAN, MILTON, *Capitalism and Freedom.* Chicago: University of Chicago Press, 1962.

HANSEN, ALVIN H., *The Postwar American Economy.* New York: W. W. Norton & Co., Inc., 1964. (paperback)

HICKMAN, BERT G., *Growth and Stability of the Postwar Economy.* Washington: The Brookings Institution, 1960.

JOINT ECONOMIC COMMITTEE, *Employment, Growth, and Price Levels.* Staff Report, Hearings (13 volumes) and 23 staff papers. 86th Congress. Washington, D.C.: Government Printing Office, 1959–60.

KENDRICK, JOHN W., *Productivity Trends in the United States.* Princeton: Princeton University Press, 1961.

KUZNETS, SIMON, *National Product in Wartime.* New York: National Bureau of Economic Research, 1945.

LEBERGOTT, STANLEY, *Men Without Work, The Economics of Unemployment.* Englewood Cliffs, N.J.: Prentice-Hall, Inc., 1964. (paperback)

MILLER, HERMAN P., *Rich Man, Poor Man.* New York: Thomas Y. Crowell, 1964.

OKUN, ARTHUR M., *The Battle Against Unemployment.* New York: W. W. Norton & Co., Inc., 1965. (paperback)

PHELPS, EDMUND S., ed., *Private Wants and Public Needs.* New York: W. W. Norton & Co., Inc., 1962. (paperback)

SCHULTZE, CHARLES L., *Recent Inflation in the United States.* Study Paper No. 1 of Joint Economic Committee's Study of Employment, Growth, and Price Levels. Washington, D.C.: Government Printing Office, 1959.

VATTER, HAROLD G., *The U.S. Economy in the 1950's.* New York: W. W. Norton & Co. Inc., 1963. (paperback)

ARTICLES

ABRAMOVITZ, MOSES, "Resource and Output Trends in the United States Since 1870," *American Economic Review*, XLVI (May, 1956), 5–23.

COCHRANE, WILLARD W., "Contributions of the New Frontier to Agricultural Reform

in the United States," *Journal of Farm Economics*, XLIV (Dec., 1962), 1167–79.

FELS, RENDIGS, "The U.S. Downturn of 1948," *American Economic Review*, LV (Dec., 1965), 1059–76.

LAMPMAN, ROBERT J., "Approaches to the Reduction of Poverty," *American Economic Review*, LV (May, 1965), 521–29.

SAMUELSON, PAUL A., and ROBERT W. SOLOW, "Analytical Aspects of Anti-Inflation Policy," *American Economic Review*, L (May, 1960), 177–94.

SCHULTZ, THEODORE W., "Investing in Poor People; An Economist's View," *American Economic Review*, LV (May, 1965), 510–20.

683

THE
UNITED STATES
ECONOMY
IN THE EARLY
POSTWAR
PERIOD

The United States Economy
in the Later Postwar Period

CHAPTER 37

National rates of economic growth depend primarily on aggregate demand in relation to aggregate supply. Aggregate supply sets a ceiling on growth, but the actual level of growth may fluctuate between the ceiling and a low or negative rate, depending on the actual level of aggregate demand. If the rate of growth is at or near the ceiling, further increases in demand will raise prices and cause inflation unless special controls are imposed on prices. In the twentieth century the long-term rate of growth of the American economy has averaged about 3 per cent per year. Because of fluctuations in aggregate demand associated chiefly with wars and depressions, the rate of growth has sometimes been higher and sometimes lower than 3 per cent. After the First World War, the decade of the twenties was above average in growth whereas the thirties was a decade of no growth at all. After the Second World War the first decade was one of above-average growth, and the second postwar decade fell below and then rose above the long-term growth rate. During both wars and in the early postwar years, aggregate demand tended to outrun aggregate supply and led to inflation. In these important respects the two-decade sequence after both wars resembled each other.

The prosperity of the first postwar decade in each instance was attributable to backlogs of demand accumulated from the war which stepped up the rate of growth until the backlogs were liquidated. After both wars prominent features of postwar prosperity were strong demands for automobiles, highway construction, residential construction, consumer durables stimulated by consumer credit, and producer plant and equipment. In both postwar periods over-optimistic expectations of the business community led to capital formation in excess of that needed to meet aggregate demand in the second postwar decade. The parallel here is between the years 1928–29 and 1956–57 in which producer durable equipment reached peaks not attained again for a number of years. The great difference between the two postwar periods is, of course, the absence after World War II of a Great Depression, which is indeed a whale of a difference. Nevertheless, it is helpful to see the slowdown after 1956 in the perspective of the interwar period.

The slowdown in the growth rate in the second postwar decade is reflected in higher unemployment rates and in weaker recoveries from recessions. Unemployment rates in the first ten years after the war averaged 4.2

per cent and in the next ten years 5.5 per cent. In the five-year period 1958–62
inclusive, unemployment averaged 6 per cent of the civilian labor force.

THE
UNITED STATES
ECONOMY
IN THE LATER
POSTWAR
PERIOD

Slower growth and higher unemployment are reflected in the recoveries
from the postwar recessions. Recoveries from the two recessions of the first
postwar decade were complete, but recoveries from the next two recessions,
in the second decade, were weak and incomplete. In the economic expansion
following the recession of 1948–49, the minimum rate of unemployment in any
month fell to 3 per cent; after the 1953–54 recession to 4.2 per cent; after the
1957–58 recession to 5.3 per cent; and after the 1960–61 recession, unemployment averaged 5.8 per cent in the four-year period 1961–64. Incomplete recoveries reflect a kind of stagnation, although a high-level stagnation compared
with that of the thirties. Aggregate demand was not strong enough between
1956 and 1963 to pull the economy back onto its potential growth path. In
recovery periods employment did not increase in proportion to output because of rising output per man-hour. For example, in the twelve months ending June, 1959, industrial production rose 15.9 per cent while employment
rose only 3.6 per cent. Output rose rapidly *in the recovery phase* of the cycle
not only because of fuller utilization of plant and equipment but also because
of a new development of the postwar period—fuller utilization of specialized
personnel, including engineers and technicians, who were kept on the payroll
through recession periods and in this sense represented labor overhead analogous to plant overhead. The forces which permit the unemployment rate to
rise *from cycle to cycle* despite rising total output are the increase in output
per worker and the increase in the number of workers in the labor force. Just
to keep the unemployment rate from rising from cycle to cycle, output must
rise enough to match the increase in productivity per man (about 2 per cent
per year) plus the increase in the size of the labor force (close to 1.5 per cent
per year), so that an aggregate rate of growth in output of 3.5 per cent per
year would be necessary to maintain a constant unemployment rate at comparable phases of the business cycle.

Private investment Investment in business plant and equipment is one
of the critical requirements for economic growth from the side of both aggregate demand and aggregate supply. On the demand side, investment is needed
to disburse purchasing power to help clear the market of consumers' goods
and services currently produced in the non-investment sector of the economy.
On the supply side, business plant and equipment provide the basis for increases in productivity and also for equipping new members of the labor force
with the capital goods required for their employment. A slowdown in the
volume of new plant and equipment developed in the second postwar decade.
From 12 per cent of real gross national product in 1947–48, it averaged 10 to
11 per cent from 1949 through 1957, and fell to 9 per cent in the following
five years. President Kennedy's Council of Economic Advisers estimated that
private investment between 10 to 11 per cent of gross national product would
be needed for a long-term growth rate of 4 per cent per year.[1] In the boom
year 1965 this figure was back to 10.5 per cent. After the early postwar crop
of babies began entering the labor market in the early 1960's, the labor force

[1] *Economic Report of the President* (Washington, D.C.: Government Printing Office,
1963), p. 62.

686

*THE
UNITED STATES
ECONOMY
IN THE LATER
POSTWAR
PERIOD*

increased on an average by 1.6 per cent per year, or more than one million new workers each year. As the labor force increased, employment also increased but by less than the labor force, with a resultant increase in unemployment. Meanwhile the excessive build-up of plant and equipment in the mid-1950's led to underutilization of existing plant and equipment. Some old factories will not be used unless new factories are currently being built to provide, not new capacity, but current demand for output.

Changing Structure of Employment

The shortage of jobs reflected a rapidly changing structure of employment as well as a deficiency of aggregate demand. Jobs producing material goods declined relative to jobs rendering services. Employment in agriculture, mining, and manufacturing declined while employment in trade, finance, and government increased.

Agriculture   American agriculture has employed a declining proportion of the total labor force almost since the beginnings of the nation, and the absolute number of persons employed in agriculture began to decline in 1910. Recently agricultural productivity has increased even more rapidly than industrial productivity. Output per man-hour in farming rose by 300 per cent in the quarter-century from the mid-thirties to the early sixties. This amazing performance was made possible by mechanization of farming and government-sponsored research operating through the United States Department of Agriculture and the experiment and extension services in land-grant colleges. With fewer farms producing a larger total output, employment in agriculture fell from 16 per cent of the labor force in 1943 to 10 per cent in 1953 and to 7 per cent in 1963. The absolute number of farm jobs in these years was, respectively, 9 million, 6.5 million, and 5 million. In 1965 the 4.5 million agricultural workers represented 5.7 per cent of the labor force.

Mining and manufacturing   Employment in mining reached a peak in the United States in 1920, and after some erratic fluctuations during the Great Depression and World War II, declined steadily after the war. Coal mining experienced the largest decrease with a reduction of 50 per cent in employment during the fifties, but miners of all types were decreasing, mainly as a result of displacement by machinery and other laborsaving devices below and above ground.

Almost from the beginning of American history the declining opportunities for agricultural employment had been compensated by increasing opportunities in manufacturing, but this also changed in recent decades. During the interwar period, manufacturing jobs as a percentage of total jobs began to decline. In November, 1943, the absolute number of jobs in manufacturing reached a peak of 18,074,000 and stagnated thereafter, with ups and downs according to the state of the business cycle. It reached a sub-peak of 17.5 million in 1953 and touched 18 million in June, 1966. Thus in the postwar period manufacturing joined agriculture as a major sector of the economy which began to decline in terms of the absolute as well as the relative number of employment opportunities.

A record number of automobiles, for example, was produced in model **687**

*THE
UNITED STATES
ECONOMY
IN THE LATER
POSTWAR
PERIOD* year 1963, with 162,000 or 22 per cent fewer blue-collar workers than in the previous peak year, 1955. Textile employment during the fifties declined by one-third. In steel, total employment fell by 14 per cent while output rose by 14 per cent between 1953, the year of peak employment, and 1964. Employment of steel production and maintenance workers fell even more than total steel employment, by 17.5 per cent during the same period, or by 108,000 down to 512,000 in 1964; [2] and with the projected rate of productivity increase exceeding the projected increase in steel output, employment among production and maintenance workers would fall another 100,000, or 20 per cent, by 1975. Moreover, in computer-controlled (automated) steel mills, many steel workers were shifted from their former highly skilled jobs to less skilled jobs at lower rates of pay.

Construction Material-goods production includes, in addition to agriculture, mining, and manufacturing, the construction industry in which employment has shown no marked trend in the postwar period, although the peak during the 1950's was 3,000,000 in 1956. However, the construction boom of the mid-1960's raised this total above 3,000,000. Productivity did not increase as rapidly in construction as in other spheres of material-goods production.

Total employment in the combined material-goods sector reached a plateau just after the Second World War, while employment in the combined service industries (trade, finance, transportation, public utilities, and government) continued to increase rapidly. Employment in services exceeded employment in material goods for the first time in 1953, and by the end of the fifties seven million and by the mid-sixties twelve million more persons were employed in producing services than in producing material goods. Within subsectors of the services industries between 1953 and 1963, employment increased in wholesale and retail trade, finance, hotels, restaurants, and state and local governments (school teachers), while it was stationary among federal government workers, and declined in transportation and public utilities.

Among the many facets of the swiftly changing pattern of employment, the most striking feature was the decline in the number of jobs in the material-goods sector of the economy. Automation and other technological advances enabled fewer workers to produce tremendous increases in physical output. In addition to meeting the demand for durable and non-durable products of the conventional type, American factories poured forth a steady stream of new gadgets which were pushed at consumers by high-pressure advertising. But all this increased output could not stay the fall in the number of jobs available in material-goods production. America in the 1950's and 1960's became an affluent society, enjoying an abundance of automobiles, housing, household furnishings, appliances, food and clothing. Apart from a submerged group in the population—those who were unskilled, poorly educated, non-white, and in households headed by non-adult male breadwinners—Americans were materially better off than any people had ever been in history.

[2] See Council of Economic Advisers, *Report to the President on Steel Prices* (Washington, D.C.: The White House, 1965), pp. 23, 31.

THE
UNITED STATES
ECONOMY
IN THE LATER
POSTWAR
PERIOD

The major economic problem of the United States in the 1930's and again in the 1960's was unemployment. As a result of the experience with unemployment during the Great Depression, Congress passed the Employment Act of 1946. Initially the sponsors of this legislation viewed it as a "full employment" bill, but as enacted it became a "maximum employment" act, which stated: "It is the continuing policy and responsibility of the Federal Government to use all practicable means . . . to coordinate and utilize all its plans, functions and resources . . . to promote maximum employment, production and purchasing power."

In pursuit of these directives the President is required to make annual recommendations to the Congress on ways and means "to promote maximum employment, production and purchasing power." Congress established a Joint Economic Committee to review the President's annual economic message and in turn to report to Congress concerning the main recommendations of the President. In order to prepare his report and to maintain continuous surveillance over the economy the President was authorized to appoint a Council of Economic Advisers. As conceived and carried out in the context of other legislative acts bearing on economic affairs, the Employment Act went far toward making the federal government responsible for the general economic health of the nation. This act stands as a charter for the dual or mixed economy, in which private enterprise is the primary instrument of employment, production and purchasing power, but in which the responsibility for satisfactory performance rests with the federal government. It was an affirmation of the policy of positive government in economic affairs inaugurated by Roosevelt's New Deal during the Great Depression of the 1930's.

Fiscal policy   Under the Employment Act, fiscal policy became the chief instrument of federal economic policy for stimulating and maintaining aggregate effective demand. Beginning with the New Deal of the 1930's, automatic stabilizers were built into the structure of the American economy, and these built-in stabilizers helped to moderate business recessions and to prevent a major depression after the Second World War. Important stabilizers included unemployment compensation, social security benefits, progressive personal income taxes, and a high level of governmental expenditures. With unemployment compensation, a worker who loses his job continues to receive income during a substantial period of unemployment. Meanwhile, he has time to look for another job. Under the old age and survivors' annuity provisions of social security a retired worker, or his widow, continues to receive income and thereby not only attains a degree of security against want but also helps to cushion the economy against loss of demand. Under the progressive income tax system, the amount of taxes paid falls more rapidly than income (when income falls) because the rate of tax is lower for lower levels of income. For example, the amount of income tax paid on a $3000 income is less than one-half the amount of income tax paid on a $6000 income in the same circumstances. Consequently, disposable (after-tax) income fluctuates less in the business cycle than personal income, national income, or gross national product. During the postwar period, disposable personal (after-tax)

income rose each succeeding year despite declines in national income during recessions.

Reducing federal tax rates Although built-in stabilizers moderated postwar business recessions, they also weakened business recoveries. They helped to prevent recoveries as well as major depressions. As employment and income rise in periods of recovery, the amount of taxes paid under progressive tax rates increases more than in proportion to income, the reverse of the $3000–$6000 example cited in the preceding paragraph. If tax rates are at a level which would produce a large surplus in the federal budget at full employment, these rates will, under normal peacetime conditions of demand, drain so much money from the income stream that economic recovery will slow down and peter out before full recovery is reached. In conditions after 1958, federal taxes acted as a brake that caused the economy to run out of gas before reaching full employment. Taxes attuned to war and inflationary pressures rose rapidly as national income rose and became too high to permit full recovery and full employment to be reached. Stated in a different way, the full-employment surplus, that is, the surplus in the federal budget *if* the economy had been at full employment, was too high. The full-employment surplus was estimated at about $5 billion in the years 1956 to 1959 and in excess of $10 billion in 1960.

Against the background of a weak and incomplete recovery from the recession of 1960–61, President Kennedy recommended to Congress a major tax cut of more than $10 billion to reduce the size of the full-employment surplus, that is, to release the tax brake and permit economic expansion to move closer to full employment. The theory behind the tax cut was as follows: A reduction in personal income tax rates would increase the take-home pay of wage and salary earners immediately. Knowing that consumers had spent 92 to 94 per cent of their after-tax personal income in every year since 1950, they presumably would spend a large part of the additional take-home pay. The increased spending would create additional demand for goods and services and create a demand for additional workers. Newly employed workers would in turn spend most of their additional income on consumers' goods and services. The direct and indirect effects of lowering the personal income tax were estimated to be approximately twice the amount of the tax cut; for each reduction of $1 billion in taxes, gross national product would increase $2 billion. A $10 billion reduction would raise gross national product by $20 billion.

A reduction in the corporation income tax would increase personal incomes through larger dividends, and also raise the after-tax rate of return to business and thus stimulate business investment. Business investment in turn would also stimulate employment and generate more income and effective demand for consumers' goods. Initially the lower tax rates would yield lower total revenue, but as gross national product rose over the years, total government revenues from lower tax rates were expected to increase and, even with no reduction in federal expenditures, to bring the government budget into balance. A gap between the potential and the actual gross national product was estimated at $50 billion in the recession of early 1961 and $30 billion during the long expansion of 1963 and 1964. This additional product

690

*THE
UNITED STATES
ECONOMY
IN THE LATER
POSTWAR
PERIOD*

could have been produced if unemployment had been reduced to 4 per cent of the labor force, a relatively modest although not easily attainable goal of national economic policy. The argument for the tax cut amounted to saying that the federal budget can be balanced only at lower tax rates applied to higher national income, and not at higher tax rates because higher rates act as a brake which restrains expansion much below full employment.

The Kennedy-Johnson income tax cut, enacted into law in March, 1964, represented an important innovation because it marked the first time a President had advocated a planned budget deficit as a step toward improving the performance of the economy. President Roosevelt was persuaded by 1937 to make a virtue of a necessity and accept budgetary deficits as desirable, but his program was one of increasing expenditures rather than lowering taxes. Under Presidents Truman and Eisenhower major tax reductions took place, but they were made as an accommodation to expenditure reductions after the Second World War and after the Korean War, respectively. They were enacted to prevent excessive budget surpluses rather than to create a budget deficit. The big excise tax cut of 1965 had purposes and consequences similar to the 1964 income tax reduction.

Size of the public debt   The most effective opposition to the Kennedy-Johnson tax cut came from those who wanted to reduce governmental expenditures as a condition for lowering tax rates. Concern with continuing deficits and the rising federal debt lay behind this point of view. Except in wartime, a large public debt, and especially an increase in it, has been a grave political liability to the party in power. However, in relation to relevant magnitudes such as national income and the size of private debt, the burden of the federal debt did not increase in the postwar period. At the end of World War II the federal government's debt equalled 131 per cent of gross national product and in 1965 it was only 48 per cent of the gross national product. Meanwhile aggregate private debt rose from 66 per cent to 133 per cent of the gross national product.[3] Combined private and public net debt in the United States passed the one-trillion dollar mark in 1962, at which time the federal government's debt constituted one-fourth of the total, whereas private corporate and personal debt constituted two-thirds of the total. (The small remaining fraction was owed by state and local governments.) From the end of the war to 1965, the *net* federal government debt increased from $252 billion to $270 billion, or by 7 per cent, while net private debt increased from $140 billion to $897 billion, or by 540 per cent. Thus public debt declined sharply in relation to gross national product and in relation to private debt during the first two postwar decades.

Public expenditures   Although tax cuts designed to stimulate the lagging economy constituted the chief innovation in postwar fiscal policy, large expenditures continued to play an important role in fiscal policy. After World War II governmental expenditures were at new peacetime highs and, by virtue of their sheer magnitude, affected the level of economic activity. National defense was by far the largest single item of expenditure in the federal budget. Because of shifting threats and crises in the Cold War, national de-

[3] See *Economic Report of the President,* 1966, pp. 272, 273.

fense expenditures fluctuated substantially and caused federal expenditures to be the most unstable of the major components of national income through the 1950's.

Increased expenditures as well as reduced taxes can stimulate economic growth. During the sixties the Kennedy-Johnson administration recommended growth-related spending for education, research, manpower training, and natural resource development, including electric power projects. A major federal highway program was pressed vigorously throughout the postwar period. The Kennedy administration urged expenditures for urban redevelopment and mass transportation for metropolitan communities, with little success in Congress, however. President Johnson enjoyed more success with health care for the aged and broad educational measures. Except as tied to military and space research and development, federal expenditures had a limited impact on raising the rate of economic growth. Many growth-promoting activities are in the domain of state governments, and federal expenditures took the form of grants to states to entice them into more vigorous action than some were accustomed to take on their own initiative.

691

THE
UNITED STATES
ECONOMY
IN THE LATER
POSTWAR
PERIOD

Monetary Policy

Next to fiscal policy, monetary policy was the most important weapon in the federal arsenal of weapons to promote economic growth and stability. In the early postwar years monetary policy was strongly conditioned by the extreme liquidity resulting from the methods used to finance the war. The Federal Reserve System continued its wartime policy of supporting the prices of government securities until March, 1951, when an "accord" was reached between the Treasury and the Federal Reserve officials. The accord relieved the Federal Reserve System of its wartime commitment to maintain low interest rates on federal securities. Since the amount of interest paid on bonds already in the hands of the public did not change, a fall in their market prices raised the effective market rate of interest. Before the 1951 accord, purchases by the Federal Reserve prevented the prices of the bonds from falling below the pegged price and hence kept the rate of interest from rising above a pegged rate. On long-term bonds, the rate of interest for ten years before the accord had been fixed at 2.5 per cent. After the accord the market rate of interest rose above 4 per cent. Congress imposed a maximum of 4¼ per cent on government securities with a maturity of more than five years, and at times this maximum was lower than the market rate of interest on such securities.

Federal Reserve officials justified higher interest rates as a necessary weapon against inflation. Monetary policy, including interest rate changes, seems to have had a noticeable effect on residential construction and on state and local governmental construction, but expenditures on business plant and equipment do not appear sensitive to monetary policy, especially to low interest rates. Although there were differences of opinion concerning the overall effectiveness of monetary policy, on balance it seems to have had limited significance as a positive weapon against inflation or unemployment. One limitation arose from the tendency for changes in the velocity of money to offset changes in the quantity of money. In the economic expansion phases of business cycles when the Federal Reserve System followed a restrictive or tight

692

THE
UNITED STATES
ECONOMY
IN THE LATER
POSTWAR
PERIOD

money policy, velocity increased; and in periods of recession when the Federal Reserve followed an easy money policy, the velocity decreased.

An important development affecting the velocity of money was the growth of non-bank financial intermediaries such as savings and loan associations, mutual savings banks, pension funds, investment trusts, insurance companies, and similar financial institutions. Assets in these intermediaries grew more rapidly than the assets of commercial banks in the postwar period and complicated monetary control. Monetary policy was also handicapped by the relatively long time lag before its impact was felt. Characteristically monetary controls are frustrated by monopolistic prices, which resist downward pressures when aggregate demand is restricted and which divert demand into higher prices rather than into output and employment when monetary conditions are relaxed. The substantial rise in interest rates dating from the accord of 1951 probably hindered expansion in the fifties and sixties.

Although the Kennedy-Johnson administration relied primarily on fiscal policy to increase aggregate demand for the purpose of raising the level of employment and growth, monetary policy was important in facilitating expansionary fiscal policy. For example, to attain maximum expansionary effect from the tax cut of 1964, the federal deficit should have been financed by selling securities to banks rather than to individuals. A non-bank purchaser of government bonds merely transfers purchasing power from himself to the government, with no net increase in the total. Since the whole objective of fiscal and monetary policy in conditions of economic slack is to increase aggregate private and public spending, the commercial banks should purchase government securities out of free reserves, either already on hand or supplied by the Federal Reserve System through open market purchases or one of the other techniques used by central banks to expand the money supply. If the central bank authorities are unwilling to use their power to expand the money supply in a period of sluggish growth and high unemployment, the government's fiscal policy can be frustrated.

The Federal Reserve System is an independent agency and therefore legally it is not directly subject to the policy decisions of the President and his administration. In hearings on the tax cut of 1964 the chairman of the Federal Reserve's Board of Governors showed reluctance to finance federal deficits created by the tax cut. Fear of inflation and of deficits in the troublesome international balance of payments during the 1960's limited the free use of fiscal policy to raise the growth rate and lower the unemployment rate.

Structural Unemployment

Even the best conceived and most skillfully administered fiscal and monetary policies cannot eliminate all unemployment, at least not without substantial price inflation. Full employment can be defined as a condition in which the number of job vacancies equals the number of unemployed workers, a condition in which unemployment is not general but specific and which in principle could be eliminated by matching the workers to the jobs available through geographical relocation, education, retraining, abolishing discrimination based on race, sex, and age, and by other means. The square pegs must be refashioned to fit into round holes. In the United States a large amount of

this so-called structural unemployment existed among teen-age school drop-outs, among unskilled and poorly educated workers of all ages, and among those further disadvantaged as members of groups discriminated against because of race, color, and sex.

With the mechanization of agriculture and the increasing automation of industry, the number of jobs available to unskilled and unschooled workers diminished rapidly. The demands of complex technology outran the education and training of the labor force. Teen-agers who dropped out of school experienced great difficulty finding jobs even though there were many unfilled positions for adequately trained and well-educated people. Unemployment among young people was accentuated by a big jump in the number of new entrants into the labor force as the crop of early postwar babies began to hit the labor market. Annual increments to the labor force increased from an average of 900,000 in the period 1956–64 to an estimated average of 1,400,000 in the years 1965–70. Unemployment among teen-agers stood at 15 per cent in the early 1960's as compared with 3 to 4 per cent among prime breadwinners, defined as married men with "wife present."

Although the percentage of youths completing high school was higher than ever before in American history, the school dropout became a serious social and economic problem in the sixties because the supply of jobs for poorly educated persons decreased faster than school dropouts. In earlier decades American youth frequently quit school to take a job on the farm or in a factory. In recent times youths who quit school have no place to go, except to the streets of cities and towns. Youth unemployment was one of the major causes of increased juvenile delinquency in the postwar period. It led in 1965 to establishment of the Job Corps, a program similar to the Civilian Conservation Corps of the 1930's.

Poorly educated older workers who lost their jobs also experienced difficulty finding new employment. Coal miners cannot easily be trained to be school teachers, nor displaced auto or steel workers to be physicians, nor railway firemen to be electrical engineers. Among workers 45 years of age and older, unemployment rates were not above the average, but older workers who lost their jobs remained unemployed longer than younger workers of comparable education and training.

The task confronting the United States was a massive upgrading of the labor force. Primary responsibility for this task rested at the local and state level in the form of improved schooling, training and retraining programs, but the federal government showed initiative in combating the problems related to structural unemployment. Among the measures taken by the Kennedy administration were the Area Redevelopment Act of 1961, the Manpower Development and Training Act of 1962, and the Vocational Education Act of 1963. In President Johnson's anti-poverty program, an attack on structural unemployment of the disadvantaged groups was a fundamental objective.

With the rapidly changing structure of industry and declining employment opportunities in coal mining, textiles, and automobiles, whole geographical areas became centers of above-average unemployment rates. The Area Redevelopment Administration was set up to assist depressed areas by providing federal funds for worker-training programs and by giving financial as-

694

**THE
UNITED STATES
ECONOMY
IN THE LATER
POSTWAR
PERIOD**

sistance to new firms locating in depressed areas. It was especially active in the Appalachian coal mining area and the New England textile area. Appalachia became a focal point in the anti-poverty program. Advocates of multibillion dollar programs for sending a man to the moon were reminded of the need to invest in Appalachia, in education, and other welfare measures to provide opportunities for disadvantaged groups.

Under the Manpower Development and Training Act grants were made to states to retrain unemployed workers for available jobs, with preference given to heads of households. Workers were permitted for the first time to receive unemployment compensation (training allowances) while participating in a full-time training program. In some communities the receipt of welfare payments was made conditional on attendance at some type of learning or training course. A further step pointed toward making the receipt of unemployment compensation beyond a minimum number of weeks conditional on attendance in an educational or retraining program. Although the manpower training program encountered numerous obstacles, it pointed the way toward a general upgrading of the American labor force essential in the age of automation. In a larger setting, manpower development formed part of a new emphasis on investment in human capital as the basis for reducing unemployment and promoting economic growth.

Manpower training programs are not very helpful unless jobs are available to workers who complete their training. Therefore manpower training is complementary to and not competitive with fiscal and monetary programs to increase aggregate demand. If the demand is strong and someone is willing to finance the training, the need for machine operatives, skilled workers, and technicians can be met—as was amply demonstrated by the American experience during World War II, when millions of workers were trained for the special jobs that needed to be done.

Fear of inflation was an impediment to strong programs to reduce unemployment in the postwar period. Historically inflation has accompanied low unemployment and, while the relation is not inevitable, neither is it entirely fortuitous. Two leading American economists, Samuelson and Solow, found that changes in unemployment rates were related to movements in the general price level. They suggested that in order to achieve a goal of 3 per cent unemployment, the American economy would experience inflation of 4 to 5 per cent per year under conditions existing in 1960. Conditions can, however, be changed. In the long run, manpower training, improved education, and greater worker mobility can lower the rate of unemployment which can be achieved without inflation.

The Kennedy administration set the "full employment rate of unemployment" at 4 per cent as a short-term target that seemed feasible within a year or two with relatively little inflation. In the longer run presumably the unemployment rate without inflation could be lowered to 3 per cent or less with appropriate policies for manpower training. Thus manpower development which provides a well-trained and mobile labor force is a weapon against inflation as well as against unemployment. An appropriate manpower policy permits fiscal and monetary policies to be pursued more vigorously with less threat of inflation.

THE
UNITED STATES
ECONOMY
IN THE LATER
POSTWAR
PERIOD

In assuming a position of world leadership after the Second World War, United States foreign policy contrasted sharply with its isolationism after the First World War. Although the Soviet Union and the United States had been Allies in World War II, in the postwar years they became leaders of contending camps in a prolonged and mutually costly Cold War. By giving foreign aid to western Europe and to underdeveloped nations, the United States used its economic and military power to check the spread of Soviet influence.

Postwar American foreign policy also had special meaning in terms of the historical evolution of the United States and western Europe as an integrated Atlantic Community, the economic aspect of which is the subject of the present volume. Under the North Atlantic Treaty Organization (NATO), formed in 1949, the United States accepted peacetime military commitments in Europe for the first time. Through the Marshall Plan, the United States took the initiative in calling for the integration of western Europe. In the Organization for Economic Cooperation and Development (OECD), formed in 1961, the United States, Canada, and eighteen European nations came together in a formal organization designed to extend world trade and to coordinate foreign aid programs to underdeveloped countries. The boldest step toward economic integration was the Common Market, formed in 1957, among six Continental countries of western Europe. Although the application of the United Kingdom for admission to the Common Market was initially rejected, this appeared to stem more from the idiosyncrasies of General de Gaulle of France than from a reversal of the historic trend toward closer economic union among the North Atlantic nations.

Marshall Plan, 1948–1951

As initially conceived, the Marshall Plan was a generous offer by the United States to aid its wartime Allies, including the Soviet Union, in recovering from the physical, financial, and organizational devastation left by the war in Europe. Fortunately for the subsequent evolution of the program, the Soviet Union chose to withdraw and to take other Communist countries with it. Continued financial support by the American Congress for the Marshall Plan stemmed from its role in rescuing western Europe from the internal and external pressures of communism. Large Communist parties in Italy and France made these two key countries particularly vulnerable to Soviet enticements and pressures.

With less money and in less time than originally contemplated the Marshall Plan succeeded in reducing the internal and external Communist threat, promoting the economic integration of western Europe, and solving the dollar shortage. Approximately $12.5 billion poured into western Europe provided the foreign exchange necessary to finance recovery. In view of the dismal interwar experience and the magnitude of the devastation in World War II the recovery of western Europe was astonishing.

696

*THE
UNITED STATES
ECONOMY
IN THE LATER
POSTWAR
PERIOD*

How Europe's Dollar Shortage Became
a Dollar Surplus

In 1950 Europe's dollar shortage appeared to many as a chronic and almost insoluble problem, yet within a decade the shortage had been reversed into a dollar surplus. Weak Europe became stronger and strong America became weaker. Europe solved its dollar shortage by importing less from the United States and by exporting more to the United States. Europe diverted purchases of wheat, cotton, tobacco, petroleum, and metals from the dollar area to third areas. In addition more wheat and metals were produced in Europe. Europe sold more automobiles, electrical appliances, and other goods to the United States. Much of the diversion involved outright discrimination in the form of quantitative restrictions on American products in order to save dollars.

More basic, however, was the shift in comparative advantage between Europe and the United States. Costs of production in European manufacturing, especially in Western Germany, fell relative to costs in the United States. This was partly a matter of European productivity rising more rapidly than American productivity during the fifties, which meant that the technological lead of the United States was narrowed as Europe adopted mass production and other advanced techniques formerly monopolized by American producers. Wages in Europe lagged behind productivity increases during the fifties, whereas wages in the United States increased as rapidly and sometimes more rapidly than productivity. By the sixties, however, European wages were rising more rapidly than American wages, and in some cases more rapidly than productivity, thus narrowing the differences in standards of living of wage-earners in Europe and the United States.

American military expenditures in the 1950's also supplied Europeans with dollars to replace the economic grants made under the Marshall Plan. Off-shore procurement, that is, the purchase of military supplies from foreign countries, became a deliberate policy of the United States government to make dollars available to Europe. Private American capital was exported to Europe, especially after growth slowed down at home, in great volume, making more dollars available to Europeans. Europe's economy grew more rapidly than the American economy and offered higher rates of return on capital invested. In the late fifties when the American economy slowed down and the newly created Common Market opened many new investment opportunities, private capital flowed into western Europe in great volume. American incentive to invest was heightened by the desire to locate branch plants inside the Common Market in order to circumvent discrimination against products shipped from outside the common tariff walls of the European Economic Community.

Deficits in the United States Balance of Payments

Chronic deficits in the United States balance of payments began in 1950, but until 1958 the deficits were modest in size. Relatively little concern was expressed about the deficits or the gold losses associated with them. During the interwar period the United States had drained the gold stocks of other countries and by 1950 held 70 per cent of the total monetary gold in the non-

Communist world. A return to orderly international trade required increases **697**

*THE
UNITED STATES
ECONOMY
IN THE LATER
POSTWAR
PERIOD* in the international reserves of the great trading countries of western Europe. A redistribution of gold stocks in their favor was a precondition for strengthening reserves. Having acquired nearly all the marbles, the United States had to pass some back if the game was to be resumed. American balance-of-payments deficits represented surpluses to Europe and a means for redistributing gold stocks. Aided by American policy under the Marshall Plan, NATO, and off-shore procurement the western European countries gained enough gold and dollar exchange by the late fifties to greatly strengthen their currencies.

Late in 1958 convertibility was restored to the European currencies. Holders of these currencies could now convert them into gold or dollars or any other currency. Convertibility occasioned a much more rapid build-up of gold reserves in European central banks and much larger gold withdrawals from the United States than in the earlier postwar years. A sudden loss of so much gold, amounting to 10 per cent of the entire United States stock, sounded the first dramatic alarm that the "good-as-gold" American dollar might be unable to continue to bear the tremendous burden imposed upon it as the world's key currency.

Under currency convertibility each country needed reserves of gold and short-term (liquid) dollar holdings adequate to meet any demands which might arise from fluctuations in its balance of payments. A satisfactory reserve position was judged primarily in relation to each country's volume of imports. Increased imports required increased reserves. Because world trade was increasing more rapidly than the supply of gold, a growing proportion of total reserves had to be provided by foreign exchange in the form of certain key currencies, especially the dollar. The British pound sterling was also a reserve currency but less important than the dollar. Filling the widening gap between total reserves and the limited supply of gold brought the United States dollar under increasing pressure. Between 1950 and 1960 gold reserves plus dollar holdings outside the United States increased $27 billion, of which nearly $6 billion represented gold losses by the United States and approximately $15 billion represented increased short-term dollar liabilities owed to foreigners. As the American gold stock declined, the volume of short-term claims against it increased. By 1960 the foreign claims against the dollar exceeded the value of U.S. gold stock. In the light of these potentially ominous signals, the deficit in the United States balance of payments became a matter of serious concern.

Analysis of the deficit in balance of payments In an international balance-of-payments statement total debits (payments) equal total credits (receipts), as in any double-entry type of balance sheet or profit-and-loss account. The important question is not whether but how the account is balanced. A country is said to have a deficit in its international payments when it achieves accounting balance by exporting gold or by drawing on its short-term balances abroad or by increasing its short-term liabilities owed to foreigners. Deficits in this sense cannot continue indefinitely because the gold stock would be exhausted in time and presumably foreigners would be unwilling to give credit indefinitely. Deficits of a chronic type call for adjustments to bring the international payments into equilibrium in the long run.

698

THE
UNITED STATES
ECONOMY
IN THE LATER
POSTWAR
PERIOD

A balance-of-payments statement contains two main segments, the current account and the capital account. The current account records total exports of goods and services and total imports of goods and services each year. Since 1884 the United States has exported more goods (merchandise) than it has imported. In nearly every year goods *and services* exports have exceeded goods and services imports, but there have been exceptions as in 1953 and 1959. Hence the current account normally shows a surplus for the United States. Income from foreign investments far exceeds the payment of income to foreigners for investments held in the United States, which is another factor besides merchandise making for a surplus in the current account. American tourists, however, spend considerably more on foreign travel than foreigners spend on travel in the United States, and this constitutes a negative item. Another major negative item in the current account since the Second World War has been military expenditures abroad for United States armed forces and for military support of the armed forces of Allied countries. On balance these items usually showed a surplus in the current account, with the amount of the surplus varying with the size of the surplus in the merchandise account. In the two years during the 1950's in which there was a deficit in the current account, the surplus in the merchandise account was small.

Since the current account in the United States balance of payments was usually in surplus, the deficits arose in an accounting sense from the capital account in which the chief items are private foreign investment and governmental foreign aid. Surpluses in the current account were not large enough to offset the outflow of dollars on foreign investment and foreign aid. Surpluses in the current account would have been larger if merchandise exports had been larger or if imports had been smaller or if military expenditure had been smaller. An increase of exports is preferable to a decrease in imports because the former expands the total volume of international trade and more nearly approximates maximum gains from regional specialization.

Large military expenditures abroad stemmed from foreign policy in the Cold War, and the deficit in the balance of payments reflected one aspect of the cost of the Cold War to the United States. Military expenditures were mainly a function of foreign policy and could not have been changed drastically without changing foreign policy. Reductions in private foreign investment or in governmental foreign aid would have diminished or eliminated the overall deficit if other items had remained unchanged. Foreign aid, like military expenditures, was a function of foreign policy and could not be changed substantially without changing foreign policy.

Foreign investment and the balance of payments   Outflows of United States private capital into foreign investments contributed significantly to the postwar deficit in the balance of payments. Foreign investment depends on the volume of investible funds available and the relative preference for investing them at home or abroad. As a wealthy nation with high savings propensities, great amounts of savings are generated in the United States at any moderate level of national income. During the first decade after the war, investment opportunities in the domestic economy absorbed a large proportion of total savings. As the United States economy sagged in the second postwar decade, the volume of foreign investment increased. Canada, Latin

America, and western Europe were the principal areas of American investments. As a result of opportunities associated with the European Common Market, the most rapid increase took place in western Europe after 1957. Manufacturing was the leading type of enterprise attracting American capital to Europe, whereas petroleum and minerals were the important types in underdeveloped areas, including the Middle East and Venezuela.

699

THE
UNITED STATES
ECONOMY
IN THE LATER
POSTWAR
PERIOD

Private investment abroad is of two main types, direct and portfolio investment. The former, consisting of capital invested in branch plants and subsidiaries of American industry, became the major form of private investment abroad. Portfolio investment, consisting of purchases of stocks and bonds of foreign enterprises by Americans, usually does not carry with it managerial control by American interests. It became less prevalent in the postwar period. Aggregate American private capital invested abroad totalled $71 billion by 1965, a fourfold increase since 1950.

Annual earnings from large American foreign investments approximated the annual outflow of new capital in the early sixties and therefore added to receipts in the balance of payments as much as the outflow of capital added to payments. Foreign investments are a source of wealth and future income to Americans, and only at the time the capital outflow occurs is there an adverse effect on the balance of payments. If new capital outflows were to cease or to diminish in amount, the income from earlier investments would continue to flow back to Americans and to strengthen the balance-of-payments position. Of course, the income is not guaranteed and might be reduced by depression, confiscation, or war.

In order to improve the United States balance of payments, President Kennedy in July, 1963, proposed an excise tax of one per cent on American purchases of foreign stocks and bonds of developed countries. This was called an Interest Equalization Tax because it had the effect of raising the rate of interest on American portfolio investment by one percentage point and was intended to equalize the lower long-term rate of interest in United States capital markets with the higher rate in foreign capital markets. The proposal did not apply to securities of underdeveloped countries. Because the proposed tax, if enacted by Congress, was to be made retroactive to the date of proposal, it immediately curbed American portfolio investments abroad and contributed significantly to a reduction in the deficit from a seasonally adjusted annual rate of $5 billion in the second quarter to $1.6 billion in the third quarter of 1963. President Johnson's exhortation to American corporations, banks, and other financial institutions to restrain themselves in foreign investments resulted in a slight, temporary surplus in the United States balance of payments in the second quarter of 1965.

Conclusions on balance-of-payments deficit   The foregoing analysis suggests that postwar deficits in the United States balance of payments have been associated with military expenditures overseas, foreign aid, and private investment abroad. However, this conclusion must be qualified because items in the balance of payments are interrelated so that changes in one item may bring changes in others of an offsetting nature and leave the overall deficit unchanged or only slightly altered. For example, outlays on foreign investment may have a buoyant effect on American exports and thus tend to raise the

700

THE
UNITED STATES
ECONOMY
IN THE LATER
POSTWAR
PERIOD

merchandise surplus. After the big increase in the deficit in 1958, government grants and loans for economic assistance to underdeveloped countries were tied to United States products and therefore could not have had much effect on the overall deficit in the balance of payments. Military spending was also tied to United States products and some foreign governments were induced to purchase their arms and military supplies in the United States as an offset to American dollar expenditures in their countries.

Despite these qualifications, it is meaningful to say that in order to balance its international accounts, the United States must have a sufficiently large surplus of commercial goods and services to pay for overseas military spending, foreign aid, and American investments abroad. To make the trade surplus large enough to offset these three deficit items, American industry must increase its efficiency relative to other countries to make it more competitive with foreign producers in overseas markets (increase exports) and in United States markets (decrease imports).

A case in point was the compact automobile. European producers successfully invaded the American market in the late fifties, but American auto manufacturers met the competition with their own compacts and regained much of the domestic market from the European producers. Japanese and European industries gained ground technologically on American industry in the fifties and early sixties, but there was no conclusive evidence that American producers could not compete successfully or that they priced themselves out of international markets.

Whatever the specific causes of the long series of deficits in the American balance of payments in the postwar period, imbalance represented a condition that had to end sooner or later. In part "natural forces" of productivity, wages, and prices—the discipline of the market—operate to bring balance in any country's international payments, and in part governmental policies must be directed toward this objective.

International Liquidity and the Dollar as International Money

Persistent deficits in the United States balance of payments presented a dilemma because, on the one hand, the deficits had to be reduced and ultimately eliminated in order to maintain confidence in the integrity of the dollar, but, on the other hand, the outflow of American gold and dollars represented by the deficits provided much of the international liquidity needed to finance expanding world trade. Some outflows of gold and dollars were necessary and desirable, but large and continued deficits in the United States balance of payments must in time reduce the gold stock so low and raise the claims against it so high that the world would cease to have confidence in the dollar. If and when such a point were reached, a gold hemorrhage from the United States would result in a collapse of the international financial structure of the non-Communist world. A somewhat similar situation precipitated the world financial panic of 1931, when the British pound sterling occupied a position comparable to the dollar in the period after the Second World War. Fundamentally the problem was more one of international liquidity than of balance of payments. A study by the Brookings Institution,

The United States Balance of Payments in 1968 (1963), concluded: "The
present problem is not primarily a balance-of-payments problem. More funda-
mentally, the problem is the basic inadequacy of the international monetary THE
UNITED STATES
ECONOMY
IN THE LATER
POSTWAR
PERIOD
mechanism in relation to requirements of the Free World."

Solutions for the liquidity problem Most suggestions for meeting the
international liquidity problem focus on an international agency such as the
International Monetary Fund (IMF). The IMF was created at the close of
the Second World War to stabilize foreign exchange rates in the short run and
to facilitate their orderly adjustment in the long run as basic adjustments become necessary. Member countries contribute quotas of gold (25 per cent)
and quotas of national currencies (75 per cent) to the Fund, which can then
assist its members as they need financing for temporary balance-of-payments
deficits arising from emergencies, such as the Suez crisis of 1956–57, as well as
seasonal disturbances.

During the first postwar decade the IMF remained largely inoperative—
except as a research organization—because its resources were inadequate for
nursing the world back to international equilibrium in exchange rates, national price levels, and balances of payments. This giant postwar task was
shouldered by the United States government through the Marshall Plan,
economic and military aid, and dollar loans and grants of many types. For the
advanced countries this goal was achieved with the convertibility of the European currencies at the end of 1958. By the sixties it became clear that the use
of the dollar or any other single national currency as the international reserve
had potentially unstable consequences and that the time had come to return
to the original source of relying primarily on an international organization to
meet the international liquidity problem.

To transfer the role of world banker from the United States to the International Monetary Fund required changes in the latter organization. Some
reformers were content to enlarge the IMF quotas and to make member borrowing from the IMF more automatic. A more radical plan called for recon-
stituting the IMF as a world central bank with authority to create new reserves of world currency for national central banks analogous to the way in
which the latter create reserves for domestic commercial banks. The latter
proposal was made in 1944 at the Bretton Woods conference by the British
economist, John Maynard Keynes, and subsequently a similar idea was put
forward by Professor Robert Triffin, who regarded the use of a national currency (the dollar) for international money as the basis for an impending gold
and dollar crisis. Triffin contended that reliance on dollar reserves must sooner
or later overburden the dollar, or any other national currency that might be
substituted for it, and lead to an international financial panic unless steps were
taken to shift the burden to a genuinely international agency such as a world
central bank.

United States Tariff Policy

Historically the United States has followed a protectionist policy, which
means that the interests of consumers have been subordinated to the interests
of producers. During the 1930's President Roosevelt and his Secretary of
State, Cordell Hull, pushed through a new policy of reciprocal trade agree-

702

*THE
UNITED STATES
ECONOMY
IN THE LATER
POSTWAR
PERIOD*

ments with other countries. Under the trade agreements the United States offered to reduce its tariffs if other countries would reduce theirs. Included in the agreements were most-favored-nation clauses, which provide that a concession granted to any one country will automatically apply to all nations with whom the United States had a most-favored-nation agreement. Tariff reductions under the Reciprocal Trade Agreements Act enabled some American exports to penetrate foreign markets. Other American producers were injured by foreign competition under lower tariffs, but the injury was minimized by escape clauses, peril points, national security amendments, and other loopholes limiting tariff cuts.

During and after World War II the United States proposed the formation of a world organization to liberalize and multilateralize international trade. In 1948 a charter was drawn up for the International Trade Organization (ITO), but the United States Congress failed to ratify the treaty establishing ITO. Some progress toward freer trade was achieved, however, when the United States and other major trading nations met in Geneva to negotiate a General Agreement on Tariffs and Trade (GATT). United States representatives participated in GATT under the President's authority granted in the Reciprocal Trade Act to reduce tariffs. Periodic tariff conferences have been conducted by the member nations of GATT.

On the domestic front, the Reciprocal Trade Agreements legislation was renewed periodically after political tussles between the successive administrations and the representatives of the tariff lobby in Congress. By the sixties substantial reductions had been achieved, and the United States ranked among the low tariff countries of the world. Nevertheless, the prevailing philosophy under reciprocal trade agreements was to force other countries to make concessions which would serve the interests of American export industries.

Trade Expansion Act of 1962   A complacent American attitude toward world trade was shaken by the unanticipated speed and success of the European Common Market. American exporters of industrial and agricultural products awakened to the fact that they would be discriminated against in the Common Market as the member countries created a large free-trade market for themselves with a common external tariff wall to be hurdled by non-members. Since about the 1870's western Europe had been the leading importer of United States wheat, meat, and many other agricultural products. American industrial products also faced a threat from the Common Market. Defense against that threat lay in having the external tariff as low as possible. Since non-member European nations also had a vital stake in bringing down the external tariff of the Common Market, American and European statesmen saw an opportunity to move toward an Atlantic Community with low tariffs. Underdeveloped nations around the world needed access to the European and American markets to strengthen their export trade and their balance of payments.

President Kennedy moved vigorously to meet this challenge by giving highest legislative priority to the Trade Expansion Act of 1962. This was the most important United States tariff legislation since the inauguration of the Trade Agreements Act of 1934 and possibly since the inception of protective tariffs in 1816. It marked, perhaps, a reversal of American protectionism and

703

THE
UNITED STATES
ECONOMY
IN THE LATER
POSTWAR
PERIOD

economic nationalism in favor of the grand design of a United States partnership with a unified western Europe in a low-tariff Western world. The United States Under-Secretary of State, George W. Ball, characterized the trade legislation as "a solemn political act taken in recognition of the undeniable fact of the interdependence of the nations of the Free World and the need for an effective Atlantic partnership if the Free World is to survive." Some of the glamour of the legislation was lost when the United Kingdom was denied admission to the Common Market in 1963.

Since the United States did not want to be squeezed out of the rich Common Market countries, it determined to use its bargaining power to force a low-tariff wall around the Common Market by agreeing to lower its own tariff wall. The Trade Act strengthened the bargaining power of the United States in negotiating for access to the European market in exchange for access to the American market. More specifically, the President was authorized to decrease by 50 per cent any rate of duty existing on July 1, 1962. In negotiations with the Common Market, tariffs could be wiped out entirely on products for which the United States and the Common Market together accounted for more than 80 per cent of the world's exports and on agricultural goods if the President determined such reductions would help to maintain or to expand United States exports. Existing ad valorem duties of less than 5 per cent could also be eliminated. Finally the President could reduce by more than 50 per cent, or eliminate altogether, duties on tropical agriculture or forestry products provided the European Economic Community would agree to do likewise. The latter provision was aimed at Europe's preferential treatment of tropical products from its former African dependencies, an arrangement which was a threat to Latin America and other non-favored tropical areas.

Some restrictive provisions of the Reciprocal Trade Agreements such as the peril point clause were eliminated in the 1962 Trade Expansion Act. Firms injured by increased imports resulting from lower tariffs could apply for loans, tax relief, and technical assistance to adjust to new conditions. Workers displaced by increased imports became eligible for retraining and cash payments to compensate for relocation. The trade adjustment assistance represented a more positive approach than the peril point and escape clause provisions, which protected and perpetuated inefficient firms and industries rather than attempting to reallocate and relocate domestic resources in the face of foreign competition. The 1962 Trade Act also empowered the President to raise duties against countries which denied equitable access to United States farm products. The first case to arise under the latter provision concerned "prohibitive" Common Market tariffs on American poultry. When the United States threatened to retaliate in the "chicken war" with high tariffs on French wines, the chicken broiler duty was submitted to negotiation. After heated debates a compromise was finally reached.

The Kennedy Round of tariff negotiations between the U.S. and Common Market   Armed with broad authority under the Trade Expansion Act, American representatives entered a long period of negotiations with the Common Market countries. This became known as the "Kennedy Round" because President Kennedy had taken the initiative which led to the tariff talks. To slash tariffs by 50 per cent on all goods traded among member nations of the

704

THE
UNITED STATES
ECONOMY
IN THE LATER
POSTWAR
PERIOD

General Agreement on Tariffs and Trade was the hoped-for objective. After a year of preliminary discussion, formal tariff negotiations began in May, 1964, in Geneva under the auspices of GATT, with 42 nations participating but with attention focused on the key bargaining between the United States and the Common Market countries.

As anticipated, numerous conflicts arose. In agriculture the French had a strong incentive to keep American farm products out of the Common Market in order that France's low-cost (for Europe) products could dominate within the common tariff wall. Inability of the Common Market countries to agree among themselves on an agricultural program—out of fear of French domination—handicapped the negotiations with the United States. American representatives threatened to refuse to negotiate on industrial products if American farm products were excluded from the European market by a high protective wall. Another difficult point was what to do where great disparities existed between the American and European tariffs which were to be reduced by 50 per cent. Some sensitive products were exempted from tariff cutting, but which products to exempt was a further point of debate. Much political significance attached to the tariff negotiations because the ability to reach a reasonable settlement after hard bargaining had political overtones which were significant for the future of the whole concept of the Atlantic partnership.

Relations with Underdeveloped Nations

During the early years following the Second World War American foreign aid focused on the recovery of western Europe, and very little aid went to the underdeveloped nations in Asia, Africa, and South America. United States aid helped to restore western Europe's productive capacity and put these countries back on the high road to self-sustaining economic growth from which they had been temporarily shunted by the devastation of war. As we noted previously, after this large injection of American aid, western Europe's economy grew faster than that of the United States during the 1950's and 1960's.

In contrast, underdeveloped nations could, at best, be expected to benefit from foreign aid slowly and over many years, even decades, because their problem was primarily one of long-term development from a low stage of development. An underdeveloped economy must first break the vicious circle of poverty whereby it is poor just because it is poor. In order to develop, a poor country must save a substantial part of its national product, but if its national product provides a bare subsistence for its people, saving is either impossible or must be at the expense of a still lower level of living for years and decades while sustained development is getting under way. This hard choice is faced by any poor country which aspires to improve its condition. Outside assistance in the form of foreign aid can ease the burden by providing foreign exchange for purchasing strategic equipment and hiring personnel. For many poor countries foreign aid was a necessary, though not a sufficient, condition for economic development.

International Bank for Reconstruction and Development (IBRD) At the Bretton Woods conference of 1944 plans were laid for the International Bank for Reconstruction and Development (IBRD), or World Bank, as a

sister organization of the International Monetary Fund, with headquarters in Washington. Its immediate postwar aim was to help finance the reconstruction of war-damaged countries, and its longer-run objective was to make loans to member countries for economic development. Loan funds were raised from contributions subscribed by member governments and from the sale of the Bank's bonds in open markets. By mid-1965 the World Bank had lent a total of nearly $9 billion to 77 countries or territories. Its loans, averaging twenty years at market rates of interest of 5 to 6 per cent, went mainly for social overhead capital, with approximately two-thirds of the total directed to electric power and transportation.

705

THE
UNITED STATES
ECONOMY
IN THE LATER
POSTWAR
PERIOD

International Finance Corporation (IFC) and International Development Association (IDA) In order to channel more capital into industrial development the World Bank created in 1956 a subsidiary, the International Finance Corporation (IFC), which could lend to private enterprises without the government guarantees required of IBRD loans to private enterprises. Another subsidiary, the International Development Association (IDA), was established in 1960 to make loans on easier terms (soft loans) for projects which could not qualify under the other two agencies. IDA loans were made for periods up to 50 years and are repayable in local (soft) currencies without interest.

United States Technical Assistance President Truman began a program of technical assistance to less developed nations in 1949. This became known as "Point Four" because it was the fourth point in Truman's inaugural address. It provided that American engineers, scientists, teachers, agronomists, and other scientific and technical experts should work abroad to raise the level of productivity in agriculture and industry in less developed countries. Unlike other foreign aid programs, technical assistance did not involve large financial outlays, but it won the plaudits of the people of underdeveloped nations as well as of a parsimonious American Congress and the tax-conscious American public.

President Kennedy's Peace Corps, which began in 1961, was a variation of technical assistance. Here the appeal was mainly to young men and women to serve abroad for two years to help other countries meet urgent needs for skilled manpower. Demand was strongest for teachers. Other personnel included nurses, engineers, mechanics, surveyors, building craftsmen, and farm specialists. The Peace Corps idea of helping others less fortunate appealed strongly to the idealism and missionary spirit of thousands of Americans.

United States foreign aid The main burden of United States foreign aid took the form of grants and loans for military assistance and for economic development. Military aid became an important aspect of the Cold War, beginning with the so-called Truman Doctrine, which provided aid to Greece and Turkey in civil wars in 1947 and was stepped up during the Korean incident in 1950. Countries friendly to the United States in the Cold War received billions of dollars in the form of weapons, equipment, food, and training. With an easing of Soviet-American international tensions in the sixties the amount of military assistance decreased relative to economic aid. Some projects such as military road building spilled over into economic aid.

706

THE
UNITED STATES
ECONOMY
IN THE LATER
POSTWAR
PERIOD

United States economic aid moved through various channels including the United Nations, the IBRD, the Export-Import Bank of Washington, technical assistance, the Peace Corps, direct military aid, military assistance, supporting assistance, farm surplus commodities and others; but the principal channel became the Development Loan Fund, the functions of which were absorbed by the Agency for International Development (AID) under the Kennedy administration. Concessionary loans were made to underdeveloped nations at low interest rates for long periods and were repayable in the currency of the borrowing countries. These "soft" loans could not meet the bankers' standards of the IBRD and the Export-Import Bank. With the onset of the balance-of-payments crisis, foreign aid loans were tied to purchases in the United States in order to remove the strain on the balance of payments. Economic aid to less developed nations was intended to raise their productivity and savings to a level at which economic growth becomes self-generating. Beyond this point they would not require further aid from outside sources, and if they did, they might provide attractive markets for private international investors. Taiwan, for example, attained this stage of development in 1965.

Domestic political opposition to American foreign aid   Military aid to prevent countries from going Communist had stronger political appeal than regular economic aid, and there was a temptation for administrators to classify as much aid as possible under the military category. With the easing of the Cold War with the Soviet Union in the 1960's, political support for military aid also weakened. Meanwhile, the strong recovery of advanced nations in western Europe plus United States balance-of-payments difficulties created a feeling that other advanced countries should bear a greater share of foreign assistance to underdeveloped nations. Through the Development Assistance Corporation (DAC), the member nations of the Organization for Economic Cooperation and Development (OECD) sought to coordinate economic aid to underdeveloped nations. European nations did increase their share of assistance. In 1962 United States bilateral economic aid totalled .84 per cent of gross national product, as compared with .60 per cent of gross national product by the eleven other members of the Development Assistance Corporation. Because the United States has a higher per capita income, it has greater ability to provide development assistance than other members of the DAC. Neither the United States nor the other members of the DAC were straining after resources to assist the poor nations of the world. In 1964 President Johnson reduced the foreign aid request to $3.4 billion, not because he felt this sum was adequate but because that was as much as he thought Congress would be willing to approve.

Poverty has always been the lot of the great majority of mankind, and stagnation has been the normal condition of economic systems. The idea of charting the course of development of a whole nation is a recent one. As the foregoing chapters have shown, the presently developed nations have taken centuries to reach their high levels of per capita income and to escape poverty for the majority of their population. Poor nations today, with the help of the rich nations, may expect to eliminate poverty in a much shorter time, but they cannot be expected to realize this dream in a few years. The Great Ascent, as Professor Heilbroner has called it, is a long, difficult, and often frustrating

road to follow. But progress thus far in the postwar period has been good, and with fortitude and a little generosity by the rich for the poor there is reason to believe that the heights can be scaled.

Summary of foreign aid   In the first twenty years after the Second World War the United States provided more than $100 billion in economic and military aid to foreign countries. In the early postwar years emphasis was on economic aid to western Europe for recovery from the ravages of war. Success came quickly and completely. During the height of the Cold War with the Soviet Union in the 1950's, the amount of military aid exceeded economic aid. South Korea, southeast Asia, nationalist China, and western Europe received the bulk of the assistance. In the 1960's, with the easing of the Cold War after the nuclear stalemate, economic aid again became more important than military aid, but the total amount of American foreign aid dropped and the chief recipients were the underdeveloped nations of southern Asia (India, Pakistan, South Korea, Vietnam) and South America. Only small amounts of aid went to Africa because of the American view that the newly liberated African states were primarily a responsibility of their former colonial masters in western Europe. Latin America felt neglected when the United States was pouring large sums of money into Europe and later into backward countries in Asia to save them from communism. With the advent of Fidel Castro in Cuba, Americans became increasingly concerned about saving Latin America from communism. In 1961 President Kennedy inaugurated the ambitious Alliance for Progress, designed to wipe out poverty in Latin America and thus eliminate the conditions in which communism is likely to germinate. The Alliance was promulgated as a multi-billion-dollar program extending over a ten-year period. It encountered economic obstacles from the start, but the political difficulties proved even greater because of the continuing pattern of military coups overthrowing incipient democratic governments which pressed for social and economic reforms. Foreign aid from the Soviet Union to underdeveloped countries was small compared with United States aid, but it tended to be concentrated in fewer countries, and thereby to have a greater impact on attitudes favorable to the Soviet Union.

SELECTED BIBLIOGRAPHY

America in the Sixties, The Economy and the Society, Fortune Magazine, eds. New York: Harper & Row, Publishers, 1960.

BARAN, PAUL A., *The Political Economy of Growth.* New York: Monthly Review Press, 1957.

BATOR, FRANCIS M., *The Question of Public Spending: Public Needs and Private Wants.* New York: Harper & Row, Publishers, 1960.

DENISON, EDWARD F., *The Sources of Economic Growth in the United States and the Alternatives Before Us.* New York: Committee for Economic Development, 1962.

ENKE, STEPHEN, *Economics for Development.* Englewood Cliffs, N.J.: Prentice-Hall, Inc., 1963.

708

THE
UNITED STATES
ECONOMY
IN THE LATER
POSTWAR
PERIOD

GINZBERG, ELI, *The Negro Potential*. New York: Columbia University Press, 1956. (paperback)

HANSEN, ALVIN H., *Economic Issues of the 1960's*. New York: McGraw-Hill, Inc., 1960. (paperback)

HEILBRONER, ROBERT L., *The Great Ascent, The Struggle for Economic Development in Our Time*. New York: Harper & Row, Publishers, 1963. (paperback)

HIGGINS, BENJAMIN, *Economic Development, Problems, Principles, and Policies*. New York: W. W. Norton & Co., Inc., 1959.

HIRSCHMAN, ALBERT C., *Strategy of Economic Development*. New Haven: Yale University Press, 1959. (paperback)

KENDRICK, JOHN W., *Productivity Trends in the United States*. Princeton: Princeton University Press, 1961.

KENEN, PETER B., *Giant Among Nations, Problems in Foreign Economic Policy*. New York: Rand McNally & Co., 1963. (paperback)

LUTZ, VERA, *French Planning*. Washington, D.C.: American Enterprise Institute, 1965. (paperback)

MILLIKAN, MAX F., and DONALD L. M. BLACKMER, eds. *The Emerging Nations, Their Growth and United States Policy*. Boston: Little, Brown & Co., 1961.

————, and WALT W. ROSTOW, *A Proposal, Key to an Effective Foreign Policy*. New York: Harper & Row, Publishers, 1957.

MONSEN, R. JOSEPH, JR., *Modern American Capitalism, Ideologies and Issues*. Boston: Houghton Mifflin Company, 1963. (paperback)

NOVACK, DAVID E., and ROBERT LEKACHMAN, eds., *Development and Society, The Dynamics of Economic Change*. New York: St. Martin's Press, 1964. (paperback)

RANIS, GUSTAV, ed., *The United States and Developing Countries*. New York: W. W. Norton & Co., Inc., 1964. (paperback)

ROSTOW, WALT W., *The Stages of Economic Growth, A Non-Communist Manifesto*. London: Cambridge University Press, 1960. (paperback)

SCHULTZ, THEODORE W., *Economic Crisis in World Agriculutre*. Ann Arbor: University of Michigan Press, 1965.

TRIFFIN, ROBERT, *Gold and the Dollar Crisis,* rev. ed. New Haven: Yale University Press, 1961. (paperback)

WARD, BARBARA, *The Rich Nations and the Poor Nations*. New York: W. W. Norton & Co., Inc., 1962. (paperback)

ARTICLES

BERNSTEIN, EDWARD M., "The Adequacy of United States Gold Reserves," *American Economic Review*, LI (May, 1961), 439–46.

DENISON, EDWARD F., "How to Raise the High-Employment Growth Rate by One Percentage Point," *American Economic Review*, LII (May, 1962), 67–75.

HICKMAN, BERT G., "The Postwar Retardation: Another Long Swing in the Rate of Growth?" *American Economic Review*, LIII (May, 1963), 490–507.

SCHULTZ, THEODORE W., "Investment in Human Capital," *American Economic Review*, LI (March, 1961), 1–17.

SOLOW, ROBERT M., "Technical Progress, Capital Formation, and Economic Growth," *American Economic Review*, LII (May, 1962), 76–86.

WILLIAMSON, JEFFREY G., "Dollar Scarcity and Surplus in Historical Perspective," *American Economic Review*, LIII (May, 1963), 519–29.

The Economic Basis
of a Great Society

CHAPTER **38**

After a long period of development on the Continent and in the British Isles a breakthrough to a successful capitalist system took place in England during the sixteenth century. The manufacture of woolen cloth was the chief industry of late medieval and early modern times. The social unrest which brought Continental capitalism to a halt in Flanders and Florence was mitigated in England by the rural setting of the cloth industry. England's success was abetted by the finest supply of domestic raw wool in the western world and by the innovation of the mechanical fulling mill, which sparked a minor industrial revolution.

By the time Columbus launched an Atlantic community with his discoveries, the feudal War of the Roses (1455–85) had ended and England had established national unity. Under the Tudors a strong central government provided the social overhead capital which permitted self-sustaining economic growth beginning in the period of mercantilism.

Although Portugal, Spain, and Holland established overseas colonies before England, the transplantation of western European economic institutions was first successful in the English colonies of North America, and marked the beginning of an Atlantic economic community. After England's mainland colonies won political independence during the eighteenth century, the United States continued to have close economic ties with Europe.

The American political revolution marked the decline of English mercantilism abroad, and the English Industrial Revolution led capitalists at home to declare their independence of laissez-faire.

When industry moved back into the towns in the late eighteenth century, urban industrialism gave rise to various forms of social protest from the wage-earning classes. The right of workers to the full produce of labor, the inequity of the private receipt of rent and interest, and finally a direct attack on all non-wage income (surplus value) were some of the revolutionary doctrines which emerged from the writings of socialists such as Robert Owen and Karl Marx. Working-class revolts in 1830, 1848, and 1871 led to abortive revolutions against capitalism in Continental Europe.

Meanwhile some social amelioration took place under the political leadership of the British land-owning class, which, having been weakened economically, supported factory legislation to vent its irritation against the rising

power and wealth of factory owners. As the base of political democracy expanded to include the right of propertyless workers to vote, middle-class governments responded sympathetically to working-class protests and legislated improvements in working and living conditions. Working-class groups began to form their own economic bargaining units to contest the dominant position of capitalist employers. In England, Germany, and France labor movements and socialist parties tended to merge in a common demand for gradual modification of capitalist institutions in the direction of socialism.

Although some of the evils of classical capitalism were eliminated through social and economic legislation, there remained well into the twentieth century one defect which working-class groups could not easily modify, the instability of unregulated capitalism. Thomas Robert Malthus, the English economist, was among the first to observe and generalize about economic instability arising from an imbalance between productive capacity on the one hand and the amount of effective demand for goods and services on the other. Recurring fluctuations of business activity, interspersed with periodic crises, characterized capitalist development during the nineteenth century. Some economists rationalized the business cycle as a necessary price of economic progress, at least under capitalism, and many went so far as to identify progress with capitalism.

Substantial modifications in capitalism resulted from a series of world-shaking events in the first half of the twentieth century: World War I, the Russian Revolution, the Great Depression, and World War II. Of these the most significant economically was the Great Depression of the 1930's, which was liquidated only by demand generated by World War II. A system which performed so badly could hardly be expected to survive without fundamental modifications. Under the pressure of widespread public opinion expressed through the ballot box in democratic capitalistic nations, far-reaching changes resulted during the Great Depression and after World War II.

The main direction of change was to shift more economic decision-making into the public sector. Governments assumed responsibility for maintaining high employment and price stability through fiscal and monetary policies, for supervising prices and wages through informal guideposts in the private sector, and for various forms of economic planning. In place of classic capitalism there emerged by the last third of the twentieth century a mixed economy in which responsibility for the overall performance of the economic system became a governmental function. The market continued to operate as an allocator of resources, but the maintenance of aggregate demand to clear the market of total goods and services became the province of discretionary fiscal policy. The relationship of economic performance to decision-making that has evolved is not easily categorized. If capitalism is thought to be a system in which economic decisions are made in the private sector, a transfer of decision-making to the public sector implies that the economic system is becoming less capitalistic. At what point it ceases to be capitalistic and becomes something else is open to question and, in the short run, not important. In the long run, the issue is nothing less than what kind of economic system, even what kind of civilization, is to prevail. The term capitalism was not invented until the nineteenth century, so there should be no urgency to apply a new name to the economic system which has been emerging in the North Atlantic community.

What does matter is recognition of how drastically the system has
changed since its classical phase in the nineteenth century. The market mechanism, the mainspring of classic capitalism until World War I, has become
increasingly subordinated to decisions based on the calculations of representatives of the economy as a whole. In general, this is what is meant by economic
planning, and it is this trend away from laissez-faire toward economic planning which has come to prevail in most countries of the world.

PRESENT STATE OF ECONOMIC DEVELOPMENT
IN EUROPE AND THE UNITED STATES

Western Europe

Creation of the Common Market was the most spectacular economic
achievement of western Europe in the twentieth century. Progress toward the
goals set by the Common Market countries in the Treaty of Rome (1956) was
more rapid than anticipated. By wiping out tariffs among the six member
nations, a giant step was taken toward economic rationality. As with all customs unions, the external tariff of the Common Market discriminates against
nonmembers. How high or how low this common tariff ultimately will be is an
important clue to the long-term significance of the Common Market. If the
external tariff is low in relation to earlier tariffs, the benefits will spread beyond
the Common Market. If the external tariff remains at about the same level as
the average of earlier tariffs of the six nations, the Common Market will make
only a limited contribution outside its member nations.

The European Free Trade Association (EFTA), consisting of Austria,
Denmark, Finland, Norway, Portugal, Sweden, Switzerland, and the United
Kingdom, was another indication of the tendency in Europe toward economic
unity and common economic policies. At the end of 1966 these eight countries
became a single market without tariffs or import quotas on industrial goods
traded among them. A real test of European economic unity will be the ability
of the Common Market to enlarge its membership to include the countries of
the European Free Trade Association. The intransigence of President de Gaulle
of France in preventing the United Kingdom's entry into the Common Market
in 1963 interrupted the advance toward European economic unity, but this
may represent merely a temporary setback to a broad historical movement.

By the 1960's western Europe was well on the way to becoming an
affluent society, characterized by mass production and mass consumption.
Business cycles were hardly perceptible in the postwar economies. Real wages
rose steadily, hours of work were shortened, and generous social security
measures removed the economic hazards of unemployment, sickness, and old
age. Poverty had been virtually wiped out in Scandinavia, and its elimination
elsewhere in Western Europe seemed feasible in the foreseeable future.

The United States

The American economy, like those of Europe, performed much better
after World War II than after World War I. In comparison with other nations,
however, its performance during the 1950's was inferior. In the first fifteen

postwar years the United States experienced four recessions with successively higher rates of unemployment. Between 1958 and 1963 economic growth slowed down, unemployment increased, and the economy performed sluggishly. New economic policies under the Kennedy and Johnson administrations injected vigor into the American economy. An expansion of record length for the United States took place following the upturn from the recession in the spring of 1961. From an annual rate of growth of less than 3 per cent in the second half of the 1950's, the growth rate rose to more than 4 per cent in the 1960's after aggregate demand was maintained at high levels through fiscal and monetary policies. In 1965 the Chairman of the President's Council of Economic Advisers could seriously assert that recessions were not inevitable. Policies which worked in Europe brought favorable results in the United States as well. The transatlantic Organization for Economic Cooperation and Development (OECD) set a goal of a 50 per cent increase in the gross national product of its member nations during the decade of the 1960's. A 4.1 per cent rate compounded annually would yield a 50 per cent increase in ten years.

At these substantial rates of growth the United States increased its absolute advantage over other countries in per capita income. Real wages grew steadily, vacations with pay for wage and salaried workers became nearly universal, profits increased even more rapidly than wages, and Americans enjoyed unprecedented prosperity. Certain economic problems persisted, however, including the decline of agriculture, the concentration of industry, certain labor problems, and the larger issue of poverty growing out of inequality of income distribution and economic opportunity.

The Farm Problem

By the mid-1960's the number of workers engaged in agriculture in the United States had fallen to less than 6 per cent of the total labor force. Although 25,000,000 people had left the farm in the twenty-five years from 1940 to 1965, there were still too many farmers in the sense that more crops were produced than could be sold profitably in domestic and foreign markets. Following the severe farm depression of the 1920's some of the costs associated with declining agriculture were shifted to taxpayers through a program of government price supports for selected farm products. This program worked badly. High price supports encouraged overproduction, led to the costly storage of huge stocks of agricultural commodities, and priced American wheat and cotton out of competitive world markets even though production was the most efficient in the world. Price supports were accompanied by attempts to restrict output, but restrictions were put on acreage rather than on output as such. By more intensive cultivation, including the application of more fertilizer per acre, larger crops were raised on a smaller acreage. Unprecedented farm surpluses persisted at the expense of the federal treasury.

Although the basic purpose of agricultural subsidies was to alleviate the distress of farmers caught in a difficult transition, a large proportion of federal payments went to well-to-do farmers whereas the small, marginal farmers living in poverty benefited very little from the expensive farm program. This anomaly arose because payments (loans) went to support prices and not to

supplement incomes of low-income farmers. Proposals to change from a system

of price supports to direct payments to low-income farmers met with strong
opposition from conservative farm groups and the farm bloc in Congress.

Price supports also had the disadvantage of raising domestic farm prices
above world levels and shutting American farm products out of competitive
world markets. In order to restore a competitive international position, export
subsidies were paid on that part of the crop entering world trade. In the case
of cotton, high domestic prices combined with low export prices enabled foreign textile manufacturers to purchase American cotton more cheaply than
American manufacturers could buy it. Consequently, further adjustments were
made to offset this disadvantage to cotton textile firms in the United States.

The overall effect of the farm program was a pervasive network of price
supports and subsidies which contributed little to solving the basic problem
of the burden on farmers during the transition of agriculture to a declining
position in the economy. Moreover, price supports led to an uneconomical
allocation of productive resources and imposed a staggering burden on the
public treasury.

Some signs of change in national agricultural policy appeared in the
1960's. Congressional redistricting on a one-man, one-vote principle as set
forth by the United States Supreme Court in 1964 weakened the political
power of the farm bloc. An urban-oriented Congress became more sensitive
to consumer interests and to the plight of the poverty-stricken marginal
farmers and less responsive to pressures from well-to-do commercial farmers
and their lobbyists. As population grew and new housing changed farms into
suburbs, the demand for food increased while the supply of farm land decreased. Substantial food surpluses went abroad to feed hungry people in
underdeveloped countries, which were unable to match the sensational increases in farm productivity achieved by American farmers.

Under the Johnson administration the system of direct payments to farm
producers, begun under the Eisenhower administration in the wool support
program, was extended to wheat, cotton, and feed grains. Lower price supports lessened overproduction and reduced the need for export subsidies. Direct payments were made to farmers who diverted cropland to other uses.
Meanwhile prosperity in the nonfarm sector enabled many poor farmers and
farm workers to migrate to more productive and higher-paying jobs outside
agriculture. Although the American farm problem remained, some light was
visible on the horizon.

Western Europe also faced the problem of what to do with too many
farmers. Price supports, export subsidies, import duties and quotas, in differing levels and amounts, characterized European farm policies. A Herculean
task which strained the foundations of the European Economic Community
during 1965 and 1966 was agreement on a common agricultural policy, including methods of financing and common price levels within the Community.
One of the stumbling blocks to British entry into the Common Market was the
British policy of letting food prices be determined in the open market with
"deficiency" payments to farmers of the difference between guaranteed prices
and the lower market prices, in contrast to the Continental preference for
prices supported above the open market. Both American and European agriculture was riddled with subsidies and special privileges which proved diffi-

cult to eliminate. A potential advantage of an Atlantic partnership between the United States and Europe, after a successful Kennedy round of tariff lowering, was the elimination of uneconomic national legislation and protection.[1]

Concentration of Industry

Concentration of economic power within the private sector is one of the important characteristics of all advanced capitalist economies. In the United States the degree of overall concentration, which had been high since the beginning of the century, increased further after World War II as a consequence of structural changes in the economy. Of 420,000 corporations, partnerships, and proprietorships engaged in manufacturing in 1962, the 20 largest firms owned assets equal to those of the 419,000 smallest firms, and 1,000 firms owned three-fourths of the total assets in manufacturing. The 200 largest manufacturing firms, with $165 billion in total assets, owned 56.8 per cent of total corporate assets in manufacturing in 1962 compared with 46.7 per cent in 1950—an increase of 7.9 percentage points, or 17 per cent in twelve years. However measured, the extent of concentration was awesome.[2]

The merger movement in the United States after World War II was distinguished by the large number of conglomerate mergers, in contrast to the more traditional horizontal and vertical mergers. A conglomerate merger is the acquisition of one firm by another firm in an unrelated product line. The Ford Motor Company's take-over of the Philco radio and television company is an example of a conglomerate merger. Another prime example is Litton Industries, Inc., which began in electronics and built up its sales to $1 billion annually in twelve years by acquiring firms producing desk calculators and typewriters, nuclear submarines, motion picture cameras, paper mills, surgical instruments, and many other diverse products. Conglomerate mergers represent part of a trend toward diversification in business.

An important question concerning concentration is its effect on the allocation of resources in particular market situations. Here the prime consideration is concentration within specific industries rather than concentration in the large. Concentration is high in some industries such as primary aluminum, steel, automobiles, cigarettes, computers, and basic steel; it is relatively low in textiles, apparel, furniture, and paper products. A high degree of concentration in a given industry generally leads to monopolistic control over the market and a distortion of resource allocation, thereby reducing the total output of the economy and limiting the total satisfaction of wants below what is potentially possible. Monopolistic firms, protected from the discipline of market competition, may be slow to innovate. The impact of conglomerate mergers on competition is complex, but some economists believe that conglomerate firms do not have the same spur to efficiency as single-industry firms because conglomerates can immunize themselves from market

---

[1] On the relation between the subsidy system and the Atlantic partnership, see Joseph Kraft, *The Grand Design, from Common Market to Atlantic Partnership* (New York: Harper & Row, Publishers, 1962).

[2] These figures are from the testimony of Dr. Willard Mueller, Director, Bureau of Economics, Federal Trade Commission, before the Senate Subcommittee on Antitrust and Monopoly. See *Economic Concentration*, Part I, *Overall and Conglomerate Aspects*, 88th Cong., 2nd sess. (Washington, D.C.: Government Printing Office, 1964), pp. 113–15.

competition by offsetting losses in some branches with profits in other branches
of the merged firm. It may be argued, however, that the entry of a large firm
from one industry into another industry will stimulate the existing firms in
that industry to more active competition. While misallocation of resources
through monopoly power is less costly than chronic unemployment, it is
nevertheless a significant shortcoming of the economic system.

In Western Europe a merger movement gained momentum under the
Common Market. Small European firms merged to protect themselves against
intense rivalry from foreign firms setting up production inside the free-trade
customs union. Merger also took place between firms in different Common
Market countries, and between Common Market firms and those in outside
countries, including the United States. A wave of mergers occurred in the
European steel industry during the 1960's in an attempt to stabilize prices in
the light of excess steel capacity generated by the world steel race. Steel
firms in Germany, France, and Luxembourg merged, and in 1966 the High
Authority of the European Coal and Steel Community approved a merger
between a steel company in Germany and one in the Netherlands.[3] Europe's
merger movement was accompanied by steel cartels in Germany, France, and
Italy.

In the future an important aspect of business concentration may be its
relation to indicative economic planning.[4] Concentration in a relatively few
giant corporations potentially enhances the feasibility of general planning.
Indicative planning is already accepted in some European countries such as
France. Leaders of big business in the United States now sit on committees
which advise government leaders on business and economic matters. Acceptance by businessmen of the idea that government is responsible for maintaining prosperity provides a setting in which indicative planning can be
embraced by the business community. Heretofore the chief barrier in the
United States has been ideological. In time, however, ideological barriers may
erode, as is illustrated by the general acceptance, after three decades, of
Keynesian deficit financing for maintaining high levels of aggregate demand.
With the improvement of analytical techniques such as econometric models
and input-output tables for making economic projections, the case for indicative planning in the United States could become as overwhelming as the
case for Keynesian fiscal policy provided business leaders saw in indicative
planning a policy for stability, growth, and increased profits.

Rapid and continuous economic growth creates problems for the business community because the expansion of total demand must be accompanied by a mix of output appropriate to the specific division of total demand.
When the mix of output does not coincide with demand, goods are produced
which cannot be sold at profitable prices. One of the flaws in the functioning
of capitalism has been periodic overproduction of particular forms of capital
investment during prosperity. Depressions have served as purgatives for correcting these maladjustments. If depressions are to be eliminated and growth
is to be continuous, the correct prediction of future demand becomes highly

[3] On the world steel race, see the "Special Report" in *Business Week* (June 4, 1966),
pp. 58–76. On mergers in the European Coal and Steel Community, see the *European Community* bulletin, No. 92 (May, 1966), p. 11.

[4] See Chapter 34.

significant. In other words, successful macro-economic planning of aggregate demand must be accompanied by successful micro-economic planning of resource allocation if real national income is to be maximized. A prediction as to how demand will be divided among sectors of the economy is hazardous at best, but it is a subject about which specialists in the functioning of the whole economy should have something to say. Under indicative planning, moreover, businessmen do not have to accept the planners' projections; they may rely on their own judgment and try to predict more accurately than the central planners the future demand for their products. Voluntary acceptance of projections is the feature of indicative planning which makes it compatible with private enterprise and individual freedom. Imperative planning of the Soviet type may be compatible with individual freedom but only under conditions of a socialized economy.

Labor Problems

The rapid growth of labor union membership which began in the United States under the New Deal in the 1930's continued through World War II and into the early postwar period. After 1953, however, union membership stagnated at about 17,000,000 despite a continuing growth in the total labor force. An important factor in the failure of unions to continue their dynamic growth was the levelling off in the number of blue-collar jobs. In order to augment total membership labor unions had to either increase the proportion of blue-collar workers belonging to unions or attract more white-collar workers. The service industries, especially retail and wholesale trade, offered the most likely source of increased union membership. Of the 12,000,000 workers in retail and wholesale trade in the United States in 1965, only 500,000 belonged to labor unions. With the displacement of small independent stores by supermarkets, clerks experience a sense of alienation from their employers which should make them more prone to join unions.

Another potential source of union membership was among wage-earners of new industries in the South. An obstacle here, however, has been the Taft-Hartley Labor-Management Relations Act passed in 1946 by a Republican Congress over the veto of President Truman. Section 14b of the Taft-Hartley Law permits individual states to pass statutes outlawing the union shop. In a union shop the employer may hire anyone he wishes but all employees must become members of the recognized union. Some twenty states, mostly in the South and Middle West, at one time or another passed these so-called right-to-work laws. They may have restricted the growth of union membership in the South where unions had always been weak. In states where unions were already strong, right-to-work laws were not passed. Senator Goldwater's advocacy of right-to-work laws in the presidential campaign of 1964 appeared to contribute to his landslide defeat. Republican senatorial and congressional candidates in industrial states feared to support Senator Goldwater because of the adverse effect this might have on labor's vote. Trade union leaders made the repeal of Section 14b the major plank in their legislative platform, and President Johnson pledged to support its repeal. Repeal legislation passed the House of Representatives in 1965 but failed in the Senate in the face of a threatened filibuster by conservative Republicans and southern Democrats.

In western Europe the postwar labor movement made its influence felt

directly through its own political parties such as the Labour Party in the

United Kingdom and the social democratic parties in Germany and the Scandinavian countries. The doctrinaire anticapitalism of earlier years gave way to milder platforms designed to appeal to the middle class electorate. Unbroken prosperity under the mixed economies of the postwar period brought major improvement to the working classes in Europe. In Germany the Social Democratic Party abandoned its support of nationalization of industry in order to appeal to middle-class voters. In the United Kingdom the Labour Party reduced its emphasis on nationalization as the basis for a rational economy. Harold Wilson's decisive re-election in 1966 indicated that the British Labour Party had a strong appeal to the middle classes as well as to the working classes.

THE ECONOMIC BASIS OF A GREAT SOCIETY

Poverty in the midst of affluence has been a paradox of capitalism since the onset of mass production in the nineteenth century brought Western society across the great divide from an age of scarcity into an age of potential plenty. In part the paradox arises from the unequal distribution of income associated with the unequal ownership of income-producing property, and in part is a consequence of business cycles which have left wide gaps between the actual and potential production of capitalist economies. Even during the prosperity phase of business cycles, however, poverty persists among large groups whose latent capacities remain undeveloped because of unequal opportunities associated with discrimination and other self-perpetuating conditions extending from generation to generation.

Poverty has always been important in the study of economics. According to Malthus, poverty is an inevitable consequence of the folly of human nature and the diminishing returns of physical nature. Because he believed the lower classes would tend to populate up to the limits of the means of subsistence, Malthus considered poverty unavoidable. Karl Marx regarded poverty as ineradicable under capitalism but was optimistic about its elimination under socialism. In the opinion of Alfred Marshall, the late Victorian English economist, poverty was the most important problem and the chief justification for the study of economics. He expressed cautious optimism that poverty might be eliminated gradually, but his economic analysis continued in the classical tradition which attributed scarcity and poverty to the limitations of human and material nature.

As in so many other respects, John Maynard Keynes broke with the main traditions of economic thinking on the reasons and remedies for poverty. He shifted the theoretical and policy emphasis from the classical economics of scarcity to the modern economics of potential plenty, and expressed the optimistic hypothesis that poverty is a consequence of social and economic institutions. "If our poverty were due to famine or earthquake or war—if we lacked material things and the resources to produce them, we could not expect to find the Means to Prosperity except in hard work, abstinence, and invention. In fact, our predicament is notoriously of another kind." [5] Keynes'

[5] *Means to Prosperity* (London: Macmillan & Co., Ltd., 1933), p. 5.

answer to the problem of poverty was his principle of effective demand, which "supplies us with an explanation of the paradox of poverty in the midst of plenty." [6]

When President Johnson declared war on poverty in his State of the Union message in 1964, one-fifth of all American families, or approximately 35,000,000 people, were living below the poverty-level income of $3000 per year—the minimum deemed necessary by American standards to sustain a family of four in decent circumstances. This somewhat arbitrary figure is far above the income of most of the families of the world, including some countries of western Europe. Raising the incomes of all American families above this level would eliminate poverty as defined by 1960 standards, but a later decade might set the sights higher. Poverty is thus both an absolute and a relative concept.

A redistribution of about $11 billion per year from families above the $3000 income level could have raised all those families below the poverty level to the $3000 minimum. This would have been a noticeable but not an intolerable burden on the affluent American taxpayer.

A proposal which combines income redistribution with work incentive is the negative income tax under which families with incomes below the poverty line would receive a payment from the government equal to a percentage of the difference between the poverty-level income and their reported income. For example, if the poverty level income for a family of four is $3000 and the negative tax rate is 50 per cent, a family of four reporting no income would receive $1500, which is 50 per cent of $3000 minus zero; and a family reporting an income of $2000 would receive $500, which is 50 per cent of $3000 minus $2000. The negative income tax is one of several proposals for a guaranteed annual income for all families. Another way to guarantee income is to guarantee employment by having an employer of last resort somewhat analogous to central banks, which are lenders of last resort in the money market. An employer of last resort would have to be the government or some agency underwritten by the government. In price support programs for farmers the government is a buyer of last resort.

Emphasis in the Economic Opportunity Act of 1964, however, was not on guaranteed income or guaranteed employment but on public expenditures directed toward eliminating the causes of poverty by helping disadvantaged groups to earn higher incomes and thereby lift themselves out of poverty. The incidence of poverty is high among the poorly educated, the elderly, small farmers, non-whites, and families headed by females.

Eliminating poverty was a critical step in achieving what President Johnson called "The Great Society." [7] A Great Society became a meaningful possibility in the United States during the 1960's, when the production of wealth appeared to be under control and a part of the annual increment in national income could be used to raise the capacities and opportunities of low-income groups. To control the production of wealth requires virtual elimination of the business cycles endemic in laissez-faire capitalism; cer-

---

[6] *The General Theory of Employment, Interest and Money* (New York: Harcourt, Brace & World, 1936), p. 30.

[7] The term Great Society was used earlier in a somewhat different context by the English Fabian, Graham Wallas, author of *The Great Society* (London, 1914).

tainly it means eliminating major depressions if not necessarily mild recessions. In this task western Europe during the 1950's enjoyed unprecedented
success, and in 1961 President Kennedy instructed his chief economic adviser to bring back from Europe the secret of its successful economic policy.

After 1961 the United States succeeded in maintaining continuous economic expansion for a longer period than at any time in its previous history.
This was accomplished by putting into practice what many economists had
been teaching since the publication of Keynes' *General Theory* in 1936. As
often happens with new ideas, Keynesian economics was impeded by the
conservative ideology of its opponents and by the intellectual timidity of its
proponents. President Kennedy gave strong support to the Keynesian policies
of his advisers to get the American economy moving. The general, though
not unanimous, opinion among economists and publicists was that the tax cuts
of 1964 and 1965 produced the results that the Keynesians predicted.

Successful fiscal policy provided the economic basis of the Great Society.
Fiscal policy was used to (1) increase the growth rate of the economy, (2) decrease the unemployment rate, and (3) increase expenditures for the war
against poverty. During the first five years of the Kennedy-Johnson administration the annual growth rate of 4.5 per cent was approximately double that
of 1953 to 1960. The unemployment rate fell from 7.0 per cent in May, 1961,
to 3.7 per cent in the spring of 1966. Federal expenditures on education,
health, manpower training, and other anti-poverty measures increased rapidly
during the Johnson administration.

Fiscal policy under Kennedy moved away from reliance on automatic
stabilizers of the business cycle to discretionary tax and expenditure measures
which would permit continuous growth at a sustainable rate. The notion of
balancing the federal budget even over the cycle was dropped in favor of the
broader concept of a balanced economy. Despite an excess of expenditures
over tax receipts, President Kennedy called for a reduction in tax rates as a
means of reducing the $40 to $50 billion gap between potential and actual
gross national product. High progressive tax rates acted as a progressive brake
on economic expansion. Given a 4 to 5 per cent annual increase in gross
national product, existing tax rates siphoned off about $7 billion of the addi-
tional $30 billion in the income stream. In order to prevent this $7 billion fiscal
drag from slowing down economic expansion, federal expenditures had to be
increased by an equivalent amount to maintain the circular flow or tax rates
had to be reduced substantially.

The policies recommended by President Kennedy and pushed through
Congress by President Johnson called for major tax cuts accompanied by increased expenditures designed to root out the causes of poverty. Opponents
of increased government spending found their arguments weakened by the
large fiscal dividends received by taxpayers in the form of tax cuts. The Great
Society was being paid for out of a fraction of the annual increment in national
product. The secret of the process was the $30 billion annual increase in gross
national product available for sharing among lower taxes, higher government
expenditures, higher wages, and higher profits. All classes were better off
each succeeding year. There was no robbing Peter to pay Paul in the Johnson
war against poverty. The theory of the expanding pie as a political and economic argument for the Great Society was, to say the least, persuasive.

Unfortunately for the war on poverty and for the fiscal dividends to tax-payers, the costly Vietnam war intervened. The fiscal drag, which in other conditions was a liability, became an anti-inflationary asset. Since fiscal policy aims at price stability as well as high employment and growth, logical consistency requires tax increases in periods of excess demand as well as tax decreases in periods of deficient demand. Strong autonomous increases in private investment or in private consumption out of given income levels could, of course, generate inflationary pressures in the absence of war-induced government spending. However, the historic characteristic of the American economy in the second and third quarters of the twentieth century was specifically not marked by such strong autonomous spending propensities either for investment or for consumption. The productive capacity of the economy and the annual increases thereto were so great as virtually to preclude the possibility of private autonomous forces being strong enough to give a general inflationary bias to the economy.

If fiscal policy provided the key that opened the door to the Great Society, education was the vestibule through which those freed from poverty make their way to the inner halls. All along the educational front during the Johnson administration federal legislation was passed to improve education from kindergartens to graduate schools. The traditional political barriers to general federal aid to education—the church-state issue and the alleged threat of federal control—were surmounted by focusing on the plight of disadvantaged children. Outside the formal educational channels, expenditures were increased for technical and vocational training, manpower development, and other types of investment in human capital. The remarkable increase in the nation's growth rate during the 1960's was stimulated by the heavy investment in human capital. This is consistent with the hypothesis that the chief source of the wealth of nations resides in people.

Mass Affluence and Some of Its Probable Consequences

The eradication of poverty in the Atlantic Community is only one aspect of the Great Society—"great" because it holds promise of a richer life for all groups. If per capita real income grows steadily at 2 per cent per year, each new generation will have twice the real income of the preceding one. Fathers with real incomes of $10,000 may normally expect their sons to have real incomes of $20,000 and their grandsons of $40,000 per year. What will people do with all this money? The prospect of such affluence titillates consumers' appetites. Some additional income will be spent for food, some for clothing, and more for housing, but even with these basic needs more adequately met, much income remains to be spent.

A good life as well as an abundant one is included in the terms of reference of the Great Society. Some increased real income will be taken in the form of added leisure, and here the accent may be less on the shorter work week and more on extended annual vacations and on year-long sabbatical leaves from work in order to travel and enjoy life according to individual tastes and appetites.

The quality and tone of life in the Great Society will depend on the en-

vironment within which individual consumption takes place. Most Americans

and Europeans live in and around great cities, and these cities as presently
constituted are incompatible with the spirit of a Great Society. They must be
transformed. The cost of urban transformation is sufficiently staggering to
dent even the wealth-producing capacity of the Great Society. In addition to
improvements in cities, vast sums need to be allocated to other collective
wants such as education, health, recreation, and beautification.

Should poverty be eliminated among Americans and West Europeans,
it will still plague some three billion people on this planet. In foreign as in
domestic life, the only lasting escape from poverty is through self-help, but
substantial outside assistance can help to break the vicious circle of poverty.
Collective decisions by Americans and Europeans will determine how much
economic assistance they will allot to the underdeveloped countries, but here
is an outlet for their surplus wealth for a long time to come. Self-interest as
well as social conscience may influence the privileged peoples of the world to
share their affluence with the poor nations. President Kennedy in his inaugural address reminded Americans of a disturbing possibility when he said:
"If a free society cannot help the many who are poor, it cannot save the few
who are rich."

Since a market system tends to underallocate resources to collective
wants and since collective wants are certain to grow rapidly in the Great
Society, economic planning becomes essential to their fulfillment. The market
is a better allocator of scarcity than it is a dispenser of abundance for the
good life. Thus mass affluence may be expected to lead to further alterations
in the relative importance of the market system and economic planning. Moreover, the motivational base of the market system, which rests on strong incentives to work, save, and accumulate material wealth, may be weakened by
mass affluence. As economic life ceases to be a struggle for physical survival
as an end in itself and becomes merely the starting point for the good life,
economic ethics may be expected to differ substantially from the market-
oriented behavior of recent centuries.

THE GRAND DESIGN

The term Grand Design refers to an Atlantic partnership between the United
States (and Canada) and a unified western Europe. Some countries of Europe
which do not border on the Atlantic Ocean are, of course, included, such as
Germany, Italy, Austria, and Greece; and in one variation of the concept, the
Grand Design includes Europe from the Atlantic Ocean to the Ural Moun-
tains. Political, cultural, and military ties are part of the concept of the Grand
Design, but consideration here is limited to the economic aspects of Atlantic
partnership.

Historically the Atlantic Community began when Columbus discovered
America and has been implicit in the economic relations of the peoples on the
eastern and western shores of the North Atlantic ever since. The Atlantic Community is the modern counterpart of the Mediterranean world of Roman times.
The Middle Ages in western Europe was the period during which the center
of Western civilization shifted from the Mediterranean Sea to the Atlantic

Ocean. Through the nineteenth century the center of power of this Atlantic Community remained in western Europe, but in the twentieth century it shifted to the United States.

Although the idea of Atlantic partnership is an old one, formalized institutional relations between the peoples of the two sides of the Atlantic were forestalled by American isolationist policies, first laid down by George Washington and continued until the Second World War. In the First World War the United States went belatedly to the defense of the Allies in western Europe, but in the 1920's the United States reverted to its historic policy of isolationism and even rejected membership in the League of Nations. In 1941 the United States again entered a world war belatedly to save the traditions of Western civilization.

Only since World War II, when the United States was thrust into a position of world leadership, has the Atlantic partnership emerged from the idea stage toward formal institutional organization. Apart from certain arrangements pertaining to economic recovery, the first formal alliance between the United States and western Europe was the North Atlantic Treaty Organization (NATO), which was nurtured by the vulnerability of western Europe to the military threat of Communism. NATO represented the initial peacetime commitment by the United States to the military defense of the nations of western Europe. It was a product of the cold war, and its cohesiveness fluctuated with the temperature of the cold war. France's withdrawal from NATO in 1966 reflected a relaxation in the military tensions between the Soviet Union and western Europe.

The strongest bid for an Atlantic partnership came from President Kennedy in his declaration of interdependence on July 4, 1962, when he said, "I will say here and now, on this day of Independence, that the United States will be ready for a declaration of interdependence, that we will be prepared to discuss with a united Europe the way and means of forming a concrete Atlantic partnership." Behind the Kennedy declaration lay fifteen years of progress toward the economic unification of western Europe, including the Marshall Plan, the Organization for European Economic Cooperation, the European Steel and Coal Community, the European Economic Community, and the European Free Trade Association. Before an economic partnership between the United States and western Europe could be established, the latter had to achieve a substantial degree of unity. President Kennedy's declaration came at a time when the United Kingdom's request for membership in the Common Market seemed likely to be granted by the six charter members and to be followed by entrance into the Common Market of other western European countries. As a major step which might lead to closer partnership with western Europe, President Kennedy proposed and Congress passed the Trade Expansion Act of 1962.[8] The American President was authorized to negotiate across-the-board reductions in tariffs. The Grand Design appeared ready to become a working concept, with the United States of America joined to a United States of Europe in a wide free trading area.

The British attitude tells much about the forces making for western European integration. When the Common Market was first proposed, the

---

[8] On the Trade Expansion Act, see Chapter 37.

British declined to become a charter member, but after its demonstrated success, the British applied for membership only to be vetoed by France. Britain's
Labour Party initially opposed its country's membership but later came to
favor it. Thus some major obstacles to Britain's admission were eliminated.
Once the United Kingdom is accepted into the Common Market, other countries of western Europe may be expected to seek affiliation.

President de Gaulle's veto of British membership in the Common Market
was a setback to the Grand Design for Atlantic partnership. The forces of
European nationalism, which centered in France in the 1960's, remain powerful and will not be overcome easily. However, it is a reasonable hypothesis
that the forces making for economic integration of the Atlantic Community
will in the long run prove stronger than the forces operating for economic nationalism. Many western Europeans who would welcome American partnership reject American leadership in Europe, and until western Europe enjoys
more economic unity than it possessed in 1963, Atlantic partnership might
mean American domination. President de Gaulle's 1963 veto was a protest
against American leadership in Europe as well as a rebuff to the United Kingdom. Under different leadership and slightly altered circumstances France
might remove the obstacles to Atlantic partnership.

Atlantic Community Integration Through Private Business Sector

Formal alliances among governments constitute only a relatively small
part of the total interdependence between western Europe and the United
States—only the visible part of the North Atlantic iceberg. Less conspicuous
but of longer duration and more comprehensive in building an Atlantic partnership has been the private sector of the economies in the Atlantic basin.
These business interrelations operate through many channels: capital markets,
labor markets, technology, research and development, travel, communication,
ideologies, and common cultural and political heritage extending back to 1492.

Although transatlantic business relations are not of recent origin, they
accelerated greatly after World War II. Massive public investment by the
United States government under the Marshall Plan was followed by massive
private investment by business corporations. American corporations became
multi-national companies with a chain of subsidiaries operating in several
countries under top American management. Most of the American corporate
giants have direct investments in western Europe. The big three in automobile
manufacture are prominent in European automobile production and distribution. From computers to soft drinks, from petroleum refining to variety stores,
American capitalists are heavy investors in Europe's economy. Direct investment to produce goods in a foreign country is a form of international trade,
but it differs radically from the conventional type involving the physical movement of goods. Sales by United States subsidiaries abroad in the 1960's exceeded the total volume of American exports.

Transatlantic business relations are a two-way affair, with European
companies investing directly in the United States and American companies
making direct investments in Europe. For example, Italy's Olivetti office ma-

chine company acquired control of the Underwood corporation in the United States in 1959, took over the management, built up a $100 million investment, and captured a substantial part of the office machine market in the United States. Olivetti rebuilt and made profitable an American company which had been losing money for years. By so doing Olivetti became part of the domestic American economy instead of merely an exporter of Italian goods made in Italy.

However, American investments in Europe have far exceeded European investments in the United States, causing resentment and fear among some Europeans. President de Gaulle spoke out against the threat of domination by the United States, and his government took some steps to curb American direct investments in France. Fear that Europe's markets would be dominated by giant American corporations arose because of the technological gap between the United States and Europe. As a partial counterbalance, the presence of American production units provided an opportunity for Europeans to learn about American technology and thereby reduce the technological gap. Since most research and development work by American corporations was done at the home office in the United States and not at their subsidiaries in Europe, some of Europe's best research scientists, attracted by high salaries, migrated to the United States in what was called the "brain drain."

More fundamentally, western Europe's lag in technology was due to slowness in adapting its system of higher education to the demands of modern economic society. The proportion of young people attending universities was substantially lower in western Europe than in the United States or the Soviet Union. Higher education is a type of investment which yields large dividends to society as well as to individuals. The correlation between university enrollments and economic productivity is most direct in the case of engineers, scientists, and business administrators, but virtually all academic disciplines have something to contribute to the wealth of nations. Because of the lag in higher education compared with the United States and the Soviet Union, Western Europe faced serious obstacles to closing the gap in research and development.

One reason for large American direct investments in Europe in the postwar period was the desire of American companies to avoid being discriminated against in the Common Market: Leaping over the external tariff wall, they set up shop within the Common Market. However, more direct investment was made in the United Kingdom than in any other single country in Europe so that the Common Market was not the only and perhaps not even the most important reason for the massive surge of American capital to Europe. At a time when Europe was just becoming a mass consumption market for automobiles, household appliances, and other mass-produced goods, the businessmen of the United States enjoyed an initial advantage because of their long experience with this type of market.

Moreover, the American capital market, being larger and more flexible than Europe's, gave an advantage to the United States, although the American capital market also enabled Europeans to obtain funds for investment anywhere in the world. The large outflow of American capital placed a strain on the balance of payments of the United States and led to restrictions on the export of American capital. This gave European capital markets an oppor-

tunity to respond to the demands of European and American investors for money capital.

Transatlantic corporations have helped to create the Atlantic partnership. In day-to-day, normal working relations the private sector has contributed directly to the economic integration of western Europe and the United States. The ease of transatlantic travel in the jet age has created a true Atlantic business community, with management experts able to divide their time between New York and Frankfurt almost as easily as between New York and San Francisco. The common cultural heritage shared by western Europe and the United States is advancing from a study of history, art, and literature and a once-in-a-lifetime grand tour of Europe by affluent Americans to matter-of-fact business relations between the people living around the Atlantic basin.

Grand Design and the Rising Nations

One of the objectives of the Grand Design is to pool the resources of the rich nations in order to mount an attack on the great economic problem of the next century, the elevation from misery of the poor nations where one-half the world's population has an average per capita income of less than $200 a year. In 1961 the North Atlantic partners formed the twenty-nation Organization for Economic Cooperation and Development to coordinate their efforts in assisting the less developed countries of the world. Because of their great wealth, the Atlantic nations are uniquely capable of disseminating technical knowledge and providing large sums of capital to the underdeveloped areas.

A grimmer aspect of the Grand Design relates to the confrontation between the East and the West in the coming decades. A strong Atlantic partnership would hold a balance of power against any foreseeable combination of other nations for a century to come. If the virtual monopoly of world power exercised by the West during the past five hundred years is relinquished gradually and wisely, the rising power of the non-West, including the Soviet-Sino blocs, may be directed into creative rather than destructive channels. Assuming nuclear weapons deterrence, the main rivalry between the great power blocs will be more economic and political than military. The West has much to contribute in science, technology, and democratic institutions to the development of the less developed countries. The United States alone cannot and should not try to control the course of world history, but in combination with Europe it can perhaps foster a peaceful transition to positions of relative equality between the peoples of the East and West.

As an idea and as an informal working arrangement, the Atlantic partnership is a fact of history. Since World War II some important steps toward the Grand Design as a community of formalized institutions have been taken. What has not yet been consummated, however, is the move from the Common Market to a formal Atlantic partnership. A major depression could wreck both the Common Market and the Great Society. While economists are almost certain that major depressions can be avoided, there is no guarantee that they will be. A strong protectionist position by the Common Market could prove a major obstacle to closer Atlantic union. Although the Common Market was intended as a low-tariff customs union, there can be no assurance that the

original intent will prevail. While there is nothing inevitable about a stronger and more formalized Atlantic partnership, this writer is convinced that the weight of history favors its ultimate success. This hypothesis is, in fact, one of the central themes of the present book.

SELECTED BIBLIOGRAPHY

BERLE, ADOLF A., *The Twentieth-Century Capitalist Revolution.* New York: Harcourt, Brace and World, Inc., 1954.

COPPOCK, J. O., *Atlantic Agricultural Unity: Is It Possible?* New York: McGraw-Hill, Inc., 1966.

COUNCIL OF ECONOMIC ADVISERS, *Annual Report to the President.* Washington, D.C.: Government Printing Office, yearly since 1946.

GALBRAITH, JOHN K., *The Affluent Society.* Boston: Houghton Mifflin Company, 1958.

GINZBERG, ELI, DALE L. HIESTAND, and BEATRICE G. REUBENS, *The Pluralistic Economy.* New York: McGraw-Hill, Inc., 1965.

HARRINGTON, MICHAEL, *The Other America, Poverty in the United States.* New York: The Macmillan Company, 1963.

HEILBRONER, ROBERT L., *The Future as History.* New York: Grove Press, Inc., 1961.

——, *The Limits of American Capitalism.* New York: Harper & Row, 1966.

HELLER, WALTER W., *New Dimensions of Political Economy.* Cambridge, Mass.: Harvard University Press, 1966.

KEYNES, JOHN M., *The General Theory of Employment, Interest and Money.* New York: Harcourt, Brace and World, Inc., 1936.

KLEIMAN, ROBERT, *Atlantic Crisis, American Diplomacy Confronts a Resurgent Europe.* New York: W. W. Norton & Co., Inc., 1964.

KRAFT, JOSEPH, *The Grand Design: From Common Market to Atlantic Partnership.* New York: Harper & Row, Publishers, 1962.

LECHT, LEONARD A., *Goals, Priorities and Dollars—The Next Decade.* New York: The Free Press of Glencoe, 1966.

LEKACHMAN, ROBERT, *The Age of Keynes.* New York: Random House, Inc., 1966.

LIPPMANN, WALTER, *Western Unity and the Common Market.* Boston: Little, Brown & Co., 1962.

MIDDLETON, DREW, *The Supreme Choice: Britain and Europe.* New York: Alfred A. Knopf, Inc., 1963.

NATIONAL COMMISSION ON TECHNOLOGY, AUTOMATION, AND ECONOMIC PROGRESS, *Technology and the American Economy,* Vol. I. Washington, D.C.: Government Printing Office, 1966.

SENATE SUBCOMMITTEE ON ANTITRUST AND MONOPOLY, *Economic Concentration,* Hearings, Parts 1–4, 88th and 89th Cong., 1964–65. Washington, D.C.: Government Printing Office, 1964–65.

SHONFIELD, ANDREW, *Modern Capitalism, The Changing Balance of Public and Private Power.* New York: Oxford University Press, 1965.

THEOBALD, ROBERT, ed., *The Guaranteed Income.* Garden City, N. Y.: Doubleday & Co., Inc., 1966.

WILCOX, FRANCIS O., and H. FIELD HAVILAND, JR., eds., *The Atlantic Community.* New York: Frederick A. Praeger, Inc., 1963.

"U.S. Business in New Europe, A Special Report," *Business Week*, May 7, 1966, pp. 94–120.

LARNER, ROBERT J., "Ownership and Control in the 200 Largest Nonfinancial Corporations, 1929 and 1963," *American Economic Review*, LVI (Sept., 1966), 777–87.

LAYTON, CHRISTOPHER, "Trans-Atlantic Investments," *Atlantic Community Quarterly* (Summer, 1966), pp. 263–67.

THISTLETHWAITE, FRANK, "Atlantic Partnership," *Economic History Review*, VII (August, 1954), pp. 1–17.

Index

Bicks, Robert A., 424
Bidwell, Percy W., 213, 320, 336
"Big Five" banks in England, 383
Big Four "D" banks in Germany, 383, 385, 399
"Big masters," 29, 43, 49, 117
Bilateral trade, 547
Bill of exchange:
  Florence, 76
  France, 19th-century, 380
  Germany, 381
  Low Countries, 78, 79
Bimetallic standard:
  Europe, 376
  United States, 216-217, 376-377
Bismarck, 281, 307, 437, 458, 468, 469, 482, 508, 509, 598
Bjork, Gordon C., 232
Black, John D., 485, 584, 611
Black Death, 59, 61-63, 64, 65, 67, 129
"Black Market," 671, 678
Black Tuesday, October, 1929, 582, 585
Blanc, Louis, 460
Bland, A. E., 13, 24, 49, 70, 144 n
Bland-Allison Act, 376
Blaug, Mark, 280
Blocked marks, 547-548
"Blue Nails," 37, 42
Bodin, Jean, 105, 106
Boer War, 491
Bogue, A. and M., 232
Boinebroke, Jean, 37, 38
Boissonade, P., 13, 49
Bonn, Moritz J., 559
Bonnen, James T., 485
Bonner, James C., 362
Bookkeeping, double-entry, 81, 84, 89, 150
Boon days, 56
Bornstein, Morris, 638
Boston Associates, 328, 335, 371
Boston Manufacturing Company, 327, 371
Boulton, Matthew, 244, 249
Bourges, 85
Bourse, 78, 159
  Bruges, 78
  distinguished from fair, 78
Bowden, Witt, 257, 317, 521, 559
Bowditch, John, 257
Bowen, Ralph H., 317
Bowen, William C., 460
Bowman, Mary Jean, 485
Boxer Rebellion, 497
Brady, Robert A., 317, 404, 428, 522, 536, 559, 666
Branch banking, 381, 383
Brandeis, Louis D., 428, 607
Brebner, J. Bartlet, 213
Brenner, Y. S., 109 n, 110
Bresciani-Turroni, Constantino, 521, 522
Bretton Woods Conference, 701
Brezhnev, 628
Bright, John, 256, 266
Brinkmann, Carl, 25, 317
Brissenden, Paul F., 460
British East India Company, 100-102, 181, 182, 370
British Steel Association, 401
Brookings Institution, 700:
  capacity study, 526
Brooks, John, 666
Brown, E. H. Phelps, 110
Brown, Robert E., 213
Brown, William A., Jr., 649 n, 666

Bruchey, Stuart W., 213
Bruges, 21, 23, 74, 76, 77, 78, 79, 80, 159
Bryan, William Jennings, 377
Bubble Act, 161, 370, 371
Bullionism, 168-169, 172-174, 177
Burn, Duncan L., 388
Burns, Arthur F., 682
Burns, Arthur R., 428, 584
"Buy American" law, 650

C

Cabot, John, 179-180
Cairnes, John E., 361
Calico, 170, 171
Calvert family, 184-185
Calvin, John, 88-89, 90
Cameron, Rondo E., 287 n, 301, 302
Campbell, Robert W., 629 n, 637
Canals:
  under mercantilism, 166-167
  United States, 322-323
Cannan, Edwin, 96
Capital:
  circulating, 35, 113-114, 115, 121:
    under slavery, 339
  "fixed," 81, 113-114, 115, 121, 122, 339
  under handicraft system, 28-29
  intangible, 10
  under putting-out system, 113-115
  under slavery, 339-340
  social overhead, 175-176, 186-187
  tangible, 29
  United States supply, 359
  Venetian merchants, 74
Capital accumulation (see Accumulation of capital and Capital formation)
Capital formation:
  effect on consumption, 579
  United States, 1920-1940, 562, 565, 575, 576-580, 609
Capital formation and the level of economic activity, 95-97, 150-151, 562, 565, 578, 579, 580, 633, 675-676, 684-685, 689
Capitalism:
  defined, 3
  as an economic system, 8
  England, 78
  Florence, medieval, 39-40
  instability, 9
  Low Countries, 77-79
  and mercantilism, 163, 179
  as a money economy, 8-9, 96, 150-152
  wage laborer contrasted with serf, 57
  and technology, 248-250
  in Venice, 72-75
Capitalist spirit, 81, 83-84
Capital market, 160, 161, 388, 724
Captains of industry, 47
Carnegie, Andrew, 413, 428
Cartels, 82, 385, 393, 395-400, 530-531, 532, 533, 557-558, 656, 715:
  Europe, postwar, 656, 715
  German, 427:
    and banks, 399-400
    Cartel Court, 400
    coal, 396-397
    legal justification, 395-396
    steel industry, 397-398, 715
  international, 530-531, 533, 535, 656
  mixed, 398-399
  tariffs, 397, 398
Cartwright, Edmund, 241, 249, 273

Joint-stock company (*Cont.*)
    in founding the North Atlantic Community, 181-184
Joint-stock ventures, 100
Jones, E. L., 148
Jones, Eliot, 429, 430
Josephson, Hannah, 327, 336
Josephson, Matthew, 429
Journeymen's gild, 44, 431
Just price, 30-32, 84

K

Kahn, Alfred E., 536
Kay, John, 241, 249
Kaysen, Carl, 430
Kelly, William, 365
Kelvin, Lord, 279
Kendrick, John W., 682, 708
Kennedy Administration, 685, 689, 690, 691, 692, 693, 694, 699, 702, 707, 712, 719, 721, 722
Kennedy-Johnson tax cut, 690, 719
Kennedy Round, 660, 665, 703-704, 714
Kerensky, Alexander, 613
Kerridge, Eric, 111
Kessler, William C., 537
Ket, Robert, 136
Keynes, John Maynard, 107, 108, 110, 178, 488 n, 519, 521, 522, 536, 540 n, 551, 559, 560, 582, 603, 604, 646 n, 667, 701, 717, 719, 726
Kimberley, 491
Kindleberger, Charles P., 287 n, 302, 549 n, 667
Kirkland, Edward C., 14, 336, 429, 430
Kleiman, Robert, 726
Klein, Burton, 668
Knapland, Paul, 502
Knight, E. C., case, 412
Knight, Frank H., 584
Knight, Melvin M., 58 n, 502
Knights of Labor, 444, 445-446, 447, 448, 452, 453, 455
Knorr, Klaus E., 214
Knowles, L. C. A., 280, 502
Kommanditgesellschaft auf Aktien, 370
Korean inflation in United States, 679
Kosminsky, E. A., 71
Kosygin, 628
Kraft, Joseph, 714 n, 726
Krause, Lawrence B., 668
Kreps, Theodore J., 309, 317
Krupp, 311, 399, 509, 529
Khrushchev, Nikita, 627, 628, 629, 635
Kuczynski, Jürgen, 442
Kuhn, Loeb, and Co., 385
Kulaks, 616, 620
Kulischer, Eugene M., 521
Kuznets, Simon, 12, 573 n,. 610, 672 n, 682

L

Labor:
    Factory Acts, England, 254-256
    forced, in colonies, 193-195
    and free competition, 250
    free, in colonies, 191-193, 194 n
    hours during Industrial Revolution, 253
    Industrial Revolution, 235-236
    organized:
        comparative analysis, 453-458

Labor (*Cont.*)
    France, 439-442
    Germany, 436-439
    Great Britain, 432-436
    United States, 444-452
    scarcity:
        in colonies, 186, 191-195
        in United States, 325
    supply:
        for French industry, 284-287
        in New England, 8
Labor force, agricultural and nonagricultural:
    Soviet Union, 631-632
    United States, 355-356
Labor movement:
    comparative analysis, 453-458
    Europe, 431-442
    France, 439-442
    Germany, 436-439
    Great Britain, 432-436
    United States, 444-458
Labor union membership, United States, 448-450, 716
Labor unions, 44, 250-251:
    British, craft union stage, 433-434
    British, formative stage, 432-433
    British, industrial union stage, 434
    compared with craft gilds, 431
    French, 439-442
    German, 436-439
    United States, craft union stage, 446-449
    United States, formative stage, 444-446
    United States, industrial union stage, 449-451
Labor unions, legal status, 432, 434, 435-436, 437, 444-445
Labor unions, under Clayton Act, 422
Labour Party, 435, 551
Labour Representation Committee, 435, 436
Labrousse, Camille Ernest, 302
"Ladies of the loom," 328-330
Laissez-faire, 259, 260, 283, 507, 576:
    and American Revolution, 207-210
    criticism of mercantilism, 176
    decline of, 256, 259
    and mercantilism, 163, 164
    and property rights, 141
    rise of, 207-210, 247, 259
    after World War I, 551
Lampman, Robert J., 683
"Land, bread, and peace," 614
Land grants for railroads, 222-224
Land hunger in Russia, 613, 614
Land redistribution in American Revolution, 206
Landes, David S., 257, 302, 303, 502, 503
Landlords, 256:
    Corn Laws, 260-261
Lando, Michele, 40
Landowners, German inflation of 1920's, 515
Lane, Frederick C., 13, 73, 92
Lange, Oskar, 636 n
Languedoc Canal, 166
Larner, Robert J., 727
Laski, Harold J., 560
Lassalle, Ferdinand, 436, 437
Latin Monetary Union, 375-376
Laurosky, V. M., 148
Lavington, Frederick, 388, 502

Private property:
 and the corporation, 322
 and the labor movement, 454-455
 under Nazis, 557, 558
Proclamation Line of 1763, 202, 206, 227
Productivity, 112, 696:
 agricultural, United States, 320, 470-473, 686
 European v. American, postwar, 696
Profit inflation, 107-109
Profits:
 during Industrial Revolution, 252
 West Indies trade, 102-103
Protectionism:
 English Corn Laws, 260-266
 under mercantilism, 170-174
 United States after Civil War, 353
 United States in 1920's, 563
Protestant ethic, 88-92
Prothero, R. E., 148, 485
Psychological factors in economic development, 91-92
Public debt:
 after American Revolution, 215-216
 United States, 690
Public expenditure to promote economic growth, 691
Public land policy, 219-226:
 farm land, 221-222
 grazing land, 224-225
 Homestead Act, 222, 225
 Jefferson's views, 220, 225
 mineral land, 225
 Preemption Act, 222
 railroads, 222-223, 225
 revenue, 221
 timber land, 224, 225
Public Utilities Holding Company Act, 601
Public works:
 under Hoover Administration, 593, 605
 under Roosevelt Administration, 593, 595, 599-600, 607
Public Works Administration (PWA), 593, 595
Puddling process, 242-243, 330-331
Pump-priming, 602
Putting-out system, 8, 96, 113-121, 123, 192, 239, 249, 250, 286:
 in colonial America, 192
 in England, 113-121

Q

Quantity theory of money, 104, 105
Quebec Act of 1774, 202
Quitrents, 185, 203, 206

R

Railroad pools, 406-408
Railroads, 84, 274-275, 291-292, 306-307, 310, 323-324, 325, 331, 348, 371, 571, 631:
 land grants, 222-224
 truck competition, 571
Raleigh, Sir Walter, 180, 181
Raskob, John Jacob, 581
Rasmussen, Wayne D., 485
Rathenau, Emil, 312
Rathenau, Walther, 312
Rationalization movement, 525, 528, 530, 535
Reaper, 320-321, 471
Recessions, postwar United States, 685

Reciprocal Trade Agreements, 701, 702, 703
Reconstruction Finance Corporation, 593, 605
Rediscounting, 382, 383, 385
Redistribution of civilian consumption in World War II, 671
Redlich, Fritz, 12
Regensburg, 80
Regrating, 31
Regulated companies, 99
Reichsbank, 381, 385, 512, 513, 542, 547
Reichsmark, 515
Rent:
 during Price Revolution, 106
 theory of, 261-263
Rentenmarks, 514-515
Reparations:
 Germany's ability to pay, 517-519
 after World War I, 513-514, 517-519
"Report on Monopolies" (1522-23), 82
Residential construction, United States, 675-676
Resource allocation in the Soviet economy, 634-637
"Return to normalcy," 523, 549, 639
Return to the gold standard, 538-540
Reveille, Thomas, 560
Revolution of 1848, 296, 305, 306-307
Rhenish-Westphalian Coal Syndicate, 396-397, 398
Rhodes, Cecil, 489, 490, 491
Ricardo, David, 246, 253, 261-265, 280, 483:
 Corn Laws, 261-264
 distribution theory, 261-263
 landlords, 261, 263
 on overproduction, 267-268
 Principles of Political Economy, 261
 profit theory, 261-262
 rent defined, 262
 rent theory, 262-264
 wages, 261
Rice in American Colonies, 189, 197, 227, 229
Rich, E. E., 18
Richards, R. D., 161, 162
Riemersma, J. C., 92
Right to work, 460
Ripley, William Z., 407 n
Robbins, Ray M., 232
Robequain, Charles, 502
Roberts, Richard, 289
Robertson, Dennis H., 560
Robertson, Ross M., 14
Robinson, Gerold T., 614, 637
Robinson, Joan, 668
Rockefeller, John D., 409-410
Rockefeller family, 419
Rogin, Leo, 337, 485
Rogow, A. A., 667
Rolt, L. T. C., 388
Roosevelt, F. D., Administration, 585, 590-610, 701
Roosevelt, Franklin D., 610
Roosevelt, Nicholas, 322
Roosevelt, Theodore, trust-buster, 415, 417
Rothschilds, 384
Rorig, Fritz, 25
Rosenberg, Nathan, 389
Ross, Arthur M., 461
Rostas, Laslow, 667

DATE DUE

MAY 15 '91			
GAYLORD			PRINTED IN U.S.A.